D1092782

PRESENTED TO

GORDON HODSON

CHAIRMAN 1997 – 2000

EAST GRINSTEAD DECORATIVE
AND
FINE ARTS SOCIETY

FROM
ALL HIS COLLEAGUES
ON THE
COMMITTEE

WINES OF THE RHÔNE VALLEY

REVISED AND EXPANDED EDITION

Also available by Robert Parker

THE WINE BUYER'S GUIDE 1996

BURGUNDY:
A Comprehensive Guide to the
Producers, Appellations and Wines

BORDEAUX:
A Comprehensive Guide

WINES OF THE RHÔNE VALLEY

REVISED AND EXPANDED EDITION

ROBERT PARKER

Drawings by
Christopher Wormell

DORLING KINDERSLEY

LONDON · NEW YORK · SYDNEY · MOSCOW

First published in Great Britain in 1988 by
Dorling Kindersley Limited, 9 Henrietta Street, London WC2E 8PS
Visit us on the World Wide Web at http://www.dk.com

Copyright © Robert Parker, 1987
Revised and expanded edition, copyright © Robert Parker 1997

All rights reserved. No part of this publication may be
reproduced, stored in a retrieval system, or transmitted in
any form or by any means, electronic, mechanical,
photocopying, recording or otherwise, without the prior
written permission of the copyright owner.

A CIP catalogue record for this book is available
from the British Library

ISBN 0-7513-1094-8

Printed in USA

ACKNOWLEDGMENTS

Two people, Joan Passman, my "Madame Everything" and Hanna Agostini, France's "La Grande Parkerette," cannot possibly be thanked enough for the enormous amount of work they did both in gathering and assisting in the verification of the vast amount of information in this book. Without their efforts I know this book would have been impossible to finish.

No author can survive mentally without considerable cooperation from their publisher. Simon & Schuster editors Gillian Sowell and Jay Schweitzer have served me well.

In the Rhône Valley, I must confess that there are many great men and women whom I have come to admire, and even call friends. In the latter instance I have tried very hard to keep an arm's distance between critic and producer, but too many trips, too many philosophical discussions, and too much delicious wine and food that they have shared with me have made it impossible to judge these people objectively. Fortunately for their wines, critical independence is still easy to maintain. These people have educated me, thrilled me, and inspired me through their words and their wines. To them, saying thank you will never fully express my appreciation and admiration for their labor. In alphabetical order they are: Paul Avril, Henri Bonneau, André Brunel, the Brunier brothers, Michel Chapoutier, Gérard Chave, Auguste Clape, Paul and Laurent Féraud, the late Jacques Ferlay, Marius Gentaz-Dervieux, Marcel Guigal, Michele and Philippe Laurent, François and Jean-Pierre Perrin, the late Jacques Reynaud, Georges Vernay, and Noël Verset.

Other Rock & Rhône enthusiasts whom I would like to thank for their support and encouragement are: "Diamond" Jim "King Cornas" Arsenault, Bruce Bassin, Christopher Cannan, Bob Cline, Jean-Luc Colombo, Paul Evans, "Fast Eddie," Lawrence and Bernard Godec, Josué Harari, Alexandra Harding, Barbara G. and Steve R. R. Jacoby, Alain Junguenet, Robert Kacher, Brenda Keller, Robert "Slowly" Lescher, Susan Lescher, "The Magnum Force," J. C. Mathes, Ron "the King" Metzer, Jay Miller, Allen Peacock, Frank Polk, Pierre-Antoine Rovani, Carlo Russo, Ed Sands, Martine Saunier, Bob Schindler, Eric Solomon, Elliott Staren, Steve "the Ho" Verlin, Peter Vezan, Karen Weinstock, Joseph Weinstock, and "the Wiz-zard."

Lastly, I am also forever indebted to the wisdom and generosity of America's and possibly the world's "second" most enthusiastic Rhône wine lover, Park B. Smith, "Le Grand Parkster."

To Pat and Maia,
and to the memory of
Jacques Ferlay and
Jacques Reynaud

CONTENTS

Do not search in a wine for the reflection of an exact science! The formulas of scientific oenology are only a thin competition which does not know how to respect the mysteries of eternal creation.

—The Late JACQUES PERRIN, Château Beaucastel,
Châteauneuf du Pape

It is sad that few people understand naturally made, individual wines. Technology has progressed to the point that far too many wines lack the taste of their place of origin and resemble one another. Terroir, more than anything, is an expression of finesse and complexity.

—GÉRARD CHAVE, Domaine J. L. Chave, Hermitage

The only way of guaranteeing quality is to take a small quantity from the vineyard.

—The Late JACQUES REYNAUD, Château Rayas,
Châteauneuf du Pape

Filtering wine is like making love wearing a condom, and adding acidity to wine is like submerging the wine's cépage, terroir, vintage character, and personality behind a suit of armor.

—MICHEL CHAPOUTIER, Chapoutier, Hermitage

I am not an oenologist; if I wanted prosperity and security, I would work for the government.

—HENRI BONNEAU, Châteauneuf du Pape

Racing men like to say that a great horse usually has a great name—impressive and euphonious—and these three wines, Côte Rôtie, Châteauneuf du Pape, and white as well as red Hermitage, bear similar cachets.

Subtlety, that hackneyed wine word, is a cliché seldom employed in writing about Rhône wines; their appeal is totally unambiguous.

—A. J. LIEBLING, *Between Meals*

When I drink a great Rhône, it is as if my heart and palate have traded places.

—ROBERT M. PARKER, JR.

The first wine in the world without a single exception.

—THOMAS JEFFERSON (writing about white Hermitage in 1787)

INTRODUCTION

After two decades of traveling to the Rhône Valley—the thousands of wines tasted, the hundreds of vineyards, cellars, and growers visited—I feel incapable of expressing, in several short paragraphs, my feelings about a region so vast, not only with wine riches, but with centuries of history and spectacular natural beauty and resources. Pictures would certainly convince anyone with an eye for beauty or adventure to visit the area. A multitude of books have documented the Rhône's remarkable history. But how could I convey to you the splendor, the majesty, the value, and the sheer pleasure of these wines? I knew the only absolute way of doing this was to hand you a glass filled with this wondrous liquid. That of course I am able to do only indirectly, through the written word, and I realize that no matter how inspired, articulate, precise, enthusiastic, or vivid I may attempt to be, this prose, by any standard of measure, is wholly inadequate in portraying the magic and experience of a Guigal Côte Rôtie; a Vernay Condrieu; a Jaboulet, Chapoutier, or Chave Hermitage; a Clape Cornas; a Châteauneuf du Pape from Rayas, Bonneau, or Beaucastel; a Gigondas from Santa Duc; a Côtes du Rhône from Gramenon or Fonsalette; or the nectarlike Muscat Beaumes de Venise from Durban, to name just a few of the extraordinary wines that transcend normal wine vocabulary and establish new tasting parameters for even the most advanced wine enthusiast.

But try I must, because these are exhilarating as well as compelling wines. For many of them, their golden age was 2,000 years ago and it coincided with the Roman conquest of France (or Gaul, as it was then known). They are the products of France's oldest vineyards and have endured centuries of being ignored, misunderstood, undervalued, and, of course, unappreciated. Yet remarkably high standards of winemaking were maintained and the decade of the eighties brought the renewed interest, praise, respect, and recognition that so many of these wonderful wines merit.

They represent France's and the world's most underrated great wines, and this is their story, from the humble generic Côtes du Rhones, to the most sublime and celestial wines of Côte Rôtie, Hermitage, Condrieu, and Châteauneuf du Pape. The wines, the producers, their personalities, the vintages, their successes and failures are covered in detail. This is a comprehensive close-up look at the Rhône Valley, one of France's and the world's most compelling and fascinating wine-producing regions. No matter how persuasive and passionate the following prose might be, it cannot do these wines justice.

An Overview of the Appellations
of the Côtes du Rhône

APPELLATION	WHITE WINE	RED WINE	ROSÉ WINE	SPARKLING	FORTIFIED SWEET WINE
Northern Rhône					
Côte Rôtie		X			
Condrieu	X				
Château Grillet	X				
Hermitage	X	X			
Cornas		X			
Crozes-Hermitage	X	X			
St.-Joseph	X	X			
St.-Péray	X			X	
Southern Rhône					
Vacqueyras	X	X	X		
Châteauneuf du Pape	X	X			
Gigondas		X	X		
Tavel		X	X		
Lirac	X	X	X		
Côtes du Rhône-Villages	X	X	X		
Beaumes de Venise		X			X
Rasteau	X	X	X		X
Côtes du Rhône	X	X	X		
Coteaux du Tricastin	X	X	X		
Côtes du Ventoux	X	X	X		

HOW TO USE
THIS BOOK

The commentaries and evaluations of the growers and producers of the wines of the Rhône Valley and Provence presented in this book are extremely comprehensive and extensive. They are a product of a love affair with these wines that started on my first visit to that region in 1970. Since then I have followed the producers and their wines very closely, and in the course of the last two decades I have spent a considerable amount of time in the Rhône Valley visiting and tasting with as many of the producers as possible. These visits, together with the numerous tastings held both in my office and at the properties of the producers, have given me an insight and an appreciation of these wines far greater than I ever imagined.

It goes without saying that in evaluating wines professionally, proper glasses and correct serving temperature of the wine must be prerequisites to any objective and meaningful tasting. Traditionally, the best glasses for critical tasting have been those approved by the International Standards Organization. Called the ISO glass, it is tulip shaped and has been designed for tasting. However, in my office I also use several other types of glasses. One, called "L'Impitoyable" (the pitiless), is a very fine tasting glass. Much larger than the ISO glass, the Impitoyable glasses exaggerate the wine's bouquet, making flaws or defects much easier to spot. They are not good glasses to drink from in normal situations because their opening is so narrow, but for critical evaluation of a wine's aromatics they are excellent. I also use the Riedel glasses, which are also superb. These glasses are made in Austria and are widely available. As for the temperature of the wine, between 60°F to 65°F is best for both reds and whites. Too warm a temperature and the bouquet becomes diffuse and the taste flat. Too cold, and there is no discernible bouquet and the flavors are completely locked in by the chilling effect on the wine.

When I examine a wine critically, there is both a visual and physical examination. Against a white background the wine is first given a visual exam for its brilliance, richness, and intensity of color. For Rhône red wines, color is extremely important. Virtually all the great vintages share a very deep, rich, dark ruby color when young, whereas the poorer vintages often have weaker, less rich-looking colors because of poor weather and rain. So a young Rhône wine that is light in color, hazy or cloudy, or both, has serious problems. Certainly in 1967, 1970, 1978, 1989, 1990, 1991, and 1995 the general color of the red wines was very dark.

In looking at an older wine, the rim of the wine next to the glass should be examined for amber, orange, rusty, or brown colors. These are normal signs of maturity, but when they appear in a good vintage of a serious wine under six or seven years old something is awry. For example, young wines that have been sloppily made and exposed to unclean barrels or air will mature at an accelerated rate and take on the look of old wines when in fact they are still relatively young in years.

In addition to looking at the color of the wines, I examine the "legs" of the wine, which are the tears or residue of the wine that run down the inside of the glass. Rich vintages tend to have "good legs" because the grapes are rich in glycerol and sugar-producing alcohol, giving the wine a viscosity that causes this "tearing" effect. Examples of vintages that produced wines with good to excellent "legs" are 1995, 1994, 1991, 1990, 1989, 1985, 1981, 1978, and 1967.

After the visual examination is completed, the actual physical examination of the wine takes place. The physical exam is composed of two parts: the smell of the wine, which depends on the olfactory senses, and the taste of the wine, which is tested on the palate. After swirling a wine, the nose must be placed into the glass (not the wine) to smell the aromas that the wine is giving off. This is an extremely critical step because the aroma and odor of the wine will tell the examiner the ripeness and richness of the underlying fruit, the state of maturity, and whether there is anything unclean or otherwise suspicious about the wine. The smell of a wine, young or old, will tell a great deal about its quality, and no responsible professional taster understates the significance of a wine's odors and aromas, often called the nose or bouquet. Emile Peynaud, in his classic book on wine tasting, *Le Goût du Vin* (Bordas, 1983), states nine principal categories of wine aromas. They are:

1. Animal odors: smells of game, beef, venison
2. Balsamic odors: smells of pine trees, resin, vanilla
3. Woody odors: smells of new wood of oak barrels
4. Chemical odors: smells of acetone, mercaptan, yeasts, hydrogen sulfide, lactic and fermentation odor
5. Spicy odors: smells of pepper, cloves, cinnamon, nutmeg, ginger, truffles, anise, mint
6. Empyreumatic odors: smells of crème brûlée, smoke, toast, leather, coffee
7. Floral odors: smells of flowers, violets, roses, lilacs, jasmine
8. Fruity odors: smells of blackcurrants, raspberries, cherries, plums, apricots, peaches, figs
9. Vegetal odors: smells of herbs, tea, mushrooms, vegetables

The presence or absence of some or all of these aromas, their intensity, their complexity, their persistence, all serve to create the bouquet or nose of a wine that can be said to be distinguished and interesting, or flawed and simple.

Once the wine's aroma or bouquet has been examined thoroughly, the wine is tasted, slushed, or chewed around on the palate while one also inhales to release the wine's aromas. The weight, richness, depth, balance, and length of a wine are apparent from the tactile impression the wine leaves on the palate. Sweetness is experienced on the tip of the tongue, saltiness just behind the tongue's tip, acidity on the sides, and bitterness at the back. Most professional tasters will spit the wine out, although a bit of wine is swallowed. The finish or length of a wine, its ability to give off aromas and flavors even though it is no longer on the palate, is the major difference between a good young wine and a great young wine. When the flavor and the aroma of the wine seem to last and last on the palate, it is usually a great, rich wine. The great wines and great vintages are always characterized by the purity, opulence, richness, depth, and ripeness of the fruit from which the wines are made. When the wines have sufficient tannin and acidity, the balance is struck. It is these traits that separate many a great 1995, 1990, 1989, 1978, or 1967 from a good 1994, 1983, or 1981.

RATING THE PRODUCERS AND GROWERS

Who's who in the world of wine becomes readily apparent after years of tasting and visiting the vineyards and wine cellars of the world's producers and growers. Great producers are, unfortunately, still quite rare, but certainly more growers and producers today are making better wine, with better technology and more knowledge. For clarity, I have rated the producers and/or their wines on a five-star system, awarding five stars and an "outstanding" to those producers deemed to be the very best, four stars to those producers who are "excellent," three stars to "good" producers, and two stars or one star to those producers rated "average" and "below average." Since the aim of the book is to provide you with the names of the very best producers, the content is dominated by the top producers.

Those few growers/producers who have received five-star ratings are indeed those who make the world's finest wines and have been selected for this rating because of the following two reasons: they make the greatest wine of their particular viticultural region, and they are remarkably consistent and reliable even in mediocre and poor vintages. Ratings, whether they be specific numerical ratings of individual wines or classifications of growers, are always likely to create controversy among not only the growers but wine tasters themselves. But, if done impartially, with a global viewpoint and firsthand, on the premises ("sur place"), with knowledge of the wines, the producers, and the type and quality of the winemaking, such ratings can be reliable and powerfully informative. The important thing for readers to remember is that those growers/producers who received either a four-star or five-star rating are producers to search out; I suspect few consumers will ever be disappointed with one of their wines. The three-star-rated growers/producers are less consistent but can be expected to make average to above-average wines in the very good to excellent vintages. Their weaknesses can be either from the fact that their vineyards are not as strategically placed, or because for financial or other reasons they are unable to make the severe selections necessary to make only the finest quality wine.

Rating the growers/producers of the world's major viticultural regions is perhaps the most important point to this book. Years of wine tasting have taught me many things, but the more one tastes and assimilates the knowledge of the world's regions, the more one begins to isolate the handful of truly world-class growers and producers who seem to rise above the crowd in great as well as mediocre vintages. I always admonish consumers against blind faith in one grower or producer, or one specific vintage, but the producers and growers rated "outstanding" and "excellent" are as close to a guarantee of high quality as you are likely to find.

TASTING NOTES AND RATINGS

Whenever possible, all of my tastings are done in peer-group, single-blind conditions (meaning that the same type of wines are tasted against each other and the producers' names are not known). The ratings reflect an independent, critical look at the wines. Neither price nor the reputation of the producer/grower affects the rating in any manner. I spend three months of every year tasting in vineyards. During the other nine months of the year, six- and sometimes seven-day workweeks are devoted solely to tasting and writing. I do not participate in wine judgings or trade tastings for many reasons, but principal among these are the following: (1) I prefer to taste from an entire bottle of wine, (2) I find it essential to have properly sized and cleaned professional tasting glasses, (3) the temperatures of the wine must be correct, and (4) I prefer to determine the time allocated to the number of wines to be critiqued.

The numerical rating is a guide to what I think of the wine vis-à-vis its peer group. Certainly wines rated above 85 are good to excellent, and any wine rated 90 or above will be outstanding for its particular type. While some would suggest that scoring is not well suited to a beverage that has been romantically extolled for centuries, wine is no different from any other consumer product. There are specific standards of quality that full-time wine professionals recognize, and there are benchmark wines against which all others can be judged. I know of no one with three or four different glasses of wine in front of him, regardless of how good or bad the wines might be, who cannot say, "I prefer this one to that one." Scoring wines is simply taking a professional's opinion and applying a numerical system to it on a consistent basis. Moreover, scoring permits rapid communication of information to expert and novice alike.

The score given for a specific wine reflects the quality of the wine at its best. I often tell people that evaluating a wine and assigning a score to a beverage that will change and evolve in many cases for up to ten or more years is analogous to taking a photograph of a marathon runner. Much can be ascertained from a picture, but, like a moving object, the wine will also evolve and change. Wines from obviously badly corked or defective bottles are retasted, since a wine from such a single bad bottle does not indicate an entirely spoiled batch. Many of the wines reviewed have been tasted several times, and the score represents a cumulative average of the wine's performance in tastings to date. Scores do not reveal the most important facts about a wine. The written commentary that accompanies the ratings is a better source of information regarding the wine's style and personality, its relative quality level vis-à-vis its peers, and its relative value and aging potential than any score could ever indicate.

Here then is a general guide to interpreting the numerical ratings:

90–100 is equivalent to an A grade and should be given for an outstanding or special effort. Wines in this category are the very best produced of their type. There is a big difference between a 90 and a 99, but both are top marks. Few wines actually make it into this top category simply because there are not that many truly great wines.

80–89 is equivalent to a B and such a wine, particularly in the 85–89 range, is very good. Many of the wines that fall into this range often are great values as well. I have many of these wines in my personal cellar.

70–79 represents a C, or average mark, but obviously 79 is a much more desirable rating than 70. Wines that receive scores between 75 and 79 are generally pleasant, straightforward wines that lack complexity, character, or depth. If inexpensive, they may be ideal for uncritical quaffing.

Below 70 is a D or F (depending on where you went to school). It is a sign of an unbalanced, flawed, or terribly dull or diluted wine that is of little interest to the discriminating consumer.

In terms of awarding points, my scoring system gives a wine 50 points to start with. The wine's general color and appearance merit up to 5 points. Since most wines today have been well made thanks to modern technology and the increased use of professional oenologists, most tend to receive at least 4, often 5 points. The aroma and bouquet merit up to 15 points, depending on the intensity level and dimension of the aroma and bouquet as well as the wine's cleanliness. The flavor and finish merit up to 20 points, and again, intensity of flavor, balance, cleanliness, and depth and length on the palate are all important considerations when awarding points. Finally, the overall quality level or potential for further evolution and improvement—aging—merits up to 10 points.

Scores are important for the reader to gauge a professional critic's overall qualitative placement of a wine vis-à-vis its peers. However, it is also vital to consider the description of the wine's style, personality, and potential. No scoring system is perfect, but a system that provides for flexibility in scores, if applied by the same experienced taster without prejudice, (1) can quantify different levels of wine quality, and (2) can be a responsible, reliable, uncensored, and highly informative account that provides the reader with one professional's judgment. However, there can never be any substitute for your own palate nor any better education than tasting the wine yourself.

THE ROLE OF A WINE CRITIC

"A man must serve his time to every trade save censure—critics all are ready made."
—Lord Byron

It has been said often enough that anyone with a pen, notebook, and a few bottles of wine can become a wine critic. And that is exactly the way I started when, in late summer 1978 I sent out a complimentary issue of my wine journal, which was then called the *Baltimore/ Washington Wine Advocate.*

There were two principal forces that shaped my view of a wine critic's responsibilities. I was then, and remain today, significantly influenced by the independent philosophy of the well-known consumer advocate, Ralph Nader. Moreover, I was marked by the indelible impression left by my law school professors who pounded into their students' heads in the post-Watergate era a broad definition of conflict of interest. These two forces have governed the purpose and soul of my newsletter, *The Wine Advocate,* and my books.

In short, the role of the critic is to render judgments that are reliable. They should be based on extensive experience and a trained sensibility for whatever is being reviewed. In practical terms, this means the critic should be blessed with the following attributes.

Independence It is imperative for a wine critic to pay his own way. Gratuitous hospitality in the form of airline tickets, hotel rooms, guest houses, and so on should never be accepted either abroad or in this country. And what about wine samples? I purchase over 75% of the wines I taste, and while I have never requested samples, I do not feel it is unethical to accept unsolicited samples that are shipped to my office. Many wine writers claim that these favors do not influence their opinions. Yet how many people in any profession are prepared to bite the hand that feeds them? Irrefutably, my target audience is the wine consumer, not the wine trade. While it is important to maintain a professional relationship with the trade, I believe the independent stance required of a consumer advocate often, and not surprisingly, results in an adversarial relationship with the wine trade. It can be no other way. In order to pursue this independence effectively, it is imperative to keep one's distance from the trade. While this can be misinterpreted as aloofness, such independence guarantees hard-hitting, candid, and uninfluenced commentary.

Courage Courage manifests itself in what I call the "democratic tasting." Judgments are to be made solely on the basis of the product in the bottle, and not the pedigree, the price, the rarity, or one's like or dislike of the producer. The wine critic who is totally candid may be considered dangerous by the trade, but an uncensored, independent point of view is of paramount importance to the consumer. A judgment of wine quality must be based on what is in the bottle. This is wine criticism at its purest and most meaningful. In a tasting, a $10 bottle of petit château Pauillac (those lesser-known and -publicized Bordeaux estates) should have as much of a chance as a $75 bottle of Lafite-Rothschild or Latour. Overachievers are to be spotted, praised, and their names highlighted and shared with the consuming public. Underachievers should be singled out for criticism and called to account for their mediocrities. Few friends from the commerce of wine are likely to be earned for such outspoken and irreverent commentary, but wine buyers are entitled to such information. When a critic bases judgments on what others think, or on the wine's pedigree, price, or perceived potential, then wine criticism is nothing more than a sham.

Experience It is essential to taste extensively across the field of play to identify the benchmark reference points and to learn winemaking standards throughout the world. This is the most time-consuming and expensive aspect of wine criticism, as well as the most fulfilling for the critic, yet it is rarely followed. Lamentably, what so often transpires is that a tasting of 10 or 12 wines from a specific region or vintage will be held. The writer will then issue a definitive judgment on the vintage based on a microscopic proportion of the wines. This is as irresponsible as it is appalling. It is essential for a wine critic to taste as comprehensively as is physically possible. This means tasting every significant wine produced in a region or vintage before reaching qualitative conclusions. Wine criticism, if it is ever to be regarded as a serious profession, must be a full-time endeavor, not the habitat of part-timers dabbling in a field so complex and time-consuming. Wine and vintages, like everything in life, cannot be reduced to black and white answers.

It is also essential to establish memory reference points for the world's greatest wines. There is such a diversity of wine and multitude of styles that this may seem impossible. But tasting as many wines as one possibly can in each vintage, and from all of the classic wine regions, helps one memorize benchmark characteristics that form the basis for making comparative judgments between vintages, wine producers, and wine regions.

Individual Accountability While I have never found anyone's wine tasting notes compelling reading, notes issued by consensus of a committee are the most insipid, and often the most misleading. Judgments by committees tend to sum up a group's personal preferences. But how do they take into consideration the possibility that each individual may have reached the decision based on totally different criteria? Did one judge adore the wine because of its typicity while another decried it for such, or was the wine's individuality given greater merit? It is impossible to know. That is never in doubt when an individual authors a tasting critique.

Furthermore, committees rarely recognize wines of great individuality. A look at the results of tasting competitions reveals, sadly, that well-made mediocrities garner the top prizes. The misleading consequence is that blandness is elevated to the status of a virtue. Wines with great individuality and character will never win a committee tasting because at least one taster will find something objectionable about the wine. Can anyone name a great red or white wine that was produced by the consensus of a committee?

I have always sensed that individual tasters, because they are unable to hide behind the collective voice of a committee, feel a greater degree of accountability.

The opinion of an individual taster—despite the taster's prejudices and predilections— if reasonably informed and comprehensive is always a far greater guide to the ultimate quality of the wine than that of a committee. At least the reader knows where the individual stands, whereas with a committee, one is never quite sure.

The Emphasis on Pleasure and Value Too much wine writing focuses on glamour wines such as France's Burgundy and Bordeaux, and California's Cabernet Sauvignon and Chardonnay. These are important, and they make up the backbone of most serious wine enthusiast's cellars. But value and diversity in wine types must always be stressed. The unhealthy legacy of the English wine writing establishment that a wine has to taste bad young to be great old should be thrown out. Wines that taste great young, such as Chenin Blanc, Dolcetto, Beaujolais, Côtes du Rhone, Merlot, and Zinfandel, are no less serious or compelling because they must be drunk within a few years rather than cellared for a decade or more before consumption. Wine is, in the final analysis, a beverage of pleasure, and intelligent wine criticism should be a blend of both hedonistic and analytical schools of thought—to the exclusion of neither.

The Focus on Qualitative Issues It is an inescapable fact that too many of the world's renowned growers/producers have intentionally permitted production levels to soar to such extraordinary levels that many wines' personalities, concentration, and character are in jeopardy. While there remain a handful of fanatics who continue, at some financial sacrifice, to reject significant proportions of their harvest to ensure that only the finest quality wine is sold under their name, they are dwindling in number. For much of the last decade production yields throughout the world have broken records, with almost every new vintage. The results increasingly are wines that lack character, concentration, and staying power. The argument that more carefully and competently managed vineyards result in larger crops is nonsense.

In addition to high yields, advances in technology have provided the savoir faire to produce more correct wines, but the abuse of practices such as acidification and excessive fining and filtration have compromised the final product. These problems are rarely and inadequately addressed by the wine writing community. Wine prices have never been higher, but is the consumer always getting a better wine? Broad qualitative issues must always be given high priority.

Candor No one argues with the incontestable fact that tasting is a subjective endeavor. The measure of an effective wine critic should be the timely and useful rendering of an intelligent laundry list of good examples of different styles of winemaking in various price categories. Articulating in an understandable fashion why the critic finds the wines enthralling or objectionable is manifestly important to both the reader and the producer. The critic must always seek to educate, to provide meaningful guidelines, never failing to emphasize to the reader that there can never be any substitute for the consumer's palate, nor any better education than tasting the wine himself. The critic has the advantage of having access to the world's wine production and must try to minimize bias, yet the critic should always share with the reader his reasoning for bad reviews. For example, I will never be able to overcome my dislike for vegetal-tasting new world Cabernets, overtly herbaceous red Loire Valley wines, or excessively acidified new world whites.

My ultimate goal in writing about wines is to seek out the world's greatest wines and greatest wine values. But in the process of ferreting out those wines, I feel the critic should never shy away from criticizing those producers whose wines are found lacking. Given the fact that the consumer is the true taster of record, the "taste no evil" approach to wine writing serves no one but the wine trade. Constructive and competent criticism has proven it can benefit consumers because it forces underachievers to improve the quality of their fare, and by lauding overachievers, it encourages them to maintain high standards to the benefit of all who enjoy and appreciate good wine.

ABOUT THE BOOK'S ORGANIZATION

This book is broken down into three major parts: Part I, The Northern Rhône; Part II, The Southern Rhône; and Part III, Visitor's Guide to the Rhône Valley.

Within each of these parts, the sections are organized by appellation, followed by a small box of facts summarizing the wines of that area, introductory text about the appellation, a chart evaluating the growers and producers, and general comments about the recent vintages for that specific appellation. Afterward, the most significant growers and producers are listed alphabetically and their wines and winemaking styles are analyzed in detail. In short, each appellation is set up as follows:

1. The name of the appellation
2. An easy-to-access "facts box" summarizing in brief the salient points of that appellation
3. A quick reference chart to that appellation's best producers, top wines, and growers
4. A summary of recent vintages
5. Introductory text for that appellation
6. An alphabetical listing of the producers with commentary, tasting notes if relevant, and evaluations of their wines

THE
NORTHERN
RHÔNE

Côte Rôtie
Condrieu and Château Grillet
Hermitage
Cornas
Crozes-Hermitage
St.-Joseph
St.-Péray

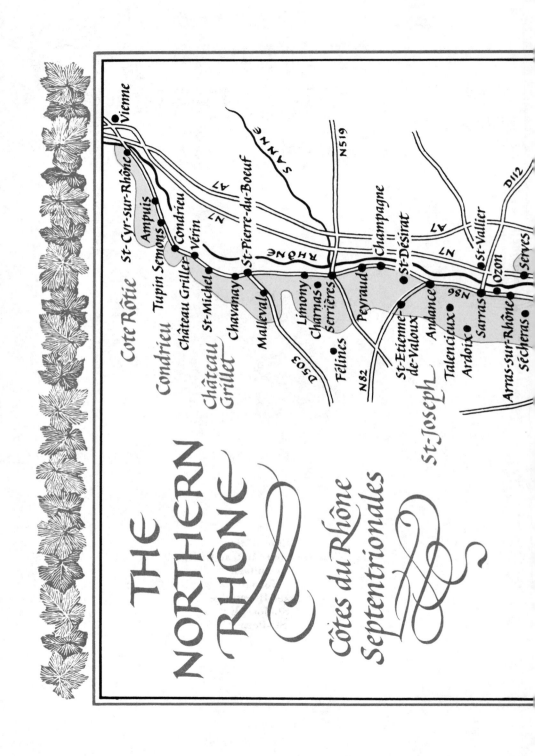

THE
NORTHERN
RHÔNE

Côtes du Rhône
Septentrionales

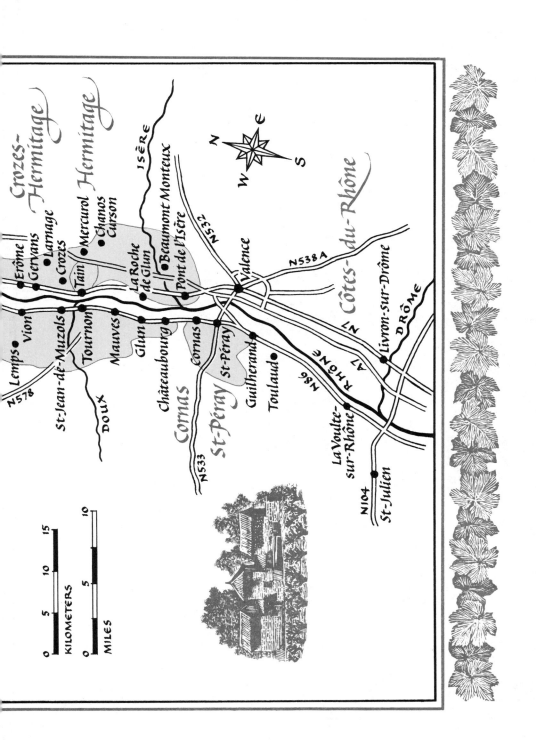

INTRODUCTION

The Rhône River starts as a trickle of water in the icy depths of Switzerland and passes in view of some of that country's best vineyards before it enters France 44 miles west of Geneva. It flows quickly through the gorges of the Jura Mountains in eastern France and then southwesterly until it intersects and absorbs the waters of another river, the Saône, at Lyons, France's second-largest city as well as a great gastronomic and commercial center. The northern viticultural region of the Rhône begins just 20 miles south of Lyons at Ampuis, where the turbulent river surges southward through steep hillsides. It is there that the wines of Côte Rôtie are made on the western bank. One hundred twenty-five miles later, at Valence, the vineyards of the northern Rhône terminate. In between there are eight major appellations and one simple Côtes du Rhône appellation. The two appellations of Hermitage and Crozes-Hermitage are the only wine zones to sit on the eastern bank of the Rhône. The others—Côte Rôtie, Condrieu, Château Grillet, St.-Joseph, Cornas, and St.-Péray—all sit on the western bank. Côte Rôtie and Cornas make only red wine. Condrieu, Château Grillet, and St.-Péray make white wine exclusively. Hermitage, St.-Joseph, and Crozes-Hermitage produce both red and white wine, with the great majority being red. Interestingly, there is no rosé made in the northern Rhône, except from the few areas entitled only to the generic Côtes du Rhône designation, although no important generic Côtes du Rhônes have been produced in the northern Rhône.

The most obvious geological characteristics of the northern Rhône are that the finest vineyards are planted on steep hillsides carved from soils made up primarily of granite. All of the best vineyards overlook the swift-moving, dangerously deep and swirling Rhône River.

The range and style of wines made here are considerable. At Côte Rôtie and Hermitage there are red wines that undoubtedly have the complexity and richness of the finest classified-growth Bordeaux or grand cru Burgundies. At Condrieu there are stunningly fragrant, exotic wines that are among the most pleasurable as well as rarest on the face of the earth. At Cornas several of the world's most massive and densest dry red table wines are produced. At the other appellations are wines of considerable value, but also boring, dull, lifeless wines. Yet all of them share one similarity: they have suffered virtual anonymity through most of this century, something that appears incomprehensible given their quality and the fact that they are made from the oldest vineyards in France as well as being produced in and around towns that have witnessed some of the most exciting history of France.

The geography, the climate, and of course the wines of the northern Rhône are very different from those of the southern Rhône. In the south, the wines can be the product of over a dozen different grape varieties, and in most cases at least three different grapes are used for making red wine and two to three for white wine. In the north, there are only four grape varieties (Marsanne, Roussanne, Viognier, and Syrah) permitted in the eight principal appellations. For red wine, the Syrah is the only accepted red varietal. For white wine, the fickle, rare Viognier is planted exclusively in Condrieu and at Château Grillet, as well as in Côte Rôtie. At St.-Joseph, Crozes-Hermitage, Hermitage, and St.-Péray, the favored white varietal is Marsanne, although ever so slowly Roussanne is making a comeback. While all of these grapes are grown in the southern Rhône, they do not play major roles in the winemaking there, but instead are supporting cast members; the Grenache, in both red and white colors, holds center stage.

The following sections will take you through the northern Rhône appellations starting in the north with Côte Rôtie and then proceeding south, terminating at St.-Péray, the final appellation of the northern Rhône. The quality of the wines, their characteristics, aging potential, as well as the quality of the growers and producers are analyzed in detail. Tasting notes of recent and older vintages are provided for all the leading producers. The northern Rhône produces three of the greatest wines in the world—the white wines of Condrieu and red wines of Côte Rôtie and Hermitage. The latter two are also remarkably long-lived. Most of my wine education started with the great classics of Bordeaux. It is these wines, from both humble and grand châteaus, that have given me such great satisfaction and pleasure in the past, and continue to do so today. However, the most exhilarating moments I have had have been not with a glass of Margaux or Pétrus in front of me, but with a mature, top Côte Rôtie or Hermitage. I believe anyone who gives these remarkable wines a chance will partake of a momentous gustatory experience.

SOME REFLECTIONS TEN YEARS AFTER THE FIRST EDITION

1. With only a handful of exceptions, particularly several single-vineyard Côte Rôties and Hermitages, and some of the prestige cuvées from the southern Rhône Valley, Rhône Valley wines continue to represent the greatest quality/price ratio of any top red wine region of the world.

Consumers must recognize that in the northern Rhône appellations of Côte Rôtie, Cornas, and Hermitage, the problem is similar to that in Burgundy—many producers making only microscopic quantities of wine. Even though this is a problem, most of the great cuvées of Hermitage can still be purchased from $35 to $50 a bottle. That is about half the price a grand cru Burgundy fetches. Even greater Syrah values exist in Cornas, as well as in Crozes-Hermitage and St.-Joseph, where a number of highly talented new producers have emerged in the last several years.

But the finest values of the entire Rhône Valley, if not all of France, for distinctive, long-lived red wines are in Châteauneuf du Pape and Gigondas. Most wines from these two scenic windswept areas still sell for a modest $18 to $25 a bottle! The prestige cuvées sell for an additional $30 to $50. For undeniable bargains, consider the top producers in the Côtes du Rhône, Côtes du Ventoux, and Côtes du Luberon. Their wines are generally available for under $15 a bottle. Most of these wines can be drunk immediately, or cellared for 4–5 years. Additionally, there are certain cuvées of Côtes du Rhône, such as the more expensive Fonsalette and Coudoulet, that can last 15–20 or more years. For example, I still have superb bottles of the 1966 and 1969 Fonsalette that exhibit no signs of decline. As wine insiders and passionate wine amateurs have long known, these profound examples remain the world's most underrated great wines.

2. Rhône Valley wines offer the broadest window of drinkability of any great wine in the world.

I continue to stress the fact that unlike young Bordeaux, virtually every red Rhône Valley wine, with the exception of Cornas and Hermitage, can generally be drunk when released.

Yet they will continue to evolve gracefully and drink well for 15–25 or more years in top vintages such as 1989, 1990, and 1995. Given their consistency in quality and performance, the top Rhône Valley wines possess a longevity potential equaled only by a handful of California Cabernets and the finest Bordeaux châteaus. In fact, among the Rhône Valley's wines, only Hermitage and Cornas are impenetrable when young, the former often needing a minimum of 10–15 years of cellaring before it can be drunk. I would safely bet that the 1989 and 1990 Jaboulet Hermitage La Chapelle, or the 1990 Hermitage from Gérard Chave, will outlive virtually any wine produced in Bordeaux in those same vintages.

3. Rhône wines offer extraordinary flexibility with food.

Diners are flocking to more casual, less pretentious restaurants such as grills, bistros, and trattorias. And why not? The service is friendly rather than haughty, and the price for a meal will not empty your pocketbook. Moreover, the food is substantial, aromatic, flavorful, and satisfying. For those same reasons, Rhône wines have always been the wines of choice among the Swiss, Belgians, French, Dutch, and Swedes. Of course, Bordeaux and top Burgundies are more prestigious, and have been fawned over by the wine press for centuries. But if you experiment with intensely flavored, aromatic dishes, you will see that Rhône wines often work better because, as a general rule, they are not encumbered by gobs of new oak, nor are they weighted down with harsh tannins. The decade of the nineties has ushered in a healthy mentality that demands total satisfaction and value. Few regions in the world are better positioned to satisfy the economic and hedonistic needs of the wine consumer than the Rhône Valley.

CÔTE RÔTIE

One of France's Most Historic
and Greatest Red Wines

CÔTE RÔTIE AT A GLANCE

Appellation creation:	October 18, 1940.
Type of wine produced:	Red wine only.
Grape varieties authorized:	Syrah and Viognier (up to 20% Viognier can be added, but as a rule few producers utilize more than 5% in their wines).
Total surface area:	497 acres.
Quality level:	At least good; at best exceptional; among the finest red wines in the world.
Aging potential:	The finest age 5–30 years.
General characteristics:	Fleshy, rich, very fragrant, smoky, full-bodied, stunning wines.
Greatest recent vintages:	1995, 1991, 1990, 1989, 1988, 1985, 1983, 1978, 1976, 1969.
Price range:	$30–$50, except for Guigal's and Chapoutier's single vineyard and/or luxury cuvées, which cost $150 or more.
Aromatic profile:	These intensely fragrant wines offer compelling bouquets showcasing scents and flavors of cassis, black raspberries, smoke, bacon fat, violets, olives, and grilled meats. For wines where a healthy dosage of new oak casks are employed, add vanillin, toast, and *pain grillé* aromas.

Textural profile: These are elegant yet authoritatively powerful wines that are often chewy and deep. They are usually medium- to full-bodied, with surprisingly good acid levels for such ripeness and power. Tannin levels are usually moderate.

The Côte Rôtie appellation's most profound wines:

Chapoutier La Mordorée
Domaine Clusel-Roch Les Grandes Places
Gentaz-Dervieux †
Jean-Michel Gérin Les Grandes Places
Guigal Château D'Ampuis
Guigal La Landonne
Guigal La Mouline

Guigal La Turque
Jean-Paul et Jean-Luc Jamet
René Rostaing Côte Blonde
René Rostaing Côte Brune La Landonne
L. de Vallouit Les Roziers
Vidal-Fleury La Chatillonne

RATING THE CÔTE RÔTIE PRODUCERS

* * * *(OUTSTANDING)

Chapoutier (La Mordorée)
Domaine Clusel-Roch (Les Grandes Places)
Marius Gentaz-Dervieux †
Guigal (Château D'Ampuis)
Guigal (La Landonne)
Guigal (La Mouline)

Guigal (La Turque)
Jean-Paul et Jean-Luc Jamet
René Rostaing (Côte Blonde)
René Rostaing (Côte Brune La Landonne)
L. de Vallouit (Les Roziers)
Vidal-Fleury (La Chatillonne)

* * *(EXCELLENT)

Bernard Burgaud
Domaine Clusel-Roch (other cuvées)
Henri Gallet
Vincent Gasse
Jean-Michel Gérin (Les Grandes Places)
Guigal (Côtes Brune et Blonde)

Michel Ogier
René Rostaing (regular cuvée)
René Rostaing (Côte Brune La Viaillère) (since 1991)
Vidal-Fleury (Côte Brune et Blonde)

* * *(GOOD)

Gilles Barge (including Pierre Barge)
Guy et Frédéric Bernard
Gérard Bonnefond
Domaine de Bonserine (Domaine de la Rousse)
Emile Champet
Joel Champet (La Viaillère)
Chapoutier (regular cuvée)

Domaine Clusel-Roch (regular cuvée)
Delas Frères (Les Seigneurs de Maugiron)
Albert Dervieux-Thaize ‡
Yves Gangloff
Jean-Michel Gérin (Champin de Seigneur)
Paul Jaboulet-Aîné (Les Jumelles)
Robert Jasmin (***/****)
Lyliane Saugère

† Gentaz retired following the 1992 vintage and his vineyard holdings are now farmed by René Rostaing, a 5-star producer.
‡ Dervieux-Thaize, retired since 1990, leases his vineyards to René Rostaing.

Côte Rôties have become among the most fashionable and popular wines of the Rhône Valley. Whether it is the extraordinary, sometimes explosive perfume often consisting of cassis, raspberries, olives, fried bacon fat, and smoke, or the cascade of velvety, berry-flavored fruit flavors, Côte Rôtie is an undeniably seductive, voluptuous wine that one needs little experience to appreciate.

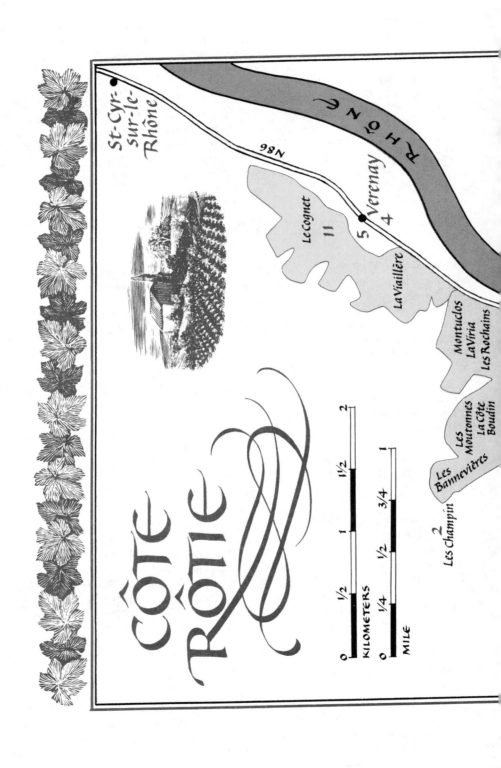

CÔTE RÔTIE

St-Cyr-sur-le-Rhône

RHÔNE

98N

Verenay
5 4
Le Cognet
11
La Viaillère
Montuclos
La Viria
Les Rochains
Les Moutonnes
La Côte Boudin
Les Bannevières
Les Champin
2

KILOMETERS
0   ½   1   1½   2

MILE
0   ¼   ½   ¾   1

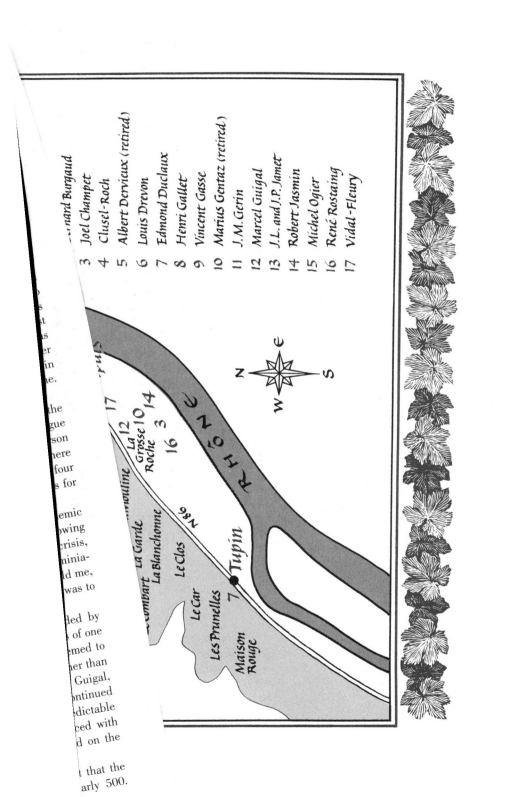

... nard Burgaud
3 Joel Champet
4 Clusel-Roch
5 Albert Dervieux (retired)
6 Louis Drevon
7 Edmond Duclaux
8 Henri Gallet
9 Vincent Gasse
10 Marius Gentaz (retired)
11 J.M. Gerin
12 Marcel Guigal
13 J.L. and J.P. Jamet
14 Robert Jasmin
15 Michel Ogier
16 René Rostaing
17 Vidal-Fleury

The first view one has of Côte Rôtie (literally translated, "the roasted hillside"), which sits on the western bank of the Rhône with a perfect southeasterly exposure, is unforgettable. Just 20 minutes by car south of Lyons is the tiny, rather drab town of Ampuis. Looming over the town are the precipitously steep terraced slopes (a 55° gradient in some spots) of Côte Rôtie. Except for some vineyards in Banyuls and along the Mosel River, there are none in Europe that appear so vertical and formidable as those of Côte Rôtie. Cultivated entirely by hand, the narrow terraces of vines and difficult footing have made the use of machines impossible. In many places even oxen and horses are useless. Undoubtedly, the huge expense of human labor has caused many a less hearty grower and winemaker to look elsewhere for a career in winemaking.

Côte Rôtie, the most northern of the Rhône Valley's appellation, has a remarkably long history and, of course, the usual legends surrounding the established facts. One school of thought attributes the origin of these vineyards to the ancient Greeks, claiming they intro-duced viticulture to Côte Rôtie in the sixth century B.C. This line of thought has its critics who claim it was the Romans, in the first century, who built the network of terraces and planted vines on these steep hillsides. It is this latter theory that seems more plausible, given the fact that Vienne is a Roman center. Vienne, only five miles away, is still a hallowed site for Roman ruins, particularly the temples of Livia and Augustus, believed to have been constructed 100 years before Christ's birth. Whichever theory is true, it seems doubtful that the look of Côte Rôtie's hillside vineyards has changed much over the last 2,000 years. There can be no doubt, however, that the size of the area under vine has increased, and will continue to do so given the great demand for this wine and the high and higher prices Côte Rôtie can command. Côte Rôtie's current-day popularity began the late seventies, benefiting enormously from the world's increased interest in fine wine. But this was not always the case.

Côte Rôtie's fame was such that in the eighteenth century Thomas Jefferson visited region, describing the vineyards of Côte Rôtie as "a string of broken hills extending a lea on the river from the village of Ampuis to the town of Condrieux." Moreover, Jeffer apparently admired the wines enough to consummate a purchase. In 1787 he wrote, "T is a quality which keeps well, bears transportation and that cannot be drunk under years." Jefferson went on to buy Côte Rôtie, having it bottled and put in wooden case shipment to his home in Paris.

About 100 years later, as the nineteenth century drew to a close, the phylloxera epid devastated Côte Rôtie, as it did nearly every major viticultural region of France. Foll the phylloxera came two world wars sandwiched around the century's worst economic the Great Depression of 1929. These events seemed to further push this backwoods, ture viticultural region to the brink of extinction. As Marius Gentaz-Dervieux once to it was easier to make a living growing apricots in the post–World War II era than it grow grapes.

However, the world's growing interest in wine, and the higher prices deman France's best products began to benefit the Côte Rôtie growers. But it was the labor Côte Rôtie producer, Etienne Guigal, and the praise these wines received, that se awaken an entire wine world to the realization that France produced great wines oth those from Champagne, Burgundy, and Bordeaux. The ascendency of the house of which coincided with the early eighties' explosive interest in fine wine, has c uninterrupted. While all the attention lavished on Guigal at first met with pr jealousy from other Côte Rôtie producers, those raw emotions have been repla respect and admiration as foreigners from around the world can now be spotte streets of the one-horse village of Ampuis.

The growing enthusiasm for the wines of Côte Rôtie is attested to by the fac acreage under vine has increased in the last 37 years from 121 acres to ne

Production has doubled from just over 40,000 cases of wine in 1987 (when the first edition of this book was published) to nearly 80,000 cases in 1995 (still far less than several châteaux from Bordeaux's famed Médoc region). This includes all of the hillside vineyards and a burgeoning, even alarming, number of new vineyards above the hills on the plateau behind the town of Ampuis. Much of the plateau is officially within the Côte Rôtie appellation boundaries, and expansion will no doubt continue in these less desirable spots. While wine produced from the plateau can be very good, it will never be as majestic as that from the slopes of Côte Rôtie. For example, the plateau vineyards yield 15–30% more juice than those from the hillsides, the density of vines per acre is much lower, and the plateau vineyards do not enjoy the near perfect south/southeasterly exposure to the sun that the hillside vineyards possess.

With respect to the hillsides, there are two of them, one called the Côte Blonde, and the other the Côte Brune. From a surface perspective, the Côte Brune is significantly larger. Both are frighteningly steep (they are almost 1,000 feet in height and have a gradient of 30–55 degrees) as well as stunningly photogenic. In addition to the sheer precipitousness of these vineyards, the old Roman terraces that snake horizontally, and sometimes vertically, across these slopes, are a majestic sight. On each terrace, the vertical pruning system, with each vine specially trained by the Guyot method, makes for additional beauty. (Guyot was a respected nineteenth-century scientist who specialized in vine growing.) Each vine must be held into these narrow escarpments by vertical stakes that cannot be driven into the rocky ground without punishing labor. When standing on one of the terraces, looking down over the slope, the impression is that should one fall off, there is a high probability of being impaled by the vertical trellising system on a lower terrace. Despite the justifiable concern about the explosion of new vineyard planting on the plateau, a young generation of growers dedicated to reclaiming more of the hillside vineyards, aided by new technology and small, powerful bulldozers, has actually led to reclamations of some of the very steep hillside slopes. In fact, more than one grower told me that most of the new planting being done in 1996 constitutes the rediscovery and resurrection of hillside slopes, rather than additional plantings on the plateau.

Local legend gets credit for giving the two slopes, the Côte Blonde and Côte Brune, their names. According to history, a feudal landlord named Lord Maugiron bequeathed these hillsides to his two daughters, one with golden blond hair and the other with dark brown. Visitors to Côte Rôtie will not find a marker dividing the line between the two hillsides, but it begins just south of a small Rhône Valley tributary, Ruisseau de Reynard, that can be spotted in the southern part of Ampuis, not far from the Guigal cellars. Certainly the soil composition of each slope is different, and the type of wine produced is profoundly marked by the dissimilar soils. The Côte Brune, the northernmost slope, has more clay and iron, the Côte Blonde more sand, granulite, and limestone. How this affects the resulting wines is usually quite obvious.

As a rule, the wines from the Côte Brune are darker in color, noticeably tannic, with more power and obvious weight. They are usually less flattering to drink in their youth, leading most observers to claim they are Côte Rôtie's longest-lived wines. The wines from the Côte Blonde are less tannic, more perfumed and fragrant, round, supple, and more easily approached when young. Côte Rôtie's appellation laws permit the use of up to 20% Viognier, the fragrant white wine grape that has made Côte Rôtie's closest vinous neighbor, the appellation of Condrieu, world famous. Virtually all of the Viognier planted in Côte Rôtie is on the Côte Blonde. This grape does not flourish in the heavy clay-and-iron-based soils of the Côte Brune. Few winemakers at Côte Rôtie use more than 5–10% in their blends, but those that do all concur that Viognier gives considerable finesse and distinction to the already majestic bouquet of a Côte Rôtie. Moreover, it adds velvet to the wine's texture. One hundred percent Syrah, the only varietal authorized in the northern Rhône, is the uncontested preference of most winemakers. Clearly the modern-day trend has been to reduce the amount of Viognier in the wine, opting instead for wines that for all intents and purposes are 100% Syrah.

The two hillsides consist of increasingly famous vineyard sites as well as equally renowned lieux-dits, or place names. There are nearly five dozen officially recognized vineyards or lieux-dits. On the Côte Blonde, the most famous vineyards are La Mouline (owned exclusively by the Guigal family), La Chatillonne (marketed under the name of Vidal-Fleury but owned by Guigal), La Garde (managed by René Rostaing), and Le Clos. On the Côte Brune, the names La Viaillère (partially owned by Dervieux-Thaize and managed by René Rostaing), La Landonne (Guigal and Rostaing are its most prominent proprietors), La Chevalière (owned by several growers, most notably Jasmin), La Turque (a Guigal vineyard), and Les Grandes Places (Clusel-Roch and J. M. Gérin designate their top wines with this vineyard's name) can all be found on bottles of Côte Rôtie. Other vineyards of Côte Rôtie include La Viria, Le Truchet, Les Triottes, Tharamon de Gron, Les Sévenières, Rosier, Les Rochains, Les Prunelles, La Pommière, Le Pavillon Rouge, Nève, Les Moutonnes, Le Moulin, Montuclos, Montmain, Le Mollar, Les Lézardes, Lancement, Les Journaries, Janville, La Guillambaude, La Balaiyat, Le Grand Taille, La Garelle, La Giroflavie, Les Germines, Les Gagères, La Fuzonne, Le Fourvier, Le Cret, La Côte Baudin, Corps des Loups, Combe de Calon, Le Combart, Le Cognet, Chez Guerard, Chez Gaboulet, Le Chavaroches, Chambretout, Le Car, La Brocarde, Les Bannevières, La Blanchonne, Bassemon, and Les Arches. Nevertheless, the vast majority of Côte Rôties on the market will not be designated by the name of a vineyard, but simply "Côte Rôtie" or "Côte Rôtie Brune et Blonde," the former referring to the fact that the wine is made from a blend of grapes from the plateau, plateau/hillside, and the latter, a wine produced exclusively from hillside vineyards.

For the last decade, the production of high-quality Côte Rôtie has been dominated by the Guigal family, who has increased their vineyard holdings and taken the quality of winemaking to the highest possible level. Their winemaking philosophy has also had a profound influence on other growers, some of whom remain vociferous in their criticism of the Guigals' introduction of new oak barrels to age Côte Rôties, and of their concept of vineyard-designated, luxury-priced Côte Rôties. Despite some philosophical disagreements of how Côte Rôtie is to be made and aged, there is no question that the overall quality of winemaking in this tiny appellation is extremely high. Guigal does indeed produce the appellation's most glamorous wines, but superb Côte Rôtie is also made by others (see my classification of producers).

There appear to be three distinct styles favored by Côte Rotie producers. I have labeled them traditionalists, liberators, and revolutionaries. *Traditionalists* are resistant to changing the way things have been done, and continue to produce Côte Rôtie the way it was made 50–100 years ago. Some of these wines can be marvelous, but they can possess off aromas, flawed because unsanitary, old barrels are used. Moreover, the refusal to destem the grapes, even in years when the stems are not ripe, also results in vegetal wines. *Liberators* are, in essence, liberals (in the traditional, nonpolitical meaning of the word), flexible and open-minded winemakers who weigh the advantages of the old methods with those of modern-day techniques. The largest group of Côte Rôtie producers falls within this category. The last group are those I call *revolutionaries*. This group has largely repudiated ancient methods in the cellar, but not in the vineyard. In fact, many of these producers are the architects behind Côte Rôtie's greatest wines. What do they share in common? They have decided to (1) reduce yields, (2) take risks by harvesting late, gathering in very ripe fruit, and (3) utilize high percentages of new oak casks for aging.

Traditionalists

Emile Champet
Joel Champet
Delas Frères
Albert Dervieux-Thaize

Marius Gentaz-Dervieux
Robert Jasmin
Vidal-Fleury

Liberators

Gilles Barge
Pierre Barge
Guy et Frédéric Bernard
Bernard Burgaud
Yves Cuilleron
Edmond Duclaux
Pierre Gaillard

Henri Gallet
Paul Jaboulet-Aîné
Jean-Paul et Jean-Luc Jamet
Michel Ogier
René Rostaing
L. de Vallouit

Revolutionaries

Domaine de Bonserine
Chapoutier
Domaine Clusel-Roch
Yves Gangloff

Vincent Gasse
Jean-Michel Gérin
Marcel Guigal
François Villard

RECENT VINTAGES

1995   For a handful of producers (Guigal, Chapoutier, and René Rostaing), 1995 turned out to be an exceptional vintage. Much like 1994, the summer was warm, even hot at times, with just barely enough rain. Like 1991, 1992, 1993, and 1994, September began on a positive note, but on September 9 the rains began. Intermittently showery weather followed for the next ten consecutive days. Those producers who felt 1995 was a replay of 1994, where the rains continued throughout the entire month of September, tended to harvest too soon, picking Syrah that was not physiologically ripe. These wines have high levels of acidity. If these same producers did not destem in 1995, they served only to increase the impression of greenness and tart acidity. While these producers have turned out good cuvées of Côte Rôtie, the sharp acidity gives the wines a shrill, compressed character. Producers who took the risk and delayed their harvests were rewarded with superb weather after September 20. Grapes picked at the end of September and the beginning of October were not only physiologically ripe, but had retained surprising levels of acidity. As Marcel Guigal has so correctly said, 1995 can be a great vintage, similar to 1985, but with more acidity. Michel Chapoutier felt that those who waited until early October to harvest, both in Côte Rôtie and Hermitage, have had an exceptionally great year, in the same mold as such legendary Rhône vintages as 1947, 1961, and 1990. The vintage's three stars, Guigal, Chapoutier, and Rostaing, all agree that yields were extremely low for their wines, with the average production down by at least 10%. All in all, this will be an inconsistent vintage, with the exceptional wines carrying, and possibly distorting, the vintage's reputation. One thing is certain, the 1995s, because of their refreshing acidity and high extraction, will be very long-lived by Côte Rôtie standards.

1994   A torridly hot summer presaged what looked to be a great vintage. On September 7 a series of weather depressions began to sweep across France, dumping tremendous amounts of rain. The rain never really stopped until the end of September, and most producers had to harvest during or between showery periods. Fortunately, the grapes were thick-skinned because of the abnormally hot summer, followed by a cold September. The quality is far from exceptional. This has turned out to be a good to very good year.

1993 Following what had been a cool summer, tumultuous weather during the month of September dumped record quantities of rain on Côte Rôtie. Rot spread quickly, resulting in the most disappointing vintage for Côte Rôtie since 1984 and 1977. Notwithstanding the group of generally dreadful wines, several producers managed to make good wines. Chapoutier's luxury cuvée, La Mordorée, is the wine of the vintage. René Rostaing produced surprisingly ripe wines for such a difficult year. Finally, it appears that Marcel Guigal has turned in good efforts with his single-vineyard Côte Rôties. Nevertheless, this remains a very distressing vintage of hollow, tannic wines that are thin, acidic, and astringent.

1992 A decent crop size survived the uncertainties of poor September weather to produce sound, medium-bodied, fruity wines that, for the most part, need to be consumed before they turn 10–12 years of age. Once again, Guigal's single-vineyard Côte Rôties, as well as Chapoutier's La Mordorée, are unbelievably concentrated and rich. They stand out well above the crowd of mediocrities. At best, 1992 is an average quality vintage with a handful of excellent to outstanding wines.

1991 Initially, when discussing this vintage with Côte Rôtie producers I was in the minority, preferring it ever so slightly to 1990. Now that the wines have had nearly six years of aging, it is apparent that 1991 has turned out to be a great vintage for Côte Rôtie, with classic, concentrated, potentially long-lived wines that are beautiful examples of the appellation. Successes can be found everywhere. This vintage has no shortage of truly profound wines. Moreover, the vintage produced a large crop, and the production of 41 hectoliters per hectare (about 2.3 tons of fruit per acre) was one of the highest ever recorded in Côte Rôtie. To put that in perspective, such yields would look absurdly tiny in Burgundy, but in Côte Rôtie, it is considered a hugely abundant crop!

1990 This vintage is just beginning to reveal secondary aromas and offer delicious drinking. The incredibly hot growing season has shaped the wines, although less than one might expect. I had always expected to taste more roasted flavors than I have found. This was a great vintage for such up-and-coming young stars as Clusel-Roch, J. M. Gérin, and Jamet. It was also a breakthrough vintage for Chapoutier's La Mordorée, and once again, Guigal led all producers with splendid single-vineyard Côte Rôties. These wines appear to be on a slightly faster revolutionary track than the 1991s. This is an excellent to outstanding vintage.

1989 A large crop of low-acid, fleshy wines was produced. Interestingly, producers either acidified (illegal under French law, but often done) or panicked because of exceptionally hot weather in September and picked too soon, when the grapes may have been ripe, but the stems were not. The result was wines with a certain greenness and more noticeably tart character. Aside from the handful of irregularities in 1989, this is a fine vintage that produced beautifully scented, fleshy wines that continue to age well. Guigal, Chapoutier, Clusel-Roch, Michel Ogier, Jamet, Gentaz-Dervieux, Vincent Gasse, and Henri Gallet produced top-flight wines. This vintage should continue to age well. It will be interesting to see how 1989 and 1990 hold up against 1991, the latter vintage being underrated vis-à-vis 1989 and 1990, but now appearing to be at least their equal.

1988 This has turned out to be an outstanding vintage with many great wines. However, it remains closed and tannic. Unlike so many of Côte Rôtie's northern neighbor's wines (the 1988 red Burgundies), the 1988 Côte Roties possess the depth, richness, and extract to stand up to their structure. The wines remain exceptionally promising, but they are still young and in need of further aging. Patience will be a virtue.

1987   Despite the fact that the summer was not particularly hot, and the month of September was not especially favorable, the 1987 Côte Rôties have consistently tasted far better than expected. In fact, Guigal's single-vineyard cuvées are exceptional, and, while fully mature, they are capable of lasting another decade. Most other Côte Rôties need to be drunk up. They are light, but surprisingly fruity and well balanced. Although this will never be considered a great vintage, it is underrated.

1986   Côte Rôtie received a great deal of rain in late August and early September, but the harvest occurred under ideal conditions. The grapes were plentiful and healthy, and while early reports that this was a very good, abundant vintage of quick-maturing wines seemed accurate in the late eighties, time has only made this vintage appear far more irregular than initially believed. While some top wines were produced by the likes of Guigal, too many wines possess astringent tannin, a hollow midsection, and a green pepper component. Overall, this is an average-quality vintage.

1985   Côte Rôtie enjoyed exceptional success in 1985, harvesting an abundant crop of very ripe fruit. The wines are splendidly concentrated, deeply colored, low in acidity, but magnificently perfumed, even when young. They have continued to develop beautifully, and nearly every Côte Rôtie producer has made top-quality wines that should continue to drink well for another 8–10 years, even longer for the single-vineyard wines of Guigal. This is one of the modern-day reference point vintages for opulent and seductive Côte Rôtie.

1984   These wines have continued to take on green flavors, and their tannin levels now tend to dominate whatever fruit they possessed. The 1984 vintage was best consumed in its youth, before the wines turned 10 years of age. Guigal's La Mouline is a singularly delicious, nearly outstanding wine, but even it needs drinking up. Overall, this is a below-average-quality year that is now largely faded.

1983   Once considered a great, classic year of tannic, concentrated, vin de garde wines, the 1983s have continued to perplex and frustrate their admirers for nearly 14 years. Patience is definitely required, and there is no shortage of revisionists beginning to decry the fact that the wines taste too tannic. Guigal's single-vineyard cuvées are perfection, and such producers as Levet and Gentaz-Dervieux turned in noteworthy efforts. The jury is still out with respect to wines from Rostaing and his father-in-law, Dervieux-Thaize. It seems highly likely that some 1983s will dry out before they ever fully blossom. The great 1983s will continue to drink well for another 10–15 + years.

1982   A huge crop of very ripe fruit was harvested under torrid weather conditions. As in 1983, there were numerous fermentation problems, but most of the top producers admirably met the challenge. The 1982s are among the most voluptuous, seductive, and flattering Côte Roties produced in the last 20 years. Acidity was low, alcohol levels were high, and the wines were delicious from birth. Guigal's 1982s are sumptuous, and should continue to drink well for another decade. Other producers, such as Gentaz-Dervieux, Barge, and Champet, fashioned very fine Côte Rôties that need to be drunk up before the end of the century.

1981   The least successful vintage for Côte Rôtie during the decade of the eighties, the 1981s have largely faded, to the surprise of no one. They began life as compact, one-dimensional wines. Among recent vintages, only 1984 and 1993 have turned out so many uninspiring wines.

1980   A terribly underrated vintage, the 1980s have been fully mature since the beginning of the nineties. The wines continue to drink surprisingly well, holding their color, fruit, and style. Guigal's La Mouline and La Landonne are exceptional wines in this vintage, with La Mouline a candidate for France's wine of the vintage (along with Burgundy's Domaine de la Romanée–Conti la Tâche). There is no reason to defer your gratification as these wines need to be drunk over the next 5–7 years.

1979   As is the tendency everywhere after a superb vintage, the subsequent year becomes lost in the hype and publicity surrounding "the great one." Such was the problem for the 1979s, conceived in the shadow of the 1978s, the northern Rhône's finest overall vintage since 1961. The Côte Rôties are all fully mature except for Guigal's La Landonne and Dervieux-Thaize's La Viaillère. The 1979s are rich, full-bodied, rather chunky wines with good character. These wines need to be drunk up, although Guigal's single-vineyard wines will keep for another 10–15 years.

1978   A memorable vintage, the 1978 Côte Rôties are splendidly concentrated, impeccably balanced, gorgeously perfumed, and will keep improving for another decade. Everyone did something special in 1978. Until the Guigal family assumed control in 1985, this was the last top vintage for the house of Vidal-Fleury. Guigal's La Mouline and La Landonne possess the stuff of legends, and are likely to be immortalized along with the 1929 and 1945 Mouton-Rothschild, or 1947 Cheval Blanc and Pétrus. 1978 is Côte Rôtie at its most magnificent—a legendary vintage!

Older Vintages

Given the minuscule production of Côte Rôtie, it appears rarely on the auction market, and the older vintages are likely to come only out of some remarkably perceptive collector's cave. Nineteen seventy-seven was a viciously cruel vintage for France, and lousy in Côte Rôtie. Nineteen seventy-six is a great vintage in Côte Rôtie and the wines can be kept for another five or so years, much like the Burgundies of that year. The 1975 vintage was a disastrously bad one, and 1974 almost as poor. Nineteen seventy-three was adequate, 1972 better than elsewhere in France, 1971 very good, but now showing signs of fatigue, and 1970 very much the same.

In the sixties, 1969 was a fabulously profound vintage for Côte Rôtie. The La Mouline of that year is one of the single finest wines I have ever tasted. Nineteen sixty-four is an excellent vintage, as is 1961, but it is very unlikely that any of these wines will be found in the marketplace.

GILLES BARGE* * *

Address: Le Carcan
         Route de Boucharey
         69420 Ampuis
Tel: 4-74-56-13-90
Fax: 4-74-56-10-98
Wines produced: Condrieu, Côte Rôtie
Surface area: 12.35 acres
Production: 30,000 bottles
Upbringing: 2 years minimum in oak
Average age of vines: oldest 50 years; half 25 years; some young vines
Percentage of Viognier: 5%

Gilles Barge, son of Pierre Barge, has assumed full control and authority over this small domaine. Gilles, who is also the president of the Côte Rôtie growers' syndicate, is one of those rare individuals who seems to sense winemaking from a global point of view. An articulate man, he spoke out strongly against filtration, which he experimented with years ago only to be saddened by the results. His wines spend two years in large wooden foudres (oak casks), although in 1985 he purchased six new Burgundy barrels, openly admitting that his use of new oak barrels was influenced by Guigal's belief in them. The Barge family owns and rents 12.35 acres of vines of which 80% are on the Côte Brune. Another 2 acres are leased from other growers. His Côte Rôtie is made with 5% Viognier. The wiry Barge thinks most vintages of his Côte Rôtie are at their best between 5 and 10 years of age, but he claims great vintages such as 1978 will keep 20 years. Gilles has also begun to produce several barrels of Condrieu each year. In most vintages Barge bottles the wine as he sells it, leading to an annoying level of bottle variation. Before 1992, he and his father offered two separate Côte Rôties under their respective names. In top years, 200–250 cases of a special cuvée called Goutillonnage are produced, but I have never seen or tasted it. This is a good source for rustic Côte Rôtie. His 1992 and 1993 Côte Rôties were, sadly, not impressive. His other successful vintages were 1983 and 1978.

VINTAGES

1991—Côte Rôtie (Gilles Barge)   Gilles Barge's excellent 1991 Côte Rôtie is typical of
·   this fine vintage. Dark ruby/purple, with a fragrant nose of underbrush, black fruits,
88   and toast, this dense, concentrated, medium- to full-bodied wine exhibits soft tannins, low acidity, and gobs of rich fruit. Drink it over the next 5–7 years. Last tasted 9/94.

1991—Côte Rôtie (Pierre Barge)   Pierre Barge, the father of Gilles Barge, produced a
·   1991 that appears slightly better than his 1990. Both are relatively light yet elegant
85   wines, with the 1991 enjoying more ripeness and fruit, as well as a longer finish. It is a soft, gentle wine that should be consumed over the next 5–6 years. Last tasted 9/94.

1990—Côte Rôtie (Gilles Barge)   The 1990 Côte Rôtie was disappointingly light, soft,
·   and fluid in cask, but now that it is in the bottle, it is displaying more grip and
85   extract. While it is hardly a great effort from Barge, it does reveal spicy oak and black-raspberry aromas in the nose, round, medium-bodied, ripe fruity flavors, soft tannins, and a pleasant but short finish. Drink it over the next 2–3 years. Last tasted 6/94.

1990—Côte Rôtie (Pierre Barge)   The 1990 has improved somewhat since I tasted it in
·   cask. It is a light, slightly diluted, pleasant, loosely knit wine that should be drunk
84   over the next 4–5 years. Last tasted 6/94.

1989—Côte Rôtie (Gilles Barge)   The 1989 exhibits an attractive sweet raspberry-scented
·   nose intermingled with the scents of earth and oak. In the mouth it is excellent,
88   with fine ripeness, deep, intense, rich fruitiness, medium body, good glycerin, enough acidity to provide focus, and a soft, medium-bodied finish. It should drink well over the next 3–5 years. Last tasted 6/94.

1989—Côte Rôtie (Pierre Barge)   This 1989 Côte Rôtie exhibits outstanding intensity
·   and extraction of flavor. A huge, spice, bacon fat, oak, and black-fruit-scented nose
90   zooms from the glass. In the mouth there is plenty of depth, gobs of fruit, nice acidity, and a long, rich, moderately soft finish. Approachable now, this flattering and precocious-tasting Côte Rôtie should drink well over the next decade. Last tasted 6/94.

1988—Côte Rôtie (Gilles Barge)   The first time I tasted the 1988 from the bottle it was
·   completely corked and impossible to judge. The second bottle displayed a slight
76   mustiness that could have been the beginning of a bad cork problem. On the palate, it was watery, light, and thin. I would hate to think that Gilles Barge had a significant problem with bad corks in 1988. Last tasted 6/93.

1988—Côte Rôtie (Pierre Barge)   The 1988 Côte Rôtie is the most structured and power-
·   ful Côte Rôtie Barge has made since 1983. The bouquet consists of smoky, vanillin
89   scents (from the use of new oak) intermingled with rich black fruits such as plums

and prunes. In the mouth, the wine is full-bodied and tannic, with more acidity and a more tightly knit feel than either the 1989 or 1990. This wine should be at its best between now and 2008. Last tasted 6/93.

1985—Côte Rôtie   Deep ruby colored, the fully mature 1985 has concentrated fruit, a
·   fragrant bouquet of blackberries, cedar, and spice, full body, and a long, ripe,
90   tannic finish. Anticipated maturity: now–2000. Last tasted 1/94.

GUY ET FRÉDÉRIC BERNARD—G.A.E.C. BERNARD* * *

Address: R.N. 86   Surface area: 10.37 acres
         69420 Tupin-et-Semons   Production: 18,000 bottles
Tel: 4-74-59-54-04   Upbringing: 18–24 months in barrels
Fax: 4-74-56-68-81   Average age of vines: 35 years
Wines produced: Côte Rôtie   Percentage of Viognier: none

VINTAGES

1995—Côte Rôtie   Bernard's 1995 is a chunky, monolithic, fleshy wine with good depth
·   and ripeness, but at present, there is no real identifiable Côte Rôtie character. It is
86   a good, well-made wine, but I would like to see more of the appellation's character-
       istics emerge. Last tasted 6/96.

1994—Côte Rôtie   The 1994 Côte Rôtie reveals just what a difference a vintage can
·   make. The wine displays an attractive deep ruby color and a rich, sweet nose of
87   smoked herbs, vanillin, and black-raspberry fruit. Medium- to full-bodied, velvety
       textured, and seductive, this is a delicious, round Côte Rôtie for drinking in its
       first 7–9 years of life. Last tasted 6/96.

1993—Côte Rôtie   The light- to medium-bodied, thin, weedy 1993 Côte Rôtie should be
·   avoided. Last tasted 11/95.
74

1990—Côte Rôtie   Although I admire the deep color and fine concentration and extrac-
·   tion, this wine tastes monochromatic. It is beefy, with a spicy, herbal, leathery
85   nose, and full-bodied, tannic flavors. Will complexity and character emerge with
       aging? It will easily last for 10–12 years. Last tasted 11/94.

1988—Côte Rôtie   The 1988, given the fine raw materials offered by that vintage, should
·   have been better. Tasted twice, it displayed an intensely herbaceous, nearly vegetal
83   bouquet, with peppery, somewhat disjointed, yet ripe flavors. There is moderate
       tannin and good acidity, but the wine's greenness suggests either young vines or
       too early a harvest date. Last tasted 6/93.

1987—Côte Rôtie   After Guy Bernard's highly successful 1986, I was not surprised to
·   see how well he performed in the underrated vintage (for Côte Rôtie) of 1987. It is
86   a soft, deliciously fruity, herb- and cassis-flavored wine, with some spicy, woody
       elements in the background. The tannins are light and velvety, the acidity is sound,
       and the concentration is very good. This is a delightful, elegant Côte Rôtie for
       drinking over the next 4–5 years. Last tasted 6/93.

DOMAINE DE BONSERINE (GEORGES DUBOEUF)* * *

Address: Proprietor: S.E.A.R., S.A.   Wines produced: Côte Rôtie
     Contact Person: Marc Allagnat   Surface area: 24.7 acres
     Verenay   Production: 45,000 bottles
     69420 Ampuis   Upbringing: 18–24 months in barrels
Tel: 4-74-56-14-27   Average age of vines: 25 years
Fax: 4-74-56-18-13   Percentage of Viognier: 3%

This domaine owns 24.7 acres of vineyards, of which 7.5 are on the hillside and the rest on the less desirable plateau of Côte Rôtie. Georges Duboeuf, the famous Beaujolais winemaker, produces his Cuvée Domaine de la Rousse from grapes grown by the Domaine de Bonserine. Although Duboeuf's wines have tended to taste richer, fuller, and more concentrated than those from Bonserine, I have been told that the cuvées are identical, but that has not been borne out in my tastings. Since this estate was acquired in 1988, Duboeuf has moved quickly to see that more attention to detail is given in the vineyards, as well as to the wine's upbringing in the cellar.

VINTAGES

1991—Côte Rôtie Domaine de la Rousse   This dark ruby/purple-colored wine remains
· youthful, with a moderately intense, cassis, leafy, herb, and spice box–scented
87 nose, medium body, excellent richness and flesh. There is not much complexity, but there is a chewy mouth feel and well-integrated tannin in the finish. The wine is approaching full maturity. Anticipated maturity: now–2003. Last tasted 8/96.

1990—Côte Rôtie Domaine de la Rousse   The 1990 Domaine de la Rousse, which is
· being aged in 50% new oak casks, is an attractive, medium-bodied, soft, fleshy
85 wine with lovely fruit, an elegant personality, and round, graceful, yet generous flavors. It should be at its best between now and 2000. Last tasted 8/94.

1989—Côte Rôtie Domaine de la Rousse   The 1989 Domaine de la Rousse displays an
· attractive bouquet of superripe raspberries, light tannin, a soft, medium-bodied,
87 supple palate, good glycerin, and a low-acid finish. In style and texture, it reminds me of some 1982 Côte Rôties. Close to full maturity, it should be drunk over the next 4–5 years. Last tasted 12/95.

1988—Côte Rôtie Domaine de la Rousse   To date, this has been the best wine produced
· at Duboeuf's Côte Rôtie estate. The wine remains deeply colored, tannic, and
89 + backward, with plenty of concentration, body, and tannin. It is a muscular, borderline rustic style of Côte Rôtie that should age effortlessly for another 10–15 years. If all the tannin melts away and the wine achieves complete harmony it will merit an outstanding score. Drink it between 1999 and 2010. Last tasted 8/96.

BERNARD BURGAUD* * * *

Address: Le Champin   Surface area: 10 acres
     69420 Ampuis   Production: 13,000 bottles
Tel: 4-74-56-11-86   Upbringing: 15 months in barrels
Fax: 4-74-56-13-03   Average age of vines: 25 years
Wines produced: Côte Rôtie   Percentage of Viognier: none

This 40-year-old winemaker's winery is located on the top of the ridge, in the hamlet of Le Champin, overlooking Côte Rôtie. His wines are to be taken seriously. When his father died in 1980, Burgaud's career as a winemaker began. He owns 10 acres, two-thirds on the hillside and one-third on the plateau. All of his wine is aged in small barrels, of which 20%

are new for each vintage. Production is just over 1,000 cases, as Burgaud continues to sell approximately one-fifth of his wine to local négociants. The wine is fermented at a very high temperature for extraction purposes, kept 15 months in small barrels, and bottled unfined and unfiltered. Burgaud appears to be one of the up-and-coming stars of this appellation. The fact that he also produces one-third of his wine from the plateau is an encouraging sign for that much-maligned segment of the Côte Rôtie appellation, although he is the first to admit that his cuvées from the plateau produce the lightest and most acidic wines. His robust style of wine is one of power and thickness, with excellent purity of flavors, and 10–15 or more years of aging potential.

VINTAGES

1995—Côte Rôtie   The 1995 Côte Rôtie, while impressively deep, dark ruby/purple in color, is hard and backward, with crisp acidity, and tons of tannin. It tasted as if it
·
87?   had just finished malolactic fermentation. I suspect this wine, which reveals fine purity and good ripeness, should be reevaluated in 6–12 months. It is certainly very good, but my judgment is intentionally conservative. Last tasted 6/96.

1994—Côte Rôtie   Bernard Burgaud's 1994 Côte Rôtie is still not bottled, but it is a rustic, tannic, deeply colored, coarse style of Côte Rôtie, with plenty of sweet, rich
·
87   fruit underneath all the tannin. Patience is definitely required, and prospective purchasers must be able to defer their gratification. The wine is tannic, backward, and in need of 4–5 years of cellaring. There appears to be enough richness, flesh, and fruit to survive the wine's power and structure. It should drink well for 10–12 years. Last tasted 6/96.

1993—Côte Rôtie   An impressively saturated color is the only positive attribute to this vegetal, hollow, tannic, unflattering Côte Rôtie. It will only dry out as the wine
·
74   ages. Drink it up. Last tasted 6/96.

1992—Côte Rôtie   Bernard Burgaud's 1992 Côte Rôtie reveals excellent deep garnet color with a purple hue, an evolved bouquet of herbs, black fruits, and damp earth,
·
87   fine fatness, excellent richness, and medium to full body. The wine's flattering, soft style suggests it should be consumed over the next 7–8 years. It is a fine effort from a vintage that has produced more good wines than I initially believed. Last tasted 6/96.

1991—Côte Rôtie   Burgaud's outstanding 1991 Côte Rôtie is a dense, opaque black/purple-colored wine with a powerful nose of black fruits, herbs, and flowers. Full-
·
90   bodied with super extraction, it offers a rich, authoritative, well-structured taste and a whoppingly long, dramatic finish. With moderate tannin and terrific concentration, it should be drinkable by the mid-nineties and last for 15 years. Last tasted 6/96.

1990—Côte Rôtie   The 1990 Côte Rôtie is showing better out of bottle than it did from barrel. It exhibits Burgaud's telltale opaque dark ruby color, as well as an herbal,
·
89 +   earthy, oaky nose intertwined with aromas of black cherries and black raspberries. In the mouth, it is one of the more concentrated 1990 Côte Rôties, with a thickness and richness that is surprising for the vintage. The long, tannic finish is impressive. Do not be surprised if this wine merits an outstanding rating in 4–5 years. Anticipated maturity: now–2010. Last tasted 6/96.

1989—Côte Rôtie   The 1989 exhibits the superb black/ruby/purple color that Burgaud claims comes from his high vinification temperature and his tendency to do numer-
·
90   ous pigéages (pushing down and breaking up the cap in the fermenting wine). This huge, blockbuster, concentrated, intense Côte Rôtie needs several years in the bottle and has the potential to last 20. Among the relatively soft, low-acid 1989

Côte Rôties, this one has gobs of everything, including acidity, a tremendous tannin level, and outstanding concentration and intensity of fruit. Last tasted 12/95.

1988—Côte Rôtie The 1988 may prove to be one of Burgaud's longer-lived wines. For
·   those with a more Bordeaux-oriented palate it is sure to have plenty of appeal. The
92 yields were low in 1988, and this wine is splendidly concentrated, opaque in color (with only some light ruby at the edge), and tannic. I have upgraded my rating of this wine as it has developed in the bottle, displaying far greater richness and intensity than I had imagined. It has proven to be a superb Côte Rôtie. Anticipated maturity: now–2010. Last tasted 1/94.

1985—Côte Rôtie By comparison with the elegantly wrought wines Burgaud produced
·   in previous vintages, the 1985 is a corpulent, dense, powerful wine that is fully
88 mature. Dark ruby-colored with moderate amber at the edge, this wine has a spicy, cassis, herb, and licorice-scented nose, good acidity, and excellent depth and length. Anticipated maturity: now–2000. Last tasted 1/94.

1983—Côte Rôtie A peppery, herbal, raspberry-scented bouquet characterizes this
·   medium-bodied yet firm and tannic wine. It will dry out over the next 5–7 years.
85 Mature: now. Last tasted 1/94.

1982—Côte Rôtie Fully mature, supple, round, and fruity, the 1982 marked Burgaud's
·   debut vintage. Though very attractive and well made in the fiery temperatures of
85 this vintage, it does not show the class and elegance of subsequent offerings. Drink it up. Last tasted 6/86.

EMILE ET JOEL CHAMPET* * *

Address: Emile Champet
22, rue du Port
69420 Ampuis

Joel Champet
Chemin de la Viaillère, Verenay
69420 Ampuis

Tel: 4-74-56-10-88
Wines produced: Côte Rôtie, Côte Rôtie La Viallère
Surface area (Emile): 0.98 acres
　　　　　(Joel): 5.68 acres
Production (Emile): 2,400 bottles
　　　　　(Joel): 14,250 bottles
Upbringing (Emile): 24 months in barrels
　　　　　(Joel): 36 months in barrels
Average age of vines (Emile): 40 years
　　　　　(Joel): 25 years
Percentage of Viognier: 6% for both Emile and Joel

The tiny, hyperactive, wiry Emile Champet could easily be mistaken for one of Steven Spielberg's devilish gremlins. He is an extremely busy man, having significant interests in the vegetable and flower business. Champet (who must be in his mid-seventies) has turned over most of his vineyards to his son, Joel. Quick-talking, fidgety, and colorful, Emile Champet still operates from an old cellar that consists of a conglomeration of small old barrels, medium-sized old barrels, and large, ancient foudres. Needless to say, it hardly inspires confidence in his winemaking, but like so many small growers in France, the decrepit cellar conditions are quite deceiving when it comes to evaluating the finished wine. Champet, who is in remarkable physical condition with a wrinkled, sun-beaten face, now makes wine only from a 1-acre parcel of 60-year-old vines on the Côte Blonde. The remainder of the vineyards (5 acres of the well-known Côte Brune La Viaillère) are cultivated and vinified by his son, Joel, who has his own cellars in Verenay. Joel keeps the wine longer in oak, but otherwise the winemaking is totally traditional, no destemming, a long upbringing in ancient wood foudres and smaller barrels, and bottling by hand with no filtration. Joel utilizes more new oak (about 25% in rich vintages) than his father. Both Champets prefer to drink their Côte Rôties between 5 and 10 years old, and are proud they make a natural wine that is never filtered. Stylistically, I find Champet's Côte Rôtie the closest thing to a big Côte de Nuits burgundy (a spicy, aggressive Chambertin comes to mind instantly) than any Côte Rôtie made by his peers. The wines from both Champets tend to be inconsistent in quality. The 1992s and 1993s from both Joel and Emile were disappointing. Unfortunately, I was not able to taste their 1994s and 1995s, two better vintages. Older top vintages are good to very good. Readers will note that the Côte Rôties of Joel Champet appear under the label "Côte Rôtie La Viaillère" whereas Emile Champet's wines appear under the name "Emile Champet."

VINTAGES

1991—Côte Rôtie La Viaillère (Joel Champet)   Joel Champet's 1991 Côte Rôtie from the
  ·   superb La Viaillère vineyard in Côte Brune offers an attractive, sweet, black-
  86   raspberry, herbal, earthy nose, medium weight, moderately concentrated flavors,
          soft tannins, low acidity, and a forward, precocious personality. Drink it over the
          next 4–7 years. Last tasted 6/94.

1990—Côte Rôtie (Emile Champet)   In 1990, Emile Champet has made a wine with an
  ·   intensely leather-scented, almost smoked-beef aroma, with medium body, plenty of
  86   tannin, but neither the expansive richness nor persistence of either the 1989 or
          1988. The low-acid, medium-bodied 1990 should be drunk up. Anticipated maturity: now–2000. Last tasted 6/94.

1989—Côte Rôtie (Emile Champet)   The rich, medium- to full-bodied 1989 offers up a
  ·   chocolaty, leathery, rustic nose, sweet, expansive, luscious flavors, softer tannins
  88   than the 1988, but a rich, tasty finish. I would opt for drinking it over the next 10
          years. Last tasted 6/94.

1988—Côte Rôtie (Emile Champet)   Champet has turned out a full-bodied, fragrant,
  ·   spicy, deep, highly extracted 1988 that is just beginning to reach full maturity. It
  88   will never shed all of its tannin, but there is also no hurry to consume it. Anticipated maturity: now–2001. Last tasted 10/93.

1985—Côte Rôtie (Emile Champet)   Champet did not have the great success that many
  ·   of his peers enjoyed in this vintage. Nevertheless, this is still a low-key, rustic,
  78   medium-bodied wine with an intensely spicy, peppery-scented aroma, adequate
          concentration, and some green tannin, as well as annoyingly high acidity. It is
          quite different in style from other 1985s. Mature now. Last tasted 11/93.

CHAPOUTIER* * */* * * * *

Address: 18, avenue du Docteur Paul Durand
        B.P. 38
        26600 Tain l'Hermitage
Tel: 4-75-08-28-65
Fax: 4-75-08-81-70
Estate wines produced: Côte Rôtie Cuvée La Mordorée
Négociant wines produced: Côte Rôtie
Surface area: 7.5 acres
Production (regular cuvée): 36,000 bottles
           (Cuvée La Mordorée): 500 cases
Upbringing (regular cuvée): 12 months in one-third new oak
           (Cuvée La Mordorée): 12 months in 100% new oak

Average age of vines (regular cuvée): 45 years
                            (Cuvée La Mordorée): 75–80 years
Percentage of Viognier: none

This famous Rhône Valley négociant and vineyard owner is discussed in depth in the chapter on Hermitage (see page 138). Chapoutier does produce a good Côte Rôtie from a blend of purchased grapes and their estate vineyards. While the quality of Chapoutier's regular cuvée of Côte Rôtie has increased significantly since Michel and Marc Chapoutier took over after their father's retirement in the late eighties, the real breakthrough in quality has been the luxury cuvée of Côte Rôtie called La Mordorée. This wine, which made its debut in 1990, is Michel Chapoutier's homage to Marcel Guigal's Côte Rôtie La Turque, La Mouline, and La Landonne. This spectacular wine is made from a selection of parcels of very old vines (averaging 75–80 years) located on the Côte Brune, adjacent to Guigal's famed La Turque vineyard. All of the Chapoutier vineyards, since 1989, have been farmed under the strict biodynamic principles of organic farming. La Mordorée is made from yields of under 25 hecoliters per hectare, aged in 100% new oak casks, and bottled with no fining or filtration. Every vintage since 1990 has been compelling, even in such difficult years as 1992 and 1993. As the following tasting notes attest, I thought the 1991 was pure perfection. Unlike the traditionalists, Michel Chapoutier and his winemaking team believe that the Syrah they harvest from their Côte Rôtie vineyards must be 100% destemmed in order to avoid excessive acidity and vegetal tastes. This firm, once in the throes of mediocrity under Michel and Marc's father, has emerged as one of the most important houses of the Rhône Valley. Certainly their regular cuvée of Côte Rôtie is improving all the time, while the Cuvée La Mordorée rivals the greatest Côte Rôties produced.

VINTAGES

1995—Côte Rôtie   Chapoutier's regular cuvée of 1995 Côte Rôtie offers a spicy, peppery,
  ·   sweet, black-raspberry-scented nose, crisp acidity, medium body, fine ripeness,
  89   and a surprising degree of elegance. The wine is aged in small oak casks. Last
            tasted 6/96.
1995—Côte Rôtie Cuvée La Mordorée   The 1995 La Mordorée may turn out to rival the
  ·   phenomenal 1991. It is the most complex, elegant, and multidimensional young
  97   Côte Rôtie I have tasted from Chapoutier. The awesome aromatics include scents of
            coffee, black raspberries, vanilla, chocolate, hickory smoke, flowers, and Provençal
            olives. Superrich, with exceptional delicacy and precision, this wine is less massive
            than the 1991, but perhaps more compelling because of its extraordinary delicacy.
            This wine's texture and complexity suggest that Côte Rôtie truly is the Musigny of
            the Rhône Valley. This is a hard wine to evaluate in terms of drinkability, but I
            suspect it will be thrilling to drink when released, and age effortlessly for two or
            more decades. Last tasted 6/96.
1994—Côte Rôtie   The 1994 (Chapoutier feels it is merely a "good" year in Côte Rôtie)
  ·   displays a sweet entry, but the tannin takes over and the wine seems structured
  86   and firm. It will be interesting to see how this wine evolves after bottling. Last
            tasted 6/96.
1994—Côte Rôtie Cuvée La Mordorée   The classic 1994 is one of the stars of the vintage.
  ·   It offers up a gorgeous, black-raspberry, cassis, olive, and violet-scented nose.
  93   Amazingly complex (as are all great Côte Rôties), the wine hits the palate with
            copious amounts of fat, smoky, cassislike fruit, medium body, sweet tannin, and a
            long, rich finish. While it is already stunningly aromatic, the flavors have yet to

catch up with the wine's super bouquet. Give it 2–3 years of cellaring and drink it over the following 10–15 years. Last tasted 6/96.

1993—Côte Rôtie   The 1993 Côte Rôtie reveals higher extraction than the 1994 and
·   1992 vintages, more new oak in its smoky, *pain grillé*–like nose, and moderate
88   tannin. It will benefit from 2–3 years of cellaring, but it is one 1993 that possesses a midpalate as well as attractive, sweet fruit. Anticipated maturity: now–2004. Last tasted 6/96.

1993—Côte Rôtie Cuvée La Mordorée   Despite having more structure and tannin than
·   the top vintages of this cuvée, the 1993 La Mordorée has turned out to be among
91   the finest wines from the northern Rhône in this dreadful vintage. It possesses an impressive dark ruby/purple color, a powerful, provocative nose of Asian spices, toasty oak, and plenty of black fruits. Medium- to full-bodied and tannic, with a fruity mid-palate, this wine is approachable, but it will benefit from another 2–4 years of cellaring; it should keep for 15 years. Last tasted 6/96.

1992—Côte Rôtie   Exhibiting sweet, herb-tinged, black-raspberry fruit, medium body,
·   subtle toasty oak, and a peppery, sweet, richly fruity bouquet, the 1992 is soft and
87+   easy to drink, with 7–8 years of aging potential. Anticipated maturity: now–2006. Last tasted 9/95.

1992—Côte Rôtie Cuvée La Mordorée   The 1992 offers a sweet, violet, cassis, smoky-
·   scented nose, sweet, rich, opulent flavors, full body, and a long, luscious, low-acid,
92   richly fruity finish. Already delicious, this full-bodied, silky-textured wine should drink well for another 15 years. Last tasted 6/96.

1991—Côte Rôtie Cuvée La Mordorée   In the same class as the great single-vineyard
·   Côte Rôties made by Marcel Guigal (i.e., La Mouline, La Turque, and La Landonne).
100   La Mordorée is most akin to La Mouline in its seductive, otherworldly fragrance and layers of sweet, expansive, velvety-textured fruit. There were 400 cases made of this saturated purple-colored wine. Its huge bouquet and spectacularly rich, layered personality offer an astonishing example of what low yields from a naturally farmed vineyard and an unfined, unfiltered winemaking philosophy can achieve. Anticipated maturity: now–2020. Last tasted 7/96.

1990—Côte Rôtie Brune et Blonde   The 1990 Côte Rôtie Brune et Blonde exhibits a
·   dark ruby color, a roasted black-raspberry-scented nose, very good richness, soft
87   tannins, low acidity, and a spicy, fleshy, voluptuously textured finish. Drink it over the next 8–10 years. Last tasted 7/96.

1990—Côte Rôtie Cuvée La Mordorée   The saturated dark ruby/purple color is followed
·   by an awesome nose that offers copious quantities of sweet black fruits, flowers,
94   toasty new oak, and smoky bacon fat. In the mouth there is superb concentration, a sweet, expansive texture, and a mind-boggling, long finish. This lavishly rich Côte Rôtie, which is already delicious, is capable of lasting for 10–15 years. Last tasted 7/96.

1989—Côte Rôtie Brune et Blonde   The powerful, intense, complex 1989 Côte Rôtie
·   exhibits a beautiful bouquet of black raspberries, spices, olives, and a touch of new
88   oak. It is pure velvet, with a rich, silky texture, soft tannin, low acidity, and an explosively rich, long finish. This beautifully made, elegantly rendered Côte Rôtie is close to full maturity. It should drink well for the next 7–8 years. Last tasted 12/95.

Older Vintages

Vintages prior to 1988, made by Marcel and Marc Chapoutier's father, Max, spent far too long in old chestnut-wood foudres. Some wines survived this upbringing and were at least good to very good. Those were the exceptions. Most of them tasted earthy, with dried-out fruit and no character of terroir or cépage. Vintages in the seventies and early eighties offered a mixed view of quality, with no outstanding wines. However, some ancient vintages from the late fifties (1959) possessed the concentration and power to age well.

DOMAINE CLUSEL-ROCH* * */* * * * *

Address: 15, route du Lacat-Verenay
        69420 Ampuis
Tel: 4-74-56-15-95
Fax: 4-74-56-19-74
Wines produced: Condrieu, Côte Rôtie, Côte Rôtie Les Grandes Places
Surface area: 7.5 acres in Côte Rôtie; 1.2 acres in Condrieu
Production: 11,000 bottles
Upbringing (regular cuvée): 18 months in barrels
        (Les Grandes Places): 24 months in barrels
Average age of vines (regular cuvée): 25 years
        (Les Grandes Places): 62 years
Percentage of Viognier: 3%

Following René Clusel's retirement, his son and daughter-in-law, Gilbert and Brigitte, run this tiny 7.5-acre Côte Rôtie estate (with an additional 1.2 acres in Condrieu). When I first met Gilbert, he was uncomfortable and reticent, but he has taken this estate to new heights, and seems more open and confident. Since 1988, Domaine Clusel-Roch has been one of the top performing estates in Côte Rôtie. Their cool, deep cellars in Verenay, at the northern edge of Côte Rôtie and Ampuis, are among the coldest in the area. Thus the wines do not suffer from severe changes in temperature. In 1988, Gilbert decided to keep the production from their 62-year-old vines of Les Grandes Places (a whopping 1.73 acres) separate, and give it 24 months in small oak casks, of which 50% are new. This wine has become one of the top wines of the appellation. Although not quite at the level of Guigal's La Mouline, La Landonne, or La Turque, or Chapoutier's La Mordorée, Clusel-Roch's Les Grandes Places is not far behind. The other Côte Rôtie from their parcels of young vines in La Viallière and Le Champon spends 18 months in casks, of which only 10–15% are new. Both wines are bottled with a light fining, but no filtration. All of the 1992s and 1993s were mediocre, not that surprising in such difficult vintages. Unfortunately, I was unable to taste Clusel-Roch's 1994s and 1995s prior to the publication of this book. Based on vintages from 1988 onward, this is one of the up-and-coming stars of the appellation.

VINTAGES

1991—Côte Rôtie   The 1991 Côte Rôtie reveals a dark ruby/purple color and a big nose
·   of violets, black raspberries, and sweet, smoky scents. The wine exhibits gorgeous
88   levels of opulent fruit, medium to full body, adequate acidity, and a chewy, rich
      finish. Drink it over the next 7–10 years. Last tasted 12/95.

1990—Côte Rôtie Les Grandes Places   The stupendous 1990 Les Grandes Places pos-
·   sesses a saturated purple/black color and a spectacular nose of grilled meats, Asian
94   spices, black fruits, and new oak. Superbly concentrated, with low acidity and
      layers of ripe, rich fruit, this full-bodied, stunningly rich, pure wine should drink
      well for 15 years. Last tasted 12/95.

1989—Côte Rôtie   The 1989 Côte Rôtie is one of the finest efforts of the vintage. The
·   wine exhibits a healthy dark ruby/purple color, as well as a sweet nose of bacon
90   fat, black raspberries, earth, and flowers. In the mouth it is expansive. The vanillin
      component suggests aging in toasty new oak. There is medium to full body, excel-

lent purity and balance, and a moderately tannic, generous finish. Drink it over the next 10–12 years. Last tasted 9/95.

1988—Côte Rôtie   The superconcentrated, tannic 1988 Côte Rôtie is more closed than the 1989, but its impressive extraction of fruit is admirable. The nose offers aromas of smoked meats, black fruits, and herbs. In the mouth, it is full-bodied, with terrific concentration, as well as a long, powerful finish. Drink it between now and 2008. Last tasted 9/95.

·

92

1985—Côte Rôtie   For a 1985 Côte Rôtie, Clusel's wine is notably less successful than others. Medium ruby, rather loosely knit, low in acidity, but soft and accessible, this wine will have to be drunk over the next 5–6 years. Last tasted 6/86.

·

84

YVES CUILLERON* *

Address: Verlieu
      42410 Chavanay
Tel: 4-74-87-02-37
Fax: 4-74-87-05-62
Wines produced: Côte Rôtie, Côte Rôtie Coteau de Bassenon, Condrieu, St.-Joseph (red and white)
Surface area: 3.7 acres
Production: 6,750 bottles
Upbringing: 18 months in barrels
Average age of vines: 15 years
Percentage of Viognier: 10%

Yves Cuilleron is discussed in more detail in the chapter on Condrieu (see page 105). His magic touch with Viognier and St.-Joseph blanc is irrefutable, but his Côte Rôtie offerings have been mixed. Cuilleron owns two parcels, one at the southern end of the Côte Rôtie appellation, in the lieu-dit Bassenon, and a tiny .9-acre parcel of 30-year-old and very young vines on the Côte Brune's La Viaillère. At present, Cuilleron's Côte Rôties are pleasant, but generally far from the top level of quality that can be obtained. Given Cuilleron's enthusiasm, energy, and overall commitment to quality, I would not be surprised to see the quality of these wines increase over the next several decades as his tiny vinyeards age.

VINTAGES

1995—Côte Rôtie Coteau de Bassenon   The 1995 Coteau de Bassenon is dominated by wood, without sufficient fruit and extract to balance out the wine's wood, tannin, and structure. Last tasted 6/96.

·

78

1994—Côte Rôtie   Cuilleron's 1994 Côte Rôtie is from a tiny 3.7-acre parcel of hillside vineyards. He added 10% Viognier, which accounts for its succulent, sexy, ostentatious nose of black fruits, honeysuckle, and apricots. Medium-bodied and elegant, with round fruit, this wine should drink well for 5–7 years. It is a seductive, graceful style of Côte Rôtie for drinking in its first 7–8 years of life. Last tasted 6/96.

·

86

1994—Côte Rôtie Coteau de Bassenon   Similar to the 1995, this wine does not possess the fruit and extract necessary to stand up to the wine's wood and tannin. Last tasted 6/96.

·

77

1993—Côte Rôtie   It should come as no surprise that Cuilleron's 1993 Côte Rôtie is a lean, hard, tough, compressed wine with little charm or ripeness. Few producers managed to overcome the difficulties of this vintage. Last tasted 9/94.

·

76

DELAS FRÈRES* */* * *

Address: 2, allées de l'Olivet
        07300 St.-Jean de Muzols
Tel: 4-75-08-60-30
Fax: 4-75-08-53-67
Wines produced: Côte Rôtie Les Ravines, Côte Rôtie Les Seigneurs de Maugiron
Surface area: 9.5 acres
Production (Les Ravines): 22,500 bottles
              (Les Seigneurs de Maugiron): 18,000 bottles
Upbringing: 14–16 months in barrels
Average age of vines: 30 years
Percentage of Viognier: 5–6%

This négociant just outside Tournon produces a small amount of uninspiring Côte Rôtie. The potential stars in the Delas house are the Hermitage Marquise de la Tourette and Hermitage Les Bessards (see page 154), as well as their excellent Condrieu. The two cuvées of Côte Rôtie are made in a modern style, fermented in stainless steel, filtered after malolactic, fined by bentonite, and filtered again before bottling. The Côte Rôtie used to spend up to two years in two- and three-year-old barrels and foudres prior to bottling, but that has been shortened to 14–16 months. The Delas cellar is air-conditioned, one of the few in the Rhône Valley to have such a luxury. The Côte Rôtie Les Seigneurs de Maugiron is made completely from vineyards on the Côte Brune, and 5% Viognier is added to the blend to add complexity and softness. Delas, once owned by the well-known champagne house of Deutz, is now under the Louis Roederer umbrella. It remains to be seen whether or not this firm will increase the quality of its Côte Rôtie to compete with the likes of Guigal, Chapoutier, or Jaboulet. At present, it lags far behind those houses, as well as that of Guigal's sister operation, Vidal-Fleury. I have tasted some outstanding bottles of Delas Condrieu and top cuvées of Hermitage, but their other offerings are merely correct, and often lack concentration and character. In a competitive marketplace, these are wines that need an infusion of quality and concentration to push them to higher levels. Let's hope higher standards will ultimately be put in place.

VINTAGES

1993—Côte Rôtie Les Seigneurs de Maugiron   Medium dark ruby colored, this hollow
·   wine has astringent tannin, no mid-palate, and plenty of acidity in the fruitless
68   finish. Last tasted 7/96.

1992—Côte Rôtie Les Seigneurs de Maugiron   A diluted wine; the light ruby color, an
·   herbal, spicy, earthy nose, and short, clipped, medium-bodied flavors are insignifi-
73   cant. Caveat emptor! Last tasted 7/96.

1990—Côte Rôtie   The 1990 Côte Rôtie exhibited a few of the telltale characteristics of
·   this appellation (smoky fruit and spice). Light and lacking concentration and depth,
76   it displayed medium body and a finish that tailed off. This is a charming, albeit
        lighter-styled Côte Rôtie for drinking before 1999. Last tasted 9/95.

1990—Côte Rôtie Les Seigneurs de Maugiron   The 1990 Les Seigneurs de Maugiron is a
·   rich, olive-scented, medium- to full-bodied wine with high acidity, but good poten-
86   tial for 10–15 years of evolution. Although not great, it is a very good wine. Last
        tasted 6/96.

1989—Côte Rôtie   In 1989, the regular cuvée of Côte Rôtie is straightforward, soft, and
·   commercial, but tasty and cleanly made. It should be drunk up. Last tasted 9/95.
78

1989—Côte Rôtie Les Seigneurs de Maugiron   The 1989 Les Seigneurs de Maugiron is
       •   more ambitious, exhibiting a great deal of toasty new oak, an attractive bacon fat
      87   nose intermingled with aromas of ripe prunes, and a long, rich, opulent finish.
               Drinkable now, it should last for another 5–7 years. Last tasted 6/93.

1988—Côte Rôtie   The 1988 is slightly less concentrated, with more acidity, and harder
       •   tannins. However, the impression is one of rich cassis fruit wrapped intelligently
      86   in new oak, with no shortage of ferocious tannin. It will keep for another decade,
               but will the fruit outlast the tannin? Last tasted 6/95.

1988—Côte Rôtie Les Seigneurs de Maugiron   This 1988 is among the most complete
       •   wines Delas has made in Côte Rôtie—full-bodied, harmonious, concentrated, and
      89   fragrant. It possesses more fruit, extract, and overall balance than the regular
               bottling. Drink it over the next 8–10 years. Last tasted 6/93.

ALBERT DERVIEUX-THAIZE* * *

At the northern end of Côte Rôtie, in the tiny town of Verenay, resides the warm, friendly,
diminutive, yet authoritative Albert Dervieux. Until his retirement, he made robust, rustic,
long-lived Côte Rôtie. He was the president of the growers' association from 1953 until his
retirement in 1990. Dervieux's last vintage was 1989, and in 1990 his son-in-law René
Rostaing began leasing Dervieux's vineyards. Dervieux's wines were the epitome of traditionally made, long-lived, rustic, sometimes flawed Côte Rôties. Dervieux used 5% Viognier
in the blend for his Côte Rôtie La Garde, and kept all of his wines in large old foudres for
30 + months. No new wood barrels were employed here since Dervieux argued they masked
the true character of Côte Rôtie. Dervieux produced 1,200–1,500 cases from three different
Côte Rôtie vineyards that totaled 8.6 acres of vines. They were La Fongent, from the Côte
Brune; La Garde, from the Côte Blonde; and his top wine, La Viaillère, from ancient vines
on the Côte Brune. His wines were egg white fined but never filtered, simply allowed to
settle and fall brilliant naturally. There is no question that Dervieux-Thaize produced some
of Côte Rôtie's most muscular and rustic wines. Yet less endowed vintages were frequently
kept too long in wood, evidence of his inflexibility. Dervieux's wines tended to be weak in
years that were plagued by rain (e.g., 1984, 1980, 1977). There is no doubt that in the top
vintages (1985, 1983, 1978) he produced wines of exceptional quality that have aged as
well as any wine produced in this appellation. In comparative tastings, Dervieux-Thaize's
Côte Rôties usually taste more tannic and brutal than those of Jasmin or Guigal. They tend
to develop into rich, full-bodied, rather virile wines with earthy, saddle leather scents
intertwined with spring flowers and ripe berry fruit. In fact, their taste confirms what
Dervieux says about them: "Je fais un vin solide et tannique."

All of these vineyards have been under the control of René Rostaing since 1990, and the
aggressive coarseness that was often a characteristic of Dervieux's wines is no longer
present. Readers are advised to read the section on René Rostaing (see page 82) for a
further analysis of how these wines are now being made.

VINTAGES

1989—Côte Rôtie La Garde   The 1989 La Garde is soft and light, and lacks concentration
       •   and grip. Drink it over the next 5–6 years. Last tasted 9/92.
      85

1989—Côte Rôtie La Fongent   The 1989 La Fongent is extremely light, with an almost
       •   metallic character, as well as a stinky lees smell that suggested a faulty upbringing
      ?   (élevage). Last tasted 9/92.

1989—Côte Rôtie La Viaillère   The 1989 La Viaillère, usually the most backward and
· impressive of Dervieux's wines, has plenty of weight. Yet the huge, aggressive,
86 astringent tannins suggest a problem of balance, and I did not think it had enough
fruit to stand up to the tannin levels. Anticipated maturity: 1998–2006. Last tasted
9/92.

1988—Côte Rôtie La Garde   Dervieux did not produce any Côte Rôtie La Fongent in
· 1988, but he did produce a La Garde. This wine is more supple than La Viaillère,
85? but is still exceptionally tannic, with the tannins possessing a coarse, astringent
edge that troubled me. In the mouth there is good ripeness and underlying concentration, but I wonder if the tannins will ultimately overwhelm the fruit? My best
guess is that it should be drunk between now and 1998. Last tasted 9/92.

1988—Côte Rôtie La Viaillère   The exuberant, chewy 1988 La Viaillère is extremely
· intense, very muscular and tannic, with loads of concentration, powerful aromas of
90 roasted black fruits and earthy, mineral scents that blossom from the glass. In the
mouth it is clearly superb, but a 5–6-year wait is mandated. Look for this wine to
be at its best between 1998 and 2010. It is comparable to the 1989, but the tannins
are tougher and the acidity is slightly higher. Last tasted 2/96.

1987—Côte Rôtie La Viaillère   A good wine from this vintage, this rough-textured, deeply
· concentrated, masculine wine has reached full maturity. It could age for another
86 5–8 years. Last tasted 5/95.

1985—Côte Rôtie La Viaillère   An excellent wine, Dervieux's 1985 La Viaillère has a
· deep ruby color with some amber at the edge, an exotic, earthy, fruity, smoked
89 herb and grilled meat bouquet, super ripeness and richness, and fine length, with
some obtrusive tannin. Anticipated maturity: now–2004. Last tasted 11/95.

1985—Côte Rôtie La Garde   In contrast to the sturdy La Viaillère from the Côte Brune,
· Dervieux's La Garde from the Côte Blonde is more supple, velvety, and fully
90 mature. It has layers of raspberry/cassis fruit, excellent intensity, a dark ruby color,
and ripe, round tannins. Anticipated maturity: now–2002. Last tasted 11/95.

1985—Côte Rôtie La Fongent   The fully mature, medium-bodied 1985 La Fongent is
· lush and concentrated, but it lacks the depth of La Garde and La Viaillère. It is a
87 very good Côte Rôtie that will drink well between now and 2000. Last tasted
11/95.

1983—Côte Rôtie La Viaillère   Dervieux's 1983 La Viaillère has continued to evolve at
· a glacial pace. Still dark ruby (some amber at the edge), firm, concentrated, and
88? robust, this wine has plenty of length and tannin to match its power, but will the
fruit hold? Anticipated maturity: now–2006. Last tasted 11/95.

1983—Côte Rôtie La Garde   Significantly less powerful and concentrated than Dervieux's
· La Viaillère, the fully mature 1983 La Garde is supple, smooth, fruity, and moder-
85 ately dark in color with some amber at the edge. Anticipated maturity: now–2000.
Last tasted 9/92.

1983—Côte Rôtie La Fongent   Deep ruby/garnet in color, with a tarry, very spicy (cinna-
· mon) sweaty horse and saddle leather bouquet, ripe and still tough, this wine from
82 Dervieux's vineyard on the Côte Brune is rustic and coarse, yet fully mature.
Anticipated maturity: now–1999. Last tasted 9/92.

LOUIS DREVON* *

Address: 3, rue des Moutonnes
69420 Ampuis
Tel: 4-74-56-11-38
Fax: 4-74-56-13-00

Wines produced: Côte Rôtie
Surface area: 17.3 acres
Production: 30,000 bottles
Upbringing: minimum of 18 months in barrels
Average age of vines: 35 years
Percentage of Viognier: 3%

Drevon continues to sell much of his wine production in bulk to Rhône Valley négociants. His estate-bottled wines have never been impressive. Moreover, in spite of his hiring the talented Jean-Luc Colombo to provide advice, the wines have not improved. Colombo, when asked about the wines' so-so quality level said, "You can give them advice, but they don't have to listen." Drevon's commercial, loosely knit wines seem to be the products of either young and/or overcropped vineyards. In short, they lack concentration. The high acidity in many vintages also seems to be symbolic of grapes picked before they have achieved full physiological ripeness. All things considered, this is an average-quality Côte Rôtie producer.

VINTAGES

1995—Côte Rôtie   Drevon's 1995 Côte Rôtie may be the finest wine I have tasted from
·   this producer. Much of his production is sold in bulk to négociants, but this is a
85   fat, ripe wine with attractive cassis fruit, medium to full body, and good density
         and character. It should drink well for 7–8 years. Last tasted 6/96.
1994—Côte Rôtie   The 1994 Côte Rôtie is extremely disappointing. Medium ruby color,
·   thin, diluted flavors, and a strong, herbaceous/vegetal component are unappealing.
72   Last tasted 6/96.
1989—Côte Rôtie   The 1989 is soft, with a touch of raspberries and new oak in the nose.
·   It exhibits round, light, undistinguished flavors. Last tasted 9/93.
80
1988—Côte Rôtie   The surprisingly insipid 1988 is similar to the 1989. Drink it over the
·   next 4–5 years. Last tasted 9/93.
75

EDMOND DUCLAUX* */* * *

Address: R.N. 86   Production: 10,000–12,000 bottles
         69420 Tupin-et-Semons   Upbringing: 2–3 years in barrels
Tel: 4-74-59-56-30   Average age of vines: 25 years
Wines produced: Côte Rôtie   Percentage of Viognier: 4–5%
Surface area: 9.4 acres

Duclaux, with his ruddy complexion and thinning hair, is one of Côte Rôtie's most enthusiastic growers. Until 1978 he sold the wine made from his 9.4 acres of vineyards located exclusively on the Côte Blonde to the likes of such firms as Guigal, Delas, and Chapoutier. Then with the encouragement of his mentor, Robert Jasmin, Duclaux began to estate-bottle his entire production. Not surprisingly, Duclaux's wines resemble those of Jasmin. They are fragrant, seductive, forward, and have ripe aromas and broad, supple flavors that suggest early drinkability and maturity. Duclaux likes to keep his wines in barrels for two years and normally uses no more than 5% Viognier in the blend. Duclaux will have none of the idea that new barrels are beneficial for his Côte Rôtie. Highly influenced by Robert Jasmin and Gentaz-Dervieux, the latter of whom has barrels that are almost 100 years old, Duclaux points out that new barrels are for winemakers who like to play tricks with their wines, thereby disguising the true flavors and concentration of fruit. Duclaux's vineyard, called the Maison Rouge, at the very southern end of the Côte Blonde, has vines that were planted in 1924, 1943, and 1963. Like many of the small growers in Côte Rôtie, Duclaux also grows vegetables and flowers to supplement his income. He has experience and good vineyards, but after some promising performances in the eighties, Duclaux's offerings in the nineties have been light in color, fruit, and body. I do not know if it is because of the vintages, or if something has changed at this estate.

PIERRE GAILLARD* *

Address: Favier
      42410 Malleval
Tel: 4-74-87-13-10
Fax: 4-74-87-17-66
Wines produced: Condrieu, Côtes du Rhône, Condrieu Clos de Cuminaille, Côte Rôtie, Côte
      Rôtie Brune et Blonde, St.-Joseph, St.-Joseph Clos de Cuminaille
Surface area: 6.7 acres
Production: 8,000 bottles
Upbringing: 18 months in oak barrels (20% new)
Average age of vines: 12 years
Percentage of Viognier: 10–15%, except in 1993 no Viognier was used due to rot

Gaillard, whose modern cellars are in the medieval village of Malleval, burst on the scene in the mid-eighties to rave reviews. However, in large part, he has not lived up to the early praise. Gaillard, who had plenty of experience, first working the vineyards for Vidal-Fleury and subsequently Guigal, seemed to have a promising start with his debut 1987 vintage. However, as things have turned out, his finest wines continue to be his white wines, generally those from St.-Joseph, followed by a delicious 100% Viognier Côtes du Rhône. His Côte Rôtie from several parcels in Viaillère and Rozier has been good, but generally unexciting. Moreover, and more worrisome, is that his best vintage of Côte Rôtie was 1988, a year he has never again equaled in a qualitative sense. Part of the reason is that the vines are only adolescents (12–13 years old). Most viticulturists recognize that growth, foliage, and canopy problems are at their worst during this age. This may be why Gaillard's Côte Rôties have been slightly vegetal over recent vintage.

Readers will find more information on Pierre Gaillard in the chapter on St.-Joseph (see page 274). I recommend concentrating on his St.-Joseph offerings, particularly his terrific whites.

VINTAGES

1995—Côte Rôtie   The light, vegetal, olive-scented, herb-flavored, thin 1995 Côte Rôtie
·   is unappealing. Last tasted 6/96.
75

1995—Côte Rôtie Brune et Blonde   The 1995 Côte Rôtie Brune et Blonde exhibits
·   similar characteristics, with more elegance than the regular cuvée, but the wine is
79   tannic, lean, hard, and charmless. Last tasted 6/96.

1990—Côte Rôtie Brune et Blonde   The 1990 Côte Rôtie Brune et Blonde reveals some
·   extraction, but the finish is lean and hard, without much ampleness or mid-palate.
83   I doubt it will improve. Last tasted 9/94.

1989—Côte Rôtie Brune et Blonde   The 1989 Côte Rôtie Brune et Blonde, which saw a
·   great deal of aging in new oak casks, is a full-bodied, rich, surprisingly tannic
86   wine, with an underlying elegance and purity that is admirable. The wine is

bursting with a black-fruit character, has great color, and a generous dosage of toasty, vanillin oakiness. It should be at its best between now and 2000. Last tasted 9/94.

1988—Côte Rôtie Brune et Blonde   The 1988 exhibits an intense ruby/purple color, and
·   a ripe cassis nose intertwined with aromas of vanilla and caramel. In the mouth it
88   displays fine richness, an attractive fatness and mid-palate depth, and long, alco-
            holic, rich, tannic flavors that suggest this wine should continue to drink well for
            10–12 years. To date, this is one of the finest Côte Rôties made by Gaillard. Last
            tasted 9/94.

HENRI GALLET* * * *

Address: Boucharey
            69420 Ampuis
Tel: 4-74-56-12-22
Fax: 4-74-56-00-08
Wines produced: Côte Rôtie, Côte Rôtie Côte Blonde
Surface area: 7.4 acres
Production: 13,500 bottles
Upbringing: 18–24 months in barrels
Average age of vines: 30–40 years
Percentage of Viognier: 5–6%

The Gallets, a robust husband-and-wife team located in Boucharey in the plateau region overlooking the steep slopes of Côte Rôtie, are increasingly bottling most of their production from their 7.5 acres split between the steep terraces and the plateau. Henri Gallet's first vintage was 1942, and until recently he sold much of his production to the Guigal firm. However, with the increased demand for Côte Rôtie, and the higher prices fetched by it, the Gallets seized the opportunity for a better economic return. The winemaking is completely traditional at this estate. Like so many small growers, they use 100% stems in the vinifica-tion, there are no new oak casks employed, and after 18–20 + months of barrel aging the wines are bottled as they are sold, an annoying and frustrating practice for consumers looking for uniformity in quality within a given vintage. Nothing gets filtered by Gallet, but his three bottlings can take place over an entire year, raising the specter of different aromas and flavors between first and last bottling.

Criticisms aside, Gallet is fashioning some marvelous Côte Rôties, as evidenced by what he accomplished in 1990 and 1991. Moreover, prices remain extremely fair for wines of such high quality.

VINTAGES

1995—Côte Rôtie   The 1995 Côte Rôtie is a soft, fruity, seductive, accessible wine that
·   is nearly Burgundian in its expansive, fragrant perfume and sweet, round, cassis
88?   flavors. The wine will not make old bones, but it should drink well for 7–8 years.
            Last tasted 6/96.

1994—Côte Rôtie   The 1994 Côte Rôtie possesses tough tannin in the finish, but other-
·   wise shares the same medium ruby-colored, ripe, round, fruity style, with smoky
87   bacon fat and cassis fruit. Last tasted 6/96.

1993—Côte Rôtie Côte Blonde   Medium dark ruby, with a pronounced herbal, spicy
·   nose, this wine has sufficient body, but high tannin, and a rather attenuated style
78   without sufficient fruit. Last tasted 7/96.

1992—Côte Rôtie Côte Blonde   It is going to be difficult to find Côte Rôties this rich and
·   complex from the rain-plagued 1992 vintage. Gallet, who made super wines in
90   1990 and 1991, has produced an open-knit, fragrant (aromas of black raspberries,
          peppers, and truffles) wine that should be drunk over the next 5–7 years. It has
          more in common with Gallet's seductive, compelling 1991 than the blockbuster,
          dense, concentrated, muscular 1990. Offering copious amounts of jammy black-
          cherry and raspberry fruit, the 1992 displays an exotic side (Gallet included about
          8% Viognier in the blend), and a medium- to full-bodied, smooth-as-silk finish.
          Last tasted 12/94.

1991—Côte Rôtie Côte Blonde   The 1991, aged in both small oak casks (about 30% new)
·   and foudres, and bottled unfiltered, represents the elegant "Musigny" style that
91   Côte Rôtie can sometimes achieve. It boasts a fragrant, intense bouquet of violets,
          cassis, cedar, herbs, and smoked duck. An exceptionally soft, velvety-textured Côte
          Rôtie, it may lack the 1990's power and extract, but it more than compensates for
          that deficiency with its finesse and perfume. I do not mean to imply this is a
          light-bodied wine lacking depth. It is a rich, complex, complete wine that is
          drinking beautifully, yet it promises to age gracefully for a decade. This is Côte
          Rôtie at its most seductive. Last tasted 12/96.

1990—Côte Rôtie Côte Blonde   Made exclusively from 40-year-old vines from the Côte
·   Blonde, this is a candidate for one of the great Côte Rôties of the good to very good
94   1990 vintage. Gallet, who used to sell all of his grapes to Marcel Guigal, bottled
          this wine after aging it in old oak foudres. The exceptionally dark color is followed
          by a sensational nose of jammy black fruits, smoke, licorice, and herbs. The
          spectacular richness, unctuousness, and viscous texture strongly suggest it is made
          from old vines and low yields. Layer upon layer of rich, jammy fruit are buttressed
          by moderate tannins and low acidity. This stunning Côte Rôtie should drink well
          for the next decade or longer. Wow! Last tasted 6/96.

YVES GANGLOFF* * *

Address: 2, chemin du Moulin
              69420 Condrieu
Tel: 4-74-59-57-04
Wines produced: Condrieu, Côte Rôtie
Surface area: 5 acres
Production: 10,500 bottles
Upbringing: 24 months minimum in barrels
Average age of vines: 3 acres more than 50 years; the rest, 6–10 years
Percentage of Viognier (from 1994): no addition to the old vines; 10% to the young vines
                  (Prior to 1994): none

   This tiny artist is quickly gaining a reputation for high quality Côte Rôtie and of course,
Condrieu. His success in such a difficult vintage as 1993 has made many of his peers
recognize his unbridled passion and commitment to excellence. It is too soon to know for
sure, but Gangloff, a wildman of sorts, gives signs of being one of the fiery new generation
of producers who can be counted on for distinctive, individualistic, high-quality wines.

VINTAGES

1993—Côte Rôtie   1993 was one of the most difficult vintages the northern Rhône Valley
·   has experienced. Few producers succeeded, but from his tiny 2-hectare vineyard
88   (5 acres), Gangloff has fashioned a surprisingly fine 1993 Côte Rôtie. The healthy

dark ruby/purple color is followed by a bouquet of vanillin (from new oak barrels), black pepper, and moderate quantities of sweet cassis fruit. There is none of the vegetal, earthy character so prevalent in many 1993s. Medium- to full-bodied, and spicy, with some hard tannin in the finish, this is a surprisingly generous, well-made, successful wine that should drink well for 7–8 years. Last tasted 5/96.

VINCENT GASSE* * * *

Address: La Roche–R.N. 86
          69420 Ampuis
Tel: 4-74-56-17-89
Wines produced: Côte Rôtie Cuvée Classique, Côte Rôtie Cuvée Vieilles Vignes, St.-Joseph;
          prior to 1992, he called his best wine Côte Rôtie Côte Brune
Surface area: 2.2 acres
Production: 3,000 bottles
Upbringing: 18–24 months in barrels (20% new)
Average age of vines: two-thirds average 12 years and one-third average 40 years
Percentage of Viognier: none

Vincent Gasse, an intelligent, articulate, wiry, bald man with a humongous black beard, is one of the few outsiders who have become successes in Côte Rôtie. Born in the famed Loire Valley village of Vouvray, Gasse moved to Ampuis in 1980, establishing a home and cellars on the Route Nationale just across the road from the entrance to Vidal-Fleury. All of his wine is estate-bottled from five parcels of vines on the slopes of Côte Rôtie. An introspective man who farms his vineyards in the biodynamic fashion, he owns several exciting parcels planted next to Guigal's La Landonne. In addition to his finest cuvée, which he calls Côte Brune, Gasse has begun to produce a Cuvée Classique and a wine from his oldest vines, which he calls Cuvée Vieilles Vignes. The wines are traditionally made in an air-conditioned, temperature-controlled cellar. There is no destemming, a relatively long maceration, and the wines are given two years in oak casks. While Gasse's regular cuvée sees about 20% new oak, his old-vine cuvée can see as much as 50% new oak in years when the richness and intensity of the wines permit it. Gasse has demonstrated the ability to make fabulous Côte Rôtie in such top vintages as 1990 and 1991, as well as good wines in such less successful vintages as 1992 and 1993. All things considered, the wine made by the candid and honest Vincent Gasse is well worth buying, particularly in Côte Rôtie's top vintages.

VINTAGES

1995—Côte Rôtie Cuvée Classique   The 1995 Côte Rôtie Cuvée Classique is good, but
  ·   it lacks the depth, richness, and intensity of the black-raspberry, smoky 1995
86   Cuvée Vieilles Vignes. Anticipated maturity: 1998–2008. Last tasted 6/96.
1995—Côte Rôtie Cuvée Vieilles Vignes   This black-raspberry-, smoky-scented 1995 is
  ·   deep, rich, and intense. Anticipated maturity: 1999–2010. Last tasted 6/96.
91
1994—Côte Rôtie Cuvée Classique   The 1994 (a vintage Vincent Gasse calls "too tan-
  ·   nic") Cuvée Classique is a lean, tough-textured, hard wine that will benefit from
87?   some egg white fining. Since Gasse does not filter, this may be the only chance to
         soften up this wine. It possesses some ripeness, but the tannins are very elevated.
         Anticipated maturity: 1998–2006. Last tasted 6/96.
1994—Côte Rôtie Cuvée Vieilles Vignes   The deeper-colored 1994 Cuvée Vieilles Vig-
  ·   nes is a richer, denser, sweeter wine, but again, the tannins in the finish are severe
89?   and not yet integrated. Anticipated maturity: 1999–2008. Last tasted 6/96.

1991—Côte Rôtie Côte Brune   This vineyard, which abuts the famed La Landonne
   ·   vineyard, has produced a black/purple-colored wine with an intense bouquet
   95   of jammy blackcurrants, herbs, smoky bacon fat, and Asian spices, particularly soy
           sauce. Full-bodied, with exceptional concentration and intensity, this layered
           wine possesses moderate tannin, and a blockbuster, chewy finish. Cellar it
           for 2–3 years and drink it over the following two decades. Bravo! Last tasted
           7/96.

1990—Côte Rôtie Côte Brune   1990 is not the great vintage in Côte Rôtie that it is in
   ·   St.-Joseph, Crozes-Hermitage, Cornas, and Hermitage. This excellent unfiltered
   91   wine has been aged in 25% new oak casks. Part of the wine is produced from a
           parcel of old vines Gasse has in the famed La Landonne vineyard. This organically
           made wine possesses a huge nose of smoky bacon fat, roasted black fruits, and
           herbs. Spicy, rich, and fleshy, with low acidity, and a good inner core of ripeness
           and fruit, medium to full body, and a soft, rich finish, it should be drunk over the
           next 7–8 years. Last tasted 10/95.

MARIUS GENTAZ-DERVIEUX* * * * *

Address: Le Vagnot
         69420 Ampuis
Tel: 4-74-56-10-83
Wines produced: Côte Rôtie
Surface area: 2.9 acres; since 1993 all except 1 acre has been leased to René Rostaing
Production: 2,000 bottles
Upbringing: 18–24 months in barrels
Average age of vines: 55 years
Percentage of Viognier: 0.1–0.2%

One of Côte Rôtie's greatest winemakers, Marius Gentaz, who is the brother-in-law of
Albert Dervieux, used to produce a mere 600–800 cases of wine from his 3 acres of vines
on the Côte Brune. Consequently, his winemaking genius was never widely known. Gentaz's
wines are now even more impossible to find since he leased to René Rostaing all of his old
vineyards except for a 1-acre parcel of 65-year old vines on the Côte Brune. Gentaz, a warm,
smiling, energetic man who is now in his seventies, eschews new oak barrels (some of his
barrels are 100 years old) and filtration, a process that he has always claimed ruined many
a wine. He keeps his wines in wood 18–24 months, fines them with several egg whites per
barrel, and then bottles them by hand! Gentaz, a very hard worker with an enthusiastic
personality, has always had to allocate his wine because of its popularity. In describing his
wine, Gentaz claims it is best drunk between 10–12 years of age, but comments that it is
often drunk earlier. I have always found his wines to be among the finest of the appellation.
They are not as powerful, oaky, and thick as those of Guigal, nor as rustic and backward as
those produced by his brother-in-law, Albert Dervieux. Yet as the following tasting notes
attest, they are marvels of both finesse and richness.

VINTAGES

1991—Côte Rôtie   The 1991 displays full body and admirable concentration, as well as
   ·   the potential for a long evolution in the bottle. The 1991 offers a deep ruby/purple
   90   color, a sweet nose of roasted black-raspberry fruit, saddle leather, ground beef,
           and damp earth. In the mouth the wine is full-bodied, with a velvety texture,
           excellent to outstanding concentration, and a long, sweet, round finish. If you object

to the leathery, meaty smells of the brett yeast, then avoid this wine. Anticipated maturity: now–2005. Last tasted 7/96.

1990—Côte Rôtie   Since bottling, the 1990 appears to have put on weight. It is not as
•   rich as the 1991, and by the standards of Gentaz, it is less interesting than his
89   1982, 1983, 1985, and 1988. However, it is a charming, medium-weight Côte Rôtie with a terrific fragrance, as well as a lovely, fat, luscious personality. Gentaz feels it is reminiscent of the 1982, although not as full-bodied and concentrated. Already drinkable, it should evolve rapidly, so I recommend drinking it over the next 6–8 years. Anticipated maturity: now–2001. Last tasted 7/96.

1989—Côte Rôtie   Gentaz's 1989 Côte Rôtie is pure finesse and seduction. Gentaz claims
•   it reminds him of his fabulous 1985, which he feels is the most complete wine he
91   has made during the last decade. With a super dark ruby color and a huge bouquet of smoky, raspberry fruit intertwined with the scent of violets and minerals, it exhibits excellent ripeness, rich, medium- to full-bodied texture, plenty of glycerin, and a long, luscious, lightly tannic finish. Anticipated maturity: now–2006. Last tasted 12/95.

1988—Côte Rôtie   The 1988 Côte Rôtie is a spectacularly rich, concentrated wine with
•   superb depth and intensity. Still very backward, this murky, dark ruby-colored
94   wine displays a huge nose of cassis, minerals, licorice, earth, and flowers. In the mouth there is astonishing concentration, terrific flavor delineation, medium to full body, plenty of tannin, and a long, spicy, tightly knit finish. This is a dazzling Côte Rôtie for ringing in the next century. Anticipated maturity: 1998–2010. Last tasted 12/95.

1987—Côte Rôtie   1987 is a surprisingly good vintage in Côte Rôtie, unlike other north-
•   ern Rhône appellations. Most top producers made impressive, even concentrated
88   wines, with soft tannins and excellent ripeness. Gentaz's 1987 is a velvety, berry, herb, olive, fruity-scented wine with medium body. This supple Côte Rôtie should be drunk up. Anticipated maturity: now–2000. Last tasted 12/95.

1985—Côte Rôtie   An exceptional wine in all respects, Gentaz feels this is his personal
•   best of the last decade. Still very dark ruby, with a flamboyant, intensely perfumed
95   bouquet of raspberry/cassis fruit, a luscious, deep, velvety texture with enough tannin for another 5–10 years of evolution, this wine is seductive, hedonistic, and a joy to drink. Anticipated maturity: now–2005. Last tasted 12/95.

1983—Côte Rôtie   Still somewhat dumb and tannic, the 1983 Côte Rôtie of Gentaz has
•   outstanding underlying richness and length, but needs further cellaring. Deep
90   garnet with some amber, the wine's spicy, leathery, smoked meat (some brett) aromatics soar from the glass. Like so many 1983s, the question is, will these tannins ever melt away? Anticipated maturity: now–2006. Last tasted 12/95.

1982—Côte Rôtie   In contrast to the stubborn, large-scaled but tough 1983, the 1982 is
•   fully mature. An open and opulent wine, with aromas of earth, meat, leather, and
93   berry fruit, this velvety-textured, chewy, rich Côte Rôtie has impressive flavor concentration. Anticipated maturity: now–1999. Last tasted 12/95.

1978—Côte Rôtie   This superb wine has a full-blown bouquet of rich plummy fruit, lush,
•   supple, deeply concentrated flavors, medium to full body, and soft tannins in the
91   lengthy finish. Drink it up. Last tasted 12/90.

JEAN-MICHEL GÉRIN* * * *

Address: 19, rue de Montmain-Verenay
              69420 Ampuis
Tel: 4-74-56-16-56
Fax: 4-74-56-11-37

Wines produced: Côte Rôtie Le Champin Junior, Côte Rôtie Champin le Seigneur, Côte
    Rôtie Les Grandes Places, Condrieu, Côtes du Rhône
Surface area (Champin le Seigneur): 9.1 acres
    (Les Grandes Places): 3.2 acres
Production (Champin le Seigneur): 20,000 bottles
    (Les Grandes Places): 5,000 bottles
Upbringing (Champin le Seigneur): 18–20 months in 25% new oak barrels and 75% in
    barrels 1, 2, and 3 years old
    (Les Grandes Places): 20 months minimum in 100% new oak barrels
Average age of vines (Champin le Seigneur): one-quarter less than 10 years, the remainder
    10–50 years
    (Les Grandes Places): one-quarter less than 10 years, the remainder
    30–60 years
Percentage of Viognier: 5%

This estate is one of the success stories of the nineties. The Gérins have long been
producers in Côte Rôtie, with Jean-Michel's father, Alfred, a well-known political figure in
the northern Rhône (onetime mayor of Ampuis and a legislator in the French government).
This estate was relatively well known in America in the late seventies and early eighties
when the wines were widely available, largely because of a group of American investors that
backed Gérin. Some of those wines were good, but too often they were extremely high in
acidity as well as vegetal.

Jean-Michel Gérin, the young, enthusiastic, exuberant son of Alfred, began his own
domaine in 1990. He had the intelligence to bring aboard the famed Cornas oenologist
Jean-Luc Colombo, and he has been drawing rave reviews for his wines ever since. There
are two cuvées of Côte Rôtie produced at this estate. The Champin le Seigneur, which is
made from a blend of parcels with both young and old vines, represents the bulk of Gérin's
production. The luxury old-vine cuvée is called Les Grandes Places, after the Côte Brune
vineyard of the same name. It is planted mostly in 80-year-old vines and a handful of
younger vines. Unlike his father, Jean-Michel believes new oak casks make a major contribution to the quality of Côte Rôtie. Les Grandes Places is aged for at least 20 months in
100% new oak casks, and bottled, like the other cuvées, with no filtration. In 1995, a
Champin Junior cuvée was introduced. It represents the production from the youngest vines
of the Gérin estate.

The jump in quality, as evidenced by the following tasting notes, began in 1991, reversed
itself with the difficult vintages of 1992 and 1993, but has continued with the 1994 and
1995 vintages. Jean-Michel Gérin is unquestionably one of the up-and-coming stars in Côte
Rôtie.

VINTAGES

1995—Côte Rôtie Le Champin Junior In 1995, another cuvée, from extremely young
   ·   vines, Le Champin Junior, was produced. The dense purple-colored 1995 Le
 89   Champin Junior exhibits more fruit and openness, as well as a more obvious
      personality with plenty of sweet, succulent, juicy fruit, but not the complexity or
      long-term potential of the Champin Le Seigneur. It should drink well when young
      and last for 7–10 years. Last tasted 6/96.

1995—Côte Rôtie Champin le Seigneur The 1995 Champin le Seigneur was displaying
   ·   less fruit than the Champin Junior. It possesses a healthy deep ruby/purple color,
 88   fine ripeness, and smoky, vanillin, toasty, cassislike fruit, but the wine is tannic
      and closed. However, it is well endowed with what appears to be sufficient fruit,

extract, and glycerin to support the wine's structure. This will not be a precocious, up-front Côte Rôtie to drink upon release. Rather, it will need 5–6 years of cellaring, after which it will age well for 15 years. Last tasted 6/96.

1995—Côte Rôtie Les Grandes Places   The 1995 Côte Rôtie Les Grandes Places is
·   always the biggest as well as richest offering. Not surprisingly, it is made from the
90   best parcels and the oldest vines. This wine is broodingly backward and unevolved, with a deep purple color, smoky oak, medium to full body, excellent to outstanding extraction, and admirable purity and length. It will require 4–5 years of cellaring and should keep for 15+ years. Last tasted 6/96.

1994—Côte Rôtie Champin le Seigneur   The deep ruby-colored 1994 Champin le Sei-
·   gneur offers a spicy, oaky nose, and silky, round flavors displaying good ripeness
86   and extract, and an abrupt finish. It is attractive, but I hope more length and character emerge with bottle age. Last tasted 6/96.

1994—Côte Rôtie Les Grandes Places   The 1994 Les Grandes Places is riper and more
·   muscular, and cuts a deeper feel on the palate. The wine exhibits a deep ruby/
87   purple color, black olive, cassis, and cedar notes in the nose, a sweet, firmly structured, powerful entry on the palate, medium body, and loads of tannin in the finish. It may always taste a trifle austere and muscular, but it is a good to excellent effort. Last tasted 6/96.

1993—Côte Rôtie Champin le Seigneur   This is a lean, slightly fruity, astringent, hard
·   1993 with no future. Last tasted 10/95.
75

1993—Côte Rôtie Les Grandes Places   The 1993 luxury cuvée Les Grandes Places
·   exhibits a darker color, more toasty oak, and some sweet fruit in the attack. It is a
82   supple, medium-bodied wine for drinking over the near term. Not a disappointment, but this wine is one-dimensional by Gérin's recent standards. Last tasted 10/95.

1991—Côte Rôtie Champin le Seigneur   The 1991 Champin le Seigneur displays a deep
·   color, a sweet herb- and black-raspberry-scented nose, sweet, soft, ripe flavors, low
89   acidity, and a ripe, round finish. Although not a blockbuster wine, nor particularly concentrated, it does possess plenty of finesse, a succulent texture, and an affable personality. Anticipated maturity: now–2003. Last tasted 6/95.

1991—Côte Rôtie Les Grandes Places   In 1991 Gérin's Les Grandes Places boasts an
·   opaque dark ruby/purple color, a superb nose of jammy black fruits, exotic spices,
93   smoke, and new oak. Rich, with layers of fruit, low acidity, and a spectacularly long finish, this voluptuously textured, rich, concentrated wine is a classic example of Côte Rôtie. Anticipated maturity: now–2007. Last tasted 7/96.

1990—Côte Rôtie Champin le Seigneur   The 1990 Champin le Seigneur is light, lean,
·   acidic, and lacking fruit, generosity, and character. It should be consumed over the
74?   near term. Mature: now. Last tasted 6/93.

GUIGAL* * * */* * * * *

Address: 1, route de Taquières or Château d'Ampuis
              69420 Ampuis
Tel: 4-74-56-10-22
Fax: 4-74-56-18-76
Wines produced: Côte Rôtie Château d'Ampuis, Côte Rôtie Brune et Blonde, Côte Rôtie La
              Landonne, Côte Rôtie La Mouline, Côte Rôtie La Turque
Surface area (Château d'Ampuis): 18–20 acres
              (Brune et Blonde): 20 acres
              (La Landonne): 6.2 acres

    (La Mouline): 3.5 acres
    (La Turque): 2.5 acres
Production (Château d'Ampuis): 28,000 bottles
    (Brune et Blonde): 20,000+ cases
    (La Landonne): 800 cases
    (La Mouline): 400 cases
    (La Turque): 400 cases
Upbringing (Château d'Ampuis): 3+ years in new oak foudres and casks
    (Brune et Blonde): 36 months in oak casks and foudres
    (La Landonne): 42 months in 100% new oak
    (La Mouline): 42 months in 100% new oak
    (La Turque): 42 months in 100% new oak
Average age of vines (Château d'Ampuis): 25–75 years
    (Brune et Blonde): 10–70 years
    (La Landonne): 10 years
    (La Mouline): 60–65 years
    (La Turque): 15 years
Percentage of Viognier (Château d'Ampuis): 5–8%
    (Brune et Blonde): 4%
    (La Landonne): none
    (La Mouline): 11%
    (La Turque): 7%

From this firm's Côtes du Rhône to excellent Châteauneuf du Pape, exquisite Condrieu, and mind-boggling, reference point Côte Rôties, there is no winemaker on planet Earth who has produced so many compelling wines irrespective of the vintage conditions as Marcel Guigal. Since I began visiting Guigal annually in the late seventies, his production must have increased more than fiftyfold, and there have been times when I feared such expansion could not occur without a decline in quality. Yet tasting annually in Guigal's cellars has proved time and time again that my fears have been unfounded. In fact, days of sniffing, swirling, and spitting in the Guigal cellars are among the most memorable and instructive days most wine enthusiasts could spend. The quality and distinctiveness of each of his wines are equaled in few other cellars in the world. Burgundy's Domaine Leroy and Alsace's Domaine Zind-Humbrecht would be two in France that come to mind immediately.

  What is the key to Guigal's success? For Guigal's own vineyards, which are cultivated organically with no chemical fertilizers or treatments, there is a notoriously late harvest aimed at picking grapes that are nearly bursting because of their supermaturity. The late harvest, plus extremely low yields, minimal intervention in the wine cellar (minimal rackings and absolutely no filtration), all combine to form spectacularly fragrant, rich, profound wines. The same prerequisites are applicable to the juice that Guigal purchases to fashion his blends of Côtes du Rhône, Hermitage, Condrieu, and Châteauneuf du Pape. He buys only from producers who have old vines and low yields and who harvest late.

  Whatever Guigal produces, his name will be forever synonymous with the appellation's most riveting examples of Côte Rôtie. Wealthy Rhône wine enthusiasts have been known to do just about everything trying to locate a bottle or two of Guigal's super-rare and expensive single-vineyard Côte Rôtie La Landonne, La Mouline, and La Turque. La Mouline is almost always the first vineyard to be harvested. From a distance, the vines look as if they are sitting in a natural Roman arena with concave slopes and terraces of vines with a full southerly exposition. That exposition and a perfect exposure to sunlight ensure that these grapes ripen several days before those of La Turque or La Landonne. Moreover, La Mouline can be harvested in a mere 3–4 hours. Once the grapes are harvested (La Mouline's vines average 60 years of age, and readers should keep in mind that there is about 11% Viognier planted on this small parcel), La Mouline is given a slow, warm, very long fermentation, but with no punching down of the cap for fear of extracting too much tannin. It is Guigal's goal to make La Mouline the most silky, elegant, and complex of his Côte Rôties, and by regularly pumping the juice gently over the cap he obtains extraordinary concentration, but no rough edges. The first vintage of La Mouline was 1966, but it was not until 1969 and 1976 that this single-vineyard wine became a superstar.

Guigal's second single-vineyard wine is La Landonne, made from a collection of small plots of land on an extremely steep slope (a gradient of 63°) that is located in the northern part of the appellation on the Côte Brune. Guigal began buying small parcels of La Landonne in 1972, and planting them in 1974. The last parcel acquired, La Petite Landonne, became part of the Guigal empire in 1985 after the purchase of Vidal-Fleury. La Landonne has a south-southeast orientation, and is usually harvested after La Mouline. A full two days are needed to pick La Landonne, largely because it is bigger than La Mouline, but also because the gradient makes harvesting frightfully difficult. In contrast to the vinification of La Mouline, La Landonne is fermented in a closed tank with a system of automatic *pigéage* to extract as much flavor and intensity as possible. There is no Viognier planted in the Landonne vineyard, and the strong iron content of the soil results in a wine that is among the most concentrated, extracted, and powerful produced in the world.

The last vineyard to be harvested is La Turque, Guigal's youngest vineyard. Situated on a convex slope with a southern orientation, La Turque enjoys sunshine throughout the day. The slope is not nearly as steep as that of La Landonne, and yields tend to be slightly higher, about 35–40 hectoliters per hectare instead of the 25–36 hectoliters at La Mouline and La Landonne. Additionally, slightly higher acidity is noticeable in La Turque, and thus Guigal perennially harvests this vineyard very late in order to have extremely high sugar levels to achieve the right acid balance. La Turque is usually harvested in one day. La Turque receives essentially the same vinification as La Landonne in closed tanks with considerable *pigéage*. Like all Guigal's Côte Rôties, destemming is rarely practiced, although in 1995 Guigal was shocked that the grapes were so physiologically ripe yet the stems were still green and full of acidity. A partial destemming was done in 1995. All three of these cuvées are put in 100% new oak casks and racked two to three times during their first year, and one to two times during the second year. During the third year of upbringing in 100% new oak casks, there is rarely more than one racking. These wines are bottled after 42 months in new oak barrels, and are neither fined nor filtered. What is so remarkable is that after 3–4 years in bottle, it is almost impossible to tell they were ever aged in new oak given their extraordinary richness and profound personalities.

What do great vintages of these wines taste like? Looking at my notes over the last 20 years, and extrapolating from the best vintages of these three extraordinary wines, this is what readers might expect:

La Mouline This is the cuvée with the highest percentage of Viognier, which can vary from 8 to 12% depending on the vintage. It is one of the world's most intensely perfumed wines, offering in the great vintages nearly otherworldly aromas of bacon fat, *pain grillé*, cassis, white flowers, black raspberries, and occasionally Provençal olives. Because of the Viognier and the vineyard's terroir, La Mouline is the most supple and seductive of Guigal's single-vineyard treasures. It is often delicious at birth and continues to offer voluptuously textured, hedonistic drinking for 15–20 years. Only the most tannic and concentrated vintages, such as 1976, 1978, 1983, 1988, and 1985, produced La Moulines that required cellaring. La Mouline is the Mozart of the Guigal portfolio.

La Landonne More like Brahms, La Landonne, coming from very steep terraces on the Côte Brune, with its distinctively high iron content, produces a wine of enormous massiveness and concentration. Since there is no Viognier in the blend (this is 100% Syrah), La Landonne is usually the most opaque purple, sometimes almost black, with extraordinary density and power, as well as a brooding backwardness that is extremely impressive, almost intimidating. La Landonne is the most tannic wine made in Côte Rôtie, and as Guigal often claims, it is meant to survive 30–40 years of cellaring. This is clearly a wine for enthusiasts who have both patience and a good, cold cellar, as it usually requires a minimum of 8–10 years of cellaring, even in lighter-weight years. Aromatically and flavor-wise, La Landonne offers much more smoke, licorice, Asian spice, grilled meat, and cassis aromas and flavors.

La Turque The newest star in the Guigal constellation, La Turque represents a synthesis in style between La Mouline and La Landonne. It comes from the Côte Brune, but the vineyard is far closer to the Côte Blonde than La Landonne. While it is not as tannic or muscular as La Landonne, it is as concentrated as the latter wine, with nearly the same compelling aromatics as La Mouline. In many respects, it tastes as if it wants to be the Rhône's answer to Burgundy's great duo of grand cru vineyards, Richebourg and Musigny. It usually possesses a saturated dark purple color (darker than La Mouline, but not as opaque as La Landonne), great flavor intensity and extraction, more structure than La Mouline, but not nearly the tannic force and power of La Landonne, with extraordinary density and richness of taste, without any heaviness. Very delicious when released, but less aromatically evolved than La Mouline, it is a wine that should, in top vintages, have 20–25 years of aging potential.

Château D'Ampuis is meant to be well above the quality of Guigal's Brune et Blonde, but without the elevated stature of his three single-vineyard wines. The first vintage was 1995 (coincidentally the first vintage that Marcel Guigal's son, Philippe, did the harvest and assisted his father in the vinification). In tasting through the six vineyards that make up this extraordinary wine, it is obvious that this is going to be one of the finest wines of the appellation. Aged both in barrel and in specially designed foudres, it has a character closer to La Turque than La Landonne or La Mouline.

Traditionally, Guigal's Côte Rôtie Brune et Blonde has been made from both his own holdings in the appellation, as well as purchased grapes and in some cases juice. With Château D'Ampuis being made entirely from estate vineyards, Guigal will be increasingly dependent on purchased grapes (and juice) for this particular cuvée. It has consistently been one of the best Côte Rôties of the appellation, and was exceptionally strong in vintages such as 1976, 1978, 1983, 1985, 1988, 1989, 1990, and 1991. Because of its long aging in cask (3 + years) and healthy percentage of Viognier, it is delicious when young, and sound advice is to drink it within 10–12 years of life, although top vintages (e.g., 1976) have aged impeccably for two decades. Guigal's production of Brune et Blonde has continued to increase, and it now represents nearly 40% of the entire production of Côte Rôtie, obviously making Guigal the undisputed king, both qualitatively and quantitatively, of the appellation.

As when any person has reached the top of their profession, it is undoubtedly fashionable to wait for the empire to tumble, or in lieu of that, be cynically critical. However, I do not believe this will happen as long as Marcel Guigal has control of this firm. With the capable assistance of his wife, and with his son, Philippe, beginning to show the dedication, seriousness, and commitment that his father and grandfather have exhibited, the elements for Guigal's continued reign of success remain in place. And one final thought. It would be very easy for someone in Guigal's position to take the Concorde to any exotic location in the world, but this is not part of the man. I have always said that one is always going to eat well in a restaurant where the chef is pale, sweaty, overweight, and sporting a dirty apron. In contrast, there have been only a few times in my life where I have eaten well when the chef was tanned and wearing a spotless apron! By analogy, Marcel Guigal is the chef who is always in the kitchen. Sporting his beret, which seems to have been planted on his head, Guigal knows the location of every barrel and foudre in his vast underground cellars, and when it was last tasted or racked. In the past 20 years I have spent visiting wineries and vignerons, I have never seen another producer so fanatical about quality as Marcel Guigal.

VINTAGES

1995—Côte Rôtie Château d'Ampuis   Guigal has decided to make a single Côte Rôtie
·   called Château d'Ampuis, all coming from a blend of six vineyards—La Pommière,
91   Pavillon, La Garde, Le Clos, La Grande Plantée, and Le Moulin. I tasted all six
        cuvées, ranking them from 89–92 to 92–94. Since only one cuvée scored below
        90, I suspect the 1995 Côte Rôtie Château d'Ampuis will merit a score in the range
        of 90–92. These are all super cuvées of rich, concentrated, formidably endowed
        wine with good underlying acidity and balance. It is the crisp acidity (a noticeable
        component in all the 1995s) that should ensure considerable longevity. Fortunately,
        the acidity is neither tart nor sharp, as it is in so many 1993 red Burgundies, and
        some 1995 northern Rhônes. This wine, which will be priced just below the
        single-vineyard Côte Roties, is significantly better than the Brune et Blonde offer-
        ing, but not quite at the qualitative level of La Mouline, La Turque, and La
        Landonne. The production will be limited to 28,000 bottles, or roughly 2,300 cases.
        Given its long aging in oak casks, and new, specially designed foudres, the 1995
        Château d'Ampuis will not be in the marketplace for several years. Last tasted 6/96.

1995—Côte Rôtie La Landonne   The opaque black-colored 1995 La Landonne was sing-
·   ing when I tasted it. The wine reveals lower acidity than many 1995 northern
95   Rhônes, good but not excessive tannin, fabulous layers of smoky, licorice, Asian
        spice, grilled-meat-scented and -flavored fruit, enormous body, and a massive
        finish. It will need 3–4 years of cellaring when released; it will keep for 25 +
        years. Last tasted 6/96.

1995—Côte Rôtie La Mouline   The 1995 La Mouline is a compelling wine. The intensity
·   of its smoky, cassis, bacon fat, and honeysuckle-scented nose, and fabulously rich,
95   sweet, opulent flavors are something to behold. Underlying everything is structure
        from the wood tannin and sound acidity. This wine is so gorgeous and hedonistic
        that I often wonder why it has not been declared illegal by antipleasure bureaucrats.
        Like most La Moulines, this wine will be delicious when released yet keep for
        15 + years. Last tasted 6/96.

1995—Côte Rôtie La Turque   The most prodigious of these three mind-boggling wines is
·   the 1995 La Turque. It is the sweetest, densest, most complete, and most exotic,
97   even eclipsing La Mouline for pure decadence in its smoky, jammy, blackcurrant,
        and raspberry-scented nose. Unctuously textured, with surprising balance for a
        wine of such size and concentration, the 1995 La Turque is a tour de force
        in winemaking. As is so often the case, these three limited-production wines
        (approximately 400–800 cases of each) are reference point wines. And yet there
        are really no secrets to their greatness—low yields, physiologically ripe fruit, and
        noninterventionist winemaking. Anticipated maturity: 2000–2018. Last tasted
        6/96.

1994—Côte Rôtie Brune et Blonde   The 1994 Côte Rôtie Brune et Blonde (I tasted six
·   separate cuvées and rated all of them between 89 and 93) is a sweet, rich, forward
90   style of Côte Rôtie with plenty of vanillin, black-raspberry, and cassislike aromas,
        a lovely, opulent texture, and a medium- to full-bodied, lush, seductive finish. It
        will be a wine to drink during its first 10–12 years of life. Last tasted 6/96.

1994—Côte Rôtie La Landonne   The 1994 La Landonne is the most backward, tannic,
·   and broad-shouldered of this group. Its black/purple color and spicy, tight, smoky
92   nose hardly hint at the richness apparent on the palate. The wine is thick and

closed, but formidably endowed. It will need 4–5 years of cellaring and will keep for two decades. Last tasted 6/96.

1994—Côte Rôtie La Mouline The 1994 Côte Rôtie La Mouline is reminiscent of the
·
94 great 1982. It possesses beautifully integrated wood and acidity, a voluptuous palate, a ruby/purple color, and exaggerated, profound aromas of honeysuckle, cassis, and jammy black raspberries. It is a gorgeously rich, concentrated wine that is already silky and approachable. It should last for 15 years. Last tasted 6/96.

1994—Côte Rôtie La Turque 1994 also appears to be another great vintage for Guigal's
·
92 La Turque. It is already amazingly sexy, with a sweet, creamy texture, a dark ruby/purple color, fabulous ripeness, and a layered inner core of sweet juice packed with extract, glycerin, and flavor. It should drink well young and keep for 12–15 years. Last tasted 6/96.

1993—Côte Rôtie Brune et Blonde The 1993 Brune et Blonde appears to be the weakest
·
78 Côte Rôtie Guigal has produced in over a decade. If it turns out to be above average I will be surprised, since all the component parts were tannic, lean, and tough-textured, with vegetal characteristics, high acidity, and an absence of fat, charm, and fruit. I am certain the wine will taste better out of bottle, a testament to the genius of Guigal's winemaking, but for now, this is a decidedly uninteresting wine. Last tasted 6/96.

1993—Côte Rôtie La Landonne The 1993 La Landonne exhibits the darkest color of
·
86 these wines, but is excruciatingly tannic, without the fat and ripe fruit behind its structure. Last tasted 6/96.

1993—Côte Rôtie La Mouline The 1993 La Mouline displays a moderately deep ruby
·
88 color and light body, with toasty notes from the vanillin-scented wood dominating the wine's personality. Initially the wine is soft, with fine ripeness and sweet fruit on the attack, but it then reveals some hollowness and a green-pepper-like character. I suspect it will require drinking within 5–8 years of its release. Last tasted 6/96.

1993—Côte Rôtie La Turque The 1993 La Turque appears to be the best of these
·
89 offerings, with a spicy, herbal, sweet, olive, Asian spice, and curranty nose. Medium-bodied, with ripe, up-front fruit, and dry, harsh tannin in the finish, it is a good wine, albeit a bit hard. Anticipated maturity: 1998–2005. Last tasted 6/96.

1992—Côte Rôtie Brune et Blonde The 1992 Brune et Blonde has turned out to be far
·
87 tastier than it appeared when I tasted the component parts prior to blending and bottling. It possesses a dark ruby color, as well as a fragrant, open-knit nose of coffee, smoke, cedar, and raspberry/currant fruit. Soft and spicy, with a sweet attack, and round flavors in its medium-bodied personality, this is a wine to drink over the next 5–7 years. Last tasted 6/96.

1992—Côte Rôtie La Landonne The 1992 La Landonne is the densest, most savage, and
·
92 animal-like of the three single-vineyard cuvées. Made from a vineyard on the steep hillside on the Côte Brune, this dark ruby/purple-colored wine reveals copious quantities of sweet black fruits in the nose intermingled with Asian spices, roasted herbs, and grilled steak. Medium- to full-bodied, powerful, and rich, with some noticeable tannin, this wine is approachable because of its low acidity. It has turned out to be another exceptional example of La Landonne. Drink it over the next 15 years. Last tasted 6/96.

1992—Côte Rôtie La Mouline The 1992 La Mouline's color is a deep dark ruby/purple,
·
91 and the nose offers a superrich fragrance of black olives, cassis, and toast. Rich, savory, and velvety textured, with copious quantities of sweet, creamy fruit, this medium- to full-bodied, luscious La Mouline should drink well for 10–12 years. Readers should remember that this is the only one of three single-vineyard bottlings that includes a percentage of Viognier (about 10%) in the blend. Last tasted 6/96.

1992—Côte Rôtie La Turque   The 1992 La Turque reveals blackcurrant, licorice, and
·   *pain grillé*–like notes in its sweet, penetrating aromatic profile. It is amazing how
93   this wine has gained weight and richness in cask. It has turned out to be a profound,
            sweet, rich, opulently styled wine with no harshness or vegetal aspects. There are
            layers of silky black fruit gently infused with smoky toast. The wine's low acidity
            and up-front, forward nature suggest it can be drunk now as well as over the next
            12–15 years. Last tasted 6/96.

1991—Côte Rôtie Brune et Blonde   The dark ruby-colored 1991 Brune et Blonde exhibits
·   the soft, succulent, precocious character of this rich, velvety-textured vintage.
90   Forward, with gobs of sweet, toasty oak intermingled with lavish quantities of
            cassis, smoke, and pepper, it is a lush, medium- to full-bodied wine with low
            acidity and ripe tannin. Already delicious, it should drink well for at least a decade.
            Last tasted 6/96.

1991—Côte Rôtie La Landonne   The 1991 La Landonne will provide multimillionaires
·   with plenty of pleasure over the next 20 years. They can also debate whether it or
99   the perfect 1990 is the better wine. The 1991's bouquet offers huge, smoky, new
            saddle leather, licorice, Asian spice, meaty, and cassis scents. Black in color, with
            layers of richness, huge body, massive extraction, and a phenomenal finish, it is
            another legend from Marcel Guigal. It will be the least precocious of the 1991s,
            needing until the turn of the century to open and develop; it should keep for 25–
            30 + years. Last tasted 6/96.

1991—Côte Rôtie La Mouline   The black/purple-colored 1991 La Mouline appears to be
·   another perfect wine in the making, with a staggering bouquet of violets, bacon fat,
100   sweet cassis fruit, and toasty oak. The wine exhibits superb density. It is tasting
            even richer and more concentrated than it did during its first several years of life.
            With 8% Viognier in the blend and made from extremely low yields (only 400
            cases produced), it is a phenomenal wine. I find it more seductive than the nearly
            perfect 1990. Anticipated maturity: now–2012. Last tasted 6/96.

1991—Côte Rôtie La Turque   The 1991 La Turque behaves as if it wants to be the
·   northern Rhône's answer to Richebourg and Musigny. However, with the exception
99   of Domaine Leroy, you cannot find a Richebourg or Musigny with the richness and
            complexity possessed by this awesome wine. The saturated dark purple color is
            followed by a wine that is surprisingly lighter in the mouth than its great flavor
            intensity and rich extraction would suggest. It is a winemaking tour de force in that
            Guigal has been able to cram phenomenal levels of fruit, complexity, and richness
            into this velvety-textured wine without causing it to taste heavy. Anticipated matu-
            rity: 1998–2015. Last tasted 6/96.

1990—Côte Rôtie Brune et Blonde   The 1990 Côte Rôtie Brune et Blonde has turned out
·   to be outstanding. It offers a sweet, expansive, smoky, bacon fat, cassis-scented
90   nose, and rich, full-bodied, opulent flavors. It is neither as tannic as the 1988 nor
            as soft as the flattering, up-front 1989.

1990—Côte Rôtie Brune et Blonde Hommage Magnum   This cuvée was bottled only
·   in magnum (the only time Guigal has ever produced a wine in this format) as a
96   special commemorative wine to honor his father. Made from a parcel of vines
            in La Pommière, this is a majestic, dense, smoky, cassis-scented wine that has
            enormous extract, an opaque purple color, and a knockout nose of jammy black
            fruit. An extremely full-bodied Côte Rôtie with an exceptional sweetness of fruit
            (from ripeness, not sugar), this rarity is largely of academic interest because
            of the microscopic production. Anticipated maturity: 1999–2015. Last tasted
            8/96.

1990—Côte Rôtie La Landonne   The 1990 La Landonne is a perfect wine! Fortunately,
·   more than 800 cases were produced. It possesses an opaque black color, and a
100   huge, truffle, licorice, cassis, and peppery-scented nose. While it is one of the most
concentrated wines I have ever poured across my palate, it is perfectly balanced,
with adequate underlying acidity, huge extraction of ripe fruit and tannin, and a
phenomenal 70-second or longer finish. This is the essence of Syrah! Give this
monumental wine 7–10 years of cellaring; it will last for 40–45 + years.

1990—Côte Rôtie La Mouline   The superconcentrated, opaque purple-colored 1990 La
·   Mouline is closer in style to the otherworldly 1988 than I would have thought.
99   Extremely rich, with a huge, bacon fat, toasty, cassis, and floral-scented nose, as
well as phenomenally rich flavors, it is a wine known for its voluptuousness and
extraordinary intensity. Anticipated maturity: 1997–2018. Last tasted 3/97.

1990—Côte Rôtie La Turque   The 1990 La Turque offers an opaque purple color, and an
·   overwhelming perfume of jammy black cherries, cassis, toast, and minerals. With
98   its sweet, generous, incredibly harmonious personality, it is an unforgettable wine.
With sweet tannin, low acidity, and one of the most velvety-textured, decadently
rich palates I have encountered, this fabulous wine has a finish that lasts more
than a minute. Anticipated maturity: 1998–2016. Last tasted 7/96.

1989—Côte Rôtie Brune et Blonde   Guigal has made a round, elegant, generously fla-
·   vored, soft and precocious 1989 Côte Rôtie Brune et Blonde. Fully mature, this is
90   a delicious, seductive, dark ruby-colored wine that should be drunk over the next
decade. Last tasted 7/96.

1989—Côte Rôtie La Landonne   The 1989 single-vineyard Côte Rôties are magnificent.
·   Reminiscent of Guigal's 1985s and 1982s, the black/purple-colored La Landonne
98   possesses fabulous concentration, and a sweet, expansive personality. It has plenty
of tannin, but there is so much fruit that the tannin is largely concealed. This is
another mammoth-sized wine with extraordinary extract. Anticipated maturity:
1999–2020. Last tasted 7/96.

1989—Côte Rôtie La Mouline   The saturated purple-colored 1989 La Mouline is an
·   explosively rich wine, with its profound perfume of violets, black raspberries, and
98   creamy, toasty new oak. Very full-bodied, with a dreamy opulence, gobs of fruit,
an unctuous texture, and powerful finish, this wine manages to balance intensity
with great elegance. Anticipated maturity: now–2016. Last tasted 7/96.

1989—Côte Rôtie La Turque   The precocious, sweet, jammy 1989 La Turque's smoky,
·   licorice, and black-raspberry aromas, as well as its phenomenal richness, make for
99   another extraordinary tasting experience. Full-bodied, dense, and thick, this wine
possesses the essence of black cherries. Still youthful, it is already gorgeous to
drink. Anticipated maturity: now–2012. Last tasted 7/96.

1988—Côte Rôtie Brune et Blonde   Guigal's regular cuvée of 1988 Brune et Blonde is
·   very fine. It has admirable levels of sweet, voluptuous, smoky, raspberry fruit,
90   intermingled with scents of new oak, bacon fat, and flowers. In the mouth it
exhibits the up-front, precocious softness and lushness of the 1985, but with more
complexity, structure, and tannin in the finish. Anticipated maturity: now–2008.
Last tasted 12/95.

1988—Côte Rôtie La Landonne   An opaque purple color and a closed but exciting nose
·   of truffles, minerals, Asian spices, and fruitcake. When the wine hits the mouth
100   with its enormous weight and extraction of flavor, one can't help but be seduced by
such enormous richness and purity. Nevertheless, there is still a remarkably high
level of tannin (sweet rather than astringent), a youthful, unevolved fruit character,
and flavors that stain the palate. After tasting this wine, one feels like brush-

ing one's teeth . . . it is that rich. Anticipated maturity: 2002–2030. Last tasted 7/96.

1988—Côte Rôtie La Mouline   Among so many exceptional La Mouline's, this is one of
· the most profound. At the same time, it is atypically backward, and has been slow
100 to evolve. Still dark purple-colored, with only a hint of the flamboyant Mouline aromatics, this thick, superconcentrated, full-bodied, tannic La Mouline is loaded with fruit, massive, and full-bodied, but still in need of time to fully shed its cloak of tannin. It is likely to be the longest-lived La Mouline since the 1978 and 1969. Anticipated maturity: 1999–2015. Last tasted 7/96.

1988—Côte Rôtie La Turque   Deep purple-colored, with grilled meat and smoky, barbe-
· cuelike aromas beginning to emerge, along with lavishly ripe scents of black plums
100 and cassis, the 1988 La Turque is not quite as suppressed aromatically as La Mouline. This thick, unctuously textured, full-bodied, monster wine is close to reaching its plateau of drinkability. The wine exhibits awesome concentration, terrific purity, and, amazingly, no evidence of the 42 months it spent in 100% new oak casks. Very full and rich, and potentially the longest-lived La Turque yet made, this wine should be legendary. Anticipated maturity: 2000–2015. Last tasted 7/96.

1987—Côte Rôtie Brune et Blonde   No appellation in the Rhône Valley had greater
· success in 1987 than Côte Rôtie. Most of the growers harvested late and picked
89 fully ripe, only slightly diluted grapes. The top wines, such as the 1987 Côte Rôtie Brune et Blonde, are wonderfully fragrant, satiny-textured wines that have great bouquets and smooth-as-silk flavors. Put Guigal's 1987 in a blind tasting against some of the 1988 grands crus of Burgundy, and I would be willing to bet it would be one of the top two or three wines, if not the very best. Always a very forward Côte Rôtie, this fully mature, deep garnet-colored wine is surprisingly concentrated, with a bouquet crammed with black raspberries, smoked herbs, and licorice. Ripe, long, concentrated, medium- to full-bodied, this luscious and opulently textured, elegant wine is close to full maturity. A sleeper vintage, this is a hedonistic glassful of Côte Rôtie that has aged remarkably well. Anticipated maturity: now–2002. Last tasted 7/96.

1987—Côte Rôtie La Landonne   Opaque purple, bordering on black in color, La Lan-
· donne's aromatics are the most subdued of the 1987s. Although still closed, this
96 wine is very powerful, rich, thick, and represents the essence of the Syrah grape. That earthy, mineral, truffle, licorice component is just beginning to poke its head through this massively framed wine. It is remarkable that this vintage produced a wine of such extraordinary concentration and richness. Anticipated maturity: 2001–2020. Last tasted 8/96.

1987—Côte Rôtie La Mouline   Guigal's 1987 La Mouline is sensational. Considering the
· vintage, this must be the greatest wine produced in France in 1987. The color is a
95 youthful purple, and the nose offers up sweet, pure aromas of jammy black raspber-ries, smoke, and honeysuckle, and vague whiffs of apricots. Thick, rich flavors coat the palate in a seamless, velvety-textured manner. This medium- to full-bodied, marvelously concentrated wine has no hard edges, and is the epitome of volup-tuousness and sumptuousness. This has been a glorious La Mouline to drink since its birth, and it shows no signs of age. Anticipated maturity: now–2007. Last tasted 8/96.

1987—Côte Rôtie La Turque   A blast of roasted herb, licorice, and black fruit scents
· jump from the glass of this full-bodied, superconcentrated 1987. Very pure, with
96 some *pain grillé* notes from new oak still present, this thick, juicy wine is soft, but its color and bouquet are more typical of a 3- or 4-year-old wine than one that is

approaching 10 years of age. The finish is long and rich, with more tannin than in La Mouline. Anticipated maturity: now–2009. Last tasted 8/96.

1986—Côte Rôtie Brune et Blonde The 1986 Brune et Blonde is a satisfying wine, but
· it needs to be drunk up. Deep garnet-colored, with a bouquet of road tar, licorice,
85 blackcurrants, and olives, it is somewhat austere and tannic, which is typical of the 1986 vintage in the northern Rhône. There is some toughness in the finish, which I doubt will ever dissipate fully. Not bad for the vintage. Anticipated maturity: now–2001. Last tasted 11/95.

1986—Côte Rôtie La Landonne The 1986 La Landonne is another outstanding wine,
· though it lacks the magical perfume of La Mouline and the indescribable, riveting
90 character of La Turque. It is more tannic and amply endowed, but among the splendid La Landonnes made during the eighties, the 1986 does not possess the size or intensity of the greatest vintages (1989, 1988, 1985, 1983, and 1982). Anticipated maturity: now–2009. Last tasted 12/91.

1986—Côte Rôtie La Mouline The 1986 La Mouline displays its characteristic exotic
· aroma of smoky oak, bacon fat, and spring flowers, which is followed by layer upon
91 layer of opulent black fruits. The color is still very dark purple, with some lightening at the edge. There is more tannin and olive-flavored fruit than one normally finds in La Mouline. For a difficult vintage, this wine is remarkable. Anticipated maturity: now–2004. Last tasted 4/95.

1986—Côte Rôtie La Turque The fully mature 1986 La Turque has a bouquet of smoke,
· new saddle leather, roasted herbs, meat, and sweet, jammy black fruit. Medium- to
92 full-bodied, ripe, and intense, without the colossal richness of the finest vintages, this still youthful wine should continue to age well. Anticipated maturity: now–2006. Last tasted 11/95.

1985—Côte Rôtie Brune et Blonde Like many northern Rhônes from this vintage, the
· 1985 regular cuvée has always been a deliciously ripe, round, precocious-tasting
90 wine, with a concentrated, creamy texture, and smoky bouquet. The amber edge and round, sweet fruit suggest full maturity. Drink it up. Mature now. Last tasted 7/96.

1985—Côte Rôtie La Landonne Once again the darkest, thickest, most powerful, and
· formidably concentrated of Guigal's single-vineyard Côte Rôties, the 1985 La
100 Landonne is also the least flattering and most intimidating. Like its two siblings, it is throwing a hefty sediment, with the inside of the bottle resembling that of a 15-year-old vintage port. The color is still a murky, inky purple. The nose offers up aromas of beef blood, vitamins (iron?), minerals, smoke, and truffles. Extremely thick, full-bodied, and massive, with noticeable tannin, this monster wine reveals no hard edges, but it does possess teeth-staining extract and power. It is a remarkable effort! Anticipated maturity: 2000–2025. Last tasted 8/96.

1985—Côte Rôtie La Mouline One of the all-time great La Moulines, this still youthful
· and unevolved wine does not have the tannic ferocity of the 1988, or the sheer
100 force and intensity of the 1978, 1976, and 1969, but it represents the epitome of this single-vineyard wine. Everything fits perfectly in this full-bodied, black/purple-colored wine that reveals no garnet or amber at the edge of its color. The nose offers up a formidable array of overripe black raspberries and cherries intertwined with scents of cedar, chocolate, olives, and toast. Extremely full-bodied, with an unctuosity and opulence that must be tasted to be believed, this velvety-textured wine's finish lasts for over a minute. It is one of the most concentrated but profoundly endowed and well-balanced wines I have ever tasted. Like so many of the wines Guigal has produced from this vineyard, no matter how hard one tries to articulate its glories, words are simply inadequate. The 1985 is just beginning to

achieve full maturity, where it should remain for another 15+ years. Anticipated maturity: now–2012. Last tasted 8/96.

1985—Côte Rôtie La Turque　The debut vintage for this wine was especially impressive
· 　　in view of the fact that the vineyard was so young. The 1985 La Turque's color
100　remains a dark purple, with no signs of amber or lightening. The nose explodes from the glass, revealing scents of jammy black fruits, licorice, lead pencil, and smoke. Sweet, thick, highly concentrated flavors contain enough acidity and soft wood tannin to give the wine a well-focused feel. This prodigiously endowed, rich wine should continue to evolve and offer accessible drinking for another 15+ years. Anticipated maturity: now–2012. Last tasted 8/96.

1984—Côte Rôtie Brune et Blonde　This wine has lost its baby fat, as well as some of its
· 　　sweet, smoky, black-raspberry fruit, now revealing earth, herbs, and green acidity.
77　It is past its prime and should be consumed. Last tasted 6/93.

1984—Côte Rôtie La Landonne　Two recent bottles have been vegetal, earthy, and dis-
· 　　jointed. The wine reveals a smoky note, as well as a stewed, underripe vegetal
76　component. There is some fruit, but this wine appears to be quickly disintegrating. Last tasted 5/92.

1984—Côte Rôtie La Mouline　The 1984 has held up, but it requires drinking before the
· 　　end of the century. For a terrible vintage, it has come close to being outstanding.
89　It still exhibits a deep garnet color with some amber at the edge. The exotic, barbecue spice, roasted herb, green olive, and black-raspberry-scented nose is intact as well as interesting. On the palate, the wine's attack offers juicy fruit, a whiff of underripe vegetables, and a compact finish. Some real sweetness and a good mid-palate are still evident, but don't push your luck. Anticipated maturity: now–1999. Last tasted 11/95.

1983—Côte Rôtie Brune et Blonde　I preferred this wine during its first 10 years of life,
· 　　as it has now lost some of its fat and succulence. Still a healthy dark ruby color,
87　with only minor amber at the edge, the nose offers a spicy, earthy, sweet red-fruit character. It possesses the dry tannin that is found in so many wines of this vintage, but some fruit remains, as well as medium to full body, and a spicy, austere finish. Anticipated maturity: now–2004. Last tasted 12/93.

1983—Côte Rôtie La Landonne　This murky, purple/garnet-colored wine offers up an
· 　　exotic nose of tea, smoked duck, licorice, truffles, and earth. Extraordinarily con-
98+　centrated, and almost too rich to be called a beverage, this viscous, compellingly endowed, massive La Landonne remains 5–7 years away from full maturity. The wine possesses excruciatingly high tannin in the finish, but awesome levels of extract and glycerin. Anticipated maturity: 2001–2025. Last tasted 6/96.

1983—Côte Rôtie La Mouline　Still backward, but beginning to throw considerable sedi-
· 　　ment and reveal some amber at the edge, this wine reveals a distinctive, violet,
100　cassis, bacon fat aroma intermixed with smoked duck and Asian spice components. Extremely full-bodied and sturdy, with noticeable tannin, this husky, powerful, concentrated La Mouline is less seductive than many vintages. In fact, in 1983, it behaves more like La Landonne. It can be drunk, but ideally it requires another 4–5 years of cellaring. Many 1983s have proven less exciting than initial predictions because of the refusal of the harsh tannins to melt away, but the tannin is clearly falling away in the 1983 La Mouline. There is still a wealth of fruit remaining. Anticipated maturity: now–2020. Last tasted 6/96.

1982—Côte Rôtie Brune et Blonde　Fully mature, this medium ruby-colored wine is
· 　　beginning to reveal considerable amber at the edge. Some sweet, earthy, berry fruit
87　is intertwined with spice box, cedar, and olive aromas. A broad, expansive sweet-

ness to the fruit is appealing, but the finish is dry and austere. The 1982 Brune et Blonde requires drinking. Last tasted 3/94.

1982—Côte Rôtie La Landonne   For such a precocious vintage, the 1982 La Landonne
· remains a backward, beefy, smoky, chewy mouthful of tannic wine. It has thrown a
95+ huge amount of sediment, and the bottle is completely stained, as if it were a 15-year-old vintage port. The wine reveals an olive, earthy, licorice, mineral, smoked-meat nose, fabulous depth, and a huge, formidably endowed personality. It is a monstrous, superconcentrated wine that should reach its apogee by the turn of the century. Anticipated maturity: 2000–2025. Last tasted 12/95.

1982—Côte Rôtie La Mouline   A fully mature example of La Mouline, the huge, smoky,
· bacon fat, cassis-scented perfume jumps from the glass of this seductive, hedonistic
99 wine. The 1982 has been delicious from birth due to its low acidity and fat, open-knit character. There is no amber or lightening at the edge of its dark ruby/purple color. The wine exhibits a thick, unctuous texture, gobs of fruit, and plenty of heady alcohol in the blockbuster finish. Anticipated maturity: now–2008. Last tasted 12/95.

1981—Côte Rôtie La Landonne   The exaggerated, smoky, stewed vegetable, black-plum-
· scented nose is controversial. The dark ruby/purple color reveals some amber, but
84 little other evidence of age. Spicy, with sweet fruit, the 1981 La Landonne tastes like an overly smoked piece of meat. Nevertheless, there is plenty of richness. Anticipated maturity: now–2002. Last tasted 12/95.

1981—Côte Rôtie La Mouline   Some vegetal, green-bean, smoked-meat characteristics
· dominate the 1981's aromatics. The wine is medium-bodied and more compact
86 than usual, with a deep, dark garnet color. Although fully mature and in need of consumption, it was a remarkable success in what was an extremely difficult vintage in Côte Rôtie. Mature now. Last tasted 12/94.

1980—Côte Rôtie La Landonne   In contrast to the open-knit, fully mature 1980 La
· Mouline, the La Landonne is just beginning to open up and reach full maturity. It
94 has thrown plenty of thick sediment, but it retains a dark murky garnet color. The huge nose of roasted meats, Asian spices, truffles, minerals, and fruitcake is thrilling. Full-bodied, with huge quantities of fruit, and a gamy, rare steak–like taste, this is a thick, masculine, chewy wine that begs to be served with aged beef. Full-bodied and exceptionally concentrated, this is a tour de force for the vintage. Along with La Mouline, it is a candidate for the greatest wine made in France in 1980. Anticipated maturity: now–2010. Last tasted 8/96.

1980—Côte Rôtie La Mouline   It is hard to believe this wine was aged for three years in
· new oak casks given the fact that it no longer exhibits any aromas of toast, vanillin,
94 or smoky new oak. The superconcentration of fruit has simply absorbed the oak, and the result is one of the top wines of the year in France. Still dark ruby/purple/garnet, with a huge, smoked-meat and black-raspberry nose, this rich, voluptuous, concentrated wine has reached full maturity, but it promises to last for several decades. A glorious tasting experience. Anticipated maturity: now–2005. Last tasted 12/91.

1979—Côte Rôtie La Landonne   Surprisingly youthful, with a dark ruby/purple color
· revealing no signs of age, this wine seems more compact and tightly knit than many
91 vintages of Guigal's Côte Rôties. Full-bodied and powerful, with good acidity and outstanding concentration and extract, this wine has aged at a glacial pace. Although not complex, and somewhat monolithic, the 1979 La Landonne is loaded with fruit, glycerin, and body. The balance is there, so perhaps it is just a question of further patience. Anticipated maturity: 1998–2015. Last tasted 5/96.

1979—Côte Rôtie La Mouline   This wine continues to turn out better than I imagined.
·   By the standards of La Mouline, it has higher acidity than normal, but that com-
93   ponent has served it well, preserving the freshness and guaranteeing a relatively
slow evolution. The wine exhibits an intense, gamy, Syrah nose, superrich, ripe
flavors, and a full-bodied, long finish. Anticipated maturity: now–2005. Last
tasted 1/92.

1978—Côte Rôtie Brune et Blonde   Medium dark ruby with some amber at the edge, this
·   spicy, earthy, sweet, jammy-scented wine is still drinking well, although it has
86   been fully mature for 10–12 years. The wine exhibits medium to full body, exuberant, rich, berry fruitiness, and attractive floral notes. Pepper, spice, and drying
tannin are noticeable in the finish. The 1978 Brune et Blonde may be just beginning to dry out. Mature now. Last tasted 6/96.

1978—Côte Rôtie La Landonne   The debut vintage for La Landonne, this formidably
·   endowed, inky-colored monster is just beginning to open up and reveal its personal-
96   ity. As with La Mouline, there is an ounce of sediment in the bottom of the bottle.
The color is a thick purple/black/garnet. The nose reveals a smoked meat, grilled
steak, earthy, truffle, black-fruit character intermixed with mineral notes. Extremely powerful, rich, slightly tannic flavors have enormous volume in the mouth.
The wine still displays a rustic side to its tannin, but there is no doubting the
excessively concentrated, prodigious amount of fruit, extract, glycerin, and character possessed by this wine. Anticipated maturity: 1998–2020. Last tasted 5/96.

1978—Côte Rôtie La Mouline   I have had this wine more than two dozen times (lucky
·   me), and it is one of the most thrilling wines I could ever drink. I loved it when it
100   was an infant, and now that it may, or may not be, fully mature, I still think it is
the quintessential expression of Guigal's La Mouline. The color remains an inky
garnet, with no perceptible lightening at the edges. The celestial aromas include
copious quantities of black raspberries, coconut, smoked duck, Asian spices, and
violets. It overloads the olfactory senses. On the palate, this wine reveals unreal
concentration, layers of thick, juicy fruit, beautifully integrated acidity and tannin,
and a sumptuous finish that lasts for more than a minute. This seamless beauty is
one of the greatest wines made in this century. If I were forced to drink just one
wine . . . let it be this! Anticipated maturity: now–2015. Last tasted 5/96.

1976—Côte Rôtie Brune et Blonde   This wine may be the finest Brune et Blonde made
·   by Guigal over the last three decades. Having had one of my last bottles for my
93   forty-ninth birthday, I was thrilled by how young, vibrant, and rich this wine
remains. The color is a deep dark ruby/garnet, and the nose offers a blast of jammy
black-raspberry fruit intertwined with smoked meat and roasted herb aromas.
Extremely full-bodied, thick, juicy, and amazingly concentrated, this is an explosive Brune et Blonde that should continue to drink well for another decade. Anticipated maturity: now–2005. Last tasted 7/96.

1976—Côte Rôtie La Mouline   The 1976 is even thicker, richer, and more jammy than
·   some of the other great vintages of La Mouline. In essence, it is something between
100   a dry red table wine and a vintage port. Of course it is not sweet, but it is so
concentrated; one simply does not see wines such as this except for 1947 Pétrus or
1947 Cheval Blanc. The wine has thrown a couple of ounces of sediment. It offers
a heavenly bouquet of sweet, floral-infused black-raspberry/cassis fruit. Extremely
unctuous and viscous, with mind-boggling concentration, this wine has always been
exceptional to drink, but it continues to defy the aging curve. I have drunk my last
bottle, so I am dependent on friends for future tastings. This is one of the legendary
wines of the century! Anticipated maturity: now–2007. Last tasted 7/96.

Older Vintages

The first vintage of La Mouline was 1966, and while I tasted the 1969 La Mouline with Marcel Guigal in June 1996 (the wine was as prodigious as ever as well as pure perfection), other vintages of La Mouline are largely at the end of their useful lives. Tastings several years ago of the 1971 and 1970 suggested that the wine could be held, but it is on the slippery downward slope. It has been years since the 1966 was tasted, but my instinct is that the wine is tired. As I indicated elsewhere in this book, the consistency and greatness of La Mouline, which was apparent in 1969, but only hinted at in other years, did not begin until the 1976 vintage. That vintage was followed by a succession of extraordinary wines, starting with 1978.

PAUL JABOULET-AINÉ* * / * * *

Address: Les Jalets
   R.N. 7, B.P. 46
   La-Roche-de-Glun
   26600 Tain l'Hermitage
Tel: 4-75-84-68-93
Fax: 4-75-84-56-14
Wines produced: Côte Rôtie, Côte Rôtie Les Jumelles
Surface area: none, a négociant wine
Production: 20,000 bottles
Upbringing: 14 months in barrels 3–4 years old
Average age of vines: none
Percentage of Viognier: 5%

This historic house, founded in 1834, is located in Tain l'Hermitage in the hamlet of La-Roche-de-Glun, in what may be one of the most unappealingly designed buildings in the Rhône. Jaboulet's fame rests in large part on the quality of their greatest red wine, the extraordinary Hermitage La Chapelle. However, like most négociants, the Jaboulets make an entire line of Rhône wines, with Côte Rôtie being one of them. (For a more detailed discussion of this firm, see page 165 in the chapter on the wines of Hermitage.)

The current generation of Jaboulets now running this house consists of the jovial father, Louis, and three family members: the proud and intense Jacques, who made the wines between 1966 and 1992 (until a scuba diving accident put him on the sidelines); gregarious Philippe, who looks after the vineyards; and the best known of all, the handsome, ruddy-faced, extremely affable Gérard, who travels extensively as an articulate spokesman for not only the wines of his family but those of the entire Rhône Valley. The Rhône could hardly ask for a better ambassador for their wines.

The Jaboulet Côte Rôtie has been inconsistent, especially since the mid-eighties. The Jaboulets own no vineyards in this appellation and therefore must depend exclusively on purchases from growers to obtain the grapes for their wine. Sources for top grapes or juice have become increasingly scarce as more and more top vignerons have begun to estate-bottle. Certainly the Jaboulet Côte Rôtie (Les Jumelles, or the Twins) is not in the same exalted class as the firm's Hermitage. It seems to be a wine made to be drunk young, usually within its first decade of life. For example, my experience with older vintages has been mixed; a 1970 and 1967 tasted in 1995 were quite tired even though they had been stored perfectly. Yet a 1959 and 1961, last drunk in 1996, were in superb condition, and among the finest Côte Rôties I have ever tasted from this firm. The Jaboulets use 5% Viognier in their blend and keep the wine 14 months in oak barrels prior to bottling. As the tasting notes demonstrate, the best recent vintages for the firm's Côte Rôtie have been 1976 and 1978, followed by 1985, 1983, and 1979.

VINTAGES

1989—Côte Rôtie Les Jumelles   The 1989 Côte Rôtie is no great wine. Soft and lacking
   ·   the concentration of Jaboulet's other 1989s, it exhibits an intense, herbaceous
  85   character in the nose that I do not find to my liking. Nevertheless, it is a round,
           decently made wine. Mature now. Last tasted 4/94.

1988—Côte Rôtie Les Jumelles   The 1988 Côte Rôtie Les Jumelles is an elegant,
   ·   straightforward, fruity wine, with no great richness or complexity. It is easy to
  79   drink, but I doubt if it will last longer than another 4–5 years. It is surprisingly
           diluted for both a Côte Rôtie and a 1988. Mature now. Last tasted 4/94.

1985—Côte Rôtie   The Jaboulets believe this to be their best Côte Rôtie since the fine
   ·   1976. It is rather low in acidity and precocious, but has heaps of lush blackberry
  86   fruit, medium to full body, and a long finish with noticeable acidity. Anticipated
           maturity: now–2000. Last tasted 4/94.

1983—Côte Rôtie   Still tannic and stern, the 1983 has a medium garnet color, a ripe
   ·   berry, somewhat gamelike smoky nose, but some astringency is worrisome. Does it
  84   have the depth of fruit to outlast the tannins? Anticipated maturity: now–2002.
           Last tasted 4/94.

1982—Côte Rôtie   Similar to the 1985, only light in style, soft and supple, this medium-
   ·   bodied wine is beginning to reveal some acidity. Drink it up. Last tasted 4/94.
  85

1979—Côte Rôtie   Ripe, rich, open-knit, toasty, soft, fruity flavors offer some berry fruit,
   ·   herbs, and spice. The amber edge to the color suggests full maturity. While the
  84   1979 could use a bit more stuffing, it is pleasant, but should be drunk up as the
           acidity is becoming more noticeable. Last tasted 4/94.

1961—Côte Rôtie Les Jumelles   Lamentably, Jaboulet does not make Côte Rôtie such as
   ·   this anymore. This spectacular wine exhibited a huge Syrah nose of hickory smoke,
  95   berries, coffee, and meat. The wine is splendidly concentrated, vividly well focused,
           and amazingly long and refreshing. This is a textbook Côte Rôtie that could easily
           evolve, perhaps even improve, for another 10–15 years. Astonishing! Last tasted
           2/92.

Older Vintages

The 1976 may well be Jaboulet's finest Côte Rôtie in the last 20 years. Very fragrant, rich, intense with all its components in balance, it is a voluptuous, delicious wine for drinking over the next 4–5 years. The 1971 and 1970 are showing fatigue, and unless the wines are from large bottle formats or from very cold cellars, they should be consumed immediately. As indicated above, should readers find well-stored bottles of 1959 or 1961, both wines are superb, with 5–6 years of life left to them.

JEAN-PAUL ET JEAN-LUC JAMET* * * * *
Address: Le Vallin
        69420 Ampuis
Tel: 4-74-56-12-57
Wines produced: Côte Rôtie
Surface area: 14.8 acres

Production: 16,000 bottles
Upbringing: 24 months in barrels
Average age of vines: 15 years
Percentage of Viognier: 0.5%

When I first visited Jamet, not only did I like the wines, I also enjoyed the company of Joseph Jamet, who must be in his late sixties and has been enjoying a well-deserved retirement for nearly a decade. His capable sons, Jean-Paul and Jean-Luc, the latter responsible for the winemaking, have been running this estate since 1985, and have continued to improve the quality of the wines. Jamet's vineyards are relatively morsellated, with most of the plantings on the hillsides still relatively young. For example, their vineyard at Chavaroche was planted in the early eighties and another parcel in the early nineties. Their oldest parcel, on the Côte Brune, is a combination of 52-year-old vines and others averaging 9 years in age. The largest holdings are in Chavaroche and the lieu-dit Le Truchet.

The wines that emerge from Jamet's cellars are very rich, concentrated, and powerful, no doubt because the brothers have been very attentive to doing a green harvest (crop thinning), keeping yields under 40 hectoliters per hectare. They have also discontinued selling large quantities of their wine to three of the major négociants, Chapoutier, Delas, and Jaboulet. One hundred percent of the crop is now estate-bottled. They utilize a small quantity of new oak barrels (about 20–25%), as well as larger wood foudres. Jamet's cellars are located in the hills of the half-horse town of Le Vallin. The wines are as natural as readers are likely to find. After having spent two years in barrel, the wines are put in the bottle without any filtration, and often without any fining. The results are very concentrated, traditional, powerful Côte Rôties, which, in top vintages are impressive and potentially long-lived. Brothers Jean-Luc and Jean-Paul have still not hit the heights in difficult rainy/wet years, which might be due to their inflexibility regarding destemming, which they refuse to do. For example, Marcel Guigal, who is against destemming, will pull off most of the stems in years where they are not physiologically mature (e.g., 1984, 1992, 1993, and, surprisingly, 1995). Nevertheless, this is an excellent, occasionally outstanding source of Côte Rôtie, and one of the most promising, youthfully run cellars in the northern Rhône.

VINTAGES

1994—Côte Rôtie   This wine has filled out considerably since I tasted it last year, and is
·   significantly better than the tannic, hollow 1993. It exhibits Jamet's telltale deep,
89   dense, saturated ruby/purple color, and an earthy, spicy, cedary, herb, fruitcake-
        scented nose with smoke and cassis in the background. Full-bodied and rich, with
        a sweet attack and moderate tannin and acidity in the finish, it needs 3–4 years of
        cellaring, and should keep for 15 + years. Last tasted 6/96.

1993—Côte Rôtie   The disappointing 1993 Côte Rôtie is typical of the vintage. It reveals
·   an excellent dark ruby/purple color, but little fruit, charm, fat, or glycerin. Ex-
72   tremely hard, with astringent tannin, a big hole in the middle, and an attenuated,
        sharp, compact finish, there is no future for this wine. Last tasted 6/96.

1992—Côte Rôtie   The 1992 Côte Rôtie, while structured and tannic, does possess
·   excellent concentration, as well as a full-bodied, powerful style. The color is deep,
88 +   and the wine is unmistakably an intense Syrah with plenty of licorice, smoky cassis
        fruit, and herbs vying for the taster's attention. The finish is long and tannic, but
        there is plenty of underlying sweet, jammy fruit and glycerin. A sleeper in this
        underrated vintage, it should be cellared until the end of the century and drunk
        over the following 10–15 years. Last tasted 9/95.

1991—Côte Rôtie   I have upgraded my opinion of this wine after having had it several
   ·   times on this side of the Atlantic. Aged in one-third new oak with one-third of the
  94   blend coming from Jamet's holdings in the La Landonne vineyard on the Côte
             Brune, the wine offers a huge, intense, spicy nose of smoked meats, black raspber-
             ries, herbs, and new saddle leather. Masculine, rich, and chewy, with massive
             flavor extraction and spicy new oak in evidence, as well as a phenomenal finish,
             this Côte Rôtie needs another 3–4 years of cellaring; it should keep for 15–20
             years. Very impressive! Anticipated maturity: 1999–2015. Last tasted 6/95.

1990—Côte Rôtie   Although the 1990 is dense and tannic, it does not have the flavor
   ·   dimension or aromatic profile of the 1991. While deep, rich, and successful for the
  89   vintage, it ranks behind the Côte Rôties Jamet produced in 1988, 1989, and 1991.
             Anticipated maturity: now–2007. Last tasted 1/94.

1989—Côte Rôtie   The 1989 Côte Rôtie is a 20 year wine, with a dark ruby/purple color,
   ·   as well as a dense, exotic nose of licorice, cassis, herbs, and spicy oak. In the mouth
  92   there is explosive richness, plenty of power, high alcohol, tremendous density, a
             chewy character, and a superopulent, even voluptuous quality to the finish. Antici-
             pated maturity: now–2015. Last tasted 6/95.

1988—Côte Rôtie   The 1988 Côte Rôtie has already thrown a heavy sediment because of
   ·   its admirable extraction level. Opaque black/purple, with an incredible knockout
  95   bouquet of cassis, leather, herbs, smoked meats, and Asian scents (soy), this
             fabulously rich, dense, chewy Côte Rôtie has a texture that reminded me of a great
             Pomerol. I have had it open for as long as three days without seeing any degree of
             oxidation. This is a profound example of Côte Rôtie. Anticipated maturity: 1998–
             2020. Last tasted 12/95.

1987—Côte Rôtie   Restaurants looking for a reasonably priced Côte Rotie that is fully
   ·   ready to drink might want to take a look at the bacon fat– and cassis-scented 1987.
  87   This smooth, medium-bodied, deliciously ripe, round Côte Rôtie is fully mature,
             but is in danger of losing its fruit. It should drink well for another 6–7 years. Last
             tasted 3/93.

1985—Côte Rôtie   Extremely concentrated, powerful, and fully mature, this wine still
   ·   possesses a saturated ruby/purple color, as well as immense fruit, full body, and
  90   impressive extract. Anticipated maturity: now–2005. Last tasted 12/95.

1983—Côte Rôtie   A typical 1983, Jamet's wine is deep ruby-colored, rich and concen-
   ·   trated, with impressive depth and length, but still tight and tannic. Will the tannins
  87   outlast the fruit? Last tasted 12/95.

1982—Côte Rôtie   Supple, flattering, and fully mature, Jamet's 1982 is richly fruity, has
   ·   a full-intensity, smoky, hickory-scented bouquet, jammy fruit, and medium to full
  87   body. Drink it over the next 5 years. Last tasted 7/94.

ROBERT JASMIN* * * / * * * *

Address: 14, rue des Maraichers   Surface area: 10 acres
           69420 Ampuis   Production: 15,000–20,000 bottles
Tel: 4-74-56-11-41   Upbringing: 12–18 months in 10% new oak
Fax: 4-74-56-01-78   Average age of vines: 35 years
Wines produced: Côte Rôtie   Percentage of Viognier: 5%

   Jasmin's vineyard holdings are spread out among seven parcels, with his oldest vines in
Les Moutonnes and La Chevalière, the former having 60-year-old vines and the latter
35-year-old vines. His other parcels include the well-situated La Garde (28-year-old vines)
on the Côte Blonde. His vinification/fermentation is totally traditional, with no destemming,
and aging of the wine in small oak casks and a few foudres. A tiny amount of new oak

barrels (usually 12–15%) is renewed each vintage. As I indicated in the first edition of this book, the problem that I have encountered with Jasmin's wines is that there are multiple bottlings, which is somewhat less of a problem today since his wines are in great demand and are usually bottled within 6–9 months of each other. But Robert Jasmin and his son, Patrick, have a tendency to drag out this process, resulting in a perplexing and, for consumers, frustrating irregularity in the wine's aromatic and taste. I am cognizant of the fact that for a small grower, economics often dictate buying the bottles and corks as the wine is sold since there is not enough capital to buy all the bottles and corks needed to do the bottling all at once. Nor is there space to stock all the bottled wines. Nevertheless, it is a characteristic of this estate that should not go unmentioned.

Jasmin's Côte Rôtie can be an intense, majestically perfumed wine that one could call the most Burgundian of this appellation. He believes in drinking it young as he claims it is at its best in five years, but certainly both his 1978 and 1976 have aged impeccably for two decades. However, both need to be drunk up.

VINTAGES

1993—Côte Rôtie   Intensely vegetal aromas mask any true Côte Rôtie character. Herbaceous, green-pepper-like flavors and high tannin tell the tale of just how difficult
·
70   this vintage was. Last tasted 7/96.

1992—Côte Rôtie   Soft and diluted, with a cranberrylike fruitiness, followed by hard
·   tannin in the finish, make this a dubious effort. Last tasted 7/96.
75

1991—Côte Rôtie   Deeper-colored than either the 1990 or 1989 (one has to go back to
·   1988 to find this intensity of color), Jasmin's 1991 exhibits sweet currant, cherry,
86   and raspberry fruit in its fragrant aromatics. High acidity on the palate is perplexing, but the wine possesses good body, extraction, and ripeness, as well as some bitterness in the finish. Time will tell if it becomes better balanced, but my instincts suggest the acidity will become more marked, and the fruit less charming. Anticipated maturity: now–2006. Last tasted 7/96.

1990—Côte Rôtie   Some attractive berry fruit intertwined with spice, wood, earth, and
·   herbs is followed by a medium-bodied wine with good rather than impressive
85   extract, elegance, and a tough-textured finish. It appears this could have been a better wine if some destemming had been done. Anticipated maturity: now–2004. Last tasted 7/96.

1989—Côte Rôtie   Somewhat of a disappointment given the vintage, Jasmin's 1989 reveals a medium ruby color, an attractive nose of cherry and raspberry fruit, with
·
84   some herbaceousness in the background. On the palate, the wine is slightly hollow, with surprising acidity, and astringent tannin in the finish. It is not one of the successes of the vintage. Drink it up. Last tasted 7/96.

1988—Côte Rôtie   This is the best wine I have tasted from Jasmin over the last decade.
·   It exhibits excellent ripeness, a rich, black-raspberry, sweet pepper, and spicy
91   nose, medium-bodied, concentrated flavors, well-integrated acidity, and firm tannin in the finish. This delicious Côte Rôtie is capable of lasting another 5–6 years. Last tasted 7/96.

1987—Côte Rôtie   The fully mature 1987 is a pleasant, correct, medium-bodied wine
·   with barely enough fruit to make it palatable. I suspect it will lose its charm
78   quickly, so readers are advised to drink it up. Last tasted 7/96.

1986—Côte Rôtie   This moderately endowed wine reveals considerable amber at the
·   edge. Some green-pepper and raspberry scents make an initial appearance, but
76   they are easily forgotten given the wine's tart acidity and tannic finish. Jasmin's 1986 appears to be drying out. Last tasted 7/96.

1985—Côte Rôtie   Jasmin once told me this was the best wine he made since his father's
  ·   1947. Fully mature, this medium ruby-colored wine exhibits an herb, oak, and
  86   raspberry-scented bouquet. However, some acidity is beginning to be intrusive and
             the wine is beginning to lose its fruit, so drink it up. Last tasted 12/94.

1978—Côte Rôtie   This has always been a sensational wine. Still deep in color with light
  ·   amber, the 1978 has a full-intensity bouquet of spice, black fruit, and spring
  92   flowers. The texture is rich, creamy, long, and impeccably balanced. Concen-
             trated, complex, yet elegant and stylish, this is a superb Côte Rôtie, the likes of
             which Jasmin has never equaled. Anticipated maturity: now–2002. Last tasted
             10/94.

1976—Côte Rôtie   Still a great wine, yet somewhat firmer and more austere than the
  ·   more succulent 1978, the 1976 remains a brawny, meaty wine that emphasizes
  90   power rather than finesse. It still offers a beautiful mouthful of wine, but it remains
             tannic. Anticipated maturity: now–2003. Last tasted 1/92.

BERNARD LEVET* *

Address: 22 et 26 boulevard des Allées
        R.N. 86
        69420 Ampuis
Tel: 4-74-56-15-39
Fax: 4-74-56-19-75
Wines produced: Côte Rôtie Brune et Blonde, Côte Rôtie La Chavaroche
Surface area: 8.6 acres
Production: 20,250 barrels
Upbringing: 2–3 years in barrels
Average age of vines: 35–40 years
Percentage of Viognier: 2–3%

Bernard Levet's cellars are located directly on the Route Nationale, which wends its way
through the tiny village of Ampuis. His winemaking is extremely traditional, with virtually
no new oak utilized, and a prolonged 2–3 years of cellaring in both barrels and foudres. I
have found Levet's wines to be extremely variable in quality, often too vegetal (destemming
might be advisable at this estate), but occasionally excellent (1983 and 1994). In recent
years, Levet has begun to bottle an unfined, unfiltered cuvée for his American importer that
bears the label "Côte Rôtie La Chavaroche Cuvée Spéciale," a wine from his parcel of vines
that sits on the Côte Brune, just across from the Côte Blonde. This is unquestionably his
finest wine, and it should age well for 10–15 years.

VINTAGES

1994—Côte Rôtie La Chavaroche   Made from old vines averaging 40–50 years in age,
  ·   the 1994 will be bottled without filtration. The wine exhibits a dark ruby color, and
  88   peppery, herbal, spicy notes intertwined with aromas of sweet black raspberries
             and smoke. Medium- to full-bodied, with considerable tannin, this is a ripe, struc-
             tured 1994 that will require 4–5 years of cellaring. It should keep for 15 + years.
             Last tasted 9/95.

1993—Côte Rôtie La Chavaroche   It is not surprising that Levet's 1993 La Chavaroche
  ·   is a rough-textured, tannic, austere, compact wine with an astringent fruit. There is
  74   not enough fruit to balance out the wine's structure. Last tasted 9/95.

1992—Côte Rôtie La Chavaroche   The 1992 exhibits a peppery, herbaceous, earthy,
·   leathery, fruity nose, medium body, considerable spice, monolithic flavors, and
86   light to moderate tannin in the finish. It is a robustly styled Côte Rôtie that requires
         1–3 more years of cellaring; it should age well for a decade. Last tasted 9/95.

1989—Côte Rôtie Brune et Blonde   This wine is medium- to full-bodied, with a big,
·   peppery, spicy, raspberry-scented bouquet, moderate tannins, relatively low acid-
87   ity, and fleshy, concentrated black fruits with an underlying taste of Provençal
         herbs. Anticipated maturity: now–2003. Last tasted 6/95.

1988—Côte Rôtie Brune et Blonde—The 1988 is a more structured wine, with better
·   acidity, slightly more aggressive tannins, but perhaps not the flamboyance and rich,
86   fleshy fruit of the 1989. It probably comes down to a matter of personal taste as to
         which wine one prefers, but I liked the openness of the 1989, and the fact that it
         will be drinkable over a broader range of years. The 1988 is a nicely concentrated,
         medium- to full-bodied wine that is well made. Drink it between now and 2003.
         Last tasted 12/94.

MICHEL OGIER * * * *

Address: Chemin du Bac
         69420 Ampuis
Tel: 4-74-56-10-75
Fax: 4-74-56-01-75
Wines produced: Côte Rôtie; Vin de pays from La Rosine vineyard
Surface area: 6.2 acres
Production: 10,000 bottles
Upbringing: 18–24 months in barrels
Average age of vines: 25 years
Percentage of Viognier: 1% maximum

Michel Ogier owns only 6.2 acres of vines, mostly on the Côte Blonde, and has been estate-bottling only since 1980. Previously he sold much of his crop to Marcel Guigal and Max Chapoutier. His vineyard, of which one-half is in old vines and the rest in vines that average 7–10 years of age, produces fragrant, sexy, supple, quintessentially elegant wines that are ideal for drinking in their first 7–10 years of life. Ogier's success is not unexpected given the fact that he owns a beautifully situated, 42-year-old vineyard in Rozier, and both young and old vines in his largest holding, Lancement. Readers of my journal, *The Wine Advocate*, have known for some time about one of Ogier's undiscovered value wines, his vin de pays made from 100% Syrah from the La Rosine vineyard just on the other side of Côte Rôtie. This wine tastes much like a good Côte Rôtie, even though it is entitled only to a vin de pays designation. Ogier's winemaking style is quasi-traditional—everything is de-stemmed, there is a 15-day cuvaison, 18–24 months of aging in small oak casks, four rackings, and a fining, but rarely any filtering. The results are exceptionally stylish Côte Rôties that may have the most finesse of any wine of the appellation.

VINTAGES

1995—Côte Rôtie   The 1995 Côte Rôtie reveals a deep color, a classic structure, with
·   obvious acidity, high tannin, and good alcohol. It has not yet developed the telltale
89   bacon fat, smoky aromas, but there is plenty of cassis fruit. The color possesses
         excellent saturation, but the wine is closed, structured, and far less flattering than

the 1994. Once again, it is an excellent, stylish, medium-bodied Côte Rôtie that is tightly knit but promising. Last tasted 6/96.

1994—Côte Rôtie   Ogier's 1994 Côte Rôtie is one of those elegant, finesse-style wines
  .   offering an intense, seductive, sexy, smoky, bacon fat, and cassis-scented nose.
 89   The wine hits the palate with a delicate, sweet ripeness, enough crisp acidity to
              provide definition, and a medium-bodied, well-knit personality. A slight shortness
              in the finish kept this wine from meriting a higher score. Readers should not be
              surprised if it fills out over the next several years, elevating my rating. It will offer
              attractive drinking now and over the next 12 years. Last tasted 6/96.

1993—Côte Rôtie   Another unsuccessful 1993, this wine's hard, chalky, astringent tan-
  .   nin makes it a dubious bet for tasty drinking. Lean, hollow, and fruitless, this wine
 74   does offer a deceptively pleasing nose of ripe Syrah fruit, but after the pleasant
              smells, the fun is over. It will continue to dry out as it evolves. Last tasted 9/95.

1992—Côte Rôtie   The 1992 Côte Rôtie is lighter, with a more noticeable herbaceous
  .   side to its cassis and smoky flavors. Soft, ripe, and medium-bodied, but lacking the
 87   concentration achieved in top years, it should be drunk over the next 5–7 years.
              Last tasted 9/95.

1991—Côte Rôtie   A sensational Côte Rôtie, this wine boasts exceptional elegance mar-
  .   ried to a velvety-textured, supple, rich fruitiness. Ogier's Côte Rôties are not as
 93   masculine or robust as others, relying more on complexity and finesse. The 1991
              displays an ethereal bouquet of ripe cassis, bacon, vanilla, and violets. This deep,
              medium-weight wine with extraordinary finesse, fragrance, and length on the palate
              would embarrass many a Musigny from Burgundy. Drink it over the next 10–12
              years. Last tasted 12/95.

1990—Côte Rôtie   The 1990 offers the smoky, berry fragrance Ogier achieves. More
  .   compact and not nearly as concentrated or complex on the palate as the 1991, this
 87   is a tasty, medium-bodied, attractive Côte Rôtie for drinking over the next 6–8
              years. Last tasted 11/94.

1989—Côte Rôtie   Ogier's 1989 Côte Rôtie exhibited an exceptional elegance and a
  .   perfume that could rival the greatest wines of Burgundy. With more tannin and
 90   structure than the 1990, as well as excellent color, it needs 2–3 years of cellaring.
              There is no doubting its magnificent fragrance of spring flowers, black fruits, oak,
              and minerals. The flavors are tightly knit, and the precociousness suggested by the
              bouquet is not followed up on the palate as the wine needs some cellaring. Last
              tasted 11/94.

RENÉ ROSTAING * * * / * * * * *

Address: Le Port
           69420 Ampuis
Tel: 4-74-56-12-00 or 4-74-59-80-03
Fax: 4-74-56-62-56
Wines produced: Côte Rôtie Cuvée Côte Blonde, Côte Rôtie Cuvée Normale, Côte Rôtie
           Côte Brune La Landonne, Côte Rôtie La Viaillère, Condrieu
Surface area (Cuvée Côte Blonde): 2.47 acres
           (Cuvée Normale): 7.4 acres
           (La Landonne): 3.7 acres
           (La Viaillère): 2.47 acres
Production (Cuvée Côte Blonde): 4,500 bottles
           (Cuvée Normale): 16,500 bottles
           (La Landonne): 6,750 bottles
           (La Viaillère): 4,500 bottles

Upbringing (Cuvée Côte Blonde): 2 years in barrels (30% new)
           (Cuvée Normale): 2 years in barrels (30% new)
           (La Landonne): 2 years in barrels (30% new)
           (La Viaillère): 2 years in barrels (30% new)
Average age of vines (Cuvée Côte Blonde): 60 years
           (Cuvée Normale): 35 years
           (La Landonne): 35 years
           (La Viaillère): 70 years
Percentage of Viognier (Cuvée Côte Blonde): 5–8%
           (Cuvée Normale): none
           (La Landonne): none
           (La Viaillère): none

Fortune is smiling on the young businessman René Rostaing. One taste of Rostaing's wine will no doubt convince anyone that he is a star of this appellation. His small underground cellar, which is beautifully equipped, as well as air-conditioned, is by the river in Ampuis, just a block away from that of Emile Champet, and near the soon to be refurbished Château d'Ampuis recently acquired by Marcel Guigal. Rostaing, a sort of French yuppie, is in the real estate business and manages apartment buildings in nearby Condrieu. An intelligent winemaker, having learned traditional techniques from his father-in-law, Albert Dervieux, he balances that knowledge with some of the benefits of modern-day technology. What is especially admirable about Rostaing is his flexibility. On such issues as fining and filtration, he will await the results of laboratory analyses in order to make a decision if the wine is healthy enough to go into the bottle with no clarification. This open-minded attitude contrasts sharply with producers who fine and filter simply because "my father and grandfather did it."

Rostaing has become one of the most important producers of high-quality Côte Rôtie. When his father-in-law, Albert Dervieux, and uncle, Marius Gentaz, retired, Rostaing inherited the responsibility for overseeing most of their vineyard holdings, thus significantly increasing his estate, as well as giving him some exceptional parcels of Côte Rôtie vineyards. His holdings include old vine parcels in La Fongent (Côte Brune), La Garde (Côte Blonde), and La Viaillère (85-year-old vines in Côte Brune). Moreover, in 1993, he acquired the right to manage the extraordinary 73-year-old vines of Marius Gentaz, also located in the Côte Brune, not far from Guigal's famed vineyard La Turque.

In Rostaing's meticulously clean cellars, there is an assortment of both new oak casks and, increasingly, the larger demi-muids, which, Rostaing is convinced, are the best size of oak vessels in which to age Côte Rôtie. His vinification, which takes place in state-of-the-art, stainless steel, rotating, automatic *pigéage* fermenters, is typical of his intelligence and flexibility. Some cuvées will be 100% destemmed, depending on the vintage and the terroir. Other cuvées will have a partial destemming. In the top years, Rostaing produces four cuvées: Cuvée Normale, Cuvée Côte Blonde, La Viaillère, and La Landonne. When the vintage is suspect, Rostaing will often blend La Landonne and La Viaillère into his Cuvée Normale. While all four cuvées are very good to excellent, the top wines are the Côte Blonde and La Landonne. When tasting in Rostaing's cellars, he often prefers to serve the Côte Blonde last, largely because of its sumptuous texture as well as extraordinary richness and intensity. It is even more outstanding than his La Landonne, even though the latter wine comes from vines older than those owned by Marcel Guigal. In fact, his three parcels of La Landonne include a young vine parcel and two parcels of 50- to 60-year-old vines, with 0.7 of an acre coming from Marius Gentaz's 63-year-old La Landonne vines!

In the 1987 edition of this book, I told the story of Rostaing's searing criticism of his fellow Frenchmen for paying so little attention to Côte Rôtie. He is still fond of citing a survey done in Lyons, one of France's three largest cities, which is only 23 miles from Côte Rôtie. According to the survey, only 1 out of 50 of Lyons's residents had ever heard of Côte Rôtie, and only 1 out of 500 claimed ever to have tasted it. It appears that study has never been far removed from Rostaing's memory as he proudly sells virtually every bottle of his Côte Rôtie outside France. A few top French restaurants and *cavistes* have begun to place orders, but Rostaing's Côte Rôties have become so renowned, he exports them as far away as Japan and Singapore.

As the following tasting notes exhibit, Rostaing has been very successful in such difficult vintages as 1992 and 1993, and in such top years as 1991 and 1995, he has produced brilliant wines that are among the finest of the appellation. They are classic Côte Roties, extremely expressive, very pure, and in the case of his top three cuvées, Côte Blonde, La Viaillère, and La Landonne, potentially very long-lived. In a short span of just over a decade, René Rostaing has become one of the superstars of Côte Rôtie.

Since so little of his Condrieu is made, I have referred to it only in the Condrieu producers' chart at the beginning of that chapter, but it is a great Condrieu. Unfortunately, only about 2,000 bottles are produced in an abundant year from his half-acre parcel on the steep hillsides of Condrieu, near Château Rozay. This is an exceptionally powerful, rich, Condrieu that may well be his best-kept secret.

VINTAGES

1995—Côte Rôtie Cuvée Côte Blonde   The dense purple-colored 1995 Côte Blonde
•   boasts an awesome, mind-boggling nose of violets, cassis, blueberries, and vanillin.
95   Sumptuous and rich on the palate despite crisp intensity, this is a wine of excep-
         tional intensity, a multilayered personality, and fabulous persistence and delinea-
         tion. It is a tour de force for Côte Rôtie. Unfortunately, quantities are extremely
         limited as the yields of just over 1 ton of fruit per acre were well below normal.
         Last tasted 6/96.

1995—Côte Rôtie Cuvée Normale   The 1995 Cuvée Classique possesses a black-
•   raspberry- and violet-scented nose, a fabulous saturated ruby/purple color, excel-
88   lent ripeness, and density, and a long, medium-bodied, crisp finish. The acidity
         gives the wine superb delineation and vibrancy. This wine should drink well for at
         least a decade. Last tasted 6/96.

1995—Côte Rôtie La Landonne   The 1995 La Landonne is another backward, tart,
•   opaque purple-colored wine that is just beginning to reveal its character. Tannic
92   and rich, with a chocolaty, smoky, blackcurrant/cassis-scented nose, this powerful,
         impenetrable wine will require cellaring until the turn of the century; drink it over
         the following 10–12 years. Last tasted 6/96.

1995—Côte Rôtie La Viaillère   The 1995 La Viaillère possesses surprisingly noticeable
•   acidity, a fresh, pure nose of blackberries, blueberries, and currants. Deeply col-
90   ored, ripe, dense, medium- to full-bodied, and tannic, this is a backward, tart, crisp
         style of Côte Rôtie that will age for 15–20 years. Last tasted 6/96.

1993—Côte Rôtie Cuvée Normale   Rostaing was one of the more successful producers in
•   the rain-plagued vintage of 1993. As the scores and following tasting notes attest,
86   Rostaing was able to obtain good levels of concentration, producing soft, seductive,
         complex, character-filled wines. He pruned 50% of his grapes in August and did a
         severe "triage" as the harvested grapes were brought in. His 1993 Côte Rôtie
         displays a medium ruby color, a smoky bouquet, elegant, adequately concentrated,
         spicy flavors, and soft tannin. It will require drinking in its first 5–7 years of life.
         Anticipated maturity: 1998–2006. Last tasted 6/96.

1993—Côte Rôtie Cuvée Côte Blonde   The most sweet and seductive of all Rostaing's
·   Côte Rôties, the 1993 Côte Blonde offers a perfumed, floral, black-cherry, and
88   cassis-scented nose, smoky, creamy-textured, ripe flavors, and soft tannin. Drink it
during its first 10 years of life. Last tasted 6/96.

1993—Côte Rôtie La Landonne   The 1993 Côte Rôtie La Landonne is an amazing wine
·   for the vintage. Made from vines averaging between 25 and 80 years old, it exhibits
89   a black color, a licorice, Asian spice, and smoky, cassis-scented nose, rich, full-
bodied, concentrated flavors, adequate acidity, and moderate tannin in the long
finish. This wine is especially admirable in view of the difficult harvest conditions.
It will age well for 10–15 years. Last tasted 6/96.

1993—Côte Rôtie La Viaillère   The 1993 Côte Rôtie La Viaillère from the famed vine-
·   yard on the Côte Brune is made and bottled by Rostaing, but still appears under
86   the label of his father-in-law, Albert Dervieux. It is a muscular, tannic, rustic wine
with excellent color. It may ultimately be overburdened because of its high acidity
and tannin. La Viaillère, a potentially great vineyard, generally hits the peaks in
years of extraordinary sunshine, heat, and ripeness. Rostaing's portion of this vineyard averages 80 years of age. Anticipated maturity: 1999-2010. Last tasted 6/96.

1992—Côte Rôtie   The 1992 Côte Rôtie generic bottling (which includes all of his
·   declassified La Landonne), exhibits a medium ruby color, a soft, cherry, earthy
86   nose, lovely, light- to medium-bodied flavors, low acidity, and an attractive finish.
Almost Burgundian in its lightness, perfume, and lushness, it should be drunk over
the next 5–7 years. Last tasted 9/95.

1992—Côte Rôtie Cuvée Côte Blonde   The peppery, herbal, and black-raspberry-scented
·   nose of the 1992 Côte Blonde is followed by smoky, medium-bodied flavors, some
87   vanillin from oak aging, and a short but pleasing fruity finish. It should drink well
for 7–8 years. Last tasted 9/95.

1991—Côte Rôtie   The 1991 Côte Rôtie is a rich, full-bodied wine, with soft tannins, low
·   acidity, and gobs of rich Syrah fruit with that telltale smoky, bacon fat–scented
88   nose, as well as luscious black fruit character. It is a wine to drink in its first 7–8
years of life. Last tasted 7/96.

1991—Côte Rôtie Cuvée Côte Blonde   The 1991 Côte Blonde is a sweeter, fatter, more
·   voluptuously styled wine with soft tannin and none of the rusticity or animal
92   character of La Viaillère. Sweet and expansive on the palate, it makes for a
seductive, generous mouthful of wine. It should drink well for 8–10 years. Last
tasted 7/96.

1991—Côte Rôtie La Landonne   Perhaps the best of the 1991s is the 1991 La Landonne.
·   As you might anticipate, there is considerable rivalry between Rostaing and his
94   neighbor, Guigal. Rostaing is quick to assert that his La Landonne vines are
considerably older than those of Guigal. This black-colored wine offers up an
exquisite perfume of licorice, violets, blackberries, and toast, staggering concentration, smooth tannin, and low acidity. It is a gorgeous, exceptionally opulent, multidimensional wine with layers of flavor. It should drink well for 10–15 years. Last
tasted 7/96.

1991—Côte Rôtie La Viaillère   The 1991 Côte Rôtie La Viaillère Côte Brune is fabulous.
·   Rostaing aged it in new oak casks (the larger demi-muids, rather than the normal
92   55-gallon barrique). Made from 80-year-old vines, this wine exhibits the animal,
meaty, earthy side of Côte Rôtie. The nearly black color is followed by huge aromas
of soy sauce, smoked game, and black raspberries intertwined with scents of toasty
new oak. Full-bodied, tannic, and loaded with extract, this voluptuous, exquisite
Côte Rôtie should drink well for 15 or more years. Last tasted 7/96.

1990—Côte Rôtie Cuvée Normale   The regular cuvée of 1990 Côte Rôtie (most of it is
·   from La Fongent vineyard) is a soft, supple, fragrant wine that is delicious. It
87   should be consumed over the next 5–7 years. It possesses toasty new oak to go
         along with its black-raspberry- and herb-scented nose. The tannins are soft and
         the finish velvety and charming. Last tasted 6/94.

1990—Côte Rôtie Cuvée Côte Blonde   The 1990 Côte Blonde (made from 30- to 60-year-
·   old vines) exhibits that penetrating, smoky, roasted Côte Rôtie aroma, sweet black-
93   raspberry-scented, supple, medium- to full-bodied flavors, and a chewy, fleshy,
         seductive finish. The tannins are covered by layers of fruit, and the acidity is low,
         so I would opt for drinking this wine over the next decade. Last tasted 6/94.

1990—Côte Rôtie La Landonne   Rostaing's 1990 La Landonne exhibits more of an
·   earthy, animal, smoky character, superb richness of fruit, gobs of glycerin and
91   extraction, soft tannins, and low acidity. Despite its considerable size, this is a
         wine that should be drunk in its first 10–12 years of life. Last tasted 6/94.

1989—Côte Rôtie Cuvée Côte Blonde   The 1989 Côte Rôties from Rostaing are delicious,
·   up-front, rich, elegant wines that just fall short of being outstanding. The 1989
89   Côte Blonde reveals a super nose of black fruits, flowers, and smoke, followed by
         chewy, ripe, elegant, medium-bodied flavors, soft tannins, crisp acidity, and a
         moderately long finish. It should drink beautifully over the next 10 years. Last
         tasted 6/94.

1989—Côte Rôtie La Landonne   While the 1989 La Landonne is, not surprisingly, exhib-
·   iting more tannin, it is still flattering to taste, with a pronounced earthy, licorice
87   and berry-scented bouquet, oak-tinged, medium-bodied, attractive flavors, and
         moderate tannins in an attractive finish. It should age gracefully for at least 10–12
         years. Last tasted 6/94.

1989—Côte Rôtie La Viaillère   The production of the 1989 La Viaillère was too abundant
·   (50 hectoliters per hectare) to produce a concentrated wine. What one gets is a
85   straightforward, richly fruity, ripe, but essentially one-dimensional wine that lacks
         the concentration and length of wines made from lower yields and older vines.
         Anticipated maturity: now–2003. Last tasted 6/94.

1988—Côte Rôtie Cuvée Côte Blonde   The 1988 Côte Blonde is a smooth, velvety-
·   textured wine with fabulous reserves of fruit that gush from the glass. Extremely
92   intense and ripe, with a raspberry, cassis-dominated bouquet touched judiciously
         by new oak, this profound, full-flavored wine is still tannic, so give it a few more
         years of cellaring. Anticipated maturity: 1998–2010. Last tasted 12/95.

1988—Côte Rôtie La Landonne   The 1988 La Landonne has a fabulously compelling
·   bouquet of black-raspberry and vanillin scents. The wine's rich, full-bodied, im-
90   peccably balanced flavors marry power with finesse. There are still some tannins to
         be resolved. Anticipated maturity: 1999–2012. Last tasted 12/95.

1987—Côte Rôtie Cuvée Côte Blonde   The medium ruby-colored 1987 Côte Blonde is
·   ripe and velvety, with a more direct and flattering, perfumed, raspberry fruitiness.
88   Fully mature, it should be drunk up. Last tasted 11/94.

1987—Côte Rôtie La Landonne   The 1987 La Landonne is tannic and tougher textured,
·   but nevertheless it is delicious, with a huge truffle- and raspberry-scented bouquet
86   intertwined with spicy, vanillin oakiness. In the mouth it is medium-bodied, con-
         centrated, has high acidity, and excellent delineation and focus. Anticipated matu-
         rity: now–2000. Last tasted 11/93.

1985—Côte Rôtie La Landonne   Deep purple in color with a very concentrated, powerful,
·   ripe feel on the palate, the 1985 La Landonne has superb extract, a fabulous
92   bouquet of black fruits and spice, medium to full body, and a vigorous, still youthful
         personality. This is a beauty! Anticipated maturity: now–2005. Last tasted 12/93.

1985—Côte Rôtie Cuvée Côte Blonde A fully mature wine, Rostaing's Côte Blonde is
·   much more velvety than the tannic La Landonne. Voluptuous on the palate, with
91   an intense bouquet of roasted nuts and ripe, jammy black-raspberry and cassis
      fruit, this wine offers a smorgasbord of exotic aromas and flavors. Anticipated
      maturity: now–2001. Last tasted 12/93.

1983—Côte Rôtie La Landonne The 1983 La Landonne remains tannic and closed, with
·   a hard, austere character. The depth of fruit may be insufficient to outlast the
85   considerable tannin. I am increasingly concerned about this wine. Anticipated
      maturity: now–2002. Last tasted 12/93.

1983—Côte Rôtie Cuvée Côte Blonde Less closed and tannic than La Landonne, this
·   wine's bouquet and flavors offer more fruit, but less body and depth. This is a
86   slightly hard-edged Côte Rôtie with vigor and fleshiness, but, again, the question
      so often posed with this vintage is the same—will the fruit outlast the tannin?
      Anticipated maturity: now–2003. Last tasted 12/93.

L. DE VALLOUIT* */* * * * *

Address: 24, rue Désiré Valette
        26240 St.-Vallier
Tel: 4-75-23-10-11
Fax: 4-75-23-05-58
Wines produced: Côte Rôtie, Côte Rôtie Les Roziers, Côte Rôtie La Vonière
Surface area (Côte Rôtie): 14.8 acres
           (Les Roziers): 4.5 acres
           (La Vonière): 5 acres
Production (Côte Rôtie): 35,000 bottles
           (Les Roziers): 7,000 bottles
           (La Vonière): 7,500 bottles
Upbringing (Côte Rôtie): 18 months in barrels (10% new)
           (Les Roziers): 30–40 months in barrels (20% new)
           (La Vonière): 30–40 months in barrels (20% new)
Average age of vines (Côte Rôtie): 40 years
                     (Les Roziers): 40 years
                     (La Vonière): 40 years
Percentage of Viognier (Côte Rôtie): 5–10%
                       (Les Roziers): 5%
                       (La Vonière): 20%

This firm is not located in Ampuis but further south in St.-Vallier. It is an established
company, having been founded in 1922, and has kept, at least in the major export markets,
a surprisingly low profile, particularly in view of the fact that Madame de Vallouit is the
proprietess of 24 acres in Côte Rôtie, making her one of the largest landowners. The firm
also operates as a négociant, producing a full range of Rhône wines from Côtes du Rhône,
Gigondas, Châteauneuf du Pape, St.-Joseph, and Hermitage. Production of Côte Rôtie
averages 4,400 cases out of the appellation's approximate total production of 80,000. I find
it interesting that little is said about this firm, yet the limited tastings I have done of their
Côte Rôties have demonstrated quite good wines that are filled with flavor and seem
uncompromisingly made and rather undervalued in the scheme of things in the northern
Rhône.

In the late 1980s, undoubtedly in response to the lavish praise being heaped on Marcel
Guigal's single-vineyard Côte Rôties, Monsieur de Vallouit began to produce two limited-
production Côte Rôties. The debut vintage for Les Roziers, from a parcel of 40-year-old

vines, was 1988. This has been, and continues to be, an outstanding wine, far above the quality of the regular cuvée made by this firm. Les Roziers was followed in 1989 by La Vonière, which contains the maximum 20% Viognier permitted under French law. This, too, is a seductive, sumptuous style of Côte Rôtie that contrasted with the masculine, full-bodied fury and power of Les Roziers. As the following tasting notes demonstrate, de Vallouit can produce exquisite wines, which for reasons unknown have been largely ignored by the wine-consuming public. Admittedly they are not easy to find, but given all the justifiable hype on some of the other limited-production Côte Rôties, de Vallouit's Les Roziers and La Vonière should merit far more attention and praise.

VINTAGES

1991—Côte Rôtie Les Roziers   The 1991 Les Roziers exhibits a deep color, a spicy,
·   smoky, black-raspberry fruitiness, full body, and a lush, succulent texture and
89   finish. The 1990 is slightly richer and more complete, with superb density, a rich,
full-bodied personality, and gobs of black fruit, glycerin, and toasty new oak, as
well as tannin. Approachable now, it should last for 10–12 years. Last tasted 6/94.

1991—Côte Rôtie La Vonière   La Vonière is a mini-cuvée of 7,500 bottles that utilizes
·   the maximum 20% Viognier permitted under French law. The result is an im-
93   mensely fragrant wine that smells as much like a Condrieu as it does a Côte
Rôtie with its peach, apricot, and honeysuckle scents, and smoky, black-raspberry
aromas. Because of the high percentage of Viognier, the wine has a dark ruby
color, a lush, velvety texture, and gobs of expansive ripe fruit. I was blown away by
the elegance and sensual qualities of the 1991. Drink it over the next 7–8 years.
Last tasted 6/94.

1990—Côte Rôtie   The standard cuvée of 1990 exhibits high acidity, plenty of tannin,
·   smoky, raspberry-scented fruit, and a medium-bodied, straightforward format.
85   Drink it over the next 5–7 years. Last tasted 6/94.

1990—Côte Rôtie Les Roziers   The 1990 Les Roziers is slightly richer and more com-
·   plete than the 1991, with superb density, a rich, full-bodied personality, and gobs
92   of black fruit, glycerin, and toasty new oak, as well as tannin. Approachable now,
it should last for 10–12 years. Last tasted 6/94.

1990—Côte Rôtie La Vonière   The similarly styled 1990 La Vonière is not as rich as the
·   1991. Soft and voluptuous, it exhibits a stunning fragrance. This is an interesting
89   idea, but the high percentage of Viognier necessitates watching the wine carefully
since it will age more quickly. Anticipated maturity: now–2002. Last tasted 6/94.

1989—Côte Rôtie   The 1989 Côte Rôtie, which displays less extraction now that it has
·   been bottled, is clearly made from ripe, more concentrated grapes than the 1990.
87   Possessing less of the herbaceous nose, and more of the smoky, bacon fat, raspberry
character, it is soft, medium- to full-bodied, with a luscious, velvety texture and a
heady, alcoholic finish. Drink it over the next decade. Last tasted 6/94.

1989—Côte Rôtie Les Roziers   The 1989 Les Roziers is less concentrated. Already soft,
·   charming, forward, and delicious, it is aromatic, but lacks the grip and depth of the
89   1990, not to mention the succulence of the 1991. Anticipated maturity: now–2006.
Last tasted 11/95.

1989—Côte Rôtie La Vonière   The 1989 La Vonière (blended with Viognier) exhibits a
·   knockout bouquet of spring flowers and raspberries, smooth, honeyed flavors, and
90   a wonderful, open-knit, round, in-your-face style. It carries its heart on its sleeve
and there is not much behind the huge opening impression this wine makes, but
wow, for drinking over the next 4–6 years, this is a real stunner. Last tasted 11/95.

1988—Côte Rôtie   The 1988 is lighter than the 1989, but is also more tannic, and more
· classically structured for the long haul. It is impressively deep in color, despite the
88 fact that de Vallouit uses the maximum 20% Viognier in the blend. The big,
raspberry-scented, exotic bouquet of red fruits and flowers is followed by a
medium-bodied wine, with good tannins, better acidity than the 1989, but not
nearly the concentration or sumptuous qualities of the more recent vintage. Anticipated maturity: now–2002. Last tasted 11/95.

1988—Côte Rôtie Les Roziers   The 1988 is magnificent. Deeply colored, with no amber
· at the edge, the huge nose of bacon fat, roasted olives, raspberries, and creamy
91 fruit soars from the glass. This multilayered wine possesses a velvety, voluptuous
texture, plenty of tannin, and lavish amounts of glycerin and extract. A superb Côte
Rôtie. Anticipated maturity: now–2012. Last tasted 7/96.

1986—Côte Rôtie Les Roziers   Amazingly rich for the vintage, the 1986 Côte Rôtie Les
· Roziers is a top-notch wine from a vintage that has largely been ignored in the
89 United States. It is a wonderfully full-bodied, heady, fragrant Côte Rôtie. Deep in
color, with a rich, expansive bouquet of black raspberries and vanillin-scented,
spicy new oak, this surprisingly soft, medium- to full-bodied wine should drink
beautifully for another 7–10 years. Last tasted 9/91.

1985—Côte Rôtie   Intense aromas of pepper and crushed raspberry fruit jump from the
· glass. On the palate, this medium-bodied wine is expansively flavored and fully
87 mature. Anticipated maturity: now–2000. Last tasted 6/90.

VIDAL-FLEURY* * * *

Address: R.N. 86
    69420 Ampuis
Tel: 4-74-56-10-18
Fax: 4-74-56-19-19
Wines produced (Estate): Côte Rôtie, Côte Rôtie La Chatillonne Côte Blonde, Côte Rôtie
    Brune et Blonde
    (Négociant): Muscat Beaumes de Venise, Châteauneuf du Pape, Condrieu,
    Cornas, Côtes du Rhône, Côtes du Ventoux, Crozes-Hermitage, Gigondas,
    Hermitage, St.-Joseph, Vacqueyras
Surface area: 25 acres
Production (Côte Rôtie): 60,000–70,000 bottles
    (La Chatillonne): 4,000 bottles
Upbringing: 36 months in barrels and foudres
Average age of vines: 25–35 years
Percentage of Viognier (Côte Rôtie): 5–8%
    (La Chatillonne): 15%

Founded in 1781, this is the oldest and, until the late seventies, one of the most respected
houses in the Rhône Valley, operating as both a négociant and grower with 25 acres of vines
in Côte Rôtie gorgeously situated on both the Côte Blonde and the Côte Brune. For decades,
Joseph Vidal-Fleury ran this house with meticulous care and great passion. His star pupil,
Etienne Guigal, left in 1946 to begin his own house. In 1976, Vidal died, and while the firm
still continued to produce some superlative wines, the great consistency of the past was
replaced by irregularity, uncertainty, and a general lack of leadership. The crusty old
cellarmaster, Monsieur Battier, appeared to become more difficult each time I paid a visit.
More troublesome was the fact that very good lots of wine were left entirely too long in the
old chestnut barrels, causing many of them to become oxidized and dried out. It was a

particularly depressing thing for this writer to realize that the great Vidal-Fleury Côte Rôties I tasted from such vintages as 1959, 1964, 1966, and 1969 were unlikely to be replicated under the winemaking practiced at this firm during this lugubrious period.

Rumors in the early eighties continually suggested that Vidal-Fleury was up for sale, a fact confirmed by its purchase in 1985 by the Guigal family, whose first vintage was, fortuitously, 1985. Marcel Guigal was quick to make it clear that both houses would retain their separate identities, and Vidal-Fleury would not become a second label for Guigal. Guigal did adopt Vidal-Fleury's best vineyard site (La Turque) for Guigal's third vineyard-designated wine, but the great La Chatillonne vineyard remained in-house. Guigal's philosophy of vinification and cellar techniques are followed in part at Vidal-Fleury, except for Guigal's use of new oak barrels. Guigal hired the talented Jean-Pierre Rochias, a former employee of the Bordeaux firm of Cordier. From 1985 to date, Rochias has run Vidal-Fleury's day-to-day affairs with considerable confidence and competence. A complete face-lift at Vidal-Fleury was completed in the mid-nineties, as evidenced by the rows of new foudres throughout the facility. It has been said that there is too little difference between the wines of Guigal and Vidal-Fleury, but that is untrue. The wines are completely different, and in many cases complementary. Vidal-Fleury has built a strong portfolio of well-made, bargain-priced red and white wines from the Côtes du Ventoux, Côtes du Rhône, and Crozes-Hermitage. Vidal-Fleury also produces a Cornas, as well as a splendid Muscat Beaumes de Venise, neither of which is produced by Guigal.

As for the Côte Rôties, Vidal-Fleury's remain among the best of the appellation. The Côte Rôtie Brune et Blonde is consistently excellent (meriting four stars), and the Côte Rôtie La Chatillonne (3,000–4,000 bottles made from a parcel of 52-year-old vines on the Côte Blonde that contains a whopping 15% Viognier) comes closest to expressing the same compelling perfume, flavors, and texture of La Mouline as well as Rostaing's Cuvée Côte Blonde. Although an exquisite wine, La Chatillonne does not appear to possess the aging potential of La Mouline. The former is best drunk during its first 10–12 years of life.

Vidal-Fleury's reputation, which suffered between 1979 and 1984, continues to rebound, as has the firm's line of négociant wines, such as their Côtes du Ventoux, Côtes du Rhône, Châteauneuf du Pape, Crozes-Hermitage, St.-Joseph, Cornas, Hermitage, and Muscat Beaumes de Venise.

VINTAGES

1994—Côte Rôtie Brune et Blonde   The 1994 Côte Rôtie Brune et Blonde is an excellent,
·   nearly outstanding wine with its smoky, black-raspberry, and bacon-scented nose,
88   and medium-bodied, concentrated, silky palate. This forward-styled Côte Rôtie should drink well for 7–8 years. Last tasted 6/96.

1994—Côte Rôtie La Chatillonne   The outstanding 1994 Côte Rôtie La Chatillonne offers
·   a superb nose of sweet, jammy black raspberries, roasted herbs, and smoke.
91   Creamy-textured, with outstanding concentration, as well as undeniable opulence, this is a gorgeously rendered, seductive wine for drinking over the next 10–12 years. Last tasted 6/96.

1993—Côte Rôtie La Chatillonne   The 1993 Côte Rôtie La Chatillonne tastes hollow,
·   tannic, hard, and tough-textured . . . an accurate representation of this charmless
79   vintage. Last tasted 6/96.

1991—Côte Rôtie Brune et Blonde   The 1991 Côte Rôtie Brune et Blonde is one of the
·   best efforts Vidal-Fleury has produced in recent years. With deeper color, more
89   perfume (bacon fat, smoke, and black raspberries), and a silky, creamy-textured feel, it is Côte Rôtie at its most seductive. Drink it over the next 10 years. Last tasted 6/96.

1991—Côte Rôtie La Chatillonne   The outstanding 1991 La Chatillonne offers a fragrant
·   personality of big, ripe scents of jammy black and red fruits, toasty oak, herbs,
92   pepper, and the appellation's famous bacon fat aroma. Voluptuously textured, with
         soft tannin and low acidity, this unctuously rich wine should drink well for 10–15
         years. Last tasted 6/96.

1990—Côte Rôtie Brune et Blonde   The regular cuvée of 1990 Côte Rôtie exhibits subtle
·   aromas of bacon fat, roasted nuts, and black raspberries, deep color, excellent
88   ripeness, and a soft, supple finish. Drink it over the next 10–12 years. Last tasted
         6/96.

1990—Côte Rôtie La Chatillonne   The 1990 displays an intoxicating perfume of cloves,
·   pepper, spice, and black fruits. Rich and medium- to full-bodied, with a shorter
90   finish than the bouquet and attack suggest, it is a complex, multidimensional wine
         for drinking over the next 10 years. Last tasted 6/96.

1989—Côte Rôtie Brune et Blonde   The 1989 Côte Rôtie Brune et Blonde is slightly less
·   impressive than the 1988. It is a rich, spicy Côte Rôtie, with a smoky, raspberry,
86   oaky-scented nose, rich, medium-bodied flavors, moderate tannins, and a good
         finish. Drink it over the next 6–7 years. Last tasted 6/96.

1989—Côte Rôtie La Chatillonne   The 1989 La Chatillonne exhibits a toasty, vanillin-
·   scented nose, plenty of red- and black-fruit scents in its bouquet, but less opulence
90   and concentration than either the 1990 or 1991. Nevertheless, I would be delighted
         to drink it on any occasion. Rich, medium- to full-bodied, and soft, it is ideal for
         consuming over the next 7 years. Last tasted 6/96.

1988—Côte Rôtie Brune et Blonde   The 1988 Côte Rôtie Brune et Blonde is nearly
·   outstanding, and may ultimately merit a better review after another one or two years
89   in the bottle. It has that classic bacon fat, smoky, roasted, raspberry fruitiness,
         rich, full-bodied, expansive flavors, an attractive richness and length, reflecting
         impeccable winemaking. Drinkable now, it should evolve nicely over the next 5–
         10 years. Last tasted 11/95.

1988—Côte Rôtie La Chatillonne   The 1988 is typical of so many northern Rhônes from
·   this vintage. A structured, muscular, tannic wine, with gobs of black-raspberry and
91   cassis fruit wrapped in smoky oak with intriguing aromas of roasted nuts and herbs,
         this wine is just beginning to open up and reach its plateau of maturity. The overall
         impression is one of superb richness, blossoming complexity, and another 10–15
         years of aging potential. This is a gorgeous Côte Rôtie. Anticipated maturity: now–
         2006. Last tasted 6/96.

1987—Côte Rôtie La Chatillonne   I have expressed numerous times how excellent the
·   1987 vintage turned out in Côte Rôtie, and this is another example. This fully
88   mature wine, with its profound bouquet of smoky, roasted plums, raspberries,
         olives, and leather, is all velvet and silk on the palate. It is a rich, smoky, concen-
         trated wine, with oodles of velvety black fruits, low acidity, and a clean, heady,
         lush finish. The amber tinge to the wine's dark ruby color suggests full maturity.
         Anticipated maturity: now–2001. Last tasted 11/95.

1986—Côte Rôtie La Chatillonne   For those consumers with patience, the 1986 La
·   Chatillonne is worth consideration. It is exceptionally tannic, but the tannins are
90   proportional to the wine's great concentration, huge, medium- to full-bodied tex-
         ture, and long, ripe, intense finish. It is an impressive yet tougher style of Côte Rôtie
         that will reward cellaring. Anticipated maturity: now–2000. Last tasted 1/90.

1985—Côte Rôtie La Chatillonne   Very ripe and fat with heaps of blackberry fruit, the
·   fully mature 1985 La Chatillonne has excellent depth and richness, low acidity,
91   but gobs of charm. It has developed quickly and needs to be drunk up. Mature
         now. Last tasted 8/96.

1985—Côte Rôtie Brune et Blonde   Nearly as good as the single-vineyard bottling of La
·　　　Chatillonne, this wine displays a dark ruby color, fine concentration, rich fruit, a
88　　creamy texture, and a soft finish. Mature now. Last tasted 8/96.

1983—Côte Rôtie La Chatillonne   The 1983 is disappointing, particularly given the
·　　　vintage; it is rather austere, quite dry and hard with barely adequate fruit, a dusty
78　　texture, and excessive tannins in the finish. It is likely only to dry out further. Last
　　　　tasted 11/88.

1978—Côte Rôtie Brune et Blonde   A great, but now variable wine, the finest bottles of
·　　　1978 have that huge bouquet of intense, jammy, cassis fruit as well as roasted nuts,
90　　licorice, tar, and herbs that makes Côte Rôtie so special. Very concentrated, lush,
　　　　and full-bodied, this impressive wine has finally reached full maturity. Last tasted
　　　　7/95.

Older Vintages

The very first great Côte Rôties I tasted were those of Vidal-Fleury. I had the 1959 only
once, in the mid-seventies, at which time it was superb, but by then had no place to go
except down. The 1966, of which I had several cases at one time, peaked in the early
seventies and has now faded. The 1969 was fully mature a decade ago, and at that time it
was quite exceptional, loaded with fruit, very fragrant, and capable of holding for another
5–6 years. I have not seen another bottle since.

OTHER CÔTE RÔTIE PRODUCERS

ANDRÉ ET JOSEPH BLANC

Address: La Brocarde
　　　　69420 Ampuis
Tel: 4-74-56-13-58
Wines produced: Côte Rôtie
Surface area: 6.2 acres

Production: 5,000 bottles
Upbringing: 20 months in barrels
Average age of vines: not disclosed
Percentage of Viognier: none

DIDIER DE BOISSEYT-CHOL

Address: R.N. 86
　　　　42410 Chavanay
Tel: 4-74-87-23-45
Fax: 4-74-87-07-36
Wines produced: Côte Rôtie

Surface area: 1.98 acres
Production: 3,000 bottles
Upbringing: 2 years minimum in barrels
Average age of vines: 55 years
Percentage of Viognier: 15%

GÉRARD BONNEFOND* * *

Address: Le Port
　　　　69420 Ampuis
Tel: 4-74-56-12-11
Wines produced: Côte Rôtie
Surface area: 6.2 acres

Production: 2,000–3,000 bottles, the rest
　　　　sold in bulk
Upbringing: 36 months in barrels
Average age of vines: 50 years
Percentage of Viognier: 8%

PATRICK ET CHRISTOPHE BONNEFOND

Address: Le Mornas
　　　　69420 Ampuis
Tel: 4-74-56-12-30
Fax: 4-74-56-17-93
Wines produced: Côte Rôtie
Surface area: 12.4 acres

Production: 27,000 bottles
Upbringing: 12 months in barrels (30%
　　　　new)
Average age of vines: 25 years, some young
vines of 4 years
Percentage of Viognier: none

CAVES COTTEVERGNE–L. SAUGÈRE* * *

Address: Quartier le Bret
   07130 St.-Péray
Tel: 4-75-40-30-43
Fax: 4-75-40-55-06
Wines produced: Côte Rôtie
Surface area: unknown

Production: 3,000 bottles
Upbringing: 6–8 months in barrels (25% new)
Average age of vines: unknown
Percentage of Viognier: 10%

BERNARD CHAMBEYRON

Address: Boucharey
   69420 Ampuis
Tel: 4-74-56-15-05
Fax: 4-74-56-00-39
Wines produced: Côte Rôtie

Surface area: 4 acres
Production: 10,500 bottles
Upbringing: 24 months in barrels
Average age of vines: 10–15 years
Percentage of Viognier: 5%

CHRISTIANE CHAMBEYRON-MANIN

Address: 23, rue de la Brocarde–Le Carcan
   69420 Ampuis
Tel: 4-74-56-11-79 or 4-74-56-11-17
Wines produced: Côte Rôtie
Surface area: 0.98 acres

Production: 2,340 bottles
Upbringing: 24 months in barrels
Average age of vines: 50 years
Percentage of Viognier: none

JEAN CLUSEL

Address: 24, route de la Roche
   69420 Ampuis
Tel: 4-74-56-13-54
Fax: 4-74-56-16-07
Wines produced: Côte Rôtie

Surface area: 1.5 acres
Production: not available—artisanal
Upbringing: 18–24 months in oak
Average age of vines: unknown
Percentage of Viognier: 5%

BERNARD DAVID

Address: Le Giraud
   69420 Ampuis
Tel: 4-74-56-14-83
Wines produced: Côte Rôtie
Surface area: 12.35 acres

Production: 1,500–2,000 bottles and 90% of the production sold in bulk
Upbringing: 15–18 months in barrels
Average age of vines: 12 years
Percentage of Viognier: 5–12%

RENÉ FERNANDEZ

Address: 8, rue de Monlis, Verenay
   69420 Ampuis
Tel: 4-74-56-10-05
Wines produced: Côte Rôtie
Surface area: 6.9 acres

Production: 135,000 bottles
Upbringing: 36 months in barrels
Average age of vines: 7–8 years
Percentage of Viognier: 15%

ANDRÉ FRANÇOIS

Address: Mornas
   69420 Ampuis
Tel: 4-74-56-13-80
Wines produced: Côte Rôtie

FRANÇOIS GÉRARD* *

Address: Côte Chatillon
      69420 Condrieu
Tel: 4-74-87-88-64
Wines produced: Côte Rôtie
Surface area: 7.5 acres

Production: 5,000–6,000 bottles
Upbringing: 18–24 in new oak barrels
Average age of vines: 20 years
Percentage of Viognier: 3%

BERNARD GUY

Address: Guy and Frédéric Bernard
      A.E.C. Bernard–
      Tupin-et-Semons
      69420 Condrieu

Tel: 4-74-59-54-04
Fax: 4-74-56-68-81
Surface area : 10.2 acres

LUCIEN LAGNIER

Address: 42410 Chavanay
Tel: 4-74-87-24-46
Wines produced: Côte Rôtie
Surface area: 1.5 acres
Production: 1,500 bottles

Upbringing: 18–24 months, half in cask
and half in barrels, no new oak
Average age of vines: 10 years
Percentage of Viognier: 10%

JEAN-PIERRE LEYMIN

Address: Planèze
      69560 St. Cyr-sur-le-Rhône
Tel: 4-74-53-42-21
Wines produced: Côte Rôtie
Surface area: 4.5 acres

Production: 1,000 bottles
Upbringing: 3 years in barrels
Average age of vines: 18 years
Percentage of Viognier: 5%

ROBERT NIERO

Address: 20, rue Cuvillère
      69420 Condrieu
Tel: 4-74-59-84-38
Fax: 4-74-56-62-70
Wines produced: Côte Rôtie
Surface area: 1.5 acres

Production: 2,500 bottles
Upbringing: 18 months, half of yield in cask
and half in barrels, with 20% in new oak
Average age of vines: 7 years
Percentage of Viognier: unknown

LOUIS REMILLIER

Address: Verenay
      69420 Ampuis
Tel: 4-74-56-17-11
Wines produced: Côte Rôtie
Surface area: 3.7 acres

Production: 3,000 bottles
Upbringing: 24 months minimum in barrels
Average age of vines: 50 years
Percentage of Viognier: 2%

ADOLPHE ROYER

Address: R.N. 86
      69420 Tupin-et-Semons

Tel: 4-74-59-52-15
Wines produced: Côte Rôtie

G.A.E.C. DANIEL ET ROLAND VERNAY

Address: Le Plany
      69560 St. Cyr-sur-le-Rhône
Tel: 4-74-53-18-26
Wines produced: Côte Rôtie
Surface area: 10.4 acres

Production: 3,000 bottles
Upbringing: 18 months in barrels
Average age of vines: 25 years
Percentage of Viognier: none

GEORGES VERNAY

Address: 1, R.N. 86
    69420 Condrieu
Tel: 4-74-59-52-22
Fax: 4-74-56-60-98
Wines produced: Côte Rôtie
Surface area: 6.9 acres

Production: 7,000 bottles
Upbringing: 24 months in barrels (30% new)
Average age of vines: 10–60 years (20% young vines)
Percentage of Viognier: 5–6%

GÉRARD VILLANO

Address: 111, R.N. 86
Tel: 4-74-59-87-64
Wines produced: Côte Rôtie
Surface area: 1.34 acres
Production: 1,000 bottles

Upbringing: 18–24 months in barrels (none new)
Average age of vines: 20 years
Percentage of Viognier: 8–10%

CONDRIEU AND CHÂTEAU GRILLET

Exotic Rarities on the Rhône

CONDRIEU AT A GLANCE

Appellation created:	April 27, 1940.
Type of wine produced:	White wine only.
Grape varieties authorized:	Viognier.
Acres currently under vine:	(Condrieu): 250, (Château Grillet): 7.6.
Quality level:	The top wines are exceptional, as this is one of the rarest and most unique wines in the world, but quality is increasingly irregular.
Aging potential:	1–4 years; Château Grillet will keep 4–8 years.
General characteristics:	An exotic, often overwhelming apricot/peach/honeysuckle fragrance is followed by low-acid, very rich wines that are usually short-lived; ironically, the less successful vintages with higher acidity age longer.
Greatest recent vintage:	1994.
Price range:	$30–$65.
Aromatic profile:	Honeysuckle, peaches, apricots, and candied tropical fruit aromas should soar from a glass of a top Condrieu.
Textural profile:	In ripe vintages, Condrieu tends to be low in acidity, but not flabby. Fleshy, decadent, dry, and gloriously fruity and layered flavors should be intense, but not heavy.

The Condrieu appellation's most profound wines:

Yves Cuilleron Condrieu Les Chaillets
  Vieilles Vignes
Yves Cuilleron Condrieu Les Eguets
  Vendange Tardive
Pierre Dumazet Condrieu Coteau de Côte
  Fournet
Yves Gangloff Condrieu
Guigal Condrieu La Doriane
Domaine du Monteillet (Antoine Montez)
  Condrieu

André Perret Condrieu Coteau du Chéry
René Rostaing Condrieu
Georges Vernay Condrieu Les Chaillées
  de l'Enfer
Georges Vernay Condrieu Coteaux du
  Vernon
François Villard Condrieu Coteaux de
  Poncin

RATING THE CONDRIEU PRODUCERS

* * * * *(OUTSTANDING)

Yves Cuilleron (Les Chaillets Vieilles
  Vignes)
Yves Cuilleron (Les Eguets)
Pierre Dumazet (Côte Fournet)
Yves Gangloff
Guigal (La Doriane)

Guigal (négociant bottling)
Domaine du Monteillet (Antoine Montez)
André Perret (Clos Chanson)
André Perret (Coteau du Chéry)
Georges Vernay (Les Chaillées d'Enfer)
Georges Vernay (Coteaux du Vernon)

* * * *(EXCELLENT)

Patrick et Christophe Bonnefond
Chapoutier
J. L. Chave
Yves Cuilleron (regular cuvée)
Delas Frères (Clos Boucher)
Pierre Dumazet (Rouelle Midi)
Philippe et Christophe Pichon

Hervé Richard
René Rostaing (* * * */* * * * *)
Georges Vernay (regular cuvée)
François Villard (Coteaux de
  Poncin) (* * * */* * * * *)
François Villard (Les Terrasses du Palat)
Gérard Villano

* * *(GOOD)

Gilles Barge
Domaine du Chêne–Marc Rouvière
Domaine Louis Chèze
Domaine Farjon
Philippe Faury

Château Grillet †
Paul Jaboulet-Aîné
Niero-Pinchon (* * */* * * *)
Vidal-Fleury

† Prior to 1979* * * * *; since 1979* * *. Château Grillet is entitled to its own appellation—a very unusual situation in France.

A visit to a fine wine shop can reveal many things. When the first edition of this book was written ten years ago, consumers were unlikely to find anything made from the Viognier grape. Perhaps a few shops, run by fanatical visionaries, had one or two examples of Condrieu, the famed and cherished white wine made from the Viognier grape, but those shops were in the minority. In 1997, the Viognier grape has become highly fashionable, and its newfound popularity is in large part attributable to the tiny, postage stamp–sized appellation of Condrieu.

Condrieu has always been one of the world's rarest white wines, in addition to being produced from what once was one of the least-known grape varietals, Viognier. Like so

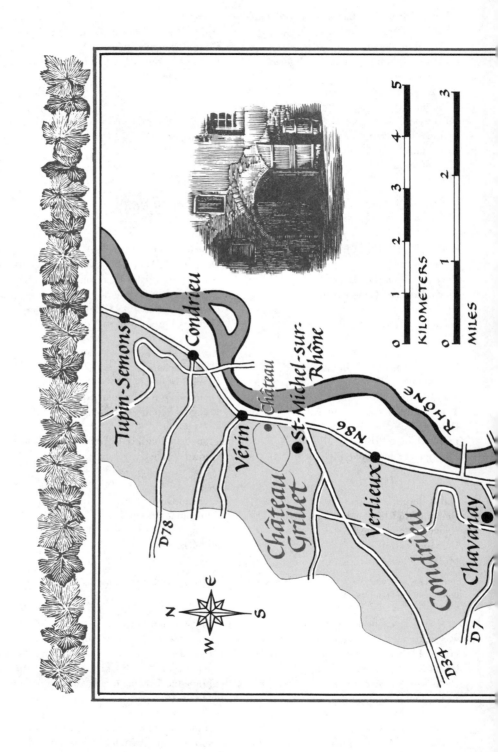

Tupin-Semons

Condrieu

Château

Vérin

St-Michel-sur-
Rhône

Château
Grillet

N86

Verlieux

D78

Condrieu

Chavanay

RHÔNE

D34

D7

N

W ──── E

S

KILOMETERS
0   1   2   3   4   5

MILES
0   1   2   3

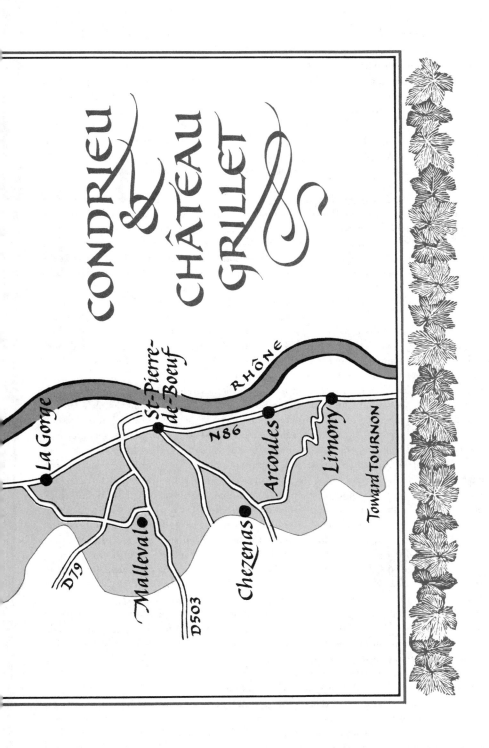

CONDRIEU & CHÂTEAU GRILLET

RHÔNE

La Gorge

St-Pierre-
de-Boeuf

N86

Arcoules

Limony

Malleval

Chezenas

D79

D503

Toward TOURNON

many other Rhône Valley appellations, there is a paucity of historical documentation on the origin of the initial plantings. Most commentators and historians have put forth convincing arguments that Viognier, along with Syrah, was probably brought up the Rhône River by Greek sailors between 600 and 400 B.C. Some of the local, old-time Condrieu storytellers like to say that it was the Romans who pirated Viognier out of Dalmatia, and transplanted it on the steep, infertile slopes behind what is now the village of Condrieu sometime during the third century A.D. Regardless of which account has more veracity, Viognier remained largely a local, insiders' wine. Although there are reports of relatively widespread plantings of Viognier in the postphylloxera era, particularly on more fertile farmlands in the northern Rhône, two world wars, and the worldwide economic crisis of the thirties virtually destroyed the small winemaking village 24 miles south of Lyons, and only 3 miles south of Ampuis, the capital of Côte Rôtie.

Viognier's ascendency is not difficult to explain, at least to anyone who has tasted a fine Condrieu. A part of Condrieu's present-day fame is attributable to great French chefs. It is irrefutable that the most renowned and influential French chef of the twentieth century was Fernand Point (1897–1955), who reigned over the kitchen of his beloved restaurant, La Pyramide, in Vienne, a few miles from both Côte Rôtie and Condrieu. Such famous gourmands as the Aga Khan, Jean Cocteau, and Winston Churchill made frequent pilgrimages to taste his art at his culinary palace. From the twenties through the mid-fifties, Point, who had a singular influence on so many of the most talented French chefs of the twentieth century (Alain Chapel, Pierre Troisgros, Paul Bocuse, Michel Guérard), was a vociferous advocate of Condrieu, which he liked to serve next to a Montrachet from Burgundy. When Point passed away, another influential chef, Jacques Pic, from his restaurant in Valence, took up the promotional cause for Condrieu. Today, the late Jacques Pic's son, Alain, continues to convert neophytes to the magic of Condrieu.

Viognier has also become the darling of other winemaking regions. In California, new Viognier plantations can be found from Santa Barbara in the south to Yolo County's Dunnigan Hills in the north. The seductive perfume of honeysuckle, peaches, and apricots, and the lush, rich fruitiness found in such a dry, concentrated wine have made Viognier à la mode. So much of this success owes its origin to Condrieu, as well as to those producers who survived the early part of the twentieth century and have slowly begun to resurrect and replant the abandoned terraces that had become overgrown with weeds and bushes. The explosion of interest in Viognier began in the mid-eighties, and reached such dangerous levels that the Institut National des Appellations d'Origine (INAO) was forced to revise completely the borders of Condrieu to be sure that new vineyards were planted only on appropriate hillsides suitable for high-quality Condrieu. Even so, no other Rhône Valley appellation save for Côte Rôtie has been permitted to expand its acreage as much as Condrieu, with perhaps the most ominous direction an increase in the maximum yield of Viognier per hectare.

Along with an increased international interest in Viognier has come a renewed interest in this grape in France. Ten years ago I reported on experimental plantings in the southern Rhône Valley, primarily at Domaine Ste.-Anne and Château Estève. Since, there have been extensive Viognier plantings in both l'Ardèche and the Languedoc-Roussillon corridor, where some surprisingly rich, interesting wines have emerged at prices one-fourth of those charged for Condrieu. Further plantations of Viognier have continued with considerable enthusiasm in the southern Rhône Valley with positive results. The upshot of all this is that Condrieu, which has enjoyed a remarkable renaissance since the mid-eighties, is now threatened by its own success and the lofty prices fetched by its wines. Many consumers have begun to wonder if a less expensive, high-quality Viognier from southern France is preferable to a high-priced Condrieu. To my taste, the appellation's most profound wines (see the list at the beginning of this chapter) do indeed justify their prices. They are the world's quintessential expressions of the Viognier grape.

No doubt the greatness of Condrieu's finest wines is the result of the soil base where the vineyards are planted. The narrow terraces of granite and a soil base that Georges Vernay calls "arzelle" (decomposed rock, granite, mica, shist, and some clay) are prerequisites for a great Condrieu. Most of the top vineyards are perched on a 13-mile stretch of real estate that hugs the western bank of the Rhône River several miles south of Côte Rôtie.

Viognier, difficult to plant in these tough soils and always prone to outbreaks of mildew, has never been an easy grape to cultivate. Most of the top hillside vineyards, such as André Perret's Coteau du Chéry, Georges Vernay's Coteaux du Vernon, Yves Cuilleron's Les Chaillets, Pierre Dumazet's Coteau de Côte Fournet, and Marcel Guigal's La Doriane are planted on terraces that are superbly oriented toward the south and southeast, where they receive the full benefit of the morning and midday sun.

The Condrieu slopes are much less forbiddingly steep than those of Côte Rôtie, Hermitage, or Cornas. Nevertheless, producers have considerable problems with soil erosion due to heavy rains. The famed arzelle soil, which contributes so much to Condrieu's fruit cocktail/flower garden/honeysuckle-like nose, can be easily washed away, and thus has to be replenished by laborious manual labor. Even though the slopes are not as steep as in other appellations, mechanical cultivation is virtually impossible save for a few isolated areas.

In addition to the extraordinary difficulty in planting and cultivating the Viognier vineyards, it is also an extremely difficult grape to vinify. When done correctly, the result is a remarkably alluring and exotic wine with an overwhelming fragrance, full body, a viscous texture, admirable length, and an alcoholic headiness. As stated by the well-known English wine writer Jancis Robinson, "Condrieu produces full-bodied, golden wines with a haunting and tantalizing, elusive bouquet." In the top vintages, Condrieu tends to be low in acidity, and thus it is best drunk within the first 2–3 years of life. Some connoisseurs, most notably France's renowned wine critic Michel Bettane, have argued that Condrieu develops well after 3–4 years of age, but with the exception of a few ancient vintages of Château Grillet, I favor drinking this decadent, opulently textured, exotically scented wine no later than three years after the vintage.

Growing, harvesting, and vinifying Viognier allow little tolerance for error. The grapes must be picked ripe or the wine tastes too acidic, with green, underripe peach and grape-fruit-like aromas. If harvested too late, Viognier is impossible to vinify dry as the sugar content soars and the natural yeasts are killed off before the vinification is completed. Most top producers make full-bodied wines, with some utilizing a small percentage of new oak to vinify a portion of the crop, and then blending this segment with the rest of the wine that has been vinified in tank. The white winemaking technique called *macération pelliculaire* (skin contact) that has done so much to raise the level of quality for Sauvignon and Semillon in Bordeaux, is used by some Condrieu producers to achieve a more intense perfume. Most Condrieus are encouraged to complete a full malolactic fermentation, but in ripe, low-acid years, a handful of producers will do a partial malolactic, blocking the remainder so the wine does not become too flabby or fat. It is not surprising that three of the finest Condrieu producers, Marcel Guigal, Georges Vernay, and André Perret, utilize some prefermentation skin contact in order to intensify their wines' aromatics. These three producers also use up to one-third new oak casks for vinifying part of the crop, and then blend that with the balance, which has been fermented and aged in stainless steel. To my palate, this tastes like the correct balance. The new oak gives the wine structure and definition, yet it should not be recognizable when tasting the wine after it has been blended.

As one might suspect, when made from fully ripened grapes, Condrieu is not a wimpy wine, as the alcohol content can often reach 13.5–14% without any hint of overripeness. At its greatest, the wine possesses extraordinary intensity, power, and richness, allied to finesse and elegance. In short, it displays something the new world Viognier producers have yet to master—intensity without heaviness.

The question about what foods to eat with such an exotic, flamboyant, distinctive wine is a subject that merits consideration. Most growers are quick to recommend salmon or the locally renowned pike quenelles with a nantua sauce. I can enthusiastically attest that this marriage of wine and food is blissful. Condrieu can also accompany sushi, Indian cuisine, and a multitude of Asian dishes. The wine's strong personality is rarely obliterated by spicy, strongly scented and flavored foods. Marcel Guigal argues that Condrieu is one of the world's few wines that complements asparagus.

RECENT VINTAGES

Only recent vintages are reviewed because a Condrieu older than 4–5 years is usually disappointing.

1995 This was a more troublesome vintage than initially believed. A handful of great wines were produced by Guigal, Vernay, Dumazet, and Cuilleron, but too many producers refused to destem and harvested too early, resulting in wines that are too high in acidity, and taste vegetal. This is a vintage in which Condrieu enthusiasts must choose carefully, but the top examples are marvelous. These wines should be consumed by the turn of the century.

1994 Overall, this is a more consistent vintage than 1995. The 1994 Condrieus are rich, flattering, opulently textured, delicious wines that should drink well until the turn of the century. Just about everybody made at least good wine, with Marcel Guigal, Georges Vernay, Pierre Dumazet, François Villard, and René Rostaing all turning in sensational efforts.

1993 Like so much of the northern Rhône, Condrieu was struck hard by harvest rains. Nevertheless, some decent wines were made, although most should have been drunk up by 1997.

1992 As bad as 1993, with rain diluting the grapes and causing difficulties and some rot, this vintage should have been consumed by the mid-nineties.

1991 A terrific vintage in Condrieu, the 1991s have drunk well since birth, but most should be consumed by the end of 1997.

1990 A very hot drought year produced enormous, massively endowed Condrieu. A number of producers made late harvest *(vendange tardive)*, semisweet wines. The latter wines should continue to drink well for 5–6 years, but the drier cuvées should have been consumed by the mid-nineties.

Note: The tasting notes for the best Condrieu producers are limited to the 1994 and 1995 vintages.

PATRICK ET CHRISTOPHE BONNEFOND* * * *

Address: Le Mornas
       69420 Ampuis
Tel: 4-74-56-12-30
Fax: 4-74-56-17-93
Wines produced: Condrieu Côte Chatillon
Surface area: 1.5 acres
Production: 1,800 bottles
Upbringing: 8–10 months, one-third in new oak and two-thirds in inox vats
Average age of vines: 10 years

This small firm is better known for its Côte Rôtie because the estate is situated in Ampuis. Since the early nineties, the Bonnefonds have produced very good, sometimes outstanding Condrieu from their small plot of vines in the superbly situated Côte Chatillon. This is an estate to look for.

VINTAGES

1995—Condrieu Côte Chatillon   Only 1,500 bottles of the unfiltered, old-vine cuvée of
·   1995 Condrieu were produced by this small grower whose cellars are in Côte Rôtie.
89   The wine exhibits considerable fatness, excellent ripeness, and fine glycerin in its apricot-laden flavors. This is a chewy, thick, muscular Condrieu for drinking over the next 5–6 years. Last tasted 6/96.

1994—Condrieu Côte Chatillon   An intense, full-bodied, rich, highly extracted, dry Condrieu crammed with honeyed apricot and peachlike fruit. There is some viscosity,
·   but the wine is neither heavy nor overbearing. Drink it over the next 1–2 years.
91   Last tasted 9/95.

CHAPOUTIER* * * *

Address: 18, avenue du Docteur Paul Durand
         B.P. 38
         26600 Tain l'Hermitage
Tel: 4-75-08-28-65
Fax: 4-75-08-81-70
Wines produced: Condrieu
Surface area: 6.2 acres
Production: 12,000 bottles (includes juice bought from other producers)
Upbringing: 8–12 months, with 25% of yield in 10% new oak, and 75% of the yield in
         inox vats
Average age of vines: 10–20 years

Michel and Marc Chapoutier farm 6.2 acres of Condrieu vines and supplement their vineyard production with juice purchased from other growers. They fashion a flinty, mineral-dominated, tasty, medium-bodied wine that emphasizes elegance and lively, fresh fruit and purity. It offers a contrast to the appellation's thicker, more unctuously styled wines. While the wines are good, they are not at the spectacular level of Chapoutier's other Rhône Valley wines.

VINTAGES

1995—Condrieu   Chapoutier's 1995 Condrieu is an exotic, ripe, mineral, apricot-scented
·   wine with crisp acidity (a characteristic of the 1995 vintage), and an elegant,
89   full-bodied, refreshing finish. Thirty percent of the wine is fermented in new oak and the rest in tank, and then blended together prior to bottling. Last tasted 6/96.

1994—Condrieu   The 1994 is a well-made, crisp Condrieu for drinking over the next
·   2–3 years. Last tasted 9/95.
87

DOMAINE DU CHÊNE (MARC ROUVIÈRE)* * *

Address: Le Pêcher
          42410 Chavanay
Tel: 4-74-87-27-34
Fax: 4-74-87-02-70
Wines produced: Condrieu, Condrieu Automnal, Condrieu Cuvée Julien
Surface area: 8.65 acres
Production: 13,000 bottles
Upbringing: 6 months, with 10–20% of the yield in new oak and the rest in inox vats
Average age of vines: 15–20 years

One of the youngest northern Rhône producers, Marc Rouvière makes wines that, while still variable, can be quite good. The firm has an important holding in Condrieu, and produces just over 1,000 cases of wine made from a blend of Condrieu aged in both new oak and stainless steel tanks. Recent vintages have been correct and serviceable, but rarely at the top level of quality. Rouvière is one of a handful of Condrieu producers who, in certain vintages, makes a sweet Condrieu, which he calls Cuvée Julien.

VINTAGES

1995—Condrieu   Rouvière's 1995 Condrieu is a successful wine for the vintage, with
·   considerable precision thanks to crisp acidity, a rich, full-bodied, penetrating,
89   honeysuckle and apricotlike fragrance and flavors, fine ripeness, and a sense of
           elegance. It should drink well for 2–4 years, possibly longer given the crisp acidity.
           Last tasted 6/96.
1995—Condrieu Automnal   The sweet 1995 Condrieu Automnal was unevolved, flabby,
·   and disjointed when I saw it. I am sure there is more to it, but the wine needs some
87?   time to settle down. Last tasted 6/96.
1994—Condrieu   This is a light, straightforward, fruity Condrieu with intriguing mineral
·   scents, but no real concentration or depth. Drink it over the next year. Last tasted
83   9/95.
1993—Condrieu Cuvée Julien   The sweet 1993 Condrieu Cuvée Julien represents this
·   domaine's *vendange tardive* style. There is excellent ripeness, a sense of freshness,
87   full body, and copious amounts of heady alcohol and sweetness in the finish. Last
           tasted 6/95.

DOMAINE LOUIS CHÈZE* * *

Address: 07340 Limony
Tel: 4-75-34-02-88
Fax: 4-75-34-13-25
Wines produced: Condrieu Coteau de Brèze
Surface area: 5 acres
Production: 9,000 bottles
Upbringing: 7 months, with 80% of the yield in new oak and 20% in inox vats
Average age of vines: 4 years

Chèze, a relative newcomer, began vinifying Condrieu in 1978, after deciding his family should no longer sell the entire production to cooperatives. He owns a small, 5-acre vineyard on the Coteau de Brèze. The vines are very young, having been planted in the late eighties. The wine, which is vinified at cold temperatures and aged in both tanks and oak casks (of which 30% are new), has been a solidly made, pleasant but uninspiring style of Condrieu.

However, there is considerable passion and enthusiasm from young Chèze, who is ably assisted by his oenologist, Jean-Luc Colombo. It is too soon to know for sure (the vines are so young), but this estate has the commitment to produce better and better Condrieu as the vineyard gets older.

VINTAGES

1994—Condrieu Coteau de Brèze   This wine is a pure, medium-bodied, dry Condrieu
·   with excellent aromatics (honeysuckle and peaches), considerable finesse, good
88   freshness, and well-integrated, crisp acidity. Although not a blockbuster, this well-
          made Condrieu will offer delicious drinking over the next 1–2 years. Last tasted
          9/95.

YVES CUILLERON* * * */* * * * *

Address: Verlieu
        42410 Chavanay
Tel: 4-74-87-02-37
Fax: 4-74-87-05-62
Wines produced: Condrieu La Côte, Condrieu Les Chaillets Vieilles Vignes, Condrieu Les
        Eguets Vendange Tardive
Surface area (La Côte): 11.2 acres
        (Les Chaillets Vieilles Vignes): 3.75 acres
        (Les Eguets Vendange Tardive): 2.5 acres
Production (La Côte): 19,500 bottles
        (Les Chaillets Vieilles Vignes): 5,250 bottles
        (Les Eguets Vendange Tardive): 1,500 bottles
Upbringing (La Côte): 6 months, with 30% of the yield in oak and 70% in inox vats
        (Les Chaillets Vieilles Vignes and Les Eguets Vendange Tardive): 7 months in
        barrels
Average age of vines (La Côte): 15 years
        (Les Chaillets Vieilles Vignes): 33–50 years
        (Les Eguets Vendange Tardive): 20 years

When it comes to white wine, Yves Cuilleron is one of the northern Rhône's superstars. His red wines have not yet demonstrated the finesse, complexity, and completeness of his whites. Since the young Cuilleron, a nephew of Antoine Cuilleron, took over his uncle's estate in 1986, the wines have soared in quality. With a whopping 22.5 acres of Condrieu vineyards (5 acres are unplanted), Cuilleron has become one of the most significant producers in this appellation. What sets his Condrieu apart is not only their exceptional perfumes, but their gorgeous purity, balance, and layered richness that is intense, but never overbearing.

Cailleron produces three cuvées of Condrieu. The regular cuvée is made from 15-year-old vines, and about 30% of it rests in oak casks and the rest in stainless steel. He does frequent *batonnage* (lees stirring), and believes his wines benefit from a full malolactic fermentation. After 6–7 months of aging, the wines are polished, and lightly filtered prior to bottling. While the regular Condrieu is a brilliant wine, the Condrieu Les Chaillets Vieilles Vignes (from vines 33–50 years old) is exquisite. Made from a 3.75 acre terraced vineyard, this is one of the great Condrieus of the appellation. It can age well for 4–5 years. As the tasting notes that follow indicate, it was a candidate for Condrieu of the Vintage in both 1994 and 1995. Cuilleron has added a Vendange Tardive (late harvest) Condrieu Les Eguets from a 2.5-acre parcel of 20-year-old vines. He claims this wine was made by his grandfather, and that the traditional harvesting date, usually around All Saints' Day (November 1), produced a slightly sweet wine that was drunk by the family as an aperitif.

In the decade since Yves Cuilleron assumed control of this family domaine, he has established himself as one of the bright shining stars of the northern Rhône. As indicated in other chapters, he also makes brilliant white wines from his holdings in St.-Joseph. While his red wines have a long way to go before they attain the quality of his whites, most of his red wine vineyards are relatively young. I believe that given his commitment to excellence, it is only a matter of time before Cuilleron's reds become as renowned as his exquisite whites.

VINTAGES

1995—Condrieu Les Chaillets Vieilles Vignes   The profound 1995 Les Chaillets is about
·   as remarkable as Condrieu can be. The huge, fruit cocktail, spring flower garden,
96   apricot/peach, and mineral-scented nose is both ostentatious and fabulously com-
        pelling. This wine tastes like concentrated incense, with unbelievable thickness
        and richness, yet fine underlying structure. It is a sensational effort. While I am
        sure some observers will claim it can be cellared for five or more years, I would opt
        for drinking it over the next 2–3 years. Last tasted 6/96.

1995—Condrieu La Côte   The 1995 La Côte is a textbook Condrieu, offering up honeyed
·   peach/apricot aromas, exotic, rich, low-acid, plump flavors with a chewy texture,
90   and admirable intensity and purity in the long, layered finish. It is a Condrieu to
        drink over the next 1–2 years. Last tasted 6/96.

1995—Condrieu Les Eguets Vendange Tardive   The 1995 Les Eguets had just been
·   bottled, and unfortunately, its personality has yet to emerge. Undoubtedly, it should
90+   be an outstanding effort given its superconcentrated, unctuous texture, and
        medium-sweet style. However, it is not yet delineated. While impressively rich and
        full on the palate, this wine requires another 6–12 months of bottle age to take on
        more personality. Last tasted 6/96.

1994—Condrieu La Côte   The regular bottling of 1994 La Côte (30% of which is vinified
·   in small barrels) is a wine of considerable richness, elegance, and style. It offers
89   up the telltale tropical fruit, honeysuckle, and peachlike aroma, crisp acidity, and
        sensational purity (a hallmark of all the Cuilleron wines). It should drink well for
        1–2 years. Last tasted 9/95.

1994—Condrieu Les Chaillets Vieilles Vignes   The 1994 Les Chaillets is made from a
·   parcel of vines that average 35 years of age. Made from tiny yields of 20 hectoliters
93   per hectare (just over 1 ton an acre), the wine exhibits superb fruit, great richness,
        crystal-clear definition, and a full-bodied, layered feel in the mouth. This spectacu-
        lar Condrieu unleashes an exotic, lavishly rich mouthful of wine that sets off nearly
        all the sensory alarms. Drink it over the next 1–2 years. Last tasted 9/95.

1994—Condrieu Les Eguets Vendange Tardive   The rare, limited-quantity (made from
·   only one-half ton of botrytised fruit per acre) 1994 Les Eguets is sweet Auslese-
95   style wine. It is oily, huge, dense, and oh, so pure and impressive. Massive and
        superconcentrated, it is the quintessential expression of Viognier. Made in a sweet
        format, this is a winemaking tour de force. It should drink well for 4–5 years. Since
        only a handful of cases will make it to America, this review is largely of academic
        interest. Last tasted 9/95.

DELAS FRÈRES* */* * * *

Address: Z.A. de l'Olivet
   B.P. 4
   07300 St.-Jean de Muzols
Tel: 4-75-08-60-30
Fax: 4-75-08-53-67
Wines produced: Condrieu, Condrieu Clos Boucher
Surface area (Condrieu): bought from other producers
           (Clos Boucher): 5 acres
Production (Condrieu): 15,000 bottles
           (Clos Boucher): 2,500 bottles
Upbringing (Condrieu): 8 months in inox vats
           (Clos Boucher): 8 months, with 15% in new oak and 85% in inox vats
Average age of vines (Condrieu): 25 years
                     (Clos Boucher): 35 years

This négociant owns one of the choicest vineyard sites in Condrieu. Called Clos Boucher, this 5-acre steep hillside vineyard produces a superb Condrieu, in spite of the tendency of this firm to process and manipulate their wines so much that they often turn out sterile and monochromatic. The Delas staff vinifies its Condrieu in stainless steel at a very low temperature, blocks the malolactic fermentation, and gives it a brief respite in small oak barrels. Although it is sterile filtered, that does not prevent some of the exquisite perfume from surviving. While most of Delas Frères' wines possess an appalling inocuousness as well as irregular quality, their Clos Boucher is a superb example of the appellation. Their other Condrieu is a product of purchased juice. It can be excellent, although it is extremely inconsistent.

VINTAGES

1994—Condrieu   The 1994 Condrieu is a gorgeously proportioned, intense wine for
   ·   drinking over the next year. Last tasted 9/95.
90

1994—Condrieu Clos Boucher   Delas Frères produces a single-vineyard-designated Con-
   ·   drieu in top years called Clos Boucher. Only 200 cases of this full-bodied, rich, fra-
91   grant wine are made. This dry wine is more unctuously textured and richer than the
           regular cuvée. The 1994 possesses enough acidity to provide vibrancy and definition
           to the wine's large proportions. Drink it over the next 1–2 years. Last tasted 9/95.

LUCIEN DÉSORMEAUX* *

Address: Le Colombier
   R.N. 86
   42410 St.-Michel-sur-Rhône
Tel: 4-74-87-21-93
Wines produced: Condrieu
Surface area: 2.5 acres
Production: 500–1,000 bottles, with the rest of the yield sold in bulk
Upbringing: 5–6 months in inox vats
Average age of vines: 10 years

Désormeaux tends to make wines much like his personality—restrained, measured, and cautious. The Condrieu from his vineyards on the Coteau du Colombier, midway between the village of Condrieu and Chavanay, are pleasant, straightforward wines that are good, but hardly worth the high price they fetch. In fact, wines such as Georges Duboeuf's Viognier from l'Ardèche and a bevy of Viogniers from the Languedoc-Roussillon that sell for one-third the price are richer and more complete wines. Some of this estate's production is sold to Marcel Guigal, with only about 100 cases being estate-bottled by Désormeaux.

PIERRE DUMAZET* * */* * * * *

Address: R.N. 86
      07340 Limony
Tel: 4-75-34-03-01
Fax: 4-75-34-14-01
Wines produced: Condrieu La Myriade, Condrieu Coteau de Côte Fournet, Condrieu Coteau
      Rouelle Midi
Surface area (Condrieu): 0.86 acres
      (Coteau de Côte Fournet): 0.99 acres
      (Coteau Rouelle Midi): 0.62 acres
Production (Condrieu): 2,000–2,200 bottles
      (Coteau de Côte Fournet): 1,200 bottles
      (Coteau Rouelle Midi): 1,600 bottles
Upbringing (all three cuvées): 13–14 months, with two-thirds in wood barrels (20% new),
      one-third in inox vats
Average age of vines (Condrieu): 20 years
      (Coteau de Côte Fournet): 65 years
      (Coteau Rouelle Midi): 5–20 years

From this microestate's humble holdings, Pierre Dumazet, a gregarious man in his late fifties, produces superb Condrieu. Dumazet's finest wine is his well-known Condrieu from the Coteau de Côte Fournet, a vineyard planted at the southern end of the Condrieu appellation in hard, granite soils. The vineyard, which was planted in 1930, produces one of the most powerful, concentrated, and intense wines of the appellation. Like his regular cuvée of Condrieu and his Condrieu Coteau Rouelle Midi (made from nearly equal parts of 5-year-old and 20-year-old vines), the Coteau de Côte Fournet is put through a full malolactic fermentation. The Côte Fournet is not made in every vintage. I have tasted only the 1989, 1990, 1991, and 1994 vintages. All three of Dumazet's wines are given both tank and cask aging. He uses more wood cask than most Condrieu producers, with 60% of his wine spending 13–14 months in wood barrels (of which 20% are new), and the rest in glass-lined stainless steel. This is another estate that does considerable *batonnage* (stirring of the lees), and believes in a light fining and cellulose pad filtration.

A small quantity of Viognier is also made from a young vineyard that Dumazet declassifies and calls simply Côtes du Rhône. There is also a vin de pays called Collines Rhodaniennes made from 100% Viognier. It is a good, reasonably priced wine.

VINTAGES

1995—Condrieu La Myriade   The 1995 La Myriade was one of the stars of my tasting. It
  ·   exhibits dry, full-bodied, lusciously rich, apricot/peach jam–like flavors, tangy
  91   acidity, full body, and ripe pearlike flavors in the finish. Complex and rich, this
      super Condrieu should age well for 4–5 years because of its higher than normal
      acidity. Last tasted 6/96.
1994—Condrieu Coteau de Côte Fournet   The 1994 Côteau de Côte Fournet (I did not
  ·   taste the 1995) is a youthful, unevolved, spectacularly rich Condrieu with copious
  91   amounts of honeysuckle-tinged, tangerinelike fruit. Good acidity provides delinea-

tion to the full-bodied wine's richness and opulence. It is an impressive wine that should drink well for 3–4 years. Last tasted 6/96.

PHILIPPE FAURY* * *

Address: La Ribaudy
        42410 Chavanay
Tel: 4-74-87-26-00
Fax: 4-74-87-05-01
Wines produced: Condrieu
Surface area: 2.5 acres
Production: 3,500 bottles
Upbringing: 9–10 months in 10% new oak, 30% in barrels 2–5 years old, and 60% in
        inox vats
Average age of vines: 5 years

Philippe Faury is part of the small but growing youth movement in Condrieu. His debut releases have been soundly made, but not exceptional, save for the splendid 1994.

VINTAGES

1994—Condrieu   Philippe Faury has fashioned a fat, soft, unctuously textured Condrieu
   ·   with a slight degree of residual sugar. A deep wine, with sensational extract and a
 90   knockout nose of overripe peaches and apricots intertwined with floral scents, it
       should be drunk over the next 12 months. It is close to being a *vendange tardive*–
       style wine. Last tasted 9/95.

PIERRE GAILLARD* */* * *

Address: 42520 Malleval
Tel: 4-74-87-13-10
Fax: 4-74-87-17-66
Wines produced: Condrieu
Surface area: 2.5 acres
Production: 3,500 bottles
Upbringing: 6 months in 10% new oak barrels
Average age of vines: 5 years

Gaillard has a large estate producing moderate amounts of St.-Joseph, Côtes du Rhône, vin de pays, and Côte Rôtie. He owns only 2.5 acres of young vines in Condrieu. He believes in aging all of his Condrieu in casks, of which 10% are new. He has won high praise from many critics, but I have found his whites from St.-Joseph and his Viognier Côtes du Rhône more interesting than his Condrieu, which is often overoaked and/or underwined.

VINTAGES

1994—Condrieu   A clean, pure, medium-bodied, finesse-style Condrieu with that unde-
   ·   niable honeysuckle/apricot/peach-like perfume, this dry, nicely proportioned, tasty
 87   wine should be drunk over the next year. Last tasted 9/95.

YVES GANGLOFF* * * * *

Address: 2, chemin du Moulin
        69420 Condrieu
Tel: 4-74-59-57-04
Fax: 4-74-59-57-04
Wines produced: Condrieu
Surface area: 3 acres
Production: 2,500 bottles
Upbringing: 10 months, fermentation is done half in oak and half in inox vats, then 8 months
        in oak
Average age of vines: 10 years

What I have tasted from Yves Gangloff has been superb, but as is so often the case, only a minuscule 200 cases are bottled at this estate. The balance is sold to Marcel Guigal. Not many Condrieus can handle the 8 months of wood aging received by Gangloff's wines, but his powerful style holds up well.

VINTAGES

1994—Condrieu   The 1994 Condrieu is an explosive fruit bomb, with full body, a huge,
  ·   honeyed, peach- and apricot-scented nose, terrific ripeness, the viscosity and unc-
  92   tuosity that are typical of a very ripe year in Condrieu, and terrific length. The wine
          is bottled unfiltered to preserve its intensity. Last tasted 9/95.

JEAN-MICHEL GÉRIN* *

Address: 19, rue de Montmain—Verenay
        69420 Ampuis
Tel: 4-74-56-16-56
Fax: 4-74-56-11-37
Wines produced: Condrieu Coteau de la Loye
Surface area: 4.4 acres
Production: 7,000 bottles
Upbringing: 10 months, one-third of yield in new oak and two-thirds in inox vats
Average age of vines: less than 10 years

Gérin owns 4.4 acres of hillside vineyards planted with young vines (8–10 years old) in an area south of the famed Coteau du Chery called Coteau de la Loye. As good as his Côte Rôties are, his Condrieu Coteau de la Loye tastes neutral and thin. I would guess it is made from very young vineyards. Final judgment on Gérin's Condrieu will have to wait until the vines mature.

VINTAGES

1994—Condrieu Coteau de la Loye   Some obtrusive toasty vanillin from new oak does
  ·   not entirely mesh with the apricot/cherry fruit in this medium-bodied, ripe, overtly
  85   spicy wine. Small amounts of new oak can add structure, but in this wine the wood
          is dominant. Drink it over the next 8–12 months before the fruit begins to fade.
          Last tasted 9/95.

CHÂTEAU GRILLET* * *

Address: S.C.E.A. Neyret Gachet
      Château Grillet
      42410 Vérin
Tel: 4-74-59-51-56
Fax: 4-78-92-96-10

Wines produced: Condrieu
Surface area: 8.4 acres
Production: 15,000 bottles
Upbringing: 18 months in old oak
Average age of vines: 40 years

The legendary Château Grillet produces not only the Rhône Valley's most famous white wine, but one of the most celebrated wines of France. It is unique in many respects. For one thing, its 8.4 acres is an appellation unto itself, making it the Rhône Valley's smallest. There is not much of it made. The vineyards, which sit 500 feet above the Rhône in a perfect amphitheater with a superb south-southeasterly exposure, are drenched in sunlight during the growing season. The grape, like that of Condrieu only a mile away, is the fickle Viognier, but at Château Grillet the soil is lighter and more fragmented, containing a great deal of mica. From this privileged, hallowed site come about 1,250 cases of a wine that sell at $50 to $75 a bottle. Once the highest-priced Condrieu, it has now been surpassed by several special cuvées of Condrieu. Château Grillet is also distinguished by its brownish-yellow bottle, the only one of its type in use in France. And close inspection will reveal that it holds only 70 centiliters, not 75 as do all other standard French wine bottles. Since 1830, Château Grillet has been owned by the Neyrat-Gachet family. The proprietor was the elderly, aristocratic-looking André Canet, who resided in Lyons but obviously spent a good deal of time at Grillet. Since the death of André Canet several years ago, his daughter, Isabelle Baratin, along with the well-known Burgundian oenologist Max Leglise, have had control and authority over Grillet's wine.

Is Château Grillet superior to the top wines of Condrieu? Absolutely not. Certainly, well-heeled collectors are drawn to this wine because of its rarity, expense, and mystique, but my experience, which includes virtually all the Grillet vintages since 1967, has proven time and time again that this wine usually fails to live up to expectations. It is ironic that Rhône wines as a general rule are notoriously undervalued and underappreciated, yet the region's most famous white wine is no doubt overpriced and overrated. Such is sometimes the state of things in the wine world.

This is not to suggest that Grillet has not made some fine wines. The 1967, 1970, 1972, and 1976 were all delicious, very good rather than stupendous expressions of winemaking art. However, recent vintages have been light, sometimes watery and underripe. Most observers (including the local cognoscenti in Condrieu) make much of the fact that Grillet has consistently harvested several weeks before the better growers, apparently unwilling to risk the chance of fall rains. Guigal in particular argues that this robs the wine of much of its richness because the grapes are not fully mature. Yields are higher than desirable, and this no doubt adds to the less than stellar performances. Finally, the continued practice of aging the wine in ancient casks for 18 months would appear to do nothing more than desiccate the wine's fruit and contribute to its lean, compressed personality. All of these factors explain why recent vintages offer little excitement. Reports continue to circulate that this domaine will eventually be sold, but much of this speculation seems nothing more than wishful thinking on the part of several powerful Rhône families who would like nothing better than to add Château Grillet to their real estate holdings. There remain plenty of apologists for Grillet's lackluster performances, particularly in the British wine press, but fame and rarity can no longer carry this wine's reputation.

VINTAGES

1994—Condrieu   A light nose of honey and green fruits is followed by a medium-bodied
·   wine with good acidity and a measured, restrained character. Although good, it is
84   one-dimensional and simple. Yes, it will keep for 10–15 years, but who really
         cares? Last tasted 6/96.

1993—Condrieu   Herbal, underripe fruit aromas are vague and reticent. Coaxing reveals
·   a wine with high acidity, hollowness, and a lean, sharp finish. It will not develop,
76   but the high acidity will ensure a modest longevity. Last tasted 6/96.

1992—Condrieu   Beginning to lose its fruit, this lean, compact wine reveals musty,
·   honeylike notes in its nose, medium body, crisp acidity, and no depth or fruit in
72   the finish. Last tasted 9/95.

1990—Condrieu   Grillet's 1990 hints at the great potential possessed by this property.
·   While most 1990 Condrieus have one foot in the grave, this wine remains young
87   and vibrant, with a moderate straw color, and plenty of fresh, honeyed fruit with
         acacia scents in the background. Medium-bodied, with good concentration, excel-
         lent freshness, and a long, spicy, crisp finish, it should continue to drink well for
         7–10 years. It is measured and streamlined but very good. Last tasted 7/96.

1989—Condrieu   Not as expressive or rich as the 1990, the 1989 is well made, with
·   honey, earth, spice, and floral notes. This medium-bodied, crisp, attractive wine
86   displays no signs of oxidation or fruit loss. It is neither flamboyant nor deep, but it
         is well made. Anticipated maturity: now–2001. Last tasted 4/94.

MARCEL GUIGAL* * * * *

Address: 1, route de Taquières
        69420 Ampuis
Tel: 4-74-56-10-22
Fax: 4-74-56-18-76
Wines produced: Condrieu La Doriane, Condrieu négociant bottling
Surface area (La Doriane): 4.5 acres
Production (La Doriane): 6,000–8,000 bottles
        (Négociant Condrieu): 45% of the appellation's production is represented by this
        Condrieu
Upbringing (La Doriane): 9–10 months in 50% new oak and 50% inox vats for both alco-
        holic and malolactic fermentation
        (Négociant Condrieu): 10 months with one-third of the yield in new oak and
        two-thirds in inox vats
Average age of vines (Condrieu La Doriane): 15 years

Of the approximately 25,000 cases of wine produced in an average Condrieu harvest,
Marcel Guigal accounts for 45% of the appellation's production. When I wrote the first
edition of this book in 1986, Guigal was a minor player in Condrieu. But even then he had
his eye on the appellation, recognizing the enormous potential and rarity of Condrieu. Since
that time, he purchased from Patrice Porte a superb 4.5-acre hillside vineyard from which
he produces his luxury cuvée La Doriane. Its debut vintage was a spectacular 1994. Only
500–600 cases of this sumptuous wine from the Côtes Colombier emerge, and there is no
likelihood of additional production since this is a single-vineyard cuvée. The rest of Guigal's
production comes from grapes (not juice) Guigal purchases in his capacity as a négociant.
    Guigal has pioneered *macération pelliculaire* (a low-temperature fermentation with the
skins of the grapes for 4–8 hours) and full malolactic fermentation for his Condrieu. He also
advocates destemming the Viognier to prevent the wine from tasting too acidic or green. The

results have been irrefutable—superb wines. His regular cuvée of Condrieu is top-notch, with one-third of it aged in new oak casks and two-thirds aged in temperature-controlled stainless steel tanks. Both wines rest in oak and steel for 10 months before bottling. La Doriane sees 50% new oak (and it is also fermented in new oak) and 50% stainless steel tanks, and then is blended.

VINTAGES

1995—Condrieu Guigal's 1995 Condrieu looks to be excellent. The wine possesses a
· penetrating fragrance of flowers, peaches, and honey. Medium-bodied, with decent
88 acidity, and copious quantities of fresh, lively fruit (some cuvées even had an element of grapefruit), this appears to be a lighter, more restrained, delicious Condrieu for drinking over the next 3–4 years. Last tasted 6/96.

1995—Condrieu La Doriane The 1995 is spectacular. It is vinified in 50% new oak and
· 50% tank and then the wine is blended together. This superb single-vineyard
93 Condrieu displays a knockout nose of minerals, licorice, honey, and ripe peaches. Full-bodied, with a silky texture, gorgeous layers of fruit, and a dry, opulent finish, this exquisite Condrieu is my early candidate for Condrieu of the Vintage. Given how well the 1994 La Doriane is aging in bottle, this wine's window of drinkability may be broader than I initially suspected—perhaps 4–6 years (although I would still opt for drinking it within 2–3 years of the vintage). Last tasted 6/96.

1994—Condrieu The 1994 (made from purchased grapes) is an elegant, fat, rich, hon-
· eyed wine with plenty of glycerin, medium to full body, and loads of fresh, lively
88 peach and apricot fruit. Although it does not possess the intensity and length of La Doriane, it is a very fine Condrieu. Anticipated maturity: now–1999. Last tasted 6/96.

1994—Condrieu La Doriane 1994 is the debut vintage of La Doriane and 10,000 bottles
· of this exquisite Condrieu were produced. The vines average 15 years of age.
94 Guigal fermented half of the wine in barrel and half in tank and then blended. The wine reveals a stunning degree of richness, intensity, and complexity. Extremely full-bodied, with an unctuous texture, considerable complexity and finesse, it displays no evidence of barrel fermentation in its huge nose of honeyed apricots, peaches, and floral scents. Layers of concentration are buttressed by enough acidity to give freshness and delineation to the wine's copious fruit components. It is an exquisite, rich Condrieu that gets my nod as one of the finest dry Condrieus of the vintage, rivaling those great wines produced by Yves Cuilleron, Georges Vernay, and André Perret. It should drink well for 1–3 more years. Last tasted 6/96.

DOMAINE DU MONTEILLET (ANTOINE MONTEZ)* * * * *

Address: 42410 Chavanay
Tel: 4-74-87-24-57
Fax: 4-74-87-06-89
Wines produced: Condrieu
Surface area: 3.7 acres
Production: 4,000 bottles
Upbringing: 10–12 months, with half of the yield in new oak and half in inox tanks
Average age of vines: 6 years

Antoine Montez owns 3.7 acres in Condrieu, all situated in the hillside vineyards of Boissey and Chanson. His sumptuous Condrieu is one of the appellation's finest . . . if it can be found.

VINTAGES

1994—Condrieu This producer's recent vintages have been impressive. The exotic,
·   smoky, honeyed, peach-scented, rich 1994 Monteillet exhibits gobs of fruit, daz-
92   zling concentration and purity, as well as a well-defined, full-bodied, long, dry
        finish. Drink this terrific Condrieu over the next several years. Last tasted 9/95.

NIERO-PINCHON* * */* * * *

Address: 20, rue Cuvillère
         69420 Condrieu
Tel: 4-74-59-84-38
Fax: 4-74-56-62-70
Wines produced: Condrieu, Condrieu Coteau du Chéry
Surface area: 6.4 acres
Production: 6,000 bottles
Upbringing: 10 months, with 80% of the yield in inox vats and 20% in 15% new oak
Average age of vines: 15–20 years, with the oldest vines 45 years

Robert Niero had the good fortune to marry the daughter of the late Jean Pinchon, one of Condrieu's most highly regarded producers. After combining those parcels he inherited through marriage, along with others he has acquired, this estate has just under 7 acres, all planted in such well-regarded vineyards as Chatillon, Coteau du Chéry, and Rozay. The vines' average age of 15–20 years is not impressive by French standards, but there are several old-vine parcels of 45 years. Robert Niero practices a cautious vinification, élevage, and bottling, with considerable manipulation and filtration. In spite of that, he has produced some very fine wines. Although he has been inconsistent, that may be due in part to the difficult vintages Condrieu experienced in 1992 and 1993. While Niero has always vinified his Coteau du Chéry separately, he has also begun to produce a Condrieu La Ronchard, from a parcel he owns in the lieu-dit Chatillon. This appears to be a good, sometimes excellent source of Condrieu that has not yet established a meaningful record for consistency. Time will tell.

VINTAGES

1994—Condrieu A green, underripe, stemmy, peachlike flavor suggests a too early har-
·   vest. Although there is decent flavor, the wine is narrow, compact, and monochro-
77   matic. Drink it over the next year. Last tasted 9/95.
1994—Condrieu Coteau du Chéry Although significantly lighter in body and flavor ex-
·   traction than the Coteau du Chéry produced by André Perret, this is a tasty, rich,
87   medium-bodied Condrieu with spring flower-garden scents intertwined with aromas
        of peaches and honey. Cleanly made with good acidity, this stylish Condrieu should
        be consumed over the next 12 months. Last tasted 9/95.

ANDRÉ PERRET* * * * *

Address: R.N. 86
         Verlieu
         42410 Chavanay
Tel: 4-74-87-24-74
Fax: 4-74-87-05-26
Wines produced: Condrieu, Condrieu Cuvée Clos Chanson, Condrieu Cuvée Coteau du
         Chéry

Surface area (Condrieu): 2.5 acres
       (Cuvée Clos Chanson): 1.25 acres
       (Cuvée Coteau du Chéry): 6.2 acres
Production (Condrieu): 2,200 bottles
       (Cuvée Clos Chanson): 1,500 bottles
       (Cuvée Coteau du Chéry): 8,000 bottles
Upbringing: all three cuvées spend 12 months in two-thirds inox vats and one-third oak
       barrels, of which 10% are new
Average age of vines (Condrieu): 10 years
       (Cuvée Clos Chanson): 30 years
       (Cuvée Coteau du Chéry): 40 years

A brilliant white wine maker and excellent red wine maker, André Perret is a name to search out for Condrieu and St.-Joseph. Friendly, warm, and easy to talk with, Perret owns 10 acres of splendidly situated vineyards on the Coteau du Chéry and in the Clos Chanson near Chavanay. His vines on the Coteau du Chéry consist of 50- and 10-year-old parcels. His famed Coteau du Chéry is made from the oldest vines. The production from the younger vines goes into his regular Condrieu. In his parcel of Clos Chanson, the average age of the vines is 30 years.

There are no secrets to André Perret's success, even in difficult vintages. Old vines, low yields, ripe fruit, and a noninterventionist winemaking philosophy result in outstanding Condrieu. Perret is willing to destem if conditions require it, and his vinification and élevage are split equally between wood casks and temperature-controlled stainless steel tanks. The wines are blended together prior to bottling, given a light fining and only a coarse pad filtration. When talking to Perret, one gets the impression that if it were not an early-bottled white wine, he would not filter it at all. His wines are uniformly superb, as well as reference points for Condrieu. While I have never been patient enough to hold one of his wines for more than 2–3 years, I believe his Condrieu might retain its fruit beyond 5–6 years.

VINTAGES

1995—Condrieu Coteau du Chéry   The 1995 Coteau du Chéry should be one of the top
·   two or three wines of the appellation in this tricky vintage for Condrieu. It exhibits
92+   crisp acidity, a complex, leesy, creamy-textured ripeness, medium to full body, great elegance, and delicious peach/apricot fruit. For all its power and intensity, the wine possesses considerable fruit, texture, and wonderful delineation as a result of excellent acidity. Last tasted 9/96.

1994—Condrieu Coteau du Chéry   The 1994 appears to be another decadently rich and
·   opulent expression of Condrieu. It was kept *sur lie* for nearly a year after being put
92   in the barrel. Full-bodied, with gobs of honeyed, rich, unctuously textured, thick peach- and apricot-flavored fruit, this wine displays blazingly clear definition and superb flavor extraction, and as a result, it does not come across as alcoholic or heavy. This is another tour de force from one of Condrieu's great producers. Last tasted 9/96.

PHILIPPE ET CHRISTOPHE PICHON* * * *

Address: Le Grand Val–Verlieu
     42410 Chavanay
Tel: 4-74-87-23-61
Fax: 4-74-87-07-27

Wines produced: Condrieu, Condrieu Moelleux
Surface area (Condrieu): 5 acres
            (Condrieu Moelleux): 1.1 acres
Production (Condrieu): 6,600 bottles
            (Condrieu Moelleux): 1,100 bottles
Upbringing (Condrieu): 8 months, with 50% of the yield in old oak and 50% in inox vats
            (Condrieu Moelleux): 6 months in inox vats
Average age of vines (Condrieu and Condrieu Moelleux): 18 years

Father, Philippe, and son, Christophe Pichon, produce elegant, slightly tart, clean Condrieu from 6.1 acres of vineyards. The wines are traditionally made, with full malolactic fermentation, and upbringing in both oak barrels and stainless steel vats. Although no new oak is used, 50% of the crop is aged in old oak, and then blended with the other 50% that is kept in stainless steel. Occasionally a sweet *(vendange tardive)* Condrieu is made from a parcel of 18-year-old vines. That wine is clearly meant to be drunk as a dessert wine. Pichon is one of the few Condrieu producers who routinely makes a sweet wine.

Recent vintages have been difficult given the troublesome 1992 and 1993 harvests, but this is a satisfactory source for good rather than great Condrieu.

HERVÉ RICHARD* * * *

Address: Verlieu
            42410 Chavanay
Tel: 4-74-87-07-75
Wines produced: Condrieu
Surface area: 6.2 acres
Production: 9,000 bottles, with half the production sold in bulk
Upbringing: 10–12 months in inox vats
Average age of vines: 10 years

Richard's 6.2 acres of vineyards in the hills behind Chavanay are not old (10 years), but he is a producer to keep an eye on. Fifty percent of his production is sold to négociants, and the other 50% estate-bottled. The Condrieus I have tasted have been veritable fruit bombs. Not surprisingly, they are aged for 10–12 months in stainless steel vats.

VINTAGES

1991—Condrieu   Hervé Richard's yields in 1991 were 25 hectoliters per hectare and the
   ·   natural alcohol in this wine was 14%. One of the most concentrated Condrieus I
   94   have tasted, this unfiltered wine exhibits a sensational nose of apricots, honey, and
                spring flowers. Extraordinarily rich yet totally dry, with great focus to its massive
                components, this is a spectacularly rich, dramatic Condrieu for drinking with rich
                fish dishes and creamy fowl and veal courses. Last tasted 12/93.

RENÉ ROSTAING* * * */* * * * *

Address: Le Port
            69420 Ampuis
Tel: 4-74-56-12-00 or 4-74-59-80-03
Fax: 4-74-56-62-56
Wines produced: Condrieu
Surface area: 2.5 acres
Production: 3,500 bottles

Upbringing: 8–10 months with one-third of the yield in oak barrels and two-thirds in
    inox vats
Average age of vines: 18 years

From his 2.5 acres of Viognier in the lieu-dit La Bonnette, just behind Georges Vernay's Coteaux du Vernon, Rostaing produces some splendidly rich, opulent wines. Unfortunately, only 200 cases are made in an abundant year. Normally, about 60% is aged in stainless steel tank, with the balance aged in oak casks. It is put through full malolactic fermentation, and bottled with only a light filtration. While Rostaing is better known for his exquisite Côte Rôties, his Condrieu is an insider's secret.

VINTAGES

1994—Condrieu La Bonnette The 1994 La Bonnette is a massive mouthful of off-dry
  ·   wine that is oozing with honeysuckle, apricot, and peachlike fruit. Extremely
  93   full-bodied, with an unctuous texture as well as exceptional purity and richness,
    this wine is remarkably well focused for its large size. Made from only 26 hectoliters
    per hectare, Rostaing's 1994 Condrieu should be drunk over the next 1–2 years.
    Last tasted 9/95.

CHÂTEAU DU ROZAY (JEAN-YVES MULTIER)* *
Address: Rozay Nord
       69420 Condrieu
Tel: 4-74-87-81-89
Fax: 4-74-87-82-92
Wines produced: Condrieu, Condrieu Cuvée Château du Rozay
Surface area (Condrieu): 5 acres
          (Cuvée Château du Rozay): 2.5 acres
Production (Condrieu): 8,000 bottles
          (Cuvée Château du Rozay): 2,000 bottles
Upbringing: both wines receive 8–10 months in 90% inox vats and 10% new oak barrels
Average age of vines (Condrieu): 12 years
          (Cuvée Château du Rozay): 45 years

High in the hills behind the town of Condrieu is Château du Rozay, a faded pink, formidably built, real château. The Multier family has lived at Château du Rozay since 1898, but it was not until 1978 that the father of the current proprietor, Jean-Yves Multier, began to estate-bottle. Since his father's premature death in 1984, Jean-Yves has guided the fortunes of this highly prestigious, renowned vineyard. In the past, I have had some extraordinary wines from Château du Rozay, but vintages since the early nineties have been decidedly mediocre. 1995 was an absolute disaster. It was so vegetal and high in acidity that I found it nearly undrinkable. Two cuvées are produced, one from 12-year-old vines planted on a 5-acre parcel in Corbery, and the other from a 45-year-old parcel of vines on the Coteau du Chéry, from which Multier produces the famed Condrieu Cuvée Château du Rozay. Both the regular Condrieu and Cuvée Château du Rozay are vinified and aged in 90% stainless steel vats, and 10% in new oak casks. As stated above, this can be an extraordinary wine, but recent vintages have had little resemblance to great vintages of the past. Of course, all of this can change, as Rozay possesses an extraordinary terroir, in addition to a proprietor who knows how to make quality wine. But possessing the knowledge and the necessary commitment to put that knowledge to good use are two different things.

CHAIS ST.-PIERRE* */* * *

Address: Place de l'Eglise
          42410 St.-Pierre-de-Boeuf
Tel: 4-74-87-12-09
Fax: 4-74-87-17-34
Wines produced: Condrieu Cuvée Le Ceps du Nébadon, Condrieu Cuvée Lys de Volan
Surface area (Cuvée Le Ceps du Nébadon): 11.1 acres
            (Cuvée Lys de Volan): 6.2 acres
Production (Cuvée Le Ceps du Nébadon): 15,000 bottles
            (Cuvée Lys de Volan): 10,000 bottles
Upbringing: both wines spend 6 months in 20% new oak and 80% inox vats
Average age of vines (Cuvée Le Ceps du Nébadon): 12–15 years
                      (Cuvée Lys de Volan): 10–15 years

Proprietor Alain Paret began this estate in 1972 after the death of his father. Behind the scenic old village of Malleval, about four miles south of Condrieu, Paret has a large 89-acre estate with 17.3 acres in Condrieu, and the balance in St.-Joseph. All of these vineyards are planted on impressively situated terraces with a south-southeasterly exposure. One of the interesting stories about this estate involves the famous French actor Gérard Depardieu. He is alleged to have been so enamored of a bottle of Paret's wine that he telephoned the estate to put in an order. Subsequently, Depardieu became Paret's partner.

I have seen Paret's red wines more frequently than his whites, but he produces two cuvées of Condrieu. Their luxury cuvée, the Lys de Volan, is named after the château of the same name that is perched prominently on a hill overlooking the medieval village of Malleval. The other cuvée, Le Ceps du Nébadon, is a straightforward Condrieu made from a vineyard planted in 1980.

The vineyards look terrific, the yields are kept low, and the winemaking is completely traditional, but there is a tendency to put the wine through too many aroma- and flavor-eviscerating filtrations. This is an estate with considerable unrealized potential.

GEORGES VERNAY* * * */* * * * *

Address: 1, R.N. 86
          69420 Condrieu
Tel: 4-74-59-52-22
Fax: 4-74-56-60-98
Wines produced: Condrieu, Condrieu Les Chaillées de l'Enfer, Condrieu Coteaux du Vernon
Surface area (Condrieu): 8 acres
            (Les Chaillées de l'Enfer): 1.9 acres
            (Coteaux du Vernon): 4 acres
Production (Condrieu): 12,000 bottles
            (Les Chaillées de l'Enfer): 2,400 bottles
            (Coteaux du Vernon): 4,500 bottles
Upbringing (Condrieu): 8 months, with 50% of the yield in inox vats, and 50% in 10% new
                       oak barrels
            (Les Chaillées de l'Enfer and Coteaux du Vernon): 15–18 months in 10% new
                       oak barrels, with assemblage in inox vats
Average age of vines (Condrieu): 10–30 years
                      (Les Chaillées de l'Enfer): 30–40 years
                      (Coteaux du Vernon): 40 years

The stocky, heavily jowled Georges Vernay is, for all intents and purposes, Mr. Condrieu. Not only is he the longstanding president of the growers' association, but he is the second-largest producer, having been bumped from the number one spot by Marcel Guigal's expansionist takeover. He owns 14 acres of vineyards, but supplements his own yields with purchases from growers. Despite 70 years of age, Vernay is always on the move, flitting around Condrieu dispensing words of encouragement, giving advice, and working extremely hard to extract from one of the wine world's most temperamental grapes as fine a wine as it is possible to make. Much like a bulldog, Vernay is relentless in his belief that Condrieu is one of the world's greatest white wines. The bulk of his production is his dry, full-bodied, delicious Condrieu, which is vinified and brought up in equal percentages of stainless steel and oak barrels (of which 10% are new). Vernay believes in an early bottling to preserve the wine's fragrance and fruit, and thus this cuvée rarely spends more than eight months aging prior to bottling. Vernay's luxury cuvée, made from 40-year-old vines on the Coteaux du Vernon (from a steep terraced vineyard situated across from the famed Condrieu restaurant-hotel, Beau Rivage), is fermented completely in cask and aged in barrels for up to 18 months. The wine is then assembled in stainless steel and bottled when Vernay believes it is appropriate. About 10% new oak casks are utilized for each new vintage. For years, Vernay's Condrieu has been the reference point, quintessential wine of the appellation. It stood alone until recently when some other producers began to make single-vineyard or luxury cuvées, most notably André Perret's Coteau du Chery and Marcel Guigal's La Doriane. Vernay, who aims for as much peach and apricot fragrance in his Viognier as possible, is a notorious late harvester. Nowhere is that more noticeable than in the Coteaux du Vernon. This is a Condrieu with the potential to last for 4–5 years, perhaps longer.

In 1992, because of the huge demand for his tiny quantities of Coteaux du Vernon, Vernay began to make a third cuvée called Les Chaillées de l'Enfer. This wine is bottled in a special tall, fluted brown bottle and has the same vinification and upbringing as the Coteaux du Vernon. I have tasted only the 1992 and 1994, but this is another terrific Condrieu from one of the appellation's legendary producers.

Although it is impossible to imagine Georges Vernay retiring, his succession is guaranteed by his handsome son, Luc, who is now intensely involved in the operation of this top-class estate.

VINTAGES

1995—Condrieu The 1995 Condrieu exhibits crisp, tart acidity, medium body, and ripe
· honeysuckle and apricot fruit that are presented in a restrained format. The wine's
86 acidity will keep it fresh and lively, but there is not as much depth as I would like.
Last tasted 6/96.

1995—Condrieu Coteaux du Vernon The 1995 Condrieu Coteaux du Vernon had just
· finished malolactic when I tasted it. It is promisingly rich, medium- to full-bodied,
88 with a waxy, honeyed, marmaladelike nose, excellent purity, zesty acidity, and a
compact finish. Last tasted 6/96.

1994—Condrieu The 1994 Condrieu reveals gobs of honeyed peach- and apricotlike
· fruit in a medium- to full-bodied, pure, tasty format. This delicious wine is best
89 consumed over the next year. Last tasted 9/95.

1994—Condrieu Les Chaillées de L'Enfer Georges Vernay has begun making an even
· more limited-production, luxury cuvée than his famed Coteaux du Vernon. Just
90+ being released, the 1994 Les Chaillées de l'Enfer (only 1,500 bottles produced) is
a stunningly rich, full-bodied, opulent Condrieu revealing an inner core of apricot/
peach fruit backed up by steely, mineral scents and flavors. Made from a vineyard

planted in 1957, and put in a specially designed bottle, this is an elegant, provocatively perfumed and flavored wine. It should be a big hit with Condrieu enthusiasts. Last tasted 6/96.

1994—Condrieu Coteaux du Vernon   Unlike most Condrieus, the Coteaux du Vernon can
   ·   age for 4–5 years. The immensely impressive 1994 is an exotic, full-bodied wine
   92   with layers of rich, chewy, honeyed fruit, enough acidity for definition, and a long,
         spicy finish that lasts for nearly 45 seconds. This is Condrieu made in its most
         lavishly rich style. Last tasted 9/95.

1993—Condrieu Coteaux du Vernon   The 1993 Condrieu Coteau du Vernon is a full-
   ·   bodied wine offering a smorgasbord of aromas such as peach blossoms, apricots,
   90   honey, and cherries. The wine exhibits excellent depth and richness, outstanding
         balance, and a long, lusty, unevolved finish. It should be drunk up. Last tasted 12/94.

FRANÇOIS VILLARD* * * */ * * * * *

Address: 42410 Chavanay
Tel: 4-74-53-11-25
Fax: 4-74-53-38-20
Wines Produced: Condrieu Coteaux de Poncin, Condrieu Les Terrasses du Palat, Condrieu
              Quintessence
Surface area: 8.6 acres
Production: 750–900 cases
Upbringing: 12–18 months in small oak casks

Villard is one of the young, serious producers who has an intellectual as well as artistic approach to making Condrieu. His wines are given extensive lees contact, with certain cuvées aged in 100% new oak, and bottled with minimal processing. They are expressionistic, firmly structured Condrieus that stand apart in a tasting for both their power and concentration.

VINTAGES

1995—Condrieu Coteaux de Poncin   The superb 1995 Coteaux de Poncin is full-bodied
   ·   and concentrated, with a leesy, honeyed nose, toasty notes, and a buttery, apricot,
 90 +   peachlike character. It gives the impression of being subdued, but as it sits in the
         glass, it reveals layers of flavors and numerous nuances. Given the wine's zesty
         acidity and outstanding extract, it may last for a decade. Last tasted 6/96.

1995—Condrieu Les Terrasses du Palat   The backward, astringent, tannic 1995 Les
   ·   Terrasses du Palat was impossible to assess. It appeared to have just finished
   ?   malolactic fermentation. It was dry and rich, but unevolved and impenetrable. Last
         tasted 6/96.

1994—Condrieu Coteaux de Poncin   The ripe 1994 Condrieu Coteaux de Poncin reveals
   ·   a Chablis-like, mineral character, as well as some noticeable astringency and
 88 +   lavish wood (100% new oak barrels are utilized). Anticipated maturity: now–2001.
         Last tasted 6/96.

1994—Condrieu Quintessence   The star of this vintage is the 1994 Condrieu Quintessence,
   ·   a Beerenauslese-style Condrieu that is fabulously rich, sweet, and unctuous, as well
   94   as gorgeously well balanced with searing acid levels in addition to an underlying
         mineral component. It should drink well for a decade or more. Last tasted 6/96.

1994—Condrieu Les Terrasses du Palat   The 1994s include the delicious 1994 Condrieu
   ·   Les Terrasses du Palat. It possesses good ripeness and fruit, crisp acidity, a
 87 +   dry, austere character, and an elegant, complex, mineral-dominated finish. In its
         measured, restrained, mineral style, it lacks some of the showboat characteristics

exhibited by some Condrieu, but it is very good. Anticipated maturity: now–2000. Last tasted 6/96.

OTHER CONDRIEU PRODUCERS

GILLES BARGE* * *

Address: Le Carcan
       Route de Boucharey
       69420 Ampuis
Tel: 4-74-56-13-90
Fax: 4-74-56-10-98
Wines produced: Condrieu
Surface area: 1.2 acres
Production: 2,550 bottles
Upbringing: 6 months in old oak barrels
Average age of vines: 50% of the vines are 20 years of age and the rest are young

PIERRE BONNARD

Address: La Petite Gorge
       42410 Chavanay
Tel: 4-74-87-21-62
Wines produced: Condrieu
Surface area: 1.9 acres
Production: Pierre Bonnard retired after the 1993 vintage and his vines are now cultivated
       by Didier Morion, but the production is sold primarily in bulk.

MICHEL BOUCHET

Address: Le Ventabrin
       42410 Chavanay
Tel: 4-74-87-23-38
Wines produced: Condrieu
Surface area: 0.74 acres
Production: 1,000 bottles
Upbringing: 8 months in oak barrels, a small percentage of which are new
Average age of vines: 5 years

PIERRE BOUCHET

Address: Domaine de la Favière
       42410 Malleval
Tel: 4-74-87-15-25
Wines produced: Condrieu
Surface area: 2.5 acres
Production: 4,000–5,000 bottles
Upbringing: 12 months in inox vats
Average age of vines: 8–10 years

DOMINIQUE BOURRIN

Address: Brossin
       42410 Roisey
Tel: 4-74-87-49-15
Wines produced: Condrieu
Surface area: 2.5 acres

Production: 3,750 bottles
Upbringing: 7–8 months with 80% of the yield in inox vats and 20% in 1-year-old barrels
Average age of vines: 7 years

FRANÇOIS BRACOUD

Address: 28, route de St. Prin
          38370 St.-Clair-du-Rhône
Tel: 4-74-56-33-24
Wines produced: Condrieu
Surface area: 1.7 acres
Production: 500–1,000 bottles, with the rest of the grapes sold in bulk
Upbringing: 18 months in oak barrels
Average age of vines: 10 years

BERNARD CHAMBEYRON

Address: Boucharey
          69420 Ampuis
Tel: 4-74-56-15-05
Wines produced: Condrieu
Surface area: 1.24 acres
Production: 3,700 bottles
Upbringing: 6 months, with 20% of the yield in new oak and 80% in inox vats
Average age of vines: 10 years

ROGER CHANAL

Address: La Combe
          42410 Pelussin
Tel: 4-74-87-83-17
Wines produced: Condrieu
Surface area: 3.2 acres
Production: 500–2,000 bottles; the rest of the yield is sold in bulk
Upbringing: 8 months in 50% inox vats and 50% old oak
Average age of vines: 10 years

GILBERT CHIRAT

Address: Le Piaton
          42410 St.-Michel-sur-Rhône
Tel: 4-74-56-68-92
Wines produced: Condrieu
Surface area: 3.7 acres
Production: 5,000 bottles
Upbringing: 6–8 months in inox vats
Average age of vines: 10 years

GILBERT CLUSEL-ROCH

Address: 15, route du Lacat–Verenay
          69420 Ampuis
Tel: 4-74-56-15-95
Fax: 4-74-56-19-74
Wines produced: Condrieu
Surface area: 1.24 acres
Production: 1,500 bottles

Upbringing: 8 months in 50% inox vats and 50% oak, few of which are new
Average age of vines: 10 years

PIERRE CORROMPT

Address: Route Nationale
   42410 Verin
Tel: 4-74-59-52-66

FRANÇOIS GÉRARD

Address: Côte Chatillon
   69420 Condrieu
Tel: 4-74-87-88-64
Wines produced: Condrieu
Surface area: 2.5 acres
Production: 2,000 bottles
Upbringing: 12 months in inox vats
Average age of vines: 15 years

ROBERT JURIE DES CAMIERS

Address: 32, chemin de la Begonnière
   69230 Genlis Laval
Tel: 4-78-56-34-02
Wines produced: Condrieu
Surface area: 3.7 acres
Production: 4,000 bottles total, with 3,000 bottles being given to André Perret as the land
   is given in *métayage* to Perret
Upbringing: 12 months in 50% new oak barrels
Average age of vines: half are 7 years old and the rest 45 years

LUCIEN LAGNIER

Address: 42410 Chavanay
Tel: 4-74-87-24-46
Wines produced: Condrieu
Surface area: 1.2 acres
Production: 1,500 bottles
Upbringing: 10 months in old oak
Average age of vines: 50 years

MICHEL MOURIER

Address: Domaine de la Pierre Blanche
   19, rue du Mont
   42000 St.-Etienne
Tel: 4-77-57-29-59
Fax: 4-77-80-68-71
Wines produced: Condrieu
Surface area: 1.1 acres
Production: 1,820 bottles
Upbringing: 6 months in inox vats
Average age of vines: 6 years

ANDRÉ PORT

Address: Place de la Maladière
       69420 Condrieu
Tel: 4-74-59-80-25
Wines produced: Condrieu

L. DE VALLOUIT

Address: 24, rue Désiré Valette
       26240 St.-Vallier
Tel: 4-75-23-10-11
Wines produced: Condrieu
Surface area: 1.6 acres
Production: 3,750 bottles
Upbringing: 8–10 months in 50% new oak and 50% inox vats
Average age of vines: 25 years

JACQUES VERNAY

Address: Le Biez
       42410 St.-Pierre-de-Boeuf
Tel: 4-74-87-11-70
Wines produced: Condrieu
Surface area: 5.5 acres
Production: 10,000 bottles
Upbringing: Usually 4 months in polyester vats, but 9 months in exceptional vintages
Average age of vines: 9–12 years

PHILIPPE VERZIER

Address: Izerat
       42410 Chavanay
Tel: 4-74-87-23-69
Wines produced: Condrieu, Condrieu Moelleux (debut vintage is 1994)
Surface area (Condrieu): 2.5 acres
       (Condrieu Moelleux): 0.86 acres
Production (Condrieu): 3,000 bottles
       (Condrieu Moelleux): 700 bottles
Upbringing (Condrieu): 10 months, with 70% of the yield in inox vats and 30% in 10% new oak
       (Condrieu Moelleux): 3 months in inox vats; the fermentation is stopped by cooling and the bottling is done early
Average age of vines (Condrieu): 6 years
       (Condrieu Moelleux): 8 years

GÉRARD VILLANO* * * *

Address: 39, grande rue de la Maladière
       69420 Condrieu
Fax: 4-74-59-87-64
Wines produced: Condrieu
Surface area: 3.8 acres
Production: 1,500 bottles
Upbringing: 8–12 months in old oak barrels
Average age of vines: 20 years

HERMITAGE

One of the World's Greatest Terroirs

HERMITAGE AT A GLANCE

Appellation created:	March 4, 1937.
Types of wine produced:	Red, white, and vin de paille, a dessert-style white wine
Grape varieties planted:	Syrah for the red wine; primarily Marsanne and some Roussanne for the white wine; up to 15% white wine grapes can be blended with the red wine, but as a practical matter, this is widely eschewed.
Acres currently under vine:	321.
Quality level:	Prodigious for the finest red wines, good to exceptional for the white wines.
Aging potential:	Red wine: 5–40 plus years; white wine: 3–25 years.
General characteristics:	Rich, viscous, very full-bodied, tannic red wines. Full-bodied white wines with a unique scent of herbs, minerals, nuts, and peaches.
Greatest recent vintages:	1995, 1991, 1990, 1989, 1979, 1978, 1972, 1970, 1966, 1961, 1959.
Price range:	$35–$55 will purchase any wine except for Chapoutier's l'Orée and Le Pavillon, and Chave's Cuvée Cathelin, which can cost $150 a bottle.
Aromatic Profile:	Red Hermitage—Cassis, black pepper, tar, and very ripe red and black fruits characterize a fine young vintage of

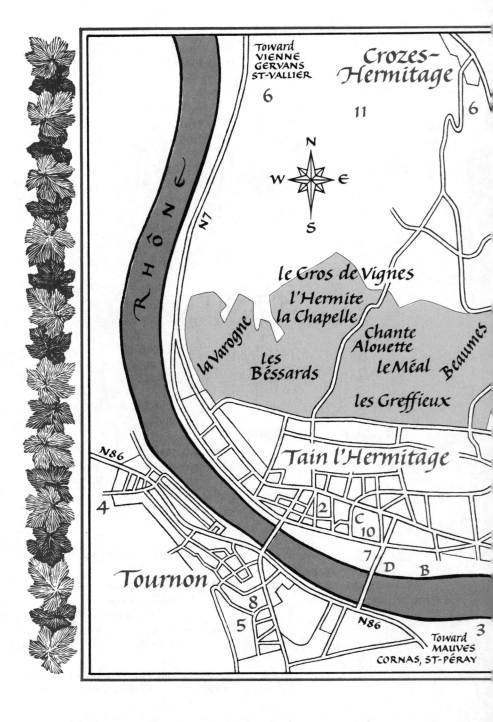

Toward
VIENNE
GERVANS
ST-VALLIER

Crozes-
Hermitage

6

11

6

N

W   E

S

N7

le Gros de Vignes
l'Hermite
la Chapelle

Chante
Alouette
le Méal

Beaumes

la Varogne

les
Béssards

les Greffieux

RHÔNE

Tain l'Hermitage

N86

4

2

C
10

7

D   B

Tournon

8

5

N86

Toward
MAUVES
CORNAS, ST-PÉRAY

3

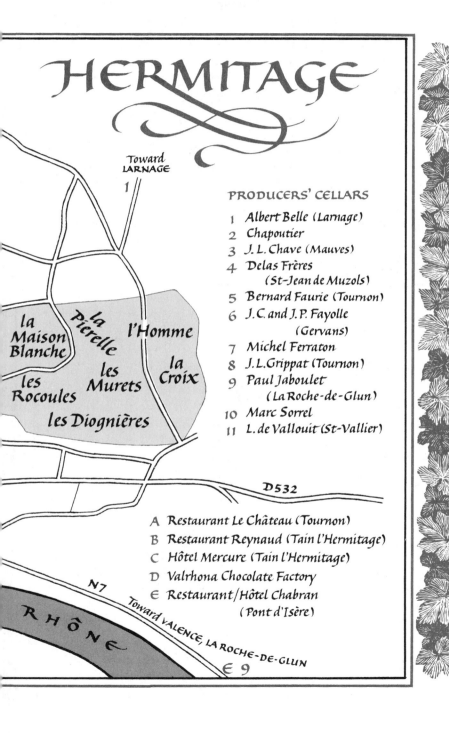

HERMITAGE

Toward
LARNAGE

1

la Maison Blanche

les Rocoules

la Pierelle

l'Homme

les Murets

la Croix

les Diognières

PRODUCERS' CELLARS

1 Albert Belle (Larnage)
2 Chapoutier
3 J. L. Chave (Mauves)
4 Delas Frères
(St-Jean de Muzols)
5 Bernard Faurie (Tournon)
6 J. C. and J. P. Fayolle
(Gervans)
7 Michel Ferraton
8 J. L. Grippat (Tournon)
9 Paul Jaboulet
(La Roche-de-Glun)
10 Marc Sorrel
11 L. de Vallouit (St-Vallier)

D532

A Restaurant Le Château (Tournon)
B Restaurant Reynaud (Tain l'Hermitage)
C Hôtel Mercure (Tain l'Hermitage)
D Valrhona Chocolate Factory
E Restaurant/Hôtel Chabran
(Pont d'Isère)

N7
Toward VALENCE, LA ROCHE-DE-GLUN

RHÔNE

E 9

red Hermitage. With a decade of bottle age, cedar, spice, and cassis can (and often do) resemble a first-growth Pauillac.

White Hermitage—Pineapple aromas intertwine with acacia flowers, peach, and honey scents. With extended age (15 or more years), scents of smoked nuts, fino sherry, and honey can be overpowering.

Textural Profile: Red Hermitage—Unusually full-bodied, powerful, and tannic, as well as resistant to oxidation, a wine that ages at a glacial pace.

White Hermitage—Fruity, full-bodied, and fragrant when young, white Hermitage closes down after 4–5 years of bottle age, only to reemerge 15–25 years later as an unctuous, dry, thick white wine.

The Hermitage appellation's most profound wines:

Chapoutier Ermitage Cuvée de l'Orée (white)

Chapoutier Ermitage Le Pavillon (red)

J. L. Chave Hermitage (red)

J. L. Chave Hermitage (white)

J. L. Chave Hermitage Cuvée Cathelin (red)

Bernard Faurie Hermitage Le Méal (red)

Delas Frères Hermitage Les Bessards (red)

Paul Jaboulet-Ainé Hermitage La Chapelle (red)

Marc Sorrel Hermitage Le Gréal (red)

RATING THE RED HERMITAGE PRODUCERS

* * * * *(OUTSTANDING)

Chapoutier (Le Pavillon)

J. L. Chave (Cuvée Cathelin)

J. L. Chave (regular cuvée)

Bernard Faurie (Le Méal)

Paul Jaboulet-Ainé (La Chapelle)

Marc Sorrel (Le Gréal)

* * * *(EXCELLENT)

Albert Belle

Chapoutier (La Sizeranne) (since 1989)

Domaine du Colombier

Delas Frères (Les Bessards)

Bernard Faurie (regular cuvée)

Marc Sorrel (Cuvéc Classique)

L. de Vallouit (Les Greffières)

* * *(GOOD)

Caves Cottevergne–L. Saugère

Bernard Chave

Dard et Ribo

Delas Frères (Marquise de la Tourette)

Desmeure

Domaine Fayolle

Ferraton Père et Fils (Cuvée Les Miaux)

Alain Graillot

Guigal

Paul Jaboulet-Ainé (Pied La Côte)

Vidal-Fleury

RATING THE WHITE HERMITAGE PRODUCERS

* * * * *(OUTSTANDING)

Chapoutier (Cuvée de l'Orée)   J. L. Chave

* * * *(EXCELLENT)

J. L. Grippat   Marc Sorrel (Les Rocoules)
Guigal
Paul Jaboulet-Aîné (Chevalier de
   Stérimberg) (since 1989)

The huge Hermitage dome, looming over a sharp bend in the Rhône River, is a formidable sight. First-time visitors to Tain l'Hermitage would be well-advised to cross over the Pont G. Toursier (the only bridge in town that permits car traffic), or park in Tain l'Hermitage, taking the walking bridge, Pont M. Séguin, across the river to Tournon sur Rhône, Tain l'Hermitage's sister town on the western bank. The view of Hermitage from the terraces of the Château de Tournon is breathtaking. From this vantage point, one can see the extraordinary southerly exposition of the three large hills of Hermitage. Another, more courageous way to get a bird's-eye view of these impressive vineyards (as well as the backbreaking labor involved in cultivating them) is to scale the hill of Hermitage. A recommended good departure point is behind the train station. Just head straight for the chapel at the top of the hill. The slippery decomposed granite found in this sector of Hermitage as well as the hill's gradient will provide a vigorous workout, even for someone in reasonably good condition. Readers should allow 30–45 minutes to reach the summit, but what a view is waiting!

Hermitage has a long and colorful history. John Livingstone-Learmonth, in his excellent book on the wines of the Rhône, states that vines were first brought to Hermitage in 500 B.C. by the Greeks. The most often quoted legend of this famous hill is that in the thirteenth century a crusader, Gaspard de Stérimberg, wounded in the wars of that period, sought refuge on top of this hill and subsequently built a chapel where he lived in self-imposed solitude. The modern, reconstructed version (St.-Christopher) sits alone near the crest of the hill and is owned by the Jaboulet family, who call their best red Hermitage "La Chapelle" and their white Hermitage "Chevalier de Stérimberg." Ironically, the vineyards surrounding the chapel are owned by a rival of Jaboulet, the Chapoutier family.

One of the earliest written references to the wines of Hermitage came from an American, Thomas Jefferson. While serving as ambassador to France, Jefferson visited Tain l'Hermitage in spring 1787. As James M. Gabler's book, *Passions—The Wines and Travels of Thomas Jefferson*, establishes, Jefferson considered white Hermitage and Champagne to be the best white wines of France. He wrote in his diary that he held white Hermitage in such esteem that he called it "the first wine in the world without a single exception." Moreover, he purchased 550 bottles. Even more revealing are Jefferson's comments about red Hermitage, which he characterized as having, "full body, dark purple color . . . exquisite flavor and perfume which is . . . compared to that of raspberry." Thomas Jefferson may have been America's first true wine connoisseur, and his comments about Hermitage could have been written today. By the early nineteenth century, Hermitage had become France's most expensive red wine. Not only did an American have an appreciation for Hermitage, Nicolas (France's best-known wine merchants) catalogs (see the illustration) indicate Hermitage fetched prices higher than such famous Bordeaux châteaus as Lafite-Rothschild and Haut-Brion. Moreover, white Hermitage was more expensive than red Hermitage. During Hermitage's glory days in the first half of the nineteenth century, it was a favorite wine of the Russian imperial court. Another little-known, but well-documented fact is that Hermitage was also sent to Bordeaux, where it was blended with high-quality Bordeaux wines to add color, strength, and structure. In fact, it was so prized as an additional component for Bordeaux that the wines were promoted as Hermitagé, and were often sold at higher prices than the unblended wines.

For all its fame in the international marketplace, Hermitage, like almost every northern

NICOLAS,
Marchand de Vins, Eaux-de-Vie & Liqueurs

MAGASIN PRINCIPAL, RUE SAINTE-ANNE, N° 53.

MAGASINS PARTICULIERS:

CLOITRE SAINT-HONORÉ, N° 1. — RUE MONTMARTRE, N° 15. — RUE SAINT-ANDRÉ-DES-ARTS, N° 30

PRIX COURANT.

Le tout rendu à domicile, franco de port, verre non compris pour tous les articles à 1 fr. et au-dessous

BONS VINS ROUGES ET BLANCS AU LITRE ET AU COURS.

VINS ORDINAIRES.

N° 3. Rouge . . . à 9 Sols la bouteille.	N° 6. Blanc . . . à 12 Sols la bouteille.
4. D°.. . . à 10 d°.	7. Bordeaux rouge . à 12 d°.
5. Blanc . . à 10 d°.	8. Mâcon rouge. . à 12 d°.

VINS ROUGES DE BORDEAUX.

	f.	s.
9. Bonnes côtes		15
10. Médoc . . .	1	.
11. Haut-Médoc . .	1	10
12. St-Emilion . .	1	10
13. St-Julien . .	2	.
14. St-Estèphe . .	2	.
15. Léoville . .	3	.
16. Rauzan . .	3	.
17. Lafite . .	5	.
18. Haut-Brion . .	5	.

VINS ROUGES DE BOURGOGNE.

	f.	s.
19. Mercurey . .		15
20. Beaune ordinaire . .	1	.
21. D° 1re qualité . .	1	10
22. Pomard . .	3	.
23. Volnay . .	3	.
24. Nuits . .	3	.
25. La Romanée . .	5	.
26. Chambertin . .	6	.
27. Clos-de-Vougeot . .	5	.

VINS ROUGES DE MACON.

	f.	s.
28. Fleury . .		15
29. Thorins . .	1	.
30. Moulin-à-Vent . .	1	10

VINS ROUGES DU RHONE ET DU MIDI.

	f.	s.
31. St-Georges vieux . .	1	.
32. Tavel vieux . .	1	.
33. Roussillon vieux . .	1	.
34. Château-Neuf vieux . .	1	.
35. Côte-Rôtie . .	4	.
36. Hermitage . .	5	.

VINS BLANCS DE BORDEAUX.

	f.	s.
37. Grave ordinaire . .		15
38. D° supérieur . .	1	.
39. Barsac . .	2	.
40. Sauterne . .	3	.
41. D° 1er cru et très vieux .	5	.

VINS BLANCS DE BOURGOGNE.

	f.	s.
42. Ordinaire . .		15
43. Chablis . .	1	.
44. D° 1re qualité . .	1	10
45. Meursault . .	2	.
46. Mont-Rachet . .	3	.
47. D° très-vieux . .	5	.

VINS BLANCS DE MACON.

	f.	s.
48. Pouilly . .	1	.
49. Pouilly-Fuissey . .	1	10

VINS DE CHAMPAGNE.

	f.	s.
50. Aï mousseux . .	3	10
51. D° 1re qualité . .	4	.
52. D° Rosé . .	4	.
53. Sillery . .	6	.

VINS BLANCS DU RHONE.

	f.	s.
54. Côte-Rôtie . .	4	.
55. Hermitage . .	6	.

VINS DE LIQUEURS.

	f.	s.
56. Muscat ordinaire . .	1	10
57. D° Lunel . .	2	.
58. D° Frontignan . .	2	.
59. D° Rivesaltes . .	3	.
60. Grenache . .	2	.

VINS ETRANGERS.

	f.	s.
61. Malaga ordinaire . .	3	.
62. D° très-vieux . .	5	.
63. Alicante ordinaire . .	3	.
64. D° très-vieux . .	5	.
65. Madère ordinaire . .	3	.
66. D° 1re qualité . .	5	.
67. Xérès . .	5	.
68. Porto . .	5	.
69. Malvoisie . .	6	.

EAUX-DE-VIE ET RHUM.

	f.	
70. Montpellier . .		9 .
71. Armagnac . .	1	10
72. Cognac ordinaire . .	1	10
73. D° vieux . .	2	.
74. D° extrêmement vieux . .	3	.
75. Rhum ordinaire . .	2	.
76. D° vieux . .	3	.
77. D° extrêmement vieux . .	4	.

FRUITS A L'EAU-DE-VIE.

	f.	s.
78. Cerises, le bocal d'un litre . .	2	.
79. Prunes, d° de 12 . .	2	.
80. Abricots, d° de 6 . .	2	.
81. Pêches, d° de 4 . .	2	.

LIQUEURS.

	f.	s.
82. Anisette de Bordeaux ordinaire.	2	10
83. D° D° 1re qualité . .	4	.
84. D° de Hollande ord. le cruchon .	8	.
85. D° D° 1re qual. d° . .	8	.
86. Curaçao de Hollande ord. . .	8	.
87. D° D° 1re qual d° . .	8	.
88. Eau de fleur d'orange, la 1/2 sac°.	1	10
89. Huile de Rose, la bouteille . .	3	.
90. D° de Rhum, d° . .	4	.
91. D° de Vanille, d° . .	3	.
92. D° de Thé, d° . .	4	.
93. D° de Venus, d° . .	3	.
94. Cassis, d° . .	3	.
95. Eau de Noyaux, d° . .	2	10
96. Absinthe Suise, d° . .	4	.
97. Kirschen-Wasser, Forêt Noire.	3	.
98. Ratafia de Grenoble, d°. . .	3	.
99. Elixir de Garus, d°. . .	4	.
100. Huile de Canelle, d°. . .	3	.

Readers should note that the wines of Hermitage were the most expensive red and white wines of France in 1828 according to this advertisement from Nicolas, the famous French wine merchant.

Rhône appellation, was devastated by phylloxera, and further stricken by the horrors of two world wars in the twentieth century, as well as by the worldwide depression of the thirties.

When I wrote the first edition of this book in 1987, I noted that Hermitage was "one of the most undervalued wines in the world." That is no longer the case as interest in these high-quality wines has skyrocketed. As the twentieth century comes to a close, Hermitage has the status of a cult wine. While prices have increased significantly, great Hermitage still sells for one-half the price of a Burgundy grand cru.

Most red Hermitage is composed of 100% Syrah, although the appellation does permit up to 15% Marsanne and Roussanne to be added. As a practical rule, this is rarely done.

White Hermitage is usually made from the Marsanne grape, although Roussanne is making a slight comeback. The great white Hermitages of Chapoutier and Chave are primarily Marsanne, although the influence of the young Jean-Louis Chave seems to favor increasing the amount of Roussanne in the white Hermitage made by him and his father. In fact, a separate cuvée in 1994 of old-vine Roussanne from l'Hermite (8 barrels/200 cases) was scheduled to be bottled separately when I was there in June 1996. It is a wine of extraordinary complexity and honeyed richness, but at the time of writing, it was uncertain whether or not the wine would be commercialized under a separate vineyard name. The Jaboulet firm utilizes the highest percentage of Roussanne in Hermitage blanc. Their Hermitage Chevalier de Stérimberg is a blend of 50% Roussane and 50% Marsanne. Roussanne is still a minority varietal because too many producers are frightened of its tendency to oxidize quickly.

Unlike the other famous northern Rhône red wine, Côte Rôtie, the size of the Hermitage appellation has remained the same. The powers that be have resisted pressure to increase the number of acres under vine, which has remained constant at 321. There are appoximately a dozen major vineyards, about half of which are of supreme importance. It is easy to understand the layout of the Hermitage appellation if one remembers that it consists of three hills. The largest granite dome, and the one with the most significant gradient, is largely covered with one of the finest vineyards, Les Bessards. Moving east, still part of the steepest sector, but with slightly less altitude, are the three major vineyards—l'Hermite, Le Méal, and Les Greffieux, the last parcel at the bottom of the slope. All of these vineyards tend to be located in the tenderloin section of Hermitage that is largely regarded as the heart and soul of the appellation. Further east, with a slightly lower elevation, is the second dome. Such principal vineyards as Maison Blanche, Les Beaumes, Les Rocoules, and Péleat are located in this sector. The third hill, with the lowest overall elevation, contains such noteworthy vineyards as Les Murets, Les Diognières, and La Croix.

The soil composition and characteristics of each of these vineyards is subject to considerable debate, but there is no greater education than tasting the specific wines made from each of these vineyards when visiting the cellars of Gérard Chave, the only Hermitage producer to possess so many separate vineyards. Moreover, the Chaves keep the wines from each vineyard separate until they blend one year after the harvest. Following are my observations after visiting and participating in tastings with Gérard Chave over the last 15 years.

Les Bessards   This is one of the largest Hermitage vineyards, with a pure granite base and topsoil of decomposed granite and sandy gravel. Situated just below Jaboulet's chapel of St.-Christopher, it lies at the most western end of the appellation, and possesses the steepest gradient of the Hermitage hillsides. It has been my experience that the wines from Les Bessards are among the richest, most concentrated, and powerful of the appellation. It is the source for Chapoutier's extraordinary Le Pavillon, as well as a large component of Chave's Hermitage (including the principal component of their Cuvée Cathelin). It plays a lesser role in Jaboulet's La Chapelle.

Les Beaumes   Located in the middle of the appellation, east of Les Bessards and Le Méal, and west of Les Murets and La Croix, Les Beaumes possesses a granite base, but limestone, clay, and stone form the topsoil. Chave's cuvée of Les Beaumes is consistently a sweet, fruity (black raspberries and cassis are abundantly present), medium- to full-bodied wine with excellent purity and fruit, but not the complexity and majesty of Les Bessards.

Les Diognières   This vineyard is situated at the eastern end of the appellation, with one of the lower elevations. Jean-Claude and Jean-Paul Fayolle make a wine from this vineyard. Guigal also purchases a large quantity of red Hermitage from this vineyard, which is an important component in the blend he fashions. Chave owns a small portion, and based on tastings there and at Fayolle, this soil, which is more gravelly and lighter, tends to produce a wine with plenty of smoky red and black fruits, as well as considerable quantities of tannin and acidity.

L'Hermite   In 1984, virtually all of this vineyard was purchased by Gérard Chave from Terrence Gray. Situated at the top of the dome, above and straddling the two great vineyards of Les Bessards and Le Méal, l'Hermite's soils contain signficant iron. The wines produced are tannic and powerful, yet they retain a sense of elegance and finesse. Chave has produced some stupendous cuvées of pure Roussanne from this location. Chapoutier began, in 1996, to produce a single-vineyard red Hermitage called l'Hermite.

Le Méal   Le Méal, directly behind the center of Tain l'Hermitage, is one of my favorite sources of great red Hermitage. I remember begging the late Henri Sorrel for the privilege of purchasing one bottle of his 1978 Hermitage Le Méal. He refused to sell me any, claiming only a tiny library stock remained for the family. The soil contains considerable amounts of limestone, with large rocks among degraded quartz. This large, steeply terraced vineyard produces one of the most exotic, smoky, sexy styles of Syrah. It is supple, voluptuously textured, and more forward and flattering than wines from other vineyards. It is by far the most important component in Jaboulet's La Chapelle, and composes 90–100% of Marc Sorrel's Hermitage Le Gréal (named thus because from time to time he blends in a tiny portion of Syrah from his holding in Les Greffieux). Chave owns several acres of old-vine Le Méal, and it plays a small role in the overall blend of his Hermitage. Interestingly, one of the great wines of Hermitage, Chapoutier's white Ermitage Cuvée de l'Orée, is made from Marsanne grown in Le Méal. In 1996, Chapoutier produced a 100% Syrah red Hermitage Le Méal.

Péleat   Located in the middle of the appellation, on the lower slopes just to the east of Les Beaumes and west of Les Rocoules, Péleat is one of the smallest of Hermitage's vineyards. It is one of the most important sources for Chave's delicious white Hermitage. The soils are brownish, sandy, degraded stones that are permeable, but possess less drainage than soils higher up the slopes. Because of the high acidity these soils produce, Péleat is deemed an ideal source for white rather than red wine.

Les Rocoules   With its mixture of sandy, stony soil and limestone, Les Rocoules, which lies in the easterly section, midway up the slopes, is considered ideal for white wine. It is the most important component of Chave's white Hermitage, as well as being the vineyard designation on Marc Sorrel's large-scaled, traditionally made white Hermitage. It also plays an important role in Jaboulet's Chevalier de Stérimberg.

Les Greffieux   Les Greffieux is at the bottom of the western end of the Hermitage hills, below Le Méal. Consisting of decomposed limestone, mixed with iron and sandy soils, this vineyard is believed to have once been part of the Rhône riverbed. This vineyard produces fruity, straightforward reds, and very good whites.

There are other important vineyards, but none as important as those itemized. As the discussions that follow indicate, most wines of Hermitage have traditionally been a blend of numerous vineyards, but the marketplace has shown a willingness to support superluxurious microvinifications of old-vine parcels. Even a traditionalist such as Chave produced a Cuvée Cathelin in 1990, 1991, and probably 1995. Faurie's Méal, Sorrel's Méal, Chapoutier's Le Pavillon, and in 1996, both a Le Méal and l'Hermite, and Delas Frères' Les Bessards were the first single-vineyard luxury cuvées. Jaboulet's La Chapelle, Chapoutier's La Sizeranne, Sorrel's Le Gréal, Delas Frères' Marquise de la Tourette, and Chave's Hermitage remain loyal to the tradition of blending different vineyards.

By and large, the small production of Hermitage is almost always made in a very traditional style. Few producers utilize more than 20–30% new oak, and virtually no one does much fining or filtration, recognizing that these wines are meant to last for decades, and most purchasers, after tasting one or two bottles early on, will have the patience to wait for them to develop. At the top level, the overall quality is both high and consistent. In fact, there is probably less difference in styles in Hermitage than in any other Rhône appellation, at least from an overall winemaking philosophy. Of course, the controversial Michel Chapoutier is the only vigneron to utilize biodynamic farming principles in the vineyard, but his winemaking is not dissimilar from that of Gérard and Jean-Louis Chave.

Like Côte Rôtie, Hermitage is in a privileged position. When it is profoundly great, it has no competition from anywhere else in the world. Increasing quantities of very good Syrah are emerging, not only from the Languedoc-Roussillon, but also from California and Australia, so other superb Syrah-based wines can be found. But for pure richness, allied to remarkable complexity and elegance, Hermitage remains unequaled.

Today's Hermitage, while still massive, is not as portlike and viscous as it may have been a century ago. As for its reputation as France's manliest wine, I would give this chauvinistic award to Cornas, the southern neighbor of Hermitage. Nevertheless, Hermitage can be a prodigious wine in the hands of the best growers and producers. The 1929 white and red Hermitages of Chave (drunk most recently in 1986), and the 1949, 1959, and 1961 La Chapelles of Paul Jaboulet-Aîné (drunk numerous times, most recently in 1996) are five wines that give irrefutable evidence to the enormous aging curve these wines possess.

RECENT VINTAGES

1995 The white wines are structured, backward, elegant wines, but they are not as powerful or concentrated as the finest 1994s. The wines possess better acidity than the 1994s, so longevity will not be an issue. The top 1995 red wine cuvées are richer, fuller, more complete, and better structured than the 1994s. Jaboulet made his finest La Chapelle since 1990, and the Chaves, who produced a marvelous wine in 1994, made a profoundly great 1995. At the time of writing, it seemed likely they would also produce a small quantity of their famed Cuvée Cathelin. Michel Chapoutier believes his two cuvées of Hermitage, La Sizeranne and Le Pavillon, will be reference point wines for his firm, even superior to the great Hermitages he produced in 1991, 1990, and 1989. Hermitage unquestionably enjoyed tremendous success in 1995, but the wines will require many years in the bottle to reach full maturity. Optimum maturity: 2005–2040.

1994 This is a very good to excellent vintage for red Hermitage, and a potentially outstanding vintage for white Hermitage. The wines are relatively low in acidity, rich, and soft. The vintage is somewhat reminiscent of 1982 and 1985, but the winemaking is better, and the selection process in top producers' cellars is more severe. Nineteen ninety-four was an extraordinarily hot summer, but September rains washed away the possibility of a great vintage, à la 1990. Nevertheless, these wines will be delicious young and keep for 15 or more years. Optimum maturity for red wines: now–2012; white wines: now–2010.

1993 Hermitage suffered an appallingly bad vintage in 1993. A so-so summer was drowned out by a horrible September. Record rainfall along with high humidity caused serious problems with mildew and rot. Most producers were devastated. They were on the verge of enjoying a good vintage when Mother Nature unleashed disastrous proportions of rot. Chave managed to produce a very good wine, largely because he sold 60% of his production to négociants. Jaboulet completely declassified La Chapelle. The story of the vintage was Michel Chapoutier, whose Ermitage Le Pavillon turned out to be the wine of the vintage. When Chapoutier ridiculed his neighbors for their addiction to chemicals, and attributed his success to his biodynamic/organic farming, controversy and jealousy reared their ugly faces, and Chapoutier was accused of showboating. Other producers did not fare as well. Guigal's Hermitage is better than most, and not far off the quality of Chave's. On paper, 1993 is a dreadful year, with even the best wines, including Chapoutier's Le Pavillon, requiring consumption before 2005.

1992 On paper a mediocre year, but in Hermitage some surprisingly fruity, lighter-styled, round, easy-to-understand wines were made. Once again, the brash, sometimes foolishly outspoken Michel Chapoutier turned in brilliant wines, but none of his neighbors have desired to compliment him on such exemplary efforts. The 1992 white wines tend to be very rich and more successful than the reds. Optimum maturity for red wines: now–2005; white wines: now. Chapoutier's luxury cuvées l'Orée and Le Pavillon will age for an additional 20–25 years.

1991 Hermitage enjoyed an excellent, nearly outstanding vintage in 1991. The crop was small and healthy, resulting in elegant but concentrated wines that have turned out to be far better than initially believed. The vintage is significantly better than such years as 1986 and 1980. While 1991 may largely be forgotten, time will prove that it has turned out many sleepers with considerable longevity. Optimum maturity for red wines: 2000–2015; white wines: now–2005.

1990 This was a great vintage throughout the Rhône Valley. It no longer seems debatable as to which appellation enjoyed the most success. Hermitage experienced a dreamlike vintage. Huge sugar readings, fabulously healthy grapes, and surprisingly high yields combined to produce the most deeply colored, fragrant, and concentrated wines since 1961. Natural alcohols came in at a whopping 13–14%. Some observers feared there would be a roasted quality to the fruit, but that has proved to be untrue. In 1991, I told readers of my journal, *The Wine Advocate*, that if they loved Rhône wines, it was a once-in-a-lifetime opportunity to stock up. Nineteen ninety was a successful vintage for everyone in Hermitage. Jaboulet's La Chapelle is perfection. It is a wine that will rival, perhaps eclipse, the legendary 1961. The two Jaboulet brothers, Gérard and Jacques, both believe the 1990 La Chapelle is the greatest wine they have ever made. Not surprisingly, Chave's two cuvées of Hermitage are magnificent, as is Chapoutier's luxury cuvée Le Pavillon. Other producers, particularly Marc Sorrel, Guigal, and the underrated Bernard Faurie also turned in superlative efforts. Faurie's Le Méal is an awesome wine. Because of the extraordinary ripeness of the fruit, the 1990 Hermitages will always possess a certain precociousness and flattering quality about them, but most of the wines are 10–15 years away from full maturity. These wines will last for 50 or more years. This is a monumental vintage for red Hermitage!

The low-acid white wines are powerful, rich, and gorgeously honeyed and thick. They are still drinking well without yet having closed down. Whether they keep for 20–30 years remains to be seen, but they are very high in alcohol. Optimum maturity for red wines: 2008–2050; white wines: now–2010.

1989 If it were not for 1990, most Hermitage producers would be touting their 1989s as great wines. This is a terrific vintage that has largely been forgotten with all the justifiable hype over 1990. The wines have closed down since bottling, but they are enormously rich, with high levels of extract, concentration, and tannin. A roasted character can be found in some wines, but it only adds to their complexity. I do not believe 1989 will ever achieve the full-throttle opulence and flamboyant richness of the 1990s, but this is a classic, long-lived, prodigious vintage for Hermitage that should age well for 30–40 years. The white 1989s have shut down, and while they are very good, they are not exceptional. Optimum maturity for red wines: 2005–2035; white wines: now–2005.

1988 The first of a trilogy of marvelous vintages, 1988 has been overshadowed by the thrilling quality of both 1989 and 1990. The red wines are deeply colored, with good size, weight, extract, and richness. Full-bodied, classically styled wines with slightly greener tannin and higher acidity than the 1989s and 1990s, this is much more than just a respectable vintage. Optimum maturity for red wines: 2007–2025; white wines: now–2010.

1987 A pleasant group of lightweight wines emerged from a vintage where September rains washed out the chance for excellence. Chave's 1987 is still a youthful, delicious, soft red Hermitage, but other producers brought out the more vegetal side of the Syrah grape. It is an inconsistent, irregular vintage, with some successes. With the exception of Chave's Hermitage, I would not push the aging curve of these wines beyond 15 years. The white wines are relatively mediocre.

1986 It was a very abundant crop in Hermitage with the white wines significantly less powerful and concentrated than the occasionally overblown, low-acid 1985s. As for the reds, they show average concentration, are medium-bodied, elegant, and fruity but early maturing. Optimum maturity: (red) now–1998; (white) now.

1985 The red wines from this vintage were not as successful as in Côte Rôtie. Nevertheless, they are intensely fruity, somewhat fat, low in acidity, but perfumed, round, and generous. They are fully mature and need to be consumed over the next decade. The one exception is Chave's red wine, the finest of the appellation, which will last another 20 years. The white wines are very, very concentrated, sometimes a trifle exaggerated, but immensely interesting, rich, full-throttle wines with somewhat elevated levels of alcohol. Chapoutier's Chante-Alouette and Chave's white wines are sensational, sumptuous wines. Optimum maturity: (red) now–2005; (white) now–2002.

1984 Again, less successful for the red wines than in Côte Rôtie; however, 1984 was a decent year for the white wines. At first they seemed lean and highly acidic, but in the bottle they have exhibited a generally lighter style, some finesse, and while they are not blockbusters, they are certainly pleasurable. The 1984 reds are quite light and will mature rapidly. Chave's white and red Hermitages are notable successes in 1984. Both mature now.

1983 This is a top vintage, but frustratingly hard and tannic in Hermitage. It does remain a true vin de garde vintage since the dry, hot summer produced modest quantities of very rich, very tannic, hard wines that will require at least another 4–5 years of cellaring. The wines were fabulous from the cask but have closed up and largely refuse to perform up to expectations, causing owners of them to become increasingly fidgety. Arguments will no doubt rage well into the next century as to whether Chave or Jaboulet produced the finest red Hermitage, but both wines are outstanding efforts that should not be touched before the year 2000. Other fine efforts were turned in by Delas Frères, Guigal, Sorrel, and Ferraton. As for the white wines, they are excellent but not as consistently exceptional as the red wines. Is 1983 better than 1978? No way! The 1978s are decidedly richer wines than the 1983s. Optimum maturity for red wines: 1993–2020; white wines: now.

1982 What was potentially an exceptional vintage was also extremely troublesome because of the torrid heat during the harvest that resulted in overheated fermentations and spoilage. The top red wines, such as those of Chave, Fayolle, and Jaboulet's La Chapelle, are velvety, rich, broadly flavored wines with considerable appeal. They should be drunk over the next 5–10 years. Rich and perfumed, but low in acidity, the wines have, as I predicted, developed quickly. As for the whites, they are all fully mature and because of low, fixed acidities, are undoubtedly beginning to break apart save for Chave's white Hermitage. Two fine growers, Ferraton and Sorrel, both made poor wines (no doubt because they were unable to control the temperature of their fermentations). Optimum maturity for red wines: now–2004; whites wines: now.

1981 To date, I find this the least attractive vintage for Hermitage in the eighties. The wines are tart, somewhat undernourished, angular, and lacking both charm and flesh. Jaboulet, who first deemed the quality insufficient to declare a La Chapelle, changed his mind, mistakenly in my view. Even Chave's 1981 is, by his standards, an austere, rather thin wine. Surprisingly, one of the best 1981s came from the small grower Michel Ferraton. Guigal also made a good wine in 1981. The white wines are more interesting, but overall still unexciting. I doubt that any of these wines will improve, so it is advisable to drink them now.

1980 An underrated vintage, the 1980s offered supple, fruity, attractive drinking for 10–15 years, but they are now beginning to fade.

1979 This is an excellent vintage for red wine and a good one for white. For the reds, 1979 was simply caught in the classic vinous scenario—a very fine year is largely forgotten because the preceding year was a compelling one. Thus 1979, coming after the superb 1978 vintage, seemed unexciting. Truth be known, the wines are not far behind the heights attained by the 1978s. As expected, they have developed more quickly than the 1978s, but they possess exceptional color and excellent depth. Jaboulet's La Chapelle, Delas's Marquise de la Tourette, and Sorrel's Le Méal will gracefully evolve into the next century in fine shape, good cellar conditions permitting. Curiously, Chave's 1979, though quite good, is not at the level one might expect. Optimum maturity for red wines: now–2005.

1978   This is the greatest vintage for Hermitage producers between 1961 and 1990. The top wines are still adolescents in terms of their evolution. Rich, profoundly concentrated, tannic yet complex, fragrant wines were produced. Most of them will keep 40–50 years. Chave made a stunning wine that will provide monumental drinking in 20 years. As sublime as Chave's 1978 is, the 1978s from Sorrel, Delas, and Paul Jaboulet's La Chapelle are equally grand. Unfortunately, the only place these wines are likely to show up is at wine auctions. Optimum maturity for red wines: now–2020.

Older Vintages

Nineteen seventy-seven was a poor vintage, 1976 rather highly regarded but vastly overrated, and 1975, 1974, and 1973 all poor to mediocre. The sleeper vintage of the seventies is the terribly underrated 1972. Jaboulet's La Chapelle is outstanding in 1972. Nineteen seventy, 1966, and 1961 were exceptional vintages in Hermitage. The latter vintage produced a La Chapelle that remains one of the three or four greatest red wines I have ever tasted. Nineteen sixty-four was also very fine. Certainly 1969 and 1962 were good, but somewhat less consistent and concentrated. Old vintages of Jaboulet's La Chapelle that turn up on the market from these years will continue to offer fine drinking if they have been cellared properly. In the fifties, 1959 is a superb vintage, with Jaboulet's 1959 La Chapelle no more than a shade below the mythical 1961.

ALBERT BELLE* * * *

Address: Les Marsuriaux
          26600 Larnage
Tel: 4-75-08-24-58
Wines produced: Hermitage (red and white)
Surface area (white): 1.2 acres
              (red): 2.47 acres
Production (white): 2,800 bottles
              (red): 5,250 bottles
Upbringing (white): Until 1993, all in inox vats for one year. From 1994, 50% in inox vats
              and 50% in 100% new oak barrels for one year.
          (red): 18 months in 50% new oak barrels
Average age of vines: (white): 25 years
                  (red): 30 years
Blend (white): 75% Marsanne, 25% Roussanne
        (red): 100% Syrah

Albert Belle, a serious, introspective man, and his son left Tain l'Hermitage's cooperative in 1990 to begin vinifiying and estate-bottling their wines. This estate is detailed more fully in the chapter on Crozes-Hermitage as the bulk of this production is from that appellation. Belle does have two small parcels of Hermitage. His white Hermitage comes from a small parcel of Les Diognières, and his red Hermitage is from Les Murets. The quality of Belle's wines appears to increase with each new vintage. Although his Hermitage is not quite up to the level of his Crozes-Hermitage Cuvée Louis Belle, they are made without any compromises. His cellar is beautifully equipped, and his goal is to make long-lived, traditionally styled wines. There is no destemming, a long three-week cuvaison, and no filtration at bottling. Belle utilizes a moderate amount of new oak, about 50% new casks for the red wine, and a blend of tank and new oak for the whites. Readers should note that a significant percentage of Roussanne is included in his white Hermitage. In the appellation, it is second only to Jaboulet's Chevalier de Stérimberg. Overall, this is an up-and-coming estate, as evidenced by the following tasting notes.

VINTAGES

1995—Hermitage   Belle's deep ruby-colored 1995 Hermitage is more restrained than the
·   Cuvée Louis Belle, with fine ripeness, medium to full body, a spicy component, a
88   crisp, acidic edge, and fine purity and balance. It will not win any awards for flamboyance, but it is an elegant, stylish Hermitage that will require drinking within its first 10–12 years of life. Last tasted 6/96.

1994—Hermitage   Although not a blockbuster, the dark ruby-colored 1994 Hermitage is
·   an elegant, medium-bodied, ripe, herbaceous, peppery-scented wine. Its sweet
88   entry and fine delineation make for an attractive, stylish Hermitage that should be drunk over the next decade. Last tasted 6/96.

1992—Hermitage   In 1992, Albert Belle made the best wines I have tasted from his
·   small estate. The 1992 Hermitage is sensational. Its huge nose of roasted herbs,
92   jammy black fruit, smoked meat, and spice soars from the glass. The wine possesses great fruit extraction, full body, low acidity, and moderate tannin. It is unevolved and grapy, so give it 3–4 years of cellaring; it will keep for 15 years. It may turn out to be one of the two or three best Hermitages in the 1992 vintage. Last tasted 6/95.

1992—Hermitage (white)   With its bouquet of pine needles, flowers, and pineapples, and
·   its full-bodied, concentrated fruitiness, Belle's 1992 white Hermitage is undeniably
87   excellent. It is an authoritatively flavored, robust, chewy white wine that should drink and evolve well for 10–12 years. Last tasted 6/95.

1990—Hermitage   I was surprised to learn that Belle's 1990 Hermitage was aged primar-
·   ily in new oak casks. The wine is so dense and rich that it was only after I learned
91   of the oak aging that I could detect any smoky, vanillin scents. Even then they are vague. The opaque color is followed by a closed, albeit promising nose offering aromas of minerals, black fruits, herbs, and truffles. In the mouth there is great extraction of fruit, a long, full-bodied, concentrated taste, plenty of power, high tannins, and enough acidity for focus. Do not touch a bottle before 1998. It should provide thrilling drinking between the late nineties and the first decade of the next century. Last tasted 9/94.

1989—Hermitage   The dark ruby/purple-colored 1989 Hermitage's sweet smell of cassis
·   fruit, combined with licorice and a roasted character, makes a considerable impact
91   on the taster. In the mouth, there is explosive richness of fruit, great concentration and length, as well as a soft, voluptuous finish. The tannins are elevated, but they are ripe and round as opposed to green and astringent. As with the 1990, I suspect this wine will mature quickly yet last for 10–15 more years. Last tasted 9/94.

CHAPOUTIER (Regular Cuvées* * */* * * *;
Single-Vineyard Cuvées* * * * *)

Address: 18, avenue du Docteur Paul Durand
      B.P. 38
      26600 Tain l'Hermitage
Tel: 4-75-08-28-65
Fax: 4-75-08-81-70
Wines produced: Hermitage Chante-Alouette, Hermitage Cuvée de l'Orée, Hermitage Le
      Pavillon, Hermitage La Sizeranne, Hermitage Vinde Paille; in 1996, two
      more luxury red Hermitage cuvées were added—Hermitage-l'Hermite
      and Hermitage-Les Méals
Surface area (white): 32.1 acres
      (red): 42 acres
Production (white): Chante-Alouette—3,400 cases
      Cuvée de l'Orée—600 cases (from Le Méal)
      (red): La Sizeranne—4,300 cases
      Le Pavillon—700 cases (from Les Bessards)
      l'Hermite—280 cases
      Les Méals—300 cases
Upbringing (white): 6–8 months, one-third in 20% new oak and 70% in inox vats
      (red): 12 months in 33% new oak barrels
Average age of vines (white): 30–80 years
      (red): 50–80 years
Blend (white): 100% Marsanne
      (red): 100% Syrah

In nearly 20 years of wine writing, I have never witnessed a more significant jump in
quality and change in winemaking philosophy than what has occurred in the Chapoutier
cellars since the 1989 vintage. This famous old firm, founded in 1808, is the proprietor of a
signficant 175 acres of vines in five Rhône Valley appellations. Chapoutier has always made
good, traditional Rhône wines, but rarely did they make superb wine. For much of the post–
World War II era, the firm was directed by the enthusiastic and animated Max Chapoutier.
However, in 1988, his youngest son, Michel, took full responsibility over the winemaking
as well as the direction of the firm with the retirement of his father. Michel's older brother,
Marc, remains responsible for the marketing of the wines. What Michel Chapoutier has
accomplished has caused ripples around the wine world. He has completely revamped the
winemaking and élevage programs for the Chapoutier wines. The results are wines that rival
the Rhône Valley's greatest wine producer, Marcel Guigal.

With respect to the white wines, Michel Chapoutier was influenced primarily by André
Ostertag and Marcel Deiss of Alsace. In essence, his basic goal was to "go back to the
earth," reducing the signature of the winemaker and raising the level of the typicity and
vineyard character of the wine. As the young Chapoutier says, "everything is in the soil and
vines." It is his intention to "kill the character of the grape, but bring up the quality of the
soil." To this end, Chapoutier decided to farm his vineyards organically, and to use only
wild yeasts for the fermentation. In both 1988 and 1989 the vineyards were pruned back
and grape bunches were cut off to reduce the yields to a conservative 30–35 hectoliters per
hectare for both the red and white wines.

Michel Chapoutier gives full credit for the direction of his red winemaking style to his
consultations with Gérard Chave and Marcel Guigal. The first thing he did was to throw out
the old chestnut foudres (a hallmark of the old Chapoutier style) and replace them with
small oak casks. The manager from the famous barrel making firm of Demptos was hired to

build small oak barrels from troncais oak. The vinification in open wood vats has been continued, with heavy reliance on mashing the wine's chapeau down into the juice. There is total destemming except for the red wines from St.-Joseph and Côte Rôtie, as well as a cuvaison that lasts from three to three and a half weeks. The two most significant changes included not only the raising of the wines in small oak barrels, but also Chapoutier's decision to neither fine nor filter his finest red or white wines prior to bottling.

In the seven years (1989–96) that Michel Chapoutier, his brother, Marc, and their brilliant oenologist, Alberic Mazoyer, have had control of the winemaking, few wine firms in the world have produced more extraordinary wines. At the same time, few firms have engendered more controversy and animosity. Michel Chapoutier is an outspoken advocate of biodynamic/organic farming, as enunciated by the guru of this agriculture practice, Rudolf Steiner, whose book *Agriculture* was the product of numerous lectures he presented in 1924 in Germany. While Chapoutier's critics tend to dismiss biodynamic farming as a cult or wizardry, more and more high-quality producers (e.g., Lalou Bize-Leroy, Nicolas Joly, and others) are moving in this direction, recognizing that decades of overdependence on chemicals, fertilizers, and sprays has wreaked enormous damage on the vineyards' health. But Michel Chapoutier, because of his vocal outbursts, has a tendency to provoke controversy wherever he goes. This is lamentable given the fact that he is the first to acknowledge the debt he owes such producers as Marcel Guigal, Gérard Chave, François and Jean-Pierre Perrin, and the late Jacques Reynaud. Yet his pursuit of quality often leads to brash statements that appear undiplomatic and, at times, scathingly critical of his colleagues. All of this is a shame, since producers, members of the wine industry, and consumers committed to quality should be Chapoutier supporters rather than detractors. While I am not sure his youthful exuberance and obsessive nature are capable of refraining from broadsides when he feels growers with top vineyards are not pursuing high quality, it is an undeniable fact that Michel Chapoutier has become one of this planet's bright shining lights.

Nearly a decade after assuming command of this firm, Michel Chapoutier is still not satisfied, pushing himself to achieve higher and higher quality. He also offers some great quotes, for example, "In 1989, I knew how to make noise . . . now I know how to make music." He obviously feels his early efforts were simply monster, massive, intensely extracted wines, but today, the extraction is there, plus more complexity and finesse. Another of his favorite quotes is that "Filtering wine is like making love with a condom." Although not politically correct, as well as evidence of Chapoutier's tendency to say things that provoke controversy, his salient point is that those producers who filter are stripping their wines of their typicity, terroir, and personality, not to mention flavor.

Chapoutier has completely renovated the cellars, installing air-conditioning and new small casks, and displaying meticulous attention to all details. This is a firm that believes in the "monocépage." Chapoutier's Côte Roties are made from 100% Syrah, his white Hermitage and St.-Joseph are 100% Marsanne, and his Châteauneuf du Pape is 100% Grenache. He is a purist who believes that blending only mutes the character of the terroir and grape.

In attempting to understand the vast array of wines now being produced at Chapoutier, readers should be aware that there are four levels of offerings.

(1) Southern France: Increasingly, the Chapoutiers are moving south, recognizing that there is enormous potential in the Languedoc-Roussillon and several of the vin de pays regions for producing high-quality wine at reasonable prices. In 1995 they acquired 7.5 acres in Banyuls. They are also looking for properties to purchase in the Côtes de Roussillon and the Coteaux d'Aix-en-Provence. In 1995 they launched their first wine from the d'Oc, a branded Syrah/Grenache/Carignan/Mourvèdre blend called Entre Nous. This excursion into southern France should continue as the Chapoutiers believe there are not enough high-quality vineyards left in the Rhône.

(2) Négociant wines—Rhône Valley: The second level of wine is their pure négociant wines that are made with purchased grapes and juice. Michel Chapoutier believes in working with specific people, and while he cannot control everything, he has consistently pushed for lower yields, reduced potassium applications, and encouraged organic viticultural practices.

(3) Estate-bottled wines—Rhône Valley: At the third level are Chapoutier's estate-bottled wines, such as the famed white Hermitage Chante-Alouette, red Hermitage La Sizeranne, Châteauneuf du Pape La Bernadine, Crozes-Hermitage Les Meysonnières, and St.-Joseph Les Deschants. The Chapoutier team has taken these wines from the throes of mediocrity to a high-quality level. In addition to the négociant wines, these are the wines readers are most likely to find in the marketplace. In 1995 Chapoutier, responding to the fact that there were several bottlings of his largest cuvées of Côtes du Rhône, Crozes-Hermitage, and Hermitage, made the necessary investment to do a maximum of two bottlings, and in most cases, only one bottling for each wine, to ensure consistent quality.

(4) Estate-bottled luxury cuvées—Rhône Valley: At the top of the Chapoutier hierarchy are the luxury cuvées made from parcels of extremely old vines, microscopic yields, and aged 100% in new oak, and usually bottled without any fining or filtration. Reference point wines for their appellations, they are among the greatest red and white wines produced in the world. From the southern Rhône comes the Châteauneuf du Pape Barbe Rac, made from a vineyard planted in 1901, not far from the famed Château La Gardine. In the north is the St.-Joseph Les Granits, an 80-year-old vineyard planted in pure granite on a hillside behind the village of Mauves, the Crozes-Hermitage Les Varonniers, the white Ermitage Cuvée de l'Orée, from ancient vines in Le Méal (often with yields of one-half ton of fruit per acre), the red Ermitage Le Pavillon, from vines 70 to 80 years old in Les Bessards, and the Côte Rôtie La Mordorée, a parcel of vines 75 to 80 years old a stone's throw from Guigal's famed La Turque. The production of these wines is frightfully small, from 400–700 cases, but the quality is prodigious.

The Chapoutiers claim they are the largest landholders in Hermitage, owning approximately 81.5 out of the total 321 acres in Hermitage. Their cuvée of Le Pavillon comes from the oldest vines in Les Bessards, a vineyard in which the Chapoutiers own a 34.3-acre parcel. Their other red wine vineyards include Les Greffieux (7.5 acres), and white grape vineyards in such lieux-dits as Chante-Alouette, Muret, Méal, and Chapelle. Chapoutier's Hermitage is always destemmed for fear of extracting too much of the stemmy, vegetal component. Until Michel Chapoutier took over the winemaking, Gérard Chave was usually the last Hermitage producer to harvest, but Chapoutier now generally harvests several days later.

VINTAGES

1995—Ermitage Le Pavillon (red)   The 1995 Ermitage Le Pavillon (Chapoutier drops the
 ·   "H" to follow the ancient spelling of Hermitage) should prove to be a perfect wine.
 99+   The harvest for this cuvée did not begin until early October, several weeks after
         the last drop of rain. The result is an opaque black/purple-colored wine that is just
         beginning to reveal its exquisite potential. It appears to possess the concentration
         of the profound 1990 and 1989, yet better acidity, resulting in a more backward
         and delineated wine. Its immense richness, huge extract, and formidable power
         and length suggest this wine needs 10–15 years of cellaring. I would not be
         surprised to see it drinking dazzlingly well in 2050. Crammed with fruit, purity,
         and depth, this is another winemaking tour de force. Last tasted 6/96.

1995—Hermitage La Sizeranne (red)   The 1995 La Sizeranne is produced from extremely
 ·   tiny yields of less than one ton of fruit per acre (about the same yields of Chapou-
 91   tier's famed Le Pavillon). It possesses an earthy, smoky, sweet blackcurrant nose;
         backward, tannic, high-acid flavors; excellent richness; and a layered feel on the

palate. Nevertheless, this is an extremely reserved wine that will be slow to evolve given its tart acidity. It will require 8–10 years of cellaring before it is ready for drinking; it will last for 20+ years. It is unquestionably the most reserved and backward La Sizeranne Michel Chapoutier has produced. Last tasted 6/96.

1995—Hermitage Chante-Alouette (white)   The 1995 Chante-Alouette exhibits a distinc-
·   tive nose of lavender, honey, pineapples, and minerals. Broad and rich, yet remark-
92   ably fresh for its large-bodied size, this is a brawny, intense white Hermitage that,
         like the 1994, should last for a decade or more. Last tasted 6/96.

1995—Ermitage Cuvée de l'Orée (white)   The 1995 is a profoundly great dry white, with
·   enormous richness, concentration, and texture that is kept in focus by crisp acidity.
98   I was shocked to learn that the wine was vinified and aged in 100% new French
         oak because there is not a hint of toast or vanillin—the wine is that thick, unctuous,
         and rich. Aromas of acacia, minerals, oranges, and honey never fade in this extra-
         ordinary effort. While it will offer spectacular drinking when young, this wine
         will close up in a few years. I may be doing a disservice to the 1995 Cuvée de
         l'Orée by not giving it a perfect score. Yields of 12 hectoliters per hectare were
         frightfully low, and the result is one of the single greatest dry white wines I
         have ever tasted. Amazingly rich, astonishingly well balanced, and extraordinarily
         complex and Montrachet-like, this liquid mineral, honeyed wine is truly a wine-
         making tour de force. Will it last 10, 20, or 30 years? I am not really sure, but it is
         unquestionably the greatest young dry white Hermitage I have ever tasted. Last
         tasted 6/96.

1994—Ermitage Le Pavillon (red)   The 1994 Le Pavillon is another blockbuster, phenom-
·   enally concentrated wine. Le Pavillon is generally among the top three or four
96   wines of France in every vintage! The 1994's opaque purple color, and wonderfully
         sweet, pure nose of cassis and other black fruits intertwined with minerals, are
         followed by a wine of profound richness, great complexity, and full body. It is
         almost the essence of blackberries and cassis. There is huge tannin in this monster
         Hermitage, that somehow manages to keep its balance and elegance. Made from a
         parcel of vines (which I have walked through), some of which predate the phylloxera
         epidemic, the 1994 Ermitage Le Pavillon should be purchased only by those who
         are willing to invest 10–12 years of cellaring. It will not reach full maturity before
         the end of the first decade of the next century, after which it will last for 30+
         years. Last tasted 6/96.

1994—Hermitage La Sizeranne (red)   The 1994 La Sizeranne (lot 6711; 1994 is the last
·   vintage to have multiple bottlings) is a structured, dense, concentrated, full-bodied
90   wine that requires 4–5 years of cellaring. It should keep for 15–20 years. The deep
         ruby/purple color is accompanied by aromas of flowers and jammy cassis. Sweet,
         ripe fruit in the attack is followed by tannin and structure. This is an impressive
         example of Hermitage, but patience is required. Last tasted 6/96.

1994—Hermitage Vin de Paille (white)   Chapoutier has produced a 1994 Hermitage Vin
·   de Paille. Only about 1,000 bottles of this unfiltered wine were produced. Aged
98+   completely in new oak, it exhibits an amber color, a sweet butterscotch, peach, tea,
         and orange marmalade-scented nose, great structure, and amazing richness and
         length. Michel Chapoutier feels this wine, which tastes like ripe apricots, will last
         at least a century. Not many readers are in a position to argue with him. Last tasted
         6/96.

1994—Hermitage Chante-Alouette (white)   The 1994 Chante-Alouette (lot 6671) is su-
·   perb, with a rich, cherry/pineapple/apricot-scented nose, unctuously thick, rich
91   flavors, a liquid mineral character, and clean, fresh, full-bodied, honeyed flavors.
         Last tasted 6/96.

1994—Ermitage Cuvée de l'Orée (white)   This wine boasts a huge, flowery, superrich
nose that is almost the essence of minerals and ripe fruit. Extremely powerful,
99   full-bodied, and unctuously textured, this staggeringly great white Hermitage
should last for 30–50+ years. Last tasted 6/96.

1993—Ermitage Le Pavillon (red)   The 1993 Le Pavillon is the Hermitage of the Vintage.
More austere than when I tasted it prior to bottling, it is one of the few 1993s with a
93   sweet inner core of fruit, as well as a dense ruby/purple color, outstanding concentration and extract, and huge tannin in the finish. It is a harder style of Le Pavillon than
the 1992, but it should turn out to be a 40- to 50-year wine. Last tasted 6/96.

1993—Hermitage La Sizeranne (red)   The black-colored 1993 La Sizeranne reveals a
huge, roasted, smoky, dense nose, superb richness and ripeness, full body, and
93   layers of flavor. This magnificent wine will need to be cellared for 5–6 years; it has
the potential to last for three decades. Last tasted 6/96.

1993—Hermitage La Sizeranne Lot 021 (red)   I, as well as many readers, have complained about the quality variation in bottles of Hermitage La Sizeranne. I intend
85   to be more attentive to lot numbers when tasting this wine, both in France and
America. Certainly the high marks I bestowed on cask samples of the 1993 and
1992 are inappropriate now, particularly for the 1993, a wine that Chapoutier feels
was bottled too late. The dark ruby-colored 1993 La Sizeranne is extremely closed,
with astringent tannin. The wine gives the impression of needing 7–10 years of
cellaring, but I do not believe the fruit will last that long. Last tasted 6/96.

1993—Hermitage Chante-Alouette (white)   The 1993 Chante-Alouette is a large-scaled,
thick, flowery, mineral, honeyed wine with a pronounced aroma of acacia flowers.
91   Deep and full-bodied, with gobs of fruit, it is a superb white Hermitage for drinking
over the next 10–20 years. Last tasted 6/96.

1993—Hermitage Chante-Alouette Lot 5931 (white)   The 1993 Chante-Alouette achieved
14% natural alcohol. It offers up a buttery, smoky, mineral-scented nose, followed
90   by a wine with considerable power, intensity, and an unctuous texture. An outstanding example from this difficult vintage, it should drink well for 10+ years.
Last tasted 6/96.

1993—Ermitage Cuvée de l'Orée (white)   The 1993 Cuvée de l'Orée has developed more
nuances, offering up liquid granitelike aromas combined with honey, smoke,
94   and flowery scents. There is even a hint of overripe peaches. The wine possesses
great fruit, a layered, viscous texture, huge quantities of alcohol and glycerin,
and a blockbuster finish. It is an utterly massive example of white Hermitage,
exceeded in size, glycerin level, and intensity only by the 1992 Ermitage Cuvée de
l'Orée. Anticipated maturity: now–2012. Last tasted 6/96.

1992—Ermitage Le Pavillon (red)   It is difficult to believe the intensity Chapoutier has
achieved in the 1992 Ermitage Le Pavillon. The black/purple color is followed by
95   a sweet, intense fragrance of licorice, peppery blackcurrants, and spices. Full-
bodied, powerful, and dense, with remarkable intensity, this is a supple wine that
should be drinkable in 6–7 years, and last for 20–25 years. It is a remarkable
achievement for the vintage. Anticipated maturity: 2000–2020. Last tasted 6/96.

1992—Hermitage La Sizeranne (red)   The deep ruby-colored 1992 La Sizeranne reveals
a green-pepper, herbaceous, blackcurranty aroma. It does possess an attractive
86   sweet, black-fruit-flavored entry, medium body, good density and concentration.
This is a smooth, ready-to-drink style of Hermitage. Anticipated maturity: now–
2007. Last tasted 6/96.

1992—Hermitage Chante-Alouette (white)   The 1992 Chante-Alouette displays the telltale tangerine, honey, acacia flower–scented nose, full body, admirable power and
90   intensity, a thick, unctuous texture, and low acidity. It is the most syrupy, layered,

and concentrated of the cuvées of Chante-Alouette. Anticipated maturity: now–2002. Last tasted 6/96.

1992—Ermitage Cuvée de l'Orée (white)   This wine reveals the viscosity of a rich Sau-
•   ternes, although it is completely dry. This full-bodied, heavyweight, massively
96   endowed monument to the Marsanne grape must be tasted to be believed. It is so
      thick and juicy that some tasters may be shocked by its intensity to the point of
      wondering what exactly is in the glass. Wines like this are rare, but I have no doubt
      that this wine will last and evolve for 30 + years. A classic! Anticipated maturity:
      1998–2025. Last tasted 6/96.

1992—Hermitage Vin de Paille (white)   The medium amber/gold-colored 1992 Hermi-
•   tage Vin de Paille exhibits a buttery, honeyed nose, viscous, thick, superrich
96 + flavors, and a syrupy finish with enough acidity to give it uplift and vibrancy. It is
      amazingly unformed. Anticipated maturity: 2005–2050. Last tasted 6/96.

1991—Ermitage Le Pavillon   This is another Le Pavillon of mythical proportions. Pro-
•   duced from extremely old vines, some dating from the mid-nineteenth century, with
100   yields averaging under 15 hectoliters per hectare, this is the richest, most concen-
      trated and profound wine made in Hermitage. The 1991 Ermitage Le Pavillon follows
      the pattern of the 1989 and 1990—it is another perfect wine. The saturated black/
      purple color is followed by a compelling bouquet of spices, roasted meats, and black
      and red fruits. Enormously concentrated yet with brilliant focus and delineation to its
      awesomely endowed personality, this extraordinary wine should age effortlessly for
      three plus decades. Very powerful and full, yet displaying silky tannin, this is a seam-
      less beauty! Anticipated maturity: 2001–2035. Last tasted 6/96.

1991—Hermitage La Sizeranne (red)   The 1991 La Sizeranne reveals a saturated color
•   and a pure nose of cassis, licorice, and roasted scents. A full-bodied, concentrated
90   wine, it is as concentrated and intense as the 1990. Compared to Le Pavillon, this
      is much more forward. Anticipated maturity: 1998–2010. Last tasted 6/96.

1991—Hermitage Chante-Alouette (white)   The 1991 Chante-Alouette, made from yields
•   of 25 hectoliters per hectare, is a brilliantly well-focused, rich, full-bodied white
90   wine with an enticing perfume of pears, flowers, and minerals, excellent richness
      and extraction, decent acidity, and a subtle touch of new oak that only adds to the
      wine's dimension and structure. Anticipated maturity: now–2009. Last tasted 6/96.

1991—Ermitage Cuvée de l'Orée (white)   Although the 1991 Ermitage Cuvée de l'Orée
•   should turn out to be compelling, the bouquet has shut down. The wine is full-
94 + bodied and stunningly rich, with a tight but promising nose of honey, peach
      blossom, acacia flower, and mineral scents. Unctuously textured, thick, rich, chewy
      flavors are buttressed by high acidity. The finish lasts for up to a minute. Antici-
      pated maturity: 2000–2025. Last tasted 6/96.

1991—Hermitage Vin de Paille (white)   Chapoutier's effort at making sweet vin de paille
•   from raisined and dried-out Hermitage grapes was highly successful in 1991. The
98   wine possesses a more roasted, honeyed marmalade character, awesome concentra-
      tion and richness, and a blockbuster finish. These wines, which are available only
      in half bottles (that should be enough to serve at least 10–15 people), will last for
      50 + years. Anticipated maturity: 2000–2050. Last tasted 6/94.

1990—Ermitage Le Pavillon (red)   The 1990 Le Pavillon is as compelling as the 1989. It
•   exhibits slightly less opulence, but more power and weight. Black colored, with an
100   extraordinary perfume of licorice, sweet blackcurrants, smoke, and minerals, it
      coats the palate with layer upon layer of decadently rich, superconcentrated, nearly
      viscous Syrah flavors. There is amazing glycerin, a chewy, unctuous texture, and
      phenomenal length. The tannins, which are considerable when analyzed, are virtu-
      ally obscured by the massive quantities of fruit. I hope I live to see the day when

Chapoutier's 1990 Ermitage Le Pavillon, Chave's 1990 Hermitage, and Jaboulet's 1990 Hermitage La Chapelle are fully mature! What a trio of wines these three producers have produced from this historic appellation! My best guess for the aging potential of the Ermitage Le Pavillon is that it is more forward than both the Chave and Jaboulet Hermitages, but should you have the good fortune to find a bottle or two, do not open it for at least 7–10 years. It should last for 30–40 years. Last tasted 12/95.

1990—Hermitage La Sizeranne (red)   The 1990 La Sizeranne, made from yields of 28
· hectoliters per hectare, has begun to close up. The color is a dark purple, and with
91 coaxing, the superripe nose of cassis, licorice, minerals, and spices has begun to emerge. This full-bodied, tannic wine was aged in 60% new oak casks. It possesses copious quantities of black fruit flavors, a chewy texture, and very fine length. I suspect this wine needs until the turn of the century to approach maturity. It should last for 25–30 years. Last tasted 12/95.

1990—Hermitage Chante-Alouette (white)   The 1990 Chante-Alouette's yellow color sug-
· gests super grape maturity. The nose displays the honeyed, hazelnut, stony,
90 peachlike aromas of a top white Hermitage. In the mouth, there is superb extraction of flavor, combined with surprisingly crisp, high acidity. This is an extremely rich and intense white Hermitage for connoisseurs. Anticipated maturity: now–2010. Last tasted 12/95.

1990—Hermitage Vin de Paille (white)   Chapoutier produced an astonishing 1990 Vin
· de Paille. Made from a microscopic 9 hectoliters per hectare, this wine (the grapes
96 spend two and a half months on straw mats before they are crushed and vinified) is an unctuous, unbelievably rich, fabulously perfumed, honeyed wine with extraordinary balance for its massive size. Unfortunately, there were only 225 cases of this nectar. These wines can be expected to age for 40–50 years. Last tasted 4/94.

1989—Ermitage Le Pavillon (red)   The 1989 Le Pavillon is a prodigious wine. Made from
· yields of 14 hectoliters per hectare, this parcel of old vines (averaging 70–80 years
100 of age) has produced an opaque black/purple-colored wine, with a hauntingly stunning bouquet of violets, cassis, minerals, and new oak. In the mouth, the similarity in texture, richness, and perfect balance to the compelling 1986 Mouton-Rothschild is striking, only this wine is richer and longer. This extraordinarily well-balanced wine will probably not be ready to drink for at least 5–10 years, but it will evolve for three decades or more. It is an enormous yet amazingly well-delineated wine. I lament the fact that there are only 600 cases of this magnificent wine. This great Hermitage was the first of a trilogy (1989, 1990, and 1991) of exquisite Le Pavillons. Last tasted 12/95.

1989—Hermitage La Sizeranne (red)   The 1989 La Sizeranne was aged in 40% new oak
· casks and was produced from yields that did not exceed 30 hectoliters per hectare.
90 It is an organically made, unfined, unfiltered wine that is drinking surprisingly well. The dark ruby/purple color exhibits no signs of age. The bouquet leaps from the glass, offering up aromas of cassis, minerals, smoky oak, and herbs. In the mouth, this rich, powerful, concentrated, superripe wine offers succulence and delineation. The tannins are noticeable, but ripe and unobtrusive. Anticipated maturity: now–2010. Last tasted 6/96.

1989—Hermitage Chante-Alouette (white)   The 1989 Chante-Alouette displays a rich,
· buttery, hazelnut-scented nose, deep, heady flavors, a lot of fatness in its chewy
90 texture, and a long, large-scaled finish. The wine has not yet developed complexity, but this is the type of white Hermitage that can evolve gracefully over two decades or more. In fact, these wines are often better after 7–10 years of aging, frequently being chunky and one-dimensional in their youth. Last tasted 6/96.

1988—Hermitage La Sizeranne (red)   The 1988 La Sizeranne is a soft but still highly
  ·   concentrated, outstanding Hermitage. It suffers only in comparison with the other-
87   worldly 1989. The bouquet is slightly more floral and includes the scent of violets to
go along with the superripe aromas of cassis and toasty oak. Generously endowed,
full-bodied, but softer and more evolved and approachable than the 1989, this
gorgeously made Hermitage should drink beautifully for the next 10–15 years. Last
tasted 10/93.

1988—Hermitage Chante-Alouette (white)   The 1988 Chante-Alouette is less concen-
  ·   trated, more spicy than flowery, but has great keeping qualities of 10–15 years. It
87   is somewhat overwhelmed by the 1989 when tasted side by side, but it is still an
impressive bottle of white Hermitage. Last tasted 10/93.

Older Vintages

Irregularity in addition to deplorable storage conditions in America were anathema to
Chapoutier's wines prior to 1980. The wines were not badly made. Under the regime of
Michel and Marc Chapoutier's father, Max, good, rustic-style red Hermitage were produced,
with the whites more consistent and superior to the reds. Max's red wine élevage often
resulted in too many oxidized wines after their lengthy sojourn in chestnut foudres. In fact,
these chestnut foudres were so despised by his sons that upon their ascension to power, they
were dismantled and, as Michel Chapoutier said, became the secret ingredient of many barbe-
cues held at the Chapoutier home. Max Chapoutier did produce nonvintage blends of wine
called Cuvée Numérotées. The wines were a blend of various high-quality vintages, with some
wine blended in from old vintages. The wines, called Ermitage Le Pavillon, Ermitage Cuvée
de l'Orée, and Châteauneuf du Pape Barbe Rac, were frequently superb. Michel Chapoutier
rightfully jettisoned the idea of a nonvintage blend. Should any of these wines show up in the
auction market, they are well worth buying, assuming they have been well stored. Approximately 400–500 cases of each of these wines were made between 1977 and 1988.

This firm also makes other very fine wines including Condrieu, St.-Joseph, Crozes-
Hermitage, Cornas, Côte Rôtie, Châteauneuf du Pape, and several Côtes du Rhônes. More
detail and tasting notes on those wines are provided in the appropriate chapters.

J. L. CHAVE* * * * *

Address: 37, avenue St.-Joseph
        07300 Mauves
Tel: 4-75-08-24-63
Fax: 4-75-07-14-21
Wines produced: Hermitage red and white, Hermitage Cuvée Cathelin, Hermitage
        Vin de Paille
Surface area (white): 12.35 acres
        (red): 25 acres
Production (white): 15,000 bottles
        (red): 25,000–30,000 bottles
        (Vin de Paille): 1,000 bottles
        (Cuvée Cathelin): 2,500 bottles (from very old vines in Les Bessards)
Upbringing (white): 18 months, 80% in oak, the rest in inox, with 10% of yield in new oak
        (red): 18–24 months in 10% new oak
Average age of vines (white): 60 years
        (red): 60 years
Blend (white): 80% Marsanne, 20% Roussanne
    (red): 100% Syrah

There can be no doubt that son, Jean-Louis, and his papa, Gérard Chave, the most recent Chaves in a family of growers that has been making Hermitage for six centuries, are among this planet's greatest winemakers. If I have trouble writing objectively about the Chaves, it is because of the fact that there is so much about them that I admire. Generous to a fault, uncommonly gracious, and bursting with a sincere joie de vivre, both Gérard and his son, Jean-Louis, are great tasters, superb chefs, and brilliant raconteurs. Gérard possesses a depth of knowledge on an amazing array of subjects, ranging from the primary causes of gout (from which he suffers) to the viability of Zinfandel planted in Hermitage's granitic soils. Chave, born in 1935, lives in the tiny one-horse village of Mauves, across the river from Tain l'Hermitage and just south of Tournon. One blink of the eye when passing through Mauves and the passerby would no doubt miss the tiny, faded and rusting, brown and white metal sign hanging from the wall of a building inconspicuously announcing the cellars of "J. L. Chave—Viticulteurs depuis 1481." The big, sad, basset hound eyes and long, pointed nose of Gérard Chave suggest sympathy and warmth immediately. For all his achievements, Chave is a remarkably modest man who remains unwaveringly committed to his passion for making wine in the same manner as his father before him, with no technological razzle-dazzle, and no compromises for consumers who want their wines to be already mature when released.

Chave is no provincial-thinking man blindly carrying on a tradition, however. Several trips to California and a keen sense of curiosity have informed him of the wonders, as well as dangers, of centrifuges and German micropore filtering machines that can clarify and stabilize a wine in a matter of minutes (as well as remove most of its flavor) so that no winemaker will ever have to worry about an unstable bottle. He will have none of these methods, which he calls "the tragedy of modern winemaking." In his deep, damp, cob-webbed cellars, over 500 vintages of the Chave family's Hermitage have been allowed to clarify and stabilize naturally without the aid of chemicals or machines. No flavors have been sacrificed, and Chave sees no reason to change because the old way, though much more troublesome and fraught with increased risk, produces wines of greater flavor, dimension, and depth.

Chave is not averse to experimentation if it can be proved that better wine will result. For instance, new oak barrels, pioneered by Marcel Guigal for his Côte Rôtie, and now à la mode in other houses in the Rhône Valley, have caused Chave to reflect. Despite the fact that Chave firmly believes that the intense richness of fruit produced at Hermitage does not require aging in new oak to give structure, he purchased *one* new barrel in 1985 to age one batch of his red Hermitage. Though a great admirer of Marcel Guigal, he believed that the toasty, vanillin character imparted by this new oak barrel to his Hermitage not only changed the character of the wine, but disguised its identity—to his Hermitage's detriment. But this 1985 experiment had an interesting conclusion. At the urging of his talented son, Jean-Louis, who spent time studying at the University of California at Davis, and who also received a master's degree in business in America, Chave aged a small amount of his red Hermitage from Les Bessards vineyard in 100% new oak casks. He agreed to do it in 1990 because the vintage was so extraordinary he knew the wine could absorb the new oak without losing its Hermitage typicity. When he blended together numerous lots of red Hermitage, this wine was kept separately and subsequently bottled in a heavy, old-fashioned bottle, with a red label. Called Cuvée Cathelin (after Chave's friend the painter Bernard Cathelin), it was also produced in 1991, and based on what I tasted in these cellars in summer 1996, it may again be produced in 1995. Interestingly, Gérard Chave continues to have mixed emotions about the importance of this deluxe cuvée, but the wine has received rave accolades from all who have been fortunate enough to taste it.

The Chave family now owns 37 acres on Hermitage hill. Production ranges between 2,000 and 3,000 cases of Hermitage, and 500 cases of red St.-Joseph are produced from the 3.7 acres Chave owns in that appellation.

There are no secrets as to why Chave's wines are great. Its because of low-yielding vines, a very late harvest producing physiologically ripe fruit, virtually no intervention in the winemaking or upbringing, and bottling with no filtration and only insignficant fining. Tasting at Chave's cellars is always educational because it is the only place where the vineyards can be tasted separately before they are blended. I have done this numerous times and it is always a thrill to see his three white wine cuvées, one from his monopole vineyard, the 3.73 acres of 50- to 85-year-old vines of Péleat, the 9+ acres of 80-year-old vines of Les Rocoules, and his tiny parcel of 60-year-old vines of La Maison Blanche. Chave also owns a tiny parcel of very old-vine Roussanne on l'Hermite, which produces an extraordinarily rich, complex, honeyed wine that manages to keep everything in balance while offering great finesse. Traditionally, this has always been blended with Chave's white Hermitage, but in 1994 it was kept separately. Chave's white Hermitage, a blend of 85% Marsanne and 15% Roussanne, aged after malolactic fermentation in both vats and barrels for 14–18 months, has benefited from an increased percentage of new oak (largely Jean-Louis's influence). It is the finest white Hermitage of the appellation. Although Chapoutier's Cuvée de l'Orée is a richer and more powerful wine, it is made in such tiny quantities as to be impossible to find in the marketplace. Chave's white Hermitage drinks beautifully for 4–5 years after its release, and it then closes down, seemingly losing its fruit and becoming more monolithic and neutral, only to reemerge 10–15 years later with a roasted hazelnut, buttery, honeyed, slight fino sherry style that is exceptional. In the great vintages it can last for 20–30 years.

Chave's red wine vineyards include a parcel of very old vines in Les Rocoules, a 5-acre parcel of 80-year-old vines in Les Bessards, relatively young vines in l'Hermite, extremely old vines in Péleat, old vines in Les Beaumes, and 50-year-old vines in Le Méal. Each of these vineyards produces an Hermitage with slightly different aromatic, textural, and flavor profiles, but the sum of their parts always turns out to be far more interesting than any individual cuvée. The one exception may be the wine from Les Bessards, part of which, in the greatest years, becomes the Cuvée Cathelin.

Like so many top winemakers, Chave is never content to rest on his reputation. Concerned about having to do several bottlings because his cellars were not large enough to store the production from an entire vintage, he constructed a beautiful underground cellar in 1990 to permit one bottling and to have sufficient room to store his entire production. In fact, there has been only one bottling of Chave Hermitage since 1983.

With respect to his red wine, perhaps the most important decision for Chave is the date to harvest. Along with Chapoutier, he is the last to harvest. He has often said that he does not need an oenologist to know when to harvest. As Chave amusingly puts it, "I don't begin to think about picking until the chestnuts on my trees start falling." His goal is to achieve super ripeness and richness, which he claims are the primary ingredients of a great red wine. Delaying the harvest is always risky because torrential rains tend to plague France in early October. Chave keeps the wines from his vineyards separate for one year and then decides what will go into the final blend, going through an elaborate, laborious exercise of making various blends to see which turns out to be the finest. It is a long and tedious process, but as I have indicated, the final product is consistently better than the individual components, a testament to Chave's formidable tasting and blending abilities. In the finest years, Chave's red Hermitage is an immortal wine. Compared to the flashy, opulent style of Jaboulet's La Chapelle, and the extraordinarily concentrated masterpieces of Chapoutier's luxury cuvées, Chave's red Hermitage begins life slowly, but it never fails to impress after 7–10 years in bottle. Will it peak in 10, 15, or 20 years? His great vintages, 1978, 1983,

1985, 1988, 1989, 1990, 1991, 1994, and 1995, are rivaled by few other producers in France.

Prior to 1978, Chave's wines were less consistent. Much of that is explained by the fact that when he took over for his father in 1970, he had to endure 1972, 1973, 1974, and 1975, all rain-plagued, extremely difficult years for Hermitage. While his 1976 did not turn out to be a successful wine, that year was also a tricky vintage given the extraordinary summer drought and heavy September rains.

Chave has also resurrected an old Hermitage practice of making a vin de paille. The tradition of taking whole bunches and leaving them on straw mats until they turn to raisins 60 + days after the harvest (usually in December), and then fermenting them, not only produces microscopic quantities of juice, but unbelievably concentrated, intense, honeyed wines that are known to have aged for more than a century. When I tasted Chave's 1974 vin de paille I was struck by its extraordinary aromas of figs, apricots, roasted nuts, and honey. That wine was never commercialized, but in 1986 and 1989, Chave intentionally set out to produce tiny quantities of vin de paille. Both vintages are extraordinary, as evidenced by the tasting notes that follow.

VINTAGES

1995—Hermitage (red) The 1995 red Hermitage would appear to possess magnificent
  · potential. Whether the wine possessed the elegant delicacy of Les Rocoules, the
95 dense, tannic power of l'Hermite, the sweet, wild-berry perfume and complexity of
  Péleat, the exotic, smoky, roasted, sexy ripeness and voluptuousness of Le Méal,
  or the extraordinary concentration, massive richness, and mineral, Richebourg-like
  complexity of Les Bessards, the 1995 red Hermitage should prove to be Chave's
  finest vintage since 1990. Frankly, I believe it will eclipse the superb 1991s
  produced by Chave. It is a wine with exceptional richness and power. Chave
  believes (and I agree), that the 1995, more than most vintages, expresses the
  eloquence and complexity of the great terroirs of Hermitage. After tasting through
  the exceptional cuvée of Les Bessards, aged in 100% new oak casks, I was convinced by the twinkle in the eyes of Jean-Louis and Gérard that there is going to
  be a Cuvée Cathelin in 1995, the first produced since the two heroic vintages of
  1990 and 1991. Last tasted 6/96.

1995—Hermitage (white) The 1995 white Hermitage appears to be one of the most
  · stupendous examples of white Hermitage Chave has made over the last decade. It
93 easily competes with 1988, 1989, and 1990, a fabulous trilogy of vintages. After
  tasting through the numerous cuvées, such as Maison Blanche, l'Hermite, Les
  Rocoules, and Péleat, it is clear that this wine merits a score in the low to
  mid-nineties. Powerful and rich, with exceptional concentration and intensity, it
  exhibits a honeyed, juicy inner core of fruit that covers the mid-palate, and a great
  finish. Now that Jean-Louis is in the cellars, part of the cuvée is being fermented
  in new oak barrels, which is then blended with the remaining wine that is fermented in older oak, as well as those cuvées kept in tank. This seems only to have
  added to the wine's richness and delineation. Last tasted 6/96.

1994—Hermitage (red) The 1994 red Hermitage appears to be superb. Last year it tasted
  · like a richer sibling of the 1985. This year it tasted significantly richer, but with
93 + the 1985's softness, elegance, and precocious appeal. The wine possesses a black/
  ruby/purple color, an intense, smoky, cassis, and mineral-scented nose, full body,
  superb density, a soft attack, good grip, and a long, impressively endowed finish. It
  is a wine of undeniable power, spice, tannin, fruit, silk, and fat—what else can

you ask for? It should be drinkable by the year 2000 and last for 25+ years. Last tasted 6/96.

1994—Hermitage (white)   The 1994 white Hermitage is one of the most seductive, per-
  ·   fumed, multilayered, and profoundly textured white Hermitages I have tasted from
 94   Chave. The unctuous texture and superb nose of honeyed white flowers and miner-
       als are followed by a wine of exceptional depth, richness, and balance. Both the
       1994 and 1995 should drink splendidly well for 4–5 years, then close completely,
       not to reemerge for a decade. It will keep for 20–30+ years. Last tasted 6/96.

1993—Hermitage (red)   This vintage, which is generally horrible (many producers de-
  ·   classified because the fruit was so rotten), is a surprising success in a few cellars.
 88   Chave's 1993, which will probably be dumped by retailers because of the vintage's
       reputation, is an excellent wine. Some acidity does poke through in the finish, but
       the wine exhibits plenty of pure, ripe black and red fruits that are neither vegetal
       nor moldy. It possesses good density and medium body, and appears to be one of
       the two finest Hermitages of this justifiably maligned vintage (the other being the
       remarkable Ermitage Le Pavillon from Chapoutier). Chave's 1993 should be drunk
       over the next 12–15 years. It is not surprising that such high quality was achieved
       because Chave declassified over two-thirds of his crop. Last tasted 6/96.

1993—Hermitage (white)   The 1993 white Hermitage is an amazing success for this
  ·   horrendous vintage. The wine exhibits good ripeness, excellent freshness, some of
 88   the honeyed, white-flower character (acacia?), medium body, and a crisp, long
       finish. Anticipated maturity: now–2000. Last tasted 6/96.

1992—Hermitage (red)   The 1992 red Hermitage exhibits a leanness combined with
  ·   bitter tannin in an otherwise medium-bodied, attractive, ripe wine. It displays some
 85   dilution from the rains that plagued the 1992 vintage. Chave's 1992 is likely to be
       a short-distance runner by the standards of this estate, lasting for no more than a
       decade. Last tasted 6/96.

1992—Hermitage (white)   The rich, full-bodied 1992 white Hermitage reveals good glyc-
  ·   erin and extract, as well as floral, honeyed, buttered nuts, and mineral aromas. It
 88   is a heady, lush, alcoholic, soft Hermitage that will provide ideal drinking over the
       next 5–6 years. Last tasted 6/96.

1991—Hermitage (red)   The beautifully elegant, stylish 1991 red Hermitage displays an
  ·   open-knit bouquet of red and black fruits, spices, flowers, and smoke. With excel-
 89   lent richness and medium to full body, this deep, graceful wine should turn out to
       be slightly richer than the 1987, and perhaps equal to the sumptuous 1982.
       Anticipated maturity: 1999–2015. Last tasted 6/96.

1991—Hermitage Cuvée Cathelin (red)   In 1991, Chave made 2,500 bottles of an Hermi-
  ·   tage Cuvée Cathelin that is significantly richer and more profound than the classic
 96   cuvée. It offers an opaque dark purple color, and a huge nose of cassis, vanillin,
       smoke, and flowers. Full-bodied, dense, and powerful, this is a deeply concen-
       trated, rich, compelling bottle of Hermitage. Anticipated maturity: 1999–2025.
       Last tasted 6/96.

1991—Hermitage (white)   The fat, rich 1991 Hermitage blanc offers a big, juicy nose of
  ·   acacia flowers and honeyed fruit, medium to full body, and loads of flavor. While it
 90   is not as broadly flavored or as powerful as the 1990 and 1989, it is a delicious,
       well-made, excellent example of white Hermitage. Anticipated maturity: now–
       2005. Last tasted 6/96.

1990—Hermitage (red)   1990 is the Hermitage appellation's greatest vintage since 1978,
  ·   and maybe since 1961. I have been tasting Chave's Hermitage since the great 1978
 99   vintage, and the black-colored 1990 is unquestionably the most massive and concen-

trated wine he has yet produced. Perhaps the real difference between it and the splendid 1989 is that the 1990 exhibits a more roasted character to its nose, as well as a bit more tannin and concentration in the mouth. Except for that, they are both mind-boggling, monumental bottles of red Hermitage. The 1990, which offers huge aromas of tar, roasted cassis fruit, and hickory, as well as astonishing concentration, will not be interesting to drink young. Anticipated maturity: 2005–2040. Last tasted 6/95.

1990—Hermitage Cuvée Cathelin (red)   The Cuvée Cathelin, more influenced by new
·   oak than the classic cuvée, is a prodigious wine. Remarkably, the new oak takes a
99   backseat to the wine's superb raw materials. The wine exhibits fabulous concentration, richness, intensity, and length, as well as a mind-boggling finish. It is not superior to the classic cuvée, just different. The Cuvée Cathelin possesses more of an international new oak signature, but awesome extract and potential. The 1990 Cuvée Cathelin should not be drunk for 10–15 years; it has the potential to last for 30–50 years! Last tasted 6/96.

1990—Hermitage (white)   This bold, rich, powerful wine exhibits a floral, honeyed, apri-
·   cot, fig, and roasted nut-scented nose. It has considerable size, as well as copious
92   fat and fruit. Still approachable, this full-bodied, rich wine is a candidate for several decades of cellaring. It had not begun to close up when last tasted. Anticipated maturity: now–2015. Last tasted 8/96.

1989—Hermitage (red)   This tannic, formidably endowed wine has already begun to close
·   down, but the black/ruby/purple color, the intensely fragrant nose of jammy cassis,
96   minerals, and spices, and the full-bodied, rich, concentrated style are unmistakable. An enormously rich, backward Hermitage, it does not share the roasted character or sheer massiveness and tannic clout of the 1990, but it is a spectacularly concentrated Hermitage that will age effortlessly for 20–30 years. Anticipated maturity: 2005–2030. Last tasted 6/96.

1989—Hermitage (white)   The 1989 Hermitage Blanc is low in acidity, expansive, and
·   weighty, and makes for a huge, chewy mouthful of white wine. The honeyed, some-
92   what unctuous personality of the wine is more dominant in the 1989 than in the 1988, but there remains the head-turning, beautiful, flowery aromas, sensational concentration, super ripeness, and low acidity. Chave believes the latter component is always a characteristic of the greatest Hermitage vintages. Last tasted 8/96.

1989—Hermitage Vin de Paille (white)   Chave's 1989 Vin de Paille is the quintessential
·   honeyed, highly extracted sweet dessert wine. I cannot say I like it any better than
98   a great Sélection de Grains Nobles from Alsace, but it is an amazingly rich, thick, unctuous wine that represents the essence of wine. A half bottle will easily serve 10–15 lucky people. Anticipated maturity: 2000–2060. Last tasted 12/95.

1988—Hermitage (red)   Even more closed than the 1989 and 1990, this opaque, dark
·   ruby/purple-colored wine reveals a tightly knit nose of cassis, minerals, and tar.
93   Full-bodied, with superb concentration, the 1988 Chave Hermitage exhibits more astringent, tougher tannin than either the 1989 or 1990. While it appears more structured, it has nowhere near the weight and dazzling opulence of its two younger siblings. Nevertheless, this is a superb Hermitage. Anticipated maturity: 2000–2020. Last tasted 6/96.

1988—Hermitage (white)   The 1988 Hermitage blanc is a delicate, subtle, rich, authorita-
·   tively flavored wine that is a fine candidate for extended cellaring. This full-bodied
90   Hermitage offers up an enticing bouquet of acacia flowers and honeyed fruit. There is brilliant precision to its rich, dense flavors, yet it is not heavy. Last tasted 8/96.

1987—Hermitage (red)   The 1987 red Hermitage is probably the finest wine of the
·   appellation. Chave's 1987 is a beautiful bottle of wine. I thought so much of it, I
88   bought several magnums. It is soft and, as Chave's wines go, extremely elegant and

feminine, but wonderfully round, rich, concentrated, and oh, so seductive. While it will become more complex with bottle age, by Chave's standards, it will not be long-lived. Anticipated maturity: now–2008. Last tasted 11/95.

1987—Hermitage (white)   The 1987 white Hermitage is light bodied, and an excellent, round, ripe wine with an attractive honeyed, peachlike bouquet intertwined with the smell of spring flowers (acacias?). In the mouth, the wine is medium- to full-bodied, with beautiful clarity, impeccable cleanliness, and a long, rich finish. It is delicious. Anticipated maturity: now–2000. Last tasted 11/95.

87

1986—Hermitage (red)   A strict selection process resulted in a deeply colored wine with a forward, precocious bouquet of smoked meat, ripe plums, and cassis. The wine is rich and soft, as well as full-bodied and long. Anticipated maturity: now–2006. Last tasted 11/95.

88

1986—Hermitage Vin de Paille (white)   This is one of the most extraordinary wines I have ever tasted. It was made with no sulfites, so it can be drunk by people who have allergies to sulfur. With its deep golden color and huge honeyed bouquet that offers a smorgasbord of decadent sweet fruits, this stunningly rich, intense, unctuous nectar must be tasted to be believed. It is nearly perfection, and probably will last 20–30 years. Last tasted 12/94.

97

1985—Hermitage (red)   Chave produced the best red Hermitage of this vintage. Yet for Chave 1985 was not a year he cares to remember. Holding back the tears, he sadly states that his beloved mother, as well as his faithful sidekick, his dog, passed away that year. A sentimentalist, Chave is likely to put little of this vintage into the huge reservoir of old vintages that his family has faithfully cellared throughout this century. His 1985 avoided the oversupple style of some of the other reds of this vintage. The wine's deep ruby color exhibits some lightening at the edge. The intense fragrance of smoked meat, cassis, and Provençal olives is followed by a rich, full-bodied, velvety-textured wine that is just beginning to reach its apogee. Anticipated maturity: now–2012. Last tasted 12/95.

91

1985—Hermitage (white)   Particularly powerful in 1985, Chave's white Hermitage is a blockbuster. The huge aroma of pineapple, wet stones, mint, spring flowers, and honey is sensational. On the palate, the wine is very intense, long, broadly flavored, lush, and extremely rich. It is a trifle low in acidity, but what a mouthful of wine! Anticipated maturity: now–2003. Last tasted 6/96.

92

1984—Hermitage (red)   This onetime elegantly wrought wine has lost some fruit, and now tastes austere, lean, and slightly vegetal. Drink it up. Mature now. Last tasted 1/93.

78

1983—Hermitage (red)   Chave has always loved the 1983 (a sentiment I share, but the tannin in the wine is worrisome). It seems to me that his 1983 has the potential to be super, but it still remains charmless and austere. Deep dark ruby in color with some amber at the edge, it has a profound concentration of ripe, smoky, berry fruit and Asian spices, full body, exceptional depth and length, as well as a formidable tannin level. Anticipated maturity: 2003–2025. Last tasted 12/95.

93?

1983—Hermitage (white)   Very aromatic with a wonderful variety of scents (honeysuckle, pineapple, stony minerals), this is a graceful wine that balances power with finesse. Chave says he will not drink it until 1995. Anticipated maturity: now–2005. Last tasted 6/95.

90

1982—Hermitage (red)   Like many of Chave's wines, the 1982 has gotten deeper and richer in the bottle after starting life a little diffuse and awkward. Fully mature, it offers a rich, silky palate with gobs of fruit, and unmistakable aromas and flavors of jammy berries, smoked barbecue, tar, and saddle leather. This is one of the most delicious Chave Hermitages to drink. Anticipated maturity: now–2008. Last tasted 7/96.

93

1980—Hermitage (red)   Soft, fruity, straightforward, and totally mature, this wine is
·   Chave's least favorite vintage of the eighties, and I must agree with him. Drink it
76   up. Last tasted 11/90.

1980—Hermitage (white)   Certainly better than the 1980 red Hermitage, this medium-
·   bodied wine shows a ripe, complex bouquet of tropical fruit and smoky nuts and
84   herbs. On the palate, it is fresh, soft, and fully ready to drink. It will not keep. Last
         tasted 6/86.

1979—Hermitage (red)   This is a perfect example of my statement about Chave's wine
·   starting off slowly. After bottling in 1981, this wine seemed light in color and rather
87   insubstantial. Two years later the color seemed deeper and more body was appar-
         ent. Fully mature by 1987, this wine remains delicious. It is elegant, ripe, round,
         medium-bodied, generously flavored, and well balanced. Drink it up. Last tasted
         11/95.

1978—Hermitage (red)   This has always been one of Chave's single greatest vintages,
·   possibly equaled in recent years by 1989, 1991, 1994, and 1995, and possibly
96   surpassed by 1990. Memorizing its aromas, its flavors, its texture, and its length is
         a quick education in what great wine is all about. Still an infant, with a murky,
         dark ruby/garnet color, this wine offers a smoky, tar, cassis, herb, and grilled meat
         set of aromatics, huge body, and mouth-searing tannin. This remains a very youthful
         wine—after nearly two decades of cellaring! Anticipated maturity: 2000–2025.
         Last tasted 11/95.

1978—Hermitage (white)   Amazingly young and vibrant, but tight, lean, closed, and
·   shockingly high in acidity, this wine may be in a dormant stage. If not, I doubt the
86   fruit is sufficient to balance out the wine's sharpness. Anticipated maturity: 2000–
         2015. Last tasted 6/96.

1976—Hermitage (red)   For whatever reason, I have found this wine excessively lean,
·   unforthcoming, and terribly tannic and dry on the palate. Perhaps I have been
77   unlucky, but I fear this wine is losing what little fruit it had. Last tasted 7/84.

1969—Hermitage (red)   Not terribly impressive, the 1969 is fully mature, seems rather
·   lightweight, and finishes short. Yet it provides a decent drink. Last tasted 5/83.
80

1967—Hermitage (red)   Medium dark ruby with an amber/orange rim, the 1967 has an
·   intense smoky, creamy, seductive bouquet, long, very generous flavors of berry fruit
91   backed up by ripe, soft tannins, and a good deal of body. The 1967 should keep
         for at least another decade. Last tasted 6/86.

1967—Hermitage (white)   Heavenly aromas of grilled nuts, dried dates, tropical fruit,
·   and exotic spices are tantalizingly marvelous. On the palate, this wine gushes with
92   generous portions of ripe fruit. Quite fresh. Last tasted 6/86.

1952—Hermitage (white)   Tasted with Chave as a prelude to his 1929, I was stunned by
·   this wine's richness and fullness as well as complexity. Is anyone other than Chave
93   prepared to cellar white Hermitage this long? Last tasted 6/86.

1935—Hermitage (red)   Chave's birth year, 1935, hardly an inspirational vintage in
·   French wine lore, produced a magnificently scented, smoky, gamy-scented wine,
92   still dark in color, and still oozing with rich, ripe fruit. An amazingly fresh wine.
         Last tasted 6/86.

1929—Hermitage (red)   Pulled directly from Chave's cellar and never recorked, this
·   medium ruby wine with a pinkish, amber edge had an ashtray, cigar-type aroma,
86   some plummy fruit on the palate, good acidity, and was still very much alive, if
         fading. Chave said he had tasted from better bottles. Next to the poorly regarded
         1935, the 1929 suffered in terms of richness, complexity, and length, but at 67
         years of age was still quite a mouthful of wine. Last tasted 6/86.

1929—Hermitage (white) The 1929 had a very deep golden color and an aroma not
· unlike a very old vintage of Yquem. Toasty hazelnut aromas, some oxidation, yet
88 dry, rich, heavy, and intense. This wine has plenty of fruit left. Again, this bottle
came from Chave's cave and had never been recorked. He served it with foie gras,
which was ideal. Quite excellent as a wine; stupendous considering its age. Last
tasted 6/86.

DOMAINE DU COLOMBIER (FLORENT ET GABRIEL VIALE)* * * *

Address: Florent et Gabriel Viale
　　　　Les Chenêts
　　　　26600 Mercurol
Tel: 4-75-07-44-07
Wines produced: Crozes-Hermitage Cuvée Gaby, Hermitage
Surface area: 3.96 acres
Production: 3,000 bottles
Upbringing: 16–18 months in cask, little new oak
Average age of vines: 50–60 years
Blend: 100% Syrah

I have had little experience with this small producer except for the 1994 and 1993, both
impressive wines. In fact, the 1993 was one of the top three wines in what was a disastrous
vintage in Hermitage. It outperformed the very good red Hermitage produced by J. L.
Chave, and ranked just behind the great Ermitage Le Pavillon made by Michel Chapoutier.
Unfortunately, proprietors Gabriel and Florent Viale make very little wine. What they do
produce from their tiny 4-acre parcel of 55-year-old vines in the Les Beaumes vineyard has
been quite impressive. This appears to be one of those tiny, virtually unknown estates that
was better known as a longtime supplier of wine to Guigal. This should be an estate to
watch, even though quantities are extremely small. The Viales also produce a very fine red
Crozes-Hermitage called Cuvée Gaby.

VINTAGES

1994—Hermitage (red) Only 80 cases were made of the 1994 Unfiltered Hermitage. This
· beautiful wine possesses an opaque purple color and a sweet, fragrant nose of pure
91 cassis, black raspberries, smoke, and minerals. Already surprisingly forward and
delicious, this full-bodied, chewy, rich Hermitage must have some tannin lurking
behind the fruit, glycerin, and alcohol. A big, surprisingly supple wine, it will
exhibit more structure as it ages over the next 10–15 + years. Last tasted 5/96.

1993—Hermitage (red) Unfortunately, only 40 cases of this special unfiltered bottling
· were made for the American importer. In what was a disastrous vintage for this
90 appellation (only two other noteworthy 1993 Hermitages were produced, Chapoutier's Le Pavillon and that of J. L. Chave), this 1993 stands out for its fine color
saturation, intensity, body, and concentration. The wine's opaque black-ruby color
is followed by an intense, fragrant nose of sweet Syrah fruit (smoke, animal, and
cassis). Dense and highly extracted, with sweet tannin and stunning richness and
length, this knockout Hermitage is the early candidate for the appellation's finest
wine of the vintage! Drink it over the next 20 + years. Last tasted 11/95.

DELAS FRÈRES* * */* * * *

Address: Z.A. de l'Olivet
          B.P. 4
          07300 St.-Jean de Muzols
Tel: 4-75-08-60-30
Fax: 4-75-08-53-67
Wines produced: Hermitage Cuvée Les Bessards, Hermitage Cuvée Les Grands Chemins,
          Hermitage Cuvée La Marquise de la Tourette (red and white)
Surface area (white): 2.47 acres
          (red): 23.3 acres
Production (white): 4,500 bottles
          (red): Cuvée Les Bessards—3,500 bottles
              Cuvée Les Grand Chemins—5,000–6,000 bottles
              Cuvée La Marquise de la Tourette—20,000 bottles
Upbringing (white): 8 months with 50% in inox vats and 50% in barrels (new oak)
          (red): 14–16 months in barrels 1–5 years old
Average age of vines (white): 30 years
          (red): 30 years
Blend (white): 80% Marsanne, 20% Roussanne
          (red): 100% Syrah

This company keeps a surprisingly low profile in spite of the fact that several of the wines are of exceptional quality. It is an old house, founded in 1836, and it remained family owned until 1978. That year, Delas was purchased by the Champagne firm of Deutz. In 1981, Delas left the quaint, touristic town of Tournon, which sits across the Rhône River opposite Tain l'Hermitage, and moved into a spacious, modern facility several miles north in St.-Jean de Muzols. In 1990, Dominique Lallier was put in charge of this appellation. Although the Deutz Champagne firm was acquired by Louis Roederer, its parent corporation, in 1993, that fact has had little influence on the direction (or lack thereof) of these wines. The pride of Delas is the estate-bottled northern Rhône wines from their 26 acres of vines in Hermitage. Delas produces an entire range of Rhône wines from the other appellations using purchased grapes and/or wine to complete the portfolio. The southern Rhône wines offered by Delas are not of the quality level of their northern Rhône estate-bottled wines, a fact that they acknowledge.

The total production of 100,000 plus cases (of which only 2,700 cases are Hermitage) belies the modest image this house promotes. The cellars are extremely modern and immaculate, with plenty of high-tech equipment, centrifuges, filters, etc. The level of wines produced here ranges considerably, from the top estate cuvées, to the bland, innocuous négociant wines. There is no doubting that Delas's flagship wines are the Hermitage Les Bessards and Hermitage Marquise de la Tourette. Once past the top cuvées, what enthusiasts taste are wines made by people obsessed with technically stable and clean wines. In pursuit of those goals, there is no malolactic fermentation for the white wines, multiple filtrations (including a sterile one), and bentonite clarifications. None of this will produce interesting, complex, or long-lived wines, but it does result in consistent, fail-safe wines made with a food-processor mentality.

That being said, the top cuvées come from well-situated vineyards in Hermitage. Delas owns nearly 15 acres in Les Bessards, from which they produce their white Marquise de la Tourette, their red Marquise de la Tourette, and in great vintages such as 1990 and 1991, their luxury cuvée Les Bessards, produced from 38-year-old Syrah vines. As the following tasting notes exhibit, Delas has produced some top vintages of red Hermitage. In comparing the Delas red Hermitage to the opulent, fleshy, exotic style of Jaboulet's La Chapelle, or the stylish, graceful, authoritatively flavored wines of Chave, or the blockbuster wines of Chapoutier, they are rich in flavor and as fleshy, but tend to have a pronounced black olive/Provençal herb scent to go along with a marked smoky, hickory, barbecue characteristic. When they are outstanding, they are undeniably overlooked and consequently underpriced, as well as capable of 10–20 years of evolution in the bottle. Vintages since 1991 have left me with the impression that Delas Frères is a candidate for the Rhône Valley's leading underachiever, and is in need of a wake-up call.

VINTAGES

1993—Hermitage Marquise de la Tourette (red)   A very hollow wine, this effort, from a
·   poor vintage, exhibits a medium ruby color, some spice and red fruit in its aromat-
73   ics, but no mid-palate or finish. It is a lean, attenuated wine. Last tasted 6/96.

1993—Hermitage Marquise de la Tourette (white)   The 1993 exhibits medium body, good
·   weight, some oaky notes, and an attractive fatness and ripeness. It requires drinking
86   over the next 5–6 years. Last tasted 9/95.

1992—Hermitage Marquise de la Tourette (red)   This is a rich wine with plenty of cassis
·   fruit, medium to full body, but not much complexity. It is a powerful, young wine
88 +   capable of lasting another 10–15 years. Last tasted 6/96.

1992—Hermitage Marquise de la Tourette (white)   Although the 1992 Marquise de la
·   Tourette is rich, honeyed, and oaky, it is on a fast evolutionary track and needs to
86   be drunk up. Last tasted 6/96.

1991—Hermitage Les Bessards (red)   The 1991 Les Bessards (named after one of the
·   tenderloin vineyards of the great dome of granite—the hill of Hermitage) is an
92 +   impressive, outstanding wine with a deep purple color, plenty of peppery cassis
         fruit and minerals in the nose, tightly wound, full-bodied flavors that exhibit terrific
         extract, and a long, muscular, powerful finish. It needs another 5–6 years of
         cellaring, and should keep for 20–30 years. Last tasted 6/96.

1991—Hermitage Marquise de la Tourette (red)   A dense, chewy, full-bodied wine with
·   considerable tannin and muscle. It needs 7–8 years of cellaring and should age
87 +   effortlessly for 20–25 years. It is an excellent rather than exceptional Hermitage.
         Last tasted 9/95.

1990—Hermitage Les Bessards (red)   The blockbuster, deep purple-colored 1990 Les
·   Bessards is dense and rich, with more opulence and sweetness than the 1991, as
93 +   well as more power and concentration. Massive and broad-shouldered, this exqui-
         site wine is the finest Hermitage I have ever tasted from Delas. Patience is required.
         Anticipated maturity: 2005–2030. Last tasted 6/96.

1990—Hermitage Marquise de la Tourette (white)   This wine exhibited admirable inten-
·   sity, an unctuous, chewy constitution, as well as rich, honeyed, apple, and nutlike
87   flavors, and a long, heady finish. I would not be surprised to see it evolve for a
         decade given the formidable aging potential of white Hermitage. Anticipated matu-
         rity: now–2004. Last tasted 6/95.

1989—Hermitage (red)   The 1989 Hermitage is light- to medium-bodied, with a fragrant
·   smell of minerals and cassis. It is a tasty, straightforward Hermitage. Mature now.
78   Last tasted 5/95.

1989—Hermitage Marquise de la Tourette (red)   The 1989 has fine flavor extraction, as
·   well as disturbingly hard tannin in the finish. It is clearly meant to be aged,
88   although it may be drinkable by the late nineties. While not as concentrated as the
         1990, it is obviously more tannic, structured, and potentially longer-lived. How-
         ever, I doubt it will ever provide the degree of pleasure the 1990 will. Anticipated
         maturity: 2000–2015. Last tasted 9/94.

1988—Hermitage Marquise de la Tourette (red)   While promising, the 1988 is closed,
·   tannic, and hard. The wine does exhibit an attractively ripe nose with scents of
87   new oak and cassis. In the mouth, the wine is rich, but the tannins have the upper
          hand at the moment, and the finish displays abundant power but also elevated
          tannins. Anticipated maturity: 1999–2010. Last tasted 6/95.

1985—Hermitage Marquise de la Tourette (red)   Deep ruby/garnet-colored, the fully
·   mature 1985 is fat, ripe, richly fruit, full-bodied, and low in acidity. The attractive
88   flavors of cassis, tar, and roasted herb remain fresh and intense. Anticipated
          maturity: now–2002. Last tasted 12/93.

1983—Hermitage Marquise de la Tourette (red)   Much more open-knit and developed
·   than many 1983s, this dark ruby/garnet-colored Hermitage has a full-blown bou-
90   quet of cured olives, smoke, fennel, and ripe berry fruit. Quite full-bodied, chewy,
          and fleshy, but surprisingly close to full maturity, this is a deep, concentrated wine.
          Delas has succeeded in producing one of the best-balanced 1983s. Anticipated
          maturity: now–2010. Last tasted 11/96.

1978—Hermitage Marquise de la Tourette (red)   A magnificent bouquet of sweet, oaky,
·   jammy, peppery, berry fruit and licorice is quite enticing. In the mouth the wine is
92   very full-bodied, even more concentrated than the outstanding 1983, has layers
          and layers of fruit, good ripe tannins, and exemplary length. Mature now. Last
          tasted 12/86.

BERNARD FAURIE* * * */* * * * *

Address: Avenue Hélène de Tournon
        07300 Tournon
Tel: 4-75-08-55-09
Fax: 4-75-08-55-09
Wines produced: Hermitage (red and white), Hermitage Le Méal, St.-Joseph
Surface area (white): 0.5 acres
             (red): 3.7 acres
Production (white): 800 bottles
             (red): 6,000 bottles
Upbringing (white): 4 week fermentation in new oak, then 12 months in old oak
             (red): 18–24 months in 10–15% new oak barrels
Average age of vines (white): 40 years
                     (red): 40–45 years
Blend (white): 100% Marsanne
      (red): 100% Syrah

Faurie, located in Tournon, has been one of the up-and-coming stars of Hermitage for
over a decade, but he continues to receive little acclaim. His winemaking style comes
closest to that of Gérard Chave. While his wines are full-flavored, they retain an elegance
and finesse and, like those of Chave, start life very slowly. Faurie produces only 500 cases
of red Hermitage and a scant 66 cases of white. He also produces 200–250 cases of
St.-Joseph. The winemaking at this estate is traditional. There is no destemming, and little
intervention in the winemaking process. I have rarely tasted his white wines, but it is
reported that they have improved immensely from the rustic, oversized examples of the past.
His red wines are fermented in open wooden tanks and given a lengthy period of skin
contact of up to 20 days. Afterward, the wine rests in wood for 18–24 months, is fined once,
but never filtered.
     Faurie, who exhibits a shy intensity, usually produces two cuvées of red Hermitage, one
from his very old vines of Syrah in Le Méal (planted in 1914), and the other made from a

blend of his other holdings. His microscopic production of white Hermitage (100% Marsanne) is made from the highly regarded Les Greffieux vineyard. The red wines have been consistently excellent, occasionally brilliant, as they were in 1988 and 1990. The finest Faurie wine is always the Hermitage Le Méal. Made in limited quantities, it can be one of the top five or six wines of the appellation. Since there are only minute quantities of this offering, and Faurie appears content to remain in the shadows of more outgoing producers, it is unlikely to receive the attention it merits. Faurie produces small quantities of St.-Joseph from three vineyard parcels totaling 4.2 acres. Almost all of this is in young vines, except for a tiny parcel on the hillside above the village of Tournon, where the Syrah vines average 35 years.

VINTAGES

1991—Hermitage (red)   This wine, 100% from Les Greffieux, reveals a deep purple color
·   with no signs of age. A big, tar, cassis, smoky-scented nose is followed by a
88+   full-bodied, rustic wine with considerable power, rich fruit, and chewiness. It needs
            2–4 more years of cellaring, and should keep for 15–20 years. If it develops more
            harmony between its fruit and tannin, it may merit an outstanding score. Anticipated maturity: 2000–2015. Last tasted 5/96.

1991—Hermitage Le Méal (red)   A spectacular black/purple color, and a sweet, roasted-
·   herb, black-fruit, smoky nose is followed by a wine with exceptional depth, full
90   body, and hard, dry tannin in the finish. This wine borders on being a blockbuster,
            but it needs better integration of the tannin. There is more sweetness and chewiness
            to Le Méal than found in the regular cuvée, but it requires another 5–6 years of
            cellaring. Anticipated maturity: 2002–2018. Last tasted 5/96.

1990—Hermitage (red)   This thick, rich, juicy wine is an outstanding success. Copious
·   amounts of fruit, considerable body, and a sweetness to the tannin not apparent in
90   Faurie's 1991s. Although accessible, it is still unevolved and grapy. Anticipated
            maturity: 2000–2015. Last tasted 5/96.

1990—Hermitage Le Méal   Unquestionably the finest Hermitage I have ever tasted from
·   Faurie, this wine's color is an opaque purple, and the nose offers up gobs of sweet,
93   cassis fruit, licorice, smoke, and pepper. Full-bodied, with marvelous concentration, silky tannin, and plenty of glycerin and extract, this blockbuster red Hermitage will be at its apogee between 2005–2020. Last tasted 5/96.

1989—Hermitage (red)   Although closed and muted aromatically, this somewhat rustic,
·   coarse wine reveals an impressive dark ruby/purple color and a roasted-herb nose.
87   Surprisingly high tannin dominates the wine's fruit, which appears to have gone
            into hiding. While the wine possesses the potential to be very good, I do not see it
            ever equaling the quality level of the 1988, 1990, and 1991. Last tasted 5/96.

1988—Hermitage (red)   This thick, juicy, rich, black/purple-colored wine remains youth-
·   ful. There is enormous richness and plenty of tannin in this well-balanced, full-
90   bodied, exuberant, powerful example of Hermitage. It may turn out to be the
            longest-lived wine of recent vintages. Anticipated maturity: 2005–2020. Last tasted
            5/96

1985—Hermitage (red)   Very deep in color, this full-bodied, powerful wine admirably
·   balances muscle and finesse. Like many 1985s there is a precocious succulent
88   appeal, but the tannins are there for longevity. Anticipated maturity: now–2001.
            Last tasted 10/86.

1983—Hermitage (red)   Deeply colored, closed, and firm as most 1983 northern Rhônes
·   are, this rich yet full-bodied, tannic wine needs plenty of time in the cellar, but
88   there can be no doubt that it has the fruit to outlast the tannin. Anticipated
            maturity: now–2005. Last tasted 10/86.

DOMAINE FAYOLLE* * *

Address: Quartier des Gamets
       26600 Gervans
Tel: 4-75-03-33-74
Fax: 4-75-03-32-52
Wines produced: Hermitage Cuvée Les Dionnières (red and white), Crozes-Hermitage
          (red and white)
Surface area (white): 0.7 acres
       (red): 3 acres
Production (white): 2,100 bottles
       (red): 6,300 bottles
Upbringing (white): 12 months in enamel vats
       (red): 2 years in 10% new oak barrels
Average age of vines (white): 15 years
         (red): 45 years
Blend (white): 100% Marsanne
     (red): 100% Syrah

The young twin Fayolle brothers, Jean-Claude and Jean-Paul, are based in the tiny hamlet of Gervans, just to the north of Tain l'Hermitage. An engaging duo, they are well known for good white and red Crozes-Hermitage. However, they can make very good, even excellent red Hermitage from a tiny 3-acre parcel within the Les Dionnières (also spelled Diognères) vineyard. The wine (of which there are about 500 cases) is always characterized by a very deep dark color and lush, deep, blackberry flavors. The problem with Fayolle's Hermitage is that far too frequently there is excessive sulfur in the nose of certain bottles, inexcusable in view of the otherwise high quality level of their fruit. A sound but uninspiring white Hermitage is produced. Fayolle is one of the important sources for Guigal's white and red Hermitage.

VINTAGES

1990—Hermitage Les Dionnières (red)   The 1990 does display some stinky lees charac-
  ·   ter, but not enough to make evaluation impossible. It is a ripe, rich, round, expan-
86   sively flavored, supermature, sweet-tasting wine with abundant fruit, superripeness,
      and low acidity. The tannins are soft. Like the 1989, it will have to be drunk in its
      first decade of life. Anticipated maturity: now–2004. Last tasted 3/90.

1989—Hermitage Les Dionnières (red)   The 1989 Les Dionnières exhibits excellent dark
  ·   ruby/purple color, a big, smoky bouquet of cassis fruit and herbs, and fat, chewy,
87   fleshy flavors. While it will not be a long-lived wine by Hermitage standards, it
      should drink well for another 7–8 years. Anticipated maturity: now–2006. Last
      tasted 12/93.

1988—Hermitage Les Dionnières (red)   The 1988 Les Dionnières had excellent deep
  ·   ruby/purple color, a big, ripe, earthy, tar and roasted black fruit-scented bouquet,
85   deep, full-bodied, muscular flavors, plenty of tannin, and a somewhat clumsy feel
      on the palate. It is admirably concentrated, but slightly coarse and disjointed.
      Anticipated maturity: 1998–2008. Last tasted 12/93.

FERRATON PÈRE ET FILS* * *

Address: 13, rue de la Sizeranne
         26600 Tain l'Hermitage
Tel: 4-75-08-59-51
Fax: 4-75-08-81-59
Wines produced: Crozes-Hermitage, Hermitage Cuvée Les Miaux, Hermitage Le Reverdy
Surface area (white): no details provided
             (red): 9.1 acres
Production (white): no details provided
           (red): 15,000 bottles
Upbringing (white): no details provided
           (red): 12–18 months with 70% of the yield in barrels and 30% in inox vats,
                  very little new oak
Average age of vines (white): no details provided
                     (red): 30 years
Blend (white): 100% Marsanne
      (red): 100% Syrah

The middle-aged, reflective, gray-haired Michel Ferraton has 9.1 acres in Hermitage from which he produces red and white Hermitage. Ferraton Père et Fils also owns 13.5 acres of vines in Crozes-Hermitage. From time to time he produces a sweet vin de paille. Ferraton, whose attractive cellar in Tain l'Hermitage is just around the corner from the city hall and immediately behind that of Marc Sorrel, is passionate about his winemaking. His white Hermitage, which is 100% Marsanne, has changed to a more modern style, emphasizing crisp, fresh fruit. Older vintages were rather ponderous, viscous, rich wines with considerable character but annoying irregularity. His white wine comes from two vineyards, Les Diognières and Les Murets. His red Hermitage, which can be very good, occasionally superb, is from the two vineyards of Le Méal and Les Beaumes. He calls his cuvée of white Hermitage "Le Reverdy" and his red Hermitage "Les Miaux." Due to problems, especially in 1982, Ferraton began to filter his red wines, but he quickly abandoned the practice in the late eighties (with the encouragement of his American importer) because too much flavor and body were being stripped. Michel Ferraton remains very much an artisan winemaker and an extremely meticulous grower who can turn out very fine wine. Readers should also realize that Ferraton's pricing remains among the fairest in the northern Rhône.

VINTAGES

1994—Hermitage Cuvée Les Miaux (red)   The 1994 Les Miaux reveals that vintage's
·   soft, low acid, fruity character (reminiscent of 1985), and is full-bodied and rich,
89   with moderate tannin in the finish. If the wine puts on a little weight, it should
           prove to be outstanding after bottling. Anticipated maturity: 1998–2010. Last
           tasted 6/95.

1992—Hermitage Cuvée les Miaux (red)   The 1992 Les Miaux exhibits a dense color,
·   pronounced aromas of earth, herbs, and black fruits, elevated tannin, soft acidity,
87   excellent ripeness, and a full-bodied, powerful finish. The wine is approachable.
           Anticipated maturity: now–2009. Last tasted 6/96.

1991—Hermitage Cuvée les Miaux (red)   The 1991 Les Miaux offers a dense, dark ruby
·   color with purple nuances. A nose of peppery, sweet, overripe black fruit is followed
88   by a medium-bodied, tannic, tough-textured, closed, austere wine. Will the high
           level of harsh tannin be a problem? Anticipated maturity: 2000–2009. Last tasted
           12/95.

1990—Hermitage Cuvée Les Miaux (red)   From what is unquestionably the greatest
·   Hermitage vintage since 1961, this wine is black in color, with a huge, developing
96   bouquet of jammy cassis, mineral, spicy, floral, and licorice scents. Massively
endowed, with frightfully high levels of glycerin, extract, and tannin, this is an
old-style, superconcentrated, beautifully pure, well-delineated Hermitage. Wow!
Anticipated maturity: 2005–2040. Last tasted 12/96.

1988—Hermitage Cuvée Les Miaux (red)   Ferraton's 1988 Les Miaux continues to dis-
·   play annoyingly high acidity but adequate concentration. For the vintage, this is a
78   smaller-scaled wine than other 1988 Hermitage. Anticipated maturity: 1998–2006.
Last tasted 4/94.

1985—Hermitage Cuvée Les Miaux (red)   The fully mature 1985 is a soft wine with a
·   thick texture and a huge bouquet of wild-berry fruit, smoky tar, and animal scents.
90   Very intense and full-bodied, it has reached its plateau of maturity, where it should
remain until 2005. Last tasted 10/94.

1985—Vin de Paille (white)   Ferraton made a minuscule quantity of this wine, which
·   statistically has 22% potential alcohol. He harvested the Marsanne grapes on
93   October 10, 1985, put them on straw mats, and pressed them on January 15, 1986.
It is a wonderfully exotic, opulent, decadently rich wine with oodles of fruit and a
staggering perfume of apricots and peaches. It should keep for 50–60 years.
Unfortunately, fewer than 100 bottles were made. Last tasted 6/86.

1983—Hermitage Cuvée Les Miaux (red)   Another severe, very structured wine, Ferra-
·   ton's 1983 is full-bodied, with a chewy texture, very good concentration, and a
88?   smoky, tar-scented bouquet that remains youthful. But the tannin in the finish is
astringent. Anticipated maturity: 2000–2010. Last tasted 10/94.

ALAIN GRAILLOT* * *

Address: Domaine les Chênes Verts
        26600 Pont de l'Isère
Tel: 4-75-84-67-52
Fax: 4-75-07-24-31
Wines produced: Crozes-Hermitage, Hermitage, St.-Joseph
Surface area: 3 acres
Production: 600 bottles
Upbringing: 18 months in old oak barrels and casks
Average age of vines: 3–80 years
Blend: 100% Syrah

I have never been a great admirer of Graillot's Hermitage. His strength lies in his
excellent wines from Crozes-Hermitage and St.-Joseph that he produces at his Domaine Les
Chênes Verts near Pont de l'Isère. While he owns a small parcel of 80-year-old vines in Les
Greffieux, he also owns another parcel planted only in 1994. His Hermitage is good, and in
some vintages (1990), close to outstanding. It generally reveals a slightly herbal, young-vine
character without depth or intensity. It is also a wine to drink young. Obviously, when the
vines attain some age, this cuvée should rival if not eclipse Graillot's Crozes-Hermitage and
St.-Joseph.

VINTAGES

1995—Hermitage (red)   For whatever reason, the 1995 Hermitage was less impressive,
·   with less color than the 1995 St.-Joseph or 1995 Crozes-Hermitage. It revealed
87   smoky, bacon fat aromas in the nose, and sweet, ripe fruit on the palate, but the

wine's high acidity only seemed to exaggerate its angular, tough-textured, tannic finish. I am sure there is more to it, but it was extremely hard to penetrate and evaluate. Last tasted 6/96.

1994—Hermitage (red)   The 1994 Hermitage (only 50 cases produced, all from Les
· Greffieux vineyard) possesses a dark ruby color, a sweet, smoky, cassis-scented
88 nose, elegant, finesse-style, supple, ripe flavors, and fine length. This is never a blockbuster Hermitage in the mold of Jaboulet's La Chapelle, Chave's Hermitage, or Chapoutier's Le Pavillon, but it should not be underestimated. It should be ready to drink in 2–3 years and last for 12–15. Last tasted 6/96.

1992—Hermitage (red)   While peppery, spicy, medium- to full-bodied, and tannic, the
· 1992 Hermitage lacks the depth and intensity expected from the finest wines of
86+ this hallowed appellation. Cellar this wine for 3–4 years (I hope the fruit doesn't fade) and drink it over the subsequent 6–7 years. Last tasted 11/94.

1990—Hermitage (red)   The 1990 is the best red Hermitage I have tasted from Graillot.
· It offers up sweet-smelling aromas of black cherries, toasty new oak, and herbs. In
89 the mouth it is dense and full-bodied, with excellent concentration, a long, moderately tannic, unevolved taste, and a spicy, moderately tannic finish. Anticipated maturity: now–2008. Last tasted 5/94.

J. L. GRIPPAT (Red* * / White* * * *)

Address: 07300 Tournon
Tel: 4-75-08-15-51
Fax: 4-75-07-00-97
Wines produced: Hermitage (red and white)
Surface area (white): 3 acres
      (red): 0.7 acres
Production (white): 4,800 bottles
      (red): 1,800–2,000 bottles

Upbringing (white): 16 months in inox vats
      (red): 16 months in oak
Average age of vines (white): 75 years
      (red): 58 years
Blend (white): 100% Marsanne
      (red): 100% Syrah

Jean-Louis Grippat's cellars are on the outskirts of Tournon, just across the Rhône River from duller and noisier Tain l'Hermitage. Grippat, who is in his early fifties, comes from a winemaking family that has been producing both Hermitage and St.-Joseph for over a century. Now assisted by his daughter, Sylvie, he is an articulate, serious, discreet man who goes to considerable lengths to explain his winemaking technique, always expressing respect for his peers, and at times denigrating his own wines. For example, he is quick to admit that his red Hermitage is light and he would like to see it more concentrated. However, as he knows full well, it is his white Hermitage, as well as his red and white St.-Joseph, that excite tasters, and must be allocated because of their quality. In a normal year he produces only 400 cases of white Hermitage from the vineyard called Les Murets. His vines there average 70 years of age. His production of red Hermitage is only 150 cases. This is approximately one-third of his total production, the rest consisting of an excellent St.-Joseph white and two St.-Joseph red wines from nearly 11 acres of well-placed hillside vineyards.

Grippat's white wines, which are not as long-lived as Chapoutier's Chante-Alouette and de l'Orée, or Chave's, are gloriously rich and fruity wines that beg to be drunk during their first four or five years of life. They are aged in tanks for up to 16 months. In 1985, Grippat purchased three new oak barrels with which to experiment, but found he did not care for the taste it imparted to his white wine. Grippat's red Hermitage will not prove disappointing, but it is the white Hermitage that one should make a special effort to find. Additional information on J. L. Grippat can be found in the chapter on St.-Joseph, since it is essentially those wines that have earned Grippat his reputation.

VINTAGES

1994—Hermitage (red)   Grippat's 1994 Hermitage is one of the few wines from this
·   appellation that can be drunk young. Its low acidity and finesse style have resulted in
87   a supple, richly fruity (cassis galore), round, generous, flattering, medium-bodied,
          concentrated Hermitage. There is some tannin, but the overall impression is one of
          up-front, flattering, sweet fruit. Drink it over the next decade. Last tasted 6/96.

1994—Hermitage (white)   The 1994 white Hermitage reveals a honeyed, citrusy fruit
·   character, outstanding ripeness, rich, layered, unctuously textured fruit, and con-
89   siderable power and intensity. The wine's low acidity suggests consumption over
          the next 5–6 years. Last tasted 6/96.

1992—Hermitage (white)   The 1992 Hermitage displays a honeyed, pineapple, and floral
·   note, unctuously textured, thick, fat flavors, low acidity, and an excellent, powerful,
88   alcoholic finish. It is a weighty although fragile wine, so I would opt for drinking it
          over the next 2–4 years. Last tasted 11/94.

1990—Hermitage (red)   Grippat's surprisingly forward 1990 red Hermitage displays an
·   impressive saturated dark ruby/purple color, and a huge nose of black cherries,
88   minerals, and herbs. In the mouth, it is medium- to full-bodied, rich and full, with
          a generous and pure taste, soft tannins, low acidity, and a soft but authoritative
          finish. It may be the most forward 1990 red Hermitage I tasted, but that will not
          prevent it from lasting for 10 or more years. Last tasted 6/94.

1990—Hermitage (white)   Grippat's 1990 white Hermitage reveals a nose of honeyed
·   peaches, minerals, an almost Chablis-like cold steel component, and rich, full-
89   bodied, beautifully delineated and focused flavors. Already enticing, it should last
          for 7–10 years. Last tasted 6/94.

1989—Hermitage (white)   The 1989 white Hermitage is extremely fresh, pure, and lively,
·   with a bouquet that roars from the glass, revealing scents of wet stones, peaches,
88   and flowers. In the mouth, this amply endowed, full-bodied wine has gobs of fruit,
          lacks a bit of acidity and clarity, but offers a succulent, juicy mouthful of white
          Hermitage for drinking over the next 2–4 years. Last tasted 11/93.

1988—Hermitage (red)   I would have liked to have had a better impression of Grippat's
·   1988 Hermitage, given how many top wines were made in this vintage. However, it
82   is a straightforward, medium-bodied, relatively light, round, and fruity wine that
          should be drunk over the next 4–5 years. It lacks structure and length, and
          therefore should be consumed sooner rather than later. Last tasted 10/92.

GUIGAL* * *

Address: 1, route de Taquières
         69420 Ampuis
Tel: 4-74-56-10-22
Fax: 4-74-56-18-76
Wines produced: red and white Hermitage, all from purchased wine

This firm produces exquisite Côte Rôtie (see page 62), but also makes a good quantity of
white and red Hermitage. The Guigal family owns no vineyards in Hermitage, but meticulously purchases wine that has been vinified by the grower according to the Guigal formula.
Guigal produces his red Hermitage from 100% Syrah, refusing to blend in the 15% white
wine permitted by law. Just under 2,000 cases of red Hermitage are produced. Guigal does
not fine the wine and will not filter it if it falls brilliant naturally by virtue of its very long
aging (three years) in wooden barrels and large foudres. He is a believer in long wood aging

for Syrah, learning from his father that extended cask and foudre aging for Syrah usually leads to a softer, more complex wine. Consequently, he is always the last to bottle his red Hermitage. The white Hermitage, of which there are usually about 600 cases per year, is normally made from a blend of 90–95% Marsanne and the rest Roussanne. Unlike Guigal's other wines, which are normally very rich, dramatic expressions of winemaking art, the white Hermitage is somewhat austere, restrained, and not as impressive as his red Hermitage. In some vintages it can taste green and severe. Among all of the successful wines in the Guigal stable, I find his white Hermitage to be the least reliable, and his red Hermitage to have an increasingly shorter and shorter lifeline. Most recent vintages (since 1985), have begun to dry out around age 10–12. Would these wines conserve more of their fruit if they were bottled earlier?

Guigal plays it close to the vest with respect to where he purchases his Hermitage juice, but the Fayolles, occasionally Bernard Faurie, and the two Sorrels (Jean-Michel and Marc) are known to be suppliers to Guigal. Marcel Guigal has also confessed to me that he will not be content until he becomes the proprietor of some Hermitage vineyards. With the vast wealth this firm has earned from its worldwide success, readers should not be surprised to find out in the future that Guigal has purchased some important vineyards in this hallowed appellation.

VINTAGES

1994—Hermitage (white)   The 1994 Hermitage blanc exhibits a nose of spring flowers, minerals, and ripe peachlike fruit. With low acidity, as well as good denseness, **89** power, and extract, it should drink well during its first 5–6 years of life. Last tasted 6/96.

1993—Hermitage (red)   The 1993 Hermitage is an amazing success in a year known for the number of hollow, astringent, and vegetal northern Rhône wines. It possesses a **88** deep ruby color, as well as good ripeness, a sweet licorice/cassis-scented nose, and medium to full body. I detected no harsh acidity, hollowness, or tough tannin in the finish. It should drink well for a decade. This is an amazing cuvée for the vintage. Last tasted 6/96.

1992—Hermitage (red)   The 1992 Hermitage reveals some green-pepper notes in the fragrant nose, but at present, they take a secondary role to the spice, earth, and **86** black fruit aromas. The wine exhibits sweet fruit up front, and then the tannin begins to dominate. Although disjointed, this is a good effort that is best drunk over the next decade. Last tasted 6/96.

1992—Hermitage (white)   Guigal's medium-bodied 1992 white Hermitage is made in a lighter, more straightforward style than usual, but the vintage has contributed to its **85** character. Last tasted 6/96.

1991—Hermitage (red)   The 1991 Hermitage, made primarily from two vineyards on Hermitage Hill called Le Méal and Les Bessards, is lighter than either the 1989 or **88** 1990. It is a medium weight, elegant, ripe wine with expansive richness and a moderately tannic finish. It should drink well for 10–15 years. Last tasted 6/96.

1991—Hermitage (white)   The 1991 white Hermitage is a softer, riper, richer wine that was made in a precocious, flattering style. Both wines are best drunk in their first **87** 7–8 years of life. Last tasted 6/96.

1990—Hermitage (red)   Although variable from bottle to bottle, this wine can be Guigal's best recent red Hermitage. Marcel Guigal believes it is the finest Hermitage made **90** at this firm since 1955. I have followed the 1990 since I first tasted its component parts. It exhibits a nose of intense peppery, jammy, black-raspberry fruit intertwined with scents of smoke, vanillin, and spices. With full body, great depth of fruit, purity, and considerable tannin in the finish, it is already approachable because of its long aging in foudres and small barrels. This is a rich, thick, concentrated wine. Anticipated maturity: now–2009. Last tasted 6/96.

1990—Hermitage (white)   Guigal's 1990 white Hermitage is a full-bodied, authoritatively
· rich wine that has managed to retain some of its flowery, honeyed, peach-scented
89 nose. With some subtle oak in the background, this firm, concentrated, chewy-textured wine can be drunk. One of the most powerful and heady white Hermitages Guigal has produced, it may turn out to be as compelling as his 1988 and 1979. Anticipated maturity: now–2000. Last tasted 4/94.

1989—Hermitage (red)   Less concentrated than the knockout 1990, the 1989 reveals a
· tight but promising nose of minerals, blackcurrants, and roasted herbs, great rich-
89 ness, full body, and significant power and tannin. Anticipated maturity: now–2001. Last tasted 12/95.

1988—Hermitage (red)   The 1988 is Guigal's best red Hermitage since the 1983. More
· concentrated than either the 1989 or 1990, it exhibits an opaque, dark ruby/purple
91 color, and a huge, relatively undeveloped but promising perfume of cassis and minerals. In the mouth there is sensational concentration, dramatic flavors that are still in their infancy, and plenty of robust tannins in the impressively long finish. Anticipated maturity: now–2005. Last tasted 12/95.

1988—Hermitage (white)   Guigal's 1988 white Hermitage offers up a bouquet of honey,
· hazelnuts, and, if Guigal is correct, acacia flowers. In the mouth, it is rich, with
88 full body, plenty of glycerin, crisp acidity, powerful flavors, and a long finish. It is a large-scaled white wine for drinking with full-flavored fish and fowl dishes. Anticipated maturity: now–2002. Last tasted 8/96.

1987—Hermitage (red)   This wine is smooth, with supple, velvety flavors, medium body,
· very good concentration and ripeness, and a satiny finish. It is a worthy effort in a
85 vintage where Hermitage was generally less successful than the appellation of Côte Rôtie. It is clearly better than Jaboulet's La Chapelle, but I would have to rank it slightly behind Gérard Chave's. Mature now. Last tasted 12/93.

1985—Hermitage (red)   This is a very good 1985, which Guigal believes resembles his
· 1982. Quite rich, very dark garnet-colored with some amber, it offers a bouquet of
87 peppery cassis fruit. This full-bodied wine's low acidity resulted in a quick maturity curve, and the wine needs to be drunk up. Anticipated maturity: now–2000. Last tasted 8/96.

1984—Hermitage (red)   By Guigal's lofty standards, this wine is a bit light and insubstan-
· tial. The wine has surprisingly good color, high acidity, angular, tart, vegetal
74 flavors, and moderate tannin. Last tasted 1/92.

1983—Hermitage (red)   Very deep garnet colored, with a bouquet of ripe cassis fruit,
· cedar, tar, and herbs, this fully mature, full-bodied, concentrated wine has an
88 unctuous texture, sweet tannin, and good balance. Anticipated maturity: now–2002. Last tasted 8/96.

1982—Hermitage (red)   Another unqualified success for Guigal, the 1982 is much more
· fruity and accessible than the tougher 1983, but has deep ruby/black color, a
88 seductive, developed bouquet of ripe cassis and black cherries, full body, an unctuous texture, and ripe, velvety fruit despite a good lashing of tannin. Mature now. Last tasted 11/89.

1979—Hermitage (red)   At one time this was the finest Hermitage of the vintage after
· Jaboulet's La Chapelle and Sorrell's Le Méal. Guigal's 1979 was a big, beefy,
86 intense wine that seemed to be evolving better than the more highly acclaimed

1978. It is still a fine effort, but fully mature and in need of being drunk up. A bouquet of smoked meat, olives, and old saddle leather is showing some age. Although full-bodied and tannic, it is beginning to dry out. Mature now. Last tasted 7/96.

1978—Hermitage (red)   Extremely impressive early on, this wine has slid downhill fast.
·   The color is deep ruby with some amber, and the aromatics are dull and faded.
74   Little fruit remains in this hollow Hermitage. Last tasted 8/96.

PAUL JABOULET-AINÉ* * * / * * * * *

Address: Les Jalets   Tel: 4-75-84-68-93
R.N. 7, B.P. 46   Fax: 4-75-84-56-14
La-Roche-de-Glun
26600 Tain l'Hermitage

Estate wines produced: Hermitage La Chapelle, Hermitage Chevalier de Stérimberg, and occasionally an Hermitage Pied La Côte, produced when the quality is not good enough for the wine to be marketed as La Chapelle. In 1993, all the Hermitage produced was sold under this label as it was not up to the required standard of quality. Other estate wines include Cornas, Crozes-Hermitage Domaine de Thalabert, Crozes-Hermitage Domaine Roure (since 1996), and Condrieu. An entire range of Rhône Valley wines is produced through négociants.

Surface area (white): 11.1 acres
(red): 51.8 acres
Production (white): 25,000 bottles
(red): 90,000 bottles
Upbringing (white): 4–8 months in barrels 1–2 years old
(red): 12–18 months in old barrels, some new oak for La Chapelle
Average age of vines (white): 10–70 years
(red): 10–70 years
Blend (white): 50% Marsanne, 50% Roussanne
(red): 100% Syrah

I would surmise that the family-owned company of Paul Jaboulet-Ainé is the world's best-known producer of high-quality Rhône wine. Their most celebrated wine is the Hermitage La Chapelle (unquestionably one of the world's greatest dry red wines), named not after a specific vineyard, but after the tiny, white, solitary chapel that sits atop the steepest part of the Hermitage hill. This famous wine comes primarily from the two vineyards known as Le Méal and Les Bessards, where the Jaboulets own 51.8 acres. In addition, they possess another 7 acres of vines that are used only to produce a regular cuvée of red Hermitage and 11.1 acres of the La Croix vineyard utilized as a component in the firm's white Hermitage, which is named after the thirteenth-century crusader Gaspard Chevalier de Stérimberg.

The Jaboulet family may be the oldest in the Rhône, but all of the documented family history was destroyed during the French Revolution. The first Jaboulet, Antoine, was born in Tain l'Hermitage in 1807, and founded this firm in 1834. Today the firm, which has opened a new, modern facility south of Tain l'Hermitage, is run with obvious gusto and brilliance by the handsome yet boyish-looking Gérard and his brother Jacques, along with cousins Philippe and Michel. The father, Louis, now approaching 85, is occasionally there (although he officially retired in 1976), and is usually full of the joie de vivre that seems a particular family characteristic. The Jaboulets, in addition to their sizeable holdings in Hermitage, own the 114-acre vineyard of Domaine de Thalabert in Crozes-Hermitage that produces one of the finest red wines of Crozes (and which could easily be called the poor man's Hermitage). As négociants they produce another 200,000 cases, which no doubt contributes to their worldwide reputation and fame, but their flagship wines come from the estate vineyard.

The increasing fame of the firm's stupendous Hermitage La Chapelle is not difficult to understand. It is an enormously concentrated wine that normally takes a decade to throw off its tannic cloak. Even then it only hints at the majestic perfume and richness that will arise. It is an almost immortal wine in terms of longevity and from the perspectives of quality and complexity is equaled only by several dozen or so Bordeaux crus classés, a half dozen or so Burgundies, and an equal number of other red Rhônes. The wine is conservatively made to last. No more than 40% of the grape bunches were destalked prior to 1988, but beginning in that vintage, 100% destemming has been the rule. Only the wild yeasts from the vineyard are used to start the fermentation. The maceration period is very long, a total of 21 days, up to 30–38 days in great years (e.g., 1990) unless the skins of the grapes are unhealthy. All of this results in a densely colored, very tannic wine. Afterward, the wine is put in small Burgundy barrels (a small percentage new), acquired from the famed Burgundy cooper François Frères, and one- and two-year old barrels formerly purchased by Jacques Jaboulet from such prominent white Burgundy producers as Leflaive and Sauzet. Although they use some new oak, the Jaboulets dislike new oak, feeling that their Hermitage needs no additional wood tannins and already has so much size and fruit that new oak would only detract from its inherent qualities. The Hermitage La Chapelle is not clarified, but is given a light filtration after malolactic fermentation. In the early eighties, the Jaboulets did a prebottling filtration as well, but this practice was halted because of the adverse impact they deemed it to have on the finished wine. Curiously, Jaboulet is among the first to bottle his Hermitage; it rarely spends more than 12–14 months in wood. Compare that with 36+ months for Guigal, and 18–24 months for Chave. Today, only Michel Chapoutier bottles his Hermitage this quickly after a vintage. Gérard Jaboulet explains that this has always been their method, and one hardly need argue, for the results speak for themselves.

Most wine enthusiasts think of Hermitage as a thick, chewy wine with a dizzying degree of alcohol. However, the Hermitage La Chapelle, when mature at 15 or 20 years, is virtually interchangeable with a great Pauillac. In addition, the alcohol content rarely exceeds 13%. Much of the enormous impact this wine makes on the palate has simply to do with its fabulous layers of fruit, which comes from vines that average 40 years of age and grow in the granite soil of Le Méal and Les Bessards. Approximately 7,500–8,500 cases of Hermitage La Chapelle are made in an abundant vintage, not nearly enough to satisfy the thirst of increasing numbers of foreign clients who are this wine's biggest fans.

As staggeringly great as the La Chapelle is, the white Hermitage, the Chevalier de Stérimberg, produced from 60% Marsanne and 40% Roussanne, was largely a disappointment until recent years. The philosophy of making white wine at Jaboulet had been to ferment at very low temperatures, block the malolactic, and bottle the wine in March and April following the vintage, without the wine's ever seeing a day in wood cooperage. Far too often this wine has lacked character and flesh, tasting like some technically perfect but flavorless new world wine. However, there seems to be an effort by the Jaboulets since the early eighties to give their white Hermitage more muscle and character. This certainly holds true for recent vintages. While I have had some marvelous old Jaboulet white Hermitage (the 1969 is superb), it was not until the eighties that Jaboulet's white Hermitage began to improve. Usually a 50–50 blend of Roussanne and Marsanne (the highest percentage of Roussanne in the appellation), the wine is now put through a full malolatic fermentation and aged in 100% new oak casks. The grapes all come from well-situated parcels planted in Maison Blanche, Les Rocoules, and La Croix. Jaboulet's white Hermitage now appears to be a wine that will last for 10–15 years, particularly in top vintages.

A question that often comes up in vertical tastings of Hermitage La Chapelle is whether recent vintages possess the profound level of richness of the finest past vintages. Undoubtedly, 1978, 1988, 1989, and 1990 are great years for this wine. In fact, the 1990 will probably equal if not surpass the legendary 1961. The 1983 has not lived up to its prebottling potential, and a similar argument can be made about the 1982 and 1985. The 1986, 1991, 1992, and 1994 are more suave, commercially oriented wines, in total contrast to the blockbuster wines of extraordinary depth and complexity produced in 1959, 1961, 1962, 1964, 1966, 1970, 1971, and 1972. There is no question that the Jaboulets' slump in the early and mid-eighties was followed by internal problems resulting from an accident suffered by Jacques Jaboulet, the firm's winemaker. Yet from 1988, this firm seems to have come through this period without any damage. When I saw Jacques in summer 1996, he was in great form. His brother, Gérard, remains one of the most articulate and enthusiastic spokespeople for all the wines of the Rhône Valley. When you add the enthusiasm and energy of Philippe and Michel into the mix, this firm has a formidable and very talented team.

While this chapter deals only with the wines of Hermitage, Jaboulet's other wines, from their brilliant Crozes-Hermitage Domaine de Thalabert, to their impressive new Cornas Domaine St.-Pierre, and their portfolio of southern Rhône Valley selections, are covered under the appropriate chapters.

Historically, Jaboulet's huge production allowed the firm to market many of its wines under other names. The two brands that regularly appeared in the marketplace were André Passat and Jaboulet-Isnard. These wines were considerably less expensive, yet reputedly were the same wines, except for the La Chapelle. The use of these secondary brands has been discontinued.

VINTAGES

1995—Hermitage La Chapelle (red)   La Chapelle is the greatest wine in the Jaboulet
· portfolio, and the 1995 is unquestionably the finest La Chapelle made since the
91 sensational quartet of 1988, 1989, 1990, and 1991. Jacques Jaboulet now believes
the 1990, which I consider to be one of the all-time great La Chapelles, will
ultimately surpass the 1961 as the greatest Hermitage ever made by this firm! The
1995, which Jaboulet compares to the 1988 and 1982, boasts a deep ruby/purple
color, and a complex set of aromatics including scents of cassis, minerals, lead
pencil, and spice. The wine possesses good acidity, full body, outstanding richness,
and a tight personality. It needs 7–8 years of cellaring to reach its plateau of
maturity, after which it should last for more than two decades. Because of its fine
acidity, the 1995 reminds me somewhat of the 1972, with some of the 1988's
character. Last tasted 6/96.

1995—Hermitage Pied La Côte (red)   Jaboulet rarely sells their Pied La Côte in America
· as it is made from younger vines, purchased juice/fruit, and from less well-situated
85 parcels on the hills of Hermitage. The charming, open 1995 Pied La Côte is
Burgundylike with its cherry, herb, and earthy personality. Medium-bodied, with
crisp acidity, and a spicy, fresh finish, it should be consumed over the next 5–7
years. Last tasted 6/96.

1995—Hermitage Chevalier de Stérimberg (white)   A 50% Roussanne–50% Marsanne
· blend fermented in 100% new French oak, this is a powerful, thick, dense, chewy
90+ wine. Look for it to close down over the next several years, and not reemerge for a
decade. These are remarkably long-lived wines that remain fairly priced because
consumers rarely have the patience to wait for them to emerge from their closed
states. This intense, honeyed Hermitage is very dry, muscular, and weighty. The
1995 is the most successful cuvée Jaboulet has made since their spectacular efforts
in the late eighties and early nineties. Last tasted 6/96.

1994—Hermitage La Chapelle (red)   The 1994 La Chapelle displays admirable intensity,
with a forward, soft, round style reminiscent of a less concentrated version of the
88   1985. Although it reveals attractive richness and intensity, the finish is austere and
tannic. It will keep for another 10–15 years. Last tasted 6/96.

1994—Hermitage Chevalier de Stérimberg (white)   The 1994 is dominated by oak, is
high in acidity, with little richness, weight, or thickness on the palate. Last tasted
77   6/96.

1991—Hermitage La Chapelle (red)   The 1991 La Chapelle, which also had a 40-day
maceration, was harvested terrace by terrace because of the unsettled weather. It
88   is successful, with a personality not far removed from the 1985. Soft and ripe, it
reveals an excellent deep purple color, a rich, unformed but intense nose, medium-
to full-bodied flavors, excellent concentration, sweet tannins, and low acidity.
Anticipated maturity: 2000–2015. Last tasted 11/96.

1991—Hermitage Chevalier de Stérimberg (white)   The 1991 Chevalier de Stérimberg, a
45% Roussanne–55% Marsanne blend, was not put through malolactic fermenta-
88   tion as was the 1990. It did, however, spend two months in new oak casks. Rich,
deep, and medium- to full-bodied, without the power and authority of the 1990, it
possesses excellent richness, a honeyed nose and texture, and luscious flavors.
These wines can last for decades, so I would not be surprised to see this offering
hold up for 20 or more years. Anticipated maturity: now–2010. Last tasted 11/96.

1990—Hermitage La Chapelle (red)   The 1990 La Chapelle is monumental. It is almost
black in color. Tasted several times in 1996 along with the 1989, 1988, 1983, and
100   1978, it was easily the most intense and complete wine of the group. The finest La
Chapelle made since the 1961 and 1959, it is even richer, deeper, and more highly
extracted than the perfect 1978. The percentage of new oak was increased to 50%
because of the wine's power. The maceration period lasted an amazing 44 days.
While Jaboulet experimented with prebottling filtration during the mid-eighties,
this wine was put in the bottle with no processing. The huge nose of pepper,
underbrush, and black fruits displays amazing intensity. In the mouth the wine has
awesome concentration, extraordinary balance and power, and a fabulously long,
huge finish that lasts for more than a minute. The tannins are considerable, but the
prodigious quantities of sweet fruit and multidimensional, layered feel to the wine
make it one of the most incredible young red wines I have ever tasted. Anticipated
maturity: 2005–2040 +. Last tasted 11/96.

1990—Hermitage Chevalier de Stérimberg (white)   No doubt this will be a long-lived,
powerful Chevalier de Stérimberg. Made from a blend of 45% Roussanne and 55%
92   Marsanne, it spent seven months in oak and was put through malolactic fermentation. It is the finest dry white wine I have tasted from Jaboulet. After having had it
three times, I wonder why there are so few aficionados of white Hermitage. I know
these wines will require patience, but the 1990 should evolve effortlessly for 15–
20 years. Readers looking for something other than Chardonnay should check out
this full-bodied, brilliantly made wine. Anticipated maturity: now–2012. Last
tasted 11/95.

1989—Hermitage La Chapelle (red)   The 1989 La Chapelle is phenomenal. The opaque
black/ruby color and the huge bouquet of coffee, hickory wood, jammy cassis,
97   minerals, and spices are the stuff of legends. In the mouth the wine is massive,
with layer upon layer of unctuous, highly extracted, and superripe fruit. The finish,
once again, offers an extraordinary explosion of fruit, glycerin, and strong but ripe
tannin. My instincts suggest the 1989 will reach maturity several years before the
1990. Both the 1989 and 1990 possess low acidity, but the tannins in the 1990
are more powerful than in the 1989. These are two monumental wines that attest to

the glory of this renowned and historic appellation. Will they prove to be modern-day replays of Jaboulet's great duo of 1959 and 1961? Anticipated maturity: 2002–2030. Last tasted 11/96.

1989—Hermitage Chevalier de Stérimberg (white)   The 1989 Chevalier de Stérimberg
·   was fermented in stainless steel vats and then moved to 100% new oak casks for
86   six months. It reveals smoky, toasty, nutty aromas, good, ripe, fruity flavors, medium
        to full body, and soft acidity in its round, generous finish. Anticipated maturity:
        now–2005. Last tasted 6/95.

1988—Hermitage La Chapelle (red)   The 1988 La Chapelle continues to evolve slowly
·   yet reassuringly. I have several friends who argue that the 1988 will ultimately turn
93   out better than the 1989! I cannot see the same astonishing depth and flavor
        dimension in the 1988, but there is no question that it is a superb La Chapelle. It
        will need more time than the 1989 to reach full maturity. Powerful and extremely
        rich, it is a classic expression of the Syrah grape. I should note again that Jaboulet,
        after experimenting with filtration in the early eighties, decided to bottle his top
        cuvées without any fining or filtration. Anticipated maturity: 2005–2025. Last
        tasted 11/96.

1988—Hermitage Chevalier de Stérimberg (white)   The 1988 Chevalier de Stérimberg is
·   even more concentrated than the 1989, no doubt because their crop size for the
87   white wines was one-half of 1989. It exhibits a great deal of toasty vanillin oakiness,
        some hazelnut and flowery-scented fruit, full body, and greater depth and better
        acidity in its finish. Anticipated maturity: now–2005. Last tasted 6/95.

1987—Hermitage La Chapelle (red)   An unimpressive ruby color retains some youth, but
·   it lacks the saturation found in top vintages of this wine. The 1987 La Chapelle
86   reveals some peppery, tar, plum, and cherry-like aromas, with background scents
        of olives. Medium-bodied and compact, with good concentration, this is a lighter-
        styled, somewhat attenuated La Chapelle that is pleasant but unexciting. Antici-
        pated maturity: now–2005. Last tasted 11/95.

1986—Hermitage La Chapelle (red)   Deep polished ruby-colored, with a polite, re-
·   strained aromatic profile, this vintage, so disappointing in the northern Rhône, has
87   turned out a surprisingly pleasant La Chapelle. Although understated when com-
        pared to the great vintages, the wine exhibits more depth and ripeness than the
        1987, medium body, sharp tannin in the finish, good purity, and some of the noted
        cassis, cedar, and pepper characteristics that this wine can offer. It can be drunk
        now, but be careful, as its potential for longevity is limited. Anticipated maturity:
        now–2005. Last tasted 11/95.

1985—Hermitage La Chapelle (red)   This wine has quickly reached full maturity. The
·   color is a dark ruby/garnet with some amber at the edge. The nose offers up
89   sweet, roasted-herb, caramel, plum, cassis, and black-cherry fruit aromas with a
        suggestion of grilled meats and animal fur. Round and velvety-textured, with more
        noticeable acidity than tannin, this wine lacks the power and richness to be great,
        but it is certainly delicious, already complex, in the elegant style of La Chapelle.
        Anticipated maturity: now–2005. Last tasted 11/96.

1985—Hermitage Chevalier de Stérimberg (white)   Perhaps the ripeness of this vintage
·   has caused this wine to taste richer and more intense than normal. Larger scaled
86   in comparison with previous efforts, this big, alcoholic wine has scents of peaches
        and apricots in its bouquet. Drink over the next 1–3 years. Last tasted 6/86.

1984—Hermitage La Chapelle (red)   This wine's color is a medium dark garnet with
·   noticeable rust/amber at the edge. The innocuous bouquet offers a whiff of melted
79   road tar, pepper, and stale coffee filters. The wine reveals soft, herbal, cherry fruit
        that quickly fades to reveal some acidity, light tannin, and not much body or finish.

This wine is drying out and becoming more compact and attenuated. It needs to be drunk up. Last tasted 5/96.

1984—Hermitage Chevalier de Stérimberg (white)   Fragrant floral, wet stone scents are
·   of light intensity. On the palate, the wine is one-dimensional, fresh, a little tart, but
72   pleasant. Drink up. Last tasted 12/86.

1983—Hermitage La Chapelle (red)   This wine is so impossibly closed, tannic, and hard
·   that it is at least 10–15 years away from full maturity. I am beginning to have
90   reservations about my initial high rating, and have consequently downgraded it.
        While it may still turn out to be spectacular (the Jaboulets still consider it their
        finest effort since 1961), it is forbiddingly tannic and backward. Anticipated matu-
        rity: 2005–2030. Last tasted 11/96.

1983—Hermitage Chevalier de Stérimberg (white)   One of Jaboulet's better efforts with a
·   white Hermitage, the 1983 is spicy, fully mature, plump, and fleshy with good fruit
85   and a pleasing, somewhat alcoholic finish. Drink up. Last tasted 4/86.

1982—Hermitage La Chapelle (red)   This wine has turned out to be a satisfying, opu-
·   lently styled, multilayered La Chapelle with plenty of glycerin, extract, and alcohol.
92   It is a fleshy, succulent wine with explosive fruitiness, deep, peppery, wild blue-
        berry, cassis aromas intermingled with cedar, truffle, and oily cured Provençal
        olive scents. Dense and chewy, with some tannin still in evidence, and a youthful,
        dark ruby/purple/garnet color with no signs of lightening, this fully mature wine
        may resemble a more modern version of the always delicious 1971. Anticipated
        maturity: now–2010. Last tasted 11/96.

1981—Hermitage La Chapelle (red)   This wine's color is a surprisingly bright ruby with
·   only a touch of amber at the edge. However, there are no aromatics save for some
68   damp cellar and stewed vegetable smells. Lean, austere, short, and obviously made
        from diluted, unripe fruit, this is increasingly a disappointing wine. Hindsight is
        everything, but this wine should have been declassified. Mature now. Last tasted
        5/96.

1980—Hermitage La Chapelle (red)   A dark garnet color with moderate ruby at the edge
·   is followed by a wine with an interesting nose of fruitcake, sweet, overripe plums,
86   smoked meats, and Asian spices. The fragrant nose is deceptive given the medium-
        bodied, compact flavors. This wine possesses a tannic bite as well as acidic sharp-
        ness, with the fruit drying out in the finish. Although it needs to be drunk up, it
        still has merit. Mature now. Last tasted 5/96.

1979—Hermitage La Chapelle (red)   This exceptional La Chapelle continues to age
·   effortlessly. The color remains a deep, dark, opaque ruby/amber. Always under-
92   rated and overlooked because of the great vintage that preceded it, 1978, the 1979
        may not possess the flamboyant aromatics of the 1978, nor the massive attack and
        richness, but it is a full-bodied, formidably endowed, rich, more compressed style
        of La Chapelle crammed with fruit, medium- to full-bodied, and more measured in
        its style. There is a lot to this wine that is just beginning to offer up aromas of
        melted road tar, cassis, plums, cedar, and smoke. Rich but still tannic, this wine is
        near full maturity, but owners need not be in a hurry to consume it. Anticipated
        maturity: 1998–2015. Last tasted 5/96.

1978—Hermitage La Chapelle (red)   Still amazingly young at nearly 20 years of age, this
·   is a great bottle of Syrah. The color remains an impenetrably dark garnet. With
100   coaxing, the nose offers up aromas of herbs, superripe cassis fruit, minerals, black
        raspberries, fruitcake, and roasted meats. In the mouth this massive, full-bodied
        wine's level of concentration is profound, but the wine is still youthful. Is it possible
        that this wine may turn out to resemble a hypothetical blend of the 1961 and 1990?
        Truly magnificent! Anticipated maturity: 2000–2020. Last tasted 11/96.

1977—Hermitage La Chapelle (red) I thought I detected the smells of my mother's
 · fruitcake in the glass. Rather light on the palate, deceptively so in view of the
76 pleasant bouquet, this wine is fully mature and offers decent, uncritical quaffing.
 Mature now. Last tasted 2/84.

1976—Hermitage La Chapelle (red) This has never been an impressive example of La
 · Chapelle, and seven tastings of it have left me unmoved. The wine is now surpris-
81 ingly light in color with considerable rust at the edge. The dusty, herbal, earthy
 nose lacks ripe fruit. On the palate, the wine is dry, tannic, and in serious decline.
 Drink it up. Last tasted 5/96.

1972—Hermitage La Chapelle (red) The wine of the vintage! Hermitage enjoyed surpris-
 · ing success in this universally maligned year. This wine has been spectacular for
93 well over 10 years, yet it continues to evolve at a snail's pace. Still dark garnet-
 colored with some amber at the edge, it offers huge aromas of smoky Syrah fruit,
 herbs, and Asian spices. In the mouth, there is tremendous concentration, plenty
 of power, and a full-bodied texture. Interestingly, the acid is remarkably high, as
 are the ripeness and extract. This fully mature wine may last for another 10–15
 years. Anticipated maturity: now–2008. Last tasted 11/96.

1971—Hermitage La Chapelle (red) This wine, which was gorgeous to drink at age four,
 · has continued to get better and better. Seemingly too soft to last long, it flows across
92 the palate with a velvety texture and huge, smoky, coffee, herb, and black-raspberry
 richness. Full-bodied and smooth as silk, this spectacular La Chapelle will last
 another 10–20 years. Anticipated maturity: now–2010. Last tasted 11/96.

1970—Hermitage La Chapelle (red) Tasted twice out of magnum in late 1995 and again
 · in 1996, this wine is fully mature even from that format. What a complex, compel-
95 ling example of La Chapelle! The color reveals considerable amber at the edge, but
 there is a good deep ruby middle. The knockout nose offers up aromas of coffee,
 cedar, melted caramel, jammy fruit, and smoke. Opulent, with an unctuous texture,
 this full-bodied, exceptionally well-balanced, expansive, chewy La Chapelle is all
 silk, with no hard edges. It is the epitome of elegance, sweetness, and richness of
 fruit. It is hard to know how long it will hold at this magical level, but well-stored
 bottles should continue to drink well for another 10–12 years. Last tasted 5/96,
 from magnum.

1969—Hermitage La Chapelle (red) This has always been a firm, tannic, structured La
 · Chapelle, and it continues to age slowly. I would assume it is fully mature, but the
89 color is a healthy dark ruby/garnet with only slight amber at the edge. The nose of
 roasted coffee, cedar, macerated ripe plums in brandy, smoke, and Asian spices is
 intense, but not flamboyant in the style of the 1970 or 1971. The wine possesses a
 firm backbone, medium to full body, excellent to outstanding concentration, and a
 tannic bite in the finish. I am not sure whether this wine will ever fully open and
 blossom. It may always be a La Chapelle that plays it close to the vest. Nevertheless, it is an excellent (some readers may score it even higher) wine that will age
 for at least another 10–15 years. Anticipated maturity: now–2010. Last tasted 5/96.

1966—Hermitage La Chapelle (red) A magnificent example of La Chapelle, this wine,
 · fully mature for more than a decade, has magically held on to all of its fruit and
94 character, without dropping anything from its full-bodied, unctuously textured,
 multidimensional personality. The color is a medium ruby/garnet with considerable
 rust and amber at the edge. The fabulous aromatics include smoked meats, jammy
 berry fruit, Provençal olives, saddle leather, and coffee. Lush, fat, and rich, with
 low acidity, and no obvious tannin, this continues to be a luxurious, lavishly rich
 La Chapelle that has resisted losing its fruit. My tasting notes on this wine over the
 last decade have been almost identical. Mature now. Last tasted 12/95.

1961—Hermitage La Chapelle (red)   This wine was inserted as a ringer in a tasting of
·   old vintages of some extraordinary Bordeaux. I was able to guess what it was, but
100   not without difficulty. At first I thought it was a 1961 Latour à Pomerol, given its
           sweet nose and expansive, lavishly rich palate. However, with airing, some of the
           wild game–like, smoked duck aromas that I associate with Syrah began to emerge.
           The wine is in extraordinary condition. Still improving, it exhibits an unctuous
           texture, unbelievable concentration, and a profound bouquet. The finish is out of
           this world. It is unquestionably one of the greatest wines ever made! Still sweet
           and compellingly rich, this monumental wine can be drunk now as well as over the
           next 20–30 years. Immortal! Last tasted 7/96.

1959—Hermitage La Chapelle (red)   Another somewhat forgotten great vintage for La
·   Chapelle, the 1959 may not possess the sheer intensity and majesty of the 1961,
98   but it is not far behind. The color is a deep, dark garnet with some amber at the
           edge. The fabulous bouquet of Asian spices, black fruits, underbrush, smoke, and
           sweet barbecue spices is followed by a wine of enormous volume. Thick, unctuous,
           and full-bodied, with high alcohol, massive fruit, and low acidity, this is one of the
           most hedonistic, decadent La Chapelles I have ever tasted. The fact that it is more
           developed and fatter than the 1961 makes for thrilling drinking. Although it has
           reached full maturity, given its size and concentration, I would have no fear of
           aging well-stored bottles for another 10–15 years. Anticipated maturity: now–
           2005. Last tasted 11/96.

1957—Hermitage La Chapelle (red)   A surprisingly deep, dark garnet color is not indica-
·   tive of this wine's age. The nose is subdued for a La Chapelle with this much time
88   in bottle. Some plum, black-cherry, herb, and leather smells emerge. High acidity
           appears to be holding the wine together, keeping it youthful and at the same time
           less expressive than one would hope and/or expect. Medium-bodied, with excellent
           concentration, a youthful vibrancy, and a spicy, moderately tannic finish, this wine
           will easily last for two to three more decades, but I am not convinced it will ever
           fully blossom. Anticipated maturity: now–2010. Last tasted 5/96.

JEAN-MICHEL SORREL* */* * *

Address: 128, avenue Jean Jaurès
        26600 Tain l'Hermitage
Tel: 4-75-08-40-94
Fax: 4-75-07-16-58
Wines produced: Hermitage (red and white), Hermitage Le Vignon
Surface area (white): 2.47 acres
Production (white): 5,000 bottles
Upbringing (white): 24 months
Average age of vines (white): 70 years
Blend (white): 100% Marsanne

   The late Henri Sorrel was not only a prodigious winemaker but also a father of four sons.
In addition to Marc Sorrel, who is running the larger part of the estate inherited from his
father, there is Jean-Michel Sorrel. Jean-Michel, a practicing lawyer, and his wife, Michelle,
do the winemaking and marketing of the wines from this tiny 2.47-acre estate. They own
superbly situated parcels of 80-year-old Marsanne vines in Les Greffieux, and 80- to
100-year-old Syrah vines in both Les Greffieux and Les Méal. The white Hermitage is
vinified in cuves and then barrels, and bottled. The red wine has been inconsistent, which
is surprising in view of the terroir. Both the red and white wines often reveal less ripeness

and completeness than those of brother Marc. Nevertheless, this estate is worth keeping an eye on as the potential is enormous, although the quantities of wine are microscopic.

VINTAGES

1991—Hermitage (white) Jean-Michel Sorrel has fashioned a 1991 white Hermitage with
· a rich, forward nose, excellent ripeness, a dense, chunky texture, and a fine finish.
87 Forward, with low acidity, this wine should be drunk over the next 6–7 years. Last tasted 6/94.

1990—Hermitage Le Vignon (red) The 1990 Hermitage Le Vignon is an opaque, black/
· purple color, with a promising nose of gamy Syrah fruit and some noticeable
87 herbaceousness. While there can be little doubt concerning the wine's exceptional richness and full body, its acids are alarmingly high, even shrill, and the tannins sear the palate because of their astringency and ferocity. My experience suggests that astringent, hard wines such as this rarely come into balance. If the fruit does not fade before the tannins, my score may look conservative. This should prove to be an uncommonly long-lived wine, even by the standards of Hermitage. Last tasted 6/94.

1989—Hermitage Le Vignon (red) The 1989 Le Vignon has a heady, alcoholic finish, a
· deep ruby color, and a complex bouquet of spices, oak, and roasted cassis. In the
87 mouth it exhibits a sizable level of alcohol, low acidity, and a long, satiny finish. It should last for up to a decade. Last tasted 6/94.

1988—Hermitage Le Vignon (red) The 1988 Le Vignon is soft, round, and ripe, but does
· not have nearly the flavor dimension, concentration, or character of the 1989. It
86 should drink well for 6–8 years. Last tasted 6/93.

MARC SORREL* * * */* * * * *

Address: 128 bis, avenue Jean Jaurès
B.P. 69
26600 Tain l'Hermitage
Tel: 4-75-07-10-07
Fax: 4-75-08-75-88
Wines produced: Crozes-Hermitage (red and white), Hermitage Cuvée Classique, Hermitage Le Gréal, Hermitage Les Greffieux (debut vintage is 1993; made from vines planted in 1984), Hermitage Les Rocoules
Surface area (white): 1.7 acres
(red): 2.2 acres
Production (white): 2,300 bottles
(red): Cuvée Classique—5,000 bottles
Le Gréal—3,900 bottles
Upbringing (white): 12 months in oak, then in inox vats before assemblage
(red): Cuvée Classique—18–22 months in oak casks 8–10 years old
Le Gréal—18–24 months in oak casks 7–8 years old
Average age of vines (white): 45 years
(red): Cuvée Classique—25 years
Le Gréal—67 years
Blend (white): 95% Marsanne, 5% Roussanne
(red): Cuvée Classique—100% Syrah
Le Gréal—92% Syrah, 8% Marsanne

One of my fondest memories is of my first visit to the Domaine Sorrel in 1980. The ancient Henri Sorrel was in very poor health at the time, yet I was treated gracefully, and was touched by his enthusiasm. Until the mid-seventies Henri Sorrel sold his wine from Le Méal, Les Greffieux, and Les Rocoules to négociants. Based on two ecstatic reports about his wines, one from Mark Williamson of Willi's Wine Bar in Paris and the other from the late Martin Bamford, I visited Sorrel and was overwhelmed by the first two vintages I tasted in 1980, a compelling 1978 and an equally impressive 1979. Henri Sorrel died in 1982 and his son Marc, in his mid-thirties, with little training or experience, assumed control over much of the estate. The result was a disastrous group of wines in 1982 that were flawed by excessive volatile acidity. The failures of that year and the documentation of them in my wine journal, *The Wine Advocate*, resulted in my banishment from the domaine for several years. Despite the problematic 1982s, Marc Sorrel bounced back in 1983 with very fine wines and has continued to build on those successes. His estate is one of the finest sources of artisanal, very traditionally made Hermitage.

There are six wines produced by Sorrel. The white Hermitage, from a 45-year-old parcel of vines in Les Rocoules, is a solid, fleshy wine with a mineral- and pineapple-scented bouquet, some oakiness, and full body. In 1995, Sorrel introduced a Hermitage Les Greffieux made from 12-year-old vines. Two red Hermitage wines are made. There is a regular cuvée (Cuvée Classique) that is good but rarely stunning, and the top-of-the-line red Hermitage called Le Gréal, made from a blend of wine from a parcel of 50-year-old vines in Le Méal and 12-year-old Les Greffieux vines. Sorrel's father called the same wine Le Méal, since 100% of his cuvée was from Le Méal. It can be a stunningly rich, potentially long-lived wine, and in vintages such as 1978, 1979, 1983, 1985, 1988, 1989, 1990, 1991, and 1995, it is certainly comparable to the finest wines of the appellation.

Everything about Marc Sorrel's winemaking process is extremely "hands off," or artisanal. There is no destemming, although Marc did exhibit some flexibility in the difficult vintage of 1993 and removed stems from his Hermitage grapes. No new oak is utilized, and the wines are bottled after as much as two years of cask aging. The white wines can be enormous, drinking fabulously well for a few years, and then shutting down completely, needing 10–15 years to reemerge. The red Hermitage, particularly Le Gréal, can possess 20–30+ years of longevity.

In the nineties, seeking to expand his estate, Marc Sorrel purchased 5 acres of 50-year-old Marsanne and 7-year-old Syrah vineyards in Crozes-Hermitage. His vineyard in Larnage has proven to produce correct, pleasant wines, although the vineyard is entirely too young to assess adequately.

As the tasting notes that follow attest, the wiry, introspective Marc Sorrel is an uncompromising winemaker, and it is a pleasure to see the success he is enjoying.

VINTAGES

1995 —Hermitage Cuvée Classique (red)   The 1995 Cuvée Classique (one-third from Les
·   Greffieux and two thirds from Méal) is a crisp, vibrant, medium-bodied red Hermi-
86   tage with more acidity than usual. The color is a dark purple, and the wine is young
           and vibrant, as well as capable of lasting 10–12 years. It lacks the depth of such
           stellar vintages as 1988, 1989, 1990, and 1991. Last tasted 6/96.

1995 —Hermitage Le Gréal (red)   The 1995 Le Gréal exhibits a dense purple color,
·   followed by a powerful, sweet nose of cassis, smoke, and minerals. Well concen-
92   trated, with a sweet attack and a tannic, tart finish, this wine reveals the vintage's
           low Ph, but with enough richness and intensity to suggest that it will be very
           long-lived. Interestingly, I learned from Marc Sorrel that 7–8% Marsanne is har-

vested along with the Syrah and added into the blend of Gréal. The 1995 Hermitage Le Gréal will require 5–6 years of cellaring, after which it will last for two decades. Last tasted 6/96.

1995— Hermitage Cuvée Classique (white)   The 1995 Cuvée Classique (all of this wine now comes from Sorrel's holdings in Les Greffieux) is an open-knit, fruity, medium-**86** bodied wine with plenty of honeyed pineapple, as well as intriguing scents and tastes of minerals. It should drink well for 5–7 years. Last tasted 6/96.

1995— Hermitage Les Rocoules (white)   The 1995 Les Rocoules (from 45-year-old vines producing 28 hectoliters per hectare in 1995) exhibits a liquid slate/mineral-like **88** nose, cherry/pineapple/honey-like flavors, excellent definition, and plenty of power combined with good acidity, giving the wine more vibrancy and delineation. Last tasted 6/96.

1994— Hermitage Cuvée Classique (red)   Compared to the 1995s, the 1994 Hermitage cuvées are more seductive, flattering, and developed. The 1994 Cuvée Classique **87** is lighter than I expected, with an evolved, medium ruby/garnet color, as well as sweet, soft, sexy, ripe, cassis aromas intermingled with herbs, pepper, minerals, and spice. The wine is round, complex, and exceptionally aromatic (almost Burgundian in that sense), with low acidity, and a round, generous finish. Already delicious, it should continue to drink well for a decade. Last tasted 6/96.

1994— Hermitage Le Gréal (red)   The outstanding 1994 Le Gréal is more forward than usual, with a voluptuous texture and copious quantities of ripe cassis fruit inter-**90** mixed with earth, truffle, and mineral scents. This rich, full-bodied, forward Hermitage reminds me of the 1979 in its infancy. It is so well balanced, with well-integrated acidity and tannin, that it can be drunk now, although it is still an infant in terms of its evolution. It should last for 15 or more years. According to Sorrel, this is the last Gréal that will include any wine from Les Greffieux in the blend. Last tasted 6/96.

1994— Hermitage Cuvée Classique (white)   The 1994 Cuvée Classique is creamier textured, more open-knit, and richer (at least for now) than the 1995. It is ripe, round, **87** and generously endowed. Last tasted 6/96.

1994— Hermitage Les Rocoules (white)   The 1994 Les Rocoules is an outstanding example of white Hermitage, exhibiting high alcohol (14% was achieved naturally), a **90+** spicy, liquid mineral, honeyed peach/pineapple-scented nose, full-bodied, expansive, ripe, seductive flavors, an open-knit style, and admirable power and glycerin in the finish. These wines tend to drink extremely well within 1–2 years of bottling, then shut down, only to reemerge after 10 or so years of aging. Last tasted 6/96.

1993— Hermitage (white)   The 1993 Hermitage (only 100 cases were produced) is a surprisingly elegant, mineral-scented and -flavored wine with medium body and **86** good ripeness. It, too, should be drunk over the near term. Last tasted 6/96.

1993— Hermitage Cuvée Classique   The only red Hermitage produced in 1993 was the Cuvée Classique (which contains the declassified Le Gréal). It is light to medium **78** ruby-colored, with decent body, some herb, earth, and berry fruit in the nose, and a soft, undistinguished finish. Drink it over the next 3–4 years. Last tasted 6/96.

1993— Hermitage Les Rocoules (white)   The 1993 Les Rocoules, from what Sorrel claims was "the worst vintage I've ever seen," has turned out well. Harvested under **89** appalling weather conditions, the wine has fleshy, earthy, mineral-dominated, spicy fruit, fine ripeness, weight, and depth, and moderate length, as well as the potential to last 5–10 years. Superrich, with 14% natural alcohol, it is full-bodied, powerful, chewy, and intense. It is a brilliant success in a miserable vintage. Last tasted 6/96.

1992—Hermitage (red)   The dark ruby-colored 1992 Hermitage reveals a peppery, her-
·   baceous, sweet, cassis, and tar-scented nose, soft, voluptuously textured flavors,
87   excellent richness, and a ripe, medium-bodied, soft finish. Already drinkable, it
        should last for a decade. Last tasted 6/96.

1992—Hermitage Cuvée Classique (red)   The 1992 Cuvée Classique is a compact, nar-
·   rowly constructed wine with sharp tannin in the finish. It appears to have quickly
77   dropped much of its fruit, and may already be beginning to dry out. Last tasted
        6/95.

1992—Hermitage Le Gréal (red)   The 1992 Le Gréal exhibits a deep ruby color, as well
·   as attractive notes of cassis, cherry, herbs, and spice in its aromatics. It is an
87 +   excellent, tannic wine revealing full body, good flavor extraction, and a spicy, long
        finish. It needs another 2–3 years of cellaring and should keep for 15 + years.
        This could turn out to be a surprisingly fine wine in this irregular vintage. Last
        tasted 6/95.

1992—Hermitage Les Rocoules (white)   The 1992 Les Rocoules is a fat, fleshy, low-acid,
·   surprisingly ripe, round wine for drinking over the next 5–6 years. In great vin-
87   tages, this wine can last for 20–30 years, but in 1992 it is a wine to drink quickly.
        Last tasted 6/95.

1991—Hermitage (red)   The 1991 Hermitage is extremely good, with a dark ruby/purple
·   color, a spicy, herb, leathery, peppery-scented nose, excellent depth, chewy, tannic
88   flavors and texture, and a spicy, tough yet long finish. It will benefit from 3–5 years
        of cellaring and keep for 15 or more years. Last tasted 6/95.

1991—Hermitage Le Gréal (red)   The spectacular, black-colored 1991 Le Gréal, made
·   from yields of under 20 hectoliters per hectare (less than in 1990), reveals a huge
93 +   bouquet of Asian spices, licorice, black fruits, earth, and vanillin. Fabulously
        concentrated and full-bodied, with moderate tannin and layers of thick, juicy Syrah
        fruit, this is a terrific Hermitage. Anticipated maturity: 2000–2020. Last tasted
        6/95.

1991—Hermitage Les Rocoules (white)   Not surprisingly, the 1991 Les Rocoules is an
·   excellent wine (1991 was the best recent vintage in the northern Rhône). It offers a
89 +   honeyed apple, citrusy, mineral-scented nose, rich, full-bodied flavors that exhibit
        excellent concentration, and a spicy, chewy finish with fine glycerin, alcohol, and
        fruit. Anticipated maturity: now–2008. Last tasted 6/95.

1990—Hermitage (red)   Sorrel's tannic 1990 reds are savage and ferocious in their back-
·   wardness and full-bodied, rustic styles. The 1990 regular cuvée displays a nearly
88   black color, and an earthy, leathery, animal-scented nose that is followed by
        full-bodied, admirably endowed tannic flavors. The wine possesses the requisite
        depth of fruit to balance out the tannins. Anticipated maturity: now–2010. Last
        tasted 10/95.

1990—Hermitage Le Gréal (red)   The 1990 Le Gréal (made from vines planted in 1928)
·   attained 13.7% alcohol naturally! This blockbuster wine reveals an opaque black/
93 +   purple color, as well as a promising nose of licorice, damp earth, leather, and black
        raspberries. An awesomely concentrated, full-bodied, and enormously weighty and
        massive wine, its tough-textured, tannic, yet impressively long finish suggests that
        considerable cellaring is required. It will prove to be an extraordinary Hermitage,
        but how many readers are prepared to wait the minimum 10–15 or more years for
        the tannins to melt away? Anticipated maturity: 2005–2040. Last tasted 6/96.

1990—Hermitage Les Rocoules (white)   The 1990 Les Rocoules, while closed, is a
·   powerful wine. Made from vines with an average age of 46 years, it is a blend of
90   90% Marsanne and 10% Roussane. Only 300–325 cases were produced. There is a

floral component to the otherwise muted nose. The big, rich, honeyed flavors exhibit considerable concentration, full body, and a slight touch of oak. A big, thick, chewy wine that needs time in the cellar, Sorrel's Hermitage will provide riveting drinking for those with the patience to wait 10–15 years. Last tasted 1/96.

1989—Hermitage (red)   The 1989 regular cuvée of Hermitage displayed significant tan-
·   nin and a backward, closed style. However, it had just been bottled when I tasted
89 +   it and may have been slightly shocked, although Sorrel does bottle without filtra-
tion. Black/ruby in color, with a reticent but blossoming bouquet of plums, hickory wood, coffee, chocolate, and cassis, in the mouth the tannins have the upper hand at the moment, but there is no doubting its weight, richness, and layers of concentration. Anticipated maturity: 1998–2010. Last tasted 6/96.

1989—Hermitage Le Gréal (red)   This wine needs at least three more years of cellaring.
·   I suspect this is one of those nearly immortal examples of the vintage that will last
95   for 40–50 years. How often can one say that about modern-day Bordeaux or Burgundies? The color is black/purple, the nose reluctantly offers up smells of tar and spices (including soy), smoke, coffee, and cassis. In the mouth, there is a heady, chewy ripeness, extraordinary presence, and an almost massive amount of weight and fruit, all crammed into a well-delineated, rich, backward, tannic, sub-lime wine that is a benchmark example of red Hermitage. Anticipated maturity: 2000–2035. Last tasted 6/96.

1989—Hermitage Les Rocoules (white)   The 1989 Les Rocoules is attractively forward
·   and precocious, with more alcohol, lower acidity, and a fleshy, chewy texture.
90   These huge white wines almost seem out of sync with today's rush to drink lighter whites, but with aging, their finesse and gracefulness emerge. They should be served with powerful, flavorful, aromatic dishes. Anticipated maturity: now–2006. Last tasted 1/96.

1988—Hermitage (red)   The 1988 regular Hermitage is ripe, rich, more supple, and
·   slightly less concentrated than the 1989. But it is still a large-scaled, intensely
88   concentrated, excellent example of Hermitage. Last tasted 6/93.

1988—Hermitage Le Gréal (red)   The 1988 Le Gréal is another great wine, as well as a
·   blockbuster Hermitage, bursting with smoky, roasted, jammy, cassis fruitiness,
92   some attractive vanillin, oaky components, and gobs of highly extracted, rich fruit flavors that can only come from low yields and old vines. Anticipated maturity: now–2012. Last tasted 6/96.

1988—Hermitage Les Rocoules (white)   I was astonished by this wine's sensational ex-
·   tract, and incredible length and richness. Like the 1989, it should last for 10–20
93   or more years. It is impressively concentrated, and as rich and deep as any white Rhône wine I have ever tasted. It tasted almost like essence of white Hermitage. I cannot urge too strongly those adventurous readers who want to taste a remarkably individualistic, great white Hermitage to latch onto a few bottles of this rarity. It shares similar aromas and tastes with the 1989, but it is more opulent and concen-trated. Anticipated maturity: 1998–2010. Last tasted 1/96.

1985—Hermitage (red)   Surprisingly elegant, soft, with plenty of black-cherry fruit, this
·   medium-bodied, stylish wine has good color, adequate acidity, and low tannins.
85   Already pleasant. Mature now. Last tasted 12/90.

1985—Hermitage Le Gréal (red)   Significantly deeper and more aromatic than the regu-
·   lar cuvée, the Le Gréal has a smoky, toasty, plummy bouquet of excellent ripeness
90   and complexity, and long, rich, very intense flavors of black cherries. This full-bodied wine is loaded with fruit. Anticipated maturity: now–2003. Last tasted 12/90.

1983—Hermitage (red)   Medium dark ruby with an amber edge, this is a spicy, peppery,
·   medium- to full-bodied wine with good color, good depth of fruit, and a hefty
86   dosage of tannin still to shed. Will it dry out before the tannin is resolved?
           Anticipated maturity: now–2005. Last tasted 1/91.

1983—Hermitage Le Gréal (red)   Add another 1983 to the list of disappointments from
·   this vintage that may turn out to be too tannic. Ruby/garnet-colored, with an earthy,
88?   olive, cedar, and plum-scented nose, this medium- to full-bodied wine still has
           plenty of tannin to lose. Lamentably, I think the fruit is beginning to dry out.
           Anticipated maturity: now–2004. Last tasted 1/91.

1979—Hermitage Le Méal (red)   This remains a youthful yet sensational Hermitage.
·   Deep ruby/black in color (no amber) with an explosive bouquet of toasty oak, tar,
94   licorice, and jammy black-cherry fruit, this full-bodied wine has stunning layers of
           fruit, plenty of tannin, and exceptional length. Tasted three times since the first
           edition of this book, it has not budged in evolution. Anticipated maturity: 2000–
           2020. Last tasted 6/96.

1978—Hermitage Le Méal (red)   This is a monumental effort! I had only tasted this wine
·   once (with Sorrel in 1980), but thanks to the generosity of France's Michel Bettane,
98 +   I had it again in 1994. After 14 years of bottle age, the wine had barely changed!
           It remains black/ruby in color, with a superb bouquet that seemed to inundate the
           olfactory senses with coffee, olives, cedar, jammy fruit, and exotic spices. Still
           immense and massive on the palate, this hugely proportioned wine may have shed
           some tannin, but little else. It had unbelievable length, and for those lucky enough
           to have this wine cellared, it should offer considerable challenge to the monumental
           wines made by Chave and Jaboulet in 1978. A profound Hermitage! Anticipated
           maturity: 2000–2025. Last tasted 6/94.

UNION DES PROPRIÉTAIRES À TAIN L'HERMITAGE* *

In the southern Rhône Valley there are numerous growers' cooperatives, but in the north there are only three. The largest northern Rhône cooperative is in Tain l'Hermitage, with 540 members producing just over 25% of this appellation's wine. It prides itself on being one of the few cooperatives in France to age its wines in small oak barrels, and it employs a cooper full-time just to make barrels.

There is an entire range of northern Rhône wines made here, and if they are to be criticized, it is not for lack of careful winemaking, but rather for their lack of individuality and blurring (no doubt due to blending) of vintage differences. The wines are soundly made, but far too frequently taste very much alike. The top wines year after year are their white Hermitage and Cornas, of which the latter seems to show the most character, but their red Hermitage wines are also competently made in a thoroughly modern style. Prices for the cooperative's wines are quite fair.

L. DE VALLOUIT* */* * * *

Address: 24, rue Désiré Valette
            26240 St.-Vallier
Tel: 4-75-23-10-11
Fax: 4-75-23-05-58
Wines produced: Hermitage (white and red), Hermitage Les Greffières
Surface area (white): 0.62 acres
             (red): regular cuvée—1.2 acres
                   Les Greffières—2.2 acres
Production (white): 1,600 bottles
             (red): regular cuvée—3,000 bottles
                   Les Greffières—4,000 bottles

Upbringing (white): 8–10 months with half of yield in new oak and half in inox vats
(red): regular cuvée—2 years in 10% new oak barrels
Les Greffières—36–40 months in 10% new oak barrels
Average age of vines (white): 40 years
(red): regular cuvée—40 years
Les Greffières—80 years
Blend (white): 85% Marsanne, 15% Roussanne
(red): regular cuvée—100% Syrah
Les Greffières—100% Syrah

De Vallouit is an interesting, albeit often misunderstood producer. The fact that the cellars are in St.-Vallier, a drab, commercial city halfway between Côte Rôtie and Hermitage, may account for the fact that it is easy to bypass. An entire line of wine is produced, most of it at the négociant level, but some luxury cuvées from estate vineyards in St.-Joseph, Hermitage, and Côte Rôtie are worthy of the most demanding connoisseur's interest. For example, such red wines as de Vallouit's St.-Joseph Les Anges, Hermitage Les Greffières, and Côte Rôtie Les Roziers were top-notch in the wonderful trilogy of Rhône Valley vintages, 1988, 1989, and 1990. Descending below this level, the de Vallouit offerings are more irregular.

The old-fashioned underground cellars at the southern end of St.-Vallier, are run by Madame de Vallouit and her husband, Louis (a dead ringer for the British actor Stanley Baker). Little new oak is used, and the cellar is an amalgam of different sized casks, demi-muids, and foudres. Everything appears to be done traditionally, with some of the regular cuvées tasting desiccated because they spend too much time in wood. While disappointments can easily be found when tasting through any large négociant's portfolio, there are some surprisingly good wines from de Vallouit, as well as some superb luxury cuvées, a fact too few Rhône wine enthusiasts seem to notice. Apparently the de Vallouits also thought this was a problem. In 1990 they bought the exquisite eleventh-century Château de Châteaubourg, the leading sightseeing attraction on the western bank of the Rhône between Tournon and St.-Péray. They have turned this into a fine-quality restaurant and, more importantly, sales and tasting room for de Vallouit's wines.

VINTAGES

1991 —Hermitage (white)   The 1991 Hermitage (of which there are only 2,000 bottles)
· reached 13.5% alcohol naturally. A full-bodied, chunky, fleshy wine with obvious
88 glycerin and alcohol, it possesses at least 8–10 years of longevity. Last tasted
6/94.
1991 —Hermitage Les Greffières (red)   De Vallouit's finest red wine is their Hermitage
· Les Greffières. For example, the 1983, the debut vintage, may surpass the Hermit-
88 ages produced by Jaboulet and Chave. Approximately 350–500 cases of Les Greffières are made from a parcel of vines that was planted between 1912 and 1922.
The wine is aged completely in small new oak casks. The 1991 is fat, spicy, long,
and supple, with some noticeable herbaceousness. It does not possess the depth or
stature of the 1989 or 1990. Anticipated maturity: 2000–2012. Last tasted 6/94.
1990 —Hermitage (red)   The hard 1990 Hermitage is spicy and well colored, with ade-
· quate concentration, but when compared with Les Greffières, it is unimpressive.
79 Last tasted 6/94.
1990 —Hermitage Les Greffières (red)   The impressive 1990 Les Greffières is nearly
· black/ruby/purple in color, with extraordinary extraction of flavor, a huge nose of
95 minerals, black olives, cassis, cherries, and toasty, smoky new oak. In the mouth

this massive wine has a roasted quality. The tannins are considerable, as is the wine's formidable richness. This is a wine to cellar for at least 8–10 years. Anticipated maturity: 2000–2030. Last tasted 6/94.

1990—Hermitage (white)   This big white wine possesses plenty of power and concentration. I am not sure most modern-day consumers are prepared to lay away a white

87   wine for as long as some of these bigger, richer, backward, white Hermitages require, but this wine should develop into something that is very good to excellent. Anticipated maturity: 1998–2006. Last tasted 6/94.

1989—Hermitage Les Greffières (red)   The 1989 is a sweet, round, generously endowed, forward style of Les Greffières, with a bouquet of black cherries, herbs, and new

90   oak. Some of the tannins it exhibited before bottling have been shed, resulting in a large-scaled, rich, chunky, but potentially complex wine. Anticipated maturity: 2000–2015. Last tasted 6/94.

1988—Hermitage Les Greffières (red)   The black/ruby-colored 1988 Les Greffières is even more backward than the 1989 and 1990. Extremely rough-textured, it is,

91   nevertheless, powerful, and unbelievably rich and concentrated. Thick cassis aromas and flavors have been gently infused with some *pain grillé* from new oak. Huge, powerful, but oh, so backward, this full-bodied wine will test readers' patience. Anticipated maturity: 2004–2020. Last tasted 6/96.

1986—Hermitage Les Greffières (red)   This offering gets my nod as the best of the 1986s from Hermitage. Dark ruby-colored with no amber, this fleshy, surprisingly ripe,

90   nicely textured 1986 will offer ideal drinking over the next decade. Last tasted 6/94.

1983—Hermitage Les Greffières (red)   Should any readers come across the 1983 Les Greffières, do not miss the opportunity to buy it. I have had it on a half dozen

93   occasions and have always rated it in the low 90s. While it is still evolving beautifully, unlike many 1983s, the tannin is gradually melting away without a loss of fruit. This wine clearly has the concentration to balance out the vintage's tannin, which is not nearly as astringent as those found in Jaboulet's 1983 La Chapelle or Chave's 1983 Hermitage. It is a gorgeous wine. Anticipated maturity: now–2010. Last tasted 1/96.

OTHER HERMITAGE PRODUCERS

CAVES COTTEVERGNE–L. SAUGÈRE* * *

Address: Quartier Le Bret
        07130 St.-Péray
Tel: 4-75-40-30-43
Fax: 4-75-40-55-06
Wines produced: Hermitage La Côte des Seigneurs
Production: 3,000 bottles
Upbringing: 18 months in barrels 2–4 years old
Blend: 100% Syrah

BERNARD CHAVE* * *

Address: 26600 Mercurol
Tel: 4-75-07-42-11
Fax: 4-75-07-47-34
Wines produced: Hermitage (red)
Surface area: 2.96 acres

Production: 3,500 bottles
Upbringing: 8 months in 20% new oak casks
Average age of vines: 15 years
Blend: 100% Syrah

DARD ET RIBO* * *

Address: Quartier Blanche Laine
26600 Mercurol
Tel: 4-75-07-40-00
Fax: 4-75-07-71-02
Wines produced: Hermitage (red)
Surface area: 0.89 acres
Production: 600 litres
Upbringing: 15–18 months in barrels, new oak not generally used
Average age of vines: youngest 5 years, and the greatest part more than 100 years
Blend: 100% Syrah

ALPHONSE ET PHILIPPE DESMEURE–DOMAINE DES REMIZIÈRES* * *

Address: Quartier des Remizières
26600 Mercurol
Tel: 4-75-07-44-28
Fax: 4-75-07-45-87
Wines produced: Hermitage (red and white)
Surface area (white): 1.3 acres
(red): 5 acres
Production (white): 3,300 bottles
(red): 12,750 bottles
Upbringing (white): 10 months in barrels, new oak not generally used
(red): 24 months in 50% new oak barrels
Average age of vines (white): 5 years
(red): 25 years
Blend (white): 100% Marsanne
(red): 100% Syrah

AIMÉ FAYOLLE

Address: Le Village
26600 Gervans
Tel: 4-75-03-30-45
Wines produced: Hermitage (red and white)
Surface area: (white): 3.7 acres
(red): 6.2 acres
Production (white): 9,000 bottles
(red): 15,000 bottles
Upbringing (white): enamel vats
(red): barrels
Average age of vines (white): 25 years
(red): 25 years
Blend (white): 100% Marsanne
(red): 100% Syrah

MARCEL HABRARD

Address: 26600 Gervans
Tel: 4-75-03-30-91
Wines produced: Hermitage (white), although very little, if any, is bottled under the estate
name. Most is sold to négociants.
Surface area: 1.1 acres
Production: 3,000 bottles
Upbringing: inox vats for 8 months
Average age of vines: 20–100 years
Blend: 100% Marsanne

DOMAINE ST.-JEMMS

Address: Les Châssis
   R.N. 7
   26600 Mercurol
Tel: 4-75-08-33-03
Fax: 4-75-08-69-80
Wines produced: Hermitage (red and white)
Surface area (white): 0.62 acres
     (red): 0.62 acres
Production (white): 1,200 bottles
    (red): 1,500 bottles
Upbringing (white): 6 months aging in old oak casks
    (red): 12–18 months in cask
Average age of vines (white): 25 years
      (red): 25 years
Blend (white): 100% Marsanne
  (red): 100% Syrah

TARDIEU-LAURENT

Address: 84160 Loumarin

This négociant firm was formed in 1994. It is dedicated to buying juice from producers known for their low yields and/or old vines. Wine broker Michel Tardieu and Burgundian baker Dominique Laurent joined forces to establish this négociant business in the Château Loumarin, which has some of the coldest cellars in the southern Rhône. Their first vintages were impressive wines. Most of the selections were from the southern Rhône, but there were excellent cuvées from Crozes-Hermitage, Cornas, Côte Rôtie, and Hermitage. The wines are all aged in small oak casks, with an important percentage new, and bottled with no fining or filtration, as well as with low levels of SO_2. Based on the two vintages I tasted in the cellars of Tardieu-Laurent in June 1996, this looks to be an exciting new source for high-quality Rhône Valley wines.

VIDAL-FLEURY* * *

Address: R.N. 86   Tel: 4-74-56-10-18
   69420 Ampuis   Fax: 4-74-56-19-19

Vidal-Fleury purchases juice from different suppliers and then blends it in large foudres in their cellars in Ampuis. While most Vidal-Fleury wines are good values as well as consistent in their relatively high quality, their cuvées of Hermitage have been more irregular, with a pronounced vegetal character in some vintages.

CORNAS

The Real Black Wines of France

CORNAS AT A GLANCE

Appellation created:	August 5, 1938.
Type of wine produced:	Red wine only.
Grape varieties authorized:	only Syrah.
Total surface area:	1,358 acres, of which 220 acres are planted.
Quality level:	Good to exceptional.
Aging potential:	5–20 years.
General characteristics:	Black/ruby in color, very tannic, full-bodied, virile, robust wines with powerful aromas and rustic personalities.
Greatest recent vintages:	1991, 1990, 1989, 1985, 1979, 1978, 1976, 1969.
Price range:	$25–$30.
Aromatic profile:	Black fruit, earth, minerals, occasionally truffles, smoked herbs, and meats are common.
Textural profile:	Massive, tannic, nearly coarse flavors have full body, intensity, length, and grip, but are often too savage and uncivilized for many tasters.

The Cornas appellation's most profound wines:

Auguste Clape

Jean-Luc Colombo Cornus Cuvée JLC

Jean-Luc Colombo Les Ruchets

Paul Jaboulet-Aîné Domaine de St.-Pierre

Noël Verset Cornas

Alain Voge Les Vieilles Fontaines

Alain Voge Cuvée Vieilles Vignes

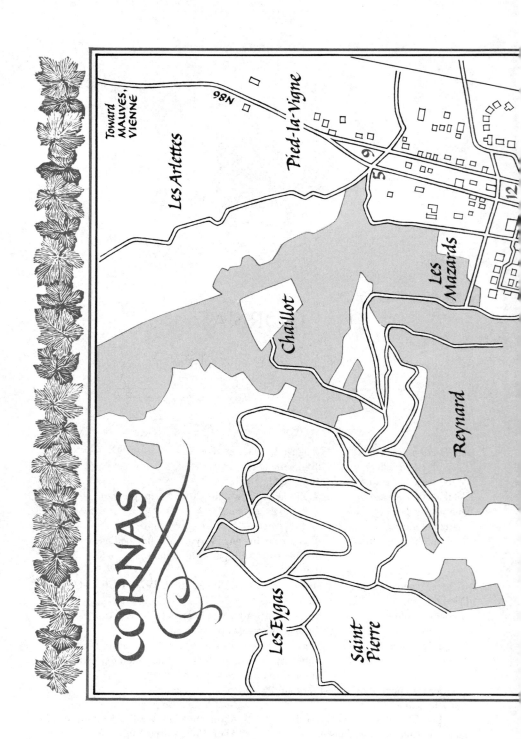

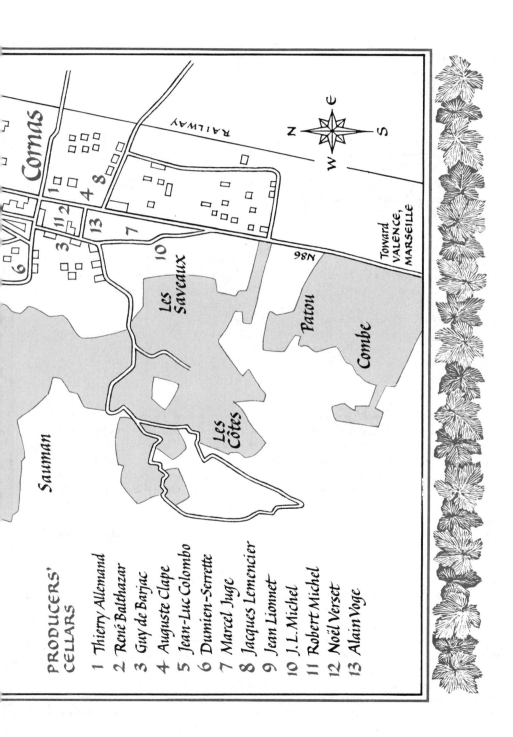

Cornas

RAILWAY

N86

Sauman

Les Saveaux

Les Côtes

Patou

Combe

Toward VALENCE, MARSEILLE

PRODUCERS'
CELLARS

1 Thierry Allemand
2 René Balthazar
3 Guy de Barjac
4 Auguste Clape
5 Jean-Luc Colombo
6 Dumien-Serrette
7 Marcel Juge
8 Jacques Lemencier
9 Jean Lionnet
10 J. L. Michel
11 Robert Michel
12 Noël Verset
13 Alain Voge

RATING THE CORNAS PRODUCERS

* * * * *(OUTSTANDING)

Auguste Clape
Jean-Luc Colombo (Cuvée JLC)
Jean-Luc Colombo (Les Ruchets)

Noël Verset
Alain Voge (Les Vieilles Fontaines)
Alain Voge (Cuvée Vieilles Vignes)

* * * *(EXCELLENT)

Thierry Allemand (Cuvée Les Chaillots)
Thierry Allemand (Cuvée Reynard)
L. et D. Courbis–Domaine des Royes
  (Champelrose)
L. et D. Courbis–Domaine des Royes (La
  Sabarotte)

Paul Jaboulet-Aîné (Domaine St.-Pierre)
Marcel Juge (Cuvée Coteaux)
Jacques Lemencier
Robert Michel (Le Geynale)

* * *(GOOD)

René Balthazar
Cave Coopérative de Tain l'Hermitage
Caves Guy de Barjac
Chapoutier
Jean-Luc Colombo (Terres Brûlées)
L. et D. Courbis (regular cuvée)
Delas Frères (Cuvée Chante-Perdrix)
Cave Dumien-Serette* * */* * * *
N. J. Durand

Domaine de la Haute Fauterie
Paul Jaboulet-Aîné (négociant bottling)
Marcel Juge (regular cuvée)
Jean Lionnet (Cuvée Rochepertuis)
Robert Michel (Cuvée des Coteaux)
Robert Michel (Cuvée le Pied du Coteau)
J. L. Thiers
Alain Voge (Cuvée Barriques)

The impenetrable black/ruby color, the brutal, even savage tannin in its youth, the massive structure and muddy sediment in the bottle are all characteristics of a wine that tastes as if it were still made in the nineteenth century. Yet for the adventurous, these wines, kept cellared for seven to twelve years, can unleash remarkable, powerful aromas of cassis, raspberries, chestnuts, and truffles. The tiny appellation of Cornas continues to survive against all odds. The best of these primitive wines are made from grapes grown on the steep hillsides of the western bank of the Rhône. This quaint, backwater viticultural area has been under the threat of a suburban housing boom from the nearby city of Valence. The inhabitants of Valence, desiring homes with a hillside location and a fabulous view of the Rhône Valley, have jeopardized more and more of the appellation. But even more dangerous to the future of Cornas is the expansion of vineyards on the valley floor beneath the steep slopes. These vineyards, planted in the overly fertile valley soil, may serve to diminish the blossoming reputation of Cornas more than French yuppies looking for a second home in the country. Wine from these valley vineyards clearly lacks the character and strength of that produced from the hillside sites.

The entire appellation of Cornas, like Côte Rôtie, lies on the western bank of the Rhône. However, the finest Cornas vineyards have a privileged situation. The sun-drenched vineyards sit in an amphitheaterlike setting with a south and southeasterly exposure, but the configuration of the surrounding hills gives Cornas protection from the severe, turbulent winds that can buffet the vineyards of Côte Rôtie and Hermitage. While this sheltered site affords relief from the powerful winds, the security from gusty winds serves only to exacerbate the effect of the summer's heat. The result is Syrah that bakes in the hot summer sun. Remarkably, temperatures are much higher in Cornas than in Hermitage seven miles to the north. Interestingly, the word Cornas is believed to originate from the ancient Celtic vocabulary and loosely translated means "burnt" or "scorched earth." The finest terroirs are mostly granite, with some limestone and clay, and, as one moves south toward the St.-Péray, more sand, and looser decomposed granite, particularly on the valley floor and lower slopes (called pied du coteau). In the northwest sector of the appellation, limestone is more prevalent. Like both Côte Rôtie and Hermitage, the hillside vineyards are buttressed by stone walls that form terraces that zigzag across the slopes. The slopes reach 800 feet in height in places and have a gradient of 45°, preventing the use of machines for cultivation. This special microclimate, the absence of any white wine in the blend to mollify the intense, powerful color, flavors, and tannin of the Syrah, as well as the ancient winemaking techniques employed by the village's growers, have resulted in what is truly France's most robust, enormously structured, and blackest-colored wine. The wines themselves, so powerful and youthful, even after a decade of cellaring, are forbiddingly raw and unapproachable in their youth. Yet the league of Cornas followers continues to grow and grow, and in top vintages, the finest producers sell out their entire crop before the wines are ever bottled. The best wines all come from the steep coteaux (or hillsides) behind the town. The grape is the Syrah and, as in Côte Rôtie, no white wine is made here. Unlike Côte Rôtie, no white wine Viognier grapes are even permitted to be grown. Given the increasing demand for Cornas, 80% of each year's crop is now exported, with the Dutch, English, Swiss, Asians, and Americans clamoring for Cornas.

Cornas is believed to be among the oldest vineyard sites in France, with references to the wines of this region appearing as long as 2,000 years ago. Local Cornas historians proudly recite the fact that Emperor Charlemagne paid the town a visit in A.D. 840 and tipped his goblet to the local growers. Despite its past and its remarkable location along the Rhône, as recently as a decade ago many growers felt there was no future in making Cornas. There were two reasons for this feeling.

First, the backbreaking labor served as an impediment to many prospective growers. Second, the prices fetched for Cornas were extremely low, forcing most growers to seek employment in the large factories across the river in Valence, or to plant fruit orchards to supplement their income. However, in the mid-seventies more and more interest began to develop in these unique wines, and the greater demand meant that higher prices could be established. Today, interest is so strong in the top wines that Cornas's best growers, such as Auguste Clape and Noël Verset, sell out a new vintage within four to six months. New vineyards have been planted and old vineyard sites left uncultivated are being reclaimed. Several large négociants with excellent reputations, particularly Paul Jaboulet-Aîné and, more recently, Chapoutier, have taken aggressive positions with respect to purchases of new vintages of Cornas, adding evidence to the belief that Cornas is an appellation whose wines are about to become fashionable. In 1993, the Jaboulets purchased 7.5 acres of steep hillside vineyards behind the village, calling their estate Domaine St.-Pierre. Yet, despite surging consumer interest, Cornas is still a remarkably undervalued wine.

This appellation runs from north to south, with the top vineyards cut out of the steep hillsides and ravines overlooking the Rhône River. The tenderloin section is immediately behind the village. These steep, terraced vineyards are the home for potentially the finest wine of Cornas. Two of the best vineyards are Reynard and La Côte. Reynard counts among its proprietors Robert Michel, Alain Voge, Auguste Clape, and Thierry Allemand. Parcels of La Côte are owned by Thierry Allemand and Auguste Clape. The well-drained, granite soils of Reynard and La Côte are prone to severe drought, so in extremely hot, dry years moisture is a precious commodity.

To the south of the village in the direction of St.-Péray the slopes are still sleep, but their orientation becomes more easterly, with some slopes actually facing north. The soils are again primarily granite, intermingled with limestone, and in the lower sectors at the foot of the hillsides, sand. The best vineyards in this area include La Combe, Sabarotte, Les Côtes, and Champelrose. Noël Verset owns important old-vine parcels in both Sabarotte and Champelrose. The fear of drought is less worrisome in these areas, and the vines are slightly less prone to the torrid heat that exists in the sheltered terraced vineyards behind the village.

The granite/limestone soils continue north of the village. The finest vineyard is Chaillots, whose prominent owners include Noël Verset, Alain Voge, Robert Michel, and Thierry Allemand. Further up the l'Ardèche hillsides, to the northwest, behind Reynard, are three lieux-dits called Les Eygas, Ruchets, and St.-Pierre (also referred to by the local cognoscenti as Les Aires). There are 25 acres of vineyards in this sector, one of the highest of the appellation. Jean-Luc Colombo has positions in all three of these parcels.

While changes occur at a glacial pace in Cornas, there has been a movement by some producers to sell multiple cuvées of wine. The most expensive is usually the hillside (or coteau) cuvée, or a single-vineyard offering from the coteaux, such as Robert Michel's Le Geynale, or the Champelrose and La Sabarotte of Laurent Courbis. The revolutionary young oenologist Jean-Luc Colombo, who has frequently stirred up emotions in the sleepy village of Cornas, calls one of his finest cuvées Les Ruchets after an old-vine parcel. Thierry Allemand is another producer to vineyard-designate his wines (Chaillots and Reynard). Other producers, such as Voge, can make as many as three cuvées; one of Voge's is called Vieilles Vignes, another Les Vieilles Fontaines. Interestingly, the two best-known and often greatest producers of the appellation, Noël Verset and Auguste Clape, produce only one cuvée of Cornas, blending their best lots together.

A word of caution is appropriate for readers anxious to rush off to their merchant to procure a bottle of Cornas. Cornas is a broodingly dark, rustic, massively proportioned, very muscular wine that can obliterate one's senses if modern, industrial, vapid, technically flawless red wines are the usual frame of reference. It is doubtful whether Cornas tastes much different today than when the Romans guzzled it down 2,000 years ago. But, if one has the patience to wait seven or up to ten years for some of its aggressive coarseness to mellow out, and for the huge, tarlike, peppery, cassis bouquet to develop nuances of truffles and saddle leather, one will be treated to a stunning gustatory treasure. It is convenient to compare Cornas to Hermitage, but in truth they are very different despite the fact that they share the same grape and are grown in much the same type of soil. Cornas is a more structured wine, yet it does not generally retain its fruit past 10–15 years as great Hermitage does. Why this should be is bewildering, for the wine seems initially to have just as much concentrated fruit as an Hermitage. Perhaps the rustic winemaking philosophy employed by virtually all the growers in Cornas precludes extended longevity for these wines. Undoubtedly, the fruit in most Cornas dries out after a decade and a half as the wine seems rarely able to support its huge tannin. Cornas is unlikely ever to resolve all of its formidable tannin, no matter how much sweet fruit it possesses. Cornas enthusiasts obviously enjoy the tannic rusticity of these wines. The top vintages of Cornas need seven to eight years to shed some of their tannin. Most Cornas should be consumed before the age of 15–20.

Few growers in Cornas ever filter their wines, so expect a five- or ten-year-old Cornas to have a tremendous amount of sediment, not only in the bottom of the bottle, but caked around the sides like a vintage port. This is one wine that demands decanting. In a village where most growers still do not own a telefax, it should come as no surprise that modern centrifuges and micropore filters, which make life easier for the winemaker, but can eviscerate the character and flavor of a wine with a switch of a button, remain largely unknown.

The overall quality of winemaking in Cornas is very good, surprisingly so in view of the antiquated winemaking techniques, ancient barrels, and dilapidated wine cellars of most growers. In spite of this high quality, and unlike other French wine villages, one could pass through Cornas without ever being aware that wine is made there. The drab village does little to promote its wines. Every grower sells wine directly to the consumer, and as a result shrewd Europeans can often be seen loading their car trunks with cases of the black wine of Cornas.

RECENT VINTAGES

1995 On paper, this looked like a very good to excellent vintage, despite two weeks of unsettled weather and intermittent showers in September. The wines have turned out to be well colored, but high acid levels give them a compact, compressed personality. Some wines taste as if they were made from underripe fruit. Such producers as Clape, Colombo, and Jaboulet turned in strong efforts, but overall Cornas was less successful in 1995 than most other Rhône Valley appellations.

1994 Despite significant rain before and during the harvest, 1994 has turned out to be a better vintage than 1995. The wines are low-acid, flattering, soft, and were already delicious to drink in 1996. The finest wines (from Clape, Courbis, Colombo, and Voge) are seductive and ideal for drinking between now and 2008. Nineteen ninety-four is an atypically soft, easy-to-understand vintage for Cornas. Neophytes take note.

1993 Like most northern Rhône appellations, this was a vintage of rain and rot. Nothing more interesting than pleasant, simple wines were produced. Most 1993 Cornas are hollow and astringently tannic, with underripe fruit flavors. It is the worst vintage for Cornas since 1977.

1992 A very irregular vintage because of rain and ripening problems, the best 1992 Cornas are easy to drink, fleshy, adequately colored wines for drinking before 2005.

1991 A very good to excellent vintage that was overlooked in all the hype over 1988, 1989, and 1990, the 1991 Cornas are among the most successful of the Rhône Valley. They are densely colored, ripe, rich, and chewy, with moderate tannin levels. This is a well-balanced vintage that will continue to provide wonderful surprises for 15 + years.

1990 On paper, 1990 looked like a great vintage, but some producers' vineyards suffered from the drought and torrid sunshine. The top wines, which possess remarkable concentration, will last for another 10–15 years. Clape made great wine, as did Juge, Lionnet, Michel, Verset, and Voge.

1989 A top vintage for everybody in this appellation, Cornas enthusiasts will have a delightful time comparing the merits of 1988, 1989, 1990, and 1991 as the wines evolve. The wines are more structured, austere, and tannic than the 1990s, but they are extremely concentrated, and in many cases massive, with plenty of body and tannin.

1988 A classic vintage for Cornas, the 1988s are muscular, broad-shouldered, massive wines with plenty of extract and tannin. The wines require further cellaring, and the top wines should easily last 20 + years.

1987 An attractive, soft, round group of Cornas was produced by the finest estates. The 1987s have been fully mature since the early nineties and need to be drunk up before the turn of the century.

1986 What looked to be a good year because of relatively healthy grapes harvested under good weather conditions has turned out to be largely disappointing. The early September rains prior to the harvest appear to have caused more dilution than initially believed. The wines are hollow, possess a vegetal streak, and seem to be drying out as they age.

1985 An excellent year for the growers of Cornas, 1985 produced a great deal of wine that is black/ruby in color, very fleshy, ripe, quite perfumed, tannic, but lower in acidity. Heat during the harvest did not cause any problems. The wines are fruitier than the tough 1983s. This has proved to be the finest vintage for Cornas between 1978 and 1991.

1984 Light-bodied, angular, and somewhat emaciated wines were produced in 1984. Few producers fared well, although Verset and Clape made very good wines that should be drunk up.

1983   Initially considered a classic year, increasingly loud grumblings about the level of astringency and high tannin content in the 1983s are now commonplace . . . and justified. For Clape, Verset, and Delas, it was an exceptional year in which one sees the requisite fruit necessary to balance out the tannin. The other wines remain nasty, astringent, and charmless. A vin de garde year, the 1983s will indeed keep for another 10–20 years, but will they ever be drinkable?

1982   This might have been a special year, but none of the growers in Cornas was equipped to cool down the fermentations. Torrid heat caused numerous problems for the growers, from overheated fermentations to total shutdowns due to excessively high temperatures. Many wines had color stability problems as well as volatile acidity. The négociants Jaboulet and Delas did better than many of the growers. Verset also made a fine 1982. In 1997, this is a dangerous year from which to buy Cornas; selection is critical.

1981   Nineteen eighty-one was much better in Cornas than in Hermitage and Côte Rôtie. The warmer microclimate gave a bit more maturity to the Syrah than elsewhere in the northern Rhône. The wines are overall more successful than the 1982s, medium weight, with considernbable tannin as well as color. The wines remain very much alive, but austere and angular.

1980   This is a very attractive vintage of relatively supple, fruity, lighter-style wines with good color, more charm and finesse than usual, and good, clean flavors. Most of the wines have been fully mature since the late eighties.

1979   An excellent vintage, 1979 was underrated at first; however, very deeply colored, rich, intense, full-bodied wines were produced that have evolved very well. The vintage is not dissimilar from 1978, a year considered great in the entire Rhône Valley. Clape, Voge, and Michel made stunning wines in 1979.

1978   As the 1978s have evolved, they appear to be slightly superior to the 1979s. They have also proven to be very long-lived, as few have reached full maturity. The wines are quite rich, dense in extract, still very tannic, and enormously long. Jaboulet produced an exceptional Cornas, as did Clape, Voge, Verset, and Juge. In overall brilliance, 1978 is one of the appellation's most magnificent vintages.

Older Vintages

Old vintages of Cornas rarely appear in the marketplace. The top vintages according to Clape were 1976, 1972, and 1969, and based on what I have tasted from Clape's cellars, I would agree. Michel and Voge claim 1969 and 1971 were tops. Barjac likes 1970. Vintages in Cornas, perhaps more than anywhere else in France, depend on the individual skills of the winemaker and his flexibility in dealing with the different climatic factors that shape each vintage.

THIERRY ALLEMAND* * * *

Address: R.N. 86
          07130 Cornas
Tel: 4-75-81-06-50
Wines produced: Cornas, Cornas Cuvée Les Chaillots, Cornas Cuvée Reynard
Surface area (Cuvée Les Chaillots): 3 acres
            (Cuvée Reynard): 3.2 acres
Production (Cuvée Les Chaillots): 5,300 bottles
            (Cuvée Reynard): 4,200 bottles
Upbringing (Cuvée Les Chaillots): 12 months, with half of yield in inox vats and half in old
            barrels
            (Cuvée Reynard): 12 months, with 40% of yield in inox vats and 60% in old
            barrels

Average age of vines (Cuvée Les Chaillots): 10–20 years
(Cuvée Reynard): 50–60 years (some 100 years)

Thierry Allemand is one of the up-and-coming stars of Cornas. In a village where most producers are in their sixties and seventies, it is refreshing to see Allemand, along with Jean-Luc Colombo, Jacques Lemencier, and Pierre-Marie Clape, forming the nucleus of a young generation of winemakers. Allemand began his career as a cellar rat for his neighbor from across the village, Robert Michel, for whom he continues to do some work. His first vintage was in 1982, but I did not taste any of his wines prior to 1990, the first year he split the production from his 6.2 acres of steeply terraced vineyards into two cuvées, Les Chaillots, from the vineyard north of Cornas, and Reynard, the superb, steeply terraced vineyard behind the village. Allemand also has a 2.5-acre parcel of St.-Joseph, which he sells to the Tain l'Hermitage cooperative. Allemand fashions blockbuster, opaque-colored, dense Cornas from small yields. They are bottled with no filtration, and often without fining. Generally, they are wines to lay away for 6–10 years.

VINTAGES

1995—Cornas Cuvée Les Chaillots   This wine exhibits a ruby/purple color, a sweet nose
·   of cassis fruit, and a crisp, tart, medium-bodied, acidic profile. It needs 2–3 years
86   of cellaring and is best drunk within 12 years of the vintage. Last tasted 6/96.

1995—Cornas Cuvée Reynard   This well-structured 1995 offers a ruby/purple color,
·   followed by a sweet nose of cassis fruit, violets, and earth. It is a medium-bodied,
88   crisp, tart wine with a long, powerful, concentrated finish. It will need 3–4 years of
cellaring and will keep for 15 years. Last tasted 6/96.

1994—Cornas Cuvée Les Chaillots   The 1994 Les Chaillots is a superb Cornas, with an
·   opaque black/purple color, and a pure, sweet nose of cassis, herbs, minerals, and
91   roasted meats. Full-bodied, with superb definition and richness, this is a large-
scaled, low-acid Cornas that should be approachable young yet keep for 15 +
years. Last tasted 6/95.

1994—Cornas Cuvée Reynard   The 1994 Reynard possesses an inner core of intense,
·   rich fruit. The wine exhibits a deep ruby/black color, wonderful purity and ripe-
89   ness, and a long, lush, low-acid, fat, unctuously textured finish. It should drink
well for 10 years. Last tasted 6/95.

1993—Cornas   This 1993 Cornas is one of the deepest, most saturated, dark ruby/purple-
·   colored wines of any of the Cornas offerings I tasted. The fine ripeness and sweet-
86   ness displayed in the nose are continued in the flavors of excellent black-cherry
fruit, licorice, and earth. There is a spicy, medium- to full-bodied finish with soft
tannin. Although it will be drinkable early, this is one 1993 Cornas with the depth
and concentration to merit serious consideration; it should last for a decade. Last
tasted 11/95.

1992—Cornas   The 1992 Cornas is also among the most concentrated wines of this
·   appellation. Dark ruby/purple, with an herbaceous, licorice, black-currant-scented
87   nose, it exhibits excellent ripeness, medium body, fine length, and an overall sense
of balance. It should be drunk in its first 7–10 years of life. Last tasted 11/95.

1990—Cornas Cuvée Reynard   Allemand's 1990 Reynard is a dazzling example of the
·   appellation. The color of this 1990 is black/purple. The nose offers up splendidly
93   ripe aromas of bacon fat and cassis. In the mouth, this wine is flamboyant and
rich, with surprisingly soft tannin for a Cornas, but fabulous concentration and a
full-bodied, lush, long finish. It should drink gorgeously for at least 10–15 more
years. Very impressive! Last tasted 1/96.

RENÉ BALTHAZAR* * *

Address: Rue Basse   Surface area: 5 acres
      07130 Cornas   Production: 10,500 bottles
Tel: 4-75-40-47-32   Upbringing: 18–24 months in old casks
Wines produced: Cornas   Average age of vines: 80 years

René Balthazar is one of the old-time traditionalists in Cornas, producing tiny quantities of wine from 5 acres of very old vines. No destemming takes place, and the wine is aged in an assortment of old foudres in Balthazar's tiny cellar. I have had little experience with this estate's wines, but recent vintages have all been strong efforts except for the weak 1993, a vintage where nearly everyone produced poor to mediocre Cornas.

VINTAGES

1995—Cornas   Balthazar's elegant, well-vinified 1995 Cornas exhibits a deep ruby/pur-
   ·   ple color, a soft suppleness, and less acidity than many of this appellation's offer-
86   ings. It is a stylish, finesse-style Cornas for drinking over the next 7–8 years. Last
     tasted 6/96.

1994—Cornas   The 1994 Cornas reveals deeper, richer fruit, plenty of cassis, an attrac-
   ·   tive, creamy, spicy oakiness, full body, round, generously endowed, low-acid fla-
89   vors, and excellent length. This is a nearly outstanding example of Cornas to drink
     over the next 10–12 years. Last tasted 6/96.

1993—Cornas   The 1993 Cornas exhibits a medium ruby color, a vegetal, dusty nose,
   ·   washed-out, hard, hollow flavors, and a tannic bite bordering on astringency in the
73   lean finish. Last tasted 9/95.

1992—Cornas   Although a successful wine for the vintage, the 1992 Cornas is less
   ·   powerful than usual. It exhibits a dark ruby color, a peppery, spicy, overripe nose,
86   fleshy, chewy fruit, and a surprisingly long, supple finish. Drink it over the next 5–
     7 years. Last tasted 9/95.

CAVE COOPÉRATIVE DE TAIN L'HERMITAGE* * *

Address: Route de Larnage
       B.P. 3
       26600 Tain l'Hermitage
Tel: 4-75-08-20-87
Wines produced: Cornas Les Nobles Rives, Cornas Les Vignerons Réunis
Production (Les Nobles Rives): 45,000 bottles
       (Les Vignerons Réunis): 30,000 bottles
Upbringing (Les Nobles Rives): 24–36 months with 70% of the yield in 1-year-old barrels
          for 12 months and the rest in inox vats
       (Les Vignerons Réunis): 24–36 months with 50% of the yields in barrels
          1–2 years old
Average age of vines (Les Nobles Rives): 35 years
       (Les Vignerons Réunis): 20–25 years

The Cave Coopérative de Tain l'Hermitage represents 15% of the production of the entire appellation. Twelve of its members own 37 acres in Cornas. Two cuvées are produced; one is called Les Nobles Rives and is sold under the name of the cooperative. The other, usually considered of lesser quality, is called Les Vignerons Réunis, and is not sold under the name of the cooperative. The main difference between the two cuvées is the age of the vines.

These are harvested and vinified separately. After fermentation, the eventual unsatisfactory portions of Les Nobles Rives are added to the Vignerons Réunis.

Wine lovers often turn up their noses at coop wines, but Cave Coopérative de Tain l'Hermitage has consistently made progress, and is unquestionably one of the better run coops in southern France.

CAVE DUMIEN-SERETTE* * */* * * *

Address: Rue du Ruisseau   Surface area: 3.2 acres
      07130 Cornas   Production: 7,500 bottles
Tel: 4-75-40-41-91   Upbringing: 18 months in old oak barrels
Fax: 4-75-40-47-27   Average age of vines: 50–80 years
Wines produced: Cornas

I have tasted only three vintages of Dumien-Serette's tiny Cornas production, but two of the three have been impressive. This estate produces interesting wines from their well-situated vines.

VINTAGES

1994—Cornas   A dark purple color is followed by a wine with a moderately intense nose of cassis, violets, pepper, and earth. The wine begins with a rich attack of ripe
88   fruit, but it lacks the weight of other 1994s, and finishes with astringent tannin. The wine's ripeness and low acidity are positive characteristics, but the hard finish is a worry. This should turn out to be a very good, possibly excellent Cornas for consuming 5–15 years after its release. Last tasted 6/96.

CAVES GUY DE BARJAC* * *

Address: 32, grande Rue   Surface area: 3.8 acres
      07130 Cornas   Production: 3,000–4,000 bottles
Tel: 4-75-40-32-03   Upbringing: 12–24 months in old oak
Wines produced: Cornas   Average age of vines: 50–92 years

The deep, baritone voice seems to go quite well with the aging but still ruggedly handsome face of Guy de Barjac, a lookalike of the late Yves Montand. When I first met him in the summer of 1986, I found him with a beer in one hand and a cigarette in the other, after what he called "a hot morning in the vines." De Barjac is drifting into semiretirement, and as he moves in that direction, he has leased out several parcels of old vines to other producers, an acre to Jean-Luc Colombo, and nearly 3 acres to Sylvain Bernard, whose Domaine de Fauterie is in St.-Péray. De Barjac's wines are deep ruby in color, robust, and capable of throwing plenty of sediment. De Barjac ages his wine in his, deep, old, cool, neatly kept cellars in very old oak barrels for 12–24 months prior to bottling. He is proud of his 3.8 acres of vines that average 50 years of age, with one parcel in the lieu-dit La Barjasse planted with 92-year-old vines. All of them are on steep hillsides. His wines are made very traditionally. There is fining but no filtration; only winter's cold weather is necessary, says de Barjac, to cause his wine to fall brilliant and be cold-stabilized naturally and gradually. He likes to drink his Cornas at five to ten years of age, and says it is ideal with game, meat, and strong cheeses. With much of his vineyards now leased to Colombo and Bernard, only 300+ cases of de Barjac's Cornas are available for the world market-place.

VINTAGES

1994—Cornas   Typical of de Barjac's wines, there is far less color saturation in his 1994
·   than in most other producers'. However, there is none of the volatile acidity or
87   mercaptan smells that often plague his wines. The 1994 is a soft, fruity, expansive,
         seductive Cornas for drinking during its first 7–8 years of life. Last tasted 6/96.

1993—Cornas   Always the last vigneron in Cornas to harvest, de Barjac could not have
·   liked his prospects in 1993 after the deluge dumped frightful quantities of rain on
85   the northern Rhône between September 25 and October 1. Nevertheless, his 1993
         Cornas has turned out to be a flattering, light-bodied, round, cleanly made wine
         with lovely fruit, low acidity, and a velvety texture. Drink it over the next 4–5
         years. Last tasted 9/95.

1992—Cornas   The 1992 Cornas exudes aromas of decaying vegetation and rot. It is a
·   major disappointment. Last tasted 9/95.
67

1989—Cornas   In the past I expressed my disappointment with the extremely light,
·   loosely knit, shallow, and fragile 1989 Cornas. Now that it is in the bottle, the
75   wine continues to reveal a lack of richness and a disjointed personality. It will
         have to be drunk over the next 2–3 years given its precarious balance. Last tasted
         11/94.

1988—Cornas   The 1988 Cornas is clearly de Barjac's best effort in the last three
·   vintages. Dark ruby colored, with soft, full-bodied, intense flavors, the 1988 exhib-
84   its some of the chewy texture one finds in Cornas, as well as spice, tannin, and
         alcohol in the finish. It will need time to resolve its tannin, and should be at its
         best between now and 2003. Last tasted 11/94.

1985—Cornas   As young Cornas wines go, the 1985 is quite flattering due to the lower
·   than normal acidity and ripe, soft tannin. It has very broad, velvety flavors, a big,
87   forward bouquet of peppery, blackberry fruit, and a sweet, long finish. It is quite
         seductive. Mature now. Last tasted 11/90.

CHAPOUTIER* * *

Address: 18, avenue du Docteur Paul Durand
         B.P. 18
         26600 Tain l'Hermitage
Tel: 4-75-08-28-65
Fax: 4-75-08-81-70
Wines produced: Cornas
Surface area: 10 acres. The wine is bought from several well-known producers, one of whom
         is Louis Verset. Chapoutier has a contract that enables its winemaking team
         to keep an eye on the vines, harvest, and vinification.
Production: 13,500 bottles
Upbringing: 12 months in 225-liter barrels, of which 25% are new
Average age of vines: 20+ years

VINTAGES

1995—Cornas   A very good, nearly outstanding 1995 Cornas, this wine is aged in small
·   oak barrels for one year before bottling. It exhibits this appellation's telltale, earthy,
89   cassis, savage, rustic character, plenty of tannin, and excellent depth, but there
         will always be a certain coarseness to the tannin in this wine, purchased from one

of the appellation's great growers. Look for this monster to last for 15 or more years. Last tasted 6/96.

1994—Cornas   Chapoutier's 1994 Cornas (most of the grapes were purchased from Louis Verset) exhibits an opaque purple color and a rich, moderately intense nose of cassis, black truffles, and minerals. Full-bodied, chewy, and tannic, this youthful, backward 1994 will benefit from 4–5 years of cellaring. Last tasted 6/95.

· **88**

1993—Cornas   The 1993 Cornas is vegetal, harsh, and charmless. Last tasted 6/95.

· **74**

1992—Cornas   A fine effort, the black-colored 1992 Cornas offers a sweet nose of roasted nuts, black cherries, and spice. Medium- to full-bodied, with moderate tannin and an alluring suppleness, this is a Cornas for drinking in its first decade of life. Last tasted 6/95.

· **89**

1990—Cornas   Chapoutier's 1990 reveals a dark purple, almost black color, a sweet, pure nose of cassis, fat, dense, full-bodied flavors, soft tannin, and a supple, velvety-textured finish. For a Cornas, it is surprisingly refined and approachable. Drink it over the next 8–10 years. Last tasted 6/94.

· **89**

AUGUSTE CLAPE* * * * *

Address: 07130 Cornas
Tel: 4-75-40-33-64
Fax: 4-75-81-01-98
Wines produced: Cornas, Côtes du Rhône, Vin des Amis (a vin de pays)
Surface area (Cornas): 10 acres
          (Other): 4.1 acres
Production: 24,000 bottles
Upbringing: 18–24 months in old oak
Average age of vines: 50–60 years

The scholarly looking Clape, who is in his sixties, has his cellars directly on the Route Nationale 86, which passes through Cornas. Like Marcel Guigal for Côte Rôtie, Gérard Chave for Hermitage, the Perrins, Henri Bonneau, the late Jacques Reynaud, and Paul Féraud for Châteauneuf du Pape, Clape is the rare winemaker who is not only the consummate craftsman, but also the passionate guardian of a tradition that in many ways he defined. No one disputes the fact that Clape's Cornas is the reference point for the appellation. Moreover, his success has created significant worldwide interest in the wines of this appellation.

Clape has one problem. Everyone wants his wine. Great French restaurants, for example the nearby Pic, Vrinat's Taillevent in Paris, and Guy Jullien's La Beaugravière in Mondragon, eagerly buy as much of his Cornas as he permits. His foreign buyers have been put on allocation, and he can no longer take new clients, for even in such a generous vintage as 1991 there is simply not enough wine to satisfy the demand.

Not that he has not tried. Clape has increased his Cornas holdings to 10 acres, of which 90% is located on the steep hillsides. His vines average 50–60 years of age, and produce an average of 2,000 cases of Cornas each year. Clape's vineyards are exceptionally well situated, just behind the heart of the village in the tenderloin sector of the appellation. He owns choice parcels of La Côte, Reynard, and, lower on the hillside, Les Mazards, and Pied la Vigne. From the latter parcel, Clape also produces a wine he calls Côtes du Rhône, but it is made of 100% Syrah from old vines at the bottom of the hillside. In short, it is a high-quality declassified Cornas. It is an especially good bargain, as is Clape's nonvintage vin de pays, called Vin des Amis. This 100% Syrah, usually from the most recent vintage, is a terrific, low-priced introduction to the Clape style. His wines spend 18–24 months in old wooden barrels and are fined once with the whites of eggs, but never filtered. Clape's wines, more consistent than Verset's, and more archetypical than Colombo's, are, in essence, the quintessential Cornas. They combine the robust, aggressive tannin and enormous structure of a Cornas, with a tremendous extraction of peppery, jammy fruit. This characteristic, plus the success of Clape in less spectacular vintages such as 1980, 1981, 1987, and 1992, has only added to his near mythical reputation. In most vintages, Clape's wines need a full six to eight years of cellaring, and in the best Cornas years, 1972, 1976, 1978, 1983, 1985, 1988, 1989, 1990, 1991, and 1994, his wine will age harmoniously for a minimum of 10 to 15 years. Fortunately for Clape, his fortyish son, Pierre-Marie, has decided to follow in his father's footsteps, a fact that fills Papa Clape with pride. Asked what he eats with his Cornas, Clape senior responds unequivocally, "Venison, rabbit, and Roquefort cheese. C'est tout."

To reiterate, the gentlemanly, articulate Auguste Clape is, more than any one person, responsible for the renewed interest in the wines of Cornas. It would be a shame for any serious wine enthusiast to pass up the opportunity to experience this man's outstanding wine.

VINTAGES

1995—Cornas   Clape's 1995 Cornas is a candidate for the wine of the vintage, although
·   the microproduction of Jean-Luc Colombo's 1995 Cuvée JLC is a worthy competi-
92   tor. Clape's 1995 exhibits an opaque purple color, and a fabulously ripe, sweet nose
             of licorice, black plums, and cassis, followed by full-bodied, dense, concentrated,
             well-balanced flavors with nicely integrated acidity and tannin. Yields were 30–32
             hectoliters per hectare (there is no secret to the high quality at this renowned
             estate). The 1995 should be a 20-year wine. Last tasted 6/96.

1994—Cornas   The 1994 Cornas is an outstanding effort, but far more open-knit, opulent,
·   and easier to drink than the 1995 at such a young age. The opaque black/ruby
90   color is accompanied by sweet aromas of truffles, black fruits, smoke, and earth. A
             voluptuous texture, great fruit, admirable ripeness, and superb purity make for a
             delicious, full-bodied, concentrated style of Cornas. It should drink well for 12–15
             years. Last tasted 6/96.

1993—Cornas   The 1993 Cornas possesses more character and a denser color, but once
·   again the shortage of fruit, glycerin, and a hollow mid-palate result in a straightfor-
78   ward tasting wine. Last tasted 9/95.

1992—Cornas   Clape's 1992 Cornas is one of the few successful wines of the vintage. It
·   reveals deep color, a licorice, mineral, and cassis-scented nose, medium body, and
87   a touch of overripe blackberries. With its deep, smoky, robust flavors, and moder-
             ately long, tannic finish, it will benefit from 1–2 years of cellaring and will keep
             for 10–12 years. Last tasted 9/95.

1991—Cornas   Cornas lovers will adore Clape's outstanding 1991. More elegant and less
·   concentrated than Noël Verset's (his friend and competitor), Clape's Cornas exhib-
90   its medium to full body, excellent depth, and a spicy, moderately tannic finish.
             Drinkable now, it should improve and last for 8–10 more years. Last tasted 11/95.

1990—Cornas   Clape's 1990 Cornas is outstanding. The color is an opaque black/purple,
·   and the nose offers up rich, ripe aromas of black fruits, licorice, and spices.
91   Superconcentrated, with a full-bodied, highly extracted, mouth-filling taste, this
             example of Cornas possesses moderate tannin, adequate acidity, and a smashingly
             long finish. It is also relatively refined for a Cornas, displaying no signs of the
             rustic tannin or funky, earthy smells many Cornas can possess. Although it can be
             drunk now, I would recommend waiting at least 3–4 years. Enjoy it over the next
             12–15 years. Last tasted 1/96.

1989—Cornas   The 1989 Cornas reveals a dark ruby/purple color, an attractive, berry
   ·   nose, substantial flavor authority, but less extraction of flavor and softer tannin than
   88   one normally expects from a Clape Cornas. Stylistically, it reminds me of a beefed-up
           1982, which was not an especially memorable vintage for Cornas. It should be ready
           to drink within 2–4 years and last for at least 12–15. Last tasted 1/96.

1988—Cornas   The 1988 Cornas is a more tender style of Cornas than I am used to from
   ·   Clape; it is not as concentrated as the 1989. It also comes across as lighter, softer,
   89   and not nearly as rich and full as most of this estate's wines tend to be. It is
           drinking surprisingly well at the moment. While some may applaud both the 1989's
           and 1988's lack of the forbiddingly raw, hard tannin that the savage wines of
           Cornas can possess, it is those characteristics that I feel make Cornas so distinctive,
           and repay those who cellar it for 10 or more years. Last tasted 1/96.

1985—Cornas   The 1985 reveals more depth of fruit and length when compared to the
   ·   1983. It is a fat, soft, lush wine with gobs of licorice, black pepper, and cassis fruit.
   90   Still a dense, dark purple color with no amber, this wine is about as ripe and round as
           Cornas gets. It is an unctuous, gorgeous Cornas that will provide tantalizing drinking
           young, but will also keep. Anticipated maturity: now–2005. Last tasted 8/96.

1984—Cornas   An exceptionally elegant Cornas, Clape's 1984 has a good bouquet of
   ·   earth, truffles, cedar, and berry fruit, adequate ripeness and length, medium body,
   86   and some acidity and tannin in the finish. Mature now. Last tasted 11/96.

1983—Cornas   Another huge, tannic, backward 1983, this wine continues to offer evi-
   ·   dence of considerable longevity. Opaque ruby/purple-colored (no amber), with a
   90   bouquet of blackcurrant fruit, pepper, and licorice, this enormously structured wine
           has outstanding depth and firm, abundant tannin. Anticipated maturity: 2000–
           2010. Last tasted 11/95.

1982—Cornas   Deep ruby-colored, with some amber, this spicy, earthy, herb, blackcur-
   ·   rant, truffle-scented wine has reached full maturity. Low in acidity, and a trifle
   85   shallow, it shows good (not great) color, a smoky, plummy nose, and mature, round
           flavors. Mature now. Last tasted 11/95.

1981—Cornas   Still deep ruby/purple in color, medium-bodied, peppery, and robust to
   ·   smell, this aggressive wine still exhibits a great deal of tannic toughness, but also
   86   fine fruit and length. It will always taste austere. Anticipated maturity: now–2000.
           Last tasted 11/96.

1979—Cornas   A very good, as well as slow to evolve vintage for Clape, the 1979 has a
   ·   ruby/purple color, a smoky bouquet with scents of roasted herbs and meat, full
   87   body, layers of flavor, good acidity, and plenty of tannin. Anticipated maturity:
           now–2008. Last tasted 11/96.

1978—Cornas   Fully mature, the 1978 reveals a deep purple color, an intense bouquet
   ·   of grilled meats and herbs intertwined with cassis, superb concentration, and firm
   90   tannin in the long finish. Anticipated maturity: now–2006. Last tasted 11/94.

Older Vintages

Clape's 1976 was outstanding. Among his top years, it is the only recent great vintage that
is close to full maturity. He also made a superb 1972. Although I have not retasted it since
1991, it exhibited a multidimensional bouquet of cedarwood, smoked meat, and oodles of
jammy blackcurrant fruit.

JEAN-LUC COLOMBO* * */* * * * *

Address: Pied de la Vigne
          07130 Cornas
Tel: 4-75-40-36-09
Fax: 4-75-40-16-49
Estate wines produced: Cornas Les Ruchets, Cornas Terres Brûlées, Cornas Cuvée JLC, and
          a vin de pays
Négociant wines produced: a range of wines made under the label Les Terroirs du Rhône
Surface area (Les Ruchets): 2.47 acres
          (Terres Brûlées): 10 acres
Production (Les Ruchets): 500 cases
          (Terres Brûlées): 1,650 cases
Upbringing (Les Ruchets): 15 months in 100% new oak
          (Terres Brûlées): 15 months in barrels 1–5 years old
Average age of vines (Les Ruchets): 80 years
          (Terres Brûlées): 20 years

The controversial oenologist Jean-Luc Colombo, in addition to doing consulting work for a significant number of Rhône Valley producers, is also a vineyard owner in Cornas. Much like Marcel Guigal 25 years ago, and Michel Chapoutier more recently, Jean-Luc Colombo is considered a radical revolutionary. Jean-Luc and his wife, Anne (both of whom hold oenological degrees), fell in love with the steep terraces of Cornas, and in 1983 formed Le Centre Oenologique des Côtes du Rhône.

Colombo's clients have increased significantly, despite all his critics. With his aggressive agenda, he has been a catalyst for major changes in many Rhône cellars. In large part, Colombo believes in complete destemming, malolactic fermentation in cask, an increased use of new oak casks, and more attention to sanitary conditions. In spite of his critics, he has garnered more than 110 clients (the number seemingly grows each week). Most objective observers would agree that Colombo has resurrected the quality of numerous famous but moribund estates (e.g., Château Fortia in Châteauneuf du Pape). Colombo is trying to accomplish what Michel Rolland and Denis Dubourdieu have achieved in Bordeaux—improving ancient winemaking practices in order to present accurately the personality of the vintage, terroir, and cépage. Are his critics willing to acknowledge how many Rhône wines were spoiled because of dirty barrel and cellar aromas? Colombo has promoted more organic farming in the vineyards, extended maceration to encourage softer tannin, and has moved toward softer bottlings with virtually no fining or filtration. Like some of his colleagues in Bordeaux, he has begun to do malolactic fermentation in barrel, which has only helped to increase the integration and subtlety of oak with the young wine.

Colombo has recognized the importance of promoting Rhône wines, a subject that tends to mortify most Rhône Valley producers. How refreshingly disarming this mentality is when compared to the massive promotion/publicity machines that exist in Bordeaux, Burgundy, and Champagne. Colombo and some of his clients have formed a group called Rhône Vignobles, and they have begun to visit other countries, including the United States, to promote their wines. Colombo has also become an increasing presence on the world scene, making presentations and tasting wines made from Rhône Valley grapes grown elsewhere in the world. He has visited California yearly, and even paid a visit to the Horton Winery, a Rhône Ranger estate in Virginia that produces Viognier.

Colombo began acquiring small parcels of vineyards in 1987, the year he purchased a superb piece of property called Les Ruchets, high up behind the village. He has added additional plots of land from Les Chaillots, Les Côtes, Les Eygats, and St.-Pierre. He also produces a vin de pays from young Syrah plantings in an area called Collines Rhodaniennes.

Additionally, Colombo leases a small parcel of vines from Guy de Barjac (an 8-acre vineyard in Chaillots). In the last few years, Colombo has begun a négociant business, buying juice and producing reasonably priced, well-made cuvées of Cornas, Côtes du Rhône, and St.-Joseph under a négociant label called Les Terroirs du Rhône.

Barbs of criticism are still directed at Jean-Luc Colombo, but in my opinion, much of it is because he is a relatively young man who can be aggressive and whose vision of the future does not tolerate a maintenance of the status quo. Like his soul mate in Tain l'Hermitage, Michel Chapoutier, he also expresses his opinions in too blunt a fashion. But if a man is to be judged by the products of his labor, his influence has been positive for producers of the Rhône. I would be remiss not to mention the importance of his wife, Anne, who, in addition to being the proprietor of the only pharmacy in the sleepy village of Cornas, helps run their oenological lab on the back streets of Cornas.

VINTAGES

1995—Cornas Cuvée JLC   The 75 cases of 1995 Cuvée JLC represent a wine made from
·   late-harvested Syrah grapes, aged in 100% new oak, and bottled with neither fining
92   nor filtering. It is a spectacular wine with gobs of black fruits, a thick, unctuous texture, and a sweet, rich finish with well-integrated tannin. It possesses enough acidity to provide definition and focus. It should drink well for two decades. Last tasted 6/96.

1995—Cornas Les Ruchets   The outstanding 1995 Les Ruchets is aged in 70% new oak
·   casks, put through a malolactic fermentation in the casks, and fined, but never
91   filtered. It exhibits a black/purple color, followed by an excellent nose of wild blueberries, cassis, earth, and vanilla. Medium- to full-bodied, deep, and rich, it is an impressive Cornas. It will require 3–4 years of cellaring, and should last for 15. Last tasted 6/96.

1995—Cornas Terres Brûlées   The 1995 Cornas Terres Brûlées is a medium-bodied,
·   black-raspberry-scented wine with fine color, nice spice, and a clean, international
86   winemaking style. Of the three Cornas 1995 cuvées, it possesses the most elevated acidity. Last tasted 6/96.

1994—Cornas Cuvée JLC   The finest wine produced by Colombo in 1994 is the Cuvée JLC.
·   The debut vintage for this wine, only microquantities were produced. Deep ruby/
91   purple-colored, with a chocolate, coffee, cassis-scented nose, opulent, sexy, evolved flavors, a chewy, sweet mid-palate, and a soft, round finish, this flattering wine is far more approachable than the 1995. Drink it over the next 5–8 years. Last tasted 6/96.

1994—Cornas Les Ruchets   Much richer and sexier than the 1994 Terres Brûlées, and
·   more austere and lean than its 1995 counterpart, the 1994 Cornas Les Ruchets is
88   a deep ruby-colored, tannic wine with gobs of ripe fruit. It is closed and backward, without the sweet, expansive mid-palate of the 1995. Last tasted 6/96.

1994—Cornas Terres Brûlées   The 1994s include this cranberry-scented and -flavored,
·   tart, but pleasing Terres Brûlées. Drink it over the next few years. Last tasted
84   6/96.

1993—Cornas Les Ruchets   In the atrocious 1993 vintage, Colombo's talent is admirably
·   displayed as he turned out two successful wines. The 1993 Les Ruchets is a sweet,
86   rich, ripe wine with medium to full body, good concentration, a healthy dark ruby color with purple tints, and a long, generous finish. It does not exhibit any of the angular qualities of the 1993 vintage, nor the bitter, astringent tannin or vegetal fruitiness. Last tasted 6/96.

1993—Cornas Terres Brûlées   The soft, round, well-colored 1993 Terres Brûlées exhibits
·   surprising ripeness and a sweet fruit-filled mid-palate (missing in most 1993s).
86   Moreover, there is a spicy, earthy, attractive black-fruit character to this medium-bodied, tannic wine. Drink it over the next 7–8 years. Last tasted 6/96.

1992—Cornas   The supple 1992 Cornas offers attractive new oak in its straightforward
·   bouquet of black cherries and roasted nuts, low acidity, and a tasty, chunky feel.
85   Drink it over the next 7–8 years. Last tasted 9/95.
1992—Cornas Les Ruchets   One of the best wines I tasted from Cornas. The wine
·   possesses an attractive, spicy, toasty, cassis-scented nose, rich, earthy, concen-
88   trated flavors, medium to full body, adequate acidity, and a soft, opulent finish.
           This is undoubtedly a top-notch success for the vintage. It should drink well for at
           least a decade. Last tasted 9/95.
1991—Cornas Les Ruchets   The 1991 Les Ruchets boasts a nearly opaque dark ruby/
·   purple color, a tremendous nose of black fruits (raspberries and plums), Provençal
92   herbs, and subtle, toasty new oak. Rich and full-bodied, with layers of fruit, low
           acidity, and a voluptuous texture, this rich, concentrated Cornas reveals surpris-
           ing finesse and complexity for a wine from this appellation. Yet it in no way loses
           what the French call "typicity." It should drink well for 10–12 years. Last tasted
           9/95.
1990—Cornas Les Ruchets   While Colombo's streamlined, compact 1990 Cornas Les
·   Ruchets is good, it lacks generosity, and its international style has a degree of
85   vagueness. Certainly the new oak has given it a distinctive style, but I do not detect
           the underlying richness that is evident in the 1991. The 1990 should be drunk
           over the next 7–8 years. Last tasted 9/95.
1989—Cornas Les Ruchets   One wonders what happened with Colombo's 1989, an exces-
·   sively oaky, medium-bodied wine that is out of balance. There is some concentra-
79   tion, but the oak has been permitted to obliterate what fruit remains. 1989 was not
           an easy vintage for the Cornas appellation, and this is an example of a wine where
           the use of new oak casks should have been eschewed. Last tasted 6/95.

L. ET D. COURBIS–DOMAINE DES ROYES* * */* * * *

Address: 07130 Châteaubourg
Tel: 4-75-40-32-12
Fax: 4-75-40-25-39
Wines produced: Cornas Champelrose, Cornas La Sabarotte, St.-Joseph (red and white)
Surface area: 10 acres
Production: 15,000 bottles
Upbringing: 14–18 months in barrel, tank, and foudre (30% new oak casks)
Average age of vines: 25 years

There is a wind of change and optimism blowing at this estate situated near the impressive
walled village of Châteaubourg. While most of Courbis's production is St.-Joseph sold under
the name of Domaine des Royes, he has begun to bottle two single-vineyard Cornas cuvées
—La Sabarotte and Champelrose—from the steep terraces south of downtown Cornas.
Courbis had the intelligence to seek outside assistance, as witnessed by his hiring of the
influential oenologist Jean-Luc Colombo. Brothers Laurent and Dominique Courbis have
demonstrated an enormous commitment to the future of Cornas and St.-Joseph by obtaining
the rights to clear and cultivate some very steep hillsides in both appellations. Based on
recent vintages, where Courbis's offerings have been among the top wines of these two
appellations, Courbis is a name to watch in the northern Rhône.
     The vinification includes completely destemming the grapes (a position taken by most of
Jean-Luc Colombo's clients), and vinification in temperature-controlled stainless steel tanks,
with a relatively long cuvaison. Approximately 30% new oak barrels are now being utilized
for the two cuvées of Cornas. It would appear that America has not yet discovered the wines
of Laurent and Dominique Courbis, as 90% of the wine is sold within France.

VINTAGES

1995—Cornas Champelrose   The 1995 Champelrose exhibits a dark ruby/purple color,
·   good spice and black fruits in the nose, as well as woody notes, but it narrows out,
84   becoming compact and compressed. It should last for a decade or more. Last tasted
        6/96.

1995—Cornas La Sabarotte   The 1995 La Sabarotte reveals a more intense purple color,
·   a sweeter, more smoky, black-fruit-dominated nose, a softer attack, medium body,
87   and well-integrated acidity with good fruit and structure. It should be consumed
        over the next 8–10 years. Last tasted 6/96.

1994—Cornas Champelrose   The 1994 Champelrose offers a deep purple color, an excel-
·   lent toasty, smoky, cassis-scented nose, fine ripeness, medium to full body, good
87   density and richness, and a low-acid, round, generously endowed finish. It can be
        drunk now or over the next 10–12 years. Last tasted 6/96.

1994—Cornas La Sabarotte   The 1994 La Sabarotte (which sees 32% new oak casks)
·   exhibits a Burgundy-like, black-cherry, cassis, *pain grillé*-scented nose, expansive,
89 +   voluptuously textured flavors, sweet ripe fruit, and an opulent finish. It is a delicious,
        appealing style of Cornas to drink over the next decade. Last tasted 6/96.

1993—Cornas Champelrose   Laurent and Dominique Courbis produced a light- to
·   medium-bodied 1993 Champelrose with attractive, moderately intense raspberry
84   and cherry fruit. Soft and already evolved, this lightweight Cornas should be drunk
        over the next 3–4 years. Last tasted 6/96.

1993—Cornas La Sabarotte   The 1993 La Sabarotte exhibits a healthy dark color, but the
·   wine is dominated by a hard, tannic personality, and compact aromatic and flavor
79   profiles. It is likely to dry out, so drink it over the near term. Last tasted 6/96.

1992—Cornas Champelrose   The 1992 Champelrose reveals more dilution, a mushroomy,
·   earthy quality (rot?), light body, and dusty, hard tannin in the finish. It lacks fruit
76   and depth. Last tasted 6/96.

1992—Cornas La Sabarotte   The 1992 La Sabarotte is cleaner, with a solid foursquare
·   personality. It should drink well for 4–6 years. Last tasted 6/96.
85

DELAS FRÈRES* * *

Address: Z. A. de l'Olivet
         07300 St.-Jean de Muzols
Tel: 4-75-08-60-30
Fax: 4-75-08-53-67
Wines produced: Cornas Cuvée Chante-Perdrix, Cornas Cuvée Les Serres
Production (Chante-Perdrix): 25,000 bottles
          (Cuvée Les Serres): 25,000 bottles
Upbringing (Chante-Perdrix): 12–14 months, with 60% of the yield in barrels 1–5 years old
          and 40% in oak casks
          (Cuvée Les Serres): 12–14 months, with 60% of the yield in barrels 1–5 years
          old and 40% in oak casks

This firm, which produces an entire range of wines from both its own vineyards in the northern Rhône and from purchased wine and grapes from growers throughout the region, used to have a small parcel of 2.5 acres in Cornas, which they sold in the early eighties. Today, their Cornas production is made 100% from purchased grapes. While I have had some good vintages of Cornas, recent examples have been largely disappointing. The perplexing nature of this firm's wines has been uninspiring.

VINTAGES

1993—Cornas Chante-Perdrix   Medium dark ruby-colored, this wine reveals no percepti-
  ·   ble fruit in its aroma, lean, austere, tannic flavors, medium body, and astringent
 71   tannin. Even if I were a masochist, I would not enjoy this wine. Last tasted 7/96.
1992—Cornas Chante-Perdrix   Thin, vegetal, and diluted, this wine is extremely disap-
  ·   pointing. Last tasted 7/96.
 68

DOMAINE DE LA HAUTE FAUTERIE* * *

Address: 07130 St.-Péray   Production: 6,000 bottles
Tel: 4-75-40-46-17   Upbringing: 18 months in barrels 1–2 years
Wines produced: Cornas, St.-Péray   old
Surface area: 3.7 acres   Average age of vines: 90–100 years

Sylvain Bernard, located in St.-Péray, has become a recent producer of Cornas, largely
because Guy de Barjac leased his entire parcel in the lieu-dit La Barjasse to Bernard. It is
one of the oldest vineyards in Cornas, having been planted between 1896 and 1904.

PAUL JABOULET-AINÉ* * * *
(Domaine de St.-Pierre)/* * * (négociant bottling)

Address: Les Jalets   Wines produced: Cornas, Cornas Domaine
    R.N. 7, B.P. 46   de St.-Pierre
    La-Roche-de-Glun   Surface area: 9.1 acres
    26600 Tain l'Hermitage   Production: 7,000 bottles
Tel: 4-75-84-68-93   Upbringing: 10–15 months in old barrels
Fax: 4-75-84-56-14   Average age of vines: 7–15 years

This famous firm significantly increased its purchases of wine from Cornas in the eighties.
For example, 75% of the appellation's production in the bountiful year of 1985 was reportedly
bought by Jaboulet. In 1993, Jaboulet's interest in Cornas was further evidenced by the purchase of the Domaine de St.-Pierre, a 9.1-acre estate of relatively young vines (7–15 years),
located behind the two renowned vineyards of Reynard and Les Chaillots, directly behind
the village. As the following tasting notes indicate, this is an impressive wine. Jaboulet also
produces a regular cuvée of Cornas (from purchased juice) that is made in a muscular, full-
bodied, old style with plenty of structure and hard tannin. Despite the lightening of some of
Jaboulet's other Rhône wines, especially their Châteauneuf du Pape Les Cèdres and their
Gigondas, this firm seems content to produce two cuvées of big, brawny, beefy Cornas.

VINTAGES

1995—Cornas   The 1995 Cornas displays copious amounts of pepper, earth, tar, and
  ·   spicy scents, as well as licorice and black-fruit notes. With medium body and
 86   moderate tannin, it is a wine to drink over the next 7–8 years. Last tasted 6/96.
1995—Cornas Domaine de St.-Pierre   The 1995 Domaine de St.-Pierre is superb. It offers
  ·   an opaque purple color, huge body and extract, and monstrous tannin in the
90 +   powerful finish. This is a Cornas to put away for 7–10 years and drink during the
        first 10–15 years of the next century. Last tasted 6/96.
1994—Cornas Domaine de St.-Pierre   The 1994 Domaine de St.-Pierre is also excep-
  ·   tional. It is sweeter, more flattering, and riper, with a deep ruby/purple color, loads
 90   of cassis fruit, and a more luscious, silky finish. It should drink well for 10–15
        years. Last tasted 6/96.

1991—Cornas   In 1991 Jaboulet's Cornas was put in small oak casks for the first time to
·   tame its savage character. The 1991 Cornas offers an attractive perfume of red and
87   black fruits as well as some toasty new oak. It is medium-bodied, round, and ideal
               for drinking over the next 7–8 years. Last tasted 11/95.

1990—Cornas   The 1990 Cornas is showing better than it did last year. It is more tannic
·   and austere, with a forceful, spicy, peppery, herb, and earth-scented nose. Medium-
86   to full-bodied, with considerable tannin but excellent concentration, this wine
               needs 5–6 years of cellaring. It should last for 12–15 years. Last tasted 5/95.

1989—Cornas   Jaboulet's 1989 Cornas is a light, aggressively tannic, somewhat eviscer-
·   ated wine that does not have nearly enough fruit and depth to stand up to its tough and
79   muscular personality. It will only get more attenuated as it ages. Last tasted 5/95.

1985—Cornas   A charming and flattering wine for a young Cornas, the 1985 is marked by
·   the low acidity of this vintage as well as a lush, rich black-cherry fruitiness. Full-
86   bodied yet supple, this wine will develop quickly. Mature now. Last tasted 12/93.

1983—Cornas   The 1983 was remarkably impressive from the cask, so much so that I
·   ordered a case of it for my cellar. After eight bottles, I have found the wine
86   stubbornly backward, astringent, and sturdy, and have begun to lose confidence in
               it. Still terribly closed, very tannic and hard, this is a large-scaled, brawny wine
               that remains impossibly unfriendly. Will the fruit hold? I doubt it. Anticipated
               maturity: now–2005? Last tasted 11/96.

Older Vintages

From the seventies, both the 1978 and 1972 are fully mature, excellent wines. I still have a
few bottles of the hard, tough 1970 in my cellar. It is good but lacks some charm and has
always had too much muscle.

MARCEL JUGE* * */* * * *

Address: Place de la Salle des Fêtes
        07130 Cornas
Tel: 4-75-40-36-68
Fax: 4-75-40-30-05
Wines produced: Cornas, Cornas Cuvée Coteaux, Cornas Sélection Coteaux, St.-Péray Blanc
Surface area: 6.2 acres
Production (Cornas): 5,000–6,000 bottles
          (Cuvée Coteaux): 10,000–12,000 bottles
          (Sélection Coteaux): 2,100 bottles
Upbringing: 2–3 years in old oak, with 18 months minimum in barrels
Average age of vines: 45 years

All three cuvées are made and raised in the cellar in the same manner. The Cuvée
Coteaux, made from grapes harvested on the vines planted in Coteaux, is made every year.
The Sélection Coteaux is a special cuvée made from grapes from the Coteaux vines that
possess an element of *surmaturité* (overripeness). This is only made when weather conditions
warrant. None of these wines is fined or filtered.

The diminutive, implike Marcel Juge is certainly the free spirit of Cornas. His cellars lie
below his modern home, right next to the school playground and Place du Marché. He
appears to be in his late fifties, but his devilish grin and playful personality make him seem
younger. Like Châteauneuf du Pape's legendary duo Jacques Reynaud and Henri Bonneau,
Juge is famous for his diatribes against France's "overloaded bureaucracy."

Juge owns 6.75 acres of vineyards (1.3 acres are in St.-Péray) of which one-half is on the

Cornas hillsides and one-half on the valley floor. The average age of his vines is 45 years, but he has a tiny parcel of seven-year-old vines, as well as one parcel of 80-year-old vines. Consequently, he makes and sells two separate cuvées of Cornas in most vintages. In such top years as 1989, 1990, and 1991, a third cuvée called Sélection Coteaux is produced. Because the appellation authorities do not allow producers to include a Coteaux designation on their labels, these special cuvées are indicated with the letter "C" for Cuvée Coteaux and "SC" for Sélection Coteaux. When I last saw Juge, he was undecided whether or not to discontinue the Sélection Coteaux, since demand for that wine exceeded the interest in his other wines.

With respect to the style of Juge's Cornas, he is a less consistent winemaker than either Clape or Verset, but when he succeeds, which is most of the time, his wines are by far the most elegant and Burgundy-like in Cornas. His wines are usually deep ruby/purple-colored, rather than opaque, and the aromas offer plenty of sweet fruit, without the piercing tannin and rusticity of other Cornas. These wines age well, as vintages from the early and mid-eighties remain in good shape in 1997. All of Juge's wine spend 24–36 months in barrel and foudre before bottling, which is done with neither fining or filtration. Perhaps because of the extended cask aging, the wines possess greater suppleness, and drink well after bottling. Obviously, his cuvées from the hillside vineyards are his finest wines. Juge also produces tiny quantities of St.-Péray blanc, but I have never tasted it.

VINTAGES

1994—Cornas   A sweet, supple Cornas, with a tarry, floral, violet, and cassis-scented
·   nose, this seductive, silky-textured wine reveals good to excellent concentration,
88   low acidity, and light tannin. Drink it during its first 7–8 years of life. Marcel Juge
        often produces a Cuvée Coteaux, which was not presented for tasting in either 1994
        or 1993. Last tasted 6/96.

1993—Cornas   This is a light-bodied, pleasant wine with a supple, clean, black-fruit
·   character, soft tannin, and low acidity. It is an attractive effort in a tough vintage.
85   Anticipated maturity: now–2000. Last tasted 4/94.

1988—Cornas   The 1988 regular cuvée is simple and straightforward. Mature now. Last
·   tasted 4/94.
79

1988—Cornas Cuvée C   The 1988 Cuvée C possesses a lovely nose of black raspberries,
·   violets, and mushrooms, but there is not much extract or length. Were the yields
84   perhaps too high? Anticipated maturity: now–2000. Last tasted 4/94.

1985—Cornas Cuvée Spéciale   This is certainly one of the finest Cornas I have tasted.
·   Only 150 cases were made. Black/ruby-colored with no amber, this concentrated
92   and perfumed (black fruits, herbs, olives, and roasted herbs) wine possesses full
        body, exceptional purity and concentration, and well-integrated acidity and tannin.
        Anticipated maturity: now–2005. Last tasted 11/95.

1985—Cornas Demi-Coteaux   A totally different wine, this 1985 is a blend of younger
·   vines on the hillside with Juge's valley vineyard. Medium ruby/purple-colored, this
84   is a fully mature, medium-bodied, finesse-style wine with soft fruit. Mature now.
        Last tasted 11/95.

JACQUES LEMENCIER* * * *

Address: Route des Granges
        07130 Cornas
Tel: 4-75-40-49-54
Wines produced: Cornas, St.-Péray Blanc
Surface area: 6.2 acres

Production: 10,500 bottles
Upbringing: 10 months in barrels 2–10 years old
Average age of vines: 10 years and 90 years

The young, wiry, long-haired Jacques Lemencier is an up-and-coming Cornas producer. He apprenticed under Robert Michel before he started his own operation. Lemencier believes in complete destemming. The wines see no new oak, and are bottled after nearly a year in barrel. Lemencier has moved toward an earlier bottling date in order to preserve as much fruit as possible. Like most Cornas producers, he never filters his wines. Lemencier produces very fine Cornas with good intensity and aging potential. Unfortunately, there is not a lot of wine to go around from his 6.2 acres of vineyards. The production, from one parcel with 10-year-old vines, and another with 90-year-old vines, is blended together. Lemencier also produces a tiny amount of St.-Péray blanc, a wine that is monolithic and one-dimensional.

VINTAGES

1990—Cornas   The 1990 appears to be fuller-bodied and more structured than the 1989, but not as concentrated as his 1988. A big wine, it is rich in color, with a spicy, stemmy earthiness, and gobs of black fruit on the palate. While it is full-bodied, raw, and tough, the potential is there. I do not think it will ever match the 1988 in quality, but it may surpass the 1989. Lemencier produces 8,000 bottles, all of which are unfined and unfiltered, so expect a heavy sediment to form with several years of aging. Last tasted 3/95.

·

87

1989—Cornas   In 1989, not the easiest vintage for the Cornas vignerons, Lemencier produced a fine example. The wine, which Lemencier calls "a cousin of 1987," displays an impressive, deep ruby/purple color, a big, spicy, earthy, mineral, and black-fruit-scented nose, a sweet, expansive palate, some noticeable tannin in the finish, as well as plenty of concentration and extract. It is a classic Cornas for drinking over the next 12–15 years. Last tasted 3/95.

·

87

1988—Cornas   In 1988, Lemencier produced a black/purple-colored wine possessing a huge, chocolaty, cassis-scented nose, rich, concentrated flavors, full body, and solid, but soft tannin in its long finish. It is a heroic effort for Cornas in this vintage. Anticipated maturity: now–2008. Last tasted 11/94.

·

90

JEAN LIONNET* */* * *

Address: Pied la Vigne
       07130 Cornas
Tel: 4-75-40-36-01
Wines produced: Cornas, Cornas Cuvée Rochepertuis
Surface area (Total): 35 acres
        (Cornas): 10 acres
        (Cuvée Rochepertuis): 10 acres
Production (Cornas): 2,500 cases
        (Cuvée Rochepertuis): 1,875 cases
Upbringing (Cornas): 18 months in barrels 1–2 years old
        (Cuvée Rochepertuis): 18 months in 20% new oak barrels
Average age of vines (Cornas): 50–60 years
        (Cuvée Rochepertuis): 80 years

Jean Lionnet, a big, warm, friendly man, has one of the most important vineyard holdings in Cornas, with a total of 20 acres of well-situated vines in Les Chaillots, Les Arlettes, and

Pied la Vigne. Another 5 acres has just come into production. In addition to his Cornas vineyards, he owns 5 acres in St.-Péray from which he produces a white wine, and just over three acres of Côtes du Rhône planted with 100% Syrah. Lionnet has become one of Jean-Luc Colombo's top clients. His cellar is one of the most modern in Cornas, with temperature-controlled stainless steel tanks, filters, etc. He follows the traditional Colombo vinification of 100% destemming, in addition to utilizing a small percentage of new oak casks (20%). His wines are bottled with fining and a light pad filtration. The wines of Lionnet are good, but rarely interesting. They are often too oaky and lack the intensity and richness found in the village's best wines. Despite the fact that he now destems, many wines possess a distinct herbaceousness that detracts from their overall charm. The Cuvée Rochepertuis, named after a craggy rock outbreak in his vineyard, is the top wine, but I have rarely given it more than an above average score. My instincts suggest that overcropping and too much processing result in wines that lack intensity and richness.

VINTAGES

1995—Cornas Cuvée Rochepertuis   Lionnet's top cuvée of Cornas, Rochepertuis, is aged
·   in small barrels, of which a high percentage are new. The 1995 Rochepertuis
84   exhibits a dark ruby color, plenty of wood in the nose, and hard, tannic, aus-
         tere, acidic flavors. I am not sure it will ever open and blossom, but it is cleanly
         made, and I will give it the benefit of the doubt until it is in bottle. Last tasted
         6/96.
1994—Cornas Cuvée Rochepertuis   The 1994 Rochepertuis reveals an old, musty, damp-
·   paper nose that made judgment impossible. It may have been a cork problem,
?   although it was not the typical musty cork smell that infects "corked" wines. Last
         tasted 6/96.
1993—Cornas Cuvée Rochepertuis   The 1993 Cornas Rochepertuis has turned out sur-
·   prisingly well for the vintage. It exhibits a dark ruby color, a sweet, vanillin,
86   curranty nose, rich, medium-bodied, ripe flavors, and a decent finish. Drink it over
         the next 6–7 years. Last tasted 6/96.
1992—Cornas Cuvée Rochepertuis   The 1992 Rochepertuis is a problematic wine. It
·   possesses a stale, mushroomy nose (rot?), light body, and a diluted, short finish.
65   Last tasted 9/95.
1991—Cornas Cuvée Rochepertuis   The compact 1991 Rochepertuis exhibits an aggres-
·   sively herbal, animal-scented nose, and decent, streamlined flavors. It should be
79   drunk over the next decade. Last tasted 9/95.
1990—Cornas Cuvée Rochepertuis   The 1990 Rochepertuis displays better color, none
·   of the herbaceousness that plagues the 1991, a spicy, earthy, black-fruit character,
85   attractive toastiness, and good, firm, medium- to full-bodied, uncomplex flavors.
         Drink it over the next decade. Last tasted 9/94.

ROBERT MICHEL* * */* * * *

Address: Grande Rue
              07130 Cornas
Tel: 4-75-40-38-70
Fax: 4-75-40-58-57
Wines produced: Cornas Cuvée des Coteaux, Cornas Le Geynale, Cornas Le Pied du Coteau
Surface area (Cuvée des Coteaux): 10 acres
                  (Le Geynale): 3.7 acres
                  (Le Pied du Coteaux): 1.24 acres

Production (Cuvée des Coteaux): 22,500 bottles
        (Le Geynale): 5,600 bottles
        (Le Pied du Coteau): 4,200 bottles
Upbringing: 6 months in inox vats and 12 months in old barrels (all 3 cuvées)
Average age of vines (Cuvée des Coteaux): 45 years
                (Le Geynale): 80 years
                (Le Pied du Coteau): 30 years

Robert Michel, a tall, balding, red-haired man in his early fifties, represents the ninth generation of Michels making wine in Cornas. Michel's cellars are right in the middle of the village, and are exceptionally damp and cold, even in the summer. He owns 14.9 acres of vineyards, of which 13.5 acres are located on the steeply terraced hillsides. His vines average an impressive 40 years in age, one tiny parcel (Le Geynale) being almost 80 years old. Michel is adamantly against filtering his black-colored, robust Cornas, but does believe in fining to soften some of its coarse tannin. This is an estate that pursues traditional winemaking—perhaps to excess. I find Michel's Cornas among the most robust and savagely raw and intense wine of the appellation. In fact, his wines are unapproachable and excruciatingly tannic to taste when young. Sadly, age does not help as much as I would like to think. Michel keeps his wine 18 months in old barrels and has no intention of using new oak. Three cuvées of Cornas are made, a single-vineyard (planted in 1910) called Le Geynale, a Cuvée des Coteaux, and a regular cuvée called Le Pied du Coteau.

VINTAGES

1995 — Cornas Cuvée des Coteaux   Both of Robert Michel's 1995 Cornas selections were
·   frightfully tannic, high in acidity, lean, and impossible to taste. I cannot imag-
77   ine there is enough fruit or glycerin to cover up the wines' acidity and tannin.
           The 1995 Cuvée des Coteaux displays an excellent ruby/purple color, low Ph-like
           texture, and a boatload of tannin. Last tasted 6/96.

1995 — Cornas Le Geynale   Similar to the 1995 Cuvée des Coteaux, it appears these 1995
·   offerings will always be tough and austere. Last tasted 6/96.
80

1994 — Cornas Cuvée des Coteaux   In total contrast to the 1995s, Michel's 1994s possess
·   sweeter fruit, deeper ruby/purple colors, and more cassis-dominated characteris-
87   tics. They are lower in acidity, which gives the wines an accessible, chewy texture.
           The 1994 Cuvée des Coteaux is a ripe, round, generous, deeply colored wine with
           a classic Cornas character of cassis, licorice, earth, and spice. There is some
           tannin, but this wine can be drunk now or over the next decade. Last tasted 6/96.

1994 — Cornas Le Geynale   The rustic 1994 Le Geynale reveals sweeter fruit, greater
·   ripeness, more tannin, and medium to full body. Its opaque purple color and
88+   outstanding ripeness suggest this wine could improve over the next decade, and
           perhaps merit a higher score. It will keep for 15 years. Last tasted 6/96.

1993 — Cornas   Readers should note that I did not taste (assuming it will be produced)
·   Michel's top cuvée of old vines, the hillside vineyard Cornas called Le Geynale.
85   The 1993 Cornas is a soft, moderately colored wine with low acidity, and an
           absence of tannin and grip. It possesses adequate ripeness, as well as moderate
           alcohol. Drink it over the next 5–7 years. Last tasted 6/96.

1992 — Cornas   The thin, compact 1992 Cornas exhibits a funky, earthy, overtly herbal
·   aroma and lacks ripeness. With airing, a touch of mushroomy rot emerges. Last
75   tasted 12/94.

1985—Cornas Le Geynale   Deep ruby/purple in color, very dense, earthy, and peppery,
·   this full-bodied wine still has considerable tannin, and is at least a decade away
87   from maturity. Mature now. Last tasted 12/94.

1985—Cornas   Dark ruby-colored, with some amber, this wine is hard and closed. Al-
·   though it exhibits decent fruit, this tough, aggressive wine is so hard that I doubt it
82   will ever be well balanced. Anticipated maturity: now? Last tasted 12/94.

1979—Cornas   A very successful 1979, this opaque garnet-colored wine remains a
·   brawny, full-bodied Cornas that has the fruit and flesh to nearly balance out its
86   huge tannin. Quite substantial on the palate, with very good length, this beefy wine
          will keep for at least another decade, but the tannin will never fully melt away.
          Mature now. Last tasted 12/95.

Older Vintages

The two older vintages of Michel's I have tasted were both very impressive. The opulent,
lush, fully mature 1971 resembled a smoky, rich, multidimensional Hermitage. It was
loaded with fruit when tasted in 1985. The 1969, tasted with Michel in 1986, was showing
some dryness and coarseness in the finish, but had a stunningly complex bouquet of exotic
spices, wild-berry fruit, and immense body.

L. DE VALLOUIT* *

Address: 24, rue Désiré   Surface area: 1.7 acres
            26240 St.-Vallier   Production: 4,500 bottles
Tel: 4-75-23-10-11   Upbringing: 18 months in 10% new oak
Fax: 4-75-23-05-58   barrels
Wines produced: Cornas   Average age of vines: 35 years

De Vallouit's Cornas is generally rustic and tannic, without the sweet fruit, completeness,
or complexity found in his top cuvées of Côte Rôtie, Hermitage, and St.-Joseph. Vintages I
have tasted have been unappealing because of excessive tannin.

NOËL VERSET* * * * *

Address: Impasse de la Couleyre   Surface area: 4.8 acres
            07130 Cornas   Production: 10,500 bottles
Tel: 4-75-40-36-66   Upbringing: 18 months in old casks
Wines produced: Cornas   Average age of vines: 80 years

The bald, elderly (he is in his early eighties), squeaky-voiced Noël Verset has essentially
retired from making Cornas. His wines were frightfully difficult to find when he owned a
whopping 6.2 acres of steeply terraced old Cornas vines. Since he sold 1.4 acres of extremely
old vines in the Reynard vineyard to Thierry Allemand, he is making even less Cornas than
in the past. Verset still owns old, gnarled, superbly situated vines, including an 80-year-old
parcel in Les Chaillots, and a 100-year-old parcel in Les Sabarottes. Another tiny parcel is
at the bottom of the hill in Champelrose.

Verset's secret for making top-notch Cornas has always been tiny yields, a late harvest,
picking fully physiologically ripe fruit, and no interventionist techniques in the cellars. His
yield per vine has always been one of the smallest in Cornas, which explains the extraordinary concentration of fruit exhibited by his wines in top vintages. His cellar, which looks
like a seventeenth-century antique, is filled with ancient barrels and large oak foudres
where he stores his wine for 18 months. He does one fining with egg whites and bottles his
wines unfiltered. Verset's production of 600 or so cases is minuscule, but he is proud of the

fact that he continues to sell virtually all of it to America, Great Britain, Holland, Switzerland, Australia, and Japan. In great vintages, Verset's wine can be drunk young, but it ages effortlessly for 15 or more years.

Prior to the decade of the nineties, Verset, along with Auguste Clape, produced the best wine of the appellation. But I am no longer convinced that is true. Creeping age and some difficult vintages, as well as the emergence of more energetic, younger producers, have made me wonder if recent vintages have not lacked some excitement. Verset's enthusiasm and animated personality remain unchanged, and he certainly has a genetic bloodline that is favorable to long life. His father, Emanuel, who died at age 100, continued to work in the winery until he was 95.

VINTAGES

1995—Cornas   The 1995 Cornas possesses a deep ruby/purple color, an excellent sweet
  ·   nose of black fruits, fine depth and ripeness, high acidity, and a lean, spicy finish.
87   It is very good. Anticipated maturity: 1999–2011. Last tasted 6/96.

1994—Cornas   Also dark ruby/purple-colored, the medium-bodied 1994 Cornas displays
  ·   fine extract, and sweet, spicy, cassislike flavors, but its short finish and lack of any
85   serious depth are surprising. It should drink well for 5–6 years. Last tasted
            6/96.

1993—Cornas   Verset owns some of the oldest and best-placed vines in Cornas, so the
  ·   fact that his wines are lighter and less concentrated than usual should demonstrate
82   to readers just what deplorable conditions producers endured in these two years.
            The medium ruby-colored 1993 Cornas displays a faint perfume of black fruits,
            minerals, and herbs. Although the attack begins well, the wine is hollow in the
            middle, with light body, and a spicy, tough finish. It may fill out with additional
            aging in Verset's ancient foudres, but don't count on it. Last tasted 6/95.

1992—Cornas   The 1992 Cornas offers a pronounced vegetal nose, ripe cassis fruit, and
  ·   hard, tough tannin in the finish. It appears more concentrated and complete than
83   the 1993, but it is frightfully tannic for its modest flavor dimensions. Last tasted
            6/95.

1991—Cornas   The 1991 (from an underrated vintage for northern Rhône appellations
  ·   such as Condrieu, Côte Rôtie, and Cornas) possesses a dense, opaque black/purple
92   color and a huge, sweet perfume of cassis, truffles, and licorice. Exceptionally
            opulent and superconcentrated with low acidity, this full-bodied wine is ideal for
            drinking over the next 10–12 years. Last tasted 11/95.

1990—Cornas   After tasting Verset's 1990 Cornas, I wrote, "The quintessence of Syrah
  ·   and of Cornas—almost like port." The wine is remarkably rich, thick, and opaque,
93   and so phenomenally intense that you could almost stand a spoon in it! Unbeliev-
            ably concentrated, Verset's yields were under 30 hectoliters per hectare. There is
            no doubting that the 1990 is a remarkable, even spectacular Cornas that may
            ultimately merit an even higher score. I would not be surprised to see it receive the
            highest rating I have ever given a Cornas once it is in the bottle. A monument!
            Anticipated maturity: now–2009. Last tasted 11/95.

1989—Cornas   The 1989 Cornas is a mere mortal wine by Verset's standards. Dark purple/
  ·   black in color, it exhibits a sweet, ripe, herbaceous, cassis-scented nose, and some
88   opulence. For the vintage, it is surprisingly tasty, round, and concentrated. Maturing
            quickly, it should be drunk over the next 7–8 years. Last tasted 6/95.

1988—Cornas   Verset's 1988 Cornas, should anyone be lucky enough to still find any, is
  ·   more structured, more tannic, and more muscular than the lush, alcoholic 1989. It
89   should be laid away for another two years. Like most of Verset's wines, it possesses

a big, black-berry, jammy bouquet of Asian spices, licorice, violets, and minerals. It is an excellent Cornas that falls just short of being outstanding. Anticipated maturity: now–2003. Last tasted 6/95.

1987—Cornas   While I rarely ever think of Cornas as a wine in which restaurants would
·   have much interest, this 1987 is an ideal wine for innovative restaurants to con-
85   sider. It has low acidity, round, tasty, generously endowed flavors, supple texture, and at least another 5–7 years of aging potential. Last tasted 6/94.

1985—Cornas   This is one of Verset's greatest efforts. Verset's 1985 has aromas of
·   smoke, violets, jammy blackberry fruit, licorice, and Asian spices. Superbly con-
91   centrated, with layers of flavor that persist and persist, this full-bodied wine pos-
sesses a voluptuous texture as well as a sweet, expansive, layered mid-palate. The extraordinary level of ripe fruit nearly conceals plenty of ripe tannin. Anticipated maturity: now–2006. Last tasted 11/95.

1983—Cornas   Although this wine is more tannic than the 1985, it is one of the better
·   balanced 1983s. Dark ruby/purple-colored, full-bodied with heaps of cassis fruit,
90   and an extremely long finish, this remains a youthful, tannic, vigorous, very rich Cornas. Anticipated maturity: 1997–2008. Last tasted 11/95.

1982—Cornas   This is the finest wine produced in Cornas in 1982. Very deep garnet-
·   colored, with a smoky, herb, truffle, and tarry-scented bouquet, and layers of
88   blackcurrant and overripe plum fruit, this full-bodied wine reveals a soft texture and a heady finish. Mature now. Last tasted 11/95.

ALAIN VOGE* * */* * * * *

Address: Rue de l'Equerre
             07130 Cornas
Tel: 4-75-40-32-04
Wines produced: Cornas, Cornas Cuvée Vieilles Vignes, Cornas Les Vieilles Fontaines,
             Cornas Cuvée Barriques
Surface area (Cornas): 4.9 acres
             (Cuvée Vieilles Vignes): 12. 4 acres
             (Les Vieilles Fontaines): This special cuvée is selected partly when the harvest
                             comes into the winery, and partly from cask tastings.
Production (Cornas): 6,000 bottles
             (Cuvée Vieilles Vignes): 30,800 bottles
             (Les Vieilles Fontaines): 3,500 bottles
Upbringing (Cornas): 12 months in barrels 2–3 years old
             (Cuvée Vieilles Vignes): 24 months in barrels 2–3 years old
             (Les Vieilles Fontaines): 32–36 months in barrels 3–5 years old
Average age of vines (Cornas): 10–20 years
             (Cuvée Vieilles Vignes): 70–80 years

Some of the greatest bottles of Cornas I have tasted were Voge's 1978, 1979, 1989, 1990, 1991, and 1994. His wines, more than any other grower's of this appellation, do indeed resemble fine Hermitage with their intense display of rich, smoky, black fruit. Voge, an ex-rugby player, has a bulldog's build and a reserved manner, but he is intense about his wines. His large domaine (relatively speaking) allows him to make at least two cuvées. In the most exceptional vintages, a special cuvée called Les Vieilles Fontaines is made from extremely old vines planted in the 1920s. This cuvée has been produced only in 1985, 1988, 1990, and 1991. Voge's wines, which are often partially destemmed, are fermented in steel tanks and then aged in wooden barrels and foudres. Like most Cornas growers, he fines his wines but rarely filters. Voge owns some superb vineyard sites, including parcels in seven of the best-known Cornas vineyards: Reynard, Les Mazards, Les Chaillots, La Côte, Patou, La Combe, and Les Sabeaux. In addition to his Cornas, Voge has 10 acres in St.-Péray where he makes both sparkling and still wine. Because of their intense, plump, succulent character, Voge's wines tend to show well at a younger age than many Cornas, yet will keep for at least 10–15 years. In the early eighties, I thought I detected a change in direction, but I believe this was due to some off-year vintages rather than any intention by Voge to change what is a very successful style of Cornas.

VINTAGES

1995—Cornas Cuvée Vieilles Vignes   Voge's 1995 offers plenty of smoky cassis fruit, as
·   well as fine density and ripeness, medium body, good acidity, and a tart, clean
88   finish. It should last for 12–15 years because of the high acidity, but it is not one
     of the more concentrated cuvées made by Voge. Last tasted 6/96.

1994—Cornas Cuvée Vieilles Vignes   The dark ruby/purple-colored 1994 is far more
·   attractive and flattering to smell, with its smoky, roasted nut, cassis-scented nose,
90   round, generous flavors, medium body, and good finish. It should drink well for a
     decade. It is unquestionably one of the finest wines made in Cornas in 1994. Fans
     of Voge should know that he just released tiny quantities of a very special cuvée of
     1991 Cornas Vieilles Fontaines. Aged for nearly three years in cask, this wine has
     only been made in selected vintages, e.g., 1990 and 1991. Anticipated maturity:
     now–2010. Last tasted 6/96.

1993—Cornas Cuvée Vieilles Vignes   The 1993 Cuvée Vieilles Vignes reveals a fine
·   deep color (it is among the darker-colored wines of this appellation), a spicy,
87   ripe, peppery, black-fruit-scented nose, round, ripe, soft, medium-bodied flavors,
     admirable concentration, some fat and flesh, and a soft finish. Drink it over the
     next 7–8 years. Last tasted 6/96.

1992—Cornas Cuvée Vieilles Vignes   The 1992 Cuvée Vieilles Vignes offers an herba-
·   ceous, black-cherry-scented nose, sweet, ripe fruit, medium body, and a moderately
86   long, supple finish. Drink it over the next 5–6 years. This is a successful wine for
     the vintage. Last tasted 9/95.

1991—Cornas   Voge can make superb Cornas and his 1991 regular cuvée (there are
·   often old-vine and new-oak cuvées as well) is a rich, earthy, black-raspberry-
90   scented wine with full body, admirable depth and ripeness, and a long, spicy finish.
     Although rustic, it is loaded with character, ripe fruit, fine richness, and moderate
     tannin. This is a Cornas for drinking over the next 7–8 years. Last tasted 9/95.

1990—Cornas Cuvée Barriques   This wine is surprisingly refined and soft for a Cornas,
·   but the new oak has tamed some of the rusticity and harsh tannin that the Syrah
87   planted on the roasted slopes of Cornas can possess. It offers up aromas of smoky,
     roasted, black fruit combined with scents of toasty new oak. In the mouth the wine
     is medium- to full-bodied and generous, with excellent ripeness, a supple, smooth
     texture, and a moderately long finish. Drink it over the next 5–7 years. Last tasted
     11/94.

1990—Cornas Les Vieilles Fontaines   This is a blockbuster Cornas. Very opaque purple-
·   colored, with a sensational jammy blueberry/blackberry/cassis-scented nose inter-
94   mixed with roasted meat and licorice aromas, this large-scaled, massive Cornas
     displays remarkable depth and balance. Still very youthful, this is one of the greatest
     Cornas I have ever tasted. Anticipated maturity: 1999–2015. Last tasted 6/96.

1989—Cornas Cuvée Vieilles Vignes   The superb 1989 Cuvée Vieilles Vignes exhibits
·   an opaque dark ruby/garnet color and a rich, sweet nose of roasted nuts, herbs, and
90   black fruits. In the mouth, it possesses the expansive, full-bodied, chewy richness

that comes from old-vine Syrah, plenty of soft tannin, low acidity, and a fat, heady, spicy, superconcentrated finish. This wine should age effortlessly for another 10–15 years. Last tasted 11/94.

1985—Cornas   A gloriously opulent 1985 Cornas, this deep-colored, full-bodied wine is
  ·   loaded with Asian spices and jammy, lush fruit. Fully mature, this smooth-as-silk
89   Cornas (a rarity) will continue to offer sumptuous drinking for another 5–6 years. Anticipated maturity: now–2002. Last tasted 11/95.

1983—Cornas   A big, hickory-scented, smoky, bacon fat, ripe, plummy bouquet seems to
  ·   gush from a glass of this dark garnet-colored Cornas. More open and advanced than
89   other wines from this vintage, Voge's Cornas shows plenty of ripe fruit, full body, excellent concentration, and another decade of cellaring potential. It is especially well balanced for a 1983. Anticipated maturity: now–2005. Last tasted 11/95.

1982—Cornas   A little diffuse and flabby with soft, one-dimensional flavors, the 1982 is
  ·   adequate but not the best example of Voge's winemaking talents. Drink up. Last
77   tasted 9/91.

1979—Cornas   Still a deep, opaque garnet/purple color, this wine possesses rich, smoky,
  ·   bacon fat aromas, an opulent, chewy mid-palate, and layers of flavor. Full-bodied,
91   velvety, intense, and extremely long, this is a hedonistic, decadently rich Cornas that has aged superbly. A brilliant wine! Last tasted 11/95.

1978—Cornas   An impressive dark garnet color with no amber is followed by an earthy,
  ·   smoky, spicy-scented and -flavored wine with very concentrated flavors. The 1978
92   is portlike with an unctuous texture and layers of toasty, jammy fruit. The creamy, lingering finish is also noteworthy. A great Cornas! Anticipated maturity: now–2008. Last tasted 11/95.

OTHER CORNAS PRODUCERS

ELIE BANCEL

Address: R.N. 86	Surface area: 2.1 acres
07130 Cornas	Production: 4,500 bottles
Tel: 4-75-40-25-53	Upbringing: 2–3 years in old barrels
Wines produced: Cornas	Average age of vines: 50 years

BERNARD BLACHON

Address: Quartier Champelrose	Surface area: 5 acres
07130 Cornas	Production: 12,000 bottles
Tel: 4-75-40-22-11	Upbringing: 18–36 months in old barrels
Wines produced: Cornas	Average age of vines: 50 years

CAVES COTTEVERGNE–L. SAUGÈRE

Address: Quartier le Bret	Wines produced: Cornas
07130 St.-Péray	Production: 4,500 bottles
Tel: 4-75-40-30-43	Upbringing: 16–18 months in barrels 2–4
Fax: 4-75-40-55-06	years old

JEAN-FRANÇOIS CHABOUD

Address: 21, rue de Vernoux	Production: 12,000 bottles
07130 St.-Péray	Upbringing: 24 months in barrels 2–5 years
Tel: 4-75-40-31-63	old
Wines produced: Cornas	Average age of vines: 30 years
Surface area: 5 acres	

CHARLES DESPESSE

Address: 07130 Cornas
Tel: 4-75-40-25-57
Wines produced: Cornas
Surface area: 0.74 acres

Production: 1,500 bottles
Upbringing: 36 months in barrels 2–3 years old
Average age of vines: oldest is 80 years

NOËL DURAND

Address: G.A.E.C. du Lautaret
07130 Châteaubourg
Tel: 4-75-40-46-78
Fax: 4-75-40-29-77
Wines produced: Cornas
Surface area: 6.2 acres

Production: 14,000 bottles, of which one-half are estate-bottled
Upbringing: 12 months in barrels 2–6 years old
Average age of vines: 10–15 years

ANDRÉ FUMAT

Address: Rue des Bouviers
07130 Cornas
Tel: 4-75-40-42-84
Wines produced: Cornas
Surface area: 3.7 acres

Production: 9,000 bottles
Upbringing: 18–24 months in 50% new oak barrels
Average age of vines: 60 years

PIERRE LIONNET

Address: Le Village
R.N. 86
07130 Cornas
Wines produced: Cornas

Surface area: 5 acres
Production: 15,000 bottles
Upbringing: 18–24 months in old oak casks
Average age of vines: 45–50 years

MARC MAURICE

Address: Grande Rue
07130 Cornas
Tel: 4-75-40-41-82
Wines produced: Cornas
Surface area: 2.47 acres

Production: only 1,000 bottles; the rest is sold in bulk
Upbringing: 24 months in old barrels
Average age of vines: 40 years

JEAN-LUC MICHEL

Address: 52, Grande Rue
07130 Cornas
Tel: 4-75-40-03-65
Wines produced: Cornas
Surface area: 7.5 acres

Production: 19,500 bottles
Upbringing: 12–15 months in oak casks 3–4 years old
Average age of vines: 23 years

G.A.E.C. LES RAVIÈRES

Address: Laurent et Dominique Courbis
07130 Châteaubourg
Tel: 4-75-40-32-12
Fax: 4-75-40-25-39
Wines produced: Cornas

Surface area: 6.2 acres
Production: 11,250 bottles
Upbringing: 12 months in old casks
Average age of vines: 40 years, and some 80 years old

DOMAINE ST.-JEMMS

Address: Les Châssis
R.N. 7
26600 Mercurol
Tel: 4-75-08-33-03
Fax: 4-75-08-69-80
Wines produced: Cornas

Surface area: 7.4 acres
Production: 15,000 bottles
Upbringing: 24 months minimum in oak casks
Average age of vines: 40 years

LOUIS SOZET

Address: Rue du Ruisseau
07130 Cornas
Tel: 4-75-40-51-13
Wines produced: Cornas
Surface area: 3.95 acres

Production: 4,500 bottles
Upbringing: 12 months in inox vats and
12–16 months in old oak
barrels
Average age of vines: oldest are 75 years

TARDIEU-LAURENT

Address: 84160 Loumarin

This négociant firm was formed in 1994. It is dedicated to buying juice from producers known for their low yields and/or old vines. Wine broker Michel Tardieu and Burgundian baker Dominique Laurent joined forces to establish this négociant business in the Château Loumarin, which has some of the coldest cellars in the southern Rhône. Their first vintages were impressive wines. Most of the selections were from the southern Rhône, but there were excellent cuvées from Crozes-Hermitage, Cornas, Côte Rôtie, and Hermitage. The wines are all aged in small oak casks, with an important percentage new, and bottled with no fining or filtration, as well as with low levels of SO_2. Based on the two vintages I tasted in the cellars of Tardieu-Laurent in June, 1996, this looks to be an exciting new source for high-quality Rhône Valley wines.

JEAN-MARIE TEYSSEIRE

Address: 07130 Cornas
Tel: 4-75-40-52-01
Wines produced: Cornas
Surface area: 6.8 acres

Production: 15,000 bottles
Upbringing: 18 months in 3-year-old
barrels
Average age of vines: 30 years

JEAN-LOUIS THIERS * * *

Address: Quartier Biguet
07130 Toulaud
Tel: 4-75-40-49-44
Wines produced: Cornas
Surface area: 1.2 acres

Production: 3,000 bottles
Upbringing: 12–15 months in barrels 2–3
years old
Average age of vines: 60 years

LOUIS VERSET

Address: R.N. 89
07130 Cornas
Tel: 4-75-40-41-23
Wines produced: Cornas
Surface area: 3.7 acres

Production: 7,500 bottles
Upbringing: 12–18 months in barrels 2–3
years old
Average age of vines: 50 years

VIDAL-FLEURY

Address: R.N. 86
69420 Ampuis
Tel: 4-74-56-10-18
Fax: 4-74-56-19-19
Wines produced: Cornas
Surface area: Wine is brought into the Vidal-Fleury cellars to age only. Vinification is done
at the producers' under control of Jean-Pierre Rochias and his team.
Production: 5,000–10,000 bottles
Upbringing: 36–48 months total, with 24–36 months in oak casks and barrels; little new
oak is used

CROZES-HERMITAGE

Budget Hermitage or Expensive
Côtes du Rhône?

CROZES-HERMITAGE AT A GLANCE

Appellation created:	March 3, 1937.
Types of wine produced:	Red and white wine.
Grape varieties authorized:	Marsanne and Roussanne for the white wine; Syrah for the red wine, which represents 90% of the appellation's production.
Acres currently under vine:	2,550.
Quality level:	Mediocre to good, occasionally excellent, a few wines are superb.
Aging potential:	White wine: 1–4 years; red wine: 3–10 years.
General characteristics:	Tremendous variability in the red wines; white wines are fleshy, chunky, solid, and rather undistinguished.
Greatest recent vintages:	1995, 1991, 1990, 1989, 1988, 1978.
Price range:	$18–$35.
Aromatic profile:	It is not dissimilar to Hermitage, but less intense, and often with more Provençal herb and olive scents. The Crozes-Hermitage terroirs are variable, and the Syrah does not achieve the exceptional ripeness found in Hermitage. The top wines are medium- to full-bodied, with attractive smoky, peppery, cassis scents and flavors that can resemble a downsized Hermitage.

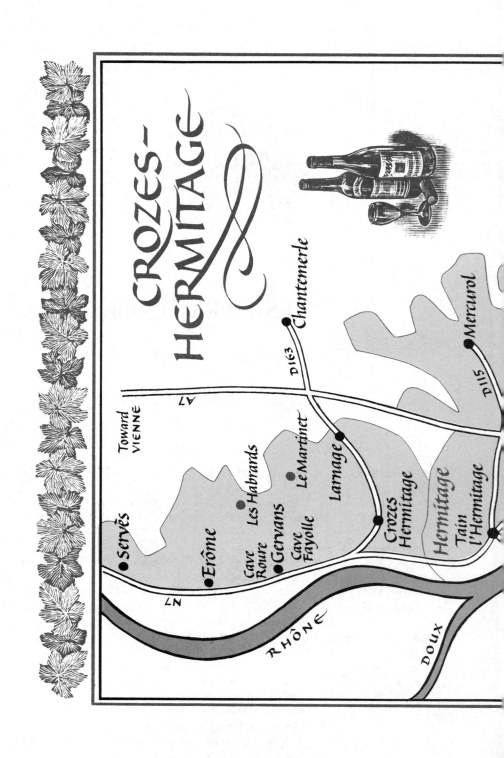

CROZES-HERMITAGE

Toward VIENNE

A7

N7

Servès

Erôme

Cave Roure   Les Habrards

Gervans

Cave Fayolle

Le Martinet

Larnage

Chantemerle

D163

Crozes Hermitage

Hermitage

Tain l'Hermitage

Mercurol

D115

RHÔNE

DOUX

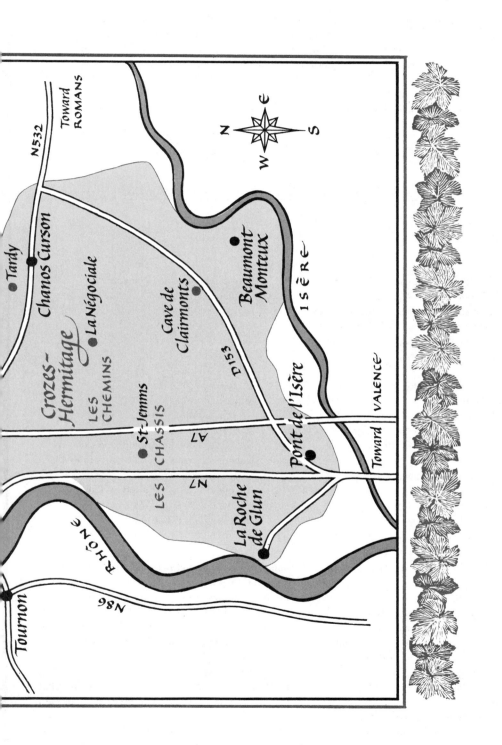

| Textural profile: | In addition to its deep ruby/purple color, this wine generally possesses medium to full body, moderate tannin, and fine depth in the best examples. It rarely rewards cellaring for more than a decade, except in vintages such as 1978, 1989, and 1990. |

The Crozes-Hermitage appellation's most profound wines:

Albert Belle Cuvée Louis Belle
Chapoutier Les Varonnières
Laurent Combier Clos des Grives
Alain Graillot La Guiraude

Paul Jaboulet-Aîné Domaine de
  Thalabert
Domaine du Pavillon Vieilles Vignes
  (Stephane Cornu)

RATING THE CROZES-HERMITAGE PRODUCERS

* * * * *(OUTSTANDING)

None

* * * *(EXCELLENT)

Albert Belle (Cuvée Louis Belle)
Chapoutier (Les Varonnières)
Domaine du Colombier (Cuvée Gaby)
Domaine Combier (Clos des Grives)
Alain Graillot (Cuvée La Guiraude)

Paul Jaboulet-Aîné (Domaine de
  Thalabert)
Domaine du Pavillon (G.A.E.C. Cornu)
  (Cuvée Vieilles Vignes)
Vidal-Fleury

* * *(GOOD)

Luc Arnavon (Domaine du Veau d'Or)
Albert Bégot
Albert Belle (Cuvée Les Pierrelles)
Chapoutier (Les Meysonniers)
Chapoutier (Petite Ruche)
Bernard Chave
Domaine Collonge
Dard et Ribo/Domaine Blanche Laine
Domaine des Entrefaux (Le Dessus des
  Entrefaux)
Domaine Fayolle (La Grande Séguine)

Domaine Fayolle (Les Voussères)
Michel Ferraton
Alain Graillot (Cuvée Classique)
Jean Marsanne
Domaines Pochon / Château de Courson
Domaine Jacques et Jean-Louis Pradelle
  (Les Hirondelles)
Raymond Roure (acquired by Paul
  Jaboulet-Aîné in 1996)
L. de Vallouit (Château du
  Larnage* * */* * * *)

The wines of Crozes-Hermitage have in name always suggested more than they have delivered. With the consent of the winemakers of Hermitage, those of Crozes were permitted to tack on, after a hyphen, the magical name of Hermitage. Despite what the name implies, most wines of Crozes-Hermitage in no way resemble those of Hermitage.

This is unfortunate, for Crozes-Hermitage is a large supplier of northern Rhône wine. The entire appellation covers a whopping 12,000 acres, but only 2,550 acres are under vine. All of the Crozes vineyards sit on the eastern side or left bank of the Rhône and completely envelop the huge granite hill of Hermitage that looms over Tain l'Hermitage. The sprawling appellation of Crozes begins six miles north of Tain at Serves-sur-Rhône, and, in what vaguely resembles a guitar shape, broadens out, terminating about eight miles south of Tain l'Hermitage, just below Pont de l'Isère.

There are five distinct sectors of the Crozes-Hermitage appellation. To the north, the best vineyard sites are in and around the village of Gervans, which has south/southwest–facing hillsides largely consisting of granite. Southeast of Gervans, in the direction of Larnage (still well north of Tain L'Hermitage), the soil is less granitic and possesses more clay, giving the wines more intensity and ripeness as well as lower acidity. South of Larnage between the village of Crozes-Hermitage and Mercurol, which is located due east of Tain l'Hermitage, behind the huge dome, the soils have more limestone and rocks. Growers believe the finest white Crozes-Hermitage is produced from this area. South of Tain L'Hermitage is where the appellation's greatest expansion has taken place over the last decade. Much of this land is flat and easily cultivated, as well as given to vineyards designed for machine harvesting. However, two of the finest estates, Jaboulet's Domaine de Thalabert and Alain Graillot's Domaine les Chênes Verts, are located in this sector, which has two stone-laden vineyards called Les Chassis and Les Sept Chemins. This area's microclimate is identical to that of Hermitage.

Some superb wines have emanated from Crozes-Hermitage, but far too many of this appellation's wines remain undistinguished. The Crozes-Hermitage growers claim they are not compensated enough for their wines, and thus there is no financial incentive to increase the quality. Undoubtedly, the influence of Jaboulet's Domaine de Thalabert, and, since the mid-eighties, the presence of Alain Graillot have helped foster and encourage a new generation of producers who are willing to make specific cuvées of Crozes-Hermitage that are richly concentrated, impressive wines that have much in common with a great Hermitage, but sell for one-third the price. More recently, young producers such as Laurent Colombier, Michel Chapoutier, and Stephane Cornu of Domaine de Pavillon, in addition to the increasingly high quality of Albert Belle's wines, have raised the reputation and image of Crozes-Hermitage.

Despite the super cuvées from the best producers (which can keep for a decade), most of the Syrahs made in Crozes-Hermitage need to be drunk within their first 5–6 years of life. One of the unexpected improvements in this appellation has been the number of tasty, elegant white wines that have emerged over recent years. None of them will ever be as profound as a great white Hermitage, or as seductive and aromatic as a Condrieu, but they are increasingly made in an easy-to-understand, straightforward, richly fruity style, and are inexpensively priced.

RECENT VINTAGES

1995 This is generally a very good to excellent vintage in Crozes-Hermitage. Alain Graillot said he had never harvested such ripe fruit with such high acidity. The wines should prove to be firm, and while less flattering at an early age than the 1994s, this vintage's best cuvées have the potential to last for 10–15 years. The white wines will need to be drunk up over the next several years. They are more acidic and less concentrated than the 1994s. Nineteen ninety-five also marked the debut vintage for Chapoutier's new luxury cuvée of Crozes-Hermitage Les Varonnières, a wine destined to be an instant legend.

1994 The rains that arrived in early September spoiled Crozes-Hermitage's chance for a great vintage. The summer had been torridly hot, but September was cool and wet. The finest wines are soft, round, fruity, and ideal for drinking over the next 5–6 years. The white wines are excellent. While they are richer, more complete, and interesting than the 1995s, they need to be consumed over the next 2–3 years.

1993 A disastrous vintage in Crozes-Hermitage, with hollow, thin wines produced by nearly everyone.

1992 Soft, slightly diluted, herbaceous, but fruity red wines were produced. They are fully mature and need to be drunk up before the end of the century. The white wines are already beginning to lose their fruit and dry out.

1991 Like so many other appellations in the northern Rhône, Crozes-Hermitage produced very fine wines that have consistently been underrated. They do not possess the massive, blockbuster power of the 1990s, but they are vastly superior to the 1992s, 1993s, and perhaps the 1994s. It is a very consistent vintage for elegant, concentrated, well-balanced wines that should drink well for another 3–4 years. The white wines were less successful.

1990 The greatest recent vintage for Crozes-Hermitage, these wines are atypically opaque-colored, rich, powerful, blockbuster wines that resemble the offerings from their big sister, Hermitage. The 1990s are aging slowly, with some of the top efforts (Graillot's La Guiraude and Jaboulet's Domaine de Thalabert) still adolescents in terms of development. This is a spectacular vintage for Crozes-Hermitage.

1989 This excellent, even outstanding vintage for Crozes-Hermitage has produced wines that are slightly less powerful and intense than in 1990, as well as firmer and more classically structured. The finest examples are deep, rich, and ageworthy. Nineteen eighty-nine and 1990 represent a magnificent duo of vintages that witnessed the production of extremely high quality wines from Crozes-Hermitage. The white Crozes-Hermitage should have been drunk by the early nineties, but the best cuvées of red wines should continue to age well through the end of the century.

Older Vintages

Older vintages are largely of academic interest, except for the top 1988s, which are still drinkable. Those wines include Jaboulet's Domaine de Thalabert and Graillot's La Guiraude. A top Crozes-Hermitage vintage that has aged well is 1978, a superb vintage for Jaboulet's Domaine de Thalabert.

Note: The only wine reviews that appear in this chapter are from those producers who turn out wines with the capacity to mature for a decade. For that reason, there are no reviews of white wines, or for producers making red Crozes-Hermitage that requires drinking within 3–4 years of the vintage.

LUC ARNAVON* * *

Address: Quartier de la Baume
26600 Mercurol
Tel: 4-75-07-43-41
Wines produced: Crozes-Hermitage (white), Crozes-Hermitage Cave Arnavon (red), Crozes-
                Hermitage Domaine du Veau d'Or (red)
Surface area (white): 3.3 acres
            (red): 11.1 acres
Production (white): 9,000 bottles
           (red): Cave Arnavon—10,500 bottles
                   Domaine du Veau d'Or—13,500 bottles
Upbringing (white): 6 months in stainless steel vats
             (red): Cave Arnavon—18 months in oak casks
                   Domaine du Veau d'Or—18 months in 2-year-old oak barrels
Average age of vines (white): 18 years
                     (red): 12–25 years
Blend (white): 100% Marsanne
        (red): 100% Syrah

Although this producer maintains a low profile, he appears intent on producing tradition-ally made wine that could benefit from less time in barrel. These rustic examples of the appellation are likely to be controversial with most modern-day tastes.

ALBERT BÉGOT* * *

Address: Le Village
      26600 Serves-sur-Rhône
Tel: 4-75-03-30-27
Wines produced: Crozes-Hermitage (red and white)
Surface area (white): 2.5 acres
      (red): 10 acres
Production (white): 6,000 bottles
      (red): 22,500 bottles
Upbringing (white): 18 months with 85% of yield in stainless steel tanks and 15% in new
      oak barrels
      (red): 2 years with 50% of the yield in stainless steel tanks and 50% of the yield
      in oak barrels (half of which are new)
Average age of vines (white): 45 years
      (red): 45 years
Blend (white): 100% Marsanne
      (red): 100% Syrah

The late Albert Bégot's widow, Marcelle, continues to fashion traditional, full-bodied, slightly coarse Crozes-Hermitage with no concessions to modern-day tastes. The wine is bottled as it is sold, but not before it has spent at least two years in both cask and stainless steel vats. It appears to me that this might be too long for less than the most concentrated wines. This vineyard is well situated, with impressive holdings of old vines, but to date its full potential has not been exploited. To Marcelle Bégot's credit, the vineyard continues to be farmed organically, as it has been for over two decades.

ALBERT BELLE* * */* * * *

Address: Les Marsuriaux
      26600 Larnage
Tel: 4-75-08-24-58
Wines produced: Crozes-Hermitage (white), Crozes-Hermitage Cuvée Les Pierrelles (red),
      Crozes-Hermitage Cuvée Louis Belle (red)
Surface area (white): 3.7 acres
      (red): Cuvée Les Pierrelles—25 acres
      Cuvée Louis Belle—16 acres
Production (white): 7,500 bottles
      (red): Cuvée Les Pierrelles—60,000 bottles
      Cuvée Louis Belle—30,000 bottles
Upbringing (white): before 1993, all in stainless steel vats for one year; from 1994, 80% in
      stainless steel vats and 20% in new oak for one year
      (red): Cuvée Les Pierrelles—12 months in oak barrels
      Cuvée Louis Belle—12 months in 25–35% new oak barrels
Average age of vines (white): 50 years
      (red): Cuvée Les Pierrelles—30 years
      Cuvée Louis Belle—50 years
Blend (white): 85% Marsanne, 15% Roussanne
      (red): Both cuvées are 100% Syrah

The Domaine Albert Belle is a relatively new creation. Belle broke away from the Tain l'Hermitage cooperative in 1990 to begin estate-bottling his production from his impressively sized holdings of 47 acres, all in Crozes-Hermitage except for a tiny 3.7 acres in the two lieux-dits of Hermitage, Les Murets and Les Diognières. When I visited Albert Belle in the early nineties, he had constructed an entirely new state-of-the-art wine cellar in the village of Larnage. Temperature-controlled stainless steel tanks, air-conditioning, and space for cask aging and bottling his entire crop at one time were all provided for in this drab but impressively equipped cave.

Belle's wines have gone from strength to strength, exhibiting rich, concentrated fruit, an old-vine intensity, and fine aging potential. In most vintages Belle does not destem. He is one of a group of northern Rhône producers who are inflexible on this particular issue. Vinification of both the red and white wines takes place in the temperature-controlled stainless steel tanks, but the special Cuvée Louis Belle (named after Albert's father) is beginning to see partial fermentation in oak casks, à la Burgundy. There is an obvious commitment to quality by both Albert and his son. The wines that have been produced since 1990, even in such difficult years as 1992 and 1993, have been among the finest of the appellation. The red wines are always bottled unfiltered.

Albert Belle is one of the bright, shining stars of Crozes-Hermitage, and this is an estate to follow.

VINTAGES

1995—Crozes-Hermitage Cuvée Louis Belle (red)   The tannic and closed 1995 Louis
·   Belle is a big, rich, intense style of wine. It is well endowed, with fine ripeness, an
88   overriding aromatic and flavor profile consisting of blackcurrants and minerals, and
       a spicy, medium-bodied, tannic finish. It should round out in 1–2 years and last
       for a decade. Last tasted 6/96.

1995—Crozes-Hermitage Les Pierrelles (red)   The 1995s do not exhibit the degree of
·   herbaceousness of the 1994s. They possess sweeter fruit and better acidity, as well
88   as more backward, structured personalities. The easiest to appreciate and most
       flattering to drink is the 1995 Les Pierrelles. A dark ruby-colored wine with purple
       nuances, it displays copious amounts of ripe, jammy, black-cherry and cassis fruit,
       medium body, some tannin, crisp acidity, and a ripe finish. It should drink well for
       7–8 years. Last tasted 6/96.

1994—Crozes-Hermitage Cuvée Louis Belle (red)   The 1994 Louis Belle is especially
·   sweet, rich, deep colored, and complete and complex. There is good density,
88   medium to full body, and a luscious, expansive, chewy richness, with gobs of
       olive-tinged, blackcurrant fruit intertwined with scents of licorice and toast. It is a
       delicious, forward Crozes-Hermitage for drinking over the next 7-8 years. Last
       tasted 6/96.

1994—Crozes-Hermitage Les Pierrelles (red)   The 1994 is a sexy, soft, green-pepper-
·   scented wine with a soft, round entry on the palate, a silky texture, and attractive
86   cassis to go along with an underlying herbaceous component. Some tannin is
       noticeable in the finish. Readers who like their Syrah with a vegetal undertone will
       appreciate this wine even more than I. Drink it over the next 5–6 years. Last tasted
       6/96.

1992—Crozes-Hermitage Cuvée Louis Belle (red)   The 1992 Louis Belle is partially aged
·   in new oak casks and bottled unfiltered (as are Belle's other red wines). It offers an
89   intense, ripe bouquet, great richness, a saturated color, and a sensationally long,
       opulent finish. This medium- to full-bodied Crozes is ideal for drinking over the
       next decade. It is impossible to find another 1992 Crozes-Hermitage this stunning!
       Anticipated maturity: now–2000. Last tasted 6/95.

1992—Crozes-Hermitage Les Pierrelles (red)   The 1992 Les Pierrelles has an intense,
·   herbal, peppery, curranty nose, supple, rich, medium-bodied, lush flavors, an
86   exuberant fruitiness, and an expansive finish. Anticipated maturity: now–1999.
      Last tasted 6/95.

1990—Crozes-Hermitage Les Pierrelles (red)   The 1990 Les Pierrelles exhibited superb
·   black/ruby color, a sweet, fragrant, undeveloped bouquet that exhibited tremendous
87   intensity of black fruits, herbs, and spices. In the mouth the wine was rich, forward,
      impressively deep, expansive, and long. The acidity was sound, the tannin levels
      high but round, and the finish impressive. This beauty should be at its best between
      now and 2000. Last tasted 11/95.

1990—Crozes-Hermitage Cuvée Louis Belle (red)   The 1990 Louis Belle possesses an
·   opaque purple color. With swirling, the tight nose offers enticing aromas of herbs,
89   tar, smoke, and black fruits. In the mouth, the wine exhibits the essence of black-
      cherry fruit, is full-bodied, dense, and rich, with considerable tannin, and a formi-
      dably long, concentrated finish. This superb Crozes should carry its Syrah fruit for
      10–15 years. Anticipated maturity: now–2003. Last tasted 11/95.

CAVE DES CLAIRMONTS* *

Address: Sylviane et Michel Borja
         26600 Beaumont-Monteux
Tel: 4-75-84-61-91
Fax: 4-75-94-56-98
Wines produced: Crozes-Hermitage (red)
Surface area: 233.4 acres
Production: 150,000 bottles (the rest is sold in bulk)
Upbringing: 18 months in cuve
Average age of vines: 27–28 years
Blend: 100% Syrah, all fined and filtered prior to bottling

This domaine, actually a consortium of four families who delegated the administration of
the firm to Michel Borja, produces only red Crozes-Hermitage from 233 acres of vineyards
spread throughout the appellation. Much of their production is sold in bulk, but they do
bottle their wines under the name Caves des Clairmonts in Beaumont-Monteux. The style is
decidedly commercial, with the wines fruity, ripe, juicy, and meant to be drunk (chilled)
within 2–3 years of the vintage. Prices are reasonable.

CHAPOUTIER* * */* * * *

Address: 18, avenue du Docteur Paul Durand
         B.P. 38
         26600 Tain l'Hermitage
Tel: 4-75-08-28-65
Fax: 4-75-08-81-70
Wines produced: Crozes-Hermitage Les Meysonniers (red and white), Crozes-Hermitage
                Petite Ruche (red and white), Crozes-Hermitage Les Varonnières (red)
Surface area (white): made from purchased grapes
               (red): Les Meysonniers and Petite Ruche—17.3 acres, with 50% of the wine
                made from purchased grapes
               Les Varonnières—6 acres
Production (white): Les Meysonniers—900 cases
                Petite Ruche—1,300 cases

             (red): Les Meysonniers—900 cases
                   Petite Ruche—1,300 cases
                   Les Varonnières—335 cases
Upbringing (white): Meysonniers—8 months in stainless steel vats, very little oak
                   Petite Ruche—6 months in stainless steel vats
             (red): Meysonniers—10–12 months in 50% stainless steel vats and 50% oak
                   barrels of which 10% are new
                   Petite Ruche—10–12 months mainly in stainless steel vats with little oak
                   Les Varonnières—12 months in 100% new oak casks
Average age of vines (white): all from purchased grapes
                   (red): Meysonniers—40–80 years
                         Petite Ruche—25 years
                         Les Varonnières—65–70 years
Blend (white): both cuvées are 100% Marsanne
      (red): all three cuvées are 100% Syrah

Most of what the Chapoutier firm produces from Crozes-Hermitage is from purchased grapes. There are two cuvées of white wine and three cuvées of red. The younger-vine cuvées of both red and white are called Petite Ruche, and the older-vine production goes into Les Meysonniers. In 1994, Michel Chapoutier launched a luxury cuvée of Crozes-Hermitage, Les Varonnières, from a low-yielding, old parcel of vines in Le Chassis, a vineyard covered with large *cailloux roulés* that resemble the football-sized stones that carpet much of the Châteauneuf du Pape appellation. The debut vintage of Les Varonnières immediately established Chapoutier as the reference point for Crozes-Hermitage. It is superior even to the top cuvées from Alain Graillot and Paul Jaboulet's Domaine de Thalabert. Although not much is made (about 335 cases), Les Varonnières demonstrates what can be achieved when a wine is made from old vines, tiny yields, and a minimally interventionist winemaking philosophy—there is no fining or filtration after a year in new oak casks.

Among Chapoutier's other Crozes-Hermitage offerings, the red and white Les Meysonniers have always been slightly superior to the Petite Ruche cuvées, which appear to be Chapoutier's concession to purchasers who want an inexpensive Crozes-Hermitage.

Chapoutier's white Crozes-Hermitage is meant to be drunk within 1–2 years of the vintage. With the exception of Les Varonnières, which gives every indication of being capable of 15–20 years of evolution, the red wines should be drunk within 3–5 years of the vintage.

VINTAGES

1995—Crozes-Hermitage Les Meysonnieres (red)   The excellent 1995 Les Meysonnieres
    •   is one of the better bargains in the Chapoutier portfolio. It boasts a sweet, black-
  86 berry, herbes de Provence, cassis-scented nose, crisp acidity, sweet, ripe, berry
    flavors, medium body, and a soft finish. Last tasted 6/96.

1995—Crozes-Hermitage Petite Ruche (red)   The 1995 Petite Ruche offers straightfor-
    •   ward licorice and cassis fruit, medium body, fine ripeness, and enough concentra-
  86 tion to suggest it will continue to drink well for 4–5 years. Last tasted 6/96.

1995—Crozes-Hermitage Les Varonnières (red)   The 1995 Les Varonnières is even
    •   greater than the mind-boggling 1994. Made from yields of 10 hectoliters per
  95 hectare, this 100% Syrah offers a monumental glass of rich, full-bodied, amazingly
    concentrated wine. Tasted blind, it could easily be mistaken for Chapoutier's
    renowned Ermitage Le Pavillon—it is that rich, complex, and prodigious. Bolstered

by fine tannin and moderate acidity, it should drink reasonably early in its life, but have considerable longevity. Anticipated maturity: 1998–2018. Last tasted 6/96.

1995—Crozes-Hermitage Les Meysonniers (white) Made from 100% Marsanne, the 1995
  · Les Meysonniers (lot 7051) exhibits a stony character, attractive orange-blossom
 87 scents, good elegance, and a crisp, dry, refreshing finish. Drink it over the next 3–
     4 years. Last tasted 6/96.

1994—Crozes-Hermitage Les Varonnières (red) This is clearly the finest Crozes-
  · Hermitage I have ever tasted. Only 4,000 bottles were produced. In essence, it is
 93 as good as, if not better than, most other producers' Hermitage. It offers thrilling
     levels of cassis fruit intermingled with aromas of licorice, smoke, flowers, and
     powdered stone. Extremely full and dense, this is a compelling example of what
     Crozes-Hermitage can achieve. Last tasted 6/96.

BERNARD CHAVE* * *

Address: La Burge
        26600 Mercurol
Tel: 4-75-07-42-11
Wines produced: Crozes-Hermitage (red and white)
Surface area (white): 3.7 acres
           (red): 14.8 acres
Production (white): 5,000 bottles
          (red): 30,000 bottles
Upbringing (white): 5% in new oak and 95% in stainless steel vats for 4 months
          (red): 20% in new oak and 80% in 2-year-old barrels for 4 months
Average age of vines (white): 20 years
                    (red): 25 years
Blend (white): 70% Marsanne, 30% Roussanne
     (red): 100% Syrah

The ruggedly handsome Bernard Chave turns out fruity, soft red Crozes-Hermitage and a small quantity of white wine. The majority of his vineyards are planted in heavy clay and sandy soils near Larnage, although he has small parcels in the rocky Les Chassis, where three of the greatest red Crozes-Hermitage—Jaboulet's Domaine de Thalabert, Alain Graillot's La Guiraude, and Chapoutier's Les Varonnières—are produced. Chave is adamantly against even a partial destemming of his crop, and the result is wines that are occasionally too vegetal. This inflexibility seems to be the downfall of many small artisan producers in the northern Rhône. In vintages such as 1990 and 1989, destemming was not necessary since the stems were fully mature, but in most vintages they are not, and they provide a pronounced olive, stemmy component that many consumers find unattractive.

Chave (no relation of Gérard Chave in Mauves, on the western bank of the Rhône) has both well-placed vineyards and low yields, and a few minor adjustments in his winemaking could elevate the quality of this estate's wines.

DOMAINE COLLONGE (GÉRARD COLLONGE)* *

Address: 26600 Mercurol
Tel: 4-75-07-44-32
Fax: 4-75-07-44-06
Wines produced: Crozes-Hermitage (red and white)
Surface area (white): 10 acres
           (red): 74 acres
Production (white): 27,000 bottles
          (red): 210,000 bottles

Upbringing (white): 3 months in enamel-lined cement vats
(red): 12 months in enamel-lined cement vats
Average age of vines (white): 20+ years
(red): 20–30 years
Blend (white): 100% Marsanne
(red): 100% Syrah

This relatively large estate is located in Mercurol. The Collonge family owns 84 acres of vineyards, from which they produce nearly 18,000 cases of red wine and 2,000 cases of white. The wines are aged in vats, bottled early, and are prized for their clean, fresh, lively fruit. Readers looking for substantial, ageworthy, concentrated wines from Crozes-Hermitage will undoubtedly find these efforts too easygoing and innocuous.

DOMAINE DU COLOMBIER (FLORENT ET GABRIEL VIALE)* * * *

Address: Les Chenêts
26600 Mercurol
Tel: 4-75-07-44-07
Fax: 4-75-07-43-47
Wines produced: Crozes-Hermitage (red and white), Crozes-Hermitage Cuvée Gaby (a special cuvée made from a selection of the finest red wine)
Surface area (white): 2.47 acres
(red): 21 acres
Production (white): 4,000 bottles
(red): 20,000 bottles
Upbringing (white): One-fifth of yield in oak cask and the rest in stainless steel vats for 5 months
(red): regular cuvée—One-third of yield in oak casks and two-thirds in stainless steel vats for 12 months
Cuvée Gaby—100% in oak casks (a small percentage new) for 12 months
Average age of vines (white): 80–100 years
(red): 35–40 years
Blend (white): 100% Marsanne
(red): 100% Syrah

Winemaker Florent Viale came to my attention because of the very fine 1993s he produced, a vintage where most of the best northern Rhône producers experienced difficulties. Viale produces two cuvées of red wine, both very good. The Cuvée Gaby is aged for 12 months in 100% new oak casks, and appears to possess the concentration and depth to support such an upbringing. The regular red wine cuvée is aged in both cask and stainless steel vat. These are impressive wines meant to be drunk within 3–4 years of the vintage. This is another estate that merits more attention.

VINTAGES

1994—Crozes-Hermitage Cuvée Gaby   The 1994 Cuvée Gaby exhibits copious quantities
·   of smoky, rich, pure cassis fruit, a lovely, ripe, sweet, round midsection, a touch of
87   toasty oak from new barrels, and a spicy, supple, well-endowed finish. Already
        accessible, it promises to drink well for 5–7 years.

DOMAINE COMBIER (LAURENT COMBIER)* * * *

Address: Clos des Grives

R.N. 7

26600 Pont de l'Isère

Tel: 4-75-84-61-56

Fax: 4-75-84-53-43

Wines produced: Crozes-Hermitage (red and white), Crozes-Hermitage Cuvée Prestige Clos des Grives (red)

Surface area (white): 2.47 acres

    (red): regular cuvée—25 acres

    Clos des Grives—5 acres

Production (white): 6,000 bottles

    (red): regular cuvée—63,000 bottles

    Clos des Grives—7,500 bottles

Upbringing (white): One-third in new oak barrels and two-thirds in stainless steel vats for 7 months

    (red): regular cuvée—80% in stainless steel vats and 20% in oak barrels 2–3 years old for 9 months

    Clos des Grives—50% in new oak barrels and 50% in 1-year-old barrels for 12 months

Average age of vines (white): 7 years and 80 years

    (red): regular cuvée—25 years

    Clos des Grives—45 years

Blend (white): 100% Marsanne

    (red): both cuvées are 100% Syrah

Maurice and Laurent Combier deserve praise for pushing their Domaine Combier into the elite of Crozes-Hermitage. The estate, consisting of 32 acres all in Crozes-Hermitage (except for 2.5 acres in St.-Joseph), has produced increasingly impressive wines over recent years. The 1995s are the finest wines Combier has yet made. They have garnered rave reviews from the French wine writing community, as well as increasing recognition in America. The new modern winery, which sits on the heavily trafficked Route Nationale, between Tain l'Hermitage and Pont de l'Isère, is equipped with temperature-controlled stainless steel tanks for fermentation, and copious quantities of small oak casks for aging their top cuvées. All of this has taken place in the short span of five years.

Father Maurice has gradually turned over most of the winemaking to his son, Laurent, who produces concentrated, rich, exuberant, fruity but intense, pure wines from their impressively situated vineyard on the Les Chassis plateau. All of Combier's vineyards are farmed organically.

There are four wines made at Combier: a fruity, straightforward white Crozes-Hermitage (the debut vintage was 1993), a small amount of red St.-Joseph, and two cuvées of red Crozes-Hermitage. The regular red Crozes-Hermitage is aged both in stainless steel tank and barrel, then blended together. The top wine, the Crozes-Hermitage Cuvée Prestige Clos des Grives, comes from a 5-acre parcel of 45-year-old vines that are aged for 12 months in 50% new oak casks. This wine is bottled without filtration.

Readers should take note of this up-and-coming star of Crozes-Hermitage.

VINTAGES

1995—Crozes-Hermitage (red)   The 1995 Crozes-Hermitage exhibits an opaque purple/
   •   black color, as well as sweet noses of blackcurrants, plums, licorice, and smoke.
88   Sweet, rich fruit, plus structure and well-integrated acidity and tannin, combine for
        an impressive palate impression. This wine should age well for a decade. Last
        tasted 6/96.

1995—Crozes-Hermitage Clos des Grives (red)   The 1995 Clos des Grives is similar to
   •   the regular cuvée, only fuller, longer, and more extracted, with sweeter, riper fruit.
90   It, too, should drink well for a decade. Last tasted 6/96.

1994—Crozes-Hermitage (red)   The 1994 Crozes-Hermitage offers a deep ruby/purple
   •   color, accompanied by a ripe, olive, cassis, vanillin-scented nose, and generous,
87   open-knit, low-acid, round, tasty, mouth-filling flavors. It should drink well for 4–
        7 years. Last tasted 6/96.

1994—Crozes-Hermitage Clos des Grives (red)   The 1994 Clos des Grives is cut from the
   •   same mold, with more black-cherry and smoky oak nuances, sweeter, riper fruit,
88   more glycerin and extract, and a layered finish. It should drink well for a decade.
        It's about time readers discover how good these reasonably priced wines are. Last
        tasted 6/96.

DARD ET RIBO/DOMAINE BLANCHE LAINE* * *

Address: Quartier Blanche Laine
        26600 Mercurol
Tel: 4-75-07-40-00
Fax: 4-75-07-71-02
Wines produced: Crozes-Hermitage (white, old-vine cuvée and young-vine cuvée), Crozes-
        Hermitage (red), Crozes-Hermitage Cuvée de Printemps (red)
Surface area (white): old-vine—0.25 acres
              young-vine—1.9 acres
        (red): 7.5 acres
Production (white): 3,800 bottles
        (red): 10,500 bottles
Upbringing (white): 6 months in barrels, no new oak
        (red): 12 months in barrels, new oak not generally used; the Cuvée de Printemps
        is bottled earlier in the spring
Average age of vines (white): old-vine—30–35 years
              young-vine—10 years
        (red): 10 years and 45 years
Blend (white): old-vine—100% Marsanne
        young-vine—20% Marsanne and 80% Roussanne
        (red): 100% Syrah

    René-Jean Dard and François Ribo formed a partnership to produce wine from 9.65 acres of vineyards, with the majority of this acreage in Crozes-Hermitage. They also own 5 acres of old-vine St.-Joseph, almost all of it on the granite slopes above Tournon and St.-Jean de Muzols. Additionally, a tiny 0.62 acre of 105-year-old vines is owned in the westernmost vineyard of Hermitage, Les Varognes.

    Low yields, a philosophy of minimal intervention in the winemaking (no filtering for the white wine, and no fining or filtering for the reds), in addition to a high percentage of Roussanne in their white Crozes-Hermitage, should produce a wine some of my colleagues call "a Parkerized wine." For whatever reason, Dard et Ribo only occasionally hit the high notes with their winemaking. The reds are somewhat coarse and rustic, and the whites are flavorful but lack vibrancy and spark. This is an interesting, sometimes very good estate, but consistency is not one of its hallmarks.

DOMAINE DES ENTREFAUX (TARDY ET ANGE)* * *

Address: La Beaume
　　　　26600 Chanos-Curson
Tel: 4-75-07-33-38
Fax: 4-75-07-35-27
Wines produced: Crozes-Hermitage (red and white), Crozes-Hermitage Le Dessus des En-
　　　　trefaux (red and white)
Surface area (white): 14.8 acres total
　　　　　　　　(red): regular cuvée—52 acres
　　　　　　　　　　　Le Dessus des Entrefaux—7.5 acres
Production (white): regular cuvée—37,500 bottles
　　　　　　　　　　Le Dessus des Entrefaux—3,000–4,000 bottles
　　　　　　　　(red): regular cuvée—90,000 bottles
　　　　　　　　　　　Le Dessus des Entrefaux—15,000 bottles
Upbringing (white): regular cuvée—7–8 months in stainless steel vats
　　　　　　　　　　　Le Dessus des Entrefaux—6 months in oak barrels and casks
　　　　　　　　(red): regular cuvée—4–5 months, with 50% of the yield in cask and 50% in
　　　　　　　　　　　barrels, of which 10% are new
　　　　　　　　　　　Le Dessus des Entrefaux—12 months, with 50% of the yield in oak
　　　　　　　　　　　barrels and 50% in oak casks, of which 30% are new
Average age of vines (white): 15–20 years
　　　　　　　　　　　(red): regular cuvée—25 years
　　　　　　　　　　　　　Le Dessus des Entrefaux—35 years
Blend (white): regular cuvée—80% Marsanne, 20% Roussanne
　　　　　　　　　Le Dessus des Entrefaux—70% Marsanne, 20% Roussanne
　　　　　(red): both cuvées are 100% Syrah

Increasingly in the Rhône Valley, as well as elsewhere, it is not uncommon for long-term members of cooperatives to decide that it is more challenging, as well as potentially more financially rewarding, to begin to estate-bottle their production, rather than have it comingled in a coop. Charles Tardy and his partner, Bernard Ange, began bottling their own wines in 1980, and they have never looked back. This is a relatively large estate of nearly 75 acres, divided between vineyards surrounding their cellars in Chanos-Curson. There is another large parcel near the L'Isère River at Beaumont-Monteux.

I have generally found the regular cuvées of white and red wine to be midlevel in quality. They are pleasant but undistinguished. This estate does produce two more ambitiously styled cuvées that they call Le Dessus des Entrefaux. In essence, these are older-vine cuvées that are given some barrel aging. The red Crozes-Hermitage Le Dessus des Entrefaux is a more substantial wine than the regular cuvée, but even in a vintage such as 1990, it is a lightweight wine when compared to the majestic richness and splendor of Jaboulet's Domaine de Thalabert or Alain Graillot's La Guiraude.

The white wine, which has its malolactic fermentation blocked and thus must be sterile-filtered, has never been a very satisfying wine, although there is clearly a demand for such one-dimensional, innocuous wines. Tardy and Ange have been attempting to give it more texture, but with little success.

DOMAINE FAYOLLE* * *

Address: Quartier des Gamets
         26600 Gervans
Tel: 4-75-03-33-74
Fax: 4-75-03-32-52
Wines produced: Crozes-Hermitage (red and white), Crozes-Hermitage Les Blancs (white),
         Crozes-Hermitage La Grande Séguine Prestige Cuvée (red), Crozes-
         Hermitage Les Pontaix (red and white), Crozes-Hermitage Les Voussères
         (red)
Surface area (white): regular cuvée—2.47 acres
         Les Pontaix—2.47 acres
         Les Blancs—3.2 acres
         (red): regular cuvée—6.2 acres
         Les Pontaix—7.4 acres
         Les Voussères—2.47 acres
         La Grande Séguine—2.7 acres
Production (white): regular cuvée—6,000 bottles
         Les Pontaix—4,500 bottles
         Les Blancs—6,000 bottles
         (red): regular cuvée—12,000 bottles
         Les Pontaix—18,000 bottles
         fLes Voussères—6,000 bottles
         La Grande Séguine—6,000 bottles
Upbringing (white): 12 months in enamel and stainless steel vats (all 3 cuvées)
         (red): 15 months in 10% new oak barrels (all 4 cuvées)
Average age of vines (white): regular cuvée—10 years
         Les Pontaix—50 years
         Les Blancs—50 years
         (red): regular cuvée—10 years
         Les Pontaix—35 years
         Les Voussères—50 years
         La Grande Séguine—20 years
Blend (white): regular cuvée—100% Marsanne
         Les Pontaix—95% Marsanne, 5% Roussanne
         Les Blancs—95% Marsanne, 5% Roussanne
         (red): 100% Syrah (all 3 cuvées)

Domaine Fayolle was one of the first Crozes-Hermitage properties to estate-bottle their wines. They began the practice in the early seventies. When I first visited this estate in 1982, I was well received by twins Jean-Paul and Jean-Claude Fayolle. This domaine's wines, which can be distressingly irregular, are produced from their nearly 27 acres of Crozes-Hermitage vineyards planted mainly on the lower slopes in and around Gervans. Fayolle also owns a small vineyard in the Hermitage vineyard of Les Diognières.

Throughout the eighties, the Domaine Fayolle wines were often plagued by mercaptanlike noses from not having been racked from one barrel/foudre to another; thus the lees' impurities tainted the wines' aromas and flavors. Recent vintages have been more consistent, but this remains an estate with more potential than realized quality.

There are three cuvées of red and an equal number of white wines produced. The white wines tend to be neutral and bland, which is typical for white Crozes-Hermitage. The red wines are generally more consistent as well as more interesting. The regular cuvée of Crozes-Hermitage, Les Pontaix, is given a relatively long aging in cask (15 months). It is a standard, middle-of-the-road Crozes-Hermitage, not too light, nor terribly concentrated. The finest Domaine Fayolle offerings are Les Voussères and La Grande Séguine, the latter being their Cuvée Prestige. These wines are made in 300-case lots, and possess more concentration and intensity. In top vintages, they are wines to drink within a decade.

MICHEL FERRATON* * *

Address: 13, rue de la Sizeranne
       B.P. 91
       26600 Tain l'Hermitage
Tel: 4-75-08-59-51
Fax: 4-75-08-81-59
Wines produced: Crozes-Hermitage Cuvée La Matinière (red)
Surface area: 13.6 acres
Production: 37,750 bottles
Upbringing: 10–12 months, with 70% of the yield in old oak barrels and 30% in stainless
       steel vats
Average age of vines: 30 years
Blend: 100% Syrah

Michel Ferraton, who is covered in more detail in the chapter on Hermitage (see page 159), owns 13.6 acres of Crozes-Hermitage vines, not far from Jaboulet's large Domaine de Thalabert estate in the rocky plateau of Les Chassis, south of Tain l'Hermitage in the direction of La-Roche-de-Glun. This traditionally made Crozes-Hermitage is occasionally rustic, but always spicy and full of flavor. In difficult vintages it can be slightly vegetal because of Ferraton's resistance to destemming. Although inconsistent, it can be one of the best wines of the appellation in top years. Moreover, it is always reasonably priced.

VINTAGES

1994—Crozes-Hermitage La Matinière   Michel Ferraton declassified his entire Hermi-
·   tage and Crozes-Hermitage production in 1993. His cuvées of 1994, which will not
86   be released for a year, include a solid, dark ruby-colored, spicy, sweet, medium-
      bodied, moderately tannic 1994 Crozes-Hermitage La Matinière. It is made in a
      muscular style that should hold up to 7–8 years of cellaring. Last tasted 6/96.

1992—Crozes-Hermitage La Matinière   The 1992 La Matinière has an excellent ruby/
·   purple color, plenty of sweet, spicy fruit, and a supple, easy-to-understand charac-
85   ter. Mature now. Last tasted 6/96.

1990—Crozes-Hermitage La Matinière   Ferraton can be inconsistent, but his deeply
·   colored 1990 La Matinière offers a forceful, gamy, spicy, herbal Syrah nose. Full-
86   bodied, rich, and concentrated, with considerable extract. Anticipated maturity:
      now–2000. Last tasted 7/94.

1988—Crozes-Hermitage La Matinière   Although the 1988 La Matinière exhibits ade-
·   quate concentration, it has high acidity, and is beginning to drop its fruit. Mature
76   now. Last tasted 7/94.

1985—Crozes-Hermitage La Matinière   Dark ruby/garnet-colored, with some orange at
·   the rim, this wine reveals a herbaceous, full-intensity bouquet of cassis fruit and
87   smoky scents. Fully mature, it is a supple, unctuous, full-bodied wine that has
      aged well. Mature now. Last tasted 7/94.

ALAIN GRAILLOT (DOMAINE LES CHÊNES VERTS) * * */* * * *

Address: 26600 Pont de l'Isère
Tel: 4-75-84-67-52
Fax: 4-75-07-24-31
Wines produced: Crozes-Hermitage Cuvée Classique (red and white), Crozes-Hermitage
          Cuvée La Guiraude (red)
Surface area (white): 7.41 acres
          (red): 42 acres
Production (white): 15,000 bottles
          (red): Cuvée Classique—80,000 bottles
          Cuvée La Guiraude—0–15,000 bottles depending on the vintage
Upbringing (white): 10 months, with 50% of the yield in stainless steel vats and 50% in oak
          barrels
          (red): Cuvée Classique—12 months, with 80% of the yield in old oak and 20%
          in cuve
          Cuvée La Guiraude—12 months in old oak
Average age of vines (white): 15 years
          (red): 20 years
Blend (white): 80% Marsanne, 20% Roussanne
          (red): 100% Syrah

Alain Graillot, who is in his early forties, never made wine until he gave up his career as
an international salesman for an agricultural firm in Paris to begin his life as a vigneron in
Crozes-Hermitage. He says he arrived in Crozes-Hermitage several weeks before the 1985
harvest, with no winemaking experience, but with a philosophy well grounded in common
sense. In just over a decade, Alain Graillot has proven to be not only one of the stars of
Crozes-Hermitage, but also one of the younger generation of Rhône Valley producers that is
reshaping the Rhône landscape with higher-quality wines. His influence has been enormous,
and he deserves all the accolades he has received.

Graillot's Domaine les Chênes Verts estate, which is also his residence, is located just
off the highly traveled Route Nationale N 7 south of Tain l'Hermitage, in the direction of
Pont de l'Isère. His vineyards are planted on the flat, rocky terrain of the broad expanse
located just to the east of La-Roche-de-Glun, and extend northward to the superb vineyard
sites of Les Chassis and Les Sept Chemins. Graillot's winemaking philosophy has been
largely acquired from his good friends Gérard Jaboulet, Gérard Chave, and Marcel Guigal
and other top-quality, highly committed French wine producers. From his first efforts in
1985 from rented vineyards, he acquired his entire 52.7-acre estate in 1988, of which 49.5
acres are in Crozes-Hermitage, with the balance in two tiny parcels in Hermitage's Les
Greffieux vineyard and in St.-Joseph.

An air-conditioned cellar, small oak casks, and a progressive approach to winemaking
have resulted in wines that are often among the finest of the appellation. Graillot believes
in keeping yields low, harvesting later than most growers, and is willing to be flexible with
the use of new oak, depending on the richness of each vintage's wine. In a region known for
an almost intransigent stubbornness about how wine is made, Graillot has a refreshing
open-minded, international point of view that is to be admired, particularly as it is backed
up with high-quality wines.

Although Graillot is high on potential for white Crozes-Hermitage, I must say that with
few exceptions I have found it to be a sterile, one-dimensional wine, although recent
improvements are noticeable. He believes in blocking malolactic, thus the wine must be
sterile-filtered. Graillot's wine lasts longer than most white Crozes-Hermitage because it is

impeccably made in his extremely sanitary cellars. While his white wine has improved, I still recommend drinking it within its first 2–3 years of life. With respect to his red wines, he demonstrates amazing flexibility. He destems 100% of his grapes from St.-Joseph, but never does any destemming with his Crozes-Hermitage. The wines, which are fermented in concrete vats, are moved into both oak casks and tank. About 80% of Graillot's red wine is aged in oak, and the other 20% in tank, and then blended together. The top cuvée, La Guiraude, is a selection of the best barrels. As Graillot says, it is simply those barrels that "I enjoy the most." The two red wine cuvées are put through a light cellulose pad filtration before bottling. Interestingly, Graillot believes that fining, which he eschews, is far more damaging to a wine than filtration. The regular cuvée of Crozes-Hermitage is best drunk in its first 6–8 years of life, but in great years such as 1990 and 1995, La Guiraude can be uncommonly long-lived; it possesses the potential to last for 15 or more years.

Alain Graillot is a rarity—a newcomer who has made an impressive contribution to the quality of Rhône wines in just over a decade.

VINTAGES

1995—Crozes-Hermitage (red) The 1995 Crozes-Hermitage looks to be superb, with a black-pepper, herb, olive, cassis-scented nose, medium to full body, outstanding
·
89 richness, huge tannin, and zesty acidity. It is a backward, youthful, vibrant wine that will require 4–5 years of cellaring before it rounds into drinking form. It should keep for 10–15 years. Last tasted 6/96.

1995—Crozes-Hermitage (white) The 1995 Crozes-Hermitage blanc is made of 80% Marsanne and 20% Roussanne. It is a ripe, creamy-textured, one-dimensional but
·
85 fruity, citrusy white wine that is meant to be drunk over the next 2–3 years. Last tasted 6/96.

1994—Crozes-Hermitage (red) Dark ruby/purple-colored, the 1994 Crozes-Hermitage reveals a meaty nose, silky-smooth flavors, and a sense of elegance and style.
·
87 Although it will drink well for 7–8 years, its charming character is hard to resist. Last tasted 6/96.

1994—Crozes-Hermitage La Guiraude (red) Graillot's top cuvée, the 1994 La Guiraude exhibits an opaque ruby/purple color, followed by a big, sweet nose of herbs,
·
89 cassis, licorice, and smoke. Round, lush, and medium- to full-bodied, this is a fat, expressive, aromatic wine that should drink well for a decade. Last tasted 6/96.

1993—Crozes-Hermitage (red) The 1993 Crozes-Hermitage exhibits an herbaceous nose, medium body, and tart, spicy flavors with high acidity. There is not much
·
76 flesh to this emaciated wine. Mature now. Last tasted 11/95.

1993—Crozes-Hermitage La Guiraude (red) The 1993 La Guiraude is more deeply colored, with more noticeable new oak, but it is lean, straightforward, medium-bodied,
·
79 and lacking fruit. A pronounced green-pepper component is also worrisome. Anticipated maturity: now–2000. Last tasted 11/95.

1992—Crozes-Hermitage (red) Graillot's 1992 red wine cuvées are not as profound as his 1990s or 1989s. They are soundly made, round, supple wines that will provide
·
83 good near-term drinking. The 1992 Crozes-Hermitage reveals a spicy, cassis-scented, ripe nose, medium-bodied flavors, and moderate tannin in the finish. Mature now. Last tasted 6/95.

1992—Crozes-Hermitage La Guiraude (red) The 1992 La Guiraude possesses more toasty new oak, a black-cherry- and herb-scented nose, rich fruit, a soft texture,
·
87 low acidity, and light tannin in the finish. Anticipated maturity: now–1999. Last tasted 6/95.

1991—Crozes-Hermitage (red)   The 1991 Crozes-Hermitage regular cuvée displays a
·   spicy, smoky, ripe, cassis-scented nose, medium body, soft tannin, and a supple,
85   fruity finish. Anticipated maturity: now–1999. Last tasted 6/95.

1991—Crozes-Hermitage La Guiraude (red)   The 1991 La Guiraude exhibits more den-
·   sity and toasty vanillin from being aged in a higher percentage of new oak barrels,
87   as well as a medium-bodied, more concentrated palate than the regular cuvée.
       Fully mature, this is an elegant, round, ripe, and fruity wine. Anticipated maturity:
       now–2002. Last tasted 6/95.

1990—Crozes-Hermitage (red)   The regular cuvée of 1990 Crozes-Hermitage tastes like
·   most producers' Hermitage. The sensational dark purple color is followed by a
91   huge bouquet of roasted, black-raspberry fruit, smoky, earthy scents, and a nice
       touch of toasty new oak. There is mind-boggling richness in this wine, as well as
       extraordinary extraction, yet the underpinnings of acidity, tannin, and alcohol are
       there. This is Graillot's finest regular cuvée of Crozes-Hermitage to date. Antici-
       pated maturity: now–2003. Last tasted 12/95.

1990—Crozes-Hermitage La Guiraude (red)   The 1990 La Guiraude is a compelling
·   example of just what heights a top producer can reach in a less prestigious appella-
93   tion. The nose of smoke, Asian spices, black fruits, and oak is enough to turn any
       wine enthusiast into a Rhône wine fanatic. On the palate, the wine exhibits a
       multidimensional personality, phenomenal ripeness and richness, decent acidity,
       and gobs of glycerin, alcohol, and extraction of flavor in a finish that must last for
       a minute. It is surprisingly approachable given its massive size, but the fruit and
       body have hidden some lofty tannin levels. Anticipated maturity: now–2006. Last
       tasted 12/95.

1989—Crozes-Hermitage (red)   The 1989 Crozes-Hermitage is a dazzling wine, with
·   at least 10–15 years of aging potential. Its ruby/purple color, sweet bouquet of
89   vanillin-scented new oak, roasted fruit (particularly cassis and black plums), excel-
       lent extract, rich, full-bodied, brilliantly focused palate impression, and super
       length make it a delicious bottle of Crozes-Hermitage. Anticipated maturity: now–
       2002. Last tasted 12/95.

1989—Crozes-Hermitage La Guiraude (red)   One of the top wines of the vintage, pos-
·   sessing an opaque ruby/purple color, a sensational bouquet of licorice, Provençal
90   herbs, vanillin, black cherries, and black raspberries, Graillot's 1989 La Guiraude
       could easily be confused with one of the better examples of Hermitage. In the
       mouth this multidimensional wine is impressively concentrated and displays more
       oak than the regular cuvée. Full-bodied, with super length and riveting depth, it is
       a superb expression of the Syrah grape. A winemaking tour de force! Bravo!
       Anticipated maturity: now–2004. Last tasted 12/95.

1988—Crozes-Hermitage (red)   The 1988 Crozes-Hermitage is a dark garnet-colored
·   wine with an extremely fragrant bouquet that suggests aromas of black raspberries,
86   Provençal herbs, and spicy, toasty oak. In the mouth this is a solidly built, muscu-
       lar, rich, concentrated wine that has plenty of soft tannins, crisp acidity, and grip
       and length. Anticipated maturity: now–2005. Last tasted 6/95.

1988—Crozes-Hermitage La Guiraude (red)   The fabulous 1988 La Guiraude offers a
·   black-pepper- and olive-scented bouquet intertwined with superripe black plums,
89   raspberries, minerals, and licorice. On the palate the wine exhibits plenty of toasty
       oak, which serves to frame its size and concentration. It is a delicious, expansively
       flavored Crozes. Anticipated maturity: now–2007. Last tasted 6/95.

PAUL JABOULET-AINÉ* * */* * * *

Address: Les Jalets
R.N. 7, B.P. 46
La-Roche-de-Glun
26600 Tain l'Hermitage
Tel: 4-75-84-68-93
Fax: 4-75-84-56-14
Wines produced: Crozes-Hermitage Mule Blanche (white), Crozes-Hermitage Les Jalets
(red), Crozes-Hermitage Domaine de Thalabert (red)
Surface area (white): 17.3 acres
(red): Domaine de Thalabert—96.3 acres
Les Jalets—produced from young vines of Domaine Thalabert, plus wine
purchased from other producers
Production (white): 35,000 bottles
(red): Domaine de Thalabert—200,000 bottles
Les Jalets—300,000 bottles
Upbringing (white): 2–3 months in barrels 1–2 years old
(red): Domaine de Thalabert—12–18 months in old oak barrels
Les Jalets—8–12 months in stainless steel vats
Average age of vines (white): 25–50 years
(red): 7–50 years
Blend (white): 50% Marsanne, 50% Roussanne
(red): 100% Syrah

Jaboulet's red Crozes-Hermitage, called Domaine de Thalabert, is indisputably among the finest wines of the appellation. It can in fact taste and smell like a lighter-weight Hermitage. Jaboulet's Domaine de Thalabert consists of 96.3 acres in Crozes, and produces approximately 17,000 cases of wine. All of it is red; there is no white wine made at this estate. The vines at Domaine de Thalabert average 25–30 years of age. The wine spends 12–18 months in oak barrels prior to being bottled. It is one of the few Crozes reds that actually will improve in the bottle for four to eight years, and can last a decade or more in vintages such as 1978, 1983, and 1990. The Jaboulets also make another red Crozes-Hermitage, Les Jalets, from a blend of purchased wine and the young vines of Thalabert. Production ranges from 25,000–40,000 cases of this red Crozes. It is usually a sound wine, but much less concentrated than Thalabert.

The Jaboulets also produce 3,000 cases of a white Crozes-Hermitage. Quaintly called La Mule Blanche, it was, like other Jaboulet white wines, neutral and boring until 1983, when the firm clearly started to incorporate more flavor and muscle into their whites. The wine is made from the Jaboulet's own 17.3-acre vineyard, and is unique because of its high percentage of Roussanne. The blend sought each year is 50% Marsanne and 50% Roussanne. It is a wine to drink within two to three years of the vintage.

With respect to the white wines, the Jaboulets have experimented with vinification techniques, as well as exposure to oak cask. The objective is to produce a fruity, vigorous, vibrant wine, and thus the malolactic fermentation is blocked, and the majority of the wine is kept in tank and given only 1–3 months' exposure to oak casks. The wines are sterile-filtered and bottled early to preserve their freshness. In some vintages, 1995 for example, this technique seems to work. It appears to me that in vintages in the nineties, Jaboulet has produced more attractive white wines, not only their Crozes-Hermitage, but also their Hermitage Chevalier de Stérimberg, St.-Joseph Le Grand Pompée, and Châteauneuf du Pape Les Cèdres.

VINTAGES

1995—Crozes-Hermitage Domaine de Thalabert (red)   The 1995 is excellent. It exhibits
·   a deep ruby/purple color, medium body, a good, spicy, herb, licorice, and cassis-
87   scented nose, excellent fruit, and an up-front, forward style. There is enough acidity
            to keep the wine fresh and well focused for 7–8 years. Last tasted 6/96.

1995—Crozes-Hermitage La Mule Blanche (white)   For drinking over the next several
·   years, readers should check out the 1995 Crozes-Hermitage La Mule Blanche. A
87   50–50 blend of Marsanne and Roussanne, this wine reveals a Viognier-like charac-
            ter in its honeyed nose and apricotlike flavors. The wine is fresh, lively, and a good
            value among Rhône Valley whites. Last tasted 6/96.

1994—Crozes-Hermitage Les Jalets (red)   The Jaboulet family declassified their famed
·   Hermitage La Chapelle and Crozes-Hermitage Domaine de Thalabert in both the
75   1992 and 1993 vintages. I was hoping for more impressive wines in 1994. The
            vegetal, light, soft, diluted 1994 Crozes-Hermitage Les Jalets is unexciting. Last
            tasted 6/96.

1994—Crozes-Hermitage Domaine de Thalabert (red)   The 1994 reveals more color satu-
·   ration, but it comes across as a foursquare, medium-bodied wine with no focal
84   point. Some olive/cassis flavors offer moderate charm. Anticipated maturity: now–
            2002. Last tasted 6/96.

1994—Crozes-Hermitage La Mule Blanche (white)   The 1994 white wines are simple and
·   medium-bodied, with barely enough fruit. I actually preferred the 1994 Crozes-
78   Hermitage La Mule Blanche to the more expensive 1994 Hermitage Chevalier de
            Stérimberg. Mature now. Last tasted 6/96.
            (*Note:* In 1993 the Crozes-Hermitage Domaine de Thalabert was declassified
            because Jaboulet was not satisfied with the quality of the wine.)

1992—Crozes-Hermitage Domaine de Thalabert (red)   A relatively diluted example of
·   Domaine de Thalabert, this spicy, herbal wine exhibits a medium ruby color, some
81   vague cassis fruit notes, coarse tannin, and none of the sweet, ripe, rich midsection
            this wine possesses in top vintages. Mature now. Last tasted 6/95.

1991—Crozes-Hermitage Domaine de Thalabert (red)   The smoky, herbal 1991 possesses
·   the sweet perfume of spicy black fruits, round, opulent, full-bodied flavors, surpris-
87   ingly good concentration, low acidity, and soft tannins in the finish. Anticipated
            maturity: now–2000. Last tasted 6/95.

1990—Crozes-Hermitage Les Jalets (red)   This wine exhibits a bouquet of black fruits,
·   herbs, smoke, and damp woodsy aromas. In the mouth it is dense, with gobs of
85   fruit, wonderful extraction, and a long, velvety finish. Anticipated maturity: now–
            1998. Last tasted 9/94.

1990—Crozes-Hermitage Domaine de Thalabert (red)   The 1990 is an unqualified win-
·   ner. My instincts suggest it will easily eclipse the 1978. The 1990 exhibits a huge,
92   roasted Syrah nose and the massive power produced by the hot sun and drought of
            this vintage. It has also benefited from an unbelievably long 40-day maceration.
            The huge, smoky, superripe nose of herbs, coffee, and cassis is followed by a
            densely packed, authoritatively rich, nearly massive, surprisingly well-balanced
            wine. Anticipated maturity: now–2005. Last tasted 12/95.

1989—Crozes-Hermitage Les Jalets (red)   The 1989 Les Jalets is more savage, with a
·   tobacco, herb, and earthy-scented nose, ripe, moderately tannic flavors, and a
82   shorter finish. It is a good, serviceable Crozes-Hermitage. Drink up. Last tasted
            11/94.

1989—Crozes-Hermitage Domaine de Thalabert (red)   A dark ruby/garnet-colored wine,
 ·   the 1989 offers up an intense bouquet of sweet, cedary spices, olives, and black
90   fruits. It is lush, richly fruity, and full-bodied, with plenty of glycerin and sweet
            tannin in the finish. Anticipated maturity: now–2004. Last tasted 6/94.

1988—Crozes-Hermitage Domaine de Thalabert (red)   The curranty, weedy, 1988 Tha-
 ·   labert is good, with a big, spicy, plummy, herbaceous bouquet, medium- to full-
85   bodied flavors, and a dense, concentrated, tannic finish. I doubt the tannin will
            ever fully melt away. Mature now. Last tasted 12/95.

1985—Crozes-Hermitage Domaine de Thalabert (red)   Much more voluptuous and opu-
 ·   lent than Jaboulet's regular bottling of Crozes, the 1985 Domaine de Thalabert has
87   a dark garnet color, full body, outstanding concentration, oodles of cassis and
            peppery, olive-flavored fruit, and a velvety finish. Mature now. Last tasted 11/94.

1983—Crozes-Hermitage Domaine de Thalabert (red)   Deep garnet-colored, with an
 ·   earthy, roasted-herb, berry-fruit aroma, the 1983 Domaine de Thalabert remains a
84   tannic wine. Still hard-edged, this medium-bodied Crozes appears to be losing its
            fruit and becoming increasingly astringent and desiccated. Mature now. Last tasted
            6/96.

Older Vintages

Last tasted in November 1995, the 1978 Domaine de Thalabert was still rich in fruit,
full-bodied, and complex, with an olive-tinged, roasted-meat, gamy quality not unlike a
smaller-scaled Hermitage. It is fully mature, yet still vibrant and delicious.

JEAN MARSANNE* * *

Address: Avenue Ozier
　　　　07300 Mauves
Tel: 4-75-08-86-26
Wines produced: Crozes-Hermitage (red)
Surface area: 1.9 acres
Production: 4,800 bottles
Upbringing: 10–15 months in old oak casks (demi-muids), then 6 months in stainless steel
　　　　vats
Average age of vines: 15–20 years
Blend: 100% Syrah

This estate, now run by André and René Marsanne following the death of their brother,
Jean Marsanne, in 1990, is better known for their richly fruity, old-style, well-made St.-
Joseph. They own nearly 2 acres of Syrah in Crozes-Hermitage. I have tasted only a handful
of vintages (none recent), but I have found them to be good efforts. I enjoyed the licorice,
Provençal herb, sweet cassis fruit this estate achieved. The Marsannes are traditional
winemakers, refusing to destem, and bottling their natural wines with no clarification. Much
of the production is sold direct.

DOMAINE DU PAVILLON (G.A.E.C. CORNU)* * * *

Address: Les Chassis
　　　　26600 Mercurol
Tel: 4-75-08-24-47
Wines produced: Crozes-Hermitage (red and white), Crozes-Hermitage Cuvée Vieilles
　　　　Vignes (red)

Surface area (white): 1.24 acres
        (red): 23.5 acres
Production (white): 3,000 bottles
        (red): 55,500 bottles, of which 15,000 are estate-bottled
Upbringing (white): 50% of the yield in stainless steel vats and 50% in cement vats for 8 months
        (red): regular cuvée—6 months in barrels 2–3 years old
        Cuvée Vieilles Vignes—6–12 months in barrels, some new
Average age of vines (white): 20 years
        (red): regular cuvée—17 years
        Cuvée Vieilles Vignes—60 years
Blend (white): 100% Marsanne
    (red): 100% Syrah (both cuvées)

This estate of nearly 25 acres was one of the major suppliers of wines to the Jaboulet firm until 1989, at which time Stephane Cornu convinced his father to begin estate-bottling more of the production. The result has been an increased level of quality. The vineyards are located in the rocky plateau soils of Les Chassis and Les Sept Chemins. The wines are made in an attractive, modern style, with enough allegiance to both the varietal and the vineyard. The estate turns out a fruity, clean, crisp white wine, and two very good cuvées of red wine. The regular cuvée is deeply colored, rich, and fruity. The Cuvée Vieilles Vignes is made from a parcel of 60-year-old Syrah vines and is aged completely in small oak casks. This is a serious estate that has only recently emerged as one of Crozes-Hermitage's top producers.

VINTAGES

1995—Crozes-Hermitage Cuvée Vieilles Vignes (red)   In 1995 Domaine du Pavillon's
   old vines produced a meager 28 hectoliters per hectare (under two tons of fruit per
89   acre). This cuvée was fashioned from a parcel of 60-year-old Syrah vines. The
   wine's opaque purple, dense, rich, sweet, cassis fruit, and medium- to full-bodied,
   flashy, as well as fleshy, texture, make for an exciting initial impression. No doubt
   proprietor Cornu is trying (and succeeding) to duplicate the style of his neighbor,
   Alain Graillot. This is a serious, full-bodied Crozes-Hermitage with low acidity and
   gobs of fruit. Drink it over the next 5–6 years. Last tasted 6/96.

DOMAINES POCHON / CHÂTEAU DE CURSON (ETIENNE POCHON)* * *
Address: Château de Curson
       26600 Chanos-Curson
Tel: 4-75-07-34-60
Fax: 4-75-07-30-27
Wines produced: Crozes-Hermitage Château Curson (red and white), Crozes-Hermitage Domaines Pochon (red and white)
Surface area (white): Château Curson—2.47 acres
        Domaines Pochon—6.2 acres
        (red): Château Curson—7.5 acres
        Domaines Pochon—20 acres
Production (white): Château Curson—6,750 bottles
        Domaines Pochon—15,000 bottles
        (red): Château Curson—6,000–18,000 bottles
        Domaines Pochon—30,000–40,000 bottles

Upbringing (white): Château Curson—4 months in 100% new oak barrels
                Domaines Pochon—6 months in stainless steel vats
         (red): Château Curson—40% of the yield spends 8 months in new oak barrels
                and 60% of the yield spends 12 months in oak barrels 1–2 years old
                Domaines Pochon—One-third of the yield spends 9 months in oak bar-
                rels, 2–6 years old and two-thirds of the yield spends 9 months in stain-
                less steel vats.
Average age of vines (white): Château Curson—20 years
                     Domaines Pochon—10–20 years
             (red): Château Curson—30 years
                     Domaines Pochon—15 years
Blend (white): Château Curson—50% Marsanne, 50% Roussanne
             Domaines Pochon—80% Marsanne, 20% Roussanne
   (red): both cuvées are 100% Syrah

The shy Etienne Pochon organically farms his 36+ acres of vineyards, turning out both white and red wines under two separate labels, Château Curson and Domaines Pochon. The Château Curson label represents the more limited cuvées that see aging primarily in oak casks, of which a high percentage is new. The Domaines Pochon wines are meant to be fruitier and are therefore aged in stainless steel tanks. By presenting two levels of wine quality, Pochon believes he satisfies consumers looking for immediately drinkable, fresh, fruity whites and reds as well as those more serious Rhône wine enthusiasts looking for fuller-bodied, more concentrated, larger-scaled wines. Pochon is one of the few Crozes-Hermitage producers to destem most of his red wine grapes, as well as one of the few to use the technique of *macération pelliculaire* to obtain complexity and aromatics in his white wines. In vintages such as 1990, 1989, and 1988 the Crozes-Hermitage Château Curson can last up to a decade, whereas the Domaines Pochon needs to be drunk in its first 3–5 years of life. Both of the white wines should be drunk in their first several years of life. This is a reliable estate producing modern-style wines that are cleanly made, fresh, lively, and in the case of the top cuvées from the best vintages, capable of modest longevity.

VINTAGES

1990—Crozes-Hermitage Château Curson (red)   The 1990 Château Curson is the best wine
·   I have yet tasted from this estate. It exhibits an opaque black/purple color, and a huge
87   nose of herbs and overripe cassis. In the mouth there is superb richness, plenty of
       tannins, a combination of elegance and fatness, and a long, spicy, roasted finish. This
       wine could easily be confused with a medium-weight Hermitage. Anticipated matu-
       rity: now–2000. Last tasted 4/95.

1989—Crozes-Hermitage Château Curson (red)   The 1989 exhibits similar substance and
·   richness, but the acids are lower and the tannins less elevated. Much like the
86   1990, this chewy, rich Hermitage should be drunk within its first 10–12 years of
       life. Last tasted 6/93.

1988—Crozes-Hermitage Château Curson (red)   The 1988 had a gorgeous black/ruby
·   color, a wonderfully up-front, seductive bouquet of black fruits and toasty new oak.
85   In the mouth it displayed good rather than great concentration, and I marked it
       down considerably for its lack of length and finish. Of course, much of the publicity
       being generated about the Château Curson wines is by Peter Vezan, the trans-
       planted American who represents them, and he is obviously not a disinterested
       party. In any event, the red Château Curson is well worth trying as it is a good,
       clean example of the Crozes-Hermitage type, but hardly the "best ever made in the
       appellation," as I had been told. Anticipated maturity: now–2000. Last tasted 6/93.

DOMAINE JACQUES ET JEAN-LOUIS PRADELLE* * *

Address: Le Village
      26600 Chanos-Curson
Tel: 4-75-07-31-00
Fax: 4-75-07-35-34
Wines produced: Crozes-Hermitage (red and white), Crozes-Hermitage Cuvée Les Hiron-
      delles (red)
Surface area (white): 10 acres
      (red): regular cuvée—35 acres
      Les Hirondelles—15 acres
Production: (white): 24,000 bottles
      (red): regular cuvée—60,000 bottles
      Les Hirondelles—30,000 bottles
Upbringing (white): 5 months in cement vats
      (red): regular cuvée—9 months with 50% of the yield in cask and 50% in old
      oak barrels
      Les Hirondelles—18 months with 50% of the yield in cask and 50% in
      old oak barrels
Average age of vines (white): 20 years
      (red): both cuvées average 20 years
Blend (white): 95% Marsanne, 5% Roussanne
      (red): both cuvées are 100% Syrah

In 1978, brothers Jacques and Jean-Louis Pradelle left the cooperative Union des Pro-
priétaires in Tain l'Hermitage, so that they could estate-bottle their own red and white
Crozes-Hermitage. Their cellars are located in the eastern part of the appellation in Chanos-
Curson. They own 50 acres of Syrah and another 10 acres of Marsanne, all of which lie in
the stony, sandy soils of Mercurol. Over two-thirds of their vines are on the plateau rather
than the hillsides. The Pradelles are a competent source for red Crozes, but their white
wine, despite the modern winemaking philosophy, lacks character and tastes tart and thin.
For all of the white wine's one-dimensional quality, the red wine is a brawny, fruit-filled,
rustic style of Crozes that offers a dramatic contrast to the innocuous white. It is aged in
casks and foudres for one year prior to bottling.

For readers willing to spend a few dollars more, I would recommend the Pradelle's Cuvée
Les Hirondelles, a wine with more intensity and riper fruit. The white wines require drinking
within 1–2 years of the vintage. The red wines will drink well for 3–8 years.

RAYMOND ROURE* * *

Address: Quartier Les Blancs
      26600 Gervans
Tel: 4-75-03-32-72
Wines produced: Crozes-Hermitage (white), Crozes-Hermitage Les Picaudières (red)
Surface area (white): 5 acres
      (red): 22 acres
Production (white): 12,000 bottles
      (red): 60,000 bottles
Upbringing (white): 18–30 months in tank and wood cask
      (red): fermentation in cement tanks with aging in cask and demi-muids for
      24–30 months
Average age of vines (white): 20 years
      (red): 50–80 years

Blend (white): 100% Marsanne
    (red): 100% Syrah

Note: In fall 1996, this estate was purchased by the firm of Paul Jaboulet-Aîné. Beginning with the 1996 vintage, the wines will be called Domaine Roure and bottled under the Jaboulet-Aîné label.

Raymond Roure, who is now in his early eighties, made profound Crozes-Hermitage in the seventies, but recent vintages have exhibited considerable irregularity. Roure owns some of the finest hillside vineyards in Crozes-Hermitage, all on the hillsides behind the huge dome of Tain l'Hermitage, extending to the north toward the village of Gervans. Old vines, low yields, and superb raw materials have never been a problem at this estate. The difficulty has been in the upbringing of the wine, which results in too many dried-out, musty, oxidized examples of both white and red Crozes-Hermitage. Undoubtedly, 24–30 months of cask aging for the white wine is excessive, and a similar argument can be made in lighter vintages for the red Crozes-Hermitage. Roure does little else wrong, as the wines are allowed to make themselves and are bottled naturally with rarely any filtration. He has also exhibited more flexibility than many of his peers in destemming the grapes in years when there is not full physiological ripeness. However, Roure's advanced age and fragile health, with no obvious successor in view, may suggest a cloudy future for this estate, which unquestionably has some of the finest terroir in the appellation.

DOMAINE ST.-JEMMS* *

Address: Les Chassis
    R.N. 7
    26600 Mercurol
Tel: 4-75-08-33-03
Fax: 4-75-08-69-80
Wines produced: Crozes-Hermitage (red and white)
Surface area (white): 7.4 acres
    (red): 79 acres
Production (white): 15,000 bottles
    (red): 15,000 cases
Upbringing (white): 8 months in enamel and fiberglass vats
    (red): At least 9 months in oak casks
Average age of vines (white): 25–30 years
    (red): 25–30 years
Blend (white): 90% Marsanne, 10% Roussanne
    (red): 100% Syrah

Robert Michelas turns out correct, chunky, frequently rustic wines from his vineyards located between Pont de l'Isère in the south and Mercurol in the north. Much of his harvest is done by machines, and in tasting the wines, I have the impression that little selection is made in the cellars. Don't get me wrong; these are not bad wines, just indifferent and blatantly commercial.

MARC SORREL* *

Address: 128 bis, avenue Jean Jaurès
    B.P. 69
    26600 Tain l'Hermitage
Tel: 4-75-07-10-07
Fax: 4-75-08-75-88
Wines produced: Crozes-Hermitage (red and white)

Surface area (white): 1.2 acres
          (red): 2.47 acres
Production (white): 1,800 bottles
          (red): 6,000 bottles
Upbringing (white): 12 months in cask, then assembled in stainless steel vats
          (red): 12 months in oak barrels and cask
Average age of vines (white): 50 years
                     (red): 5–7 years
Blend (white): 90% Marsanne, 10% Roussanne
     (red): 100% Syrah

Marc Sorrel has made only a handful of Crozes-Hermitage vintages, so it is uncertain how good these wines will ultimately be. There is no question that his white Crozes looks to be a slightly better wine than the red, but Sorrel is the first to admit that his red Crozes-Hermitage is produced from very young vines (5–7 years old), and the vineyard clearly needs to increase in age before its full potential can be judged. The white wine is produced from a parcel of 50-year-old vines made up of 90% Marsanne and 10% Roussanne. The vineyard is planted in the Larnage sector. Given how brilliant Sorrel's red and white Hermitage can be, it is not unreasonable to expect these wines to improve in quality over the next few years.

VINTAGES

1995—Crozes-Hermitage (red)   The 1995 and 1994 red Crozes-Hermitage are made from
  ·   Syrah vines 5–6 years old, with modest yields of 40 hectoliters per hectare. These
 78   are light ruby-colored, medium-bodied wines to drink over the next 3–4 years. The
        1995 is more acidic, leaner, and compact on the palate. All of Sorrel's red wines
        are bottled with no fining or filtration. Last tasted 6/96.
1995—Crozes-Hermitage (white)   Both the 1994 and 1995 Crozes-Hermitage blanc (90%
  ·   Marsanne/10% Roussanne) exhibit solid, stony, pineapplelike fruit, medium body,
 84   and good, clean winemaking with low but adequate acidity. Last tasted 6/96.

L. DE VALLOUIT* * */* * * *

Address: 24, rue Désiré Valette
         26240 St.-Vallier
Tel: 4-75-23-10-11
Fax: 4-75-23-05-58
Wines produced: Crozes-Hermitage (red and white), Crozes-Hermitage Château du Larnage
               (red)
Surface area (white): 3.7 acres
             (red): regular cuvée—11.1 acres
                    Château du Larnage—3.7 acres
Production (white): 6,000 bottles
           (red): regular cuvée—25,000 bottles
                  Château du Larnage—8,000 bottles
Upbringing (white): 8–10 months with 50% of the yield in stainless steel vats and 50% in
                    oak barrels
           (red): regular cuvée—18 months in 10% new oak barrels
                  Château du Larnage—30 months in 10% new oak barrels
Average age of vines (white): 30 years
                     (red): regular cuvée—30 years
                            Château du Larnage—50 years

Blend (white): 90% Marsanne, 10% Roussanne
(red): 100% Syrah (both cuvées)

The firm of L. de Vallouit owns an important 18.5 acres in Crozes-Hermitage. A traditional vinification results in straightforward, standard-quality red and white wines. The new limited-production, old-vine cuvée called Château du Larnage (named after a vineyard in the Larnage sector), has the potential to be one of the finest wines of the appellation. For example, the 1990 (the most recent vintage I have tasted of this cuvée) was rich, concentrated, and far better than the uninspiring, straightforward, pleasant regular cuvées of red and white Crozes-Hermitage.

VIDAL-FLEURY* * * *

Address: R.N. 86
      69420 Ampuis
Tel: 4-74-56-10-18
Fax: 4-74-56-19-19
Wines produced: Crozes-Hermitage (red and white)
Production (white): 5,000–10,000 bottles
      (red): 75,000 bottles
Upbringing (white): 6 months in stainless steel vats
      (red): 24–36 months in oak casks
Blend (white): 100% Marsanne
      (red): 100% Syrah

Vidal-Fleury purchases all of its wine and ages it in foudres in their cellars. I must admit that under the administration of Jean-Pierre Rochias, this firm's Crozes-Hermitage can be one of the better wines of the appellation. In some vintages it has a tendency to taste too vegetal (1994), but in other years (1989, 1988, and 1985), the wine possesses surprisingly fine color, rich, olive- and cassis-scented fruit, medium body, and a velvety texture. It is a wine that generally has a long upbringing in large wood foudres.

OTHER CROZES-HERMITAGE PRODUCERS

JEAN-LOUIS BUFFIÈRES

Address: Les Sept Chemins
      26600 Pont de l'Isère
Tel: 4-75-07-32-85
Wines produced: Crozes-Hermitage (red and white)
Surface area (white): 2.5 acres
      (red): 19.8 acres
Production (white): 7,500 bottles, of which 2,200 bottles are estate-bottled
      (red): 60,000 bottles, of which 15,000 bottles are estate-bottled
Upbringing (white): 8–10 months in barrels 2–4 years old
      (red): 12 months in barrels 2–4 years old
Average age of vines (white): 15 years
      (red): 15–25 years
Blend (white): 100% Marsanne
      (red): 100% Syrah

CAVES COTTEVERGNE–L. SAUGÈRE

Address: Quartier le Bret
        07130 St.-Péray
Tel: 4-75-40-30-43
Fax: 4-75-40-55-06
Wines produced: Crozes-Hermitage Les Arbalètes (red)
Production: 12,000 bottles
Upbringing: 12 months in barrels 2–4 years old
Blend: 100% Syrah

GABRIEL CHOMEL

Address: Le Village   Tel: 4-75-03-32-91
        26600 Gervans

MAXIME CHOMEL

Address: Quartier les Blancs
        26600 Gervans
Tel: 4-75-03-32-70
Fax: 4-75-03-37-58
Wines produced: Crozes-Hermitage (red and white)
Surface area (white): 3.7 acres
          (red): 13.6 acres
Production (white): 9,000 bottles
          (red): 30,000 bottles
Upbringing (white): 8–9 months in stainless steel vats
          (red): 12–18 months in barrels 2–3 years old
Average age of vines (white): 35 years
                (red): 10 and 50 years
Blend (white): 100% Marsanne
        (red): 100% Syrah

DELAS FRÈRES

Address: Z.A. de l'Olivet
        B.P. 4
        07300 St.-Jean de Muzols
Tel: 4-75-08-60-30
Fax: 4-75-08-53-67
Wines produced: Crozes-Hermitage Les Launes (red and white), Crozes-Hermitage Cuvée
        Tour d'Albon (red)
Production (white): Les Launes—12,000 bottles
        (red): Cuvée Tour d'Albon—12,000 bottles
                Les Launes—82,200 bottles
Upbringing (white): 8 months, with 20% of the production in oak barrels 1–3 years old and
        80% in stainless steel vats
        (red): both cuvées spend 14–16 months in oak barrels 1–5 years old
Blend (white): 80% Marsanne, 20% Roussanne
        (red): 100% Syrah (both cuvées)

ALPHONSE ET PHILIPPE DESMEURE–DOMAINE DES REMIZIÈRES* *

Address: Quartier des Remizières   Tel: 4-75-07-44-28
      26600 Mercurol   Fax: 4-75-07-45-87

OLIVIER DUMAINE

Address: 26600 Larnage
Tel: 4-75-08-22-24
Fax: 4-75-08-13-75
Wines produced: Crozes-Hermitage (red and white)
Surface area (white): 6.2 acres
         (red): 11.1 acres
Production (white): 5,250 bottles
         (red): 15,000 bottles
Upbringing (white): 8–9 months in stainless steel vats
         (red): 12 months, with two-thirds of the yield in cement vats and one-third in
            old oak barrels
Average age of vines (white): 60 years
         (red): 60 years
Blend (white): 100% Marsanne
      (red): 100% Syrah

AIMÉ FAYOLLE

Address: Le Village
      26600 Gervans
Tel: 4-75-03-30-45
Wines produced: Crozes-Hermitage (red and white)
Surface area (white): 5 acres
         (red): 6.2 acres
Production (white): 15,000 bottles
         (red): 18,750 bottles
Upbringing (white): in enamel vats
         (red): in oak barrels
Average age of vines (white): 25 years
         (red): 25 years
Blend (white): 100% Marsanne
      (red): 100% Syrah

Note: None of the production is estate-bottled. Most is sold to Marcel Guigal.

ROBERT FLANDIN

Address: Quartier les Balmes
      26600 Crozes-Hermitage
Tel: 4-75-08-39-98
Wines produced: Crozes-Hermitage (red and white)
Surface area (white): 0.62 acres
         (red): 5.6 acres
Production (white): 1,500 bottles
         (red): 2,500 bottles
Upbringing (white): 6 months in old oak barrels
         (red): 18 months in old oak barrels
Average age of vines (white): 50 years
         (red): 50 years

Blend (white): 100% Marsanne
(red): 100% Syrah

RAYMOND FONFREDE

Address: Les Chenets
26600 Mercurol
Tel: 4-75-07-44-24
Wines produced: Crozes-Hermitage (red and white)
Surface area: (white): 8.6 acres
(red): 14.8 acres
Production (white): 18,000 bottles
(red): 37,500 bottles
Upbringing (white): 8 months in stainless steel vats
(red): 9–12 months in oak barrels, of which 40% are new
Average age of vines (white): 15 years
(red): 15 years
Blend (white): 100% Marsanne
(red): 100% Syrah

MARCEL HABRARD

Address: Le Village
26600 Gervans
Tel: 4-75-03-30-91
Wines produced: Crozes-Hermitage (red and white)
Surface area (white): 5.4 acres
(red): 12.4 acres
Production (white): 4,500 bottles
(red): 37,500 bottles
Upbringing (white): 8 months in stainless steel vats
(red): 8 months in old oak barrels
Average age of vines (white): 70–100 years
(red): 40 years
Blend (white): 100% Marsanne
(red): 100% Syrah

ERIC ROCHER

Address: Domaine de Champal
07370 Sarras
Tel: 4-75-23-08-51
Fax: 4-78-34-30-60
Wines produced: Crozes-Hermitage (red)
Surface area: 3 acres
Production: 10,500 bottles
Upbringing: 6 months, with 75% of the yield in stainless steel vats and 25% in old oak
barrels
Average age of vines: 6 years
Blend: 100% Syrah

ROBERT ROUSSET

Address: Le Village
        26600 Erôme
Tel: 4-75-03-30-38
Wines produced: Crozes-Hermitage (red and white)
Surface area (white): 6.2 acres
            (red): 13.5 acres
Production (white): 12,000 bottles, of which 7,500 are estate-bottled
            (red): 30,000 bottles, of which 18,000 are estate-bottled
Upbringing (white): 4 months in stainless steel vats
            (red): 12 months, with 60% of the yield in stainless steel vats and 40% in oak
                barrels 1–3 years old
Average age of vines (white): 50 years
                    (red): 25 years
Blend (white): 100% Marsanne
        (red): 100% Syrah

ST.-JOSEPH

In Search of an Identity

ST.-JOSEPH AT A GLANCE

Appellation created:	June 15, 1956.
Types of wine produced:	Red and white wine.
Grape varieties planted:	Marsanne and Roussanne for the white wine; Syrah for the red wine.
Acres currently under vine:	1,729.
Quality level:	Average to excellent.
Aging potential:	White wine: 1–5 years; red wine: 3–8 years.
General characteristics:	The red wines are the lightest, fruitiest, and most feminine of the northern Rhône. The white wines are perfumed and fleshy with scents of apricots and pears.
Greatest recent vintages:	1995, 1990, 1989, 1978.
Price range:	$18–$25.
Aromatic profile (white wines):	At the top level, the finest white wines are medium-bodied, refreshing, peach/apricot, sometimes pear-scented wines with good citrusy acidity that are delightful to drink within their first 2–3 years of life. Unfortunately, only a small percentage of dry whites meet these criteria. The majority of white St.-Joseph tend to be neutral, monolithic wines lacking charm and personality.
Aromatic profile (red wines):	Syrah can be at its fruitiest, lightest, and most charming in this appellation. A good St.-Joseph red should display

a Burgundy-like black-cherry, raspberry, and occasionally cassis-scented nose with medium body, light tannin, and zingy acidity. These are the Rhône Valley's lightest reds, and are thus best drunk in their first 5–6 years of life.

Textural profile (white wines): Light to medium body is the prevailing rule, with not much weight. Good freshness, crisp acidity, and uncomplicated fruit give these wines an appealing lightweight character.

Textural profile (red wines): Good fruit presented in a medium-bodied, zesty format is the hallmark of a fine St.-Joseph red. They should not possess tannin for support, but rather, crisp acidity.

The St.-Joseph appellation's most profound wines:

Chapoutier Les Granites (red and white)
J. L. Chave (red)
Domaine Louis Chèze Cuvée Prestige de Caroline
Yves Cuilleron (white)
Paul Jaboulet-Ainé Le Grand Pompée (red)
J. L. Grippat Vignes de l'Hospices (red)
J. L. Grippat (white)

Domaine du Monteillet–Antoine Montez Cuvée de Papy (red)
André Perret (white)
André Perret Cuvée Les Grisières (red)
Pascal Perrier Domaine de Gachon (red)
Pascal Perrier Cuvée de Collonjon (red)
Raymond Trollat (red)
L. de Vallouit Les Anges (red)

RATING THE ST.-JOSEPH PRODUCERS

* * * * *(OUTSTANDING)

Chapoutier (Les Granites) (red)

* * * *(EXCELLENT)

Chapoutier (Les Granites) (white)
J. L. Chave (red)
Domaine du Chêne (Cuvée Anaïs) (red)
Domaine Louis Chèze (Cuvée Prestige de Caroline) (red)
Yves Cuilleron (white)
Yves Cuilleron (Cuvée Prestige Le Bois Lombard) (white)
Bernard Faurie (red)
Alain Graillot (red)
J. L. Grippat (white)

Paul Jaboulet-Ainé (Le Grand Pompée) (red)
Domaine du Monteillet–Antoine et Monique Montez (Cuvée du Papy) (red)
André Perret (white)
André Perret (Les Grisières) (red)
Pascal Perrier (Domaine de Gachon) (red)
Pascal Perrier (Cuvée de Collonjon) (red)
Raymond Trollat (red)
L. de Vallouit (Les Anges) (red)

* * *(GOOD)

Clos de l'Arbalestrier (red)
Roger Blachon (red)
Chapoutier (Les Deschants) (red and white)
Domaine du Chêne (red)
Domaine Louis Chèze (red)
Domaine Collonge (red)
Maurice Courbis (red and white)

Pierre Coursodon (Paradis St.-Pierre) (red)
Pierre Coursodon (l'Olivaie) (red)
Yves Cuilleron (red)
Yves Cuilleron (Cuvée Prestige) (red)
Bernard Faurie (white)
Philippe Faury (red)
Bernard Grippa (red)

Bernard Grippa (Cuvée Le Berceau)
  (white and red)
J. L. Grippat (red)
Paul Jaboulet-Ainé (white)
Jean Marsanne (red)
Domaine du Monteillet–Antoine et
  Monique Montez (red)
Alain Paret (Chais St.-Pierre l'Arm de
  Père) (red)

Alain Paret (Chais St.-Pierre Domaine de
  la Couthiat) (red)
André Perret (red)
St.-Désirat Cave Coopérative (red and
  white)
Vidal-Fleury (red)

This is the northern Rhône's most confusing appellation. The entire appellation of St.-Joseph is vast, stretching from just south of Les Roches de Condrieu, all the way south to the doorstep of Cornas. Within the appellation's parameters, all on the western bank of the Rhône River, there is the potential for a whopping 7,420 acres of vines, but to date, only 1,729 acres are planted. Admittedly, many of these areas are undesirable for top-quality vineyards. This is apparent as one drives south on the route Nationale from Condrieu to Châteaubourg, where St.-Joseph vineyards are planted on fertile, flat-bottom valley soils, as well as on steep, granite hillsides. This extraordinary diversity in vineyard selection is undoubtedly the reason why St.-Joseph can vary from mediocre to charming and seductive.

Most growers agree that the finest St.-Joseph comes from within the original appellation's boundary lines established in 1956. Six communes, all north of Cornas, including Mauves, Tournon, St.-Jean de Muzols, Lemps, Vion, and Glun, are within a seven-mile stretch, from Vion, just to the north of Tain l'Hermitage, to Glun, just south of Tain l'Hermitage. It is within this seven miles that the finest St.-Joseph hillside vineyards are located. For blatantly commercial reasons, the appellation was extended in 1971 from its original 222 acres to the present-day 7,420! In the early nineties there was a movement by the syndicate of St.-Joseph to have the borders redrawn a third time, cutting back the size of the appellation.

St.-Joseph, like Côte Rôtie, has no village of the same name. The St.-Joseph name is derived from a vineyard site on the steep hillsides behind Tournon. John Livingstone-Learmonth, in his excellent book *The Wines of the Rhône*, provides considerable detail on the origins of this wine, stating that the first references to St.-Joseph were under the reign of Louis XII (1498–1515) and King Henry II (1519–1559). This wine was also mentioned by the renowned French author Victor Hugo (1802–1885) in his classic *Les Misérables*. Certainly the vineyards predate all these references. It is well known that the Carmelite monks, who were an important presence in Tournon, cultivated vineyards with their spartan work ethic on the steep hillsides as early as the thirteenth century.

Today, St.-Joseph needs to establish an identity. Wine enthusiasts are justifiably perplexed as to just what sort of wine St.-Joseph delivers. The following chapter chronicles the finest producers and their top wines. Many of these emerge from the original appellation borders, particularly in and around the villages of Mauves, and to the north, Tournon and St.-Jean de Muzols. Much of what is produced in St.-Joseph is mediocre. When I wrote the first edition of this book in 1987, I believed this appellation had immense potential to provide copious amounts of good-quality, reasonably priced wines. Yet in the last decade, the quality has remained stagnant, while other Rhône Valley appellations have measurably improved the quality of their wines.

What is the future for St.-Joseph? Undoubtedly this appellation needs to have its boundaries redrawn. Whether the French government is willing to go that far is debatable, but at the minimum a system of vineyard classification, much like what exists in Burgundy, would help consumers recognize the best vineyards—at least from a perspective of potential. If neither of these options is enacted, consumers can expect St.-Joseph to continue to muddle along, offering perplexing and distressingly irregular wines.

RECENT VINTAGES

1995 This is generally a very good to excellent vintage in St.-Joseph. The wines should prove to be firm, and while less flattering at an early age than the 1994s, this vintage's best cuvées have the potential to last for 10–15 years. The white wines will need to be drunk up over the next several years. They are more acidic and less concentrated than the 1994s.

1994 The rains that arrived in early September spoiled St.-Joseph's chance for a great vintage. The summer had been torridly hot, but September was cool and wet. The finest wines are soft, round, fruity, and ideal for drinking over the next 5–6 years. The white wines are excellent. While they are richer, more complete, and interesting than the 1995s, they need to be consumed over the next 2–3 years.

1993 A disastrous vintage in St.-Joseph, with hollow, thin wines produced by nearly everyone.

1992 Soft, slightly diluted, herbaceous, but fruity red wines were produced. They are fully mature and need to be drunk up before the end of the century. The white wines are already beginning to lose their fruit and dry out.

1991 Like so many other appellations in the northern Rhône, St.-Joseph produced very fine wines that have consistently been underrated. They do not possess the massive, blockbuster power of the 1990s, but they are vastly superior to the 1992s, 1993s, and perhaps the 1994s. It is a very consistent vintage for elegant, concentrated, well-balanced wines that should drink well for another 3–4 years. The white wines were less successful.

1990 The greatest recent vintage for St.-Joseph, these wines are atypically opaque-colored, rich, powerful, blockbuster wines that resemble the offerings from their big sister, Hermitage. The 1990s are aging slowly, with some of the top efforts still adolescents in terms of development. This is a spectacular vintage for St.-Joseph.

Older Vintages

I know of no St.-Joseph white wine that will improve beyond two to three years in the bottle. As for the red wines, they are at their best when they have the exuberant raspberry, peppery fruitiness well displayed. This is usually when they are between three and six years old. Despite the close proximity to Hermitage, the wines of St.-Joseph do not evolve well in the bottle once they are over six or seven years of age. The only exception would be a great vintage such as 1978.

CLOS DE L'ARBALESTRIER (DR. D. FLORENTIN)* * *

Address: 32, avenue St.-Joseph
07300 Mauves
Tel: 4-75-08-12-11
Fax: 4-75-55-83-10
Wines produced: St.-Joseph (red and white)
Surface area (white): 2.47 acres
(red): 10 acres
Production (white): 4,500 bottles
(red): 18,000 bottles
Upbringing (white): 2 years in old oak barrels
(red): 3 years in old oak barrels
Average age of vines (white): one-third 15 years and two-thirds 50 years
(red): 50 years
Blend (white): 67% Roussanne, 33% Marsanne
(red): 100% Syrah

This traditionally run estate appears to be finally recognizing that it is the twentieth century, rather than the eighteenth. The property has long been run by the ancient Dr. Florentin, a Paris physician (who must be in his late eighties), who believes in biodynamic farming and traditional winemaking to an extreme. This 13-acre estate owns 8.5 acres within a *clos* (a completely walled vineyard) south of Mauves. Planted on flat, decomposed, sandy, granite, and clay soils, the vines are 50+ years of age. From this site extremely rustic, old-style whites and reds have been produced. Florentin has handed the reins of this estate to his son, Dr. Dominique Florentin, and one of his daughters, Françoise, both of whom are refining some of the ancient methods of winemaking. In the past, an occasionally impressive, full-bodied, large-scaled, blockbuster red would emerge, but generally the wines were stale, oxidized whites, and coarse, tannic, chewy but savage reds. Dr. Florentin's son and daughter appear to be making some concessions to more modern-day tastes. Nevertheless, the white wines spend two years and the red wines three years in barrels. Even with their small yields of under 2 tons of fruit per acre (well below the yields of most of this appellation's producers), this is entirely too long a sojourn in old wood casks. When combined with the fact that no sulfur is used, the results are decidedly irregular. Nevertheless, the raw materials can be fascinating. I suspect a few more concessions to the twentieth century could propel this domaine into the upper echelon of St.-Joseph producers.

The only recent wines I have tasted from Clos de l'Arbalestrier include an over-the-hill, oxidized 1989 white St.-Joseph, and an impressively rich, full-bodied, earthy, prune, black-cherry, and tobacco-scented 1990 red. The latter wine survived the overly long élevage without losing its fruit, but remember, it was produced from what was the greatest vintage in the northern Rhône since 1961. I suspect lighter-weight years such as 1992, 1993, and 1994 cannot handle such a long cask aging without irreparable damage.

CHAPOUTIER* * */* * * * *

Address: 18, avenue du Docteur Paul Durand
        B.P. 38
        26600 Tain l'Hermitage
Tel: 4-75-08-28-65
Fax: 4-75-08-81-70
Wines produced: St.-Joseph Les Deschants (red and white), St.-Joseph Les Granites (red and white)
Surface area (white): 10 acres
        (red): 10 acres
Production (white): Les Deschants—1,600 cases
        Les Granites—500 cases
        (red): Les Deschants—3,000 cases (includes the equivalent of 7.5 acres worth of wine bought from other producers)
        Les Granites—500 cases
Upbringing (white): Les Deschants—6 months, with 20% of the yield in barrels 2–3 years old and 80% in stainless steel vats
        Les Granites—6 months in new oak casks and tank
        (red): Les Deschants—12 months in barrels 2–5 years old
        Les Granites—12 months in 100% new oak, no fining or filtration
Average age of vines (white): Les Deschants—25–30 years
        Les Granites—50–60 years
        (red): Les Deschants—35–40 years
        Les Granites—60–70 years
Blend (white): 100% Marsanne (both cuvées)
        (red): 100% Syrah (both cuvées)

This large, well-known firm in Tain l'Hermitage has 20 acres of hillside vineyards in St.-Joseph from which they produce two separate cuvées of both red and white wines. Their regular cuvée, called Les Deschants, is made from both their own vineyards and purchased grapes. The white wine has improved immensely in quality since the late eighties, with Michel Chapoutier attempting to get more of the mineral character into the wine's bouquet and flavors. In my opinion, he has succeeded. The St.-Joseph Les Deschants red is a fruity, well-made wine offering good value.

In 1994, Chapoutier decided to produce an old-vine cuvée that would represent the "quintessential St.-Joseph red and white." Made from tiny yields of old-vine Marsanne for the white and old-vine Syrah for the red, both wines come from Chapoutier's best parcels of hillside vineyards near Mauves. They are unquestionably the finest wines I have ever tasted from St.-Joseph. They are made in extremely limited quantities. Like most Chapoutier wines, there is a huge difference in quality between the luxury cuvées and the regular bottlings. Readers desiring to taste what is possible in this appellation where no compromises are made should try to secure a few bottles of Chapoutier's St.-Joseph Les Granites.

VINTAGES

1995—St.-Joseph Les Deschants (red)   The 1995 Les Deschants from the granitic soils
•   of the hillside vineyards of St.-Joseph reveals a mineral note in its ripe cassis fruit.
85   Elegant, with tart acidity, it is reminiscent of the lean, tart 1993 red Burgundies.
          When I inquired about the Ph, I was told it was a very low 3.3. Last tasted 6/96.

1995—St.-Joseph Les Deschants (white)   The 1995 white Les Deschants is a Chablis
•   lookalike. With a flinty, orange-scented, fruity nose, admirable precision, and rich,
89   medium-bodied, concentrated flavors, this is a wine of exceptional purity and
          finesse. Moreover, it is a terrific bargain. Drink it over the next 3–4 years. Last
          tasted 6/96.

1995—St.-Joseph Les Granites (red)   The red 1995 Les Granites boasts an opaque black/
•   purple color, a profound bouquet of essence of cassis and minerals, awesome
93   intensity, layers of flavor, and exceptional length. Tasting notes are nearly ridicu-
          lous when tasting at this level of quality since these wines are so singularly
          prodigious. The 1995 Les Granites should be drinkable when released, and keep
          for 20–30 years. Last tasted 6/96.

1995—St.-Joseph Les Granites (white)   The new luxury cuvée of St.-Joseph called Les
•   Granites is a selection from an ancient 80-year-old, 5-acre vineyard planted on a
94   hillside behind Gérard Chave's house in Mauves. It is a wine of extraordinary
          intensity. Yields were 15 hectoliters per hectare, and the wine was vinified com-
          pletely in small barrels. Its liquid mineral/apricot-like aromas and flavors jump
          from the glass. The underlying crisp acidity provides delineation to this massive,
          100% Marsanne wine, which tastes as if some Viognier were added to the blend.
          Only 250 cases were produced of what is the greatest dry white wine I have ever
          tasted from St.-Joseph. It should last for 15–20 years. Last tasted 6/96.

1994—St.-Joseph Les Deschants (red)   The 1994 Les Deschants possesses a deep black/
•   ruby/purple color, powerful, sweet Syrah aromas of cassis, smoke, and pepper,
86   excellent intensity, and a rich, sweet mid-palate. Last tasted 6/96.

1994—St.-Joseph Les Deschants (Lot 5641) (white)   The 1994 Les Deschants Lot 5641
•   exhibits a light straw color, excellent orange-peel, mineral, and acacia-scented
86   notes, good concentration, and plenty of pure, ripe fruit. Last tasted 6/96.

J. L. CHAVE * * * *

Address: 37, avenue St.-Joseph
      07300 Mauves
Tel: 4-75-08-24-63
Fax: 4-75-07-14-21
Wines produced: St.-Joseph (red)
Surface area: 3.7 acres

Production: 5,000–6,000 bottles
Upbringing: 16–18 months in old oak
     barrels
Average age of vines: 25 years
Blend: 100% Syrah

No longer a well-kept secret, Gérard Chave and his son, Jean-Louis, produce 400–500 cases of gorgeously fruity, elegant, supple, medium-bodied red St.-Joseph. The wine, which used to be sold almost exclusively to Chave's British importer, the highly esteemed wine merchant in Wiltshire, Robin Yapp, and to Alice Waters' Berkeley restaurant, Chez Panisse, now gets broader distribution. This fine example of St.-Joseph is best drunk within its first 4–5 years of life. When I last saw Chave in the summer of 1996, he and Jean-Louis were contemplating the possibility of doing a négociant bottling of St.-Joseph to try to alleviate the stress caused by the incredible demand for their wines.

VINTAGES

1995—St.-Joseph   Readers desiring an introduction to the Chave mystique are well ad-
· vised to check out his red wine made from the hillsides of St.-Joseph. It will not
86 last more than a decade, but it is a deliciously ripe, pure, elegant, cassis- and cherry-scented wine with plenty of fruit and charm. The 1995 St.-Joseph should drink well for 5–8 years. Last tasted 6/96.

1990—St.-Joseph   The dark purple-colored 1990 is bursting with flavor. Readers are
· likely to come across a bottle only while dining at the Berkeley restaurant Chez
89 Panisse. It is so easy to drink that it is tempting to conclude it will not age, but I would not be surprised to see it last for more than a decade. However, much of its appeal is its youthful purity and fruity intensity, so why wait? Last tasted 6/96.

1989—St.-Joseph   The 1989 is a hedonistic, exuberantly rich, fruity wine, bursting with
· scents and flavors of cassis and Provençal herbs. Drink this lovely wine over the
88 next 5–7 years. Last tasted 6/96.

DOMAINE DU CHÊNE (MARC ROUVIÈRE)* * */* * * *

Address: Le Pêcher
      42410 Chavanay
Tel: 4-74-87-27-34
Fax: 4-74-87-02-70
Wines produced: St.-Joseph (red and white), St.-Joseph Cuvée Anaïs (red) (a selection of
        the finest regular red cuvées)
Surface area (white): 3.7 acres
        (red): 14.8 acres
Production (white): 9,000 bottles
        (red): 36,000 bottles
Upbringing (white): 8–10 months, with 10–20% of the yield in new oak and the rest in
        stainless steel vats
        (red): 12–18 months in barrels
Average age of vines (white): 15 years
        (red): 35 years
Blend (white): 100% Marsanne
        (red): 100% Syrah

Marc Rouvière has continued to refine his winemaking skills. He turns out a very good, fruity St.-Joseph white wine made from 100% Marsanne. His good red St.-Joseph is best drunk in its first 3–4 years of life. Rouvière also produces approximately 600 cases of Cuvée Anaïs, which is a selection of his most concentrated wine that is aged in oak barrels, of which a small percentage is new. The latter wine has given signs of being atypically long-lived for a St.-Joseph, with most of the better vintages suggesting a lifeline of 8–10 years.

VINTAGES

1994—St.-Joseph Cuvée Anaïs (red)   The 1994 Anaïs is an excellent, nearly outstanding
·   wine. Deep ruby-colored, with a spicy bouquet of toasty new oak and cassis, this
89   medium- to full-bodied wine exhibits outstanding ripeness and richness, and a
       long, spicy, concentrated finish. Drink this supple, forward beauty over the next 7–
       8 years. Last tasted 6/96.

Older Vintages

Marc Rouvière produced very fine cuvées of Anaïs in 1989, 1990, and 1991, all but the 1989 meriting scores in the upper eighties. They all should be drunk by the end of this century. In 1992, a very difficult vintage, Rouvière produced a supple, fruity Cuvée Anaïs.

DOMAINE LOUIS CHÈZE* * */* * * *

Address: 07340 Limony
Tel: 4-75-34-02-88
Fax: 4-75-34-13-25
Wines produced: St.-Joseph (red and white), St.-Joseph Cuvée Prestige de Caroline (red)
Surface area (white): 2.47 acres
                (red): regular cuvée—14.8 acres
                        Cuvée Prestige de Caroline—5 acres
Production (white): 6,000 bottles
              (red): regular cuvée—37,500 bottles
                        Cuvée Prestige de Caroline—9,750 bottles
Upbringing (white): 7 months, with 60% of the yield in old oak barrels and 40% in stainless
                steel vats
              (red): regular cuvée—14–18 months, with 80% of the yield in old oak barrels
                and 20% in stainless steel vats
                        Cuvée Prestige de Caroline—18–24 months, with 80% of the yield in
                        new oak and 20% of the yield in oak barrels 2–3 years old
Average age of vines (white): 10 years
                (red): regular cuvée—10–15 years
                        Cuvée Prestige de Caroline—25–30 years
Blend (white): 100% Marsanne
        (red): 100% Syrah (both cuvées)

This is one of the up-and-coming estates in St.-Joseph. Founded only in 1978, Louis Chèze decided that his father's practice of selling his production to négociants should be discontinued. The top wine is his Cuvée de Caroline (named after his daughter born in 1986). In 1994 there was also a Cuvée de Ro-Rez, which is not as intense as the Cuvée de Caroline. The Cuvée de Caroline has been very good in years such as 1995 and 1994, and nearly outstanding in 1991.

Everything made in the modern Chèze cellars is controlled by the estate's oenologist,

Jean-Luc Colombo. The reds are completely destemmed and fermented at a relatively high temperature to extract more color and intensity. Colombo has also refined Chèze's heavy hand with fining and filtration, and the wines are now bottled more softly, with the idea of capturing as much of the fruit, texture, and body as possible.

This estate also makes a small quantity of Condrieu from a 5-acre parcel on the Coteau de Breze. It is an elegant wine made from a vineyard planted only in 1988 and 1989. Additionally, there is a tiny quantity of inexpensive, serviceable Gamay entitled to a vin de table designation.

MAURICE COURBIS (G.A.E.C. LES RAVIÈRES)* * *

Address: 07130 Châteaubourg
Tel: 4-75-40-32-12
Fax: 4-75-40-25-39
Wines produced: St.-Joseph (red and white), Cuvée Spéciale Les Royes (red)
Surface area (white): 11.2 acres
        (red): 30.1 acres total
            Cuvée Spéciale Les Royes—selected from vines planted on 10.4 acres
Production (white): 4,800 bottles
        (red): regular cuvée—4,800 bottles
            Cuvée Spéciale Les Royes—4,500 bottles
Upbringing (white): 6 months, with 25% of the yield in 1-year-old oak barrels and 75% in
            stainless steel vats
        (red): regular cuvée—14–18 months in old oak barrels
            Cuvée Spéciale Les Royes—14–18 months in old oak barrels
Average age of vines (white): 40 years
        (red): regular cuvée—25 years
            Cuvée Spéciale Les Royes—20 years
Blend (white): 95% Marsanne, 5% Roussanne
     (red): both cuvées are 100% Syrah

Courbis produces three cuvées of St.-Joseph. All are good, but the finest is the St.-Joseph Les Royes. The Courbis family has been making wine from their cellars in Châteaubourg since 1587. Their top hillside vineyard, Domaine des Royes, is located here. Courbis is another of the growing league of young Rhône Valley producers who have chosen Jean-Luc Colombo as their oenologist. Readers should also note the Cornas wines produced by L. et D. Courbis (the sons of Maurice) under their own label (see page 200).

VINTAGES

1995—St.-Joseph (white)   This is a crisp, lemony, citrusy, medium-bodied, dry wine that
·   is meant to be drunk over the next two years. Last tasted 6/96.
85
1995—St.-Joseph Les Royes (red)   The oaky, muscular, tannic 1995 Les Royes will
·   benefit from 1–3 years of cellaring and should be drunk over the subsequent 7–8
86   years. Last tasted 6/96.
1994—St.-Joseph Les Royes (red)   Slightly better is the 1994 Les Royes, a richly fruity,
·   toasty, sweet, dark ruby-colored wine with copious amounts of fruit and character.
87   Last tasted 6/96.

PIERRE COURSODON* * *

Address: Place du Marché
07300 Mauves
Tel: 4-75-08-18-29
Fax: 4-75-08-75-72
Wines produced: St.-Joseph (red and white), St.-Joseph Paradis St.-Pierre (red and white),
     St.-Joseph l'Olivaie (red)
Surface area (white): 5 acres total
          (red): regular cuvée—19.8 acres
                 Paradis St.-Pierre—2.47 acres
                 l'Olivaie—2.47 acres
Production (white): regular cuvée—7,500 bottles
                 Paradis St.-Pierre—2,250 bottles
          (red): regular cuvée—45,000 bottles
                 Paradis St.-Pierre—3,500–4,500 bottles
                 l'Olivaie—3,500–4,500 bottles
Upbringing (white): regular cuvée—6 months in stainless steel vats
                 Paradis St.-Pierre—80 months in barrels 2–3 years old
          (red): regular cuvée—18 months in oak barrels
                 Paradis St.-Pierre—18 months in oak barrels
                 L'Olivaie—18 months in 20% new oak barrels
Average age of vines (white): 40 years
                 (red): regular cuvée—40 years
                        Paradis St.-Pierre—50–70 years
                        l'Olivaie—50–70 years
Blend (white): 100% Marsanne (both cuvées)
      (red): 100% Syrah (all three cuvées)

This estate's 30 acres of vineyards are all within the St.-Joseph appellation. There are
two cuvées of white produced, and three cuvées of red, all of which have improved since
Gustave Coursodon's son, Pierre, took over the winemaking. The white wines are typical of
the appellation. Pierre is flexible enough to do a partial malolactic, not wanting the wine too
acidic, nor too flabby. The results are citrusy, fruity white St.-Josephs to drink within 1–2
years of the vintage. The 200 or so cases of the Paradis St.-Pierre white spends eight months
in old oak casks, giving the wine more fat and a more developed character than the regular
cuvée, which is aged in stainless steel tanks.

There are three red wine cuvées, ranging in quality from the regular cuvée, to the Paradis
St.-Pierre (an old-vine cuvée), to the top-of-the-line l'Olivaie (also an old-vine cuvée). The
Paradis St.-Pierre is made from a selection of the best barrels of old-vine parcels, whereas
the l'Olivaie is from a 2.47-acre parcel of vines 50–70 years old located on the decomposed
granitic soils on the hillsides above the town of St.-Jean de Muzols. The only criticism I
have of the reds is that 18 months in barrels appears to be an unusually long time.
Nevertheless, in vintages such as 1989 and 1990, the top cuvées are more than capable of
standing up to this élevage. These are relatively masculine, bigger-style red St.-Josephs that
can keep for a decade or more. I have noticed significant improvement in the consistency of
Coursodon's wines since the late eighties.

YVES CUILLERON* * */* * * *

Address: Les Prairies
        R.N. 86
        42410 Chavanay
Tel: 4-74-87-02-37
Fax: 4-74-87-05-62
Wines produced: St.-Joseph Cuvée Izeras (white), St.-Joseph Cuvée Prestige Le Bois Lom-
            bard (white), St.-Joseph (red), St.-Joseph Cuvée Prestige (red), St.-Joseph
            l'Amarybelle (red)
Surface area (white): Cuvée Izeras—2.47 acres
                Cuvée Prestige Le Bois Lombard—1.2 acres
        (red): regular cuvée—14.8 acres
                Cuvée Prestige—6.2 acres
Production (white): Cuvée Izeras—6,000 bottles
                Cuvée Prestige Le Bois Lombard—3,000 bottles
        (red): regular cuvée—30,000 bottles
                Cuvée Prestige—10,500 bottles
Upbringing (white): Cuvée Izeras—6 months, with 30% of the yield in oak and 70% in
            stainless steel vats
                Cuvée Prestige Le Bois Lombard—7 months, with 30% of the yield in
                oak and 70% in stainless steel vats
        (red): regular cuvée—16 months in cask and barrels
                Cuvée Prestige—20 months in casks and barrels
Average age of vines (white): Cuvée Izeras—20 years
                Cuvée Prestige Le Bois Lombard—40 years
        (red): regular cuvée—15 years
                Cuvée Prestige—35–50 years
Blend (white): 100% Marsanne (both cuvées)
        (red): 100% Syrah (both cuvées)

Yves Cuilleron's talent is described in more detail in the chapter on Condrieu (see page 105). Some of his top white wines, and certainly his finest reds, all emerge from the appellation of St.-Joseph. There are two red wine cuvées and two whites. Cuilleron is a master white wine maker, and readers are advised to seek out either his Cuvée Izeras or Cuvée Prestige Le Bois Lombard. As the tasting notes that follow demonstrate, these are delicious, dry whites that are among the reference point whites of the northern Rhône.

While Cuilleron has rarely shown the same talent in red winemaking, his St.-Josephs, from a small hillside plantation of Syrah, have been surprisingly rich, well-balanced, and delicious wines for drinking during their first five or so years of life. Cuilleron is one of the few undeniable stars of St.-Joseph, and one of the few who is equally successful with both white and red wines.

VINTAGES

1995—St.-Joseph l'Amarybelle (red)   The finest of Cuilleron's current and upcoming
    ·   releases is the 1995 l'Amarybelle, a wine with a sweet, pure nose of black cherries,
    86   crisp, elegant, tart, medium-bodied flavors, and a vibrant, lively personality. It
            should drink well for 4–5 years. Last tasted 6/96.
1995—St.-Joseph Izeras (white)   The 1995 Izeras reveals a citrusy/pineapple-scented
    ·   nose, gobs of fruit, medium to full body, and a clean, refreshing finish with just enough
    87   acidity to provide zest and vibrancy. Drink it over the next year. Last tasted 6/96.

1995—St.-Joseph Le Bois Lombard (white)   The 1995 Le Bois Lombard exhibits dense,
·   chewy, full-bodied flavors that are the result of exceptionally low yields and ripe
89   fruit. A honeyed-pineapple component dominates both the aromatics and flavors in
          this lush, juicy wine made from 100% Marsanne. White St.-Joseph just does not
          get any better than this. Drink it over the next 2–3 years. Last tasted 6/96.

1994—St.-Joseph l'Amarybelle (red)   This wine is austere, lean, and undernourished.
·   Last tasted 6/96.
78?

1994—St.-Joseph Cuvée Prestige (red)   Cuilleron's 1994 Cuvée Prestige exhibits a deep
·   color, as well as attractive toasty, new oak, black-cherry, and cassis aromas. This
86   low-acid, soft, ripe wine offers a delicious, elegant, supple mouthful of Syrah fruit.
          Drink it during its first 7–8 years of life. Last tasted 6/96.

1992—St.-Joseph Cuvée Prestige (red)   Terrific, as well as reasonably priced, the 1992
·   Cuvée Prestige is made from Cuilleron's oldest vines. Its healthy dark ruby/purple
89   color is accompanied by a broad aromatic display of black fruits, herbs, and
          vanilla. Wonderfully rich, expansive, and concentrated, this is a full-bodied, vel-
          vety-textured wine. Anticipated maturity: now–1998. Last tasted 9/95.

1991—St.-Joseph Cuvée Prestige (red)   There is a spicy, peppery, herbal side to the
·   abundant quantities of cassis fruit found in the 1991 Cuvée Prestige. The wine is
89   finely tuned, with admirable underlying acidity, excellent concentration, and a
          rich, medium to full-bodied, long, moderately tannic finish. Anticipated maturity:
          now–2002. Last tasted 9/95.

DELAS FRÈRES* *

Address: 2, allées de l'Olivet
        07300 St.-Jean de Muzols
Tel: 4-75-08-60-30
Fax: 4-75-08-53-67
Wines produced: St.-Joseph Cuvée Ste.-Epine (white and red), St.-Joseph Cuvée Les Chal-
        leys (white and red), St.-Joseph Cuvée François de Tournon (red)
Surface area (white): 2.47 acres
              (red): 7.4 acres
Production (white): 15,000 bottles (total production, including that bought from other pro-
              ducers)
              Cuvée Ste.-Epine—2,500 bottles
              Cuvée Les Challeys—8,000–9,000 bottles
          (red): 90,000 bottles (total production, including that bought from other pro-
              ducers)
              Cuvée Ste.-Epine—2,500 bottles
              Cuvée Les Challeys—55,000 bottles
              Cuvée François de Tournon—12,000 bottles
Upbringing (white): 8 months, with 50% of the yield in new oak and 50% in old oak barrels
              (red): 12–14 months in barrels 2–5 years old
Average age of vines (white): 15–20 years
              (red): 15–20 years
Blend (white): 90% Marsanne, 10% Roussanne
        (red): 100% Syrah

    A bevy of St.-Joseph cuvées is made at Delas Frères, all of it representing varying degrees
of mediocrity. Until this well-financed négociant in St.-Jean de Muzols becomes more
serious about quality, these wines are unlikely to provide much excitement.

BERNARD FAURIE* * */* * * *

Address: Avenue Hélène de Tournon
         07300 Tournon
Tel and fax: 4-75-08-55-09
Wines produced: St.-Joseph (red and white)
Surface area (white): 0.42 acres
             (red): 3.7 acres
Production (white): 800 bottles
           (red): 6,000 bottles
Upbringing (white): fermentation in new oak for 4 weeks, then 9 months in old barrels
           (red): 14–18 months in oak barrels with a maximum of 10% new oak
Average age of vines (white): 10 years
                     (red): 10 years and 30 years
Blend (white): 100% Marsanne
      (red): 100% Syrah

Faurie does not produce much St.-Joseph, and although his white wine cuvée has improved over recent years, it remains more neutral than enticing. His red St.-Joseph is sold under two different labels, a Cuvée Jeunes Vignes and a Cuvée Vieilles Vignes. Each represents about 125 cases of wine. Both are good, but the Cuvée Vieilles Vignes possesses more color, as well as more intense aromas of blackberries and cassis, and more structure. It is a wine to drink within 3–6 years of the vintage.

ALAIN GRAILLOT (DOMAINE LES CHÊNES VERTS)* * * *

Address: 26600 Pont de l'Isère
Tel: 4-75-84-67-52
Fax: 4-75-07-24-31
Wines produced: St.-Joseph (red)
Surface area: 5 acres
Production: 10,000 bottles
Upbringing: 12 months with 80% of the yield in oak and 20% in stainless steel vats
Average age of vines: 20 years
Blend: 100% Syrah

Alain Graillot leases 4 acres of hillside St.-Joseph vineyards near Tournon, from which he produces very fine, rich, concentrated wine. Although not much is made, it is well worth seeking out. For more detailed information on Graillot and his winemaking, readers should refer to the chapter on Crozes-Hermitage.

VINTAGES

1995—St.-Joseph (red)   The 1995 St.-Joseph reveals an inky/black color, a classic nose
·   of ripe cassis, smoke, and minerals, crisp acidity, superb definition, and a tannic,
88   backward personality. Stylistically it reminded me of the 1988. This wine will
         require several years of cellaring before it reaches full maturity, but it should last
         for a decade. Last tasted 6/96.
1994—St.-Joseph (red)   The 1994 St.-Joseph is a classic example of what high-quality
·   winemaking can achieve. It is a deep ruby/purple-colored wine with gobs of cassis
87   fruit. Buy this delicious wine by the case, should you be lucky enough to find any.
         Last tasted 6/96.

1993—St.-Joseph (red)   One of the most disappointing wines I have ever tasted from this
·   high-quality producer is the 1993 St.-Joseph. It is a hard, hollow wine with no fruit
67   or ripeness. The fact that Alain Graillot produced wines such as this is a sign of
         just how difficult the 1993 vintage was. Last tasted 6/95.

1991—St.-Joseph (red)   For pure elegance and a satiny-smooth texture, check out
·   Graillot's 1991 St.-Joseph. This lush St.-Joseph offers gobs of pure black-cherry
87   and cassis fruit, medium body, light tannin, and a heady, opulently textured, long
         finish. Anticipated maturity: now–1999. Last tasted 11/95.

1990—St.-Joseph (red)   Graillot's 1990 St.-Joseph is nearly opaque purple, displaying a
·   huge nose of licorice, black fruits, and minerals. It is stuffed with unctuous layers
89   of creamy currant fruit, has decent acidity, plenty of tannin, and an explosively
         long, velvety finish. Anticipated maturity: now–2000. Last tasted 4/94.

BERNARD GRIPPA* * *

Address: 5, avenue Ozier
         07300 Mauves
Tel: 4-75-08-14-96
Fax: 4-75-07-06-81
Wines produced: St.-Joseph (red and white), St.-Joseph Cuvée Le Berceau (red and white)
Surface area (white): 7.4 acres
             (red): 14.8 acres
Production (white): regular cuvée—18,000 bottles
                    Cuvée Le Berceau—1,200 bottles
             (red): regular cuvée—30,000 bottles
                    Cuvée Le Berceau—700–2,000 bottles
Upbringing (white): Both cuvées receive 6 months, with 80% of the yield in stainless steel
                    vats and 20% in new oak barrels.
             (red): regular cuvée—12 months in 10% new oak barrels
                    Cuvée Le Berceau—12 months in 25% new oak barrels
Average age of vines (white): 30–40 years
                      (red): 30 years, with some vines 70 years of age
Blend (white): 100% Marsanne
      (red): 100% Syrah

This moderately sized estate of 22.2 acres is, except for 2.47 acres, all in St.-Joseph.
Bernard Grippa, a balding yet handsome, enthusiastic man, has some of the best situated
vineyards of St.-Joseph, with two parcels of very old vines planted on the steep hillsides of
Tournon and Mauves. Bernard, the fourth generation to produce wine under the Grippa
name, produces two cuvées of white and two cuvées of red wine. The regular cuvée is the
one most likely to be encountered, but the red and white Cuvée Le Berceau ("cradle") are
selections made from old-vine parcels that produce wine of much higher concentration and
quality. This wine is not produced in each vintage.

Everything about the vinification is completely traditional. While the white wine is
primarily fermented in tank, a small percentage, usually under 20%, is vinified in wood.
The red grapes are not destemmed, although there are ongoing discussions with their
oenologist, Jean-Luc Colombo, about moving toward complete destemming, so this may
change. The red wine is aged in small oak casks, of which never more than 25% are new,
and then only for the Cuvée Le Berceau.

I have found the wines of Grippa, particularly the reds, to be consistently very good, with
the more intense Cuvée Le Berceau characterized by its dark ruby/purple color and attrac-

tive black-raspberry and cassis fruit. It is a wine to drink within 6–7 years of the vintage. The regular cuvée is best drunk within 4–5 years of the vintage. The white wines are far better than the overall quality level of most white St.-Joseph. They possess peach and apricot aromas, medium body, good fruit, and clean, fresh flavors.

For whatever reason, Grippa's 1994s and 1995s did not show well in tastings in the Rhône Valley in summer 1996.

VINTAGES

1990—St.-Joseph Le Berceau (red)   The 1990 Le Berceau exhibits plenty of toasty new
·   oak, as well as an opaque dark ruby/purple color. In the mouth there is attractive,
87   ripe, black-raspberry and cassis fruit, an expansive, chewy texture, soft tannins, and a long finish. It may ultimately merit a higher score. Anticipated maturity: now–2000. Last tasted 9/94.

J. L. GRIPPAT* * */* * * *

Address: 07300 Tournon
Tel: 4-75-08-15-51
Fax: 4-75-07-00-97
Wines produced: St.-Joseph (red and white) St.-Joseph Cuvée des Hospices
Surface area (white): 3.4 acres
              (red): 10.6 acres
Production (white): 9,000 bottles
              (red): 21,000 bottles (of which a tiny quantity is the Cuvée des Hospices)
Upbringing (white): 16 months in stainless steel vats
              (red): 3–4 months in stainless steel vats and 10–12 months in oak
Average age of vines (white): 50 years
                      (red): 20 years
Blend (white): 100% Marsanne
       (red): 100% Syrah

The ebullient Grippat, who makes great white Hermitage and unexciting red Hermitage (see page 161), devotes most of his time and energy to producing white and red St.-Joseph. He owns 14 acres of vines superbly situated on the hillside above Tournon (where he maintains his cellars) and in Mauves. In addition, he rents from Tournon's hospital 1 acre of 100-year-old vines that zigzag up the precipitously steep hillside near the medieval tower overlooking Tournon and Tain l'Hermitage. From this plot of vines he produces 125 cases of his St.-Joseph Cuvée des Hospices, unquestionably one of the appellation's finest red wines. Unfortunately, it is virtually impossible to find in the marketplace.

Grippat's other red St.-Joseph wines are elegant, soft, fairly light wines that one is apt to like for their charm and lightness rather than power or intensity. However, he makes St.-Joseph's best white wine, which is very aromatic with vivid aromas of peaches and apricots. It is a very pleasurable wine to seek out for both its quality and modest price.

VINTAGES

1994—St.-Joseph (red)   The 1994 would have merited a higher score save for its green-
·   pepper/vegetal-scented nose. It resembled a Loire Valley Chinon more than a wine
85   from the northern Rhône. Once past the vegetal component, the wine exhibits

plenty of cassis fruit. Readers who prefer intensely herbaceous St.-Joseph will appreciate this wine more than I did. Last tasted 6/96.

1994—St.-Joseph (white)   I have always been an admirer of Grippat's beautiful whites
·   and stylish reds. His 1994 white St.-Joseph is honeyed and apricot-scented. This
87   tasty wine exhibits medium to full body, excellent purity, and a soft, succulent style that begs for consumption over the next several years. Last tasted 6/96.

1994—St.-Joseph Cuvée des Hospices   The 1994 des Hospices (from one of the steepest
·   and best vineyard sites of St.-Joseph) reveals a deep ruby color, and an attractive
86   black-cherry, herb, and smoky-scented nose. This elegant, round, medium-bodied wine is bursting with fruit and charm. Drink it over the next 4–6 years. Last tasted 6/96.

Older Vintages

Should readers find any of Grippat's gorgeous 1990 Cuvée des Hospices, it is well worth checking out. The finest red St.-Joseph I have ever tasted from Grippat, it offers a huge, black-raspberry and truffle-scented nose, and full-bodied, lusciously rich flavors. It is a sumptuous example of just what heights St.-Joseph can achieve. I last tasted it in November 1994, and it was stunning.

PAUL JABOULET-AINÉ* * */* * * *

Address: Les Jalets
        R.N. 7, B.P. 46
        La-Roche-de-Glun
        26600 Tain l'Hermitage
Tel: 4-75-84-68-93
Fax: 4-75-84-56-14
Wines produced: St.-Joseph Le Grand Pompée (red and white)
Surface area (white): none, all wine is purchased for this blend
            (red): none, all wine is purchased for this blend
Production (white): 4,000 bottles
            (red): 100,000 bottles
Upbringing (white): 6–8 months in oak casks
            (red): 10 months in oak casks
Blend (white): 100% Marsanne
      (red): 100% Syrah

Consumers looking for a good St.-Joseph at a reasonable price should search out Jaboulet's fruity, exuberant-styled St.-Josephs called "Le Grand Pompée" (named after one of Charlemagne's favorite generals). Jaboulet produces nearly 8,500 cases of this modern-style, cleanly made red wine that is best drunk during its first 5–6 years of life. Over recent years this firm has begun to turn out a small quantity (about 330 cases) of a delicious, 100% Marsanne white wine, of which a small percentage sees some fermentation in new oak casks and is then aged for six months in used wood. The most recent vintage, the 1995, has been delicious, although it is a wine to drink within its first 1–2 years of life.

VINTAGES

1995—St.-Joseph Le Grand Pompée (white)   The 1995 Le Grand Pompée (100% Mar-
·   sanne) exhibits lovely tangerine and grapefruitlike characteristics, Mandarin
87   orange/apricot flavors, good body and richness, and a straightforward, crisp finish. This wine should be drunk over the next several years. Last tasted 6/96.

1990—St.-Joseph Le Grand Pompée (red)   The 1990 Le Grand Pompée is a rich wine
  ·   that is about as concentrated as Jaboulet's St.-Joseph can be. The saturated purple
  89   color is followed by a nose of blackcurrants and minerals, full-bodied, highly
             extracted flavors, good acidity, sweet tannin, and a lush finish. Anticipated matu-
             rity: now–2000. Last tasted 6/95.

JEAN MARSANNE* * *

Address: Avenue Ozier
         07300 Mauves
Tel: 4-75-08-86-26
Wines produced: St.-Joseph (red and white)
Surface area (white): 0.86 acres
             (red): 10 acres
Production (white): 1,950 bottles
             (red): 19,500 bottles
Upbringing (white): 6–8 months in stainless steel vats
             (red): 10–15 months in old oak casks, followed by 6 months in stainless steel vats
Average age of vines (white): 4 years
             (red): 30–50 years
Blend (white): 100% Marsanne
      (red): 100% Syrah

Marsanne, who resides above his wine cellars in Mauves, produces very small quantities
of red St.-Joseph, and, since 1994, tiny quantities of white. He earns most of his living from
his fruit tree orchards. Marsanne's red wine is traditionally made and aged 16–21 months
in both tank and large foudres. It is one of the biggest St.-Joseph reds, yet is always
loaded with fruit. Its style reminds me of the beefy, more full-bodied St.-Joseph red produced by Pierre Coursodon, a neighbor of Jean Marsanne. I have never tasted his white
St.-Joseph.

DOMAINE DU MONTEILLET
(ANTOINE ET MONIQUE MONTEZ)* * */* * * *

Address: 42410 Chavanay
Tel: 4-74-87-24-57
Fax: 4-74-87-06-89
Wines produced: St.-Joseph (red and white), St.-Joseph Cuvée du Papy (red)
Surface area (white): 1.7 acres
             (red): regular cuvée—7.4 acres
                   Cuvée du Papy—3.7 acres
Production (white): 3,000 bottles
             (red): regular cuvée—15,000 bottles
                   Cuvée du Papy—5,000 bottles
Upbringing (white): 10–12 months with 50% of the yield in old oak barrels and 50% in
                   stainless steel vats
             (red): regular cuvée—12 months with 50% of the yield in old oak casks and
                   50% in old oak barrels
                   Cuvée du Papy—18–24 months in 100% new oak barrels
Average age of vines (white): 20 years
             (red): regular cuvée—25 years
                   Cuvée du Papy—40 years
Blend (white): 100% Marsanne
      (red): 100% Syrah (both cuvées)

Antoine Montez is stirring up interest in high-quality St.-Joseph with his performances over recent vintages. With the exception of several of Pascal Perrier's Domaine Gachon and Michel Chapoutier's new Les Granites, readers will not find a more concentrated and formidably endowed St.-Joseph than those from Antoine and Monique Montez. The regular cuvée is excellent. The Cuvée du Papy is aged in 100% new oak casks for nearly two years. The only other St.-Joseph to see as much new oak is Chapoutier's Les Granites. The Cuvée du Papy can easily support the oak given its superconcentration and intensity. The Domaine du Monteillet is one of the bright new shining stars of St.-Joseph.

VINTAGES

1992—St.-Joseph (red)   Made from yields of 35 hectoliters per hectare, and bottled
·   unfiltered for the American importer, Monteillet's St.-Joseph exhibits a dense,
90   saturated, black/purple color, and a huge nose of black cherries, herbs, and under-
         brush. Fabulously concentrated, with amazing richness, ripeness, and length, this
         full-bodied wine is an exquisite bargain. Anticipated maturity: now–2005. Last
         tasted 9/95.
1991—St.-Joseph (red)   Domaine du Monteillet has made quite a first impression! The
·   1991 Rhône Valley vintage was strongest in Condrieu and Côte Rôtie, but
90   this wine is a candidate for the best 1991 from St.-Joseph. New oak was not em-
         ployed, so you can imagine the richness of the peppery, blackcurrant-flavored
         Syrah fruit in this wine. There is a deep, viscous texture, sweet, chewy fla-
         vors, and gobs of fruit in the finish. Anticipated maturity: now–2004. Last tasted
         9/95.

ANDRÉ PERRET* * */* * * *

Address: R.N. 86
         Verlieu
         42410 Chavanay
Tel: 4-74-87-24-74
Fax: 4-74-87-05-26
Wines produced: St.-Joseph (red and white), St.-Joseph Les Grisières (red)
Surface area (white): 1.2 acres
              (red): 8.6 acres
Production (white): 1,500 bottles
           (red): 15,000 bottles
Upbringing (white): 12 months in oak barrels
           (red): 12–18 months with 50% of the yield in 10% new oak barrels and 50% in
                  oak casks
Average age of vines (white): 12 years
                     (red): 20 years
Blend (white): 100% Marsanne
      (red): 100% Syrah (both cuvées)

André Perret, who makes exquisite Condrieu, often demonstrates a fine hand with his white St.-Joseph from a 1.2-acre parcel of Marsanne planted in both young and old vines. He produces two red wine cuvées from 8.6 acres of Syrah. The best lots are designated Les Grisières. This cuvée receives more time in toasty new oak, and the fruit is riper and more concentrated. It is an excellent St.-Joseph for drinking in the first 7–8 years of life. The most successful vintages of Les Grisières have been 1989, 1990, and 1991. Perret's regular cuvée of red St.-Joseph tends to be irregular in quality, with the ripest vintages producing the best wines. The white St.-Joseph has been consistently well made, as one might expect from this talented winemaker.

VINTAGES

1995—St.-Joseph Les Grisières (red)   The seductive, sexy 1995 Les Grisières reveals a
·   dark ruby color, excellent ripeness, fine precision, a sweet attack, and a classic,
87   pure, cherry- and vanillin-flavored finish. It should drink well for 7–8 years. Last
            tasted 6/96.

1994—St.-Joseph (red)   The 1994 St.-Joseph is a ripe, fruity, delicious cherry- and
·   raspberry-scented and -flavored wine that loses points and quality in its hard, lean,
84   compact finish. The wine's aromatics and attack are lovely, but after that it's tough
            going. Last tasted 6/96.

1994—St.-Joseph Les Grisières (red)   The 1994 Les Grisières offers elegant, sweet,
·   black-cherry fruit, medium body, excellent purity, and a long, ripe finish with fine
85   fruit and body. This well-made wine is ideal for drinking over the next 3–6 years.
            Last tasted 6/96.

PASCAL PERRIER (DOMAINE DE GACHON)* * * *

Address: Rue de l'Eglise
      07370 Gachon
Tel: 4-75-23-24-10
Wines produced: St.-Joseph Domaine de Gachon (red), St.-Joseph Cuvée de Collonjon (red)
Surface area (Domaine de Gachon): 12.4 acres
          (Cuvée de Collonjon): 2 acres
Production (Domaine de Gachon): 25,500 bottles
          (Cuvée de Collonjon): 3,780 bottles
Upbringing (both cuvées): 24 months, with 12 spent in barrels, a small percentage of which
      are new
Average age of vines (Domaine de Gachon): 15 years
          (Cuvée de Collonjon): 8 years
Blend: 100% Syrah (both cuvées)

This 14.4-acre estate produces only red St.-Joseph, of which there are two cuvées. The regular cuvée, Domaine de Gachon, is immensely impressive. I have never seen, much less tasted, the Cuvée de Collonjon. Pascal Perrier obviously believes in very intense, concentrated wines, and these are among the biggest, richest wines of the appellation, particularly the cuvée selected by the American importer that he requests be bottled unfiltered. It is those wines that are reviewed in the following tasting notes.

Pascal Perrier's bright shining potential was aborted by a tragedy in 1993. In the deluge that occurred prior to the harvest, the hillside above his winery collapsed, causing an avalanche, which virtually destroyed Perrier's entire winery and wine storage area. I am sad to say he has yet to recover, having sold off what remained of the 1993 as well as 1994 vintages in bulk to négociants.

VINTAGES

1991—St.-Joseph Domaine de Gachon   Aged in 20% new oak casks and bottled unfil-
·   tered for the American importer, this magnificently scented (black cherries, herbs,
90   licorice, and Asian spices), full-bodied, super-concentrated wine is one of the finest
            St.-Josephs I have tasted. The wine's purity and intensity of flavor are wonderful to

behold, and the finish lasts for over a minute. Approachable now, it promises to last for two decades. Anticipated maturity: now–2004. Last tasted 12/94.

1990—St.-Joseph Domaine de Gachon   The 1990 may turn out to be outstanding. It is
·   almost opaque black/purple-colored, with a huge, unevolved bouquet of cassis,
89   licorice, and herbs. In the mouth there is astonishing richness for a St.-Joseph, a
      full-bodied, almost massive display of fruit, as well as long, supple tannins in the
      dramatic finish. Anticipated maturity: now–2002. Last tasted 12/94.

1989—St.-Joseph Domaine de Gachon   The 1989 Domaine de Gachon is impressive,
·   with more richness and promise than the 1990. The color is opaque black/purple.
90   The bouquet suggest mint, cassis, Provençal herbs, and hickory wood. In the
      mouth there is an explosion of fruit, wonderful, chewy, fleshy texture, and a long,
      superconcentrated finish. If this wine develops slightly more complexity, it may
      turn out to be among the best St.-Joseph I have ever tasted. Anticipated maturity:
      now–2005. Last tasted 12/94.

ST.-DÉSIRAT CAVE COOPÉRATIVE* * *

Address: 07340 St.-Désirat
Tel.: 4-75-34-22-05
Fax: 4-75-34-30-10

This is one of the better cooperatives in France, turning out a full range of Rhône Valley wines. The basic cuvées are satisfactory, if somewhat light and one-dimensional. The finest wines, such as the St.-Joseph Cuvée Côte Diane, are well-endowed, rich, concentrated wines that rank among the better efforts of the appellation. There is no shortage of potential for this coop, which is brilliantly run by Jean-Luc Chaleat. The membership includes more than 100 growers, most producing Syrah and Marsanne. In the state-of-the-art winery there are rows of temperature-controlled stainless steel vats, and a barrel-aging room where plenty of new oak casks are utilized for the most concentrated cuvées. I realize it is fashionable to downplay the quality of coop wines, but St.-Désirat Cave Coopérative is a seriously run, ambitious coop that often produces wines that are better than all but the top three or four wines of the appellation.

VINTAGES

1990—St.-Joseph Côte Diane (red)   Aged in small oak casks, the 1990 Côte Diane is an
·   impressive example from this underrated appellation on the western flank of the
87   Rhône river. Its deep, opaque, ruby/purple color is followed by a moderately
      intense bouquet of toasty new oak and blackcurrants, medium to full body, rich,
      sweet, fruit, soft tannin, and a long, concentrated finish. While drinkable now, it
      will age gracefully for 8–10 years.

RAYMOND TROLLAT* * * *

Address: Quartier Aubert
         07300 St.-Jean de Muzols
Tel: 4-75-08-27-17
Wines produced: St.-Joseph (red and white)
Surface area (white): 0.4 acres
           (red): 5 acres
Production (white): 1,050 bottles
           (red): 12,000 bottles

Upbringing (white): 10–12 months in old oak barrels
          (red): 18 months in old oak barrels
Average age of vines (white): 40–80 years
                         (red): 40–80 years
Blend (white): 100% Marsanne
        (red): 100% Syrah

Trollat is one of the legendary producers of St.-Joseph. His 5.4-acre estate, with some of the oldest, thickest, most gnarled vines of St.-Joseph, can only be reached by a tortuous drive up the slopes outside St.-Jean de Muzols. Trollat is another old-fashioned Rhône vigneron cut from the same mold as the late Jacques Reynaud and Henri Bonneau of Châteauneuf du Pape. With his ruddy cheeks and oversized nose, Trollat could be the French version of America's slapstick comedian Ernest. He is full of one-liners that poke fun at both the French government and modern-day oenology. From these steep, granite slopes Trollat produces intense, concentrated, muscular wines that require time in the bottle. In great years such as 1989 and 1990, his red wines benefit from 18 months in barrel, but even with low yields and ripe fruit, vintages such as 1987 and 1993 cannot support such a long sojourn in wood. A tiny quantity (under 100 cases) of white wine is made. Bottled earlier, it is a chunky, fleshy, full-bodied white St.-Joseph that is not far removed in style and quality from the white Hermitage made by Trollat's dear friend and old school buddy, Gérard Chave. The red wines can be awesome. From time to time there is a barrel or two of spectacular, world-class old-vine Syrah that Trollat bottles separately. I have never seen any in the marketplace—not surprising since it is almost impossible to find his regular cuvée.

In years where there is not great ripeness, Trollat's wines often reveal a stemmy, herbaceous character, as this traditional winemaker will never destem. Recent top vintages have been 1994, 1992 (remarkable wine for the vintage), 1991, 1990, and 1989. All of the red wines from those vintages are capable of lasting well beyond the turn of the century.

L. DE VALLOUIT* * * *

Address: 24, rue Désiré Valette
             26240 St.-Vallier
Tel: 4-75-23-10-11
Fax: 4-75-23-05-58
Wines produced: St.-Joseph (red and white), St.-Joseph Les Anges (red)
Surface area (white): 1.2 acres
                  (red): regular cuvée—2.47 acres
                          Les Anges—2.47 acres
Production (white): 3,000 bottles
            (red): regular cuvée—6,000 bottles
                    Les Anges—5,000 bottles
Upbringing (white): 8–10 months with 50% of the yield in new oak barrels and 50% in
                     stainless steel vats
              (red): regular cuvée—18 months in 10% new oak barrels
                      Les Anges—30 months in 10% new oak barrels
Average age of vines (white): 40 years
                         (red): regular cuvée—40 years
                                 Les Anges—60 years
Blend (white): 80% Marsanne, 20% Roussanne
        (red): 100% Syrah (both cuvées)

De Vallouit produces one white and two red cuvées of St.-Joseph, but only the special cuvée of St.-Joseph Les Anges is of interest. Produced from 60-year-old Syrah vines, and aged for 30 months in small casks, of which 10% are new, this wine represents the chewier, more robust, concentrated style of St.-Joseph. It was especially impressive in 1988, followed by very good efforts in 1989 and 1990. The other de Vallouit cuvées are modestly proportioned, low-key wines of no particular focus or excitement.

OTHER ST.-JOSEPH PRODUCERS

ROGER BLACHON* * *

Address: Chemin des Goules
       07300 Mauves
Tel: 4-75-08-51-12
Wines produced: St.-Joseph (red and white)
Surface area (white): 1.7 acres
       (red): 9.4 acres
Production (white): 3,750 bottles
       (red): 22,000 bottles
Upbringing (white): all in polyester vats, either 6–8 months or 12 months
       (red): 12 months in barrels 1–2 years old
Average age of vines (white): 10 years
       (red): 20–25 years
Blend (white): 100% Marsanne
       (red): 100% Syrah

DIDIER DE BOISSEYT-CHOL

Address: R.N. 86
       42410 Chavanay
Tel: 4-74-87-23-45
Fax: 4-74-87-07-36
Wines produced: St.-Joseph (red); one cuvée is the normal St.-Joseph and the other is called St.-Joseph Trois Ans Fûts de Chêne
Surface area: 12.4 acres
Production: 20,000 bottles
Upbringing: 2–3 years in oak barrels
Average age of vines: 35 years
Blend: 100% Syrah

JEAN-LOUIS BONNARDEL

Address: 07340 Vinzieux
Tel: 4-75-34-86-94
Wines produced: St.-Joseph (red)
Surface area: 1.4 acres
Production: 3,600 bottles
Upbringing: 6 months in old oak barrels
Average age of vines: 15–20 years
Blend: 100% Syrah

PIERRE BOUCHER

Address: Domaine de la Favière
       42520 Malleval
Tel. and fax: 4-74-87-15-25
Wines produced: St.-Joseph (red and white)
Surface area (white): 1.2 acres
       (red): 6.2 acres

Production (white): 2,000 bottles
        (red): 8,000–10,000 bottles
Upbringing (white): 10 months in stainless steel vats
        (red): 12 months with 50% of the yield in stainless steel vats and 50% in oak
           barrels, little new oak
Average age of vines (white): 12–15 years
        (red): 12–15 years
Blend (white): 100% Marsanne
   (red): 100% Syrah

MICHEL BOUCHET

Address: Le Ventabrin
       42410 Chavanay
Tel: 4-74-87-23-38
Wines produced: St.-Joseph (red and white)
Surface area (white): 0.5 acres
        (red): 3.7 acres
Production (white): 1,000–1,200 bottles
        (red): 10,500 bottles
Upbringing (white): 5–6 months in oak barrels, little new oak
        (red): 18 months in oak barrels, little new oak
Average age of vines (white): 12 years
        (red): 15–20 years
Blend (white): 100% Marsanne
   (red): 100% Syrah

DOMINIQUE BOURRIN

Address: Brossin
       42410 Roisey
Tel: 4-74-87-49-15
Wines produced: St.-Joseph (red and white)
Surface area (white): 0.62 acres
        (red): 5 acres
Production (white): 1,800 bottles
        (red): 15,000 bottles
Upbringing (white): 12 months in 1-year-old barrels
        (red): 1–2 years with 25% of the yield in stainless steel vats and 75% in old
           oak barrels
Average age of vines (white): 12 years
        (red): 10 years
Blend (white): 100% Marsanne
   (red): 100% Syrah

CAVES COTTEVERGNE

Address: Quartier le Bret
       07130 St.-Péray
Tel: 4-75-40-30-43
Fax: 4-75-40-55-06
Wines produced: St.-Joseph Chandarcet (red)

Production: 9,000 bottles
Upbringing: 12 months in barrels 2–4 years old
Blend: 100% Syrah

DOMAINE COLLONGE* * *

Address: 26600 Mercurol
Tel: 4-75-07-44-32
Fax: 4-75-07-44-06
Wines produced: St.-Joseph (red and white)
Surface area (white): 3.7 acres
       (red): 11.6 acres
Production (white): 9,000 bottles
       (red): 25,500 bottles
Upbringing (white): 3 months in enamel vats
       (red): 12 months with one-third of the yield in enamel vats and two-thirds in old
         oak barrels
Average age of vines (white): 10–15 years
       (red): 15+ years
Blend (white): 100% Marsanne
   (red): 100% Syrah

MIREILLE COMBE

Address: Les Vessettes
     42410 Chavanay
Tel: 4-74-87-26-26
Wines produced: St.-Joseph (red and white)
Surface area (white): 1.2 acres
       (red): 7.5 acres
Production (white): 2,700 bottles
       (red): 18,000 bottles
Upbringing (white): 8–10 months in stainless steel vats
       (red): 18–20 months with one-third of the yield in oak barrels up to 5 years old
         and two-thirds of the yield in cement vats
Average age of vines (white): 20 years
       (red): 30 years
Blend (white): 100% Marsanne
   (red): 100% Syrah

DARD ET RIBO (DOMAINE BLANCHE LAINE)

Address: Quartier Blanche Laine
     26600 Mercurol
Tel: 4-75-07-40-00
Wines produced: St.-Joseph (red and white)
Surface area (white): 0.5 acres
       (red): 5 acres
Production (white): 1,200 bottles
       (red): 9,000 bottles
Upbringing (white): 6 months in old oak barrels
       (red): 15–18 months in old oak barrels
Average age of vines (white): 45 years
       (red): 40–45 years
Blend (white): 100% Roussanne
   (red): 100% Syrah

PHILIPPE DESBOS

Address: Gouye
          07300 St.-Jean de Muzols
Tel: 4-75-08-58-24
Wines produced: St.-Joseph (red and white)
Surface area (white): 0.82 acres
              (red): 7.5 acres
Production (white): 900 bottles
            (red): 10,500 bottles
Upbringing (white); 12 months in stainless steel vats
            (red): 14 months in old oak barrels
Average age of vines (white): 20 years
                      (red): 35 years
Blend (white): 100% Marsanne
       (red): 100% Syrah

MICHEL DESESTRET

Address: Domaine de la Côte Ste.-Epine
          07300 St.-Jean de Muzols
Tel: 4-75-08-85-35
Wines produced: St.-Joseph (red and white)
Surface area (white): 0.25 acres
              (red): 10 acres
Production (white): 600 bottles
            (red): 4,500 bottles
Upbringing (white): 6–8 months in old oak barrels
            (red): 18 months in barrels 3–4 years old
Average age of vines (white): 7–50 years
                      (red): 50–150 years
Blend (white): 100% Marsanne
       (red): 100% Syrah

NOËL DURAND

Address: G.A.E.C. du Lautaret
          07130 Châteaubourg
Tel: 4-75-40-46-78
Fax: 4-75-40-29-77
Wines produced: St.-Joseph Cuvée Générique (young vines, red), St.-Joseph Sélection des
                Coteaux (red)
Surface area: 12.4 acres
Production (Cuvée Générique): 3,000 bottles
            (Sélection des Coteaux): 10,000 bottles
Upbringing: 6–12 months with 20–40% of the yield in stainless steel vats and 60–80% in
            oak barrels 1–5 years old
Average age of vines: 15 years
Blend: 100% Syrah

PHILIPPE FAURY* * *

Address: La Ribaudy
        42410 Chavanay
Tel: 4-74-87-26-00
Fax: 4-74-87-05-01
Wines produced: St.-Joseph (red and white)
Surface area (white): 2.47 acres
            (red): 10 acres
Production (white): 6,000 bottles
            (red): 22,500 bottles
Upbringing (white): 10 months with 30% of the yield in old oak barrels and 70% in stainless
            steel vats
            (red): 12–18 months in 10% new oak barrels
Average age of vines (white): 25 years
                    (red): 20–25 years
Blend (white): 80% Marsanne, 20% Roussanne
      (red): 100% Syrah

PIERRE FINON

Address: 07340 Charnas
Tel: 4-75-34-08-75
Wines produced: St.-Joseph (red and white)
Surface area (white): 1 acre
            (red): 10 acres
Production (white): 2,250 bottles
            (red): 22,500 bottles
Upbringing (white): 10 months with 60% of the yield in polyester vats and 40% in one-third
            new oak barrels
            (red): 16 months with 40% of the yield in polyester vats, 45% in old barrels,
            and 15% in new oak barrels
Average age of vines (white): 5–6 years
                    (red): 12–13 years
Blend (white): 100% Marsanne
      (red): 100% Syrah

GILLES FLACHER

Address: Le Village
        07340 Charnas
Tel: 4-75-34-06-97
Wines produced: St.-Joseph (red and white)
Surface area (white): 1.2 acres
            (red): 10 acres
Production (white): 1,000 bottles
            (red): 8,000–9,000 bottles
Upbringing (white): 6 months with 30% of the yield in new oak and 70% in stainless steel
            vats
            (red): 10–14 months in 30% new oak barrels
Average age of vines (white): 6 years
                    (red): 15 years
Blend (white): 100% Marsanne
      (red): 100% Syrah

ELIZABETH FOGIER

Address: La Roue
07300 St.-Jean de Muzols
Tel: 4-75-08-22-13
Wines produced: St.-Joseph (red)
Surface area: 4.9 acres

Production: 7,500 bottles, of which 2,700 are estate-bottled
Upbringing: 12 months in old oak barrels
Average age of vines: 10–100 years
Blend: 100% Syrah

PIERRE GAILLARD

Address: Favier 42520 Malleval
Tel: 4-74-87-13-10
Fax: 4-74-87-17-66
Wines produced: St.-Joseph (red and white)
Surface area (white): 2.47 acres
          (red): 16 acres
Production (white): 2,200 bottles
          (red): 18,000 bottles
Upbringing (white): 6 months in old oak casks
          (red): 18 months in 20% new oak barrels
Average age of vines (white): 5 years
          (red): 15 years
Blend (white): 100% Roussanne
          (red): 100% Syrah

VINCENT GASSE-LAFOY

Address: R.N. 86
La Roche
69420 Ampuis
Tel: 4-74-56-17-89
Wines produced: St.-Joseph (red)
Surface area: 0.7 acres

Production: 1,000 bottles
Upbringing: 18–24 months in 20% new oak barrels
Average age of vines: 12 years
Blend: 100% Syrah

PIERRE ET JEAN GONON

Address: Rue des Launays
07300 Mauves
Tel: 4-75-08-07-95
Fax: 4-75-08-65-21
Wines produced: St.-Joseph Les Oliviers (white), St.-Joseph (red)
Surface area (white): 3.7 acres
          (red): 11 acres
Production (white): 5,000–6,000 bottles
          (red): 15,000–18,000 bottles
Upbringing (white): 11 months in barrels 4–10 years old
          (red): 14–16 months in old oak casks
Average age of vines (white): 30 years
                (red): 28 years
Blend (white): 75% Marsanne, 25% Roussanne
          (red): 100% Syrah

PAUL GRUAS

Address: 8, avenue de Nîmes
     07300 Tournon
Tel: 4-75-08-15-36
Wines produced: St.-Joseph (red)
Surface area: 1 acre

Production: 1,500 bottles
Upbringing: 12 months in old oak barrels
Average age of vines: 4 and 50 years
Blend: 100% Syrah

PIERRE GUILLERMAIN

Address: La Tuilière
     R.N. 86
     07300 Lemps
Tel: 4-75-08-11-50
Wines produced: St.-Joseph (red and white)
Surface area (white): 1.2 acrres
          (red): 6.2 acres
Production (white): 700 bottles
         (red): 1,200–1,500 bottles
Upbringing (white): 6–8 months in old oak barrels
        (red): 12–18 months (sometimes 24 months) in old oak barrels
Average age of vines (white): 20 years
              (red): 20 years
Blend (white): 95% Marsanne, 5% Roussanne
     (red): 100% Syrah

DOMAINE DE LA HAUTE FAUTERIE

Address: 07130 St.-Péray
Tel: 4-75-40-46-17
Wines produced: Usually two cuvées are produced: the Cuvée Tradition and the Cuvée Sélection. If the quality is not good enough, the whole production is bottled as Cuvée Tradition.
Surface area: 12.35 acres
Production: 23,000 bottles
Upbringing: 8–12 months in old oak barrels
Average age of vines: 12 years
Blend: 100% Syrah

GEORGES LAGNIER

Address: Verlieu
     42410 Chavanay
Tel: 4-74-87-24-74
Wines produced: St.-Joseph (red and white)
Surface area (white): 0.37 acres
         (red): 1.2 acres
Production (white): 2,250 bottles
         (red): 3,000 bottles
Upbringing (white): 9–10 months in old oak barrels
        (red): 12 months in old oak barrels
Average age of vines (white): 40–50 years
           (red): 40–50 years
Blend (white): 100% Marsanne
     (red): 100% Syrah

GUY LANTHEAUME

Address: 80, avenue de St.-Joseph   Tel: 4-75-08-00-20
07300 Mauves

JEAN-YVES LOMBARD

Address: Chalaix   Tel: 4-75-08-66-86
07300 Mauves

ANDRÉ MARGIRIER

Address: Cessieux
07300 St.-Jean de Muzols
Tel: 4-75-08-67-02
Wines produced: St.-Joseph (red and white)
Surface area (white): 0.7 acres
          (red): 4.9 acres
Production (white): 750 bottles
          (red): 6,000 bottles
Upbringing (white): 12 months in epoxy vats
          (red): 6 months in stainless steel vats and 12 months in old oak
Average age of vines (white): 20 years, with the oldest being 80 years
          (red): 25 years, with the oldest being 90 years
Blend (white): 100% Marsanne
          (red): 100% Syrah

LAURENT MARTHOURET

Address: Les Rotisses
07340 Charnas
Tel: 4-75-34-03-55
Fax: 4-75-34-15-91
Wines produced: St.-Joseph (red)
Surface area: 6.2 acres
Production: 15,000 bottles, of which 7,500 are estate-bottled
Upbringing: 12 months in barrels 2–6 years old
Average age of vines: 10–15 years
Blend: 100% Syrah

MICHEL MOURIER

Address: Domaine de la Pierre Blanche   Surface area: 2.47 acres
19, rue du Mont   Production: 6,450 bottles
42000 St.-Etienne   Upbringing: 10 months in new oak barrels
Tel: 4-77-57-29-59   Average age of vines: 4–7 years
Fax: 4-77-80-68-71   Blend: 100% Syrah
Wines produced: St.-Joseph (red)

ALAIN PARET (CHAIS ST.-PIERRE)* * *

Address: Place de l'Eglise   Tel: 4-74-87-12-09
42410 St.-Pierre-de-Boeuf   Fax: 4-74-87-17-34

PHILIPPE PICHON

Address: Le Grand Val
    Verlieu
    42410 Chavanay
Tel: 4-74-87-23-61
Fax: 4-74-87-07-27
Wines produced: St.-Joseph (red)
Surface area: 0.94 acres
Production: 5,700 bottles
Upbringing: 6 months with 25% of the yield in old oak casks and 75% in stainless steel
    and epoxy vats
Average age of vines: 20 years
Blend: 100% Syrah

JACQUES ET JEAN-LOUIS PRADELLE

Address: Le Village
    26600 Chanos-Curson
Tel: 4-75-07-31-00
Fax: 4-75-07-35-34
Wines produced: St.-Joseph (red)
Surface area: 1.5 acres
Production: 3,000 bottles
Upbringing: 12 months in old oak casks
Average age of vines: 5 years
Blend: 100% Syrah

HERVÉ RICHARD

Address: Verlieu
    42410 Chavanay
Tel: 4-74-87-07-75
Wines produced: St.-Joseph (red and white)
Surface area (white): 1.7 acres
    (red): 7.4 acres
Production (white): 3,750 bottles
    (red): 18,000 bottles
Upbringing (white): 10–12 months in stainless steel vats
    (red): 18 months in 10% new oak barrels
Average age of vines (white): 15 years
    (red): 15 years
Blend (white): 80% Marsanne and 20% Roussanne
    (red): 100% Syrah

DANIEL ROCHE

Address: Le Village
    07340 Charnas
Tel: 4-75-34-05-50
Wines produced: St.-Joseph (red and white), St.-Joseph Cuvée Spéciale (red, made only
    when the product of the oldest vines is considered satisfactory. Otherwise,
    it is added to the normal cuvée).
Surface area (white): 0.7 acres
    (red): regular cuvée—6.2 acres
    Cuvée Spéciale—2.47 acres
Production (white): 1,800 bottles
    (red): regular cuvée—18,000 bottles
    Cuvée Spéciale—4,000 bottles

Upbringing (white): 6 months with 70% of the yield in stainless steel vats and 30% in oak
    barrels 1–2 years old
      (red): 1–2 years in oak barrels, little new oak (both cuvées)
Average age of vines (white): 17 years
              (red): regular cuvée—15 years
                  Cuvée Spéciale—25 years
Blend (white): 100% Marsanne
   (red): 100% Syrah (both cuvées)

ERIC ROCHER

Address: Domaine de Champal
    07370 Sarras
Tel: 4-75-23-08-51
Fax: 4-78-34-30-60
Wines produced: St.-Joseph (red and white)
Surface area (white): 5 acres
       (red): 32 acres
Production (white): 10,500 bottles
       (red): 75,000 bottles
Upbringing (white): 4 months in stainless steel vats
       (red): 6 months with 75% of the yield in stainless steel vats and 25% in old oak
           barrels
Average age of vines (white): 7 years
              (red): 7 years
Blend (white): 50% Marsanne, 50% Roussanne
   (red): 100% Syrah

DOMAINE ST.-JEMMS

Address: Les Châssis–R.N. 7
    26600 Mercurol
Tel: 4-75-08-33-03
Fax: 4-75-08-69-80
Wines produced: St.-Joseph (red and white)
Surface area (white): 2.47 acres
         (red): 10 acres
Production (white): 6,750 bottles
        (red): 22,500 bottles
Upbringing (white): 8 months in stainless steel vats
        (red): 12 months in oak casks
Average age of vines (white): 15 years
              (red): 15 years
Blend (white): 100% Marsanne
   (red): 100% Syrah

FERNAND SALETTE

Address: Chemin de Corneilhac
    07340 Vinzieux
Tel: 4-75-34-86-94
Wines produced: St.-Joseph (red)
Surface area: 8.6 acres

Production: 18,000 bottles
Upbringing: 12 months in old oak casks
Average age of vines: 15–18 years
Blend: 100% Syrah

ETIENNE SAUZAT

Address: Les Eguets
       42410 Chavanay
Tel: 4-74-87-21-44
Wines produced: St.-Joseph (red)
Surface area: 3.7 acres

Production: 700 bottles
Upbringing: 12–14 months in 4-year-old barrels
Average age of vines: 25 years
Blend: 100% Syrah

MARCEL TOMASINI

Address: Jassoux
       42410 St.-Michel-sur-Rhône
Tel: 4-74-87-26-57
Wines produced: St.-Joseph (red and white)
Surface area (white): 0.27 acres
           (red): 0.64 acres
Production (white): 675 bottles
          (red): 1,800 bottles
Upbringing (white): 12 months in stainless steel vats
         (red): 12 months in old oak casks
Average age of vines (white): 35 years
          (red): 35 years
Blend (white): 100% Marsanne
(red): 100% Syrah

LOUIS VALLET

Address: 07340 Serrières
Tel: 4-75-34-04-64
Wines produced: St.-Joseph (red and white)
Surface area (white): 1.2 acres
         (red): 10 acres
Production (white): 400 bottles
         (red): 18,000 bottles
Upbringing (white): 6 months with 50% of the yield in stainless steel vats and 50% in new oak barrels
        (red): 12 months in oak barrels, of which 10% are new and 90% are 3–4 years old
Average age of vines (white): 12–15 years
         (red): 18 years
Blend (white): 95% Marsanne, 5% Roussanne
(red): 100% Syrah

GEORGES VERNAY

Address: 1, R.N. 86
       69420 Condrieu
Tel: 4-74-59-22-22
Fax: 4-74-56-60-98
Wines produced: St.-Joseph (red)

Surface area: 2.47 acres
Production: 3,000 bottles
Upbringing: not available
Average age of vines: 25–50 years
Blend: 100% Syrah

PHILIPPE VERZIER

Address: Izerat
        42410 Chavanay
Tel: 4-74-87-23-69
Fax: 4-74-87-07-77
Wines produced: St.-Joseph (red and white), St.-Joseph Cuvée La Madone (red)
Surface area (white): 1.5 acres
            (red): regular cuvée—7.9 acres
                Cuvée La Madone—1.2 acres
Production (white): 300 bottles
            (red): regular cuvée—15,000 bottles
                Cuvée La Madone—2,500 bottles
Upbringing (white): 10 months in enamel vats
            (red): regular cuvée—12–18 months in old oak barrels
                Cuvée La Madone—12–18 months in oak barrels 2–5 years old
Average age of vines (white): 20 years
                (red): regular cuvée—15 years
                    Cuvée La Madone—30 years
Blend (white): 100% Marsanne
    (red): 100% Syrah (both cuvées)

GUY VEYRIER

Address: 07340 St.-Désirat
Tel: 4-75-34-23-05
Wines produced: St.-Joseph (red and white)
Surface area (white): 0.98 acres
            (red): 10 acres
Production (white): 2,250 bottles
            (red): 18,750 bottles
Upbringing (white): 6 months in enamel and fiberglass vats
            (red): 18 months in enamel and fiberglass vats
Average age of vines (white): 7–12 years
                (red): 3 years and 25 years
Blend (white): 100% Marsanne
    (red): 100% Syrah

VIDAL-FLEURY* * *

Address: R.N. 86   Tel: 4-74-56-10-18
        B.P. 12   Fax: 4-74-56-19-19
        69420 Ampuis

GEORGES VILLANO

Address: 111, R.N. 86   Production: 1,500 bottles
        69420 Condrieu   Upbringing: 18–24 months in old oak
Tel: 4-74-59-87-64   barrels
Wines produced: St.-Joseph (red)   Average age of vines: 20 years
Surface area: 2.47 acres   Blend: 100% Syrah

ST.-PÉRAY

The Jurassic Park of the Rhône

ST.-PÉRAY AT A GLANCE

Appellation created:	December 8, 1936.
Type of wine produced:	Still and sparkling white wines, the latter representing 60% of the production.
Grape varieties planted:	Marsanne and Roussanne.
Acres currently under vine:	160.
Quality level:	Below average to average.
Aging potential:	2–4 years.
General characteristics:	Dull, somewhat odd, uninteresting wines that are heavy and diffuse.
Greatest recent vintages:	None.
Price range:	$15–$20.
Aromatic profile:	The acceptable examples—sadly, there are too few—offer a vague lemony/peach-like smell, with neutral fruit flavors. The majority of the wines are acidic, heavy, and lacking fruit.
Textural profile:	The sparkling wines are crisp, and at times refreshing, but in a low-brow sense. The still wines can be flabby, full-bodied, chewy wines with no real vibrancy. There are no profound St.-Péray wines.

RATING THE ST.-PÉRAY SPARKLING WINE PRODUCERS

* * *(GOOD)

Jean-François Chaboud   Jean-Marie Teysseire
Pierre et Guy Darona   Jean-Louis Thiers

RATING THE ST.-PÉRAY STILL WINE PRODUCERS

* * *(GOOD)

Auguste Clape   Jean-Marie Teysseire
Jean-René Lionnet   Jean-Louis Thiers

St.-Péray, the last of the northern Rhône appellations, is situated across from Valence on the west bank of the Rhône, just south of but contiguous to Cornas. The wine offers little to get excited about. The town itself is undistinguished, yet a hike or drive to the ruins of the Château de Crussol, which sits on a craggy outcropping of granite that dominates the town, will provide an exhilarating view of Valence and the Rhône River basin. If the pollution from Valence is not too bad, you can see the Alps. Also not to be missed is a drive west up the perilous, twisting D287 in the direction of St.-Romain-de-Lerps, which offers splendid views of the Rhône Valley. Further, one will encounter a gorgeous, tranquil countryside after crossing onto the plateau above St.-Péray. In spite of these tourist diversions, it is the wine that has made St.-Péray famous. There is plenty of historical documentation giving credit to the monks of the tenth century for planting the vines on the steep, terraced slopes behind the town. The local growers all seem to be in agreement that in 1795 Napoleon, who was a cadet stationed in Valence, developed a taste for the wines of St.-Péray. But this story pales in comparison with the other widely quoted tale that the famous German composer Richard Wagner, while in the midst of composing *Parsifal*, ordered 100 bottles of St.-Péray be sent to him in Bayreuth.

Only white wine is made at St.-Péray. It comes in two types, dull still wines and dull sparkling wines. The two white grape varietals used are the Marsanne and the Roussanne. Over 80% of the wine made here is sparkling. It is produced in the traditional manner and is naturally fermented in the bottle. To say it is adequate would be disingenuous. Heavy, prone to oxidation, and never, in my experience, lively or interesting, sparkling St.-Péray is a curiosity piece that seems doomed in the highly competitive, quality-conscious wine world of today. The still wines are marginally better, but they too have little commercial viability since they tend to be heavy and very low in acidity.

In my opinion, there is no future for this appellation in either of these wines. The granite slopes above the town would no doubt prove much more desirable for Syrah, which is grown with great success on these same slopes only one mile north in Cornas. However, it is unlikely that Syrah will get a foothold here because housing developers have begun aggressively to develop the scenic hillsides. The middle-aged, bald Jean-François Chaboud is this appellation's most famous producer, and even he seems to recognize that the end is near. His fears are based not so much on the lack of appeal of St.-Péray's wines but on the increasing competition in France from lower-priced sparkling wines produced in greater and greater amounts in areas such as Alsace, Limoux, the Loire Valley, and Burgundy. The growth of the sparkling wine business from these areas will do more to put producers out of business than will any inherent deficiencies in these wines. Chaboud readily acknowledges that good money is also to be made by any grower who wants to sell his vineyards to the eagerly awaiting housing developers.

St.-Péray is the only dinosaur of the Rhône Valley viticultural districts. Because of its unique sparkling wines and historic tradition, one would like to see this tiny appellation of 160 acres survive, but the intrinsic quality of the wines made here does not merit anything more than curiosity.

For the adventurous, most of St.-Péray's wines are not inexpensive. They cost a little less than a good nonvintage champagne, but more than a better sparkling wine from Alsace, the Loire, or Burgundy. They are wines that require drinking up within two to three years of the vintage. Whether it is the primitive winemaking technique or the use of Marsanne and Roussanne to make the wine, many of the wines taste bizarre and sometimes oxidized upon release. They are not wines that can be recommended.

JEAN-FRANÇOIS CHABOUD* * *

Address: 21, rue de Vernoux

      07130 St.-Péray

Tel: 4-75-40-31-63

Wines produced: St.-Péray (still and sparkling)

Surface area: 22 acres

Production (still): 24,000 bottles

      (sparkling): 37,500 bottles

Upbringing (still): 6–8 months in stainless steel vats

      (sparkling): 5–6 months in stainless steel vats and 3 years in bottle

Average age of vines: 45 years

Blend (still): 80% Marsanne, 20% Roussanne

      (sparkling): 100% Marsanne

From Chaboud's 22 acres of vines, he produces both sparkling and still wine, but mostly the former. His family has been making wine in St.-Péray since 1715. His underground cellars are impressive and he claims to have a very bustling direct-sale business to tourists who pass through the area. Chaboud is very skeptical of the future of St.-Péray's wines, but claims he has no problem selling any of his wine.

PIERRE ET GUY DARONA* * *

Address: Les Faures

      Route de Toulaud

      07130 St.-Péray

Tel: 4-75-40-34-11

Wines produced: St.-Péray (still and sparkling)

Surface area: 22.2 acres

Production (still): 12,000 bottles

      (sparkling): 45,000 bottles

Upbringing (still): 12 months in stainless steel vats

      (sparkling): 6 months in stainless steel vats and 18–24 months in bottle

Average age of vines: 30–40 years

Blend: 90% Marsanne, 10% Roussanne

Darona has a modest-sized vineyard of 22 acres and, like Chaboud, 80% of his production (3,800 cases) is in sparkling wine. His sparkling wines are less identifiable as textbook St.-Pérays, and for that reason seem to be less bizarre and unusual to taste. Nevertheless, Darona's sparkling wines, which are cleanly made, lack a focal point in flavor interest and fall into the bland, one-dimensional category. I prefer the still wine here to the sparkling.

JEAN-MARIE TEYSSEIRE* * *

Address: 07130 Cornas
Tel: 4-75-40-52-01
Wines produced: St.-Péray (still and sparkling)
Surface area: 4.2 acres
Production: 8,250 bottles, which varies between still and sparkling
Upbringing (still): 18 months in enamel vats
            (sparkling): 7 months in enamel vats and 12–24 months in bottle
Average age of vines: 80 years
Blend: 100% Marsanne

Teysseire, who also makes Cornas, has 4.2 acres of vines in St.-Péray. I prefer his still to his sparkling wine, but that is hardly a compliment.

OTHER ST.-PÉRAY PRODUCERS

CAVE LES VIGNERONS DE ST.-PÉRAY

Address: Avenue du 11 Novembre
            07130 St.-Péray
Tel: 4-75-40-31-17
Fax: 4-75-81-06-02
Wines produced: St.-Péray (still and sparkling)
Production (still): 15,000 bottles
            (sparkling): 35,000–40,000
Upbringing (still): 8–10 months in stainless steel vats
            (sparkling): 6 months in stainless steel vats and 30 months in bottle
Blend: normally 100% Marsanne

CAVES COTTEVERGNE (L. SAUGÈRE)

Address: Quartier le Bret
            07130 St.-Péray
Tel: 4-75-40-30-43
Fax: 4-75-40-55-06
Wines produced: St.-Péray Beauregard (still), St.–Péray Golden Hill (sparkling)
Surface area: 7.4 acres
Production (Beauregard): 6,750 bottles
            (Golden Hill): 6,750 bottles
Upbringing (Beauregard): 3–4 months in 30% new oak barrels
            (Golden Hill): 6–8 months in stainless steel vats and a minimum of 24 months
                        in bottle
Average age of vines: 25 years
Blend: 100% Marsanne

AUGUSTE CLAPE* * *

Address: 07130 Cornas
Tel: 4-75-40-33-64
Fax: 4-75-81-01-98
Wines produced: St.-Péray (still)
Surface area: 0.7 acres

Production: 2,200 bottles
Upbringing: 6–8 months in stainless steel vats
Average age of vines: 60 years
Blend: 100% Marsanne

BERNARD GRIPPA

Address: 5, avenue Ozier
  07300 Mauves
Tel: 4-75-08-14-96
Fax: 4-75-07-06-81
Wines produced: St.-Péray (still)
Surface area: 2.47 acres
Production: 5,700 bottles
Upbringing: 8 months with 90% of the yield in stainless steel vats and 10% in oak barrels, little new
Average age of vines: 50 years
Blend: 80% Marsanne, 20% Roussanne

DOMAINE DE LA HAUTE FAUTERIE

Address: 07130 St.-Péray
Tel: 4-75-40-46-17
Wines produced: St.-Péray Cuvée Tradition (still), St.-Péray Cuvée Sélection (still). If the quality is not good enough, the whole production is bottled as Cuvée Tradition.
Surface area: 7.5 acres
Production: 18,000 bottles
Upbringing: 8 months in stainless steel vats
Average age of vines: 8–10 years
Blend: 70% Marsanne, 30% Roussanne

MARCEL JUGE

Address: Place de la Salle des Fêtes
  07130 Cornas
Tel: 4-75-40-36-68
Fax: 4-75-40-30-05
Wines produced: St.-Péray (still)

Surface area: 0.86 acres
Production: 1,600 bottles
Upbringing: 12 months in old oak
Average age of vines: 40 years
Blend: 50% Marsanne, 50% Roussanne

JACQUES LEMENCIER

Address: Route des Granges
  07130 Cornas
Tel: 4-75-40-49-54
Wines produced: St.-Péray Cuvée Traditionnelle (still), St.-Péray Cuvée Boisée (still)
Surface area: 1.2 acres
Production (Cuvée Traditionnelle): 1,500 bottles
  (Cuvée Boisée): 1,500 bottles
Upbringing (Cuvée Traditionnelle): 7–8 months in enamel vats
  (Cuvée Boisée): 6–8 months in new oak barrels
Average age of vines: 60 years
Blend: 100% Marsanne

JEAN-RENÉ LIONNET* * *

Address: Pied la Vigne
  07130 Cornas
Tel: 4-75-40-36-01
Wines produced: St.-Péray (still)
Surface area: 4.9 acres

Production: 12,000 bottles
Upbringing: 8 months with 40% of the yield in 20% new oak barrels and 60% in stainless
        steel vats
Average age of the vines: 60 years
Blend: 80% Marsanne, 20% Roussanne

JEAN-LOUIS THIERS* * *

Address: Quartier Biguet
        07130 Toulaud
Tel: 4-75-40-49-44
Wines produced: St.-Péray (still and sparkling)
Surface area: 12.4 acres
Production (still): 4,000–5,000 bottles
        (sparkling): 20,000 bottles
Upbringing (still): 6–8 months in stainless steel vats
        (sparkling): 6 months in stainless steel vats and 18 months in bottle
Average age of vines: 4–5 years and 50 years
Blend: 100% Marsanne

ALAIN VOGE

Address: Rue de l'Equerre
        07130 Cornas
Tel: 4-75-40-32-04
Wines produced: St.-Péray (still), St.-Péray Cuvée Boisée (still), St.-Péray Ultra Brut
        (sparkling), St.-Péray Brut (sparkling)
Surface area: 17.3 acres
Production (St.-Péray): 22,500 bottles
        (Cuvée Boisée): 8,000 bottles
        (Ultra Brut): 2,000 bottles
        (Brut): 8,000 bottles
Upbringing (St.-Péray): 12 months, with 50% of the yield in enamel vats and 50% in 50%
        new oak barrels
        (Cuvée Boisée): 12 months in 50% new oak barrels
        (Ultra Brut): 6 months in stainless steel vats and 5 years in bottle
        (Brut): 6 months in stainless steel vats and 2 years in bottle
Average age of vines: 30–40 years
Blend: 100% Marsanne

THE SOUTHERN RHÔNE

Vacqueyras
Châteauneuf du Pape
Gigondas
Tavel
Lirac
Côtes du Rhône-Villages
Côtes du Rhône
Esoteric Rhône Wines

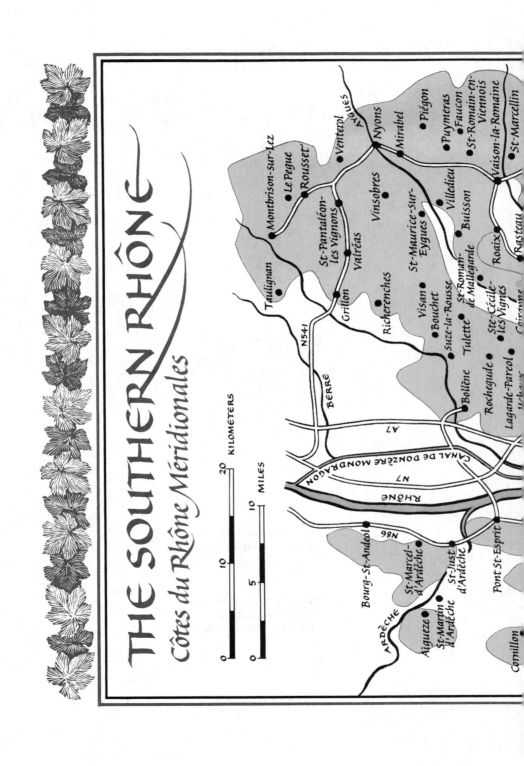

THE SOUTHERN RHÔNE
Côtes du Rhône Méridionales

KILOMETERS
20
10
0

MILES
10
5
0

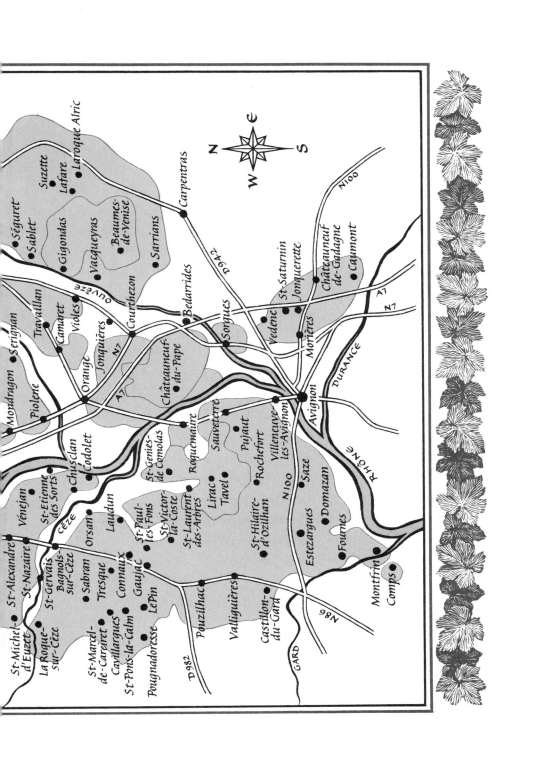

INTRODUCTION

The northern Rhône's viticultural region (often referred to by the French as the Côtes du Rhône Septentrionales) ends after the appellation of St.-Péray, located just west of the large commercial city of Valence. For all intents and purposes, the viticultural region of the southern Rhône Valley (referred to by the French as the Côtes du Rhône Meridionales) does not begin until one reaches the outskirts of Orange, approximately 60 miles south of Valence.

While the distance between Valence and Orange is not great, the differences in climate and geography are striking and vividly divergent, regardless of how many times one travels between the two cities. Aside from the huge, rather forbidding nuclear power plants that dominate the landscape between Montélimar and Orange, the vegetation becomes notably less lush, and the topography reflects the windswept and sun-drenched climate of the southern Rhône. In climatic terms, the southern Rhône has a much drier, hotter, breezier Mediterranean-influenced climate than the north. The aromas of Provençal herbs and *garrigue* (an earthy herb scent peculiar to this region) are more than just imaginary flights of olfactory fancy; these scents are virtually everywhere. It should come as no surprise that these same aromas can be found in both the wines and the cuisine of this region.

In the northern Rhône, nearly every vineyard is within view of the Rhône River, and all the best growing sites are on the steep, terraced hillsides that flank the river. In the south, there are plenty of hillside plantations, but no steep, terraced vineyards the likes of which are found in Côte Rôtie, Hermitage, and Cornas.

The Rhône River passes through the region, but the vast viticultural area composing the southern Rhône fans out both east and west for many miles. On the right bank is Lirac, a promising appellation that has yet to fulfill its potential, Tavel, the home of France's most expensive and occasionally its best rosé wines, and a handful of Côtes du Rhône-Villages, the best of which is St.-Gervais.

The bulk of the southern Rhône wines are made on the left bank or eastern side of the Rhône. This area is also among the most scenic and most traveled in France. In truth, this is Provence. From Valréas and Vinsobres, northeast of Orange, to Châteauneuf du Pape, vineyards on flat plains and gentle slopes coexist with the charming medieval hill towns filled with artists and artisans. The scenery is spectacular, and the climate idyllic, save for the ferocious mistral winds. Near Châteauneuf du Pape, the southern Rhône's most famous appellation, is Gigondas, which also produces very high-quality, chewy, full-bodied wines. Within view of Gigondas is Beaumes de Venise, known for its opulent fortified dessert wines. With few exceptions, this eastern sector has a monopoly on the finest Côtes du Rhônes-Villages. Quaint towns such as Vaison-la-Romaine, Rochegude, Lagarde-Paréol,

Ste.-Cecile-les-Vignes, Séguret, Cairanne, Rasteau, Vacqueyras, and Carpentras, to name a few, sit scenically and strategically amid an ocean of vineyards. Each of them has its own charm, and its share of uncomplicated but generous and satisfying wines. This area of sun-scorched, lazy hill towns is fertile territory not only for the frequent tourist or amateur photographer but also the shrewd wine enthusiast either looking for a bargain or on a chase for something great.

One of the stumbling blocks to understanding the wines of the southern Rhône is the number of grape varieties utilized by the growers. As in the northern Rhône, there is Syrah, but it is far less important in the south, where some growers argue that it overripens and raisins in the intense heat and sun of this region. Yet when planted in the right terroir, Syrah has produced some superb examples. Grenache is the dominant red wine grape in the south. It produces fleshy, ripe, alcoholic wines without much character when its yield is not controlled. When pruned severely to curtail the yield, the Grenache is capable of producing magnificent wines. Only a few wines made in the southern Rhône are 100% Grenache; most reds are the result of a blend of at least four varietals. Other grape varieties used for these blends are the Mourvèdre, which has the disadvantage of ripening very late but offers some color, plenty of structure, and additional aromatic complexity to any blend. Cinsault, which is widely planted in the Rhône because it is easy to grow, is relatively prolific, and adds aromatic complexity and acidity, but because of the qualitative revolution, its popularity continues to plummet. In addition, the permitted red wine varietals that are less commonly encountered include Muscardin, Terret, Counoise, and Vaccarèse. The last two are believed to have immense potential.

For the white wines made in the south, three grapes found in the north—the ubiquitous Marsanne, the fickle Roussanne, and the fascinating Viognier—are also planted in the southern Rhône, but to a much lesser extent. The workhorse white wine varietals in the south remain Grenache Blanc, Clairette, and Bourboulenc. While Picardin and Picpoul have lost popularity, interest in Viognier and Roussanne has soared, so much so that many new vineyards are dedicated to these two varietals.

With such an assortment of grape varietals, it is no wonder that the type and style of each producer's wine in the southern Rhône can vary enormously depending on the percentage of a particular grape used in the blend. To facilitate your comprehension, the major grape varietals used in the southern Rhône are listed below with their telltale personality traits.

A SUMMARY OF THE SOUTHERN RHÔNE VARIETALS

White Wine Varietals

Bourboulenc This grape offers plenty of body as well as some much needed acidity in the hot southern Rhône. The local cognoscenti also attribute the scent of roses to Bourboulenc, though I cannot yet claim the same experience. Bourboulenc is thought to be a vine of Greek origin. It is most commonly found in Châteauneuf du Pape, but also in the Côtes du Rhône, Lirac, and, to a certain extent, in Tavel.

Clairette Until the advent of cold fermentations and modern equipment to minimize the risk of oxidation, the Clairette produced heavy, alcoholic, often deep yellow wines that were thick and ponderous. Given the benefit of state-of-the-art technology, it now produces soft, floral, fruity, light- to medium-bodied wines that must be drunk young. With the increasing interest in Roussanne, Clairette Blanc appears to be falling out of favor with many southern Rhône white wine producers.

Grenache Blanc Deeply fruity, highly alcoholic yet low-acid wines are produced from Grenache Blanc. When fermented at cool temperatures and the malolactic fermentation blocked, it can be a vibrant, delicious wine capable of providing more texture and, at times, an alluring perfume of narcissus flower. Texturally, the wine varies from medium to full bodied, with plenty of alcohol and glycerin.

Marsanne   Marsanne planted in the southern Rhône is believed to produce chunky wines, and it must receive help from other varietals. It cannot stand alone as it can in the north. Jancis Robinson claims it smells "not unpleasantly reminiscent of glue." This seems a bit unfair, but clearly Marsanne is much more successful in the north than the south.

Picardin   This grape has fallen out of favor largely because the growers felt it added nothing to their blends. Apparently its neutral character as well as low acidity was its undoing, but the white Châteauneuf du Pape Les Cèdres from the Jaboulet firm has an unmistakable smell of apricots and peaches. However, Jacques Jaboulet claims low-yielding, old-vine Picardin smells similar to Viognier!

Picpoul   Frankly, I have no idea what this grape tastes like. I have never seen it isolated or represented in sufficiently hefty a percentage to be identifiable. Today it is rarely used in the southern Rhône. Old-timers claim it provided a floral component to a wine's aroma, and added structure because Picpoul has tannin in its skin.

Roussanne   For centuries, this grape was the essence of white Hermitage in the northern Rhône, but its small yields and proclivity to disease led to its being largely replaced by Marsanne. It has made a strong comeback in the southern Rhône. It has the most character of any of the white wine varietals. With aromas of honey, coffee, flowers (iris), and nuts, it produces a powerful, unctuously textured wine that can be very long-lived, an anomaly for a white wine from the southern Rhône. The famous Châteauneuf du Pape estate Beaucastel uses 80% Roussanne in their regular cuvée of white Beaucastel. In 1986, they launched a luxury cuvée of 100% old-vine Roussanne, unquestionably the southern Rhône's most compelling and complex dry white wine. New plantings of Roussanne can be seen throughout Châteauneuf du Pape, as well as the Côtes du Rhône. In Châteauneuf du Pape, Château de la Nerthe as well as a bevy of other producers have taken up the cause for this grape, which has immense potential.

Viognier   As has already been indicated in the chapter on Condrieu, Viognier produces a very distinctive and potentially great wine, but one that must be consumed young. Viognier is synonymous with Condrieu and Château Grillet in the northern Rhône. In the south, the experimental plantings of the late seventies and early eighties have been so successful that Viognier is now *très à la mode*. Fine examples of Viognier can be found in almost every village in the Côtes du Rhône. Even where it is not bottled as a separate varietal, it provides an intriguing and enticing component to southern Rhône blends. It has become an important part of many generic Côtes du Rhône blends from major négociants, particularly Guigal. This grape, which is ideally suited for the hot, sunny, windy weather of the region, appears to have a fabulous future. Along with Roussanne, it holds the key for the development of great dry whites from the southern Rhône.

Red Wine Varietals

Cinsault   All the growers seem to use a small amount of Cinsault. It ripens very early, gives good yields, and produces wines that offer a great deal of fruit. It seems to offset the high alcohol of the Grenache and the tannins of the Syrah and Mourvèdre. Despite its value, it seems to have lost appeal in favor of Syrah or Mourvèdre, yet it remains a valuable asset in a blend. While Cinsault can rarely stand alone, tasting low-yielding, old-vine Cinsault in the Rayas cellars before it is blended into Jacques Reynaud's Côtes du Rhône Fonsalette has often left me wanting to purchase a couple of cases of pure Cinsault. It can smell of both roses and almonds. Unfortunately, if yields are kept to 15–20 hectoliters per hectare as Reynaud does, it is not commercially viable to make a 100% Cinsault wine.

Counoise   Very little of this grape exists in the south because of its capricious growing habits. However, I have tasted it separately at Château Beaucastel in Châteauneuf du Pape where the Perrin family has augmented its use. It has great finesse and provides deep, richly fruity flavors and a complex perfume of smoked meat, nutmeg, green pepper, flowers, and berry fruit. The Perrins feel Counoise has at least as much potential as a high-quality ingredient in their blend as Mourvèdre.

Grenache   A classic hot climate grape varietal, Grenache is for better or worse the dominant grape of the southern Rhône. The quality of the wines it produces ranges from hot, alcoholic, unbalanced, coarse wines, to rich, majestic, very long-lived, sumptuous wines. The differences are largely caused by the yield of juice per acre. Where Grenache is pruned back and not overly fertilized, it can do wondrous things. The sensational Châteauneuf du Pape, Château Rayas, is a poignant example of that. At its best, it offers aromas of kirsch, blackcurrants, raspberry jam, pepper, licorice, and roasted peanuts.

Mourvèdre   Everyone seems to agree on the antioxidant virtues of the Mourvèdre, but few people want to take the risk and grow it. It flourishes in the Mediterranean appellation of Bandol, but only Château Beaucastel and Château de la Nerthe in Châteauneuf du Pape have made it an important part of their blend. It gives color, a complex aroma, and superb structure. Moreover, it is very resistant to oxidation. However, it ripens very late and unlike other grape varietals has no value until it is perfectly mature. When it lacks maturity, the growers say it gives them nothing, as it is colorless and acidic. Given the eccentricities of this grape, it is unlikely that anyone other than adventurous or passionately obsessed growers will make much use of it. Its telltale aromas are those of foresty undergrowth, animal fur, leather, truffles, fresh mushrooms, and tree bark. The provocative animal side of Mourvèdre has often caused many new world tasters to suspect that a wine contains the yeast brettanomyces (often called brett). This particular yeast, when present in high quantities, does give a wine an unpleasant sweaty, saddle, musty, animal smell, but it should not be confused with the more focused aromatics of the Mourvèdre grape.

Muscardin   More common than Terret Noir, Muscardin provides a floral perfume while imparting a solidarity and a good measure of alcohol and strength to a wine. Beaucastel uses Muscardin, but by far the most important plantings of Muscardin at a serious winemaking estate were at Chante-Perdrix in Châteauneuf du Pape. For whatever reason, the Nicolet family has reduced the percentage of Muscardin in their wine.

Syrah   Syrah, the only game in town in the northern Rhône, is relegated to an accessory role in the south. However, its role in providing needed structure, backbone, and tannin to the fleshy Grenache is incontestable. Some growers believe it ripens too fast in the hotter south, but it is, in my opinion, a very strong addition to many southern Rhône wines. More and more of the Côtes du Rhône estates are producing special bottlings of 100% Syrah wines that show immense potential. The finest Syrah made in the southern Rhône is the Cuvée Syrah from the Château de Fonsalette, a wine that can last and evolve for 25–30 years. Its aromas are those of berry fruit, coffee, smoky tar, and hickory wood. Other Côtes du Rhône estates are also incorporating more Syrah in their blends. Even in Châteauneuf du Pape, Syrah has become an increasingly important component, with the renowned Château Fortia utilizing over one-third Syrah in recent blends. The key to cultivating top-quality Syrah is to find cooler microclimates and/or northern-oriented vineyards.

Terret Noir   Little of this grape is now found in the southern Rhône, though it remains one of the permitted varieties. It was used to give acidity to a wine and mollify the strong character provided by the Grenache and Syrah. None of the best estates employs it any longer.

Vaccarèse   It is again at Beaucastel where I tasted the wine produced from this grape, which the Perrins vinify separately. It is not as powerful or as deep as Syrah, nor as alcoholic as Grenache, but it has its own unique character that I would describe as giving aromas of flowers, tobacco, and licorice. It offers little in either body or texture.

There are exceptionally great wines made in the southern Rhône, and the potential for high quality is enormous. The climate is the most consistent and favorable of all France's viticultural regions (save for the Languedoc-Roussillon). The dry heat and persistent gusty winds (called le mistral) serve as a natural antibiotic, inhibiting the dreaded rot that causes so many problems elsewhere in France. The legally permitted yields of juice per acre remain very conservative, and lead routinely to a production per acre that is less than half of that now produced in Burgundy or Bordeaux. Machine harvesters are prohibited in appellations such as Châteauneuf du Pape and Gigondas. Unlike the tiny amounts of wine produced in the northern Rhône, quantities of the top wines from the south are far more plentiful and easier to find. The prices for these wines qualify them as among the greatest bargains in serious red wine in the world. Furthermore, most of the wines have the virtue of being drinkable, or are at least accessible, when released. However, the top Châteauneuf du Papes can last and evolve 15–20 years, the best Gigondas 8–12 years, and even a good Côtes du Rhône 2–5 years.

There is a vast amount of enjoyment to be discovered in the southern Rhône for only a modest amount of money, for these are some of the most sumptuous and pleasure-giving wines produced in the world.

VACQUEYRAS

Not Just a Petit Châteauneuf du Pape or Gigondas

VACQUEYRAS AT A GLANCE

Appellation created:	August 9, 1990.
Type of wine produced:	Red wine represents 95% of the production, with 4% rosé and 1% white.
Grape varieties planted:	Grenache, Syrah, Mourvèdre, and Cinsault for the red and rosé wines, and Grenache Blanc, Clairette, and Bourboulenc for the white wines.
Acres currently under vine:	3,211.
Quality level:	Average to good, but increasing.
Aging potential:	4–12 years.
General characteristics:	Powerful, rustic, full-bodied red wines that tend to lack the complexity and finesse of Gigondas or Châteauneuf du Pape.
Greatest recent vintages:	1995, 1990, 1989.
Price range:	$10–$16.
Aromatic profile:	A classic Provençal/Mediterranean nose of herbes de Provence, *garrigue*, red and black fruits, earth, and olives.
Textural profile:	Unbridled power, as well as coarse tannin and a fleshy personality, make for a substantial and mouth-filling glass of wine.

RATING THE VACQUEYRAS PRODUCERS

* * * * *(OUTSTANDING)

None

* * * *(EXCELLENT)

Domaine des Amouriers   Domaine de Montvac
Domaine de la Charbonnière   Tardieu-Laurent
Domaine du Couroulu   Domaine de la Tourade
Domaine la Fourmone   Château des Tours

* * *(GOOD)

La Bastide St.-Vincent   Château de Montmirail
Domaine de Boissan   Château des Roques
Domaine Chamfort   Domaine le Sang des Cailloux
Domaine le Clos des Cazaux ***/****   Domaine de Verquière
Domaine de la Garrigue   Vidal-Fleury
Paul Jaboulet-Ainé

Vacqueyras, even more than Gigondas, is the classic Provençal village. Yet it is easy to bypass when taking the Route du Vin (D 7) from Carpentras in the direction of Vaison la Romaine. This wine road passes through the undistinguished outskirts of Vacqueyras. It is mandatory to make a turn into the village and experience its considerable charms. As in so many of the villages in this gorgeous landscape, there is a collection of yellow/rust/brown homes all topped off with the telltale brick-colored tiles common in this part of France. The village's lazy atmosphere, shady, narrow streets, groups of old men playing *pétanque*, and the omnipresent marketplace aromas of herbs, olives, fruits, and vegetables are straight out of a Marcel Pagnol novel. Moreover, there seem to be as many caveaux in Vacqueyras as in the village of Châteauneuf du Pape.

Vacqueyras was elevated from a Côtes du Rhône-Village to its own appellation in 1990, leaving several excellent Côtes du Rhône-Villages (Séguret, Sablet, and Cairanne) to wonder why they were not also entitled to a promotion. Over 50% of Vacqueyras is dominated by the local cooperative, which claims as members 130 of the 160 vignerons. The other 30 produce and estate-bottle their wine, which is certainly more than a petit Châteauneuf du Pape or Gigondas.

Situated in the Vaucluse and protected by the Dentelles de Montmirail, Vacqueyras is only a few miles north of Gigondas, and the two wines share similar characteristics. However, Vacqueyras can be even more blatantly robust and coarse, without the purity and sweetness of fruit found in the finest Gigondas. Vacqueyras's terroirs are relatively homogeneous, with the most important vineyard sectors on the Plateau des Garrigues, in the direction of Sarrians, and the others spread out on the plain, where there is red, sandy soil, as well as the famed *galets roulés* that are so prominent in Châteauneuf du Pape. This area possesses searing heat exacerbated by the severe mistral winds.

Grenache is king in Vacqueyras, but there are increasing plantations of Syrah and Mourvèdre, with Cinsault and Carignan largely being eliminated from modern-day blends. Virtually all the wine made in Vacqueyras is red. A tiny bit of indifferent rosé is produced, as well as minuscule quantities of white wine. However, there are new plantings of Roussanne, which have shown high quality, causing enthusiasm among several of the growers. There is no reason why this varietal should not excel in the terroirs of Vacqueyras.

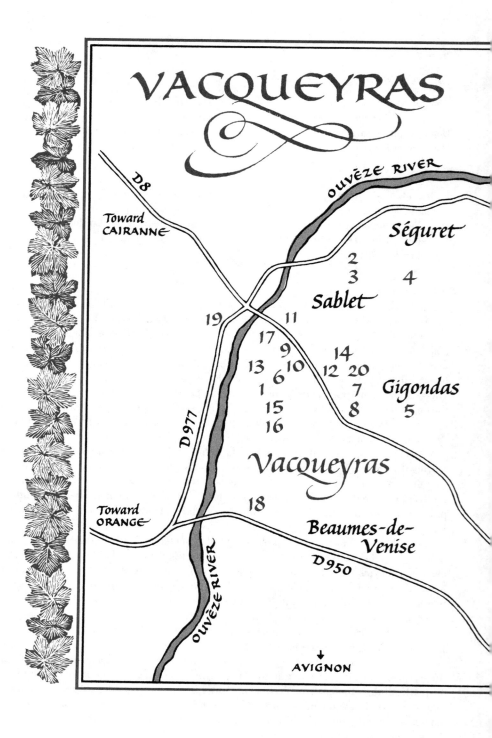

Toward
VAISON-
LA-ROMAINE

D977

Dentelles
de-
Montmiral

N
W E
S

Toward
CARPENTRAS

LOCATION OF CELLARS

1 Domaine des Amouriers
2 La Bastide St-Vincent
3 Domaine de Boissan
4 Domaine Chamfort
5 Domaine le Clos de Caveau
6 Domaine le Clos des Cazaux
7 Domaine de la Colline St-Jean
8 Domaine le Couroulu
9 Domaine la Fourmone
10 Domaine des Lambertins
11 Domaine du Mas des Collines
12 Château de Montmirail
13 Domaine de la Monardière
14 Domaine de Montvac
15 Château des Roques
16 Domaine le Sang des Cailloux
17 Domaine de la Tourade
18 Château des Tours
19 Domaine de Verquière
20 Cave des Vigerons

Winemaking in Vacqueyras can be traced to the early fifteenth century. The village is proud to claim the famed twelfth-century Provençal troubadour, Raimbaud, as a native son. Part of the modern-day image of Vacqueyras stems from the fact that there has been no famous personage since Raimbaud to become a leader in this appellation. Of the 30 producers who estate-bottle, no one makes exceptional wine, but increasing numbers are fashioning excellent Vacqueyras. They have resisted the temptation, even with their new status as a single appellation, to raise prices. The future of Vacqueyras depends on one of these estates emerging as a superstar—essential for garnering international attention. The most likely candidates are Domaine la Fourmone, Château des Tours, Domaine le Couroulu, or Domaine des Amouriers, all among the current reference point producers of the appellation. With excellent terroirs, an impressive percentage of old vines, and a superb climate, there is no reason why Vacqueyras cannot push overall quality to a higher plateau.

It is hard to determine what the future holds for Vacqueyras. The potential exists for top-quality wines, but someone needs to emerge as a leader to create more interest in foreign markets. Yet, there can be no question that at the top level, these wines are underrated and undervalued.

DOMAINE DES AMOURIERS* * * *

Address: Les Garrigues
       84190 Vacqueyras
Tel: 4-90-65-83-22
Fax: 4-90-65-84-13
Wines produced: Vacqueyras Cuvée Signature, Vacqueyras Cuvée Les Genestres, Vacqueyras Cuvée Les Truffières, Vacqueyras Cuvée Hautes Terraces, Vacqueyras Cuvée Normale
Surface area: 16 acres
Production (Cuvée Signature): 1,500 cases
          (Cuvée Les Genestres): 812 cases
          (Cuvée Les Truffières): 312 cases
          (Cuvée Hautes Terraces): 225 cases (9 barrels)
Upbringing (Cuvée Signature): 12–18 months in stainless steel and enamel vats
          (Cuvée Les Genestres): 12–18 months in stainless steel and enamel vats
          (Cuvée Les Truffières): 8 months in new oak barrels
          (Cuvée Hautes Terraces): 100% aging in new oak casks
Average age of vines: 40 years
Blend (Cuvée Signature): 60% Grenache, 30% Syrah, 6% Cinsault, 4% Mourvèdre
       (Cuvée Les Genestres): 50% Grenache, 40% Syrah, 6% Cinsault, 4% Mourvèdre
       (Cuvée Les Truffières): 47% Grenache, 40% Syrah, 9% Cinsault, 4% Mourvèdre
       (Cuvée Hautes Terraces): 75% Syrah, 25% Grenache

Proprietor Jocelyn Chudzikiewicz and his oenologist, Gérard Philis, have emerged as one of the most significant producers of high-quality Vacqueyras. Although he only owns 16 acres in Vacqueyras, the estate is far larger, with another 30 acres of Côtes du Rhône vineyards. A young, enthusiastic, mustached man, Chudzikiewicz's grandparents immigrated from Poland in 1928 to work in the local mines, but their attention quickly turned to viticulture, and after planting vineyards, they became important members of the local cooperative.

The traditional vinification is carried out in cement vats, with no destemming. There has been experimentation with new oak, with such success for the most concentrated cuvées that Domaine des Amouriers' Cuvée Les Truffières and microproduction of Cuvée Hautes Terraces are now aged primarily in new oak. Given the fact that the entire production was sold to the cooperative until 1985, this estate has quickly emerged as one of the potential leaders of the future. All the wines are delicious, pure, concentrated, and impeccably made. Under the inspired administration of Jocelyn Chudzikiewicz, Domaine des Amouriers appears to be one of the potential candidates to lead Vacqueyras into a new era of quality.

VINTAGES

1995—Vacqueyras Cuvée Genestres   The 1995 Cuvée Genestres (a blend of 40% Syrah
·   and 60% Grenache) reveals gobs of black cassis fruit, along with cherries, herbs,
88   and earth notes. Medium- to full-bodied, with excellent definition, and a spicy,
            peppery, long finish, it should drink well for 4–5 years. Last tasted 6/96.

1995—Vacqueyras Cuvée Hautes Terraces   The opaque black/purple-colored Hautes
·   Terraces offers a lavish display of jammy blackcurrant fruit intermingled with
89   scents of thyme, licorice, and spices. Full-bodied, powerful, and concentrated, with
            layers of flavor, this low-acid wine is a terrific example of a Syrah-based Côtes du
            Rhône. Reminiscent of the outstanding Cuvée Syrah made by Château de Fonsa-
            lette, it could be called the Hermitage of Vacqueyras. Drink it over the next 10–
            15+ years. Last tasted 6/96.

1995—Vacqueyras Cuvée Signature   The 1995 Cuvée Signature (85% Grenache from
·   40-year-old vines, 5% Syrah from 25-year-old vines, and 10% Cinsault) is a dense,
87   chocolaty, wine scented with herbs, and black cherry, with a deeper color than the
            Côtes du Rhône, as well as more power and ripeness. It is a fresh, pure, elegant
            Vacqueyras for drinking over the next 4–5 years. Last tasted 6/96.

1994—Vacqueyras Cuvée Normale   Made from a blend of 60% Grenache, 20% Mour-
·   vèdre, and 20% Syrah, the 1994 reveals a deep ruby color, a big, forceful, peppery
87   nose with scents of black cherry and Provençal herbs, ripe, medium- to full-bodied,
            spicy flavors, an attractive suppleness, and a smooth, rich finish. It should drink
            well for 4–5 years. Last tasted 9/95.

1993—Vacqueyras Cuvée Normale   The 1993, a blend of approximately 60% Grenache,
·   30% Mourvèdre, and 10% Syrah, is a full-bodied, chewy, exuberant, peppery,
88   fruity Rhône wine. It is fully mature and should be drunk up. Last tasted 6/96.

LA BASTIDE ST.-VINCENT* * *

Address: Route de Vaison-la-Romaine
         84150 Violès
Tel: 4-90-70-94-13
Fax: 4-90-70-96-13
Wines produced: Vacqueyras
Surface area: 12.4 acres
Production: 1,625 cases
Upbringing: 12–18 months in cement or enamel vats
Average age of vines: 25 years
Blend: 65% Grenache, 25% Syrah, 10% Mourvèdre

This very good though inconsistent estate, superbly situated on the *garrigues* of Sarrians, produces a full-bodied, robust, exuberant wine. Guy and Brigitte Daniel produce a ripe, peppery wine exhibiting plenty of the redcurrant, jammy, black-cherry character found in many wines of the southern Rhône. The success of this estate is evidenced by the fact that 100% of the production is estate-bottled. By replacing the ancient wood foudres, this property could easily move up in the quality hierarchy as the raw materials are top class. Only the élevage is suspect.

CAVES DES VIGNERONS DE VACQUEYRAS* */* * *

Address: Le Troubadour
      84190 Vacqueyras
Tel: 4-90-65-84-54
Fax: 4-90-65-81-32
Wines produced: Vacqueyras Château Hautes Ribes, Vacqueyras Domaine Soleiade, Vacqueyras Cuvée Fonseguille, Vacqueyras Cuvée Fontimple, Vacqueyras Cuvée Vieillie en Fûts de Chêne, Vacqueyras Cuvée du Président, Vacqueyras Cuvée Vieilles Vignes
Surface area (Château Hautes Ribes): 74 acres
      (Domaine Soleiade): 86 acres
Production (Château Hautes Ribes): 10,000 cases
      (Domaine Soleiade): 12,500 cases
      (Cuvée Fonseguille): 50,000 cases
      (Cuvée Fontimple): 25,000 cases
      (Cuvée Vieillie en Fûts de Chêne): 18,750 cases
      (Cuvée du Président): 6,250 cases
      (Cuvée Vieilles Vignes): 2,500 cases
Upbringing (Château Hautes Ribes) 12 months in stainless steel vats
      (Domaine Soleiade): 12 months in stainless steel vats
      (Cuvée Fonseguille): 7–8 months in cement vats
      (Cuvée Fontimple): 7–8 months in cement vats
      (Cuvée Vieillie en Fûts de Chêne): 15–18 months in oak casks
      (Cuvée du Président): 15–18 months in oak casks
      (Cuvée Vieilles Vignes): 18 months total, with 6 months in new oak barrels
Average age of vines (Château Hautes Ribes): 35 years
      (Domaine Soleiade): 35 years
      (Cuvée Fonseguille): 30 years
      (Cuvée Fontimple): 30 years
      (Cuvée Vieillie en Fûts de Chêne): 30 years
      (Cuvée du Président): 30–35 years
      (Cuvée Vieilles Vignes): 50 + years for the Grenache
Blend (Château Hautes Ribes): 65% Grenache, 25% Syrah, 5% Mourvèdre, 5% Cinsault
      (Domaine Soleiade): 65% Grenache, 25% Syrah, 5% Mourvèdre, 5% Cinsault
      (Cuvée Fonseguille): 65% Grenache, 15% Syrah, 20% Mourvèdre and Cinsault
      (Cuvée Fontimple): 65% Grenache, 25% Syrah, 10% Mourvèdre and Cinsault
      (Cuvée Vieillie en Fûts de Chêne): 70% Grenache, 20% Syrah, 10% Mourvèdre
      (Cuvée du Président): 70% Grenache, 15% Syrah, 15% Mourvèdre
      (Cuvée Vieilles Vignes): 65% Grenache, 25% Syrah, 5% Mourvèdre, 5% Cinsault

As readers might expect, with so many different cuvées produced, the quality at this cooperative, which controls 1,111 acres of vineyards, and produces 187,000 + cases of wine, is variable. However, the finest cuvées reveal plenty of fruit and character, in addition to being extremely value-priced. All the wines are made in an up-front, fruity, clean style that invites consumption within 2–5 years of the vintage.

DOMAINE CHAMFORT* * *

Address: La Pause
      84111 Sablet
Tel: 4-90-46-95-95
Fax: 4-90-46-99-86
Wines produced: Vacqueyras

Surface area: 19.8 acres
Production: 3,750 cases
Upbringing: 6 months in old oak casks
Average age of vines: 25 years
Blend: 75% Grenache, 25% Mourvèdre

This is a relatively new estate run by Denis Chamfort. He had the misfortune of debuting in 1991, a year that posed insurmountable difficulties because of mutiple deluges during the harvest. That vintage was followed by the catastrophic flooding of the Ouvèze River during the 1992 harvest, and damp, cold weather during the 1993 harvest. Nevertheless, this serious, energetic young man appears to be intent on producing high-quality Vacqueyras. With the 1994 and 1995 vintages, I believe Domaine Chamfort will begin to make some waves in Vacqueyras.

DOMAINE DE LA CHARBONNIÈRE (MICHEL MARET)* * * *

Address: Route de Courthézon
        84230 Châteauneuf du Pape
Tel: 4-90-83-64-59
Fax: 4-90-83-53-46
Wines produced: Vacqueyras
Surface area: 10 acres
Production: 1,750 cases
Upbringing: A traditional vinification with no destemming and minimal intervention
Average age of the vines: 50–60 years
Blend: 50% Grenache, 50% Syrah

Michel Maret, one of the up-and-coming stars of Châteauneuf du Pape (see page 380), also produces a small quantity of excellent Vacqueyras from a parcel of old vines. As the following tasting notes demonstrate, these are high-class, rich, chewy wines made from an intriguing blend of 50% Grenache and 50% Syrah. The wine is bottled unfiltered for the American importer. If readers can find any, this is one of the finest wines of the appellation.

VINTAGES

1995—Vacqueyras The 1995 Vacqueyras reveals a dense, dark purple color, a big,
·   peppery, spicy, jammy black-cherry-scented nose, full body, fine power, and a
88   long, rustic, large-scaled finish. It is an excellent wine that should drink well for
       5–7 years. Last tasted 6/96.

1994—Vacqueyras This offering is a noteworthy effort from the 1994 vintage. With its
·   deep ruby/purple color, intense nose of Provençal herbs, pepper, spice, and black
88   fruits, this husky, rich, medium- to full-bodied, velvety-textured Vacqueyras is
       already delicious, yet it promises to keep for another 3–4 years. Last tasted 6/96.

DOMAINE LE CLOS DES CAZAUX* * */* * * *

Address: 84190 Vacqueyras
Tel: 4-90-65-85-83
Fax: 4-90-65-83-94
Wines produced: Vacqueyras Cuvée Les Clefs d'Or (white), Vacqueyras Cuvée St.-Roch,
        Vacqueyras Cuvée des Templiers
Surface area (Cuvée Les Clefs d'Or): 3.7 acres
        (Cuvée St.-Roch): 19.8 acres
        (Cuvée des Templiers): 25 acres
Production (Cuvée Les Clefs d'Or): 375 cases
        (Cuvée St.-Roch): 1,875 cases
        (Cuvée des Templiers): 2,187 cases
Upbringing: 24 months in stainless steel vats (all three cuvées)
Average age of vines (Cuvée Les Clefs d'Or): 20–30 years
               (Cuvée St.-Roch): 25–40 years
               (Cuvée des Templiers): 25 years

Blend (Cuvée Les Clefs d'Or): 70% Clairette, 15% Grenache Blanc, 15% Roussanne
    (Cuvée St.-Roch): 60% Grenache, 35% Syrah, 5% Mourvèdre
    (Cuvée des Templiers): 60% Syrah, 30% Grenache, 10% Mourvèdre

Maurice and Jean-Michel Vache are young, ambitious men who are turning out fine, full-bodied, textbook Vacqueyras. Father Maurice and son Jean-Michel believe in taking only small quantities from the vineyard and doing as little as possible to intervene in the making of the wine. This estate has begun to produce perhaps the best dry white wine of Vacqueyras. The Les Clefs d'Or is a blend of 70% Clairette, 15% Grenache Blanc, and 15% Roussanne.

There are two cuvées of red wine. The Cuvée St.-Roch is a solid, chunky, wine that is rich, full-bodied yet supple, and ideal for drinking during its first 5–7 years of life. The Cuvée des Templiers is a blend of 60% Syrah, 30% Grenache, and 10% Mourvèdre. It is a deeply colored wine, with copious quantities of cassis fruit and a chewy finish. There is no destemming before vinification. The wines are essentially allowed to make themselves. Domaine le Clos des Cazaux is a very good, reliable Vacqueyras estate.

DOMAINE DE LA COLLINE ST.-JEAN* */* * *

Address: 84190 Vacqueyras
Tel: 4-90-65-85-50
Wines produced: Vacqueyras
Surface area: 44 acres
Production: 8,125 cases
Upbringing: 24 months total, with at least 6 months in old oak barrels
Average age of vines: 50–80 years
Blend: 75% Grenache, 15% Syrah, 5% Mourvèdre, 5% Cinsault

The Alazard family produces a rustic, old-style Vacqueyras from its holdings on the limestone terraces and rocky plateau soils. This estate has not made many changes over the years, still relying on a high percentage of Grenache, with a small quantity of Syrah, and tiny amounts of Mourvèdre and Cinsault for their blend. Moreover, the wine is often desiccated by too long a sojourn in old wood. Only about 30% of the production is estate-bottled. This is a wine to drink during its first 4–5 years of life, just don't expect a great deal of finesse.

DOMAINE LE COUROULU* * * *

Address: 84190 Vacqueyras
Tel: 4-90-65-84-83
Fax: 4-90-65-81-25
Wines produced: Vacqueyras Cuvée Jeune Fruite, Vacqueyras Vieilli en Foudre
Surface area (Cuvée Jeune Fruite): 12.3 acres
    (Vieilli en Foudre): 27 acres
Production (Cuvée Jeune Fruite): 2,250 cases
    (Vieilli en Foudre): 4,400 cases
Upbringing (Cuvée Jeune Fruite): 6 months in old oak casks
    (Vieilli en Foudre): 18 months in old oak casks
Average age of vines (Cuvée Jeune Fruite): 20 years
    (Vieilli en Foudre): 40–50 years
Blend (Cuvée Jeune Fruite): 60% Grenache, 30% Syrah, 10% Mourvèdre
    (Vieilli en Foudre): 60% Grenache, 25% Mourvèdre, 15% Syrah

Proprietor Jean Ricard produces a beautiful, supple, fleshy, plump Vacqueyras. This relatively large estate also turns out very fine Côtes du Rhône. The vineyards, all planted on limestone as well as the rocky *galets roulés,* average an impressive 40–50 years. There is no destemming, and the vinification combines about 10% carbonic maceration with the remaining 90% vinified by the whole-berry system. To Ricard's credit, the fruit from young vines (20 years) is separated from the older vines and sold for a lower price. It is a tasty wine. Over recent years, Domaine le Couroulu has augmented the percentage of Mourvèdre and Syrah. In the top cuvée, Mourvèdre can represent as much as 25% of the blend and Syrah 15%. These traditionally made, classic examples of Vacqueyras age beautifully for 5–7 years. The only negative is the multiple bottlings done as the wine is sold. My experience suggests the first bottling is far superior to subsequent ones, which have lost some fruit.

DOMAINE LA FOURMONE (ROGER COMBE)* * * *
Address: 84190 Vacqueyras
Tel: 4-90-65-86-05
Wines produced: Vacqueyras Trésor du Poète, Vacqueyras Sélection Maître de Chais,
           Vacqueyras Cuvée des Ceps d'Or, Vacqueyras Cuvée Fleurantine (white)
Surface area (Trésor du Poète): 19.8 acres
           (Sélection Maître de Chais): 24.7 acrres
           (Cuvée des Ceps d'Or): 5 acres
           (Cuvée Fleurantine): 3.7 acres
Production (Trésor du Poète): 3,125 cases
           (Sélection Maître de Chais): 4,375 cases
           (Cuvée des Ceps d'Or): 500 cases
           (Cuvée Fleurantine): 625 cases
Upbringing (Trésor du Poète): 4–6 months in oak
           (Sélection Maître de Chais): 24 months total, with 12 months in oak
           (Cuvée des Ceps d'Or): 36 months total with 18 months in oak
           (Cuvée Fleurantine): 6 months in stainless steel vats
Average age of vines (Trésor du Poète): 30 years
                  (Sélection Maître de Chais): 30 years
                  (Cuvée des Ceps d'Or): 50 years
                  (Cuvée Fleurantine): 20 years
Blend (Trésor du Poète): 85% Grenache, 15% Syrah
       (Sélection Maître de Chais): 70% Grenache, 15% Syrah, 15% Mourvèdre
       (Cuvée des Ceps d'Or): 100% Grenache
       (Cuvée Fleurantine): 50% Grenache Blanc, 50% Clairette

Roger Combe has been long associated with high-quality Gigondas, and while he slowly inches his way toward retirement, his daughter, Marie-Thérèse, has taken command of this fine estate. This is a relatively large domaine, producing four separate cuvées. It is one of the few properties in Vacqueyras that produces a white wine. Fourmone's Cuvée Fleurantine, made from 50% Grenache Blanc and 50% Clairette, is a solid rather than exciting white Vacqueyras.

The red wines are classic examples of Vacqueyras—full, exuberant, robust, purely made, and relatively ageworthy. The two wines most readers are likely to encounter include the Trésor du Poète, prized for its rich, up-front, black-cherry, plumlike fruitiness. It is a wine to drink within 4–5 years of the vintage. The Sélection Maître de Chais is a more seriously endowed wine, largely because of the presence of 15% Mourvèdre in the blend. It also spends more time in wood and is bottled 12 months later than the Trésor du Poète. It is often more concentrated, as well as more rustic and artisanal than the Trésor du Poète, but always mouth-filling and substantial. The limited production Cuvée des Ceps d'Or is a recent addition to the Combe portfolio. This blockbuster, 100% old-vine Grenache is loaded with character, but in my opinion, it is bottled later than it should be. All things considered, this is one of the best estates in Vacqueyras, and it can be counted on for consistency and textbook wines from this part of the southern Rhône.

VINTAGES

1995—Vacqueyras Sélection Maître de Chais (red)   There is little difference between the
·   1994 and 1995 Vacqueyras Maître de Chais cuvées. The 1994 is more developed,
86   sweeter, and more seductive, but both are delicious, round, fruity, fleshy wines to
         drink over the next 4–5 years. Last tasted 6/96.

1995—Vacqueyras Trésor du Poète (red)   The 1995 Vacqueyras Trésor du Poète exhibits
·   a deep ruby/purple color, fine density and richness, and sweet, ripe fruit. Antici-
86   pated maturity: now–2003. Last tasted 6/96.

1994—Vacqueyras Sélection Maître de Chais (red)   Plump, round, and precocious, this
·   herb-tinged, spicy Vacqueyras is medium- to full-bodied, and fully mature. Drink
87   it up. Last tasted 6/96.

1994—Vacqueyras Trésor du Poète (red)   The ambitiously made 1994 Vacqueyras Trésor
·   du Poète is structured, but lacking in charm, with only a medium ruby color. Drink
85   it up. Last tasted 6/96.

DOMAINE DE LA GARRIGUE* * *

Address: Château Tallaud
         B.P. 23
         84190 Vacqueyras
Tel: 4-90-65-84-60
Wines produced: Vacqueyras (red and rosé)
Surface area: 165.5 acres
Production: 7,500 cases
Upbringing: 24 months in cement vats; no filtration
Average age of vines: 45 years
Blend: 75% Grenache, 15% Syrah, 5% Mourvèdre, 5% Cinsault

This is one of the largest properties in Vacqueyras. Pierre-Albert Bernard and his wife (also the proprietors of the excellent restaurant Les Florets in Gigondas) produce a serious, tannic, spicy Vacqueyras that has a penchant for being excessively astringent and coarse. At best, this is a rustic example of the appellation. A small quantity of dry rosé is also produced.

VINTAGES

1993—Vacqueyras (red)   A rustic style of wine, this earthy, spicy, black-cherry-scented
·   wine reveals a deep ruby color with amber at the edge. Medium- to full-bodied,
87   with moderate tannin, a large framework, and rich fruit, this is an intensely spicy,
         peppery Vacqueyras. Anticipated maturity: now–1996. Last tasted 6/95.

PAUL JABOULET-AINÉ* * *

Address: Les Jalets
   R.N. 7, B.P. 462
   La-Roche-de-Glun
   26600 Tain l'Hermitage
Tel: 4-75-84-68-93
Fax: 4-75-84-56-14

The famous northern Rhône négociant Paul Jaboulet-Ainé of Tain l'Hermitage consistently produces a good Vacqueyras from purchased wine. It is heavily dependent on Grenache, although the Jaboulets have been insisting on more Syrah in the blends of their southern Rhônes. Most vintages of the Jaboulet Vacqueyras can last for up to a decade. In particular, the 1990 and 1989 were excellent wines with 10 years of ageability. I drank a 1978 Vacqueyras with Jacques Jaboulet in June, 1996, and the wine was fully mature, but surprisingly complex and tasty.

CHÂTEAU DE MONTMIRAIL* * *

Address: B.P. 12
   84190 Vacqueyras
Tel: 4-90-65-86-72
Fax: 4-90-65-81-31
Wines produced: Vacqueyras Cuvée des St.-Papes, Vacqueyras Cuvée de l'Ermite, Vacqueyras Cuvée des Deux Frères
Surface area: 50 acres
Production (Cuvée des St.-Papes): 3,125 cases
   (Cuvée de l'Ermite): 2,500 cases
   (Cuvée des Deux Frères): 3,125 cases
Upbringing (Cuvée des St.-Papes): 18 months in enamel vats
   (Cuvée de l'Ermite): 15–18 months in enamel vats
   (Cuvée des Deux Frères): 18 months in enamel vats
Average age of vines: 40 years
Blend (Cuvée des St.-Papes): 70% Grenache, 15% Syrah, 15% Mourvèdre and Cinsault
   (Cuvée de l'Ermite): 50% Grenache, 50% Syrah
   (Cuvée des Deux Frères): 70% Grenache, 15% Syrah, 15% Mourvèdre and Cinsault

Maurice Archimbeault, a somewhat legendary figure in Vacqueyras with a bigger-than-life personality, and his daughter, Monique, produce multiple cuvées of fleshy, full-bodied Vacqueyras. These wines are among the finest of the appellation, exhibiting spicy, peppery flavors of roasted herb and jammy red and black fruit. They are delicious young but can keep for 7–8 years. There are three cuvées; the Cuvée des Deux Frères and Cuvée des St.-Papes are Grenache-based wines, and the Cuvée de l'Ermite is a blend of equal parts Grenache and Syrah. Everything is aged in enamel vats, with a small quantity of wine kept in wood foudres. My experience has shown the Cuvée des St.-Papes to be a light, but richly fruity Vacqueyras that is easy to understand and drink. The Cuvée des Deux Frères is slightly fuller, more robust, and ageworthy, and the Cuvée de l'Ermite is the most concentrated, inky, thick wine.

DOMAINE DE MONTVAC* * * *

Address: 84190 Vacqueyras
Tel: 4-90-65-85-51
Fax: 4-90-65-82-38
Wines produced: Vacqueyras Domaine de Montvac, Vacqueyras Cuvée Vincila

Surface area (Domaine de Montvac): 35 acres
        (Cuvée Vincila): 15 acres
Production (Domaine de Montvac): 5,625 cases
        (Cuvée Vincila): 1,875 cases
Upbringing (Domaine de Montvac): 12–24 months, normally all in cement vats; sometimes,
                        depending on the vintage, aging is done in oak casks
        (Cuvée Vincila): 36 months total, with 10 months in old oak casks
Average age of vines (Domaine de Montvac): 30–35 years
        (Cuvée Vincila): 65–70 years
Blend (Domaine de Montvac): 60% Grenache, 35% Syrah, 5% Mourvèdre
        (Cuvée Vincila): 60% Grenache, 40% Syrah

This estate, run by Monique and Jean Dusserre, is quickly emerging as one of the most serious and ambitious in Vacqueyras. These are impeccably made (Jean Dusserre is an oenologist), deeply-colored wines that represent a blend of the more rustic, traditional style of Vacqueyras with the modern, rich, fruity, pure examples. I have never tasted the special Cuvée Vincila, but given the quality of the regular wine, it could be extra-special.

CHÂTEAU DES ROQUES* * *

Address: B.P. 9
        84190 Vacqueyras
Tel: 4-90-65-85-16
Fax: 4-90-65-88-18
Wines produced: Vacqueyras (red and white)
Surface area (red): 91.4 acres
        (white): 7.4 acres
Production (red): 16,250 cases
        (white): 1,250 cases
Upbringing (red): 12 months in cement vats and 12 months in 3-year-old barrels
        (white): 6–8 months in stainless steel vats
Average age of vines (red): 30–35 years
        (white): 30 years
Blend (red): 80% Grenache, 20% Syrah and Mourvèdre
        (white): 70% Marsanne, 30% Roussanne, Bourboulenc, and Viognier

Physically, Edouard Dusser resembles a nose tackle in the National Football League, and he tends to make wines in his own image. The large quantities of his red Vacqueyras are bottled as the wine is sold. About 60% of his total production is sold off in bulk. A small amount of rosé is also made, and this is one of the few Vacqueyras estates to produce a white wine. Dusser's white may be the village's single best dry white wine. Château des Roques' wines are typical, old-style Vacqueyras—rustic and coarse, but flavorful and filled with personality, although rarely complex or elegant.

DOMAINE LE SANG DES CAILLOUX* * *

Address: Route de Vacqueyras
        84110 Sarrians
Tel: 4-90-65-88-64
Fax: 4-90-65-88-75
Wines produced: Vacqueyras
Surface area: 39.5 acres
Production: 6,875 cases

Upbringing: 6–8 months in old oak casks
Average age of vines: 28–30 years
Blend: 70% Grenache, 20% Syrah, 5% Mourvèdre, 5% Cinsault

This Vacqueyras estate has long made a potent, fiery wine. The wines have been irregular, as well as excessively fined and filtered at the insistence of the estate's oenologist. In spite of this, in vintages such as 1989, 1990, and 1995, Le Sang des Cailloux can be counted on to produce a forceful Vacqueyras that will age well for a decade.

TARDIEU-LAURENT* * * *

Address: Chemin de la Marquette
84360 Lauris
Tel: 4-90-08-32-07
Fax: 4-90-08-26-57

This négociant, with its cellars in Château Loumarin, specializes in buying concentrated, old-vine cuvées from several Vacqueyras producers. The wine is aged in small oak casks, of which 50% are new. It is one of the appellation's most flamboyant, intense, dramatic wines.

VINTAGES

1995—Vacqueyras   The impressive 1995 Vacqueyras (aged in 50% new oak) is made
·   primarily from 70-year-old Grenache vines. This wine is stacked with sweet, ripe,
88   peppery, herb-tinged, black-cherry fruit. Full-bodied and fleshy, with an inner core
          of sweetness and ripeness, this is a mouth-filling, full-bodied Vacqueyras to drink
          over the next 5–6 years. Last tasted 6/96.
1994—Vacqueyras   The 1994 Vacqueyras exhibits spice, as well as a vague notion of
·   garrigue (a nebulous, earthy, herbes de Provence smell that seems to permeate this
87   region's enchanted countryside in the spring and summer). This wine also reveals
          toasty oak, plenty of ripe, peppery fruit, medium body, good density, and an
          attractive texture—a hallmark of wines that enjoy extensive lees contact and
          minimal racking. It should drink well for 5–6 years. Last tasted 6/96.

DOMAINE DE LA TOURADE* * * *

Address: Hameau Beaumette
84190 Gigondas
Tel: 4-90-70-91-09
Fax: 4-90-70-96-31
Wines produced: Vacqueyras
Surface area: 14.8 acres
Production: 1,500 cases
Upbringing: 36 months total; with 12–18 months in old oak casks
Average age of vines: 30 years
Blend: 65% Grenache, 15% Syrah, 10% Mourvèdre, 10% Cinsault

This serious estate, run with considerable passion by André Richard and his wife, produces relatively massive, strong, muscular Vacqueyras that requires cellaring, especially in such top vintages as 1989, 1990, and 1995. Richard aims for maximum extraction. To preserve all of the force and fury (significant in the above-mentioned vintages), these wines are bottled without fining or filtration, a rarity in this village.

CHÂTEAU DES TOURS* * * *

Address: Quartier des Sablons
Tel: 4-90-65-41-75
Fax: 4-90-65-38-46
Wines produced: Vacqueyras
Surface area: 37 acres
Production: 5,600 cases
Upbringing: 24 months total; fermentation in stainless steel and cement vats; part of the
          yield spends 3–6 months in old oak casks, depending on the vintage; storage
          in stainless steel and cement vats
Average age of vines: 35–40 years
Blend: 95% Grenache, 5% Syrah

Readers looking for a Vacqueyras made in the image of the renowned Châteauneuf du Pape from Château Rayas should seek out the wines of Château des Tours, a 37-acre Vacqueyras estate situated directly on Route D 950, between the Côtes du Rhône-Villages of Sarrians and Jonquières. There are another 56 acres of vineyards located outside Vacqueyras that are entitled to either a Côtes du Rhône or vin de pays designation. The proprietor of Château des Tours is Bernard Reynaud, the brother of the late Jacques Reynaud of Château Rayas. He has gradually turned over the winemaking responsibilities to his son, Emmanuel, a quiet, serious, and conservative man who is attempting to make Château des Tours the leader of Vacqueyras. He is well on his way to succeeding. After apprenticing with both his father and his idiosyncratic Uncle Jacques, it is safe to say that Emmanuel is producing the most concentrated and potentially complex wine of Vacqueyras. The selection is severe, with only one-third of the crop bottled as Vacqueyras and the rest declassified and blended with the Côtes du Rhône. Emmanuel's wine, much like his uncle's, relies on intense, late-harvested, jammy Grenache to provide complexity, character, and a sumptuous texture. Yields are among the lowest in the appellation (also true of his vin de pays and Côtes du Rhône), and the results have been a powerful, rich, concentrated style of Vacqueyras that gives every indication of aging for a minimum of 10 years in great vintages (e.g., 1989, 1990, 1995). In fact, I would not be surprised to see Château des Tours' Vacqueyras drinking well at age 20. Readers should remember the name of Emmanuel Reynaud as he is building Château des Tours into the top estate of the appellation. Moreover, it would not surprise me if he were the successor to the inimical Jacques Reynaud at Château Rayas.

VINTAGES

1992—Vacqueyras   The rich, powerful, alcoholic 1992 offers a saturated deep ruby color,
 ·   a handsome bouquet of earthy, herb, and black-cherry scents, medium to full body,
 86   a lovely, supple texture, and a heady, lusty finish. Drink it over the next 5–6 years.
          Last tasted 6/96.

1990—Vacqueyras   This wine's huge, ripe nose of black-raspberry fruit and roasted nuts
 ·   is dazzling. In the mouth, there is immense body, gobs of chewy, intense flavors,
 90   moderate tannin, and a voluptuous, explosively long finish. This Rayas lookalike
          should easily last through the first decade of the next century. Anticipated maturity:
          now–2008. Last tasted 6/96.

1989—Vacqueyras   If this wine were tasted blind, the first thing any Rayas aficionado
 ·   would think is that this must be the 1985 or 1988 Rayas. It is that rich, dense, and
 91   bursting with overripe Grenache fruit. With an explosive richness and unbelievable
          concentration and depth, I would not be surprised to see it last for 15–20 years. It
          is that impressive and intense. Drink it between now and 2005. Last tasted 6/96.

DOMAINE DE VERQUIÈRE* * *

Address: 84110 Sarrians
Tel: 4-90-46-90-11
Fax: 4-90-46-99-69
Wines produced: Vacqueyras
Surface area: 6.2 acres
Production: 937 cases
Upbringing: 6–8 months in old oak barrels
Average age of vines: 15 years
Blend: 70% Grenache, 15% Syrah, 15% Cinsault

Proprietor Bernard Chamfort has most of his holdings in the Côtes du Rhône-Villages, but he owns a tiny 6.2-acre estate in Vacqueyras that produces just under 1,000 cases of wine. The vineyard is young, but these wines deserve attention for their purity, balance, and nicely integrated, complex style. It is too soon to know if Domaine de Verquière will be one of the stars of the appellation, but to date, it exhibits considerable promise.

VIDAL-FLEURY* * *

Address: R.N. 86
          69420 Ampuis
Tel: 4-74-56-10-18
Fax: 4-74-56-19-19
Wines produced: A complete line-up of négociant wine, including Vacqueyras
Surface area: All grapes and/or juice purchased
Production: 5,500 cases
Upbringing: 36–48 months total, with 24–36 months in old oak casks
Blend: 70% Grenache, 20% Syrah, 10% Mourvèdre

This négociant in Ampuis, run with considerable talent by Jean-Pierre Rochias, purchases wine from multiple Vacqueyras proprietors to fashion a blend. Rochias prefers a blend of 70% Grenache, 20% Syrah, and 10% Mourvèdre. The wine is then aged for 6–8 months in large wood foudres in Vidal-Fleury's cellars in Ampuis. Over recent years this has been a consistently noteworthy Vacqueyras, with strong efforts in the difficult vintage of 1992, and even better wines produced in 1990, 1989, and 1988. It is a powerful, rich Vacqueyras with distinctive aromas of roasted herb, cassis, and earth. It is a forceful, full-bodied, mouth-filling Vacqueyras to drink within 5–7 years of the vintage.

OTHER VACQUEYRAS PRODUCERS

DOMAINE DE BOISSAN

Address: 84110 Sablet
Tel: 4-90-46-93-30
Fax: 4-90-46-99-46
Wines produced: Vacqueyras
Surface area: 3.8 acres
Production: 700 cases
Upbringing: 24 months in cement vats
Average age of vines: 6 years
Blend: 80% Grenache, 20% Syrah

DOMAINE BOULETIN

Address: 84190 Beaumes de Venise
Tel: 4-90-62-95-10
Wines produced: Vacqueyras
Surface area: 25 acres

Production: 2,500 cases
Upbringing: 12 months in cement vats
Average age of vines: 10 years
Blend: 55% Grenache, 15% Mourvèdre, 15% Syrah, 10% Cinsault, 5% Clairette

DOMAINE LA BRUNELLY

Address: 84260 Sarrians
Tel: 4-90-65-41-24
Fax: 4-90-65-30-60
Wines produced: Vacqueyras
Surface area: 49 acres
Production: 8,125 cases
Upbringing: 36 months in cement vats
Average age of vines: 30 years
Blend: 70% Syrah, 25% Grenache, 5% Mourvèdre and Cinsault

EDMONDE BURLE

Address: La Beaumette
       84190 Gigondas
Tel: 4-90-70-94-85
Wines produced: Vacqueyras
Surface area: 10 acres
Production: 1,550 cases
Upbringing: 24 months total, with 6 months in old oak barrels
Average age of vines: 70 years
Blend: 80% Grenache, 15% Syrah, 5% Clairette and Cinsault

DOMAINE DES CARDELINES

Address: 84190 Vacqueyras
Tel: 4-90-65-88-27
Wines produced: Vacqueyras
Surface area: 19.8 acres
Production: 2,500 cases
Upbringing: 36 months in cement vats
Average age of vines: 30 years
Blend: 70% Grenache, 30% Syrah

CAVE VINICOLE DE SERRES

Address: Route de Malaucène
       84200 Carpentras
Tel: 4-90-63-00-85
Fax: 4-90-63-06-41
Wines produced: Vacqueyras
Production: 625 cases
Upbringing: 6–12 months in cement vats
Average age of vines: 15 years
Blend: 80% Grenache, 20% Syrah
    Note: This cave coopérative buys the harvest of two Vacqueyras producers.

DOMAINE DE CHANTEGUT

Address: 436, boulevard du Comte d'Orange
Tel: 4-90-65-46-38
Wines produced: Vacqueyras
Surface area: 49 acres
Production: 8,750 cases
Upbringing: 18 months minimum in cement vats

Average age of vines: 30 years
Blend: 75% Grenache, 20% Syrah, 5% Mourvèdre

DOMAINE LE CLOS DE CAVEAU

Address: 84190 Vacqueyras
Tel: 4-90-65-85-33
Wines produced: Vacqueyras
Surface area: 28.4 acres
Production: 3,750 cases
Upbringing: 16–18 months in epoxy vats
Average age of vines: 5–10 years
Blend: 70% Grenache, 25% Syrah, 5% Cinsault

CLOS DU JONCUAS

Address: 84190 Gigondas
Tel: 4-90-65-86-86
Fax: 4-90-65-83-68
Wines produced: Vacqueyras
Surface area: 12.4 acres (all cultivated organically)
Production: 1,875 cases
Upbringing: 18–24 months total, with 12 months in old oak casks
Average age of vines: 30 years
Blend: 65% Grenache, 20% Syrah, 15% Mourvèdre

DOMAINE DU COLOMBIER

Address: 84190 Vacqueyras
Tel: 4-90-65-85-84
Wines produced: Vacqueyras
Surface area: 37 acres
Production: 7,500 cases
Upbringing: 18–24 months in cement vats
Average age of vines: 30–50 years
Blend: 70% Grenache, 20% Syrah, 10% Cinsault, Mourvèdre, and Carignan

DOMAINE DE LA CYPRIÈRE

Address: 84260 Sarrians
Tel: 4-90-65-88-11
Wines produced: Vacqueyras
Surface area: 19.8 acres
Production: 3,125 cases
Upbringing: 24 months in cement vats
Average age of vines: 20 years
Blend: 80% Grenache, 20% Syrah

DELAS FRÈRES

Address: Z. A. de l'Oliver
B.P. 4
07300 St.-Jean de Muzols
Tel: 4-75-08-60-30
Fax: 4-75-08-53-67
Wines produced: Domaine des Genets Vacqueyras
Production: 2,000 cases
Upbringing: 12–18 months with 30% of the yield in oak barrels and 70% in oak casks
Blend: 80% Grenache, 10% Mourvèdre, 10% Syrah

Note: The vinification and bottling of purchased wines are done under the control of the Delas Frères team.

DOMAINE DU GRAND PRIEUR (GABRIEL MEFFRE S.A.)

Address: Cave des Troubadours
         84190 Vacqueyras
Tel: 4-90-65-80-80
Fax: 4-90-65-81-81
Wines produced: Vacqueyras
Surface area: 61.8 acres
Production: 6,250 cases
Upbringing: 9 months total, with 8 months in enamel vats
Average age of vines: 20 years
Blend: 70% Grenache, 25% Syrah, 5% Cinsault

LES GRANDS CYPRES (GABRIEL MEFFRE S.A.)

Address: Cave des Troubadours
         84190 Vacqueyras
Tel: 4-90-65-80-80
Fax: 4-90-65-81-81
Wines produced: Vacqueyras
Surface area: 61.8 acres
Production: 2,500 cases
Upbringing: 9 months total, with fermentation in stainless steel vats, and 8 months in
        enamel vats
Average age of vines: 15–20 years
Blend: 75% Grenache, 25% Syrah

DOMAINE DE LA JAUFRETTE

Address: Chemin de la Fironde
         84100 Orange
Tel: 4-90-34-35-34
Wines produced: Vacqueyras
Surface area: 25 acres
Production: 4,400 cases
Upbringing: 3–4 years total; 18–21 days of fermentation in cement vats, then 6–8 months
        in old oak casks and barrels, followed by storage in epoxy vats until bottling
Average age of vines: 40–50 years
Blend: 80% Grenache, 10% Syrah, 10% Mourvèdre

DOMAINE DES LAMBERTINS

Address: La Grande Fontaine
         84190 Vacqueyras
Tel: 4-90-65-85-54
Fax: 4-90-65-83-38
Wines produced: Vacqueyras
Surface area: 52 acres
Production: 5,625 cases
Upbringing: 24 months total with 6 months in old oak casks
Average age of vines: 30–40 years
Blend: 65% Grenache, 25% Syrah, 5% Mourvèdre, 5% Cinsault

DOMAINE DU MAS DES COLLINES

Address: Les Hautes Garrigues
         84190 Gigondas
Tel: 4-90-65-90-40

Wines produced: Vacqueyras
Surface area: 16 acres
Production: 2,500 cases
Upbringing: 36 months total, with 12 months in old oak casks
Average age of vines: 50 years
Blend: 90% Grenache, 7% Syrah, 3% Cinsault

DOMAINE DE LA MONARDIÈRE

Address: Quartier des Grès
   84190 Vacqueyras
Tel: 4-90-65-87-20
Fax: 4-90-65-82-01
Wines produced: Vacqueyras Cuvée des Monardes, Vacqueyras Cuvée Vieille Vigne, Vac-
   queyras Rosé
Surface area (Cuvée des Monardes): 35 acres
     (Cuvée Vieille Vigne): 2.47 acres
     (Rosé): 2.47 acres
Production (Cuvée des Monardes): 6,250 cases
     (Cuvée Vieille Vigne): 375 cases
     (Rosé): 375 cases
Upbringing (Cuvée des Monardes): 6 months in epoxy vats
     (Cuvée Vieille Vigne): 6 months in oak
     (Rosé): 5–6 months in epoxy vats
Average age of vines (Cuvée des Monardes): 45 years
      (Cuvée Vieille Vigne): 55 years
      (Rosé): 25–30 years
Blend (Cuvée des Monardes): 80% Grenache, 10% Syrah and 10% Mourvèdre
   (Cuvée Vieille Vigne): 70% Grenache, 30% Syrah
   (Rosé): 60% Grenache, 20% Cinsault, 20% Mourvèdre

DOMAINE DE LA MUSE (GABRIEL MEFFRE S.A.)

Address: 84190 Gigondas
Tel: 4-90-65-80-80
Fax: 4-90-65-81-81
Wines produced: Vacqueyras
Surface area: 6.2 acres
Production: 1,000 cases
Upbringing: 6–8 months in stainless steel vats
Average age of vines: 20 years
Blend: 70% Grenache, 30% Syrah

DOMAINE DU PONT DE RIEU

Address: 84190 Vacqueyras
Tel: 4-90-65-86-03
Wines produced: Vacqueyras
Surface area: 37 acres
Production: 6,250 cases
Upbringing: 36 months total, with 18 months in old oak casks
Average age of vines: 40 years
Blend: 80% Grenache, 10% Syrah, 10% Mourvèdre

DOMAINE DES RICHARDS

Address: Route d'Avignon
        84150 Violès
Tel: 4-90-70-93-73
Fax: 4-90-70-90-74
Wines produced: Vacqueyras
Surface area: 12.5 acres
Production: 1,875 cases
Upbringing: 6 months in cement vats and 4–5 months in new oak barrels
Average age of vines: 15–20 years
Blend: 80% Grenache, 20% Syrah

DOMAINE ST.-FRANÇOIS XAVIER

Address: 84190 Gigondas
Tel: 4-90-65-85-08
Wines produced: Vacqueyras
Surface area: 10 acres
Production: 1,500 cases
Upbringing: 18 months total, with 6–12 months in old oak casks; no fining or filtration
Average age of vines: 40 years
Blend: 70% Grenache, 10% Syrah, 10% Cinsault, 10% Mourvèdre

VIEUX CLOCHER

Address: 84190 Vacqueyras
Tel: 4-90-65-84-18
Fax: 4-90-65-80-07
Wines produced: Vacqueyras Vieux Clocher, Vacqueyras Seigneur de Lauris, Vacqueyras
        La Nuit des Temps, Vacqueyras Lestour Clocher
Surface area (Vieux Clocher): 74 acres
            (Seigneur de Lauris): 25 acres
            (La Nuit des Temps and Lestour Clocher): 37 acres
Production (Vieux Clocher): 12,500 cases
            (Seigneur de Lauris): 3,125 cases
            (La Nuit des Temps and Lestour Clocher): 6,250 cases
Upbringing (Vieux Clocher): Normally 8–12 months in old oak casks, but in some cases a
        first bottling is done as early as May following the vintages.
        (Seigneur de Lauris): 18–24 months in old oak casks; the wines are kept in the
        cellars for 2 years after bottling.
        (La Nuit des Temps and Lestour Clocher): Normally 8–12 months in old oak
        casks, but in some cases a first bottling is done as early as May following the
        vintages.
Average age of vines (Vieux Clocher): 35 years
            (Seigneur de Lauris): 60 years
            (La Nuit des Temps and Lestour Clocher): 40 years
Blend (Vieux Clocher): 75% Grenache, 12% Mourvèdre, 10% Syrah, and 3% Cinsault
        (Seigneur de Lauris): 80% Grenache, 10% Mourvèdre, 10% Syrah
        (La Nuit des Temps and Lestour Clocher): 80% Grenache, 17% Syrah, 3% Cinsault
Note: La Nuit des Temps and Lestour Clocher are made from grapes purchased from
other estates. They are actually the same wine sold under two different brand names.

CHÂTEAUNEUF
DU PAPE

The Heart and Soul of
the Rhône and Provence

CHÂTEAUNEUF DU PAPE AT A GLANCE

Appellation created:	May 15, 1936.
Type of wine produced:	Red, 93%; white, 7%.
Grape varieties planted:	Thirteen (actually 14 if the white clone of Grenache is counted) varieties are permitted; for red wines, Grenache, Syrah, Mourvèdre, Cinsault, Muscardin, Counoise, Vaccarèse, and Terret Noir; for white wines, Grenache Blanc, Clairette, Bourboulenc, Roussanne, Picpoul, and Picardin.
Acres currently under vine:	8,100.
Quality level:	Red wine—at the estate-bottled level, very good to exceptional; at the négociant level, mediocre to very good. White wine—mediocre to exceptional.
Aging potential:	Red wine, depending on the style, 5–20 years; white wine: 1–3 years, except for Beaucastel and La Nerthe's Beauvenir.
General characteristics:	Red wine—considerable diversity in stylistic approach can result in full-bodied, generous, rich, round, alcoholic, and long-lived wines, to soft, fruity wines that could be called the Beaujolais of Provence. White wine—floral, fruity, straightforward, and fresh if drunk within two years of the vintage.

Greatest recent vintages:	1995, 1990, 1989, 1981, 1979, 1978, 1970, 1967, 1961.
Price range:	$18–$25, with special old-vine and/or single-vineyard cuvées costing considerably more; $50–$85 is not an unusual price for such rarities.
Aromatic profile:	Red wines—Given the enormous diversity of winemaking styles in this appellation, the following is a simplified view. Producers who use carbonic maceration are aiming for very early bottling and easy-to-understand red and black fruit aromas that are jammy and appealing. Those producers aiming for fuller-bodied, more classically made Châteauneuf du Pape produce wines with a vast array of aromatics, ranging from black cherries, blackcurrants, and blueberries, to roasted herbs, the noted Provençal *garrigue* smell (an earthy herbes de Provence aromatic concoction), overripe peaches, and raspberry jam.
Aromatic profile:	White wines—The great majority of Châteauneuf du Pape white wines have their malolactic fermentation blocked, and are made in a style that sees no oak and very early bottling (usually within 3–4 months of the vintage). These wines are meant to be consumed within 1–2 years. They offer floral, tropical fruit aromas in a pleasing but uncomplicated bouquet.
Textural profile:	Red wines—The lighter-style red wines that have seen partial or full carbonic vinifications can be full-bodied, but tend to be soft and fruity, with the appellation's lusty alcohol present, but not the weight and layered, multidimensional personality. More classical offerings vary from muscular, full-bodied, concentrated wines, to those of immense proportions, that are chewy and thick, with high glycerin and alcohol. They saturate the palate, and fall just short of staining the teeth.
Textural profile:	White wines—The modern-style, nonmalolactic, early bottled whites are surprisingly full-bodied and alcoholic, as well as plump and mouth-filling. Their size suggests longevity, but they are meant to be consumed quickly. The few producers who practice full malolactic fermentation and later bottling produce honeyed, unctuously textured, thick, juicy wines that can be special if they are bottled without oxidizing.

The Châteauneuf du Pape appellation's most profound wines:

White Wines

Château Beaucastel Cuvée Classique

Château Beaucastel Roussanne Vieilles
  Vignes

Clos des Papes

Font de Michelle

Domaine de la Janasse

Domaine du Marcoux

Domaine de Nalys

Château de la Nerthe Clos de Beauvenir

Château Rayas

Domaine du Vieux-Télégraphe

Red Wines

Château Beaucastel Cuvée Classique
Château Beaucastel Hommage à Jacques
  Perrin
Domaine de Beaurenard Cuvée
  Boisrenard
Domaine Henri Bonneau Réserve des
  Célestins
La Bosquet des Papes Cuvée
  Chantemerle
Les Cailloux
Les Cailloux Cuvée Centenaire
Chapoutier Barbe Rac
Domaine de la Charbonnière Mourre des
  Perdrix
Domaine de la Charbonnière Cuvée
  Vieilles Vignes
Gérard Charvin
Clos du Mont Olivet Cuvée Papet
Clos des Papes
Font de Michelle Cuvée Etienne Gonnet

Château Fortia (since 1994)
Château de la Gardine Cuvée des
  Générations
Domaine de la Janasse Cuvée Chaupin
Domaine de la Janasse Cuvée Vieilles
  Vignes
Domaine de Marcoux Cuvée Vieilles
  Vignes
Domaine de la Mordorée Cuvée de la
  Reine des Bois
Château de la Nerthe Cuvée des Cadettes
Domaine du Pégau Cuvée Réservée
Domaine du Pégau Cuvée Laurence
Château Rayas
Domaine Roger Sabon Cuvée Prestige
Domaine St.-Benoît Grande Garde
Domaine St.-Benoît La Truffière
Le Vieux Donjon
Domaine du Vieux-Télégraphe

RATING THE RED CHÂTEAUNEUF DU PAPE PRODUCERS

* * * * *(OUTSTANDING)

Château Beaucastel
Château Beaucastel (Hommage à
  Jacques Perrin)
Domaine de Beaurenard (Cuvée
  Boisrenard)
Domaine Henri Bonneau (Réserve des
  Célestins)
Le Bosquet des Papes (Cuvée
  Chantemerle)
Les Cailloux
Les Cailloux (Cuvée Centenaire)
Chapoutier (Barbe Rac)
Clos du Mont Olivet (Cuvée Papet)
Clos des Papes
Font de Michelle (Cuvée Etienne Gonnet)
Château de la Gardine (Cuvée des
  Générations)

Domaine de la Janasse (Cuvée Chaupin)
Domaine de la Janasse (Cuvée Vieilles
  Vignes)
Domaine de Marcoux (Cuvée Vieilles
  Vignes)
Domaine de la Mordorée (Cuvée de la
  Reine des Bois)
Château de la Nerthe (Cuvée des Cadettes)
Domaine du Pégau (Cuvée Réservée)
Domaine du Pégau (Cuvée Laurence)
Château Rayas
Domaine Roger Sabon (Cuvée Prestige)
Le Vieux Donjon
Domaine du Vieux-Télégraphe

* * * *(EXCELLENT)

Pierre André
Paul Autard (Cuvée La Côte Ronde)
Paul Autard (Cuvée Mireille)
Lucien Barrot

Domaine de Beaurenard (Cuvée Classique)
Domaine Bois de Boursan
Henri Bonneau (Cuvée Marie Beurrier)
Le Bosquet des Papes (Cuvée Classique)

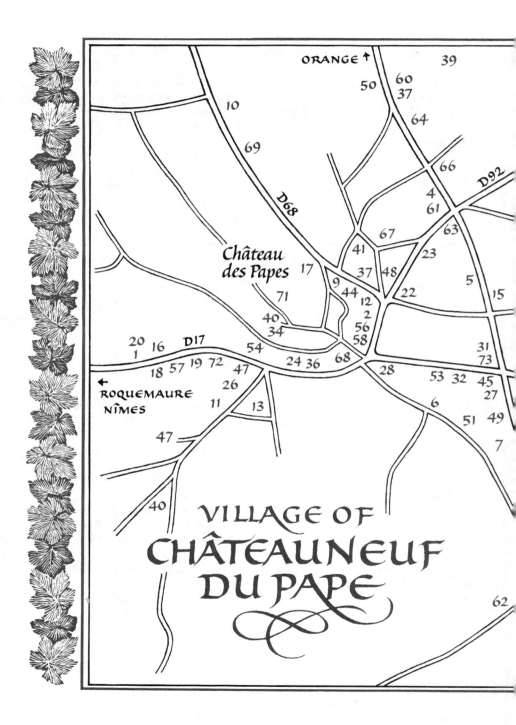

ORANGE ↑

39

50   60
     37

10

64

69

66

D92

D68

4
61

Château
des Papes   17

67

63

41

23

5

9 44

37 48

22

15

12

71

2

40

56

34

58

31
73

20   16   D17

54

24 36   68

28

53 32   45

1

18 57 19 72   47

27

← ROQUEMAURE
   NÎMES

26

11   13

6

51   49

47

7

40

VILLAGE OF
CHÂTEAUNEUF
DU PAPE

62

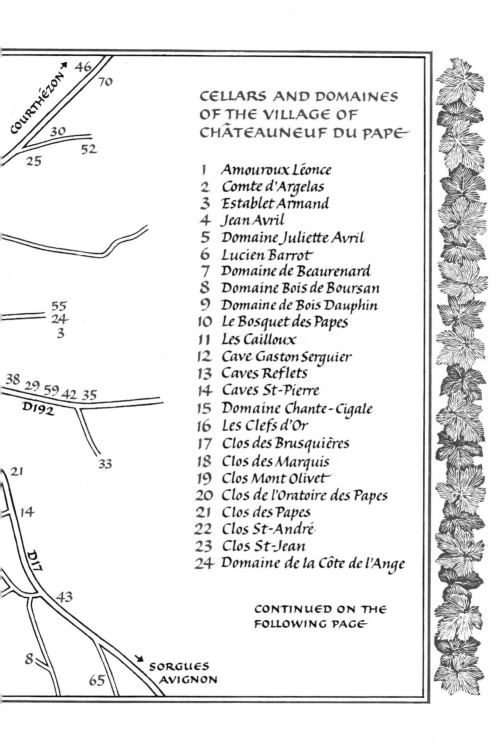

CELLARS AND DOMAINES OF THE VILLAGE OF CHÂTEAUNEUF DU PAPE

1 Amouroux Léonce
2 Comte d'Argelas
3 Establet Armand
4 Jean Avril
5 Domaine Juliette Avril
6 Lucien Barrot
7 Domaine de Beaurenard
8 Domaine Bois de Boursan
9 Domaine de Bois Dauphin
10 Le Bosquet des Papes
11 Les Cailloux
12 Cave Gaston Serguier
13 Caves Reflets
14 Caves St-Pierre
15 Domaine Chante-Cigale
16 Les Clefs d'Or
17 Clos des Brusquières
18 Clos des Marquis
19 Clos Mont Olivet
20 Clos de l'Oratoire des Papes
21 Clos des Papes
22 Clos St-André
23 Clos St-Jean
24 Domaine de la Côte de l'Ange

CONTINUED ON THE FOLLOWING PAGE

CONTINUED FROM THE PREVIOUS PAGE

CELLARS AND DOMAINES OF CHÂTEAUNEUF DU PAPE

SEE MAP ON THE FOLLOWING PAGE

1 Pierre André
2 Paul Autard
3 Domaine les Barulettes
4 Domaine la Bastide
    St-Dominique
5 Château Beaucastel
6 Domaine Berthet-Rayne
7 Domaine de la Biscarelle
8 Château Cabrières
9 Cellier des Princes
10 Domaine de Chanssaud
11 Domaine de Chante-Perdrix
12 Domaine de la Charbonnière
13 Gérard Charvin
14 Domaine Clos du Caillou
15 Clos St-Michel
16 Clos Val Seille
17 Domaine de Cristia
18 Cuvée de Boisdauphin
19 La Fagotière
20 Château des Fines Roches
21 Château des Fines Roches
    et du Bois de la Garde
22 Château des Fines Roches
    (Domaine Mousset)
23 Château de la Font du Loup
24 Font de Michelle
25 Lou Fréjau
26 Château de la Gardine
27 Les Grandes Serres
28 Domaine Grand Veneur

29 Château de Husson
30 Domaine de la Janasse
31 Domaine de la Jaufrette
32 Mas de Bois Lauzon
33 Mas Chante Mistral
34 Château Maucoil
35 Domaine de la Mereuille
36 Domaine de la Millière
37 Domaine de Mont Redon
38 Château du Mont Thabor
39 Fabrice Mousset
40 Château de la Nerthe
41 Domaine de Nalys
42 Domaine de Palestor
43 Du Peloux
44 Roger Perrin
45 Domaine de la Pinède
46 Domaine St-Laurent
47 Domaine de St-Prefert
48 Château St-Roch
49 Domaine de St-Siffrein
50 Domaine de la Solitude
51 Domaine Terre Ferme
52 Domaine Tour Saint Michel
53 Jean-Pierre Usseglio
54 Domaine la Vallée du Mistral
55 Château Vaudieu
56 Domaine de la Vieille Julienne
57 Domaine de la
    Vieux-Télégraphe
58 Domaine de Villeneuve

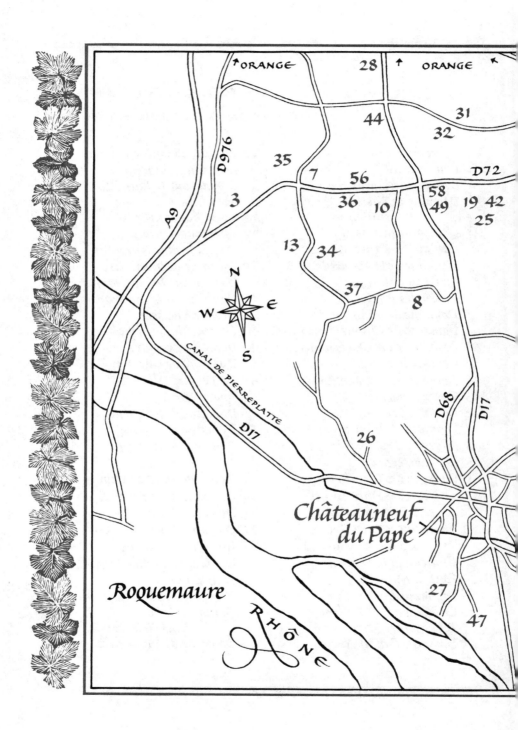

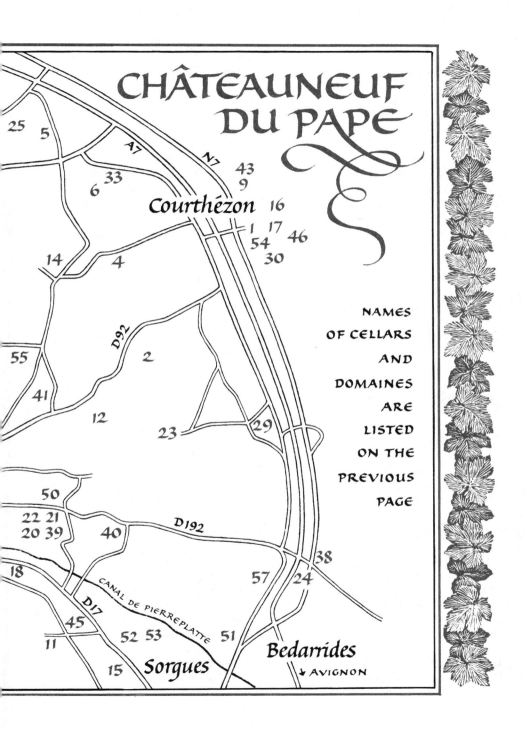

CHÂTEAUNEUF DU PAPE

25 5

A7

N7 43
9

6 33

Courthézon 16

1 17
54 46
30

14 4

NAMES
OF CELLARS
AND
DOMAINES
ARE
LISTED
ON THE
PREVIOUS
PAGE

D92

55 2

41

12

23 29

50

22 21
20 39 40

D192

18 38

57 24

CANAL DE PIERREPLATTE

D17

45

11 52 53 51

Bedarrides

15 Sorgues ↓AVIGNON

RATING THE RED CHÂTEAUNEUF DU PAPE PRODUCERS (cont.)

* * * *(EXCELLENT) (cont.)

Domaine de Chante-Perdrix
Domaine de la Charbonnière
Gérard Charvin (****/*****)
Domaine les Clefs d'Or
Domaine Clos du Caillou
Clos du Mont Olivet (Cuvée Classique)
Clos St.-Michel
Henriet Crouzet-Féraud
Cuvée de Boisdauphin
Cuvée du Vatican
Font du Loup (Le Puy Rolland)
Font de Michelle (Cuvée Classique)
Château Fortia (since 1994)
Château de la Gardine
Domaine Haut des Terres Blanches
Domaine les Hautes Brusquières
Domaine de la Janasse (Cuvée Classique)
Domaine de Marcoux (Cuvée Classique)
Mas de Bois Lauzon
Domaine de Montpertuis (Cuvée Tradition)

Domaine de la Mordorée (Cuvée Classique)
Domaine de Nalys
Château de la Nerthe (Cuvée Classique)
Père Caboche (Cuvée Elisabeth Chambellan)
Domaine Roger Perrin (Réserve de Vieilles Vignes)
Domaine de la Présidente
Château Reyas Château Pignan
Domaine de la Roquette
Domaine Roger Sabon (Cuvée Réservée)
Domaine St.-Benoît (Grande Garde)
Domaine St.-Benoît (La Truffière)
Domaine de St.-Siffrein
Domaine des Sénéchaux
Château Simian
Tardieu-Laurent
Raymond Usseglio
Domaine de la Vieille Julienne
Domaine de Villeneuve

* * *(Good)

Paul Autard
Jean Avril
Domaine de Bois Dauphin
Château Cabrières (Cuvée Prestige)
Domaine de Chanssaud
Domaine Chantadu
Domaine Chante-Cigale
Chapoutier (La Bernadine)
Clos St.-Jean
Domaine de Cristia
Cuvée du Belvedere (***/****)
Domaine Durieu
Château des Fines Roches
Lou Fréjau
Domaine du Galet des Papes (***/****)
Domaine du Grand Tinel
Domaine Grand Veneur
Guigal
Domaine Haut des Terres Blanches
Paul Jaboulet-Ainé (Les Cèdres)
    (***** prior to 1970)
Domaine Mathieu
Château Maucoil (**/***)
Château Mongin

Domaine de Mont Redon
Domaine de Montpertuis (Cuvée Classique)
Moulin-Tacussel
Domaine de Palestor
Père Anselme
Père Caboche (Cuvée Classique)
Domaine du Père Pape (***/****)
Roger Perrin
Domaine de la Pinède
Domaine Pontifical (***/****)
Domaine des Relagnes
Domaine Riche
Domaine Roger Sabon (Les Olivets)
St.-Benoît (Cuvée Elise)
St.-Benoît (Soleil et Festins)
Domaine de la Solitude
Domaine Terre Ferme
Domaine Trintignant
Jean-Pierre Usseglio
Pierre Usseglio
Château Vaudieu
Vidal-Fleury

RATING THE WHITE CHÂTEAUNEUF DU PAPE PRODUCERS

* * * * *(OUTSTANDING)*

Château Beaucastel (Roussanne Vieilles
  Vignes)

* * * *(EXCELLENT)*

Château Beaucastel (Cuvée Classique)   Domaine de Nalys
Clos des Papes   Domaine de la Nerthe (Cuvée Beauvenir)
Font de Michelle   Château Rayas
Domaine de la Janasse   Domaine du Vieux-Télégraphe
Domaine du Marcoux

* * *(GOOD)*

Domaine de Beaurenard   Château de la Nerthe
Les Cailloux   Domaine du Père Caboche
Château de la Gardine   Domaine de la Roquette
Domaine de Mont Redon   Domaine Trintignant (La Reviscoulado)

Let me make this short and simple—I love a great Châteauneuf du Pape. For nearly 20 years in my wine journal, *The Wine Advocate,* I have proselytized the virtues of the best wines from this sun-drenched region of Provence. In the first edition of this book, I subtitled the Châteauneuf du Pape chapter "The Bordeaux of the Rhône," and said "Châteauneuf du Pape has the potential to consistently produce some of the finest and longest-lived red wines in the world." Its glorious perfume, which is reminiscent of an open-air produce market in a Provençal hill town, expansive, generous, well-endowed flavors, sumptuous texture, and heady alcohol content evoke an image of hedonism. Like hunger, fear, and lust, Châteauneuf du Pape, when it is great, has an almost addictive attraction to one's basic instincts. In spite of having an amazingly diverse taste for so many different kinds of wine, I drink more Châteauneuf du Pape than any other type of wine. Moreover, visitors to my private cellar can attest to the fact that my stock of Châteauneuf du Pape is proportional to my voracious taste for the appellation's finest wines. I have often posed the question—why it is that Châteauneuf du Pape is so often the centerpiece wine when I am having a dinner with dear friends, whereas Bordeaux seems to be reserved for other occasions?

My affection and criticism (of the village's underachievers) have not gone unnoticed in this large appellation of 8,100 acres, with just over 300 proprietors. In 1995, I became one of a handful of people in this century to be made an honorary citizen (citoyen d'honneur) of the village. Lest any readers think this has softened my position as a critic, let me make it very clear that of the 300 or so Châteauneuf du Pape proprietors, less than four dozen are making world-class wines. The enormous potential that exists in this appellation continues to go largely unrealized, but nowhere else in France are there such magnificent terroirs, an unbelievable percentage of very old vines, and the exquisite microclimate necessary to produce such fine wine.

Châteauneuf du Pape, from the perspective of both volume and potential, is the Rhône Valley's most important appellation. Additionally, the name is well known in the global wine market, although one rarely refers to Châteauneuf du Pape with the same awe and respect that is reserved for such glamorous French viticultural regions as Bordeaux, Burgundy, and Champagne. According to the village's two syndicates, in 1996 there were over 300 growers, of which 235 were estate-bottling all or a part of their production. Unlike Bordeaux and Burgundy, where virtually every major and minor estate has been scrupulously studied, analyzed, and written about in one book after another, there is very little information or analysis of the leading Châteauneuf du Pape producers. Indicative of the blatant ignorance of many fine estates was a cover story in the August 1996 issue of *The Wine Spectator*, the glitzy, nationally known wine magazine. The article, which featured profiles of "great American cellars," arrived in my office when I had finished about three-fourths of this chapter. What was so disheartening was that none of the eight collectors and their multimillion-dollar cellars that were profiled even acknowledged (if they did, then the writer failed to mention the wines) the existence of any Châteauneuf du Pape in their cellars. I suppose wine drinkers can take some pride in the fact that these eight trophy hunters ignored such treasures.

If Châteauneuf du Pape did not produce so much fine wine it would still be a worthy tourist destination because of its charming village sprawled over a hillside just underneath the impressive ruins of an ancient château. Châteauneuf du Pape derives its name from the rich history of the area and its close proximity to the hallowed walled city of Avignon. Between 1309 and 1378, the Roman popes established themselves at Avignon as a result of tumultuous and strained relations between the king of France and the papacy of Rome. When a Frenchman, Clement V, was installed as pope in 1305, he did what any good Frenchman would do—he moved the papacy to Avignon (in 1309). Vineyards had long existed in this region, and Clement V was no stranger to vineyard operations, having planted the famous Graves vineyard, Pape-Clement.

Yet it was Clement's successor, Pope John XXII, who left the most enduring legacy in Châteauneuf du Pape. Pope John built a summer residence in the area in order to escape from the congestion and heat of Avignon (which was apparently as hot and noisy in the fourteenth century as it is today). His immense castle, which survived centuries of warfare as well as the ravages of marauding bandits, was used for munitions storage by the Germans in World War II. During a retreat from this area in August 1944, the castle was blown up. All that remains are the impressive wall and tower that dominate the village spread out below.

The idea of the papal palace being in France did not last long, and this period of history, known as the Babylonian Captivity, ended in 1378. After this notorious period, little is known about the fortunes of Châteauneuf du Pape until the late nineteenth century, when there were references to this area as "Châteauneuf du Pape-Calcernier," so named after the nearby limestone quarries. By the beginning of the twentieth century, Châteauneuf du Pape, like so much of France, had suffered the ravages of phylloxera. Furthermore, the destruction of a generation of young Frenchmen in the appallingly mind-numbing trench warfare of World War I created a shortage of manpower. As a result, nearly half of the appellation remained unplanted following World War I, with many growers forced to abandon their vineyards. Châteauneuf du Pape fell into such low regard that overproduction as well as sales of grapes to other wine regions, particularly Burgundy, led the late Baron Le Roy of Château Fortia, one of the finest estates of the appellation, to develop in 1923 a series of controls for improving the quality and image of Châteauneuf du Pape. These self-imposed guidelines were ultimately of monumental significance and subsequently became the basis for the entire French appellation contrôlée system. Baron Le Roy was a visionary, and had hoped the adoption of these regulations would exploit the full potential of this privileged area of southern France. He stipulated that in order for a wine to be entitled to the name Châteauneuf du Pape, it had to satisfy the following criteria:

1. They had to be produced from a precise delineation for the area in which the vineyards were to be planted.
2. Only specific grape varieties could be grown within this area.
3. The cultivation techniques for the vines were to be controlled.

4. The wine had to contain a minimum alcoholic degree of 12.5%.
5. At harvest time, 5% of the crop had to be discarded, regardless of quality—a sort of mandatory selection process.
6. No rosé wine could be made, and all wines were to be submitted to a tasting panel before they were allowed to bear the name Châteauneuf du Pape.

There seems to be no doubt that the regulations encouraged an increase in quality. In his book *Documents pour servir à l'historie Châteauneuf du Pape* (written and published in 1932), Baron Le Roy wrote that as of 1932, the finest Châteauneuf du Pape estates were Les Cabrières, Fines-Roches, Fortia, La Nerthe, Rayas, Vaudieu, Clos des Papes, and Nalys. These eight estates all exist today, and while they have had ups and downs, they remain among the most significant producers of the appellation.

Today Baron Le Roy would be proud of the fact that the appellation is fully planted. Other than a few forested areas and some uncivilized scrub brush on the *garrigues*, there is little land that could be reclaimed for additional vineyards. The village of Châteauneuf du Pape, which is superbly placed not far from the physical center of the appellation, teems with vignerons and tourists. Except for the months of January, February, and March, Châteauneuf du Pape, with its maze of small streets, corridors, and caves, is one of the most desirable stops on a tourist's itinerary of Provence.

While other renowned viticultural regions of France can boast of a rich history and produce high-quality wines, two other factors contribute to the distinctive quality or signature of these wines, and to the uniqueness of Châteauneuf du Pape. First and foremost is the choice of grapes used in making Châteauneuf du Pape. Grenache, that highly maligned varietal that most Americans naively associate with rosé wine, reaches its most noble heights in Châteauneuf du Pape. It accounts for 80% of the vineyard plantings, in addition to being the grape that shapes the aromatics, flavors, and textures of most of the appellation's greatest wines. But this is no monocépage appellation. In Châteauneuf du Pape 13 varietals are permitted. In addition to Grenache, red wine grapes include Mourvèdre, Syrah, Cinsault, Vaccarèse, Counoise, Muscardin, Terret Noir, and Picpoul Noir. The white wines, which represent only 5–7% of the total production, are made from Grenache Blanc, Clairette, Bourboulenc, Roussanne, Picpoul, and Picardin. This interesting concoction was legislated by the appellation laws adopted in 1936.

The second factor that makes a major contribution to Châteauneuf du Pape is the terroir. Châteauneuf du Pape's vineyards are about 8.5 miles in length and 5 miles wide. The west is bounded by the Rhône River, and the east by the modern A 7 autoroute. To the north, there is Orange, and to the south Route Nationale N 7, and the drab town of Sorgues. The most prominent characteristic of these vineyards is the carpet of huge stones, ranging in size from cantelopes to footballs (called *galets roulés*). These rust-colored boulders are a vestige left by Alpine glaciers that once covered this region. The entire appellation is not covered with such stones (at Rayas there are very few), but on the plateau north and northwest of the village, the vineyards of Mont Redon, Cabrières, and Maucoil are noted for their ocean of rocks. Similar outcroppings can also be spotted east of the village, in the direction of Courthézon and Bédarrides. The lower part of Châteauneuf du Pape, in the direction of Sorgues, has very few of these boulders, as the soil is mostly gravelly decomposed rock intermixed with both clay and sand.

Visitors to any of these rock-and-roll vineyards should try to walk 30 yards or so through a row of vines. The attention and pressure on both knee joint and spine seems to suggest strongly that harvesting grapes in such vineyards can be backbreaking. The stones serve one purpose, though. In the glaring Provençal sunshine, they absorb heat and reflect it back to the vines in the early evening hours.

Throughout all these sectors, visitors cannot help but notice the extremely old average

age of the vines. Resembling old, gnarled dwarfs, these "head-pruned" vineyards are trained very low to the ground for one reason—this is the playground for the fierce mistral, the wind that emerges from the Alps, sweeping south and gaining speed before it explodes into the azure waters of the Mediterranean. The mistral, which can blow up to 50 miles an hour, may be unsettling (it blows mercilessly for an average of 125–150 days a year), but it is the appellation's homeopathic cure for a multitude of vineyard illnesses. Given the low humidity, hot sun, and frequent windy conditions, it is no surprise that most of the Châteauneuf du Pape vineyards are cultivated organically.

Châteauneuf du Pape is made in many different styles. Of primary importance is understanding the blend of grapes used by the different estates, and what each grape contributes to the wine's aromas and flavors. One of the top Châteauneuf du Papes, Beaucastel, possesses the lowest percentage of Grenache in the appellation and tends to favor a very high percentage of Mourvèdre, whereas Rayas utilizes nearly 100% Grenache. Both make profoundly great wines, but they could not be more different.

Several estates that tend to use 80–100% Grenache in the blend include Rayas, Chapoutier for Barbe Rac, André Brunel for Les Cailloux, and Henri Bonneau for Réserve des Célestins. Château Fortia tends to use a high percentage of Syrah, whereas Château La Nerthe employs a significant proportion of Mourvèdre in their Cuvée des Cadettes. Beaucastel uses the highest percentage of Mourvèdre, thus making the appellation's most atypical wine. As a general rule, most estates use 65–70% Grenache, and blend it with 10–15% Mourvèdre and Syrah. During the sixties, at the encouragement of the Ministry of Agriculture and the Institute of Appellation, growers were encouraged to plant Cinsault. Two of the Rhône Valley's most prominent authorities, Pierre Charney (also an author) and Philippe DuFays, went along with what turned out to be appallingly bad advice. Cinsault produced wine that lacked color, and it diminished the typicity of the Grenache-based Châteauneuf du Papes, the signature wines of the appellation. Much of those Cinsault plantings have now been pulled up by furious growers feeling misled by both the government and their own local authorities. In the seventies and eighties, Mourvèdre and Syrah have become more fashionable, as has Roussanne for white Châteauneuf du Pape. It is believed, with some justification, that a small dosage of Mourvèdre adds structure, definition, and aromatic complexity to a Grenache-based Châteauneuf du Pape, whereas Syrah adds color, a notion of ripe black fruits (cassis), and additional complexity. Roussanne, which has proven to produce sumptuous, Montrachet-like, old-vine cuvées at Beaucastel, gives white Châteauneuf du Pape a more honeyed, unctuous texture. Despite all the rhetoric about Grenache possibly losing out to some of the more fashionable grapes such as Mourvèdre and Syrah, a survey done in the early 1990s by the Fédération des Vignerons concluded that the following were the average plantations of each varietal in Châteauneuf du Pape: 79.25% Grenache Noir, 5.6% Syrah, 4.7% Mourvèdre, 3.3% Cinsault, 2.3% Clairette, 2% Grenache Blanc, with the remaining 2.85% of vineyard space utilized for the esoteric varietals Counoise and Vaccarèse for the red wines, and Roussanne for the whites. For the great majority of Châteauneuf du Pape estates, Grenache remains king, and that is as it should be, because this varietal reaches majestic heights in the southern Rhône that are unequaled anywhere else in the world except Spain.

For any readers who could possibly still be skeptical about the pleasures of Grenache, consider the fact that wine made from this varietal was so prized by top Burgundian négociants to round out, add weight and fruit to, and "ameliorate" the quality of premiers and grands crus of the Côte d'Or, that until the mid-seventies, many of Châteauneuf du Pape's most renowned estates routinely sold their wine in bulk to Burgundy producers (old-timers in nearby Gigondas also remember selling "tanker trucks" of wine to Burgundy producers), who, with the addition of 5–25% old-vine Grenache, magically transformed an acidic, sharp, diluted Clos de Vougeot, Chambertin, or Musigny into a hedonistic, textural marvel. I distinctly remember a tasting with a well-known Burgundy wholesaler/importer where he excitedly poured me a 1959 Musigny, saying, "Just wait until you taste this!" I loved the wine, but I told him it was not a Musigny, but one of the "best damn Châteauneuf du Papes I had ever tasted." I suppose it is not surprising that more than a few knowledgeable wine insiders have observed that modern-day Burgundy's irregularity and disappointingly short life span can perhaps be attributed to the fact that so much of it is no longer "ameliorated."

In attempting to comprehend this complex appellation, it is also important to understand the various styles of Châteauneuf du Pape. While there are innumerable variations on any of these themes, I have divided the three schools of Châteauneuf du Pape winemaking into traditionalists, modernists, and contrarians. How is this grouping determined? First of all, it is important to realize that virtually all of these producers have certain techniques or philosophies that could place them in one of the other categories, but overall, I define these categories as follows.

Traditionalists tend to be those producers who make Châteauneuf du Pape in large measure the way their fathers, grandfathers, and great-grandfathers produced wine. Most of these producers are averse to destemming, tend to age all of their wine in large wood foudres rather than smaller barrels or demi-muids, and rarely can be accused of rushing the wine into bottle. No new oak casks are likely to be found in these cellars, and the wines, while lightly fined and sometimes lightly filtered (or not filtered), will be traditional, full-bodied Châteauneuf du Papes that vary in concentration depending on the age of the vineyard and the producer's intentions. Most of these producers make wines solidly based on Grenache, with 60–80% Grenache and the balance a combination of Mourvèdre and Syrah. One aggravating, inflexible position most of these producers take is to bottle a vintage as it is sold, often leading to multiple bottlings over extended periods of time. Some producers keep this period short to guarantee uniformity in their wines, but others (Clos du Mont Olivet, Hauts des Terres Blanches, and Grand Tinel, for example) can bottle the same vintage over a period of 2–6 years, sometimes longer. Lastly, very few traditionalists ever utilize the carbonic maceration style of vinification to make Châteauneuf du Pape, preferring to make wines with an aging potential of at least 10–15 years in the top vintages.

Modernists tend to be producers who share certain general philosophies of winemaking. Most believe that Châteauneuf du Pape should be a fruity, easily accessible wine that is bottled quickly. While some do practice carbonic maceration for part or all of their crop, most tend to do full cluster fermentations, with minimal crushing. Most modernist producers destem part or all of their crop. These producers tend to process their wines more, since one of their objectives is to produce an easily drinkable, fruity wine that can be bottled within 12–16 months of the vintage. In order to reach that objective, a certain degree of processing must be accomplished. In general, modernists produce some of the lightest and most one-dimensional Châteauneuf du Papes, but producers such as Font de Michelle, Beaurenard, and La Roquette produce wines with excellent to outstanding intensity that are capable of lasting 10–15 years, even though they may be delicious upon release. Ironically, some of Châteauneuf du Pape's most famous and best known estates with magnificent terroirs— Mont Redon, Les Cabrières, La Solitude, Clos de l'Oratoire, Vaudieu, and Nalys—do not produce wines as rich, generous, and typical of Châteauneuf du Pape as they did two or three decades ago. The blend utilized by most modernists is basically no different from that of the traditionalists, although certain estates, such as La Nerthe, Vieux-Télégraphe, Mont Redon, and a handful of others, have multiple cépages planted, not just Grenache, Syrah, and Mourvèdre.

Contrarians are a group of Châteauneuf du Pape producers who march to the beat of their own drums. This group includes producers who believe in using 100% Grenache (Chapoutier, Domaine de la Janasse for Cuvée Chaupin, Les Cailloux for Cuvée Centenaire, and

Rayas). Others include those who believe that no more than 50% Grenache should be used (Beaucastel and, increasingly La Nerthe for Cuvée des Cadettes, and Château Fortia). It also includes those who believe in aging part of their wine in new oak casks (La Nerthe for Cuvée des Cadettes, Beaurenard for Cuvée Boisrenard, J. Marchand's Clos des Pontifes, Château de la Gardine for Cuvée des Générations, Les Cailloux for Cuvée Centenaire, and Beaucastel (in the latter case the Syrah and Roussanne are aged in small oak barrels). This group also includes the appellation's legendary, idiosyncratic recluse, Jacques Reynaud of Rayas, and the inimitable Henri Bonneau. Until his death in January 1997, Reynaud liked to flaunt authority, and produced wines from microscopic yields of 100% Grenache that have been aged in a bevy of wood vessels, from small old barrels to large wood foudres. The same can be said of Henri Bonneau, who utilizes a minimum of 80% Grenache, and would rather compliment the efficiency of the French bureaucracy than purchase a new oak cask. This group also includes producers dedicated to making as rich and concentrated a Châteauneuf du Pape as possible. Special cuvées of either 100% Grenache (as in the case of La Janasse's Chaupin, Les Cailloux Centenaire, and Chapoutier's Barbe Rac). Some of these producers destem, while others, such as Reynaud and Bonneau, do not. Additionally, most of these producers are adamantly against manipulation and excessive processing of their wines. Virtually all of these producers bottle their wines without filtration, and in some cases without fining. They are vehemently opposed to the philosophy espoused by the modernists, at least for their top wines. Although they are most closely allied to the traditionalists, they have moved beyond that style to something that in many ways epitomizes the greatest heights Châteauneuf du Pape can achieve.

What does the future hold for Châteauneuf du Pape? For nearly twenty years I have been advocating the best wines of this appellation as something of an insider's secret—decadent, hedonistic, complex, and full wines that are frightfully underpriced and underestimated. The most profound Châteauneuf du Papes are among the most enjoyable wines in the world. But the appellation of Châteauneuf du Pape needs to find satisfactory solutions to the following issues in order to maximize its extraordinary potential.

1. The appellation must come to grips with the fact that so many estates bottle their wine as it is sold, leading to inexcusable and unacceptable bottle variation. When an estate bottles a given vintage 18 months after the harvest and also five years after the harvest, can anyone doubt that there is a significant difference in character, flavor, and quality? The later bottling is often (but not always) dried out and unrepresentative of the vintage.

2. The large and moderately sized estates must begin to make a selection, selling off excess production to négociants, or offering the wine under a second label at a greatly reduced price. Many of the finest producers already do this. Vieux-Télégraphe and others have begun to offer a second label, and most of the other top five-star and four-star estates sell increasing percentages of their production to négociants in order to strengthen what remains to be bottled as an estate wine. But this practice has to extend beyond the top 30 or so estates.

3. To exploit and demonstrate the awesome potential possessed by this appellation, I believe most estates should consider producing luxury, old-vine, or single-vineyard cuvées that are bottled with minimal processing (little fining or filtration). The wine world has proven time and time again that it will enthusiastically support a high price for wines of exemplary quality, and the truly passionate Châteauneuf du Pape enthusiasts have strongly supported the luxury cuvées since they began to emerge in the late eighties. This allows a producer the flexibility of producing a more commercial, fruity style that is meant to be drunk during its first 7–8 years of life and that will please the majority of Rhône wine enthusiasts, as well as a special cuvée that represents the essence of a particular producer's cépage, terroir, etc., and can be sold at a much higher price.

4. The two syndicates that control the promotion and regulation of the Châteauneuf du Pape estates need to be more aggressive and export oriented. They need to educate the world about the magnificent terroirs, single vineyards, and diversity of styles that exist in this appellation. While most wine lovers can quickly rattle off a dozen or so prominent Burgundy or Bordeaux vineyards, how many old-vine vineyards or producers of Châteauneuf du Pape can most enthusiasts recite?

5. The appellation of Châteauneuf du Pape as well as France's Ministry of Agriculture must fight the increasing danger emanating from European bureaucrats sitting in Brussels who want wines to be more uniformly made, lower in alcohol, and sterilized. One of the great attributes of Châteauneuf du Pape is its explosive richness and lusty power and opulence. Consider what Mother Nature benevolently affords these wines. Châteauneuf du Pape is produced under the glorious sunshine and strong mistral winds of Provence. It is a wine of singular stature and character unrivaled or challenged by lookalike wines from the new world. The increasing standardization advocated by European bureaucrats must be resisted at every level.

6. White Châteauneuf du Pape, which represents a very small percentage of the appellation's production, is better than ever, but it remains a relatively monolithic, uninteresting wine save for a half dozen or so glorious cuvées. The authorities have been adamantly against the introduction of Viognier in Châteauneuf du Pape, yet it flourishes just outside the appellation's boundaries. In order to give the white Châteauneuf du Papes more aromatic complexity and interest, I believe Viognier should be a permitted varietal in this appellation.

7. In addition to promoting the fabulous vineyards and multiple styles of Châteauneuf du Pape, the appellation authorities should promote the following: (a) yields are among the lowest in France, (b) the appellation cannot be expanded, (c) no machine harvesters can be used, and (d) most of Châteauneuf du Pape's vineyards are farmed organically, something that should not be taken lightly in view of how many vineyard owners elsewhere have become addicted to chemicals and fertilizers.

RECENT VINTAGES

1995 On paper, the 1995 vintage is an irrefutably promising year. In large part a replay of 1994, 1995 enjoyed a hot summer (but less torrid than 1994). At the beginning of September, as in 1994, there was widespread optimism for a great vintage if the September weather was good. Lightning can strike twice in the same place, and on nearly the same date as in 1994, the heavens opened, dumping two weeks of heavy showers on the Rhône Valley between September 7 and September 20. But there was one significant difference. In 1994, early harvesters usually had more success because the grape maturity was so advanced at the time of the rains. Delaying the harvest meant potential rot. In 1995, the grapes were 1–2 weeks behind the maturity curve of the 1994s, thus the rain was less of a reason to harvest early. Moreover, there was significantly less rain in September 1995, than in September 1994. Unlike 1994, the rain was finished by the end of the third week of September, and several weeks of clear, dry, warm, windy weather followed, allowing late harvesters to bring in very ripe, healthy fruit that, surprisingly, possessed a high degree of acidity for the degree of physiological ripeness. While the 1995 vintage can clearly be called exceptional in the south, it is not as profound as 1989 or 1990.

1994 This could have been a great Châteauneuf du Pape vintage except for the heavy rains that began September 9 and continued throughout the month. Until that time, the summer had been torridly hot and dry, and producers were hoping for a vintage such as 1990 or 1989. The early harvesters were the most successful in 1994. Producers who waited rarely made as good wines as the early harvesters, just the reverse of 1995. A small crop was achieved, both because of the summer drought and by the selection process practiced by the better estates. Before bottling the wines appeared to be very good to excellent, but after bottling there was less consistency than I had hoped. Nevertheless, 1994 is a very good year for Châteauneuf du Pape, with a number of outstanding wines produced. The finest wines are forward and soft, with an unmistakable *garrigue* smell, good body, low acidity, and early accessibility. It should turn out to be as satisfying as 1988, 1985, and 1983.

1993 This vintage, largely a disaster in the northern Rhône, produced reasonably good but irregular wines in the south. The most appealing Châteauneuf du Papes possess good color and fruit, but tend to taste austere and tannic, at least in 1996. The finest wines are well above average, and promise to be long-lived. The downside of this vintage is that some 1993s could turn out to be a replay of the hollow, tannic, lean, austere 1986s. An average to above average vintage, but 1993 is a year that needs to be closely monitored.

1992 The torrential rains that caused severe flooding in and around Gigondas, were not nearly as severe in Châteauneuf du Pape. This was a year of high yields and a damp September. On paper, the vintage appeared to be well below average, but I have been consistently surprised by how delicious, fruity, and well made many of the 1992 Châteauneuf du Papes have turned out to be. They will not make old bones as only a handful possess the concentration to age, but they are plump, low-acid, fruity wines for drinking in the first 10–12 years following the vintage.

1991 This vintage was written off before anyone tasted the wines, and after tasting through all of them, it would appear that the early soothsayers were largely correct. A handful of decent wines were produced, but overall this is a thin, hollow, nasty vintage of Châteauneuf du Pape that is best forgotten.

1990 A debate among Châteauneuf du Pape producers will no doubt rage on for another two decades as to whether 1990 or 1989 is the greater vintage. If 1989 turns out to be a replay of 1978, 1990 may be a replay of 1967 or 1959. It is a fabulous vintage, with virtually everybody producing wines of enormous richness, power, weight, and lofty alcohol levels. The wines are quintessential Châteauneuf du Pape—robust, superconcentrated, very rich, and immensely appealing. In spite of their concentration, size, and potential for longevity, their low acidity and high levels of glycerin have ensured a precocious, sweet style that have made these wines unforgettable from birth. While drinkable and accessible, the great 1990 Châteauneuf du Papes should prove to be uncommonly long-lived because three of the necessary components for longevity—extract, alcohol, and tannin—are all present in copious quantities. This is a great vintage!

1989 A memorable vintage for Châteauneuf du Pape, the 1989s are slightly more classically structured, with less of the flamboyant, ostentatious character found in the 1990s. The 1989s resemble the 1978s in their huge power and concentrated richness, but backward, tannic, structured personality. They are loaded with potential, but when tasted side by side with the 1990s, most 1989s appear more closed and restrained. This is a uniformly great vintage for all the top producers. As I wrote in my journal, *The Wine Advocate*, in 1991, lovers of gloriously decadent Châteauneuf du Pape should purchase as many 1989s and 1990s as they can afford, since this is an unprecedented and glorious duo of vintages.

1988 This is one of the three finest vintages of the decade of the eighties, surpassed only by the richness and potential greatness of the 1989s, and by the opulence and lusty intensity of the 1981s. This vintage initially met with some restraint, but it has proven to be more rewarding than the quick-to-mature 1985. The wines are structured, with deep colors, and are aging well. Most of the 1988s can be consumed with considerable pleasure, but this is a vintage that should age well, particularly for those top estates that followed a classical vinification and élevage. In all the hyperbole over 1989, 1990, and more recently 1995, 1988 remains a somewhat underrated vintage.

1987 Not as dreadful as 1991, but certainly a below-average-quality vintage, 1987 was spoiled by a mediocre summer and a rainy harvest. The vintage was famous for one of the most unusual occurrences in Châteauneuf du Pape history—a blanket of fog that enveloped the vineyards during the month of September—never seen before, even by the village's octogenarians. This promoted rot and mold. Most of the 1987s should be drunk up by age 10.

1986 After a relatively hot summer, September began with large quantities of rain as a result of several severe thunderstorms. However, the weather quickly cleared, and the rest of September as well as early October experienced beautiful weather. For that reason, many observers felt this would be an excellent vintage. As it turned out, too many producers panicked during the early September deluge and picked much of their crop. The result, as is increasingly apparent in the wines, is a hollowness, astringent green tannin, and a lack of fat, glycerin, and ripeness. Not everybody made a mistake, as those who have tasted Henri Bonneau's incredible Réserve des Célestins, Paul Féraud's Pégau, or the 1986 from Domaine Durieu can attest. However, this vintage, once well received, is at best mediocre as well as exceptionally irregular, save for a handful of terrific wines made by those who harvested very late.

1985 There is a tendency today to be mildly let down by how the highly hyped 1985s have performed. The hot summer, with just enough rain, and a fine September created considerable excitement that this would be the finest vintage in Châteauneuf du Pape since 1978. From an overall perspective, 1985 is more consistent than 1981, but the finest wines of 1981 clearly overshadow anything produced in 1985. The wines are low in acidity, with very good concentration, and fine color. While they have always drunk well, they have evolved quickly. In 1996, many 1985s were just beginning to head down the slippery slope —to their extinction. The finest examples that have been kept in cool cellars are still fruity, open-knit, round, flattering wines that will drink well through the end of the century. Only a handful of wines (Henri Bonneau's Réserve des Célestins, Beaucastel, Clos des Papes, and perhaps Vieux-Télégraphe) will age gracefully into the first decade of the next century. Owners of 1985s should not defer their gratification any longer.

1984 A below-average-quality vintage, although not as bad as initially believed. A cool summer and damp September kept the grapes from reaching full maturity. Many producers harvested very late (October), and still did not pick physiologically mature grapes. Not many 1984s have turned out to be interesting, and those that did should have been consumed by now.

1983 This harvest produced a small crop, largely because the Grenache crop was severely reduced by *coulure* (a natural phenomenon that results in the vine prematurely dropping its berries) during and after the flowering in June. The summer was hot, almost tropical, which complicated the vintage. Producers not accustomed to smaller than normal quantities of Grenache often produced blends that were unbalanced. Plenty of very good to excellent wines were produced, most of which still provide delicious drinking. However, like 1985, the finest 1983s have matured quickly and need to be drunk up before the turn of the century.

1982 A gigantic crop produced wines that have always tasted diluted and flabby. Crop thinning should have been employed in 1982. The torrid temperatures during the harvest, which raisined many of the grapes, created nightmare situations for many of the smaller growers who do not have the capacity to cool down their fermenters. The best 1982s were open-knit, fruity, alcoholic, and delicious when young, but they have not aged well. They should have been consumed within the first decade of the vintage.

1981 Initially considered to be above average in quality, the 1981s have shed their early backwardness, and have developed into the second best vintage of the eighties. A moderately sized crop produced wines that were rich and alcoholic, as well as firmly tannic and structured. After 5–6 years of cellaring, the tannin began to melt away, and it became obvious there were glorious quantities of fruit, glycerin, and intensity to these full-bodied, dramatic wines. The finest 1981s have continued to strengthen in the bottle, but even those efforts were fully mature by 1996. Nevertheless, the most concentrated and fullest of the 1981 Châteauneuf du Papes have another decade or more of life. Beaucastel, followed by Rayas, Pégau, Vieux-Télégraphe, and Clos des Papes produced the wines of the vintage. This is an excellent to outstanding vintage that often shows up in rare-wine auctions at attractive prices.

1980   In Châteauneuf du Pape, 1980 was far better than in many other areas of France. Most of the 1980s turned out to be midweight, slightly herbal wines with enough succulent fruit and texture to provide delicious drinking during their first 10–12 years of life. The 1980s need drinking up.

1979   1979 was largely forgotten after the hoopla over 1978. As so often happens, the 1979s turned out to be a fine vintage of rich, concentrated, structured Châteauneuf du Papes that have aged slowly. Because of the relatively cool summer, the wines will never possess the aromatic profile of 1981, 1989, and 1990, but neither are they restrained or understated. Most of the best 1979s still reveal surprisingly deep colors, with little signs of age, and remain tight and structured, as well as concentrated and long. At best, this is an elegant, authoritatively flavored, excellent vintage for Châteauneuf du Pape. Rayas made a great wine in 1979 that comes close to being as compelling as their legendary 1978.

1978   This is the greatest Châteauneuf du Pape vintage between 1967 and 1989/1990. The wines have aged at a glacial pace, and well-stored bottles remain remarkably powerful, rich, youthful wines with a vigor and intensity rarely encountered. The summer was warm, but not excessively hot, and the crop size was moderate. The wines have always been very full-bodied and, when young, densely-colored and tannic. The tannin has melted away, leaving a bevy of extraordinary Châteauneuf du Papes. Just about all the top producers made reference point examples for their estates and the appellation. Personally, I rarely buy wines at auction, but I scrutinize auction catalogs to see what 1978 Châteauneuf du Papes might be available. Stylistically, 1989 and perhaps 1995 may turn out to be modern-day clones of this great vintage.

Older Vintages

In Châteauneuf du Pape, 1976, 1975, 1974, and 1973 were all difficult years. Nineteen seventy-two has provided its share of surprises (Beaucastel and Vieux-Télégraphe made exceptional wines). Nineteen seventy-one, while initially plump, rich, and delicious, is on its last legs. Well-kept 1970s can be marvelous, as this was an exceptional vintage in Châteauneuf du Pape. Nineteen sixty-nine was better in Châteauneuf du Pape than in most of France. Nineteen-sixty-eight was a disaster. In 1967, the troubles experienced by Burgundy and Bordeaux are well known, and thus most followers of French wine tend to think every producer in France had a so-so vintage. Châteauneuf du Pape and Alsace enjoyed great vintages in 1967. The 1967 Châteauneuf du Papes, some of which can still be found today, were marvelously rich, exotic, decadent wines with low acidity, huge body, and massive quantities of fruit, glcyerin, and alcohol. Beaucastel made a great 1967, but the most profound wine of the vintage, as well as one of the greatest Châteauneuf du Papes I ever tasted, was from the northern Rhône négociant Paul Jaboulet-Aîné. Their 1967 Châteauneuf du Pape Les Cèdres (called La Grappe de Pape outside the American marketplace) was made from 100% old-vine juice produced at Château de la Nerthe. I must have drunk nearly three cases of this wine since its release. When I last had it in 1996, I found it to be every bit as prodigious as in the past. For my palate, it is one of the greatest Châteauneuf du Papes ever made. Nineteen sixty-six was a top-notch year, as were 1961, 1959, 1957, and 1953. Unless exceptionally well stored in cold cellars, wines from these vintages are likely to be over the hill, although occasionally great bottles of 1961, 1955, and 1949 Mont Redon do appear in the auction market.

WHO'S WHO IN CHÂTEAUNEUF DU PAPE

Traditionalists

Pierre André
Lucien Barrot
Bois de Boursan
Le Bosquet des Papes
Les Cailloux
Chante-Perdrix
La Charbonnière
Gérard Charvin
Les Clefs d'Or
Clos du Caillou
Clos du Mont Olivet
Clos des Papes
Clos St.-Jean
Crouzet-Féraud
Cuvée du Belvedere
Cuvée de Boisdauphin
Cuvée du Vatican
Durieu
Font du Loup
Lou Fréjau
Galet des Papes
Grand Tinel
Guigal
Haut des Terres Blanches
Les Hautes Brusquières
De Marcoux

Mas de Bois Lauzon
Mathieu
Millière
Monpertuis
Moulin-Tacussel
Palestor
Pégau
Père Anselme
Père Pape
La Pinède
Pontifical
La Présidente
Riche
Roger Sabon
St.-Siffrein
Château Simian
Tardieu-Laurent
Terre Ferme
Jean-Pierre Usseglio
Pierre Usseglio
Raymond Usseglio
Vidal-Fleury
La Vieille Julienne
Le Vieux Donjon
Villeneuve

Modernists

Juliette Avril
Michel Bernard
Berthet-Rayne
Bois Dauphin
Château Cabrières
Chanssaud
Chantadu
Chante-Cigale
Clos de l'Oratoire des Papes
Cristia
Fines Roches
Font de Michelle
Grand Veneur
Paul Jaboulet-Ainé (Les Cèdres)
Comte de Lauze

Lauzon
Maucoil
Mongin
Mont Redon
Nalys
Père Caboche
Roger Perrin
Relagnes
La Roquette
St.-Benoît
Sénéchaux
La Solitude
Trintignant
Vaudieu
Vieux Lazaret

Contrarians

Paul Autard
Beaucastel
Beaurenard (Cuvée Boisrenard)
Clos des Pontifes
Henri Bonneau
Les Cailloux (Cuvée Centenaire)
Chapoutier (Barbe Rac)
Chapoutier (La Bernardine)

Charbonnière (Mourre Perdrix)
Château Fortia (since 1994)
La Gardine
De la Janasse
La Mordorée
La Nerthe
Rayas
Vieux-Télégraphe

PIERRE ANDRÉ* * * *

Address: Faubourg St.-Georges
        84350 Courthézon
Tel: 4-90-70-73-25
Fax: 4-90-70-75-73
Wines produced: Châteauneuf du Pape (red and white)
Surface area (white): 1.2 acres
         (red): 37 acres
Production (white): 200 cases
      (red): 5,625 cases
Upbringing (white): fermentation of 10–15 days, then 6–8 months in stainless steel vats
      (red): fermentation of 15–21 days in cement and enamel vats, then 18 months
         in old oak casks
Average age of vines (white): 60 years
         (red): 60 years
Blend (white): 40% Clairette, 30% Bourboulenc, 20% Roussanne, 10% Grenache Blanc
     (red): 78% Grenache, 10% Syrah, 10% Mourvèdre, 2% Cinsault, Muscardin, Picpoul,
        and Counoise

This is a reliable producer of textbook Châteauneuf du Pape. While it rarely hits the summit of quality, à la Rayas or Henri Bonneau's Réserve des Célestins, Pierre André rarely misses either. The red wines, made from Grenache, Syrah, Mourvèdre, and a tiny percentage of Cinsault and other miscellaneous varietals, are full-bodied, alcoholic, big, classic Châteauneuf du Papes that drink surprisingly well young, no doubt because of the tendency to bottle the wine 18–20 months after the harvest. Pierre André, a diminutive, enthusiastic, youthful man approaching 70 years of age, is competently assisted by his daughter, Jacqueline. Like many properties in Châteauneuf du Pape, this estate is mor-sellated, and the soils vary from lighter, sandy/clay soil, to more limestone in the higher parts of the appellation in the direction of André's cellars in Courthézon. Everything is traditional, from a resistance to destemming, to bottling the wine with only a light egg white fining, and no filtration. Readers looking for typical, delicious, full-bodied, flavorful Châteauneuf du Pape should remember Pierre André as one of the appellation's more consistent and satisfying producers.

I have tasted only a few vintages of André's white wines (200 cases produced). More Roussanne has been included in the blend since I last had the wine, but it is usually a competent, albeit unexciting effort.

VINTAGES

1994—Châteauneuf du Pape (red)   While I did not see Pierre André's 1995 offering, the
  ·   1994 is unquestionably an impressive example of the vintage. It displays a deep
 89   garnet color, ripe as well as sweet, heady aromas of herbs, cherries, spice, and
       pepper. Gloriously fruity and full-bodied, with loads of alcohol, glycerin, and ex-
       tract, this lush, exuberant Châteauneuf du Pape is already delicious; it should keep
       for a decade. Last tasted 6/96.

1990—Châteauneuf du Pape (red)   Pierre André's 1990 is an intriguing wine. The deep
  ·   ruby/purple color is followed by a lovely mélange of sweet red and black fruits
 88   intermingled with strong aromas of olives and Provençal herbs. The wine is full-
       bodied, fat, and succulent, with wonderful opulence, a velvety texture, and a
       smooth, ripe, luscious finish. Delicious now, wines such as this have a tendency to
       last longer than one initially suspects. However, potential purchasers should con-
       sider it a wine to drink over the next 7–8 years. Last tasted 9/95.

1989—Châteauneuf du Pape (red)   More backward than the 1990, without the dramatic,
  ·   sweet, overripe nose of red and black fruits and Provençal herbs, the 1989 exhibits
88 + a deep ruby color with purple nuances but no signs of age. Firmly structured,
       full-bodied, powerful, rich, and in need of another year of cellaring, this is an
       impressive, potentially long-lived wine that should offer considerable pleasure over
       the next decade. Anticipated maturity: now–2006. Last tasted 9/95.

PAUL AUTARD* * */* * * *

Address: Route de Châteauneuf
          84350 Courthézon
Tel: 4-90-70-73-15
Wines produced: Châteauneuf du Pape (red and white), Châteauneuf du Pape Cuvée La
Côte Ronde (red)
Surface area (white): 2.47 acres
              (red): regular cuvée—25 acres
              Cuvée La Côte Ronde—5 acres
Production (white): 3,000–4,000 bottles
              (red): regular cuvée—6,000–40,000 bottles
              Cuvée La Côte Ronde—1,000–5,000 bottles
Upbringing (white): 7 months with 40% of the yield in stainless steel vats and 60% in new
              oak barrels
              (red): regular cuvée—12 months, with 30–40% of the yield in old oak casks,
              10% of yield in new oak barrels, and 50% in barrels 1–5 years old;
              storage in tanks before bottling; fermentation of 28 days
              Cuvée La Côte Ronde—18 months total, with 50% of the yield in new
              oak barrels for 12 months; bottling after storage in tanks; fermentation in
              cement vats for 28 days
Average age of vines (white): 60 years
              (red): regular cuvée—50 years
              Cuvée La Côte Ronde—70–95 years
Blend (white): one-third each Grenache, Clairette, and Roussanne
       (red): regular cuvée—60–70% Grenache, 10% Syrah, 10% Cinsault, and other
              varietals
              Cuvée La Côte Ronde—40–50% Syrah, 20–30% Grenache, and Cinsault,
              Mourvèdre, Counoise, Muscardin, Vaccarèse

There is a quasi-traditional approach to winemaking at this domaine of 32.5 acres. Jean-Paul Autard appears to be moving toward richer, more concentrated wines than the more delicate style he produced a decade ago. One of the few producers to systematically destem much of his crop, and moving in the direction of the appellation's contrarians, Autard is now producing four cuvées of red Châteauneuf du Pape in top vintages. These include the Cuvée Tradition, which is the lightest and easiest to drink young, the Cuvée La Côte Ronde, in essence a single-vineyard wine made from a parcel of vines located north of the village of Châteauneuf du Pape, and, beginning in 1995, two new prestige cuvées called Cuvée Mireille and Cuvée Michele. The Cuvée La Côte Ronde is from a sedimentary, sandy subsoil, and the Cuvée Tradition is produced from vineyards planted in the *galets roulés*. The Cuvée Mireille and Cuvée Michele are selections made from specific barrels; both are extremely limited in quantity. Recent vintages have been very successful, and this estate appears to be a potential star of the future.

Jean-Paul and Joachim Autard produce a satisfactory white Châteauneuf du Pape. They also own a 36-acre estate in the Côtes du Rhône that produces a good, solid, juicy wine for drinking within 2–3 years of the vintage.

VINTAGES

1995 — Châteauneuf du Pape Cuvée La Côte Ronde (red)   The dense 1995 La Côte Ronde is not yet displaying much evidence of aging in new oak. While it is impressively
·
89   constituted, full-bodied, ripe, and promising, the wine appears to be very backward, as if it had just finished its malolactic fermentation. Its personality is subdued, but I suspect there may be more to this wine than my tasting notes and score suggest. Last tasted 6/96.

1994 — Châteauneuf du Pape (red)   The 1994 Châteauneuf du Pape exhibits spicy, toasty oak, along with aromas of new saddle leather, pepper, and ripe, curranty/cherry
·
86   fruit. The wine is medium- to full-bodied, somewhat monolithic, but solidly built, and capable of lasting for 7–8 years. Last tasted 6/96.

1994 — Châteauneuf du Pape Cuvée La Côte Ronde (red)   The 1994 La Côte Ronde reveals sweet *pain grillé* and jammy black-cherry fruit notes. The wine is full-
·
90   bodied and concentrated, with good structure, excellent purity, and a long, deep, concentrated finish with admirable fruit, extract, glycerin, and sweet tannin. Give it 2–3 years of cellaring and drink it over the following 10–12 years. Last tasted 6/96.

1993 — Châteauneuf du Pape (red)   Although not the most muscular or extracted wine of the vintage, the 1993 Châteauneuf du Pape offers a seductive, delicious, elegant
·
87   blend of rich cherry fruit, spice, Provençal herbs, and dried flowers. Medium-bodied, silky-soft, and well-balanced, this stylish, flattering Châteauneuf du Pape should be drunk over the next 5–6 years. Last tasted 9/95.

1993 — Châteauneuf du Pape Cuvée La Côte Ronde (red)   The smoky, sweet, oaky, *pain grillé*-scented 1993 La Côte Ronde exhibits a dark, impressively saturated color
·
88+   and rich, structured, medium- to full-bodied flavors with lavish new oak in evidence. Displaying excellent depth, purity, and grip, it should improve with 2–3 years of cellaring and drink well for 10–15 years. Last tasted 9/95.

1990 — Châteauneuf du Pape (red)   Autard's 1990 Châteauneuf du Pape is excellent. With a black/ruby/purple color and an intense nose of black cherries and smoke,
·
87   it has serious flavor, a considerable amount of soft tannin, and a spicy, earthy fruitiness. There is significant glycerin and copious quantities of sweet fruit in this full-bodied, smooth, gutsy wine. Anticipated maturity: now–2004. Last tasted 6/94.

1990—Châteauneuf du Pape Cuvée La Côte Ronde (red) The 1990 La Côte Ronde
·   has obviously seen some aging in new oak casks. The opaque ruby/purple color,
91   multidimensional nose of black fruits, minerals, and toasty vanillin, and the full-
bodied, gloriously extracted flavors of chocolate, herbs, and coffee generously fill
the mouth. There is excellent structure, as well as a delineated feel to the wine.
Anticipated maturity: now–2005. Last tasted 6/94.

1989—Châteauneuf du Pape (red) The 1989 displays an impressive deep, dark ruby/
·   purple color, and a spicy, tight nose of oak, cassis, and herbs. In the mouth there
87   is plenty of richness, but the wine remains well structured, dense, and almost
Bordeaux-like in its toughness and austerity. Anticipated maturity: now–2016.
Last tasted 4/94.

1988—Châteauneuf du Pape (red) The medium ruby-colored 1988 is a fragrant wine,
·   with a bouquet of tobacco, black raspberries, pepper, and Provençal herbs. In the
88   mouth, it is full-bodied, round, and plump, with a gorgeous texture oozing with
ripeness and richness, soft tannin, as well as a long, heady, alcoholic finish.
Anticipated maturity: now–2001. Last tasted 6/94.

JEAN AVRIL * * *

Address: Avenue Impériale
        84230 Châteauneuf du Pape
Tel: 4-90-83-73-83
Fax: 4-90-83-50-21
Wines produced: Châteauneuf du Pape (red)
Surface area: 49.4 acres
Production: 850 cases
Upbringing: 18 months total; fermentation in cement tanks for 3 weeks, and 12 months in
        old oak casks. The wine is then stored in tank until bottling.
Average age of vines: 50–60 years
Blend: 85% Grenache, 15% Cinsault and Syrah, and some Mourvèdre and Counoise

Virtually the entire production of Jean Avril is sold to négociants before bottling. He does
bottle approximately 850 cases of wine that is made primarily from Grenache. I have tasted
only a handful of vintages in addition to 1989 and 1990, and have found it to be a loosely
knit, ripe, fat style of wine made in a commercial manner, and meant to be drunk in its first
4–5 years of life.

VINTAGES

1994—Châteauneuf du Pape The 1994 Châteauneuf du Pape exhibits a healthy dark
·   ruby/purple color, as well as the vintage's lavishly rich, sweet, abundant fruit, low
88   acidity, plenty of glycerin, and a mouth-filling, corpulent style that is flattering and
seductive. Drink it over the next decade. Last tasted 6/96.

1993—Châteauneuf du Pape The 1993 Châteauneuf du Pape reveals more tannin, firm-
·   ness, and grip than the 1994, as well as gobs of peppery, herb-tinged black-cherry
88+   fruit in the nose and flavors. The excellent ripeness achieved makes a sweet
impression in this fleshy, long, delicious wine. There are moderately high tannin
levels in the finish. Give the 1993 two more years of cellaring and drink it over the
following 15 years. Last tasted 6/95.

DOMAINE JULIETTE AVRIL* *

Address: 8, avenue Louis Pasteur
            84230 Châteauneuf du Pape
Tel: 4-90-83-72-49
Fax: 4-90-83-53-08
Wines produced: Châteauneuf du Pape (red and white)
Surface area (white): 5 acres
                (red): 47 acres
Production (white): 800 cases
              (red): 8,350 cases
Upbringing (white): Fermentation of 8–10 days, and 6–8 months in stainless steel vats
              (red): 12 months total; fermentation of 10–20 days in stainless steel vats, then
                   the yield goes 3–6 months in old oak casks. The wine is stored in stainless
                   steel vats before bottling.
Average age of vines (white): 7 years
                        (red): 50 years
Blend (white): 40% Grenache, 20% Roussanne, 20% Clairette, 20% Bourboulenc
        (red): 80% Grenache, 10% Syrah, 5% Cinsault, 5% Mourvèdre

The wines I have tasted from this estate have been competently made, modern-style, fruity, processed Châteauneuf du Papes that are meant to be bottled early, and sold and drunk quickly. Since I have never tasted the wine prior to bottling, I do not know if there may be more richness that is stripped at bottling by overzealous fining and filtration, but this is clearly not one of the leaders of Châteauneuf du Pape.

LUCIEN BARROT* * * *

Address: Chemin du Clos
            84230 Châteauneuf du Pape
Tel: 4-90-83-70-90
Fax: 4-90-83-51-89
Wines produced: Châteauneuf du Pape (red)
Surface area: 47 acres (10 acres are leased)
Production: 6,900 cases
Upbringing: Fermentation for 21–24 weeks in cement vats, then 2–3 years in old oak casks
Average age of vines: 50 years
Blend: 80% Grenache, 10% Syrah, 10% Cinsault and Mourvèdre

The Barrot family has been residing in Châteauneuf du Pape since the fourteenth century. However, it is only recently that they have been estate-bottling their wine. Lucien Barrot, one of the members of the small group of artisan producers called Prestige et Tradition, fashions delicious, textbook Châteauneuf du Papes that have given me immense pleasure over the years. I was first smitten with Barrot's wines when I tasted the 1979. As a fan of his bold, blockbuster, but never hard style of Châteauneuf du Pape, I have purchased almost every top vintage, and I have never been disappointed with their quality or development in the bottle. As a general rule, Barrot's wines are drinkable young, but capable of lasting for 15–16 years.

This is a traditional estate, with all of their parcels of vines situated on the famous bed of *galets roulés*. The wine is made from a high percentage of Grenache (80%). Fermentation is long, as Barrot tries to obtain plenty of richness and extract through a relatively hot vinification. Perhaps the most noticeable aspect of Barrot's wines is their gloriously seductive, flamboyant bouquets of Provençal herbs, jammy red and black fruits, and spices. Unfortunately, Barrot, like many small growers, does not have the financial resources necessary to bottle his entire vintage at once. Consequently, numerous bottlings are done as the wine is sold. To his credit, the wine is bottled with minimal processing. Only a light filtration is used in vintages where the wine does not fall brilliant.

Lucien Barrot produces no white wine, which is unusual for a Châteauneuf du Pape producer. Readers who have old bottles of Barrot's Châteauneuf du Pape in their cellars may wonder why recent vintages do not include his Cuvée de Tastevin designation on the label. The Burgundians and their Confrérie des Chevaliers de Tastevin sued Barrot a few years ago, claiming the use of these three words caused confusion and infringed on their use of the same words for their selections made in Burgundy. One would think such an expenditure of energy would be better directed in the pursuit of higher quality, rather than wasted on such frivolous matters.

As the following tasting notes attest, this is a highly consistent, top-notch producer of classic, full-bodied Châteauneuf du Pape.

VINTAGES

1995—Châteauneuf du Pape   Compared to the 1994, the 1995 Châteauneuf du Pape
·   exhibits more purple nuances in its deep ruby color. The fruit is sweeter, and the
89   wine reveals more glycerin, alcohol, and tannin. It is more powerful, larger-scaled, and bigger, with good structure, and a touch of toasty vanillin (as if a new barrel or two may have been used in this wine's upbringing). The 1995 is a potentially outstanding example from Lucien Barrot, an underrated Châteauneuf du Pape producer whose wines remain very reasonably priced for such quality. The 1995 will be drinkable when released next year and last for 10–15 years. Last tasted 6/96.

1994—Châteauneuf du Pape   Lucien Barrot's 1994 is made in a forward style, displaying
·   a deep ruby/purple color, exotic spices, jammy black cherries, and medium to full
88   body. The wine is lush and powerful, as well as surprisingly elegant and well balanced. It possesses a fat, forward character that is reminiscent of the delicious 1988. Drink it now and over the next 7–8 years. Last tasted 6/96.

1993—Châteauneuf du Pape   The 1993 possesses an intriguing nose with scents of
·   iodine, licorice, chocolate, and roasted coffee, admirable fat and glycerin, full
88   body, and a lusty, sweet, high-alcohol, viscous finish. This forward wine is more typical of the 1994 vintage than the structured 1993. Drink it over the next 7–8 years. Last tasted 6/95.

1992—Châteauneuf du Pape   The 1992 offers cherry fruit, gobs of glycerin, high alcohol,
·   low acidity, and an easygoing, plump personality. It is a success for this irregular
86   year, but it requires drinking. Mature now. Last tasted 6/95.

1990—Châteauneuf du Pape   Barrot has fashioned an exceptionally seductive 1990. The
·   deep ruby/purple color is followed by a wine with a spicy, precocious, peppery,
90   smoky, tar, and berry-scented nose. I also detected the apricot and peach scents of supermaturity. In the mouth there is wonderful richness, a velvety texture, and gobs of ripe, luscious fruit. The wine does not possess either the structure or tannic grip of the 1989, but for drinking over the next 10 years, this heady, fat, somewhat decadent style of Châteauneuf du Pape will prove hard to resist. Anticipated maturity: now–2003. Last tasted 9/94.

1989—Châteauneuf du Pape   The 1989 is a sweet, round, velvety-textured wine. As
·   large-scaled and rich as the 1988, it is a precocious, decadently hedonistic, flavor-
90   ful Châteauneuf du Pape. The tannins are soft and the acidity slightly lower than

in the 1988, but there is an abundance of rich, smoky, cedary, chocolaty fruit in this fleshy, powerful wine. Anticipated maturity: now–2005. Last tasted 6/96.

1988—Châteauneuf du Pape   The 1988 is an excellent, full-bodied wine, with a natural
·   alcohol content of 13.5%. Typical of the Barrot style, it is deeply colored, with
89   highly extracted, chewy, muscular, rich, yet pure, impeccably balanced flavors. This intense, traditionally made Châteauneuf du Pape should age gracefully for up to a decade. Anticipated maturity: now–2001. Last tasted 8/96.

Older Vintages

Barrot's 1985 was highly successful, but it is now fully mature and needs to be drunk up before the end of the decade. The fully mature 1983 is more complex than the 1985, with a slightly longer evolutionary curve, but I would still recommend drinking it by the turn of the century. The 1981 is one of my favorite Barrot wines. It is a rich, blockbuster, powerful wine that has aged superbly. It remains a deep garnet color, with gorgeous Provençal aromatics, and gobs of sweet, rich fruit, all presented in a chewy, full-bodied format. I have gone through nearly two cases of this wine, with several bottles remaining in my cellar, and it shows no signs of cracking up. Nevertheless, I would not push my luck past another 5–6 years. The excellent 1979 is more compact and austere, but certainly built for longevity. I lament the fact that I have never tasted the 1978; I am sure it must be a superb wine from this producer.

CHÂTEAU BEAUCASTEL (PERRIN)* * * * *

Address: Chemin de Beaucastel
              84350 Courthézon
Tel: 4-90-70-41-00
Fax: 4-90-70-41-19
Wines produced: Châteauneuf du Pape (red and white), Châteauneuf du Pape Cuvée Rous-
              sanne Vieilles Vignes (white), Châteauneuf du Pape Hommage à Jacques
              Perrin (red)
Surface area (white): Cuvée Tradition—13.6 acres
                      Cuvée Vieilles Vignes—5 acres
          (red): regular cuvée—173 acres
                 Hommage à Jacques Perrin—5 acres
Production (white): Cuvée Tradition—1,625 cases
                    Cuvée Vieilles Vignes—300–325 cases
          (red): regular cuvée—20,000–24,000 cases
                 Hommage à Jacques Perrin—400–425 cases
Upbringing (white): Cuvée Tradition—Fermentation of 15–60 days, with 80% of the wine
                    in stainless steel vats and 20% in both old and new oak barrels. Bottling
                    is done 10–12 months after assemblage.
                    Cuvée Vieilles Vignes—12 months total. Fermentation of 15–60 days,
                    with 50% of the yield in stainless steel tanks and 50% in 1-year-old
                    barrels.
          (red): regular cuvée—24 months total; fermentation of 3 weeks in cement tanks,
                 the wine then goes into old oak casks for 8–18 months
                 Hommage à Jacques Perrin—fermentation of 3 weeks in cement tanks,
                 then the wine goes into old oak casks for 8–18 months. Bottling after 24
                 months.
Average age of the vines (white): Cuvée Tradition—30 years
                                  Cuvée Vieilles Vignes—70 years
              (red): regular cuvée—50 years
                     Hommage à Jacques Perrin—65–90+ years

Blend (white): 80% Roussanne, 15% Grenache Blanc, 5% Clairette, Bourboulenc, Picardan
    Cuvée Vieilles Vignes—100% Roussanne
    (red): 30% Grenache, 30% Mourvèdre, 10% Syrah, 10% Counoise, 5% Cinsault, and
    other varietals, mainly Vaccarèse and Muscardin
    Hommage à Jacques Perrin—70% Mourvèdre, 15% Syrah, 10% Grenache, 5%
    Counoise

The fact that Beaucastel produces the longest-lived red wine of the southern Rhône is irrefutable. However, this estate also produces one of the Rhône Valley's greatest and most distinctive wines. The wine is made by totally organic methods. No chemicals are used in the vast 272-acre vineyard located in the northernmost sector of Châteauneuf du Pape near the town of Courthézon. Over 500 tons of manure are dumped on these vineyards whose vines, through a meticulously planned rotational replanting formula, maintain an average age of 50 years. The late Jacques Perrin, considered by many to be one of the Rhône Valley's most brilliant and philosophical winemakers, believed adamantly in three principles: (1) a wine must be made naturally, (2) the percentage of Mourvèdre in the blend must be significant, and (3) the wine's character and intrinsic qualities could not be compromised by concessions to modern technology. Jacques Perrin died in 1978, but his two sons, François and Jean-Pierre, were well indoctrinated with their father's beliefs, and have not only carried on his methodology but have further increased the quality of Beaucastel.

The vineyards of Beaucastel are one of three major estates to have all 13 permitted varietals planted. The others are Mont Redon and Domaine de Nalys. For red wines, Beaucastel is marked by the high percentage of Mourvèdre. The preferred blend here is 30% Grenache, 30% Mourvèdre, 10% Syrah, 10% Counoise, 5% Cinsault, and the rest Muscardin and Vaccarèse. They are augmenting the percentage of Mourvèdre and Counoise in their new plantings. For their white wine, they remain unique as well, using an unusually high percentage of 80% Roussanne, and the rest Bourboulenc, Clairette, and Grenache Blanc. Except for Château de la Nerthe, no other estate in this appellation uses this much Mourvèdre for its red wine.

It is ironic that Beaucastel, though America's best-known Châteauneuf du Pape, is undeniably the appellation's most atypical wine. The high percentage of Mourvèdre, combined with Counoise, Muscardin, and Vaccarèse, as well as the low percentage of Grenache, result in a wine that the Châteauneuf du Pape cognoscenti often call the antithesis of what is considered classic for the appellation. Yet the results are stunning, if unusual for a wine from this appellation. In top vintages, the red wine is usually a black/ruby or purple color, loaded with layers of fruit, tannin, and a multitude of fascinating scents and aromas. Since Mourvèdre tends to give Châteauneuf du Pape more structure and tannin, as well as an unmistakable perfume of animal and mushroomlike, tree bark scents, readers can understand why not everyone loves Beaucastel. Moreover, the finest vintages are often unflattering to drink young, but as with a great thoroughbred, age, usually a minimum of six to ten years, brings forth the distinctive aromatic profile, and the sweetness and richness of fruit. Most top vintages of Beaucastel improve and last in the bottle for a minimum of two decades. Some critics of Beaucastel have argued that the wine possesses an unacceptably high level of brettanomyces (often called brett), an airborne yeast that tends to inhabit almost every winery. Critics say that when huge populations of brett are present in a finished wine, the wine possesses an unusual, off-putting smell of sweaty saddle leather and horse dung. Some vintages of Beaucastel have had levels of brett that would horrify tasters weaned on sterile-filtered, monochromatic wines, yet, interestingly, bottles of finished wine that have been analyzed by laboratories have revealed a level of brett that is far lower than Beaucastel's critics suggest. Nevertheless, Mourvèdre, Counoise, and some brett make for a very distinctive style of wine that is not everyone's cup of tea, especially new world drinkers who are looking for fruit and new oak. Admittedly, brettanomyces is an issue that is not discussed even among French wine consumers or, for that matter, most wine drinkers in western Europe.

This meticulously run estate remains remarkably open-minded, as brothers François and Jean-Pierre Perrin are consummate professionals of their craft. One unusual technique utilized during the fermentation is the Perrins' controversial *vinification à chaud*. It is a process of heating the incoming grapes to very high temperatures (30° centigrade for just over one minute) and then immediately cooling them down (to 20° centigrade) as they go into the fermentation tanks. This process, first pioneered by the Perrins' grandfather and perfected by their father, is believed to accomplish several things: (1) It halts the natural tendency of grapes to oxidize. (2) It extracts deeper, richer color, aromas, and flavor from the skins of the grapes. (3) It prolongs and slows the fermentation. (4) It precludes the necessity of using much sulfur during the fermentation. The results speak for themselves, but critics call it a flash pasteurization.

All the grape varietals at Beaucastel are handled separately, with most of the Mourvèdre and Syrah being destemmed. Syrah is the only varietal to see any new oak, since experiments conducted by the Perrins have deemed that the Syrah benefits from fermentation in small oak casks. The rest of the component varietals are vinified and aged separately until late spring following the vintage when the selection process and final blends are made.

As visitors to Beaucastel can attest, the rows of huge foudres in the air-conditioned, underground cellars are visually impressive. After blending, the wine spends a year in these foudres until the bottling takes place. Because of the traditional practice of bottling as the wine is sold, resulting in bottle variation, Beaucastel constructed an underground storage facility beginning with the 1980 vintage. Since then, all 18,000–25,000 cases of Beaucastel are bottled at the same time, thus guaranteeing uniformity of quality from bottle to bottle. In keeping with the artisanal approach to viticulture and winemaking, Beaucastel is bottled after an egg white fining; it is never filtered.

François Perrin, a youthful-looking, trim, articulate individual, and his handsome brother, Jean-Pierre (the more outspoken and fiery of the brothers), both provide provocative information when discussing the issue of filtration. Both have experimented with filtration and have been shocked by the negative effect it has on a wine's bouquet, richness, body, and potential for development. It is not surprising that after three or four years of bottle age, most Beaucastels will shed considerable sediment, with the richer, more concentrated vintages caking the inside of the bottle and dropping a significant amount of *dépôt* (sediment).

The red cuvée of Beaucastel, which has had such an illustrious history, was joined by a special cuvée, called Hommage à Jacques Perrin, in the 1989, 1990, 1994, and 1995 vintages. The debut vintage, 1989, was inaugurated as a dedication to François and Jean-Pierre's father, Jacques, who had an enormous influence on them, and had steadfastly supported the use of Mourvèdre in the appellation. It is a super-concentrated blend of 60% Mourvèdre, 20% Grenache, 10% Syrah, and 10% Counoise that is aged in foudre, and bottled later than Beaucastel's Châteauneuf du Pape. Given its thrilling level of quality, in addition to the tiny quantity produced, it became immortal from the release of the first vintage.

The Perrins, contrarians under my schematic of producers, are supporters of the Mourvedre grape in Châteauneuf du Pape, and Château de la Nerthe is following in their path. Beaucastel is also opposed to the prevailing philosophy of making white wine, preferring the fickle, often difficult-to-cultivate Roussanne to the more popular Grenache Blanc, Clairette, and Bourboulenc. There are two cuvées of white Beaucastel, both of them the finest wines made in the appellation. Not only do they both have considerable longevity by the standards of white Châteauneuf du Pape, but they are also the region's richest and most complex white wines. Both are Roussanne-based wines, with the regular cuvée made from

80% Roussanne, 15% Grenache Blanc, and the remaining 5% composed of Bourboulenc, Clairette, and Picpoul. This wine is augmented by a limited-production 100% old-vine Roussanne from a 10-acre parcel of 65-year-old vines. This wine, priced at a level that competes with grand cru white Burgundy, is vinified in both wood casks (some of which are new) and stainless steel, and then blended together. It is put through full malolactic fermentation. It may be the world's greatest expression of Roussanne. The debut vintage was 1986. Every year has produced a compelling wine with at least 10–20 years of aging potential.

Beaucastel is obviously the flagship estate of the Perrin family, but they also produce one of the finest white and red Côtes du Rhône, Coudoulet, from a vineyard adjoining Beaucastel just outside the Châteauneuf du Pape boundaries. Additionally, they produce a Côtes du Rhône called Le Grand Prébois from an estate that also serves as the home of François Perrin and his family. Jean-Pierre Perrin also has a négociant firm, La Vieille Ferme. The latter has become one of the most successful branded red and white wines in many foreign markets because of the high quality-price rapport.

Not content to limit their investments in France, François and Jean-Pierre Perrin formed a partnership with the well-known American importer Robert Haas, and purchased 125 acres of potential vineyard property in California's sun-drenched, arid region of Paso Robles. That project was just beginning to come to fruition when this book went to press, with the first wines being released in 1997, and the estate wines scheduled for release at the turn of the century. Not surprisingly, all the wines are being produced from Rhône Valley varietals planted in California soils.

What is so obvious with all of these ventures is the high level of professionalism and commitment to the best that nature can provide. The well-deserved success of Beaucastel has meant that François and Jean-Pierre Perrin have come to represent more than just qualitative proprietors in the Rhône Valley. They symbolize such virtues as honesty, excellence, dedication, and hard work. They have not only preserved the very finest aspects of Rhône Valley traditions but have built upon them, and in the process have earned worldwide fame for their wines, for the Rhône Valley, and for France.

VINTAGES

1995—Châteauneuf du Pape (red)   Beaucastel's 1995 Châteauneuf du Pape had not been
·   assembled at the time of my visit, but tasting through all of its component parts
93   revealed a very ripe, concentrated, and impressively endowed wine. None of my
           ratings for the component parts was below 90, with most in the 92–95 range. This
           is another thick, rich, juicy Châteauneuf du Pape with that telltale black nose of
           raspberry, cherry, smoked herbs, roasted coffee, and licorice that is profoundly
           complex. The wine is full-bodied and concentrated, as well as slightly riper and
           more alcoholic than the 1994. It should evolve effortlessly for 15–20 years. Last
           tasted 6/96.

1995—Châteauneuf du Pape (white)   The 1995 Châteauneuf du Pape blanc (80% Rous-
·   sanne, 15% Grenache Blanc, and 5% various other white wine varietals) sees 25%
92   small oak casks. It is a rich, dense, opulently styled wine with copious quantities
           of honeyed fruit, considerable power, and a rose petal/honeyed richness with a
           touch of toast and spice. Drink this long, delicious, thick Beaucastel over the next
           few years before it closes down. Last tasted 6/96.

1995—Châteauneuf du Pape Hommage à Jacques Perrin (red)   The 1995 Châteauneuf
·   du Pape Cuvée Jacques Perrin reveals a black/purple color, and a huge nose of
95   Provençal herbs, smoked olives, grilled meats, and sweet, jammy black-cherry and

black-raspberry fruit. Full-bodied, and oozing with extract and glycerin (nearly concealing the wine's formidable tannin levels), this blockbuster Châteauneuf du Pape will need a minimum of 10–12 years of cellaring; it should keep through the first half of the next century. Last tasted 6/96.

1995—Châteauneuf du Pape Roussanne Vieilles Vignes (white) The 1995 Roussanne
· Vieilles Vignes is a wine of Montrachet-like stature. It possesses the texture of the
95 greatest white Burgundies, amazing concentration, low acidity, huge thickness, and
an unctuous, chewy finish. It offers a large-scaled, concentrated, husky mouthful
of Roussanne that must be tasted to be believed. The debut vintage of this cuvée
was 1986, and my experience has shown that they become more and more delineated and civilized with cellaring. This wine was made from yields of under 1 ton of
fruit per acre. Readers lucky enough to latch on to both the 1994 and 1995
Roussanne Vieilles Vignes will have fun deciding which one is better. Both are
great examples of this cuvée. Last tasted 6/96.

1994—Châteauneuf du Pape (red) The 1994 Châteauneuf du Pape is a black/ruby/
· purple wine with sweet, expansive, chewy fruit. It reminds me of a more concen-
93 trated 1985, with nearly the character and size of the prodigious 1989. It possesses
the lowest percentage of Grenache (30%) of any Châteauneuf du Pape, and the
highest percentage of Mourvèdre (40%). For example, the 1993 Beaucastel, which
was so tasty early in life, is now locked in a profoundly dumb stage. I am not sure
the 1994 will ever close down as much because it is such a sweet, rich, thick,
chewy wine with full body, and a superb nose of smoky black fruits, Asian spices,
licorice, olives, and herbs. Full, concentrated, and lush, it should drink well for
15–20 years. Last tasted 6/96.

1994—Châteauneuf du Pape (white) The 1994 Châteauneuf du Pape blanc is more
· honeyed and rich than the 1995. It is full-bodied and intense, with gobs of cherry-
93 like fruit. Structured yet dense, it is a formidable example of Beaucastel's white
wine. It will age for 10–15 or more years. Last tasted 6/96.

1994—Châteauneuf du Pape Hommage à Jacques Perrin (red) There will be about 300
· cases of the 1994 Hommage à Jacques Perrin (a 70% Mourvèdre, 15% Grenache,
95 and the rest Counoise-Syrah blend). The wine's opaque purple color is followed by
a tight but promising nose of black raspberries, smoke, herbes de Provence, new
saddle leather, coffee, and earth. Exceptionally tannic, powerful, and concentrated,
with lofty levels of glycerin and extract, this is an enormously endowed, backward,
massive wine that will require a decade of cellaring; it is a 30- to 40-year wine.
Last tasted 6/96.

1994—Châteauneuf du Pape Roussanne Vieilles Vignes (white) The 1994 Roussanne
· Vieilles Vignes is sensational, and perhaps even more fragrant and unctuous than
96 the 1995. The nose, which offers up aromas of honey, roses, *pain grillé*, and white
flowers, is followed by a wine of exceptional body, thickness, richness, and purity.
It is a splendidly rich, flamboyant wine that will undoubtedly close down and
appear more structured with another year or two in the bottle. It should keep for
15–20 years. Last tasted 6/96.

1993—Châteauneuf du Pape (red) When I tasted the 1993 Beaucastel in Châteauneuf
· du Pape, the wine was far more showy, flashy, and open-knit than bottles tasted
87? stateside, admittedly right after reaching these shores. I backed off my initial high
rating a bit and added the question mark because of how tannic, backward, and
firm the wine showed on two separate occasions from a case I purchased. It
certainly possesses a dense color, as well as plenty of body and intensity. However,
the rich, sweet, open-knit bouquet has gone into hibernation, leaving a tightly knit
wine that is frozen in place, reluctantly offering up aromas of black fruits and

smoke. Tannic, austere, and more in step with the 1988, this appears to be a vintage that will require more initial cellaring than I had anticipated. It will be interesting to retaste this wine after it has had 4–6 months of rest on these shores. Last tasted 11/96.

1993—Châteauneuf du Pape (white)   The 1993 Beaucastel blanc (80% Roussanne) is
·   fat, unctuous, and full-bodied with layers of honeyed fruit. It is a massive dry white
90   wine that is best paired with powerfully scented Provençal cuisine. Last tasted
7/96.

1993—Châteauneuf du Pape Roussanne Vieilles Vignes (white)   The 1993 Roussanne
·   Vieilles Vignes (only 4,000 bottles produced) exhibits a huge cherry- and rose-
96   scented nose, tropical fruit flavors, great richness and concentration, medium to
full body, and wonderful, vibrant, zesty acidity. This rarity, produced from a small parcel of vines averaging 50–60 years, is undoubtedly the finest dry white wine made in the southern Rhône. Last tasted 7/96.

1992—Châteauneuf du Pape (red)   Sadly, the only two bottles purchased of this wine had
·   to be opened and both were cooked. They revealed no signs of heat damage, with
74   good fills and no protruding corks or stained labels, and they had been resting
comfortably in my cold cellar since I purchased them. However, the wine tasted hollow, with tarlike aromas, an absence of fruit, and a baked character. I will report on this wine again once I have had a chance to purchase several more bottles. The 1992 Beaucastel was one of the best wines of an average-quality vintage in Châteauneuf du Pape, so it is distressing to see that along the route from Avignon to America someone negligently fried the wine. Last tasted 1/96.

1992—Châteauneuf du Pape (white)   The 1992 blanc exhibits a floral, honeyed bouquet
·   and medium-bodied, firm, chewy flavors. It should drink well for 10–15 years. Last
89   tasted 6/95.

1992—Châteauneuf du Pape Roussanne Vieilles Vignes (white)   The 1992 Roussanne
·   Vieilles Vignes possesses an exotic, honeyed, roasted nut, and floral-scented nose,
91   intense, full-bodied flavors, superb concentration, and a long, lush, pure finish.
These wines tend to drink beautifully for 2–3 years after bottling and then close up. The Perrins believe they can be aged for 15–20 + years. Last tasted 6/95.

1991—Châteauneuf du Pape (red)   Despite the fact that 50% of the crop was sold off to
·   négociants, this is an emaciated, thin, vegetal Beaucastel without enough fruit and
77   glycerin to cover its skeletal structure. Given its lack of fruit, charm, and pleasure,
it has no place to go but down. Last tasted 12/95.

1990—Châteauneuf du Pape (red)   Beaucastel made another great Châteauneuf du Pape
·   in 1990. In stylistic terms, it is completely different from the profound 1989. The
94   color is opaque black/ruby/purple. The perfume of smoked meats, coffee, hickory,
Asian spices, and black raspberries is sensational. In the mouth the wine, while concentrated, full-bodied, and extremely rich, displays slightly harder tannins, higher acidity, and comes across as a more muscular, less opulent example than the 1989. It is a profound wine, but I would rate it inferior to the 1989 and 1981, yet easily equivalent to the 1983 and 1985. Both François and Jean-Pierre Perrin compare their 1990 to the renowned 1967, and both brothers prefer it to their 1989 —high praise! Unlike the 1989, it will not be as flattering to drink when young. It should age for at least 30 years. Last tasted 12/95.

1990—Châteauneuf du Pape (white)   The 1990 blanc exhibits a great deal of strength
·   and muscle in a full-bodied, well-balanced, ripe, heady, nicely textured style. The
88   wine is less concentrated than the 1989, but it is still an impressive mouthful of
wine. As I have stated in the past, if you are going to buy this wine, drink it within 2–3 years of the vintage, or be prepared to cellar it for 10 years. It tends to be best

several years after bottling, at which time it closes up, not to emerge for 7–8 years. Last tasted 11/94.

1990—Châteauneuf du Pape Hommage à Jacques Perrin   The 1990 Hommage à Jacques
·   Perrin possesses an increased percentage of Mourvèdre (60%), along with Gren-
100   ache (20%), Counoise (10%), and Syrah (10%). It is a superconcentrated, mammoth-
sized wine with black/purple color, and a huge, fragrant perfume of smoked meat, black fruits, earth, and Asian spices. Muscular and tannic, with tremendous amounts of glycerin and concentration, this super cuvée should reach its peak by the end of the century and last for 20–30 years. Last tasted 12/95.

1990—Châteauneuf du Pape Roussanne Vieilles Vignes (white)   The 1990 Roussanne
·   Vieilles Vignes has that distinctive bouquet of honey, smoky hazelnuts, and pine-
90   apples. In the mouth, it is closed but rich and full, with an intriguing texture, as well as a firm but promising finish. In comparison to the 1989, it is more structured, and not as soft and opulent, but is as concentrated. It may merit an even higher score in ten years' time. Last tasted 12/96.

1989—Châteauneuf du Pape (red)   The sumptuous 1989 possesses an intense black/
·   ruby/purple color. The nose offers a veritable smorgasbord of jammy cassis,
97   Provençal herbs, Asian spices, fruitcake, coffee, and hickory wood. The wine is sensationally concentrated and well balanced, with soft tannin and enough acidity to provide balance and freshness. Full-bodied, with layers of fruit and glycerin, it can be drunk now because of its lavish richness, yet it should age for 20+ more years. It should exceed the quality of the superb 1981. Last tasted 12/95.

1989—Châteauneuf du Pape (white)   The 1989 Beaucastel blanc seems surprisingly
·   forward, round, richly fruity, ripe, and luscious on the palate, with at least 10–12
86   years' evolution ahead of it. It is drinking well now, but I suspect it will close up within the next several years. Last tasted 4/95.

1989—Châteauneuf du Pape Hommage à Jacques Perrin   The 1989 Hommage à Jacques
·   Perrin is a profound wine. The dense, saturated, almost opaque black/purple color
99   suggests superripeness and intensity. The nose has begun to close up (in total contrast to the more open 1990 Jacques Perrin), but it still offers smoky aromas of minerals, licorice, black fruits, and even an intriguing floral component. The wine is exceptionally full-bodied and tannic, as well as awesomely concentrated and magnificently well balanced. This wine looks to be more backward and less flattering in its youth than the 1990. Anticipated maturity: 2002–2020. Last tasted 12/95.

1989—Châteauneuf du Pape Roussanne Vieilles Vignes (white)   The 1989 Roussanne
·   Vieilles Vignes has a wonderfully expansive, intense bouquet of smoky hazelnuts,
90   wet stones, and pineapples. In the mouth it is full-bodied, rich, very concentrated, somewhat similar to the 1986, but slightly lower in acidity. It should keep for 12–15 years. Last tasted 1/96.

1988—Châteauneuf du Pape (red)   The 1988 Beaucastel has evolved from a surprisingly
·   forward, supple style to one that is now revealing more tannin and structure.
90 +   Nevertheless, the wine already has accessibility and charm. It exhibits a healthy dark ruby/purple color with no signs of age. Medium- to full-bodied, with plenty of earthy, sweet, ripe fruit, a dosage of brett (a sweaty horse/old leather scent), and a long, rich, concentrated, moderately tannic finish. The wine will evolve for another 12–15 years and last even longer. Last tasted 12/95.

1988—Châteauneuf du Pape (white)   The 1988 Beaucastel blanc has a spicy, almost
·   peppery bouquet that suggests a red wine more than a white wine. In the mouth it
87   is fat, full-bodied, deep, and rich, with excellent length. While the Perrins prefer the 1989, I prefer the 1988. Last tasted 6/92.

1988—Châteauneuf du Pape Roussanne Vieilles Vignes (white)   The 1988 Roussanne
 ·   Vieilles Vignes is a marvelous example of a southern Rhône white wine, with its
90   bouquet of grilled almonds, buttery pineapple, and minerals. I also detected in the
1988, but not in the 1989, an intense scent of spring flowers, which reminded me
of acacia. The 1988 has a more honeyed as well as richer texture and better acidity. I
would be happy to own either the 1988 or 1989 Roussanne Vieilles Vignes. Like the
1989, the 1988 should drink and evolve for at least 12–15 years. Last tasted 1/96.

1987—Châteauneuf du Pape (red)   This wine offered some soft, fruity, light- to medium-
 ·   bodied, vegetal flavors in its first 4–5 years of life, but it is now displaying more
73   tannin and austerity than charm or pleasure. It is drying out and losing what little
appeal it once possessed. Drink it up. Last tasted 12/95.

1986—Châteauneuf du Pape (red)   My tasting notes on the 1986 Beaucastel reveal
 ·   alarming irregularity. The wine has gone through numerous stages, but I have con-
78   cluded that this wine continues to perform less well than it did during its first 3–4
years of life. All my recent notes have indicated a leanness, toughness, and excessive
austerity without the fruit, flesh, and fat necessary to give the wine balance. The last
bottle from my cellar exhibited a healthy dark ruby/purple color, a muted aromatic
profile (some dust, earth, and red fruits did finally emerge), and a tough, tannic, hard
personality. The color remains sound, but the wine is closed, tannic, and uninspiring.
Although I disagree with them, the Perrin brothers believe the wine needs more
time and will reemerge from its current state of dormancy. Last tasted 12/95.

1985—Châteauneuf du Pape (red)   One of the most consistent wines, and among the
 ·   easiest Beaucastels to assess, the 1985 was delicious before bottling, after bottling,
93   and has routinely offered an opulent, rich, savory style of wine with a spicy,
earthy, black-fruit, animal-scented nose, gamy, ripe, chewy, concentrated flavors,
considerable body, low acidity, and a lush, velvety-textured finish. There are no
signs of color degradation or loss of fat. It should continue to drink well for at least
another decade. A natural beauty! Last tasted 12/95.

1985—Châteauneuf du Pape (white)   Somewhat reminiscent of the 1982, this full-bodied,
 ·   rich wine has scents of nuts and pineapples, is very concentrated, extremely long,
90   and should keep for at least a decade. Anticipated maturity: now–2000. Last tasted
1/87.

1984—Châteauneuf du Pape (red)   This wine has turned out very well. Deep in color, al-
 ·   though by standards here it is not opaque. A rich, fragrant bouquet of spring flowers
87   and broad cherry fruit is intense. Full-bodied, surprisingly concentrated with some
tannin to lose, this is an elegantly wrought Beaucastel. Mature now. Last tasted 1/87.

1983—Châteauneuf du Pape (red)   Certain Beaucastel vintages possess more intense
 ·   aromas of the brett yeast (aged beef, sweaty animal–like smells) than other vin-
91   tages. The 1978, 1983, and 1990, and to a lesser extent 1981, are Beaucastel's
candidates with the largest brett population. Most Europeans love this smell, which
is reminiscent of well-hung game (as the English would say), but to Americans
weaned on pristine, pure, red- and black-fruit aromas, it can be an ungodly characteristic. Since the only ways of getting rid of it are with huge doses of flavor-
stripping SO_2, or by a sterile filtration (i.e., a wine lobotomy), it is best managed by
a winery keeping the brett population as small as possible. A little brett can add
remarkable complexity, as demonstrated by the great red Burgundies of Domaine
Roumier and Domaine Leroy, and such renowned Bordeaux as Lynch Bages and
L'Evangile. However, there is no question that when brett dominates the wine's
fruit, it is a flaw. That being said, the 1993 Beaucastel takes its level of brett (for
my palate) to the limit, but I still love the wine for its rich, flashy display of red
and black fruits, licorice, Provençal herbs, and the subtle, sweet smell of aged

beef. This full-bodied, fully mature wine should be drunk over the next 5–7 years. Last tasted 12/95.

1982—Châteauneuf du Pape (red)   This wine has never been a heavyweight, nor a distin-
•   guished effort, but it has held up longer than I would have suspected. It still
82   reveals a medium ruby color, some vegetal components, an attractive, earthy, spicy, black-pepper, and cherry-scented nose, medium body, and some fruit in a compact, compressed format. Drink it up. Last tasted 12/95.

1981—Châteauneuf du Pape (red)   A spectacular Beaucastel that came into its plateau
•   of full maturity in the mid- to late eighties, the flamboyant 1981 exhibits a knockout
94   nose of truffles, leather, cedar, black and red fruits, herbs, and pepper. Full-bodied, with layers of sweet, jammy fruit, and high glycerin, drinking this soft, velvety-textured Beaucastel is akin to eating Mourvèdre/Grenache cotton candy. There is significant amber and rust at the edge of the wine's color, so don't push fate—drink it over the next 5–7 years. Last tasted 12/96.

1980—Châteauneuf du Pape (red)   Now reaching full maturity, the 1980 Beaucastel is
•   not terribly concentrated or powerful, but has a soft, fruity, well-developed charac-
85   ter, good length, and no tannins or astringence in the finish. Drink over the next 3–5 years. Last tasted 10/86.

1979—Châteauneuf du Pape (red)   There is a Barolo-like, asphalt, melted road tar,
•   truffle-like nose to this wine, which has remained youthful and concentrated.
90   Medium- to full-bodied and compact (particularly when compared to the 1981), this is a powerful, rich, surprisingly youthful Beaucastel. The underrated 1979 may never hit the peaks of the great vintages, but it is consistent from bottle to bottle. Drink it over the next 10–15 years. Last tasted 12/95.

1978—Châteauneuf du Pape (red)   Guess which vintage of Beaucastel I purchased more
•   of than any other? The 1978 continues to perplex me. I remember the massive
90   richness and intensity it possessed both prior to bottling and for several years after bottling. It then did a complete reversal and retreated into its shell, revealing little more than a tannic, hard, charmless, severe style. Four bottles opened during the month of December (one was corked) offered little relief from the agonizing memory of the exceptional reviews I bestowed on this wine in its youth. The color remains a dark ruby with purple tints (a good sign). Although tight, the nose offers up some dusty red fruits (very little brett, thankfully), and a suggestion of ripeness. The wine hits the palate with a mass of tannin, narrowing out to a dry, austere, angular finish that is increasingly cause for concern. Nineteen seventy-eight is undoubtedly one of the slowest-maturing vintages Châteauneuf du Pape has ever had, and if I had not seen so many outstanding examples of this wine, I could easily dismiss it. Will 10 more years of bottle age reveal what I have always believed to be one of the great classic Beaucastels? Will this wine open and blossom, or will it lose its fruit and become increasingly more tannic, charmless, and austere? For now, hold on to that 1978 Beaucastel, with fingers crossed and a rabbit's foot placed close to the cellar door. Last tasted 12/95.

1976—Châteauneuf du Pape (red)   This wine reveals considerable rust and amber at the
•   edge. It possesses an earthy nose with an absence of ripe fruit. The wine remains
78   excruciatingly tannic as well as a bit dried out and desiccated, and without enough fruit, fat, or charm. It should be drunk up. Last tasted 8/96.

1973—Châteauneuf du Pape (red)   This soft, fragrant, fruity wine drank extremely well
•   in 1975–76—so well that I never dreamed it would last. Now it shows a great deal
84   of orange at the rim, but still has a good measure of soft, smoky fruit. Drink it up. Last tasted 6/85.

1972—Châteauneuf du Pape (red)   This wine was at its peak from the late seventies
· through the late eighties. It has just now begun to lose some of its sweet fruit
88 and complexity. Always a successful wine, this deep, full-bodied Beaucastel still
possesses plenty of earthy, animal, smoke, prune, and tarlike aromas and flavors.
Good underlying acidity has kept the wine fresh, but the drying tannin suggests it
is slightly past its plateau of full maturity. The wine is well structured and austere.
Drink it up. Last tasted 8/96.

1970—Châteauneuf du Pape (red)   Consistently one of the great vintages of Beaucastel,
· the last few bottles in my cellar sport the old Beaucastel label with the words
91 Domaine de Beaucastel, rather than Château de Beaucastel. The color is an impressive, opaque garnet, with some amber at the edge. The nose offers up classic
Beaucastel aromatics of soy sauce, sweet, chocolaty black fruit intermixed with
truffles, tar, animal fur, and new saddle leather. Full-bodied yet structured and
extremely well delineated, this is a gorgeously rich, vibrant, healthy Beaucastel
that should continue to drink well for another decade. Readers should recognize
that this tasting note came from bottles stored in my cellar, which were purchased
in the mid-seventies and kept at temperatures in the upper 50s. Anticipated
maturity: now–2001. Last tasted 8/96.

Older Vintages

How wines from older vintages have been stored is the key to whether or not they are still
drinkable. In a vertical tasting of Beaucastel in 1992, old vintages that came directly from
the winery did not survive the trans-Atlantic shipping. Where the wines have been purchased and stored properly, the 1967, 1966, 1961, and 1959 are undeniably great examples.
I suspect more bottles have at least one foot in the grave, unless they have come from very
cold cellars. My favorite of this trio has always been the 1959, a blockbuster, intense wine.
Other vintages that were good in their day were 1964 and 1962. Disappointing wines I have
tasted include 1954 (tasted multiple times, and, unfortunately, the birth year of François
Perrin).

CHÂTEAU BEAUCHÈNE (DOMAINE MICHEL BERNARD)* *
Address: Route de Sérignan
84100 Orange
Tel: 4-90-34-35-17
Fax: 4-90-34-87-30
Wines produced: Châteauneuf du Pape (red and white), Châteauneuf du Pape Vignobles de
la Serrière
Surface area (red): 14.8 acres
Production (red): 1,400 cases
Average age of vines: 70 years
Blend (white): 70% Clairette, 30% Grenache Blanc
(red): 80% Grenache, 10% Mourvèdre, 10% Syrah

Michel Bernard, a large négociant in the southern Rhône, acquired in the late eighties
this ancient estate that dates from the fifteenth century. This is a potentially excellent
terroir, with very old vines, and relatively dense plantings for Châteauneuf du Pape (5,000
vines per hectare—1 hectare equals 2.47 acres). The vinification is quasi-traditional, with
some stem removal and an upbringing in both foudre and small barrels. As the tasting notes
that follow suggest, the wines are straightforward, one-dimensional Châteauneuf du Papes.
They appear to be rather processed, with intense finings and filtrations. Nevertheless, there

is considerable potential given the location of this estate, and its outstanding exposition, terroir, and limestone soil base.

VINTAGES

1995—Châteauneuf du Pape Vignobles de la Serrière (red)   Although the 1995 Vignobles
  ·   de la Serrière is a medium-weight, moderately endowed wine with ripe fruit, as
83   well as an attractive, sweet palate, yet simple and one-dimensional. It should drink
        well for 4–5 years. Last tasted 6/96.

1994—Châteauneuf du Pape Vignobles de la Serrière (red)   The 1994 Vignobles de la
  ·   Serrière displays loads of herbaceous, cedary scents in its spicy nose. On the
78   palate, the wine is cleanly made, but it lacks concentration and possesses a com-
        pact, quick-to-evaporate finish. Drink it over the next 3–4 years. Last tasted 6/96.

1993—Châteauneuf du Pape Vignobles de la Serrière (red)   This is one of the more
  ·   straightforward Châteauneuf du Papes among the 1993s and 1994s I tasted. The
83   wine reveals a medium ruby color, a cherry-scented nose, medium body, a compact
        personality, and a ripe but short finish. Drink it over the next 3–4 years. Last
        tasted 9/95.

DOMAINE DE BEAURENARD (PAUL COULON)
(Cuvée Classique* * * * Cuvée Boisrenard* * * * *)

Address: 10, route d'Avignon
        84230 Châteauneuf du Pape
Tel: 4-90-83-71-79
Fax: 4-90-83-78-06
Wines produced: Châteauneuf du Pape Cuvée Classique (red), Châteauneuf du Pape Cuvée
        Boisrenard (red), Châteaux du Pape (white)
Surface area (Cuvée Classique): 67 acres
            (Cuvée Boisrenard): 7.5 acres
Production (Cuvée Classique): 10,500 cases
           (Cuvée Boisrenard): 1,800 cases
Upbringing (Cuvée Classique): 12 months in 5% new oak casks and barrels
           (Cuvée Boisrenard): 12–15 months in 20% new oak casks and barrels
Average age of vines (Cuvée Classique): 40 years
                     (Cuvée Boisrenard): 65–90 years
Blend (Cuvée Classique): 70% Grenache, 10% Syrah, 10% Mourvèdre, 7–8% Cinsault,
                         2–3% other varietals
      (Cuvée Boisrenard): 85% Grenache, 10% Mourvèdre, 5% other varietals

Domaine de Beaurenard is one of the leading estates of Châteauneuf du Pape. Proprietor Paul Coulon and his enthusiastic son, Daniel, run this large estate, which has always made classic, charming, supple Châteauneuf du Papes. And in the time since the cellars were completely modernized in the late eighties, the quality of the wine has gone from excellent to often exceptional, especially in the top vintages. The aim has always been to produce a medium-weight, smoothly textured wine. Some carbonic maceration is still done, but not as much as in the past. The grapes are never destemmed, and a portion of each crop is crushed, with the rest going into the tanks untouched. Under the influence of Daniel, Beaurenard has extended the vinification and maceration to extract more density and richness, without compromising the wine's intrinsic suppleness, charm, and silky texture.

In 1990, the Coulons began producing a luxury cuvée called Boisrenard. Approximately 1,800 cases are produced from a 7.5-acre plot of vines 65–90 years old, which are primarily

Grenache (85%) and the rest Mourvèdre, with a few unidentified, extremely old vines that are too ancient to determine precisely what they are. The Cuvée Boisrenard is aged for 12–15 months in oak casks, of which 20% are new. While there is a tendency to criticize wines such as this as being too international in style, this wine is one of the great wines of Châteauneuf du Pape, yet it has retained the typicity and character of the appellation despite its new world-ish vinification and upbringing.

The Coulons also make a white Châteauneuf du Pape. Although it has improved over recent years, it is not at the same quality level of their two red wine cuvées. They also produce a delicious, budget-priced Côtes du Rhône from their 112-acre estate in the Vaucluse, near Rasteau.

The Domaine de Beaurenard Châteauneuf du Pape estate, which is 75 acres in size, is not as morsellated as many properties. The Coulons possess four separate terroirs, but all of them are either rocky, stony soils, or they are clay/limestone based. Remarkably, there are 25 separate parcels, all located in the northwestern sector of the appellation in the lieux-dits Beaurenard, Cabrières, and Pradel. This estate is proud of its success, and visitors can be assured of a warm greeting by anyone from the Coulon family. It is also one of the few modestly sized Châteauneuf du Pape estates to be more promotion oriented as they have an interesting Musée du Vigneron adjoining their sales room. The regular cuvée is one of my favorite Châteauneuf du Papes for introducing readers to the gloriously fruity, exuberant pleasures of the wines of southern France. The Cuvée Boisrenard is a world-class, great example of the appellation, and it has been made without compromising the richness, elegance, and appeal of the regular cuvée.

VINTAGES

1995—Châteauneuf du Pape (red)   The 1995 Châteauneuf du Pape reveals the ripe fruit
· that was routinely obtained in this vintage. Its black-raspberry, licorice, smoky,
89 peppery-scented nose is captivating. Full and voluptuous, with layers of fruit, this is a lush, classic Châteauneuf du Pape that can be drunk young, or cellared for a decade or more. Last tasted 6/96.

1995—Châteauneuf du Pape Cuvée Boisrenard (red)   The 1995 Cuvée Boisrenard pos-
· sesses great fruit, plenty of tannin, higher acidity than the 1994, wonderful ele-
92 gance, and full-bodied, rich, black-raspberry, cherry, and oak-tinged aromatic and flavor profiles. This wine, the Musigny of Châteauneuf du Pape, requires another 2–3 years of cellaring, and should keep for 15 + years. Last tasted 6/96.

1994—Châteauneuf du Pape (red):   The 1994 Châteauneuf du Pape is a sexy, sweet,
· rich, black-fruit-scented wine with a whiff of Provençal herbs. It is round, generous,
89 and richly fruity, but behind the fruit and flesh are good structure and focus. This is a delicious Châteauneuf du Pape to drink over the next 7–8 years. Last tasted 6/96.

1994—Châteauneuf du Pape Cuvée Boisrenard (red)   The 1994 Cuvée Boisrenard was
· aged in small oak casks and represents this estate's most concentrated wine.
90 + Although closed and tannic, some toasty, vanillin and black-cherry scents emerge with airing. Full-bodied, concentrated, austere, and backward, this large-scaled, rich, tannic wine begs for another 2–3 years of cellaring. It should keep for 15 years. Although not as flattering initially as some of the previous vintages, good extract and richness are present. Last tasted 6/96.

1993—Châteauneuf du Pape (red)   The 1993 Châteauneuf du Pape is one of the top
· wines of the vintage. It exhibits a deep, highly extracted purple color, and a super
88 nose of sweet, jammy, black-raspberry and cassis aromas intertwined with subtle scents of herbs and spice. The lavishly rich texture avoids both heaviness and

cloyingness. It is a full-bodied, expansively flavored, well-delineated, silky-textured Châteauneuf du Pape that can be drunk now and over the next 7–8 years. Anticipated maturity: now–2002. Last tasted 6/96.

1993—Châteauneuf du Pape Cuvée Boisrenard (red)   The 1993 Châteauneuf du Pape
  ·   Boisrenard (made from a selection of the top cuvées and given some aging in new
89 +   wood) was closed when I tasted it in September. The unevolved, young-looking dense ruby/purple color is followed by toasty *pain grillé* and ripe black-cherry scents that emerge with airing. The attack offers plenty of sweet, ripe fruit, and the overall impression is one of considerable elegance and richness presented in a medium- to full-bodied, classic format. The new oak is more dominant than it was last year, but the wine could have been in a reticent state when I saw it. Anticipated maturity: 1998–2008. Last tasted 8/96.

1992—Châteauneuf du Pape (red)   The delicious 1992 Châteauneuf du Pape represents
  ·   a modern style of Châteauneuf in its wonderfully pure, black-cherry, peppery, and
86   herb-scented nose, round, soft, expansive, medium- to full-bodied flavors, and a moderate finish. Mature now. Last tasted 12/95.

1990—Châteauneuf du Pape (red)   The forward 1990 Châteauneuf du Pape looks to be
  ·   one of the best wines Beaurenard has made in over a decade. It possesses an
89   impressive dark ruby color, a huge bouquet of cloves, spice, cinnamon, black cherries, and tobacco. In the mouth, there are superrich, soft, opulent fruit flavors, a smooth-as-silk texture, and a long, luscious finish. Anticipated maturity: now–2001. Last tasted 11/94.

1990—Châteauneuf du Pape Cuvée Boisrenard (red)   This wine continues to drink splen-
  ·   didly well. Displaying no hard edges, it offers a strikingly deep ruby/purple color,
94   stunning aromatics of vanilla, and copious quantities of jammy cassis. This is followed by a lavishly rich, multidimensional, layered wine with an expansive, chewy texture, great purity and intensity, and a stunningly long finish. There is unbridled opulence and purity to this beautifully made luxury cuvée of Châteauneuf du Pape, which represents a selection of old-vine parcels of Grenache and Mourvèdre that have been aged in both small and larger oak casks. Anticipated maturity: now–2009. Last tasted 7/96.

1989—Châteauneuf du Pape (red)   The 1989 is another highly seductive, charming Châ-
  ·   teauneuf du Pape. Although it does not have the intensity of fruit and depth of the
89   1990, it is medium- to full-bodied, round, generous, and perfumed (coffee, hickory, berry, and herbs dominate), with a supple, juicy finish. Anticipated maturity: now–2000. Last tasted 6/95.

1988—Châteauneuf du Pape (red)   The fully mature 1988 is a delicious, round, amply
  ·   endowed wine that exhibits plenty of smoky, berry scents and flavors. Some creep-
87   ing rust to its deep ruby color suggests full maturity. Last tasted 11/94.

Older Vintages

For whatever reason, Beaurenard's vintages from the early eighties seemed loosely knit and lacked concentrated and focus. The only vintage I have tasted recently is the 1981, which seems to be losing its fruit and headed downward. The 1978 was always very good, but not one of the top wines of the vintage. Among the older vintages, 1967 was superb at nearly 20 years of age, but I have not tasted it since 1986.

DOMAINE BERTHET-RAYNE* */* * *

Address: Route de Roquemaure
        84350 Courthézon
Tel: 4-90-70-74-14
Fax: 4-90-70-77-85
Wines produced: Châteauneuf du Pape (red and white), Châteauneuf du Pape Cuvée
        Vieilles Vignes (red)
Surface area (white): 2.47 acres
        (red): 30 acres
        Cuvée Vieilles Vignes—3.7 acres
Production (white): 375 cases
        (red): 3,200 cases
        Cuvée Vieilles Vignes—416 cases
Upbringing (white): fermentation of 30 days, then 12–14 months in stainless steel tanks
        (red): fermentation of 21 days in cement and stainless steel vats, then 18 months
        in stainless steel vats
        Cuvée Vieilles Vignes—fermentation of 21 days in stainless steel vats,
        then 12–18 months in oak barrels, of which 30% are new and 70% are
        2–3 years old. Storage in stainless steel vats before bottling.
Average age of vines (white): 20–25 years
        (red): 30 years
        Cuvée Vieilles Vignes—50–60 years
Blend (white): 30% Grenache Blanc, 30% Clairette, 30% Bourboulenc, 10% Roussanne
        (red): 60% Grenache, 20% Syrah, 20% Counoise
        Cuvée Vieilles Vignes—60% Grenache, 20% Syrah, 20% Counoise

This estate tends to be one of the more innovative in Châteauneuf du Pape. They have increased the percentage of Roussanne in their white wine and Counoise in their red, are using some new oak, and are trying different methods to produce a more modern-style Châteauneuf du Pape. I have found the wines to be light, with a resiny, piny component. When examining the vinification and upbringing of the wines, nothing appears unusual and, in fact, the wines should be better. I am perplexed as to why they have not performed well in my tastings. Nevertheless, my instincts suggest this estate could turn things around under proprietor Christian Berthet-Rayne.

VINTAGES

1995—Châteauneuf du Pape (red)   This small domaine, with exceptionally old vines
·   (planted in 1902, 1908, and 1930), has been estate-bottling only since 1980.
86   Grenache dominates their vineyards, making up 60% of the plantings, with the
remainder being equal proportions of Syrah, Mourvèrde, Cinsault, and increasing quantities of Counoise. This deep ruby-colored, medium- to full-bodied wine reveals good ripeness, an attractive, sweet, spicy, resiny, herb-scented nose, forward flavors, and enough extract and fruit to carry it for 7–8 years. Last tasted 6/96.

1990—Châteauneuf du Pape (red)   The 1990 displays a considerable amount of tannin. I
·   found it to be a fleshy, somewhat one-dimensional wine, without the underlying
82   concentration or personality of many 1990s. Anticipated maturity: now–2000. Last
tasted 6/94.

1989—Châteauneuf du Pape (red)   The 1989 is surprisingly light and lacks concentra-
·   tion. Lean, tart, herbal, and lacking depth and character, it is not typical of the
77   vintage. Drink it up. Last tasted 6/94.

1988—Châteauneuf du Pape (red)   The 1988 has good ripeness and fruit, but is still soft,
·   straightforward, and essentially one-dimensional. It will have to be drunk over the
82   next 3–4 years. Last tasted 6/94.

DOMAINE BOIS DE BOURSAN* * * *

Address: Quartier St.-Pierre
              84230 Châteauneuf du Pape
Tel: 4-90-83-73-60
Fax: 4-90-34-46-61
Wines produced: Châteauneuf du Pape (red and white)
Surface area (white): 1.7 acres
                    (red): 27 acres
Production (white): 166 cases
                  (red): 4,125 cases
Upbringing (white): 4 months total, fermentation of 3–4 weeks in stainless steel vats, then
                  3 months in stainless steel vats, filtration before bottling
                  (red): 24–36 months total, fermentation of 3 weeks in cement and stainless steel
                  vats. The best lots are aged for 24 months in old oak casks.
Average age of vines (white): 40 years
                          (red): 40–80 years
Blend (white): 40% Clairette, 30% Grenache Blanc, 15% Bourboulenc, 15% Roussanne
      (red): 65% Grenache, 15% Mourvèdre, 15% Syrah, 5% other varietals

This estate has come on strong over the last decade. Proprietor Jean Versino created this
modestly sized estate in 1955. Interestingly, his father came from Piedmont, and Versino
readily admits his affection for the Nebbiolo cépage and a great Barolo. Domaine Bois de
Boursan owns 15 separate vineyard parcels, representing virtually every type of soil base
found in Châteauneuf du Pape, from the rocky, boulder-strewn soils to the more sandy parts
of the appellation. The wine is a consistent, traditionally made, rich Châteauneuf du Pape.
I have found the white wine irregular, but the red is well worth seeking out. It can usually
be aged for a decade or more. Domaine Bois de Boursan is an underrated estate making
very traditional, yet accessible wines.

VINTAGES

1995—Châteauneuf du Pape (red)   The 1995 is excellent, possibly outstanding. The wine
·   exhibits a deep ruby/purple color, sweet, jammy, cassis and cherry aromas, pure,
88   well-etched, full-bodied flavors, and impressive extract as well as length. There are
          no hard edges to be found in this Châteauneuf du Pape. Drink it over the next 10–
          15 years. Last tasted 6/96.
1994—Châteauneuf du Pape (red)   Although the 1994 seems less concentrated than it
·   did prior to bottling (too much fining and filtering?), it is still a very good to
89   excellent example of the appellation and the vintage. The color is a healthy dark
          ruby/garnet. The fragrant, moderately intense bouquet of herbs, olives, cedar,
          plums, and cherries is followed by a spicy, sweet, expansively flavored, medium-
          to full-bodied, forward, accessible wine. Drink it over the next 7–8 years. Last
          tasted 6/96.
1993—Châteauneuf du Pape (red)   The 1993 displays a dark ruby color with plenty of
·   purple tints. The flashy nose of ground pepper, Provençal herbs, and ripe black-
88   cherry fruit is followed by a full-bodied wine with admirable depth and richness,
          as well as light to moderate tannin. Although a structured style of Châteauneuf du

Pape, it is flattering to drink at present. Consume it over the next 10–12 years. Last tasted 6/95.

1990—Châteauneuf du Pape (red)   The 1990 offers up a vague but overripe nose of
· peaches, apricots, and black cherries. In the mouth it is a tasty, soft, loosely knit
85 wine that is ideal for drinking over the next five years. Given its spit-polished look and clipped finish, this wine must have received a serious filtration. Anticipated maturity: now–1999. Last tasted 9/94.

1989—Châteauneuf du Pape (red)   The 1989 is better balanced, with an impressive deep,
· ruby/purple color, a reticent but blossoming bouquet of herbs, vanilla, red and
89 black fruits, and a slightly resinous (pine trees?) component. Powerful, with plenty of richness, a dried-cherry fruit flavor, elevated tannins, and a heady, spicy, finish, this is a very fine 1989. Anticipated maturity: now–2006. Last tasted 11/95.

1988—Châteauneuf du Pape (red)   The 1988 is equally supple, with more of a herba-
· ceous, saltwater-scented bouquet, smooth, velvety flavors, and a moderately long
86 finish. Anticipated maturity: now–2000. Last tasted 6/94.

DOMAINE DE BOIS DAUPHIN (JEAN MARCHAND)* * *

Address: 21, route d'Orange
        84230 Châteauneuf du Pape
Tel: 4-90-83-70-34
Fax: 4-90-83-50-83
Wines produced: Châteauneuf du Pape (red and white), Châteauneuf du Pape Clos des Pontifes (red and white)
Surface area: 76.6 acres
Production (white): 1,250 cases
          (red): 7,500 cases
Upbringing (red): 2–4 years in tank and foudre; the Clos des Pontifes is aged in small
          oak casks
Average age of vines: 80 years
Blend (white): 60% Clairette, 20% Roussanne, 20% Grenache Blanc
      (red): 80% Grenache, 20% Syrah, Cinsault, and Mourvèdre

Domaine de Bois Dauphin (note that Bois Dauphin is two words, rather than one word as in Pierre Jacumin's Cuvée de Boisdauphin) has existed under proprietor Jean Marchand since the founding of the estate in 1920. It is named after the vineyard adjacent to the cellars. The well-known northern Rhône Valley oenologist Jean-Luc Colombo has encouraged Marchand to move toward a softer bottling, with less fining and filtration. The results have been mixed, but the wine is a modern-styled, fruity, soft Châteauneuf du Pape that sometimes lacks concentration but can be charming in its youth. In recent years, Marchand has begun to produce a luxury cuvée called Clos des Pontifes. This wine has benefited from partial aging in new oak, resulting in a wine with more intensity, richness, and character made in an international style. The best vintage to date has been the 1990.

VINTAGES

1993—Châteauneuf du Pape Clos des Pontifes (red)   This is the prestige cuvée from
· proprietor Jean Marchand's Domaine du Bois Dauphin. Producer Marchand tends
91 to make a light, fruity, almost carbonic maceration style of Châteauneuf du Pape for his regular cuvées, but this deluxe cuvée is a more serious wine. This cuvée, aged in a high percentage of new oak casks, is less typical of the appellation because of its new world-like style. For a Châteauneuf du Pape, I can understand

the criticism from traditionalists, but as a wine, there is much to admire. The color is a saturated dark ruby/purple, and the nose offers up scents of *pain grillé*, lush, very ripe black cherries, and floral notes. Impressively concentrated with layers of sweet, jammy fruit, this full-bodied, pure wine possesses good delineation and a long, unctuously textured finish. Anticipated maturity: now–2006. Last tasted 6/96.

1991—Châteauneuf du Pape Clos des Pontifes (white)   This is one of the two best white
  ·   wines I tasted from the otherwise uninspiring 1991 vintage. It reveals a ripe,
  87   flowery, honeyed nose, and rich, full-bodied, concentrated, impressively endowed
         flavors with a subtle touch of new oak. This offering is well above the quality of
         most 1991 white Châteauneuf du Papes. Last tasted 6/95.

1990—Châteauneuf du Pape Clos des Pontifes (red)   The 1990 exhibited considerable
  ·   tannins, a deep, purple color, fat, rich, raspberry and black-cherry fruitiness inter-
  87   twined with aromas of Provençal herbs. Drink this beefy, lusty Châteauneuf du
         Pape over the next 10 years. Last tasted 4/96.

1989—Châteauneuf du Pape Clos des Pontifes (red)   The 1989 offers a concoction of red
  ·   and black fruits in its moderately intense nose. In the mouth, there is fine ripeness,
  87   attractive suppleness, deep, well-knit flavors, and some moderate tannins in the
         long, alcoholic finish. Anticipated maturity: now–2002. Last tasted 11/93.

DOMAINE HENRI BONNEAU
(Cuvée Marie Beurrier* * * */Réserve des Célestins* * * * *)

Address: 35, rue Joseph Ducos
          84230 Châteauneuf du Pape
Tel: confidential
Fax: confidential
Wines produced: Châteauneuf du Pape (red), Châteauneuf du Pape Réserve des Célestins,
          Châteauneuf du Pape Cuvée Marie Beurrier
Surface area: 14.8 acres
Production: 1,500 cases
Upbringing: 3–4 years of aging in small barrels, and larger demi-muids and foudres. The
          wine is bottled without filtration when Henri Bonneau deems it ready.
Average age of vines: 30–45 years
Blend: 80–90% Grenache, 10–20% other varietals

It is probably no coincidence that the idiosyncratic Henri Bonneau's hodgepodge of cellars are located at the *top* of the village of Châteauneuf du Pape. His wine, like that of Rayas, belongs in a class by itself. Although totally different from Rayas, both estates rely on shy-bearing old vines of Grenache for their power and richness. Bonneau's top cuvée, the Réserve des Célestins, is a formidable and massive wine (the biggest, most forceful and powerful wine of the southern Rhône Valley), but, wow, what a thrill it gives, provided you can get your hands on a bottle or two from the 800–1,000 cases of Réserve des Célestins. A visit with the wry Henri Bonneau should be counted as one of life's more memorable encounters. He is one of the most fascinating wine personalities I have ever met. His noted Provençal twang, vicious sense of humor (particularly when aimed at the French government), and encyclopedic knowledge of cuisine are added benefits when one considers just how extraordinary his wines are. In fact, if the question is posed as to what is the quintessential Châteauneuf du Pape at the highest quality level, the answer can only be Henri Bonneau's Réserve des Célestins. The Bonneau family has been in Châteauneuf du Pape since the late eighteenth century.

Needless to say, tasting in this cellar is an experience not to be missed. Bonneau's cellar sets new standards for dinginess and crampedness. Excavation for Roman ruins below the cellar have left these caverns dotted with large black holes that can be crossed only by walking carefully across wood planks that keep visitors from falling 20–30 feet into a dark abyss. Like the late Jacques Reynaud, Bonneau is a legend in Châteauneuf du Pape, where he is widely admired as both a great winemaker and one of the village's most forceful personalities. Henri is now aided by his son, Marcel. His tiny domaine of nearly 15 acres includes most of his old vines (13 acres) in what many vignerons consider the finest terroir of Châteauneuf du Pape, La Crau. Bonneau's yields are reasonably low, but his explanation of how he makes the wines does not reveal the secrets to obtaining the extraordinary complexity, richness, and intensity they possess. Bonneau's finest vintages have a distinct taste of concentrated beef blood, combined with a powerful, thick, and viscous texture. Given Henri's admiration of great food (he is a "copain" of one of France's great gourmands, Gérard Chave), it is no surprise that he often seems more comfortable discussing his favorite foods (e.g., goat testicles) than his wines.

Unlike many wines, particularly Burgundies, as impressive as the wines are in cask, a Châteauneuf du Pape from Bonneau always tastes even better out of bottle. Bonneau is willing to declassify his cuvées of Célestins and Marie Beurrier if conditions warrant. For example, neither wine was produced in 1987, 1991, or 1993. Like his friend Jacques Reynaud, Bonneau is a late harvester, and he can be burned badly if he gets caught by October rains. So little of his wine is made that it is almost impossible to find, but I consider it a personal triumph that when I first met him a decade ago he was unwilling to sell even one bottle in America, and now several hundred cases of his liquid treasure make it to these shores. As one might expect, this has not endeared me to his clients in other countries.

Most of Bonneau's wines are enormous in concentration and character (much like the man's personality). These wines are almost immortal in terms of ageability. While I have enjoyed many memorable discussions with Henri Bonneau, one of the most remarkable events of my career was the evening spent several years ago at the wonderful La Beaugra-vière restaurant in Mondragon with Bonneau, Jacques Reynaud, noted New Jersey wine merchant Carlo Russo, and French importer Alain Junguenet. Prior to that dinner I accompanied Bonneau to Jacques Reynaud's cellar, only a mile or so away. Remarkably, it was the first time in his life that Henri Bonneau had visited Rayas.

VINTAGES

1995—Châteauneuf du Pape (Cuvées One and Two, probably Marie Beurrier)   Bonneau
    ·   is not yet sure which designations he will use for his 1994s or 1995s, but I suspect
    89   there will be both a Marie Beurrier and Réserve des Célestins. Bonneau's lighter
          cuvées of 1995 are stunning—sweet, rich, and ripe, with a concentrated essence of
          beef blood, herbes de Provence, black cherry, and cassis fruit. This is a full-bodied,
          expansive, rich, chewy wine that will drink well for 15 or more years. Last tasted
          6/96.

1995—Châteauneuf du Pape (Cuvées Three and Four, probably Réserve des
    ·   Célestins)   In his modest manner, Bonneau claims 1995 to be a "bon millésime"
    93   (vintage). Usually when Henri Bonneau says "bon" it means great. The more
          concentrated cuvées appear to merit a Réserve des Célestins classification as they
          are black/purple-colored, extremely broad, full-bodied, with huge alcohol, and
          unctuous textures. These wines should turn out to be as good as his 1988s, but
          Bonneau claims they are not the equal of his three greatest vintages, 1978, 1989,
          and 1990. Last tasted 6/96.

1994—Châteauneuf du Pape (a composite note for all the barrels)   The 1994s possess
    ·   slightly coarser tannin, but wonderfully sweet, rich, concentrated fruit, huge body,
    92   and old-vine intensity and power. Henri Bonneau's is one of the few cellars where

the bottled wines are significantly superior to the individual component parts tasted in the cellar (it's just the reverse in Burgundy). The 1994s are powerful, rich wines with the potential to be among the longest-lived and most massive wines of the vintage if the top cuvées are kept separate and bottled as Célestins, rather than blended together and bottled only as a Marie Beurrier. Last tasted 6/96.

1993—Châteauneuf du Pape   Bonneau's least favorite vintage of the last four years is
·   1993. He calls it "my vintage of worry." The 1993, which may be classified a
89   Cuvée Marie Beurrier, is soft, with no trace of rot or vegetal fruit. It reveals a deep ruby color, full body, a sweet, expansive chewiness, and earthy, truffle-like, spicy flavors. The 1993 appears to be a 10- to 12-year wine, which by Bonneau standards is short-lived. Last tasted 6/96.

1993—Châteauneuf du Pape (Cuvées One and Two)   The 1993 is an austere, thin, hard
·   wine, although several cuvées had some fruit, ripeness, and medium body. Bonneau
77   despises the vintage, using words to describe his wines that I dare not repeat. Anticipated maturity: 1998–2005. Last tasted 6/96.

1992—Châteauneuf du Pape Réserve des Célestins   This wine possesses an element of
·   overripeness, and extraordinarily sweet, black-cherry fruit intermixed with cedar,
92   smoke, grilled meat, barbecue, and chocolate aromas. Rich and full-bodied, with a fat, unctuous texture, Bonneau's top 1992 cuvées are easily the most compelling wines made in this vintage in Châteauneuf du Pape (Michel Chapoutier's Barbe Rac is the other outstanding wine of the vintage). Anticipated maturity: 1998– 2012. Last tasted 6/96.

1991—Châteauneuf du Pape   Bonneau's 1991 Châteauneuf du Pape is a major success
·   for what was a dreadful vintage in this appellation, comparable to such notoriously
89   bad years as 1984 and 1975. Bonneau declassified his Marie Beurrier and Célestins in 1991. To prove he is capable of dealing with the worst weather conditions possible, Bonneau opened a bottle of 1975 from his private stock. It unquestionably merited a 90-point score. Well-placed vineyards, low yields, and totally natural winemaking do indeed account for much of this estate's success. The 1991 displays a surprisingly intense color, a rich, leathery, meaty, herby, and black-cherry-scented nose, alcoholic, chewy flavors, and considerable body and depth. This amazing wine is the finest 1991 produced in Châteauneuf du Pape. Anticipated maturity: now–2007. Last tasted 6/96.

1990—Châteauneuf du Pape Réserve des Célestins   This is a massively endowed, thick,
·   full-bodied wine revealing an otherworldly combination of power, extract, and
100   balance. I would not trade a bottle of the small quantities of this wine to anybody, for anything. The titanic 1990 is off the charts simply because it has not yet begun to shut down and is revealing massive quantities of smoky, peppery, red and black fruits combined with an essence like liquefied beef. This full-bodied, awesomely endowed monster is more like a sauce than a beverage. Anticipated maturity: now– 2020. Last tasted 8/96.

1990—Châteauneuf du Pape Cuvée Marie Beurrier   The 1990 Cuvée Marie Beurrier is
·   nearly as profound. Bonneau feels it is lighter than his Célestins, but in Bonneau's
94   vocabulary, "light" means "massive!" This huge, concentrated wine possesses much of the same character as the 1990 Célestins, but it is slightly less tannic and powerful. However, it is unquestionably a wine of extraordinary size and enormous extract and richness. Anticipated maturity: now–2008. Last tasted 8/96.

1990—Châteauneuf du Pape Cuvée Spéciale   For the first time, Henri Bonneau produced
·   a Cuvée Speciale in 1990. The vintage was so extraordinary he let one parcel of
96   Grenache vines hang until the sugars were over 30%. In essence, this is a late-

harvest Châteauneuf du Pape with 16.5% natural alcohol and 3 grams residual sugar. It took three years to ferment on its wild yeasts and, after aging in cask and foudre for more than four years, it was bottled without filtration. To say this wine will last for 25–30 years is an understatement. When I asked Bonneau what he would serve with such a powerful, rich wine, he spent the next 20 minutes fantasizing about possible matchups. If readers want to taste the quintessential Henri Bonneau style, as well as how exciting (and exaggerated) Grenache can be when made from such a degree of ripeness and tiny yields, this wine should not be missed. Although too massive to drink now, it should become surprisingly civilized with aging. Sit on it for 7–10 years and drink it over the following two decades. For Rhône wine enthusiasts, it will likely become a collector's item worth its weight in gold. Anticipated maturity: 2001–2040. Last tasted 6/96.

1989—Châteauneuf du Pape Réserve des Célestins   If the 1990 is close to perfection,
· the 1989, 1988, and 1986 are hardly far behind. The 1989 has closed down since I
98 + first tasted it. Dark ruby/purple-colored, this wine is a huge, animalistic, prodigious Châteauneuf du Pape, with great balance, purity, and character. The massive 1989 is oozing with extract, glycerin, and personality, but like many Châteauneuf du Papes of this vintage, it is quite backward. It will benefit from another 5–10 years of cellaring. Anticipated maturity: 2002–2025. Last tasted 8/96.

1989—Châteauneuf du Pape Cuvée Marie Beurrier   The 1989 Marie Beurrier reveals a
· dark plummy color, a huge, sweet nose reminiscent of brandy-soaked fruitcake,
89 opulent, full-bodied flavors that exhibit excellent concentration and a powerful, heady, intensely spicy finish. In spite of its size, this broad-shouldered wine can be drunk now. Anticipated maturity: now–2006. Last tasted 6/96.

1988—Châteauneuf du Pape Réserve des Célestins   The 1988 Réserve des Célestins has
· always tasted better out of bottle than when I tasted it from the large foudres in
95 Bonneau's tiny, cramped, underground cellars. Much like his 1989, it is one of the greatest Châteauneuf du Papes I have ever had. The 1988, a wine of enormous depth, richness, and complexity, was drinkable early in life, but it has subsequently shut down. It has the potential to rival some of Bonneau's legendary efforts, and will probably last and develop more complexity for another 25–30 years. This is another wine of mind-boggling richness that must be placed at the top of the Châteauneuf du Pape hierarchy. Anticipated maturity: 2002–2022. Last tasted 5/96.

1988—Châteauneuf du Pape Cuvée Marie Beurrier   Though Bonneau considers the
· Cuvée Marie Beurrier to be less intense than his other cuvées, most tasters will
90 find it a wine of enormous richness and thickness. It is a great bottle of Châteauneuf du Pape, with an exotic bouquet of herbs, chocolate, red fruits, and leather. In the mouth it is velvety, rich, and a true old, heady, blockbuster style of Châteauneuf. Anticipated maturity: now–2007. Last tasted 5/96.

1986—Châteauneuf du Pape Réserve des Célestins   The 1986 Réserve des Célestins is
· unquestionably the Rhône Valley's "wine of the vintage." It is massive, nearly as
95 grand as the 1990, with more noticeable tannin, as well as layers of jammy, concentrated fruit that seems so at odds with the style of this vintage. It has barely budged since I first tasted it after bottling. Like the 1988, 1989, and 1990, it will last and evolve for another 20–30 + years. Last tasted 1/96.

1981—Châteauneuf du Pape Réserve des Célestins   Still youthful, this dark ruby/garnet-
· colored wine displays an immense nose of a smoky barbecue pit, black fruits,
93 truffles, and aged beef. With a blast of glycerin, alcohol, and extract, this monster Châteauneuf du Pape has remarkable balance for its immense size. The color

exhibits no signs of rust at the edge, only a slight lightening. Thick, juicy, and succulent, this is a lusty, hedonistic Châteauneuf du Pape that can be drunk now or cellared for another 20 years. Last tasted 6/94.

1978—Châteauneuf du Pape Réserve des Célestins   When drunk with Henri Bonneau at
·   his home, this wine was so remarkably young as to defy belief. A clone of the
99   1989–1990 blend, this structured, tannic, profoundly concentrated wine represents the essence of Châteauneuf du Pape. The huge nose of smoked herbs, olives, beef blood, and black fruits is intense. The enormous concentration, freshness, and superb balance are hallmarks of this classically profound vintage for Châteauneuf du Pape. The wine reveals amazing extract and intensity, as well as a striking youthfulness. Still young, yet complete and complex, the 1978 should prove to be uncommonly long-lived, even by Henri Bonneau's standards. Anticipated maturity: now–2020. Last tasted 6/94.

1975—Châteauneuf du Pape Réserve des Célestins   Henri Bonneau opened this wine
·   simply to prove that with time, even the most unappealing vintages (e.g., 1991,
90   1993) can do surprising things in the bottle. From a dreadful Châteauneuf du Pape vintage, this wine, from Bonneau's personal stock, exhibited an exotic, herb, *garrigue*, fruitcake, smoky-scented nose, thick, juicy, fat, ripe flavors, noticeable acidity, and a whoppingly long finish. This fully mature wine exhibits far more ripe fruit than one would expect. Anticipated maturity: now–2002. Last tasted 6/95.

1970—Châteauneuf du Pape Réserve des Célestins   Similar to the 1978, although even
·   more fragrant, the 1970 reveals some amber at the edge of its opaque garnet color.
98   The smoky, roasted-meat-scented nose is followed by a wine of immense depth, with huge quantities of glycerin and tannin. This enormously endowed wine still possesses a vigor and freshness that are more akin to a wine 5–8 years old. Anticipated maturity: now–2015. Last tasted 6/94.

Older Vintages

I might be persuaded to do just about anything to taste Henri Bonneau's 1967, 1961, 1959, 1957, etc., but the only ancient vintage I have had the privilege of tasting is the 1935, drunk with extraordinary pleasure beside the great man himself. Although fully mature and revealing some hot alcohol, the 1935 was remarkably intact, rich, deep, and, believe it or not, fruity. Miracles do not occur in this cellar by accident—this man is a phenomenal winemaker!

LE BOSQUET DES PAPES (MAURICE BOIRON)
(Cuvée Classique* * * */Cuvée Chantemerle* * * * *)

Address: Route d'Orange
        84230 Châteauneuf du Pape
Tel: 4-90-83-72-33
Fax: 4-90-83-50-52
Wines produced: Châteauneuf du Pape Cuvée Classique (red and white), Châteauneuf du
        Pape Cuvée Chantemerle (red)
Surface area (white): 3.7 acres
        (red): 54 acres
                Cuvée Chantemerle—8.6 acres
Production (white): 500 cases
        (red): 7,500 cases
                Cuvée Chantemerle—800 cases

Upbringing (white): 6 months in enamel vats
          (red): 24 months total. Fermentation of 21 days in cement vats, then 12–18
          months in old oak casks, then storage in cement tanks before bottling.
          Cuvée Chantemerle—24 months total. Fermentation of 21 days in cement
          vats, then 12–18 months in old oak casks, then storage in cement tanks
          before bottling.
Average age of vines (white): 45–50 years (oldest is 90 years)
          (red): 45 years
          Cuvée Chantemerle—90 years
Blend (white): One-third each Grenache, Clairette, Bourboulenc
          (red): 70% Grenache, 10% Syrah, 10% Mourvèdre, 10% Cinsault
          Cuvée Chantemerle—70% Grenache, 10% Syrah, 10% Mourvèdre, 5% Cin-
          sault, 5% Vaccarèse

This modest-sized estate of 57 acres is located just behind the village of Châteauneuf du Pape on the road (D 68) to the ruins of Pope John's castle. Le Bosquet des Papes is a member of the growers' association called Prestige et Tradition. The estate produces both red and white wine. The white wine is adequate but dull. The red wine is one of the appellation's better wines, possessing a breadth of flavor and depth that is quite profound. The wine is made from a blend of 70% Grenache, with the rest equal parts of Syrah, Mourvèdre, and Cinsault. The wine is vinified in the classic manner and aged 18 months in large oak casks. Madame Josette Boiron, who seems to know all the goings-on in Châteauneuf du Pape, and her shy husband run this family-owned estate with a great deal of care. I have no experience with any vintages older than 1978, but I see no reason not to expect Le Bosquet des Papes to last at least a decade in the top vintages. The wine has also demonstrated excellent consistency in so-called off years.

The vinification and upbringing of Bosquet des Papes are totally traditional. Nothing is destemmed, and the wine is aged in old wood foudres and small oak casks prior to multiple bottlings. The red wine receives a light filtration at the cellars of Prestige et Tradition, the high-quality growers' group that the Boirons joined years ago. The white wine has its malolactic blocked and is sterile-filtered. Le Bosquet des Papes' vineyards are primarily situated in the northern part of the appellation, with the rockier vineyards near Cabrières, and those on gravelly, more sandy and claylike soil near Vaudieu and Rayas, and in the southeastern part of the appellation toward Sorgues.

In 1990, the Boirons launched a luxury cuvée called Chantemerle, produced from parcels of 90-year-old Grenache. The 1990 was an awesome Châteauneuf du Pape, undoubtedly one of the greatest examples of this superb vintage. That wine has been followed by a bevy of exceptional wines, including the 1993, 1994, and 1995. Unfortunately, the small production of 800 cases makes this wine difficult to find.

VINTAGES

1995—Châteauneuf du Pape (red)   The 1995 Châteauneuf du Pape reveals a purple hue
·   to its color, great ripeness, and admirable glycerin, structure, and power. It is a
89   full-bodied, concentrated, powerful Bosquet des Papes that should be the finest
     regular cuvée made at this estate since 1989 and 1990. Last tasted 6/96.
1995—Châteauneuf du Pape Cuvée Chantemerle (red)   The 1995 Cuvée Chantemerle
·   exhibits that special overripe aroma of kirsch, jammy black cherries, and raspber-
91   ries. There is an element of *surmaturité*, as well as a sweet, thick, unctuously
     textured attack, full body, significant structure and tannin, and outstanding purity.

This large-scaled, young as well as unevolved wine should hit its peak by the turn of the century and last for 10–15 years. Last tasted 6/96.

1994—Châteauneuf du Pape (red)   The 1994 Châteauneuf du Pape exhibits plenty of
·   sweet black-cherry fruit, the unmistakable scents of Provençal herbs and *garrigue*,
88   excellent density, admirable glycerin and ripeness, and a long, full-bodied, heady finish. This rich, chewy wine tastes far better out of bottle than it did from foudre. Drink it now and over the next 6–8 years. Last tasted 6/96.

1994—Châteauneuf du Pape Cuvée Chantemerle (red)   The 1994 Cuvée Chantemerle
·   boasts an intense nose of black raspberries, smoked meats, licorice, and wood.
90   There is considerable structure and tannin to this full-bodied, powerful, exceptionally concentrated wine. It was closed when I saw it, leading me to believe that there is even more to it than my positive notes suggest. This wine requires 2–3 years of cellaring, and it should keep for 15+ years. I am sure the alcohol easily exceeds 14%. Last tasted 6/96.

1993—Châteauneuf du Pape (red)   The 1993 Châteauneuf du Pape reveals a dark ruby
·   color with some garnet at the rim. The wine possesses moderately high tannin,
87   plenty of grip and structure, as well as good ripeness and richness. It is an excellent Châteauneuf du Pape that should evolve nicely over the next 2–3 years and remain drinkable for a decade after its release. I have a slight reservation about the tannin, but Le Bosquet des Papes' track record has been exemplary for producing well-balanced, ageworthy Châteauneuf du Pape. Anticipated maturity: 1998–2008. Last tasted 7/96.

1993—Châteauneuf du Pape Cuvée Chantemerle (red)   The dark, saturated ruby/purple-
·   colored 1993 Cuvée Chantemerle offers a tight but promising nose of roasted
90   Provençal herbs, *garrigue*, and sweet berry fruit. Full-bodied, spicy, dense, and moderately tannic, this backward 1993 requires 3–5 years of cellaring. It is one of the richest and most complete wines of the vintage. Anticipated maturity: 1999–2012. Last tasted 7/96.

1992—Châteauneuf du Pape (red)   The 1992 Châteauneuf du Pape is a round, delicious
·   wine with surprising robustness and power for a Châteauneuf from this medium-
86   weight vintage. The wine exhibits a sweet, jammy fruitiness and medium to full body. Mature now. Last tasted 11/95.

1990—Châteauneuf du Pape (red)   The 1990 red Châteauneuf du Pape is marginally
·   superior to the 1989. The color is a saturated opaque purple, and the nose offers
92   up beautifully pure, superripe aromas of black cherries, cassis, herbs, and pepper. In the mouth there is splendid ripeness, a rich, full-bodied texture, as well as a long, moderately tannic, structured, immensely impressive finish. Anticipated maturity: now–2007. Last tasted 12/95.

1990—Châteauneuf du Pape Cuvée Chantemerle (red)   The opaque purple/black-colored
·   1990 Cuvée Chantemerle is a spectacular wine with a staggering perfume of black
98   fruits, minerals, pepper, and flowers. Exceptionally rich, with stupendous concentration and a viscous texture suggesting low yields and old vines, this profound Châteauneuf du Pape is outrageously delicious, even decadent; it should last for two decades or more. An exceptional effort! Anticipated maturity: now–2012. Last tasted 12/95.

1989—Châteauneuf du Pape (red)   The 1989 is a potentially long-lived wine. Having lost
·   much of its baby fat, it is displaying a more structured, tannic, backward style than
90   it did during its first year in cask. The opaque dark ruby/purple color and the huge bouquet of cassis, herbs, and spices are followed by powerfully built, dense, concentrated flavors that exhibit the potential for at least 15 or more years of aging. Unlike the 1983 and 1985 Bosquet des Papes, this will not be a forward, preco-

cious, or flattering style of Châteauneuf du Pape to drink young. It is, rather, a wine that will require 3–5 years in the cellar before it reaches maturity. Structurally, texturally, and aromatically, the 1989 Bosquet des Papes is the finest wine this domaine has made since their fabulous 1978, which is just now reaching its apogee. Anticipated maturity: 1999–2007. Last tasted 12/95.

1988—Châteauneuf du Pape (red)   The 1988 is a much more flattering style of wine, offering a bouquet redolent with aromas of blackcurrants, tobacco, and cedar. A **88** velvety-textured wine, this rich, full-bodied, admirably concentrated wine, with flavors that suggest fruitcake, should drink well young but last for up to a decade. Anticipated maturity: now–2004. Last tasted 1/95.

1985—Châteauneuf du Pape (red)   Moderately deep ruby in color, this fully mature wine has an herb, olive, and black-cherry-scented bouquet, robust, round, soft flavors, **87** plenty of length, and a loosely knit finish. It is at its peak of maturity and needs to be drunk up. Mature now. Last tasted 1/96.

1983—Châteauneuf du Pape (red)   Maturing gracefully, as well as more slowly than the 1985, the 1983 Châteauneuf du Pape reveals a ruby/garnet color, an expansive **90** fragrance of tobacco, Provençal herbs, smoke, and spices. This finely crafted, medium- to full-bodied, rich wine is fully mature, but in no danger of losing its fruit. Mature now. Last tasted 6/96.

Older Vintages

I have not tasted the 1982 in many years, but it is undoubtedly now past its prime. The 1981 was drinking well in the late eighties, but no bottles remain in my cellar. The 1978 was an outstanding wine when last tasted in 1986.

CHÂTEAU CABRIÈRES (LOUIS ARNAUD)* * */* * * *

Address: Route d'Orange
        84230 Châteauneuf du Pape
Tel: 4-90-83-73-58
Fax: 4-90-83-75-55
Wines produced: Châteauneuf du Pape (red and white), Châteauneuf du Pape Cuvée Prestige (red)
Surface area (white): 7.4 acres
            (red): 62 acres
                  Cuvée Prestige—12.4 acres
Production (white): 1,125 cases
            (red): 9,400 cases
                  Cuvée Prestige—875 cases
Upbringing (white): 4–5 months in stainless steel vats
            (red): fermentation of 3 weeks in stainless steel and earthenware-lined vats, then 12–18 months in old oak casks
                  Cuvée Prestige—fermentation of 3 weeks in stainless steel vats, then 12–24 months in oak barrels, of which 30–50% are new and the rest are 1–2 years old. The wine is stored in stainless steel vats until bottling.
Average age of vines (white): 35 years
                   (red): 45 years
                         Cuvée Prestige—90 years
Blend (white): 30% Clairette, 30% Grenache Blanc, 30% Bourboulenc, 10% Roussanne
       (red): 50% Grenache, 12% Syrah, 12% Mourvèdre, 8% Cinsault, 18% other varietals
             Cuvée Prestige—a mixture of all 13 varietals

The Domaine de Cabrières is situated on the plateau near Mont Redon. Virtually everyone agrees that this area has the best potential for producing great Châteauneuf du Pape. It is an especially stony area, and the vineyards adjacent to Cabrières are among the most forbidding looking yet fascinating in the entire appellation.

The winemaking philosophy at Cabrières is clearly inspired by state-of-the-art technology. Both the winery and the wines have that new world feel of being the products of technical razzle-dazzle where statistics and stability are the primary ends sought. The results are, of course, wines where the vintage differences are muted and much of the character and flavor eviscerated by too much fining and filtration. After filtering the wines twice at Cabrières, M. Arnaud says proudly, "We guarantee that all the germs and microbes harmful to the wine are removed." Yet tasting the current wines proves that this is not all that has been exorcised from the wine—it has lost its soul as well. This is all rather sad; old vintages of Cabrières such as the 1961, 1966, and 1967 are still splendidly rich and complex, hardly examples of bad wine ruined by a few microbes or germs.

The red wines being produced today are very cleanly made with moderately intense aromas and flavors of cherry fruit and spices. They are good wines that exhibit consistency from vintage to vintage. Yet given the potential of their vineyards, the fact that their Châteauneuf tastes much like many others produced in this style is undeniably sad. Cabrières spends 12 to 18 months in small oak casks and large foudres. The Arnauds have begun to employ some new oak barrels for aging part of their red wine.

The wines here are good, but the older vintages of Cabrières, produced before the advent of dual filtration and the centrifuge, are indeed remarkable wines with character and majestic flavors. While the same cannot be said for the likes of the contemporary vintages, I believe the Arnauds have been trying to put more intensity and character into recent vintages. Certainly the Cuvée Prestige, from a 12.4-acre parcel of 90-year-old vines, has been very good to nearly outstanding over recent vintages.

This wine is popular in Europe, where consumers and restaurant sommeliers do not want to take the time to deal with wines containing a *dépôt* (sediment).

VINTAGES

1995—Châteauneuf du Pape (red)   The 1995 reveals a less flattering style than the 1994.
·   It offers a spicy, peppery nose, better acidity, but not the richness or intensity of
84   the 1994. It will certainly age longer given its structural profile. Last tasted 6/96.

1995—Châteauneuf du Pape Cuvée Prestige (red)   The 1995 Cuvée Prestige (made from
·   the estate's oldest vines) is a dense, rich, full-bodied wine, with an opaque dark
88   ruby/garnet color, decent acidity, a smoky, roasted-herb character, and copious
     quantities of sweet red and black fruit. The wine boasts good glycerin, high alcohol,
     and a well-delineated personality. Anticipated maturity: 1998–2006. Last tasted
     6/96.

1994—Châteauneuf du Pape (red)   From bottle, this wine is not nearly as rich and
·   impressive as it was from barrel. I suspect an aroma- and flavor-stripping fining
86   and/or filtration did the damage. Nevertheless, enough of the wine has survived to
     merit a recommendation. It possesses an attractive ripe nose of sweet cherry fruit,
     Provençal herbs, and pepper. Medium- to full-bodied, with excellent ripeness and
     an open-knit, soft, creamy texture, this medium to dark ruby-colored wine should
     be drunk over the next 7–8 years. If only someone could persuade Château Ca-
     brières to abandon fining and filtration (at least for those cuvées sent to America),
     I am sure this wine would be far more impressive. Anticipated maturity: now–
     2002. Last tasted 6/96.

1992—Châteauneuf du Pape Cuvée Prestige (red)   This wine exhibits aromas of black
·   olives, cassis, and Provençal herbs, a spicy, medium- to full-bodied palate, excel-
88   lent richness, and a chewy texture. Long and succulent, with decent acidity and
light tannin, it should be drunk over the next 7–8 years. Last tasted 6/95.

1990—Châteauneuf du Pape (red)   The 1990 offers a superripe nose of apricot, peach,
·   and black-cherry fruit. In the mouth, the element of *surmaturité* continues with a
86   sweet, jammy red-fruit character. Low in acidity, crammed with glycerin and rich
fruit, this should be a seductive red wine for drinking over the next 5–7 years. Last
tasted 6/94.

1990—Châteauneuf du Pape Cuvée Prestige (red)   One would have to go back to their
·   exquisite 1961 to find a Châteauneuf du Pape from Cabrières as superb as their
90   1990 Cuvée Prestige. This selection from their oldest vines is superb. But I wonder
if the bottling that arrives in America will be as profound as what I tasted in
France? What I tasted was exquisite. It had obviously seen some new oak given
the subtle vanillin, smoky character in the fabulously dramatic, earthy, black-fruit-
scented, sweet nose. In the mouth the wine displays full body, exquisite depth
and richness, as well as fine grip and focus. This flashy, immensely impressive,
velvety-textured wine can be drunk young, but it should easily last for 15 or more
years. Last tasted 6/94.

1989—Châteauneuf du Pape Cuvée Prestige (red)   The 1989 Cuvée Prestige, a blend of
·   50% Grenache, 14% Syrah, 12% Mourvèdre, 10% Cinsault, and the rest a field
89   blend of other varietals, is one of the best Châteauneuf du Pape Cabrières has
made since their profound 1961. The huge, smoky, hickory, black-cherry, and
herb-scented nose is followed by a rich wine that adroitly marries power and
finesse. There is expansive, sweet, ripe fruit, decent acidity for focus, and moderately high tannin levels in the long, lusty finish. How encouraging it is to see this
great domaine turn out a wine of such stature. Anticipated maturity: now–2006.
Last tasted 6/95.

Older Vintages

Cabrières 1959 and 1961 were superb Châteauneuf du Papes, but it has been nearly a
decade since I tasted either. Made in the old, rich, full-bodied style, they possessed more
intensity when fully mature than most younger vintages. I have tasted the 1967 twice, and
the most recent tasting, marred by a slightly corked bottle, was certainly a very good effort,
as was the 1966. I have not tasted either vintage in over a decade. Other more recent
vintages, such as the 1985, 1983, 1982, 1981, 1979, and 1978, were competent, correct
wines, but not exciting. Well-stored vintages, such as 1961 and 1959, would no doubt be
fairly priced if they appeared in wine auctions.

LES CAILLOUX (ANDRÉ BRUNEL)* * * * *

Address: 6, chemin du Bois de la Ville
        84230 Châteauneuf du Pape
Tel: 4-90-83-72-62
Fax: 4-90-83-51-07
Wines produced: Châteauneuf du Pape (red and white), Châteauneuf du Pape Cuvée Cen-
        tenaire (red)
Surface area (white): 4.9 acres
        (red): 47 acres
        Cuvée Centenaire—5.6 acres

Production (white): 750 cases
                 (red): 6,900 cases
                         Cuvée Centenaire—500 cases
Upbringing (white): fermentation of 15–21 days in stainless steel vats, then 5 months in
                 stainless steel vats.
                 (red): fermentation of 3–4 weeks in enamel vats, then a percentage of yield goes
                 into oak barrels, of which one-third are new and two-thirds 1–2 years old.
                 The rest of the yield remains in enamel-lined cement vats for 18 months.
                 Cuvée Centenaire—Fermentation of 3–4 weeks in enamel vats, then 50%
                 of the yield goes into new oak barrels for 18 months, and the rest stays in
                 enamel vats.
Average age of vines (white): 30 years
                 (red): 60 years
                         Cuvée Centenaire—100+ years (vineyard planted in 1889)
Blend (white): 30% Grenache Blanc, 30% Roussanne, 30% Clairette, 10% Bourboulenc
     (red): 65% Grenache, 20% Mourvèdre, 10% Syrah, 5% other varietals
           Cuvée Centenaire—90% Grenache, 10% other varietals

André Brunel, who resembles the movie actor William Hurt, must be in his early fifties, but he looks ten years younger. He has always been one of the more serious producers in Châteauneuf du Pape, and I am thrilled to write that since I first reported on his wines 10 years ago, the quality at Les Cailloux has risen higher and higher. From this 52-acre estate, André Brunel produces powerful yet rich, elegant, concentrated wines that have gone from strength to strength since the late eighties. His vineyards are morsellated, but a large segment is planted near Mont Redon, on the famed *galets roulés*. Brunel, who took over from his father in the early seventies, comes from a family that has lived in Châteauneuf du Pape since the eighteenth century. His enthusiasm and leadership qualities have not gone unnoticed in the village, where he has a prominent position with one of the two syndicates that govern the appellation, as well as his own growers' group, Les Reflets.

Brunel has never been content to rest on his accomplishments, always challenging the old ways while examining and questioning newer methods. He has gradually increased the percentage of Roussanne in the very good white wine made at Les Cailloux, and in the red, Syrah and Mourvèdre have taken on increasing importance in the final blend. In 1989 Brunel launched a limited-production Cuvée Centenaire, made from a 5.6-acre parcel of vines that were planted in 1889. This wine is primarily Grenache.

The flexible approach to winemaking that exists at Les Cailloux extends to Brunel's position on destemming. Since Brunel recognized that the stems were often not physiologically mature and imparted too much acidity and bitterness, virtually all of the Mourvèdre and most of the Syrah and Grenache have been destemmed. Prior to 1988, Brunel kept an open mind with respect to fining and filtration. In vintages where the wine did not fall bright and clear, he did a minimal fining and filtering. In those years where there were no suspended protein or haziness, the wines were bottled unfiltered. However, since the 1988 vintage, Brunel decided to eliminate both fining and filtration for his red wines. The Cuvée Centenaire has always been bottled unfiltered.

Brunel's wines were good though lacking consistency in the seventies and early eighties, but they have been in top form since the late eighties. His Châteauneuf du Pape is usually drinkable when released, but it is capable of 10–15 years of aging. The Cuvée Centenaire, made in 1989, 1990, and 1995, is a wine of extraordinary opulence and richness, and although very drinkable young, it is capable of lasting for two decades or more. André Brunel is one of the bright shining lights of Châteauneuf du Pape.

Note: The reviews that follow are from the cuvée of Les Cailloux exclusively selected and sold in the American market by importer Robert Kacher. This cuvée is different than the cuvée of Les Cailloux sold elsewhere in the world. The American cuvée consists of 1,500 cases that see a higher percentage of new oak, with the Mourvèdre and Syrah aged in 25% new oak casks, and the rest in older barrels and foudres. The Cuvée Centenaire is the same wine in America as elsewhere.

VINTAGES

1995—Châteauneuf du Pape (red)   The 1995 Châteauneuf du Pape comes close to rival-
· ing Brunel's magnificent 1990. The wine displays a deeper ruby/purple color than
92 the 1994, as well as outstanding ripeness, exceptional richness, an inner core of sweet, highly extracted fruit, and a long, cassis-flavored finish. This pure, moder- ately tannic, impressively built wine explodes on the back of the palate. It will be accessible when released, and will last for 15 years. Last tasted 6/96.

1994—Châteauneuf du Pape (red)   Brunel has produced one of the finest 1994 Châ-
· teauneuf du Papes, a full-bodied, impressively textured and concentrated wine that
90 is not far off the mark of his great 1989 and 1990. The 1994 exhibits a deep ruby/ purple color, a wonderful Provençal nose of seaweed, black olives, and copious quantities of black and red cherries and raspberries. Full-bodied, with a soft, silky texture, and outstanding purity, this is a long, well-balanced, harmonious wine to drink over the next 10–12 years. Last tasted 6/96.

1993—Châteauneuf du Pape (red)   The 1993 may never reach the level of the sumptuous
· 1990, but it is equal to Brunel's 1988. The wine reveals an impressive dark ruby/
90 purple color, a fragrant, textbook nose of *garrigue*, and sweet, black-cherry fruit. Ripe and full-bodied, with an inner core of sweetness and richness, this admirable Châteauneuf du Pape is soft enough to drink now, but it can be cellared for 10–12 years. Last tasted 6/96.

1992—Châteauneuf du Pape (red)   The 1992 (remember, the cuvée I am describing is
· the one sold to the American importer) represents 850 cases of Brunel's oldest
92 vines aged in 15–20% new oak. The wine is one of the superstars of what is an average to slightly above average vintage. It reveals an impressively saturated dark ruby/purple color, a profound, sweet, exotic nose of black raspberries, spices, and sweet vanillin. Full-bodied, dense, and concentrated, with gobs of glycerin, extract, and high alcohol, this decadently styled Châteauneuf du Pape should be drunk over the next 10 years. Last tasted 12/95.

1990—Châteauneuf du Pape (red)   The sumptuous 1990 Châteauneuf du Pape, with its
· slightly higher alcohol and more open-knit style, tends to be more open and less
93 structured than the equally impressive but more backward 1989. Don't forget that many 1990s attained 14.5–15% natural alcohol. The 1990 exhibits a dark ruby color with purple nuances. The nose offers knockout proportions of jammy black- cherry fruit intertwined with sweet fruitcake and Provençal herb aromas. The wine is full-bodied, rich, well balanced, and concentrated, with gorgeously integrated acidity, tannin, and an alcohol level that surpasses 14%. This sumptuous, juicy, full, flavorful wine is drinking well, yet it is capable of lasting for another 10–12 years. This is a superb Châteauneuf du Pape. Last tasted 8/96.

1990—Châteauneuf du Pape Cuvée Centenaire (red)   This is a fabulous wine. The opaque
· dark ruby/purple color suggests fine extraction of flavor. The nose displays an
96 almost Guigal Côte Rôtie La Mouline profoundness. A floral, sweet black-raspberry character in the bouquet, combined with smoky new oak and minerals, provides

excitement. In the mouth, the wine is full-bodied and exceptionally generous, with a sweet taste due to the fabulous ripeness and richness of the fruit. The finish is opulent, voluptuously textured, and long. While the 1990 is not as robust and concentrated as the 1989, it offers more complexity and finesse in a more up-front style. The new oak adds a subtle dimension to the wine's lavish fruit and richness. I would love to see how this wine would perform in a blind tasting of 1990 grand cru Burgundies, particularly from the appellation of Richebourg. The 1990 Cuvée Centenaire should provide fabulous near-term drinking and last for 12–15 years. Last tasted 1/96.

1989—Châteauneuf du Pape (red)   The 1989 Les Cailloux is a superb wine, with a black/
·   purple color, a huge nose of leather, cedar, exotic spices, and red and black fruits.
93   In the mouth it is richer and fuller-bodied than the 1990, with considerably more tannin. It is Brunel's best effort since his splendid 1978. The finish is long, concentrated, and impressive. Give this wine at least 4–5 years in the cellar; it will last for up to two decades. Last tasted 1/96.

1989—Châteauneuf du Pape Cuvée Centenaire (red)   For those lucky enough to run
·   across any of Brunel's prestige cuvée, the 1989 Les Cailloux Cuvée Centenaire is
95   truly extraordinary. There were a number of monumental Châteauneuf du Papes made in 1989, but this is one of the best. As great as the regular cuvée is, the 1989 Cuvée Centenaire is even richer, deeper in color, with even more layers of concentrated fruit built into its massive framework. All of this comes together in a remarkably well-balanced format for such a rich, full wine. The finish must last for well over a minute. What is so impressive is the penetrating, explosive bouquet of minerals, licorice, black fruits, and Asian spices. This Châteauneuf du Pape is approachable now, but like so many of the great wines of the appellation, it will improve for at least another 10–15 years and last for 20 or more. Fabulous! Last tasted 1/96.

1988—Châteauneuf du Pape (red)   The 1988 offers a complex bouquet of peppers, spices,
·   black fruits, and herbs, followed by a rich, medium- to full-bodied, velvety-textured
89   wine that is complex yet more forward and less concentrated than the 1989. Anticipated maturity: now–2004. Last tasted 4/96.

1985—Châteauneuf du Pape (red)   Like so many 1985 Châteauneuf du Papes (Beaucastel
·   and Henri Bonneau are noteworthy exceptions), Les Cailloux's offering has turned
86   out to be a good but uninspiring wine. The baby fat possessed by so many 1985 Châteauneufs when young quickly fell away to reveal wines with less body than originally believed. The 1985 Les Cailloux is soft and herbaceous, with good fruit, medium to full body, and a smooth, round texture. Drink it up as its color has begun to reveal significant amber and rust. Last tasted 1/96.

1983—Châteauneuf du Pape (red)   This wine has developed well. Undoubtedly a success
·   for the vintage, the wine has a good, deep color, a spicy, black-cherry-scented
87   bouquet, some subtle herbaceousness, full body, and considerable length. Antici-pated maturity: now–2000. Last tasted 12/93.

1978—Châteauneuf du Pape (red)   Finally, this vintage has reached full maturity. Deep
·   garnet-colored, with smoky, cedary, tobacco, and jammy cherry-scented aromas,
90   this is a classic, full-bodied, deep, succulent wine. Mouth-filling and complex, it will drink well for another 10 years. Last tasted 4/96.

CAVE SAINT-PIERRE* *

Tel: 4-90-83-72-14
Fax: 4-90-83-77-23

This huge négociant offers a diverse array of wines, including southern Rhône wines, wines from Provence, and miscellaneous Languedoc-Roussillon offerings entitled only to a vin de pays designation. They produce a competent, medium- to full-bodied, chunky, husky Châteauneuf du Pape. It is neither insipid nor compelling. It is easy to criticize vast, commercial concerns such as Cave St.-Pierre, but the bottom line is that the quality of the wines is at least acceptable, and occasionally above average.

CELLIER DES PRINCES* *

Tel: 4-90-70-21-44
Fax: 4-90-70-27-56

The only cooperative in Châteauneuf du Pape, the Cellier des Princes (founded in 1924) has over 500 members and controls more than 588 vineyards within the appellation. The average age of the vines is 30 years. According to their records, they are exploiting vineyards that on an average contain 80% Grenache, 10% Mourvèdre and Syrah, and 10% miscellaneous varietals. This is not an exciting Châteauneuf du Pape. While it is acceptable, it hardly raises the image of Châteauneuf du Pape. Competently made, fruity, and soft, it requires drinking during its first 5–6 years of life. If tasters concentrated very hard, they would find aromas of *garrigue*, herbes de Provence, and pepper.

DOMAINE DE CHANSSAUD* * *

Address: 84100 Orange
Tel: 4-90-34-23-51
Fax: 4-90-34-50-20
Wines produced: Châteauneuf du Pape (red and white)
Surface area (white): 5.1 acres
    (red): 96 acres
Production (white): 750 cases
   (red): 15,000 cases
Upbringing (white): 4 months total; fermentation of 15 days in cement and epoxy vats, then
    4 months in cement vats
   (red): 18–20 months total; fermentation of 15–20 days in epoxy vats, then 15%
    of the yield goes into demi-muids (some new oak, the oldest casks are 3
    years) for 8–12 months. The rest of the yield stays in cement vats.
Average age of vines (white): 20 years
    (red): 60 years
Blend (white): 70% Clairette, 20% Grenache Blanc, 10% Bourboulenc, Roussanne, and
    other varietals
   (red): 80% Grenache, 8–10% Syrah, 6% Mourvèdre, 4% Cinsault

Proprietor Patrick Jaume's cellars are located halfway between Châteauneuf du Pape and Orange. The origins of this estate date from 1772. Like so many estates in this appellation, there are many parcels (15 in this case) of vines, with almost all on clay/stony soils. My tastings have revealed a commercial, modern style of Châteauneuf du Pape that is fruity, soft, and best drunk within the first 5–7 years after the vintage. I have very limited experience with the white Châteauneuf du Pape, but those vintages I have tasted have been one-dimensional.

VINTAGES

1995—Châteauneuf du Pape (red)   The 1995 Châteauneuf du Pape was just emerging
·   from malolactic fermentation when I tasted it, so this note may turn out to be too
77   severe given the fact that wines are notoriously difficult to judge immediately after
   malolactic. The wine tastes lean and tannic, with surprisingly high acidity. Last
   tasted 6/96.

1994—Châteauneuf du Pape (red)   Prior to bottling, the 1994 Châteauneuf du Pape
·   exhibited a lot more flesh and richness, but as is the tendency of so many Châ-
85   teauneuf du Pape estates, Chanssaud has undoubtedly undergone a fining and
   filtration, robbing it of considerable potential. Readers can blame the oenologists
   of the village who advocate such techniques, as well as the uneducated wine
   consumers who do not want any sediment in their wines. The pleasant, soft, round,
   forward 1994 possesses attractive olive and jammy cherry scents, a medium ruby
   color, and low acidity. It is ideal for drinking over the next 3–4 years. Last tasted
   6/96.

1993—Châteauneuf du Pape (red)   The soft, fruity, midweight 1993 Châteauneuf du Pape
·   should be consumed over the next 5–6 years. Last tasted 9/95.
85

1990—Châteauneuf du Pape (red)   This 1990 offers a sweet, almost apricot- and rasp-
·   berry jam–scented nose that suggests that proprietor Jaume harvested later than
85   others. In the mouth the wine is expansive, slightly sweet, with round, soft flavors.
   An enjoyable, commercial style of Châteauneuf du Pape, it is ideal for drinking
   over the next 4–6 years. Last tasted 6/93.

1989—Châteauneuf du Pape (red)   The 1989 is surprisingly light, straightforward, and
·   one-dimensional. Last tasted 6/93.
76

1988—Châteauneuf du Pape (red)   The 1988 was medium-bodied and spicy, with ade-
·   quate fruit, but was overall a one-dimensional wine lacking depth and concentra-
82   tion. Last tasted 6/92.

DOMAINE CHANTADU* * *

Address: 84230 Châteauneuf du Pape
Tel: 4-90-83-72-87
Fax: 4-90-83-50-93
Wines produced: Châteauneuf du Pape (red and white)
Surface area: 40 acres
Production: 3,500 cases
Upbringing (red): 12–14 months in oak foudres
Average age of vines: 35 years
Blend (white): 60% Grenache Blanc, 40% Clairette
      (red): 80% Grenache, 10% Cinsault, 10% Syrah

This estate, owned by Jean Comte de Lauze, was founded in 1976. Another morsellated estate, with most of the vineyards possessing a northerly or southerly exposure, and planted on limestone and clay soils, Domaine Chantadu tends to produce light, fruity, soft wines that have consistently scored in the mid-eighties. The best vintage I have tasted to date was the 1990, which should have been drunk within the first 6–7 years of the vintage.

VINTAGES

1990—Châteauneuf du Pape (red)   Domaine Chantadu's 1990 Châteauneuf du Pape, the
  ·   second-prize winner in the annual Festival of St.-Marc, displays overripe aromas
  86   of oranges, apricots, and peaches. In the mouth the wine exhibits some richness,
        soft tannins, medium to full body, as well as plenty of heady alcohol. I continue to
        be surprised by the fact that the wines that frequently win this festival (the produc-
        ers of Châteauneuf du Pape serve as the judges) are usually made in an up-front,
        commercial, medium- to full-bodied, alcoholic style. I should also point out that
        three of this village's superstars, Rayas, Bonneau, and Beaucastel, do not partici-
        pate in the festival. Last tasted 9/94.

1989—Châteauneuf du Pape (red)   The 1989 is a relatively commercial, open-knit, soft,
  ·   direct style of Châteauneuf du Pape, with a bouquet of pepper, herbs, and berries.
  82   In the mouth there is medium body, soft, ripe fruit, and a round, alcoholic finish.
        Drink it over the next 3–5 years. Last tasted 9/94.

1988—Châteauneuf du Pape (red)   The 1988 is also ripe and alcoholic, but has more
  ·   focus to its heady, fleshy, chocolaty flavors. It is a very good example of a modern
  85   style Châteauneuf du Pape that is ideal for drinking over the next 4–5 years. Last
        tasted 6/93.

DOMAINE CHANTE-CIGALE* * *

Address: Avenue Louis Pasteur
        84230 Châteauneuf du Pape
Tel: 4-90-83-70-57
Fax: 4-90-83-51-28
Wines produced: Châteauneuf du Pape (red and white), Châteauneuf du Pape Cuvée Spéci-
        ale (white)
Surface area (white): 15 acres
              (red): 86 acres
                  Cuvée Spéciale—2.47 acres
Production (white): 2,500 cases
              (red): 12,500 cases
                  Cuvée Spéciale—438 cases
Upbringing (white): 4 months in stainless steel vats
              (red): 24–28 months total; fermentation of 3 weeks; then the yield spends 12–
                  24 months in old oak casks, and then is stored in stainless steel vats;
                  bottling is done all at one time.
                  Cuvée Spéciale—4 months in 100% new oak barrels for alcoholic fermen-
                  tation
Average age of vines (white): 15 years
                      (red): 30 years
                  Cuvée Spéciale—15 years
Blend (white): 30% Grenache Blanc, 40% Clairette, 15% Bourboulenc, 15% Roussanne
      (red): 80% Grenache, 10% Syrah, 5% Cinsault, 5% Mourvèdre
              Cuvée Spéciale—100% Roussanne

The charmingly named Domaine Chante-Cigale (the singing grasshopper) is run by Christian Favier, the son-in-law of Noël Sabon, who has fathered many a winemaker in Châteauneuf-du-Pape. This is a relatively large estate of 104 acres planted with 80% Grenache,
10% Syrah, 5% Mourvèdre, and 5% Cinsault for the red wine. There are two cuvées of
white wine, including 2,500 cases of a standard-quality dry white made from 30% Grenache

Blanc, 40% Clairette, 15% Bourboulenc, and 15% Roussanne. In recent years, Favier launched a luxury cuvée of white Châteauneuf du Pape made from 100% Roussanne and fermented in 100% new oak casks, where the wine rests for an additional four months. Unfortunately, I have never tasted this special cuvée, but if it is similar to the 100% Roussanne Vieilles Vignes produced by Beaucastel, it is undoubtedly quite special.

This is another domaine that tends to do mutiple bottlings, resulting in a frustrating array of bottle variation. Chante-Cigale used to produce traditional, blockbuster, intense wines that were exotic, concentrated, and ageworthy. Since the early eighties, the wines have been fruity, soft, and modern-style, with 6–8 years of aging potential. Multiple filtrations as well as a fining produce a wine meant for early consumption. This is a fruity, soft, appealing wine, but do not expect anything profound, at least since the late seventies.

No recent vintages have been tasted, largely because of what is perceived of as overly critical reviews of the wines. However, I have enthusiastic notes for the 1989 and 1990, although both wines varied from bottle to bottle, depending on when they were bottled and who was the importer. Older vintages include a good 1988, and mediocre wines in 1985, 1982, and 1980.

DOMAINE DE CHANTE-PERDRIX (NICOLET FRÈRES)* * * *

Address: 84230 Châteauneuf du Pape
Tel: 4-90-83-71-86
Fax: 4-90-83-53-14
Wines produced: Châteauneuf du Pape (red and white)
Surface area (white): 2.47 acres
     (red): 42 acres
Production (white): 562 cases
     (red): 6,875 cases
Upbringing (white): 8 months in enamel vats
     (red): 30 months total; fermentation of 15 days in cement vats; yield then goes into oak oak casks for 18–24 months; storage for 6 months in enamel vats before bottling
Average age of vines (white): 25 years
     (red): 45 years
Blend (white): 70% Grenache Blanc, 10% Clairette, 10% Bourboulenc, 10% Roussanne
     (red): 80% Grenache, 6% Syrah, 6% Muscardin, 6% Mourvèdre, 2% other varietals

The domaine of the "singing partridge," Chante-Perdrix, produces one of the more exotic and intriguing wines of Châteauneuf du Pape. In top vintages such as 1989, this is an undeniably flamboyant and dramatic wine. The estate is modestly sized (45 acres), and the red wine is made from a traditional blend of 80% Grenache, 6% Syrah, 6% Muscardin, 6% Mourvèdre, and 2% other varietals. I have never tasted the white wine. The average age of proprietors Guy and Frédéric Nicolet's vineyards is an impressive 45 years. Additionally, this is one of the few single-estate vineyards with the entire vineyard located in the southern part of the appellation, in the sector known as Condorcet. The soil is lighter, with more gravel, and fewer cobblestones and small boulders. The Nicolets are members of the growers' union called Les Reflets. Guy Nicolet, a quiet and unassuming man, diminutive in stature, produces wines that are the reverse of his personality. Enormously fruity, voluptuous in texture, and extroverted, they represent Châteauneuf du Pape at its most seductive. Fanciers of this style are best advised to drink Chante-Perdrix within its first 10–15 years of life. Although not one of the appellation's longest-lived wines, it is one of the most delicious.

VINTAGES

1994—Châteauneuf du Pape (red)   The 1994 displays an evolved medium to dark ruby
·   color with a garnet tinge already in evidence. The big, spicy, herb, smoky, roasted-
84   coffee nose is followed by a modestly concentrated, lighter-styled wine than the
        1993. I wonder if the Nicolets harvested too late in 1994? Last tasted 6/95.

1993—Châteauneuf du Pape (red)   The 1993 is a textbook wine from the Nicolet family.
·   It is an exotic, coffee- and chocolate-scented wine with gobs of overripe black
89   cherry, apricot, and peachlike fruit, and those telltale Provençal herbs for complex-
        ity. The wine is flashy, velvety-textured, and loaded with fruit. This soft wine is
        ideal for drinking over the next 10–12 years. Last tasted 6/95.

1990—Châteauneuf du Pape (red)   After the success Chante-Perdrix enjoyed with their
·   glorious 1989, the 1990 is less exciting. While it is undoubtedly a good Châteauneuf
86   du Pape, it lacks the concentration, complexity, and aging potential of the 1989.
        The color is a medium dark ruby, and the nose offers intense aromas of herbs,
        licorice, and red and black fruits. In the mouth the wine is medium- to full-bodied,
        with an attractive, unctuous, fleshy texture, good rather than great depth, and a
        smooth, silky finish. Quite evolved for its age, it is already revealing slight amber at
        the edge, so I would opt for drinking it over the next 5–6 years. Last tasted 4/95.

1989—Châteauneuf du Pape (red)   Chante-Perdrix's 1989 is one of the vintage's most
·   decadently rich and exotic wines. I bought several cases because it was such a
94   super value. The wine still reveals a healthy dark ruby/purple color, followed by a
        splendidly intense bouquet of dried flowers, jammy black fruits, Asian spices, smoke,
        and Provençal herbs. Full-bodied and lavishly rich, with a voluptuous texture,
        layers of fruit that ooze over the palate, this viscous, superconcentrated, luscious
        Châteauneuf du Pape has been delicious since birth. It shows no signs of decline.
        Given its size it should continue to drink well for another decade. A thrilling
        glass of Châteauneuf du Pape! Anticipated maturity: now–2005. Last tasted 3/97.

Older Vintages

Chante-Perdrix's finest older vintages include a wonderful 1983, a very good 1981, and a
superb 1978. It has been more than five years since I tasted these three vintages, but they
were in fine condition in 1990.

CHAPOUTIER (Barbe Rac* * * * * / La Bernardine* * *)

Address: 18, avenue du Docteur Paul Durand
        B.P. 382
        26600 Tain l'Hermitage
Tel: 4-75-08-28-65
Fax: 4-75-08-81-70
Wines produced: Châteauneuf du Pape La Bernardine (red and white), Châteauneuf du
        Pape Barbe Rac
Surface area: 74 acres
Production (white): 600 cases
        (red): 2,000 cases
Upbringing (white): 6 months in stainless steel vats
        (red): 12 months in barrels and demi-muids
Average age of vines: 40–90 years
Blend (white): 80% Grenache Blanc, 20% Clairette
    (red): 100% Grenache

Chapoutier's estate in Châteauneuf du Pape is called La Bernardine. This 74-acre estate is unusual in the sense that this red wine vineyard is planted with 100% Grenache. Michel Chapoutier believes in what he calls "monocépage" wines. He believes that if yields are restricted, these wines are the finest expressions of the terroir. This estate, purchased in 1938, consists of several parcels, with the largest pieces in the northern part of the appellation, near La Gardine, and on the eastern side of the appellation, near Vieux-Télégraphe and the village of Bédarrides. The oldest parcel, 90-year-old vines planted in 1901, is on the western side of the appellation. Since 1989 this parcel has been culled from the La Bernardine blend and made into a luxury cuvée called Barbe Rac. This 100% old-vine Grenache is designed to be a massive, huge, quintessential expression of Grenache, much like that of Jacques Reynaud's Château Rayas. Production of Barbe Rac varies from 500 to 700 cases per year, whereas La Bernardine produces up to 7,500 cases in a generous vintage. There is also a tiny quantity of white La Bernardine.

The vinification of both La Bernardine and Barbe Rac has changed since Michel Chapoutier took over the estate. The grapes are all destemmed, and a long vinification and maceration are practiced in order to extract as much color and intensity as possible. The wine spends 12 months in small oak casks and demi-muids before bottling. While Barbe Rac has been bottled without fining or filtration since it debut vintage in 1989, La Bernardine was traditionally given more clarification and processing prior to bottling. However, that changed in 1995 when Chapoutier decided to bottle the red La Bernardine without fining or filtration. Additionally, in order to guarantee consistency between bottles, Chapoutier has begun to do only one bottling of La Bernardine, rather than bottle it as it was sold.

The quality of these wines has soared in Michel Chapoutier's capable hands, with La Bernardine being a very good to excellent Châteauneuf du Pape, and Barbe Rac one of the appellation's most exquisite wines.

VINTAGES

1995—Châteauneuf du Pape Barbe Rac (red) Production in 1995 was 10 hectoliters per
· hectare (about two-thirds of a ton of fruit per acre). The 1995 is reminiscent of a
95 young 1978. The huge nose of kirsch, black raspberries, and minerals is followed by a backward, dense, powerful Châteauneuf du Pape of legendary richness, as well as striking intensity and depth. This opaque purple-colored wine is massive in the mouth, as well as somewhat tannic. It is a magnificent example of old-style Châteauneuf du Pape, the likes of which are rarely seen. Anticipated maturity: 2001–2025. Last tasted 6/96.

1995—Châteauneuf du Pape La Bernardine (red) The 1995 La Bernardine displays a
· deep ruby/purple color, and a sweet, expansive nose of *garrigue*, cedar, black and
90 red fruits, and roasted peanuts. Full-bodied, rich, and structured, this outstanding wine will prove to be long-lived. Anticipated maturity: 1998–2010. Last tasted 6/96.

1995—Châteauneuf du Pape La Bernardine (white) The 1995 La Bernardine blanc (lot
· 7011) is made from nearly 100% Grenache. It offers a perfumed tangerine, citrusy,
87 mineral-scented nose and flavors. Fleshy, medium-bodied, and elegant, it should drink well for 1–3 years. Last tasted 6/96.

1994—Châteauneuf du Pape Barbe Rac (red) The 1994 Barbe Rac possesses a textbook
· Provençal bouquet of lavender, *garrigue*, herbs, black olives, and jammy black-
93 cherry scents. Powerful flavors bursting with extract and glycerin provide immense volume and force in the mouth, as well as a surprising sense of elegance and finesse. This full-bodied Châteauneuf du Pape will come around much sooner than the 1995 (4–6 years), yet it will drink well for two decades. Last tasted 6/96.

1994—Châteauneuf du Pape La Bernardine (red)   The 1994 possesses a licorice, pep-
  ·   pery, black-cherry/kirsch-scented nose, spicy, full-bodied, tannic, structured fla-
 89   vors, outstanding depth, and copious amounts of alcohol and glycerin in the long
         finish. Give it 2–3 years of cellaring and drink it over the following 20 years.
         Chapoutier is moving toward one bottling of La Bernardine, but in 1994 there will
         be a second bottling. It is the exact same blend, but it will not be bottled until the
         first 8,000 cases of lot 6731 (this wine) are sold. Last tasted 6/96.

1993—Châteauneuf du Pape Barbe Rac (red)   Thick, rich, and tannic, the 1993 Barbe
  ·   Rac (from yields of 10 hectoliters per hectare, or 0.8 tons per acre) is a terrific
 92   wine. It boasts a saturated dark ruby/purple color, massive body, layers of jammy
         sweet fruit, an unctuous texture, and huge, nearly ferocious tannin in the finish.
         This is a gargantuan-styled Châteauneuf du Pape that has been designed for
         long-term cellaring. Anticipated maturity: 2000–2020. Last tasted 6/96.

1993—Châteauneuf du Pape La Bernardine (red)   The 1993 Châteauneuf du Pape La
  ·   Bernardine is less impressively endowed out of bottle than when I tasted it from
 88   cask. While the tannin is more noticeable, the wine remains a backward, rich,
         medium- to full-bodied Châteauneuf du Pape with excellent richness, considerable
         structure, and an aging potential of 12–15 years. Last tasted 6/96.

1992—Châteauneuf du Pape Barbe Rac (red)   The 1992 Barbe Rac offers a sweet,
  ·   forward, jammy nose of roasted herbs, black fruits, and spice. Full-bodied yet
 90   velvety textured, with high alcohol, this rich, medium to dark ruby-colored wine
         should be drunk over the next 10–12 years. Last tasted 8/96.

1992—Châteauneuf du Pape La Bernardine (red)   The purple-colored 1992 La Bernar-
  ·   dine offers a perfumed bouquet of exotic spices, herbs, pepper, leather, and black
 88   fruits. Made from only 15 hectoliters per hectare, this dense, concentrated wine pos-
         sesses fine ripeness, copious quantities of rich, chewy fruit, and a long, heady finish.
         It is soft enough to be drunk. Anticipated maturity: now–2005. Last tasted 9/95.

1991—Châteauneuf du Pape Barbe Rac (red)   The 1991 Barbe Rac is one of the two or
  ·   three best wines I tasted in Châteauneuf du Pape from this dreadful vintage. It
 87   displays a deep ruby color, a spicy, herbaceous-scented nose, and rich, curranty
         fruit. Although it possesses a narrow flavor profile, there is medium to full body, as
         well as excellent concentration and ripeness. With more noticeable tannin than the
         1992 and 1993, it will benefit from 2–3 years of cellaring; it should keep for 15
         years. Last tasted 6/96.

1990—Châteauneuf du Pape Barbe Rac (red)   In 1990 (less than 5,000 bottles produced),
  ·   the yields were a microscopic 15 hectoliters per hectare, or roughly one-half ton of
97+   grapes per acre. The wine was cold macerated for several days before fermentation.
         The cuvaison lasted for a month! The result is one of the most awesome red wines
         I have ever tasted. The opaque dark ruby/purple color is followed by a nose that is
         at first reticent and backward. With airing, powerful aromas of black raspberries,
         chocolate, roasted nuts, herbs, and earth eventually emerge. In the mouth there is
         extraordinary richness, gobs of glycerin, a full-bodied, unctuous texture, and a
         finish that reveals stunning extraction of flavor and high tannins. My instincts
         suggest a probable 25–35 years of longevity. If Michel Chapoutier is aiming for a
         style of Châteauneuf du Pape that emulates the renowned Château Rayas, but even
         more concentrated and intense, he has achieved that goal with the 1990 Barbe
         Rac. Anticipated maturity: 1998–2020. Last tasted 12/95.

1990—Châteauneuf du Pape La Bernardine (red)   A deep dark ruby/garnet color is
  ·   followed by a huge nose of sweet, roasted, raspberry fruit intermingled with scents
 89   of peanuts, fruitcake, and spicy pepper. This rich, expansive, full-bodied wine
         exhibits an unctuous texture, excellent concentration, and a long, moderately tannic

finish. An intense, velvety wine, it should continue to provide exciting drinking for at least 12–14 years. Last tasted 12/95.

1989—Châteauneuf du Pape Barbe Rac (red)   The 1989 Barbe Rac is made from minus-
·   cule yields of 14 hectoliters per hectare, which may be the most conservative
93   production of the entire appellation. The sad news is that there are only 600 cases of this magnificent wine. With a huge bouquet of herbs, licorice, chocolate, and berry fruit, it is extraordinary. In the mouth it displays exceptional density, concentration, high tannins, and an overall impression of layers of richness and remarkable persistence on the palate. The wine does not taste alcoholic despite its considerable size and power. This is a sensational expression of Châteauneuf du Pape. Anticipated maturity: 1998–2022. Last tasted 12/95.

1989—Châteauneuf du Pape La Bernardine (red)   While the 1989 La Bernardine was
·   splendid prior to bottling, I have found the wine to be lighter and not nearly as
88   profound as I had once hoped. Nevertheless, this is an excellent wine, with a big, spicy, berry-scented nose intermingled with the scent of herbs, almonds, and gobs of red fruits. In the mouth there are voluptuous, nicely concentrated, supple flavors. The finish is long and heady. Anticipated maturity: now–2005. Last tasted 6/96.

Older Vintages

Prior to the winemaking revolution that took place with Michel Chapoutier's ascendency, La Bernardine was an irregular wine, often too rustic and dried out by the time it was bottled. Michel's father, Max, believed in keeping the wines for several years in his ubiquitous chestnut wood foudres, which often resulted in musty, thin, desiccated wines, particularly in vintages that were not formidably endowed. While Max did produce the luxury cuvée Barbe Rac, it was never vintage dated, being a blend of several vintages. Readers fortunate enough to find any of this wine should taste it. It is impossible to know which bottling is on the market, but those I have tasted have all been significantly richer and more complex, complete wines than the regular cuvée of La Bernardine.

DOMAINE DE LA CHARBONNIÈRE* * * *

Address: Route de Courthézon
        84230 Châteauneuf du Pape
Tel: 4-90-83-64-59
Fax: 4-90-83-53-46
Wines produced: Châteauneuf du Pape (red and white), Châteauneuf du Pape Mourre des Perdrix (red), Châteauneuf du Pape Cuvée Vieilles Vignes (red)
Surface area (white): 2.47 acres
        (red): 17 acres
                Mourre des Perdrix—12.4 acres
                Cuvée Vieilles Vignes—7.5 acres
Production (white): 437 cases
        (red): 2,812 cases
                Mourre des Perdrix—2,200 cases
                Cuvée Vieilles Vignes—1,250 cases
Upbringing (white): 3–5 months total with 90% of the yield vinified in stainless steel vats, and 10% in new oak barrels
        (red): 3 weeks' fermentation in stainless steel vats, then 12–18 months in old oak casks and barrels; assemblage is done in cement vats where the wine is stored before bottling

Mourre des Perdrix and Cuvée Vielles Vignes—the same as for the regular cuvée of red wine, except that 50% of the yield is in oak barrels and 50% in oak casks, with 15% new oak

Average age of vines (white): 10 years

(red): 25–30 years

Mourre des Perdrix—25–30 years

Cuvée Vieilles Vignes—80+ years

Blend (white): 25% each of Roussanne, Grenache Blanc, Bourboulenc, and Clairette

(red): 75% Grenache, 25% Syrah and Mourvèdre

Mourre des Perdrix—75% Grenache, 20% Mourvèdre, 5% Cinsault

Cuvée Vieilles Vignes—100% Grenache

This property has been a marvelous discovery. Proprietor Michel Maret continues to display considerable confidence as a winemaker, producing better wines with each new vintage. While most of the production from this estate's 49.5 acres is in red wine, a tiny quantity of pleasant, dry white is made from an intriguing blend. Maret's white wines are well above the average level of quality for white Châteauneuf du Pape, and the red wines are among the finest of the appellation.

There are three red wine cuvées produced—a cuvée classique, the Mourre des Perdrix (from the lieu-dit vineyard of the same name), and his special cuvée of Vieilles Vignes made from 80-year-old parcels. With the exception of the Cuvée Vieilles Vignes, this estate has increased the percentage of Mourvèdre in the final blend, which is now 20–25% in certain vintages. Maret's vineyards, which are morsellated like most in Châteauneuf du Pape, are located in all four sectors of the appellation, from the hillsides, to the plateau, to the stony carpets of the northern part of the appellation, to the more sandy, lighter soils in the southeast.

The vinification at this estate is classic, with no destemming, and usually an upbringing of 12–18 months in both small oak casks and larger demi-muids and foudres. Over the last decade, Maret has increased the percentage of new oak casks to approximately 15% for his two top cuvées, Mourre des Perdrix and Vieilles Vignes. As the tasting notes that follow suggest, these are classic, textbook Châteauneuf du Papes that combine the best of traditional winemaking with a certain nod in the direction of the modernists. The wines are pure, rich, complex, and while approachable young, give evidence of aging well for 10–15 or more years. This is an impressive, largely unknown estate.

VINTAGES

1995—Châteauneuf du Pape Mourre des Perdrix (red)   The 1995 Châteauneuf du Pape
·   Mourre des Perdrix offers sweeter fruit, a more unctuous texture, outstanding
90   purity, adequate acidity, and a full-bodied, ripe, rich style that does not yet reveal
          any of the ocean/saltwater scents. It should drink well for 12–15 years. Last tasted
          6/96.

1995—Châteauneuf du Pape Vieilles Vignes (red)   The 1995 Châteauneuf du Pape Vieil-
·   les Vignes is reminiscent of a young, classic 1989 Châteauneuf du Pape. It is a
91   true vin de garde in its tannic, backward, formidable style. The color is opaque
          purple, and the wine is rich, pure, and impressive, but it is not meant for those
          wanting an up-front, flattering, delicious Châteauneuf du Pape for immediate con-
          sumption. Based on my tasting in June, this wine needs another 4–5 years of
          cellaring. It is one of those rare Châteauneuf du Papes that will improve and age
          well for 15–20 years. Last tasted 6/96.

1994—Châteauneuf du Pape (red)   The 1994 Châteauneuf du Pape (classic cuvée) exhib-
·   its a pungent, steak au poivre–scented nose intermixed with roasted Provençal
88   herbs. Softer, fatter, and more flattering than the classically structured and delineated 1993, the plush 1994 possesses an intense set of aromatics, as well as
good to excellent concentration. Drink it over the next 7–8 years. Last tasted
8/96.

1994—Châteauneuf du Pape Mourre des Perdrix (red)   The outstanding 1994 Mourre des
·   Perdrix possesses a dark ruby color with purple nuances, as well as an expressive
90   set of aromatics that includes notes of seaweed, black cherries, roasted herbs, and
spice. The wine exhibits excellent density, a sweet, expansive mid-palate, full
body, and loads of flavor. It explodes on the back of the palate, suggesting there is
even more hidden beneath the tannin and sound structure. This is an impressive,
rich Châteauneuf du Pape for drinking over the next 10–12 years. Last tasted
8/96.

1994—Châteauneuf du Pape Cuvée Vieilles Vignes (red)   The dark ruby/purple-tinged
·   1994 Cuvée Vieilles Vignes offers up a broad, sweet bouquet of smoked meats,
91   roasted herbs, and gobs of rich black-cherry and raspberry fruit. Expansive and
attractively textured, this deep, full-bodied, powerful wine needs 2–3 years of
cellaring; it can be drunk over the following decade and a half. It is an impressively
rich wine made from vines averaging 60 years in age. Last tasted 8/96.

1993—Châteauneuf du Pape (red)   The impressively constituted, full-bodied, generous,
·   rich, and concentrated 1993 Châteauneuf du Pape reveals fine sweetness and
88 + length. The wine's grip and tannic structure suggest several years of cellaring will
be beneficial. This concentrated wine is one of the more backward and potentially
long-lived examples of the 1993 vintage. Drink it between 1997–2010. Last tasted
12/95.

1993—Châteauneuf du Pape Cuvée Vieilles Vignes (red)   The richer, fuller 1993 Cuvée
·   Vieilles Vignes exhibits more noticeable tannin. It should drink well for a decade.
87   Last tasted 12/95.

1992—Châteauneuf du Pape (red)   The 1992 Châteauneuf du Pape reveals a moderately
·   saturated ruby color and a flattering, perfumed bouquet of jammy red and black
86   fruits, herbs, and spice. Soft, fat, fleshy, and chewy, this is a low-acid, heady wine
for drinking over the next 5–6 years. Last tasted 12/95.

1992—Châteauneuf du Pape Cuvée Vieilles Vignes (red)   The 1992 Cuvée Vieilles Vig-
·   nes possesses a dark ruby color, as well as an impressively rich fragrance of black
88   and red fruits, leather, cedar, and herbs, excellent extraction, full body, adequate
acidity, and light tannin in the finish. This multidimensional wine is among the
more concentrated efforts of the vintage. Drink it over the next 10–12 + years.
Last tasted 12/95.

1990—Châteauneuf du Pape (red)   The 1990 displays a pleasing richness, attractive,
·   herb and black-cherry scents, as well as ripe, round, supple cherry and cassis
87   flavors that are presented in an easy-to-drink, medium- to full-bodied format. This
is an attractive, well-made, moderately full Châteauneuf for drinking over the next
5–7 years. Last tasted 9/94.

1989—Châteauneuf du Pape (red)   The 1989 is a fleshy, full-bodied, large-scaled Châ-
·   teauneuf du Pape with excellent concentration, ripeness, surprisingly good acidity
87   for the vintage, and soft tannins in its robust finish. It should be at its best between
now and 2002. Last tasted 9/94.

1988—Châteauneuf du Pape (red)   The 1988 displayed excellent extract, a rich, concen-
·   trated, broad, expansive, nearly sweet palate impression, spicy, peppery, currany
87   flavors intertwined with flavors of thyme and pepper. The 1988 is probably every

bit as good as the 1989, and may even last longer. Drink it over the next 10 years. Last tasted 6/93.

GÉRARD CHARVIN* * * */* * * * *

Address: Chemin de Maucoil
　　　　84100 Orange
Tel: 4-90-34-41-10
Fax: 4-90-51-65-59
Wines produced: Châteauneuf du Pape (red)
Surface area: 19.8 acres
Production: 2,750 cases
Upbringing: 18 months total; fermentation of 17 days in cement or enamel vats; 6 months
　　　　minimum in old demi-muids, then storage in cement vats
Average age of vines: 45 years, with the oldest 70 years
Blend: 90% Grenache, 5% Mourvèdre, 5% Vaccarèse and other white varietals

One of the most enjoyable aspects of doing comprehensive tastings in such areas as Châteauneuf du Pape is that small vignerons like Gérard Charvin, who previously never sold a bottle of Châteauneuf du Pape in the United States, are now represented. Charvin has enjoyed considerable success with his sumptuously styled, authoritatively flavored wines. He made a terrific 1990 (I bought a case), and his recent vintages have produced top wines. Charvin, perhaps the only Châteauneuf du Pape producer to indicate boldly on the front label that his wine is *nonfiltré*, fashions Châteauneuf du Pape that comes closest in style to that of Rayas. There is a splendidly pure, black-raspberry fruitiness to his wines, a wonderfully sweet, deep, concentrated mid-palate, and layers of flavor that unfold on the palate. Great Burgundy should possess a similar texture and purity, but it rarely does. Charvin, who has not yet been discovered by the masses, may indeed produce the Richebourg of Châteauneuf du Pape—for a very reasonable price.

Charvin's 19.8 acres produce only red wine and a handful of "white grapes." The wine spends 6 months in demi-muids (no new oak is to be found in these cellars), then stored in cement vats until bottling, which, as indicated on the label, occurs without filtration. Charvin's vineyard parcels are exceptionally well located in the Maucoil, Mont Redon, and La Gardine sectors. The soil is mainly rocky stones covering a limestone/clay base. Charvin, who has traditionally sold much of his production to several well-known négociants, continues to estate-bottle more of his liquid treasure. As I have written in my journal, *The Wine Advocate*, this is a dazzling source of top-notch Châteauneuf du Pape that deserves more recognition.

VINTAGES

1995—Châteauneuf du Pape   The 1995 reveals an opaque ruby/purple color, a pure but
·　　restrained nose of black raspberries and kirsch, considerable body, fine tannin and
91　acidity, outstanding concentration, and a structured, restrained, and backward
　　　style. The 1995 will need several years of cellaring, but it has the potential to last
　　　longer (15 or more years) than the 1994. But readers should not forget—the 1995
　　　will not possess the forward charm of the 1994. Anticipated maturity: 2000-2015.
　　　Last tasted 6/96.

1994—Châteauneuf du Pape   The 1994 exhibits that telltale sweet, fragrant, black-
·　　raspberry/kirsch-scented nose, sweet, expansive, chewy fruit, superb purity, an
91　excellent marriage of power and elegance, and a soft, round, generous finish. This
　　　is a well-balanced, symmetrical Châteauneuf du Pape. Anticipated maturity: now–
　　　2008. Last tasted 6/96.

1993—Châteauneuf du Pape   Charvin's 1993 Châteauneuf du Pape reveals a healthy
   · purple color with impressive opacity. A gorgeously rich, jammy, black-raspberry
91 nose (a hallmark of Charvin's wines) soars from the glass. Full-bodied, sweet yet
   well delineated, this well-proportioned, generously endowed wine coats the palate
   with a viscous richness, but it is never heavy or tiring to drink. Lurking behind the
   splendid display of fruit is moderate tannin. Anticipated maturity: now–2006. Last
   tasted 12/95.

1992—Châteauneuf du Pape   The 1992 Châteauneuf du Pape exhibits Charvin's telltale
   · bouquet of ripe, pure, rich, raspberry fruit. Full-bodied, with excellent depth, an
87 expansive, supple texture, low acidity, and a velvety finish. Anticipated maturity:
   now–2000. Last tasted 6/96.

1990—Châteauneuf du Pape   This wine was one of the stars of my tastings of 1990
   · Châteauneuf du Papes. It is a blockbuster wine. The dark, saturated ruby color is
93 followed by an unevolved, superrich nose of roasted herbs, nuts, black fruits, and
   Asian spices. Spectacularly rich, with an unctuous, multidimensional flavor profile,
   and a chewy, robust finish, this big wine (14.5% alcohol) exhibits marvelous
   balance, as well as the potential to last for 10–15 years. Charvin's style is close in
   spirit to that of Château Rayas and Henri Bonneau. Last tasted 7/96.

DOMAINE LES CLEFS D'OR (JEAN DEYDIER)* * * *

Address: Avenue St.-Joseph
      84230 Châteauneuf du Pape
Tel: 4-90-83-70-35
Fax: 4-90-83-50-57
Wines produced: Châteauneuf du Pape (red and white)
Surface area (white): 5 acres
      (red): 54 acres
Production (white): 625 cases
      (red): 8,750 cases
Upbringing (white): 4 months in enamel vats
      (red): fermentation of 20 days in cement vats, then 16–20 months in old oak
      casks; there are several bottlings directly from the casks
Average age of vines (white): 40 years
      (red): 40 years
Blend (white): one-third each of Grenache Blanc, Bourboulenc, and Clairette
      (red): 80% Grenache, 15% Mourvèdre, and 5% Syrah and Mourvèdre

    At the foot of the ruins of the old papal château, on the tiny, twisting back streets of the
village of Châteauneuf du Pape, are the home and cellars of the Deydier family. This is a
highly regarded Châteauneuf du Pape, made from 54 acres of vineyards planted with 80%
Grenache, and the rest a field blend of Syrah and Mourvèdre. The vines average 40 years in
age, and Deydier rarely filters his wines. He makes 625 cases of very good white wine from
equal proportions of Bourboulenc, Grenache Blanc, and Clairette. His vines are admirably
situated on the plateau, one parcel near Mont Redon, another further east toward Vieux-
Télégraphe. His wine can last 10, 15, even 20 years in great vintages such as 1978. These
are traditionally styled wines, but also seem to have an elegance and breeding that set them
apart.

    The vinification combines the traditional, classic method with the newer, modern, whole-
berry style. Two-thirds of the grapes are crushed and given the classic long, hot vinification.
The other one-third are destemmed and put in the tank whole. This is another estate that

bottles its wine as it is sold, a practice that inevitably leads to some bottle variation. Jean Deydier's son, Pierre, has assumed control and has no intention of changing a thing about this very well-made, popular Châteauneuf du Pape. Seventy percent of Deydier's production is exported because he says "the foreigners know more about fine wine than the French."

VINTAGES

1995—Châteauneuf du Pape (red)   I was perplexed by the 1995 Châteauneuf du Pape. It
·   exhibits a dark ruby/purple color and a reticent but promising nose of black fruits,
88   flowers, spices, and a whiff of pepper. The initial attack of good richness and sweet fruit falls off to reveal tannin, acidity, and a monolithic personality. This wine should develop into a very good Châteauneuf du Pape, but I doubt it will ever merit an outstanding score. Last tasted 6/96.

1994—Châteauneuf du Pape (red)   Jean Deydier has produced an excellent 1994 Châ-
·   teauneuf du Pape. It boasts a healthy dark ruby color, and a reserved, backward
88   yet promising nose of black raspberries and cherries. A sweet, round, medium- to full-bodied attack is followed by a wine with moderate tannin, and a more structured, vin de garde style than found in many 1994 Châteauneuf du Papes. The wine displays very good to excellent concentration, as well as clean winemaking. Another 1–3 years of bottle age will be beneficial; it should keep for 10–12 years. Last tasted 6/96.

1993—Châteauneuf du Pape (red)   The 1993 is a textbook Châteauneuf du Pape, with a
·   rich, ripe, sweet, black-cherry nose intermingled with scents of Provençal herbs,
88   spices, and pepper, smoky, ripe, richly fruity flavors, full body, excellent purity, and a velvety texture. It should drink well for 10–12 + years. Last tasted 9/95.

1992—Châteauneuf du Pape (red)   The easygoing 1992 Châteauneuf du Pape is a light-
·   bodied wine with adequate concentration and a smooth finish. Drink it before the
84   turn of the century. Last tasted 6/95.

1990—Châteauneuf du Pape (red)   The 1990 exhibits the power, richness, and structure
·   of a top-notch year. Backward, with an interesting and penetrating bouquet of
88   blackberries, spring flowers, earth, and herbs, in the mouth there is plenty of fat and tannin. More backward than most 1990s, the wine appears to have more elegance and balance than many of the larger-scaled wines from this vintage. If the finish had been longer, it would have merited an outstanding rating. Anticipated maturity: now–2005. Last tasted 6/95.

1989—Châteauneuf du Pape (red)   The 1989 offers a bouquet of sweet, nearly overripe
·   raspberry fruit intermingled with scents of licorice and flowers. In the mouth,
90   it was exceptionally rich, with gobs of glycerin, plenty of tannin, and a long, well-structured, impressive finish. The wine tastes surprisingly backward, even for a Châteauneuf du Pape. For the record, Deydier continues to bottle his wines with minimal fining and filtering in order to preserve all of their richness and aging potential. Anticipated maturity: now–2007. Last tasted 12/94.

1988—Châteauneuf du Pape (red)   The 1988 is one of the stars of that excellent vintage.
·   The bouquet of plums, blackberries, violets, and other spring flowers could easily
90   be confused with a grand cru from the Côte de Nuits in Burgundy. In the mouth, however, I know of few Burgundies that would exhibit such fat, ripe, concentrated, full-bodied power, as well as such a high level of glycerin. The result is an opulently styled, gorgeously-textured, rich, fleshy Châteauneuf du Pape. Anticipated maturity: now–2004. Last tasted 2/95.

Older Vintages

I have had significant tasting experience with this wine as it has been available in the American market for decades. The fully mature 1985, like so many wines of this vintage, is very good, but not as exciting as it promised when young. It needs to be drunk up. The 1983 and 1981 are both fully mature, and both should be drunk before the end of the century. In fact, one could argue that they might be starting to lose some fruit, but they are still intact, medium- to full-bodied, elegant, yet authoritatively flavored Châteauneuf du Papes. The 1979 has always been somewhat attenuated and compact, but the 1978 remains the finest wine the Deydiers have made over the last 25 years. I was fortunate enough to buy the latter wine in 750 ml as well as magnum format, and the magnums remain remarkably fresh and lively, with a gorgeous bouquet of flowers and ripe raspberry fruit, with a vague notion of Provençal herbs and pepper. Perhaps the fullest and richest Les Clefs d'Or of recent history, the fully mature 1978 should continue to drink well for another 5–7 years. I last had it in December 1995.

DOMAINE CLOS DU CAILLOU* * * *

Address: 84350 Courthézon
Tel: 4-90-70-73-05
Fax: 4-90-70-76-47
Wines produced: Châteauneuf du Pape (red and white)
Surface area (white): 2.47 acres
        (red): 15 acres
Production (white): 375 cases
        (red): 2,500 cases
Upbringing (white): 6 months in stainless steel vats
        (red): 36 months total: fermentation for 18–23 days in cement vats; no destemming; upbringing for 12 months in cement vats, then 6 months in stainless steel vats, after which the yield goes into oak casks for 12–18 months
Average age of vines (white): 20 years
        (red): 30–35 years
Blend (white): 60% Grenache Blanc, 30% Roussanne, 10% Clairette
        (red): 80% Grenache, 15% Syrah, 5% Mourvèdre

Claude Pouizin's 17.5 acres of vineyards sit in the northeast sector of the appellation, adjacent to those of Château Beaucastel. The vineyards are well situated on cobblestone-like beds as well as slopes. I discovered this estate in 1990, and bought some of the splendid 1988, which was awarded second place in the annual wine tasting festival of St.-Marc, eclipsed only by the 1988 Vieux-Télégraphe. His wines, which display admirable purity, as well as plenty of deep, alcoholic, rich, heady fruit, are real head-turners when he gets everything right. The blend used is 80% Grenache, 15% Syrah, and 5% Mourvèdre. The wines spend 12–18 months in wood foudres and are bottled unfiltered. Proprietor Claude Pouizin makes Châteauneuf du Pape in what could be called a Chopin–Groffier/Henri Jayer style. These are immensely seductive, fragrant, velvety-textured, full-bodied wines with excellent color and layers of luscious fruit. Readers should not expect these to be blockbuster Châteauneuf du Papes. Rather, they are wines of considerable elegance and fragrance. They are rich, smooth, stylish wines for drinking during their first decade of life. Pouizin sold much of his 1993 crop to négociants, saving a small quantity of his finest juice for his estate-bottled wine.

VINTAGES

1995—Châteauneuf du Pape (red)   The structured 1995 Châteauneuf du Pape exhibits
·   acidity, plenty of sweet, ripe fruit, and a touch of toasty new oak. This medium- to
88   full-bodied wine displays fine depth, as well as considerable character. It may
merit close to 90 points after bottling. It should keep for 10–12 years. Last tasted
6/96.

1994—Châteauneuf du Pape (red)   This estate tends to make sexy, up-front, juicy, succu-
·   lent, velvety-textured Châteauneuf du Papes that I find hard to resist. I would not
89   push their aging potential beyond 7–8 years, except in the most extraordinary
vintages, but for pure hedonistic appeal, they are hard to surpass. The 1994
Châteauneuf du Pape offers a flamboyant nose of jammy black-cherry fruit, along
with hickory, smoky, barbecue scents, and tangy, herblike aromas. The wine possesses a voluptuous texture, copious quantities of fruit, terrific ripeness, an expansive, chewy mid-palate, and a heady, alcoholic finish. It is a lusty Châteauneuf du
Pape for drinking over the next 5–6 years. Last tasted 6/96.

1993—Châteauneuf du Pape (red)   The 1993 will not be a long-lived wine, but who can
·   resist the intense perfume and glorious display of rich black-cherry fruit infused
90   with copious quantities of glycerin, extract, and alcohol? Anticipated maturity:
now–2000. Last tasted 12/95.

1990—Châteauneuf du Pape (red)   Pouizin's 1990 red Châteauneuf du Pape is a fruity,
·   lush, hedonistic wine, with enormous quantities of sweet red and black fruits. The
91   bouquet of black raspberries and flowers is both intense and captivating. In the
mouth, it is crammed with highly extracted, rich fruit, possesses a chewy, enticing
texture, and a long, rich, softly tannic finish. This is a sumptuous Châteauneuf du
Pape. Anticipated maturity: now–2004. Last tasted 2/96.

1989—Châteauneuf du Pape (red)   The 1989 is not nearly as impressive as either the
·   1990 or 1988. Richly fruity, straightforward, round, and generous, it suffers in
86   comparison only with the 1988 and 1990. It is a chunky, generously endowed
Châteauneuf du Pape for drinking over the next 5–7 years. Last tasted 11/94.

1988—Châteauneuf du Pape (red)   The full-bodied and fully mature 1988 is one of the
·   top wines of the vintage. It has a generous bouquet of chocolate, cedar, black
92   plums, and black cherries. In the mouth it is concentrated, rich, and full-bodied,
with a velvety texture, and a long, heady, amazingly extracted finish. Anticipated
maturity: now–2000. Last tasted 8/96.

CLOS DU MONT OLIVET (JOSEPH SABON)
(Cuvée Classique* * * */Cuvée du Papet* * * * *)
Address: 15, avenue St.-Joseph
84230 Châteauneuf du Pape
Tel: 4-90-83-72-46
Fax: 4-90-83-51-75
Wines produced: Châteauneuf du Pape Cuvée Classique (red and white), Châteauneuf du
Pape Cuvée du Papet (red)
Surface area (white): 5.6 acres
(red): 54 acres
Cuvée du Papet—5 acres
Production (white): 875 cases
(red): 8,100 cases
Cuvée du Papet—562 cases

Upbringing (white): 8 months in stainless steel vats; malolactic is stopped by cooling
        (red): fermentation of 18–21 days in cement vats; wines spend 18 months to 5
        years in oak casks as the wine is bottled according to demand; no fining
        or filtration
        Cuvée du Papet—fermentation of 18–21 days; then 18 months in oak
        casks, after which the wine is all bottled at the same time; no fining or
        filtration
Average age of vines (white): 50 years
        (red): 60+ years
        Cuvée du Papet—60–80 years
Blend (white): 30% Clairette, 30% Bourboulenc, 25% Roussanne, 15% Grenache Blanc
        (both red wine cuvées): 90–92% Grenache, 2–3% Syrah, the rest other varietals
Note: The Cuvée du Papet is a selection of old vines that is made only in exceptional
years (e.g., 1989 and 1990).

One of the very best Châteauneuf du Papes, Mont Olivet is made by Pierre, Jean-Claude, and Bernard Sabon, the three sons of the legendary Joseph Sabon. They produce a splendidly rich, old-style Châteauneuf du Pape from ancient vines (an average age of 60 years) from 60 acres of vineyards. Another 19 acres of Côtes du Rhône (near Bollène) is also farmed by the Sabon brothers. The blend of cépages is 90–92% Grenache, a tiny portion of Syrah, and a dose or two of assorted varietals. As superb as the red wine can be, the white wine produced here has been green, acidic, and mediocre, although more recent vintages have shown improvement. As for the red, my only criticism of the Sabons is their practice of "bottling upon ordering," meaning that the same vintages may spend different amounts of time in the large oak foudres. For example, the 1978 was bottled over a period of eight years! Lest anyone think I do not understand the difficulty for small domaines that have neither the financial capacity nor the space to buy all the corks, labels, and bottles to do one bottling, it is incumbent upon the powers that be in Châteauneuf du Pape to recognize that this issue needs to be resolved. Given the potential for exquisite wines in this appellation, it is a shame that the French government and producers have not allocated enough resources to provide a solution to this problem. Nevertheless, I believe if you purchase the early bottlings, truly remarkable wines can emerge in Sabon's great years, such as 1967, 1970, 1971, 1976, 1978, 1979, 1985, 1988, 1989, 1990, 1994, and 1995. The wines of this estate will keep a good 10–15+ years in the top vintages, even longer in great years such as 1978, 1989, and 1990.

The vinification practiced by the Sabons is totally traditional or classic. The incoming grapes are not destemmed, but are crushed and given a hot, lengthy fermentation and maceration. Since 1989, the wine has not been fined nor filtered prior to bottling. Except for their practice of different bottling dates *(mise en bouteille)* for their wines, Clos du Mont Olivet is a wine to purchase without hesitation. It seems to deftly marry the robustness of an old-style Châteauneuf du Pape with a measure of finesse and elegance. Moreover, the Sabons are members of the growers' association Les Reflets, an association of quality-oriented producers who charge modest prices for their wines.

The Sabons can boast four generations of winemakers (the name of the estate comes from a notary public that owned a vineyard of the same name in 1547). The morsellated vineyard parcels are almost all on clay/limestone–based soil with a rocky carpet. The top parcels are in the north, the eastern sector, and in the southern section near the lieu-dit Les Gallimardes. The "clos" of Mont Olivet is a specific vineyard of nearly 20 acres, all on the plateau just north of Domaine la Solitude. From this parcel of old vines, the Sabons produce their famed Cuvée du Papet (named after the grandfather) from very old vines. The Cuvée du Papet was only produced in 1989 and 1990, and as the tasting notes that follow enthusiastically attest, it is an exquisite wine. Approximately 600 cases were made.

VINTAGES

1995—Châteauneuf du Pape (red)   The deep ruby/purple color is followed by straight-
·   forward, ripe aromas of raspberries, cherries, and pepper. Dense, concentrated,
90   full-bodied, and tannic, with more acidity than the 1994, the 1995 should turn out
        to be at least excellent, but will it equal the 1994? The 1995 does not possess the
        up-front charm of the 1994, and will require 3–5 years of cellaring. Anticipated
        maturity: 2001–2015. Last tasted 6/96.

1994—Châteauneuf du Pape (red)   The 1994 Châteauneuf du Pape is one of the top
·   wines of the vintage. Dark ruby/purple-colored, it exhibits a textbook Châteauneuf
91   du Pape bouquet of black olives, salty sea breezes, *garrigue*, and masses of black-
        cherry/plum-like fruit. Extremely full-bodied, with high extraction, admirable
        glycerin, a dense, supple attack, and a chewy mid-palate, this is a layered, concen-
        trated, impressively long Châteauneuf du Pape. Anticipated maturity: now–2007.
        Last tasted 6/96.

1993—Châteauneuf du Pape (red)   The 1993 offers a dark, saturated ruby color with
·   some garnet at the edge. The wine exhibits sexy sweet, red and black fruits, as well
89   as smoky/roasted Provençal herbs in its fragrant aromatics. Rich, full-bodied,
        round, and remarkably supple for such a young Clos du Mont Olivet Châteauneuf
        du Pape, it is a delicious 1993. Anticipated maturity: now–2001. Last tasted 9/95.

1992—Châteauneuf du Pape (red)   The 1992 possesses a spicy, roasted, cherry-scented
·   nose, surprisingly fine grip and structure for a 1992, medium body, and good depth
85   and ripeness in the moderately long finish. Drink it over the next 7–10 years. Last
        tasted 9/95.

1990—Châteauneuf du Pape (red)   The 1990 is a highly concentrated, backstrapping,
·   muscular, big wine. The color is a dark ruby/purple. With swirling, a spicy, peppery
90   nose of herbes de Provence and cassis fruit is apparent. Full-bodied and impres-
        sively endowed, this large-scaled wine is just beginning to shed its cloak of tannin.
        Anticipated maturity: now–2010. Last tasted 2/96.

1990—Châteauneuf du Pape Cuvée du Papet (red)   The Cuvée du Papet exhibits far
·   more tannin and rusticity, as well as some of the weedy, herbal, *garrigue* character
95   of Provence. With massive body, and exhilarating concentration and extract, the
        1990 displays more openness and even greater ripeness than the spectacular
        1989. This is a splendid, formidably endowed, old-style Châteauneuf du Pape.
        Anticipated maturity: 2000–2025. Last tasted 8/96.

1989—Châteauneuf du Pape (red)   Lovers of Châteauneuf du Pape will have immense
·   pleasure comparing Clos du Mont Olivet's 1989 and 1990. The 1989 has begun to
90+   close down, but it is a beautifully made, intense, full-bodied wine with some of the
        Provençal *garrigue* character, along with smoke, jammy black cherries, and dusty
        tannin. The wine is full-bodied and highly extracted, with plenty of purity, richness,
        and length. It reveals more delineation, but perhaps less jamminess when compared
        to the 1990, but this is splitting hairs. Anticipated maturity: 1998–2012. Last
        tasted 8/96.

1989—Châteauneuf du Pape Cuvée du Papet (red)   The 1989 Cuvée du Papet offers up
·   huge aromas of Provençal herbs, roasted nuts, and sweet, jammy, exotic fruits. In
94   the mouth its decadence and opulence must be tasted to be believed. This unctu-
        ous, wonderfully rich wine makes for splendid drinking at present, but it promises
        to be even better with bottle age. It is an astonishing, old-style, traditionally made
        Châteauneuf du Pape, the likes of which are rarely seen in today's high-tech world
        where wines are so often made within strictly formulated parameters. Anticipated
        maturity: 1998–2020. Last tasted 8/96.

1988—Châteauneuf du Pape (red)   The 1988 has a super bouquet of Asian spices, black
  ·   cherries, cedar, chocolate, and coffee. It is extremely full-bodied, and possibly as
 90   concentrated as the 1989 and 1990. With intense, rich, wonderfully pure fruit, this
          wine is well-balanced and impressive. Anticipated maturity: now–2008. Last tasted
          8/96.
1986—Châteauneuf du Pape (red)   A highly successful 1986, this deep ruby/purple-
  ·   colored wine reveals an intense bouquet of raspberries, thyme, and currants. This
 88   is another old-fashioned, rich, deep, chewy, full-bodied, massive wine built to age.
          Anticipated maturity: now–2005. Last tasted 12/93.
1985—Châteauneuf du Pape (red)   I have had some great bottles of the 1985 Clos du
  ·   Mont Olivet Châteauneuf du Pape, but none of them have come from those I
85–92?purchased, which were imported by Robert Kacher. At its finest, this wine, which
          won first prize in the Festival of St.-Marc, is one of the top 1985s. Other bottlings
          have been lighter-weight, more diluted, straightforward cuvées that barely resemble
          the wine that won so many raves in Châteauneuf du Pape. Depending on which
          1985 you have, it is either a wine that can be drunk over another 7–10 years, or
          one that should be consumed immediately. Last tasted 1/96.
1983—Châteauneuf du Pape (red)   The aromas of *surmaturité* peaches, apricots, as well
  ·   as berry fruit are wonderfully present in this wine. On the palate, it is almost
 87   Burgundy-like with supple, broad, velvety flavors, full body, and a delicious, long
          finish. Maturity now. Last tasted 11/90.
1982—Châteauneuf du Pape (red)   The color shows a watery edge, the bouquet has some
  ·   pleasant berry fruit, but also the hotness of high alcohol. Somewhat disjointed, this
 76   is a palatable wine that is precariously balanced. Mature now. Last tasted 6/86.

Older Vintages

Older vintage of Clos du Mont Olivet can be immensely rewarding, but buying them is akin
to purchasing the proverbial pig in a poke. The multiple bottlings over such a long period
of time causes considerable bottle variation. Top vintages include brilliant wines in 1978
and 1967.

CLOS DE L'ORATOIRE DES PAPES (MADAME AMOUROUX)* *

Address: Avenue St.-Joseph
        84230 Châteauneuf du Pape
Tel: 4-90-83-70-19
Fax: 4-90-83-51-24
Wines produced: Châteauneuf du Pape (red and white)
Surface area (white): 10 acres
        (red): 99 acres
Production (white): 1,200 cases
        (red): 12,500 cases
Upbringing (white): 8 months in temperature-controlled stainless steel vats
        (red): fermentations of 10–15 days in temperature-controlled stainless steel
        vats; then the wines stay 6–8 months in stainless steel vats for malolactic
        and then go into old oak casks for 18–20 months; earliest bottling is done
        after 24 months
Average age of vines (white): 15 years
        (red): 40 years
Blend (white): 25% each Clairette, Bourboulenc, Grenache Blanc, and Roussanne
        (red): 60% Grenache, 20% Mourvèdre, 10% Syrah, and 10% other varietals

This historic estate has existed in Châteauneuf du Pape since the eighteenth century. Thirty years ago it produced one of the most impressive wines made in the appellation, but over the last three decades, the wine has been made in an ultramodern style. A large estate of 109 acres, with well-situated hillside parcels, this fruity, pleasant, charming wine is meant to be drunk within 3–4 years of bottling. While I have seen new vintages bottled within 8–10 months of the vintage, the information I requested from the estate suggests the wines are aged for two years before bottling, so perhaps a change has recently been instituted.

Certainly, the wines are models of risk-free winemaking—one-dimensional, soft, and overtly commercial, but tasty. They offer a good introduction to Châteauneuf du Pape for those who are not looking for more forceful examples of the appellation.

CLOS DES PAPES (PAUL AVRIL)* * * * *

Address: 13, avenue Pierre de Luxembourg
        84230 Châteauneuf du Pape
Tel: 4-90-83-70-13
Fax: 4-90-83-50-87
Wines produced: Châteauneuf du Pape (red and white)
Surface area (white): 7.5 acres
             (red): 72 acres
Production (white): 1,050 cases
           (red): 9,650 cases
Upbringing (white): 6–8 months in enamel tanks; malolactic is stopped and the wines are
                filtered before bottling
           (red): 14–16 months in barrel and large foudres; bottling without filtration
Average age of vines (white): 30 years
                     (red): 30 years
Blend (white): equal proportions of Grenache Blanc, Roussanne, Clairette, Bourboulenc,
        and Picpoul
      (red): 65% Grenache, 20% Mourvèdre, 10% Syrah, 5% other varietals

The Avril family has been making wine in Châteauneuf du Pape since the beginning of the eighteenth century. The current master of ceremonies is Paul Avril, now aided by his talented son, Vincent. Clos des Papes has always been one of the appellation's reference point wines. Sometimes such a distinction does not mesh with one's tasting experiences, but at Clos des Papes, the wines are brilliant. Moreover, Paul, Vincent, and Madame Avril are three of the most generous and gracious vignerons in the southern Rhône. This is an estate that visitors to the region should not hesitate to visit, not only for the quality of the wines, but because of the warm welcome extended by the Avrils.

In the office hangs a map showing a morsellated domaine of 18 separate parcels. The estate's name derives from the vineyard's name, which was once part of the old papal vineyard located within the walls of what is now a ruined château. The other parcels are spread out over the entire Châteauneuf du Pape appellation, from the sandy soils to the west and southeast, to the rocky plateau limestone/clay soils of the north and northeast. Paul Avril has gradually decreased the amount of Grenache in his blend, while increasing the Syrah and Mourvèdre. In principle, the wine is largely made of Grenache, Syrah, and Mourvèdre, but this is one estate that has other plantations, particularly Muscardin, Counoise, and Vaccarèse. A dollop of each of these varietals is usually included in the blend. Vinification is traditional, with usually no destemming, except for the Mourvèdre and Syrah, although flexibility is the operative mode of action at this estate. In 1995, the Avrils, recognizing that the stems were not as mature as they liked, destemmed a large percentage of Grenache.

Only one red and one white wine are produced, as the Avrils do not believe in making a luxury cuvée, saying that anything not acceptable is sold in bulk to négociants. The wines, which were always bottled without fining or filtration, did go through both of these processes in the early and mid-eighties. The Avrils were disappointed at the negative impact it had on the wine and abandoned filtration starting with the 1988 vintage. Generally they do not even fine the wine if it does not taste too tannic. While the red wine has always been one of the finest of the appellation, the Avrils have had considerable success with their white wines. Recent vintages have been among the better wines of the appellation, but they require drinking very young. Additionally, the Avrils make a nonvintage wine called Le Petit d'Avril, which is usually a blend of the three most recent vintages. About 1,200 cases are made each year from their young vines and cuvées of wine deemed not rich enough for Clos des Papes. It is a noteworthy value.

Clos des Papes is one of the few Châteauneuf du Papes that is rarely flattering to drink young, with most top vintages needing 5–8 years to blossom. Not surprisingly, Clos des Papes is one of the appellation's longest-lived wines—a wine for passionate amateurs of Châteauneuf du Pape.

VINTAGES

1995—Châteauneuf du Pape (red)   The 1995 Châteauneuf du Pape achieved an average
·   natural alcohol of 14%, which is not far off the record 14.3% obtained in 1990.
92   Yields were a modest 25 hectoliters per hectare. Not surprisingly, this has turned
           out to be a spectacularly dense, black/ruby/purple-colored wine with a fabulous
           nose of Asian spices, black cherries, raspberries, smoke, cedar, and spice. Full-
           bodied, with plenty of muscle, richness, and moderate tannin, this should be one
           of the longest-lived and most powerful Châteauneuf du Papes of the vintage. It will
           need 4–5 years of cellaring and should keep for two decades. Last tasted 6/96.

1994—Châteauneuf du Pape (red)   The 1994 Châteauneuf du Pape has turned out to be
·   one of the most successful wines of the vintage. It exhibits a sweet nose of kirsch,
91   cedar, and spice, full body, outstanding ripeness, and an exotic, spicy, smoked-
           meat component. The wine is chewy and fleshy, with moderate tannin in the finish.
           Readers should keep in mind that this estate utilizes a relatively high percentage
           of Mourvèdre in the final blend, which is usually 65% Grenache, 20% Mourvèdre,
           10% Syrah, and the rest a blend of such diverse varietals as Counoise and Muscar-
           din. The 1994 should be cellared for 2–3 years and drunk over the following 15
           years. Last tasted 6/96.

1993—Châteauneuf du Pape (red)   The impressive 1993 is one of the vintage's stars. The
·   dark ruby/purple color is followed by classic aromas of black cherries and cassis
90   with considerable sweetness and dimension. The wine is full-bodied, moderately
           tannic, with an expansive, chewy mid-palate, and excellent glycerin, concentration,
           and finish. The wine is firm, but impressively endowed. Cellar it for 3–4 years and
           enjoy it over the subsequent two decades. Last tasted 6/96.

1992—Châteauneuf du Pape (red)   One of the most concentrated wines I tasted from the
·   vintage, the 1992 Châteauneuf du Pape exhibits a dark ruby/purple color, a big,
89 +   spicy, black-cherry and cedary-scented nose, superb richness, a chewy, unctuous
           texture, and moderate tannin in the long finish. Anticipated maturity: now–2008.
           Last tasted 6/96.

1990—Châteauneuf du Pape (red)   The 1990 is Avril's finest wine since his terrific 1978.
·   It exhibits an impressive opaque, dark ruby/purple color, a pronounced nose of
94   sweet cassis and black-cherry fruit, an attractive, expansive sweetness and ripeness
           on the palate, and a powerful, long finish, with plenty of tannin, glycerin, and

alcohol. This wine, a classic, authoritatively flavored wine, is much more backward than many 1990s. Anticipated maturity: 2000–2015. Last tasted 6/96.

1989—Châteauneuf du Pape (red)   Although impressive, the 1989 remains closed, struc-
·   tured, tannic, and just beginning to hint at its enormous potential. The wine
90 +   exhibits a deep, dark ruby color, a tight but jammy black-cherry bouquet inter-
        twined with the scent of Provençal herbs. Extremely full-bodied and concentrated,
        it is a classic Châteauneuf du Pape built to last. Anticipated maturity: 1999–2015.
        Last tasted 6/96.

1988—Châteauneuf du Pape (red)   The finesse-styled 1988 offers a peppery, spicy nose,
·   intense, richly fruity flavors, medium to full body, and moderate tannins in the
88   finish. Anticipated maturity: now–2006. Last tasted 6/95.

1985—Châteauneuf du Pape (red)   Made during the period when, by their own admission,
·   the Avrils were doing too much fining and filtering, this wine has turned out well,
88   but it is fully mature. It exhibits a deep ruby color with plenty of rust and orange
        at the edge, followed by a spicy nose with scents of Provençal herbs, *garrigue*, and
        sweet cherry fruit. The wine has lost some of its fatness, and now tastes medium-
        bodied, with good length but low acidity. It needs to be drunk up before the turn of
        the century. Last tasted 8/96.

1983—Châteauneuf du Pape (red)   The 1983 reveals a deep garnet color, a smoky, sweet,
·   jammy, black-cherry, and herb-scented nose, and ripe, medium- to full-bodied
89   flavors that still exhibit copious amounts of fruit, glycerin, and extract. Some firm
        tannin is noticeable in the finish. The 1983 is fully mature, yet capable of holding
        for another 8–10 years. Last tasted 8/96.

1981—Châteauneuf du Pape (red)   Drinking better than ever, the 1981 has blossomed
·   gorgeously in the bottle. A huge nose of sweet red and black fruits, caramel, smoke,
92   roasted herbs, and olives is followed by a full-bodied, flamboyant wine with gobs
        of fruit. The color remains a youthful deep ruby with no amber at the edge.
        Powerful, yet elegant and mouth-filling, this is a sumptuous example of Clos des
        Papes. Anticipated maturity: now–2004. Last tasted 6/96.

1979—Châteauneuf du Pape (red)   Very dark in color, the 1979 has the wild, gamelike,
·   smoky character I associate with Mourvèdre and Syrah. Very full-bodied, rich, and
88   powerful on the palate, the 1979 is just beginning to show some signs of reaching
        maturity. It has thrown a great deal of sediment. Anticipated maturity: now–2002.
        Last tasted 6/86.

1978—Châteauneuf du Pape (red)   Absolutely fabulous, the 1978 has reached full matu-
·   rity. This was always the finest Clos des Papes since the 1961, but I am hoping the
95   1990 will equal if not surpass it. The 1978 exhibits a dark, almost opaque garnet
        color, followed by a huge, smoky, herb, roasted-meat, and sweet truffle and black-
        fruit-scented nose. Massively rich, with great body, and layers of concentrated,
        highly extracted fruit, this supple, fleshy, awesome example of Châteauneuf du
        Pape should continue to drink well for at least another decade. Last tasted 6/96.

Older Vintages

Since the last edition of this book, I have not had the opportunity to retaste the great 1970 or 1966, so I have no idea how they have matured over the last decade. Well-stored bottles of these wines are likely to be intact.

CLOS DU ROI

Address: Le Prieure St.-Joseph
        84700 Sorgues
Tel: 4-90-39-57-46
Fax: 4-90-39-15-28
Wines produced: Châteauneuf du Pape (red)
Surface area: 52 acres
Production: 7,500 cases
Upbringing: 12–14 months in barrel and foudre
Average age of vines: 40 years
Blend: 60% Grenache, 10% Mourvèdre, 10% Clairette, 10% Cinsault, 10% Picpoul

This estate was created in 1930 and has been owned by the Mousset family for many years. The wine seems to have improved over recent years, but it tends to be a relatively one-dimensional, concentrated, but processed Châteauneuf du Pape for drinking during its first 5–6 years of life.

CLOS ST.-JEAN (G. MAUREL)* * *

Address: 8, chemin de la Calade
        84230 Châteauneuf du Pape
Tel: 4-90-83-71-33
Fax: 4-90-83-50-56
Wines produced: Châteauneuf du Pape (red)
Surface area: 4 acres
Production: 12,500 cases
Upbringing: No destemming; after vinification, the wines are kept for two years in wood
        foudres, then fined with egg whites and filtered prior to bottling.
Average age of vines: 40 years
Blend: 75% Grenache, 15% Syrah, 10% Cinsault, Mourvèdre, Vaccarèse, Muscardin, and
        Picpoul

This old-style, traditional Châteauneuf du Pape producer owns well-situated vineyards, with the two largest parcels in the northern part of the appellation between Fines-Roches and the town of Bédarrides. Some of the production is sold to négociants, but their fame lies in the fact that they do not release their wines until they believe they are at the "peak of perfection." Consequently, vintages such as 1989 and 1990 had not yet been released in the mid-nineties. The wine is not sold until the owners decide upon a release date.

The vintages I have tasted have been rustic, old-style Châteauneuf du Papes with a distinctive tar, leather, animal, earthy component that tended to overwhelm the fruity/floral side of the wines' aromatics and flavors. This style of wine is controversial, but there is something admirable about an estate where the proprietor, in this case Madame Guy Maurel, continues to do business in an unmistakably traditional manner. Most vintages, even those that are 10–12 years old upon release, give every sign of lasting for another 15–20 years, but do not expect a great deal of well-integrated, sweet tannin, or refinement, as these are aggressive, rustic wines.

CLOS ST.-MICHEL* * * *

Address: Le Prieure St.-Joseph
        84770 Sorgues
Tel: 4-90-39-57-46
Fax: 4-90-39-15-28

Wines produced: Châteauneuf du Pape (red), Châteauneuf du Pape Cuvée Réservée (red),
Châteauneuf du Pape Vignes Nobles Guy Mousset (red)
Surface area: 40 acres
Production: 6,850 cases
Upbringing: 12–16 months in oak foudres and steel tanks
Average age of vines: 20 years
Blend: 60% Grenache, 20% Syrah, 10% Mourvèdre, 5% Cinsault, 4% miscellaneous
varietals

Guy Mousset's son Franck, assisted by the omnipresent Châteauneuf du Pape oenologist
Noël Rabot, has improved the quality of this wine. It is a deep, thick, chewy Châteauneuf
du Pape made from well-situated parcels on the periphery of the appellation, in the direction
of Sorgues. This estate destems about 50% of the grapes, aims for high extraction of fruit
and color, and ages the wines in foudres until bottling, usually after 12–16 months. All
things considered, Clos St.-Michel is the best wine being made under the Mousset umbrella
of estates.

VINTAGES

1995—Châteauneuf du Pape   The 1995 possesses plenty of fat, ripe fruit, a sweet, expan-
· sive mid-palate, some complexity, and a heady, sweet, rich finish. It should drink
87 well young and last for a decade. Last tasted 6/96.

1995—Châteauneuf du Pape Cuvée Réservée   The 1995 Cuvée Réservée shares the
· 1994's intensity, along with riper fruit and higher acidity and tannin. The overall
88 emphasis is on the overripe black-fruit character, without the seaweed/iodine component. This large-scaled, husky Châteauneuf may not achieve the complexity of
the 1994, but it is an excellent wine that should last for 10-15 years. Last tasted
6/96.

1994—Châteauneuf du Pape Cuvée Réservée   Made from ripe, rich, jammy fruit, the
· 1994 Cuvée Réservée may turn out to be the most complete wine, with its complex
89+ set of aromatics, ranging from salty, iodine, sealike aromas, to those of jammy
black cherries, pepper, and herbs. It is a highly extracted, rich, tannic wine with a
smoky, roasted character that offers considerable promise. Given its structured,
backward personality, this wine requires 2–3 more years of cellaring, after which
it may merit an outstanding rating. Last tasted 6/96.

1994—Châteauneuf du Pape Vignes Nobles Guy Mousset   The 1994 displays the vin-
· tage's richness. Full-bodied, with fat, black-cherry, silky-smooth flavors that linger
88 on the palate, it is a pure, well-made, immensely satisfying wine that can be drunk
early or cellared for 7–8 years. Last tasted 6/96.

1993—Châteauneuf du Pape Cuvée Réservée   Franck Mousset also turned in a fine effort
· with the 1993 Cuvée Réservée. It offers a dark ruby color with purple tints, as well
89 as a ripe, sweet, persistent, cassis-scented nose. Loaded with glycerin and jammy
fruit, the wine possesses that lavish, chewy mouth feel that makes Châteauneuf du
Pape so seductive. Drink it over the next 7–8 years. Last tasted 6/95.

1993—Châteauneuf du Pape Vignes Nobles Guy Mousset   The 1993 exhibits a Provençal
· mélange of spice, pepper, and black-cherry fruit. This dark ruby-colored wine
87 reveals medium to full body, good richness, and light to moderate tannin in its
well-delineated, spicy finish. The wine will benefit from 1–3 years of cellaring and
drink well for 10–12 + years. Last tasted 6/95.

DOMAINE DE CRISTIA* * *

Address: 33, faubourg St.-Georges
          84350 Courthézon
Tel: 4-90-70-89-15
Wines produced: Châteauneuf du Pape (red and white), Châteauneuf du Pape A. Grangeon
          Sélection (red)
Surface area (white): 2.47 acres
               (red): 24.7 acres
Production (white): 333 cases
             (red): 1,250–1,660 cases
             A. Grangeon—416 cases
Upbringing (white): 14–16 months total, with 90% of the yield in stainless steel vats and
               10% in old oak barrels; assemblage is done just before bottling
          (red, regular cuvée and A. Grangeon): 36 months total; fermentation of 3 weeks
                         in cement tanks, then 24 months in old
                         oak casks; storage in cement vats before
                         bottling
Average age of vines (white): 70 years and 12 years for the Grenache Blanc vines
                        (red): 50 years
Blend (white): 40% Grenache Blanc, 30% Clairette, 20% Bourboulenc, 10% Roussanne
        (red): 70% Grenache, 10% Syrah, 10% Mourvèdre, 5% Cinsault, 5% Muscardin
          A. Grangeon—100% Grenache
Note: The A. Grangeon Sélection is made in the way of a Bordeaux *tête de cuvée*, from a
selection of the best terroir and top fruit. There is a further selection after fermentation and
the finest vats are reserved for this cuvée.

Proprietor Alain Grangeon consistently turns out good Châteauneuf du Pape from his 26
acres of vineyards. I have had only a few vintages of the red Domaine de Cristia, and have
found it well made, but lacking intensity and length. Although it is a good example of the
appellation, it is meant for drinking during its first 5–7 years of life. Sadly, I have never
tasted the special cuvée, A. Grangeon Sélection, which is a cellar selection of 100% old-vine
Grenache.

HENRIET CROUZET-FÉRAUD* * * *

Address: 4 bis, chemin de Bois de la Ville
          84230 Châteauneuf du Pape
Tel: confidential
Wines produced: Châteauneuf du Pape (red)
Surface area: 12.5 acres
Production: 1,250 cases
Upbringing: no destemming, at least 14–20 months in foudre prior to bottling with no
          filtration
Average age of vines: 60 years
Blend: 80% Grenache, 20% miscellaneous varietals

I have had little experience with the wines of this estate, but those I have tasted have
been impressive. Traditional, powerful, concentrated wines, Crouzet-Féraud's Châteauneuf
du Papes are not dissimilar from the wines of Laurent and Paul Féraud. In spite of the tiny
production, this estate merits more attention.

CUVÉE DU BELVEDERE (ROBERT GIRARD)* * */* * * *

Address: Le Boucou
       84230 Châteauneuf du Pape
Tel: 4-90-83-70-08
Fax: 4-90-83-50-45
Wines produced: Châteauneuf du Pape Le Boucou (red)
Surface area: 10 acres
Production: 800 cases, of which a certain percentage is sold to négociants
Upbringing: no destemming; vinification in 100-hectoliter tanks for 3–4 weeks, with a
       maximum temperature of 30–32° centigrade; the wine spends 12–20 months
       in tank before bottling
Average age of vines: 40 years
Blend: 80% Grenache, 15% Counoise, 5% Syrah

Proprietor Robert Girard, a wiry, inquisitive man, with a gnarled appearance that resembles a bit some of the 70-year-old head-pruned vines in Châteauneuf du Pape, owns only 10 acres of vines that form a single parcel called Le Boucou. His vineyards are primarily Grenache (80%), but they also contain an unusually high amount of Counoise (15%), and 5% Syrah. Girard is not a very well-known winemaker, but his wines, particularly 1978, 1979, 1983, and 1989, have given me considerable pleasure. He uses the classic, old-time vinification—no destemming, and bottling after a reasonable amount of time in old wood foudres. In some vintages, the wines are almost Burgundian because of their black-cherry-scented noses and intense fragrance. I remember a "blind" tasting where the 1985 Cuvée du Belvedere was inserted with a group of 1985 Côte d'Or premiers and grands crus for noted New Jersey wine merchant Carlo Russo, and the huge crowd ranked Cuvée du Belvedere first, well ahead of the Burgundies, a group of much more expensive wines. Moreover, no one picked the wine out as a Rhône wine!

Recent vintages have given me the impression that Girard has lightened his style as the wines have lacked the concentration and expressiveness of earlier vintages. It will be sad if my instincts are correct, as this has traditionally been one of the most charming, seductive, and elegant styles of Châteauneuf du Pape.

VINTAGES

1995—Châteauneuf du Pape Le Boucou   To my surprise, the light ruby-colored 1995 Le
·   Boucou did not possess the depth of the 1994. It lacks body and extract, and
76   possesses a superficial finish, with no underpinning of depth or intensity. It is
    pleasant but uninspiring. Anticipated maturity: now–2000. Last tasted 6/96.

1994—Châteauneuf du Pape Le Boucou   Here is where I began to be concerned about
·   Girard's lightening his style. The 1994 Châteauneuf du Pape exhibits a Burgun-
86   dian, seductive nose of red cherries, floral scents, and spice. Although not a boldly
    styled wine, it is seductive, round, fruity, and easy to drink. Anticipated maturity:
    now–2001. Last tasted 6/96.

1993—Châteauneuf du Pape Le Boucou   The 1993 Le Boucou is astringent and hollow,
·   although there is enough fruit to provide some pleasure and charm. This wine is
83   likely to dry out with 3–4 more years of cellaring, so drink it over the near term.
    Last tasted 9/95.

1990—Châteauneuf du Pape Le Boucou   The 1990 is tasting far richer out of bottle than
·   it did from cask. Medium deep ruby, with an intensely fragrant bouquet of jammy
88   raspberries, flowers, and earth, this opulent, fleshy, satiny-smooth wine displays

full body, low acidity, and a long, sweet, voluptuously textured finish. Drink it over the next 6–8 years. Last tasted 12/95.

1989—Châteauneuf du Pape Le Boucou   The well-balanced, deep ruby-colored 1989
·   offers a graceful, rich, plummy bouquet, intertwined with scents of raspberries and
89   chocolate. In the mouth there is elegance, rich fruit, good structure, and noticeable tannins in the long, heady, lush finish. As most of Girard's Châteauneufs tend to be, the wine is gorgeously fruity and up front at the moment, giving the mistaken impression that it will not last. Anticipated maturity: now–2003. Last tasted 6/95.

1988—Châteauneuf du Pape Le Boucou   This wine has the bold, dramatic bouquet that
·   Girard routinely obtains in his wines. If the 1989 has more of the character of a Vol-
88   nay, the 1988 tastes more like a Pomerol. It is luscious, rich, and full-bodied, and while not as concentrated nor as flamboyantly fragrant, it is a sexy, terrific bottle of Châteauneuf du Pape. Anticipated maturity: now–2002. Last tasted 12/95.

1985—Châteauneuf du Pape Le Boucou   This was a delicious, up-front wine that drank
·   beautifully young, but is now beginning to lose its fruit and take on a more attenuated,
87   compact style. The medium ruby color reveals considerable lightening at the edge. The wonderful jammy raspberry and cherry fruit this wine once possessed has fallen away to reveal some herbs, earth, spice, and a hint of red fruits. The wine exhibits hot alcohol in its soft, flaccid finish. It needs to be drunk up. Last tasted 11/95.

1983—Châteauneuf du Pape Le Boucou   In complete contrast to the 1985, Girard's 1983
·   has always been a rich, luscious Châteauneuf du Pape that seemed ready to drink
89   at birth. It has not lost any of its copious quantities of smoky, black-cherry fruit. The wine is medium- to full-bodied, soft, but focused and well balanced. Owners should not push their luck. Mature now. Last tasted 11/95.

Older Vintages

In the early nineties, when I last tasted the 1981, which was once a fine wine, it appeared to be drying out. Owners of the 1979 and 1978 Cuvée du Belvedere will be delighted to hear that both wines remain in very good condition. The 1979 reveals a certain rustic character, with more of the earthy, animal side of Châteauneuf du Pape than the rich, creamy, raspberry and black-cherry fruit Girard usually obtains. The 1978 has always been a stunning, full-bodied, expansive wine from this exceptional vintage. I have not tasted it since 1990, but the last bottle I had was superb.

CUVÉE DE BOISDAUPHIN (PIERRE JACUMIN)* * * *

Address: Route de Sorgues
           84230 Châteauneuf du Pape
Tel: 4-90-83-70-34
Fax: 4-90-83-50-83
Wines produced: Châteauneuf du Pape (red and white)
Surface area (white): 2.47 acres
                (red): 15 acres
Production (white): 438 cases
                (red): 1,500 cases
Upbringing (white): 6–8 months total, with 80% of the yield in stainless steel and enamel vats, and 20% of the yield in oak barrels, of which 20% are new, for 4 months.
                (red): Fermentation of 20 days in cement vats. The yield then goes into 10% new oak casks and barrels, and the assemblage is done just before bottling.
Average age of vines (white): 35 years
                (red): 35 years

Blend (white): 50% Grenache Blanc, and one-third each Picpoul, Clairette, and Roussanne
(red): 65% Grenache, 10–15% Mourvèdre, 10–15% Syrah, 10% other varietals

Readers should be sure not to confuse this estate, Cuvée de Boisdauphin, with the
Domaine de Bois Dauphin of Jean Marchand. They are very different styles of wine. The
Cuvée de Boisdauphin, owned by Pierre Jacumin, is a much smaller estate, producing
intense wines that exhibit the telltale Provençal *garrigue* scent, along with plenty of power
and richness. As with many Châteauneuf du Pape estates, the vineyards are sprinkled
throughout the appellation, with various types of soils, from the *galets roulés* to the more
sandy/limestone soils. Jacumin, a serious, balding man, who gives the impression of being
quite confident about his winemaking abilities, seems to have more flexibility than many of
the region's producers. His red wine blend, which has begun to include larger percentages
of Mourvèdre and Syrah, is made in an interesting fashion. The Grenache is not destemmed
and vinified in a classic manner, but the Mourvèdre is completely destemmed, as is some of
the Syrah. The latter grape is put through a carbonic maceration vinification as Jacumin
believes this gives the wine more fruit and intensity, and less tannin, an idea that has merit
since the Mourvèdre provides the wine's structural delineation. This is a small but noteworthy estate producing well-made, traditional Châteauneuf du Pape that can age for 10–15
years in the top vintages.

VINTAGES

1995—Châteauneuf du Pape (red)   The outstanding 1995 exhibits an opaque ruby/purple
       ·   color, accompanied by a sweet, heady nose of cedar, Provençal herbs, black and
       91   red fruits, and earth. With layers of ripe, chewy fruit, this rich, sumptuously
                textured yet structured, full-bodied Châteauneuf is a beauty. It will be flattering
                when released, yet it will age impeccably for 12–15 years. Last tasted 6/96.

1994—Châteauneuf du Pape (red)   Cuvée de Boisdauphin's 1994 is closed by the stan-
       ·   dards of this vintage. Its healthy dark ruby color is followed by reluctant aromas of
       89   fruitcake, cedar, spice, olives, and black cherries. The wine is medium- to full-
                bodied, powerful, with excellent richness, an overall structured feel on the palate,
                and a spicy, long, alcoholic finish. It can be drunk now, but it promises to be even
                better in 2–3 years; it will keep for 10–12 years. Last tasted 6/96.

1993—Châteauneuf du Pape (red)   It is no surprise that the 1993 is excellent. It pos-
       ·   sesses a healthy dark ruby/purple color that is among the most saturated of the
       89   vintage. The restrained aromatics open with coaxing to reveal sweet layers of
                black-cherry fruit, cedar, Provençal herbs, and roasted meats. Deep, dense, and
                full-bodied, with plenty of spice, this is a large-scaled, forward, structured 1993
                Châteauneuf du Pape that will easily stand up to a decade of cellaring. Anticipated
                maturity: 1997–2008. Last tasted 12/95.

1990—Châteauneuf du Pape (red)   Although slightly less profound than the 1989, the
       ·   1990 offers a husky mouthful of wine. There is an earthy, cherry-scented nose,
       88+   rich, thick, tannic-laden flavors, and a full-bodied, big, alcoholic finish. Antici-
                pated maturity: now–2006. Last tasted 6/96.

1989—Châteauneuf du Pape (red)   Jacumin's 1989 is one of the top examples of the
       ·   vintage. The wine remains youthful and relatively unevolved. It displays a provoca-
       91   tive, licorice, peppery, herb, and sweet, jammy black-cherry-scented nose. With a
                rich, opulent, full-bodied texture, high alcohol, and moderate tannin, this is a
                large-scaled, concentrated wine that is typical of the 1989 vintage. While accessi-
                ble and enjoyable, this wine will continue to age well for another 10–15 years.
                Anticipated maturity: now–2010. Last tasted 7/96.

CUVÉE DU VATICAN (FELICIEN DIFFONTY)* * * *

Address: Route de Courthézon
                84230 Châteauneuf du Pape
Tel: 4-90-83-70-31
Fax: 4-90-83-50-36
Wines produced: Châteauneuf du Pape (red and white)
Surface area (white): 2.47 acres
                (red): 38 acres
Production (white): 333 cases
                (red): 5,400 cases
Upbringing (white): 5–6 months in temperature-controlled stainless steel vats
                (red): 24–36 months total; fermentation of 22 days in stainless steel vats at 28–
                        33° centigrade; then 6 months in cement tanks for malolactic, followed by
                        18–30 months in old oak casks
Average age of vines (white): 5 years
                (red): 5 years
Blend (white): 35% Clairette, 25% Roussanne, 25% Grenache Blanc, 15% Bourboulenc
                (red): 70% Grenache, 15% Syrah, 12% Mourvèdre, 3% Cinsault

The Diffontys, like the Sabon family, possess a famous name in Châteauneuf du Pape. Diffonty's brother, Rémy, runs another estate in Châteauneuf, Domaine Haut des Terres Blanches. This well-known family, which produced one of the mayors of Châteauneuf du Pape earlier in this century, makes traditional Châteauneuf du Pape from 38 acres of vines. Of this, only 2.5 acres are dedicated to making white wines. Diffonty and his son, Marius, have increased the percentage of Roussanne in the white wine, which should increase its quality.

The red wine is a traditional blend of 70% Grenache, 15% Syrah, 12% Mourvèdre, and 3% Cinsault aged in oak casks (nothing new at this estate), and bottled after two to three years of aging. I have had some marvelous wines from this estate that are full-bodied, powerful, rich, and oozing with an unmistakable Provençal character, as well as packing a hefty alcoholic clout. Because of the long cask aging and high alcohol, the wines tend to be drinkable and plump when released.

There are few concessions to modern oenology, except for a telltale filtering machine. No destemming takes place, and the wines' intensity is a result of the long fermentation done at a relatively high temperature, designed to produce full-bodied, powerful wines. While these wines do not achieve the appellation's highest level of quality, they are never disappointing. As the following tasting notes reveal, these are robust Châteauneuf du Papes to drink within their first 6–10 years of life.

VINTAGES

1995—Châteauneuf du Pape (red)   The 1995 reveals a smoky, roasted herb, and jammy
    ·   black-cherry-scented nose, sweet, dense, chewy fruit flavors, excellent length, and
    88   plenty of body and alcohol in the long finish. It also possesses that unmistakable
            salty, earthy, herb, *garrigue* characteristic that is a part of so many wines from the
            southern Rhône. Anticipated maturity: now–2003. Last tasted 6/96.
1994—Châteauneuf du Pape (red)   The 1994 exhibits a medium dark ruby/garnet color,
    ·   a spicy, cigar box, herb, curranty, and cherry-scented nose, medium to full body,
    87   admirable richness, and an easygoing, plump finish with noticeable alcohol. Antici-
            pated maturity: now–2002. Last tasted 6/96.

1990—Châteauneuf du Pape (red)   The 1990 exhibits an intensely spicy, cherry, roasted
·   nut, kirsch-scented nose, sweet, alcoholic, supple, chewy flavors, plenty of ripe-
87   ness, and sweet tannins in the long, succulent, lusty finish. This is a decadently
           styled, exotic Châteauneuf du Pape. Anticipated maturity: now–2003. Last tasted
           9/95.

Older Vintages

I have had considerable experience with Cuvée du Vaticans going back to 1966. The finest
wines were the 1966, 1970, and 1978. I suspect almost all of these vintages are now on
their last legs.

DOMAINE DURIEU (PAUL DURIEU)* * *

Address: 10, avenue Baron Le Roy
               84230 Châteauneuf du Pape
Tel: 4-90-83-70-86
Fax: 4-90-37-76-05
Wines produced: Châteauneuf du Pape (red and white)
Surface area (white): 1.9 acres
               (red): 49 acres
Production (white): 250 cases
               (red): 8,750 cases
Upbringing (white): 2–3 months total; fermentation in stainless steel and enamel vats at low
               temperatures
               (red): 24–36 months total; fermentation of 3 weeks in cement vats; no destem-
               ming; then 6–18 months in oak casks, followed by storage in enamel vats
               prior to bottling
Average age of vines (white): 10 years
               (red): 15–90 years
Blend (white): 80% Roussanne, 10% Bourboulenc, 10% Grenache Blanc
       (red): 70% Grenache, 10% Syrah, 10% Mourvèdre, 10% Counoise

The "caves," and that is exactly what they appear to be, of the Domaine Durieu are in
the middle of the busy little wind-beaten village of Châteauneuf du Pape. The tasting room
is reached after descending underground via some steep steps. Durieu's cellars stretch into
the bowels of the earth, where one is amazed to find the huge wooden foudres and large
fermentation tanks that had to be brought into these caves piece by piece and then assembled. The handsome, black-haired (with increasing strands of gray) Paul Durieu has 51
acres of vines ranging in age from 10 to 90 years old. He is as critical of the light
Beaujolais-styled wines of Châteauneuf du Pape as he is of the heavy, oxidized, overly
muscular style that was more widely practiced 30–40 years ago. He tries to strike a balance
between these two extremes and, I believe, succeeds.

Durieu has three parcels, one located near Maucoil, one not far from Beaucastel, and the
largest (35 acres) gorgeously situated on the plateau, sandwiched between Les Cabrières
and Mont Redon. Durieu has tended to experiment with winemaking styles more than most
French winemakers. After some false starts, he has settled into a style that produces
powerful yet concentrated wines that have been consistent, and especially reliable in difficult vintages. For example, his 1986 is one of the finest of that year. While he experimented with destemming, he refrains from that practice today, and tends to age his wine
longer in large oak casks than was done in the past. His Châteauneuf du Pape generally reveals a more animal character than many examples, with the Mourvèdre and Counoise

more expressive in spite of the fact that neither represents more than 10% of the final blend.

Durieu has also begun producing a white Châteauneuf du Pape that I have not had the opportunity to taste. However, with 80% Roussanne, I suspect it could turn out to be one of the more intriguing dry whites of Châteauneuf du Pape.

Durieu has made a special cuvée in certain vintages. In 1990, a tiny quantity of Cuvée Lucille Avril (named for Durieu's wife) was produced, but I have not seen this wine in any vintage since.

This is an interesting, high-quality estate that has not yet fully exploited its potential. Already excellent, these wines could improve, pushing Durieu to an even higher level of quality.

VINTAGES

1995—Châteauneuf du Pape (red)   Extremely unevolved, the 1995 Châteauneuf du Pape
  ·   displays a dark ruby color, high tannin, and a closed, awkward personality that
87   does not reveal the sweetness and ripeness suggested by the nose. All the component parts are in place, but this is a vin de garde. Anticipated maturity: 2002–
         2015. Last tasted 6/96.

1994—Châteauneuf du Pape (red)   The 1994 Châteauneuf du Pape possesses a deep
  ·   ruby/garnet/purple color, a big, smoked meat, Asian spice, licorice, herb, and
88   black-fruit-scented nose, full body, excellent concentration, moderate tannin, and
         plenty of glycerin. This is a rustic but impressively endowed wine. Anticipated
         maturity: 1998–2009. Last tasted 6/96.

1990—Châteauneuf du Pape (red)   Paul Durieu is an excellent winemaker, but he contin
  ·   ues to perplex me, often doing just the opposite of the majority of Châteauneuf du
87   Pape producers. For example, his 1986 was better than his 1985, and his 1983
         (his personal best during the decade of the eighties) was better than his 1981.
         Moreover, he produced a so-so 1989, not that easy to accomplish in such a super
         vintage. Durieu produced two cuvées in 1990. The 1990 regular cuvée displays a
         dark ruby color, spicy, earthy (a touch of brett yeast), leathery aromas, meaty,
         sweet, expansive, full-bodied flavors, and a long, lush, alcoholic finish. Anticipated
         maturity: now–2002. Last tasted 9/95.

1990—Châteauneuf du Pape Cuvée Lucille Avril (red)   The 1990 Cuvée Lucille Avril is
  ·   potentially outstanding, with a huge nose of smoked meats, leather, ripe black-
88+   cherry fruit, and herbs. In the mouth, the wine is full-bodied, intense, alcoholic,
         and very tannic. Impressive but rustic, this wine exhibits considerable stuffing and
         structure. Anticipated maturity: 1998–2009. Last tasted 9/95.

1989—Châteauneuf du Pape (red)   Durieu's 1989 is a green, hard, meagerly endowed
  ·   wine, lacking richness and character. It is difficult to imagine what happened with
79   this exceptional vintage. Last tasted 2/93.

1988—Châteauneuf du Pape (red)   The youthful 1988 is medium- to full-bodied, spicy
  ·   and heady, with an earthy, cinnamon, raspberry-scented bouquet, and juicy, meaty
86   tannic flavors. Not particularly concentrated, this wine needs to be drunk up.
         Mature now. Last tasted 3/95.

1986—Châteauneuf du Pape (red)   In a year known for more disappointments, and wines
  ·   that have turned out more hollow and austere than anyone expected, Durieu made
90   one of the vintage's most impressive wines. The deep ruby/garnet-colored 1986
         remains youthful. The provocative earthy, licorice, roasted meat and herb-scented
         nose is followed by a powerful, full-bodied, concentrated wine with plenty of muscle

and extract. Despite throwing considerable sediment, the wine seems several years away from full maturity. Anticipated maturity: 1999–2011. Last tasted 1/96.

Older Vintages

Durieu's 1985 was light and surprisingly diluted for a wine from this vintage. The terrific 1983 was one of the finest wines he has ever produced. The 1982 was light, and the 1981 surprisingly thin for the vintage. The oldest wine I have ever tasted from this estate, 1978, was very good, but I have not tasted it in a decade.

CHÂTEAU DES FINES ROCHES* * *

Address: 1, avenue Baron Le Roy
    84230 Châteauneuf du Pape
Tel: 4-90-83-73-10
Fax: 4-90-83-50-78
Wines produced: Châteauneuf du Pape (red and white)
Surface area (white): 10 acres
     (red): 94 acres
Production (white): 1,500 cases
     (red): 16,250 cases
Upbringing (white): 4–6 months in stainless steel vats
     (red): 6–12 months total; fermentation of 20 days in stainless steel tanks; then 6 months in old oak casks; followed by storage in cement, epoxy, and stainless steel tanks
Average age of vines (white): 9 years
     (red): 45–50 years
Blend (white): 60% Grenache Blanc, 35% Clairette and Bourboulenc (variable), 5% Roussanne
     (red): 60% Grenache, 15% Syrah, 10% Mourvèdre, 10% Cinsault, and 5% various varietals

Visitors leaving Avignon and taking D 17 in the direction of Châteauneuf du Pape cannot miss the Château des Fines Roches, which is on the right about one mile before the entrance to Châteauneuf du Pape. This building, which resembles a downsized version of the Excalibur Hotel on Las Vegas's famous strip, boasts a tiny, high-class hotel and excellent restaurant. There are not many rooms, but the food is good, as the two chefs that oversee the kitchen are Henri Estevin and his son.

Although Château des Fines Roches has long been one of the leading names of Châteauneuf du Pape, it has been many years since I tasted a profound wine from this estate. This is not meant in a pejorative sense, since the wines, which are made by a modified carbonic maceration, are fruity, ripe, tasty, and delicious if drunk in their first 5–6 years of life. While they are acceptable, this estate possesses a great terroir. If more traditional winemaking methods were utilized, this could be a classic Châteauneuf du Pape with 15–20 years of aging potential. Isn't this the style of wine that enhances the image of Châteauneuf du Pape? But obviously the fruity, open-knit wines of Fines Roches are adored by the masses.

My tasting notes continue to reveal the same fruity, open-knit, commercial style despite reports that this property was making more intense wines. Purchasers of Fines Roches should be prepared to drink it within 5–7 years of the vintage.

Readers might well imagine the potential this property has given the fact that it possesses a gorgeously situated vineyard sandwiched between two of the appellation's most famous estates, Château Fortia and Château de la Nerthe. The two parcels that comprise most of Fines Roches' vineyard holdings are situated on the large *galets roulés*.

VINTAGES

1990—Châteauneuf du Pape (red)　The 1990 is soft, round, and tasty, but generally
　·　　one-dimensional. It is ideal for drinking over the next 5–6 years. Last tasted
82　6/94.

1989—Châteauneuf du Pape (red)　The 1989 exhibits a ruby/purple color, a big, black-
　·　　cherry, intensely perfumed nose, gobs of soft, luscious fruit, plenty of alcohol, and
86　moderate tannins in the finish. There is good reason to believe this wine will
　　　evolve nicely over the next 7–10 years. Nevertheless, given the financial resources
　　　available to the Mousset family and the superb vineyard location, this is Châ-
　　　teauneuf du Pape's most notable underachiever. Last tasted 6/94.

1988—Châteauneuf du Pape (red)　The 1988 is disappointingly light, medium-bodied,
　·　　and distressingly insipid. Last tasted 3/93.
80

FONT DU LOUP (CHARLES MELIA)* * * *

Address: Route de Châteauneuf du Pape
　　　　　84350 Courthézon
Tel: 4-90-33-06-34
Fax: 4-90-33-05-47
Wines produced: Châteauneuf du Pape (red and white)
Surface area (white): 2.47 acres
　　　　　　　　(red): 52 acres
Production (white): 438 cases
　　　　　　　(red): 4,400–9,200 cases
Upbringing (white): 6 months in stainless steel vats
　　　　　　　(red): 18–36 months total; fermentation of 21 days, followed by 12–18 months
　　　　　　　　　in old oak casks; then storage in stainless steel vats
Average age of vines (white): 15 years
　　　　　　　　　　　(red): 60 years
Blend (white): 50% Grenache Blanc, 50% various varietals
　　　(red): 80% Grenache, 20% various varietals

The Domaine Font du Loup is located in the northeastern sector of the appellation of Châteauneuf du Pape not far from Vieux-Télégraphe. It is run by the handsome, serious Charles Melia and his artist wife. The soil in this area is very sandy, certain parcels being covered with a blanket of the smooth, large stones *(galets roulés)* so common in Châteauneuf du Pape. This domaine was purchased by Melia's grandparents in 1942, and since 1977 has been run by Charles. He is a very dedicated winemaker who makes it clear that since his time is spent in the vineyard and wine cellars, he has little time for visitors. His vineyard has many old vines (the average age is 60 years) and the blend he uses is 80% Grenache, with the balance Syrah, Cinsault, and Mourvèdre. He intends to incorporate Muscardin into this formula as his acre of Muscardin comes into production. His white wine is among the more tasty of the appellation, but he only makes 438 cases of it from 50% Grenache Blanc with the balance equally split between Bourboulenc, Roussanne, and Clairette.

Melia argues that a strict selection is essential to get the highest quality. Each vintage he claims his yield is among the lowest, and he sells off to négociants those lots of wine he does not want. He complains that few of his clients seem to care about this when they argue that his Châteauneuf du Pape is more expensive than many others. The wines of Font du Loup are dense and less open and flattering than many other Châteauneuf du Pape. Melia dearly desires to produce a vin de garde that possesses more elegance and finessse than those of his peers.

In the following tasting notes, readers will note that Melia produces another Châteauneuf du Pape called Le Puy Rolland. This wine emerges from a 10-acre vineyard adjacent to Font du Loup.

VINTAGES

1995—Châteauneuf du Pape (red)   The 1995 Châteauneuf du Pape reveals some toasty
· vanillin in the nose, as if a few new barrels have made their way into the Melia
89 cellars. The wine exhibits an impressively saturated ruby/purple color, and a terrific nose of black cherries and raspberries, combined with toasty notes from the new wood. It is a deep, rich, full-bodied wine with outstanding delineation and terrific purity. Once again, excellent winemaking plus high-quality raw materials have been translated into something special. Melia appears to have the ability to obtain considerable richness, but also keep his flavors well focused and pure, without their becoming overweight or too extracted. Anticipated maturity: 2002–2012. Last tasted 6/96.

1995—Châteauneuf du Pape Le Puy Rolland (red)   The 1995 Le Puy Rolland is a
· tannic, backward, vin de garde style of Châteauneuf du Pape with an impressively
90 saturated, dark ruby/purple color, plenty of spice, ripeness, extract, and richness, as well as surprising grip and moderately high tannin. It is a wine to lay away. Anticipated maturity: 2005–2015. Last tasted 6/96.

1994—Châteauneuf du Pape (red)   The 1994 Châteauneuf du Pape boasts a dark ruby/
· purple color, and a reticent, backward, but promising nose of sweet berry fruit.
88 Full-bodied, with grip, structure, and ripeness, this wine possesses a Burgundy-like black-cherry fruitiness and floral character. Pure, rich, and beautifully proportioned, it requires cellaring. Anticipated maturity: 1998–2010. Last tasted 6/96.

1994—Châteauneuf du Pape Le Puy Rolland (red)   Behind the attractive artist's label is
· a well-endowed, dark ruby/purple-colored wine with excellent purity and intensity.
88 A sweet nose of red and black fruits, spice, and minerals is followed by a wine with moderate tannin, rich, medium- to full-bodied flavors, and a long, clean finish. Anticipated maturity: now–2010. Last tasted 9/95.

1990—Châteauneuf du Pape (red)   Melia's dark ruby-colored 1990 exhibits plenty of
· black fruit, herbs, and minerals in its aroma. In the mouth it displays multidimen-
89 sional flavors, as well as an attractive unctuous quality that serves its rich, concentrated, ripe, opulent style well. It should drink well for the next 10 years. Last tasted 9/95.

Older Vintages

Font du Loup made two cuvées of wine in 1989—a very good regular cuvée, and a luxury cuvée that I have never seen in the marketplace. It may have been an experimental venture, but it was a wine of enormous richness, massive, full body, an unctuous texture, and extraordinary focus for its size and power. I thought it was the most exciting wine I had ever tasted from Melia, but it was not commercialized, so my comments are of academic interest only. Melia's 1988 was very good, and the 1985 elegant and light, now fully mature. Another noteworthy success is the 1981. One of the few wines I have found disappointing from Melia was his 1983.

FONT DE MICHELLE (GONNET FRÈRES)
(* * * *Cuvée Classique/* * * * *Cuvée Etienne Gonnet)

Address: 14, impasse des Vignerons
        84370 Bédarrides
Tel: 4-90-33-00-22
Fax: 4-90-33-20-27
Wines produced: Châteauneuf du Pape (red and white), Châteauneuf du Pape Cuvée Etienne
        Gonnet (red and white)
Surface area (white): 6.2 acres
                Cuvée E. Gonnet—a cellar selection
        (red): 74 acres
                Cuvée E. Gonnet—a cellar selection
Production (white): 1,000 cases
                Cuvée E. Gonnet—250 cases
        (red): 10,000 cases
                Cuvée E. Gonnet—1,000 cases
Upbringing (white): 3–4 months in stainless steel vats
                Cuvée E. Gonnet—The Roussanne is fermented in new oak barrels for
        4 months and is assembled with an equal amount of the normal cuvée
        prior to bottling.
        (red): 15–18 months total; fermentation of 18–20 days in temperature-
        controlled stainless steel vats; 30% of the harvest is destemmed; then 8–
        12 months in old oak casks followed by storage in stainless steel vats
                Cuvée E. Gonnet—18 months total; fermentation of 18–20 days in
        temperature-controlled cement tanks; then 12 months in new oak and oak
        barrels 2–3 years old; this cuvée is then assembled with 25% of the
        normal cuvée before bottling
Average age of vines (white): 40 and 15 years
                (red): 35–40 years
Blend (white): 50% Grenache Blanc, 25% Clairette, 20% Bourboulenc, 5% Roussanne
                Cuvée E. Gonnet—50% Roussanne, 50% of the normal cuvée
        (red): 65% Grenache, 15% Cinsault, 10% Syrah, 10% Mourvèdre
                Cuvée E. Gonnet—65% Grenache, 15% Cinsault, 10% Syrah, 10% Mourvèdre

The youthful Gonnet brothers, inspired by their mentor and uncle, Henri Brunier of Vieux-Télégraphe, have quickly built a reputation for a modern-style, interesting, distinctive white (one of the appellation's best) and red Châteauneuf du Pape. The estate is of good size, 80 acres, and has a fairly typical blend of grapes for its red wine. More than three-fourths of the production is exported. Much of the Gonnets' vineyard holdings are near the famous Vieux-Télégraphe on pure clay/limestone soils blanketed with small boulders and cobble-stones. The white wine, one of the finest of the appellation, is bottled early, but despite having its malolactic fermentation blocked, is not sterile-filtered. Perhaps that is why it possesses such wonderful aromatics, flesh, and fruit. Nevertheless, it requires drinking within the first several years of life. Recently, the Gonnets introduced an oakier style of wine, the Cuvée Etienne Gonnet, made with 50% Roussane and 50% of the blend for their regular white wine. It is a cellar selection, and possesses more fat as well as more oak. I still have reservations about it, and continue to have a preference for the nonoaked, regular cuvée.

The red wine vinification is quasi-traditional. The Syrah is vinified by the carbonic maceration method, while the other grape varieties are not destemmed, but crushed and fermented in the classic manner. The wine spends no more than 18 months in large wooden foudres. During this period, the Gonnets taste and make a selection of the finest cuvées, which is then culled out and part of it moved to small oak casks, of which a certain percentage are new. This wine becomes the luxury cuvée, Cuvée Etienne Gonnet, which debuted with the 1988 vintage. Unlike many luxury cuvées, it is not an old-vine selection or from a single vineyard; rather it is a selection made in the cellars.

Despite the similarities between the Gonnets' wine and Brunier's Vieux-Télégraphe (even the equipment in each cellar is similar), Font de Michelle is a less weighty wine, as well as less powerful and alcoholic. Certainly the Cuvée Etienne Gonnet is their densest, richest wine, and generally one of the finest of the appellation. All the Font de Michelle wines are consistently well made, and among the most reasonably priced of the appellation.

VINTAGES

1995—Châteauneuf du Pape (red)   The dense purple-colored 1995 Châteauneuf du Pape
•   offers a sweet, black-cherry/raspberry, licorice, and smoky-scented nose, lush,
89   peppery, concentrated flavors, full body, and an expansive palate with no hard
           edges. It is an immensely seductive style of Châteauneuf du Pape. Anticipated
           maturity: 1998–2007. Last tasted 6/96.

1995—Châteauneuf du Pape Cuvée Etienne Gonnet (red)   The backward, admirably
•   endowed, massive 1995 Cuvée Etienne Gonnet reveals some evidence of aging in
91   small oak casks, but the wine is dominated by huge quantities of fruit, glycerin,
           and extract. Full-bodied, powerful, and rich, with surprising tannin levels and
           excellent acidity, it is a youthful, dense wine. Anticipated maturity: 1999–2012.
           Last tasted 6/96.

1994—Châteauneuf du Pape (red)   The 1994 Châteauneuf du Pape confirms my high
•   praise given last year from barrel tastings. The attractive dark ruby/purple color is
88   accompanied by aromas of olives, herbes de Provence, and sweet, jammy, black-
           cherry and raspberry fruit. The wine is full-bodied, chewy, lush, and generously
           endowed. It should drink well for a decade. Anticipated maturity: now–2004. Last
           tasted 6/96.

1994—Châteauneuf du Pape Cuvée Etienne Gonnet (red)   The deep ruby/purple-colored
•   1994 Cuvée Etienne Gonnet exhibits copious amounts of smoky underbrush, *gar-*
91   *rigue,* olive, peppery aromas, along with attractive roasted-meat characteristics.
           Full-bodied, with layers of jammy fruit, high glycerin, and a blockbuster finish,
           this is a rich, broad-shouldered Châteauneuf du Pape. Anticipated maturity: 1998–
           2012. Last tasted 6/96.

1993—Châteauneuf du Pape (red)   The 1993 Châteauneuf du Pape exhibits a healthy
•   dark ruby/purple color, plenty of peppery, herb, *garrigue,* and coffee-scented, spicy
88   aromas, round, rich, full-bodied flavors, and light tannin in the finish. It possesses
           a chewy, Provençal herb personality. Anticipated maturity: now–2003. Last tasted
           6/95.

1993—Châteauneuf du Pape Cuvée Etienne Gonnet (red)   The 1993 reveals the essence
•   of cherries in its nose, as well as scents of overripe fruit intertwined with cedar,
89   smoke, pepper, and herbs. This is a highly extracted, supple, full-bodied, lush, and
           mouth-filling wine. Anticipated maturity: 1998–2007. Last tasted 6/95.

1992—Châteauneuf du Pape (red)   The 1992 Châteauneuf du Pape boasts a wonderfully
•   sweet bouquet of cedar, herbs, coffee, and cherries. Medium- to full-bodied, with
86   supple texture, this is a generously endowed, concentrated, plump wine. Mature
           now. Last tasted 9/94.

1992—Châteauneuf du Pape Cuvée Etienne Gonnet (red)   The 1992 Cuvée Etienne
·   Gonnet displays an attractive olive, black-cherry, and herb-scented nose, excellent
88   ripeness, full-bodied, soft tannin, and a heady finish. Anticipated maturity: now–
          2004. Last tasted 9/94.

1990—Châteauneuf du Pape (red)   The 1990 Châteauneuf du Pape is the Gonnets' best
·   wine since their heroic 1978. With a splendid black/ruby color, as well as a terrific
89   bouquet of crushed, jammy, raspberry fruit, it displays a full-bodied, concentrated
          palate, and gobs of fruit, glycerin, and spices in its long finish. Anticipated matu-
          rity: now–2008. Last tasted 10/95.

1990—Châteauneuf du Pape Cuvée Etienne Gonnet (red)   This wine tastes marvelously
·   rich, fat, and full-bodied, with terrific floral, herb, black-cherry, and pepper aromat-
91   ics. Full-bodied, with excellent concentration, this is a juicy, succulent Châ-
          teauneuf du Pape. This particular selection, first inaugurated by the Gonnet
          brothers in 1989, is given a slightly different upbringing, with more small casks
          utilized than for their regular cuvée. Anticipated maturity: now–2007. Last tasted
          6/96.

1989—Châteauneuf du Pape (red)   The regular 1989 Châteauneuf du Pape is a tasty
·   wine with an herbaceous, peppery nose, rich red and black fruit flavors, full body,
86   and brobust tannins in its long finish. Anticipated maturity: now–2004. Last tasted
          2/95.

1989—Châteauneuf du Pape Cuvée Etienne Gonnet (red)   The toasty, vanillin scent of
·   wood is present in the wine's aroma, but these subtle scents add a degree of
88   complexity. The wine is more structured, slightly richer and riper, full-bodied, and
          larger framed than the 1989 regular cuvée. Anticipated maturity: now–2006. Last
          tasted 5/95.

Older Vintages

Other than the brilliant 1978, most other good vintages of Font de Michelle (1981, 1983,
and 1985) were good rather than exciting wines. There was a tendency in the decade of the
eighties to make the wines too *facile* (easy), as the French would say, and some vintages
lacked richness and staying power. This changed after the 1988 vintage, with richer, more
complete, and well-endowed wines.

CHÂTEAU FORTIA (BARON LE ROY DE BOISEAUMARIE)
(* * * * *before 1978/* *from 1978–93/* * * *since 1994)

Address: 84230 Châteauneuf du Pape
Tel: 4-90-83-72-25
Fax: 4-90-83-51-03
Wines produced: Châteauneuf du Pape (red and white)
Surface area (white): 5 acres
              (red): 62 acres
Production (white): 416 cases
              (red): 5,420 cases
Upbringing (white): 6 months in temperature-controlled stainless steel vats
              (red): 24–36 months total; fermentation of 22 days in cement tanks; then 18
                  months in old oak casks, followed by 6 months storage in enamel tanks
Average age of vines (white): 15–20 years
              (red): 50 years
Blend (white): 50% Roussanne, 43% Clairette, 6% Grenache Blanc, 1% Bourboulenc
      (red): 70% Grenache, 20% Syrah, 7% Mourvèdre, 3% Counoise

Historically, the ivy-covered, impressive, turreted Château Fortia is the most important property of Châteauneuf du Pape. The late Baron Pierre Le Roy developed in 1923 a set of stringent wine-producing regulations that in 1936 became the basis for all of France's appellation contrôlée laws. His son, Henri, also called Baron Le Roy, succeeded here in 1967, and proceeded largely to ruin the reputation of this estate's wines during his 25-year tenure. Despite the quality of the terroir, multiple visits to Fortia between 1978 and 1994 always left me with the vivid impression that Baron Henri Le Roy was not at all content with either the wine of Fortia or the wine of Châteauneuf du Pape, an appellation that he claimed was "going to hell." Seemingly tired of working and feuding with the other owners, he castigated their expensive new destemmer-crushers (it does not crush the grapes enough), excoriated the village's obsession with Grenache (he wanted more Mourvèdre and Counoise), and always said that if he didn't get his way, he was going to retire. His personality, in addition to the quality of wine he produced, made my annual visit to Fortia about as much fun as being audited by the IRS. This curmudgeon, largely out of touch with reality, ceded administrative control to his youngest son, Bruno, in 1994. And guess what? The oxidized, woody, eviscerated, and diluted wines made during Henri's reign of mediocrity quickly became history.

Bruno, an enthusiastic young man who appears to be well aware of the huge job he has ahead of him to resurrect this property, began his tenure by immediately bringing in the renowned oenologist Jean-Luc Colombo. Colombo sensed that this could be an enormous opportunity to showcase his talent, for Fortia already had an exquisite terroir in addition to its historical importance. A strict selection was made with the first two vintages vinified under Colombo's supervision (1994 and 1995), and the percentage of Syrah in the final blend was increased to a whopping 40%. The results have been stunning, as in both 1994 and 1995 Château Fortia produced the two finest red wines since the prodigious 1978. All of this bodes well for the future. The young Bruno, with his father pushed out to pasture, and with Colombo well installed, has taken several gigantic steps toward reestablishing the reputation of Château Fortia.

VINTAGES

1995—Château du Pape (red) Fortia's 1995 Châteauneuf du Pape is a more struc-
·   tured, backward, muscular rendition of the 1994. It will not be as delicious and
90   flattering young, but it has the potential to surpass the 1994. It will turn out to be
a 15- to 20-year wine. The color is an opaque deep purple, and the wine offers up a tight but promising nose of sweet cassis and blueberry fruit. Purely made, with a wonderful texture, a structured feel, and plenty of grip, this is a full-bodied, admirably endowed, backward wine with terrific flavor intensity. I also admired its focus and delineation. Anticipated maturity: 2000–2015. Last tasted 6/96.

1994—Châteauneuf du Pape (red) The exceptional 1994 Châteauneuf du Pape boasts a
·   deep ruby/purple color, as well as aromas of jammy cassis fruit allied to smoky
90   notes. The wine is sweet, rich, fleshy, and full-bodied with gobs of wild-blackberry
fruit intermingled with cassis. There is soft tannin, low acidity, and a large, full-bodied, opulent, sumptuous finish. This should turn out to be a terrific Châteauneuf du Pape. Anticipated maturity: now–2010. Last tasted 6/96.

1993—Châteauneuf du Pape (red) The 1993 is supple and round, with plenty of black
·   fruits intermingled with scents of Provençal herbs, smoke, and earth. It is a
87   medium-bodied wine with fine concentration and ripeness, a smooth-as-silk personality, and a long, heady, alcoholic finish. Anticipated maturity: now–2002. Last tasted 6/95.

1992—Châteauneuf du Pape (red)   The 1992 Châteauneuf du Pape displays earthy,
·   spicy, diluted flavors of dried fruit, tobacco, and herbs, medium body, and a simple,
74   compact finish. What a shame! Last tasted 6/95.

1990—Châteauneuf du Pape (red)   The herb-tinged 1990 red Châteauneuf displays some
·   ripeness, but it is diffuse, lacks concentration, and finishes with a flabby fruitiness
82   and excessive alcohol. Anticipated maturity: now–2002. Last tasted 9/94.

1989—Châteauneuf du Pape (red)   The 1989 displays plenty of tannin and glycerin. It
·   was the richest, ripest, and most promising Fortia made during the decade of the
87   eighties. It offers an interesting, spicy, jammy, sweet nose, a Burgundy-like, velvety
     texture, backed up by considerable alcohol. Drink it between now and 2008. Last
     tasted 8/96.

1988—Châteauneuf du Pape (red)   The 1988 exhibited a medium ruby color, a dense,
·   alcoholic, spicy taste, some notes of truffles, leather, and ground beef, a soft texture,
84   and a round, gentle finish. Anticipated maturity: now–2001. Last tasted 11/95.

1986—Châteauneuf du Pape (red)   The fully mature 1986 displays an exotic, Asian
·   spice, sweet pruny fruit nose, rich, velvety texture, and plenty of smoky, juicy fruit
84   in its finish. Mature now. Last tasted 11/95.

1985—Châteauneuf du Pape (red)   Medium garnet with an amber edge, this fully mature
·   1985 reveals a spicy, fruitcake sort of nose, and very low acidity. The fat has
82   melted away, and what is left is an alcoholic, fruity wine that is beginning to dry
     out. Drink it up. Last tasted 4/94.

Older Vintages

Virtually everything produced in the early eighties is now over the hill. The 1978 remains a compelling, majestic Châteauneuf du Pape that reveals what a sensational terroir Fortia possesses. I have drunk several cases of this wine, and with only a handful of bottles left in my cellar, I am still amazed by how much richness, fruit, and complexity this wine offers. The color remains a deep opaque garnet with plenty of ruby remaining. The wine is loaded with fruit, glycerin, and extract, with gorgeous delineation. It is full-bodied, rich, and impressive. I frequently look for this wine at auctions, but I have had no success in finding more bottles.

LOU FRÉJAU* * *

Address: Chemin de la Gironde
          84100 Orange
Tel: 4-90-34-83-00
Fax: 4-90-34-48-78
Wines produced: Châteauneuf du Pape (red and white)
Surface area (white): 1 acre
              (red): 18 acres
Production (white): 375 cases
           (red): 2,875 cases
Upbringing (white): 2–4 months in stainless steel tanks
           (red): 15–28 months in wood foudres
Average age of vines (white): 20 years
                     (red): 45–50 years
Blend (white): 40% Clairette, 40% Bourboulenc, 20% Grenache Blanc
      (red): 70% Grenache, 20% Mourvèdre, 10% various varietals

The Chastans, who run the Lou Fréjau estate, are one of the better-known families of Châteauneuf du Pape. Their origins are in the northern part of the appellation, just south of

Orange. This estate makes a fresh, one-dimensional white wine, and a medium-bodied, spicy, attractive but easygoing red. Lou Fréjau's (Fréjau is Provençal for the boulders and stones that blanket so much of the appellation) parcels are in the northern part of the appellation on rocky, clay-based soils. Over recent years, the percentage of Mourvèdre has been increased to give the wine more structure. Chastan has demonstrated a high degree of flexibility with respect to destemming. He will often destem part of his harvest if conditions warrant. Normally, this is a wine to drink within 7–10 years of the vintage.

VINTAGES

1995—Châteauneuf du Pape (red)   The 1995 displays good grip, tannin, acidity, ripeness, and richness. Medium-bodied, with attractive cherry and herbaceous fruit, enough
·
86   glycerin to provide an interesting texture, and a spicy finish, it should drink well for 7–8 + years. Last tasted 6/96.

1994—Châteauneuf du Pape (red)   The 1994 possesses a spicy, peppery, black-olive-scented nose, medium body, average concentration, good purity, and a spicy,
·
82   herbaceous finish. Anticipated maturity: now–2000. Last tasted 6/96.

1993—Châteauneuf du Pape (red)   This is one of the few domaines where I preferred the 1993 to the 1994. The 1993 gives evidence of sweet, ripe fruit, full body, and a
·
87   supple, velvety texture with admirable length and power. Anticipated maturity: now–2000. Last tasted 9/95.

1990—Châteauneuf du Pape (red)   The 1990 offers a big, nicely scented, herbal, jammy nose, as well as ripe, unctuous, full-bodied flavors reminiscent of black cherries
·
87   and fruitcake. The finish is sweet, round, spicy, and alcoholic. It will not make old bones. Mature now. Last tasted 9/95.

1989—Châteauneuf du Pape (red)   This charming yet one-dimensional 1989 is fragrant and soft, with attractive berry fruitiness, medium to full body, and a round, slightly
·
85   tannic finish. There are some elements of apricot and peach jam, suggesting the grapes had reached *surmaturité*. Mature now. Last tasted 9/95.

1988—Châteauneuf du Pape (red)   The 1988 had an exuberant, chocolaty, black-raspberry, cedary bouquet, deep, rich, medium- to full-bodied flavors, and a soft,
·
87   velvety texture. Mature now. Last tasted 9/95.

DOMAINE DU GALET DES PAPES* * */* * * *

Address: Route de Bédarrides
        84230 Châteauneuf du Pape
Tel: 4-90-83-73-67
Fax: 4-90-83-50-22
Wines produced: Châteauneuf du Pape (red and white), Châteauneuf du Pape Cuvée
        Vieilles Vignes (red)
Surface area (white): 2.47 acres
        (red): 25 acres
        Cuvée Vieilles Vignes—7.4 acres
Production (white): 250 cases
        (red): 3,250 cases
        Cuvée Vieilles Vignes—1,125 cases
Upbringing (white): 6 months in enamel vats
        (red): 18–24 months total; fermentation of 15 days in stainless steel and enamel vats; then 6 months in oak casks; then 6–12 months' storage in stainless steel tanks
        Cuvée Vieilles Vignes—same as for the regular red wine cuvée

Average age of vines (white): 30 years
                              (red): 40 years
                                    Cuvée Vieilles Vignes—60 years, with some vines 90–100
                                    years old
Blend (white): 60% Grenache Blanc, 20% Clairette, 20% Bourboulenc
      (red): 80% Grenache, 5% Vaccarèse, 5% Cinsault, 5% Mourvèdre, 5% Syrah
            Cuvée Vieilles Vignes—60% Grenache, 30% Mourvèdre, 10% Syrah

This moderately sized estate, owned by Jean-Luc and Roger Mayard, has been producing better and better wines. There are two red wine cuvées and one white from the estate's 18 vineyard parcels located in three sectors of Châteauneuf du Pape—the rocky, boulder-laden area of the southwest, the clay/limestone soils of the north, and the sandy, rocky soils of the northeast. The cuvée from parcels of old vines can be an exceptional wine. This is a traditionally made wine that relies heavily on Grenache, but with some Syrah and Mourvèdre. Interestingly, some young vineyards of Counoise and Vaccarèse will be coming into production. The red wine is bottled without filtration, although the white wine has to be sterile-filtered because malolactic is blocked. The red wine is typical of the appellation's better examples, with its jammy, cherry, herbes de Provence, *garrigue*, smoky, spicy, forceful personality and fleshy texture. The Cuvée Vieilles Vignes is deeper and richer. This estate appears to be on the upswing, producing more impressive wines with each new good vintage. Prices have tended to lag behind those of other stars of the appellation, so readers are advised to put that information to good use.

The white Châteauneuf du Pape is pleasant, but like many of the white wines of this appellation, its rarity as well as quality makes it overpriced.

VINTAGES

1995—Châteauneuf du Pape (red)   The 1995 Châteauneuf du Pape displays a deep ruby/
·   purple color, with sweet cherry flavors, a thick texture, some unctuousness, and fat,
89   body, and extract in the long, ripe finish. It should drink well for 8–10 years. Last
         tasted 6/96.
1995—Châteauneuf du Pape Cuvée Vieilles Vignes (red)   The 1995 Cuvée Vieilles Vignes
·   possesses a backward, unevolved style. Although closed, it is an impressive wine
90   exhibiting a deep purple color, a considerable amount of tannin, and outstanding
         concentration and potential. Anticipated maturity: 2000–2012. Last tasted 6/96.
1994—Châteauneuf du Pape (red)   I have noticed in the past that Jean-Luc Mayard's
·   wines tend to show better after bottling. Certainly the 1994 Châteauneuf du Pape
88   was impressive from the barrel and it appears to have lost little in the bottling
         process. It exhibits a deep ruby color, an expressive, spicy, cherry, Provençal herb,
         smoky-scented nose, round, rich, sweet, fruity flavors, medium to full body, a
         velvety texture, and a spicy, clean, fleshy finish. Anticipated maturity: now–2003.
         Last tasted 6/96.
1994—Châteauneuf du Pape Cuvée Vieilles Vignes (red)   The 1994 Cuvée Vieilles
·   Vignes offers a dark ruby/garnet color, followed by a fragrant, flamboyant nose of
89+   Provençal herbs, smoked meats, fruitcake, and cherry jam. Full-bodied, with rich,
         chewy fruit, this soft, round, generously endowed wine should drink well for 10–
         12 years. It is a hedonistic, up-front, admirably endowed Châteauneuf du Pape.
         Anticipated maturity: now–2003. Last tasted 6/96.
1993—Châteauneuf du Pape (red)   The 1993 Châteauneuf du Pape represents the es-
·   sence of Bing cherry fruit presented in a medium- to full-bodied, seductive style.
86   The color is a healthy medium to dark ruby and the wine reveals layers of round,

generous fruit that caresses the palate. Anticipated maturity: now–2000. Last tasted 9/95.

1993—Châteauneuf du Pape Cuvée Vieilles Vignes (red)   The 1993 Cuvée Vieilles Vig-
·   nes offers very good concentration, body, glycerin, and tannin. Accessible, full,
88   and rich, it reveals gobs of black-cherry aromas intermingled with scents of herbs, smoke, spice, and earth. Anticipated maturity: now–2005. Last tasted 9/95.

1992—Châteauneuf du Pape (red)   The 1992 Châteauneuf du Pape reveals a sweet, juicy,
·   herb, black-cherry, and earthy-scented nose, medium- to full-bodied, expansive,
86   round flavors exhibiting glycerin and fatness, and a soft, pleasant finish. Mature now. Last tasted 6/95.

1992—Châteauneuf du Pape Cuvée Vieilles Vignes (red)   The 1992 Cuvée Vieilles Vig-
·   nes is more backward and structured, with excellent saturated dark ruby color, a
87+ spicy, restrained but rich nose, and full-bodied, tannic yet concentrated flavors. Anticipated maturity: now–2001. Last tasted 6/95.

1990—Châteauneuf du Pape (red)   The 1990 exhibits an attractive dark ruby color and a
·   ripe, sweet, jammy nose of black fruits and herbs. In the mouth the wine is medium-
86   to full-bodied and monolithic, but dense, nicely concentrated, with considerable tannin and alcohol in the finish. Will more character and complexity emerge? Anticipated maturity: now–2001. Last tasted 6/94.

1989—Châteauneuf du Pape (red)   The 1989 reveals that wonderful inner core of sweet,
·   black fruits, a tight but blossoming bouquet of minerals, licorice, tobacco, fruitcake,
89   and black fruits, and an impressively deep purple color. The acids in the 1989 were lower than in the 1990, and the alcohol level was higher. This impressive wine may merit an outstanding rating with another 3–4 years of bottle age. Anticipated maturity: now–2005. Last tasted 6/94.

LES GALETS BLONDE* * * *

This wine represents a special cuvée purchased by Paris-based wine broker Patrick Lesec. As the tasting note indicates, it is purchased from Monsieur Maurel's Clos St.-Jean estate. In essence, it is a selection sold to Lesec, and then bottled unfined and unfiltered for his clients. The only vintage I have tasted (1995) suggests that this is at least a four-star cuvée, but sources for such wines change, and the wines are often not purchased in less than top vintages. It is a wine that should be noted, but readers are advised that future sources for this blend may be different.

VINTAGES

1995—Châteauneuf du Pape (red)   Made by Monsieur Maurel, this 1995 Châteauneuf du
·   Pape is from a Grenache vineyard 80–85 years old planted in the commune of
91   Bédarrides, not far from the well-known vineyards of Vieux-Télégraphe. The wine is made from primarily Grenache, with a small amount of Syrah and Mourvèdre. It is not racked until it is assembled for bottling, which is scheduled to be done without any fining or filtration. Fortunately, there are 500 cases of this powerful, rich, multilayered Châteauneuf du Pape that is bursting with black fruit. This sweet (from ripeness not sugar), full-bodied, concentrated wine should turn heads with its hedonistic display of fruit, glycerin, and alcohol. It is a big, rich, accessible style of Châteauneuf du Pape that should drink marvelously well for 12–15+ years. Last tasted 6/96.

CHÂTEAU DE LA GARDINE (GASTON BRUNEL)
(* * * *Château de la Gardine/* * * * *Cuvée des Générations)

Address: 84230 Châteauneuf du Pape

Tel: 4-90-83-73-20

Fax: 4-90-83-77-24

Wines produced: Châteauneuf du Pape Château de la Gardine (red and white), Châteauneuf du Pape Cuvée Vieilles Vignes (white), Châteauneuf du Pape Cuvée des Générations (red)

Surface area: Château de la Gardine (white)—7.5 acres
Cuvée Vieilles Vignes—3.7 acres
Total red wine surface area—141 acres

Production: Château de la Gardine (white)—1,125 cases
Cuvée Vieilles Vignes—562 cases
Château de la Gardine (red)—16,500 cases
Cuvée des Générations—250–1,000 cases

Upbringing: Château de la Gardine (white)—4–6 months in stainless steel tanks
Cuvée Vieilles Vignes—9 months in new oak barrels for alcoholic and malolactic fermentations
Château de la Gardine (red)—24 months total; fermentation of 15–21 days in stainless steel tanks, then 9–12 months in 15% new oak barrels (depending on the vintage), then storage in cement tanks
Cuvée des Générations—24 months total; fermentation of 15–21 days in stainless steel vats; then 9–18 months in 100% new oak barrels; then storage in cement vats

Average age of vines: Château de la Gardine (white)—15 years
Cuvée Vieilles Vignes—35 years
Château de la Gardine (red)—30 years
Cuvée des Générations—35–38 years

Blend: Château de la Gardine (white)—25% each Grenache Blanc, Roussanne, Bourboulenc, Clairette
Cuvée Vieilles Vignes—60% Roussanne, 40% divided evenly between Grenache Blanc, Bourboulenc, and Clairette
All three red wine cuvées—60% Grenache, 15% Syrah, 12% Mourvèdre, and 13% various varietals

Note: The white Cuvée Vieilles Vignes is made from the oldest vines located on a specific plot of land. The blend differs from the normal cuvée, with a larger proportion of Roussanne.

The Cuvée des Générations is produced only in vintages where its quality is considered well above that of the normal cuvée (none was produced in 1988, 1991, or 1992). Otherwise, it is assembled with the normal Château de la Gardine. This special cuvée is produced from older vines planted on a special terroir.

Château de la Gardine is made in the manner of a Bordeaux second wine. It is essentially produced from the younger vines. The vineyard is being replanted in certain places and this accounts for the large variability in the production of this cuvée, as much as 24,000 bottles in certain years.

Contrary to what is done at most Châteauneuf du Pape estates, there is no separate vinification by blend. The grapes are picked according to maturity and there can be several passages in the vineyards so that grapes of identical maturity are collected and fermented together. The Château de la Gardine wants to renew an old tradition of Châteauneuf—in the last century there existed mixed plantations and there was no sorting of the different cépages.

Since the late seventies and early eighties, Château de la Gardine has soared in quality, becoming one of the great estates of Châteauneuf du Pape. The late Gaston Brunel, who acquired this estate, was one of Châteauneuf du Pape's great champions. The soil is lighter and shallower here, and not as highly regarded as the other sections of Châteauneuf du Pape. In hot drought years this soil often causes severe stress to the vineyards. However, Brunel, through an extensive rehabilitation program, enlarged this domaine to 152 acres, planted it with an interesting blend of 60% Grenache, a significant portion of Syrah (15%), 12% Mourvèdre, and 13% Muscardin and Cinsault. There are plans to increase the percentage of Mourvèdre while decreasing the amount of Grenache. The vines average 35–38 years of age.

Gaston Brunel, the author of a major book on the region published in 1980, died tragically in the summer of 1986 in a fishing accident, the first time in his life he had ever gone fishing. His two sons, Maxime and Patrick, were well prepared by their father and now run the property.

The Brunel brothers have proven to be dynamic and flexible, and in essence have infused a new commitment to quality into this major estate, located behind the village of Châteauneuf du Pape in the western sector, with a clear view of the Rhône River and the town of Roquemaure. The hillside vineyards are planted in cobblestone and *galets roulés* soils, although the *galets roulés* are not as thick as on the plateau between Mont Redon and Cabrières, or in the eastern part of the appellation near Vieux-Télégraphe. Unlike so many Châteauneuf du Pape estates, the Château de la Gardine's vineyard holdings are all in one parcel, as opposed to being morsellated throughout the appellation.

Many changes have occured under the leadership of Maxime and Patrick Brunel. The amount of Roussanne plantations has been increased, and there are now two cuvées of white wine (with a total production of approximately 1,700 cases). The regular cuvée, a blend of equal proportions of Grenache Blanc, Roussanne, Bourboulenc, and Clairette, is made in a fruity yet powerful style that has increased in quality over recent vintages. The Cuvée Vieilles Vignes is produced from 60% Roussanne and the rest Grenache Blanc, Bourboulenc, and Clairette. This wine is fermented and aged for up to 9 months in new oak casks. The first vintage was atrociously overwooded, but recent vintages have shown far better integration of wood with the rich, honeyed Roussanne fruit. Readers should pay more attention to this up-and-coming cuvée of white Châteauneuf du Pape.

The true glories of Château de la Gardine are the cuvées of red wine. This is an estate that marches to the beat of a different drummer (à la Rayas). It has eschewed the use of the traditional Châteauneuf du Pape bottle with the embossed papal keys. The de la Gardine bottle is a specially embossed brown, somewhat crooked-looking bottle that I find esthetically unpleasing and eccentric. However, no one drinks the bottle, and what is inside has been consistently excellent to outstanding since the late eighties. In keeping with both tradition and a progressive approach to new techniques, in 1989, La Gardine installed ten stainless steel tanks with the ability to do automatic *pigéage* (this is the same system employed at Beaurenard and La Nerthe). Additionally, this estate has an untraditional view on the issue of destemming. In any given year, at least 80%, sometimes 100%, of the varietals are destemmed, as the Brunels are adamant about avoiding the astringency of stem tannin. Their approach to vinification and maceration is almost Bordeaux-like in their extended maceration to extract sweet tannin and as much color and intensity as possible.

There are three red wines made. There is a second wine made from lots of wine not deemed sufficiently concentrated for either the Cuvée Tradition or Cuvée des Générations.

This is rare in Châteauneuf du Pape as most quality producers tend to sell their production from young vines to négociants. Gardine's Cuvée Tradition is aged in both cement tank and small oak casks from the Demptos firm in Bordeaux. However, no more than 15% new oak is used for the Cuvée Tradition in any vintage. In certain vintages—1985, 1989, 1990, 1994, and 1995—the Brunels produce 250–1,000 cases of their Cuvée des Générations, a superrich Châteauneuf du Pape aged for two years in 100% new Bordeaux casks. It is a dedication cuvée to their father, Gaston, and their grandfather Philippe. While critics have noted its new world–ish, international style (I don't necessarily disagree), this wine does retain plenty of Châteauneuf du Pape typicity.

Because of the respect for old traditions, as well as the willingness to experiment with modern techniques, de la Gardine makes for one of the more interesting visits in Châteauneuf du Pape. The wines are top-notch, and the Brunels are consistently trying to improve the quality with each new vintage. This estate has become one of the appellation's leaders, and its success in the international marketplace is well earned.

VINTAGES

1995—Châteauneuf du Pape Cuvée Tradition (red)   The 1995 Cuvée Tradition displays
·   considerable structure and tannin, ripe fruit, a deep ruby/purple color, and an
87   attractive, sweet inner core of fruit. I was surprised by the wine's tannic ferocity
         and structure, as well as its crisp acidity. It will need 4–5 years of cellaring, and
         will keep for 10–15. It should be a true vin de garde. Last tasted 6/96.

1995—Châteauneuf du Pape Cuvée des Générations (red)   Although backward and
·   dense, the 1995 Cuvée des Générations offers an opaque purple color, high tannin,
92   and impressive levels of ripeness, extract, and fruit. The 1995 reveals less oak
         influence, but it has not yet been bottled, so perhaps more vanillin and *pain grillé*
         aromas will emerge. This is a structured, classic, rich, superb Châteauneuf du
         Pape for passionate Rhône wine lovers who possess the patience to wait several
         years for it to develop. Anticipated maturity: 2001–2018. Last tasted 6/96.

1994—Châteauneuf du Pape Cuvée Tradition (red)   The 1994 Cuvée Tradition possesses
·   an impressively saturated dark ruby/purple color, a spicy, elegant nose with scents
87   of melon, black cherry, and cassis, medium to full body, moderate tannin, with a
         structured, layered feel. It is a very good to excellent Châteauneuf du Pape for
         drinking between 1998 and 2008. Last tasted 6/96.

1994—Châteauneuf du Pape Cuvée des Générations (red)   The opaque purple-colored
·   1994 Cuvée des Générations offers up a restrained but blossoming nose of sweet
91   vanillin, toasty oak, jammy black cherries, herbs, and chocolate. Rich and full-
         bodied, with a spicy, peppery component, layers of rich, concentrated flavors,
         and a structured, moderately tannic finish, this is a large-scaled, muscular wine
         with significant aging potential. Anticipated maturity: 1999–2015. Last tasted
         6/96.

1993—Châteauneuf du Pape (red)   The 1993 Châteauneuf du Pape exhibits a Bordeaux-
·   like structure, sweet, toasty new oak in the nose, an impressive ruby/purple color,
89+   ripe, sweet, rich fruit, medium to full body, and a long, tannic, persuasive finish.
         This young, backward wine should be cellared for 1–2 years; it will drink well for
         15 years. Last tasted 6/96.

1993—Châteauneuf du Pape Cuvée des Générations (red)   The 1993 Cuvée des Généra-
·   tions reveals a Pauillac-like lead pencil, vanillin, and cassis-scented nose. Loaded
90   with richness, the wine is highly extracted, pure, and clean. In 2–3 years, the
         wine's sweet, rich, intense fruit will soak up any hints of new oak that may be
         displayed over the next several years. Given its grip, intensity, and unevolved state,

it will benefit from several years of cellaring. Anticipated maturity: 1998–2010. Last tasted 6/96.

1992—Châteauneuf du Pape (red)   The 1992 is one of the most tannic, concentrated,
· intense wines I tasted from the vintage. In fact, most 1992 Châteauneuf du Papes
89 + are ready to drink, but de la Gardine's will benefit from additional cellaring given its ferocious tannin level. A top-flight effort for the vintage, it possesses a saturated, dark ruby color, a fragrant, black-cherry, herb, leather, and toasty nose, full body, excellent concentration, and a long, spicy, closed finish. Anticipated maturity: 1998–2006. Last tasted 6/96.

1990—Châteauneuf du Pape (red)   The fully mature 1990 Châteauneuf du Pape reveals
· a deeply saturated purple color, a tight but blossoming bouquet of sweet black
88 fruit, and a tannic, well-structured, full-bodied feel on the palate. The finish is long and pure. Anticipated maturity: now–2005. Last tasted 4/96.

1990—Châteauneuf du Pape Cuvée des Générations (red)   The 1990 Cuvée des Généra-
· tions is black/purple-colored, with a closed but promising bouquet of vanillin,
93 + smoke, minerals, and blackcurrants. The concentration and length are dazzling in this large-scaled, tannic, blockbuster wine that will last for 20–25 years. Antici- pated maturity: 1998–2014. Last tasted 8/96.

1989—Châteauneuf du Pape (red)   The 1989 Châteauneuf du Pape exhibits a black-
· cherry, smoke, herb, and toasty, vanillin-scented bouquet. The dense purple color
90 suggests exceptional ripeness and richness. In the mouth, it is even more tannic and muscular than the 1990. This exceptionally young, promising, and backward wine may ultimately merit a score several points higher when the wine reaches its apogee. The impressive extract levels clearly stand up to the wine's tannins. Patrick Brunel feels the 1989 and 1990 are the finest de la Gardines made since their exceptional 1952, which I had an opportunity to taste 10 years ago. At that time it was still an extraordinary mouthful of wine. Anticipated maturity: 1999–2019. Last tasted 8/96.

1988—Châteauneuf du Pape (red)   The 1988 is extremely rich and full-bodied. It offers
· a bouquet reminiscent of superripe black plums intertwined with aromas of toasty
89 new oak, licorice, and violets. Full-bodied, broodingly dense and tannic, this is a wine made more in the style of a Bordeaux than a Châteauneuf du Pape. Antici- pated maturity: now–2008. Last tasted 12/95.

1985—Châteauneuf du Pape (red)   The 1985 has reached full maturity. Made during a
· period when the wines were less intense, as well as victims of mutiple filtrations
85 and severe fining, it exhibits a deep ruby color with some amber at the edge. The nose offers up sweet cherry fruit, earth, licorice, and herbs. Medium-bodied and round, but beginning to flatten out, this wine needs to be drunk up. Last tasted 12/95.

Older Vintages

The vintages of the 1970s and 1980s were made in a lighter, more open-knit, less concen- trated style. All of them peaked around 7–8 years of age and lasted for 12–15 years. For all the top Châteauneuf du Pape vintages (1983, 1981, 1979, 1978, 1970), my best tasting note was for the 1978, which I rated 87, but I have not tasted it since 1986. It was fully mature a decade ago. The 1952 was an extraordinary wine when I had it 10 years ago. I would quickly bid on it if well-stored bottles became available at auction.

DOMAINE DU GRAND TINEL (ELIE JEUNE)* * *

Address: B.P. 58

84230 Châteauneuf du Pape

Tel: 4-90-34-68-70

Fax: 4-90-34-43-71

Wines produced: Châteauneuf du Pape (red and white)

Surface area (white): 5 acres

(red): 131 acres

Production (white): 750 cases

(red): 18,750 cases

Upbringing (white): 6 months in stainless steel vats

(red): 18–24 months total; fermentation of 15–18 days in stainless steel and cement tanks; then 12–18 months in old oak casks; then storage in stainless steel vats until bottling

Average age of vines (white): 15 years

(red): 45–50 years

Blend (white): 40% Grenache Blanc, 30% Clairette, 30% Bourboulenc

(red): 80% Grenache, 10% Syrah, 10% Mourvèdre, Counoise, and Cinsault

This large estate of 136 acres, planted with 80% Grenache and the rest Syrah, Mourvèdre, Counoise, and Cinsault, produces a very traditional Châteauneuf du Pape that emphasizes power, body, leathery, spicy, exotic scents over the pure berry fruit found in the wines from the more modern school of Châteauneuf producers. The average age of the vines is quite old (45–60 years). Most of its vineyards are located in the eastern half of the appellation, one near Courthézon, one near La Petite Gardiole, one near Montalivet, and one superbly placed near La Nerthe. Jeune is a fine winemaker, but he, like some other producers in Châteauneuf, continues the practice of bottling when the wine is sold. Thus, the bottling of one vintage can be spread over six or more years. This practice saves space and money initially, but wines kept too long in the large wooden foudres and then bottled lack the freshness and fruit of earlier bottlings. Jeune makes excellent, often outstanding, wine, but I wish he would do his entire *mise en bouteille* at the same time, as is done at the very best domaines serious about putting approximately the same wine in all the bottles. To his credit, Jeune produces a second wine, Les Caves St.-Paul.

The wine of Grand Tinel, very classically made, extremely powerful, and aged in oak foudres for two to three years before bottling, is one of the most forceful, alcoholic, and distinctive of the appellation, but I would advise buying the first releases of a given vintage (normally released two to three years after the vintage) and staying away from the old vintages that have just been bottled and put on the market.

VINTAGES

1995—Châteauneuf du Pape (red)   The 1995 Châteauneuf du Pape offers more structure
· than the 1994 because of higher acidity. The wine is spicy, ripe, generously
87 endowed, full-bodied, not complex, but satisfying. It should drink well for 7–8 years. Last tasted 6/96.

1994—Châteauneuf du Pape (red)   This estate seems to produce an authentic style of
· Châteauneuf du Pape regardless of vintage conditions. It tends to be a peppery,
87 roasted-peanut-scented, kirsch-flavored, generously styled wine that is high in alcohol but savory and mouth-filling. The 1994 Châteauneuf du Pape possesses all of those characteristics, as well as a velvety texture and plenty of alcohol. It is an ideal restaurant Châteauneuf du Pape. Anticipated maturity: now–2003. Last tasted 6/96.

1993—Châteauneuf du Pape (red)   The monolithic, flavorful, rustic, and closed 1993
·   Châteauneuf du Pape exhibits a dark ruby color, vague whiffs of Provençal herbs,
86   pepper, and black-cherry fruit, medium to full body, noticeably hard tannin, and
        good depth. Anticipated maturity: now–2003. Last tasted 6/96.

1992—Châteauneuf du Pape (red)   The plump, full-bodied, fleshy 1992 Châteauneuf du
·   Pape exhibits a distinctive olive, herb, and currant nose and plenty of alcohol and
85   glycerin. Mature now. Last tasted 6/95.

1990—Châteauneuf du Pape (red)   The 1990 displays Grand Tinel's in-your-face, full-
·   throttle, high-alcohol, gaudy style that wine snobs might criticize, but there is no
86   doubting the satisfying personality of this wine. The extroverted bouquet of jammy
        red-berry fruit and Provençal herbs is followed by a fleshy, fat wine with a dizzying
        level of alcohol, plenty of unctuous, thick fruit flavors, a weighty, chunky texture,
        and a hot finish. Anticipated maturity: now–2001. Last tasted 6/95.

1989—Châteauneuf du Pape (red)   Although the 1989 is structured and tannic, it is a
·   large-scaled, concentrated wine with an explosive, jammy, black fruit personality.
89   Opulent, with powerful flavors, but lacking finesse, it should provide rewarding
        drinking over the next 10–12 years. Readers should buy the first bottling and avoid
        all the subsequent cuvées that may appear in the marketplace. Anticipated matu-
        rity: now–2004. Last tasted 6/95.

1988—Châteauneuf du Pape (red)   The 1988 is as impressive as the 1989. It is not as
·   overwhelmingly weighty and thick, but one has to admire its dense color, big,
89   chocolaty, fruitcake, meaty aromas, and powerful, bold flavors. There are significant
        tannins in its long finish, but this wine can be drunk now or cellared. Anticipated
        maturity: now–2007. Last tasted 6/95.

1985—Châteauneuf du Pape (red)   With alcohol tipping the scales at 14.7%, the 1985
·   has reached full maturity. The wine is made in the classic Grand Tinel style—
90   huge alcohol and a robust, exuberant personality with plenty of size, weight, and
        clout. The wine exhibits peppery, black-cherry and raspberry fruit intermingled
        with scents of Provençal herbs, olives, and roasted meats. Full-bodied, soft, fat,
        and fleshy, this wine's low acidity suggests it should be drunk over the next 4–5
        years. Anticipated maturity: now–2002. Last tasted 6/95.

Older Vintages

The comments that follow relate to the first bottling of each vintage, which is generally the
best, although the most robust vintages can hold up to longer aging in foudres. The top two
vintages for Grand Tinel in the seventies and eighties were the 1978 and 1981. Both of
these wines were retasted in Châteauneuf du Pape in 1993. While I would not rate them
exceptional, as I did a decade ago, they are still excellent, fully mature, chewy, big, massive
Châteauneuf du Papes with plenty of guts, alcohol, and character. Both should be drunk
before the turn of the century. Other successful vintages include 1983 and 1979. Although
not at the level of the 1978 and 1981, they are both very good Châteauneuf du Papes. Given
the fact that Proprietor Elie Jeune has been making Châteauneuf du Pape only since 1969,
this estate has come a long way, yet I suspect the quality could be pushed even higher given
the overall philosophy of Jeune and his excellent terroir.

DOMAINE GRAND VENEUR* * *
Address: Route de Châteauneuf du Pape
        84100 Orange
Tel: 4-90-34-68-70
Fax: 4-90-34-43-71

Wines produced: Châteauneuf du Pape (red and white), Châteauneuf du Pape Cuvée Lafontaine (white)
Surface area (white): 6.2 acres
(red): 32 acres
Cuvée Lafontaine—1.2 acres
Production (white): 833 cases
(red): 4,375 cases
Cuvée Lafontaine—166 cases
Upbringing (white): 6 months in temperature-controlled stainless steel vats
(red): 18 months total; fermentation of 18–20 days in stainless steel vats; then
60% of the yield is aged in oak barrels (one-fifth new oak and the rest 1–
4 years old) for 6 months and 40% of the yield in stainless steel vats;
storage in stainless steel and enamel tanks until bottling, which is all
done at one time
Cuvée Lafontaine—6 months in 100% new oak barrels; malolactic is
blocked
Average age of vines (white): 15 years
(red): 45 years
Cuvée Lafontaine—18 years
Blend (white): One-third each Grenache Blanc, Clairette, and Roussanne
(red): 65% Grenache, 15–20% Syrah, 10% Mourvèdre, 5–10% other varietals
Cuvée Lafontaine—100% Roussanne

This forward-looking estate is run by Alain Jaume. His entire 42.5 acres of vineyards are in
the northeast sector of the appellation, south of Orange. The soils are variable, with rocks as
well as clay and iron. This sector has a reputation for producing rustic-styled wines, and as a
consequence, Jaume believes in complete destemming of all his red wine cépage. While his
family has been making wine since 1826, this estate is relatively new in Châteauneuf du Pape
terms, having its debut vintage in 1979. The wines have improved over recent years, emphasizing very forward, clean, pure fruit. Jaume has moved toward a white wine that is one of the more
perfumed and intense of the appellation. He recently added a Cuvée Lafontaine, which is
100% Roussanne, vinified in 100% new oak, with its malolactic fermentation blocked. It
appears to be a good wine, but, interestingly, it is not as good as his gorgeous Côtes du
Rhône made outside the appellation, which include a healthy percentage of Viognier.
The red wine is a good, modern-styled Châteauneuf du Pape that is meant to be drunk
within its first 5–8 years of life. It would be interesting to see how these wines would taste
if they did not have to endure multiple filtrations. When tasted prior to bottling, the red
wines often seem more stuffed and complete. It appears that the intensity level and overall
quality of the red wine could be improved by less processing. Nevertheless, this is an
attractive, easygoing, up-front, modern style of Châteauneuf du Pape.

VINTAGES

1995—Châteauneuf du Pape (red)   The 1995 Châteauneuf du Pape reveals sweet, ripe
· fruit, a high level of glycerin, extract, and alcohol, with some underlying tannin
88 and sound acidity. But will the wine become processed and eviscerated at bottling?
I wish the American importer could convince Jaume to bottle these wines naturally,
as the raw materials are very good. Last tasted 6/96.
1994—Châteauneuf du Pape (red)   Jaume continues to gradually increase the extract,
· complexity, and overall quality of his wines. I thought the 1994 Châteauneuf du
84 Pape to be slightly more concentrated before bottling. Fining and filtration are

the most likely culprits . . . again. The wine exhibits medium to full body, ripe black-cherry fruit, a sweet attack, a good mid-palate, and dry, sharp, attenuated tannin in the finish. Anticipated maturity: now–2000. Last tasted 6/96.

1993—Châteauneuf du Pape (red)   This is another example of a wine that exhibited more
·   fruit, body, and intensity prior to bottling. It is still a good wine, with a deep ruby
86   color, a big, sweet nose scented with cherry, earth, and herbs, medium body, some
        tannin, and fine purity. Unlike many 1993s, it is neither hollow nor excessively
        tannic. Anticipated maturity: now–2000. Last tasted 6/96.

1990—Châteauneuf du Pape (red)   The 1990 reveals slight overripeness in its pruny,
·   plummy, herb-scented nose. This medium dark ruby-colored wine exhibits power-
87   ful, concentrated, rich, unctuous, chewy flavors, as well as a long, heady, alcoholic
        finish. The wine is almost overdone in its superripe, fleshy style. Anticipated
        maturity: now–1999. Last tasted 6/95.

1989—Châteauneuf du Pape (red)   The 1989 is a full-bodied, excellent Châteauneuf du
·   Pape with chewy, black-raspberry fruit, moderate acidity, an attractively clean,
87   pure, berry fragrance, and a soft, heady finish. Anticipated maturity: now–2001.
        Last tasted 6/95.

1988—Châteauneuf du Pape (red)   The 1988 is lighter, less concentrated, and smaller
·   scaled, as well as straightforward and well made. It should be drunk up. Last tasted
84   6/95.

GUIGAL (E. GUIGAL)* * *

Note: Négociant—Guigal's entire production is a blend of purchased wine.

This superb producer and vineyard owner from Ampuis in the northern Rhône purchases juice from growers in Châteauneuf du Pape for his bottlings from that appellation. In most vintages, this wine is capable of at least 10 years of cellaring. Guigal refuses to reveal his sources for juice, but he keeps the wine in tank, foudre, and barrel for two to three years before its release. He has successfully incorporated more Syrah and Mourvèdre in the blend to give the wine (in his opinion) more aromatic complexity as well as structure.

With Guigal's marvelous Côte Rôties and fine Côtes du Rhône selections, in addition to all the fine Châteauneufs from the top growers, it is tempting to overlook the quality of Guigal's Châteauneuf. Don't make that mistake.

VINTAGES

1994—Châteauneuf du Pape   The 1994 Châteauneuf du Pape is medium-bodied, soft,
·   and round, with ripe black-cherry fruit intermingled with scents of pepper and
86   cedar. Although forward and fleshy, it does not possess the weight and richness of
        the 1990. Anticipated maturity: now–2001. Last tasted 6/96.

1991—Châteauneuf du Pape   Guigal decided not to make any Châteauneuf du Pape in
·   1992 and 1993, stating bluntly that there was nothing of quality. The 1991 Châ-
83   teauneuf du Pape is modestly constructed. The vintage was extremely difficult and
        this wine reflects the fact that not even a magician such as Guigal can make
        the proverbial sow's ear into a silk purse. Nevertheless, this is a solid Château-
        neuf du Pape, with peppery, herbal, cherry fruit, some spice, and medium body,
        but a compact, angular personality. Anticipated maturity: now–2000. Last tasted
        6/96.

1990—Châteauneuf du Pape   Marcel Guigal was shrewd enough to recognize the great-
·   ness of this vintage and bought heavily from all his sources in Châteauneuf du
90   Pape, resulting in one of the finest Châteauneufs this firm has produced. Already
        delicious, it is a full-bodied, rich, thick, boldly flavored wine with gobs of fruit.

With over 14% alcohol, it is a blockbuster in terms of its power and fiery richness. Anticipated maturity: now–2005. Last tasted 6/96.

1989—Châteauneuf du Pape   The 1989 would receive more attention if it were not for
·   the blockbuster 1990. The 1989 reveals a dark ruby color, a big, dusty, black-
88   cherry, pepper, and herb-scented nose, excellent depth and richness, full body,
       soft tannin, and a chewy finish. Anticipated maturity: now–2001. Last tasted 8/96.

1988—Châteauneuf du Pape   The deep, full-bodied 1988's big, black/ruby color, and
·   herb, plum, and cassis flavors make for an attractive, meaty glassful of wine.
89   Anticipated maturity: now–2000. Last tasted 11/95.

1986—Châteauneuf du Pape   The 1986 is a more tannic, tougher-textured wine, lacking
·   the generosity of the 1988 and finishing with some astringency. However, there is
84?   good underlying depth, and for those who have the patience, it may come around.
       Last tasted 11/95.

Older Vintages

Guigal's older vintages have generally been good to very good in the top years, but they are clearly wines to be drunk within the first 7–8 years of their release (usually 2–3 years after the vintage). Since there are usually 2–3 bottlings, with the first bottling spending 2–3 years in his patented élevage, it is advisable to try to get the first bottling, although it is impossible to know from the label which wine is being drunk. Among the older vintages, 1981 was a chunky, rustic wine, 1979 was good, and 1978 was consistently dull, and slightly oxidized with a tarry, musty barrel/foudre smell. The 1967, drunk in September 1996, was still very rich and impressive, but fully mature. Like Guigal's Hermitage, which is also made from purchased juice, these wines generally require earlier drinking than his Côte Rôties.

DOMAINE HAUT DES TERRES BLANCHES (RÉMY DIFFONTY)* * * *
Address: Les Terres Blanches
        84230 Châteauneuf du Pape
Tel: 4-90-83-71-19
Fax: 4-90-83-51-26
Wines produced: Châteauneuf du Pape (red), Châteauneuf du Pape Domaine de la Glacière
Surface area: 131 acres
Production: 20,625 cases
Upbringing: 36 months total; fermentation of 21 days in cement tanks, then 12 months in
        old oak casks; then storage in enamel or epoxy tanks prior to bottling
Average age of vines: 50 years, with the oldest vines 100 years
Blend: 75% Grenache, 10% Syrah, 10% Mourvèdre, 5% Cinsault

High up on a hill to the east of the village of Châteauneuf du Pape are the home and cellars of Rémy Diffonty and his son Joel. From this spot is undoubtedly one of the best vistas in the environs of Châteauneuf. Diffonty owns a major vineyard parcel in the northern part of Châteauneuf du Pape, in the area called Les Pradels, and a well-placed parcel in the northwestern part of the appellation, just south of the plateau region dominated by the vineyards of Mont Redon and Les Cabrières. His wine tends to fall in between the high-alcohol, concentrated, old style of properties such as Grand Tinel and the floral, berry-fruit-scented, more modern-style wines such as Vieux Lazaret. This wine is never very dark in color or especially concentrated, yet it always seems to have broad, expansive flavors and a fiery, in-your-face charm . . . so to speak.

Given the fact that 20,000 cases of Châteauneuf du Pape emerge from Haut des Terres Blanches, readers should not be surprised that there appear to be mutiple cuvées, as well as a tendency to bottle the vintage over a long period of time (5–6 years). While this does afford the opportunity to do a mini-vertical in the cellars, as well as buy older vintages, it also leads to bottle variation.

Diffonty also produces Châteauneuf du Pape under several other labels. He owns a vineyard called La Glacière, also in the northwestern sector of the appellation, from which he turns out powerful, ripe, classic Châteauneuf du Pape. In addition, there are secondary labels that are often sold exclusively to specific importers.

VINTAGES

1993—Châteauneuf du Pape   The 1993 displays gobs of raspberry fruit, an elegant
·   personality, medium to full body, and a soft, ripe, round finish. Anticipated matu-
87   rity: now–1999. Last tasted 6/95.

1993—Châteauneuf du Pape Domaine de la Glacière   This tasty, rich, full-bodied Châ-
·   teauneuf du Pape possesses plenty of peppery, spicy, thick, black-cherry fruit, fine
88   ripeness, full body, and a long, lusty finish. Drink it over the next 5–6 years. Last
        tasted 6/96.

1992—Châteauneuf du Pape   The 1992 exhibits sweet, jammy, raspberry flavors well
·   displayed in an easy-to-appreciate format. Mature now. Last tasted 6/95.
86

1990—Châteauneuf du Pape   Diffonty's wines are not the most massive style of Châ-
·   teauneuf du Pape, but they possess a sweet raspberry fruitiness and gracefulness
88   that render them stylish, elegant, and suave. The 1990 is all of those things, as well
        as round, gorgeously perfumed, with a cedary, perfumed, sweet black-raspberry
        fruitiness. Though its tannin is soft and its acid low, this is undoubtedly a seduc-
        tive, succulent wine. Anticipated maturity: now–2001. Last tasted 6/95.

1989—Châteauneuf du Pape   The dark ruby-colored 1989 displays an attractive, over-
·   ripe, sweet, raspberry-scented nose (much like the 1990 although more opulent). It
88   reveals delicious, richly fruity, round, totally hedonistic flavors, soft tannins, and a
        velvety texture. Anticipated maturity: now–2002. Last tasted 6/95.

1988—Châteauneuf du Pape   The medium ruby-colored 1988 has a big, chocolaty,
·   roasted black-raspberry-scented bouquet, ripe, long, hedonistic flavors, low acidity,
88   and a lush, velvety texture. Anticipated maturity: now–2000. Last tasted 6/95.

Older Vintages

Older vintages can be bought at the estate and are often seen in the auction market. This estate made very fine wines in 1985, 1983, and 1970. I suspect all of these wines are at the end of their useful drinking life, but in larger formats from cold, damp cellars, I suspect they may still be excellent.

DOMAINE LES HAUTES BRUSQUIÈRES* * * *

Note: This wine is an importer selection (Eric Solomon of America's European Cellars) that is made from one of Châteauneuf du Pape's finest estates. The wine is selected in the cellar and bottled unfined and unfiltered specifically for the American importer. There are only two vintages to date, both of which are outstanding.

VINTAGES

1995—Châteauneuf du Pape (red)   The 1995 Châteauneuf du Pape is similar to this
·   estate's excellent 1994, but slightly richer, with more body, extract, and acidity.
90   Anticipated maturity: 1998–2008. Last tasted 6/96.

1994—Châteauneuf du Pape (red)   With its aromatic herbes de Provence–scented nose
   ·   intermixed with jammy black cherries, this medium ruby/purple-colored wine of-
   90   fers an enticing bouquet, as well as opulent, supple-textured, full-bodied flavors
               oozing with jammy black-cherry fruit. Low acidity, high alcohol, and copious
               glycerin give the wine additional weight, and contribute to its creamy texture. This
               is an attractive, fleshy, textbook, Châteauneuf du Pape. Anticipated maturity: now–
               2001. Last tasted 6/96.

PAUL JABOULET-AINÉ (* * */prior to 1970* * * * *)

Address: Les Jalets
            R.N. 7, B.P. 462
            La-Roche-de-Glun
            26600 Tain l'Hermitage
Tel: 4-75-84-68-93
Fax: 4-75-84-56-14
Wines produced: Châteauneuf du Pape Les Cèdres (red). *Note:* the same wine is sold in the
               French market under the name La Grappe des Papes; a small quantity of
               white Les Cèdres was introduced in 1994 and 1995.
Production: 6,000 cases
Upbringing: 10 months in barrels 2–3 years old
Blend: 65% Grenache, 20–25% Cinsault, 10–15% Syrah

   I have sought out, drunk with great pleasure, and cellared as many cases of Paul Jaboulet's exquisite 1957, 1961, 1962, 1966, 1967, and 1969 Châteauneuf-du-Pape Les
Cèdres as I could find and afford. Except for the 1957 and 1966, which are fading,
these wines were and continue to be quintessential examples of full-bodied, sumptuous,
magnificently perfumed wines. However, vintages since the seventies have become lighter
and lighter, and in the eighties the wines are nothing more than vapid, characterless,
commercial specimens. Fortunately, the Jaboulets, during the decade of the nineties, have
begun to build more depth and intensity into these wines.
   Part of the problem is undoubtedly the fact that the Jaboulets own no vineyards in
Châteauneuf du Pape and must buy juice from selected growers. During the fifties and
sixties, this was a relatively simple procedure. It is a well-known fact that much of the juice
came from the finest old-vine vineyards in the appellation. For example, the colossal 1967
Les Cèdres was made totally from old-vine cuvées purchased by Jacques Jaboulet from
Château de la Nerthe. With the advent of more estate bottling by Châteauneuf du Pape's
growers, the availablity of high-quality, old-vine juice was significantly reduced, resulting
in only a trickle of wine available for négociant blends in the mid-nineties.
   Jaboulet's wine has traditionally been dominated by the Grenache grape, but over the last
decade the percentage of Syrah has been increased. While the older Les Cèdres were 85%
to nearly 100% Grenache, the newer wines tend to include no more than 60–65% Grenache,
with at least 25–35% Syrah in the blend. In addition to a relatively early bottling, the
Jaboulets' flirtation with excessive filtration during the early and mid-eighties has been
reduced. The wine is now filtered only once prior to bottling.

VINTAGES

1995—Châteauneuf du Pape Les Cèdres (red)   The deep ruby-colored 1995 is an elegant,
   ·   black-cherry-scented and -flavored wine with medium body and attractive fruit, but
   86   it is not an exceptional example of Châteauneuf du Pape. A pretty wine, but it's no
               1967! Anticipated maturity: now–2002. Last tasted 6/96.

1995—Châteauneuf du Pape Les Cèdres (white)   The 1995 Les Cèdres blanc exhibits an
  ·   apricot/peach-scented nose, ripe fruit, and plenty of power, body, and alcohol.
 88   Interestingly, the Jaboulets believe the small percentage of Picardin (one of the rarest
      of the permitted southern Rhône varietals) takes on a Viognier character when fer-
      mented at cold temperatures, and both the 1995 and 1994 taste as if some Viognier
      were included in the blend. Anticipated maturity: now–1998. Last tasted 6/96.

1994—Châteauneuf du Pape Les Cèdres (white)   I had a slight preference for the 1994
  ·   over the 1995 Les Cèdres. With its luscious honeysuckle, richly fruity, flamboyant
 89   nose and full-bodied, ripe, heady, alcoholic flavors, it offers a delicious mouthful
      of dry white wine. Anticipated maturity: now–1998. Last tasted 6/96.

1990—Châteauneuf du Pape Les Cèdres (red)   The 1990 Châteauneuf du Pape, a 65%
  ·   Grenache/35% Syrah blend, with 14% natural alcohol, reveals an impressive dark
 88   ruby/purple color, a big, spicy, earthy, jammy nose, deep, unctuous, full-bodied
      flavors, and a dense, long, moderately tannic finish. Unevolved, young, and back-
      ward, this wine will benefit from some cellaring. Anticipated maturity: now–2004.
      Last tasted 6/96.

1989—Châteauneuf du Pape Les Cèdres (red)   The 1989 Les Cèdres, made from 75%
  ·   Grenache, 10% Mourvèdre, and 15% Cinsault (no Syrah in this vintage), is a
 87   seductive, rich, generously endowed wine, with soft tannins and gobs of intense
      fruit. Unctuous and velvety, it is ideal for drinking over the next decade. Antici-
      pated maturity: now–2000. Last tasted 4/95.

1985—Châteauneuf du Pape Les Cèdres (red)   This one-dimensional wine is a far cry
  ·   from the wines made in the sixties. Medium deep ruby, with a grapy, straightforward
 84   bouquet, this wine is fat, soft, quite pleasant, and full-bodied. Mature now. Last
      tasted 9/94.

1983—Châteauneuf du Pape Les Cèdres (red)   A modest cherry fruit character intermin-
  ·   gled with *garrigue* scents suggest a good Côtes du Rhône. On the palate, the wine
 79   is medium-bodied and spicy, but light and simple. Mature now. Last tasted 10/94.

1982—Châteauneuf du Pape Les Cèdres (red)   Light medium garnet-colored with some
  ·   rust, the 1982 is a soft, loosely knit, fully mature wine that is losing its fruit. Drink
 76   it up. Last tasted 10/94.

1978—Châteauneuf du Pape Les Cèdres (red)   This has always been a disappointing
  ·   wine considering the greatness of this vintage. It reveals a medium garnet color, a
 83   dusty, herbal, animal-scented nose, medium body, some sweet fruit, and a lean,
      attenuated style. It seems to be drying out. Drink it up. Last tasted 10/94.

1969—Châteauneuf du Pape Les Cèdres (red)   Just beginning to start its downward slide,
  ·   the dark garnet-colored 1969 exhibits a smoky, tarry, truffle-like smell, medium to
 86   full body, and some noticeable tannin and alcohol. It is still intact, but the fruit is
      drying out. Drink it up. Last tasted 10/94.

1967—Châteauneuf du Pape Les Cèdres (red)   Having gone through nearly three cases
  ·   of this wine, I can unequivocally say that it has been one of the great treasures in
 95   my cellar. Few other wines have been as consistently brilliant and spectacular as
      the 1967 Les Cèdres. This wine is made 100% from old vines of Château de la
      Nerthe (the Cuvée des Cadettes). With nearly 15% alcohol, the wine retains a
      huge, unctuous texture, thick, juicy fruit, and Asian spices, smoky, cedar, and
      black-fruit aromas and flavors. It has always been so thick and rich that it tasted
      almost sweet. This glorious Châteauneuf du Pape is one of the monumental wines
      of the appellation. How much longer will it keep? For the last 20 years I have been
      wrong about this wine's marvelous ability to hold on to most of its fruit and continue
      to develop, so I may be incorrect, but I would opt for drinking it over the next few
      years. Last tasted 8/96.

1966—Châteauneuf du Pape Les Cèdres (red) From magnum, this wine can still be
· glorious, but the regular bottles are in decline. It was a gloriously sweet, perfumed,
87 exotic, full-bodied, thick Châteauneuf du Pape without the same degree of richness
as the 1967, but still high-class, with marvelous concentration and intensity. Today,
the wine reveals considerable rust and amber. It is beginning to lose much of its
fruit, displaying a dusty, earthy component, a lack of sweet fruit, and high alcohol
in the finish. Drink it up. Last tasted 8/96.

1962—Châteauneuf du Pape Les Cèdres (red) Another great effort from Jaboulet that is
· now in decline, the 1962's color reveals a pronounced orange/rust, with some
85 bottles resembling tea. This was an exceptional wine for much of its life, but it is
now a mere shadow of its former self. It possesses a leafy, herb, earthy, musty nose,
an absence of sweet fruit (once a hallmark of the 1962 vintage), and an alcoholic,
tannic finish. Drink it up. Last tasted 8/96.

1961—Châteauneuf du Pape Les Cèdres (red) One of the most magnificent wines made
· in Châteauneuf du Pape, the 1961 Les Cèdres was nearly as profound as the 1967.
90? It is still in fine condition, although clearly on its last legs. The deep garnet color
reveals considerable rust and amber at the edge. The wine possesses a sweet,
cedary, fruitcake, smoky nose, and full body, but the immense thickness and
richness have begun to fade. Although still powerful, alcoholic, and full-bodied,
the 1961 is dropping its fruit. Don't push fate any longer. Last tasted 8/96.

Older Vintages

The last few tastings of the 1957 (all from magnum) revealed a wine in serious decline.

DOMAINE DE LA JANASSE
(* * * *Cuvée Classique/* * * * *Cuvée Chaupin and Cuvée Vieilles Vignes)
Address: 27, chemin du Moulin
84350 Courthézon
Tel: 4-90-70-86-29
Fax: 4-90-70-75-93
Wines produced: Châteauneuf du Pape (red and white), Châteauneuf du Pape Cuvée Chau-
pin (red), Châteauneuf du Pape Cuvée Vieilles Vignes (red)
Surface area (white): 4.4 acres
(red): 11 acres
Cuvée Chaupin—7.4 acres
Cuvée Vieilles Vignes—7.5 acres
Production (white): 333 cases
(red): 833 cases
Cuvée Chaupin—833 cases
Cuvée Vieilles Vignes—500 cases
Upbringing (white): the Roussanne is vinified in 100% new oak barrels for 6 months
(no malolactic fermentation); the other varietals spend 6 months in
temperature-controlled enamel tanks; an assemblage is done before
bottling
(red): 18 months total; fermentation of 20 days in cement tanks; then 85% of
the yield is put in oak casks and 15% in 5% new oak barrels for 12
months; then storage in epoxy tanks before bottling
Cuvée Chaupin—18 months total; fermentation of 21–23 days in cement
and stainless steel tanks; then 90% of the yield goes into oak casks and
10% into old barrels; then storage in epoxy tanks before bottling

> Cuvée Vieilles Vignes—18 months total; fermentation of 23–25 days in stainless steel vats; then 85% of the yield goes into old oak casks and 15% of the yield goes into 5% new oak barrels; then storage in epoxy vats before bottling

Average age of vines (white): 40 years

             (red): 40 years

             Cuvée Chaupin—80 years

             Cuvée Vieilles Vignes—80+ years

Blend (white): 40% Roussanne, 40% Grenache Blanc, 20% Clairette

      (red): 80% Grenache, 15% Syrah, 5% other varietals

      Cuvée Chaupin—100% Grenache

      Cuvée Vieilles Vignes—90% Grenache, 10% other varietals

This modestly sized property of just over 30 acres has emerged in the last five years to become one of the most intelligently run estates of Châteauneuf du Pape. Father Aimé Sabon and his yuppie, impeccably dressed son, Christophe, deserve all the credit. Aimé had sold the entire production to cooperatives until 1973 when he began to estate-bottle. Christophe, who is in his early thirties, took over the administration of the estate in 1991 and has provided a degree of energy and enthusiasm that has been translated into a bevy of superb wines. The Châteauneuf du Papes from Domaine de la Janasse are becoming so popular they are allocated, but readers should also be aware that this family makes very fine Côtes du Rhône from a 48-acre estate, as well as an impressive vin de table from another 30-acre property in the southern Rhône.

The Domaine de la Janasse owns some superb vineyard parcels. Like most Châteauneuf du Pape estates, they are morsellated, with 15 separate parcels. This has led to three cuvées of wine. The regular cuvée (cuvée classique) comes from relatively old vine parcels including a parcel of Le Crau, to the more sandy, claylike soil in the northeastern section, not far from Courthézon. The Cuvée Chaupin comes from a parcel of Grenache vines planted in 1912. The Cuvée Vieilles Vignes comes from multiple parcels with an average age of 80 years. All these wines are Grenache dominated. Since Christophe is continually experimenting with new techniques, I would not be surprised to see more innovative additions to this portfolio of fine wine. He has begun to do some destemming, although he remains open-minded about how important destemming is in a very ripe year. The wines have moved away from heavy filtering, to virtually no processing, with the American cuvées unfiltered, and those sold elsewhere given only the lightest filtration possible. Crop thinning in abundant years is routinely employed. Additionally, a tiny percentage of new oak (about 5%) is used for the Cuvée Vieilles Vignes, but small casks are widely employed for the non-Grenache varietals. The results are some of the purest, authoritatively flavored, yet undeniably elegant, suave, and graceful wines being made in Châteauneuf du Pape. They have the intensity of the old-style traditionalists, but the purity of a modernist. The Sabons have achieved a classic, rich, complex Châteauneuf du Pape without compromising its exuberance and intensity.

Christophe Sabon has also revived the white wine program at Janasse. As with many forward-looking Châteauneuf du Pape estates, new plantations of Roussanne have added immensely to the character and personality of the white wine. Today Roussanne represents 40% of the blend, along with 40% Grenache Blanc and 20% Clairette. The Roussanne is vinified (à la Beaucastel) in 100% new oak casks and then blended with the white wine that has been vinified in tank. The results have been unquestionably successful.

As I stated earlier, this is a brilliantly run Châteauneuf du Pape estate that has just reached the top qualitative level of the appellation's hierarchy. The wines are becoming international superstars. The chapter on Côtes du Rhône provides more information on

Domaine de la Janasse's offerings from this generic appellation; this estate is also making some of the most delicious red and white Côtes du Rhône in the southern Rhône Valley.

VINTAGES

1995—Châteauneuf du Pape (red)   The 1995s tasted extremely young, exhibiting less of
·   the herbes de Provence/*garrigue* character, but more of the black-fruit characteris-
88   tics. All three 1995s are powerful, with good structure, and better acidity than their
1994 counterparts. The 1995 Châteauneuf du Pape should turn out to be nearly as good as the 1994, perhaps more structured and less precocious, but without the overall plumpness and fat of its older sibling. Some patience will be required. Anticipated maturity: 1998–2008. Last tasted 6/96.

1995—Châteauneuf du Pape Cuvée Chaupin (red)   The black/ruby-colored 1995 Cuvée
·   Chaupin displays superb richness, admirable power, and a restrained, measured,
91   elegant style. It could pass for a grand cru Burgundy from the Côtes de Nuits in a blind tasting. This is a gorgeous, multidimensional, rich yet beautifully balanced wine. Anticipated maturity: 1998–2010. Last tasted 6/96.

1995—Châteauneuf du Pape Cuvée Vieilles Vignes (red)   The 1995 Cuvée Vieilles Vig-
·   nes is the essence of black-raspberry jam. It is the most closed and structured
91   young Châteauneuf du Pape I have tasted from Domaine de la Janasse. Full-bodied, powerful, and rich, with a sound underpinning of acidity and tannin, it is an impressively endowed wine that will require patience, somewhat atypical for a Sabon wine. Anticipated maturity: 2000–2015. Last tasted 6/96.

1994—Châteauneuf du Pape (red)   The 1994 Châteauneuf du Pape is an attractive,
·   open-knit, full-bodied wine with no hard edges. The color is a deep ruby with
89   purple nuances. The sweet nose of black raspberries, cherries, cedar, and spice jumps from the glass. Round and velvety textured, with luscious levels of fruit, this generously endowed, silky wine is already delicious. Anticipated maturity: now–2003. Last tasted 6/96.

1994—Châteauneuf du Pape Cuvée Chaupin (red)   The 1994 Cuvée Chaupin reveals an
·   intense, seductive nose of jammy cherries, kirsch, smoke, and herbes de Provence.
90   Round, with good body, copious quantities of glycerin, and layers of fruit, this wine seems too delicious to last, but there is enough structure and acidity to provide another decade of hedonistic consumption. It also offers a whiff of that unmistakable Provençal *garrigue* smell. Anticipated maturity: now–2006. Last tasted 6/96.

1994—Châteauneuf du Pape Cuvée Vieilles Vignes (red)   The 1994 Cuvée Vieilles Vig-
·   nes is a fuller-bodied, deeper wine with greater stuffing, more glycerin, smoke,
92   kirsch, and cherry fruit, as well as more alcohol. It is a terrific young Châteauneuf du Pape that is already surprisingly developed and delicious. The wine hits the palate broadside with fruit, followed by plenty of ripeness, richness, and purity. There is some tannin, but the overall impression is one of gloriously ripe, rich fruit presented in a velvety-textured, beautifully well-focused format. Anticipated maturity: 1998–2010. Last tasted 6/96.

1993—Châteauneuf du Pape (red)   The rich, well-proportioned 1993 Châteauneuf du
·   Pape offers a healthy dark ruby color with purple tints, a firm structure, moderate
87   tannin, and a sweet, berry-scented perfume with hints of black olives, Provençal herbs, and cherry/cassis. Anticipated maturity: now–2006. Last tasted 6/96.

1993—Châteauneuf du Pape Cuvée Chaupin (red)   The outstanding deep ruby-colored
·   1993 Cuvée Chaupin (from a lieu-dit) is extremely concentrated and full-bodied,
90   with great purity of black-cherry and cassis fruit. Long and opulent, it has a viscous texture, surprising for a 1993. Anticipated maturity: now–2006. Last tasted 6/96.

1993—Châteauneuf du Pape Cuvée Vieilles Vignes (red)   The less evolved 1993 Cuvée
· Vieilles Vignes is the most backward of Sabon's 1993s. It displays a saturated dark
90 + ruby/purple color, and a tight but promising nose of spices, black fruits, and ground
pepper. Moderately tannic, with a structured, backward personality, this is a hefty
yet stylish Châteauneuf du Pape. Anticipated maturity: 1998–2007. Last tasted
6/96.

1993—Châteauneuf du Pape Cuvée Vingtième (20th) Anniversaire (red)   The superb
· 1993 Cuvée Vingtième (20th) Anniversaire is extremely young and tannic, but it
92 possesses magnificent richness, as well as gobs of black-cherry fruit intermingled
with subtle scents of Provençal herbs, *garrigue,* smoked meats, and black cherries.
Concentrated and full-bodied, this is a knockout Châteauneuf du Pape. Anticipated
maturity: 1998–2012. Last tasted 11/95.

1992—Châteauneuf du Pape Cuvée Chaupin (red)   The 1992 Cuvée Chaupin exhibits a
· saturated ruby color, a spicy, pruny, earthy nose, sweet, expansive, generous fla-
85 vors, medium body, and rustic, coarse tannin in the finish. Although it lacks
harmony and balance, it possesses good raw materials. Anticipated maturity: now–
2002. Last tasted 6/95.

1990—Châteauneuf du Pape (red)   The last vintage vinified by Aimé Sabon before his
· son, Christophe, took over, the 1990 offers a ruby/garnet color, and an attractive
85 and evolved bouquet of black cherries, leather, spices, and smoke. It is medium-
bodied, soft, and pleasant, but simple and straightforward, particularly when compared to the other 1990s. Mature now. Last tasted 11/94.

1990—Châteauneuf du Pape Cuvée Chaupin (red)   The dark ruby/purple-colored
· 1990 Cuvée Chaupin displays a flamboyant nose of fiery black raspberries,
90 roasted herbs, and chocolate. The wine has excellent concentration, gobs of glycerin and extraction, plenty of alcohol, and a long, moderately tannic finish. Anticipated maturity: now–2008. Last tasted 11/94.

1990—Châteauneuf du Pape Cuvée Vieilles Vignes (red)   The dark ruby-colored 1990
· Cuvée Vieilles Vignes is a massive, highly extracted, densely colored wine with
92 gobs of tannin and excellent aging potential. It boasts a whopping 15% natural
alcohol. Still youthful, this is a noteworthy 1990. Anticipated maturity: now–2009.
Last tasted 6/96.

1989—Châteauneuf du Pape (red)   The 1989 Châteauneuf du Pape is full-bodied, with a
· ruby/purple color, a ripe nose of cassis, herbs, and other black fruits, excellent,
89 nearly outstanding stuffing, and an impressive, chewy, highly concentrated, ripe
finish. Anticipated maturity: now–2008. Last tasted 6/96.

COMTE DE LAUZE* *

Address: 7, avenue des Bosquets
        84230 Châteauneuf du Pape
Tel: 4-90-83-72-87
Fax: 4-90-83-50-93
Wines produced: Châteauneuf du Pape (red and white)
Surface area (white): 2.47 acres
            (red): 45 acres
Production (white): 187 cases
            (red): 6,250 cases
Upbringing (white): 6 months in termperature-controlled stainless steel and cement vats
            (red): 18 months total; fermentation of 12 days in cement vats; then 12 months
            in old oak casks, barrels, and demi-muids; then storage in cement tanks
            until bottling

Average age of vines (white): 40 years
                        (red): 40 years
Blend (white): 70% Clairette, 30% Grenache Blanc
        (red): 70% Grenache, 10% Syrah, 10% Mourvèdre and Muscardin, 10% Cinsault

Ghislène Carre is also the proprietor for the Châteauneuf du Pape estate of Chantadu. The wines from Comte de Lauze can be soft, fruity, and lacking concentration and length. Some vintages (1990) have been successful, but this is an inconsistent estate that tends to turn out overly processed, lighter-styled Châteauneuf du Papes.

VINTAGES

1995—Châteauneuf du Pape (red)   The 1995 tastes diluted, with simple cherry fruit
·   flavors, medium body, and little finish. It is a pleasant, simple, uninspiring effort.
79   Anticipated maturity: now–2000. Last tasted 6/96.
1994—Châteauneuf du Pape (red)   The evolved medium garnet-colored 1994 displays a
·   salty, sea breeze, *garrigue*, herbaceous-scented nose, medium body, and a lack of
82   depth and extract. The wine is open, round, spicy, and fully mature. Last tasted 6/96.
1990—Châteauneuf du Pape (red)   The 1990 exhibits a dark ruby/purple color, followed by
·   a full-intensity bouquet of roasted peanuts, herbs, and black cherries. The wine dis-
89   plays great fruit, as well as a long, opulent, moderately tannic, rich finish. It is the
        finest wine I have tasted from this estate. Anticipated maturity: now–2002. Last
        tasted 6/94.
1989—Châteauneuf du Pape (red)   This 1989 offers up a pronounced peppery, herbal,
·   smoky nose, good tannin and structure, attractive richness, medium to full body, and
86   a long, well-structured finish. Anticipated maturity: now–2005. Last tasted 6/94.
1988—Châteauneuf du Pape (red)   The 1988 was robust and round, but one-dimensional
·   and a little rustic and coarse. Mature now. Last tasted 4/94.
84

DOMAINE DE MARCOUX (PHILIPPE ARMENIER)
(* * * *Cuvée Classique/* * * * *Cuvée Vieilles Vignes)
Address: 7, rue A. Daudet
        Chemin de la Gironde
        84100 Orange
Tel: 4-90-34-67-43
Fax: 4-90-51-84-53
Wines produced: Châteauneuf du Pape Cuvée Classique (red and white), Châteauneuf du
        Pape Cuvée Vieilles Vignes (red)
Surface area (white): 2.9 acres
            (red): 40 acres
                Cuvée Vieilles Vignes—9.8 acres
Production (white): 500 cases
            (red): 5,000 cases
                Cuvée Vieilles Vignes—750 cases
Upbringing (white): vinification in stainless steel vats and bottling after 4–6 months mini-
                mum; malolactic fermentation is blocked
            (red): 18–24 months total; fermentation of one month in stainless steel vats;
                30% of the yield stays in stainless steel and 70% spends 3 months in old
                oak casks and barrels
                Cuvée Vieilles Vignes—the same as for the regular red wine cuvée

Average age of vines (white): 15 years
(red): 40–50 years
Cuvée Vieilles Vignes—90 years
Blend (white): 40% Bourboulenc, 40% Roussanne, 20% Clairette
(red): 80% Grenache, 5% Cinsault, 5% Syrah, 5% Mourvèdre, 5% other varietals
Cuvée Vieilles Vignes—80% Grenache, 10% Mourvèdre, 10% other varietals

There are not many Frenchmen who tower at six feet, five inches in height, but Philippe Armenier, who has run the Domaine de Marcoux for nearly two decades, is one of them. An intense, serious winemaker who has evolved greatly since I first met him 20 years ago, the imposing Armenier is making some of the most compelling wines of the region. A disciple of biodynamic farming, inspired by Lalou Bize-Leroy, Nicolas Joly, and Michel Chapoutier, Armenier cultivates his 53 acres of vineyards following the astrological/homeopathic writings of the famed German professor Rudolf Steiner. Yields are kept very low and, not surprisingly, the quality is exceptionally high.

The Armenier family, who can trace its origins in Châteauneuf du Pape to the fourteenth century, has an impressive old-vine average of 40–50 years for the red wine grapes, with several parcels over 90 years. There are at least 10 separate parcels, with the oldest vines located in Les Charbonnières, a vineyard in the eastern sector of the appellation, just west of the famed La Crau. Another parcel of extremely old vines is in Les Esquirons, a vineyard planted on sandy soil, just behind the château ruins. Fruit from these two parcels, plus another in the southern part of the appellation, covered with the famed *galets roulés*, make up the Vieilles Vignes cuvée. This can be one of the greatest red wines made in the world (the 1989 and 1990, for example), if not the single most phenomenal wine of Châteauneuf du Pape. It possesses a level of concentration and a vivid blackberry/blueberry fruitiness that are mind-boggling. Even lighter years, such as 1992 and 1993, are surprisingly powerful wines. This cuvée, which sees no new oak, but rather old barrels, foudres, and tanks, is always bottled without fining or filtration.

The regular cuvée of Marcoux is no wimpy wine either. In top vintages, it is a powerful Châteauneuf du Pape that is given the same élevage and, at least for the American importer, is bottled with no fining or filtering. Even the cuvée sold elsewhere in the world is given only a light filtration.

All of the cellar activity is guided by the stars (the ones in the sky), and there is virtually no manipulation of the wine. The grapes are not destemmed, and vinification, in spite of the lunar cycle, is traditional. With the extraordinary intensity it obtains, one would think that maceration must last a month or more, but that is rarely the case. In fact, in great years such as 1989 and 1990, the cuvaison was relatively short (two weeks), and in lighter years, such as 1993, it lasted for nearly a month. The red wines contain 80% Grenache, but Armenier has planted Vaccarèse, Counoise, Muscardin, Terret Noir, in addition to the regular line-up of Cinsault, Syrah, and Mourvèdre.

Domaine de Marcoux's white wine has always been one of the finest whites of the appellation, even before producers began to understand the importance of Roussanne in the overall blend. Marcoux's white always possessed more aromatics and fruit than most, and it continues to be a very good example of dry white Châteauneuf du Pape. Like other producers, Armenier has incorporated more Roussanne in the blend (40%), along with 40% Bourboulenc and 20% Clairette.

While it is fashionable to rave about recent vintages of Philippe Armenier, his father, Elie, who died in 1980, also produced some classic Châteauneuf du Papes. Should you come across such older vintages as 1966, 1967, 1970, and 1978, do not hesitate to buy them, as they were classic, high-octane, superbly endowed Châteauneuf du Papes. This is a superb reference point estate for Châteauneuf du Pape.

VINTAGES

1995—Châteauneuf du Pape (red)   Armenier's 1995 Châteauneuf du Pape exhibits a
•   dark ruby/purple color, and pure, sweet aromas of cassis, black cherries, and
89   truffles. Aromatically, it reminds me of the Château Fortia, which is interesting in
             view of the high percentage of Syrah in Fortia's blend (which is not the case with
             Marcoux). This rich wine offers a sweet attack, full body, excellent definition, good
             ripeness and extract, and a clean, round, opulently textured finish. Anticipated
             maturity: 1998–2006. Last tasted 6/96.

1995—Châteauneuf du Pape Cuvée Vieilles Vignes (red)   The 1995 Cuvée Vieilles Vig-
•   nes is another blockbuster wine that represents the essence of old-vine Châ-
94   teauneuf du Pape. The grapes are harvested when very ripe, with an element of
             what the French call *surmaturité*, overripeness. In English, this has a negative
             connotation, but in the French language, it is used in a positive sense. The 1995
             appears to be the greatest Cuvée Vieilles Vignes since the monumental 1990. The
             opaque purple color is followed by aromas of licorice, jammy cassis, spicy under-
             brush, and a suggestion of white flowers. An extremely rich, full-bodied Châ-
             teauneuf with fabulously concentrated flavors that amount to a liquid skyscraper
             on the palate, this is a stupendous example of Châteauneuf du Pape that is remark-
             ably well balanced despite its massive size. This wine's thick, almost excessive
             richness nearly obscures its formidable tannin and structure. Anticipated maturity:
             2002–2020. Last tasted 6/96.

1994—Châteauneuf du Pape (red)   The 1994 Châteauneuf du Pape displays an advanced,
•   dark ruby color with some garnet hues at the edge. The controversial, spicy aroma
88   of allspice, vitamin tablets, and overripe red and black fruits is sure to find a mixed
             reception, even from Rhône wine enthusiasts. With rich, sweet, jammy fruit and
             low acidity, this is a mouth-filling, fleshy, distinctively styled Châteauneuf du Pape.
             Anticipated maturity: now–2004. Last tasted 6/96.

1994—Châteauneuf du Pape Cuvée Vieilles Vignes (red)   The 1994 Cuvée Vieilles Vig-
•   nes appears to be an awesome wine. The opaque dark ruby/purple color is accom-
93   panied by a sensational nose of crushed black fruits, licorice, and truffles.
             Full-bodied, with magnificent extraction of fruit and a layered, viscous texture,
             this unctuous, superconcentrated wine has plenty of tannin lurking behind the
             ostentatious display of richness. This is a dazzling Châteauneuf du Pape! Antici-
             pated maturity: 1998–2012. Last tasted 6/96.

1993—Châteauneuf du Pape (red)   The 1993 exhibits intense aromas of cinnamon, cher-
•   ries, pepper, and herbal tea, as well as an advanced, medium dark, ruby/garnet
88   color, sweet, round, medium- to full-bodied flavors, and a soft, lush finish. Surpris-
             ingly evolved for the vintage, it is best drunk over the next 4–5 years. It is a
             controversial wine. Last tasted 6/96.

1993—Châteauneuf du Pape Cuvée Vieilles Vignes (red)   The 1993 Cuvée Vieilles Vig-
•   nes offers an exotic, gingery, cinnamon, jammy, black-cherry-scented nose, and
90   excellent, sweet, rich, late harvest–styled flavors that ooze viscous cherry fruit.
             This wine may be Châteauneuf du Pape's answer to the famous Pomerol estate
             Lafleur. Although not as impressive as the 1989 and 1990, it is thick and rich but
             appears fragile and surprisingly forward. Anticipated maturity: now–2003. Last
             tasted 6/96.

1992—Châteauneuf du Pape (red)   The exuberant, in-your-face 1992 Châteauneuf du
•   Pape is a jammy, decadently styled wine with a sweet, cedary, Provençal herb, and
87   cherry-scented nose, lush, voluptuously textured flavors, low acidity, and copious
             amounts of alcohol. Anticipated maturity: now–2001. Last tasted 9/96.

1992—Châteauneuf du Pape Cuvée Vieilles Vignes (red) A pronounced musty, stale tea
  ·   aroma has marred several tastings of this wine. But other bottles, as evidenced by
94?   the following tasting note, are outrageously delicious. Except for its high level of
      alcohol, the 1992 Cuvée Vieilles Vignes could easily be mistaken for the great
      Pomerol Lafleur. It boasts a phenomenal purple color, a huge nose of jammy black
      raspberries, flowers, and minerals, amazing concentration and unctuosity, and a
      staggeringly long finish with so much extraction and depth that the moderate tannin
      level is hardly noticeable. It already offers superb drinking. The clean bottles
      represent one of the greatest wines of this average to above-average quality vintage.
      Anticipated maturity: now–2005. Last tasted 8/96.

1990—Châteauneuf du Pape (red) The 1990 reveals a dark ruby/purple color, and a
  ·   huge nose of jammy, sweet black fruits and herbs. In the mouth, the sweetness,
90   glycerin, high alcohol, and gorgeous extract levels make for a sumptuous drinking
      experience. The tannins are silky and the finish is formidable. Anticipated matu-
      rity: now–2006. Last tasted 8/96.

1990—Châteauneuf du Pape Cuvée Vieilles Vignes (red) The 1990 Cuvée Vieilles Vig-
  ·   nes is opaque black/purple in color, with a nose of superripe cassis, blueberries,
100   spring flowers, and licorice. In the mouth it is awesomely rich and concentrated,
      with a thick, unctuous texture, plenty of tannin, and some heady alcohol in the
      finish. A profound wine, with multiple levels of interest and flavor, the 1990 should
      prove to be an immortal classic Châteauneuf du Pape. Anticipated maturity: 2000–
      2025. Last tasted 7/96.

1989—Châteauneuf du Pape (red) The 1989 Châteauneuf du Pape is soft, round, gener-
  ·   ously endowed, with low acidity, as well as a fleshy, meaty personality. Primarily it
85   is a straightforward, richly fruity Châteauneuf du Pape. Anticipated maturity: now–
      2000. Last tasted 6/96.

1989—Châteauneuf du Pape Cuvée Vieilles Vignes (red) The 1989 Cuvée Vieilles Vig-
  ·   nes exhibits an opaque black/purple color, with a huge, undeveloped bouquet of
99   cassis, black raspberries, and licorice. This smashingly rich, exceptionally con-
      centrated wine is one of the most compelling Châteauneuf du Papes I have ever
      tasted. The awesome extract levels, massive concentration, and amazing length
      are rarely encountered today. It is a monument to Châteauneuf du Pape and the
      Grenache grape. Absolutely awesome. Anticipated maturity: 2000–2020. Last tasted
      7/96.

1988—Châteauneuf du Pape (red) The 1988 tastes surprisingly soft, shallow, fruity, and
  ·   straightforward. Drink it up. Last tasted 12/93.
82

Older Vintages

Since I do not have any older vintages of Domaine de Marcoux left in my cellar, it has been
years since I have tasted the older successful vintages. The 1983 and 1981 were not as good
as one might have hoped given the vintage conditions. The 1978 was excellent but not
outstanding, which is surprising in view of the vintage. The 1970, 1967, and 1966 were all
superb, but it has been more than a decade since I have tasted them.

MAS DE BOIS LAUZON* * * *

Address: Quartier Bois Lauzon
      Route D 68
      84110 Orange
Tel: 4-90-34-46-49
Fax: 4-90-34-46-61
Wines produced: Châteauneuf du Pape (red and white), Châteauneuf du Pape Réserve
      Suzeraine
Surface area (white): 2.47 acres
      (red): 24.7 acres
Production (white): 375 cases
      (red): 3,750 cases
Upbringing (white): Fermentation of 8 days, then 3 months in stainless steel tanks
      (red): Fermentation of 10 days in cement vats, then 24 months in old oak casks,
      bottling after 12 months' storage in stainless steel vats
Average age of vines (white): 25 years
      (red): 50–60 years
Blend (white): One third each Grenache Blanc, Clairette, and Bourboulenc
      (red): 90% Grenache, 10% other varietals

VINTAGES

1995—Châteauneuf du Pape (red) I had never before tasted the wines of Mas de Bois
· Lauzon, made by Monique and Daniel Chaussy in Orange, the ancient Roman
88 village just north of Châteauneuf du Pape. Both the 1995 and 1994 are impressive
offerings. The 1995 Châteauneuf du Pape offers sweet fruit, good body, and a long
finish. It possesses a healthy dark ruby color with purple nuances, excellent extract,
good fruit, an expansive, chewy texture, full body, serious depth, and a long, spicy,
peppery, rich finish with significant alcohol and glycerin. It should drink well
young, and keep for a dozen or more years. Last tasted 6/96.

1994—Châteauneuf du Pape (red) The 1994 Châteauneuf du Pape exhibits a healthy
· dark ruby/garnet color, followed by a rich, chocolaty, cherry, and herb-scented
87 nose, and powerful, medium- to full-bodied flavors, with fine ripeness, density, and
structure. This wine should improve with 1–2 years of cellaring, and keep for 10–
12 years. Last tasted 6/96.

DOMAINE MATHIEU* * *

Address: Route de Courthézon
      B.P. 32
      84230 Châteauneuf du Pape
Tel: 4-90-83-72-09
Fax: 4-90-83-50-55
Wines produced: Châteauneuf du Pape (red and white)
Surface area (white): 0.5 acre
      (red): 46 acres
Production (white): 375 cases
      (red): 7,500 cases
Upbringing (white): Vinified and aged in tank with malolactic blocked and bottled after 4–
      5 months following a sterile filtration
      (red): 12–20 months in old wood foudres before bottling without fining or filtra-
      tion

Average age of vines (white): 60 years
                           (red): 60 years
Blend (white): 50% Clairette, 30% Grenache Blanc, 8% Picpoul, 7% Bourboulenc, 5%
      (red): 80% Grenache, 8% Mourvèdre, 3% Cinsault, 2% Syrah, 7% various varietals

This historic estate, which has been making wines in Châteauneuf du Pape since 1600, owns a whopping 45 separate parcels of vines scattered throughout the Châteauneuf du Pape appellation. I imagine that the harvest strategy at this estate is not unlike planning a major military invasion. Virtually every type of soil is represented, but the one constant is the high percentage of Grenache in almost all the parcels. The wines are traditionally made, with no destemming, vinified in tanks, and bottled after 12–20 months of aging in old wood foudres. The bland white Châteauneuf du Pape is crisp and fresh but one-dimensional.

The red wines have been irregular, but in top years they can be very good Châteauneufs that are meant to be drunk in their first 7–8 years of life. My emotions about this estate have been on a roller-coaster ride, with my enthusiasm for several vintages crushed by indifferent performances in other years. No doubt fine wines emerge from proprietors Charles, Jacqueline, and André Mathieu, but this estate lacks the consistency shown by top domaines.

VINTAGES

1995—Châteauneuf du Pape (red)   After Domaine Mathieu's rich, concentrated, promis-
  ·   ing 1993, I was disappointed with indifferent efforts in 1994 and 1995, both
 82   better vintages. The 1995 Châteauneuf du Pape is made in an obvious, open-knit,
      modern-day style. It is fruity, pure, ripe, and cleanly made, but it possesses little
      depth and individual character. Anticipated maturity: now–2000. Last tasted 6/96.

1994—Châteauneuf du Pape (red)   The 1994 Châteauneuf du Pape is made in a soft,
  ·   commercial style, with good fruit, spicy, fruitcake aromas, and a decent finish.
 80   Drink this medium-bodied, easygoing wine over the next 3–4 years. Last tasted
      6/96.

1993—Châteauneuf du Pape (red)   The 1993 is a distinctive, full-bodied, generous,
  ·   succulent Châteauneuf du Pape with considerable complexity. Its style is reminis-
 88   cent of top Chante-Perdrix vintages. The earthy, truffle, Asian spice, herb, and
      jammy black-fruit-scented nose is followed by a full-bodied, ripe wine with copious
      quantities of fruit, glycerin, and alcohol. Although undeniably rich, seductive, and
      mouth-filling, it is unlikely to be a long-termer. Anticipated maturity: now–2001.
      Last tasted 6/96.

1990—Châteauneuf du Pape (red)   The ruby-colored 1990 Châteauneuf du Pape is a
  ·   jammy, spicy, richly fruity wine with soft tannins, fleshy quantities of glycerin,
 87   formidable alcohol, low acid, and an element of *surmaturité*. It exhibits explosive
      cherry aromas, and a powerful combination of chewy fruit, alcohol, and tannin. I
      would opt for drinking this soft, low-acid wine over the next 7–10 years. Last tasted
      6/95.

1989—Châteauneuf du Pape (red)   The 1989 exhibits an intense aromatic character,
  ·   suggesting spicy, herbaceous-scented raspberries and smoky tobacco. In the mouth
 87   it is deep, round, and sweet. This is a wine for hedonists—obvious but enjoyable.
      Mature now. Last tasted 6/95.

1988—Châteauneuf du Pape (red)   The 1988 exhibits a seductive, soft, expansive, sweet-
  ·   tasting palate, a cedary, cassis-scented bouquet, and a long, elegant finish. Its soft
 86   texture suggests that it should be consumed over the next 4–5 years. Last tasted
      6/94.

CHÂTEAU MAUCOIL (PIERRE QUIOT)* */* * *

Address: Chemin de Maucoil
        84230 Châteauneuf du Pape
Tel: 4-90-34-14-86
Fax: 4-90-34-71-88
Wines produced: Châteauneuf du Pape Réserve Suzeraine (red and white)
Surface area (white): 2.47 acres
              (red): 47 acres
Production (white): 300 cases
            (red): 6,875 cases
Upbringing (white): 6 months in epoxy vats
            (red): 24 months total; 12–18 months minimum in old oak casks
Average age of vines (white): 55 years
                      (red): 55 years
Blend (white): 70% Grenache Blanc, 20% Clairette, 10% Roussanne
       (red): 50% Grenache, 20% Syrah, 5% Mourvèdre, 25% other varietals

Château Maucoil takes its name from the vineyard in the very northwestern section of the appellation. This estate has as much history as any in Châteauneuf du Pape. Wine has been made here since at least the sixteenth century, and some argue that traces of Roman implements found on the property suggest that winemaking was practiced 2,000 years ago. The current proprietor, Pierre Quiot, is one of the leading political figures in Châteauneuf du Pape, as well as the Rhône Valley. The administration of this estate has been turned over to Carol Maimone, who continues the estate's practice of producing modern, uncomplicated, fruity, cherry-flavored Châteauneuf du Pape that is meant to be drunk in its first four or five years of life. This is clearly an estate that processes the wine in order to get it into the bottle as quickly as possible. Filtering and fining are done after malolactic fermentation, and another filtration prior to bottling. The potential of the raw materials could make Château Maucoil one of the leaders of the appellation, but they have chosen a safe, risk-free, commercial style that no doubt has its fans.

A tiny percentage of straightforward white wine is made at Château Maucoil.

VINTAGES

1995—Châteauneuf du Pape Réserve Suzeraine (red)   The 1995 Réserve Suzeraine is
  ·   sweet and expansive, but lighter-bodied than the 1994, with less concentration
  82   and more acidity. Although pleasant, it is one-dimensional and simple. Last tasted
          6/96.

1994—Châteauneuf du Pape Réserve Suzeraine (red): At this estate, the 1994 offering
  ·   turned out better than the 1995. The 1994 Réserve Suzeraine exhibits an attractive
  86   dark ruby/purple color as well as a sweet nose of herbs, pepper, olives, and black
          cherries. Medium- to full-bodied, with good concentration, a soft, easygoing texture,
          and an adequately long finish, this is a wine to drink over the next 7–8 years. Last
          tasted 6/96.

1993—Châteauneuf du Pape Réserve Suzeraine (red)   The excellent 1993 Réserve Suzer-
  ·   aine offers a healthy deep ruby/purple color, and sweet, pure, black-cherry fruit
  86   intermixed with scents of herbs and spice. Medium- to full-bodied, with fine depth,
          a soft attack, and a spicy finish, this wine can be drunk now as well as over the
          next 6–7 years. Last tasted 6/96.

DOMAINE DE LA MILLIÈRE* *

Address: Quartier Cabrières
        84100 Orange
Tel: 4-90-34-53-06
Fax: 4-90-51-14-60
Wines produced: Châteauneuf du Pape (red and white), Châteauneuf du Pape Cuvée Vieilles Vignes (red)
Surface area (white): 1.7 acres
             (red): 12.4 acres
                   Cuvée Vieilles Vignes—29.7 acres
Production (white): 250 cases
           (red): 1,875 cases
                 Cuvée Vieilles Vignes—2,625 cases
Upbringing (white): 8 months in enamel tanks
           (red): 36–42 months total; fermentation of 20 days in cement tanks; then 18 months in old oak casks, followed by storage in stainless steel and enamel tanks
                 Cuvée Vieilles Vignes—36–42 months total; fermentation of 25 days; then 18 months in old oak casks, followed by storage in stainless steel and enamel tanks
Average age of vines (white): 60 years
                     (red): 75 years
                           Cuvée Vieilles Vignes—95 years
Blend (white): 80% Grenache Blanc, 15% Clairette, 5% Bourboulenc
      (red): 70% Grenache, 15% Cinsault, 10% Mourvèdre, 5% Syrah
            Cuvée Vieilles Vignes—70% Grenache, 15% Cinsault, 10% Mourvèdre, 5% Syrah

This estate, with most of its vineyards south of Orange, produces a pleasant but one-dimensional white wine and two cuvées of red wine. The regular Châteauneuf du Pape is in essence the property's second wine, with the bulk of the production going into their Cuvée Vieilles Vignes, a wine that, sadly, I have never tasted. The regular cuvée is of average quality. The Cuvée Vieilles Vignes is made from 90-year-old vines, of which 70% are Grenache, and the rest Cinsault, Mourvèdre, and Syrah. The vinification practiced is traditional, with no destemming, and an upbringing in small oak casks and larger oak foudres for 18 months prior to bottling.

VINTAGES

1995—Châteauneuf du Pape (red)   The 1995 Châteauneuf du Pape displays a darker
  ·   ruby color than the 1994, sweeter, riper fruit, medium body, and a restrained,
 83   moderately concentrated style. It should drink well for 4–5 years. Last tasted 6/96.
1994—Châteauneuf du Pape (red)   This estate has turned out a correct, spicy, herba-
  ·   ceous, but thin, medium-bodied 1994 Châteauneuf du Pape. Correct but uninspir-
 76   ing, it will provide adequate drinking for 3–5 years. Last tasted 6/96.
1990—Châteauneuf du Pape (red)   The 1990 red Châteauneuf du Pape is a straightfor-
  ·   ward, robust wine, with moderate tannins, an attractive black-cherry, herb, and
 85   spicy-scented nose, and medium- to full-bodied, concentrated flavors that exhibit
      firm tannins. While it lacks excitement, it is a competent example of Châteauneuf
      du Pape that should be drunk over the next 5–7 years. Last tasted 6/95.

CHÂTEAU MONGIN* * *

This small estate is managed by the Lycée Viticole d'Orange, a school for burgeoning winemakers. The vineyard is situated near the school, which is a modern, state-of-the-art facility just south of Orange. The wines are modern style, but well made and reasonably priced. They deserve more recognition than they have enjoyed to date.

VINTAGES

1994—Châteauneuf du Pape (red) This is a fine example of Châteauneuf du Pape. The
·   wine exhibits medium body, sweet black-cherry fruit, a soft, velvety texture, and a
87   long, lush finish. While it may be too obvious and open-knit, it offers a delicious
       mouthful of Châteauneuf du Pape. Anticipated maturity: now–2000. Last tasted
       6/96.

1993—Châteauneuf du Pape (red) 1993 was the first vintage I tasted from this graduate
·   school for wine-makers/oenologists. It is a well-made wine produced in a modern,
87   up-front, fruity style with clean aromas and flavors, medium to full body, and soft,
       sweet tannin. Anticipated maturity: now–2000. Last tasted 6/95.

DOMAINE DE MONT REDON (FABRE/ABEILLE)* * *

Address: 84230 Châteauneuf du Pape
Tel: 4-90-83-72-75
Fax: 4-90-83-77-20
Wines produced: Châteauneuf du Pape (red and white)
Surface area (white): 25 acres
       (red): 247 acres
Production (white): 6,000 cases
     (red): 30,000 cases
Upbringing (white): 4–5 months tank vinification with malolactic blocked; sterile-filtered at
     bottling
    (red): Almost 100% destemming, and the wines are vinified in modern
     temperature-controlled tanks and then moved to both oak foudres and
     small oak casks, of which a small percentage are new. The wine stays in
     wood for 18 months prior to bottling.
Average age of vines (red): 45 years
Blend (white): 40% Grenache Blanc, 25% Bourboulenc, 20% Clairette, 10% Picpoul, 5%
    Roussanne
    (red): 65% Grenache, 15% Syrah, 10% Cinsault, 5% Mourvèdre, 5% other varietals

Mont Redon is one of the most historic estates in Châteauneuf du Pape. Historians have established that vineyards were planted as early as 1334. The modern-day era dates from 1921, when Henri Plantin set about to resurrect Mont Redon's vineyards after decades of neglect. This property is one of the most splendidly situated of Châteauneuf du Pape. It is located directly on the stony plateau north of the village. The large estate (247 acres) is impeccably and enthusiastically run by Jean Abeille and Didier Fabre, grandsons of the late Henri Plantin.

Mont Redon was once known for its reference point wines. The 1947, 1949, 1955, and 1961 (the last two vintages were on the wine list of the famous Paris restaurant Taillevent for nearly a decade; I did my duty in nearly exhausting their stock) were classic, blockbuster, hefty but remarkably complex Châteauneuf du Papes that aged effortlessly for 20–30 years. Under Abeille and Fabre, Mont Redon has moved to a lighter style of wine, so much so that the wine was frequently insipid and innocuous in the late seventies and early eighties.

While denials of such a change in Mont Redon are to be expected, the truth is that Mont Redon was perhaps Châteauneuf du Pape's most conspicuous underachiever during the decade of the eighties.

It appears that there has been a movement (albeit a limited one) to beef up the wine, with more flesh, muscle, and aromatic complexity, but the proprietors cannot break away from their obsessive food-processor mentality, i.e., mutiple filtrations, and fining. In short, this wine remains a relatively unexciting, simple, fruity, commercial-style Châteauneuf du Pape. Admittedly, tasters who have never had a glass of Rayas, Beaucastel, Henri Bonneau, or Pégau are unlikely to react as critically, because the wine is cleanly made, pure, and charming, if not dissimilar from thousands of other commercially fruity red wines made throughout the world. But protests fall on deaf ears at Mont Redon because the estate's fame has ensured that it is the best-known Châteauneuf du Pape of the appellation.

On such issues, I have talked at length with Abeille and Fabre, but it is like chatting with a scrub bush on a lonely Provençal *garrigue*. It appears to me that the solution would be to produce a small quantity of old-vine Mont Redon that recalls the classics of the forties, fifties, and early sixties. Let that wine be the ultimate expression of this great terroir, in addition to being symbolic of Mont Redon's long history. It would satisfy the league of Châteauneuf du Pape connoisseurs looking (and willing to pay) for something more than just a full-bodied Beaujolais. There would still be plenty of wine to sell to the masses, thus providing the estate its impressive cash flow. Despite such a suggestion, my feeling is that nothing will change as long as the current administration remains.

Ironically, there has been progress in the quality of Mont Redon's white wines. Once the most prominent example of the abuses of modern-day technology—a nonwine, with no aromatics or flavors save for an impression of acidity and alcohol—this wine has improved immensely over recent years. It is now a good example of the appellation. It is sterile-filtered because it has its malolactic blocked, but the wine possesses more fatness and ripeness than in the past.

Another interesting irony is that Mont Redon has a fine 50-acre Côtes du Rhône estate that makes a fruity, soft, clean, commercial wine that tastes similar to their Châteauneuf du Pape, but can be purchased for one-third the price.

Mont Redon, an estate with a fabulous terroir and exquisite potential, as well as producers of legendary wines in the forties, fifties, and early sixties, is today the appellation's most conspicuous underachiever. It also remains a sterling example of what modern-day oenology, when carried to extremes, can do (or undo) to a great terroir.

VINTAGES

1993—Châteauneuf du Pape (red)   A medium-bodied, cleanly made, mainstream, commercial wine, the 1993 Châteauneuf du Pape exhibits an attractive, moderately intense, ripe, black-fruit personality, accompanied by a weedy, peppery component. With good depth and a soft, straightforward finish, it should drink well for 10–12 years. Last tasted 6/95.
•
86

1992—Châteauneuf du Pape (red)   The 1992 Châteauneuf du Pape is similarly sized, with a likeable black-cherry, herb, and cedary nose, peppery, ripe, medium-bodied flavors, soft texture, and a juicy finish. Mature now. Last tasted 6/96.
•
86

1990—Châteauneuf du Pape (red)   The 1990 displays deep ruby color, a ripe, medium- to full-bodied, highly structured feel on the palate, plenty of tannin, and a closed, firm style. After bottling, there is significantly less to the wine than prior to its filtration. Anticipated maturity: 1998–2005. Last tasted 11/95.
•
85

The careful management of the vineyard and the impeccable winemaking practiced in the cellars, not to mention the character of the vineyard and vintage, have all been compromised by a sterile filtration. When will producers who have extraordinary terroirs, old vines, and the potential to make riveting wines of profound complexity and richness realize that the serious wine consumers of the world will no longer pay the price for compromised wines?

1989—Châteauneuf du Pape (red)   The 1989 is a pure, well-structured wine, and a
   •   classic example of Mont Redon's modern style. There is considerable tannin, as
   87   well as a touch of new oak in its closed bouquet of black fruits, spices, minerals, and licorice. Medium-bodied, rich, and concentrated, this wine should last for 20 years. Having tasted this wine from tank in 1990 following its completion of malolactic, the raw materials were awesome. While the wine is still very good, I imagine 50% of the aromatics, body, and flavor were stripped out by the numerous filtrations this wine had to endure. Mature now. Last tasted 6/95.

1988—Châteauneuf du Pape (red)   The 1988 Mont Redon is a more structured, more
   •   austere style of Châteauneuf du Pape. While it does not possess the flamboyance
   86   and dramatic qualities of the 1989, it is good but restrained. I wonder how much more fruit and perfume it would have had if it had it not been fined and filtered prior to bottling? Mature: now–2002. Last tasted 6/95.

Older Vintages

The vintages of the eighties are pathetic. The fully mature 1985 is dropping its fruit; the disappointing 1983, 1982, and 1981 are all light-bodied, stripped, eviscerated wines that are still alive but have little to offer. The same thing can be said for the compact, attenuated 1979, and the desiccated 1978. The latter wine was the first wine to be subjected to the new system of mutiple filtrations. Although the wine is still alive, it displays virtually no aromatic profile, a neutral taste, and no real typicity or character. The 1976 is austere and harshly tannic. Perhaps the last of the old-style Mont Redons, the 1971 possesses a glorious bouquet of coffee, *garrigue*, and sweet jammy fruit, followed by lush, full-bodied, chunky flavors. It is no 1961, but certainly far superior to anything that has been made since. I last had the 1971 at a French restaurant in 1990, and it was in terrific condition.

Other older vintages that may show up at auction and merit buying (the old-style Mont Redon could easily evolve for 25–30 years), include the 1970, 1967, the magnificent 1961, and the colossal 1949 and 1947. The last bottle I had of 1955, drunk at Taillevent, was starting to fade, but these old vintages are true treasures, and offer a complete contrast to the mediocre standards of today.

DOMAINE DE MONTPERTUIS
(* * *Cuvée Classique/* * * *Cuvée Tradition)

Address: 7, avenue St.-Joseph
         84230 Châteauneuf du Pape
Tel: 4-90-83-73-87
Fax: 4-90-83-51-13
Wines produced: Châteauneuf du Pape (white), Châteauneuf du Pape Cuvée Classique
                (red), Châteauneuf du Pape Cuvée Tradition (red)
Surface area (white): 7.4 acres
             (red): Cuvée Classique—24.7 acres
                    Cuvée Tradition—13.6 acres
Production (white): 800–950 cases
           (red): Cuvée Classique—3,750 cases
                  Cuvée Tradition—1,125 cases

Upbringing (white): 6 months in termperature-controlled stainless steel vats

      (red): Cuvée Classique—fermentation for 3 weeks in cement vats; followed by storage for 3 months in cement vats; then 10–12 months in old oak barrels; several bottlings, the earliest after 18 months

      Cuvée Tradition—fermentation for 30–45 days in cement vats; then 3 months storage in stainless steel vats; then 20 months in oak casks; bottling done all at one time

Average age of vines (white): 25 years

      (red): Cuvée Classique—40 years

      Cuvée Tradition—60–110 years

Blend (white): 40% Grenache Blanc, 20% Clairette (white and pink), 20% Bourboulenc, 20% Roussanne

      (red): Cuvée Classique—60% Grenache, 20% Mourvèdre, 10% Syrah, 10% other varietals

      Cuvée Tradition—90% Grenache, 10% other varietals except Syrah

Run by Proprietor Paul Jeune, this estate produces traditional Châteauneuf du Papes that, atypically, often need 4–5 years of cellaring to reveal their potential. The white wines are correct but one dimensional. The two cuvées of red wine elicit far more interest. Jeune produces a Cuvée Classique that is meant to be drunk during its first 10–15 years of life and, in top vintages, a Cuvée Tradition from lower yields and older vines. The latter wine is 90% Grenache with a dollop of other varietals. The Cuvée Classique is 60% Grenache, buttressed by Mourvèdre, Syrah, and miscellaneous grapes.

There is something old-fashioned about the Montpertuis wines, and I do not mean that in a pejorative sense. They appear to be made by someone who will not make any concessions for modern-day tasters who want the fruit up front and an uncomplicated simplicity to a wine. There is no destemming, a standard vinification, and aging in oak casks for 18–20 months prior to bottling, which is done with no filtration.

Montpertuis's red wines are difficult to judge when young, often tasting closed, tightly strung, and reticent, but my experience has demonstrated that the great years of Montpertuis do come forth at around 6–8 years of age. At that age they taste better than they did immediately after bottling. These wines consistently reveal an umistakable scent and flavor of Bing cherries. This morsellated estate (there are a whopping 42 parcels) has its largest vineyards in such sectors as Les Cabrières, Montpertuis, La Crau, and La Croze.

VINTAGES

1995—Châteauneuf du Pape Cuvée Classique (red)   The excellent 1995 Cuvée Classique
·
88   exhibits a dark ruby/purple color and an attractive, pure nose of vibrant red cherries, with a whiff of herbs and earth. Impressive depth, ripeness, and extraction are found in this well-balanced, youthful wine. It will be less flattering in its youth than the 1994, but it possesses the potential to last for 10–12 + years. Last tasted 6/96.

1994—Châteauneuf du Pape Cuvée Classique (red)   The 1994 offers copious amounts of
·
87   sweet, ripe, berry aromas accompanied by attractive scents of pepper and herbs. This round, sweet, pure wine is more precocious than Jeune's offerings are normally, with medium to full body, excellent fruit, and a dense, attractive, spicy, full-bodied finish. Anticipated maturity: 1998–2006. Last tasted 6/96.

1993—Châteauneuf du Pape Cuvée Classique (red)   The 1993 Cuvée Classique exhibits
·
87   a medium to dark ruby color, spicy, sweet, black-cherry fruit, medium to full body, a clean, well-structured, moderately tannic personality, and fine length.

Approachable now, it can be drunk over the next 10–12 + years. Last tasted 6/96.

1992—Châteauneuf du Pape Cuvée Classique (red)   Proprietor Paul Jeune made no
·   Cuvée Tradition in 1992. The unfiltered 1992 Cuvée Classique, which includes all
87   of the old-vine production, possesses a deep ruby color, a ripe, sweet, lovely nose,
         fat, chewy, black-cherry and herb-scented flavors, and a moderately long, spicy,
         heady finish. Anticipated maturity: now–2006. Last tasted 6/95.

1990—Châteauneuf du Pape Cuvée Classique (red)   The 1990 Cuvée Classique is ready
·   to drink, with a soft, up-front, herbal, berry fragrance, tasty, medium- to full-
86   bodied, generously endowed flavors, low acidity, and plenty of alcoholic punch in
         the finish. Anticipated maturity: now–2004. Last tasted 6/96.

1990—Châteauneuf du Pape Cuvée Tradition (red)   Readers may still be able to find
·   some of Jeune's spectacular 1990 Cuvée Tradition, which has begun to display
92   even more character than it did when first bottled. The deep ruby/purple color is
         followed by a big, spicy, herb, black-cherry, black-raspberry, peppery-scented
         nose, full body, and gobs of glycerin and richness, as well as moderate tannin in
         the finish. Anticipated maturity: 1998–2015. Last tasted 12/95.

1989—Châteauneuf du Pape Cuvée Tradition (red)   The 1989 (14.8% alcohol) should
·   prove to be one of the blockbuster, great, long-lived stars of the vintage. It reminded
91   me of a blend of the 1989 Clefs d'Or and the 1989 Rayas—incredibly high praise.
         Black/ruby in color, a fabulous bouquet of minerals, licorice, and pure black
         raspberries is followed by a wine with awesome concentration, full body, gobs
         of tannin, and decent acidity. This is a true vin de garde that will have to be put
         away in the cellar for at least 4–5 years. It has the potential to last for at least
         two decades. Jeune told me that the natural alcohol in the wine is 14.8%.
         What is amazing is that the huge concentration of fruit completely covers any trace
         that the wine has alcohol this high. Anticipated maturity: now–2010. Last
         tasted 5/96.

1988—Châteauneuf du Pape Cuvée Classique (red)   The 1988 Cuvée Classique is an-
·   other classically made, potentially long-lived Châteauneuf du Pape. From its spicy,
89   black-cherry-scented bouquet to its intense, muscular, full-bodied flavors, this is
         an impressively built and structured Châteauneuf du Pape. Anticipated maturity:
         1998–2008. Last tasted 5/96.

DOMAINE DE LA MORDORÉE
(* * * *Cuvée Classique/* * * * *Cuvée de la Reine des Bois)

Address: 30126 Tavel

Tel: 4-66-50-00-75

Fax: 4-66-50-47-39

Wines produced: Châteauneuf du Pape Cuvée Classique (red), Châteauneuf du Pape Cuvée
         de la Reine des Bois (red)

Surface area: 7.5 acres

Production: 1,125 cases

Upbringing: 24 months total; 50% of the yield in new oak barrels and 50% in stainless steel
         vats for 9 months

Average age of vines: 60 years

Blend: 70% Grenache, 10% Mourvèdre, 5% Cinsault, 5% Syrah, 5% Counoise, 5%
         Vaccarèse

Note: The Cuvée de la Reine des Bois is a very limited bottling of a special selection of
the most concentrated wine; it is produced only in the most exceptional vintages.

Domaine de la Mordorée is a well-known producer in Lirac, the appellation west of Châteauneuf du Pape on the other side of the Rhône River. They have a tiny 7.5 acreage of 60-year-old vines that consists of three parcels superbly situated in La Crau, Les Cabrières, and Bois la Ville. Christophe Délorme has brought a modern philosophy to this wine's vinification, which is completely destemmed and aged in small oak casks. La Mordorée has emerged as one of the top wines of the appellation, rather remarkable in view of the fact that the first vintage was 1989. This is a pure, full-bodied Châteauneuf du Pape with superb texture. It is accessible young, but possesses the requisite concentration and intensity to last for 10–15 years. The Cuvée de la Reine des Bois is unquestionably a five-star wine, and the regular cuvée a consistent four-star wine. Another admirable aspect of La Mordorée is that the wines have been extremely successful in such difficult vintages as 1992 and 1993.

VINTAGES

1994—Châteauneuf du Pape   La Mordorée's 1994 Châteauneuf du Pape won first prize
·   at the Festival of St.-Marc, where most of the Châteauneuf du Pape growers offer
90   their wines in a blind tasting of the newest vintage. This 1994 is an impressive, modern-style, deliciously rich wine with scents of black raspberry, cherry, and pepper. Like so many of this estate's wines, its hallmark is its purity, excellent balance, and ripe, decadently rich fruit. Anticipated maturity: now–2005. Last tasted 6/96.

1994—Châteauneuf du Pape Cuvée de la Reine des Bois   Even more special is the dark
·   ruby/purple-colored 1994 Cuvée de la Reine des Bois. Tasted for the first time,
93   this cuvée is obviously made from older vines and the ripest fruit. An element of *surmaturité* personifies its character. The wine possesses immense body, superb extract, a sweet, flamboyant nose of black-cherry jam, fruitcake, and smoke. Unctuous, thick, and full-bodied, with some tannin lurking in the background, this is a large-scaled yet drinkable Châteauneuf du Pape. Anticipated maturity: now–2010. Last tasted 6/96.

1993—Châteauneuf du Pape   The 1993 Châteauneuf du Pape possesses a dark ruby
·   color with purple tints, a sweet, ripe, exceptionally pure, well-delineated nose of
89   black cherries and curranty fruit, full body, light but noticeable tannin, considerable richness and thickness, and admirable length. Anticipated maturity: now–2006. Last tasted 6/96.

1992—Châteauneuf du Pape (red)   The 1992 Châteauneuf du Pape caused producers in
·   the village to recognize just what progress Domaine de la Mordorée had made. It
90   took first place in the producers' annual tasting of Châteauneuf du Papes, the prize of St.-Marc (making this winery the first-prize winner for two of the last three years). This outstanding Châteauneuf du Pape is made in a user-friendly, full-bodied, expansive, fragrant style with gobs of red and black fruits, considerable glycerin, high alcohol, and a noteworthy velvety finish. It is a joy to drink. Anticipated maturity: now–2003. Last tasted 6/95.

MOULIN-TACUSSEL* * *

Address: 10, avenue des Bosquets
        84230 Châteauneuf du Pape
Tel: 4-90-83-70-09
Fax: 4-90-83-50-92
Wines produced: Châteauneuf du Pape (red)

Surface area: 21 acres

Production: 3,000 cases

Upbringing: 24–26 months total; fermentation of 15–20 days in epoxy vats, then storage in tiled vats for 5–6 months, then 12–18 months in old oak casks; bottling is done all at once

Average age of vines: 60 years

Blend: 80% Grenache, 20% Mourvèdre, Cinsault, and Syrah

This property takes its name from the current proprietor, Moulin, and the late Henri Tacussel, who was a friend of the late Baron Le Roy. It has been estate-bottling only since 1985. They own several parcels of vines, all covered with the rounded stones that are part of Châteauneuf du Pape's fame. No white wine is made. The red wine is made traditionally, with no destemming, a classical vinification, and an upbringing in both small barrels and large foudres for up to two years. As the tasting notes that follow indicate, one of the more intriguing characteristics of Moulin-Tacussel has been what I perceive as a distinctive eucalyptus scent similar to that of certain California Cabernet Sauvignons, particularly the famed Heitz Martha's Vineyard Cabernet from the western sector of Napa Valley.

Moulin-Tacussel's wines were very good in the wonderful trilogy of 1988, 1989, and 1990 vintages, but subsequently, this estate's efforts have been disappointing. My instincts suggest this is another Châteauneuf du Pape domaine that could cut back on fining and filtration.

VINTAGES

1995—Châteauneuf du Pape   The 1995 Châteauneuf du Pape reveals chalky, hard tannin, and a metallic personality that detracts from the wine's overall impression.
78   The finish is short, hard, and lacking ripeness and fruit. This estate has produced some very fine Châteauneuf du Papes, but this example performed poorly. Last tasted 6/96.

1994—Châteauneuf du Pape   Before bottling, the 1994 Châteauneuf du Pape was significantly better than when I tasted it in June 1996. The wine is variable from
86?   bottle to bottle. Some are seemingly light, while other bottles have shown more fruit intensity and character. Last tasted 6/96.

1993—Châteauneuf du Pape   The 1993 exhibits a medium ruby color, the telltale minty nose, and round, soft flavors that quickly slide over the palate. This indifferent
83   effort should be drunk over the next 5–6 years. Last tasted 6/95.

1992—Châteauneuf du Pape   In the 1992 Châteauneuf du Pape the minty characteristic is accompanied by ripe black-cherry fruit intertwined with scents of tar. Medium-
85   bodied and fruity, with decent glycerin and alcohol, this soft, easy-to-drink, medium-weight Châteauneuf should be consumed over the next 4–5 years. Last tasted 6/95.

1990—Châteauneuf du Pape   There is a tart, crisp edge to this wine, a bouquet redolent with the scents of mint and cassis, rich, long, full-bodied, structured and tannic
87   flavors, and a spicy, tightly knit finish. While this distinctive, unusually styled Châteauneuf du Pape can be drunk at present, it ideally needs 3–4 years of cellaring. Anticipated maturity: now–2002. Last tasted 11/95.

1989—Châteauneuf du Pape   Again the tart, crisp edge to this wine, and a huge bouquet of mint and cassis, rich, long, full-bodied, structured and tannic flavors,
89   and a spicy, tightly knit finish. I thought the 1989 exhibited more depth and

concentration, but the differences between it and the 1990 are negligible. This distinctive, unusually styled Châteauneuf du Pape tastes amazingly like a top California Cabernet—strange but true! Anticipated maturity: now–2006. Last tasted 11/95.

1988—Châteauneuf du Pape   The 1988 possessed a less concentrated but still impressively minty, rich, cassis bouquet, full-bodied, fleshy, chewy flavors, with moderate
·
87   tannins, good acidity, definition, and focus. Anticipated maturity: now–2004. Last tasted 11/95.

DOMAINE DE NALYS (DUFAYS)* * * *

Address: Route de Courthézon
        84230 Châteauneuf du Pape
Tel: 4-90-83-72-52
Fax: 4-90-83-51-15
Wines produced: Châteauneuf du Pape (red and white)
Surface area (white): 25 acres
             (red): 106 acres
Production (white): 4,375 cases
            (red): 17,500 cases
Upbringing (white): 4 months in temperature-controlled stainless steel vats; malolactic is
                not stopped
             (red): fermentation of 10 days in stainless steel vats; then the wine is transferred
                to cement tanks for malolactics; then 6–8 months in 3-year-old oak casks
                before bottling
Average age of vines (white): 40 years
                      (red): 40 years
Blend (white): equal parts Grenache Blanc, Clairette, and Bourboulenc
       (red): 55% Grenache, 15% Syrah, 15% Cinsault and Mourvèdre, 15% other varietals

The late Dr. Philippe DuFays was the southern Rhône's most ardent proponent of the carbonic maceration method for producing red wines. DuFays died in 1978 and his beloved domaine was sold to a syndicate. The winemaking has not changed, however, and at Nalys all 13 of the permitted grape varieties are planted. The current size of the estate is 131 acres; the ages of the vines range from 20 to 80, with the average age around 40 years. The red wine is a result of a blend that features 55% Grenache, 15% Syrah, 15% Cinsault and Mourvèdre, and the remainder other varietals. The white wine, which is excellent and which, along with Vieux-Télégraphe, represents the finest of the modern, fruity, perfumed style, is a delicious wine to drink in its first two to four years and keeps better than the others made in this style.

The controversial carbonic maceration method of vinification is said to sacrifice the wine's depth and potential for longevity in favor of youthful, exuberant fruitiness. Virtually all my experience with red Châteauneuf-du-Papes made in this manner is that they are delicious, charming, round, fruity wines to drink between four to six years, after which they decline rapidly. Even the estate's oenologist, Pierre Pelissier, argues for drinking Nalys within seven to eight years of the vintage. There is one exception that sticks in my mind. The 1967 Nalys, drunk with one of the late Dr. DuFay's disciples, André Roux of the Château de Trignon, was sheer hedonistic pleasure when drunk in 1986. Was this an isolated example or is there some merit to Dr. DuFay's belief that these wines do age? In summary, the white wine here is sure to provide fine drinking and I cannot recommend it enthusiastically enough. The red wine is also disarmingly lush, seductive, and delicious. Except for a few freakish vintages,

1967, for example, it is a wine to drink within four to six years of the vintage. It is the ideal picnic Châteauneuf du Pape.

VINTAGES

1994—Châteauneuf du Pape (red)   The medium ruby-colored (Domaine de Nalys's offer-
·   ings are never saturated in color), silky 1994 offers rich, ripe, seductive fruitiness.
88   It appears to have adequate stuffing, high alcohol, and good length. Anticipated
maturity: now–2000. Last tasted 6/96.

1993—Châteauneuf du Pape (red)   The 1993 is deceptively easy to drink with loads of
·   soft, black-cherry fruit, an elegant perfume of herbs, pepper, and cherries, and an
86   attractive, medium-bodied, smooth-as-silk finish. Anticipated maturity: now–1998.
Last tasted 6/96.

1992—Châteauneuf du Pape (red)   The 1992 Châteauneuf du Pape reveals a deep ruby
·   color, and an excellent nose of tobacco, cedar, prunes, and jammy black cherries.
87   It is fat and chewy, with copious amounts of alcohol in the finish. Mature now. Last
tasted 12/95.

1990—Châteauneuf du Pape (red)   Domaine de Nalys's 1990 Châteauneuf du Pape is a
·   richly fruity (raspberries galore!), round, succulent wine with soft tannins, low
86   acidity, and a velvety texture. The color is dark ruby, and the overall impression is
of a grapy, fruity, exuberant wine that will provide considerable enjoyment. Anticipated maturity: now–1998. Last tasted 6/94.

CHÂTEAU DE LA NERTHE (SOCIÉTÉ CIVILE)
(* * * *Cuvée Classique/* * * * *Cuvée des Cadettes)

Address: 84230 Châteauneuf du Pape
Tel: 4-90-83-70-11
Fax: 4-90-83-79-69
Wines produced: Châteauneuf du Pape (red and white), Châteauneuf du Pape Clos de
Beauvenir (white), Châteauneuf du Pape Cuvée des Cadettes (red)
Surface area (white): 12.4 acres
            Clos de Beauvenir—7.5 acres
    (red): 190 acres
            Cuvée des Cadettes—12.4 acres
Production (white): 2,000 cases
            Clos de Beauvenir—400 cases
    (red): 27,500 cases
            Cuvée des Cadettes—1,000 cases
Upbringing (white): 4–5 months in stainless steel vats with malolactic stopped
            Clos de Beauvenir—Fermentation of 1 month in new oak barrels and
            1-year-old barrels with malolactic stopped; then 12 months in the same
            barrels prior to bottling.
    (red): 24–26 months total. Fermentation of 20–24 days in several kinds of vats;
            one-third of the yield then goes into new oak barrels, one-third in old oak
            casks, and one-third in tanks for 12–18 months, depending on the vintage;
            then assemblage and storage in tanks prior to bottling.
            Cuvée des Cadettes—Fermentation of 24 days minimum in wooden tanks;
            pigéage is systematic; then 80% of the yield goes into new oak barrels
            and 20% of the yield into 1-year-old oak barrels for 12 months; storage
            and assemblage in vats before bottling.

Average age of vines (white): 15 years
Clos de Beauvenir—15 years
(red): 40 years
Cuvée des Cadettes—80–100 years

Blend (white): equal parts of Bourboulenc, Grenache Blanc, Clairette, and Roussanne
Clos de Beauvenir—60% Roussanne, 40% Clairette

(red): 55% Grenache, 17% Syrah, 15% Mourvèdre, 7% Cinsault, 3% Counoise, 3% other varietals
Cuvée des Cadettes—60% Grenache, 30% Mourvedre, 10% Syrah

Note: The Clos de Beauvenir, besides having a different cépage and finer upbringing, is a specific plot of land surrounded by a small wall. Also, the Cuvée des Cadettes is produced only in very good years. It is a selection of old vines, especially Grenache.

Historically, this is the most renowned property of the appellation. The vineyards and château sit on the southeastern side of the village, well marked from the road, but hidden by a large outcropping of trees. Wine has been made here continuously since the sixteenth century. Records show that a merchant in Boston, Massachusetts, actually ordered barrels of La Nerthe in the late eighteenth century. The famous French poet Frédéric Mistral, who gave his name to the fierce, persistent winds of the region, called the wine of La Nerthe "un vin royal impérial et pontifical." During World War II, the German air force used La Nerthe as its command control and the property was badly damaged in the subsequent liberation of the area by the British. Until 1985, the estate was owned by the Dereumaux family and the wine was highly prized for its immense size and enormous palate-pleasing pleasure. In 1985 this famous property was purchased by the Ricaud family and a négociant firm, David and Foillard. Extensive renovations costing millions were made, and Alain Dugas was brought in to administer the resurrection of La Nerthe. Today, La Nerthe is the showpiece château of the southern Rhône Valley. In fact, it is the only château with the stature and grandeur of a top Médoc estate. The vineyards have been completely reconstituted with the exception of the old-vine parcels that are still used to produce the famed Cuvée des Cadettes. The vineyard surface area includes 20 acres for the two white wine cuvées, and 202 acres for the two red wines. In 1991 this acreage was increased dramatically by the acquisition of another Châteauneuf du Pape estate, La Terre Ferme.

La Nerthe was one of Châteauneuf du Pape's legendary wines during the sixties and seventies. I remember my first taste of the 1978 Cuvée des Cadettes, a wine that must have topped 15% alcohol. It was black in color, and to this day remains one of the most memorable Châteauneuf du Papes I have ever tasted. However, this style has been abandoned, first in favor of a more commercially oriented style. Gradually administrator Alain Dugas began moving in a direction that suggests only the highest quality will be accepted, a refreshing perspective in view of the corporate mentality that often prizes quantity over quality. Dugas, an intense individual, seems to require perfection at all levels. The cellars are immaculate, and one can sense there is an element of precision about everything being done at La Nerthe, in complete contrast to the pre-1985 era.

The winemaking technique is relatively modern, with destemming, and vinification carried out in assorted tanks and vats. What is nontraditional is that the regular cuvée of Château La Nerthe then goes into both barrel and tank, with two-thirds being put in oak casks (one-half of which are new) and one third in tank. The wines are then blended prior to bottling. The regular cuvée has seen its percentage of Grenache decrease under the new ownership. Today it is a blend of 55% Grenache with Syrah, Mourvèdre, Cinsault, Counoise, and a few dollops of other grapes. The Cuvée des Cadettes continues to be made from the original 12.4-acre parcel of vines 80–100 years old. It is a blend of 60% Grenache with Mourvèdre and Syrah, and is aged in new oak casks, of which 80% are new and 20% are one-year-old barrels. Since 1993, Alain Dugas has bottled the two red wine cuvées without any filtration. There is no question that the fabulous raw potential of both the 1989 and 1990 Les Cadettes was compromised by both an overly zealous fining and filtration at bottling. That is not likely to happen again, and for that reason I believe this estate is ready to take its position with the very top properties in Châteauneuf du Pape.

The white wine vinification is aimed at achieving wines with freshness, as well as more fat and richness than are generally found in white Châteauneuf du Pape. The regular cuvée is a Bourboulenc, Grenache Blanc, Clairette, and Roussanne blend aged in tank, with its malolactic fermentation halted, then bottled quickly to preserve its freshness and fruit. The Clos de Beauvenir is a 60% Roussanne/40% Clairette blend from a 15-year-old vineyard. It is fermented and aged for one year in new oak casks. Malolactic is blocked, thus requiring a sterile filtration, but the wine, because of low yields and very ripe fruit, is a powerful, intense, concentrated, dry white Châteauneuf that can age for 5–10 years.

Château de la Nerthe is also one of the few Châteauneuf du Pape estates that has a secondary label, Clos de la Granière. With the purchase of the 62-acre estate of Pierre Bérard (La Terre Ferme) in 1991, La Nerthe now owns a huge single block of vineyard land fanning out over the southeastern sector of the appellation into the famed La Crau in the eastern sector. The soils are a mix of sand, clay, and the ever-present rust-colored *galets roulés*.

After a decade of new ownership, La Nerthe is beginning to make wines that reflect its terroir and historic reputation. Although the wines are not the finest of the appellation, they are moving in that direction, and the fears I expressed 10 years ago in the first edition of this book about modern technology dominating the wine and producing a sculptured, innocuous, "elegant," modern style of wine have fortunately not proved to be true.

VINTAGES

1994—Châteauneuf du Pape Cuvée Classique (red)   The 1994 Cuvée Classique is a
·   dark ruby/purple-colored wine with a smoky, vanillin, sweet, black-cherry and
89   raspberry-scented nose, medium to full body, outstanding purity of fruit, a sweet,
         expansive mid-palate, and a long, ripe, structured, moderately tannic finish. Antici-
         pated maturity: 2000–2010. Last tasted 6/96.

1994—Châteauneuf du Pape Cuvée des Cadettes (red)   The 1994 Cuvée des Cadettes
·   (10,000 bottles produced) reveals an opaque dark ruby/purple color, superb ripe-
92   ness, and a layered, textured feel with an opulence and richness that transcend the
         Cuvée Classique. Powerful and dense, with well-integrated acidity and moderate
         tannin, this may turn out to be the finest Cuvée des Cadettes yet made under the
         administration of Alain Dugas. Anticipated maturity: 1999–2012. Last tasted 6/96.

1994—Châteauneuf du Pape Clos de Beauvenir (white)   I am pleased with the progress
·   Château de la Nerthe has achieved. The 1994 and 1993 are two of the best dry
90   white wines La Nerthe has yet produced. Unfortunately, there are only 9,000
         bottles (750 cases) of each vintage. The 1994 is a full-bodied, rich, concentrated,
         white Châteauneuf du Pape with considerable fragrance, personality, and dimen-
         sion. I am not generally a partisan of white Châteauneuf du Pape, but what has
         been accomplished at Beaucastel and La Nerthe merits considerable praise and
         attention. This dense, powerful wine exhibits Roussanne's honeyed, cherry fruit, a
         nicely integrated touch of new oak, in addition to Burgundy-like fleshy textures.
         Long, rich, and concentrated, this dry white wine should be drunk over the next
         3–4 years. Last tasted 6/96.

1993—Châteauneuf du Pape (red)   Filters were finally eliminated with the 1993s, and
·   consequently the estate's Châteauneufs have a more natural richness and chewier
89   mouth feel. The 1993 Cuvée Classique exhibits a deep ruby/purple color, sweet,

black-cherry and cassis fruit, full body, excellent concentration, and a long, savory, velvety-textured finish. Anticipated maturity: now–2008. Last tasted 6/96.

1993— Châteauneuf du Pape Cuvée des Cadettes (red)   The 1993 Châteauneuf du Pape
•   Cuvée des Cadettes is made from the estate's oldest vines and is aged in 50% new
91   oak casks and 50% large wood foudres. It is a more profoundly concentrated, structured, and ageworthy wine because of the elevated percentages of Syrah and Mourvèdre. The 1993 possesses an impressive, saturated dark purple color, and a sweet, jammy nose of black fruits, toasty oak, and roasted Provençal herbs. Dense, full-bodied, with an alluring, chewy texture (plenty of glycerin to be found), this is an outstanding wine. Anticipated maturity: now–2009. Last tasted 6/96.

1992— Châteauneuf du Pape (red)   The 1992 Châteauneuf du Pape is an elegant, me-
•   dium- to full-bodied wine with moderate tannin, adequate depth, and spicy, black-
86   cherry and raspberry fruit. Drink this stylized yet tasty Châteauneuf du Pape over the next 7–8 years. Last tasted 6/95.

1992— Châteauneuf du Pape Cuvée des Cadettes (red)   The 1992 Cuvée des Cadettes is
•   forward, rich, and full-bodied, with plenty of smoky, herb, and red- and black-fruit
89   aromas and flavors. It should be consumed over the next 7–8 years. Last tasted 6/95.

1991— Châteauneuf du Pape   No Cuvée des Cadettes was made in 1991. The regular
•   1991 Châteauneuf du Pape is a successful wine from a dreadfully difficult vintage.
78   Although more herbaceous and compact than normal, it exhibits adequate ripeness, straightforward, medium-bodied black-cherry fruit, and a spicy finish. Drink it over the next 5–6 years. Last tasted 6/95.

1990— Châteauneuf du Pape (red)   Nearly 20,000 cases were made of the regular cuvée
•   of 1990 Châteauneuf du Pape. It possesses a tight, backward nose. There is a
85   brilliant, spit-polished ruby color, a tannic, compact palate, and plenty of acidity and tannin in the somewhat lean finish. Prior to bottling, this was an outstanding (potentially 90–93 points) wine, but excessive filtration stripped it. Last tasted 6/95.

1990— Châteauneuf du Pape Cuvée des Cadettes (red)   From cask, the 1990 Cuvée des
•   Cadettes was dazzling, a wine that I believed could merit a rating in the mid- to
90+   upper nineties. I remember it as a huge, massive wine, with extraordinary richness and intensity, a chocolaty, black-raspberry, spicy nose, and long, profoundly rich, tannic flavors. After the bottling process, the wine is still outstanding, but not as exciting. What one now gets is still a deeply colored wine, but one that smells like Bordeaux. The individual character of such cépages as Grenache and Mourvèdre has been muted by considerable new oak smells. What is left is the scent of ripe fruit and a ton of sweet oak. In the mouth this wine still possesses admirable richness, an attractive oakiness, medium to full body, and a highly structured, crisp finish. If one had never tasted this wine prior to bottling, he or she would no doubt be pleased with this international style of Châteauneuf du Pape. Anticipated maturity: now–2008. Last tasted 6/95.

1989— Châteauneuf du Pape (red)   The 1989 Châteauneuf exhibits an impressive dense
•   black/ruby/purple color, a huge bouquet of violets, black raspberries, and minerals,
87   full-bodied, intensely concentrated flavors, plenty of tannin, decent acidity, and a long, promising finish. Anticipated maturity: now–2007. Last tasted 11/95.

1989— Châteauneuf du Pape Cuvée des Cadettes (red)   A profoundly great wine prior to
•   bottling, an aggressive fining and filtration partially denuded the 1989 Cuvée des
89   Cadettes. It is sweet on the palate, with a developed, penetrating bouquet of cassis, vanillin from the new oak barrels, and spices. In the mouth, it is well balanced,

with excellent depth of flavor, a surprisingly well-focused personality given its size, and a moderately tannic finish. Like the 1990, greatness was sacrificed at bottling. What a shame! Anticipated maturity: now–2006. Last tasted 8/94.

Older Vintages

The first vintages made at Château de la Nerthe under the new ownership have not aged well, losing their fruit at an advanced pace. Immediately prior to the change in ownership, the wines began to suffer from the difficult economics of the proprietor, and vintages such as 1983, 1980, and 1979 should have been far better, but they were aged in old musty foudres and casually bottled. The last great efforts from La Nerthe were the two cuvées of 1978, both wines still remarkable today. The regular bottling of 1978 has thrown considerable sediment, but it offers a fabulous raspberry/blueberry perfume along with *garrigue* and spicy fruitcake aromas. Full-bodied, rich, and lush, it has been fully mature for five or six years, but it shows no signs of decline. It is an enormous, full-bodied Châteauneuf du Pape that I drank with great pleasure on my birthday in July 1996. I have not had the 1978 Cuvée des Cadettes since 1991, but it is one of the most remarkable, intense, thick, and unctuously textured Châteauneuf du Papes I have tasted. I imagine it is still youthful, and I hope one day to find a case or two at auction.

DOMAINE DE PALESTOR* * *

Address: 84100 Orange
Tel: 4-90-34-50-96
Fax: 4-90-34-69-93
Wines produced: Châteauneuf du Pape (red)
Surface area: 7.5 acres
Production: 1,100 cases
Upbringing: fermentation of 15–21 days in cement vats; then 2 months storage in tanks and 12 months in oak casks; bottling is done over a period of 6–12 months
Average age of vines: 40 years
Blend: 80% Grenache, 20% Mourvèdre

Unfortunately, I have tasted too few vintages of this small estate located in the northern part of the appellation, with vineyard parcels south of Orange and Courthézon. No white wine is made at this estate. The only vintage I can comment on is the 1978, drunk from magnum in 1994. It was very good, but hardly exceptional for this great vintage. It exhibited no signs of advanced maturity.

DOMAINE DU PÉGAU* * * * *

Address: Avenue Impériale
         84230 Châteauneuf du Pape
Tel: 4-90-83-72-70
Fax: 4-90-83-53-02
Wines produced: Châteauneuf du Pape (white), Châteauneuf du Pape Cuvée Réservée (red),
                Châteauneuf du Pape Cuvée Laurence (red)
Surface area (white): 2.47 acres
              (red): 30 acres
Production (white): 125 cases
                    Cuvée Réservée—5,600 cases
                    Cuvée Laurence—650 cases

Upbringing (white): There are two different upbringings; either (1) fermentation in cement vats; then 6 months in oak barrels 1–4 years old (done in 1994), or (2) fermentation in stainless steel vats and bottling after 3 months (done in 1995).

Cuvée Réservée—15 days' fermentation in cement vats; then 2 years in oak casks; then part of the yield is bottled

Cuvée Laurence—same as for the Cuvée Réservée, except that the wine spends more than 2 years in oak casks

Average age of vines (white): 20 years

(red): 50–60 years

Blend (white): 60% Grenache Blanc, 20% Clairette, 10% Bourboulenc, 10% Roussanne

(red): 80% Grenache, 17% Syrah, 3% Mourvèdre and other varietals

The 32-acre estate of Laurence Féraud and her father, Paul, produces one of Châteauneuf du Pape's most majestic, old-style, robust, superconcentrated, blockbuster wines. Not surprisingly, Paul Féraud was a high school classmate and chum of Henri Bonneau, and they remain dear friends to this day. I suppose that it is not just a coincidence that of all the wines of Châteauneuf du Pape, Pégau's Cuvée Réservée and Cuvée Laurence come closest to achieving the same glory as Henri Bonneau's Cuvée des Célestins.

Father and daughter could not have more different personalities. Paul, a diminutive, sinewy man with a strong Provençal twang to his speech, looks as though he sprouted from one of the stone-covered Châteauneuf du Pape vineyards. He exudes the style of a man who works in the vineyards. His daughter, charming, articulate, and university educated, is clearly in charge of the business side of Pégau. Although quite different, the two complement each other, and on my last visit to Pégau it was Laurence rather than Paul who was climbing the ladder to extract juice from the large old wood foudres in the cellars next to the family's home in downtown Châteauneuf du Pape.

This morsellated estate, with holdings sprinkled throughout three sectors, Courthézon, La Solitude, and Bédarrides, possesses many old vines. The two finest parcels include one planted in 1902, in the northwestern sector, not far from La Gardine, and an old-vine parcel planted in 1905, in the heart of La Crau. Until 1987 (when Laurence became able to assist her father), this estate sold much of its production to négociants. This is winemaking with no compromises. These wines are made from physiologically ripe grapes, low yields, and are left to sit on their lees in the large foudres until Paul and Laurence decide it is time to bottle. Moreover, the wines suffer no bottle shock, because sulfur additions are low, and, more importantly, there is no fining or filtration for any Pégau red wine.

The white wines, which are now benefiting from the addition of Roussanne in the blend (a tiny parcel of Roussanne planted in 1901 was recently acquired), were in a state of flux at the time of writing. Laurence is clearly exhibiting her influence, and is not sure whether to produce a typical white Châteauneuf du Pape with malolactic blocked, thus requiring the wine to be sterile-filtered, or one where the wine is allowed to go through malolactic and bottled more naturally. Pégau's white Châteauneuf du Pape is solid and correct, but hardly at the level of the inspirational reds.

I have long been a huge fan of this estate, and have put my money where my mouth is, having purchased all of Pégau's vintages since 1979. Remarkably, a tasting I did for this book of all the Pégau wines I own did not reveal one wine that had passed its plateau of maturity. Accessible, if somewhat fiery and forceful, when young, Pégau's Châteauneuf du Papes are among the most classic and long-lived of the appellation. The great vintages, 1981, 1985, 1989, 1990, 1994, and 1995 (all potential legends), can easily age well for two decades.

The Cuvée Laurence (about 650 cases produced in top vintages) is kept in cellars several miles away from those most visitors are shown. This wine is largely identical to the Cuvée Réservée, but it is kept two to three years longer in small oak casks (no new oak is ever used). I have tasted the available vintages blind against the Cuvée Réservée, and in most cases I have a slight preference for the more intense fruit and grapiness of the Cuvée Réservée, but the Cuvée Laurence is noticeably more complex and evolved because of its longer sojourn in wood. It is not meant to be a luxury cuvée, simply a wine that reflects the oldest traditions of Châteauneuf du Pape when the wine was often kept four or five years before being bottled.

VINTAGES

1995—Châteauneuf du Pape Cuvée Réservée (red)   The 1995 Cuvée Réservée exhibits
·   an opaque black/purple color, and extraordinary rich, intense aromas of smoke,
94   black raspberries, kirsch, and spice. Exceptionally full-bodied, with an unctuous texture, and a thick, rich, expansive mid-palate, this superbly concentrated wine appears to be a worthy rival to this estate's phenomenal 1989 and 1990. Interestingly, the average alcohol level achieved by Domaine du Pégau in 1995 was 14.5–15.5%. This is a blockbuster Châteauneuf du Pape. Anticipated maturity: 2001–2020. Last tasted 6/96.

1994—Châteauneuf du Pape Cuvée Réservée (red)   The superb 1994 is one of the top
·   wines of the vintage. It reveals a deep ruby/purple color, followed by an expres-
92   sive nose of black cherries, smoked meats, black olives, and Provençal herbs. Thick, rich, and full-bodied, as well as sweeter and softer than the more structured 1995, this is a huge wine for the vintage. Anticipated maturity: now–2015. Last tasted 6/96.

1993—Châteauneuf du Pape Cuvée Réservée (red)   The exuberant and virile 1993 Châ-
·   teauneuf du Pape Cuvée Réservée is a typical wine from this estate—powerful,
90   full-bodied, rich, dense, and tannic, with intense, chewy, peppery fruit, a muscular personality, and impressive flavor extraction. Anticipated maturity: 1998–2010. Last tasted 6/96.

1992—Châteauneuf du Pape Cuvée Réservée (red)   The already delicious 1992 exhibits
·   a huge, earthy, herbal, black-cherry, and chocolaty, exotic nose, superrich, full-
90   bodied flavors, a saturated color (it is one of the darkest 1992s I tasted), low acidity, and a fleshy, alcoholic, intense finish. Anticipated maturity: now–2008. Last tasted 11/95.

1991—Châteauneuf du Pape Cuvée Réservée (red)   The Férauds have always been proud
·   of this wine, but having tasted it a half dozen times, I am just not that impressed.
78   The wine exhibits a decent ruby color, a good, spicy, peppery, *garrigue*-scented nose, medium body, and a somewhat attenuated taste with a lack of flesh, volume, and sweetness of fruit. It will last for another decade, but it will become increasingly desiccated as it ages, with the tannin, acidity, and alcohol taking over. Last tasted 7/96.

1990—Châteauneuf du Pape Cuvée Laurence (red)   Bottled at what I suspect is the whim
·   of Paul Féraud, the 1989 and 1990 Châteauneuf du Pape Cuvée Laurence were
95   tasted side by side with the Cuvée Réservée. Although the Cuvée Laurence is no better than the Cuvée Réservée, it is more evolved, with more complexity from the extended cask aging. Ultimately, I think the Cuvée Réservée will surpass it, since the development of that wine will take place in the bottle, not in wood. Anticipated maturity: now–2020. Last tasted 6/96.

1990—Châteauneuf du Pape Cuvée Réservée (red)   The 1990 Cuvée Réservée is one of
· the appellation's superstars. After bottling, the color is still an impenetrable, black/
96 purple color. The huge nose of truffles, tar, superripe black fruits, licorice, tobacco,
and spices is profound. In the mouth there is sweet, expansive fruit, a superconcentrated, powerful, tannic taste, lavish amounts of glycerin and body, as well as a
finish that lasts well over a minute. With plenty of tannin, this wine is destined to
have 20–25 years of evolution. And yes, this wine was bottled unfined and unfiltered, so expect considerable sediment to occur. Anticipated maturity: 2000–2020.
Last tasted 6/96.

1989—Châteauneuf du Pape Cuvée Réservée (red)   Féraud's 1989 resembles something
· between a dry red table wine and vintage port. Its dark purple/black color, excep-
92 tional concentration, great extract, and huge body loaded with glycerin and tannin
make it one of the most immense wines of this superlative vintage. Surprisingly
forward (blame the superb ripeness and relatively low acidity of the 1989 vintage),
this is a prodigious Châteauneuf du Pape. Anticipated maturity: 1998–2018. Last
tasted 6/96.

1989—Châteauneuf du Pape Cuvée Laurence (red)   The 1989 Cuvée Laurence is slightly
· sweeter, richer, and more opulent than its younger sibling. However, both wines
95 are enormously constituted, thick, rich, classic, old-style Châteauneuf du Papes
the likes of which are rarely seen today. Anticipated maturity: now–2018. Last
tasted 6/96.

1988—Châteauneuf du Pape Cuvée Réservée (red)   Dark ruby-colored with a slight
· lightening at the edge, the 1988 Pegau has always been a more tightly strung, more
89 closed, and less generous style of wine. It is not to say this is a light wine (this
estate does not produce light cuvées), but it is not nearly as exuberant, forceful,
and expressive as most other vintages. The wine is firmly structured, spicy, and
peppery, with some of the Provençal *garrigue* (herb/earth tones) apparent. Full-
bodied, muscular, rich, and still youthful, this wine may merit an outstanding score
with another 1–2 years of bottle age, but it will never be as generous and exuberant
as Pégau's finest vintages. Anticipated maturity: 1998–2010. Last tasted 7/96.

1985—Châteauneuf du Pape Cuvée Réservée (red)   Most 1985 Châteauneuf du Papes
· matured quickly, and in most cases did not achieve the heights of richness and
93 complexity predicted when they were young. Pégau's 1985 is an exception. The
color is still an opaque ruby/purple with no lightening at the edge. The nose
resembles a 3- to 5-year-old wine, rather than one that is nearly 12. Its huge fruit,
muscular, thick, full-bodied, corpulent personality, and stunning length make for
a rich, powerful glass of Châteauneuf du Pape. The wine, however, while impressive because of its unctuous texture and thickness, is still unevolved and in
need of several more years of cellaring. Anticipated maturity: 1998–2012. Last
tasted 7/96.

1983—Châteauneuf du Pape Cuvée Réservée (red)   In complete contrast to the superpow-
· erful, rich yet backward 1985, the 1983 appears to have reached full maturity. The
90 color is a deep ruby with some amber/orange at the edge, and the flamboyant nose
offers up oodles of sweet cedar, herbes de Provence, smoked meats, and jammy
cherry fruit. Full-bodied, fleshy, and mouth-filling, this powerful yet soft, expansive, velvety-textured wine makes for a delicious glassful of Châteauneuf du Pape.
Anticipated maturity: now–2005. Last tasted 7/96.

1981—Châteauneuf du Pape Cuvée Réservée (red)   This has always been a magnificent
· example of the vintage. After having gone through nearly two cases, except for one
93 corked bottle, I have found this to be consistently a thrilling wine. It has tasted

fully mature since 1990, but the wine displays no loss of fruit, and continues to gain in terms of its aromatic development and complexity. The color is a deep dark garnet with some amber at the edge. The huge, flashy, ostentatious nose of smoked meats, jammy berry fruit, Asian spices, and truffles is followed by an enormously constituted, big, fleshy, full-bodied wine that is crammed with glycerin, extract, and alcohol. This is a blockbuster, velvety-textured, decadent Châteauneuf du Pape that should continue to drink well for another 10–12 years. Last tasted 7/96.

1979—Châteauneuf du Pape Cuvée Réservée (red)   Typical of the vintage, Pégau's 1979
·   is more compact and firmly structured than other vintages. Many 1979 Châ-
89   teauneufs have an almost Bordeaux-like structural profile and austerity. This deep ruby-colored wine is generous, rich, and still young. It reveals attractive licorice, tar, spice, earth, and black-fruit scents and flavors. Full-bodied, but without the sweetness and thick glycerin of the 1981 or 1985, this is an extremely well-made Châteauneuf du Pape that should continue to drink well for another 10–12 years. Last tasted 7/96.

PÈRE ANSELME (P. BROTTE)* * *

Address: B.P. 1
         84230 Châteauneuf du Pape
Tel: 4-90-83-70-07
Fax: 4-90-83-74-34
Wines produced: Châteauneuf du Pape
   Note: This négociant purchases wine from throughout the appellation, producing blends that are sold under the name Père Anselme.

   Just before one enters the village of Châteauneuf du Pape are the cellars, wine museum, and offices of Père Anselme, a large négociant. This business specializing in wine from the entire southern Rhône is run by the Brotte family. Their total production is just under 200,000 cases of wine. The Brottes also own the village's well-known restaurant, La Mule des Papes, where the wine list is composed entirely of their wines. Their Châteauneuf du Pape is criticized by many, largely I believe because it is a négociant's wine, but it is not at all a bad wine. In fact, the vintages I have tasted, 1978 through 1995, were all sound, deeply colored, burly, chunky wines that offered aggressive, meaty, tarry-scented fruit and a hefty dose of alcohol. If not sublime, they are quite satisfactory. They call their Châteauneuf du Pape La Fiole du Pape, and offer it in a funny-looking, misshapen, charcoal-colored bottle covered with fake dust. Their wine deserves better than this gimmicky bottle.

   This house also vinifies, bottles, and commercializes the wines from the 17.3-acre Clos Bimard estate. Made from a blend of 90% Grenache, 5% Cinsault, and 5% Syrah, these wines are quite good.

VINTAGES

1995—Châteauneuf du Pape (red)   The wines produced by négociant Laurent-Charles
·   Brotte reflect a significant increase in quality. The deeply-colored 1995 Châ-
85   teauneuf du Pape packs more density and power than the 1994. This medium-bodied, open-knit, forward wine is meant to be drunk young. It is pleasing to see such progress. Last tasted 6/96.

1994—Châteauneuf du Pape (red)   The 1994 Châteauneuf du Pape exhibits a medium
·   dark ruby color, an open, easygoing, coffee/cherry-scented nose, spicy, round, silky
85   flavors, good depth, and medium body. Although fully mature, it will last for another 3–4 years. Last tasted 6/96.

1990—Châteauneuf du Pape (red)   A surprisingly ripe, attractive wine with plenty of
·   sweet, roasted peanut, and cassis-scented fruit, medium to full body, a chewy
85   texture, and a supple, long finish. Anticipated maturity: now–2000. Last tasted 6/94.
1989—Châteauneuf du Pape (red)   The 1989 regular cuvée is a round, fruity, solidly
·   made wine, with some succulent, roasted, black-cherry flavors, and soft tannins.
85   Anticipated maturity: now–1999. Last tasted 6/94.
1988—Châteauneuf du Pape Cuvée Prestige (red)   The 1988 Cuvée Prestige is a more
·   powerful wine than the regular cuvée in 1989. Quite spicy and rich, with a mineral-
86   scented, roasted bouquet, this is a full-bodied, flavorful wine with moderate tannin
         in its finish. Anticipated maturity: now–2001. Last tasted 6/94.

PÈRE CABOCHE (JEAN-PIERRE BOISSON)
(* * *Cuvée Classique,* * * *Cuvée Elisabeth Chambellan)

Address: Route de Courthézon
         84230 Châteauneuf du Pape
Tel: 4-90-83-71-44
Fax: 4-90-83-50-46
Wines produced: Châteauneuf du Pape Cuvée Classique (red and white), Châteauneuf du
        Pape J.P. Boisson Vielles Vignes Elisabeth Chambellan (red)
Surface area (red): 80 acres
Production (white): 2,500 cases
           (red): 11,500 cases
Upbringing (white): fermented at cold temperatures in stainless steel; malolactic is blocked;
           the wine is bottled 3–4 months after the vintage to secure its freshness
           and fruit
        (red): the grapes are not destemmed, and are vinified separately by varietal; the
           Syrah is the only varietal vinified with carbonic maceration; the wines are
           then moved to barrel and large wood foudres for 6–18 months for aging
Average age of vines (red): 40 years
Blend (white): 40% Bourboulenc, 25% Clairette, 25% Grenache Blanc, 10% Roussanne
        and Picpoul
        (red): 70% Grenache, 15% Syrah, 7% Mourvèdre, 8% Cinsault, Counoise, Muscar-
           din, Vaccarèse, and Terret Noir
Note: The Cuvée Elisabeth Chambellan, which represents about 10% of the total produc-
tion, is made from vines 60–80 years old planted on the plateau of La Crau. It has the same
upbringing as the regular red wine cuvée, but is made from smaller yields and older vines.

This 80-acre vineyard is run with enthusiasm by the loquacious Jean-Pierre Boisson, also
the current mayor of the village. Père Caboche produces light, fruity, easy-to-drink red and
white wines, as well as a cuvée prestige, the old-vine Elisabeth Chambellan (named after
the Chambellan family, who first planted this vineyard in the seventeenth century). It is the
fullest, richest wine made at Père Caboche, and although it is clearly a product of a modern
vinification, it is an expressive, rich, concentrated wine that can be drunk young and usually
lasts for a decade.

This estate does do a lot of processing of their wine, with the red wine given dual
filtrations, through the Kisselguhr system (diatomaceous earth is used as the clarifying
material) after malolactic and through the German micropore system prior to bottling. It is
also fined by egg whites. As I have said so many times in the past in both *The Wine Advocate*
and the first edition of this book, I cannot help but conclude that this excessive degree of
clarification robs the wine of a significant portion of its color, body, extract, and aroma.
Tasting here before all the processing takes place often reveals very impressive raw materi-

als. However, that is often the case not only in Châteauneuf du Pape, but elsewhere in the world where modern-day oenology holds a strong grip over so many estates. Nevertheless, this is still an excellent wine. The Cuvée Elisabeth Chambellan can often be an outstanding wine. Moreover, this is a Châteauneuf du Pape estate that almost gives its wine away, with prices that are among the most modest of the appellation. Even the Cuvée Elisabeth Chambellan sells for a remarkably fair price.

The white wine is typical of so many white Châteauneuf du Papes—clean, fresh, with considerable body, but not a great deal of character.

VINTAGES

1995—Châteauneuf du Pape (red)   The 1995 is similar to the 1994. Ripe and fat, with
·   more structure because of a better acid profile, the wine reveals good lushness,
86   an open-knit style, and enough fruit concentration to ensure modest longevity. Anticipated maturity: 1998–2005. Last tasted 6/96.

1995—Châteauneuf du Pape Cuvée Elisabeth Chambellan (red)   The 1995 Cuvée Elisa-
·   beth Chambellan reveals the darkest ruby/purple color of this quartet, as well as
88   more tannin and acidity. With an expansive, sweet inner core of ripe fruit, and some tannin in its full-bodied finish, this wine will offer a husky mouthful of Châteauneuf du Pape. Anticipated maturity: 1999–2007. Last tasted 6/96.

1994—Châteauneuf du Pape (red)   The 1994 is an attractive, delicious, hedonistic style
·   of Châteauneuf du Pape made for drinking over the next 5–7 years. The soft, fruity,
87   jammy 1994 Châteauneuf du Pape exhibits a medium dark garnet color, a sexy, lush personality, medium to full body, low acidity, abundant alcohol, and copious quantities of rich, juicy fruit in the finish. It tastes like a Châteauneuf du Pape candy bar. Anticipated maturity: now–2003. Last tasted 6/96.

1994—Châteauneuf du Pape Cuvée Elisabeth Chambellan (red)   The 1994 Cuvée Elisa-
·   beth Chambellan is riper and more expressive, with more glycerin and body. Round
89   and expansive, with a silky style that's easy to understand and appreciate, it possesses gobs of sweet berry fruit, herbs, pepper, and spicy scents. This is an alcoholic, open, crowd-pleasing Châteauneuf du Pape. Anticipated maturity: now–2003. Last tasted 6/96.

1993—Châteauneuf du Pape (red)   The 1993 Châteauneuf du Pape reveals an excellent
·   color, and gobs of sweet, jammy red and black fruit allied with that unmistakable
87   Provençal spicy, herbaceous, peppery, earthy, *garrigue* scent. Supple and velvety textured, with layers of seductive richness, this is a user-friendly, lush, hedonistic wine. Anticipated maturity: now–2000. Last tasted 6/96.

1990—Châteauneuf du Pape Cuvée Elisabeth Chambellan (red)   The most concentrated
·   wine I have tasted at this estate after bottling, the deep ruby-colored 1990 Cuvée
88   Elisabeth Chambellan exhibits some of the distinctive Provençal *garrigue,* olive, and jammy black-cherry fruit. Full-bodied, with high alcohol, gobs of fruit and glycerin, a silky-smooth finish, and a lusty, hedonistic personality, this deliciously fruity Châteauneuf du Pape is an excellent example of the modern style. Antici- pated maturity: now–2002. Last tasted 6/96.

1989—Châteauneuf du Pape (red)   The 1989 exhibits an interesting nose of balsam wood,
·   black cherries, and roasted peanuts. In the mouth there is plenty of delicious red
85   fruit, a delicate herbaceous character, and a full-bodied, lush finish. It should be drunk up. Last tasted 6/94.

1988—Châteauneuf du Pape (red)   The medium ruby/garnet-colored 1988 has a distinct
·   aroma of licorice, herbs, and cassis. The wine is soft, ripe, medium- to full-bodied,
85   and low in acidity as well as tannin. It should be drunk up. Last tasted 6/94.

Older Vintages

Because of the style of the wines produced at Père Caboche, it would be foolish to keep the whites more than 18 months or the reds more than 8–10 years. Most vintages must be drunk within 5–7 years, with only the most exceptional vintages, such as 1990 or 1995, lasting longer.

DOMAINE DU PÈRE PAPE* * */* * * *

Address: 24, avenue Baron Le Roy
　　　　84230 Châteauneuf du Pape
Tel: 4-90-83-70-16
Fax: 4-90-83-50-47
Wines produced: Châteauneuf du Pape (red and white), Châteauneuf du Pape Clos du Calvaire (red)
Surface area (white): 10 acres
　　　　　　　(red): 96 acres
Production (white): 3,000 cases
　　　　　　　(red): 12,100 cases
Upbringing (white): malolactic is blocked, and the wine is bottled after 3 months in tank
　　　　　　　(red): very traditional, no destemming, and 8–14 months' aging in tank and foudre
Average age of vines: 40 years
Blend (white): equal parts Grenache Blanc, Clairette, Bourboulenc, Roussanne, and Picpoul
　　　　　(red): 70% Grenache, 20% Syrah, 10% Cinsault and Mourvèdre

By the standards of Châteauneuf du Pape, the Domaine du Père Pape is relatively young, tracing its origins only to 1864. Much of the present-day property is the result of mutiple acquisitions by proprietor Maurice Mayard, who began to expand the estate in the mid-seventies, after several inheritances. One of the most important acquisitions was the 42-acre Domaine de Grand Coulet in 1989. This acreage was added to the 12 acres already owned by Mayard to form what is called the Clos du Calvaire, a superb piece of terroir situated between Domaine de Nalys and Vieux-Télégraphe in the eastern sector. This is an area of hillside vineyards covered with *galets roulés,* with an excellent exposition.

This estate appears to be just beginning to exploit its potential, as vintages from the late eighties have shown more and more intensity and flavor authority. The white wine is relatively monochromatic and uninteresting. The two cuvées of red wine are classic examples of Châteauneuf du Pape. The Clos du Calvaire is a single-vineyard wine, and the regular cuvée is a blend from proprietor Mayard's holdings. The wines are traditionally made, with no destemming, and 8–14 months in tank and foudre before blending. No new oak is used in the wines' upbringing.

Given recent performances of Domaine du Père Pape, this should be an estate to keep an eye on.

VINTAGES

1994—Châteauneuf du Pape (red)   This impressively endowed, possibly outstanding
　·　　Châteauneuf du Pape offers a deep, saturated purple color, a sweet nose scented
　89　　with chocolate, roasted herb, and black cherry, excellent flavor concentration, full
　　　　body, and an unctuously thick, long finish that nearly masks the light tannin.
　　　　Anticipated maturity: now–2004. Last tasted 6/96.

1990—Châteauneuf du Pape Clos du Calvaire (red)   The dark ruby-colored 1990 exhibits
· spicy, herbaceous, Bing cherry fruit, soft, full-bodied, earthy flavors that are some-
87 what reminiscent of truffles, velvety texture, and an alcoholic finish. The tannins
are present, but they are largely concealed by the jammy fruit. Anticipated maturity: now–2000. Last tasted 6/95.

1989—Châteauneuf du Pape Clos du Calvaire (red)   The 1989 Clos du Calvaire promises
· to be an outstanding bottle of wine. It is a massive style of Châteauneuf du Pape,
88 with rich, alcoholic, almost late-harvest flavors of apricots, peaches, and jammy
black cherries. In the mouth, it is splendidly deep and full, with wonderful purity, and a long, heady, alcoholic finish. The tannin level is high, but they are
soft tannins, and the fruit is oh-so-sweet. Anticipated maturity: now–2005. Last
tasted 6/95.

1988—Châteauneuf du Pape Clos du Calvaire (red)   The 1988 Clos du Calvaire is
· soft, fruity, medium to full-bodied, with good concentration. Mature now. Last
83 tasted 6/94.

ROGER PERRIN* * */* * * *

Address: La Berthaude
Route de Châteauneuf du Pape
84100 Orange
Tel: 4-90-34-25-64
Fax: 4-90-34-88-37
Wines produced: Châteauneuf du Pape (red and white), Châteauneuf du Pape Réserve de
Vieilles Vignes
Surface area (white): 3.7 acres
(red): 26 acres
Production (white): 625 cases
(red): 2,200 cases
Upbringing (white): 3–4 months in temperature-controlled stainless steel tanks; malolactic
is stopped
(red): 18–20 months total. Fermentation of 18–24 days in stainless steel vats;
wines stay in enamel vats for 4 months afterward for malolactic; then 50%
of the yield goes into oak casks for 9–12 months, 15% into oak barrels
(some new, some 1–2 years old) for 12–14 months, and the rest of the
yield stays in enamel vats; assemblage and storage in enamel vats prior
to bottling.
Average age of vines (white): 40 years
(red): 65 years
Blend (white): 45% Grenache Blanc, 30% Clairette, 20% Roussanne, 5% Bourboulenc
(red): 70–75% Grenache, 10–15% Syrah, 6–8% Mourvèdre, 5–6% Cinsault and
Clairette, and the rest Counoise and Vaccarèse

Proprietor Luc Perrin was suddenly thrust into the job of owner/winemaker in 1986 when
his father was accidently killed while working in the vineyard. There are two cuvées of
traditionally made red wine. However, the Réserve de Vieilles Vignes sees some aging in
small oak casks, of which about 33% are new. It possesses a new world style, without losing
its Châteauneuf du Pape typicity. Luc Perrin has had a tendency to fine and filter his wines
excessively, under the advice of the omnipresent Châteauneuf du Pape oenologist Noël
Rabot. The excellent raw materials I have tasted prior to bottling possess less texture,
intensity, and perfume after bottling. This is sad, but the goal of the oenologist is 100%
security, and the Europeans seem more concerned about a few specks of sediment in the

bottle than the English or Americans, who actually seek it out as a sign of a naturally made, unprocessed wine.

This domaine could easily move into the four-star category with a slightly less interventionist, manipulative approach to winemaking.

VINTAGES

1995—Châteauneuf du Pape (red)   The 1995 Châteauneuf du Pape exhibits sweet fruit,
· an elegant, restrained, international style, medium to full body, and good, clean
86 winemaking. Although not as expressionistic as one might hope, it is a good wine
that should take on more character with additional age. Anticipated maturity: 1998–2006. Last tasted 6/96.

1995—Châteauneuf du Pape Réserve de Vieilles Vignes (red)   In 1995 a Réserve de
· Vieilles Vignes cuvée was produced from very old vines composed of 80% Gren-
88 ache and 20% Syrah. Aged in small oak casks, of which one-third were new, this
wine is reminiscent of the luxury Cuvée des Générations from Château de la Gardine. The Réserve de Vieilles Vignes possesses the potential to merit an outstanding rating. It exhibits an impressive dark ruby/purple color, and attractive vanillin/*pain grillé* scents to go along with plenty of ripe black-cherry and curranty fruit. There is an underlying mineral character to this full-bodied, stylish, oaky wine. Anticipated maturity: 1999–2007. Last tasted 6/96.

1994—Châteauneuf du Pape (red)   Roger Perrin has fashioned a medium ruby-colored,
· spicy, stemmy, cherry-scented and -flavored 1994 Châteauneuf du Pape. The wine
85 possesses a firm underpinning of structure, but the overall impression is of a soft,
medium- to full-bodied, ripe, herbaceous wine for drinking over the next 3-4 years. Last tasted 6/96.

1993—Châteauneuf du Pape (red)   The 1993 reveals evidence of aging in new oak casks
· given the sweet vanillin and ripe cherry-scented nose. The wine exhibits lovely
87 ripeness, medium to full body, admirable fruit and depth, and a soft, lush finish.
Anticipated maturity: now–2000. Last tasted 6/96.

1992—Châteauneuf du Pape (red)   The fat 1992 displays evidence of extraction and
· ripeness in its black-cherry, peppery, and herb-scented nose, and lush, medium-
87 to full-bodied, succulent flavors. Forward and delicious, it is ideal for drinking over
the next 6–7 years. Last tasted 6/95.

1990—Châteauneuf du Pape (red)   Perrin's 1990 red Châteauneuf is excellent. It pos-
· sesses a deep, opaque black/ruby/purple color, a rich cassis- and black-cherry-
88 dominated nose, dense, chewy, concentrated flavors, and an authoritative, long,
chewy finish. Anticipated maturity: now–2002. Last tasted 6/94.

1989—Châteauneuf du Pape (red)   The 1989 exhibited dry, hard tannins and good con-
· centration, but its backward, impenetrable style made judgment less certain. Antic-
85 ipated maturity: now–2001. Last tasted 6/94.

Older Vintages

Perrin's Châteauneuf du Papes are midweight wines, particularly following the processing they must go through prior to bottling. They are generally best drunk within their first decade of life. The only older vintages I have tasted included an old, mature, fading 1985 (tasted in 1992), and a disappointing, diluted 1988 (tasted in 1993).

DOMAINE DE LA PINÈDE* * *

Address: Route de Sorgues
              84230 Châteauneuf du Pape
Tel: 4-90-83-71-50
Fax: 4-90-83-52-20
Wines produced: Châteauneuf du Pape (red and white)
Surface area (white): 2.47 acres
                  (red): 19.8 acres
Production (white): 375 cases
                  (red): 3,125 cases
Upbringing (white): 3–4 months in stainless steel vats; malolactic is stopped
                  (red): 18 months total; fermentation of 3 weeks in enamel vats, where the wines
                  remain for their entire upbringing
Average age of vines (white): 10 years
                  (red): 30 years
Blend (white): 40% Grenache Blanc, and the rest evenly divided between Clairette, Rous-
              sanne, and Bourboulenc
      (red): 60% Grenache, 10% Syrah, 10% Cinsault, 20% Mourvèdre and Muscardin

This estate can trace its origins to 1870, but proprietor Georges-Pierre Coulon began estate-bottling wine only in 1982. Made in a traditional manner, the red wine grapes are not destemmed, and are aged in both foudre and tank for up to 18 months prior to bottling. The few vintages of white La Pinède I have tasted have been well above average for white Châteauneuf du Pape.

VINTAGES

1994—Châteauneuf du Pape (red)   I have tasted some good wines from this estate, but
   ·   the 1994 exhibits a washed-out, herbal, spicy-scented nose. Deficient in fruit, this
  77   tart, lean, angular wine does not possess the requisite meat or flesh to cover its
         bony structure. Last tasted 6/96.
1992—Châteauneuf du Pape (red)   A smoky, cedary, pine needle, herb, and black-
   ·   cherry-scented nose is followed by a fat, lush wine with full body, low acidity, and
  87   soft tannin. It is a delicious Châteauneuf for drinking over the next 6–8 years. Last
         tasted 6/95.
1990—Châteauneuf du Pape (red)   Georges Coulon made a finer red wine in 1990 than
   ·   he did in 1989. The huge bouquet of pepper, spice, herb, tobacco, chocolate, and
  87   salty ocean water is followed by a rich, long, fat, sweet, expansively flavored wine
         with super extract, and an alcoholic, heady finish. Although soft, it possesses some
         structure, muscle, and concentration. Anticipated maturity: now–2002. Last tasted
         6/95.
1989—Châteauneuf du Pape (red)   The 1989 is ripe, tasty, and generously endowed, but
   ·   one-dimensional. Furthermore, it does not have the structure and profound depth
  85   found in the 1990. Anticipated maturity: now–1999. Last tasted 6/95.

DOMAINE PONTIFICAL (FRANÇOIS LAGET)* * */* * * *

Address: 19, avenue St.-Joseph
              84230 Châteauneuf du Pape
Tel: 4-90-83-70-91
Fax: 4-90-83-52-97

Wines produced: Châteauneuf du Pape (red and white)
Surface area (white): 2 acres
        (red): 35.8 acres
Production (white): 250 cases
        (red): 5,500 cases
Upbringing (white): 6 months minimum in stainless steel tanks
        (red): 18 months total; fermentation for 10–15 days in cement vats; then 12
        months in old oak casks
Average age of vines (white): 5 years
        (red): 40 years
Blend (white): 35% Roussanne, 30% Bourboulenc, 18% Clairette, 17% Grenache Blanc
    (red): 70–75% Grenache, 25–30% Mourvèdre, Syrah, Counoise, and Cinsault

My first experience with Domaine Pontifical's wine was the 1989, which I found to be superb. Perhaps I became too excited about the potential quality of this estate based on the 1989, because no vintage since has exhibited as much potential. Certainly the estate, which has been in the Laget-Royer family since the early twenties, is typical of Châteauneuf du Pape, with 30 separate parcels spread throughout all sectors of the appellation—a nightmare at harvest. There are vineyards planted on sandy soil, limestone, clay, and on the stony carpets.

The wine is traditionally made, with no destemming, and an upbringing in small barrels, tanks, and foudres for 12 months prior to bottling. Based on most vintages, except for the 1989, this appears to be a midweight Châteauneuf du Pape to drink within 8–10 years of the vintage. The 1989 seems atypically powerful, rich, and long-lived.

VINTAGES

1995—Châteauneuf du Pape (red)   Based on what I tasted, proprietor François Laget-
·   Royer appears to have produced a far better wine in 1994 than in 1995. The 1995
80? Châteauneuf du Pape is short and compressed, without the volume and intensity of
      the 1994. Perhaps it was going through an awkward stage, but the wine was
      one-dimensional and simple when I tasted it. Last tasted 6/96.

1994—Châteauneuf du Pape (red)   The 1994 displays an open, chocolaty, herbaceous,
·   smoky, cherry jam–scented nose suggesting extremely ripe fruit was harvested.
87   That impression is confirmed with the sweet, low-acid, generous, seductive palate
      impression. This is a forward, savory, complex Châteauneuf du Pape. Anticipated
      maturity: now–2001. Last tasted 6/96.

1992—Châteauneuf du Pape (red)   The 1992 offers a pruny, peppery, spicy nose, jammy,
·   overripe flavors, and hard tannin in the finish. Its elements are not in harmony and
85   its future may be problematic given the ferociousness of the tannin. Anticipated
      maturity: now–1999. Last tasted 4/95.

1990—Châteauneuf du Pape (red)   Though the 1990 Châteauneuf du Pape will not make
·   old bones, it will be ideal for drinking over the next 7–8 years. It displays a deep
87   ruby color, a seductively fragrant perfume of sweet berry fruit, long, lush, supple
      flavors, full body, low acidity, and a fleshy finish, but neither the depth nor structure
      of the superb 1989. Anticipated maturity: now–2002. Last tasted 6/95.

1989—Châteauneuf du Pape (red)   The 1989 is magnificent, with an opaque, dark ruby/
·   purple color, an immensely impressive nose of pepper, herbs, cassis, and tobacco,
92   and full-bodied, rich flavors with impressive levels of glycerin and extract. There
      is abundant power, moderate tannins, and a sensationally long (60 seconds or more)

finish. A great Châteauneuf du Pape. Anticipated maturity: now–2007. Last tasted 8/96.

DOMAINE DE LA PRESIDENTE (M. AUBERT)* * * *

Max Aubert is a well-known personality in the southern Rhône, with his Domaine de la Présidente cellars in the Côtes du Rhône village of Ste.-Cécile-les-Vignes. Although best known for his Côtes du Rhône and his estate-bottled Cairanne, Aubert also produces small quantities of a top-class Châteauneuf du Pape called La Nonciature Réserve. Released late into the marketplace, based on the three vintages I have tasted, it is a powerful, rich, full-bodied style of Châteauneuf du Pape that can age for 15 or more years.

VINTAGES

1995—Châteauneuf du Pape La Nonciature Réserve (red)   This is the top Châteauneuf du Pape cuvée produced by the well-known broker-négociant Max Aubert. In 1995 **89** I gave ecstatic reviews to both the 1989 and 1990 La Nonciature Réserve wines, which were released late into the marketplace. Should you come across either of those wines languishing on retailers' shelves, I highly recommend buying them . . . assuming they have been well stored. The 1995 La Nonciature Réserve is a powerful, tannic, structured wine with loads of dense Bing cherry fruit, dusty, peppery, earthy scents, full body, good tannin and acidity, and a spicy, structured finish. Give it 3–4 years of cellaring and drink it over the subsequent 10–15. This wine is usually released late into the marketplace, so do not expect to see the 1995 La Nonciature Réserve for several more years. Last tasted 6/96.

1990—Châteauneuf du Pape La Nonciature Réserve (red)   Dense purple in color, with an authentic Provençal-scented nose (smoke, herbs, chocolate, *garrigue*, and ripe **92** black cherries), this large-scaled, full-bodied wine reveals outstanding complexity and intensity. Drink it over the next 7–10 years. The 1990 is very rich and alcoholic, in short, a classic, hefty, large-scaled Châteauneuf du Pape. Last tasted 7/96.

1989—Châteauneuf du Pape La Nonciature Réserve (red)   Interestingly, Aubert's 1989 is similar to the 1990 (the 1989s are often more tight and closed, and the 1990s **91** more flamboyant, at least when tasted in 1996). The 1989 reveals a healthy dark ruby/purple color with no signs of age. A big, smoked, olive, herb-scented nose includes plenty of jammy fruit that soars from the glass. Full-bodied, with more noticeable tannin than the 1990, and perhaps a degree less alcohol, the 1989 is a robust, chewy, large-scaled Châteauneuf du Pape that is typical of the finest examples of the appellation. Anticipated maturity: now–2005. Last tasted 7/96.

CHÂTEAU RAYAS (JACQUES REYNAUD)* * * */* * * * *

Address: 84230 Châteauneuf du Pape
Tel: 4-90-83-73-09
Fax: 4-90-83-51-17
Wines produced: Rayas Châteauneuf du Pape (red and white), Château Pignan Châteauneuf
          du Pape (red)
Surface area (white): 5 acres
          (red): Rayas—19.8 acres
          Pignan—7.5 acres
Production (white): 375 cases
          (red): Rayas—2,000 cases
          Pignan—800 cases

Upbringing (white): 9 months in stainless steel vats, although before the 1995 vintage it was
        kept in old oak barrels
        (red): Rayas and Pignan—24 months total; fermentation in cement tanks, then
        12–22 months in old oak barrels
Average age of vines (white): 25 years
        (red): Rayas—30 years
        Pignan—30 years
Blend (white): 50% Grenache Blanc, 50% Clairette
        (red): Rayas—98% Grenache, 2% other varietals
        Pignan—98% Grenache, 2% other varietals

The wines from this extraordinary estate run by the eccentric and charmingly devilish Jacques Reynaud has given me some of the greatest tasting experiences of my life. In my personal collection there are a few wines with which I would never part. Among the few "untouchables" are the finest vintages of Rayas. In great vintages, Rayas reaches a level of sumptuousness and extraordinary intensity, allied with an opulence in texture and flavor, that can even humble a great Bordeaux or Burgundy.

No one would suspect that inside the drab, unpainted building that houses Château Rayas (sitting unmarked at the end of a deteriorating dirt road in the appellation of Châteauneuf du Pape) are some of the world's most distinctive wines. The credit goes to Jacques Reynaud and his late father, Louis, who passed away in 1978. Jacques Reynaud (he reminds me of a cross between Dr. Seuss's Grinch and Yoda from the *Star Wars* trilogy) is the brilliant, unassuming genius behind these wines, which are made from low yields from some of the oldest vines in the southern Rhône Valley. Reynaud is assisted by his sister, Françoise, who is cut from the same eccentric mold as her brother.

Château Rayas is the antithesis of modern-day winemaking. No stainless steel, no temperature controls, no new oak, and no oenologists are to be found in the Rayas cellar, which contains a hodgepodge of barrels, demi-muids, and foudres. The stories I could tell about Jacques Reynaud could fill a book, but behind his decidedly antifame, anti-twentieth-century facade is an extremely well-read gentleman with exceptional knowledge and a love of many things, including fine food, as I discovered over several meals with him at the nearby La Beaugravière.

Getting precise information on what goes on at Château Rayas is not an easy task. Despite having visited and tasted with Reynaud more than a dozen times during the last decade, I still have not figured out what magic takes place in these cellars. Given the extraordinary quality that emerges in the finest years, I can live without the answers. We have gotten to know each other reasonably well, and I will convey a few stories to give readers a glimpse of Reynaud's impish character. Early in my tasting experience with him, I became irritated after tasting through four different barrels without Reynaud's saying one word about what was in each barrel. Finally, I asked what we were tasting. His response was, "You're the expert. You tell me." Another example of his sense of humor emerged over dinner at La Beaugravière while we were sharing a magnificent bottle of Chave Hermitage. I asked him whom he admired the most. His deadly serious response was, "You."

What I have learned over the last decade is that Château Rayas is a 56-acre estate, of which 37 acres are in vine. From those 37 acres, less than 3,000 cases of Châteauneuf du Pape are produced. When you consider that Château Pétrus produces an average of 4,500 cases from 28 acres, readers can understand just how small the yields are at Rayas. From this estate, Jacques Reynaud produces two red wines, Rayas and Pignan. A controversial white Rayas is also made.

While Jacques Reynaud likes to play the role of a reclusive loner, the fact that he has never turned down a dinner invitation from me indicates that there is much more to the man than he likes to let on. Visitors to Rayas are advised to make an appointment, if possible, through the estate's American importer. Once an appointment has been secured, there is no guarantee that visitors will be able to find the property. This is one of the few cellars (Henri Bonneau's is another) that is unmarked. The best advice I can provide is to follow the signs for Château Vaudieu, or take the road out of Châteauneuf du Pape in the direction of Orange (D 68), passing Bosquet des Papes on the right and the ruined papal château on the left. Proceed another mile or so toward Orange and take a right at the unmarked road that sharply veers right in a easterly direction. About one mile back on this road, Château Vaudieu can be spotted to the southeast, and on a small wooden sign will be the word "Rayas." The dark, drab cellars are nearly hidden behind the large trees. A mile or two to the west the plateau of Châteauneuf du Pape begins, and the famed *galets roulés* blanket the vineyards, but this part of Châteauneuf du Pape is noticeably different, with more sandy, red soils, and a marked absence of the large football- and melon-shaped boulders. A tasting inside the low-slung, two-story, drab cellars is never going to produce a great deal of technical detail about just how these marvelous wines are made. In these cellars, Reynaud makes Rayas and his second wine, Pignan, as well as his Côtes du Rhône Fonsalette and other miscellaneous cuvées that have been culled out for his all-purpose La Pialade. Reynaud is unlikely to provide much help, but his basic response to any winemaking inquiry is essentially, "It's the vineyard and small yields, stupid." His yields are considered commercial madness by his peers, but to a person, I have never met anyone in Châteauneuf du Pape who does not regard Reynaud and his spiritual sidekick, Henri Bonneau, with extraordinary admiration and respect. In these cellars, tasting the component parts is never as satisfying as tasting the wine after it is bottled. How refreshing that is, as in Burgundy it is just the reverse.

While everyone raves about Rayas, it is easy to forget that the Pignan, made from a selection chosen after the Rayas selection has been made, can also be a terrific wine. In fact, the 1990 Pignan is more powerful and concentrated than the 1990 Rayas, but without the latter wine's complexity. In fact, in vintages such as 1990 and 1989, Pignan can eclipse most of the top Châteauneuf du Papes.

One wine that is controversial, even among Rayas enthusiasts, is the white Rayas, made from 100% Clairette. This wine, which is an old-style Châteauneuf du Pape aged in various wood vessels for 10–16 months, can be magically rich and sensationally well endowed, whereas in other vintages it is oxidized and distressingly irregular. The wine is usually put through malolactic fermentation, but in some vintages this has been blocked. Reynaud claims he "does what the wine tells me to do." Jacques Reynaud's father, Louis, occasionally produced a flowery, sweet Marc Liquoreux, which I had the privilege to taste once (the 1945) at the restaurant La Beaugravière. To my knowledge, Jacques Reynaud has never produced this wine.

In the Rayas cellars, Jacques Reynaud tends to bottle his white cuvée of Rayas and white cuvée of Fonsalette first, followed by Rayas, Fonsalette Côtes du Rhône, and Fonsalette Côtes du Rhône Syrah. After that, those cuvées deemed not good enough for Rayas are bottled under the Pignan name. Everything else left in the cellar is bottled as a Côtes du Rhône called La Pialade, which is the least distinguished wine of the Reynaud portfolio. Rayas, which has a cooler microclimate and terroir, is usually harvested last, after every other Châteauneuf du Pape estate. In the great vintages, it is this late harvest that gives Rayas the extraordinary essence of cherries and raspberries. There is no other wine I have ever tasted in the world, save perhaps for the old-vine Merlot and Cabernet Franc of Château Lafleur in Pomerol, that gives such a quintessentially raspberry/cherry/framboise liqueur intensity as does Château Rayas. As limited in quantity as Rayas and its vinous siblings tend to be, it would be a shame to go through life without tasting at least one great vintage of this prodigious wine. For example, at a birthday party for a dear friend in 1996, a 1978 Rayas and a 1978 Domaine de la Romanée–Conti la Tâche (one of the greatest red Burgundies I have tasted) were opened. Within 15 minutes, not a drop of Rayas remained in anyone's glass, but many glasses still contained plenty of La Tâche. Doesn't this say everything one needs to know?

Reynaud has inspired and motivated a young generation of French winemakers to rediscover the methods of the past, and to recognize the legitimacy of Grenache. Finally, Jacques Reynaud, part recluse, part philosopher, part gourmet, part superb winemaker, and part myth and legend, has left an indelible imprint on this author and, I suspect, on all of those who have been touched by him or his extraordinary wines.

On January 14, 1997, one day before his seventy-third birthday, Jacques Reynaud, while shopping for shoes in Avignon (probably his only materialistic addiction), collapsed and died from a heart attack. He was a *real* legend, and I shall miss him.

VINTAGES

1995—Rayas Châteauneuf du Pape (red)   The outrageously profound 1995 Rayas Châteauneuf du Pape is a glorious example of what heights Grenache can achieve.
97+   Made from yields of 12–15 hectoliters per hectare, the tiny quantities produced in 1995 will make this wine even more difficult than usual to find. It does not possess the unrestrained opulence and overripeness of the 1990. To me it tastes like a hypothetical blend of the 1978, 1989, and 1990. The color is a dense, rich purple, and the nose offers up unmistakable scents of kirsch, cassis, and roasted peanuts. Full-bodied, with magnificent concentration yet striking definition, this is a Rayas that offers all the power and hedonistic richness of the great vintages, but manages to infuse the wine's massive richness with a sense of elegance and focus. I do not know what the 1978 tasted like at nine months, but there is a structure, inner strength, and intensity to this 1995 that might equal the legendary 1978. It is a superconcentrated, gorgeously made, seamless wine that will propel Rayas freaks into fits of ecstasy. It will need five to six years of cellaring (the acidity level is surprising given its high extract and richness). Expect the 1995 Rayas to age well for two decades. Last tasted 6/96.

1994—Rayas Châteauneuf du Pape (red)   The 1994 Rayas has turned out to be a classic. Resembling the 1988, but more forward and sweeter, it displays a deep ruby/purple
92+   color, and a gorgeously fragrant nose of framboise, kirsch, and black raspberries. Dense and full-bodied, with a sweet midsection, this well-proportioned, stylish, yet authoritatively rich and powerful Rayas has turned out to be a noteworthy success. It should drink well for 12–16 years. Last tasted 9/96.

1993—Rayas Châteauneuf du Pape (red)   Open and fragrant, this light to medium ruby-colored wine possesses peppery, berry fruit, medium body, light tannin, and a soft,
86   pleasant, uncomplicated personality. It lacks the concentration inherent in the finest vintages, and will dry out and become increasingly austere over the next 7–8 years. Last tasted 12/95.

1992—Rayas Châteauneuf du Pape (red)   Another fruity, soft, round style of Rayas, the 1992 exhibits more depth than the 1993. This medium ruby-colored wine offers
86   dusty, earthy, cherry fruit intermingled with scents of pepper and herbs. This medium-bodied, fleshy wine has barely enough fruit, glycerin, and body to cover its fiery alcohol. Drink it over the next 4–6 years. Last tasted 12/95.

1992—Rayas Châteauneuf du Pape (white)   The 1992 Rayas blanc possesses crisp acidity, medium body, but little depth or character. Last tasted 6/95.

·

78

1991—Château Pignan Châteauneuf du Pape (red)   The 1991 Pignan is a better bargain than Rayas, as it contains all of the declassified Rayas. While it is extremely tannic (unusual for a wine from Reynaud), the opaque ruby/purple color, and big, sweet, leathery, licorice, and black fruit-scented nose are impressive. There is huge fruit and amazing extract, as well as ferocious tannin in this impressive, well-built, large-scaled wine. It will easily merit an outstanding score if the tannin melts away before the fruit fades. Drink it between 1997 and 2010. Last tasted 6/96.

·

89

1990—Rayas Châteauneuf du Pape (red)   The 1990 Rayas may be the most prized wine in my personal collection. I would not trade it for anything less than a pristine bottle of 1921, 1929, 1961, or 1947 Pétrus! Produced from an extremely late harvest, with awesome sugar readings and ripeness, Reynaud's 1990 Rayas is quintessential Rayas, and one of the greatest young red wines I have ever tasted. It is exceptionally opulent, thick, and juicy, with an overripe kirsch/cherry intensity that has not yet begun to take on secondary aromas or character. Massive, viscous, and exceptionally full-bodied and alcoholic (it must be pushing 15%), this luscious, unctuously textured wine is spectacular to drink, even though it has not yet begun to take on any of the mature gamy characteristics its closest rival, the phenomenal 1978, has possessed for over a decade. Life is too short not to drink as much of this wine as possible! Anticipated maturity: now–2010. Last tasted 9/96.

·

100

1990—Rayas Châteauneuf du Pape (white)   The 1990 Rayas blanc proved to be astonishing when drunk at a restaurant near Orange. Reynaud suggested that the 1990 Rayas blanc needs 10–15 years just to reach full maturity! When I last had it, the wine revealed a huge nose of honey and pears, expansive, unctuous flavors, gorgeous extraction of fruit, and a long, alcoholic finish. It should drink well for 15–20 years. Last tasted 2/97.

·

91

1990—Château Pignan Châteauneuf du Pape (red)   Pignan is an actual terroir or lieu-dit that sits to the west and north of the narrow band of sandy/clay soil that composes the Rayas vineyard. While it is a separate vineyard, in practice, Pignan is the second wine of Rayas. Its extraordinary showing in such recent vintages as 1989 and 1990 have led some skeptics to suggest that Reynaud may be putting his best juice in Pignan, using Rayas as a second label. This is untrue, but there is no doubting that Pignan, especially in 1989 and 1990, is a wine of extraordinary richness and intensity that can be purchased for less than half the price of Rayas. The 1990 Pignan is a thick, fruity ball of overripe black-cherry Grenache fruit. Thick and juicy, with high alcohol and glycerin, this knockout, full-bodied, portlike wine should drink well for another 15+ years. Last tasted 12/95.

·

95

1989—Rayas Châteauneuf du Pape (red)   While not as obviously massive as the 1990, the 1989 Rayas may turn out to be a more classically proportioned example of this wine, similar to the 1978. The 1989 reveals a dark ruby/purple color, as well as Rayas's telltale aromatics of roasted fruits, kirsch, earth, and smoke. More noticeably structured, this is a highly extracted, thick Rayas for drinking over the next 20+ years. Although it may not rival the 1990 for power, extract, and weight, this is an exquisite Rayas, and clearly one of the finest wines made at the estate in the last 30 years. Last tasted 9/96.

·

96

1989—Château Pignan Châteauneuf du Pape (red)   Similar to the 1990, although slightly less portlike and without the color saturation of that wine, the full-throttle, robust, intense, rich 1989 Pignan coats the palate with layers of viscous fruit flavors, high alcohol, and an impressive velvety sweetness. This high-octane wine exhibits no

·

93

signs of going into a closed stage; it should continue to drink splendidly well for another 12–15+ years.

1988— Rayas Châteauneuf du Pape (red)   Tasted beside the 1989 and 1990, the 1988
   ·   Rayas appears polite and civilized. However, this is no shy wine. By itself, it is an
94+   enormously constituted, juicy example of Rayas, thus the sometimes misleading nature of vertical tastings. The wine's color is a healthy dark ruby. The nose is less open than in either the 1989 or 1990, but it reveals the essence of black-cherry fruit in that kinky, undeniably Rayas style. Full-bodied and rich, with more tannin and structure than even the 1989, this large-scaled Rayas will always take a backseat to the flamboyant 1989 and legendary 1990. Nevertheless, it is an extremely worthy, high-quality Châteauneuf du Pape that will evolve beautifully and eventually outdistance some of the fully mature top vintages of Rayas such as 1985, 1983, and 1981. Last tasted 12/95.

1986— Rayas Châteauneuf du Pape (red)   This wine has been fully mature since its release
   ·   and continues to drink well, although owners are advised to consume it before the
86   turn of the century. Not one of the most successful 1986s (a difficult as well as irregular vintage in Châteauneuf du Pape), it displays a medium ruby color with no signs of amber or orange. A peppery, herbaceous, celery-scented note competes with ripe cherry/kirsch aromas. Although medium- to full-bodied, with good glycerin and a velvety texture, the wine lacks the sweet mid-palate and inner core of extraction and depth found in the greatest Rayas vintages. Drink it up. Last tasted 12/95.

1985— Rayas Châteauneuf du Pape (red)   The 1985 is a tricky wine to evaluate. The
   ·   wine has always shown extremely well, displaying a dark ruby color, plenty of
90?   peppery, black-cherry fruit, full body, excellent power and thickness, and a juicy attack, mid-palate, and finish filled with glycerin, fruit, extract, and alcohol. For whatever reason, it continues to reveal a monolithic character, without the definition or focus of such great vintages as the 1988, 1989, and 1990. My instincts suggest that some of the baby fat is rolling back, revealing more alcohol. I would opt for drinking this wine over the next 5–8 years, rather than hoping more magic will develop. It is unquestionably an excellent, maybe outstanding example of Rayas, but its balance appears fragile, despite the fact there is no color degradation. Last tasted 12/95.

1985— Rayas Châteauneuf du Pape (white)   I have never been greatly enamored of the
   ·   white wine of Rayas, but I must admit the 1985 appears to be one of this estate's
86   better efforts. Quite rich, full-bodied, and alcoholic, it is a very big, unctuous wine that should be drunk over the next 3–4 years. Last tasted 6/86.

1983— Rayas Châteauneuf du Pape (red)   The 1983 has been fully mature since the late
   ·   eighties, yet it continues to hold at a sumptuous level of drinkability. The color is
92   a dark ruby/garnet, with some noticeable amber at the edge. The intoxicating aromatic profile of black pepper, red and black fruits, spices, herbs, and earth is especially appealing. Soft, velvety-textured, sweet, and round, with no hard edges, this has been a consistently delicious wine for nearly a decade. Owners are advised to drink it before 2002, before the fat and fruit begin to fade. Last tasted 12/95.

1983— Château Pignan Châteauneuf du Pape (red)   For one half, sometimes one-third
   ·   the price of Rayas, Pignan represents a great value. Very similar to the 1983
89   Rayas, Pignan is deep in color with vast, sweet berry flavors, a peppery, raspberry fruitiness, and lush finish. Mature now. Last tasted 2/87.

1981— Rayas Châteauneuf du Pape (red)   Similar in style to the 1983, although more
   ·   alcoholic and heady, the 1981 began to drink fabulously well in the late eighties
92   and has continued to offer splendidly opulent, rich, creamy-textured, jammy, cherry flavors combined with smoke, pepper, and herbs. Full-bodied and soft, with

more underlying definition and focus than found in the 1983 or 1985, this fully mature Rayas should be drunk over the next 4–5 years. It's a beauty! Last tasted 12/95.

1981—Château Pignan Châteauneuf du Pape (red)   A great Châteauneuf du Pape, the
·   1981 Pignan is deeper in color than the 1983, has a roasted nut and plummy
90   bouquet, intense, very concentrated, full-bodied flavors, and a long, tannic finish. Anticipated maturity: 1989–1998. Last tasted 2/87.

1979—Rayas Châteauneuf du Pape (red)   Occasionally, this wine rivals the otherworldly
·   1978. The 1979 has always been a sleeper, underrated vintage for Rayas (except
96   in my writings), and I have drunk more than two cases since its release in the early eighties. The recent vintage that most resembles the 1979 is the 1988, at least at this stage. The wine's dark garnet color with slight amber hues is followed by a huge, smoky, black-raspberry, cherry, licorice, and fruitcake-scented nose, lush, full-bodied flavors, considerable glycerin, extract, and thickness, and slight tannin in the massive finish. This is an enormously constituted, rich Rayas, which, despite some amber in its color, reveals no signs of losing its fruit. The 1979 Rayas is another example of what makes terrific Châteauneuf du Pape so splendid—the huge window of drinkability. Owners are advised to not let the rapture pass them by; drink it over the next 4–5 years. Last tasted 12/95.

1978—Rayas Châteauneuf du Pape (red)   It remains to be seen if the 1989, 1990, and
·   1995 live up to the sumptuous quality of the 1978 Rayas. My gut feeling is that
100   the 1990 should surpass this monumental wine, the 1995 and 1989 should rival it, and the 1988 might come close to equaling it. The 1978 has provided me with some of the most decadent nectar of my life. It is one of the most precious wines in my collection, and I would not trade it for anything less than a 1961 Château Latour à Pomerol! The wine began life as a massive but structured, backward Rayas and came into full bloom during the mid-eighties. It has not lost any of its huge concentration of jammy black-raspberry/kirsch/cherry fruit. The dark garnet color reveals some amber at the edge. The smoky, earthy, gamy nose that interplays with the extraordinary quantity of fruit is a hedonist's dream. Thick, juicy, and succulent, with no hard edges, this high-octane, marvelously proportioned and concentrated wine is Rayas at its greatest. Drink it over the next 7–8 years, as the finest Châteauneuf du Papes from this vintage have proven to have uncommon ageability. Last tasted 8/96.

1976—Rayas Châteauneuf du Pape (red)   The 1976 has been in decline since the mid-
·   to late eighties, and it continues to take on more orange/amber at the edge. The
76?   nose is losing some of its once modest quantities of jammy, cherry fruit, taking on a more earthy, herbaceous, washed-out character. The wine is soft, angular, and beginning to display an austere character as the fruit continues to dry out. Time has not been kind to either the 1976 Châteauneuf du Pape vintage, or to Rayas. Last tasted 12/95.

1971—Rayas Châteauneuf du Pape (red)   Medium ruby with a great deal of brown at the
·   edge, the 1971 Rayas has been fully mature since 1978. Broad, expansive, sweet,
85   plummy fruit is very appealing. Ripe and round but beginning to fade, this wine was better and more concentrated 2–3 years ago. It must be drunk up. Last tasted 7/86.

1969—Rayas Châteauneuf du Pape (red)   At its apogee, the 1969 Rayas is in better
·   condition than either the 1971 or 1976. A smoky, complex, Asian spice, bouquet
88   is followed by an equally intriguing wine with full body, a broad layer of sweet fruit, full body, and a sumptuous finish. This is a joy to drink. Last tasted 7/86.

1967—Rayas Châteauneuf du Pape (red)   The aromas of roasted nuts, Provençal herbs,
·   smoked meats, and intense candied fruit swell in the glass. On the palate, the
91   unctuous texture from the heaps of fruit, glycerin, and alcohol makes for a won-
         derfully hedonistic drinking experience. This should be drunk up. Last tasted
         6/86.

1966—Rayas Châteauneuf du Pape (red)   Less expansive and sweet than the 1967, the
·   1966 is, however, a classic Rayas with a very fragrant, full-intensity bouquet,
89   chewy, portlike flavors, and a long aftertaste. Last tasted 7/86.

1964—Rayas Châteauneuf du Pape (red)   Like the 1967, this wine cannot get any better
·   or evolve any further and therefore should be drunk up. The telltale bouquet of
87   smoky nuts, Asian spices, and very ripe fruit is all one could ask for. On the palate,
         the wine is just beginning to lose some fruit and show its hefty alcohol level. Last
         tasted 6/85.

1962—Rayas Châteauneuf du Pape (red)   Very light color and washed-out flavors; I
·   drank this bottle in mid-1986 and found the wine in serious decline. Two years
65–90   earlier I had a splendidly preserved bottle of 1962 Rayas that was as good as the
         1967. Storage conditions are extremely important when drinking a wine this old.
         Last tasted 6/86.

1961—Rayas Châteauneuf du Pape (red)   Despite the fading color, this wine is still
·   loaded with heaps of ripe, sweet fruit. The palate impression is akin to a 20-year-
92   old tawny port. This wine is ripe, hedonistic, and a privilege to drink. Last tasted
         6/86.

DOMAINE DES RELAGNES (CUVÉE VIGNERONNE) (HENRI BOIRON)* * *
Address: Route de Bédarrides
         84230 Châteauneuf du Pape
Tel: 4-90-83-73-37
Wines produced: Châteauneuf du Pape (red and white)
Surface area: 32.1 acres
Production (white): 375 cases
           (red): 5,000 cases
Upbringing: Traditional—no destemming and cellaring in foudre
Average age of vines: 60 years
Blend (white): 45% Grenache Blanc, 45% Clairette, 10% Bourboulenc
      (red): 85% Grenache, 8% Mourvèdre, 7% Cinsault and Syrah

This 30-acre estate, of which 85% is planted with Grenache and the rest Mourvèdre, Syrah, and Cinsault, has very old vines that average 60 years in age. While this estate can make rich, deep Châteauneuf du Pape, the style has lightened up from the rather robust, full-bodied, chewy-textured wine of the late seventies. Boiron has begun to do two filtrations on his wine because "consumers want their wines without sediment." He also sells the same wine under the names Cuvée Vigneronne and Cuvée Henri Boiron.

Boiron's estate is spread thoughout the appellation on sandy, clay, and stony soils. His vinification is completely traditional, with no destemming except for Syrah, which is 100% destemmed. While his wines became considerably lighter during the eighties, over the last five or six years, there appears to be a movement to increase the wines' richness and intensity. Even Boiron expressed disappointment at what fining did to his wine. While he will not eliminate filtration, fining is no longer practiced. This has resulted in wines with deeper colors, as well as more body.

Overall Boiron produces a fruity, somewhat commercial but tasty, soft-textured Châteauneuf du Pape that is best drunk in its first five to eight years of life. Henri Boiron is the cousin of Maurice Boiron, who, along with his wife, are the proprietors of the excellent Le Bosquet des Pape.

VINTAGES

1995—Châteauneuf du Pape (red)   The 1995 Châteauneuf du Pape exhibits fine inten-
·   sity, a deep ruby color, good fatness in its midsection, with sweet black cherry
88   dominating the olfactory senses as well as palate. The wine possesses excellent
         ripeness, better delineation than the 1994, and a fine finish. It will be an accessible,
         beefier wine than its older sibling. Anticipated maturity: now–2004. Last tasted
         6/96.

1994—Châteauneuf du Pape (red)   Proprietor Henri Boiron's 1994 Châteauneuf du Pape
·   has turned out to be an attractive, medium dark garnet-colored wine with a
86   spicy, cherry/herbal-scented nose. Soft, round, medium-bodied flavors that pos-
         sess an intriguing cinnamon component, fine ripeness, a fleshy feel, good alcohol,
         and a spicy finish fill the mouth. Anticipated maturity: now–2001. Last tasted
         6/96.

1993—Châteauneuf du Pape (red)   The 1993 exhibits a surprisingly evolved color already
·   displaying some garnet/amber. Fat, round, and diffuse, this tasty, mouthfilling wine
86   is almost pruny in its jammy, cherry fruitiness. Mature now. Last tasted 6/96.

1992—Châteauneuf du Pape (red)   The medium to dark ruby-colored 1992 Châteauneuf
·   du Pape reveals an expansive, sweet, floral, jammy nose, and broad, chewy fla-
87   vors. It is a very seductive style of Châteauneuf du Pape. Mature now. Last tasted
         6/95.

1990—Châteauneuf du Pape (red)   The 1990 red cuvée exhibits medium ruby color, a
·   pleasant spicy, herb, and red-fruit-scented nose, moderately endowed flavors, good
84   body, a soft texture, and the telltale peppery, nut smell of superripe Grenache.
         Mature now. Last tasted 6/95.

1989—Châteauneuf du Pape (red)   The 1989 is Henri Boiron's best wine since 1981.
·   Deep ruby/purple, with a bouquet of Provençal herbs, black raspberries, roasted
88   peanuts, and pepper, this is a full-bodied, soft, velvety-textured wine. Anticipated
         maturity: now–2000. Last tasted 6/94.

1988—Châteauneuf du Pape (red)   The 1988 is a good, light ruby-colorerd Châteauneuf
·   du Pape, with a peppery, spicy, intensely herbaceous bouquet, and round, soft,
84   somewhat flabby flavors. Mature now. Last tasted 6/94.

Older Vintages

Both the 1985 and 1983 fell apart within 5–6 years of the vintage. Should readers come across either the 1981 or 1978, both should be very good examples of Domaine des Relagnes.

DOMAINE RICHE* * *

Address: 27, avenue de Général de Gaulle
            84230 Châteauneuf du Pape
Tel: 4-90-83-72-63
Wines produced: Châteauneuf du Pape (red and white)
Surface area (white): 2.5 acres
            (red): 31.6 acres
Production (white): 1,800 cases
            (red): 5,000 cases

Upbringing (white): fermentation at low temperatures in tank; then bottled in December or
January after the vintage
(red): after destemming, the grapes are crushed and the subsequent wine is aged
12–18 months in an assortment of foudres
Average age of vines (white): 30 years
(red): 30 years
Blend (white): 50% Grenache Blanc, 30% Clairette, 20% Bourboulenc
(red): 70% Grenache, 10% Cinsault, 10% Mourvèdre, and 10% Syrah

This little-known estate has a good track record for producing textbook Châteauneuf du
Pape that relies heavily on Grenache, and exhibits the telltale *garrigue*, herbes de Provence,
black-cherry aromatic profile, and good, plump, succulent fruit. The wines are not meant to
be long-lived, but rather to be consumed in their first 5–8 years of life. My experience with
Domaine Riche has revealed very good wines in the better vintages.

VINTAGES

1995—Châteauneuf du Pape (red)   A fine effort from Domaine Riche, the 1995 is a
·   forward, plump, slightly commercial style of Châteauneuf du Pape that is meant to
87   be drunk during its first 5–8 years of life. It displays a dark ruby color, good
structure and acidity, fine richness and definition, and an easygoing, sweet, black-
cherry, herbes de Provence aromatic and flavor profile. Anticipated maturity: now–
2004. Last tasted 6/96.
1994—Châteauneuf du Pape (red)   The 1994 exhibits a medium dark ruby/garnet color,
·   a spicy, sweet, cherry, earthy, leather, and olive-scented nose, rich, medium to
86 +   full-bodied, velvety-textured flavors, good alcohol and glycerin, and a low-acid,
heady finish. Anticipated maturity: now–2002. Last tasted 6/96.
1993—Châteauneuf du Pape (red)   The medium ruby-colored 1993 is a ripe, well-made,
·   commercially oriented Châteauneuf du Pape with warmth, generosity, and fat,
86   herbal, peppery, cherry flavors. Exhibiting lushness, glycerin, and fatness, it should
be drunk over the near term. Anticipated maturity: now–1999. Last tasted 6/96.
1992—Châteauneuf du Pape (red)   The light, shallow 1992 offers decent fruit, medium
·   body, and an undistinguished, compact finish. Drink it up. Last tasted 6/95.
77
1989—Châteauneuf du Pape (red)   The dark garnet/ruby 1989 exhibits ripeness, concen-
·   tration, medium to full body, a supple texture, and plenty of spice and pepper. It is a
86   good wine from a great vintage. Anticipated maturity: now–2000. Last tasted 6/95.
1988—Châteauneuf du Pape (red)   The 1988 is light, straightforward, soft, fruity, and
·   one-dimensional. Mature now. Last tasted 6/94.
83

DOMAINE DE LA ROQUETTE (DANIEL BRUNIER)* * * *
Address: 2, avenue Louis Pasteur
84230 Châteauneuf du Pape
Tel: 4-90-33-00-31
Fax: 4-90-83-71-25
Wines produced: Châteauneuf du Pape (red and white)
Surface area (white): 7.5 acres
(red): 67 acres
Production (white): 1,875 cases
(red): 11,250 cases

Upbringing (white): 8 months in enamel vats
>   (red): 24 months total. Fermentation of 12–15 days in cement vats, where the
>   wines stay for one year; then 8 months in old oak casks. Bottling is done
>   all at once without fining or filtration.

Average age of vines (white): 10 years
>   (red): 40 years

Blend (white): equal parts Grenache Blanc, Bourboulenc, Roussanne, and Clairette
>   (red): 70% Grenache, 20% Syrah, 10% Mourvèdre

Until 1986, René Laugier produced both red and white Châteauneuf du Pape from his domaine of 74 acres. Then Laugier sold his estate to Henri Brunier, the owner of Vieux-Télégraphe. Grenache dominates his plantings with 70%. Production is just under 13,500 cases of wine.

Since the acquisition of this estate by the Bruniers, the young brothers, Daniel and Frédéric, have immensely improved the quality of Domaine de la Roquette, renovating the cellars and beginning to destem. The wines have moved toward a more modern but authoritatively flavored style of Châteauneuf du Pape. The estate has a fine terroir consisting of three separate parcels, all situated on the rocky plateau north of the village. With the average age of the vines a healthy 40 years, it is not surprising what the Bruniers have been able to accomplish. Moreover, recent refinements have included the abandonment of any fining or filtration prior to bottling in order to present a wine that is the true essence of this old vineyard.

The white wine has also improved. It is an elegant, fruity, stylish, dry white Châteauneuf du Pape that has benefited immensely from the incorporation of 25% Roussanne in the blend. As the following tasting notes demonstrate, this is an underrated, reasonably priced Châteauneuf du Pape that merits more attention.

VINTAGES

1995—Châteauneuf du Pape (red)   The Brunier family of Vieux-Télégraphe has done a
·   marvelous job in upgrading the quality of this estate's wines. Compared to the
90   1994, the 1995 Châteauneuf du Pape from Roquette reveals a deeper color, more
structure (higher acidity and more tannin), outstanding richness and ripeness, and a broad, fat, thick palate. It should prove to be longer-lived, but not as flattering early on as the 1994. Anticipated maturity: 1998–2007. Last tasted 6/96.

1994—Châteauneuf du Pape (red)   The 1994 Châteauneuf du Pape, which was bottled
·   with no filtration, is a 70% Grenache, 15% Syrah, and 15% Mourvèdre blend. This
89   dark ruby/purple-colored wine exhibits plenty of black fruits, a sweet mid-palate,
full body, a supple, round, generously endowed personality, and a spicy, long, peppery finish. It is a delicious, forward style of Châteauneuf du Pape. Anticipated maturity: now–2004. Last tasted 6/96.

1993—Châteauneuf du Pape (red)   The tannic and backward 1993 exhibits a classic
·   Châteauneuf du Pape nose of roasted herbs, black pepper, and sweet black-cherry
88 +   fruit. It is a densely concentrated, big, full-bodied, muscular wine with moderate
tannin in the long finish. The color is a healthy, saturated, dense ruby/purple. This is one 1993 that will benefit from cellaring. Anticipated maturity: 1998–2007. Last tasted 6/96.

1992—Châteauneuf du Pape (red)   The medium- to full-bodied 1992 Châteauneuf du
·   Pape displays a bouquet of prunes, overripe black cherries, and herb/peppery
86   scents, tarry, chewy flavors, low acidity, and plenty of alcohol in the heady finish.

Although slightly overripe, it provides a solid, chewy mouthful of wine. Anticipated maturity: now–2000. Last tasted 6/95.

1990—Châteauneuf du Pape (red)   This wine exhibits an attractive sweet smell of over-
·   ripe black fruits, spicy herbs, a touch of coffee and tobacco, as well as rich, plump,
90   smooth flavors in a velvety-textured format. Though it will not prove to be the longest-lived Châteauneuf du Pape, it can provide immense pleasure. Anticipated maturity: now–2002. Last tasted 9/95.

1989—Châteauneuf du Pape (red)   The 1989 is an ambitiously styled, big, rich, agewor-
·   thy wine. Less flattering than the 1990, there is no doubting its intense black-
90   cherry, herb, licorice, and earthy-scented fruitiness, sweet, exotic, black-fruit flavors, gobs of glycerin, and its rich, powerful, long finish. Anticipated maturity: now–2004. Last tasted 9/95.

Older Vintages

Domaine la Roquette was disappointingly light and short-lived before the Brunier acquisition. The only positive note I have from 1978 on is the 1988, which should still be in fine form.

DOMAINE ROGER SABON (ROGER SABON)
(Les Olivets* * */Cuvée Réservée* * * */Cuvée Prestige* * * * *)

Address: Avenue Impériale
    B.P. 57
    84230 Châteauneuf du Pape
Tel: 4-90-83-71-72
Fax: 4-90-83-50-51
Wines produced: Châteauneuf du Pape (red and white), Châteauneuf du Pape Les Olivets (red), Châteauneuf du Pape Cuvée Réservée (red), Châteauneuf du Pape Cuvée Prestige (red)
Surface area (white): 3.7 acres
        (red): 37 acres (some which is within Lirac and Côtes du Rhône appellation)
            Les Olivets—21 acres
            Cuvée Réservée—7.5 acres
            Cuvée Prestige—6 acres
Production (white): 560 cases
        (red): 5,750 cases
            Les Olivets—3,750 cases
            Cuvée Réservée—1,250 cases
            Cuvée Prestige—750 cases
Upbringing (white): 6–7 months in enamel vats
        (red): After fermentation, the three special red wine cuvées are tasted, and those not good enough to be part of those cuvées are declassified into the regular cuvée.
            Les Olivets—14 months total, with 6 months in old oak casks
            Cuvée Réservée—14 months total, with 6 months in old oak casks
            Cuvée Prestige—14 months total, with 6 months in old oak casks
Average age of vines (white): 40 years
        (red): 40–90 years
            Les Olivets—50 years
            Cuvée Réservée—60–70 years
            Cuvée Prestige—90 years

Blend (white): 30–40% Clairette, 20% Grenache Blanc, 20% Bourboulenc, 15% Rous-
sanne, 4–5% Picpoul plus a field blend of different grapes that constitute
15–20%
Les Olivets—80% Grenache, 10% Syrah, 10% Cinsault
Cuvée Réservée—70% Grenache, 10% Syrah, 10% Cinsault, 10%
Mourvèdre
Cuvée Prestige—55–60% Grenache, 10–15% Syrah, 10% Mourvèdre, and
the rest other varietals

Roger Sabon is one of the more intellectual and forward-thinking vignerons in Châteauneuf
du Pape. Perhaps because the Sabon name has been associated with Châteauneuf du Pape
since the early seventeenth century, he seems more concerned about the future than many
vignerons. Sabon, who produces a solid white wine and three cuvées of red Châteauneuf du
Pape, owns a moderately sized estate of 41 acres. His vineyards are in such superbly situated
sectors as Les Cabrières, La Crau, Courthézon, and Nalys. While the soils are slightly diverse,
what they all have in common is the famed *galets roulés*. The overall Grenache percentage
remains at 70%, but in the Cuvée Prestige, this is reduced to 55–60% of the blend.

Sabon is a traditional winemaker. He has moved toward raising his red wines in small
oak casks (all old since he does not like the effect of new oak). After being pressured by his
oenologist and European clients to do more fining and filtering, Sabon decided to make a
qualitative rather than business decision, and for the last half decade or so has refused to
filter any of his wines. In fact, he is an outspoken critic of those oenologists who consistently
advocate an intense filtration, not recognizing that it can harmfully remove much of the
aromatics, body, and flavors of a wine. Sabon's wines are classic Châteauneuf du Papes,
and, as one might imagine, they increase in intensity from the traditional cuvée of Les
Olivets, to the Cuvée Réservée, and Cuvée Prestige. The latter wine is made from the
estate's oldest vines (close to 100 years old).

This estate has been making exceptionally high-quality wines for years, but recent vintages seem to have risen to a new level of quality. Moreover, Sabon's wines have not yet
been discovered by the masses, so prices are surprisingly reasonable.

Readers should also be aware that Roger Sabon produces a very delicious Côtes du
Rhône and Lirac from vineyard holdings in those appellations.

VINTAGES

1995—Châteauneuf du Pape Cuvée Prestige (red)   The 1995 Cuvée Prestige boasts great
· sweetness, a pronounced black-fruit character, a high degree of ripeness, and
90 admirable glycerin and alcohol. It is a dense, promising, formidably endowed
Châteauneuf du Pape. Anticipated maturity: 1998–2012. Last tasted 6/96.

1995—Châteauneuf du Pape Cuvée Réservée (red)   The 1995 Châteauneuf du Pape
· Cuvée Réservée displays more of a black-fruit character, with less of the olive,
89 leathery component. There are copious quantities of fruit, a denser personality, full
body, and a structured, well-delineated, spicy, tannic finish. Anticipated maturity:
1998–2009. Last tasted 6/96.

1995—Châteauneuf du Pape Les Olivets (red)   The 1995 Les Olivets offers up an attrac-
· tive, spicy, peppery, jammy black-cherry-scented nose, sweet, round, generously
87 endowed flavors, medium to full body, and a low-acid, lush finish. Anticipated
maturity: now–2005. Last tasted 6/96.

1994—Châteauneuf du Pape Cuvée Prestige (red)   The dark garnet-colored 1994 Cuvée
· Prestige possesses a powerful fragrance of olives, cedar, red and black fruits, spice,
90 and pepper. Heady, thick, and full-bodied, with layers of flavor, this beautifully

made, rich, complex Châteauneuf du Pape can be drunk now. Anticipated maturity: now–2007. Last tasted 6/96.

1994—Châteauneuf du Pape Cuvée Réservée (red)   The 1994 Cuvée Réservée exhibits a
·   dark ruby/purple color, and a pronounced nose of black olives, cedar, new saddle
88   leather, and ripe, jammy cherry and currant fruit. Full-bodied, with tannin in the background, this is a plump, generous, classic Châteauneuf du Pape. Anticipated maturity: now–2006. Last tasted 6/96.

1993—Châteauneuf du Pape Cuvée Prestige (red)   The 1993 Cuvée Prestige is more
·   tannic and concentrated, with a more saturated ruby/purple color and gobs of rich
89 +   fruit in its aromatics. Full-bodied, expansive, and opulent, this is a large-scaled, concentrated Châteauneuf du Pape with chewy, intense fruit that conceals what appears to be light to moderate tannin. Anticipated maturity: now–2006. Last tasted 6/96.

1993—Châteauneuf du Pape Cuvée Réservée (red)   The 1993 Cuvée Réservée displays
·   a healthy dark ruby/purple color followed by a big, sweet nose of black cherries,
88   cedar, herbs, and spice. Full-bodied, rich, and creamy-textured, this generously endowed, silky-smooth Châteauneuf du Pape can be drunk now. Anticipated maturity: now–2003. Last tasted 6/96.

1993—Châteauneuf du Pape Les Olivets (red)   The 1993 Les Olivets reveals a saturated
·   dark ruby color, a sweet, jammy nose of black cherries, herbs, and pepper, and a
88   voluptuously rich, chewy palate with excellent depth and length. Anticipated maturity: now–2002. Last tasted 6/96.

1992—Châteauneuf du Pape Cuvée Prestige (red)   The outstanding, decadently styled
·   1992 Cuvée Prestige (unfiltered) offers lavish quantities of jammy red and black
90   fruits, roasted herbs, smoked nuts, and pepper in the bouquet. Full-bodied, rich, fat, and unctuous, this is a lusty, no-holds-barred Châteauneuf for drinking over the next 7–8 years. Last tasted 6/95.

1992—Châteauneuf du Pape Cuvée Réservée (red)   The lusty 1992 Cuvée Réservée
·   exhibits a generous, roasted nut and herb-scented, richly fruity nose, copious
86   quantities of chunky fruit, loads of alcohol, and an appealing, mouth-filling personality. Anticipated maturity: now–2000. Last tasted 6/95.

1990—Châteauneuf du Pape Cuvée Prestige (red)   Sabon's 1990 Cuvée Prestige has
·   less Grenache and more Syrah and Mourvèdre included in the blend, which is
90   produced from some of Sabon's oldest vineyards. The 14.5% alcohol is well concealed beneath a cascade of sweet black-cherry fruit. The nose soars from the glass, offering up loads of fruit and peppery spices, as well as interesting bacon fat and roasted peanut aromas. In the mouth, the wine is dense and full-bodied, with an enticing texture, soft tannins, and low acidity. The finish is rich, full, and well balanced. Anticipated maturity: now–2006. Last tasted 6/94.

1990—Châteauneuf du Pape Cuvée Réservée (red)   The 1990 Cuvée Réservée is higher
·   in alcohol, as well as richer, with a more fleshy texture, deep scents of red and
86   black fruit in its spicy, earthy nose, and full-bodied, voluptuous flavors that linger on the palate. Again, the acidity is low and the alcohol high, but the overall impression is one of a fleshy, velvety-textured wine. Anticipated maturity: now–2003. Last tasted 6/94.

1990—Châteauneuf du Pape Les Olivets   The 1990 Les Olivets offers a medium to dark
·   ruby color, and an attractive spicy nose with aromas of overripe cherries and
85   oranges. In the mouth, it is full-bodied, solid, and straightforward, with good depth, soft tannins, and plenty of up-front appeal. Anticipated maturity: now–2002. Last tasted 6/94.

1989—Châteauneuf du Pape Cuvée Réservée (red)   The 1989 Cuvée Réservée offers a
·   Bing cherry, herb-scented nose, round, full-bodied flavors, and some noticeable
85   alcohol in the finish. The overall impression is one of generosity and softness.
        Anticipated maturity: now–1999. Last tasted 6/94.

Older Vintages

Sabon admits that the performance of his wines during the eighties influenced him to stop
filtering and do only the lightest fining possible. Those wines have not held up to cellaring,
and Sabon recognizes that he stripped the wines by overprocessing them at the advice of
the village's oenologist. Vintages such as 1985, 1983, and 1981 were all fatigued and losing
their fruit after only 5–7 years in the bottle.

DOMAINE ST.-BENOÎT
**(Cuvée Elise* * */Soleil et Festins* * */Grande Garde* * * */
La Truffière* * * *)**

Address: Quartier St.-Pierrre
         84230 Châteauneuf du Pape
Tel: 4-90-83-51-36
Fax: 4-90-83-51-37
Wines produced: Châteauneuf du Pape (white), Châteauneuf du Pape Cuvée Vieilles Vignes
        (white), Châteauneuf du Pape Cuvée Elise (red), Châteauneuf du Pape
        Soleil et Festins (red), Châteauneuf du Pape Grande Garde (red), Châ-
        teauneuf du Pape La Truffière (red)
Surface area (white): 6.8 acres
Production (white): 1,000 cases
              Cuvée Vieilles Vignes—50 cases
      (red): Cuvée Elise—1,000 cases
          Soleil et Festins—2,125 cases
          Grande Garde—1,500 cases
          La Truffière—250 cases
Upbringing (white): Each varietal is vinified separately in temperature-controlled stainless
        steel vats; after 4 months the assemblage is done, and the wines are
        then stored for 6–7 months in stainless steel vats until bottling; malo-
        lactic is blocked.
        Cuvée Vieilles Vignes—30–50% of the yield is vinified in new oak
        barrels and the rest in temperature-controlled stainless steel tanks;
        assemblage takes place after 9 months; bottling is all done at one time.
    (red): Cuvée Elise—Each varietal is vinified separately for 20 days, with the
        Grenache in stainless steel vats and the other varietals in cement vats;
        then all varietals spend 12 months in stainless steel vats prior to bottling.
        Soleil et Festins—Each varietal is vinified separately for 20 days, with
        the Grenache in stainless steel vats and the other varietals in cement
        vats; then all varietals spend 18 months in oak casks prior to bottling.
        Grande Garde—Each varietal is vinified separately for 20 days, with the
        Grenache in stainless steel vats and the other varietals in cement vats;
        then all varietals spend 18–24 months in oak casks prior to bottling.
        La Truffière—Each varietal is vinified separately for 20 days, with the
        Grenache in stainless steel vats and the other varietals in cement vats;
        then all varietals spend 18 months in oak barrels prior to bottling.

Average age of vines (white): 15 years
            Cuvée Vieilles Vignes—47 years
            (red): Cuvée Elise—40+ years for the Grenache vines
            Grande Garde—70+ years for the Grenache vines
Blend (white): various proportions of Grenache Blanc, Clairette, Roussanne, and Picpoul
            Cuvée Vieilles Vignes—100% Roussanne
       (red): Cuvée Elise—various proportions of Grenache, Clairette rosé, Syrah, and Cinsault
            Soleil et Festins—90% red varietals and 10% white varietals, including Clairette rosé, Grenache Blanc, Cinsault, Mourvèdre, Syrah, and Picpoul
            Grande Garde—various proportions of Mourvèdre and Grenache
            La Truffière—50% Grenache, 25% Mourvèdre, 25% Syrah

This is a new estate created only in 1989 as a result of the grouping of three separate proprietors under the Domaine St.-Benoît name. Proprietors Paul Courtil, Madame Cellier, and Pierre Jacumin joined their 45 separate parcels of Châteauneuf du Pape and began to produce St.-Benoît.

The wines are made in a modern style, with half the Grenache and all the Syrah vinified with a modified carbonic maceration. The yields are kept reasonable and the wines have gotten better and better in this estate's short history. There are two cuvées of white wine and three cuvées of red wine, with a fourth, La Truffière, made only for the American market. The regular cuvée of white Châteauneuf du Pape has been of standard quality, and I have not yet had an opportunity to taste the debut vintage of the 100% Roussanne Cuvée Vieilles Vignes, which is modeled after the famed old-vine Roussanne of Beaucastel.

The four red wine cuvées begin with the Cuvée Elise, the fruitiest, most accessible offering, bottled after 12 months of tank aging. The Soleil et Festins is made primarily from Grenache, and is aged in oak casks for 18 months prior to bottling. The third cuvée, Grande Garde, comes from 70-year-old Grenache vines, with a tiny portion of Mourvèdre in the blend. The wine spends 18–24 months in oak casks, and is usually the richest, fullest-bodied, and densest of the St.-Benoît wines. The fourth cuvée, La Truffière, was introduced with the 1995 vintage. An unfined and unfiltered cuvée made for the American importer, it appears to be a hugely successful wine.

It is hard to pigeonhole the style of St.-Benoît since there are multiple cuvées, but with only a short history, my instincts suggest these wines tend to be made in a modern style, but with more intensity, richness, and potential longevity for the top two cuvées, Grande Garde and La Truffière, than most modern-style Châteauneuf du Papes offer. All things considered, this appears to be a promising newcomer to the hierarchy of quality Châteauneuf du Pape estates.

VINTAGES

1995—Châteauneuf du Pape Grande Garde (red)   The 1995 Grande Garde possesses a
  ·   saturated ruby/purple color, sweet, fragrant, attractive aromatics loaded with berry
  89   fruit, considerable body, potentially outstanding density, and a layered, rich, struc-
           tured feel. It is a forceful, broad-shouldered, muscular Châteauneuf du Pape meant
           to be cellared for 3–4 years. Anticipated maturity: 2000–2015. Last tasted 6/96.

1995—Châteauneuf du Pape Cuvée Elise (red)   The 1995 Cuvée Elise is made in an
  ·   overtly fruity style, with plenty of ripe black-cherry fruit, an easygoing, fat, round,
  86   generous, open-knit personality, low acidity, and a spicy, ripe finish. Anticipated
           maturity: now–2001. Last tasted 6/96.

1995—Châteauneuf du Pape Soleil et Festins (red)   The 1995 Soleil et Festins reveals
· good ripeness, medium to full body, fine purity, and a structured, lightly tannic
87 finish. Anticipated maturity: now–2003. Last tasted 6/96.

1995—Châteauneuf du Pape La Truffière (red)   Opaque purple, with extremely low acid-
· ity and high alcohol, the unctuous, creamy-textured, full-bodied 1995 La Truffière
92 possesses gobs of black-cherry and cassis fruit in its bouquet, thick, juicy, almost
sweet (from ripeness, not sugar) flavors, and a plump, hedonistic finish. Anticipated
maturity: now–2006. Last tasted 6/96.

1994—Châteauneuf du Pape Grande Garde (red)   Like the 1995, the 1994 Grande Garde
· is a classic, full-bodied Châteauneuf du Pape with layers of flavor and excellent
90 structure and spice. It exhibits a dark ruby color with purple nuances. The youthful
nose offers exuberant, vibrant, pure aromas of black cherries, raspberries, pepper,
and spice. Full-bodied and rich, with grip and tannin, this is a textbook Châteauneuf du Pape. Anticipated maturity: 1998–2010. Last tasted 6/96.

1994—Châteauneuf du Pape Cuvée Elise (red)   The 1994 Cuvée Elise exhibits a medium
· garnet color, an attractive, moderately intense nose of cherries and spice, and good
86 extraction and balance, but it tastes more evolved and less concentrated than it did
prior to bottling. It is an attractive Châteauneuf du Pape for near-term drinking.
Anticipated maturity: now–2001. Last tasted 6/96.

1994—Châteauneuf du Pape Soleil et Festins (red)   The 1994 Soleil et Festins offers up
· a fragrant, peppery, earthy, licorice, spicy, red-cherry-scented nose, as well as
87 medium body, and some tannin. A spicy *garrigue* character dominates the wine's
moderately well-endowed flavors. Anticipated maturity: now–2002. Last tasted
6/96.

1993—Châteauneuf du Pape Grande Garde (red)   The outstanding 1993 Grande Garde
· reveals that unmistakable Provençal nose of *garrigue*, crushed black pepper, sweet
90 black fruits (primarily cherries), and Asian spice notes in the background. Big,
forceful, and intense, this full-bodied, moderately tannic Châteauneuf du Pape is
highly extracted, rich, and in need of 3–5 years of cellaring. It may last for 20
years. Anticipated maturity: 1998–2012. Last tasted 6/96.

1993—Châteauneuf du Pape Cuvée Elise (red)   The 1993 Cuvée Elise exhibits a dark
· color, and a Pinot Noir–like nose of damp earth, black fruits, and floral notes.
86 Some tannin is noticeable on the palate, but this is a round, generous, richly fruity,
stylish Châteauneuf du Pape. Anticipated maturity: now–2001. Last tasted 6/96.

1993—Châteauneuf du Pape Soleil et Festins (red)   With fine color saturation, denseness,
· extraction, a sweet entry and mid-palate, and noticeable tannin in the finish, the
87 1993 Soleil et Festins will benefit from cellaring. Anticipated maturity: 1998–
2007. Last tasted 6/96.

1992—Châteauneuf du Pape Grande Garde (red)   The 1992 Grande Garde's aromatics
· display interesting spicy, peppery, black-cherry aromas, and the flavors are
86 medium- to full-bodied with adequate concentration, and moderate acidity and tannin. Anticipated maturity: now–2003. Last tasted 6/95.

1992—Châteauneuf du Pape Cuvée Elise (red)   The 1992 Cuvée Elise offers plummy
· fruit intertwined with scents of leather, pepper, and herbs. Round and medium-
84 bodied, with decent ripeness and moderate tannin, it is a straightforward, medium-
weight Châteauneuf du Pape. Mature now. Last tasted 6/95.

1992—Châteauneuf du Pape Soleil et Festins (red)   The 1992 Soleil et Festins has
· demonstrated bottle variation. When I tasted it in France it appeared to be a deep,
? rich, soft, straightforward wine made in a plump style. It was somewhat commercial,
but easy to understand and appreciate. Several bottles tasted this side of the
Atlantic were less concentrated and angular. Last tasted 6/95.

1990—Châteauneuf du Pape Grande Garde (red)   The 1990, an exceptionally rich, force-
·   ful, concentrated wine, was bottled unfined and unfiltered for the American im-
91   porter. The huge nose of black pepper, jammy fruit, tobacco, Provençal herbs, and
roasted meats is followed by a wine with great stature, good balance, and a muscular, rich finish. Anticipated maturity: now–2005. Last tasted 6/94.

1989—Châteauneuf du Pape (red)   The 1989's dark ruby/purple color is followed by a
·   wine with a spicy, black-cherry, and blackberry nose that displays evidence of new
88   oak aging in the vanillin notes. It is ripe and opulent in the mouth, with soft
tannins, plenty of glycerin, and a smooth, heady, alcoholic finish. Anticipated
maturity: now–2001. Last tasted 6/94.

DOMAINE DE ST.-SIFFREIN (CLAUDE CHASTAN)* * * *

Address: Route de Châteauneuf du Pape
        84100 Orange
Tel: 4-90-34-49-85
Wines produced: Châteauneuf du Pape (red)
Surface area: 42 acres
Production: 5,000 cases
Upbringing: no destemming; fermentation takes place in cement cuves for 18–20 days; the
        wine is then moved to wood foudres where it rests for 20–24 months
Average age of vines: 50 years
Blend: 70% Grenache, 12% Syrah, 10% Mourvèdre, 5% Cinsault, 1% Clairette, 1% Bour-
        boulenc, 1% Picpoul
Note: The few white wine grapes are blended in with the red wine.

This domaine has been in the Chastan family since its creation in 1880. It is located in
the northern part of the appellation on *galets roulés*. The wine is sold largely in Europe, but
the vintages I have seen since the early nineties have been powerful, full-throttle, dense
wines that are impressively constituted. In addition, they appear to be wines capable of
lasting 10–15 years.

VINTAGES

1995—Châteauneuf du Pape   The 1995 is impressively extracted, powerful, rich, and
·   dense, with gobs of fruit, as well as noteworthy tannin and acidity. This is a big,
89   deep, backward, rustic Châteauneuf du Pape that begs for 4–5 years of cellaring;
it should keep for 12–15 + years. If the acidity and tannin become better integrated, this will easily merit a 90-point score. Anticipated maturity: 1999–2008.
Last tasted 6/96.

1994—Châteauneuf du Pape   In bottle, the 1994 confirms the high quality I predicted
·   for it. The wine's deep dark ruby/garnet color is accompanied by an exotic, fragrant
88 +   nose of salty sea breezes, herbs, olives, *garrigue,* and jammy black cherries.
Medium- to full-bodied, with excellent richness, and a muscular, rustic, powerful
style, this burly, husky Châteauneuf du Pape needs cellaring. Anticipated maturity:
1998–2007. Last tasted 6/96.

1993—Châteauneuf du Pape   I have reservations about the saturated dark ruby/purple-
·   colored 1993 as it may be too tannic. Offering rich, black-cherry, chocolaty, herb-
87   scented fruit, the wine is full-bodied and concentrated, but extremely structured
and tightly knit. There is plenty of intensity, but the 1993 requires 5–6 years of
cellaring and should last for 15 + years. Let's hope the tannin melts away gracefully without any loss of fruit. Anticipated maturity: 2000–2007. Last tasted 6/96.

1990—Châteauneuf du Pape   I remember seeing this wine before bottling and was not
· that impressed with it because a mustiness pervaded its aromatics. However, since
87 bottling, the wine appears to have cleaned up its act. While it is not as impressive
as the vintage would suggest, this is a jammy, medium- to full-bodied, richly fruity
wine with high alcohol, low acidity, and a plump, ripe style. Anticipated maturity:
now–2003. Last tasted 6/96.

1989—Châteauneuf du Pape   The dark ruby/purple-colored 1989 is evolving at a glacial
· pace. The wine exhibits some earthy, black-cherry, pepper, and spice scents, rich,
90 expansive, chewy, full-bodied, unctuous flavors, and light to moderate tannin in
the long, lusty, high-alcohol finish. This wine is far more concentrated and delineated than the 1990. Anticipated maturity: now–2007. Last tasted 6/96.

DOMAINE DES SÉNÉCHAUX* * * *

Address: 3, rue de la Nouvelle Poste
            84230 Châteauneuf du Pape
Tel: 4-90-83-73-52
Fax: 4-90-83-52-88
Wines produced: Châteauneuf du Pape (red and white)
Surface area (white): 5 acres
            (red): 62 acres
Production (white): 600 cases
            (red): 5,500 cases
Upbringing (white): 6 months in stainless steel vats
            (red): 12–18 months in 10% new oak casks
Average age of vines (white): 40 years
            (red): 70 years
Blend (white): 40% Grenache Blanc, 40% Clairette, 20% Bourboulenc
            (red): 90% Grenache, 5% Syrah, 3% Mourvèdre, and 2% other varietals

At this ancient domaine winemaking can be traced back to the fourteenth century.
Sénéchaux, the Provençal word for "woods," is a 67-acre estate with all 13 permitted
varieties planted. Grenache is again dominant, accounting for 90% of the blend, with the
rest consisting of Mourvèdre, and a field blend.

This estate, which was in the Raynaud family, inhabitants of Châteauneuf du Pape since
the fourteenth century, was sold in 1993 to the Roux family, who are best known for their
Côtes du Rhône wines sold under the label Château du Trignon. From the old, traditional,
somewhat rustic style of wine made at Sénéchaux, there has been a complete transformation
to a more modern style, which is accessible but concentrated and appealing. I also suspect
the irregularity that existed under the previous administration will be eliminated under the
more careful viticulture and vinification of the Roux family.

While Pascal Roux has only produced three vintages, this would appear to be a medium-
weight, richly fruity, textbook Châteauneuf du Pape made to be drunk during its first 7–8
years of life.

VINTAGES

1995—Châteauneuf du Pape (red)   The 1995 Châteauneuf du Pape is made in an easygo-
· ing, up-front, fruity, peppery, smoky, herb-tinged, cherry-flavored style. This is a
87 soft, round, medium- to full-bodied style of wine. Anticipated maturity: now–2003.
Last tasted 6/96.

1994—Châteauneuf du Pape (red)   The 1994 displays a healthy dark ruby color, a sweet,
  ·   ripe, black-cherry, and smoked-herb-scented bouquet, sweet, round, seductive
  87   flavors, a voluptuous texture, low acidity, and a lush, herb-tinged, black-cherry
          finish with adequate levels of glycerin, extract, and alcohol. Anticipated maturity:
          now–2001. Last tasted 6/96.

1993—Châteauneuf du Pape (red)   The 1993, the first vintage made under Monsieur Roux's
  ·   regime, is a very fine Châteauneuf du Pape. It reveals the telltale peppery, *garrigue*,
  88   spicy, sweet, jammy, black-cherry fruit that defines the quality of a top red wine from
          Provence. Full-bodied, intense, supple, and accessible, this is a hedonistically styled
          Châteauneuf du Pape. Anticipated maturity: now–2001. Last tasted 6/95.

1990—Châteauneuf du Pape (red)   This slightly eviscerated, medium ruby-colored wine
  ·   appears to have been stripped at bottling. It offers a vague nose of herbs and fruit,
  79   medium to full body, dusty, coarse tannins, and some round, ripe fruit. A fragile
          wine, it should be drunk up. Mature now. Last tasted 6/94.

1989—Châteauneuf du Pape (red)   The 1989 is intensely concentrated, and a richer,
  ·   fuller wine than either the 1990 or 1988. It is low in acidity, and comes across as
  87   somewhat flabby, but there is plenty of fleshy, rich, peppery, cassis and black-
          cherry fruit, full body, and a soft, heady finish. Anticipated maturity: now–2000.
          Last tasted 6/94.

1988—Châteauneuf du Pape (red)   The fully mature, medium garnet-colored 1988 is
  ·   round and soft, and not as substantially proportioned as I might have thought given
  86   the vintage. Medium-bodied and fruity, it needs to be drunk up. Anticipated
          maturity: now–1999. Last tasted 6/94.

CHÂTEAU SIMIAN* * * *

Address: 84420 Piolenc
Tel: 4-90-29-50-67
Fax: 4-90-29-62-33
Wines produced: Châteauneuf du Pape (red and white)
Surface area (white): .5 acre
              (red): 10 acres
Production (white): 125 cases
              (red): 1,700 cases
Upbringing (white): malolactic blocked and aging in tank with early bottling
              (red): a traditional vinification with no destemming and 8–14 months in oak
                  foudres
Average age of vines: (white): 15 years
              (red): 45 years
Blend (white): 100% Clairette
        (red): 80% Grenache, 20% Syrah

This tiny estate of 10 acres, owned by Yves and Jean-Pierre Serguier, is beautifully
situated on the plateau behind the village, between the stony vineyards of Château Cabrières
and Château Mont Redon.

VINTAGES

1994—Châteauneuf du Pape (red)   The 1994 is an attractive, soft, well-endowed Châ-
  ·   teauneuf du Pape with plenty of *garrigue*, herbes de Provence, black-cherry fruiti-
  86   ness, low acidity, a round, savory mouth feel, good purity and ripeness, and a

peppery, alcoholic finish. It will not make old bones, but it is a pleasurable wine to drink over the next 5–7 years. Last tasted 6/96.

1993—Châteauneuf du Pape (red)   An impressive 1993 Châteauneuf du Pape was pro-
·   duced by Château Simian. The healthy dark ruby/purple color is accompanied by
88   aromas of overripe cherries and plums intertwined with scents of roasted Provençal herbs, chocolate, and spice. With a youthful, full-bodied mouth feel and excellent concentration, this wine has a plush, sweet, chewy entry and finish. Anticipated maturity: now–2004. Last tasted 6/96.

1990—Châteauneuf du Pape (red)   This 1990 Châteauneuf du Pape exhibits a moderately
·   intense bouquet of cherries and raspberries, with some vague aromas of Provençal
85   herbs in the background. In the mouth the wine displayed a spicy ripeness, medium- to full-bodied flavors, and a soft, up-front, precocious style. Anticipated maturity: now–2001. Last tasted 6/95.

1989—Châteauneuf du Pape (red)   The 1989 Châteauneuf du Pape possessed a good
·   ruby/purple color, an intense bouquet of hickory smoke, black cherries, and choco-
89   late. In the mouth the wine displayed fine ripeness, a generously endowed, opulent texture, and soft tannins in its heady, impressive finish. Drink it over the next 8–10 years. Last tasted 6/95.

1988—Châteauneuf du Pape (red)   The 1988 has a huge, fragrant, fruitcake sort of
·   bouquet, rich, intense, chewy, alcoholic flavors, a full-bodied, intensely concen-
89   trated feel on the palate, and a long, spicy, moderately tannic finish. It is as impressive as the 1989. Anticipated maturity: now–2003. Last tasted 6/95.

DOMAINE DE LA SOLITUDE (LANÇON)* * *

Address: Route de Bédarrides
        84230 Châteauneuf du Pape
Tel: 4-90-83-71-45
Fax: 4-90-83-51-34
Wines produced: Châteauneuf du Pape (red and white)
Surface area (white): 14.8 acres
             (red): 86 acres
Production (white): 1,850 cases
          (red): 15,000 cases
Upbringing (white): The Roussanne is fermented and aged in 100% new oak and the other varietals in stainless steel tanks for a total of 6 months; no malolactic; assemblage is done just before bottling in March or April following the harvest.
        (red): Fermentation of 18–25 days in cement and stainless steel tanks; 10% of the yield spends 6–8 months in new oak barrels, and the rest in stainless steel vats for 6–8 months; assembled and stored in stainless steel tanks until bottling.
Average age of vines (white): 30 years
                    (red): 40 years
Blend (white): 40% Grenache Blanc, 30% Roussanne, 20% Clairette, 10% Bourboulenc
      (red): 60% Grenache, 20% Syrah, 15% Mourvèdre, 5% Cinsault

This 197-acre domaine (100 acres in vine) has experimented with new oak, different grape varietals, and innovative vinification techniques. Proprietor Lançon was one of the first of the appellation to begin utilizing new oak barrels for both the white and red wines, with admittedly mixed results. Vintages from the sixties, which were made in a serious manner, were followed by a disappointing period of almost two decades when the wines were made by carbonic maceration, resulting in light, feeble, and characterless Châteauneuf du Pape. There appears to be a change for the better with recent releases from Lançon.

Domaine de la Solitude is one of Châteauneuf du Pape's most historic and ancient estates. It has been making wine continuously since 1604. Remarkably, La Solitude can prove that it did an estate bottling prior to the French Revolution, a fact whose significance stands out when one realizes that the first Lafite-Rothschild was not bottled until 1797, after the Revolution. Domaine de la Solitude was also the first Châteauneuf du Pape estate to export their offerings, selling wine to Austria and England in the nineteenth century.

With such a distinguished history it is hard to fathom what took place in this century during the seventies and most of the eighties, a period that saw a succession of pathetic wines that fell apart after 4–5 years in the bottle. However, Pierre Lançon, now helped by his sons, Jean and Michel, after experimenting widely, has begun to put more intensity into the wines. The result is a product much improved over what consumers would have found 10–15 years ago. Much of the vinification is no longer done by carbonic maceration, and the Lançons have increased the percentage of both Syrah and Mourvèdre in the final wine, cutting back on the Grenache, from a high of 80% to only 60%. The grapes are destalked, and a selection is done, with the best wine being sold as Domaine de la Solitude. New oak is still utilized, but because it has gained in concentration, the wine seems less oaky. No more than 15% of the red wine spends any time in new oak, and the rest is aged in the traditional foudres used throughout Châteauneuf du Pape. There is still too much fining and the ever-present filters at La Solitude, but under the younger generation, this estate is gradually moving toward producing a more substantial and intense modern-style Châteauneuf du Pape that can age for 10–12 years. No, the wines are still not comparable to the majestic Châteauneuf du Pape made here in 1967, 1964, and 1961, but at least there is a movement in that direction.

Domaine de la Solitude has immense potential as their vineyard is one of the rockiest in Châteauneuf du Pape. Moreover, it consists of one large parcel, rather than being morsellated with patches of vines sprinkled throughout the appellation. The entire clay/limestone soil base is covered with the ubiquitous *galets roulés*, which can often reach football size at La Solitude.

The white wine has been helped greatly by the addition of 30% Roussanne in the final blend. It is a fresh, lively wine with more body and honeyed notes than in the past. Like the red wine, it appears to be moving in a direction that offers more flavor and complexity. It is made under the modern school of winemaking, with malolactic blocked and bottling 3–4 months after the harvest.

Domaine de la Solitude is a solid three-star Châteauneuf du Pape estate, but with a little less manipulation and processing, this estate could easily return to its glory days of the fifties and sixties and once again become a five-star estate.

VINTAGES

1995—Châteauneuf du Pape (red) Proprietor Pierre Lançon has fashioned a fruity, rich,
· spicy, concentrated yet elegant 1995 Châteauneuf du Pape that is Burgundy-like
87 in its creamy, cherry flavors that reveal a hint of vanillin and spice. There is
adequate acidity, good richness, and fine equilibrium. Anticipated maturity: now–
2003. Last tasted 6/96.

1990—Châteauneuf du Pape (red) La Solitude's 1990 signals a partial return of this
· famous domaine to the forefront of Châteauneuf du Pape's finest producers. Dis-
90 playing an opaque black/ruby/purple color, an impressive vanillin, black-cherry,
and cassis-scented nose, and rich, robust, herblike flavors, this big, untraditional
style of wine was aged in small oak casks. It should drink well for 10–15 years.

This is the finest La Solitude since the fabulous 1964 and 1967. Last tasted 5/94.

1989—Châteauneuf du Pape (red)   The 1989 exhibits aromas of smoky new oak. On the
·   palate it displays wonderfully rich, tobacco-scented, raspberry fruit, medium to full
87   body, and a long, spicy, yet supple finish. Anticipated maturity: now–2003. Last
           tasted 5/94.

1988—Châteauneuf du Pape (red)   The attractive, fully mature 1988 is less concentrated
·   and flamboyant than the 1989. It exhibits a judicious use of smoky, toasty oak,
85   ripe, pleasant, chewy flavors, medium body, and a soft, attractive finish. It does not
           possess the aging potential of the 1989. Mature now. Last tasted 5/94.

Older Vintages

Just about anything produced from the early seventies through 1985 was made in a light, fruity Beaujolais style. Most of these vintages, even 1985, 1983, 1981, and 1978, began to fall apart within 4–5 years of the vintage. Should any of the glorious old Domaine de la Solitudes (1967, 1966, 1964, and 1961) show up in the auction market, readers should not hesitate to buy them, assuming they have been impeccably stored.

TARDIEU-LAURENT* * * *

This new négociant operation, run by the Rhône Valley's Michel Tardieu and Burgundy's Dominique Laurent, is dedicated to producing concentrated wines that are bottled with minimal intervention and extremely low levels of SO_2. Readers may be familiar with the name of Dominique Laurent as he has created a storm of controversy with his négociant cellars in Nuits St.-Georges. There he has garnered remarkable praise from consumers and wine writers for the concentration and naturalness of his wines. Investing in the southern Rhône Valley, with cellars in an ancient château in the beautiful hillside village of Loumarin, Laurent has teamed up with Michel Tardieu, who is responsible for finding cuvées of old-vine wines from various appellations. Their cellar in the Château Loumarin possesses one of the coldest underground caves in the southern Rhône. All of the wines are aged in small oak barrels. Since Laurent believes in extensive barrel aging, considerable lees contact, no fining or filtration, and minimal SO_2, most of these wines are expressive. None of the following wines had yet been bottled, but since they are bottled barrel by barrel, with no fining or filtration, these notes should be relatively reflective of the different qualitative levels.

VINTAGES

1995—Châteauneuf du Pape (red)   The superb 1995 Châteauneuf du Pape displays gobs
·   of black-raspberry, black-cherry, and herb-tinged fruit, good fat and glycerin, lofty
90   alcohol, and a ripe, chewy, structured finish. The wine is intensely concentrated,
           and obviously made from low-yielding, old vines. It will be accessible young.
           Anticipated maturity: now–2009. Last tasted 6/96.

1994—Châteauneuf du Pape (red)   I was very impressed with Tardieu-Laurent's 1994
·   Châteauneuf du Pape. Aged in 50% new oak casks, this is a structured, full-bodied,
90   richly concentrated Châteauneuf offering up copious amounts of black cassis fruit,
           a chewy texture, considerable power, and light tannin in the finish. Anticipated
           maturity: now–2006. Last tasted 6/96.

DOMAINE TERRE FERME (BÉRARD)* * *

Note: In 1991, this entire estate was sold to Château de la Nerthe. The following information is provided for historical purposes.

I shall never forget a luncheon I had with three dozen of Châteauneuf du Pape proprietors.

Presiding over this group, much like a godfather, was the boisterous, loud, loquacious Monsieur Bérard, the owner of Terre Ferme. In 1986 he sold part of his interest in the estate. Sadly, he passed away several years ago. In 1991, the balance of the estate was sold to La Nerthe. This was an underrated property in Châteauneuf du Pape. The cellars and vineyard were located near Vieux-Télégraphe in the eastern sector of the appellation. The blend for their flavorful yet very elegant red wine was 70% Grenache, 12% Syrah, 15% Mourvèdre, and 3% Cinsault. The Grenache and Cinsault were crushed and vinified classically, the Syrah and Mourvèdre vinified by the carbonic maceration method. The red wine spent up to 30 months in foudres and was given a light filtration prior to bottling. The white, also quite good, was made from 70% Grenache Blanc, 20% Bourboulenc, 3% Roussanne, and 7% Clairette.

Several vintages of the red Châteauneuf du Pape tasted from Terre Ferme have had an almost Volnay-like fruit and texture.

VINTAGES

1990—Châteauneuf du Pape (red)   From cask, I reported that Terre Ferme's 1990 Châteauneuf du Pape was a voluptuously styled, explosively rich, broad-shouldered
82   wine loaded with extraction and character. After bottling, which I fear was accomplished through an intense filtration, the color is significantly lighter, the nose straightforward and clipped, and the great depth that was apparent out of foudre is no longer present. The wine is pleasant in a medium- to full-bodied, soft, round, uninspiring manner. I suspect much of this wine's soul and character were left in the filter. Last tasted 6/94.

1989—Châteauneuf du Pape (red)   The 1989 has begun to close up, although the bouquet
does display some elements of overripeness, as suggested by its peach, apricot, and
88   jammy scents. In the mouth, there is a streak of herbaceousness, firm tannins, and plenty of ripe, unctuous fruit. This is a large-scaled yet backward Châteauneuf that needs 4–5 years in the cellar. Anticipated maturity: now–2010. Last tasted 6/95.

DOMAINE TRINTIGNANT* * *

Address: Place de la Fontaine
        B.P. 64
        84230 Châteauneuf du Pape
Tel: 4-90-83-73-23
Fax: 4-90-83-52-30
Wines produced: Châteauneuf du Pape (red and white)
Surface area (white): 3.5 acres
             (red): 15.8 acres
Production (white): 625 cases
           (red): 2,750 cases
Upbringing (white): fermentation and upbringing in temperature-controlled stainless steel
                vats for 3–4 months; malolactic is blocked
           (red): fermentation of 18–21 days in cement tanks where the wines stay for one
                month for malolactic; then 50% of the yield stays in vats and 50% goes
                into oak casks 3–4 years old and barrels for 1–6 months; numerous
                bottlings are done
Average age of vines (white): 30 years
                     (red): 50 years
Blend (white): 35% Grenache Blanc, 35% Roussanne, 20% Clairette, 10% Picpoul
      (red): 70% Grenache, 15% Syrah, 10% Cinsault, 5% Mourvèdre

This tends to be a midweight, fruity, appealing style of Châteauneuf du Pape that is meant to be drunk within the first 5–8 years of the vintage. From time to time, several different cuvées are offered, one called La Reviscoulado (named after an old farm), and another cuvée that is meant to be the richer wine, La Réserve de Vigneron. Much of this estate's wine is sold directly to European clients, and I get the impression that proprietor Jean-Philippe Trintignant continues to experiment with his winemaking (note the 1989 Cuvée Fut Neuf). The vinification is traditional, with no destemming, and a standard 2- to 3-week maceration, followed by an upbringing in wood foudres.

A small quantity of white wine is also produced, which seems to have gotten better over recent years with the addition of Roussanne in the blend.

VINTAGES

1990—Châteauneuf du Pape (red)   The 1990 regular cuvée of red Châteauneuf du Pape
•   exhibits aromas of *surmaturité,* or jammy, cherry, apricot and peach-flavored fruit.
86   In the mouth, it is a long, fat, chewy, luscious, thick wine without much finesse. I
      would opt for drinking it over the next decade. Last tasted 6/95.

1989—Châteauneuf du Pape Fut Neuf (red)   The 1989 Cuvée Fut Neuf was bottled with
•   no fining or filtration. It is a blockbuster. A black/purple-colored Châteauneuf du
89   Pape oozing with roasted cassis fruit, it is full-bodied, highly extracted, and pos-
      sesses moderate tannin levels that are amazingly well concealed by the gobs of
      extract. Anticipated maturity: now–2003. Last tasted 6/94.

1989—Châteauneuf du Pape La Reviscoulado (red)   The 1989 La Reviscoulado is ex-
•   tremely forward and supple, a bit commercial in style, but deeply flavored, and
85   ideal for drinking over the next 5–6 years. Last tasted 6/94.

JEAN-PIERRE USSEGLIO* * *

Address: Route d'Avignon
            84700 Sorgues
Tel: 4-90-39-58-10
Wines produced: Châteauneuf du Pape (red and white)
Surface area (white): 2.47 acres
                (red): 29.6 acres
Production (white): 250 cases
                (red): 4,400 cases
Upbringing (white): 3 months in temperature-controlled stainless steel vats
                (red): 30–36 months total; fermentation of 15–20 days in cement vats where the
                    wine remains for malolactic, then wines spend 2 years minimum in old
                    oak casks
Average age of vines (white): 35 years
                (red): 55 years
Blend (white): 30% Grenache Blanc, and equal portions of Bourboulenc, Clairette, and
                Picpoul
                (red): 75–80% Grenache, 10% Syrah, 10% Cinsault, Mourvèdre, and others

The Usseglio family is almost Burgundian in its multiple families and estates. Jean-Pierre produces wines very similar to Pierre Usseglio—full-bodied, traditional, alcoholic, rich, chunky, textbook Châteauneuf du Papes. Virtually his entire production is sold direct to European clients. I have tasted only two vintages, 1990 and 1989, and both tasted similar to those of Pierre Usseglio. All three Usseglios share the same oenologist, Monsieur Lauriol, and their vinification and upbringing techniques are virtually identical. This is undoubtedly another fine source for traditional Châteauneuf du Pape.

PIERRE USSEGLIO* * *

Address: Route d'Orange
84230 Châteauneuf du Pape
Tel: 4-90-83-72-98
Wines produced: Châteauneuf du Pape (red and white)
Surface area (white): 2.47 acres
(red): 32 acres
Production (white): 350 cases
(red): 5,000 cases
Upbringing (white): 3–4 months in temperature-controlled stainless steel vats
(red): fermentation of 15 days in cement vats; then for malolactic wines remain in tanks for 4 months, followed by 18 months in oak casks
Average age of vines (white): 20 years
(red): 40 years
Blend (white): equal portions of Grenache Blanc, Clairette, and Bourboulenc
(red): 70% Grenache, 20% Syrah, 10% Mourvèdre, Cinsault, and Muscardin

Perhaps the only difference between the wines of Pierre Usseglio and Jean-Pierre Usseglio is that Pierre still sells a percentage of his crop to négociants, especially his white wine production. The red wines are made like those of the other Usseglios, but are aged completely in small oak casks rather than foudres. These are full-bodied Châteauneuf du Papes to drink within their first decade of life.

RAYMOND USSEGLIO* * * *

Address: Route de Courthézon
84230 Châteauneuf du Pape
Tel: 4-90-83-71-85
Fax: 4-90-83-50-42
Wines produced: Châteauneuf du Pape (red and white), Châteauneuf du Pape Cuvée Vieilles Vignes (red)
Surface area (white): 2.47 acres
(red): 37 acres
Cuvée Vieilles Vignes—2.47 acres
Production (white): 350 cases
(red): 4,200 cases
Cuvée Vieilles Vignes—250 cases
Upbringing (white): fermentation in temperature-controlled stainless steel tanks and upbringing in stainless steel tanks for 5–6 months
(red): fermentation of 21 days in cement and epoxy vats; then two and a half months in cement vats for malolactic, followed by 16–24 months in oak casks; 3–4 bottlings
Cuvée Vieilles Vignes—same as for the regular red wine cuvée
Average age of vines (white): 30 years
(red): 50 years
Cuvée Vieilles Vignes—90 years
Blend (white): equal parts of Grenache Blanc, Clairette, Bourboulenc, and Roussanne
(red): 75% Grenache, 15% Syrah, 10% Mourvèdre
Cuvée Vieilles Vignes—95% Grenache, 5% Cinsault

Of the three Usseglios, Raymond produces the richest and fullest wines. His traditionally made Châteauneuf du Pape exhibits plenty of the *garrigue,* herbes de Provence character in its smoky, jammy, cherry flavors. Usseglio looks for some degree of overripeness and produces a juicy, plump, chewy style of Châteauneuf du Pape that can drink well for a decade.

A tiny quantity of white wine is made, but I have never encountered a bottle. Usseglio also makes a very small quantity of Cuvée Vieilles Vignes, but, again, I have never seen it. He claims it is made only in certain years, and no more than 250 cases are produced, all of it sold directly to his best clients in Europe.

VINTAGES

1995—Châteauneuf du Pape (red)   Rarely do I have an opportunity to taste the wines of
·   Raymond Usseglio, but I admire this producer, who sells much of his production
89   to private clients and merchants in western Europe. The dense ruby/purple-colored
1995 Châteauneuf du Pape tastes accessible with its display of flashy black-cherry fruit and spice. Full-bodied, rich, and intense, with zesty acidity and moderate tannin, this wine has not yet begun to exhibit the aromatic components displayed by the 1994. Anticipated maturity: 1999–2009. Last tasted 6/96.

1994—Châteauneuf du Pape (red)   The 1994 Châteauneuf du Pape is reflective of the
·   traditional, old-style vinification practiced by Usseglio. A muscular, full-bodied,
90   powerfully extracted wine, it is vaguely reminiscent of such wines as those pro-
duced by Pegau and Henri Bonneau. It displays a seaweed, spicy, cedar, iodine/ peppery nose, and rich, full-bodied flavors exhibiting thick, unctuously textured fruit. There is also an underbrush, herbes de Provence/*garrigue* component to this rustic wine's flavors. Anticipated maturity: now–2007. Last tasted 6/96.

1990—Châteauneuf du Pape (red)   I immensely admired Usseglio's 1990 red Châ-
·   teauneuf du Pape, which is typical of the big, opulent, high-alcohol, lusty style of
88   wine that requires consumption in its first 7–8 years of life. The huge nose of
jammy red and black fruits, roasted nuts, black olives, and spices is a real turn-on. In the mouth, there are gobs of sweet, succulent fruit, low acidity, at least 15% alcohol, and a gutsy, chewy, fiery finish. It is not a Châteauneuf du Pape for the timid, but it does provide immense satisfaction in an up-front, precocious manner. Anticipated maturity: now–2003. Last tasted 4/95.

CHÂTEAU VAUDIEU (MEFFRE)* * *

Address: 84230 Châteauneuf du Pape
Tel: 4-90-83-70-31
Fax: 4-90-83-51-97
Wines produced: Châteauneuf du Pape (red and white)
Surface area (white): 25 acres
             (red): 148 acres
Production (white): 3,750 cases
             (red): 22,500 cases
Upbringing (white): 3–4 months with 10% of the yield in new oak casks and 90% in
             stainless steel vats
        (red): 24 months total in underground stainless steel vats; 20% of the yield
             spends 4–5 months in old oak casks; the wines are then assembled before
             bottling
Average age of vines (white): 25 years
             (red): 30–40 years

Blend (white): 60% Grenache Blanc, 20% Roussanne, 10% Clairette, 10% Picardan and Bourboulenc

(red): 80% Grenache, 10% Syrah, 5% Mourvèdre, 5% Cinsault

If it were not for the majestic glory of Château de la Nerthe, Vaudieu would be Châteauneuf du Pape's most celebrated "real" château. Vaudieu's history dates from 1767, when construction of the château was begun by the Gerini family from Florence. The gorgeous château cannot be seen from the road. The best way of approaching it is to take D 68 north toward Orange and take the first righthand turn as you clear the village. The château sits just south of the Rayas vineyard. Another way is to take the road to Courthézon (D 92) and look for the sign for Château Vaudieu.

This estate tends to produce a modern-style red wine, but the light, Beaujolais-like wines of the seventies and early eighties have given way to richer, more complete and substantial wines. The Meffre family, a well-known family with extensive property holdings throughout the southern Rhône, have run this estate since 1953. They should be commended for improving the quality over recent years. This fruity, midweight Châteauneuf du Pape requires drinking within five to seven years of the vintage. The grapes are completely destemmed, and the wine is given more processing and filtering than necessary, but security is one of the primary objectives at Vaudieu.

VINTAGES

1995—Châteauneuf du Pape (red)   This modern-styled 1995 is well made, fruity, ripe,
· and best enjoyed within 5–7 years of the vintage. Cut from the same mold as the
86 1994, the 1995 Châteauneuf du Pape exhibits more density, fuller body, and more color. Anticipated maturity: now–2002. Last tasted 6/96.

1994—Châteauneuf du Pape (red)   Readers will no doubt find the 1994 Châteauneuf du
· Pape an attractively spice, herb, cherry, and pepper-scented wine with good body
86 and ripeness, and a rich, mouth-filling character. Anticipated maturity: now–2001. Last tasted 6/96.

1990—Châteauneuf du Pape (red)   Although this estate has a tendency to stylize their
· wines according to the tenets of high-tech winemaking, there is no question that
87 the 1990 has come through its manufacturing process with significant charm and appeal. The color is a brilliant, polished medium ruby, and the largely intact nose offers gobs of sweet black-raspberry fruit. In the mouth, this full-bodied, hedonistic wine offers opulent, chunky, jammy black fruits, low acidity, a lush, chewy texture, and heady levels of alcohol and glycerin in the long, chewy finish. Although not the most complex Châteauneuf du Pape, one has to admire its abundant, even lavish quantities of fruit. Anticipated maturity: now–2000. Last tasted 6/94.

1989—Châteauneuf du Pape (red)   The 1989 Vaudieu is full-bodied, rich, clean, some-
· what straightforward, with an attractive fat, fleshy character, but lacking complexity
85 and individuality. It will provide pleasurable drinking. Anticipated maturity: now–2000. Last tasted 6/94.

1988—Châteauneuf du Pape (red)   The fully mature 1988, which reveals some amber at
· the edge, is robust and medium-bodied, with a spicy, peppery, jammy, cassis
85 bouquet, soft tannins, and low acidity. Mature now. Last tasted 6/96.

Older Vintages

Even such great years as 1978 and to a lesser extent 1981 were wines meant to be drunk in their first 5–6 years of life. Anything older than 7–8 years is likely to be in serious decline.

VIDAL-FLEURY* * *

Address: R.N. 86
     69420 Ampuis
Tel: 4-74-56-10-18
Fax: 4-74-56-19-19

Note: This is a négociant wine made from purchased juice that is aged in large foudres.

The name Vidal-Fleury evokes the northern Rhône, particularly Côte Rôtie. However, this négociant has been a longtime producer of well made and reasonably priced Châteauneuf du Pape.

VINTAGES

1992—Châteauneuf du Pape (red)   This is a disappointingly vegetal, thin, lean, and
·   hollow 1992 Châteauneuf du Pape. Last tasted 6/96.
74

1990—Châteauneuf du Pape (red)   A slightly fuller-bodied, opulent, powerful 1990, this
·   chewy, fully mature, low-acid wine is excellent. Anticipated maturity: now–2002.
89   Last tasted 6/95.

1989—Châteauneuf du Pape (red)   The dark ruby-colored 1989 Châteauneuf du Pape is
·   hard, tannic, and medium- to full-bodied. It is a very good to excellent, firmly
87   structured wine that should evolve well. Anticipated maturity: now–2004. Last
     tasted 6/95.

1988—Châteauneuf du Pape (red)   Vidal-Fleury's 1988 Châteauneuf du Pape is as good
·   as their tasty 1985, with plenty of ripe black-cherry and raspberry fruit, a nice,
86   spicy, peppery nose, and a full-bodied, alcoholic finish. It lacks some complexity,
     but it is an attractive, robust, chunky wine. Anticipated maturity: now–2000. Last
     tasted 9/94.

1985—Châteauneuf du Pape (red)   This is a wonderfully pure, beefy, rich, full-bodied,
·   juicy wine with peppery, spicy fruit, soft tannin, and low acidity. Anticipated
86   maturity: now–1999. Last tasted 9/94.

DOMAINE DE LA VIEILLE JULIENNE (ARNAUD-DAUMEN)* * * *

Address: Le Grès
     84100 Orange
Tel: 4-90-34-20-10
Fax: 4-90-34-10-20
Wines produced: Châteauneuf du Pape (red and white), Châteauneuf du Pape Cuvée
     Réservée
Surface area (white): 1 acre
     (red): 27 acres
Production (white): 185 cases
     (red): 4,400 cases total (much is sold in bulk)
     Vieille Julienne—2,500 cases
     Cuvée Réservée—65–250 cases

Upbringing (white): Vinifications for the Clairette (picked rather overripe) are carried out in new oak barrels; the other varietals are vinified in enamel tanks; no malolactic; bottling after 4 months; assemblage is done 1 month before bottling.

(red): Fermentation of 3 weeks at an average temperature of 28° centigrade, except for the last 5–6 days when it is allowed to rise to 33° centigrade in order to ensure better extraction of tannins. This process is carried out in enameled cement vats. The wines then spend 12–18 months, with one-third in new oak barrels, one-third in oak casks, and one-third in tanks; some fining but no filtration; only one bottling is done.

Cuvée Réservée—Same as for the regular red wine cuvée, except that all the wine is put in new oak barrels for 12–18 months.

Average age of vines (white): 40 years

(red): 55 years

Cuvée Réservée—70 years, with some 100-year-old vines

Blend (white): equal parts Grenache Blanc, Clairette, and Bourboulenc

(red): 60% Grenache, 15% Syrah, 10% Mourvèdre, 10% Counoise, 5% Cinsault

Cuvée Réservée—40% Grenache, 30% Syrah, 15% Counoise, 15% Mourvèdre

This has been an interesting estate to follow. When I first tasted the wines more than a decade ago, they were frustratingly irregular, at best, the quintessentially old, heavy, black-colored mode of Châteauneuf du Pape. However, there was a casual approach to winemaking, as well as bottling, with some vintages spending 7–10 years in large foudres, and bottled as they were sold. The finest wines were enormous in body, high in alcohol, and tannic, but not always harmonious examples of winemaking. In fact, they could be outrageously rustic. At other times, the wines were thin and diluted.

Much has changed since Jean-Paul Daumen took over for his father in 1990. The cellars have been cleaned up, and all the red wine is now being aged in foudres. The old practice of leaving all the stems on has given way to 100% destemming. Additionally, the multiple bottlings have been replaced by a single bottling per vintage, and, if possible, the wines are not filtered. A secondary label, Grangette des Grès, for young vines and cuvées deemed not rich enough to be bottled under the Vieille Julienne name, has also been created. In fact, everything here appears to be set for a bright future, if Mother Nature cooperates.

The property and cellars are located in the northern part of the appellation, in the sector known as Le Grès. Named after the Julienne family that developed the vineyard in the seventeenth century, this estate is poised to move into the top echelon of Châteauneuf du Pape, primarily because of the enthusiasm and commitment to quality exhibited by Jean-Paul Daumen.

VINTAGES

1995—Châteauneuf du Pape (red) Although the deep ruby-colored 1995 Châteauneuf du Pape exhibits good tannin, fruit, and color, as well as more acidity than the 1994, it possesses a monolithic, foursquare character. I look for more character to develop. Anticipated maturity: 2000–2007. Last tasted 6/96.

·

86 +

1994—Châteauneuf du Pape (red) La Vieille Julienne's 1994 Châteauneuf du Pape reveals an exotic, coffee, herb, chocolaty, spicy nose, sweet, round, seductive, black-cherry fruit, low acidity, and a plump, fleshy finish. It is a soft, easygoing wine. Anticipated maturity: now–2002. Last tasted 6/96.

·

86

1994—Châteauneuf du Pape Cuvée Réservée (red)   The 1994 Cuvée Réservée (to my
· knowledge, this is the first old-vine cuvée produced at this estate) possesses toasty
90 vanillin notes from new oak casks, as well as gobs of sweet, chocolate, cherry,
herb, olive, and coffeelike aromas. The hickory and jammy black-cherry flavors
offer significant extract, glycerin, and power. This is a bold, rich, chewy, dense,
slightly rustic, but impressively endowed Châteauneuf du Pape. Anticipated maturity: 1997–2007. Last tasted 6/96.

1993—Châteauneuf du Pape (red)   The light-bodied 1993 Châteauneuf du Pape exhibits
· a nose with scents of roasted nut and berry fruit, but the wine's lack of concentra-
82 tion is obvious on the palate. Anticipated maturity: now–2000. Last tasted 6/96.

1990—Châteauneuf du Pape (red)   The 1990 displays a chocolate, smoke, cassis-scented
· nose, and peppery, rich, powerful, full-bodied flavors that are oozing extract, glyc-
89+ erin, and tannin. It is impressive for its size and potential longevity. The overbearing, coarse, sometimes volatile, dirty style that characterized so many older vintages
from this domaine is, fortunately, a thing of the past. Anticipated maturity: now–
2007. Last tasted 6/95.

1989—Châteauneuf du Pape (red)   The 1989 is a massive, quintessential, old-style Châ-
· teauneuf du Pape with huge, chewy, enormously extracted flavors that resemble
90 grilled meat and wild game. It is sensationally ripe, yet nearly overbearing because of
its concentration and rustic style. It will make a great bottle of Châteauneuf du Pape
for drinking in the cold of winter. Anticipated maturity: now–2008. Last tasted 6/95.

Older Vintages

Older vintages of La Vieille Julienne can be problematic. The bottling was often dragged
out over 6–8 years, and the property was incredibly inconsistent, hitting the bull's-eye with
some vintages, and failing miserably with others. The one terrific old vintage worth checking
out is the 1978, an overwhelmingly rich, tannic wine that will keep for 30 years.

LE VIEUX DONJON (LOUIS MICHEL)* * * * *

Address: 9, avenue St.-Joseph
      84230 Châteauneuf du Pape
Tel: 4-90-83-70-03
Fax: 4-90-83-50-38
Wines produced: Châteauneuf du Pape (red and white)
Surface area (white): 2.47 acres
          (red): 30 acres
Production (white): 600 cases
          (red): 4,200 cases
Upbringing (white): 3–4 months in temperature-controlled stainless steel vats
          (red): fermentation of 18–21 days in cement vats; then 2 months in cement
              tanks for malolactic; then 2 years minimum in oak casks before bottling
Average age of vines (white): 6 years
          (red): over 75% of the vines are 80–90 years
Blend (white): equal parts Clairette, Roussanne, and Grenache Blanc
      (red): 80% Grenache, 10% Syrah, 10% Mourvèdre and Cinsault

This is one of the great unheralded estates of Châteauneuf du Pape. It is a relatively new
creation, having been founded after the marriage of Lucien Michel and Marie Jose in 1979.
The 32.5 acres include many old vines, with 25 acres of the estate possessing vines over 80
years of age, all on the plateau near Mont Redon and Les Cabrières (the sector covered with

the famed *galets roulés*). In 1990, the Michels planted one hectare with equal parts of Clairette, Roussanne, and Grenache Blanc, from which they have begun to make a fruity, dry white Châteauneuf du Pape. However, the real glory from this estate is their majestic red wine.

The red wine is put through a traditional vinification, with no destemming, a relatively long maceration, and—perhaps the biggest factor of all—low yields from ancient vines. Moreover, the wine is one of the handful in Châteauneuf du Pape to be bottled with no fining or filtration. The modest, enthusiastic Michels farm their vineyard organically, harvest much later than most in Châteauneuf du Pape (except for Henri Bonneau and Jacques Reynaud), and let the wine make itself. The upbringing in wood casks can last for two years before the first bottling. The only criticism that can be made of Vieux Donjon is that they bottle as the wine is sold. At this estate that is less of a problem since virtually the entire harvest is now being sold as soon as it is ready to bottle, eliminating the tendency to bottle the wine over a long period of time.

Vieux Donjon wines are some of the great classics of the appellation, and are very long-lived. The estate has been remarkably consistent in lighter years. Moreover, prices have remained essentially stable for almost a decade!

VINTAGES

1995—Châteauneuf du Pape (red)   The 1995 Châteauneuf du Pape displays an opaque
· purple color, followed by a pungent, fragrant nose of overripe black cherries, sweet
91 barbecue smoke, roasted herbs, and meats, and an enthralling chocolaty, cherry
component. Thick, unctuous, and powerful, with layers of flavor, this wine is obviously made from extremely ripe fruit and low yields. These wines are bottled with neither fining nor filtration. Anticipated maturity: 2000–2015. Last tasted 6/96.

1994—Châteauneuf du Pape (red)   The opaque dark ruby/purple-colored 1994 Châ-
· teauneuf du Pape exhibits a fabulous nose of sweet, jammy black cherries, raspber-
91 ries, smoke, and a vague hint of licorice and Provençal herbs. Full-bodied, with excellent concentration, power, and a sweet, expansive, chewy mid-palate, this is an outstanding example of Châteauneuf du Pape from what continues to be the most underrated great estate of the appellation. Anticipated maturity: now–2010. Last tasted 6/96.

1993—Châteauneuf du Pape (red)   The 1993 is one of the top wines of the vintage.
· The healthy, impressive, opaque dark ruby/purple color is accompanied by rich,
90 concentrated, superripe scents and flavors (blackcurrants, cherries, licorice, herbs, chocolate, and coffee). Approachable now, this wine is presented in a full-bodied, supple, beautifully proportioned style, reflecting flawless winemaking. Anticipated maturity: 1998–2009. Last tasted 6/96.

1992—Châteauneuf du Pape (red)   The 1992 Châteauneuf du Pape is excellent for the
· vintage. One of the deepest-colored 1992s, it possesses a surprisingly saturated
88 color, an attractive, ripe nose of cassis fruit, Provençal herbs, and cedar, sweet, expansive, attractively endowed flavors, full body, low acidity, and light tannin. It should provide seductive drinking for at least a decade. Last tasted 6/96.

1990—Châteauneuf du Pape (red)   The black/ruby-colored 1990 is the best Châteauneuf
· du Pape I have tasted from this estate. It is extremely powerful and concentrated,
93 with a sensational nose of Provençal herbs and jammy black-cherry and cassis fruit. Powerful and full-bodied, with exceptional intensity, this wine smells and tastes of old vines and low yields. Anticipated maturity: now–2010. Last tasted 8/96.

1989—Châteauneuf du Pape (red)   The impressive 1989 is opaque dark ruby/purple-
· colored, with a tight but ripe nose of cassis, black cherries, herbs, and licorice, this
91 superbly balanced, highly extracted wine exhibits layer upon layer of ripe fruit,

brilliant clarity and definition to its flavors, and a long, moderately tannic finish. Anticipated maturity: now–2008. Last tasted 8/96.

1988—Châteauneuf du Pape (red)　The elegant 1988 is lighter than the 1989, with a
·　　 lovely berry-scented bouquet intertwined with aromas of herbs and coffee. In the
87　　 mouth it is medium- to full-bodied, richly fruity, but seems to fall short of having the flavor dimension and impressive constitution of the 1989. Anticipated maturity: now–2002. Last tasted 11/95.

1985—Châteauneuf du Pape (red)　The fully mature 1985 is good, but like many wines
·　　 of that vintage, it is somewhat monolithic and foursquare without the richness,
86　　 exuberance, and definition of the 1990. Although a successful wine, it has no place to go, as its amber/orange rim and the mature nose of pepper, spice, old leather, and cherry fruit confirm. Last tasted 1/96.

1983—Châteauneuf du Pape (red)　Again the hallmark of this wine, like the other wines
·　　 from Vieux Donjon, is a healthy, deep color and heaps of the rich plummy fruitiness
89　　 that gives a suggestion of Pomerol. Deep ruby-colored with some amber, and more tannic than the 1985, this fully mature, full-bodied wine shows excellent balance and depth. Anticipated maturity: now–2000. Last tasted 12/95.

1981—Châteauneuf du Pape (red)　The nose of jammy raspberry fruit explodes from the
·　　 glass of this dark garnet-colored wine. Very deep, concentrated, seductively opu-
90　　 lent and luxuriant flavors fill the mouth. Smooth and velvety, but balanced, this wine has reached full maturity, but it displays no signs of losing its fruit. It is another high-class, distinctive wine from Vieux Donjon. Anticipated maturity: now–2000. Last tasted 11/95.

VIEUX LAZARET (JÉROME QUIOT)* */* * *

Address: Avenue Baron Le Roy
　　　　 84230 Châteauneuf du Pape
Tel: 4-90-83-73-55
Fax: 4-90-83-78-48
Wines produced: Châteauneuf du Pape (red and white)
Surface area (total): 212.5 acres
Production (white): 3,600 cases
　　　　　 (red): 27,500 cases
Upbringing (white): Vinified in a modern manner, with malolactic fermentation blocked. The wine is sterile-filtered prior to bottling.
　　　　　 (red): Occasionally destemmed, but vinified traditionally with an upbringing in tank and foudre for 12–14 months.
Average age of vines (white): 16 years
　　　　　 (red): 35 years
Blend (white): 49% Grenache Blanc, 29% Bourboulenc, 18% Clairette, 4% Roussanne
　　　 (red): 75% Grenache, 15% Syrah, 5% Cinsault, 1% Mourvèdre, 1% Terret Noir, 1% Counouis, 1% Muscardin, 1% Vaccarèse

One of the strongest proponents of the fruity, simple, modern style of Châteauneuf is Vieux Lazaret, a large property owned by Jérome Quiot and family. Quiot, an important personality in the southern Rhône, as well as in the appellation system in France, believes that the wines should be drunk within 4–5 years as "no one really cellars wine anymore." His white wine is relatively neutral, but the red wine can be counted on for immediate drinkability in a supple, berry fruit, medium-bodied style. Offering immediate gratification, these wines are obviously meant to exploit the commercial side of Châteauneuf du Pape.

DOMAINE DU VIEUX-TÉLÉGRAPHE (HENRI BRUNIER)* * * * *

Address: 3, route de Châteauneuf du Pape
      84360 Bédarrides
Tel: 4-90-33-00-31
Fax: 4-90-33-18-47
Wines produced: Châteauneuf du Pape (red and white), Vieux Mas des Papes (red)
Surface area (white): 12.4 acres
      (red): 111 acres
          Vieux Mas des Papes—62 acres
Production (white): 1,800 cases
      (red): 17,000 cases
          Vieux Mas des Papes—3,200 cases
Upbringing (white): 8 months total. Fermentation of 1 month with 80% of the yield in temperature-controlled stainless steel vats and 20% of the yield in oak barrels 3–5 years old. After fermentation, assemblage is done and the wines are returned to stainless steel vats for their upbringing; there is no oak aging and the wines are bottled after 8 months.
      (red): 24 months total. Fermentation of 12–15 days in stainless steel vats; then 12 months in cement vats and another year in old oak casks. Bottling is done all at one time directly from cask without any fining or filtering.
      Vieux Mas des Papes—18 months total. Fermentation of 12 days in stainless steel vats, then one year in stainless steel, followed by 6 months in oak casks. Bottling is done all at one time without any fining or filtering.
Average age of vines (white): 35 years
      (red): 55 years
          Vieux Mas des Papes—25 years
Blend (white): 40% Clairette, 30% Grenache Blanc, 15% Roussanne, 15% Bourboulenc
      (red): 70% Grenache, 15% Syrah, 5% Cinsault, 10% other varietals
          Vieux Mas des Papes—100% Grenache

Vieux-Télégraphe is unquestionably one of Châteauneuf du Pape's most famous estates. It was named after a telegraph tower erected on the property in 1792 by Claude Chappe (the inventor). No doubt the large production from the estate's 180-acre vineyard accounts for the effective distribution of this wine throughout the world's finest wine circles. Owned by the Brunier family since the early part of this century, Vieux-Télégraphe has one of the most privileged terroirs of Châteauneuf du Pape. Along with the two famous estates on the plateau of Châteauneuf du Pape, Mont Redon and Les Cabrières, Vieux-Télégraphe's vineyard is considered to possess one of the finest microclimates and vineyards. Located in the eastern section of the appellation, in an area covered with large, football-sized *galets roulés*, the entire vineyard is in a sector known as La Crau. Vieux-Télégraphe's vineyards enjoy an extremely hot microclimate, enabling the Bruniers to harvest 7–10 days before many other estates in the appellation. Their early harvest is largely responsible for the property's success in years where other estates have failed (e.g., 1993).

For most of the latter part of the twentieth century, the fortunes of Vieux-Télégraphe were guided by Henri Brunier, whom I first met in the late seventies. Gregarious, open, and always tanned and well-chiseled (another vigneron with more than a vague similarity to the appellation's old, gnarled vines), Brunier retired in the late eighties, turning over the operation of Vieux-Télégraphe to his two capable sons, Daniel and Frédéric. Everything I have seen since these two enthusiastic young men have taken over suggests that Vieux-Télégraphe is pushing the envelope of quality to an even higher level.

From the old vineyards (the average age of the vines is 40 years, with one-third an impressive 60 years of age) emerges a wine made from a traditional blend of 60–70% Grenache, 15–18% Syrah, 15–18% Mourvèdre, and a tiny dollop of Cinsault. Since the two brothers have taken over there has been an effort made to decrease the percentage of Grenache and use slightly more Syrah and Mourvèdre. Yields are always conservative, with 30 hectoliters per hectare being the norm.

The winemaking style of Vieux-Télégraphe did go through a metamorphsis of sorts when the sparkling new cuverie was constructed in 1979. In my 1987 book on the wines of the Rhône Valley, I lamented the fact that Vieux-Télégraphe's winemaking style had moved away from their textbook, classic, ageworthy, thick, burly Châteauneuf du Papes best exemplified by the magnificent 1978 and excellent 1972, to a more modern, fruity style that was immensely appealing but lacked the longevity of the pre-1979 vintages. That style has gradually been refined, with most of the changes occuring in the nineties. A second wine, Vieux Mas des Papes, (named after the residence of Daniel) was introduced in 1994. This 100% Grenache Châteauneuf du Pape is made from younger vines. In 1994, the estate introduced a Cuvée Spéciale, bottled only in magnum, from a blend containing a high percentage of Mourvèdre. Very little of this wine was produced, and the Bruniers have adamantly insisted that this wine is only to be tasted with friends or wine-tasting professionals. It will not be commercialized. Another apparent change is that since the late eighties, Vieux-Télégraphe has been bottled unfiltered. The Bruniers had been doing several filtrations, a Kisselguhr filtration after malolactic, and a prebottling filtration. The latter has been eliminated for fear of losing too much extract and body.

From a vinification perspective, the wines are impeccably handled. The Bruniers are flexible regarding destemming, never removing the stems from their old-vine Grenache, but destemming the young-vine Grenache, as well as a hefty percentage of the Mourvèdre and Syrah. The wines never see any new oak, but they are vinified and raised in spotless stainless steel tanks buried in a hill underneath the famed Autoroute de Soleil. After eight to ten months in tanks, the wines are moved to large wooden foudres until deemed ready for bottling. Nearly 20,000 cases of Vieux-Télégraphe are made, and several thousand cases of the second wine, Vieux Mas des Papes. There are also about 1,000 cases of a white Châteauneuf du Pape, a blend of Clairette, Grenache Blanc, Roussanne, and Bourboulenc. This wine has had its ups and downs, but it is usually one of the finest white wines of the appellation, displaying a moderately intense, floral, citrusy, fruity bouquet. However, like most of the nonmalolactic white Châteauneuf du Papes, it is best drunk in its first two years of life.

The question that remains is whether Vieux-Télégraphe ever produced a wine of the profound stature of the 1978. Even with the flirtation with a lighter style during the eighties, those wines have held up, proving that Vieux-Télégraphe can produce wines of surprising richness and longevity. However, nothing produced in the eighties can match the extraordinary intensity and majestic richness and complexity of the 1978. In the nineties, I thought the 1994 and 1995 were the finest wines made at this estate since the 1978. The style of Vieux-Télégraphe is one that appeals to both neophytes and connoisseurs of Rhône Valley wines, and this renowned estate has achieved its worldwide popularity the hard way—it has earned it.

VINTAGES

1995—Châteauneuf du Pape (red)   The 1995 Châteauneuf du Pape continues Vieux-
  ·   Télégraphe's surge in quality. It possesses riper fruit, a deeper purple color, and
  93   similar unctuosity, sweetness, and suppleness. A glorious nose of roasted meats,
          licorice, Provençal herbs, and gobs of jammy black fruits (cherries and plums) is

followed by a thick, full wine with high glycerin, good acidity, and a moderately tannic finish. It should prove to be another great Châteauneuf du Pape. Anticipated maturity: now–2009. Last tasted 6/96.

1995—Châteauneuf du Pape Vieux Mas des Papes (red)   Vieux-Télégraphe has begun to
·   produce a second cuvée, keeping their oldest vines for the estate's *grand vin*. The
88   second wine, Vieux Mas des Papes, is supple, rich, and ideal for drinking within
the first 7–8 years of life. The excellent 1995 exhibits gobs of sweet licorice, Provençal herb, and jammy black-cherry fruit. This ripe, plump, low-acid wine possesses a velvety texture as well as an alcoholic finish. Although not complex, it represents a delicious, jammy mouthful of pure fruit. Anticipated maturity: now– 2005. Last tasted 6/96.

1994—Châteauneuf du Pape (red)   The 1994 Châteauneuf du Pape is an outstanding
·   success. The color is a healthy dark purple, and the nose offers up copious quanti-
92   ties of jammy, sweet, black cherries, licorice, smoke, pepper, and herbs. It is
full-bodied, with superb purity, a layered, concentrated mid-palate, and an opulent, thick, rich finish. In spite of its size, the wine does not come across as heavy or overly alcoholic (although the alcohol is well above 14%). This is a rich, thick, juicy, succulent yet structured Châteauneuf du Pape that may be the finest wine made at this estate since their unreal 1978. Anticipated maturity: now–2009. Last tasted 6/96.

1994—Châteauneuf du Pape Cuvée Prestige (red)   Only 100 magnums of the Cuvée
·   Prestige (the final name is yet to be determined) will be produced. Made from 50%
95   Grenache, 30% Mourvèdre, and 20% Syrah, it represents the estate's oldest vines,
ranging from 50 to 80+ years. Although the wine possesses Vieux-Télégraphe's massive richness of fruit, it is atypical because of its firm, powerful, tannic struc- ture. The elevated percentage of Mourvèdre will require owners of this wine to be patient. It is a far less flattering wine to drink than the 1994 regular Châteauneuf. The opaque purple-colored Cuvée Prestige tastes like a hypothetical blend of a great Bandol from the likes of Domaine Pradeaux and Beaucastel's Hommage à Jacques Perrin. A mammoth wine of enormous richness, it will need 8–10 years of cellaring after its release (presumably in 1996). Last tasted 6/96.

1993—Châteauneuf du Pape (red)   In 1993, Vieux-Télégraphe was able to harvest virtu-
·   ally all of its crop at sugar levels that produced a wine of 14% alcohol. The
90   outstanding 1993 reveals an impressively saturated dark ruby/purple color, and a
spicy, Provençal herb, pepper, black-cherry and raspberry-scented nose with a touch of licorice. Full-bodied, with firm tannin and structure (reminiscent of the 1989), as well as layered richness, this Châteauneuf du Pape has 10–15 years of aging potential. Last tasted 8/96.

1993—Châteauneuf du Pape Vieux Mas des Papes (red)   This 1993 is the inaugural
·   cuvée of Vieux-Télégraphe's second wine, Vieux Mas des Papes. The Brunier
88   family is committed to raising the first wine's level of intensity. In order to accom-
plish that, they are making a second wine from Vieux-Télégraphe's younger vines. There are 2,500 cases of this 100% Grenache cuvée. The dark ruby/purple color is followed by an impressive wine exhibiting gobs of black fruits and glycerin. Expansive and round on the palate, there is no noticeable harshness, and a mouth- filling, full-bodied, exuberant finish. It is all that a full-bodied, velvety-textured Châteauneuf du Pape should be. Drink it over the next 7–8 years. Last tasted 6/96.

1992—Châteauneuf du Pape (red)   The 1992 Vieux-Télégraphe is an excellent example
·   from this average to slightly above-average vintage. The wine reveals a medium to
86   dark ruby color, a spicy, herb, and black-cherry-scented nose, medium- to full-
bodied, expansive flavors that possess an attractive sweetness and lushness, low

acidity, and a ripe, corpulent, heady finish. Drink it over the next 5–7 years. Last tasted 12/95.

1991—Châteauneuf du Pape (red)   Herbaceous, vegetal, peppery aromas dominate this
·   meagerly endowed, medium-weight wine that reveals some attractive cherry fruit,
76   but comes across as skinny and emaciated. Over the next several years, it will lose what little baby fat it possesses and dry out. Last tasted 12/95.

1990—Châteauneuf du Pape (red)   I have had several outstanding bottles of this wine,
·   but in most tastings this wine just misses meriting top marks. It is full-bodied,
90   alcoholic, and fleshy, with plenty of Vieux-Télégraphe's telltale nose of herbs, olives, black pepper, iodine, and sweet, jammy fruit. Soft, round, and generous, the 1990 should be drunk over the next 7–8 years. Last tasted 12/95.

1989—Châteauneuf du Pape (red)   This wine is performing better than it did early in
·   life. It could use more extract, but it is an excellent, spicy Vieux-Télégraphe with
88   sweet, jammy, tobacco, olive, fruitcake, and cherry aromas and flavors. Full-bodied and velvety textured, with chewy glycerin, this plush, savory wine should be drunk over the next 5–6 years. Last tasted 12/95.

1988—Châteauneuf du Pape (red)   More structured, tannic, and backward than the open-
·   knit 1989 and 1990, the 1988 Vieux-Télégraphe exhibits a healthy dark ruby color
87   and a subdued but spicy nose of red and black fruits, earth, and Provençal herbs. Medium- to full-bodied, restrained but concentrated, this should turn out to be a long-lived Vieux-Télégraphe, lasting through the first 5–6 years of the next century. It is less flattering to drink than either the 1989 or 1990, so readers may want to drink the two younger vintages while waiting for the 1988 to soften. Last tasted 12/95.

1987—Châteauneuf du Pape (red)   The 1987 comes across as skinny, even anorexic,
·   when compared to the 1988 and 1989. It has decent fruit, an underlying, intense,
78   vegetal, peppery streak, and finishes short on the palate. On its own, it is quite quaffable, but when you taste it in the company of the 1988 and 1989, it appears to be distinctly second-rate and uninteresting. Last tasted 3/93.

1986—Châteauneuf du Pape (red)   As these tasting notes suggest, Vieux-Télégraphe's
·   performance during the eighties was consistent—rarely disappointing, but, lamen-
86   tably, not reaching the highest standards of the appellation. Nineteen eighty-six is the youngest vintage to reveal amber and rust hues at the edge. A seaweedlike, smoky, herb, and olive-scented nose is followed by an austere, medium- to full-bodied wine that is just beginning to shed its fruit and reveal signs of losing its balance. I would opt for consuming it over the next 2–3 years. Last tasted 12/95.

1986—Châteauneuf du Pape (white)   A splendidly perfumed bouquet of tropical fruit and
·   floral scents is gloriously appealing. Lovely, ripe, rich fruit fills the mouth with this
90   unctuous, full-bodied wine. Mature now. Last tasted 2/87.

1985—Châteauneuf du Pape (red)   A consistently delicious example of Vieux-
·   Télégraphe, this spicy, fruity, exuberant, flamboyant wine is full-bodied, juicy, and
88   succulent. Although it lacks the extra dimension of flavor and complexity necessary to merit an outstanding score, it consistently provides a pleasing, mouth-filling glass of textbook Vieux-Télégraphe. Drink it over the next 2–3 years. Last tasted 12/95.

1985—Châteauneuf du Pape (white)   Now beginning to fade, the 1985 was superb in
·   October 1986, but three months later the fruit had begun to come out, proving just
87   how important it is to drink these wines very, very young. Last tasted 2/87.

1984—Châteauneuf du Pape (red)   A strong effort, the 1984 Vieux-Télégraphe is deep in
·   color, loaded with spicy, peppery, berry fruit, quite full-bodied for the vintage, but
86   more elegant and significantly less alcoholic than the full-throttle 1985. Mature now. Last tasted 12/86.

1983—Châteauneuf du Pape (red)   One of the top successes for this property during a
·   period of very good rather than outstanding winemaking, the 1983 is spicy, pep-
90   pery, and earthy, with a fragrant, in-your-face aromatic profile. This full-bodied,
          corpulent, muscular Vieux-Télégraphe is one of the few wines made during the
          estate's high-tech period that displays some of the old, burly, thick character of
          pre-1979 vintages. Some amber/orange is creeping along the edge, but the wine
          reveals no loss of fruit. This fully mature wine should last another 4–5 years. Last
          tasted 12/95.

1982—Châteauneuf du Pape (red)   Fully mature, the 1982 is quite high in alcohol, but
·   manages to deliver enough plump, succulent, ripe fruit to keep the wine from
85   tasting hot and unbalanced. Drink it up. Last tasted 10/86.

1981—Châteauneuf du Pape (red)   Another strong effort from Vieux-Télégraphe that falls
·   just short of being outstanding, the 1981 is full-bodied, soft, and velvety, with
89   considerable amber at the edge of its color. The high alcohol is beginning to
          nudge through the chewy, fleshy fruit. The wine is a gutsy, spicy, peppery, mature
          Châteauneuf du Pape that should be consumed before the end of the century. Last
          tasted 12/95.

1980—Châteauneuf du Pape (red)   Soft, unctuous, fruity flavors, full body, and an inter-
·   esting scent of herbs and salty seaweed make for an intriguing concoction of
84   aromas. This is fully mature and should be drunk up. Last tasted 6/86.

1979—Châteauneuf du Pape (red)   The first vintage made in the estate's new production
·   facility, the 1979 has aged well. The wine retains its youthful exuberance, as well
87   as plenty of the telltale seaweed, iodine, fruitcake, spicy, jammy fruit, medium to
          full body, an austerely structured underpinning, and a clean, crisp, peppery finish.
          It is a very good, though monolithic example of Vieux-Télégraphe. Drink it over
          the next 4–5 years. Last tasted 12/95.

1978—Châteauneuf du Pape (red)   I am almost embarrassed to say I have drunk nearly
·   four cases of this compelling and remarkably consistent wine, none of which was
96   less than spectacular (nor was any bottle ever corked)! The 1978 Vieux-Télégraphe
          remains a benchmark for the heights Châteauneuf du Pape can attain. The color
          remains an opaque dark ruby/garnet with no amber or rust. The huge nose of
          underbrush *(garrigue)*, pepper, black fruits, truffles, and smoked meats is sensa-
          tional. On the palate the wine exhibits the thickness, viscosity, and extraordinary
          extraction of a classically great vintage, as well as good structure, a youthful
          exuberance, and immense flavor concentration and intensity. This wine was bottled
          unfiltered, and as a result, close to 2 ounces are lost despite careful decanting.
          This remains the quintessential Vieux-Télégraphe. I have high hopes that the 1994
          is a movement back in this direction. The 1978 has been fully mature since the
          mid-eighties, but there is no hurry to consume it as it will last for another 10+
          years. A classic. Last tasted 12/95.

Older Vintages

Based on a tasting done in 1994, the once extraordinary 1972, 1971, and 1967 have begun
to fade.

DOMAINE DE VILLENEUVE* * *

Address: Route de Courthézon
            84100 Orange
Tel: 4-90-51-61-22
Wines produced: Châteauneuf du Pape, Châteauneuf du Pape Cuvée Vieilles Vignes (red)
Surface area: 21.5 acres

Production: 3,125 cases
Upbringing: Traditional, with no destemming and aging in foudre and tank.
Average age of vines: 40 years
Blend: 75% Grenache, 5% Syrah, 5% Roussanne, 5% Cinsault, and 10% miscellaneous varietals

This is a relatively recent creation, although the Domaine de Villeneuve can trace its origins to the late nineteenth century. Under proprietor Madame Veuve Arnoux, this wine has only been estate-bottled since 1987. Situated in the northern part of the appellation, not far from Orange, there are three vineyard parcels, all on what is referred to as the sector of Le Grés. The vinification is traditional, and based on the three vintages I have tasted, the wines are impressive. This looks to be a powerful, old-style Châteauneuf du Pape that is meant to be a vin de garde.

VINTAGES

1995—Châteauneuf du Pape Cuvée Vieilles Vignes   The 1995 Cuvée Vieilles Vignes is
· an impressive offering. Although still in barrel, this blockbuster, opaque-colored,
91 rich Châteauneuf du Pape possesses superb raw materials. In addition to its terrific color, the wine exhibits a blossoming nose of truffles, smoked herbs, and black fruits. It is highly extracted, powerful, and rich, with moderate tannin in the long finish. This wine reveals all the components necessary for something special. I'll keep my fingers crossed that it is bottled without excessive fining and/or filtration that will eviscerate the aroma, flavor, and body. Anticipated maturity: 1999–2010. Last tasted 6/96.

1994—Châteauneuf du Pape Cuvée Vieilles Vignes   The 1994 Cuvée Vieilles Vignes
· (which was perplexing when tasted last year) is now in bottle, and I am pleased to
87 + say it is a very good, possibly excellent, Châteauneuf du Pape. It possesses a dark ruby/purple color, a rustic, earthy, black-raspberry-scented nose, medium to full body, good purity and ripeness, an attractive, sweet palate, and moderate tannin in the long, rustic finish. It requires 1–2 years of cellaring, after which it will drink well for 7–8 years. Last tasted 6/96.

1993—Châteauneuf du Pape Cuvée Vieilles Vignes   The 1993 is a young, grapy, mono-
· lithic style of Châteauneuf du Pape with excellent purity, and gobs of sweet black
88 + fruit, but its extremely youthful personality has not yet begun to reveal any complexity. One of the youngest-tasting 1993s, it displays impressive color saturation, full body, and plenty of extract. If more delineation and complexity evolve, this wine will merit an outstanding rating. It is a candidate for 10–15 years of cellaring. Last tasted 6/96.

OTHER CHÂTEAUNEUF DU PAPE PRODUCERS

COMTE D'ARGELAS

Address: 9 et 11, rue de la République   Tel: 4-90-83-74-01
84230 Châteauneuf du Pape   Fax: 4-90-83-50-93

This négociant firm makes a selection of wines in each appellation and the labels bear both the trademark "Comte d'Argelas" and the producer's name and address. Their selection in Vacqueyras is called Domaine de Fontavin; in Gigondas, Domaine des Paillières; in Tavel, Domaine de Roc Epine; in Lirac, Domaine Devoy; and in Muscat de Beaumes de Venise, the Cave Coopérative.

DOMAINE LA BASTIDE ST.-DOMINIQUE

Address: 84350 Courthézon
Tel: 4-90-70-85-32
Wines produced: Châteauneuf du Pape (red and white)
Surface area 19.8 acres
Production (white): 312 cases
    (red): 2,000 cases
Upbringing: no destemming and aging in tank and foudre
Average age of vines: 50 years
Blend: (white): 40% Grenache Blanc, 40% Clairette, 20% Bouboulenc
  (red): 70% Grenache, 10% Syrah, 10% Mourvèdre, 5% Cinsault, 5% Clairette

DOMAINE DE LA BISCARELLE

Address: Quartier du Grès
   84100 Orange
Tel: 4-90-34-64-71
Wines produced: Châteauneuf du Pape (red)
Surface area: 10 acres
Production: 1,700 cases
Upbringing: 24–36 months total; fermentation and storage in cement tanks followed by 12–18 months in oak casks
Average age of vines: 30 years
Blend: 90% Grenache, 10% Cinsault

DOMAINE DE BOIS LAUZUN

Address: Route de Ste.-Cécile
   84830 Sérignan
Tel: 4-90-70-01-60
Wines produced: Châteauneuf du Pape (red)
Surface area: 5 acres
Production: 625 cases (only 225 estate-bottled)
Upbringing: 36 months total; fermentation of 13–20 days in cement tanks; then 24 months in old oak casks, followed by storage in stainless steel vats until bottling
Average age of vines: 30–40 years
Blend: 90% Grenache, 10% Cinsault

CHÂTEAU DU BOIS DE LA GARDE

Address: 1, avenue Baron Le Roy
   84230 Châteauneuf du Pape
Tel: 4-90-83-73-10
Fax: 4-90-83-50-78
Wines produced: Châteauneuf du Pape (red)
Surface area: 153 acres
Production: 35,000 cases
Upbringing: 6–12 months total; fermentation of 20 days in stainless steel vats; then 6 months in oak casks; followed by storage in cement, stainless steel, and epoxy vats until bottling
Average age of vines: 45–50 years
Blend: 55% Grenache, 15% Syrah, 10% Cinsault, 10% Mourvèdre and Carignan, and the remainder various varietals

CLOS DES BRUSQUIÈRES

Address: 15, rue Vieille Ville
        84230 Châteauneuf du Pape
Tel: 4-90-83-74-47
Wines produced: Châteauneuf du Pape (red)
Surface area: 14.8 acres
Production: 2,500 cases
Upbringing: 24–36 months total; fermentation of 20 days in cement tanks; then 24 months
        in old demi-muids; storage in cement and enamel vats prior to bottling
Average age of vines: 30–40 years and 80–100 years
Blend: 80% Grenache, 10% Syrah, 5% Mourvèdre, 5% other varietals

CLOS DES MARQUIS

Address: 23, avenue St.-Joseph
        84230 Châteauneuf du Pape
Tel: 4-90-83-52-74
Fax: 4-90-83-52-75
Wines produced: Châteauneuf du Pape (red and white)
Surface area (white): 1.9 acres
        (red): 11 acres
Production (white): 320 cases
        (red): 1,625 cases
Upbringing (white): fermentation in temperature-controlled enamel vats for a minimum of 4
        months; no malolactic fermentation
        (red): 24 months total; fermentation of 15–21 days in cement vats; then one-
        third of the yield spends 9–12 months in old oak casks, and the rest stays
        in stainless steel tanks; after assemblage, storage in stainless steel tanks
        until bottling
Average age of vines (white): 30 years
        (red): 50–100 years
Blend (white): Equal parts Grenache Blanc, Bourboulenc, and Clairette
        (red): 80% Grenache, 10% Syrah, 10% other varietals

CLOS ST.-ANDRÉ

Address: 4 et 6, avenue Général de Gaulle
        84230 Châteauneuf du Pape
Tel: 4-90-83-72-26
Fax: 4-90-83-53-85
Wines produced: Châteauneuf du Pape (red)
Surface area: 49 acres
Production: 8,700 cases
Upbringing: 24–30 months total; fermentation of 15–20 days in stainless steel vats; then
        12–24 months in oak casks; storage in stainless steel vats until bottling
Average age of vines: 50 years
Blend: 70% Grenache, 15% Mourvèdre, 10% Syrah, 5% other varietals

DOMAINE DE LA CÔTE DE L'ANGE

Address: Quartier de la Font du Pape
        84230 Châteauneuf du Pape
Tel: 4-90-83-72-24
Fax: 4-90-83-54-88
Wines produced: Châteauneuf du Pape (red and white)

Surface area (white): 2.47 acres
            (red): 25 acres
Production (white): 375 cases
            (red): 3,750 cases
Upbringing (white): 6 months in cement tanks
            (red): 24 months total; fermentation of 15 days in cement vats; then 18 months
                in old oak casks, followed by storage in cement tanks until bottling
Average age of vines (white): 30 years
                      (red): 30 years
Blend (white): equal parts of Grenache Blanc, Clairette, and Bourboulenc
      (red): 75% Grenache, 10% Syrah, 15% Mourvèdre and Cinsault

DOMAINE LA CRAU DES PAPES
Address: Route de Courthézon
        84230 Châteauneuf du Pape
Tel: 4-90-83-72-39
Fax: 4-90-83-53-01
Wines produced: Châteauneuf du Pape (red)
Surface area: 56 acres
Production: 10,000 cases
Upbringing: 12 months total; fermentation of 3 weeks in cement tanks, where the wine
        remains until it is bottled, within 1 year
Average age of vines: Some young, and some as old as 100 years
Blend: 85% Grenache, 10% Syrah, 5% Cinsault and Mourvèdre

DELAS FRÈRES
Address: Z. A. de l'Olivet
        B.P. 4
        07300 St.-Jean de Muzols
Tel: 4-75-08-60-30
Fax: 4-75-08-53-67

Delas Frères produces approximately 3,000 cases of Les Hauts Pierres and 3,000 cases of Les Calcerniers. These wines are brought into the Delas cellars only for bottling. They are vinified and brought up by a team of suppliers.

LA FAGOTIÈRE
Address: Domaine de Palestor
        84100 Orange
Tel: 4-90-34-51-81
Fax: 4-90-51-04-44
Wines produced: Châteauneuf du Pape (red)
Surface area: 49 acres
Production: 7,500 cases
Upbringing: 24 months total; fermentation of 3 weeks in cement and enamel vats; then
        12–18 months in oak casks, followed by storage in stainless steel vats until
        bottling
Average age of vines: 30–50 years and older
Blend: 70% Grenache, 7% Cinsault, 7% Mourvèdre, 1% Syrah, 1% Clairette, 0.5%
        Counoise, and the rest other varietals

CHÂTEAU DE FONTAVIN

Address: 1468, route de la Plaine
        84350 Courthézon
Tel: 4-90-70-72-14
Fax: 4-90-70-79-39
Wines produced: Châteauneuf du Pape (red)
Surface area: 25 acres
Production: 4,000 cases
Upbringing: 24 months total; fermentation of 15 days in stainless steel vats; then 20% of
        the yield goes into 3-year-old oak barrels for 6 months, and the rest is stored
        in cement tanks; assemblage just prior to bottling
Average age of vines: 50 years, with the oldest 100 years
Blend: 70% Grenache, 30% Syrah

DOMAINE DE FUSAT

Address: 20, avenue des Oliviers
        B.P. 14
        84230 Châteauneuf du Pape
Tel: 4-90-83-73-58
Fax: 4-90-83-75-55
Wines produced: Châteauneuf du Pape (red)
Surface area: 50 acres
Production: 6,250 cases
Upbringing: 12 months total; fermentation of 3 weeks in stainless steel and cement vats;
        then 6–12 months in old oak casks; no storage before bottling

DOMAINE GIMOND

Address: La Désirade
        Quartier du Bosquet
        84230 Châteauneuf du Pape
Tel: 4-90-83-73-49
Wines produced: Châteauneuf du Pape (red)
Surface area: 10.4 acres
Production: 1,500 cases
Upbringing: 24 months total; fermentation of 3 weeks in enamel vats; then 6–12 months in
        old oak casks; storage in enamel vats until bottling
Average age of vines: 40 years
Blend: 80% Grenache, 20% Mourvèdre and Cinsault

DOMAINE PIERRE GIRAUD

Address: Avenue Impériale
        84230 Châteauneuf du Pape
Tel: 4-90-83-73-49
Fax: 4-90-83-52-05
Wines produced: Châteauneuf du Pape Cuvée des Gallimardes (red and white)
Surface area (white): 3.7 acres
        (red): 49 acres
Production (white): 500 cases
        (red): 7,500 cases
Upbringing (white): 6 months in enamel tanks
        (red): 24 months total; fermentation of 21 days in enamel and cement tanks;
        then 6–12 months in old oak casks

Average age of vines (white): 10 years
                      (red): 60–70 years
Blend (white): Equal parts Grenache Blanc, Bourboulenc, Roussanne, and Clairette
       (red): 80% Grenache, 10% Syrah, 5% Mourvèdre, 5% Cinsault

CHÂTEAU DE HUSSON

Address: 2031, chemin des Stes.-Vierges
         84350 Courthézon
Tel: 4-90-33-02-96
Fax: 4-90-33-16-82
Wines produced: Châteauneuf du Pape (red and white)
Surface area (white): 8.6 acres (only 5 acres in production)
             (red): 52 acres
Production (white): 685 cases
           (red): 7,500 cases (only 625 cases, from the oldest vines, are estate-bottled)
Upbringing (white): 2–3 months in stainless steel vats
           (red): 24–36 months total; fermentation of 15–20 days in temperature-
               controlled stainless steel vats; assemblage is done after malolactic and
               the yield then spends 5–6 months in old oak casks; storage in cement
               vats until bottling
Average age of the vines (white): 10 years
                         (red): 70–80 years
Blend (white): 70% Grenache Blanc, 20% Clairette, 10% Bourboulenc
       (red): 70–75% Grenache, 5% Cinsault, the rest Syrah and Mourvèdre

DOMAINE ALAIN JACUMIN

Address: Le Moulin à Vent
         84230 Châteauneuf du Pape
Tel: 4-90-83-73-58
Fax: 4-90-83-75-55
Wines produced: Châteauneuf du Pape (red)
Surface area: 25 acres
Production: 2,875 cases
Upbringing: 12 months total; fermentation of 3 weeks in stainless steel and cement vats;
           then 6–12 months in oak casks
Average age of vines: 40 years
Blend: 65% Grenache, 12% Mourvèdre, 10% Syrah, 6% Cinsault, the rest various varietals

DOMAINE DE LA JAUFRETTE

Address: Chemin de la Gironde
         84100 Orange
Tel: 4-90-34-35-34
Wines produced: Châteauneuf du Pape (red)
Surface area: 6.2 acres
Production: 875 cases
Upbringing: 3–4 years total; fermentation of 18–21 days in cement vats; then 6–8 months
           in old oak casks and barrels; storage in epoxy vats until bottling
Average age of vines: 50 years
Blend: 99% Grenache, 1% other varietals

MAS CHANTE MISTRAL

Address: 1880, route de Caderousse
        84230 Châteauneuf du Pape
Tel: 4-90-70-72-65
Wines produced: Châteauneuf du Pape (red)
Surface area: 30 acres, but only 1.2 acres are used for bottling purposes
Production: 3,000 bottles, most of which is sold in bulk
Upbringing: 12 months total; fermentation of 15–20 days in stainless steel vats; then 6
            months in oak barrels 3–4 years old, followed by storage in stainless steel vats
            until bottling
Average age of vines: 40 years
Blend: 70% Grenache, 15% Cinsault, 15% Mourvèdre

CHÂTEAU DU MONT THABOR

Address: Le Mont Thabor
        84370 Bédarrides
Tel: 4-90-33-16-21
Fax: 4-90-33-00-04
Wines produced: Châteauneuf du Pape (red)
Surface area: 10 acres
Production: 1,500 cases
Upbringing: 10–24 months total; fermentation of 15 days in cement vats; then 12 months in
            cement vats before going into old oak barrels for 6 months; bottling is done
            without fining or filtration
Average age of vines: 70 years
Blend: 80% Grenache, 15% Syrah and Mourvèdre, 5% Cinsault

DOMAINE DU MOULIN BLANC

Address: 3026 Tavel
Tel: 4-78-34-25-06
Fax: 4-78-34-30-60
Wines produced: Châteauneuf du Pape (red)
Surface area: 3.2 acres
Production: 500 cases
Upbringing: 12 months total; with 6 months in oak casks
Average age of vines: 9 years
Blend: 80% Grenache, 20% Syrah

FABRICE MOUSSET

Address: 84230 Châteauneuf du Pape
Tel: 4-90-83-73-10
Fax: 4-90-83-74-79
Wines produced: Châteauneuf du Pape (red and white)
Surface area: 10 acres
Production (white): 875 cases
            (red): 875 cases
Upbringing (white): cold-fermented with malolactic blocked; sterile-filtered and bottled in
                January following the vintage
            (red): 6–18 months in foudres and tanks; 70% of the grapes are destemmed
Average age of vines: 5 years
Blend (white): equal parts Roussanne, Bourboulenc, Grenache Blanc, Clairette
        (red): 80% Grenache, 20% Mourvèdre

OGIER ET FILS

Address: La Grande Marine
        Avenue Louis Boudin
        B.P. 64
        84800 L'Isle-sur-la-Sorgue

This huge négociant produces a Châteauneuf du Pape (among other Rhône Valley wines) that I have always found cooked and uncharacteristic of the appellation.

DOMAINE PERGES

Address: 8, avenue St.-Joseph
        84230 Châteauneuf du Pape
Tel: 4-90-83-71-34
Wines produced: Châteauneuf du Pape (red)
Surface area: 19.8 acres
Upbringing: no destemming; aged in tanks and foudres for a year before bottling
Average age of vines: 40 years
Blend: 75% Grenache, 10% Muscardin, 10% Mourvèdre, 5% other varietals

RÉSERVE DES DIACRES

Address: Quartier des Terres Blanches
        84230 Châteauneuf du Pape
Tel: 4-90-83-70-84
Wines produced: Châteauneuf du Pape (red and white)
Surface area (white): .7 acre
           (red): 30 acres
Production (white): 185 cases
           (red): 2,850 cases
Upbringing (white): vinified at a cold temperature, with malolactic blocked, and bottled
        within 3–4 months of the vintage
        (red): made without destemming in cuves and then moved to large old oak
        foudres for 6–12 months
Average age of vines (white): 20 years
           (red): 60 years
Blend (white): equal parts Grenache Blanc, Clairette, and Bourboulenc
        (red): 80% Grenache, 10% Cinsault, 10% Mourvèdre and Syrah

DOMAINE ST.-GAYAN

Address: Le Trignon
        84190 Vacqueyras
Tel: 4-90-65-90-33
Fax: 4-90-65-85-10
Wines produced: Châteauneuf du Pape (red)
Surface area: 1.8 acres
Production: 300 cases
Upbringing: 30 months total, with 12 months in old oak barrels and casks
Average age of vines: 50 years
Blend: 90% Grenache, 10% Syrah, Cinsault, and Mourvèdre

DOMAINE ST.-LAURENT

Address: 1375, chemin de St.-Laurent
        84350 Courthézon

Tel: 4-90-70-87-92

Fax: 4-90-70-78-49

Wines produced: Châteauneuf du Pape (red and white)

Surface area (white): 1.2 acres

         (red): 6.2 acres

Production (white): 250 cases

         (red): 1,000 cases

Upbringing (white): vinification and upbringing in enamel vats for 12 months; malolactic fermentation is not blocked

         (red): 18–24 months total; fermentation of 15–20 days in cement or stainless steel tanks; then 20% of the yield spends 12–18 months in new oak barrels and the rest remains in enamel tanks; storage in stainless steel vats until bottling

Average age of vines (white): 25 years

         (red): 25–30 years

Blend (white): 80% Clairette, 20% Roussanne and Bourboulenc

   (red): 90% Grenache, 10% Syrah

DOMAINE DE ST.-PAUL

Address: B.P. 58

       84230 Châteauneuf du Pape

Tel: 4-90-83-70-28

Fax: 4-90-83-78-07

Wines produced: Châteauneuf du Pape (red)

Surface area: 32 acres

Production: 4,375 cases

Upbringing: 20 months total; fermentation of 20 days in stainless steel vats; then 12 months in 3-year-old oak barrels, followed by storage in stainless steel vats until bottling

Average age of vines: 25 years

Blend: 80% Grenache, 20% equal portions of Syrah, Cinsault, and Muscardin

CHÂTEAU ST.-ROCH

Address: 30150 Roquemaure

Tel: 4-66-82-82-59

Fax: 4-66-82-83-00

Wines produced: Châteauneuf du Pape (red)

Surface area: 4.2 acres

Production: 560 cases

Upbringing: 42 months total, fermentation in stainless steel vats, then 18 months in oak casks and 6 months in oak barrels, followed by storage in stainless steel vats until bottling

Average age of vines: 60 years

Blend: 90% Grenache, 10% other varietals

DOMAINE DE VALORI

Address: Domaines Meffre

Wines produced: Châteauneuf du Pape (red)

Surface area: 19.8 acres

Production: 3,000 cases

Upbringing: 2 years minimum in stainless steel and cement vats

Average age of vines: 30–35 years

Blend: 80% Grenache, 20% Syrah

GIGONDAS

Hearty, Robust Wines
for a Cold Winter's Night

GIGONDAS AT A GLANCE

Appellation created:	January 6, 1971.
Type of wine produced:	Red wine represents 97% of the production. The only other wine permitted is rosé.
Grape varieties planted:	Grenache, Syrah, Mourvèdre, and Cinsault are the dominant varietals.
Acres currently under vine:	2,569.
Quality level:	Average to exceptional.
Aging potential:	5–15 years.
General characteristics:	A robust, chewy, full-bodied, rich, generous red wine; light, vibrant, fresh, underrated rosé.
Greatest recent vintages:	1995, 1990, 1989, 1985, 1979, 1978.
Price range:	$18–$25.
Aromatic profile:	Earth, *garrigue* (that earthy, Provençal herb mélange), pepper, sweet black cherry, blueberry, and cassis fruit are evident in top examples of Gigondas.
Textural profile:	Light, fruity, soft, commercially styled wines are produced, but classic Gigondas also possesses a full-bodied, muscular, unbridled power that is fine-tuned in the best examples, and rustic to the point of being savage in the more uncivilized styles.

The Gigondas appellation's most profound wines:

Domaine de Cayron	Château Redortier
Domaine de Font-Sane Cuvée Futée	Château de St.-Cosme Cuvée Valbelle
Domaine les Goubert Cuvée Florence	Domaine Santa Duc Cuvée des Hautes
Les Hauts de Montmirail	Garrigues
Moulin de la Gardette Cuvée Spéciale	Domaine Santa Duc Cuvée Classique

---

RATING THE GIGONDAS PRODUCERS

---

* * * * *(OUTSTANDING)

Domaine de Cayron	Domaine Santa Duc
Les Hauts de Montmirail (Daniel Brusset)	

* * * *(EXCELLENT)

Domaine de Font-Sane	Domaine de Piauger
Domaine de la Garrigue	Domaine Raspail (Dominique Ay)
Domaine les Goubert****/*****	Château Redortier****/*****
Domaine du Gour de Chaule	Château de St.-Cosme****/*****
Domaine de Longue-Toque	Domaine St.-Gayan
Moulin de la Gardette	Tardieu-Laurent
Domaine les Pallieroudas (Edmonde Burle)	Domaine du Terme

* * *(GOOD)

La Bastide St.-Vincent	Château de Montmirail
Domaine la Bouissière	L'Oustau Fouquet
Domaine de Cassan	Domaine les Pallières***/****
Caves des Vignerons de Gigondas	Domaine du Pesquier
Domaine le Clos des Cazaux	Château Raspail (Meffre family)
Clos du Joncuas	Domaine Romane-Machotte
Domaine des Espiers	Domaine Roucas de St.-Pierre
Domaine Grand-Romane	Domaine les Teyssonières
Domaine du Grapillon d'Or	Domaine de la Tourade
Guigal	Domaine des Tourelles***/****
Paul Jaboulet-Ainé	Château du Trignon
Domaine de la Mavette	Vidal-Fleury

The sleepy village of Gigondas, which seems to have as many dogs and cats as human inhabitants, sits on a sheltered spot at the foot of a craggy set of limestone needles that seem to have exploded upward from the earth. They are called the Dentelles de Montmirail, and they look as if they are part of a Hollywood set for a Steven Spielberg movie.

Gigondas came of age in 1971 when it was given its own appellation status, rather than being just another village of the Côtes du Rhône appellation. The vineyard area, which extends over 2,369 acres, is composed largely of three sectors. On the relatively flat plain fanning out to the west as one approaches Gigondas, the soil is a combination of gravel and clay (terre rouge). The most torrid microclimate of Gigondas, this is the portion of the appellation from which many of the most robust and powerful wines emerge. As one heads east toward the village of Gigondas, the lower slopes of the formidable Dentelles Mountains possess less clay and more sand and gravel, although some areas have more of the *terre rouge* commonly found in the flatter vineyards. Behind the village of Gigondas are numerous hillside vineyards, often cut from the slopes of the mountains. These vineyards are planted at an altitude of 900–1200 feet, a good 700–800 feet above those on the plain. These craggy sites, not dissimilar from a lunar landscape, possess a cooler microclimate, and the soils are primarily limestone and splintered rock, as well as some clay. Although the growers argue on behalf of wherever their vines are planted, top-quality Gigondas emerges from all three expositions: the plains, the lower terraces, and the hillside vineyards.

It is sad that much of the fame of Gigondas (le Médecin, "the doctor") rests largely on the fact that it was often used to doctor (fortify and enrich) Burgundy much like Châteauneuf du Pape. However, Gigondas was cheaper than Châteauneuf du Pape, so it should not be surprising that vignerons in Châteauneuf du Pape claim their wine was used to augment the quality of grands crus and premiers crus, whereas Gigondas was used to augment lesser Burgundies. Gigondas old-timers fondly retell stories of the tanker trucks that would come to their village from Burgundian firms in search of high-powered, concentrated, ripe, fruity wines to put some fat and weight in the weaker Burgundies. Presumably, today such fraudulent practices are less of a problem, yet it would appear reprehensible that some large Burgundian négociants still offer Gigondas along with their portfolio of Burgundies.

Aside from the robust, fiery wines made in Gigondas, this is one of the most scenic, attractive, sleepy Provençal hill towns. This wine village sits under both the aforementioned needles of the Dentelles Mountains and its own ruined Château. A tiny village, with narrow sidewalks inching up the Dentelles, more tractors and minitrucks than cars, a hodgepodge of houses and caveaux, and shade trees aligned strategically around the village's square (where a game of boules is usually in progress), this is the classic Provençal hill town. Gigondas was once the site of impressive Roman villas, as artifacts from the Roman occupation of France have been found throughout the village and surrounding vineyards. In fact, the word *gigondas* is believed to be a bastardization of the Latin word *jocundits*, which meant "merry city." Could this be an ancient reference to the firepower Gigondas possessed 2,000 years ago?

Until 1971, Gigondas was just another Côtes du Rhône village, but through the efforts of Hilarion Roux (of Domaine les Pallières), Pierre Amadieu, and Edmond Chauvet, Gigondas was awarded its own appellation status. While some white wine was once made in Gigondas, the production today is essentially 93% red wine and 7% rosé. Grenache Noir is the grape of choice, representing 65–80% of the blend in most Gigondas cuvées. However, Syrah and Mourvèdre have taken on increasing importance in appellation plantings, and can constitute between 15% and 35% of a blend. It is fashionable to compare Châteauneuf du Pape to Gigondas and, in fact, they do have similarities, but Gigondas has a cooler microclimate than Châteauneuf du Pape, and consequently the harvest is often 10–15 days later. This can prove to be their undoing in years where the harvest is inundated by weather depressions sweeping across France. In years where an "Indian summer" weather condition emerges, Gigondas benefits as much as any appellation of the southern Rhône. It is rare for the Gigondas harvest to occur earlier than late September/early October.

I have been visiting Gigondas for nearly twenty years, each year doing a tasting of virtually all the estate wines, as well as selections from the village's cooperative. In one sense this has been frustrating, because so often the stunning raw materials that emerge from the vineyards are spoiled by defective upbringings in old, musty Gigondas cellars. Too many wines begin life with fabulous potential, great purity of fruit, and an unmistakable character that would give them great international appeal, but are (1) spoiled in part by unsanitary cellar conditions, (2) bottled too late, and/or (3) excessively fined and filtered at the command of oenologists whose only objective is stability, without any regard for the consumer's search for pleasure. It seems to me some attention to cellar hygiene, an earlier bottling, and bottling the entire harvest at one or two bottlings without as much processing would be a major improvement over today's approach.

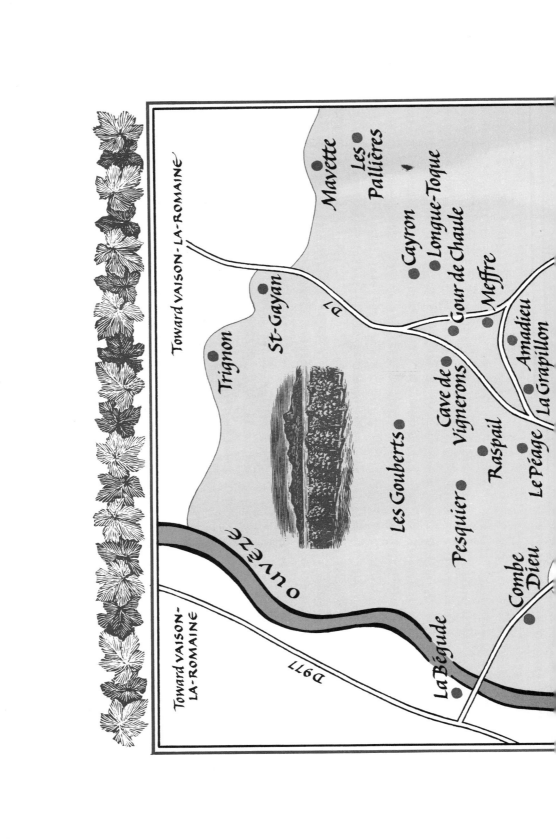

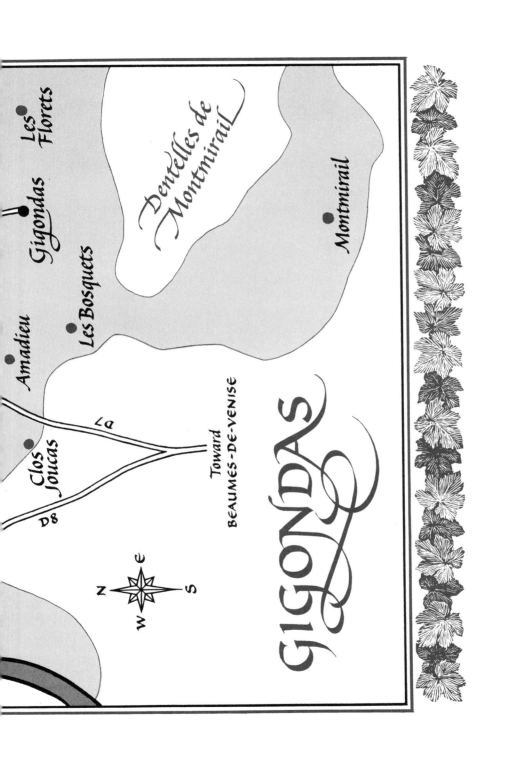

Yet the top Gigondas estates have seen interest in their wines soar, and justifiably so. Many of the better properties, e.g., Daniel Brusset's Les Hauts de Montmirail, Santa Duc, Font-Sane, and Les Goubert, have begun making old-vine or luxury cuvées that now spend some time in new oak casks and are bottled with minimal clarification. As one might expect, the response to these wines has been splendid.

A top Gigondas can last for up to two decades, but my experience has been that they are best drunk in their first 7–8 years. Much of their virtue lies in their powerful, lusty, heady character, and fiery style. The wine is prized for these distinct characteristics, all of which become tamer after 10–12 years in the bottle. While a 15-year-old Gigondas may be a more subtle wine, it often seems to lack the extroverted character and personality it possessed as a younger wine. As in any appellation, there are a variety of styles, ranging from small cask-aged, international lookalikes, to the old-fashioned, slightly oxidized, Grenache-based wines still produced by estates such as Domaine les Pallières. Having loved many of these wines in the past, I must admit that recent vintages have seemed somewhat stale and less interesting when compared to some of the other wines. There are also plenty of light, soft, fruity cuvées ready to drink upon release, but unquestionably there is less diversity in Gigondas than in neighboring Châteauneuf du Pape.

Regardless of style, Gigondas remains one of the wine world's great bargains. Most regular cuvées can still be purchased for $15-$18 a bottle, and even the luxury small-cask or old-vine cuvées are rarely more than $25 a bottle. With a few overall improvements in quality, Gigondas could become one of the most sought-after wines in southern France.

To reiterate, Gigondas is never a shy or subtle wine. Its appeal is its robust, frank, generous, extroverted character, in addition to its value. It is to be savored and admired because of these virtues.

RECENT VINTAGES

1995   In 1995, Gigondas may turn out to be the most successful appellation in southern France, even surpassing Châteauneuf du Pape. Even those estates and négociants that tend to produce lighter-styled wines fashioned black/purple-colored wines with exceptionally ripe fruit, good structure and acidity, and superb concentration. Most Gigondas producers bottle their wine as it is sold, often aging their wine too long in musty old foudres. This is hardly conducive to producing the best wine, but that's the way it is. However, the raw materials in 1995 are superb, and I am hoping that most of these wines get into the bottle before the end of 1997. This vintage has the potential to be as good, if not superior to, 1989 and 1990.

1994   This is generally a very good vintage in the southern Rhône, but for whatever reason, the wines of Gigondas have turned out to be very irregular, and often lacking the concentration and ripeness that one can find in nearby Côtes du Rhône villages such as Cairanne and Vacqueyras, and in Châteauneuf du Pape. It is an average to above-average vintage because Gigondas looks to be the weakest southern Rhône appellation in 1994.

1993   One of the ironies of wine tasting is that on paper, 1994 should be better than 1993, but when tasting the wines, the latter vintage is at least as good as its younger sibling. The 1993 Gigondas are solid, robust, well-endowed wines, but without the fat and density of great years like 1995, 1990, and 1989. The 1993s should age well for a decade.

1992   This was an atrocious vintage in Gigondas. Heavy rains and flooding created havoc in the vineyards, resulting in some of the most deplorable, thin, diluted, rotten wines produced in this appellation since the appalling 1975 vintage. Everyone was overwhelmed by the wrath of Mother Nature.

1991   A small amount of decent wine was produced. The wines are more compact, compressed, and generally of average quality. 1991 is not the disaster that 1992 was, but neither did it produce exciting wines.

1990 Every appellation in the southern Rhône enjoyed a great vintage in 1990, and Gigondas was no exception. A hot, dry growing season produced wines of enormous color, ripeness, body, richness, and dizzyingly high alcohol contents. The wines were still tasting youthful, yet formidably endowed and immensely promising in the mid-nineties. This vintage should last for 15–20 years. This may be one vintage where a Gigondas 12–15 years old is every bit as fabulous as it was at eight or nine years.

1989 Although a hot summer put stress on the vineyards, generous, full-bodied, powerful, textbook Gigondas was produced in 1989. As a general rule, the wines tend to be slightly firmer and more structured than the enormously fruity, opulent 1990s, but 1989 is a top, high-quality vintage.

1988 A very good vintage, overshadowed by the two years that followed, the 1988s were a product of a hot, dry summer, with some rain prior to the harvest. The wines possess good structure and tannin, as well as fine richness, and that round, generous, satisfying mouth feel that makes Gigondas so appealing.

1987 This is a poor to average quality vintage spoiled by very heavy rains in late September and October. The better cuvées were soft, herbaceous, and vegetal when released. Most of these wines should have been drunk by the mid-nineties.

1986 This intriguing year looked top-notch on paper, but while some very good 1986s were produced, the wines possess an unflattering toughness, austerity, and hollowness. They are keepers, and no doubt will last for another decade or more, but I am not sure any of these wines will offer much charm, richness, or intensity.

1985 A super vintage in Gigondas, it is interesting that the finest producers tended to make wines that have aged slightly better, with more balance and freshness than their more esteemed neighbors to the west, Châteauneuf du Pape. The fully mature 1985s are delicious, fleshy, full-bodied, and charming.

1984 A difficult vintage in Gigondas, the 1984s should have been drunk by the mid-nineties.

1983 Because of problems with the Grenache, a tiny crop was produced, resulting in wines with good power, richness, and high alcohol. Many rustic but flavorful, full-bodied wines were produced. Most reached full maturity by 1990, but they are holding on nicely. However, they should be drunk before the turn of the century.

1982 Overripeness and torrid heat during the harvest created significant problems. Many wines had color stability problems, volatile acidity, and exaggerated degrees of alcohol, without the balancing fat, fruit, and extract. The 1982s aged quickly and is now on its last legs.

1981 A poor vintage.

Older Vintages

It was a very good vintage in 1979, and as in virtually every appellation in the Rhône Valley, 1978 was a magnificent year for full-bodied, intense, occasionally overblown wines that have all reached their apogee. They are reference point wines for Gigondas that have been equaled, perhaps surpassed, by 1989, 1990, and, if handled properly, 1995.

LA BASTIDE ST.-VINCENT* * *

Address: Route de Vaison-la-Romaine
       84150 Violès
Wines produced: Gigondas
Surface area: 14.8 acres
Production: 1,875 cases
Upbringing: 12–18 months in cement or epoxy vats. Since 1994, 10% of the yield spends 12 months in new oak barrels before blending.

Average age of vines: 25 years
Blend: 70% Grenache, 20% Mourvèdre, 10% Syrah

Proprietor Guy Daniel has a small estate located on both the terraces and the plateau of Gigondas. The wine is traditionally made, with no destemming, and after fermentation in cuve the wine is brought up in 225-liter foudres. The blend of 70% Grenache, 20% Mourvèdre, and 10% Syrah is standard for Gigondas. New oak was introduced with the 1994 vintage, resulting in wines with slightly more definition and focus. This is an up-and-coming Gigondas estate that merits attention.

VINTAGES

1995—Gigondas This dark purple-colored 1995 Gigondas tasted as if it had just finished
  · malolactic fermentation, so it may be better than my notes indicate. The nose is
86 just beginning to offer hints of black raspberries and cherries. There is sweet ripe fruit in the attack, as well as some unresolved CO_2, and a youthful, backward finish. I suspect there is more to this wine than I thought (tasting right after malolactic is difficult), but for now, the 1994 is tasting better. Anticipated maturity: 1999–2007. Last tasted 6/96.

1994—Gigondas The 1994's dark plummy color is accompanied by sweet, jammy, ripe,
  · herb, pepper, and black-cherry aromas. Good ripeness, power, and a chewy, fleshy
87 texture make for a delicious, forward Gigondas for drinking over the next 5–6 years. Last tasted 6/96.

1990—Gigondas This 1990 Gigondas represents a straightforward, commercial style of
  · Gigondas with plenty of up-front charm. The ripe black fruit nose, tasty, fat, chewy
86 flavors, supple texture, and clean, smooth fruit are appealing. If I were in the restaurant business, this is the sort of wine I would be suggesting to customers. It should be drunk within 5–6 years of the vintage. Last tasted 6/95.

1989—Gigondas The 1989 Gigondas is clean, plump, ripe, and fruity, but essentially
  · straightforward and commercial in style. It should drink nicely for the next 4–7
83 years. Last tasted 6/94.

1988—Gigondas The 1988 is fuller, more alcoholic, but also deeper and longer on the
  · palate. The low acidity and soft tannins suggest it should be drunk over the next 5
85 years. Last tasted 9/94.

DOMAINE DES BOSQUETS* */* * *

Address: 84190 Gigondas
Tel: 4-90-65-86-09
Fax: 4-90-65-81-81
Wines produced: Gigondas
Surface area: 62 acres
Production: 9,000–10,000 cases
Upbringing: stainless steel vats for fermentation, then 2–3 years in underground enamel vats; from the 1995 vintage on, the wines will age in oak barrels and casks
Average age of vines: 30 years
Blend: 75% Grenache, 10% Syrah, 10% Cinsault, 5% Mourvèdre

In spite of the very fine performance in 1995, this estate tends to produce old-style Gigondas without the requisite backbone of concentration and intensity to support the long cask aging. Domaine des Bosquets' vineyards possess various expositions, but they are primarily located on the clay/limestone soils of the plain and terraces.

VINTAGES

1995—Gigondas   An excellent, nearly outstanding example of 1995 Gigondas, Bosquets'
·   wine exhibits the vintage's telltale opaque purple color, rich, sweet, uncomplicated
87   black-raspberry and cassis aromas, deep, medium- to full-bodied flavors, excellent
      texture and purity, and surprising length. It should drink well for 10–12 years.
      Last tasted 6/96.

1994—Gigondas   The 1994 Gigondas possesses a dark plummy/garnet color, a Bing
·   cherry, herbes de Provence, peppery-scented nose, crisp, pleasant, medium-bodied
81   flavors of above average concentration, and a clean finish. It requires drinking over
      the next 3–4 years. Last tasted 6/96.

1990—Gigondas   At the verge of being unacceptable, this thin, watery wine offers no
·   concentration, surprisingly light body, and a diluted finish. In a vintage such as
70   1990, it is hard to believe that such an undistinguished wine could emerge. Last
      tasted 6/94.

1989—Gigondas   The 1989 is a light, soft, fruity, straightforward wine with decent con-
·   centration, but little complexity, flavor dimension, or length. Drink it up. Last
80   tasted 6/93.

DOMAINE LA BOUISSIÈRE* * *

Address: Rue du Portail
        84190 Gigondas
Tel: 4-90-65-87-91
Wines produced: Gigondas, Gigondas La Font de Tonin
Surface area (regular cuvée): 17.3 acres
            (La Font de Tonin): 1.2 acres
Production (regular cuvée): 3,100 cases
            (La Font de Tonin): 160 cases
Upbringing (regular cuvée): 36 months total, with 12–18 months in old oak casks
            (La Font de Tonin): 36 months total, with 15–21 months in oak barrels 2–3
                years old
Average age of vines (regular cuvée): 35 years
            (La Font de Tonin): 45 years
Blend (regular cuvée): 70% Grenache, 20% Syrah, 10% Mourvèdre
        (La Font de Tonin): 85% Grenache, 15% Syrah

Following the death of their father, Antonin Faravel, sons Gilles and Thierry have begun
to push the level of quality of this moderately sized estate to a higher level. The estate's
name is a Provençal word for the groves of trees that were cut down in order to plant the
vines on the terraces at the foot of the Dentelles de Montmirail. The Faravels produce two
wines. Their regular cuvée is a rustic Gigondas with raspberry fruit and plenty of earthy
overtones. Their cuvée spéciale, La Font de Tonin, is made from older vines with no
Mourvèdre in the blend. The potential at this estate remains largely unexploited, but these
traditionally made wines have displayed more strength and intensity over the last 7–8 years.

VINTAGES

1995—Gigondas   An opaque ruby/purple color is followed by a wine with a backward yet
·   pure black-cherry, framboise, licorice-scented nose, excellent depth, good power
87   and intensity, and a tannic, spicy, concentrated, rich finish. Anticipated maturity:
      1998–2010. Last tasted 6/96.

1995—Gigondas La Font de Tonin   This opaque purple-colored wine offers up an ambi-
  •   tious, powerful, full-bodied, black-cherry, cassis, roasted-herb-scented nose. This
  89   immense, seriously-endowed Gigondas will age well for 15 years. Wines such as
           this give evidence that 1995 is the finest vintage for Gigondas since 1978. Antici-
           pated maturity: 2000–2010. Last tasted 6/96.

1993—Gigondas   The dark-colored, backward, spicy, medium- to full-bodied 1993 Gi-
  •   gondas exhibits above-average quality, fine depth, and a spicy, moderately long
  86   finish. Anticipated maturity: now–2001. Last tasted 6/95.

1992—Gigondas   The 1992 Gigondas reveals a pruny, herbal, tea-scented nose with
  •   hints of raspberry fruit. The wine is attenuated, with a compact flavor profile, and
  79   a short finish. Drink it up. Last tasted 6/94.

1989—Gigondas   The 1989 has plenty of concentration, but there were significant levels
  •   of tannins that might present a problem of balance in the future. For now, it appears
  87?   to be an old-style vin de garde, with plenty of aging potential. But I wonder if there
           is enough underlying fruit to support such astringent tannins? This could turn out
           to be impressive. Anticipated maturity: 1998–2004. Last tasted 6/94.

1988—Gigondas   The 1988 is totally unlike the 1989. It has neither the concentration
  •   nor the tannin level of the 1989, and is made in a softer, more forward style. It
  86   should provide tasty drinking over the next 4–5 years. Anticipated maturity: now–
           2000. Last tasted 6/93.

DOMAINE DE CASSAN* * *

Address: 84190 Lafare
Tel: 4-90-65-87-65
Fax: 4-90-65-80-83
Wines produced: Gigondas
Surface area: 18.5 acres
Production: 3,125 cases
Upbringing: 18 months in old oak casks
Average age of vines: 25–30 years
Blend: 65% Grenache, 10% Syrah, 15% Mourvèdre

This small estate's vineyards are completely on clay/limestone soils with a full southern
exposition. The few vintages I have tasted have been well-made, traditionally styled Gigondas that are supple enough to be drunk when released, yet capable of lasting for 7–8 years.

VINTAGES

1994—Gigondas   Domaine de Cassan's Gigondas is one of the more interesting 1994s I
  •   tasted. A dark ruby/purple color is followed by a wine with a jammy, cherry,
  87   licorice, smoky-scented nose, elegant yet powerful flavors, low acidity, and a sense
           of surmaturité. The wine possesses some tannin, as well as excellent richness, a
           good attack, and a slight narrowing in the finish. Anticipated maturity: now–2001.
           Last tasted 6/96.

1990—Gigondas   This 1990 Gigondas exhibits attractive black-cherry fruit to go along
  •   with toasty oak smells in its ripe, medium-bodied style. Anticipated maturity: now–
  85   2000. Last tasted 6/94.

CAVES DES VIGNERONS DE GIGONDAS* * *

Address: 84190 Gigondas

Tel: 4-90-65-86-27

Fax: 4-90-65-80-13

Wines produced: Gigondas Cuvée Signature, Gigondas Cuvée Signature Rosé, Gigondas Cuvée du Président, Gigondas Cuvée Le Pavillon de Beaumirail, Gigondas La Seigneurie de Fontange Vielles Vignes

Surface area: 617.5 acres

Production (Cuvée Signature): 29,000–30,000 cases
        (Cuvée Signature Rosé): 3,350 cases
        (Cuvée du Président): 3,300 cases
        (Le Pavillon de Beaumirail): 1,000 cases
        (Le Seigneurie de Fontange): 3,300 cases

Upbringing (Cuvée Signature): 12 months in underground cement vats, and 12–18 months in old oak casks
        (Cuvée Signature Rosé): 8–10 months in stainless steel vats
        (Cuvée du Président): 12 months in cement vats
        (Pavillon de Beaumirail): 12 months in new oak barrels
        (Seigneurie de Fontange): 36 months minimum total, with 18 months in oak casks, depending on the vintage

Average age of vines: 40 years, except for the Seigneurie de Fontange, 50 years

Blend (Cuvée Signature, Cuvée Signature Rosé, Cuvée du Président, and Seigneurie de Fontange): 80% Grenache, 15% Syrah and Mourvèdre, 5% Cinsault
        (Pavillon de Beaumirail): 80% Grenache, 20% Syrah and Mourvèdre

This is one of the better-run cooperatives in southern France. They produce a huge range of cuvées, from light, fruity, Beaujolais-styled Gigondas, to cuvées from very old, terraced vineyards that are concentrated, full-bodied, and ageworthy. The finest wines are their Seigneurie de Fontage Vieilles Vignes and Le Pavillon de Beaumirail. The Cuvée du Président is made to be drunk young and fresh. Readers should note that these wines are very reasonably priced for such quality. If the wines are not quite at the level of a Santa Duc, Les Hauts Montmirail, or Domaine de Cayron, they are often better than many other estates turning out indifferent Gigondas.

While it is fashionable to cast dispersions on coop-produced wines, this coop makes very good wines. Certainly the quality has improved over recent years under the talented administration of Madame Annie Gleize.

DOMAINE DE CAYRON* * * * *

Address: Rue de la Fontaine
        84190 Gigondas

Tel: 4-90-65-87-46

Fax: 4-90-65-88-81

Wines produced: Gigondas

Surface area: 35 acres

Production: 5,000 cases

Upbringing: 36 months total, with 18 months in old oak casks

Average age of vines: 40 years

Blend: 70% Grenache, 16% Cinsault, 12% Syrah, 2% Mourvèdre

As one enters the sleepy town of Gigondas, the first cellar on the left is that of the Faraud family. Georges Faraud, a gray-haired, very elderly man, has been assisted by his handsome, athletic son, Michel, for over a decade. Faraud's family has been making one wine, an extremely concentrated, intense Gigondas, for over 150 years. The 35 acres of vines that average 40 years of age are situated at the foot of the Dentelles Mountains that loom over the town.

Faraud's wines are the richest, most exotic, and often the most dramatic of the appellation. On occasion, their explosive richness and rustic set of aromas can be a bit overwhelming. His wines, made in one of the few underground cellars in Gigondas, are never fined or filtered but are allowed to settle naturally by virtue of a two- to three-year sojourn in ancient wooden foudres. He uses 70% Grenache and incorporates with that Syrah, Cinsault, and Mourvèdre. His wines do not lack for power; they normally reach 14% alcohol naturally. The squeaky-voiced Faraud recommends that people give his wines one to two hours' breathing because of their size and style. Stating that there is no need to rush to drink them, he says they will improve for 10–15 years. I might add that they should also be decanted, given their enormous amount of sediment.

Faraud's wines are such forceful examples of Gigondas that they, more than any other wine of this appellation, require rich stews, cassoulets, and game to absorb their strong personalities. Properly served and matched up with the right culinary offering, they are memorable wines that can take one on a pleasant trip to the nineteenth century.

VINTAGES

1995—Gigondas   Domaine de Cayron's 1995 tasted as if it had just completed malolactic
·   fermentation. The wine revealed an opaque purple color, fine acidity, an unevolved
91   personality, and massive amounts of fruit and extract. While it is deep and formidably endowed, it is also backward and youthful. Give it 3–4 years in the cellar to
soften. Anticipated maturity: 2000–2015. Last tasted 6/96.

1994—Gigondas   The 1994 offers plenty of licorice, blackberry, and blueberry-like fruit,
·   good fatness for a 1994, medium to full body, a seductive, open-knit character, and
87   a round, glycerin-imbued, luscious finish. Although not complex, it is a tasty,
easy-to-understand wine. Anticipated maturity: now–2004. Last tasted 6/96.

1993—Gigondas   The 1993 Gigondas should turn out to be nearly outstanding, although
·   I cannot see it equaling the quality of proprietor Faraud's 1988, 1989, 1990, or
88   1995. The 1993 exhibits a saturated black/purple color, highly extracted, earthy,
truffle-like, roasted herb and black-cherry-scented nose, rich, concentrated fruit,
super length and ripeness, and a lush texture. Anticipated maturity: now–2004.
Last tasted 6/96.

1992—Gigondas   The 1992 Gigondas had a singed, raisiny, vegetal nose, sweet, soupy
·   flavors, and a lack of grip and focus. Even a master winemaking team such as
?   Michel and Georges Faraud could not overcome the difficulties posed by the floods
of 1992. Last tasted 6/95.

1990—Gigondas   Faraud's 1990 exhibits a black/ruby color. The big, spicy, earthy,
·   licorice nose and opulent, fat, chewy flavors nearly conceal the considerable tannin
90   levels. This in-your-face, full-throttle Gigondas is quasi-civilized, but absolutely
delicious. Anticipated maturity: now–2006. Last tasted 11/95.

1989—Gigondas   The 1989 reveals even greater richness. The kinky, exotic, smoked-
·   meat fragrance, gobs of thick, chewy, chocolate, hickory-flavored fruit, and mouth-
90   coating glycerin and tannin levels make for an interesting, even provocative glass
of wine. Anticipated maturity: now–2005. Last tasted 11/95.

1988—Gigondas   The dark garnet-colored 1988 possesses huge, peppery, fruitcake, her-
·   baceous, olive and smoky flavors and aromas. Expansive and nearly sweet on the
90   palate, there is no doubting the extract levels that must have been obtained to hide

a wine that has an alcohol level of over 14%. This thrill-a-sip Gigondas should continue to turn heads, raise eyebrows, and horrify puritans. Anticipated maturity: now–2005. Last tasted 11/95.

1986—Gigondas   The deep plum/garnet-colored 1986 is slightly less concentrated and
·   less alcoholic than the 1985, but it is still perfumed, rich, and intense. Fully
90   mature, this fleshy, corpulent wine is a noteworthy success in an otherwise undis-
            tinguished vintage. Anticipated maturity: now–2000. Last tasted 11/95.

1985—Gigondas   This Gigondas has always been a mind-blowing, decadent example of
·   Gigondas. That some grower could pack so much succulent, hedonistic, peppery,
90   blackberry and cherry fruit into a wine is hard to believe. But there are lavish
            amounts of seductively smooth fruit in this full-bodied, heady wine with a dazzling
            perfume of Asian spices and red fruits. Fully mature, this wine offers a textbook
            lesson in what Gigondas is all about. Anticipated maturity: now–2004. Last tasted
            11/95.

1984—Gigondas   Very deep in color, the 1984 also has a peppery, blackcurrant bouquet,
·   rich, spicy flavors, very good depth and balance, and "only" 13.3% alcohol. This
86   is a top success for the vintage. Mature now. Last tasted 6/86.

1983—Gigondas   The stunningly complex bouquet of cedar, pepper, olives, berry fruit,
·   and truffles is top rank. On the palate, a trace of coarseness keeps the rating down,
87   as does the 14.8% alcohol level. Extremely full-bodied, this is a brawny, muscular
            wine, the likes of which one rarely sees today. Mature now. Last tasted 6/86.

1982—Gigondas   Another blockbuster, the 1982, with 14.5% alcohol, has a full-intensity
·   bouquet of fruitcake, pepper, and herbs. Portlike and lush with a trace of sweetness,
87   this is a large-scaled, very lush, generously flavored wine that offers a big mouthful
            of wine. Mature now. Last tasted 6/86.

1981—Gigondas   This is a very good Gigondas, spicy, earthy, and Provençal herb–
·   scented. Deep in color, quite concentrated, full-bodied, and well made, this is a
86   gutsy, powerful Gigondas oozing with character. Mature now. Last tasted 1/87.

Older Vintages

In November 1995, I tasted the excellent 1979 and the huge, massive 1978. The 1979 is exotic, jammy, and loaded with the scents and flavors of truffles and jammy fruits. The 1978 has thrown off its funky character, leaving a huge wine with layers of extract and personality.

DOMAINE LE CLOS DES CAZAUX* * *

Address: 84190 Vacqueyras
Tel: 4-90-65-85-83
Fax: 4-90-65-83-94
Wines produced: Gigondas La Tour Sarrazine
Surface area: 25 acres
Production: 2,188 cases
Upbringing: 18–24 months in stainless steel vats
Average age of vines: 30–40 years
Blend: 80% Grenache, 15% Syrah, 5% Mourvèdre

The Archimbau-Vache family runs this relatively large estate, which is better known for an excellent Vacqueyras. This operation has been estate-bottling only since 1980, despite the fact that more than five generations of this family have owned vineyards in Gigondas and Vacqueyras. I tasted most of the Clos des Cazaux vintages in the eighties, but nothing since. The wines were well-made, traditionally styled Gigondas meant to be drunk in their first 5–7 years of life. There is a long cask aging of nearly two years, and, fortunately, bottling without fining or filtration. However, I have always found their Vacqueyras to be a more interesting wine. Perhaps Vacqueyras's warmer microclimate, which allows the vineyards to be harvested 10–14 days prior to those in Gigondas, has favored that appellation more than the cooler terraces and hillside vineyards in Gigondas.

CLOS DU JONCUAS* * *

Address: 84190 Gigondas
Tel: 4-90-65-86-86
Fax: 4-90-65-83-68
Wines produced: Gigondas, Gigondas Cuvée F. Chastan, Gigondas Cuvée Prestige
Surface area: 27 acres
Production (regular cuvée): 4,375 cases
         (Cuvée F. Chastan): 825 cases
         (Cuvée Prestige): amount varies, produced only in very good vintages
Upbringing: 18–24 months total, with 12 months in old oak casks
Average age of vines: 40 years
Blend: 80% Grenache, 10% Cinsault, 10% Mourvèdre

This is a traditionally made wine, with aging in small casks, and bottling as the wine is sold. Unfortunately, in the nineties I have seen wines only from difficult vintages in Gigondas. The 1992 was disappointing, but the 1993 was a good, old-style, rustic wine. Proprietor Fernand Chastan produces three cuvées—a regular cuvée, Cuvée F. Chastan, and tiny quantities of a Cuvée Prestige that is made only in top vintages. This is a good source for rustic, full-bodied Gigondas for aging 10 or more years in top vintages.

VINTAGES

1993—Gigondas   The deeply colored, surprisingly tannic, full-bodied, chewy, one-
•   dimensional but immensely mouth-filling 1993 Gigondas should be a 10-to-15-year
86   wine. Last tasted 6/95.
1992—Gigondas   A leafy, vegetal component accompanies the 1992's coffee, spicy, fruit-
•   cake flavors, hard tannin, and pruny, high-alcohol finish. Although awkward and
76   perplexing, it is not unlikable. Drink it over the next 4–5 years. Last tasted 6/95.

DOMAINE DES ESPIERS* * *

Address: 84190 Gigondas
Tel: 4-90-65-87-98
Wines produced: Gigondas
Surface area: 5 acres
Production: 800–1,000 cases
Upbringing: a traditionally produced Gigondas with no destemming, and storage in old wood
        foudres until bottling
Average age of vines: 40 years
Blend: 85% Grenache, 15% Syrah

I have tasted only a few wines from this tiny domaine of 5 acres in Gigondas. The vines have an impressive average age of 40 years, and the wine is made primarily from Grenache, with a small quantity of Syrah added for structure and complexity.

VINTAGES

1995—Gigondas   The sample of 1995 was very impressive, and indicative of a wine that
·   could turn out to be outstanding. Nineteen ninety-five is an outstanding vintage in
89   Gigondas. This wine exhibits an opaque black/purple color, a fabulously rich nose
of flowers, black fruits, and minerals, extraordinary intensity, thick, unctuously
textured flavors, good acidity for such ripeness, and a medium- to full-bodied, long
finish. Anticipated maturity: 1999–2010. Last tasted 6/96.

1994—Gigondas   The 1994 Gigondas is disappointingly thin, high-acid, compact, and
·   compressed. Last tasted 6/96.
78

1989—Gigondas   The medium dark garnet-colored 1989 displayed a roasted, ripe bou-
·   quet of black raspberries, soft, fat, alcoholic flavors, and low acidity. It is fully
86   mature. Last tasted 6/94.

DOMAINE DE FONT-SANE* * * *

Address: Quartier Tuilières
          84190 Gigondas
Tel: 4-90-65-86-36
Fax: 4-90-65-81-71
Wines produced: Gigondas, Gigondas Cuvée Futée
Surface area: 35 acres
Production (regular cuvée): 3,000 cases
          (Cuvée Futée): 325 cases
Upbringing (regular cuvée): 24 months total, with 8–10 months in old oak casks
          (Cuvée Futée): 24 months total, with 8–12 months in new oak barrels
Average age of vines: 35 years
Blend (regular cuvée): 75% Grenache, 10–15% Syrah, the rest Cinsault and Mourvèdre
          (Cuvée Futée): 75% Grenache, 25% Syrah

Since the mid-eighties, Domaine de Font-Sane has emerged as one of the top producers
of Gigondas. This 35-acre estate has long been owned by the Peysson family. Gilbert
Peysson's daughter, Véronique Cunty, has run the estate with precision and enthusiasm
over the last five years. The name Font-Sane comes from a local source for water. The
moderately sized vineyard has its best parcels of Grenache in the terraces at the foot of
the Dentelles (limestone and clay soils), and on the flat plateau that extends away from the
Dentelles, where the microclimate is much hotter, and the gravelly soil includes more sand.
Madame Cunty has some of the lowest yields in Gigondas, rarely averaging more than 2 tons
of fruit per acre.

This traditionally vinified wine is always deeply colored, pure, and expressive. Two
cuvées are offered. The regular cuvée is excellent, and the Cuvée Futée is superb. The
latter wine is aged for 24 months in 100% new oak casks and bottled unfiltered. It is
produced only in the finest vintages (1986, 1988, 1989, and 1990). I suspect there will be
a Cuvée Futée released in 1995.

It is unusual in a small appellation to find two estates run by dynamic women, but in
addition to Domaine de Font-Sane there is Domaine du Gour de Chaule, directed by
Madame Beaumet and Madame Bonfils.

VINTAGES

1995—Gigondas   The Domaine de Font-Sane's 1995 unquestionably outperformed the
  ·   1994. Its deep ruby/purple color, sweet, peppery, jammy nose of red and black
 88   fruits, medium to full body, and uncomplicated but fleshy, pure fruit flavors, with
           good glycerin and length, should provide a fine bottle of Gigondas. Anticipated
           maturity: 1999–2009. Last tasted 6/96.

1994—Gigondas   The dark plum-colored 1994 possesses medium body, and considerable
  ·   austerity, without the fat, ripeness, and sweet fruit I would have expected of this
 80   high-quality producer. Anticipated maturity: now–2001. Last tasted 6/96.

1993—Gigondas   Domaine de Font-Sane was successful in 1993. The dark ruby/purple-
  ·   colored 1993 Gigondas offers an excellent nose of cassis, licorice, and flowers,
 88   medium- to full-bodied flavors, moderate tannin, and excellent purity and ripeness.
           It should drink well for 10–12 years. Last tasted 6/96.

1992—Gigondas   The 1992 Gigondas exhibits a surprising amount of purple in its color
  ·   (it is one of the darkest wines of the vintage), admirable ripeness, medium body,
 87   moderate tannin, and a rich, chewy finish. Unquestionably, this is a top success for
           what was an appallingly bad year in Gigondas. Anticipated maturity: now–2000.
           Last tasted 6/95.

1990—Gigondas   The 1990 Gigondas exhibits an impressive purple color, a pure bouquet
  ·   of cassis and black raspberries, full-bodied, lusciously fruity, fat flavors, and a long
 87   finish. The tender tannins and low-acid result is a wine that should drink well for
           6–7 years. Last tasted 6/95.

1990—Gigondas Cuvée Futée   Deep ruby/purple-colored, the 1991 Cuvée Futée displays
  ·   an excellent nose of sweet black-cherry and cassis fruit, plenty of toasty new oak
 91   with a touch of lead pencil, full body, outstanding purity and ripeness, and a
           layered, multidimensional feel. It is powerful and rich, as well as elegant. Antici-
           pated maturity: now–2006. Last tasted 6/96.

1989—Gigondas   The 1989 Gigondas exhibits a black/purple color, as well as a huge
  ·   bouquet of spring flowers, ripe blackcurrants, herbs, and minerals. In the mouth
 89   there is that voluptuous texture so evident in the top 1989s, low acidity, big, rich,
           chewy flavors, and a long, intense finish. Anticipated maturity: now–2003. Last
           tasted 9/95.

1989—Gigondas Cuvée Futée   Deep ruby/purple-colored, with a more closed aromatic
  ·   profile than the 1990, the 1989 is full-bodied, impressively endowed, rich, tannic,
 90   cleanly made, and backward. The wine is still closed and will benefit from addi-
           tional cellaring. Anticipated maturity: 1998–2009. Last tasted 6/96.

1988—Gigondas   The fully mature, garnet-colored 1988 Gigondas displays a fragrant,
  ·   roasted, Provençal herb character in the nose, round, generously endowed, full-
 87   bodied flavors, and a soft finish. Anticipated maturity: now–2000. Last tasted
           6/95.

1988—Gigondas Cuvée Futée   The 1988 Cuvée Futée, which was aged in 100% vosges
  ·   oak barrels, is a deeper-colored, more richly extracted Gigondas, exhibiting copious
 90   amounts of new oak in its nose and flavors. With superb underlying richness and
           fruit, this wine is marvelous to drink. Anticipated maturity: now–2004. Last tasted
           9/95.

1986—Gigondas Cuvée Futée   The 1986 Futée (the debut vintage for this wine) is a rich,
  ·   full-bodied, attractively scented wine (smoky aromas combined with cassis) that
 87   has reached full maturity. Although it reveals a certain austerity, it remains very
           fresh. Anticipated maturity: now–2000. Last tasted 9/95.

DOMAINE DE LA GARRIGUE* * * *

Address: B.P. 23
       84190 Vacqueyras
Tel: 4-90-65-84-60
Wines produced: Gigondas
Surface area: 7.4 acres
Production: 1,125 cases
Upbringing: 24 months in cement vats
Average age of vines: 45 years
Blend: 75% Grenache, 15% Syrah, 5% Cinsault, 5% Mourvèdre

One of the most charming places to dine in Provence is the Restaurant Les Florets, which is idyllically situated on a hillside behind the village of Gigondas. The restaurant's owners, the Bernard family, own a small 7.4 Gigondas vineyard. They also oversee 100 acres in Vacqueyras. Their Gigondas is an unfined, unfiltered, blockbuster, powerful wine that sometimes errs on the side of being to rustic, but it is filled with personality and character. Most of the top vintages (1988, 1989, 1990) should not have been drunk before they attain 5–6 years of age. Given the tiny production of just over 1,000 cases, a large percentage of which is understandably reserved for Restaurant Les Florets, not much of this wine makes it outside the village.

VINTAGES

1990—Gigondas   This thick garnet/purple-colored Gigondas offers up aromas of
  ·   Provençal herbs, smoked olives, beef blood, and sweet, jammy red and black fruits.
  90   Full-bodied, opulent, and massive on the palate, with plenty of tannin, this is a
          husky, fiery style of Gigondas that should drink well for a decade or more. Antici-
          pated maturity: now–2008. Last tasted 6/96.
1989—Gigondas   A ferociously tannic, spicy, dark garnet-colored wine, the 1989 Do-
  ·   maine de la Garrigue Gigondas is full-bodied, well endowed, and tightly knit,
  89   especially when tasted next to the more open 1990. It is an old-fashioned, rustic
          wine with plenty of firepower and flavor. Anticipated maturity: 1998-2009. Last
          tasted 6/96.

DOMAINE LES GOUBERT* * * */* * * * *

Address: 84190 Gigondas
Tel: 4-90-65-86-38
Fax: 4-90-65-81-52
Wines produced: Gigondas, Gigondas Cuvée Florence
Surface area (regular cuvée): 24 acres
          (Cuvée Florence): 13.6 acres
Production (regular cuvée): 1,800 cases
          (Cuvée Florence): 375–400 cases
Upbringing (regular cuvée): 23 months in cement vats
          (Cuvée Florence): 24 months total, with 9–18 months in 25% new oak barrels;
                  since 1993, 50% new oak is utilized
Average age of vines (regular cuvée): 35 years
          (Cuvée Florence): 100 years
Blend (regular cuvée): 62% Grenache, 25% Syrah, 10% Mourvèdre, 3% Cinsault
          (Cuvée Florence): 80% Grenache, 19% Syrah, 1% Clairette

Jean-Pierre Cartier is certainly capable of producing some of the finest Gigondas of the appellation. For example, his 1985, 1981, and 1979 were *hors classe* for their respective vintages. Cartier, a bald man in his early fifties who is often seen sporting an American baseball cap rather than the traditional French beret, has built this estate into one of the most successful in Gigondas. He owns more than 50 acres of vines spread throughout Gigondas, Beaumes de Venise, and the Côtes du Rhône village of Sablet. Cartier, who is justifiably proud of the fact that his family has made wine since 1636, named his estate after the Goubert sector of Gigondas where their winery and home are located. Cartier's wife, Mireille, is heavily involved in running this estate, as well as serving as secretary for the syndicate of Gigondas. The estate's luxury cuvée, Cuvée Florence, is named after their only child, the brilliantly red-haired Florence, who was born in 1985.

Despite all the success Jean-Pierre Cartier has enjoyed, the quality of his wines seemed to dip after the first edition of this book was written a decade ago. Too high a production and a somewhat misdirected fear of sediment caused many wines to be excessively fined and filtered. Fortunately, the nineties have seen Cartier return to a more natural winemaking approach, with a softer bottling. With the 1993 vintage, he eliminated all filtrations of the red wines.

There are two Gigondas cuvées produced, a very good *cuvée tradition* that is aged entirely in concrete vats, and the renowned Cuvée Florence, the first wine made in Gigondas to be exposed to new wood casks. It spends up to two years in small oak casks, of which 25–50% are new. Both of these wines come from a multitude of vineyards, with the bulk of them planted in the sandy, gravelly soil surrounding the winery, and the rest from the rocky clay/limestone soils of the terraces in the Dentelles de Montmirail, and the gravelly red clay of the lower slopes. Having been a big fan of the Domaine les Goubert's wines of the early and mid-eighties, I can say without hesitation that the top cuvées age beautifully for 10–12 years. I can also say that one of the insider wines from Cartier is his excellent red Côtes du Rhône made from the village of Beaumes de Venise. Additionally, Cartier is producing increasingly interesting Côtes du Rhône white wines as he has begun to incorporate more Viognier into the blend.

This is an excellent estate that went through a slump in the early nineties, but has rebounded to the form that established Les Goubert as one of the appellation's reference point wines.

VINTAGES

1990—Gigondas   The forward 1990 Gigondas regular cuvée tastes ripe, soft, and me-
  ·   dium-bodied, but lacking the concentration and intensity I have come to expect
85   from Jean-Pierre Cartier's wines. Anticipated maturity: now–1999. Last tasted
       6/95.

1990—Gigondas Cuvée Florence   The 1990 Gigondas-Cuvée Florence was terrific from
  ·   cask, but since bottling, the wine has tasted austere and a trifle eviscerated (too
87   much fining and filtration?). It reveals toasty new oak aromas combined with an
       attractive fragrance of black-cherry and cassis fruit. In the mouth, there was less
       of the superripe character of the 1989, more structure, and a surprisingly quick
       finish. After a serious discussion with Cartier about excessive fining and filtration,
       I sensed he regretted the degree to which he filtered his 1990s. Anticipated
       maturity: now–1999. Last tasted 6/95.

1989—Gigondas   The regular cuvée of 1989 Gigondas offers up an open-knit, attractive,
  ·   spicy, peppery, curranty nose, intermingled with the scent of Provençal herbs. In
87   the mouth it is sweet, ripe, and fleshy, with moderate tannins and a chewy, concen-
       trated finish. Mature now. Last tasted 11/95.

1989—Gigondas Cuvée Florence   The dark ruby-colored 1989 Cuvée Florence exhibits
· more toasty, spicy, new oak in its nose, but there are also intense smells of
89 herb-scented cassis and overripe plums. This medium-bodied, voluptuously textured, opulent wine displays soft tannin, a nice touch of vanillin and smoky new
oak, as well as a long finish. Anticipated maturity: now–2000. Last tasted 6/95.

1988—Gigondas   Offering delicious drinking, the 1988 regular cuvée is a big, alcoholic,
· rich, impeccably clean, but muscular style of Gigondas that has a relatively high
87 alcohol content and a heady, lusty finish. Mature now. Last tasted 1/95.

1988—Gigondas Cuvée Florence   The 1988 Gigondas Cuvée Florence has a dark ruby/
· purple color, a highly extracted bouquet of violets, black raspberries, and toasty,
91 smoky oak. In the mouth it is rich, full-bodied, and amply endowed, with soft
tannins and moderate acidity. Finally approaching full maturity, this wine should
prove especially long-lived. Anticipated maturity: now–2005. Last tasted 6/95.

1986—Gigondas Cuvée Florence   The hot, dry year of 1986 resulted in larger-structured,
· more tannic and less flattering wines than in 1985. The youthful-looking Cuvée
90 Florence is a rich, multidimensional wine loaded with an intense bouquet of black
fruits, lead pencil, minerals, and smoke, as well as an admirable old-vine flavor
intensity. It is just beginning to reach its plateau of maturity. Anticipated maturity:
now–2003. Last tasted 12/95.

1985—Gigondas Cuvée Florence   This blend of 88% Grenache, 10% Syrah, and 2%
· Mourvèdre seems to have benefited immensely from its sojourn in new oak barrels.
92 Very fragrant and complex, rich and full-bodied, and not lacking acidity and
structure as are many 1985s, this wine has drunk beautifully since the late eighties.
It is beginning to exhibit some amber, but while fully mature, it appears capable of
lasting a few more years. Anticipated maturity: now–2003. Last tasted 12/95.

DOMAINE DU GOUR DE CHAULE* * * *

Address: Quartier Ste.-Anne
            84190 Gigondas
Tel: 4-90-65-85-62
Fax: 4-90-65-82-40
Wines produced: Gigondas (red and rosé)
Surface area: 25 acres
Production (red): 4,000 cases
            (rosé): 375 cases
Upbringing (red): 1 year in stainless steel and cement vats and 12–18 months in old oak
            casks
            (rosé): 4 months in stainless steel and cement vats
Average age of vines: 35 years
Blend (red): 80% Grenache, 20% Syrah and Mourvèdre
            (rosé): 45% Grenache, 45% Clairette, 10% Mourvèdre

This estate keeps a very low profile yet makes very delicious, velvety, richly fruity
Gigondas. The estate is 25 acres in size and the blend used for their well-bred Gigondas is
80% Grenache and 20% Syrah and Mourvèdre. The wine is aged one year in cement tanks,
then 14–16 months in large wooden foudres. This is quite a serious domaine, impeccably
looked after by Madame Bonfils. Why the wines are not better known is a mystery.

VINTAGES

1995—Gigondas   This well-run estate fashioned a black/purple-colored, youthful 1995
·   Gigondas with medium to full body, fine underlying acidity, and excellent potential.
88   The wine is firm and tightly knit, yet pure and well defined. Could the 1995
            Gigondas turn out like a 1978? Anticipated maturity: 2000–2010. Last tasted 6/96.
1994—Gigondas   The 1994 Gigondas exhibits a medium dark ruby color, an attractive nose
·   of pepper, ripe plums, and cherries, a good attack, some sweetness, and a medium-
85   bodied, uninspiring finish. Anticipated maturity: now–2002. Last tasted 6/96.
1993—Gigondas   The medium-weight 1993 is a ripe, well-made wine that lacks the
·   depth, power, and intensity of other efforts from this producer. Last tasted 6/96.
77

Older Vintages

This estate had a strong decade in the eighties, with top-notch efforts in 1981, 1983, 1985
(superlative, and gorgeous to drink in 1996), 1986 (one of the best wines of the vintage for
this appellation), 1988, and 1989. The 1990 is a powerhouse Gigondas, yet still youthful,
promising, and delicious when drunk in 1996. This estate's wines can easily last 10–12
years in top vintages.

DOMAINE GRAND-ROMANE* * *

Address: 84190 Gigondas
Tel: 4-90-65-84-08
Fax: 4-90-65-82-14
Wines produced: Gigondas
Surface area: 148 acres
Production: 18,750 cases
Upbringing: 24 months total; for 6 months 20% of the yield is in new oak barrels, 10% of
            the yield is in barrels 2–3 years old, and the remaining 70% stays in stainless
            steel
Average age of vines: 30–35 years
Blend: 65% Grenache, 25% Syrah, 10% Mourvèdre and Counoise

   The Domaine Grand-Romane, part of the Jean-Pierre Amadieu empire, is a sizable
domaine planted primarily with Grenache, as well as important percentages of Syrah and,
surprisingly, Counoise, a grape varietal rarely seen except in Châteauneuf du Pape, and
then only at top domaines such as Beaucastel and Mont Redon. These are rustic, muscular
wines that can age well for 10–12 years.

VINTAGES

1995—Gigondas   This 1995 Gigondas was not one of the most concentrated and impres-
·   sive wines I tasted from this well-endowed vintage. While it is well made, with
86   clean fruit and medium body, it was made to be drunk during its first 5–6 years of
            life. Last tasted 6/96.
1994—Gigondas   The 1994 Gigondas is lean and herbal, with an advanced color and not
·   much intensity or fat. It needs to be drunk up quickly. Last tasted 6/96.
78
1990—Gigondas   A huge nose of spicy, herbal, and earthy-scented black fruit is followed
·   by a deep, rich, full-bodied wine that cuts a formidable impression on the palate.
89   As one might expect from such a broad-shouldered wine, the color is opaque ruby/

purple. Although it is not yet exhibiting much complexity, for pure flavor power and a tremendously full mouth feel, this Gigondas has considerable appeal, and will offer robust drinking. Anticipated maturity: now–2001. Last tasted 6/96.

1989—Gigondas   Dark ruby/purple in color, with a complex bouquet of spicy, toasty new
·   oak, rich, ripe, cassis fruit, pepper, and licorice, in the mouth, the 1989 is full-
88   bodied, velvety, and generously endowed, with a long, heady finish. It is an excel-
           lent, impeccably clean Gigondas that should age gracefully for 7–8 years. Last
           tasted 6/95.

DOMAINE DU GRAPILLON D'OR* * *

Address: Le Péage
        84190 Gigondas
Tel: 4-90-65-66-37
Fax: 4-90-65-82-99
Wines produced: Gigondas
Surface area: 37 acres
Production: 5,625 cases
Upbringing: 36 months total, with 12–14 months in old oak casks
Average age of vines: 30 years
Blend: 80% Grenache, 15% Syrah, 5% Cinsault

This is a traditional (so what's new?) Gigondas made from a multitude of parcels owned by proprietor Bernard Chauvet, the president of the syndicate of Gigondas. If the wine tends toward a certain rusticity, it is because everything is done the same way it was a century ago. There is no destemming of the old-vine, low-yielding grapes. The wines are kept in foudre until Chauvet deems them ready for bottling, usually 12 months or more of cellaring. They are bottled with neither fining nor filtration, and consequently will throw a very heavy sediment. Although a little more complexity would elevate this estate to an even higher level, there is no doubting the full-blooded, robust style of these powerful wines. Chauvet, who is assisted by his son, makes Gigondas they way it was in the old days, and most top vintages can easily handle 10–12 years of cellaring.

VINTAGES

1995—Gigondas   The 1995 Gigondas exhibits a dense purple color, sweet, uncompli-
·   cated aromas of blackberries and cherries, medium to full body, excellent richness,
86   a chewy texture, and good purity and length. It should turn out to be a very good
           example of Gigondas. Anticipated maturity: now–2001. Last tasted 6/96.

1994—Gigondas   The soft 1994 Gigondas displays a plummy/garnet color, sweet black-
·   cherry fruit, medium body, and an easygoing, round, straightforward but satisfying
85   personality. It should be drunk during its first 5–6 years of life. Last tasted 6/96.

1993—Gigondas   The light, pleasant, medium-bodied, soft 1993 Gigondas should be
·   drunk over the next 5–7 years. Last tasted 6/96.
84

1992—Gigondas   This 1992 Gigondas displays the light, dusty garnet color of the vintage,
·   raisiny fruit, light body, and an alcoholic finish. Last tasted 6/95.
73

1990—Gigondas   Some slight mustiness quickly blows off in the 1990's otherwise attrac-
·   tive, roasted, chocolaty, herb, and olive-scented nose. Highly extracted, with an
86   earthy, black-raspberry fruitiness, this soft wine should be drunk over the next 7–
           8 years. Last tasted 6/94.

1989—Gigondas   The flattering, jammy 1989 displays good purity, an attractive, roasted,
   ·   chocolaty, herb, olive, red- and black-fruit-scented nose, and a soft, luscious
   86   texture. Anticipated maturity: now–2001. Last tasted 6/94.

GUIGAL* * *

Address: 1, route de Taquières and Château d'Ampuis
         69420 Ampuis
Tel: 4-74-56-10-22
Fax: 4-74-56-10-96
Wines produced: Gigondas
Production: 10,800 cases
Upbringing: 3 years in old oak casks
Blend: 50% Grenache, 35% Mourvèdre, 15% Syrah

This northern Rhône vineyard owner and négociant reaches into the southern Rhône to purchase grape juice for its good, sometimes excellent Gigondas. Marcel Guigal spends considerable time tasting in the growers' cellars, believing that if one is willing to pay cash on the spot for certain good lots, a fine Gigondas can be made from the component parts. Guigal has increased the quality of his Gigondas, which is powerful, jammy, and authoritative. Guigal has gradually increased the percentage of Syrah and Mourvèdre, while reducing the amount of Grenache. It is a wine best drunk within five to ten years of the vintage.

VINTAGES

1990—Gigondas   The 1990 Gigondas (made from one-third Mourvèdre and two-thirds
   ·   Grenache) possesses a deep, dark ruby color, a big, spicy, leathery, black-fruit-
   87+   scented nose, sweet, fat, full-bodied flavors, firm structure, moderate tannin, and
          an excellent finish. Anticipated maturity: now–2002. Last tasted 6/96.
1989—Gigondas   The gorgeous 1989 Gigondas offers a precocious, evolved nose of black
   ·   fruits, cedar, Provençal herbs, and damp earth. In the mouth it is full-bodied,
   90   with a deep, unctuous, chewy texture, and a splendid ripe, heady, supple finish.
          Anticipated maturity: now–1999. Last tasted 6/94.
1988—Gigondas   The 1988 Gigondas is a structured, tannic wine, without the intense,
   ·   superripe black fruit character of the 1989 and 1990. For those who prefer a more
   86   linear, less expansive style of Gigondas, the 1988 is a good choice. Anticipated
          maturity: now–2001. Last tasted 6/96.

Older Vintages

While it is best to drink Guigal's Gigondas within a decade of the vintage, that is not to say the wine will not last longer. Guigal produced solid wines in 1983, 1979, and 1978 that are probably still holding on. I remember drinking a delicious 1969 and 1971 in 1986; both wines were in fine condition.

LES HAUTS DE MONTMIRAIL (DANIEL BRUSSET)* * * * *

Address: Place du Village
         84190 Gigondas
Tel: 4-90-70-91-60 or 90-30-82-16
Fax: 4-90-30-73-31
Wines produced: Gigondas Les Hauts de Montmirail, Gigondas Cuvée Tradition

Surface area: 46 acres
Production: 6,250 cases
Upbringing (Les Hauts de Montmirail): 18 months total, with 12 months in 100% new oak
    (Cuvée Tradition): 18 months in foudres
Average age of vines: 25 years
Blend (Les Hauts de Montmirail): 55% Grenache, 20% Syrah, 20% Mourvèdre, 5% Cinsault
    (Cuvée Tradition): 70% Grenache, 25% Syrah, and 5% Cinsault

Daniel Brusset, a tall, chiseled man with cellars in the nearby Côtes du Rhône village of Cairanne, owns 45.7 acres spread out over steeply terraced vineyards behind the spiky needles of the Dentelles de Montmirail. These terraces, covered with broken rocks and boulders, whose vineyards are planted on pure limestone, produce one of the most concentrated, magical wines of the appellation.

This is not an old estate, as Daniel's father started it in 1947 from his cellars in Cairanne. From just over 20 acres, it has gradually grown to nearly 205 acres, the bulk of the acreage being in Côtes du Rhône and Cairanne. In the provincial village of Gigondas, Brusset has always been looked upon as an outsider, even though his cellars are less than a 10-minute drive from the village square. He also incurred the village's skepticism when he began utilizing 100% new oak casks for his top cuvée, the Gigondas Les Hauts de Montmirail. Perhaps the real reason for the village's jealousy is that his wines perform so well in blind tastings; they are usually among the best of the appellation.

No one works harder than Brusset and his son, Laurent, as evidenced by anyone who takes the highly recommended drive up through the Dentelles de Montmirail. The Brusset vineyards can be reached only by following the road through the village, and circling above the village. From this perspective, there is an incredible vista of stone-covered, windswept, surreal-looking vineyards that can be cultivated only by intensive labor. Brusset would never plant a vineyard on anything but a steep terrace. He owns 68 separate terraced vineyards behind the craggy Dentelles. His vinification consistently reveals his flexibility. While nothing is destemmed, Brusset has gradually moved to 40–45% whole-berry fermentation. He is adamantly against any filtration unless the wine is unstable.

This is also a fine source for Brusset's regular cuvée of Gigondas, as well as a good selection of Côtes du Rhône. There is also some Viognier being added to his white Côtes du Rhône, making it even more appealing. Visitors to the region should recognize that Daniel Brusset is also one of the most promotion-conscious vignerons, with three separate caveaux (locations where his wines can be bought). One is in the Gigondas village square, another, called the Caveau du Plan de Dieu, at the crossing of D 8 and D 975, and the third at his home cellars in the village of Cairanne.

VINTAGES

1995—Gigondas Les Hauts de Montmirail   The 1995 Les Hauts de Montmirail appears
·   to be another outstanding wine from Brusset. His Gigondas is aged in new oak
90   casks made from a variety of French woods (vosges, nevers, and allier). The 1995 offers copious amounts of seductive, sweet, rich black fruit (raspberries, cherries, and currants) and vanilla in its flattering bouquet. Backward, dense, concentrated, and obviously tannic, with finesse allied to power, this is one of the more structured wines I tasted from Gigondas. Clearly in need of 4–5 years of cellaring, it should hit its peak around the turn of the century and last for a decade or more. It is a beautifully pure wine, with plenty of black fruit presented in a toasty, vanillin-scented, full-bodied style. Like all of the serious red wines produced by Brusset, this wine was bottled without filtration. Last tasted 6/96.

1994—Gigondas Les Hauts de Montmirail   The 1994 Gigondas is an intense, medium-
·   to full-bodied, deep ruby/purple-colored wine made in an elegant style. The wine's
88+   Mourvèdre component dominates, but I suspect the Grenache and Syrah will move
          to the forefront with more time in bottle. The wine possesses fine structure, some
          of Mourvèdre's animal and tree bark–like scents, an expansive, chewy mid-palate,
          and loads of tannin and structure in the long finish. Although the wine achieved
          13.5% alcohol naturally, it is closed and tight. Give it another 1–2 years of bottle
          age, and drink it over the next 10–12 years. Last tasted 6/96.

1993—Gigondas Les Hauts de Montmirail   Deep ruby-colored, with a pronounced black-
·   cherry, spicy, vanillin nose, this tasty, round, elegant yet chewy wine was produced
88   with more Grenache in the blend than usual. Brusset felt the Mourvèdre was too
          vegetal to use in the 1993. This is undoubtedly one of the most successful wines in
          what was a difficult vintage for Gigondas. Anticipated maturity: now–2003. Last
          tasted 6/96.

1992—Gigondas Les Hauts de Montmirail   The following notes apply only to the cuvée
·   sold to the American importer. The wine reveals a dark ruby color, a forceful
90   bouquet of sweet vanillin, toasty new oak, black fruits, herbs, and roasted nuts.
          Ripe and full-bodied, with layers of jammy fruit, this supple, generously endowed
          Gigondas exhibits none of the dilution or vegetal character revealed by many wines
          of this appellation. This is an exceptional effort for the vintage. Anticipated matu-
          rity: now–2004. Last tasted 6/96.

1991—Gigondas Les Hauts de Montmirail   Nineteen ninety-one was a dreadful vintage
·   in the southern Rhône, so one can imagine what a severe selection, not to mention
89   the winemaking talent, it must have taken to fashion such an impressive wine.
          Produced from yields of only 18 hectoliters per hectare, this 1991 Gigondas dis-
          plays a profound deep black/ruby color, and a huge, chocolaty, black-cherry, and
          herb nose that offers up sweet aromas of ripe, undiluted fruit. Full-bodied, with
          layers of fruit and richness, this sumptuously ripe wine is an amazing achievement
          given the vintage! Anticipated maturity: now–2004. Last tasted 6/95.

1990—Gigondas Les Hauts de Montmirail   The black-colored 1990 Les Hauts de Mont-
·   mirail exhibits lavish quantities of toasty new oak, along with superripe scents of
90   cassis. Exceptionally rich, as well as round and soft, this dramatic, full-throttle
          Gigondas is a real head-turner. I do not see it having the aging potential of the
          1989, but who really cares? Anticipated maturity: now–2006. Last tasted 11/95.

1989—Gigondas Les Hauts de Montmirail   The 1989 Les Hauts de Montmirail is a
·   spectacular wine for this appellation. My notes said, "essence of wine." Superrich,
93   with a huge bouquet that soars from the glass, it offers up aromas of cassis, vanillin,
          smoke, minerals, and licorice. In the mouth it exhibits huge extraction of flavor,
          gobs of ripe tannins, and a sweet, expansive, superb finish. This is a Gigondas to
          buy by the case. Anticipated maturity: now–2007. Last tasted 8/96.

1988—Gigondas Les Hauts de Montmirail   The 1988 is almost as good as the 1989.
·   Nineteen eighty-eight was an excellent vintage in Gigondas, and this wine looks to
91   be marginally the finest of the vintage, along with the great efforts of the likes of
          Domaine les Goubert and Domaine de Cayron. The huge, mineral, toasty, black-
          currant-scented bouquet is enthralling. In the mouth this full-bodied wine has great
          presence, super depth and length, slightly better acidity, and more definition than
          the 1989. This is a terrific Gigondas. Anticipated maturity: now–2002. Last tasted
          8/96.

1987—Gigondas   Given the deplorable vintage conditions, Brusset has turned out a soft,
·   fruity, spicy, adequate Gigondas. Mature now. Last tasted 11/96.
82

PAUL JABOULET-AINÉ* * *

Address: Les Jalets
      R.N. 7, B.P. 46
      26600 Tain l'Hermitage
Tel: 4-75-84-68-93
Fax: 4-75-84-56-14
Wines produced: Gigondas, Gigondas Cuvée Pierre Aiguille
Production: 1,675 cases
Upbringing: 8–10 months in oak barrels 2–3 years old
Blend: 90% Grenache, 10% Cinsault and Mourvèdre

The famous Jaboulet firm of Tain l'Hermitage has always made very good Gigondas. In fact, until 1980 it was usually one of the top five or six wines of the appellation. It also had superb aging potential. Bottles of the 1964, 1967, 1969, and 1970 are still in very good condition. However, since 1980 the style has clearly changed, and the Jaboulets apparently have decided to produce a more modern-style, very clean, filtered, and polished commercial wine that has a shelf life of four to six years, at most. This is all rather regrettable, but things may be changing for the better. Jaboulet began to produce a superconcentrated Gigondas Cuvée Pierre Aiguille in recent vintages that may be the answer to providing a satisfying, mouth-filling, classic, ageworthy Gigondas to Rhône wine enthusiasts, leaving his regular cuvée for the supermarkets and consumers looking for a fruity, straightforward wine.

VINTAGES

1995—Gigondas Cuvée Pierre Aiguille   The 1995 Pierre Aiguille is a more rustic wine, with an herbes de Provence/*garrigue*, earthy component, deep ruby color, a spicy,
·
86   medium-bodied personality, and good fruit and length. Tasted side by side with the Côtes du Rhône Villages and Côtes du Rhône Parallel 45, I would opt for the latter two wines over the more expensive Gigondas. Anticipated maturity: now–2003. Last tasted 6/96.

1990—Gigondas   Jaboulet's 1990 Gigondas, also made primarily from Grenache, is a big, lusty, rustic style of wine with a saturated black/purple color, and a tight but
·
88   promising nose of black fruits, licorice, and herbs. In the mouth there is super concentration, as well as tons of tannin. Anticipated maturity: now–2005. Last tasted 12/95.

1989—Gigondas   Jaboulet's dark ruby-colored 1989 Gigondas offers a mouthful of relatively simple, but jammy, rich, concentrated, and roasted blackberry fruit, heady,
·
86   alcoholic flavors, and a lush, soft finish. It is not a complex wine, but for those who like a full-throttle, muscular, unctuous style of Gigondas, this wine will provide immense satisfaction over the next 5–8 years. Last tasted 12/96.

1989—Gigondas Cuvée Pierre Aiguille   I was knocked out by the spectacular 1989 Pierre Aiguille. Made from 100% Grenache, this black/ruby-colored wine exhibits
·
90   a bouquet that soars from the glass, offering up aromas of roasted nuts, chocolate, black cherries, raspberries, and minerals. In the mouth it makes a super impression, with a full-bodied, sensationally concentrated texture. This wine is crammed with fruit, and displays a heady, spicy, and alcoholic finish. This is Jaboulet's finest Gigondas since their 1967. Anticipated maturity: now–2006. Last tasted 12/95.

Older Vintages

Vintages between 1979 and 1985 were disappointing, with light, thin wines made in 1985, 1983, 1982, and 1981. Should the 1978 show up in the auction market, it has always been a peppery, spicy, rich, full-bodied, old style Gigondas the likes of which Jaboulet consistently made in the sixties and seventies. Even older vintages, such as the wonderful 1967, 1969, and 1971, could still be in good shape if they have been well stored.

DOMAINE DE LONGUE-TOQUE* * * *

Address: Route de Sablet
        84190 Gigondas
Tel: 4-90-12-39-31
Fax: 4-90-12-39-32
Wines produced: Gigondas Cuvée Elégance, Gigondas Cuvée Prestige, Gigondas Cuvée
        Excellence
Surface area: 44.5 acres
Production (Cuvée Elégance): 1,875 cases
        (Cuvée Prestige): 1,875 cases
        (Cuvée Excellence): 1,875 cases
Upbringing (Cuvée Elégance): fermentation of 15 days in cement tanks; grape varietals are
        vinified separately; in November, there is a first assemblage
        and afterward the wines return to tanks for 3 months and are
        then transferred into old oak casks for 2 years; after 1 year
        in barrel, the final assemblage is done and the wine then
        spends 1 more year in cask
        (Cuvée Prestige): fermentation of 15 days in cement tanks; the 50-year-old
        Grenache and Syrah are fermented together in cement tanks;
        the assemblage and aging are the same as for the Cuvée
        Elégance
        (Cuvée Excellence): fermentation of 15 days in cement tanks; the 100-year-old
        Grenache and Syrah are vinified separately; the assem-
        blage and aging are the same as for the Cuvée Elégance
Average age of vines: 50–100 years
Blend (all 3 cuvées): 80% Grenache, 20% Cinsault, and a dollop of Mourvèdre

In 1995, the renowned 44.5-acre Domaine de Longue-Toque was sold by the diminutive, soft-spoken, hippie-ish Serge Chapalain to Madame Glenat. Founded by Chapalain's father in 1962, this has been one of the better estates in Gigondas. Chapalain's wine was made in an individualistic style, with an expressive, supple, opulently fruity, silky personality that had more in common with a top-class Burgundy than a rustic Gigondas.

Chapalain, who marched to the beat of his own drum, was spiritually and commercially similar to Châteauneuf du Pape's recently deceased Jacques Reynaud. He will no doubt be missed, but Madame Glenat has brought a new enthusiasm and vigor to the estate. She has decided to produce three separate cuvées to take advantage of the oldest parcels of Grenache. The 50-year-old parcels will go into the Cuvée Prestige, and the 100-year old parcels into the Cuvée Excellence. All three cuvées will contain 80% Grenache, 20% Syrah, and a tiny bit of Mourvèdre. None of the wines vinified and raised under Madame Glenat have been bottled, but the new ownership appears ready to build on the quality established over the last 35 years by Serge Chapalain and his father.

For readers fortunate enough to find any of Chapalain's wines in the marketplace, the 1990 and 1989 Gigondas, both released four years after their respective vintage, were the two finest wines produced by Chapalain since the early eighties. Both wines have 7–8 years of longevity and should be consumed by the end of the century.

DOMAINE DE LA MAVETTE* * *

Address: Quartier des Paillères
        Route de Lancieux
        84190 Gigondas
Tel: 4-90-65-85-29
Wines produced: Gigondas, Gigondas Cuvée Prestige
Surface area (regular cuvée): 13.6 acres
          (Cuvée Prestige): 2.47 acres
Production (regular cuvée): 1,875 cases
          (Cuvée Prestige): 312 cases
Upbringing (regular cuvée): Cement vats, then 12–24 months in old oak casks
          (Cuvée Prestige): Cement vats, then 24–36 months in old oak casks
Average age of vines (regular cuvée): 60 years
          (Cuvée Prestige): 100 years
Blend (regular cuvée): 70% Grenache, 20% Syrah, 5% Cinsault, 5% Mourvèdre
     (Cuvée Prestige): 70% Grenache, 20% Syrah, 5% Cinsault, 5% Mourvèdre

This estate has impressive hillside vineyard sites in addition to very old vines, so the potential for brilliant wines is obvious. To date, the wine has been an old-style, slightly oxidized Gigondas that is heavy and forceful. The 1995s may be a sign that more freshness and an earlier bottling are making some inroads at this property.

VINTAGES

1995—Gigondas   Domaine de la Mavette's 1995s are unquestionably the best wines I
·   have tasted from this estate. The 1995 Cuvée Tradition is a backward wine, with a
85?   deep ruby/purple color, a sweet, crushed, jammy blackcurrant nose, some austerity
       and dry tannin, but good purity, ripeness, and spice. My only reservation is whether
       the tannin may turn out to be too powerful for the wine's fruit. Anticipated maturity:
       2000–2007. Last tasted 6/96.

1995—Gigondas Cuvée Prestige   This is the finest wine I have tasted from Domaine de
·   la Mavette. It needs 3–4 years of cellaring, but it reveals a deep ruby/purple color,
88   a big-boned, structured, tannic feel in the mouth, plenty of depth and ripeness,
       oodles of jammy black-cherry and curranty fruit, and ferocious tannin in the finish.
       Anticipated maturity: 2000–2008. Last tasted 6/96.

1994—Gigondas   Medium ruby-colored, with a simple, jammy nose of red fruits, this
·   spicy, peppery, herbal Gigondas needs to be drunk young. Anticipated maturity:
82   now–1999. Last tasted 6/96.

1994—Gigondas Cuvée Prestige   The 1994 Cuvée Prestige is a more backward, deeper,
·   fuller-bodied wine than the regular cuvée. It exhibits a dark color, not much
86   complexity, but good spice, and attractive sweet, ripe fruit in a medium-weight
       format. Anticipated maturity: now–2001. Last tasted 6/96.

1989—Gigondas   The problem with the 1989 Gigondas from the Domaine de la Mavette
·   is that once past the herbal, peppery, spicy nose, there are short, malnourished,
76   soft flavors that lack grip and concentration. Drink it up. Last tasted 11/94.

1988—Gigondas   The 1988 has some ripe fruit in evidence, but the tannin levels are too
·   elevated for the wine's balance. Medium-bodied, with some attractive spicy fruit,
79   overall, this wine is an uninspiring, indifferent winemaking effort. Last tasted 6/94.

CHÂTEAU DE MONTMIRAIL* * *

Address: B.P. 12
        84190 Vacqueyras
Tel: 4-90-65-86-72
Fax: 4-90-65-81-31
Wines produced: Gigondas
Surface area: 74 acres
Production: 12,500 cases
Upbringing: 18 months minimum in enamel or cement vats
Average age of vines: 30 years
Blend: 75% Grenache, 15% Syrah, 10% Mourvèdre and Cinsault

    This moderate-sized estate has its cellars in the quaint Côtes du Rhône-Villages Vacqueyras, and is run with obvious enthusiasm by Maurice Archimbaud and his son-in-law, Jacques Bouteiller. They own 74 acres in Gigondas with the vineyards well situated on the sun-drenched terraces. The Gigondas spends 18 months aging in wooden foudres and cement cuves prior to bottling. Archimbaud does not want to risk any oxidation and is a great believer in early bottling to effect this end. His wines are not fined, but given a light filtration prior to bottling. The Gigondas called Cuvée Beauchamp is one of only four red wines made at Montmirail. They also make three different cuvées of Vacqueyras from their vineyards surrounding that village. Their Gigondas is, however, the firm's best wine and is always rather deep in color and jammy, with plenty of fruit; it lacks the complexity and power of the top Gigondas, but it has broad commercial appeal because it is so easy to understand and drink. It is a wine that usually requires drinking young, normally before it attains seven or eight years of age.

MOULIN DE LA GARDETTE* * * *

Address: 84190 Gigondas
Tel: 4-90-65-81-51
Fax: 4-90-65-85-92
Wines produced: Gigondas Cuvée Classique, Gigondas Cuvée Spéciale, Gigondas Rosé
Surface area (regular cuvée): 12.4 acres
                (Cuvée Speciale): 5 acres
Production (regular cuvée): 1,560 cases
              (Cuvée Spéciale): 500 cases
              (rosé): 110 cases
Upbringing (regular cuvée): 18 months total, with 6–12 months in old oak casks
              (Cuvée Spéciale): 18 months total, with 8 months in oak barrels 2–3 years old
              (rosé): 5 months in stainless steel vats
Average age of vines (regular cuvée): 60 years
              (Cuvée Spéciale): 60–100 years
              (rosé): 20 years
Blend (regular cuvée): 80% Grenache, 15% Syrah, 5% Cinsault, Mourvèdre, and Clairette
    (Cuvée Spéciale): 80% Grenache, 20% Syrah
    (rosé): 70% Syrah, 30% Cinsault

    Proprietor Jean-Baptiste Meunier owns a small estate of 17.4 acres from which he produces a classic Gigondas. His vineyards are located on limestone and clay soils on both the terraces and hotter plateau. From very old vines (averaging 60 years) and low yields, Moulin de la Gardette produces powerful, concentrated wines that may lack finesse, but compensate with their full-blown fury. Most vintages possess high alcohol levels, so this is not a

Gigondas for readers who enjoy wimpy wines. They give every indication of lasting for at least a decade, with the rarely produced Cuvée Spéciale possessing the ability to age gracefully for 15+ years. Some years occasionally turn out too rustic and coarse, but this estate is capable of making robust, satisfying, artisanal wines that deserve more recognition.

VINTAGES

1995—Gigondas Cuvée Classique   The 1995 Gigondas boasts an opaque purple color,
·   crisp acidity, amazing fruit ripeness and concentration (astonishing given the tart
91   acids), a sweet, rich, powerful attack, and long, muscular, full-bodied flavors that finish in a youthful manner. It is an expressionistic, large-scaled Gigondas that is just beginning to develop. Anticipated maturity: 2000–2012. Last tasted 6/96.

1994—Gigondas Cuvée Classique   The 1994 Gigondas Cuvée Classique exhibits an at-
·   tractive spicy, peppery, mineral, and earth-scented nose, medium-bodied, ripe
85   flavors, and an easygoing finish. In contrast to the monster 1995, this wine is open and flattering. Anticipated maturity: now–2003. Last tasted 6/96.

1994—Gigondas Cuvée Spéciale   The 1994 Cuvée Speciale offers a deep ruby/purple
·   color and an earthy, exotic, Asian spice, sweet, black-cherry-scented nose with
88+   background scents of truffles and licorice. Dense, tannic, and structured, with excellent concentration, this wine may turn out to be even better than my score indicates. Anticipated maturity: 1999–2008. Last tasted 6/96.

1993—Gigondas Cuvée Classique   The 1993 Gigondas exhibits a floral, licorice, earthy,
·   cherry-scented nose, medium- to full-bodied, spicy flavors with fine concentration
86   and glycerin and moderate tannin. A success for the vintage, it should be drunk over the next decade. Last tasted 6/96.

1992—Gigondas Cuvée Classique   This disappointing 1992 Gigondas has plenty of com-
·   pany in this horrific vintage for Gigondas. The wine displays a stale vegetable,
72   faded rose, weedy, burnt coffee aroma, and thin, harshly tannic flavors. Last tasted 6/95.

1990—Gigondas Cuvée Classique   The 1990 Moulin de la Gardette Gigondas performed
·   admirably in a blind tasting with its peers. The color is an opaque dark ruby/
88   purple, and the nose offers up sweet vanillin aromas as well as copious quantities of black raspberries. In the mouth this opulent, full-bodied wine exhibits superb concentration, a big, muscular, chewy texture, and a long, concentrated, alcoholic finish. The low acidity gives it accessibility, but this bruiser is so well constituted that it should last for at least 10–12 years. Last tasted 6/95.

1989—Gigondas Cuvée Classique   Although this was a backward, tough-textured, tannic,
·   and closed style of Gigondas, with airing it displayed a considerable amount of ripe
87   fruit and ample concentration. I would not be surprised to see this wine merit a higher score after it sheds some tannin as my rating may be conservative. Antici- pated maturity: 1998–2010. Last tasted 6/95.

L'OUSTAU FOUQUET* * *

Address: Domaine de la Fourmone
   84190 Vacqueyras
Tel: 4-90-65-86-05
Wines produced: Gigondas, Gigondas Cuvée Cigaloun
Surface area (regular cuvée): 12.4 acres
    (Cuvée Cigaloun): 10 acres
Production (regular cuvée): 2,000 cases
    (Cuvée Cigaloun): 1,625 cases

Upbringing (regular cuvée): 36 months total, with 12 months in oak casks
    (Cuvée Cigaloun): 36 months total, with 18 months in oak casks
Average age of vines (regular cuvée): 30 years
    (Cuvée Cigaloun): 35 years
Blend (regular cuvée): 80% Grenache, 10% Syrah, 10% Mourvèdre and Cinsault
    (Cuvée Cigaloun): 70% Grenache, 30% Mourvèdre

Roger Combe, whose cellars lie midway between the ancient village of Gigondas and the prettier town of Vacqueyras, produces only red wine from both appellations. Combe and his family own 59 acres, of which 22.4 are in Gigondas. The wine produced here is quite traditionally made. Produced from 80% Grenache and the rest of a field blend of Syrah, Mourvèdre, and Cinsault, it is a wine that is never filtered or fined, and spends 8–12 months in cement tanks and wooden foudres before being bottled. All of the Gigondas vineyards are on the hillsides of Mt. Montmirail. This is a good source for reliable, rarely exciting, but soundly made, very reasonably priced Gigondas.

VINTAGES

1993—Gigondas   The elegant 1993 Gigondas displays fine body and ripeness, and a
·   spicy, clean, berrylike fruitiness. Mature now. Last tasted 6/95.
86
1992—Gigondas   The light ruby/rusty-colored 1992 Gigondas reveals a vague bouquet of
·   cedar and earthy fruit. Watery, soft, and light-bodied, the wine's quality reflects
74   the torrential rains that nearly destroyed the Gigondas vignerons in 1992. Last
    tasted 6/94.

DOMAINE LES PALLIÈRES* * */* * * *
Address: 84190 Gigondas
Tel: 4-90-65-85-07
Wines produced: Gigondas
Surface area: 62 acres
Production: 10,625 cases
Upbringing: 36 months total, with 24 months in old oak casks, and the remainder in cement
    vats
Average age of vines: 50–55 years
Blend: 65% Grenache, 17% Syrah, 15% Mourvèdre, 2% Cinsault, 1% other varietals

I have fond memories of the visits I have made to Domaine les Pallières. This was the first domaine in Gigondas to begin estate-bottling, and it remains a classic example of the appellation in terms of the old, oxidized style of Grenache that is aged from 2–6 years in old cement tanks prior to bottling. This estate continues to be run by Pierre Roux, who is somewhat of a recluse, particularly since his partner and brother, Christian, passed away. This is one of the more splendidly situated properties in Gigondas, with vineyards planted on the clay/limestone terraces tucked under the craggy needles of the Dentelles de Montmirail.

I have had some marvelous Domaine les Pallières wines over the years, all of them possessing aged, complex, smoky, tobacco-scented noses, and soft, round, generous, warm flavors. However, with modern-day tastes moving toward the grapy style of winemaking, it is understandable that wines such as this have fallen from favor. Moreover, I do not believe recent vintages of Les Pallières, for whatever reason, even after their long sojourn in concrete vats and wood foudres prior to bottling, are as concentrated as they were in the seventies and early eighties. This was always a robust, full-flavored Gigondas, but recent vintages have not exhibited a similar character.

Pierre Roux will no doubt continue to run this estate, but neither he nor his deceased brother ever married, thus raising questions about succession. I would not be surprised to see a wealthy third party come in and snatch this estate up, because the vineyard is impressively situated, with the average age of the vines a healthy 50–55 years.

As the following tasting notes demonstrate, this wine can be the most authoritative example of an old-style Gigondas. Since the wine is usually not bottled for 3–4 years after the vintage, I have not included notes on the 1994 or 1995. The 1994 was surprisingly soft and shockingly deficient in intensity, but the 1995 looked to be an excellent, possibly outstanding example from Pierre Roux. However, it will probably not be bottled until the end of the century.

VINTAGES

1990—Gigondas   I have tasted many classic examples of Gigondas from this producer,
·   so I am perplexed about the more austere, less concentrated, and far less interesting
84   style of wine that has emerged in recent vintages. No doubt this estate, like many
                 of the larger southern Rhône domaines, tends to bottle as the wines are sold, which
                 can result in an enormous variation in quality, but even the first-bottled cuvées
                 were lacking the muscle and intensity that made Les Pallières renowned in the
                 sixties and seventies. That being said, I thought the 1990 to be pleasant, essentially
                 soft and fruity, but lacking weight, extract, and body. It will have to be drunk in its
                 first 5–7 years of life. Last tasted 6/95.

1989—Gigondas   The 1989 displays that big, animal, almost savage, smoked-meat smell
·   typical of an old-style Gigondas that puts some people off. In the mouth there are
88   powerful, chewy, alcoholic flavors that clearly demonstrate that proprietor Roux's
                 vines are quite old (three-fourths of his vines are over 70 years old, with the rest in
                 their mid-teens). Full-bodied, spicy, but somewhat coarse and rustic, this broadly
                 flavored, expansive Gigondas will no doubt drink well during its first 10–15 years
                 of life. Last tasted 6/95.

1988—Gigondas   The 1988 reveals some amber/orange at the edge. It displays a peppery,
·   herb, and berry-scented nose, medium-bodied, soft, spicy, adequately endowed
85   flavors, and a short, tannic finish. This wine lacks intensity and richness. Antici-
                 pated maturity: now–2000. Last tasted 6/94.

1985—Gigondas   There is no doubt that the early-bottled 1985 Les Pallières is a deli-
·   cious wine, and one of the great successes of the southern Rhône in this vintage.
90?   Dense ruby/garnet, with an exceptionally intense fragrance of Provençal herbs,
                 black·pepper, raspberry fruit, and violets, this is a full-bodied, powerful, and
                 harmonious wine. Subsequent bottlings exhibited considerable anise and rust
                 colors, and significantly less fruit and extract, no doubt having become desiccated
                 by their long sojourn in these cellars. Anticipated maturity: now–1999. Last tasted
                 11/95.

Older Vintages

I have drunk more than a case of the 1983 Les Pallières, and it has always been a big, smoky, cedary-scented wine with plenty of fruit, good freshness, and a full-bodied, lusty palate. In many ways it is a quintessential, old-style Gigondas without an excess of oxidation. The wine was drinking exceptionally well when last tasted in 1995. Other old vintages to look for include the superb 1978, and nearly as impressive 1979. It has been a decade since I had either of those wines.

DOMAINE LES PALLIEROUDAS (EDMONDE BURLE)* * * *
Address: La Beaumette
　　　　　84190 Gigondas
Tel: 4-90-70-94-85
Wines produced: Gigondas Les Pallieroudas
Surface area: 4.9 acres
Production: 685 cases
Upbringing: 24 months total, with 6 months in old oak barrels
Average age of vines: 60 years
Blend: 80% Grenache, 20% Mourvèdre

　　The stocky, self-deprecating Edmonde Burle owns some impressively old vines on the plateau and terraces of Gigondas. From his chaotic, dilapidated cellars, some spectacular wine has emerged, particularly in 1989 and 1990. However, irregularity is a hallmark of this estate. The Burle wines have the potential to be among the most concentrated and intense Gigondas—classic, fiery, old-style monsters that are increasingly rare—but some cuvées are spoiled by volatile acidity and the presence of brett yeast. All the wine is aged for up to two years, and depending on Burle's financial condition, a varying percentage of the crop is sold to négociants. This is a potentially outstanding estate, if it becomes more consistent. Some organization and modernization in the cellars would unquestionably help. Nevertheless, for flavor and intensity, Burle's Les Pallieroudas (in spite of its garish neon orange label), represents one of the appellation's classic wines . . . but be sure to taste before buying.

VINTAGES

1990—Gigondas　The 1990 offers an opaque black/purple, and a bouquet of sweet,
　·　　　　smoky, ripe black-cherry/black-raspberry fruit that soars from the glass. In the
　92　　　mouth, the wine is massively concentrated, yet opulent and silky given the sweet-
　　　　　　ness and ripeness of the tannins. The finish is voluptuous, long, and heady. Antici-
　　　　　　pated maturity: now–2006. Last tasted 6/96.
1989—Gigondas　The 1989 is bursting with exhilarating levels of vividly pure, sweet black
　·　　　　fruits intermingled with flavors of Provençal herbs. Undoubtedly the alcohol level is
　93　　　well over 14%. The yields from Burle's vineyard must have been minuscule to pro-
　　　　　　duce such levels of extraction. Anticipated maturity: now–2006. Last tasted 6/96.

DOMAINE DU PESQUIER* * *
Address: 84190 Gigondas
Tel: 4-90-65-86-16
Fax: 4-90-65-88-48
Wines produced: Gigondas
Surface area: 39.5 acres
Production: 6,250 cases
Upbringing: 12 months in cement vats and 18–24 months in old oak casks
Average age of vines: 35–40 years
Blend: 75% Grenache, 20% Syrah, 5% Mourvèdre

　　Proprietor Raymond Boutière has always made one of the most robust wines of Gigondas. Most of the vineyard is on the plateau, fanning out from the Dentelles, and thus benefits from this torridly hot, dry microclimate. Raymond is inching into retirement as his son, Guy, takes over the operation of this estate. The Boutières ferment all the wine in concrete and old wood vats, and then bottle the wine following a minimum of 18 months of aging. While some wine is still sold to négociants, increasing quantities are estate-bottled. They are full-blown, rich, spicy Gigondas that, like so many wines in this village, can be irregular, but when they get everything right, they are riveting examples of old winemaking and big, muscular, chewy wines for those with nineteenth-century palates.

VINTAGES

1995—Gigondas   The 1995 revealed a backward ruby/purple color, and plenty of tannin,
·   acidity, extract, and sweet ripe fruit. The wine is rustic, coarse, and unrefined at
88   present, but there is significant raw potential in Pesquier's 1995 Gigondas. Al-
         though it may always taste somewhat uncivilized, it should develop into an excel-
         lent wine. Anticipated maturity: 2000–2009. Last tasted 6/96.

1994—Gigondas   The medium ruby-colored 1994 exhibits an olive, *garrigue*, light
·   cherry-scented nose, good fruit, and a soft, diffuse character. Anticipated maturity:
84   now–2000. Last tasted 6/96.

1993—Gigondas   A medium-weight, moderately tannic, good Gigondas produced from
·   the forward-tasting 1993 vintage, this wine is lighter than expected, but it exhibits
85   a peppery, black-fruit character and a spicy finish. Anticipated maturity: now–
         2000. Last tasted 6/96.

1992—Gigondas   The 1992 Gigondas reveals a meaty, prune, and underbrush-scented
·   nose, disjointed flavors, and a soft, tannic, awkward finish. Last tasted 6/95.
75

1990—Gigondas   This domaine has long been known for its rustic, traditional, old-style
·   Gigondas. The robust, rich, chewy, massive 1990 displayed the dried pit fruit,
90   spicy, peppery, cherry flavors, robust tannins, and high-alcohol style that has
         increasingly fallen out of fashion. The 1990 should prove to have uncommonly long
         life, even for a Gigondas, and last for up to 20 years. This pure, old-style wine,
         which displays the essence of Bing cherries in its superextracted, husky style, it
         reminiscent of the old-vine, superripe style that Rayas extracts from their Gre-
         nache. It unquestionably warrants attention. Anticipated maturity: now–2005. Last
         tasted 6/95.

Older Vintages

Domaine du Pesquier produced a surprisingly light 1989, but the 1985 and 1981 were very strong efforts. Although I have not tasted either wine in over five years, they were going strong when last drunk in the southern Rhône Valley.

DOMAINE DE PIAUGER * * * *
Address: La Daysse des Dulcy
        84110 Sablet
Tel: 4-90-46-90-54
Fax: 4-90-46-99-48
Wines produced: Gigondas
Surface area: 8.9 acres
Production: 1,500 cases
Upbringing: 18 months in cement vats
Average age of vines: 40 years
Blend: 70% Grenache, 20% Mourvèdre, 10% Syrah

Praise for this small but consistently high-quality producer of both Côtes du Rhone and Gigondas is the result of the intelligence and capable efforts of proprietor Jean-Marc Autran. The Autrans have a modern approach to making wines, resulting in Gigondas that is pure, with less of the oxidized character and hefty, chunky personalities of so many of their peers. To date, these have been impressive, rich, authoritatively flavored, elegantly styled Gigondas that are capable of lasting for a decade. Proprietor Marc Autran generally utilizes surprisingly low yields of 30 or less hectoliters per hectare. Unfortunately, the Gigondas estate is small, but the Autrans also produce high-quality wines from their Côtes du Rhône holdings, particularly in Sablet, the village where their cellars are located.

VINTAGES

1995—Gigondas　The 1995 Gigondas's deep purple color is typical of the vintage's top
·　　　　wines. It possesses super fruit, powerful, forceful flavors, high extraction, and
88　　　excellent purity and length. This is an impressive Gigondas that will age for 10–
　　　　15 years. Last tasted 6/96.

1994—Gigondas　The 1994 Gigondas is a lower-keyed, leaner wine with a plum/garnet
·　　　　color, attractive cherry fruit, and a narrow palate. A compressed and compact wine,
81　　　it requires drinking over the next 3–4 years. Last tasted 6/96.

1990—Gigondas　The expansive 1990 is exceptionally pure, very supple, and deeply
·　　　　colored, with gobs of rich, spicy, roasted cassis fruit, an impressive deep purple
87　　　color, and a long, chewy, intense finish. Anticipated maturity: now–2003. Last
　　　　tasted 7/94.

1989—Gigondas　The deep ruby-colored, opulent 1989 possesses low acidity and an
·　　　　extremely flattering, impressive, up-front ripeness and richness. Readers should
88　　　note the sweet, rich, black-cherry fruit and medium- to full-bodied personality.
　　　　Anticipated maturity: now–2002. Last tasted 6/94.

1988—Gigondas　The dark garnet-colored 1988 is a more tannic and structured wine
·　　　　than either the 1989 or 1990. It is still youthful but fresh, and crammed with rich,
89　　　chunky fruit. Anticipated maturity: now–2003. Last tasted 6/94.

CHÂTEAU RASPAIL (MEFFRE FAMILY)* * *

Address: Domaines Meffre
　　　　　84190 Gigondas
Tel: 4-90-65-88-93
Wines produced: Gigondas
Surface area: 98.9 acres
Production: 15,000 cases
Upbringing: 18–24 months in stainless steel vats
Average age of vines: 25 years
Blend: 60% Grenache, 35% Syrah, 5% Mourvèdre

Château Raspail is owned by the Meffre family, whose empire was built by the late Gabriel Meffre. In the post–World War II period, Meffre forged the largest holding of appellation controlée vineyards in France. At present, there are 2,222 acres of AOC vines, with estates such as Château Raspail, Domaine de la Daysse, Domaine des Bosquets, and Domaine de la Chapelle all producing Gigondas. In Châteauneuf du Pape, Château Vaudieu is part of the Meffre empire, run by a daughter, Sylvette Brechet. The late Gabriel Meffre completely transformed much of the Gigondas landscape by using heavy equipment to terrace and blast away any of the scrub bushes or trees that precluded planting a vineyard. This family, along with the Amadieu family, dominates the total volume of Gigondas. The

Meffres have even larger holdings in the vast sector of Vaucluse known as the Plan du Dieu. In this area the Meffre family owns six estates, with approximately 1,250 acres of vines. It is not surprising that a consumer's chance of running across one of the Meffre Rhône Valley wines is far higher than for any other producer.

Because of the huge size of this enterprise, it has its share of critics, but truth be known, the quality of the wines has been sound. Château Raspail is the Meffre's 100-acre flagship Gigondas estate. The Grenache, Syrah, and Mourvèdre vineyards that average 25 years in age are planted on clay/limestone terraces, as well as what the French call the Jurassic *marne*, with a south-southwest exposure. Unlike at most Gigondas estates, there is 100% destemming at Château Raspail, but otherwise the vinification and upbringing are totally traditional.

While much of the Meffre production is middle-of-the-road, mainstream wines prized largely because of an absence of defects rather than for a particular character, recent vintages of Château Raspail have performed well.

VINTAGES

1995—Gigondas   Château Raspail has fashioned a potentially outstanding 1995 Gigon-
·   das. This concentrated, powerful, youthful wine possesses a bright purple color,
89   zesty acidity, moderate tannin, and oodles of fruit and extract. This wine will
         remain backward and unformed for several years. Anticipated maturity: 2000–
         2008. Last tasted 6/96.

1994—Gigondas   The medium-bodied 1994 Gigondas offers a light intensity nose of
·   *garrigue*, earth, and ripe cherry fruit. There is good purity, adequate acidity, and
85   firm tannin in the moderately long finish. Anticipated maturity: now–2000. Last
         tasted 6/96.

1990—Gigondas   The 1990 is an alcoholic, husky Gigondas with touches of plummy,
·   prune, and herb scents to its bouquet, and thick, chewy, soft flavors that reveal an
84   elevated degree of alcohol. Anticipated maturity: now–1998. Last tasted 6/95.

1989—Gigondas   The 1989 is a perplexing wine to follow. Two tastings revealed an
·   extremely full-bodied, dense, rich, highly concentrated style of Gigondas, with an
88?   herb- and cherry-dominated nose, and full-bodied, rustic flavors. Several other
         tastings have suggested a much lighter style of wine, giving rise to the question of
         whether there was a harmonious blending prior to bottling, or if there are several
         bottlings made from different cuvées? The best bottlings of this wine are excellent,
         and may be outstanding with another several years of aging. Last tasted 6/96.

1988—Gigondas   The intense 1988 possesses gobs of extract and tannin, as well as
·   powerful, roasted, peppery, black-fruit flavors. It is an impressive, full-bodied,
87   chewy, slightly rustic style of Gigondas. Anticipated maturity: now–2001. Last
         tasted 5/96.

DOMAINE RASPAIL (DOMINIQUE AY)* * * *

Address: 84190 Gigondas
Tel: 4-90-65-83-01
Fax: 4-90-65-89-55
Wines produced: Gigondas
Surface area: 44 acres
Production: 6,250 cases
Upbringing: 36 months total, with 18–24 months in old oak barrels and casks
Average age of vines: 30 years
Blend: 70% Grenache, 15% Syrah, 6% Mourvèdre, 5% Clairette, 4% Cinsault

Domaine Raspail, managed by the articulate, serious-minded, obsessive-compulsive Dominique Ay, can be one of the leading wines of the appellation. Although irregular in the late eighties, this is usually an impeccably made wine that can age for up to 20 years, one of the few Gigondas to possess this sort of longevity.

The deeply colored, rich, fragrant wine produced by Monsieur Ay is vinified in temperature-controlled stainless steel tanks after a complete destemming, a rarity in this village. The wine is given a long maceration lasting three weeks, and then aged 18–24 months in large wood foudres. It settles naturally and is neither fined nor filtered, so a heavy sediment will precipitate in the highly concentrated vintages. Ay uses a blend of 70% Grenache, 15% Syrah, with the rest a mixture of Mourvèdre, Clairette, and Cinsault. The average age of his vines is 30 years. Ay's Raspail is undoubtedly a textbook Gigondas. The deep color, the peppery, raspberry-scented bouquet, full-bodied, fleshy texture, and heady alcoholic punch admirably represent the corpulent, thunder-and-lightning school of Gigondas winemaking.

VINTAGES

1995—Gigondas   After a shaky period in the late eighties and early nineties, this estate
  ·   appears to have made a 1995 Gigondas that recalls their glory vintages. The superb
 91   opaque black/purple color is followed by a powerfully scented wine with gobs of
       overripe black-fruit scents, full-bodied, luscious, intense, and highly extracted
       flavors, admirable acidity, moderate tannin, and a blockbuster finish. This is a real
       vin de garde in need of 3–4 years of cellaring. How nice it is to see one of my
       favorite estates produce such a super wine. Anticipated maturity: 2000–2015. Last
       tasted 6/96.

1994—Gigondas   In contrast to the 1995, the 1994 Gigondas is an elegant, more re-
  ·   strained, medium-weight Gigondas with attractive peppery, cherry fruit, but not
 85   much concentration or intensity. Anticipated maturity: now–2002. Last tasted 6/96.

1993—Gigondas   The 1993 Gigondas is extremely light for this property, with medium
  ·   body and soft, fruity flavors exhibiting a peppery, red-fruit character. The wine
 82   lacks depth, focus, and richness. Drink it over the next 5–6 years. Last tasted
       6/96.

1992—Gigondas   The soft 1992 Gigondas is disappointingly short, light, and diluted. It
  ·   requires consumption. Last tasted 6/95.
 73

1990—Gigondas   The 1990 Domaine Raspail looks to be the best wine from this estate
  ·   since the 1985. The saturated black/ruby/purple color suggests superripeness and
 90   high extraction of flavor. The nose offers up intense, roasted, mineral, cassis aromas
       intermingled with the scents of Provençal herbs. In the mouth this wine reveals
       full-bodied, deep, concentrated flavors, excellent intensity and depth, as well as
       moderate tannins in the long finish. There is a sense of structure to go along with
       the lavish richness and intensity. This well-delineated Gigondas is one of the stars
       of the vintage. Anticipated maturity: now–2007. Last tasted 11/95.

1989—Gigondas   The 1989 is dark ruby-colored, with a spicy, herb, and black-cherry-
  ·   scented nose. In the mouth the wine is full-bodied, with fine concentration, a sweet
 86   mid-palate, but gobs of hard tannins in the finish. The wine is very good, but not
       comparable to the splendid 1990. Anticipated maturity: now–2004. Last tasted
       11/95.

1988—Gigondas   The medium ruby/garnet 1988 is a spicy, herb, earth, and raspberry-
  ·   scented wine, although it is tough-textured, hard, and possibly too tannic. Antici-
 85?   pated maturity: 1998–2006. Last tasted 6/94.

Older Vintages

The 1979, 1981, and 1983 Domaine Raspail wines are not nearly as concentrated and intense as I would have expected. I have known these wines since my days as a college student when I stocked up on vintages such as 1964, 1966, and 1967. The 1985 was the best wine made at this estate during that decade. A rich, sumptuous, fat, juicy Gigondas, it was still going strong when I last had it in 1993. In the seventies, Raspail produced a number of terrific wines, including the 1978, of which there are a handful of bottles remaining in my cellar. This wine has always been a full-bodied, powerful vin de garde, with plenty of spice, pepper, and black-cherry fruit intermingled with scents of truffles and *garrigue*. Although fully mature (finally), it remains full-bodied and rich, and should keep for another 5–6 years. I last had it in December 1995. The old classics from 1971, 1970, 1967, and 1964 are probably past their prime, but I would not be surprised to learn that magnums of these wines are still in terrific condition.

CHÂTEAU REDORTIER* * * */* * * * *
Address: 84190 Suzette
Tel: 4-90-65-85-83
Fax: 4-90-65-83-94
Wines produced: Gigondas (red)
Surface area: 12.4 acres
Production: 1,875 cases
Upbringing: 24–36 months in cement vats
Average age of vines: 15 years
Blend: 60% Grenache, 40% Syrah

Even more than Daniel Brusset of Les Hauts de Montmirail, Etienne de Menthon is undoubtedly an outsider in Gigondas. A native of the lovely French Alpine city of Annecy, in the early eighties Menthon moved south, building a Provençal farmhouse and carving out a vineyard in the Beaumes de Venise region. His predilection for vineyard planting continued with the acquisition of what has become 12.4 acres of high-altitude terraced vineyards in Gigondas. From his small Gigondas estate, Menthon, an intelligent, articulate man, produces one of the most impressive wines of the appellation. Perhaps because he is looked upon as an outsider, few locals seem inclined to volunteer information about his Gigondas, but it is one of the finest of the appellation. The wine is traditionally made, although a relatively high percentage of Syrah is included in the blend, giving the wine a deeper color and an unmistakable black-fruit character. The wine is kept for up to three years in cement vats (Menthon detests the taste of wood in Gigondas), and is bottled without filtration.

Château Redortier's Gigondas is usually delicious when released, but it is so well endowed, concentrated, and powerful that it will easily last for a decade or more, particularly in top vintages. This is a small but outstanding Gigondas estate that deserves significantly more attention.

VINTAGES

1994—Gigondas   This wine possesses a dark garnet/ruby color, a sweet nose of roasted
·   herbs, blackberries, and cherries, and sweet, round, alcoholic flavors with good
87   intensity and medium to full body. It is a delicious, flattering style of Gigondas that
        fills the mouth. This is one of the finest 1994s. Anticipated maturity: now–2004.
        Last tasted 6/96.

1993—Gigondas   From one of Gigondas's emerging stars, Château Redortier's 1993 of-
·   fers a saturated color, a big, chunky, fleshy, peppery, black-cherry-scented nose
87   with a touch of Provençal herbs, and full-bodied, tasty, concentrated flavors. Antici-
      pated maturity: now–2003. Last tasted 6/96.

1992—Gigondas   This is the wine of the vintage, and a major accomplishment in this
·   rain-soaked year. An intense, old-vine aroma of overripe black fruits is followed by
89   a clean, pure wine displaying none of the vegetal, pruny, mushroomy character
      afflicting so many of the 1992s from Gigondas. The wine is powerful, with fine
      density, dark color, and low acidity. It does appear fragile, suggesting it should be
      drunk earlier rather than later. Anticipated maturity: now–2000. Last tasted 6/95.

1990—Gigondas   The 1990 is nearly as impressive as the 1989, although it is softer,
·   with a great deal of alcohol in the finish. Nevertheless, there is plenty to admire in
89   its ruby/purple color, intense bouquet of herbaceous, overripe black cherries,
      concentrated, thick flavors, and long, velvety-textured finish. It should age grace-
      fully for a decade. Anticipated maturity: now–2005. Last tasted 6/95.

1989—Gigondas   The 1989 is one of the stars of Gigondas in what is undoubtedly this
·   appellation's best vintage between 1978 and 1990. Deep opaque black/ruby/purple
91   color, with a huge nose of olives, Provençal herbs, cassis, and licorice that is
      intensely fragrant, the wine coats the palate with glycerin and exceptional concen-
      tration of fruit. Because of the vintage, the acids are low and the tannins are ripe
      and round, so this wine can be drunk now. Anticipated maturity: now–2005. Last
      tasted 6/95.

1988—Gigondas   The medium ruby-colored 1988 suffers in comparison with its two
·   younger siblings. It displays a spicy, peppery, herb-scented nose, but the color
84   lacks the pigmentation and saturation of the 1989 and 1990, and the wine is soft
      and already fully mature. Drink it up. Last tasted 6/95.

DOMAINE ROMANE-MACHOTTE (JEAN-PIERRE AMADIEU)* * *

Address: 84190 Gigondas
Tel: 4-90-65-84-08
Fax: 4-90-65-82-14
Wines produced: Gigondas (red and rosé)
Surface area: 148 acres
Production (red): 15,625 cases
            (rosé): 2,000 cases
Upbringing (red): 48 months total, with 36 months in old oak barrels
            (rosé): 3 months in stainless steel vats
Average age of vines: 30–35 years
Blend (red): 70% Grenache, 30% Syrah
      (rosé): 80% Grenache, 10% Syrah, 10% Cinsault

Jean-Pierre Amadieu is one of the largest Gigondas producers, controlling over 225 acres of vineyards. Amadieu also owns Grand-Romane, which is located next to Romane-Machotte. Both are high-altitude, terraced vineyards planted at approximately 1,200 feet. Amadieu feels the quality of Grand-Romane is slightly higher because the terroir is better and they practice a more severe selection. As good as this wine is, it could be even better with less processing and filtration.

VINTAGES

1995—Gigondas   An impressive, sweet, seductive, black/ruby/purple-colored wine with
·   aromas of blueberries and kirsch, with a touch of licorice and pepper, this full-
89   bodied, evolved, voluptuously textured wine should be drinkable when released
         next year. Anticipated maturity: 1998–2008. Last tasted 6/96.

1990—Gigondas   This 1990 is light and somewhat stemmy, but soft and medium- to
·   full-bodied, with some attractive spicy, cherry fruitiness. Drink it up. Last tasted
80   6/94.

DOMAINE ROUCAS DE ST.-PIERRE* * *

Address: 84190 Gigondas
Tel: 4-90-65-00-22
Wines produced: Gigondas
Surface area: 12.4 acres
Production: 1,875 cases
Upbringing: 3 years minimum in underground cement vats
Age of vines: 10–40 years
Blend: 80% Grenache, 20% Syrah

This is a domaine with which I have had little experience. It is a small property of 12.5
acres planted primarily with Grenache and a small quantity of Syrah. The age of the vines
varies from 10 to 40 years. Production in recent years has been a modest 30 hectoliters per
hectare, or 2 tons of fruit per acre. This could be an estate to watch more closely, especially
if the winemaking sheds its irregular tendencies.

VINTAGES

1995—Gigondas   Roucas de St.-Pierre has fashioned an impressive, full-bodied, power-
·   ful 1995. Some tart acidity, a hallmark of this vintage, gives the wine delineation
89   and vibrancy in spite of its size. The color is a deep purple, and there is an
         inner core of sweet, chewy fruit to this broad-shouldered, full-bodied Gigondas.
         Anticipated maturity: 1999–2008. Last tasted 6/96.

1994—Gigondas   Although the medium ruby-colored 1994 Gigondas possesses a spicy
·   nose, the diluted, fecal flavors and lack of charm and fat are off-putting. It is
76   perplexing how one vintage (1995) could be so promising, and another so disap-
         pointing. Last tasted 6/96.

1989—Gigondas   The impressive 1989 reveals a black/ruby/purple color, an intense,
·   jammy, peppery, raspberry-like bouquet, full-bodied, concentrated, highly ex-
87   tracted, ripe, luscious flavors, low acidity, and plenty of heady alcohol in the finish.
         Anticipated maturity: now–2002. Last tasted 6/94.

CHÂTEAU DE ST.-COSME* * * */* * * * *

Address: 84190 Gigondas
Tel: 4-90-65-86-97
Wines produced: Gigondas, Gigondas Cuvée Valbelle Fut de Chêne, Gigondas Pavillon de
            St.-Cosme (sold only in the United Kingdom)
Surface area: 37 acres
Production (regular cuvée): 1,500 cases
            (Cuvée Valbelle): 916 cases
            (Pavillon de St.-Cosme): 1,250 cases

Upbringing (regular cuvée): 18 months total, with 75% of the yield in stainless steel vats
and 25% in 4-year-old barrels for 12 months
(Cuvée Valbelle): 18 months total, with 12 months in 30% new oak barrels
(Pavillon de St.-Cosme): 18 months in stainless steel vats
Average age of vines (regular cuvée): 40–50 years
(Cuvée Valbelle): 80 years
(Pavillon de St.-Cosme): 30 years
Blend (regular cuvée): 80% Grenache, 15% Syrah, 5% Cinsault
(Cuvée Valbelle): 70% Grenache, 25% Syrah, 5% Cinsault
(Pavillon de St.-Cosme): 100% Grenache

While son Louis Barruol has been in charge of this estate since the early nineties, and has justifiably insisted that more of the production from the old vines be estate-bottled, his father was one of the most spicy, outspoken characters of the village. I suspect the reason why Château de St.-Cosme is not better known is because a considerable quantity of the production was sold to négociants. As recently as 1995, shrewd négociants were pounding on the door, trying to get Louis to sell them wine.

Louis is taking this estate to a higher quality level. New oak (about 30% new casks) is now being used for their prestige cuvée, Valbelle. That wine also has malolactic done in new oak, resulting (at least in 1995) in a remarkably flashy, intense wine that could be called the Château Le Pin of Gigondas. Louis Barruol has also resisted any attempt by local oenologists to insist on fining and filtration, and has introduced a second wine made up of declassified batches from either the Cuvée Valbelle or the regular cuvée of Gigondas that he sells exclusively to the United Kingdom. It may be premature to write this, but my instincts suggest Louis Barruol is going to push Château de St.-Cosme into the five-star echelon of Gigondas producers.

VINTAGES

1995—Gigondas   The 1995 exhibits an attractive, ripe, black-cherry component, good
· fat and depth, and a spicy, pure, layered finish. This rich Gigondas will be drink-
89 able early, but should prove ageworthy. Anticipated maturity: 1998–2007. Last
tasted 6/96.

1995—Gigondas Cuvée Valbelle Fut de Chêne   The 1995 Valbelle Fut de Chêne, a
· cuvée made from vines 40–80 years old and aged in 40% new oak casks, is a
92 spectacular Gigondas. The opaque purple color is followed by sweet aromas of
black fruits, white flowers, pepper, and toast. Rich and full-bodied, with surprising
power as well as well-integrated acidity and tannin, this is a sumptuously-styled,
blockbuster Gigondas. Anticipated maturity: 1999–2012. Last tasted 6/96.

DOMAINE ST.-GAYAN* * * *

Address: Le Trignon
84190 Vacqueyras
Tel: 4-90-65-86-33
Fax: 4-90-65-85-10
Wines produced: Gigondas
Surface area: 39.5 acres
Production: 6,000 cases
Upbringing: 30 months total, with 12 months in old oak barrels and casks
Average age of vines: 60 years
Blend: 75% Grenache, 15% Syrah, 5% Mourvèdre, 5% other varietals

Roger Meffre is a warm, friendly, extremely confident and optimistic man in his early sixties. The former president of the Gigondas growers' association, he decided to take a quasi-retirement in the early nineties, turning over the administration of this estate to his talented son, Jean-Pierre. This family has been making wine at St.-Gayan since 1400, so along with Gérard Chave in Mauves (whose family of winemakers dates from 1481) he has winemaking genetically programmed into his blood. Meffre has an exuberance when talking about the potential for Gigondas that is infectious. He points out that mechanical harvesters are forbidden, and that the yield of juice per acre is restricted to one-third that of what growers in Burgundy and châteaux in Bordeaux are routinely producing today. He claims the local cooperative is concentrating more on quality, and that finally Gigondas is getting some respect for their wines. With quality such as is produced at St.-Gayan, Gigondas deserves to get much more attention and respect.

Meffre owns 39.5 acres of Gigondas vineyards, which are lined with rows of vines that average 60 years old. His wines, which are consistently rich and full-bodied, spend two years in cement cuves, followed by one year in wood foudres. He fines his wines prior to bottling but never filters them, saying, "To make a great wine one must take risks." Meffre's Gigondas, which seem to peak at about six or seven years and begin to fade around age 12, are among the richest wines of the appellation. They are characterized by an intense, almost portlike, jammy, berry fruit that Meffre attributes to his very old vines.

This is an excellent estate dedicated to making robustly styled, natural wines that are always among the best of the traditional heavyweights of Gigondas. Readers looking to save a few dollars should also search out the St.-Gayan Côtes du Rhône and the powerful, concentrated Côtes du Rhône-Villages Rasteau.

VINTAGES

1995—Gigondas   This purple-colored wine was still in cask when I tasted it in the
  ·   summer of 1996. It revealed copious quantities of sweet berry fruit, fine density,
88 +   good acidity, and a boatload of rustic tannin. It is a well-endowed, concentrated
          wine that appears to be a true vin de garde that should age for 10–15 years. Last
          tasted 6/96.

1994—Gigondas   The 1994 Gigondas exhibits good color, but a tough, hard, tannic
  ·   overlay. Is there enough fruit to survive the wine's tannic structure? Last tasted
83   6/96.

1993—Gigondas   It was pleasantly surprising to see just how well the 1993 Gigondas has
  ·   turned out. This is a so-so year, with abundant disappointments, but Meffre has
86   produced a deep garnet-colored Gigondas with a smoky, meaty, overripe plum-
          scented nose with notes of pepper and herbes de Provence. The wine possesses
          good density and ripeness, as well as a chunky personality; it should drink well for
          5–6 years. Last tasted 6/96.

1992—Gigondas   The thin, tannic, rustic, charmless 1992 Gigondas is distinctly inferior
  ·   to the 1993. Last tasted 6/96.
76

1991—Gigondas   The 1991 is surprisingly well made, round, and fruity. Drink it up. Last
  ·   tasted 6/96.
84

1990—Gigondas   The real star is St.-Gayan's 1990 Gigondas, an opaque purple/garnet-
  ·   colored wine with a huge bouquet of smoked olives, herbs, black fruits, and gamy
90   scents. Full body, an unctuous texture, thick, rich flavors, and loads of concentra-
          tion have combined to create a terrific Gigondas. Anticipated maturity: now–2006.
          Last tasted 6/96.

1989—Gigondas   The 1989 Gigondas is superb. It is a blockbuster Gigondas, with an
·   opaque dark ruby/purple color, a huge nose of roasted meats, black raspberries,
91   Asian spices, herbs, and pepper. In the mouth there is sensational concentration,
a massive, full-bodied, unctuous texture, adequate acidity to provide grip and
delineation, and a whoppingly long, rich finish. Anticipated maturity: now–2005.
Last tasted 6/96.

1988—Gigondas   The 1988 Gigondas exhibits more structure and tannin, but not quite
·   the opulence of fruit that both the 1989 and 1990 possess. It is a deep, rich wine
89   with a more reticent nose, which, with coaxing, gives up aromas of peppery black
fruit, herbs, and truffles. In the mouth it is full-bodied, with more noticeable tannin
and better acidity than either the 1989 or 1990. Anticipated maturity: now–2002.
Last tasted 6/96.

1985—Gigondas   This wine performed very well young (as did most 1985s), but it has
·   quickly attained full maturity. Deep ruby/garnet with a full-intensity, portlike
87   bouquet of jammy, berry, herb-tinged fruit, the 1985 is full-bodied, lush, and long.
The wine's low acidity suggests additional cellaring is fraught with worry. Mature
now. Last tasted 6/96.

Older Vintages

There is no shortage of older stars from this estate. The 1978, 1979, and even 1980 were
classic, full-blown, earthy, rich, rough-and-tumble wines that could easily take the chill off
a cold winter's night. Nineteen eighty-one was good. The 1983, which was somewhat
disappointing in the context of the vintage, was eclipsed by the surprisingly opulent, fat
1982. The wines of St.-Gayan can last, especially when well stored.

DOMAINE SANTA DUC* * * * *

Address: Quartier des Hautes Garrigues
      84190 Gigondas
Tel: 4-90-65-84-49
Wines produced: Gigondas Cuvée Classique, Gigondas Cuvée des Hautes Garrigues (pro-
      duced only in top vintages)
Surface area (regular cuvée): 25 acres
      (Cuvée des Hautes Garrigues): 12.4 acres
Production (regular cuvée): 6,875 cases
      (Cuvée des Hautes Garrigues): 935 cases
Upbringing (regular cuvée): 18–24 months total, with 12 months in old oak casks
      (Cuvée des Hautes Garrigues): 18–24 months total, with 30% of the yield
      spending 12 months in new oak barrels, the
      other 70% remaining in stainless steel vats
Average age of vines (regular cuvée): 40 years
      (Cuvée des Hautes Garrigues): 50 years
Blend (regular cuvée): 70% Grenache, 15% Syrah, 15% Mourvèdre
      (Cuvée des Hautes Garrigues): 70% Grenache, 15% Syrah, 15% Mourvèdre (blend
      sometimes has as much as 30% Mourvèdre)

The Domaine Santa Duc has emerged in just over a decade as the number one estate for
quality in Gigondas. Much of the credit for this must go to Yves Gras, a tall, good-looking
young man who is probably in his mid-thirties, but looks even younger. He took over when
his father, Edmond Gras, retired in 1985. Until then, virtually the entire production was
sold to various négociants. Yves, fresh and enthusiastic, with the vigor of youth, decided the

estate had to take a different direction, and begin to estate-bottle most of the production from its vineyards.

Santa Duc has become not only an important estate in Gigondas (37.4 acres of vines), but also a noteworthy producer of high-quality Côtes du Rhône and Vacqueyras from the family's 17 acres of vineyards sprinkled in and around Vacqueyras, Séguret, and Roaix.

I believe I was the first writer to discover these wines. I do a blind tasting with the syndicate each year, and for several years in a row the number one and number two wines in my tastings were Santa Duc's regular cuvée of Gigondas, or their special luxury cuvée called Hautes Garrigues. The latter wine has been produced only in 1989, 1990, 1993, and 1995. The Gras cellars, which are located on the plateau of Gigondas two miles from the village center, hardly give evidence of the magic that is practiced inside. This estate has moved forward in a progressive manner, utilizing small casks for aging one-third of their Gigondas crop. Another third is aged in tank, and the rest in foudre. The three components are blended prior to bottling. In the great years, Yves Gras makes his Cuvée des Hautes Garrigues from a 50-year-old parcel of hillside vineyards (planted with 70% Grenache, 15% Syrah, 15% Mourvèdre) that tends to yield a shockingly low one-half ton of fruit per acre. This wine, which sees more new oak than the regular cuvée (30% is aged in 100% new oak casks), also contains a healthy whollop of Mourvèdre (sometimes as much as 30%). All of the Gras vineyards are on either the plateau of Gigondas that faces the Côtes du Rhône village of Sablet to the north, or on the terraced limestone/clay hillsides of Les Hautes Garrigues. The low yields that are a hallmark of this estate's wines tend to produce Gigondas that reaches 13–14% alcohol for the cuvée classique, and in vintages like 1989 and 1990, 15% alcohol for the Cuvée des Hautes Garrigues. If that sounds intimidating, what is even more remarkable is that the alcohol is not noticeable given the wines' intensity of fruit and extract.

Today, over 90% of Santa Duc's wines are sold in the export market. It is not unusual for Yves to get requests for his exquisite Gigondas from such far-flung locations as Singapore, Australia, and South America. Because of the popularity of his wines, Yves Gras is quickly moving toward doing only one bottling to ensure complete uniformity of quality (Hautes Garrigues is always bottled at one time). Gras never fines, but he does use a plaque (filter pad #3), which in essence amounts to a negligible filtration since this is a very porous cellulose filter pad designed for those growers who want some security but do not want to remove the wine's aromatics, flavors, or body.

Is this the finest estate in Gigondas in 1997? As the following tasting notes demonstrate, Santa Duc combines the muscle, richness, and fire of a classic Gigondas with a degree of elegance and purity that many wines of this appellation lack. For me, Santa Duc is the reigning champion of Gigondas.

VINTAGES

1995—Gigondas Cuvée Classique   The 1995 Gigondas Cuvée Classique is a blend of 75% Grenache, 15% Syrah, and 10% Mourvèdre. The wine reveals an opaque

88 purple color, good structure, enough vibrant acidity to provide focus, full body, outstanding concentration, and a sweet, rich, long finish. Although youthful and unformed, it is a potentially outstanding Gigondas. Anticipated maturity: 1998– 2008. Last tasted 6/96.

1995—Gigondas des Hautes Garrigues   The 1995 Cuvée des Hautes Garrigues (made from 70% Grenache and 30% Mourvèdre, with 40% of the blend aged in new oak

91 casks) was harvested at degrees of sugar resulting in a wine with nearly 16% alcohol. This wine has only been produced in 1989, 1990, 1993, and 1995. The 1995 boasts an opaque purple color, and a backward but promising nose of floral scents, and pure, black-raspberry fruit. Full-bodied and powerful, with considerable tannic clout, this is an enormously endowed Gigondas that is meant to be laid away for 5–6 years until it can resolve its tannin and exhibit its sweet, rich fruit. Anticipated maturity: 2000–2010. Last tasted 6/96.

1994—Gigondas Cuvée Classique   The 1994 Gigondas is forceful and robust, with excel-
   ·   lent depth, purity, and size. Still youthful and exuberant, this is a Gigondas that
   89   marries finesse with power. Anticipated maturity: now–2005. Last tasted 6/96.

1993—Gigondas Cuvée des Hautes Garrigues   The estate's prestige cuvée is amazing for
   ·   the vintage. Made from 75% Grenache and 25% Mourvèdre, and aged in small oak
   90   casks, this black/purple-colored wine offers wonderful ripeness, a dense, viscous,
          thick texture, full body, and a sumptuous, concentrated style. Anticipated maturity:
          1998–2007. Last tasted 6/96.

1993—Gigondas Cuvée des Hautes Garrigues   The 1993 Cuvée des Hautes Garrigues is
   ·   the finest Gigondas I tasted from this vintage. The wine displays a black color and
   92   a superrich nose of raspberries, jammy cherries, and spice. Full-bodied, with
          splendid concentration, moderate tannin, and loads of glycerin, it should prove to
          be a large-scaled, impressively concentrated Gigondas for drinking during its first
          15 years of life. Last tasted 6/96.

1992—Gigondas Cuvée Classique   Nineteen ninety-two was a very difficult vintage in
   ·   Gigondas. Most of the 1992s I tasted have been unimpressive. However, that
   88   cannot be said about Santa Duc's 1992 Gigondas. It offers a sweet, jammy nose of
          roasted nuts, Provençal herbs, and black-cherry fruit. Medium- to full-bodied, with
          expansive, sweet fruitiness, moderate tannin, and admirable structure, this is a seri-
          ous, well-endowed Gigondas. Anticipated maturity: now–2001. Last tasted 9/95.

1991—Gigondas Cuvée Classique   Gras's genius for turning out high-quality wines in
   ·   dreadful years is even more apparent in 1991. Only one-third of his production
   88   was estate-bottled. The dark ruby-colored 1991 Gigondas exhibits an enticing
          chocolaty, cedary, Provençal herb–scented nose, sweet, jammy, black-cherry fruit,
          fruitcakelike flavors, and a spicy, medium-bodied, soft finish. It is a super effort
          from this undistinguished vintage. Drink it over the next 5–6 years. Last tasted
          9/95.

1990—Gigondas Cuvée Classique   The 1990 regular cuvée is an opaque black/purple-
   ·   colored wine with a wonderfully pure nose of black raspberries and minerals. In
   89   the mouth, this full-bodied, superconcentrated wine is long, opulent, powerful, and
          impeccably well balanced. Approachable now for its sheer intensity of sweet fruit,
          it will easily last for up to a decade. Last tasted 11/95.

1990—Gigondas Cuvée des Hautes Garrigues   Santa Duc's 1990 cuvée prestige was aged
   ·   in small oak casks, but the oak enhances rather than dominates the extraordinary
   93   richness and opulence of this wine. The huge nose of cassis, vanillin, smoke,
          flowers, and minerals is followed by a deeply concentrated, full-bodied wine with
          soft tannins, considerable complexity, and a voluptuous, explosively long, rich
          finish. It can be drunk now, but wow, what a future this wine possesses. Anticipated
          maturity: now–2008. Last tasted 8/96.

1989—Gigondas Cuvée Classique   The 1989 regular Gigondas is a dynamite wine, with
   ·   a sensational opaque black/ruby/purple color, a superintense nose of violets, cassis,
   90   smoke, and minerals, rich, almost extravagantly intense, ripe flavors, plenty of
          glycerin, an unctuous texture, and a spectacularly long, explosive finish. This
          dazzling bottle of Gigondas can be drunk young because of the soft tannins and
          low acidity. It promises to keep for at least 12–15 years. Last tasted 11/95.

1989—Gigondas Cuvée des Hautes Garrigues   The 1989 Cuvée des Hautes Garrigues
   ·   displays more tannin than the regular cuvée, generous, smoky, vanillin, toasty,
   92   cassis-scented aromas, enticingly rich black/purple color, and huge flavors of cof-

fee, chocolate, herbs, and superripe black fruits. In the mouth there is the same opulence, but the use of new barrels has resulted in a more muscular, structured, tannic wine. Very impressive! Anticipated maturity: 1998–2010. Last tasted 12/95.

1988—Gigondas Cuvée Classique   The 1988 Gigondas from Santa Duc is an excellent, nearly outstanding wine. Concentrated, with an opaque, dark ruby/purple color, **88** this spicy, peppery, richly fruity wine is full-bodied, displays some toasty, vanillin, oaky aromas from being aged in small casks, and offers stunning length and balance. It is an impeccable wine from the appellation, and its price makes it one of the best bargains in the marketplace. Anticipated maturity: now–2005. Last tasted 6/95.

TARDIEU-LAURENT* * * *

Address: Chemin de la Marquette
      84360 Lauris
Tel. 4-90-08-32-07
Fax: 4-90-08-26-57

This négociant, with its cellars in the beautiful Château Loumarin, depends on purchased juice from specific growers to fashion their blends. Additional information on Tardieu-Laurent, a firm that produces wines from most Rhône Valley appellations, can be found on page 484. Their first vintages of Gigondas were very impressive wines made from juice purchased from the estate of Louis Barruol of Château de St.-Cosme. The quality of these wines is clearly four-star.

VINTAGES

1995—Gigondas   The ruby/purple-colored 1995 Gigondas exhibits kirsch/black-cherry aromatics, medium to full body, and excellent density and concentration. Antici-**89** pated maturity: 1998–2005. Last tasted 6/96.

1995—Gigondas Vieilles Vignes   The 1995 Vieilles Vignes (70% Grenache, 30% Mourvèdre) achieved 14.7% natural alcohol. It is a spectacular wine, with fabulous **91** ripeness, layers of sweet, jammy fruit, good structure, and some tannin in the finish. It is a large-scaled, big, juicy, pure Gigondas that will have many fans. Anticipated maturity: 1998–2008. Last tasted 6/96.

1994—Gigondas   The tough-textured, traditional, dense, tannic, spicy, medium- to full-bodied 1994 Gigondas boasts an impressive ruby/purple color. This backward wine **87** offers up aromas of tree bark and spices. Not surprisingly, it contains 15% Mourvèdre in the blend, giving the wine its formidable structure and backward style. If it blossoms, it will merit an even higher rating. At present, it is austere, although well-endowed. Anticipated maturity: 1998–2005. Last tasted 6/96.

DOMAINE DU TERME* * * *

Address: 84190 Gigondas
Tel: 4-90-65-86-75
Fax: 4-90-65-80-29
Wines produced: Gigondas (red and rosé)
Surface area: 27 acres
Production (red): 3,125 cases
        (rosé): 625 cases
Upbringing (red): 36 months total, with 12 months in enamel vats, 6–8 months in old oak. After bottling, the wines remain in the cellar for 6 months.

Average age of vines: 30 years
Blend (red): 80% Grenache, 15% Syrah, 5% Mourvèdre and Cinsault
    (rosé): 80% Grenache, 20% Mourvèdre and Cinsault

The handsome Rolland Gaudin, the current president of the Syndicat des Vignerons, makes a traditional, robust, tannic style of Gigondas that can age well for 10–12 or more years. When tasted young, the wine often seems coarse because of its tannic astringence, but there is plenty of underlying fruit and intensity. As one might expect in a village known for artisan-styled wines, the president of the syndicate makes wine very traditionally.

VINTAGES

1993—Gigondas   The 1993 possesses an opaque saturated purple color, a dense, black-cherry-scented nose, and long, rich, medium- to full-bodied flavors with moderate
  ·
  87?   tannin. It should be one of the more concentrated and structured wines of the 1993 vintage. Anticipated maturity: 2000–2008. Last tasted 6/95.
1992—Gigondas   Domaine du Terme produced a sweet, soft, fruitcake-scented, grapy, alcoholic 1992 Gigondas that has avoided the vegetal, pruny, damp, woodsy quality
  ·
  85   exhibited by many of the rain-plagued 1992s. A fine effort, it should be consumed over the next 3–4 years. Last tasted 6/95.
1990—Gigondas   This wine exhibits considerable fatness, a fleshy, ripe, fruitiness, and a supple, chewy texture, but lacks complexity. It should make delicious drinking
  ·
  82   over the next 4–6 years. Last tasted 6/94.
1989—Gigondas   The deep garnet-colored 1989 is intense, concentrated, and full-bodied, with deep, ripe, concentrated flavors of black and red fruits, *garrigue*, and
  ·
  87   pepper. With soft tannin, plenty of alcohol, and low acidity, it should drink well for 5–7 years. Last tasted 6/94.
1988—Gigondas   The fully mature, rustic, nearly savage 1988 was similarly chewy, dense, and intensely concentrated, with excellent ripeness, full body, crisp acidity,
  ·
  87   and aggressive tannin. This is a hefty, spicy, old-styled Gigondas. Anticipated maturity: now–2006. Last tasted 6/94.

DOMAINE LES TEYSSONIÈRES* * *

Address: 84190 Gigondas
Tel: 4-90-65-86-39
Wines produced: Gigondas, Gigondas Cuvée Alexandre
Surface area (regular cuvée): 27 acres
            (Cuvée Alexandre): 2.47 acres
Production (regular cuvée): 4,275 cases
            (Cuvée Alexandre): 291 cases
Upbringing (regular cuvée): 36 months total, with 18 months in old oak casks
            (Cuvée Alexandre): 18 months total, with 12–18 months in old oak casks
Average age of vines (regular cuvée): 60 years
            (Cuvée Alexandre): 65 years
Blend (regular cuvée): 80% Grenache, 15% Syrah, 5% Mourvèdre
    (Cuvée Alexandre): 80% Grenache, 20% Syrah

Domaine les Teysonnières produces a traditionally made wine from their vineyard holdings that are essentially all on clay soils south of the terraced hillsides. Vintages I have tasted have been good, midweight Gigondas that exhibit the typicity of the appellation, and moderate longevity.

VINTAGES

1995—Gigondas   The 1995 Gigondas reveals the black/ruby color consistently apparent
·   in these young wines, as well as cherry, *framboise*, flower, and spice scents. This is
87   a medium-weight, elegantly wrought wine with purity and style. There is enough
acidity to provide definition to this classy, intense, flavorful yet finesse-style Gigondas. Anticipated maturity: 1998–2006. Last tasted 6/96.

1994—Gigondas   The 1994 Gigondas exhibits a dark ruby color, medium body, attractive
·   fruit, and a short finish. I also notice scents of toasty new oak in its smoky, *pain*
86   *grillé* character. Anticipated maturity: now–2001. Last tasted 6/96.

1989—Gigondas   The 1989 offering was watery, angular, light-bodied, and diluted. Ma-
·   ture now. Last tasted 6/95.
71

1988—Gigondas   The 1988 displayed an attractive ripe berry fruitiness, medium body,
·   soft tannins, and overall good balance, but it lacked depth and concentration.
84   Drink it up. Last tasted 6/94.

DOMAINE DE LA TOURADE* * *

Address: Hameau Beaumette
       84190 Gigondas
Tel: 4-90-70-91-09
Wines produced: Gigondas, Gigondas Cuvée Font des Aieux
Surface area (regular cuvée): 9.9 acres
      (Cuvée Font des Aieux): 5 acres
Production (regular cuvée): 1,875 cases
      (Cuvée Font des Aieux): 750 cases
Upbringing (regular cuvée): 36 months total, with 12–18 months in old oak casks
      (Cuvée Font des Aieux): 18 months total, with 12–18 months in old oak casks
Average age of vines (regular cuvée): 40 years
      (Cuvée Font des Aieux): 40 years
Blend (regular cuvée): 80% Grenache, 10% Syrah, 10% Mourvèdre
      (Cuvée Font des Aieux): 80% Grenache, 15% Syrah, 5% Cinsault

This estate, which is run by André Richard, produces two Gigondas cuvées, a regular
cuvée from vineyards on the plateau, and their limited-production Cuvée Font des Aieux,
from a 5-acre parcel of 40-year-old vines. There is no destemming, and the wines are
vinified traditionally and aged in small casks for 18 months. My limited exposure to this
estate has revealed a moderately endowed, midweight Gigondas that is faithful to tradition,
but is not a huge, blockbuster/bruiser wine.

VINTAGES

1995—Gigondas   Tourade's 1995 exhibits the supermature fruit achieved by many Gi-
·   gondas producers in this vintage. The dark ruby/purple color is followed by
87   straightforward but ripe, sweet, jammy cherry, kirsch, and roasted-herb aromas.
Fat and rich, but unevolved, this is a very good example of Gigondas. Anticipated
maturity: now–2006. Last tasted 6/96.

1994—Gigondas   The 1994 reveals an advanced garnet/plum-like color. Medium-bodied,
·   soft, and ripe, with a peppery, spicy component, and sweet fruit on the attack, it is
85   a wine for near-term consumption. Anticipated maturity: now–2001. Last tasted
6/96.

1990—Gigondas   This 1990 Gigondas is a success. Clearly made from exceptionally ripe
    (perhaps even overripe) Grenache, given the nose of jammy cherries, prune, and
85   kirsch, the wine is medium- to full-bodied, fat, and tasty, with little tannin, as well
    as alarmingly low acidity. This wine offers uncomplicated, delicious drinking.
    Anticipated maturity: now–2000. Last tasted 6/94.

DOMAINE DES TOURELLES* * */* * * *

Address: Le Village
            84190 Gigondas
Tel: 4-90-65-86-98
Fax: 4-90-65-89-47
Wines produced: Gigondas
Surface area: 19.8 acres
Production: 3,250 cases
Upbringing: 36 months total, with 12–18 months in old oak casks
Average age of vines: 45 years
Blend: 80% Grenache, 10% Syrah, 5% Cinsault, 5% Mourvèdre

This estate appears to be gradually improving the quality of the wines under the administration of André Cuillerat. Part of the production is still sold to négociants, but Cuillerat has increased the quantity of estate-bottled wine from his terraced vineyards composed of limestone/clay. The wines reveal good weight, more elegance than most, and clean, fresh flavors, but admittedly, my experience has been limited to recent vintages.

VINTAGES

1995—Gigondas   An impressive 1995, Domaine des Tourelles' offering possesses an
    opaque dark ruby/purple color, plenty of extract, fine power, and crisp underlying
89   acidity. There is enough sweet fruit to support the acid and tannin in this wine,
    which should evolve slowly. It will need several years of cellaring. Anticipated
    maturity: 1999–2008. Last tasted 6/96.
1994—Gigondas   The 1994 is a nicely packaged, dark ruby-colored wine with sweet plum
    and cherry fruit, medium body, some roundness, and a fine attack. Some compactness
86   in the finish held down my score. It should drink well for 4–5 years. Last tasted 6/96.

CHÂTEAU DU TRIGNON* * *

Address: 84190 Gigondas
Tel: 4-90-46-90-27
Fax: 4-90-46-98-63
Wines produced: Gigondas
Surface area: 54.3 acres
Production: 7,000 cases
Upbringing: 18 months in cement vats
Average age of vines: 40 years
Blend: 60% Grenache, 20% Syrah, 10% Mourvèdre, 8% Cinsault, 2% other varietals

On a visit to Château du Trignon, the round, friendly, welcoming face of André Roux was always enough to put even the most foul-dispositioned visitor in a good mood. Roux retired in 1987, turning over the reins to his nephew, Pascal, who runs the Château du Trignon in Sablet, one of the Côtes du Rhône-Villages. Roux produces a number of Rhône wines, but his best is his Gigondas. André Roux was one of the Rhône Valley's most vocal exponents of the whole berry semi-carbonic maceration method of fermentation. He worked under the famous Dr. Nalys of the Domaine Nalys, a well-known estate in Châteauneuf-du-Pape that practices this method of making red wine. Wines made by the carbonic maceration method are usually delightfully fresh, fruity wines that must be consumed when young. Starting in 1993, Pascal Roux replaced the semi-carbonic maceration with at least 60 percent of the harvest being vinified in a traditional manner. In addition, some new oak casks with foudres are used in the aging process. However, my experience has been that the Trignon Gigondas does not improve much or even last beyond four to five years, and thus has been a wine to consume in its exuberant youth. Roux thinks that the answer is to add more and more Syrah and Mourvèdre to the blend, which he has gradually done.

Château du Trignon has done some serious empire building since the late eighties. Under the leadership of Pascal Roux, the wine quality, which seemed to have slipped in 1991 and 1992, has rebounded, with strong efforts in 1994 and 1995. Moreover, the wines have taken on greater richness, more natural textures, and are bottled with less trauma. Fining and filtration appear to have been reduced considerably in favor of putting in the bottle essentially the same wine that was made in the vineyard. Given the increased intentisy of the Trignon wines, these wines, usually best drunk within their first 4–5 years of life, give every indication in top vintages since 1995 of lasting for a decade or more. All of this is a very positive development.

VINTAGES

1995—Gigondas   The massive, opaque black/purple-colored 1995 Gigondas is the rich-
·   est, most concentrated wine I have ever tasted from Château du Trignon. This
89   estate generally produces fruity, well-made wines that are delicious young, but
               rarely carry enough stuffing to last for more than 5–7 years. The 1995 possesses
               fine underlying acidity, masses of fruit, and a nearly overripe, black-raspberry,
               kirsch character intermingled with earth and licorice. Anticipated maturity: 1998–
               2006. Last tasted 6/96.

1994—Gigondas   The dark ruby/plum-colored 1994 Gigondas offers elegant scents of
·   cherries and pepper. Medium-weight, attractive, soft, and commercial, this is an
85   easygoing, tasty Gigondas to drink over the next 4–5 years. Certainly the 1994
               appears more typical of this estate's style than the 1995. Last tasted 6/96.

VIDAL-FLEURY* * *

This négociant tends to produce very good wines from purchased juice. All the Vidal-Fleury Gigondas is moved to Ampuis and aged in the large foudres that fill the underground cellars of this famous northern Rhône négociant.

VINTAGES

1992—Gigondas   The 1992 Gigondas is superior to more than 90% of the estate-bottled
·   wines. It possesses a chocolaty, smoky, black-cherry-scented nose, ripe, round,
86   medium- to full-bodied flavors, no vegetal elements, and plenty of sweet, ripe fruit
               in the finish. It should drink well for 4–5 years. Last tasted 6/96.

1990—Gigondas   The 1990 Gigondas displays a deep ruby/purple color, followed by a
·   rich nose of licorice, cassis, herb, and pepper. This long, voluptuous, deep wine is
87   a top-notch Gigondas for drinking over the next decade. Last tasted 6/95.

1989—Gigondas   Vidal-Fleury's 1989 Gigondas offers plenty of cassis fruit, dusty tannin,
·   excellent intensity, and medium to full body. The 1990 Gigondas is even better.
85   With deep ruby/purple color, a rich nose of licorice, cassis, herb, and pepper, this
               is a solid Gigondas for drinking over the next decade. Last tasted 9/95.

1988—Gigondas   The 1988 Gigondas is smoky and tasty, but one-dimensional. While correct in style, it lacks the extra spark that makes one want to drink a second glass. Last tasted 9/95.

· 82

1985—Gigondas   For those readers looking for a wonderfully pure, beefy, rich, full-bodied, juicy Rhône wine that supports hearty bistro cooking, this 1985 Gigondas is a full-bodied, peppery, spicy, richly fruity wine with soft tannin and low acidity. It is ideal for drinking over the next 3–4 years. Last tasted 9/95.

· 86

OTHER GIGONDAS PRODUCERS

DOMAINE DU BOIS DES NÉGES

Address: 84190 Gigondas
Tel: 4-90-70-92-95
Fax: 4-90-70-97-39
Wines produced: Gigondas
Surface area: 1.2 acres
Production: 300–500 cases
Upbringing: The wine is brought up in both cement cuves and small oak barrels, of which a small percentage are new.
Average age of vines: 25 years
Blend: 75% Grenache, 25% Syrah

DOMAINE DE BOISSAN

Address: 84110 Sablet
Tel: 4-90-46-93-30
Fax: 4-90-46-99-46
Wines produced: Gigondas
Surface area: 29.6 acres
Production: 5,625 cases
Upbringing: 24 months in cement vats
Average age of vines: 30 years
Blend: 75% Grenache, 25% Syrah

CAVE LE GRAVILLAS

Address: 84110 Sablet
Tel: 4-90-46-90-20
Fax: 4-90-46-96-71
Wines produced: Gigondas
Surface area: 74 acres
Production: 10,000 cases
Upbringing: 36–48 months total, with 50% of the wine spending 12–24 months in oak and the rest in cement vats; no destemming
Average age of vines: 35 years
Blend: 80% Grenache, 10% Syrah, 10% Mourvèdre

DOMAINE LES CHÊNES BLANCS

Address: 84190 Gigondas
Tel: 4-90-65-85-04
Fax: 4-90-65-82-94
Wines produced: Gigondas
Surface area: 25 acres
Production: 3,125 cases
Upbringing: 12 months in cement vats, then 12 months in enamel vats, then 12 months in old oak casks
Average age of vines: 50 years
Blend: 80% Grenache, 15% Syrah, 5% Clairette

DOMAINE DE LA COLLINE ST.-JEAN

Address: 84190 Vacqueyras
Tel: 4-90-65-85-50
Wines produced: Gigondas
Surface area: 6.6 acres
Production: 925 cases
Upbringing: 36 months total, with a minimum of 6 months in old oak barrels
Average age of vines: 10–60 years
Blend: 75% Grenache, 25% Mourvèdre

DOMAINE DE COYEAUX

Address: B.P. 7
          84190 Beaumes de Venise
Tel: 4-90-62-97-96
Fax: 4-90-65-01-87
Wines produced: Gigondas
Surface area: 2.47 acres
Production: 438 cases
Upbringing: 18 months total, with 9 months in one-third new oak barrels (since 1988)
Average age of vines: 25 years
Blend: 50% Grenache, 20% Syrah, 20% Mourvèdre, 10% Cinsault

DOMAINE DE LA DAYSSE* * *

Address: Domaines Meffre
          84190 Gigondas
No information available

DELAS FRÈRES

Address: Z. A. de l'Oliver
          B.P. 4
          07300 St.-Jean de Muzols
Tel: 4-75-08-60-30
Fax: 4-75-08-53-67
Wines produced: Gigondas sold under the label Les Reinages, made from purchased wine
Production: 2,000 cases
Upbringing: normally 12–18 months with 60% of the yield in oak casks and 40% in oak
          barrels
Blend: 80% Grenache, 10% Mourvèdre, 10% Syrah

DOMAINE DE FONTSEREINE

Address: 84190 Gigondas
Tel: 4-90-65-86-09
Fax: 4-90-65-81-81
Wines produced: Gigondas
Surface area: 11.1 acres
Production: 1,625 cases
Upbringing: 2–3 years in enamel vats
Average age of vines: 30 years
Blend: 75% Grenache, 10% Syrah, 10% Cinsault, 5% Mourvèdre

DOMAINE DU GRAND MONTMIRAIL

Address: 84190 Gigondas
Tel: 4-90-65-00-22
Wines produced: Gigondas (red and rosé)
Surface area (red): 44.5 acres
          (rosé): 5 acres
Production (red): 6,875 cases
          (rosé): 625 cases
Upbringing (red): 3 years minimum in underground cement vats
          (rosé): 6–8 months in stainless steel vats
Average age of vines (red): 10–50 years
          (rosé): 10–15 years
Blend (red): 80% Grenache, 20% Syrah
     (rosé): 50% Grenache, 50% Mourvèdre

DOMAINE DE LA JAUFRETTE

Address: Chemin de la Gironde
          84100 Orange
Tel: 4-90-34-35-34
Wines produced: Gigondas
Surface area: 12.4 acres
Production: 2,125 cases
Upbringing: 3–4 years in all, with 6–8 months in old oak casks and barrels and the
          remainder in epoxy vats
Average age of vines: 60–80 years
Blend: 80% Grenache, 10% Syrah, 10% Mourvèdre

DOMAINE DU MAS DES COLLINES

Address: Les Hautes Garrigues
          84190 Gigondas
Tel: 4-90-65-90-40
Wines produced: Gigondas
Surface area: 44.5 acres
Production: 6,875 cases
Upbringing: 36 months total, with 12 months in old oak casks
Average age of vines: 50 years
Blend: 90% Grenache, 7% Syrah, 3% Cinsault

DOMAINE DE MONTVAC

Address: 84190 Vacqueyras
Tel: 4-90-65-85-51
Fax: 4-90-65-82-38
Wines produced: Gigondas
Surface area: 10 acres
Production: 1,625 cases
Upbringing: 10 months in cement vats and 12 months in oak casks
Average age of vines: 40–45 years
Blend: 60% Grenache, 35% Syrah, 5% Mourvèdre

DOMAINE LOU MOULIN D'OLI

Address: Le Moulin
       84150 Violès
Tel: 4-90-70-93-71
Wines produced: Gigondas
Surface area: 1.9 acres
Production: 337 cases
Upbringing: 12–18 months in enamel vats
Average age of vines: 30 years
Blend: 80% Grenache, 20% Syrah

DOMAINE NOTRE DAME DES PAILLÈRES

Address: Route de Lencieux
       84190 Gigondas
Tel: 4-90-46-93-82
Wines produced: Gigondas
Surface area: 37 acres
Production: 5,000 cases
Upbringing: 42 months in enamel vats
Average age of vines: 40 years
Blend: 80% Grenache, 15% Mourvèdre, 5% Cinsault and Syrah

DOMAINE DU PARANDOU

Address: Route d'Avignon
       84110 Sablet
Tel: 4-90-46-90-52
Fax: 4-90-46-99-05
Wines produced: Gigondas
Surface area: 5 acres
Production: 875 cases
Upbringing: 24 months in stainless steel vats
Average age of vines: 20–25 years
Blend: 70% Grenache, 30% Syrah

DOMAINE LE PÉAGE

Address: 84190 Gigondas
Tel: 4-90-70-96-80
Wines produced: Gigondas
Surface area: 42 acres
Production: 6,250 cases
Upbringing: 24 months in cement vats
Average age of vines: 25 years
Blend: 80% Grenache, 15% Syrah, 5% Mourvèdre and Cinsault

DOMAINE DU POURRA

Address: Quartier des Abeilles
       84110 Sablet
Tel: 4-90-46-93-59

Fax: 4-90-46-99-66
No information available

CHÂTEAU ST.-ANDRÉ

Address: 84190 Gigondas
Tel: 4-90-65-84-03
Fax: 4-90-65-83-11
Wines produced: Gigondas
Surface area: 131 acres
Production: 22,500 cases
Upbringing: 12 months total, with 6 months in old oak casks
Average age of vines: 15–20 years
Blend: 70% Grenache, 15% Syrah, 10% Mourvèdre, 5% Cinsault

DOMAINE ST.-DAMIEN

Address: La Beaumette
         84190 Gigondas
Tel: 4-90-70-96-80
Wines produced: Gigondas
Surface area: 54 acres
Production: 8,250 cases
Upbringing: 24 months total, with 12 months in oak casks
Average age of vines: 30–35 years
Blend: 80% Grenache, 15% Syrah, 5% Mourvèdre

DOMAINE ST.-FRANÇOIS XAVIER

Address: 84190 Gigondas
Tel: 4-90-65-85-08
Wines produced: Gigondas
Surface area: 37 acres
Production: 5,625 cases
Upbringing: 18 months total, with 6–12 months in old oak casks
Average age of vines: 30 years
Blend: 70% Grenache, 10% Syrah, 10% Cinsault, 10% Mourvèdre

DOMAINE DE ST.-GENS

Address: 84190 Gigondas
Tel: 4-90-65-00-22
Wines produced: Gigondas
Surface area: 12.4 acres
Production: 1,875 cases
Upbringing: 36 months minimum in underground cement vats
Average age of vines: 10–40 years
Blend: 80% Grenache, 20% Syrah

DOMAINE ST.-PIERRE

Address: 84150 Violès
Tel: 4-90-70-92-64
Wines produced: Gigondas
Surface area: 2.47 acres
Production: 375 cases
Upbringing: 24–36 months total, with 18–24 months in old oak casks
Average age of vines: 30 years
Blend: 80% Grenache, 20% Syrah

DOMAINE DE LA TUILIÈRE

Address: 84190 Gigondas
Tel: 4-90-65-86-51
Wines produced: Gigondas
Surface area: 9.8 acres
Production: 1,250 cases
Upbringing: 18 months total, with 12 months in old oak casks and barrels
Average age of vines: unknown
Blend: 80% Grenache, 18% Syrah, 2% Mourvèdre

L. DE VALLOUIT

Note: This négociant owns no vineyards, and produces a thin, high-acid, vegetal Gigondas that is not to my liking.

VIEUX CLOCHER

Address: 84190 Vacqueyras
Tel: 4-90-65-84-18
Fax: 4-90-65-80-07
Wines produced: Négociant Gigondas
Production: 1,250 cases
Upbringing: 18–24 months in oak casks, then kept in the cellars for 2 years after bottling
Blend: 75% Grenache, 15% Syrah, 10% Mourvèdre

TAVEL

France's Most Famous, Expensive,
and Overrated Rosé

TAVEL AT A GLANCE

Appellation created:	May 15, 1936.
Type of wine produced:	Dry rosé only—the sole appellation in France to recognize rosé as the only authorized wine.
Grape varieties planted:	There are nine authorized varieties; Grenache and Cinsault dominate, followed by Clairette, Syrah, Bourboulenc, Mourvèdre, Picpoul, Carignan, and Calitor.
Acres currently under vine:	2,340.
Quality level:	Average to very good rosé wines.
Aging potential:	1–3 years.
General characteristics:	The finest Tavels are dry, full-bodied, and boldly flavored.
Greatest recent vintages:	1995.
Price range:	$14–$22.
Aromatic profile:	Strawberries, cherries, and a vague scent of Provençal *garrigue.*
Textural profile:	Dry, sometimes austere, full-bodied wines can taste surprisingly rugged and shocking to those weaned on semisweet, soft, flabby, new world rosés.

There are no profound Tavel wines.

RATING THE TAVEL PRODUCERS

* * * * *(OUTSTANDING)

None

* * * *(EXCELLENT)

None

* * *(GOOD)

Château d'Acqueria	Guigal
Domaine Canto-Perdrix	Domaine Méjan-Taulier
Domaine Corne-Loup	Domaine de la Mordorée
Domaine de la Forcadière	Domaine de Roc Epine
Domaine de la Genestière	Château de Trinquevedel

Just eight miles west of Châteauneuf du Pape, across a barren, dry landscape of scrub bush and sharp rock outcrops called *garrigues,* is the tiny wine village of Tavel. The local cooperative has proudly embellished across its roof line a huge sign proclaiming "Tavel 1er Rosé de France." Perhaps it should add the words "Most Expensive and Frequently Undistinguished." Tavel is like no other rosé wine. Does it really taste so good because it is the only thing that brings relief in the relentless hot sun and slashing wind that seem even worse in Tavel than in nearby Châteauneuf du Pape? Or is it that this famous wine, championed by Louis XIV, mentioned with admiration by French writers such as Daudet and Balzac, and guzzled with pleasure by the bon vivant gastronome Brillat-Savarin, is really exceptional? Certainly its fame, past and present, has given the growers a great deal of leverage in getting the prices they want, but today few Tavels justify their lofty price. Regardless of how one answers that question, there is no argument that the wine is distinctive, although it does have its critics, notably Hugh Johnson, who claims "never to have been attracted to its dry, full-bodied style."

The tiny village of Tavel, which seems to exist only to produce wine, is full of tasting rooms and "caves." The rosé wine can be made in one of two ways. Most Tavel is produced not from blending white and red together as many people imagine, but from stacking up the freshly picked whole grapes in stainless steel tanks, letting their weight do a light crushing, and then permitting the juice to sit with the skins for one or two days, just long enough to give Tavel its vibrant salmon color. All of this must be done carefully at cool temperatures to prevent the oxidation of the aromatic intensity and freshness of Tavel's bouquet. The second method, commonly employed elsewhere in the world, but not used with great enthusiasm in Tavel, is what the French call *saigner.* This is the process of bleeding off the top of a vat when the wine's color has sufficient pink to be a rosé. In the latter method, the balance of this wine mass continues to macerate with the skins, resulting in a red wine. In tasting through a range of Tavels, the color varies from producer to producer. It can range from a light, pale pink salmon color, to a deep, vibrant light ruby. If the color becomes too deep in the ruby tone, the local cognoscenti consider the wine vulgar and poorly vinified.

Over the last 10 years, the biggest change in Tavel has been the abdication of winemaking responsibility by the growers to a handful of prominent oenologists. With this has come the new, crisp, lighter styles of Tavel. Malolactic fermentation is blocked, then the wines are sterile filtered and bottled within four to six months of the vintage. Some of these wines still retain enough typicity, punch, and power to recall the glorious Tavels of yesteryear, but, lamentably, many of them taste no different than most rosés made elsewhere in the world.

TAVEL

Toward
VALLIGUIÈRES

D4

Roc Epine

La Vau et Clau

Les Joncie

Le Malaven

Forêt de Tavel

N
W   E
S

A9

Toward
REMOULINS

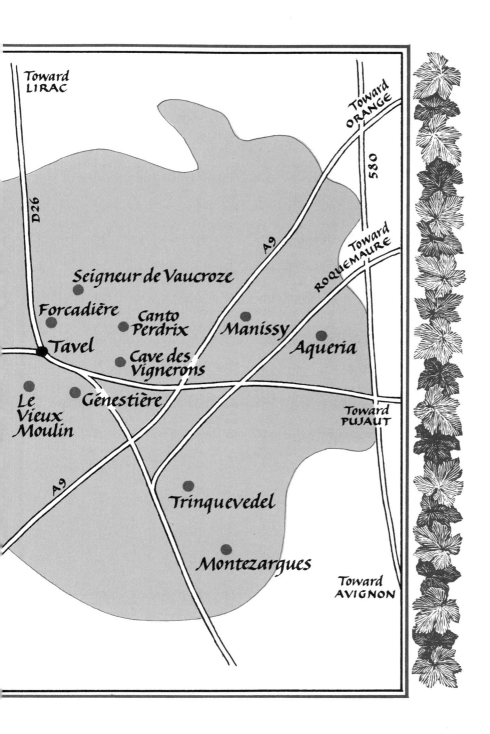

Toward
LIRAC

Toward
ORANGE

580

D26

A9

Toward
ROQUEMAURE

Seigneur de Vaucroze

Forcadière

Canto
Perdrix

Manissy

Aqueria

Tavel

Cave des
Vignerons

Le
Vieux
Moulin

Génestière

Toward
PUJAUT

A9

Trinquevedel

Montezargues

Toward
AVIGNON

Since Tavel sells at a price double, sometimes triple, what other good rosé wines fetch, marketing difficulties cannot be far away.

The locals claim that Tavel has moderate aging potential because of its lusty alcohol content of 13% to 14%, high for a rosé. I have never, I repeat never, enjoyed one of these wines that was more than three years old. To me, a fine rosé wine, as distinct from the cheap, cloyingly sweet varieties that populate the shelves of many retailers, must be drunk during its youth. Tavel in particular seems to suffer once the gush of fresh strawberry or cherry fruit fades and the ugly level of alcohol is exposed. However, drunk young it can be a deliciously heady wine. Rosés are usually prized for their freshness, vibrancy of fruit, crisp acidity, and balance. A fine Tavel adds body and depth to this formula, and the result can be an impressively layered, rich, and powerful wine. Tavel when young has tremendous fruit and body, possessing a deep fragrance of flowers and berry fruit. Rather shockingly, it also feels deep and long on the palate, because of its body and alcoholic clout. If the wine does not have freshness and good fruit, it is not pleasant. Perhaps the most useful purpose for Tavel is as an accompaniment to the often peppery, spicy, distinctive Provençal cuisine. Anyone who has tasted such Provençal specialties as ratatouille, the peppery charcuterie, or the herb-infused meat and fish dishes will understand that these particular foods overpower many wines, save for a dry, full-bodied, austere Tavel.

What does the future hold for Tavel? With so many terrific rosés emerging from France's Languedoc-Roussillon and from neighboring Spain, most of which sell for one-third to one-half the price of a Tavel, it remains unlikely that this appellation can continue to rest on its historic reputation. Its mythical character, fostered by thousands of tourists who have visited this region, has served it well for centuries, but today, competition from other areas makes Tavel look like an overpriced oddity.

RECENT VINTAGES

1995   Since Tavel requires drinking within three years of the vintage, 1996 and 1995 are the only vintages that should be consumed in 1997 and 1998. As I have said so many times, there is only one rule when it comes to vintages older than three years for any rosé, including Tavel: caveat emptor.

CHÂTEAU D'AQUERIA (PAUL DEBEZ)* * *

Address: 30126 Tavel
Tel: 4-66-50-04-56
Fax: 4-66-50-18-46
Wines produced: Tavel
Surface area: 118.6 acres
Production: 25,000 cases
Upbringing: fermentation in stainless steel vats at 20° centigrade; after the wine is assembled it spends 6 months in stainless steel vats
Average age of vines: 35 years
Blend: 45% Grenache, 20% Clairette, 15% Cinsault, 7% Mourvèdre, 13% Bourboulenc and Syrah

Outside the tiny village of Tavel in the direction of Roquemaure is the beautiful Château d'Aqueria. The production is large, but the wine is among the finest of the appellation. It often carries 14% alcohol, and is known for its power and provocative display of red fruits, primarily cherries and strawberries.

DOMAINE CORNE-LOUP (J. LAFOND)* * *

Address: 30126 Tavel
Tel: 4-66-50-34-37
Fax: 4-66-50-31-36
Wines produced: Côtes du Rhône, Tavel
Surface area (Côtes du Rhône): 67 acres
         (Tavel): 54 acres
Production (Côtes du Rhône): 13,750 cases
         (Tavel): 8,000 cases
Upbringing: 4 months in stainless steel and epoxy vats
Average age of vines: 30–35 years
Blend: 60% Grenache, 20% Cinsault, 5% Syrah, 15% Clairette, Mourvèdre, and Carignan

This estate of 54 acres produces 8,000 cases of Tavel under the meticulous care of Jacques Lafond. The rosé is usually a bright salmon color, very fruity and perfumed. It is quite dry as well as full-bodied. Lafond believes in bottling his Tavel as early as possible to preserve the freshness and fragrance of the fruit. Normally the wine is in the bottle by the end of March following the vintage. This is a good producer who seems to be making better and better Tavel.

DOMAINE DE LA FORCADIÈRE (ROGER MABY)* * *

Address: Rue St.-Vincent
        B.P. 8
        30126 Tavel
Tel: 4-66-50-03-40
Fax: 4-66-50-43-12
Wines produced: Tavel
Surface area: 44 acres
Production: 9,400 cases
Upbringing: 6–12 months in stainless steel vats
Average age of vines: 25 years
Blend: 50% Grenache, 20% Cinsault, 5% Mourvèdre, 25% Syrah, Mourvèdre, Clairette,
    Picpoul, and Bourboulenc

Roger Maby continues a tradition established by this well-known Tavel family of producing one of the most popular wines of the appellation. Customers for Maby's Tavel exist throughout the world, as it is a crisp, well-balanced, full-bodied, generously alcoholic wine that never disappoints. While Maby claims it will last for five or more years, it is best drunk within the first two to three years of the vintage, a fact agreed upon by this estate's clients since the wine normally sells out within six months of release.

DOMAINE DE LA GENESTIÈRE* * *

Address: 30126 Tavel
Tel: 4-66-50-07-03
Fax: 4-66-50-27-03
Wines produced: Tavel
Surface area: 91.4 acres
Production: 16,250 cases
Upbringing: 6–12 months in cement and stainless steel vats
Average age of vines: 20–25 years
Blend: Primarily Grenache with small portions of Cinsault, Carignan, Syrah, and Clairette

When this estate was owned by George Bernard it unquestionably produced one of the finest Tavels. However, the property has been sold to Monsieur Garcin, who controls the sales of rootstock and vines to area growers. This has always been a fruity, deeply colored, more elegantly styled Tavel than some of the bigger rosés, but with new owners, the style may change.

GUIGAL* * *

Address: 1, route de Taquières
        69420 Ampuis
Tel: 4-74-56-10-22
Fax: 4-74-56-18-76
Wines produced: Tavel (négociant)
Production: 3,400 cases
Upbringing: 6 months in stainless steel vats
Blend: 35% Cinsault, 35% Grenache, 15% Syrah, 10% Clairette, 5% Mourvèdre

Guigal does so many things right, it is easy to overlook his dry rosé. He makes an excellent Côtes du Rhône and a very good, classic Tavel that rarely gets the attention it deserves. It is a wine to drink within 2–3 years of the vintage.

DOMAINE MÉJAN-TAULIER* * *

Address: S.C.E.A. Méjean-Taulier
        30126 Tavel
Tel: 4-66-50-04-02
Fax: 4-66-50-21-72
Wines produced: Tavel
Surface area: 67 acres
Production: 16,250 cases
Upbringing: 6–12 months in stainless steel vats
Age of vines: 8–50 years
Blend: 50% Grenache, 10% Syrah, 10% Mourvèdre, 10% Cinsault, 20% Bourboulenc,
        Picpoul, and Clairette

One of the best wines of the appellation, proprietor André Méjan fashions fresh, vivid, medium- to full-bodied rosés that are crisp, austere, and flavorful.

DOMAINE DE LA MORDORÉE* * *

Address: 30126 Tavel
Tel: 4-66-50-00-75
Fax: 4-66-50-47-39
Wines produced: Tavel
Surface area: 22 acres
Production: 4,375 cases
Upbringing: 4–6 months in stainless steel vats
Average age of vines: 40 years
Blend: 60% Grenache, 10% Cinsault, 5–10% Mourvèdre, 3–5% Bourboulenc, 15–22%
        other varietals

As I have written elsewhere in this book, proprietor Christophe Délorme has pushed this estate's level of quality to impressive heights. One of the most reliable southern Rhône producers, Domaine de la Mordorée turns out exquisite Châteauneuf du Pape, excellent Lirac (red and rosé), and a full-bodied, intensely strawberry-scented, elegant, dry Tavel. Moreover, it is reasonably priced, making it a Tavel well worth seeking out.

DOMAINE DE ROC EPINE (LAFOND)* * *

Address: Route des Vignobles
       30126 Tavel
Tel: 4-66-50-24-59
Fax: 4-66-50-12-42
Wines produced: Tavel
Surface area: 91.4 acres
Production: 20,000 cases
Upbringing: 6–12 months in stainless steel vats, followed by 6 months' cellaring after
       bottling
Average age of vines: 25 years
Blend: 60% Grenache, 10% Cinsault, 5% Syrah, 3% Carignan, 2% Mourvèdre, 2%
       Clairette, 18% other varietals

This is another reliable Tavel producer making a modern, medium-bodied, deeply colored wine bursting with aromas of fresh red fruits. It is bottled early and meant to be drunk within a year of its release.

CHÂTEAU DE TRINQUEVEDEL (F. DUMOULIN)* * *

Address: S.C.E.A. Demoulin
       30126 Tavel
Tel: 4-66-50-04-04
Fax: 4-66-50-31-66
Wines produced: Tavel
Surface area: 79 acres
Production: 13,750 cases
Upbringing: 9 months in stainless steel vats
Average age of vines: 36 years
Blend: 40% Grenache, 20% Cinsault, 18% Clairette, 3% Bourboulenc, 2% Syrah, 1%
       Mourvèdre, and the remainder other white varietals

The historic estate of Trinquevedel, whose origins date back to the French Revolution, is just outside the village of Tavel. The wine is made by carbonic maceration of red and white grapes and then pulled off the skin when the right color has been obtained. It is a perfumed and powerful wine that consistently ranks among the best of the appellation.

LES VIGNERONS DE TAVEL

Address: Route de la Commanderie
       B.P. 3
       30126 Tavel
Tel: 4-66-50-03-57
Fax: 4-66-50-46-57
Wines produced: Tavel Cuvée Royale, Tavel Cuvée du Roi, Tavel Cuvée du Tableau, Tavel
       Carte d'Or
Surface area: 988 acres
Production (total): 237,000 cases
            (Cuvée Royale): 4,200 cases
            (Cuvée du Roi): 5,800 cases
            (Cuvée du Tableau): 2,500 cases
            (Carte d'Or): 85,000 cases
Upbringing: all the cuvées spend 6 months in stainless steel vats
Average age of vines: 30–35 years

Blend: 55% Grenache, 15% Cinsault, 15% Clairette, and 15% Picpoul, Bourboulenc, Syrah, Mourvèdre, Grenache Blanc, and Carignan

This cave coopérative has 140 producers who own 988 acres in Tavel, representing nearly half of the appellation. The total production is 237,000 cases. Four separate cuvées are produced and the selection is done after fermentation when the pieces are set apart. Part of the production is sold in bulk. Every year one special cuvée is sent to the annual competition where the best Tavel is designated. This wine is sold under the name Cuvée du Roi. Production of the Cuvée du Tableau began with the 1993 vintage. The Cuvée Carte d'Or is the coop's generic cuvée.

The production of the Cave Coopérative de Tavel is the most representative of the appellation. The three distinct parts of Tavel are represented equally by the members of the coop. The soil in the plains is alluvial and sandy, and the plateau consists of pebbles and round stones similar to the *galets roulés* found in Châteauneuf du Pape. In the third area, the terraces and coteaux, the land is arid with a calcareous subsoil. The yields are very low (under 2 tons per acre), and the vines in this region give very concentrated wines.

This cave coopérative is the place to go to taste a wide range of different cuvées of Tavel. The quality is variable, but the best cuvées offer a quaffable, competent, juicy style of Tavel. The locals all agree that the Cuvée du Roi is the wine that best demonstrates the character of this appellation.

OTHER TAVEL PRODUCERS

DOMAINE DES AMANDINES

Address: Rue des Carrières
            30126 Tavel
Wines produced: Tavel
Surface area: 29.6 acres
Production: 7,500 cases
Upbringing: 6 months total; vinification in stainless steel vats and conservation in cement vats
Average age of vines: 25 years
Blend: 60% Grenache, 25% Cinsault, 15% Syrah and Mourvèdre

DOMAINE BALAZU DES VAUSSIÈRES

Address: Rue des Vaussières
Tel: 4-66-50-44-22
Wines produced: Tavel
Surface area: 6.6 acres
Production: 1,550 cases
Upbringing: 6 months in stainless steel vats
Average age of vines: 4–5 years and 80 years
Blend: 50% Grenache, 30% Cinsault, 2% Syrah, 2% Bourboulenc, 2% Clairette, 14% other varietals

DOMAINE DU BOIS LAURE

Address: 30126 Tavel
Tel: 4-66-50-45-97
Wines produced: Tavel
Surface area: 12.4 acres

Production: 2,250 cases
Upbringing: 6 months in cement vats
Average age of vines: 20 years
Blend: 50% Grenache, and equal parts Cinsault, Mourvèdre, Bourboulenc, and Clairette

DOMAINE DES CARABINIERS

Address: 30150 Roquemaure
Tel: 4-66-82-62-94
Fax: 4-66-82-82-15
Wines produced: Tavel
Surface area: 12.4 acres
Production: 2,500 cases
Upbringing: 6 months in cement vats
Average age of vines: 30 years
Blend: 50% Grenache, 20% Cinsault, 10% each of Clairette, Picpoul, and Syrah

CHAPOUTIER

Address: 18, avenue du Docteur Paul Durand
        B.P. 38
        26600 Tain l'Hermitage
Tel: 4-75-08-28-65
Fax: 4-75-08-81-70
Wines produced: Tavel
Production: 2,500 cases
Upbringing: 4–6 months in stainless steel vats
Blend: Cinsault and Grenache
   Note: All of the Chapoutier Tavels are bought young from their suppliers.

DOMAINE LE CHEMIN DU ROY

Address: Rue de la Fontaine
        30126 Tavel
Tel: 4-66-50-07-93
Fax: 4-66-50-17-02
Wines produced: Tavel
Surface area: 17.3 acres
Production: 3,750 cases
Upbringing: 6–7 months in enamel vats
Average age of vines: 20 and 50 years
Blend: 50% Grenache, 30% Cinsault, 15% Clairette, 3% Syrah, 2% Bourboulenc and
       Carignan

DELAS FRÈRES

Address: Z.A. de l'Oliver
        B.P. 4
        07300 St.-Jean de Muzols
Tel: 4-75-08-60-30
Fax: 4-75-08-53-67
Wines produced: Tavel La Comballe
Production: 1,800–2,000 cases
Blend: 60% Grenache, 40% Cinsault
   Note: The wines are vinified and brought up under control of the Delas oenologists, and
bottled by Delas Frères.

DOMAINE DES LAMBRUSQUES

Address: Vieux Chemin de Lirac
   30126 Tavel
Tel: 4-66-50-06-89
Wines produced: Tavel
Surface area: 14.8 acres
Production: 3,125 cases
Upbringing: 6 months in epoxy vats
Average age of vines: 20–25 years
Blend: 50% Grenache, 20% Mourvèdre, 20% Cinsault, 10% Carignon, Clairette, and Picpoul

DOMAINE DE LANZAC

Address: Route de Pujaut
   30126 Tavel
Tel: 4-66-50-22-17
Fax: 4-66-50-47-44
Wines produced: Tavel
Surface area: 27 acres
Production: 6,250 cases
Upbringing: 4 months minimum in stainless steel vats
Average age of vines: 30 years
Blend: 50% Grenache, 20% Cinsault, 10% Carignan, 10% Clairette, 10% Picpoul, Bourboulenc, and other varietals

CHÂTEAU DE MANISSY

Address: 30126 Tavel
Tel: 4-66-50-04-16
Wines produced: Tavel
Surface area: 74 acres
Production: 15,000 cases
Upbringing: 12 months minimum in old oak casks (the 1989 spent 5 years in oak)
Average age of vines: 60 years
Blend: 50–60% Grenache, 10–20% Cinsault, 5–7% Clairette, 2–3% Picpoul, and other varietals

PRIEURÉ DE MONTEZARGUES

Address: 30126 Tavel
Tel: 4-66-50-04-48
Fax: 4-66-50-30-41
Wines produced: Tavel
Surface area: 79 acres
Production: 12,500 cases
Upbringing: 6 months in stainless steel vats
Average age of vines: 30 years
Blend: 55% Grenache, 20% Cinsault, 8% Clairette, 6% Carignan, 5% Bourboulenc, 4% Mourvèdre, 2% other varietals

DOMAINE DU MOULIN BLANC

Address: 33, rue du 11 Novembre
        69160 Tassin-la-Demi-Lune
Tel: 4-78-34-25-06
Fax: 4-78-34-30-60
Wines produced: Tavel
Surface area: 8.6 acres
Production: 2,000 cases
Upbringing: 6 months in stainless steel vats
Average age of vines: 15 years
Blend: 50% Cinsault, 40% Grenache, 10% Carignan

DOMAINE PELAQUIÉ

Address: 7, rue Vernet
        30290 St.-Victor-la-Coste
Tel: 4-66-50-06-04
Fax: 4-66-50-33-42
Wines produced: Tavel
Surface area: 1.5 acres
Production: 325 cases
Upbringing: 4–6 months in stainless steel vats
Average age of vines: 25 years
Blend: 60% Grenache, 40% Cinsault

DOMAINE DU PETIT AVRIL

Address: Rue du Pressoir
        30126 Tavel
Tel: 4-66-50-28-05
Fax: 4-66-50-07-61
Wines produced: Tavel
Surface area: 37 acres
Production: 5,600 cases
Upbringing: 4 months in epoxy vats
Average age of vines: 40 years
Blend: 50% Grenache, 15% Cinsault, 10% Clairette, 10% Carignan, 15% Bourboulenc,
    Clairette, Picpoul, and Mourvèdre

DOMAINE ST.-FERREOL

Address: 11, rue St.-Louis
        30126 Tavel
Tel: 4-66-50-47-10
Fax: 4-66-50-42-20
Wines produced: Tavel
Surface area: 7.9 acres
Production: 1,800 cases
Upbringing: 6 months in epoxy vats
Average age of vines: 35 years minimum
Blend: 50% Grenache, 20% Syrah, 20% Cinsault, 10% Mourvèdre, Bourboulenc, and
    Clairette

DOMAINE SEIGNEUR DE VAUCROSE

Address: S.C.A. Leveque
   Route de Lirac
   30126 Tavel
Tel: 4-66-50-04-37
Fax: 4-66-50-17-04
Wines produced: Tavel
Surface area: 74 acres
Production: 11,250 cases
Upbringing: vinification of 3 months in stainless steel vats, followed by 2 years in enamel
   vats

DOMAINE DE TOURTOUIL

Address: B.P. 06
   30126 Tavel
Tel: 4-66-50-05-68
Fax: 4-66-50-21-11
Wines produced: Tavel
Surface area: 49.4 acres
Production: 9,375 cases
Upbringing: 5–6 months in stainless steel or cement vats
Average age of vines: 30 years
Blend: 60% Grenache, 20% Cinsault, 20% Syrah, Clairette, and Mourvèdre

DOMAINE DES TROIS LOGIS

Address: G.A.E.C. Charmasson Plantevin
   Rue de Tourtouil
   30126 Tavel
Tel: 4-66-50-05-34
Fax: 4-66-50-45-31
Wines produced: Tavel
Surface area: 49 acres
Production: 11,250 cases
Upbringing: 4 months in stainless steel vats; no filtration
Average age of vines: 35–40 years
Blend: 60% Grenache, 15–20% Cinsault, the rest is Bourboulenc, Clairette, and Picpoul

DOMAINE DE LA VALINIÈRE

Address: Rue de Valinière
Tel: 4-66-50-36-12
Wines produced: Tavel
Surface area: 17.3 acres
Production: 3,750 cases
Upbringing: 6 months in enamel and cement vats
Average age of vines: 40 years
Blend: 50% Grenache, 20% Cinsault, 7–8% Carignan, 5% Syrah, 5–8% Clairette, the rest
   Bourboulenc and Picpoul

DOMAINE DU VIEUX MOULIN

Address: Rue des Lavandières
     30126 Tavel
Tel: 4-66-50-07-79
Fax: 4-66-50-10-02
Wines produced: Tavel
Surface area: 91 acres
Production: 20,625 cases
Upbringing: 9–12 months in stainless steel vats
Average age of vines: 35 years
Blend: 60% Grenache, 25% Cinsault, 10% Clairette, Bourboulenc, Picpoul, and Grenache
    Blanc, 5% Syrah, Mourvèdre, and Carignan

DOMAINE DU VIEUX RELAIS

Address: Route de la Commanderie
     30126 Tavel
Tel: 4-66-50-36-52
Fax: 4-66-50-35-92
Wines produced: Tavel
Surface area: 22 acres
Production: 6,250 cases
Upbringing: 5–6 months in cement vats
Average age of vines: 40 years
Blend: 50% Grenache, 50% Syrah, Clairette, Mourvèdre, and Cinsault

LIRAC

The Forgotten Appellation

LIRAC AT A GLANCE

Appellation created:	October 14, 1947.
Type of wine produced:	Red, rosé, and white wines, of which 75% of the production is red, 20% rosé, and 5% white.
Grape varieties planted	(red): Grenache Noir, Syrah, Mourvèdre, Cinsault, and Carignan; (white): Grenache Blanc, Clairette, Bourboulenc, Ugni Blanc, Picpoul, Marsanne, Roussanne, and Viognier.
Acres currently under vine:	1,037.
Quality level:	Mediocre to good, but improving.
Aging potential:	2–8 years.
General characteristics:	Soft, very fruity, medium-bodied red wines; neutral white wines; exuberantly fresh, fruity rosés (the frugal consumers' Tavel).
Greatest recent vintages:	1995, 1994, 1990, 1989.
Price range:	$10–$15.
Aromatic profile:	Similar to a Côtes du Rhône, with scents of red fruits, spices, and herbes de Provence.
Textural profile:	Soft, fruity, generally medium-bodied red wines, and relatively innocuous, one-dimensional white wines. The rosés can be excellent, and are not dissimilar from a top Tavel.

The Lirac appellation's most profound wine:
Domaine de la Mordorée

RATING THE LIRAC PRODUCERS

* * * * *(OUTSTANDING)

None

* * * *(EXCELLENT)

Domaine de Cantegril   Château St.-Roch
Domaine de la Mordorée****/*****   Château de Ségriès
Domaine Roger Sabon

* * *(GOOD)

Château Boucarut***/****   Domaine de la Forcadière
Domaine Canto-Perdrix   Domaine des Garrigues
Domaine des Causses et de St.-Eymes   Domaine Jean Marchand
Domaine les Costes   Domaine de Roc Epine

About three miles north of Tavel is the sleepy village of Lirac, which, like the wines made there, seems not only unsure of its potential but also unable to find the energy needed to even promote its products. The contrast with the festive, promotion-oriented village of Tavel is remarkable. Appellation status was given to Lirac in 1947, and while that village bears the name of the wine, the area within the appellation borders includes the nearby town of Roquemaure, as well as St.-Laurent-des-Arbres and St.-Génies-de-Comolas north of Roquemaure. The vineyards in and around Lirac tend to be on gradually sloping hillsides; those near Roquemaure are on a stony plateau not unlike that of Châteauneuf du Pape, which sits only a mile away on the east bank of the Rhône River. This is the southernmost appellation of the Rhône Valley, as well as the dividing line between that area and France's Languedoc-Roussillon.

Given the beneficial climate, well-drained gravel, and stone-studded soil, the potential for excellent wine is obvious. In fact, the top estates of Lirac, such as Domaine de la Mordorée, Domaine de Ségriès, and Château St.-Roch, do indeed produce delicious wines that sell for very low prices given their quality in top years such as 1989, 1990, and 1995. Yet the rank-and-file producers of Lirac seem content to turn out a bevy of one-dimensional wines.

Today the red wine is usually the most attractive of Lirac. It has its own unique character, much lighter in body, more flowery and more obviously fruity than the nearby reds from the Côtes du Rhône-Villages or of course Châteauneuf du Pape. The white wine of Lirac is fairly neutral tasting, although the Château St.-Roch turns out a surprisingly tasty, tropical fruit–scented, agreeable white wine. The rosé can be gloriously refreshing, vibrant, and flavorful, and a worthy competitor to a nearby Tavel at half the price. However, only a handful of producers are making Lirac rosé of this quality.

The local cooperative dominates the production in Lirac. Unlike many other appellations, there seems to be no effort here by small growers to break away from the coop and begin estate-bottling their finest wines. Lirac possesses the most unexploited potential of any appellation in the département of Gard, and an argument can be made that a handful of estates need to emerge as leaders. Perhaps Domaine de la Mordorée or Château St.-Roch will take charge and produce the quality of wine essential to bring international attention to this forgotten appellation. If not, then Lirac will continue to creep along with its low profile

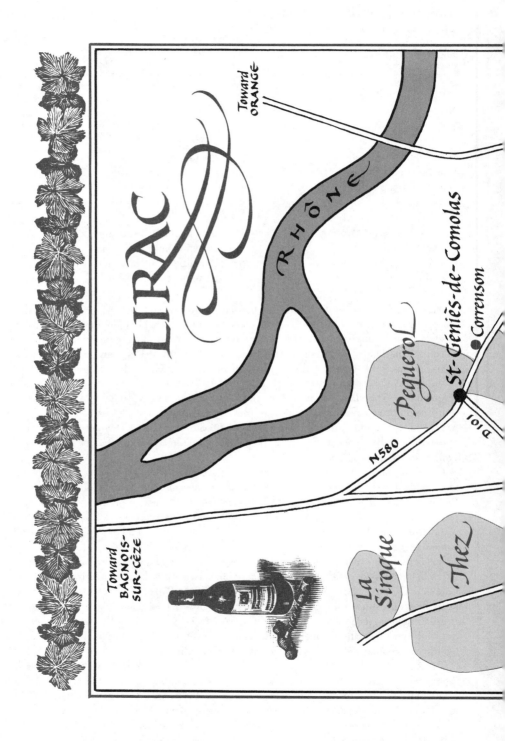

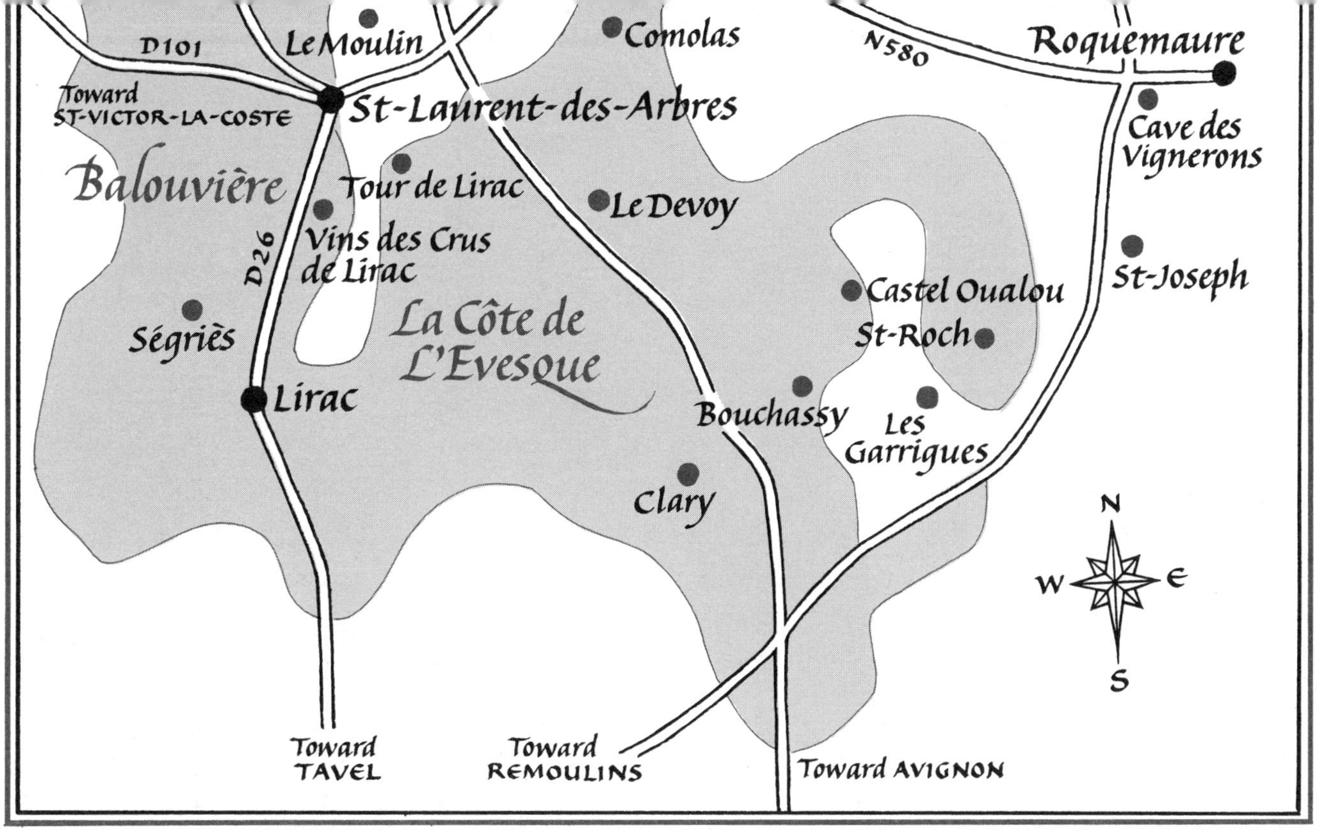

Roquemaure

N580

Cave des Vignerons

St-Joseph

Castel Oualou

St-Roch

Les Garrigues

Bouchassy

Clary

Comolas

St-Laurent-des-Arbres

Le Devoy

La Côte de L'Evesque

Le Moulin

Tour de Lirac

Vins des Crus de Lirac

Lirac

Balouvière

Ségriès

D101

A26

Toward ST-VICTOR-LA-COSTE

Toward TAVEL

Toward REMOULINS

Toward AVIGNON

N
E
S
W

status, which I find sad in view of this appellation's potential to produce high-quality wines at modest prices.

RECENT VINTAGES

1995 This is the finest vintage in Lirac since 1990. The wines exhibit deep colors, pure fruit, enough acidity for focus, and perhaps more aging potential than usual. The finest cuvées should drink well for 5–7 years.

1994 Although the wines are less consistent than the 1995s, and more herbaceous, tasty Liracs were made by those producers who harvested early and did a green harvest, cutting back the potential size of the crop.

1993 An extremely irregular year because of harvest rain, the 1993 Liracs range from hollow, austere, charmless wines to those that possess good fruit and 3–5 years of aging potential.

Older Vintages

Except for the richest cuvées of 1989 and 1990, the general rule is to drink any Lirac within 5–7 years of the vintage. The white and rosé wines need to be consumed within 12–18 months of the vintage.

CHÂTEAU BOUCARUT* * */* * * *

Address: 30150 Roquemaure
Tel: 4-66-50-40-91
Wines produced: Lirac (white, red, and rosé)
Surface area (white): 1.8 acres
           (red and rosé): 27 acres
Production (white): 312 cases
           (red): 3,125 cases
           (rosé): 312 cases
Upbringing (white): 12–15 months in stainless steel vats
           (red): 18 months total; 40% of the yield spends 8–10 months in old oak casks;
                fermentation and storage are done in stainless steel and epoxy vats
           (rosé): 6–12 months in stainless steel vats
Average age of vines (white): 40 years
                     (red and rosé): 30 years
Blend (white): 50% Grenache Blanc and 50% Clairette
      (red): 60% Grenache, 30% Syrah, 10% Cinsault
      (rosé): 80% Grenache, 20% Cinsault

This estate is coming on strong under proprietor Christophe Valat. Recent red wine offerings have been particularly impressive. The blockbuster Liracs produced in 1989 and 1990 are the two most concentrated wines I have ever tasted from this appellation. This appears to be an up-and-coming estate worth watching.

CHÂTEAU DE BOUCHASSY* *

Address: Route de Nîmes
         30150 Roquemaure
Tel: 4-66-82-82-49
Fax: 4-66-82-87-80
Wines produced: Lirac (white, red, and rosé)

Surface area (white): 2.47 acres
        (red and rosé): 17.3 acres
Production (white): 375 cases
        (red): 2,500 cases
        (rosé): 1,000 cases
Upbringing (white): 9 months in enamel vats
        (red): 36 months minimum, with the wines spending 6–8 months in barrels 2–4
            years old
        (rosé): 6–9 months in enamel vats
Average age of vines (white): 40 years
        (red and rosé): 40 years
Blend (white): 30% Grenache Blanc, 30% Clairette, 20% Bourboulenc, 10% Roussanne,
        10% Viognier
    (red): 60% Grenache, 20% Syrah, 20% Mourvèdre
    (rosé): 65% Grenache, 25% Cinsault, 5% Syrah, 5% Mourvèdre

Proprietor Gérard Degoul produces nearly 4,000 cases of white, red, and rosé Lirac from vineyards near Roquemaure. The red wine, which can be powerful and rich for a Lirac, possesses the distinctive *garrigue*, jammy cherry/plum-like flavors, and surprising power. Degoul's best vineyard slopes are situated on the *galets roulés* on the plateau of Lirac, not far from the well-known estate of Cantegril. There is a tendency at Château de Bouchassy to keep every vintage of red wine in wood for at least three years, resulting in dried-out wines in lighter years that cannot handle such a long exposure to oak.

DOMAINE DE CANTEGRIL* * * *

Address: 30150 Roquemaure
Tel: 4-66-82-82-59
Fax: 4-66-82-83-00
Wines produced: Lirac (red, white, and rosé)
Surface area (white): 6.2 acres
        (red and rosé): 30 acres
Production (white): 375 cases
        (red): 7,500 cases
        (rosé): 500 cases
Upbringing (white): 6 months in stainless steel vats
        (red): 12 months in stainless steel vats
        (rosé): 12 months in stainless steel vats
Average age of vines (white): 15 years
        (red and rosé): 17–20 years
Blend (white): 50% Clairette, 50% Grenache Blanc
    (red): 60% Grenache, 20% Syrah, 10% Cinsault, 10% Mourvèdre
    (rosé): 50% Grenache, 50% Cinsault

Domaine de Cantegril is owned by the Verda family, who are better known for the wines they produce from their Domaine St.-Roch estate in Roquemaure. The Cantegril Liracs, which are similar in style to those of St.-Roch, are vinified and brought up in the St.-Roch cellars.

CASTEL OUALOU* *

Address: 30150 Roquemaure
Tel: 4-66-82-65-65
Fax: 4-66-82-86-76
Wines produced: Lirac (white and rosé), Lirac Cuvée Traditionnelle (red), Lirac Cuvée
        Syrah (red), Lirac Syrah élevé bois (red)
Surface area (white): 9.9 acres
      (red and rosé): 12.4 acres
Production (white): 1,500 cases
      (rosé): 3,125 cases
      (red): Cuvée Traditionnelle—6,875 cases
            Cuvée Syrah—6,750 cases
            Syrah élevé bois—750 cases
Upbringing (white): 4–5 months in stainless steel vats
      (rosé): 6 months in enamel vats
      (red): Cuvée Traditionnelle—9 months in underground vats
            Cuvée Syrah—9 months in underground vats
            Syrah élevé bois—20 months total; 6 months in new and 1- to 2-year-old
            oak barrels; storage in stainless steel vats
Average age of vines (white): 30 years
               (red and rosé): 30 years
Blend (white): 40% Clairette, 20% Viognier, 20% Grenache Blanc, 10% Picpoul
    (rosé): 80% Cinsault, 18% Grenache, 2% Syrah
    (red): Cuvée Traditionnelle—60% Grenache, 20% Syrah, 10% Cinsault, 10% other
      varietals
      Cuvée Syrah—60% Syrah, 40% other varietals
      Syrah élevé bois—60% Syrah, 40% other varietals

This is another estate owned by Jean-Claude Assemat (also the proprietor of the Domaine des Causses et de St.-Eymes, and Domaine des Garrigues). Castel Oualou has an impressive single vineyard in Roquemaure planted on stony soil with an excellent exposure. The estate produces a light, easygoing red Lirac that needs to be drunk within 4–5 years of the vintage. I actually prefer the rosé, which possesses more crispness and intensity.

DOMAINE DES CAUSSES ET DE ST.-EYMES* * *

Address: R.N. 580
       30150 Roquemaure
Tel: 4-66-82-65-52
Fax: 4-66-82-86-76
Wines produced: Lirac white, Lirac Rouge d'Eté (white), Lirac rosé, Lirac Cuvée Tradition
        (red), Lirac Cuvée Type Syrah (red), Lirac Syrah éléve bois (red)
Surface area (white): 7.5 acres
      (red and rosé): 59 acres
Production (white): 1,250 cases
        Rouge d'Eté—1,875 cases
      (rosé): 1,875 cases
      (red): Cuvée Tradition—1,875 cases
            Cuvée Type Syrah—6,250 cases
            Syrah élevé bois—625 cases
Upbringing (white): 6 months in stainless steel vats
            Rouge d'Eté—Fermented in tank—whole berry clusters

(rosé): 6 months in underground enamel vats

(red): Cuvée Tradition—9 months in underground enamel vats

Cuvée Type Syrah—20 months in underground enamel vats

Syrah élevé bois—20 months total; 6 months in new and 1- to 2-year-old oak barrels; storage in underground vats

Average age of vines (white): 20 years

(red and rosé): 20 years

Blend (white): equal parts Grenache Blanc, Picpoul, and Clairette

Rouge d'Eté—60% Cinsault, 35% Grenache, 5% Syrah

(rosé): 70% Cinsault, 25% Grenache, 5% Syrah

(red): Cuvée Tradition—60% Grenache, 20% Syrah, 10% Cinsault, 10% other varietals

Cuvée Type Syrah—60% Syrah, 40% other varietals

Syrah élevé bois—60% Syrah, 40% other varietals

This estate, one of a number owned by Jean-Claude Assemat, produces numerous cuvées of red Lirac, as well as a white and rosé. Readers looking for an interesting, Cinsault-based wine should check out the Rouge d'Eté, a wine meant to be drunk in summer for its light, fruity, Beaujolais style. There are also more serious cuvées produced, including a Cuvée Type Syrah, made from 60% Syrah and the rest a blend of Grenache and Cinsault, and a small production of Syrah aged for six months in new oak barrels before being moved to other barrels prior to bottling.

CHÂTEAU DE CLARY* *

Address: 30150 Roquemaure

Tel: 4-66-82-62-88

Wines produced: Lirac (red, rosé, and white)

Surface area: 135.9 acres

Production: Variable, depending on how much is sold to négociants

Upbringing: In various foudres

Average age of vines: 35 years

Blend: Grenache, and equal parts Mourvèdre, Cinsault, and Syrah

Château de Clary is an old, historic property located in a forest near Tavel. It was here that Roman ruins were found, suggesting that wine was made at this château in ancient days. Run by Madame Veuve-Mayer and her daughter Nicole, this is thought to be the oldest wine domaine in Lirac. A huge amount of acreage in the Forest de Clary remains one of the prime sites for hunting enthusiasts. Much of Château de Clary's wine is sold to négociants, but they estate-bottle some of the production. The half dozen vintages I have tasted have been inconsistent. The wine does not live up to its renowned name.

DOMAINE LE DEVOY-MARTINE* *

Address: 30126 St.-Laurent-des-Arbres

Tel: 4-66-50-01-23

Fax: 4-66-50-43-58

Wines produced: Lirac (white, rosé, and red)

Surface area (white): 4.9 acres

(red and rosé): 98.8 acres

Production (white): 1,000 cases

(red): 20,000 cases

(rosé): 3,125 cases

Upbringing (white): 6 months in stainless steel vats
            (red): 2 years in cement vats
            (rosé): 5–6 months in stainless steel vats
Average age of vines (white): 15 years
                    (red and rosé): 25 years
Blend (white): equal parts Grenache Blanc, Clairette, Bourboulenc, and Roussanne
        (red): equal parts Syrah, Cinsault, Grenache, and Mourvèdre
        (rosé): 40% Cinsault, 30% Grenache, 30% Mourvèdre

This estate is capable of making fine wines from their single vineyard located northwest of St.-Roch. The wines tend to be more rustic, tighter knit, and more ageworthy than many Liracs, largely because of the surprisingly high percentage of Syrah (25%) and Mourvèdre (25%), which is blended with 25% Grenache and 25% Cinsault. It contains significantly less Grenache than most Liracs. These wines tend to be appreciated by those with a high tolerance for tannin and structure, and thus are less appealing to casual drinkers.

DOMAINE DE LA FORCADIÈRE* * *
Address: Rue St.-Vincent
        B.P. 8
        30126 Tavel
Tel: 4-66-50-03-40
Fax: 4-66-50-43-12
Wines produced: Lirac (red and white), Lirac Cuvée Prestige (red and white)
Surface area (white): 19.8 acres
            (red): 42 acres
Production (white): 3,375 cases
        (Cuvée Prestige white): 375 cases
        (red): 8,375 cases
        (Cuvée Prestige red): 250–330 cases
Upbringing (white): 6 months in stainless steel vats
            Cuvée Prestige—12 months in new oak barrels
        (red): 1 year in stainless steel vats, then 1 year with part of the wine in oak casks and part in new oak barrels, then 1 year in underground cellars after bottling
            Cuvée Prestige—the same as for the regular red cuvée, but with 1 year in new oak barrels
Average age of vines (white): 20 years
                    (red): 20–25 years
Blend (white): 40% Clairette, 30% Grenache Blanc, 30% Picpoul; beginning with the 1996 vintage some Viognier will be added to the white wines
        (red): 50% Mourvèdre, 40% Grenache, 10% Syrah and Carignan

This domaine, which also makes one of the finest Tavels, turns out delicious red Lirac as well as a small quantity of white wine. The white is pleasant, but generally one-dimensional and simple. The red wines are increasingly fruity, supple, and ideal for modern-day tastes. Recently, proprietor Roger Maby added a small quantity of Cuvée Prestige to his portfolio. The Cuvée Prestige (both red and white) is aged in 100% new oak for one year, and can age for up to a decade. The regular cuvée is meant to be drunk within 5–6 years. This is another estate that has diminished the quantity of Grenache in the red blend (it now represents 40%), and has moved toward Mourvèdre, which represents a whopping 50% of the blend in both the regular and Prestige Cuvée.

DOMAINE DES GARRIGUES* * *

Address: 30150 Roquemaure
Tel: 4-66-82-65-52
Fax: 4-66-82-86-76
Wines produced: Lirac (rosé), Lirac Cuvée Tradition (red), Lirac Cuvée Type Syrah (red)
Surface area: 39.5 acres
Production (rosé): 1,500 cases
         (red): Cuvée Tradition—1,250 cases
           Cuvée Type Syrah—5,000 cases
Upbringing (rosé): 6 months in enamel vats
         (red): Cuvée Tradition—9 months in underground vats
           Cuvée Type Syrah—20 months in underground enamel vats
Average age of vines: 30 years
Blend (rosé): 80% Cinsault, 15% Grenache, 5% Syrah
      (red): Cuvée Tradition—60% Grenache, 20% Syrah, 10% Cinsault, 10% other
      (red): varietals
      Cuvée Type Syrah—60% Syrah, 40% Grenache and Cinsault

Les Garrigues is one of the estates owned by Jean-Claude Assemat. It produces a more elegant, lighter-style Lirac than those from Assemat's Domaine des Causses et de St.-Eymes.

DOMAINE DE LA MORDORÉE* * * */* * * * *

Address: 30126 Tavel
Tel: 4-66-50-00-75
Fax: 4-66-50-47-39
Wines produced: Lirac (red), Lirac Cuvée de la Reine des Bois (red)
Surface area: 64 acres
Production (regular cuvée): 5,625 cases
         (Cuvée de la Reine des Bois): 1,250 cases
Upbringing (regular cuvée): 6–12 months in old oak casks
         (Cuvée de la Reine des Bois): 6–9 months in new oak barrels
Average age of vines: 40 years
Blend (regular cuvée): 50% Grenache, 50% Syrah
      (Cuvée de la Reine des Bois): equal parts Grenache, Mourvèdre, and Syrah

Under the inspired leadership of Christophe Delorme, Domaine de la Mordorée has surged to the forefront in Lirac. While some excellent Tavel is produced, as well as a superb Châteauneuf du Pape (see page 442), the wines most readily available are the estate's delicious reds. The regular cuvée of Lirac is undoubtedly the finest wine being made in the appellation. It is a blend of 50% Grenache and 50% Syrah. Interestingly, Mordorée avoids the more animal-like, tannic character of the Mourvèdre, preferring to use jammy Grenache and buttress it with the deep, black fruits and tannin of Syrah. This has been an undeniable success, producing a Lirac that tastes like a slightly downsized Châteauneuf du Pape. It is capable of lasting for a decade.

In superb vintages a limited quantity of a luxury cuvée, La Reine des Bois, is made. It incorporates Mourvèdre in equal portions with Grenache and Syrah. Delorme believes Mourvèdre gives the wine another 5–10 years of aging potential, and it is meant to mature over a period of 10–15 years—uncommonly long for a Lirac. Recent vintages, even the irregular 1993, have been immensely impressive. The wines have revealed deep ruby/purple colors, aromas of black cherries and roasted Provençal herbs, and surprisingly expansive, succulent, medium- to full-bodied personalities. La Reine des Bois, which is a selection made in the cellar, usually from a parcel of vines 55–60 years old, is made from equal parts Grenache, Syrah, and Mourvèdre. It is a large-scale, boldly styled, rich Lirac and the single finest wine of the appellation.

CHÂTEAU ST.-ROCH* * * *

Address: 30150 Roquemaure
Tel: 4-66-82-82-59
Fax: 4-66-82-83-00
Wines produced: Lirac (red, white, and rosé), Lirac Ancienne Viguerie (red)
Surface area (white): 12.4 acres
             (red and rosé): 86 acres
Production (white): 1,875 cases
           (rosé): 2,500 cases
           (red): 11,250 cases
                 Ancienne Viguerie—1,250 cases
Upbringing (white): 6 months in stainless steel vats
           (rosé): 6 months in stainless steel vats
           (red): 2 years total; 1 year in stainless steel and epoxy vats for fermentation and
                 storage, and 1 year in old oak casks
                 Ancienne Viguerie—2 years total; 1 year in stainless steel vats, 6 months
                 in old oak casks, and 6 months in new oak barrels
Average age of vines: 20 years
Blend (white): equal portions of Grenache Blanc, Clairette, and Bourboulenc
      (rosé): 60% Cinsault, 40% Grenache
      (red): 60% Grenache, 20% Syrah, 20% Cinsault
            Ancienne Viguerie—50% Grenache, 25% Syrah, 25% Mourvèdre

Proprietor Antoine Verda is one of the stars of Lirac, and his domaine, located north of Roquemaure, is probably one of the most important in the appellation. Truly a family domaine, father Antoine is joined by his sons, Jean-Jacques, who looks over the vinification and élevage, and André, who is responsible for the viticulture. The estate is not old, having been, brought together through multiple purchases since the mid-fifties. The first vintage was 1960.

Most of the wines of St.-Roch should be drunk within 5–6 years of the vintage, even sooner in lighter years such as 1992 and 1993. This estate also makes a special cuvée, Ancienne Viguerie, that is meant to age for 10–12 years in great vintages (e.g., 1990 and 1995). Just over 1,000 cases of this wine are produced from a blend of 50% Grenache, 25% Syrah, and 25% Mourvèdre. The Mourvèdre gives the wine structure, tannin, and some formidable antioxidant characteristics.

In addition to the Château St.-Roch label, the Verda family produces a wine called Château Cantegril (see page 583) from a single estate purchased by the Verda family near Roquemaure. The wines of Cantegril are vinified and brought up in the cellars of St.-Roch. They are similar in character to the St.-Roch offerings.

CHÂTEAU DE SÉGRIÈS* * * *

Address: 30126 Lirac
Tel: 4-66-50-44-72
Wines produced: Lirac (red, white, and rosé)
Surface area (white): 3.7 acres
             (red): 33.4 acres
             (rosé): 10 acres
Production (white): 625 cases

(red): 6,000 cases

(rosé): 188 cases

Upbringing (white): 8 months in enamel vats

(red): 12 months in cement vats

(rosé): 12–24 months in cement vats

Average age of vines: 20 years and 50 years

Blend (white): 50% Clairette, 25% Bourboulenc, 25% Ugni Blanc

(red): 60% Grenache, 20% Syrah, 20% Cinsault and Mourvèdre

(rosé): 50–60% Grenache, 30–40% Cinsault, 10% Syrah

Domaine de Ségriès is run by the Comte de Regis and his son, François, who are among the pioneers of the Lirac appellation. Prior to the influx of French Algerians following the revolution in that country in the mid-fifties, Domaine de Ségriès, along with St.-Roch and Château de Clary, was one of the best-known estates of Lirac. With east- and west-facing vineyards, this estate often produces some of the finest raw materials in Lirac. However, aging the red one year in old cement vats never results in as much fruit and intensity in the bottled wine as expected. Nevertheless, this is a good, traditional, unfiltered Lirac with plenty of the herbes de Provence/*garrigue* character to give it a decidedly Provençal character. The white wine is an old-fashioned white Lirac—monolithic, dull, and simple.

Son François appears to be moving toward a shorter vatting time for the red wines, so perhaps fresher, livelier fruit will show up in the bottle.

OTHER LIRAC PRODUCERS

CHÂTEAU D'ACQUERIA

Address: 30126 Tavel

Tel: 4-66-50-04-56

Fax: 4-66-50-18-46

Wines produced: Lirac (red and white)

Surface area (white): 10 acres

(red): 32 acres

Production (white): 1,875 cases

(red): 4,375 cases

Upbringing (white): 5 months in stainless steel vats

(red): 18 months total, with 6–8 months in oak casks

Average age of vines (white): 8 years

(red): 20 years

Blend (white): 45–50% Grenache Blanc, 25% Bourboulenc, 15% Clairette, 10% Roussanne

(red): 45% Grenache, 35% Mourvèdre, 10% Cinsault, 10% Syrah

DOMAINE DES AMANDINES

Address: Rue des Carrières

30126 Tavel

Tel: 4-66-50-04-41

Wines produced: Lirac (red)

Surface area: 14.8 acres

Production: 3,125 cases

Upbringing: 18–20 months total; vinification in stainless steel vats followed by 16–18 months in old oak casks

Average age of vines: 30 years

Blend: 50% Grenache, 35% Syrah, 15% Mourvèdre

DOMAINE BALAZU DES VAUSSIÈRES

Address: Rue des Vaussières
        30126 Tavel
Tel: 4-66-50-44-22
Wines produced: Lirac (red)
Surface area: 3.1 acres
Production: 250 cases
Upbringing: 18–24 months total, with one-third of the yield in oak barrels for 10 months
        and the rest in stainless steel vats
Average age of vines: 40 years
Blend: 100% Grenache

DOMAINE CANTO-PERDRIX* * *

Address: S.C.E.A. Méjean-Taulier
        30126 Tavel
Tel: 4-66-50-04-02
Fax: 4-66-50-21-72
Wines produced: Lirac (red)
Surface area: 11.1 acres
Production: 1,000 cases
Upbringing: 3–4 years in stainless steel vats
Average age of vines: 5–6 years
Blend: 60% Grenache, 20% Syrah, 20% Mourvèdre and Cinsault

DOMAINE DES CARABINIERS

Address: R.N. 580
        30150 Roquemaure
Tel: 4-66-82-62-04
Fax: 4-66-82-82-15
Wines produced: Lirac (red and white)
Surface area (white): 5 acres
        (red): 37 acres
Production (white): 1000 cases
        (red): 6,250 cases
Upbringing white): 6 months in cement vats
        (red): 24 months total; with 70% of the yield in cement vats and 30% in
        2-year-old barrels for 12 months
Average age of vines (white): 15 years
        (red): 35 years
Blend (white): 30% Grenache Blanc, 30% Clairette, 30% Bourboulenc, 10% Roussanne
        (red): 50% Grenache, 20% Mourvèdre, 20% Syrah, 10% Cinsault

CAVES DES VIGNERONS DE LIRAC

Address: 30126 St.-Laurent-des-Arbres
Tel: 4-66-50-01-02
Fax: 4-66-50-37-23
Wines produced: Lirac (white), Lirac Cuvée Générique (red), Lirac Cuvée Vieilles Vignes
        (red), Lirac Cuvée Jean XXII (red), Lirac Monseigneur de la Rovère (red)
Surface area: 197 acres
Production (white): 750 cases
        (red): Cuvée Générique—3,750 cases

Cuvée Vieilles Vignes—10,000 cases
Cuvée Jean XXII—12,500 cases
Monseigneur de la Rovère—6,250 cases
Upbringing (white): 5 months in stainless steel vats
(red): Cuvée Générique—12 months in epoxy vats
Cuvée Vieilles Vignes—12 months in epoxy vats
Cuvée Jean XXII—12 months in epoxy vats
Monseigneur de la Rovère—12 months in epoxy vats
Average age of vines (red): Cuvée Générique—30 years maximum
Cuvée Vieilles Vignes—35 years minimum
Cuvée Jean XXII—undetermined
Monseigneur de la Rovère—undetermined
Blend (white): 50% Grenache Blanc, 25% Clairette, 25% Bourboulenc
(red): Cuvée Générique—60% Grenache, 40% other varietals
Cuvée Vieilles Vignes—60% Grenache, 40% other varietals
Cuvée Jean XXII—60% Grenache, 25% Mourvèdre, 15% other varietals
Monseigneur de la Rovère—60% Grenache, 25% Syrah, 15% other varietals
except Mourvèdre

CAVE DES VIGNERONS DE ROQUEMAURE

Address: 30150 Roquemaure
Tel: 4-66-82-82-01
Fax: 4-66-82-67-28
Wines produced: Lirac (red, white, and rosé), Lirac Cuvée Sélection (red)
Surface area: 198 acres
Production (white): 688 cases
(red): 12,500 cases
(rosé): 6,250 cases
Upbringing (white): 4–5 months in cement vats
(red): 12 months in cement vats
Cuvée Sélection—14 months total, with 6–12 months in old oak barrels
and casks
(rosé): 5 months in cement vats
Average age of vines (white): 20–25 years
(red): 20–25 years
Cuvée Sélection—over 25 years
(rosé): 20–25 years
Blend (white): 60% Grenache Blanc, 20% Bourboulenc, 20% Clairette
(red): 55–60% Grenache, 20% Cinsault, 10% Mourvèdre, 10% Syrah
(rosé): 60% Grenache, 20% Cinsault, 10% Mourvèdre, 10% Syrah

DOMAINE CHAMBON

Address: 30290 St.-Victor-la-Coste
Tel: 4-66-50-45-88
Wines produced: Lirac (red and rosé)
Surface area: 19.8 acres
Production (red): 2,500 cases
(rosé): 1,875 cases
Upbringing (red): 36 months total; fermentation and storage in cement vats, with 6 months
in oak casks
(rosé): 3 months in cement vats

Average age of vines: 40 years
Blend (red): 60% Grenache, 40% equal portions of Cinsault, Syrah, and Mourvèdre
(rosé): 60% Grenache, 20% Clairette, 10% Cinsault, 10% Mourvèdre

DOMAINE LES COSTES* * *

Address: Rue du Stade
30150 St.-Génies-de-Comolas
Tel: 4-66-50-05-28
Wines produced: Lirac (red, white, and rosé), Lirac Cuvée Syrah (red)
Surface area (white): 2.47 acres
(red): 19.8 acres
(rosé): 5 acres
Production (white): 500 cases
(red): 2,500 cases
Cuvée Syrah—1,250 cases
(rosé): 1,125 cases
Upbringing (white): 4 months in epoxy vats
(red): 9 months in cement vats, with 10% of the yield in old oak casks for 3 months (both cuvées)
(rosé): 6 months in epoxy vats
Average age of vines (white): 20 years
(red): 40 years
Blend (white): 50% Clairette, 50% Grenache Blanc
(red): 70% Grenache, 20% Syrah, 10% Cinsault
Cuvée Syrah—60% Grenache, 40% Syrah
(rosé): 60% Grenache, 40% Cinsault

DOMAINE DE LA CROZE

Address: 13, rue Bécatillon
30150 Roquemaure
Tel: 4-66-82-56-73
Wines produced: Lirac (red)
Surface area: 10 acres
Production: 500 cases
Upbringing: 14 months total; with 12 months in barrels, of which 10% are new
Average age of vines: 50–60 years
Blend: 60% Grenache, 20% Syrah, 10% Mourvèdre, 10% Cinsault

DOMAINE DUSEIGNEUR

Address: 30126 St.-Laurent-des-Arbres
Tel: 4-66-50-02-57
Fax: 4-66-50-43-57
Wines produced: Lirac (red, white, and rosé)
Surface area (white): 2.47 acres
(red and rosé): 28.4 acres
Production (white): 250 cases
(red): 1,875 cases
(rosé): 1,250 cases
Upbringing (white): 4 months in stainless steel vats
(red): fermentation and storage in cement vats for 1 year, as well as 3–6 months in old oak barrels and casks
(rosé): 6 months in stainless steel vats

Average age of vines (white): 20–25 years
      (red and rosé): 20–25 years
Blend (white): 60% Bourboulenc, 30% Clairette, 10% Grenache Blanc
  (red): 50–60% Grenache, 20% Cinsault, the rest Syrah and Mourvèdre
  (rosé): 50% Grenache, 40% Cinsault, 5% Syrah, 5% Clairette

DOMAINE DE LA GENESTIÈRE

Address: 30126 Tavel
Tel: 4-66-50-07-03
Fax: 4-66-50-27-03
Wines produced: Lirac (red and white)
Surface area: 27 acres
Production (white): 375 cases
   (red): 4,000 cases
Upbringing (white): 6–12 months in enamel vats
   (red): 2 years total, with 6 months in oak casks
Average age of vines: 15–20 years
Blend (white): Grenache Blanc, Clairette, Picpoul, Bourboulenc
  (red): Grenache, Cinsault, Carignan, Syrah, Clairette

DOMAINE DES JONCIERS

Address: Rue de la Combe
   30126 Tavel
Tel: 4-66-50-27-70
Fax: 4-66-50-34-07
Wines produced: Lirac (red, white, and rosé)
Surface area (white): 4.9 acres
   (red and rosé): 74 acres
Production (white): 375 cases
   (red): 15,000 cases
   (rosé): 1,250 cases
Upbringing (white): 6 months in enamel vats
   (red): 2 years in underground cement vats
   (rosé): 6 months in cement vats
Average age of vines (white): half are 25 years old and half are 1 year old
     (red and rosé): 25 years
Blend (white): 50% Bourboulenc, 25% Roussanne, 25% Marsanne (because of recent plan-
    tations, the actual production at present is really a 100% Bourboulenc wine)
  (red): 50% Grenache, 20% Syrah, 20% Cinsault, 10% Mourvèdre
  (rosé): 50% Cinsault, 45% Grenache, 5% Syrah

DOMAINE LAFARGUE

Address: 30126 St.-Laurent-des-Arbres
Tel: 4-66-50-05-21
Wines produced: Lirac (red, white, and rosé)
Surface area (white): 7.4 acres
   (red and rosé): 17.3 acres
Production (white): 1,500 cases
   (red): 1,625 cases
   (rosé): 1,625 cases

Upbringing (white): 6 months in stainless steel vats
   (red): 12 months in cement and stainless steel vats
   (rosé): 6 months in stainless steel vats
Average age of vines (white): 20 years
     (red and rosé): 35 years
Blend (white): 50% Clairette, 25% Grenache Blanc, 25% Ugni Blanc
  (red): 50% Grenache, 20% Cinsault, 15% Mourvèdre, 15% Syrah
  (rosé): 50% Grenache, 30% Cinsault, 20% other varietals, including Syrah

DOMAINE DE LANZAC

Address: Route de Pujaut
   30126 Tavel
Tel: 4-66-50-22-17
Wines produced: Lirac (red)
Surface area: 14.9 acres
Production: 2,500 cases
Upbringing: 12 months total, with 6–8 months in old oak casks
Average age of vines: 20 years
Blend: 50% Grenache, 30% Syrah, 20% Cinsault

DOMAINE JEAN MARCHAND* * *

Address: 21, route d'Orange
   84230 Châteauneuf du Pape
Tel: 4-90-83-70-34
Fax: 4-90-83-50-83
Wines produced: Lirac (red)
Surface area: 12.4 acres
Production: 2,500 cases
Upbringing: 6 months in enamel vats
Average age of vines: 25 years
Blend: 80% Grenache, 20% Clairette

DOMAINE DU MOULIN BLANC

Address: 30126 Tavel
Tel: 4-78-34-25-06
Fax: 4-78-34-30-60
Wines produced: Lirac (red and rosé)
Surface area (red): 4.9 acres
   (rosé): 2.47 acres
Production (red): 1,000 cases
   (rosé): 562 cases
Upbringing (red): 12 months total, with 6 months in oak casks
   (rosé): 6 months in stainless steel vats
Average age of vines (red): 25 years
    (rosé): 10 years
Blend (red): 60% Grenache, 30% Syrah, 10% Mourvèdre
 (rosé): 100% Grenache

DOMAINE PELAQUIÉ

Address: 7, rue du Vernet
   30290 St.-Victor-la-Coste
Tel: 4-66-50-21-88
Wines produced: Lirac (red and rosé)
Surface area (red): 3.4 acres
   (rosé): 1.5 acres

Production (red): 837 cases
       (rosé): 375 cases
Upbringing (red): 15–18 months in stainless steel vats
       (rosé): 5–8 months in stainless steel vats
Average age of vines (red): 20 years
                (rosé): 20 years
Blend (red): 60% Grenache, 40% Mourvèdre
       (rosé): Equal parts Grenache, Cinsault, and Mourvèdre

DOMAINE DE ROC EPINE or DOMAINE LAFOND* * *

Address: Route des Vignobles
         30126 Tavel
Tel: 4-66-50-24-59
Fax: 4-66-50-12-42
Wines produced: Lirac (red and white) (the debut vintage for the white wines is 1995)
Surface area (white): 3.7 acres
             (red): 24.7 acres
Production (white): 750 cases
           (red): 5,000 cases
Upbringing (white): 6–12 months in stainless steel vats
           (red): 18 months total, with 4–5 months in old oak casks
Average age of vines (white): 4 years and 25 years
                     (red): 25 years
Blend (white): 40% Grenache Blanc, 20% Viognier, 20% Roussanne, 20% Clairette
       (red): 60% Grenache, 30% Syrah, 10% Carignan and Cinsault

DOMAINE ROGER SABON* * * *

Address: Avenue Impériale
         84230 Châteauneuf du Pape
Tel: 4-90-83-71-72
Fax: 4-90-83-50-51
Wines produced: Lirac (red and white)
Surface area (white): 1.2 acres
             (red): 34 acres
Production (white): 150 cases
           (red): 3,750 cases
Upbringing (white): 4–5 months in enamel vats
           (red): 14 months total, with 6 months in old oak casks and the remainder in
                cement vats
Average age of vines (white): 25 years
                     (red): 40 years
Blend (white): 30% Viognier, 25% Clairette, 25% Bourboulenc, 20% Grenache Blanc
       (red): 60% Grenache, 20% Syrah, 10% Mourvèdre, 10% Cinsault

CHÂTEAU ST.-MAURICE

Address: 30290 Laudun
Tel: 4-66-50-29-31
Fax: 4-66-50-40-91
Wines produced: Lirac (red)
Surface area: 10 acres
Production: 1,500 cases

Upbringing: 18 months minimum, with 40% of the yield in old oak casks for 8–10 months, and the remainder in stainless steel and epoxy vats
Average age of vines: 35 years
Blend: 70% Grenache, 30% Syrah

DOMAINE TOUR DES CHÊNES

Address: 30126 St.-Laurent-des-Arbres
Tel: 4-66-50-34-19
Fax: 4-66-50-34-69
Wines produced: Lirac (red, white, and rosé)
Surface area (white): 1.4 acres
       (red and rosé): 72 acres
Production (white): 312 cases
       (red): 8,750 cases
       (rosé): 3,750 cases
Upbringing (white): 6 months minimum in cement vats
       (red): 18 months in cement vats
       (rosé): 4 months in cement vats
Average age of vines (white): 20–25 years
       (red and rosé): 20–25 years
Blend (white): 40% Clairette, 35% Grenache Blanc, 25% Ugni Blanc
      (red): 50% Grenache, 25% Cinsault, 20% Syrah, 5% Mourvèdre
      (rosé): 65% Cinsault, 35% Grenache

DOMAINE DU VIEUX MOULIN

Address: 30126 Tavel
Tel: 4-66-50-07-79
Fax: 4-66-50-10-02
Wines produced: Lirac (red)
Surface area: 19.8 acres
Production: 4,000 cases
Upbringing: 24 months minimum, with at least 6 months in very old oak casks
Average age of vines: 25 years
Blend: 40% Grenache, 25% Syrah, 20% Cinsault, 15% Mourvèdre

CÔTES DU RHÔNE-VILLAGES

Caveat Emptor! Terrible to Terrific

CÔTES DU RHÔNE-VILLAGES AT A GLANCE

Type of wine produced:	Red, white, and rosé.
Grape varieties planted:	Twenty-four varietals are permitted, of which 14 are considered major players and 10 accessory. In practice, the red wines are dominated by Grenache, Syrah, Mourvèdre, Cinsault, and Carignan, and the whites by Grenache Blanc, Clairette, Bourboulenc, and, increasingly, Roussanne and Viognier.
Acres currently under vine:	Just over 12,500 acres are entitled to be called Côtes du Rhône-Villages. This area spans both banks of the Rhône River, as well as three French départements, Vaucluse, Gard, and Drôme.
Quality level:	Poor to excellent.
Aging potential	(white): 1–2 years.
	(rosé): 1–2 years.
	(red): 3–5 years, with a few top wines capable of 10–15 years of evolution.
Top villages to seek out:	About 85% of the wines made in the Côtes du Rhône-Villages appellation have one of the sixteen villages' name annexed to the words Côtes du Rhône-Villages. In alphabetical order, the villages are: Beaumes de Venise, Cairanne, Chusclan, Laudun,

Rasteau, Roaix, Rochegude, Rousset-les-Vignes, Sablet, St.-Gervais, St.-Maurice-sur-Eygues, St.-Pantaléon-les-Vignes, Séguret, Valréas, Vinsobres, and Visan. Knowing individual producers is more important than knowing villages, but the overall quality tends to be highest in Beaumes de Venise, Cairanne, Rasteau, Sablet, and Séguret.

The remaining 15% or so of the production from this appellation is from villages that are not entitled to attach their names to the words Côtes du Rhône, but they can call their wine Côtes du Rhône-Villages. Some of this wine can be very good.

General characteristics:	The quality and style of white, red, and rosé Côtes du Rhône-Villages varies enormously.
Greatest recent vintages:	1995, 1990, 1989.
Price range:	$9–$20, with the most expensive wines representing old-vine or single-varietal cuvées made from Syrah, Viognier, or Roussanne.

Within the gigantic southern Rhône region, the French government, in particular the INAO, National Institute of Appellations of Origin, determined that 16 "villages" or communes had particularly good soil and microclimates and therefore produced superior wine. These 16 "villages" are entitled Côtes du Rhône-Villages, and their wines can be identified by either that appellation on the label or the name of the village preceded by the words "Côtes du Rhône."

The controls governing the vineyard area—permitted yield per acre, grape varieties, and alcohol content—are more strictly limited and regulated for wines called Côtes du Rhône-Villages than Côtes du Rhône. This should ensure that the consumer will get a better wine when purchasing a Côtes du Rhône-Villages rather than a Côtes du Rhône. Ironically, while there are many fine Côtes du Rhône-Villages wines, the two greatest wines made with a Côtes du Rhône appellation are not "Villages" wines. These two wines, the Cru de Coudoulet of the Perrin family and Château de Fonsalette of Jacques Reynaud, are obvious exceptions to the rule, but more on them and the generic Côtes du Rhône in the next chapter.

The appellation Côtes du Rhône-Villages was first granted in 1953 only to Cairanne, Chusclan, Laudun, and Gigondas. (The last, Gigondas, was elevated in 1971 to a full-fledged appellation of its own.) The other villages have asked for and received "Villages" status, except Vacqueyras, which was also elevated to its own appellation. It would be foolish to assume that all the village wines are of equal merit. In the course of the vast amount of tasting and visiting of domaines conducted in researching this book, it was apparent to me that certain villages produced better wines than others. Generally, I found the least successful Côtes du Rhône-Villages wines to come from the three villages in the Drôme département. Here in the northeastern quarter of the southern Rhône viticultural area are the official villages of Rochegude, Rousset-les-Vignes, St.-Maurice-sur-Eygues, St.-Pantaléon-les-Vignes, and Vinsobres. There is very interesting countryside to see here, but only a few of the wines I tasted from these villages seemed to merit a special "Villages" AOC status. Most of the wines produced in these one-horse towns are made by cooperatives.

On the western bank of the Rhône is the Gard département, which has three official Côtes du Rhône-Villages—Chusclan, Laudun, and St.-Gervais. For my palate, only the last merits Côtes du Rhône-Villages status.

Unquestionably the finest Côtes du Rhône-Villages wines come from the scenic, heavily visited Vaucluse département. Amidst a landscape of vines and Provençal hill towns, official Côtes du Rhône-Villages such as Beaumes de Venise (also entitled to its own AOC for its sweet, fortified Muscat wine), Cairanne, Rasteau (which has its own AOC, too, for its fortified sweet wine), Sablet, and Séguret, produce vast quantities of very good, full-bodied, honest, sometimes exceptional wine that generally represents a fine value. The Côtes du Rhône-Villages are reviewed in alphabetical order.

BEAUMES DE VENISE

Type of wine produced:	The appellation is most famous for its sweet vins doux naturels, which are essentially fortified sweet wines made from the Muscat grape, but dry red, white, and rosé are also produced, some of it excellent.
Grape varieties planted:	All permitted southern Rhône varietals, as well as the only legal plantations of Muscat à Petits Grains in the Rhône Valley (both the white and black variety).
Acres currently under vine:	1,087.
Quality level:	Good to exceptional.
Aging potential:	2–4 years.
General characteristics:	The Muscat is a sweet, alcoholic, extraordinarily perfumed and exotic, rich, decadent dessert wine. The best examples of red wine are classic Côtes du Rhône-Villages with plenty of red and black cherry fruit, peppery, Provençal-herb-scented noses, and gutsy, lusty flavors.
Greatest recent vintages:	1995.
Price range	(Muscat de Beaumes de Venise): $15–$30. (Côtes du Rhône-Villages Beaumes de Venise red): $10–$16.
The village's best-kept secret:	The excellent dry red wines produced by Domaine de Fenouillet, Domaine les Goubert, and Château Redortier.

RATING THE MUSCAT BEAUMES DE VENISE PRODUCERS (Sweet Wine)

* * * * *(OUTSTANDING)

Domaine de Baumalric   Paul Jaboulet-Aîné
Domaine de Durban

* * * *(EXCELLENT)

Domaine des Bernardins   Domaine de Fenouillet
Chapoutier   Château St.-Sauveur
Domaine de Coyeaux   Vidal-Fleury

* * *(GOOD)

Caves des Vignerons de Vacqueyras
Vignerons de Beaumes de Venise

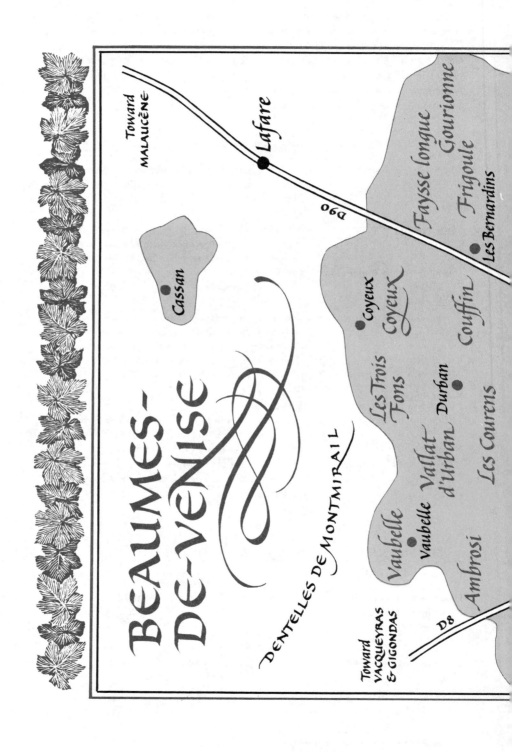

BEAUMES-DE-VENISE

DENTELLES DE MONTMIRAIL

Toward
MALAUCÈNE

Lafare

D90

Cassan

Faysse longue

Gourionne

Frigoule

Les Bernardins

Coyeux

Coyeux

Couffin

Les Trois
Fons

Durban

Les Courens

Vallat
d'Urban

Vaubelle

Vaubelle

Ambrosi

Toward
VACQUEYRAS
& GIGONDAS

D8

Font Sante
Roguabinaud
Vignaux
La Gière   St-Véran
St-Sauveur
Bosquet

N
E
W
S

Beaumes-
de-Venise

D90

D81

St-Sauveur

Aubignan

Toward CARPENTRAS

D7

Mornas
Payard
Coste Belle
Cave des Vignerons

Bousquet
Imbrescades
L'Estagnon

This sleepy hillside village is largely known for its decadently fragrant and perfumed "vin doux naturel," or Muscat de Beaumes de Venise. However, this village is also a very fine source for red Côtes du Rhône. Beaumes de Venise is a five-minute drive south of Gigondas, and is tucked up against the Dentelles de Montmirail mountains. It is an ancient village founded by the Romans, who were known to use the sulfur springs at nearby Montmirail. It remains the only area of the Rhône Valley where the Muscat à Petits Grains is grown.

The Muscat de Beaumes de Venise is one of the world's greatest and most underrated sweet dessert wines; I disagree completely with the local cognoscenti who quaff this full-bodied, 21% alcohol wine as an apéritif. Its weakness is its inability to last or improve in the bottle. In short, Muscat de Beaumes de Venise must be drunk within three to four years of the vintage. Consumed young, before it loses its freshness and heady fragrance, Muscat de Beaumes de Venise inundates the taster with a veritable tidal wave of aromas ranging from scents of apricots, peaches, and coconuts, to amaretto, roasted nuts, and oranges. The unctuous, opulent, exotic flavors and staggering level of fruit hide far too easily the hefty alcoholic content. This is a wine to drink as a dessert, or with a very basic food companion —open-face fruit pies and tarts do magnificently. Another virtue of this wine is that the unfinished portion, if refrigerated, can be kept for five to seven days without fear of oxidation.

Since the first edition of this book, the popularity of Muscat de Beaumes de Venise has grown significantly. In a normal vintage, approximately 175,000 cases are produced, of which 135,000 cases come from the huge cooperative (120 members). The virtues of Beaumes de Venise, which I have long extolled, have been recognized as far away as Singapore and Japan, where the popularity of these wines seems to increase with each new vintage. Fortunately, prices for Beaumes de Venise have remained relatively stable, making them one of the best values in sweet wine.

DOMAINE DE BAUMALRIC* * * * *

Address: Quartier St.-Roch, B.P. 15
        84190 Beaumes de Venise
Tel: 4-90-65-01-77
Fax: 4-90-62-97-28
Wines produced: Beaumes de Venise
Surface area: 17.3 acres
Production: 1,250 cases
Upbringing: 12 months in stainless steel and cement vats
Average age of vines: 30–40 years
Blend: 100% Muscat à Petits Grains Blanc

This is one of the up-and-coming stars of Beaumes de Venise. Proprietor Daniel Begouaussel broke away from the appellation's cooperative in 1991 and began to estate-bottle his wine, even though he was only a youthful 35 years old. By keeping his yields low (23 hectoliters per hectare rather than the allowed 30), and utilizing 100% Muscat à Petits Grains, Begouaussel has fashioned some of the most elegant, refreshing, lighter-styled but authoritatively flavored sweet wines of Beaumes de Venise. Unlike those that tilt the scales at 20 + % alcohol, Domaine de Baumalric rarely has more than 15%. The 1994 and 1995 were impressive for their extraordinary purity, freshness, and lovely apricot fruit. Daniel Begouaussel also produces a red Côtes du Rhône and Beaumes de Venise, as well as some Côtes du Ventoux.

DOMAINE DES BERNARDINS* * * *

Address: Quartier St.-Anne
      84110 Beaumes de Venise
Tel: 4-90-62-94-13
Wines produced: Muscat de Beaumes de Venise
Surface area: 12.4 acres
Production: 6,250 cases
Upbringing: 6 months in stainless steel vats
Average age of vines: 10–40 years
Blend: 75% Muscat à Petits Grains Blanc, 25% Petits Grains Noir

Madame Renée Castaud is quick to point out that this estate, also known as Domaine Castaud-Maurin, is one of the few in Beaumes de Venise still to produce Beaumes de Venise in a traditional manner, with no centrifuges. The result is an old-style Muscat with more color than most, and a thicker, more unctuously textured, ripe, chewy, heavyweight style. While I disagree with Madame Castaud when she says this wine can age for two decades, it is certainly a big, viscous style of Beaumes de Venise with a more oxidized character than most.

CAVES DES VIGNERONS DE VACQUEYRAS* * *

Address: Le Troubadour
      84190 Vacqueyras
Tel: 4-90-65-84-54
Fax: 4-90-65-81-32
Wines produced: Muscat de Beaumes de Venise
Surface area: 16.1 acres
Production: 2,185 cases
Upbringing: 6 months minimum in stainless steel vats
Average age of vines: 10 years, and 15–20 years
Blend: 100% Muscat à Petits Grains Blanc

This small cooperative in nearby Vacqueyras has only six members owning 16.1 acres. The average age of the vines is young (about 10 years) except for one tiny parcel where the vines average 15–20 years. The wine produced is a pleasant, straightforward example of the appellation.

CHAPOUTIER* * * *

Address: 18, avenue du Docteur Paul Durand
      B.P. 38
      26600 Tain l'Hermitage
Tel: 4-75-08-27-43
Fax: 4-75-08-28-65

The stylish, elegant, refreshingly fruity, rich cuvée purchased by Chapoutier from growers in Beaumes de Venise is made from 100% Muscat à Petits Grains, and vinified in the growers' cellars under the supervision of Chapoutier. The production averages around 1,875 cases, which have gone from strength to strength under the administration of Michel and Marc Chapoutier.

DOMAINE DE COYEAUX* * * *

Address: B.P. 7
        84190 Beaumes de Venise
Tel: 4-90-62-97-96
Fax: 4-90-65-01-87
Wines produced: Muscat Beaumes de Venise
Surface area: 124 acres
Production: 17,500 cases
Upbringing: 12 months in stainless steel vats, and 6–18 months in bottle
Average age of vines: 30 years
Blend: 100% Muscat à Petits Grains Blanc

The charming, confident, friendly Yves Nativelle, a Parisian who worked at the well-known French pharmaceutical giant Rhône-Poulenc, acquired this gorgeous estate high in the hills above the village in 1978. He produced his first Beaumes de Venise in 1982. Nativelle, who has a habit of calling Muscat either the "nectar of the Pope" or "nectar of God," fashions a fresh, lively wine. It possesses an orangeish color, and plenty of clean, pure fruit. Although not the most complex Muscat, it is consistently delicious, and made in a lighter, less powerful and opulent style than, for example, Domaine des Bernardins or Domaine de Durban. Nativelle also produces modern-style, one-dimensional red Beaumes de Venise, and he owns a small estate in Gigondas.

DOMAINE DE DURBAN* * * * *

Address: 84190 Beaumes de Venise
Tel: 4-90-62-94-26
Wines produced: Muscat Beaumes de Venise
Surface area: 62 acres
Production: 10,000 cases
Upbringing: Minimum of 4 months in stainless steel vats
Average age of vines: 30–40 years
Blend: 100% Muscat à Petit Grains Blanc

The 62-acre Muscat vineyard of Domaine de Durban produces what many observers feel is the finest Muscat Beaumes de Venise of the appellation. It is always an extroverted and flamboyant wine, even in rain-plagued, lighter vintages. The Domaine de Durban, run by Bernard and Jean-Pierre Leydier, is perched on a steep hillside above the village, with a spectacular view of the countryside. While the Leydiers have lightened the style produced by their father, this remains an intense, concentrated, viscous Beaumes de Venise with striking flavors and a haunting fragrance. For years this wine was sold without a vintage, but in 1985 the Leydiers began to vintage date the wine, a critical as well as intelligent modification given not only the short shelf life of these wines, but also the vintage consciousness of most purchasers. If anyone doubts the popularity of Beaumes de Venise, try buying a bottle of Domaine de Durban three or four months after the wine has been released—it rapidly disappears from the marketplace.

DOMAINE DE FENOUILLET* * * *

Address: 84190 Beaumes de Venise
Tel: 4-90-62-95-61
Fax: 4-90-62-90-67
Wines produced: Muscat Beaumes de Venise
Surface area: 18.2 acres

Production: 2,500 cases
Upbringing: 7–8 months in epoxy and cement vats
Average age of vines: 30 years
Blend: 100% Muscat à Petits Grains Blanc

The Soard family is one of the unheralded stars of Beaumes de Venise. Their sweet wine is one of the finest of the appellation, although not quite at the level of Paul Jaboulet-Ainé, Domaine de Durban, and Domaine de Baumalric. Their red wines also merit attention. They produce one of the finest dry red Beaumes de Venise wines, as well as a bevy of other Côtes du Rhônes. This energetically run estate has emerged in the nineties as one of the more serious players in the southern Côtes du Rhône.

PAUL JABOULET-AINÉ* * * * *

Address: Domaine de Thalabert
        Les Jalets, R.N. 7
        26600 La-Roche-de-Glun
Tel: 4-75-84-68-93
Fax: 4-75-84-56-14
Wines produced: Muscat Beaumes de Venise
Production: 3,500 cases

The Jaboulets have always produced a brilliant Muscat Beaumes de Venise. They visit the large cooperative, Vignerons des Beaumes de Venise, and make a selection of what they feel are the best cuvées. The wines are shipped in bulk to Jaboulet's cellars south of Tain l'Hermitage and bottled early to preserve their freshness and fruit. This is a consistently delicious, light peach-colored wine bursting with flavor.

CHÂTEAU ST.-SAUVEUR* * * *

Address: G.A.E.C. Les Héritiers de Marcel Rey
        84810 Aubignan
Tel: 4-90-62-90-39
Fax: 4-90-62-60-46
Wines produced: Muscat Beaumes de Venise
Surface area: 16 acres
Production: 2,250 cases
Upbringing: 6 months in stainless steel vats
Age of the vines: 6–35 years
Blend: 100% Muscat à Petits Grains Blanc

The Rey family produces a stylish, elegant, lighter Beaumes de Venise that tends to be less alcoholic than most other wines of the appellation, averaging about 15% alcohol. A very good example of the appellation, it is meant to be drunk within 1–2 years of the vintage.

VIDAL-FLEURY* * * *

Address: 69420 Ampuis
Tel: 4-74-56-10-18
Fax: 4-74-56-19-19
Wines produced: Muscat Beaumes de Venise
Production: 1,750 cases
Upbringing: 1–2 years maximum in stainless steel vats
Blend: 100% Muscat à Petits Grains Blanc

Administrator Jean-Pierre Rochias consistently turns out a fine Beaumes de Venise from purchased juice. It is aged in stainless steel vats for 1–2 years, and is always made from 100% Muscat à Petits Grains Blanc.

VIGNERONS DES BEAUMES DE VENISE * * *

Address: Quartier Ravel
       84190 Beaumes de Venise
Tel: 4-90-12-41-00
Fax: 4-90-65-02-05
Wines produced: Muscat Beaumes de Venise Cuvée Tradition, Muscat Beaumes de Venise
       Cuvée Carte d'Or, Muscat Beaumes de Venise Cuvée Bois Doré
Surface area: 815 acres
Production (Cuvée Tradition): 93,750 cases
       (Cuvée Carte d'Or): 31,250 cases
       (Cuvée Bois Doré): 1,875 cases
Upbringing (Cuvée Tradition): 3–6 months in stainless steel vats
       (Cuvée Carte d'Or): 3–6 months in stainless steel vats
       (Cuvée Bois Doré): 3–6 months in oak barrels, with 30% of the yield in
       new oak
Average age of vines (Cuvée Tradition): 25–30 years
       (Cuvée Carte d'Or): 20–30 years
       (Cuvée Bois Doré): 35–40 years
Blend: 95% Muscat à Petits Grains Blanc, 5% Muscat à Petits Grains Noir (all 3 cuvées)

There are three separate cuvées produced by this cooperative, which produces wine from 815 acres owned by 120 vignerons living in or around the village of Beaumes de Venise. The total production of 132,000 cases seems to fly out of the cellars, either in bulk to négociants, or to the ocean of tourists that reveal a fondness for this Provençal nectar. The coop's wines are well made, with the Cuvée Tradition a midweight Muscat Beaumes de Venise, the Cuvée Carte d'Or slightly riper, sweeter, and more viscous, and the Cuvée Bois Doré a more structured and delineated wine as a result of spending some time in small oak casks, of which one-third are new. Much of the credit must go to President Alain Ignace for the consistently sound quality of these wines.

OTHER MUSCAT BEAUMES DE VENISE PRODUCERS

DOMAINE BOULETIN

Address: 84190 Beaumes de Venise
Tel: 4-90-62-95-10
Wines produced: Muscat Beaumes de Venise
Surface area: 11.1 acres
Production: 1,875 cases
Upbringing: 6 months in cement vats
Average age of vines: 20 years
Blend: 90–95% Muscat à Petits Grains Blanc, 5–10% Muscat à Petits Grains Noir

DELAS FRÈRES

Address: Z.A. de l'Olivier
      B.P. 4
      07300 St.-Jean de Muzols
Tel: 4-75-08-60-30
Fax: 4-75-08-53-67
Production: 2,000 cases
Upbringing: Fermentation of 21 days in stainless steel vats; there is a fining and filtration, and only one bottling.
Blend: 100% Muscat à Petits Grains Blanc

DOMAINE DES RICHARDS

Address: Route d'Avignon
      84150 Violès
Tel: 4-90-70-93-73
Fax: 4-90-70-90-74
Wines produced: Muscat Beaumes de Venise
Surface area: 24.8 acres
Production: 3,438 cases
Upbringing: 6–8 months in stainless steel vats
Average age of vines: 15–20 years
Blend: 100% Muscat à Petits Grains Blanc

CAIRANNE

Top Producers

Domaine de l'Ameillaud (Nick Thompson)****
Domaine Laurent Brusset****
Domaine de l'Oratoire St.-Martin (Frédéric Alary)****/*****
Domaine Rabasse-Charavin (Corinne Couturier)***/****
Marcel Richaud****

The scenic village of Cairanne is spread across a rock outcropping, as are many villages in this area of France. Once a fortified village, Cairanne offers an attractive photographic opportunity, particularly as it is approached from the south. Sitting amidst an ocean of vines, Cairanne is one of the oldest villages of Vaucluse, as well as a noteworthy candidate to be the next village elevated to its own appellation. South of Cairanne are the well-known *garrigues* that are so much a part of Provence. These stony outbreaks support not only vines but lavender, thyme, rosemary, and juniper as well. North and east of the village are the lower slopes where the balance of the Cairanne vineyards are planted. Both of these areas are brutally abused by the mistral winds, as evidenced in the very low pruning of the vines.

Cairanne wines are forceful, big, rich Côtes du Rhônes that are mouth-filling and peppery. The finest estates have elevated winemaking to a point where their wines are no longer just rustic and merely substantial, but are rounded, rich, elegant, fleshy, and purely made. The Cave des Coteaux de Cairanne is one of the finest cooperatives in the southern Rhône. Founded in 1929, it produces over 75% of the village's wines. It is refreshing to see a coop turning out a bevy of good-quality, reasonably priced wines.

DOMAINE DE L'AMEILLAUD* * * *

Address: 84290 Cairanne
Tel: 4-90-30-82-92
Fax: 4-90-30-74-66
Wines produced: Côtes du Rhône-Villages (white), Vin de Pays (red), Côtes du Rhône (red),
       Côtes du Rhône-Villages-Cairanne (red)
Surface area (white): Côtes du Rhône-Villages—7.5 acres
       (red): Vin de Pays—42 acres
              Côtes du Rhône—42 acres
              Côtes du Rhône-Villages-Cairanne—29.6 acres
Production (white): Côtes du Rhône-Villages—100 cases
       (red): Vin de Pays—8,700 cases
              Côtes du Rhône—8,750 cases
              Côtes du Rhône-Villages-Cairanne—5,000 cases
Upbringing (white): Côtes du Rhône-Villages—fermentation in temperature-controlled
       stainless steel vats; bottling after 4 months, before malolactic
       (red:) Vin de Pays—a traditional fermentation of 7–12 days in cement vats;
       storage in cement and stainless steel tanks for 6–8 months; there is a
       fining and filtration
       Côtes du Rhône—a traditional fermentation of 10–15 days in cement
       vats; storage in cement and stainless steel tanks for 6–8 months; there is
       a fining and filtration
       Côtes du Rhône-Villages-Cairanne—fermentation of 3 weeks in stainless
       steel and cement tanks; 5–10% of the yield is transferred into new oak
       for 4 months; assemblage and bottling after 12 months
Average age of vines (white): Côtes du Rhône-Villages—7–8 years
       (red): Vin de Pays—20–25 years
              Côtes du Rhône—25–30 years
              Côtes du Rhône-Villages-Cairanne—40 years
Blend (white): Côtes du Rhône-Villages—40–45% Bourboulenc and the rest divided
       equally between Grenache Blanc and Marsanne
       (red): Vin de Pays—60–65% Grenache, 15% Syrah, 10–15% Carignan, and the
       rest Cinsault
       Côtes du Rhône—60–65% Grenache, 15–20% Syrah, 15% Carignan, and the
       rest Mourvèdre
       Côtes du Rhône-Villages-Cairanne—60% Grenache, 20–25% Syrah, 10%
       Carignan, and the rest Mourvèdre

Proprietor Nick Thompson fashions an excellent Côtes du Rhône-Villages-Cairanne and Côtes du Rhône, but he is probably best known for his budget-priced vin de pays made from Grenache, Syrah, Carignan, and Cinsault. The latter wine, which I have often seen priced under $8 a bottle, is a delicious, round, generous, Provençal red for drinking within 2–3 years of the vintage. The Côtes du Rhône-Villages-Cairanne is a highly extracted, rich, mouth filling wine meant to stand up to a decade of aging. The 1995 is terrific, and the 1994 very good. Moreover, the 1995 has the potential to age well for 6–7 years.

An experimental dry white wine, made from Bourboulenc, Grenache Blanc, and Marsanne, is made from young vines and limited in availability, but early efforts have exhibited promise.

DOMAINE LAURENT BRUSSET* * * *

Address: 84290 Cairanne
Tel: 4-90-70-91-60
Fax: 4-90-30-73-31
Wines produced: Cairanne Les Hauts de Montmirail, Côtes du Rhône
Surface area: 74 acres
Production: 10,600 cases
Average age of vines: 27 years
Blend: 55% Grenache, 20–25% Syrah, 5–10% Mourvèdre, 5–10% Cinsault and Carignan

Daniel Brusset is best known for his lavishly wooded Gigondas, but his home and cellars are in the village of Cairanne. Additional information about Daniel Brusset and his son, Laurent, can be found in the chapter on Gigondas. The bulk of Domaine Brusset's production is in Côtes du Rhône and Côtes du Rhône-Villages-Cairanne. These are rich, well-made wines with plenty of flavor. The Cuvée des Templiers, which is available only in top vintages, contains nearly 25% Mourvèdre in addition to 60% Syrah and 15% Grenache. It is meant to age well for a decade. There is also the Côteaux de Travers, all from a mistral-beaten, terraced vineyard planted on the *garrigues*. It is a peppery, spicy, rich wine. All of Brusset's wines have consistently been among the best of Cairanne as well as the Côtes du Rhône.

Brusset is proud of the improvement in quality demonstrated by his white wine cuvée. The first vintage to show real improvement was the 1992, which included more Viognier in the blend. Today this wine reveals greater aromatics, plumpness, and fat as a result of the increasing percentage of Viognier in the blend.

DOMAINE DE L'ORATOIRE ST.-MARTIN* * * */* * * * *

Address: Route de St.-Romain
        84290 Cairanne
Tel: 4-90-30-82-07
Fax: 4-90-30-74-27
Wines produced: Cairanne (white), Côtes du Rhône (white), Côtes du Rhône (red), Réserve
        des Seigneurs (red), Cuvée Prestige (red), Cuvée Haut Coustias (red)
Surface area (white): Cairanne—6.2 acres
        Côtes du Rhône—6.2 acres
    (red): Côtes du Rhône—25 acres
        Réserve des Seigneurs—17.3 acres
        Cuvée Prestige—7.4 acres
        Cuvée Haut Coustias—5 acres
Production (white): Cairanne—540 cases
        Côtes du Rhône—540 cases
    (red): Côtes du Rhône—2,500 cases
        Réserve des Seigneurs—2,000 cases
        Cuvée Prestige—1,000 cases
        Cuvée Haut Coustias—500 cases
Upbringing (white): Cairanne—10 months in oak casks
        Côtes du Rhône—4–5 months in tanks
    (red): Côtes du Rhône—traditional fermentation of 6–8 days; then 6 months'
        storage in vats; no fining or filtering
        Réserve des Seigneurs—a 12-day traditional fermentation for the Gre-
        nache with *pigéage* for the other varietals, followed by 12 months' storage
        in tanks; fining but no filtering

Cuvée Prestige—fermentation of 12 days with *pigéage*, followed by 12 months' storage in tanks; fining but no filtration

Cuvée Haut Coustias—fermentation for 12 days, followed by 18 months in 1-year-old oak barrels; no filtration

Average age of vines (white): Cairanne—50 years
 Côtes du Rhône—10 and 30 years
 (red): Côtes du Rhône—30 years
 Réserve des Seigneurs—50 years
 Cuvée Prestige—90 years
 Cuvée Haut Coustias—60 years

Blend: (white): Cairanne—45% Marsanne, 45% Roussanne, 5% Viognier, 5% Muscat
 Côtes du Rhône—50% Roussanne, 45% Clairette, 5% Viognier
 (red) Côtes du Rhône—80% Grenache, 20% Syrah
 Réserve des Seigneurs—60% Grenache, 30% Mourvèdre, 10% Syrah
 Cuvée Prestige—60% Grenache, 40% Mourvèdre
 Cuvée Haut Coustias—50% Mourvèdre, 50% Syrah

Domaine de l'Oratoire St.-Martin is one of the southern Rhône Valley's most conspicuous overachievers, making wines that are far above their humble appellations. The rise in quality began under Bernard Alary, but his son Frédéric has pushed the quality further. To date there are two cuvées of white wine. The Côtes du Rhône is heavily dependent on Roussanne, and the Cairanne is primarily a blend of Roussanne and Marsanne, with small quantities of Viognier and Muscat. Both are gorgeously fresh, lively dry whites, textbook examples of just how good a dry white Côtes du Rhône can be. If the Côtes du Rhône could produce more dry whites such as this, consumers throughout the world would be thrilled.

The red wines have always been Domaine de l'Oratoire St.-Martin's strong suit. These include the Grenache-Mourvèdre-Syrah–based Réserve des Seigneurs, the Grenache-Mourvèdre Cuvée Prestige, and limited quantities of a Mourvèdre and Syrah blend called Cuvée Haut Coustias, from 60-year-old vines. All of these wines go into the bottle with no filtration and only a light fining. These have been consistently strong efforts since the mid-eighties, with delicious wines in 1985, followed by excellent results in 1989, 1990, 1994, and 1995. This is the type of estate that brings smiles to consumers who happen upon their wines. They are reasonably priced and qualitatively equivalent to wines selling at two or three times the price.

DOMAINE RABASSE-CHARAVIN* * */* * * *

Address: Les Coteaux St.-Martin
 84290 Cairanne
Tel: 4-90-30-70-05
Fax: 4-90-34-74-42
Wines produced: Vin de table, Côtes du Rhône (red and white), Côtes du Rhône-Villages-Cairanne (red and white), Côtes du Rhône-Villages-Cairanne Cuvée Laure-Olivier, Côtes du Rhône-Villages-Cairanne Cuvée d'Estevenas
Surface area: 168 acres
Production: 10,000–15,000 + cases
Upbringing: traditionally made, spending 12–18 months in old wood foudres and bottled without any filtration
Age of the vines: 15–100 years
Blend (red wines): 70% Grenache, 10% Syrah, 10% Cinsault, 10% Mourvèdre
 (white wines): 65% Bourboulenc, 35% Clairette

Another fine estate in the southern Côtes du Rhône, I have had many a good bottle of wine from Rabasse-Charavin, both from father Abel and since 1985, from daughter Corinne Couturier, who apprenticed with her father until 1985, at which time she took over the making of the wines. Like many large Côtes du Rhône estates, they produce a bevy of wines, including a vin de table, red and white Côtes du Rhône, several cuvées of Cairanne, including an excellent, rich, stylish, peppery, black-cherry-flavored Côtes du Rhône-Villages-Cairanne, the sumptuous, thick, juicy, opulent Côtes du Rhône-Villages-Cairanne Cuvée Laure-Olivier, and a Côtes du Rhône-Villages-Cairanne Cuvée d'Estevenas. A tiny quantity (about 250 cases) of Côtes du Rhône-Villages-Cairanne white is also made from a 50-50 blend of Bourboulenc and Clairette.

All of these wines come from multiple vineyard parcels spread out over Cairanne, Côtes du Rhône, and nearby Rasteau (about 69 acres). The wines are traditionally made, aged 12–18 months in old wood foudres, and, since Corinne took over, bottled without any filtration. It is tempting to argue whether it is the Cairanne or Rasteau cuvées that are better, but frankly, virtually everything that emerges from Rabasse-Charavin, particularly in top years such as 1989, 1990, 1994, and 1995, possesses plenty of fruit, character, and quality. Most of the wines are best drunk within 2–4 years of the vintage, but the Cuvée Laure-Olivier and Cuvée d'Estevenas can age for up to a decade.

MARCEL RICHAUD* * * *

Address: 84290 Cairanne
Tel: 4-90-30-85-25
Fax: 4-90-30-71-12
Wines produced: Côtes du Rhône (red), Côtes du Rhône-Villages-Cairanne (red and white), Vin de Table Vaucluse, Vin de Pays Vaucluse, Côtes du Rhône-Villages-Cuvée L'Ebrescade
Surface area: 37 acres owned, 62 acres rented
Production: 6,000–8,000 cases
Upbringing: various wood barrels and foudres
Age of the vines: 15–97 years
Blend (red): primarily Grenache (65–75%), with the balance of Syrah, Mourvèdre, and Cinsault
(white): Roussanne, Marsanne, Grenache Blanc, Clairette, and Viognier (percentage change with each vintage)

Marcel Richaud, a handsome, graying vigneron in his early forties, represents the new generation that is breaking away from the coop and accomplishing small miracles in the southern Rhône. Richaud could easily have been another anonymous member of one of the local coops, comingling all the production from his old-vine vineyards in some huge fermentation tank with other producers' wine. Instead, he has been estate-bottling for over 20 years. He makes a bevy of wines from 37 acres of Côtes du Rhône-Villages-Cairanne, in addition to another 62 acres that are rented out under the French agreement called *métayage*. From these vineyards emerges a solid, robust Vin de Table, an interesting Vin de Pays de Vaucluse, a red Côtes du Rhône, a red Côtes du Rhône-Villages-Cairanne, and a special old-vine cuvée of Grenache called Côtes du Rhône-Villages-Cairanne-Cuvée L'Ebrescade.

There are also increasing quantities of a tasty white wine. Like so many of the forward-thinking southern Rhône vignerons, Richaud has immensely improved his white wine by the addition of Roussanne and Viognier to the standard blend of Grenache Blanc, Clairette, and Marsanne. It is one of the better dry whites being made in the south. Richaud understands the value of the gorgeous fruit obtained from old-vine terroirs in the southern Rhône. None of his wines ever see a barrel, or even a foudre. They are aged in tank, and assembled and bottled with minimum processing. The results in top vintages such as 1989, 1990, 1994, and 1995 are bursting with fruit, and are undeniably seductive and delicious. Readers need to remember Marcel Richaud; he is one of a bevy of progressive, high-quality vignerons in the Rhône, and particularly in Cairanne, who are going to push the authorities in France to give Cairanne its own appellation in the near future.

CHUSCLAN

Top Producer

Cave Coopérative de Chusclan**

On the right, or western, bank of the Rhône, the village of Chusclan is situated a mere six miles west of Orange. This is a relatively forgotten part of the Rhône Valley, but in 1953 when the French authorities gave four villages the authority to annex their names to the Côtes du Rhône appellation, Chusclan was one of that quartet. The area has a rich history, having had vineyards cultivated by the Romans and subsequently Benedictine monks. Rosé was long the village's claim to fame, but though it once accounted for over half of the production, it now represents about 12% of the total production, with red wine dominating, followed by a tiny quantity of white.

In many other Côtes du Rhône villages, small vignerons have broken away from the local cooperative, but that has not yet happened in Chusclan. The Cave Coopérative de Chusclan essentially controls everything in the village. Its 140 + growers cultivate nearly 2,000 acres of vineyards, from which emerges virtually all of the Chusclan wine. The rustic wines produced are of standard quality. The cooperative's most renowned bottling is their Cuvée de Marcoule, a decent rosé named, inexplicably, after the nearby nuclear power plant!

LAUDUN

Top Producer

Domaine Pelaquié***

Laudun, a quaint Provençal village six miles southwest of Chusclan, also sits on the western bank of the Rhône in the department of Gard. Like its northern neighbor, this was one of the four villages (the other two being Cairanne and Gigondas) that were promoted to Côtes du Rhone-Villages in 1953. Laudun remains one of the least-promising villages in which to find high-quality wine. History dominates much of the chatter when it comes to Laudun, since Julius Caesar had a military encampment in this area, as evidenced by artifacts found in the vineyards. Without the charm of other Provençal villages, Laudun seems content to continue to permit the Cave des Quartier Chemins, the local cooperative, to dominate the wine production. With 282 members, it controls over 95% of this village's production. The wines from the Cave des Quartier Chemins are serviceable but unexciting. The only estate that seems to make wine worthy of attention has been Domaine Pelaquié.

DOMAINE PELAQUIÉ

Address: 7, rue de Vernet
        30290 St.-Victor-la-Coste
Tel: 4-66-50-06-04
Fax: 4-66-50-33-32

Surface area: 160 acres
Wines produced: Côtes du Rhône-Village
Production: 4,000–5,000 cases
Blend (red): 60% Grenache, 40% Syrah, Mourvèdre, Cinsault, and Counoise
    (white): Clairette, Grenache Blanc, Bourboulenc, Marsanne, Roussanne, Viognier

Over the last 10–15 years, Luc Pelaquié has lightened the style of wine produced by his father. This estate produces a correct, pleasant, rustic, peppery red wine that can be powerful in top years, but is generally a spicy, attractive red for drinking during its first 5–6 years of life. Recent vintages of the white wine have been seductively aromatic, elegant, and attractive, no doubt because of the introduction of Viognier and Roussanne into the blend.

RASTEAU

Top Producers

Domaine de Beaumistral (Jean-Marc Brun)***
Domaine des Coteaux de Travers (Robert Charavin)***
Domaine des Papillons (Didier Charavin)***
Domaine Rabasse Charavin (Corinne Couturier)****
Domaine de la Soumade (André Romero)*****
Domaine du Trapadis****
Château du Trignon (Pascal Roux)***
Domaine de Verquière (Bernard Chamfort)***

Rasteau is another tiny village perched against the hills of Provence just north of Séguret and south of Vaison-la-Romaine. This is a prime tourist area in the heart of the southern Rhône and northern Provence.

Rasteau is actually two separate appellations. One is the Côtes du Rhône-Villages-Rasteau, an appellation dedicated primarily to red wine with some rosé and a tiny quantity of white wine. The red wines are made from standard southern Rhône varietals—Grenache, Syrah, Cinsault, and Mourvèdre. The other appellation in this oblong-shaped village is the Rasteau-Village Vin Doux Naturel, named for the white and red sweet wines, produced exclusively from the Grenache grape. The white wines represent 70% of the entire production. Created in 1944, this appellation covers about 247 acres, with an annual production of approximately 25,000 cases of this sweet, fortified, Grenache-based, alcoholic wine. The reds tend to resemble a rustic, tawny/ruby port, and the whites, a white port. These are clearly wines that require some cuddling up with to get used to the fiery alcohol, unctuous texture, and slightly oxidized, herbal, chocolaty, roasted aromatics.

André Romero of the Domaine de la Soumade, the only five-star producer in this village, makes the finest example of Rasteau; his greatest wines are his dry reds.

DOMAINE DE LA SOUMADE* * * * *

Address: Route d'Orange
       84110 Rasteau
Tel: 4-90-46-11-26
Fax: 4-90-46-11-69
Wines produced: Côtes du Rhône-Villages-Rasteau Cuvée Normale, Côtes du Rhône-Villages-Rasteau Cuvée Prestige, Côtes du Rhône-Villages-Rasteau Cuvée Confiance, Rasteau Vin Doux Naturel Doré, Rasteau Vin Doux Naturel Rouge

Surface area (Cuvée Normale): 14.8 acres
   (Cuvée Prestige): 25 acres
   (Cuvée Confiance): 5 acres
   (V.D.N. Doré): 12.5 acres
   (V.D.N. Rouge): 10 acres
Production (Cuvée Normale): 2,750 cases
   (Cuvée Prestige): 4,375 cases
   (Cuvée Confiance): 750 cases
   (V.D.N. Doré): 1,500 cases
   (V.D.N. Rouge): 1,375 cases
Upbringing (Cuvée Normale): 12 months in old oak casks
   (Cuvée Prestige): 12 months in old oak casks
   (Cuvée Confiance): 12 months in old oak casks
   (V.D.N. Doré): 1–2 years in 1,000-liter oak casks
   (V.D.N. Rouge): 1–2 years in 1,000-liter oak casks
Average age of vines (Cuvée Normale): 5–20 years
   (Cuvée Prestige): 40 years
   (Cuvée Confiance): 95 years
   (V.D.N. Doré): 40 years
   (V.D.N. Rouge): 40 years
Blend (Cuvée Normale): 60% Grenache, 20% Syrah, 10% Cinsault, 10% other varietals
   (Cuvée Prestige): 60% Grenache, 20% Syrah, 10% Cinsault, 10% other varietals
   (Cuvée Confiance): 80% Grenache, 20% Syrah
   (V.D.N. Doré): 100% Grenache
   (V.D.N. Rouge): 90% Grenache, 10% Syrah

The superstar of Rasteau is André Romero of the Domaine de la Soumade. Romero produces five cuvées of drop-dead, delicious red wine. There are three cuvées of dry red wine, and two of the renowned late-harvest vin doux naturel. The dry red cuvées are blockbuster wines, particularly in top vintages such as 1995 and, to a lesser extent, 1994. The fact that Romero makes a reasonable quantity of wine from his 67.3 acres of vineyards is good news for consumers looking for unheralded, rich, concentrated, complex wines from southern France. His vinification is traditional, but since he hired the northern Rhône oenologist-maven Jean-Luc Colombo, he has been destemming more of his grapes, resulting in even blacker-colored wine with more sweet fruit. Romero has plenty of old vines, as well as a sure touch when it comes to making great wine. Like Henri Bonneau, Jacques Reynaud, and dozens of other enormously talented southern Rhône Valley vignerons, Romero is self-taught, and the better for it.

VINTAGES

1995—Cuvée Confiance The 1995 Cuvée Confiance exhibits an opaque purple color, a
 · chewy texture, aromas of cassis and kirsch, superb definition, and gobs of fruit and
 89 body in the long finish. Anticipated maturity: now–2006. Last tasted 6/96.
1995—Cuvée Fleur de Confiance The 1995 Cuvée Fleur de Confiance is an enormous,
 · Henri Bonneau–like wine of massive concentration and power. It should evolve
 90 well for 10–15 years! Last tasted 6/96.
1994—Cuvée Confiance The dark purple-colored 1994 Cuvée Confiance possesses great
 · fruit, copious quantities of Provençal herb and black-cherry fruit aromas, full body,
 90 a sweet, round, juicy as well as succulent texture, and a lush, soft finish. It should

be drunk over the next 5–8 years, while waiting for the 1995s to reach full maturity. Last tasted 6/96.

1994—Cuvée Prestige   Almost identical to the 1994 Cuvée Confiance, this opaque purple-
·   Colored wine is packed and stacked with fruit, glycerin, and extract. Expansive
90   and full-bodied, this is an explosively rich Côtes du Rhône. Drink it over the next
            decade. Last tasted 6/96.

Several other producers to keep an eye on in Rasteau include Jean-Marc Brun's **Domaine de Beaumistral.** His dry red Rasteau is produced from 40% Grenache, 30% Syrah, 20% Mourvèdre, 5% Carignan, and 5% Cinsault, and aged for eight months in old oak barrels. The wine appears to have taken on more character over recent vintages. This is another noteworthy estate to follow more closely.

The **Domaine des Coteaux de Travers** of proprietor Robert Charavin is another high-quality Rasteau estate. Charavin owns 19.8 acres, from which he produces 3,200 cases of sturdy, husky—or as the French say, *solide*—red wine. There is a regular cuvée of rustic Rasteau aged 6–12 months in cement vats, and bottled with minimal clarification. There is also a small quantity of red Cuvée Prestige that spends time in demi-muids and small oak casks, of which 10% are new. Charavin is the only Rasteau producer to make a dry white Rasteau-Village. It is an interesting and promising blend of equal parts Marsanne, Roussanne, Viognier, and Grenache Blanc. It is a wine that could prove to be one of the better dry whites in the southern Rhône. Unfortunately, Charavin has only 2.47 acres planted with these grapes and the production to date has been under 400 cases.

Another Charavin, Didier, runs the promising estate of **Domaine des Papillons.** He produces high-quality dry red wine, including a Village Rasteau aged in cement vats, and a Cuvée Prestige made from vines 40–80 years old. Both wines are made from a blend of 70% Grenache, 25% Syrah, and 5% Carignan. The Cuvée Prestige is aged for eight months in demi-muids and bottled with only a light clarification. Domaine des Papillons also makes a very good Vin Doux Naturel Doré, which is not far off the quality achieved by André Romero at Domaine de la Soumade.

Readers looking for wines of unbridled power and fury should check out the superconcentrated, slightly rustic, but immensely impressive offerings of Helen Durand's **Domaine du Trapadis.** Durand made super 1994s and 1995s, but, sadly, the production from this estate's six acres is minuscule. There are three cuvées produced, including a Rasteau, from 60% Grenache, 25% Carignan, and 15% Syrah, and a remarkable Cuvée Prestige from 70-year-old vines (40% Mourvèdre, 40% Grenache, and 20% Syrah). The third cuvée is the Vin Doux Naturel Doré. All three wines are aged in cement vats and are bottled with no fining or filtration. With a few refinements to these massive wines, Domaine du Trapadis could be a five-star producer.

Other noteworthy Rasteau estates include **Domaine Rabasse-Charavin,** run by proprietor Corinne Couturier in Cairanne. This estate, which is one of the leading domaines in the southern Rhône, has 19.8 acres of Côtes du Rhône-Villages-Rasteau, from which they produce 2,500 cases of a rustic, flavorful, mouth-filling, fleshy red wine from a blend of 60% Grenache and 40% Mourvèdre. One of the more structured wines of the appellation, it gives every sign of aging for up to a decade or more in years such as 1995.

Other producers who make good dry red wines in Rasteau are **Château du Trignon** (Pascal Roux) and **Domaine de Verquière** (Bernard Chamfort).

Important Rasteau Addresses

Domaine de Beaumistral
Contact: Jean-Marc Brun
Address: Place du Village
    84110 Rasteau
Tel: 4-90-46-16-90

Domaine Bressy-Masson
Contact: Marie France et Thierry Masson
Address: 84110 Rasteau
Tel: 4-90-46-10-45

Domaine Chamfort
Contact: Denis Chamfort
Address: La Pause
    84110 Sablet
Tel: 4-90-46-95-95
Fax: 4-90-46-99-86

Domaine des Coteaux de Travers
Contact: Robert Charavin
Address: 84110 Rasteau
Tel: 4-90-46-10-48
Fax: 4-90-46-15-81

Domaine des Girasols
Contact: Catherine Joyet
Address: La Brune
    84110 Rasteau
Tel: 4-90-46-11-70
Fax: 4-90-46-16-82

Domaine du Grand Nicolet
Contact: Maurice Leyraud
Address: 84110 Rasteau
Tel: 4-90-46-11-37

Domaine des Nymphes du Grand Jas
Contact: Jean-Louis Meyer
Address: 84110 Rasteau
Tel: 4-90-46-14-13

Domaine des Papillons
Contact: Didier Charavin
Address: Route de Vaison-la-Romaine
    84110 Rasteau
Tel: 4-90-46-15-63
Fax: 4-90-46-16-22

Domaine Rabasse-Charavin
Contact: Corinne Couturier
Address: Les Coteaux St.-Martin
    84290 Cairanne
Tel: 4-90-30-70-05
Fax: 4-90-34-74-42

Château du Trignon
Contact: Pascal Roux
Address: 84190 Gigondas
Tel: 4-90-46-90-27
Fax: 4-90-46-98-63

Domaine de Verquière
Contact: Bernard Chamfort
Address: 84110 Sablet
Tel: 4-90-46-90-11
Fax: 4-90-46-99-69

Vignerons de Rasteau
Contact: Jean-Jacques Dost
Address: 84110 Rasteau
Tel: 4-90-10-90-10
Fax: 4-90-46-16-65

Domaine Wilfried
Contact: Jean-Luc Pouzoulas et Emile Charavin
Address: Quartier Blovac
    84110 Rasteau
Tel: 4-90-46-10-66

ROAIX

Just north of the splendidly picturesque hill town of Séguret is Roaix, a medieval village with immense photogenic interest. The **Cave Coopérative de Roaix-Séguret** produces the wine made here. It is not one of the better-run cooperatives, and the wines reflect a lack of direction, little attention to detail, and not much commitment to quality. Fortunately, most of Roaix is sold in bulk for blending with who knows what, a justifiable destination for the uninspiring wine produced. Readers should visit Roaix for its scenic charm, not its wine.

ROCHEGUDE

Perhaps the only reason to make the eight-mile drive north of Orange is to stay at the luxurious hotel located here, the Château de Rochegude, a seventeenth-century edifice that dominates this tiny village. However, this is also an official Côtes du Rhône-Villages. It is alleged that Thomas Jefferson enjoyed the village wines, but I wonder why. The **Cave Coopérative Vinicole de Rochegude** is the only producer of red wine; it turns out sound, chunky, foursquare wines that offer decent value for uncritical quaffing. They also produce run-of-the-mill, generic rosé and dull white Côtes du Rhône.

SABLET

Top Producers

Domaine de Boissan***
Domaine les Goubert***
Domaine de Piauger****

Château du Trignon**
Domaine de Verquière***

The fortified village of Sablet's prominent bell tower dominates the view as one heads north on Route D 7 from nearby Gigondas. It is in the heart of some of the most beautiful countryside of Provence, with the Ventoux Mountains only a 30-minute drive to the east, the Dentelles de Montmirail overlooking the village, and the huge vineyard plateau extending west from Sablet in the direction of Violès to the suburbs of Orange. There are just over 1,000 acres under vine in Sablet, and 95% of the production is red wine. The balance consists of tiny quantities of white and rosé. Sandwiched between Gigondas (two or three miles south) and Séguret (about two miles north), this village, with its narrowing, winding, medieval alleys, tiny shops, fountains, and shade trees interspersed with multiple tasting caves *(les caveaux des gustations)*, could easily serve as a backdrop for a Hollywood film set in southern France. The village can also lay claim to inventing the machine for grafting American rootstock to French vines.

Like so many of these Côtes du Rhône-Villages, much of the production has been dominated by the local cave coopérative, called **Le Gravillas**. Founded in 1935, this is one of the more modern cooperatives, producing a multitude of cuvées, many quite well made. The quality of Sablet's wines has long been known, and it received a promotion to Côtes du Rhône-Villages-Sablet in 1974. Many insiders believe it is a strong candidate to receive its own appellation during the next decade. There is no doubting that the overall quality of winemaking in Sablet is very good.

There are five leading producers of Côtes du Rhône-Villages-Sablet. Christian Bonfils, of the 99-acre **Domaine de Boissan,** has succeeded his father, Hubert. He produces a Grenache-based wine that is richly colored, fruity, medium- to full-bodied, with all the pepper and *garrigue* smells one expects of a southern Côtes du Rhône. It is one of the more powerful wines of the village.

Jean-Pierre Cartier lives in nearby Gigondas. He produces a tasty white Sablet, as well as a lush, opulent red made from a blend of 65% Grenache and 35% Syrah.

Perhaps the longest-lived and most concentrated wine of Sablet is the wine from **Domaine de Verquière.** For decades run by father Louis Chamfort, this estate is now managed by his son, Bernard. The father often kept the wines five or six years in foudre before bottling, but Bernard has shortened that period, recognizing that in less than perfect years the fruit cannot stand up to such a long sojourn in old wood. Today the wine is usually bottled within two to three years of the vintage. It is one of the more rustic, peppery, spicy, muscular wines of the village.

Other good Sablet wines are made by the **Château du Trignon's** Pascal Roux.

DOMAINE DE PIAUGER* * * *

Address: La-Daysse-des-Dulcy
           84110 Sablet
Tel: 4-90-46-90-54
Fax: 4-90-46-99-48
Wines produced: Côtes du Rhône-Villages-Sablet Les Briguières (red), Côtes du Rhône-
                Villages-Sablet Montmartel (red), Côtes du Rhône-Villages-Sablet (white)
Surface area (Les Briguières): 9.8 acres
            (Montmartel): 6.2 acres
            (white): 2.47 acres
Production (Les Briguières): 1,875 cases
            (Montmartel): 1,000 cases
Upbringing (Les Briguières): fermentation of 1 month in cement tanks, followed by bottling
                            after 18 months. There is no destemming; one fining after
                            malolactics, but no filtration.
                            (Montmartel): same as for Les Briguières
Average age of vines (Les Briguières): 45 years
                    (Montmartel): 40 years
Blend (Les Briguières): 80% Grenache, 20% Mourvèdre
       (Montmartel): 80% Grenache, 20% Mourvèdre
       (white): 50% Grenache Blanc, 25% Clairette, 25% Viognier

Perhaps the emerging star of Sablet is Domaine de Piaugier, an estate that also makes fine Gigondas under the inspired youthful enthusiasm of Jean-Marc Autran. This estate garners considerable praise from the French press, all of which is justified. The wines are well made, pure, ripe, and capable of lasting for 5–7 years. Jean-Marc has increased the percentage of Mourvèdre in the blend to give this Grenache-based wine more structure and aging potential. These two well-made wines possess rich fruit, plenty of peppery, black-cherry character, more lushness and purity than most, and supple textures. They have been especially strong over recent vintages.

A tiny quantity of white Côtes du Rhône-Villages-Sablet is also produced from 50% Grenache Blanc, 25% Viognier, and 25% Clairette.

While I have not tasted it, Autran introduced a third cuvée of Côtes du Rhône-Villages-Sablet in 1994 and 1995. It is called Tenebi.

Readers should not forget that Jean-Marc Autran also produces a very fine Gigondas (see that chapter). Even better values are his Côtes du Rhône-Villages wines, Les Briguières and Montmartel.

ST.-GERVAIS

Top Producer

Domaine Ste.-Anne (G. Steinmaier)****

Above the town of St.-Gervais is one of the best estates in the entire Rhône Valley. The **Domaine Ste.-Anne**, the 64-acre estate of Guy Steinmaier, is superbly located on a hilltop with a vast view of the southern Rhône River basin. The thin, balding Steinmaier is an innovative as well as serious winemaker; his description of his wine as "an intermediary wine between Gigondas and Châteauneuf du Pape" hardly does it justice. He has impeccably high winemaking standards. Should you find a bottle of Ste.-Anne's Viognier, it is stunning—not only the most successful Viognier made in the southern Rhône, but similar to a very fine Condrieu. However, Ste.-Anne's bevy of red wine selections, while typical of the richly fruity, clean, modern style of winemaking, also possesses plenty of personality. Steinmaier has increased the importance of Mourvèdre and Syrah in his red wines. The regular cuvée of Domaine Ste.-Anne Côtes du Rhône is made from approximately 50% Mourvèdre, 25% Syrah, and 25% Grenache. The wine could easily be called a mini-Beaucastel and/or Bandol because of its leathery, earthy, animal-scented nose and ripe berry fruit. The Cuvée Notre Dame de Cellettes is made from about 60% Grenache, with the balance Syrah and Mourvèdre. It is a typical Côtes du Rhône, with telltale aromas of pepper, kirsch, roasted herbs, and berry fruit. The hallmarks of both Steinmaier's white and red Côtes du Rhône are their natural textures, unfiltered styles, and emphasis on pure, ripe fruit.

Unfortunately, St.-Gervais has no other producers at the level of Domaine Ste.-Anne. The **Cave Coopérative de St.-Gervais** dominates the production from the other growers, turning out uninspiring, dull, monochromatic wines.

ST.-MAURICE-SUR-EYGUES

The French authorities made another questionable selection for a Côtes du Rhône-Villages with the nomination of St.-Maurice-sur-Eygues. The local cooperative, **La Cave des Coteaux de St.-Maurice-sur-Eygues,** is essentially the only wine producer in the village, although the French press has been promoting the wines from the **Domaine de Deurre,** a property that has begun to display some potential under the proprietorship of Jean-Claude Valayer and his son Hubert, an oenologist. I was unmoved by the 1995s and 1994s I tasted from this estate. The coop wines are undistinguished. Even more lamentable, this is perhaps the most uninteresting and dull village of the southern Rhône Valley.

ST.-PANTALÉON-LES-VIGNES AND ROUSSET-LES-VIGNES

These two Côtes du Rhône-Villages are well worth visiting because of the gorgeous drive through the countryside and their touristic appeal, but, sadly, not because of the wines. The **Union des Producteurs de St.-Pantaléon-les-Vignes et Rousset-les-Vignes** controls the entire wine production. The rosé is bland, the white sterile and neutral, and the red charmless, hollow, and insipid. However, the drive to remote St.-Pantaléon-les-Vignes village is a great way of taking in some savage mountain scenery while traversing some of the least traveled roads in what is otherwise an overly visited part of the southern Rhône/ Provence. Go for the scenery, not the wine. Once there, be sure to take Route D 538 through Rousset-les-Vignes, another postcard/picture-perfect drive.

SÉGURET

Top Producers

Domaine de la Cabasse***   Paul Jaboulet-Ainé***

The windswept village of Séguret appears to be carved from the cliff on which it sits. If there is one view of the Rhône Valley not to be missed, it is from either the restaurant or bedrooms of Séguret's fine hotel and restaurant, La Table du Comtat. The vista westward, particularly at sunset, is magnificent. With a bottle of the Séguret produced by the Domaine de la Cabasse at your side, the view and experience are sublime. Run by the dynamic Nadine Latour, **Domaine de la Cabasse** produces textbook red, white, and rosé Côtes du

Rhône-Villages wines. They are meant to be drunk young, but are full of flavor, round, and, if not complex, always immensely satisfying.

Although the label does not indicate Séguret as the source, the **Paul Jaboulet-Aîné** Côtes du Rhône-Villages is made entirely from wine produced from vineyards in the Séguret area. It is a very reasonably priced, plump wine that requires drinking within its first 5–6 years of life.

VALRÉAS

Top Producers

Domaine des Grands Devers (René Sinard)***
Domaine Mireille et Vincent***
Le Val des Rois (Romain Bouchard)***

Valréas, a hilltop village situated in rather forbidding countryside, is technically in the department of Vaucluse, but given its northerly location, the microclimate is much cooler and essentially it should be considered as part of the Drôme. The village has plenty of appeal to tourists, with its impressive Hôtel de Ville, its eleventh- and twelfth-century Provençal church, the Eglise Notre Dame de Nazareth, and the attractive ancient homes sprinkled throughout the village. Visitors lucky enough to arrive on market day will find this one of the more lively market towns of the region. But be warned, the drive to Valréas from Orange over the narrow, circuitous road seems much farther than 20 miles.

As in so many Côtes du Rhône-Villages, the local coop, the **Cave Coopérative la Gaillarde,** controls most of the production. It turns out a correct, but essentially one-dimensional, wine. The top producers include the Bouchard family's **Le Val des Rois,** René Sinard's **Domaine des Grands Devers,** and the wines from the Bizard family, whose cellars for the **Domaine Mireille et Vincent** are in Valréas, although the wine comes from vineyards outside the appellation and is simply called Côtes du Rhône.

VINSOBRES

Top Producers

Domaine les Aussellons***   Domaine de Coriançon**
Cave Coopérative la Vinsobraise**   Château de Deurre***
Caves C. N. Jaume***   Domaine de Moulin**

Southeast of Valréas is the old Roman village of Vinsobres. It is easy to forget just how far east this Côtes du Rhône-Villages is, only a few miles west of Nyon and the viticulture area known as the Coteau de Tricastin. The cool, northerly, almost mountainous village is sheltered better than Valréas from the blast of the mistral winds. The village, which received Côtes du Rhône-Villages status in 1957, takes its name from the words of a seventeenth-century bishop of nearby Vaison-la-Romaine, the highly touristed former Roman settlement, when the bishop said, "sober wine or wine of sobriety, take it soberly."

Two cooperatives, **Cave Coopérative la Vinsobraise** and **La Cave du Prieuré,** dominate this village's production. Vinsobres's promising potential is evidenced by the increasing number of vignerons who are breaking away from the local coops and estate-bottling their production. The finest estates include **Domaine les Aussellons** (over 40 acres), **Caves C. N. Jaume** (67 acres, much of it impressively terraced, slopeside vineyards), and the 50-acre estate of **Château de Deurre.** These three estates tend to produce the most consistent red wine of the village, although it should be noted that the Jaumes, because of a change in appellation regulations, can no longer call their wine Vinsobres, and thus it is simply called Côtes du Rhône. Denis Vinson's **Domaine de Moulin** (48 acres) can also produce good wine, but it is less consistent. In top vintages, the best cuvées that emerge from Cave Coopérative la Vinsobraise are good Côtes du Rhône-Villages.

The wines of Vinsobres tend to possess less Grenache than their Côtes du Rhône-Villages neighbors to the south—Cairanne, Sablet, Rasteau, Beaumes de Venise, and Séguret— because the climate is slightly cooler in Vinsobres. Among all the northern Côtes du Rhône-Villages, Vinsobres has the best potential, but it is far from my favorite source for rich, complete, complex, and satisfying Côtes du Rhône. The white wines are generally too acidic, and the rosés are bland. However, competent reds are well above the quality level produced at St.-Pantaléon-les-Vignes and Valréas to the north, or Visan and St.-Maurice-sur-Eygues to the south.

VISAN

Top Producers

Domaine de la Cantharide (J. Roux)***   Clos du Père Clément (H. Depeyre)***

Southwest of Valréas and west of Vinsobres is another medieval village filled with winding passageways, endless photogenic charm, and Provençal peasants, many of whom look like the colorful *santons* (clay Christmas figurines) for which the region is famous. The red wines produced in Visan come from rich clay soil, and have a tendency to possess flavors that remotely recall raspberries, as well as the peppery, undeniable herbaceous element that sometimes dominates these wines in less than ideal vintages. The two best estates, the Laget-Roux family's **Domaine de la Cantharide,** and the Depeyre family's **Clos du Père Clément,** turn out modern, fruity, round, medium-bodied wines with good depth, and enough character to merit interest. The **Cave Coopérative les Coteaux Visan** tends to produce average-quality, one-dimensional wines. All things considered, this is a worthwhile tourist destination, but the implication of higher-quality wine, since this is a Côtes du Rhône-Villages, is not realized when objectively tasting the wines.

CÔTES DU RHÔNE

Fertile Hunting Ground
for Great Wine Values

CÔTES DU RHÔNE AT A GLANCE

Appellation created:	November 19, 1937.
Types of wine produced:	Red, white, and rosé, although over 95% of the production is red wine.
Grape varieties planted:	Twenty-four grapes are authorized, 14 designated as primary varietals and 10 as accessory, but for all practical purposes, the predominant red wine grape is Grenache, followed by Syrah, Mourvèdre, and Cinsault. For the white wines, Grenache Blanc, Clairette, Bourboulenc, and, increasingly, Viognier and Roussanne are the principal grapes.
Acres currently under vine:	110,495.
Quality level:	At the cooperative level, which accounts for 75–80% of the entire generic Côtes du Rhône production, quality ranges from insipid and sterile to very good or excellent; at the estate-bottled level, the quality ranges from below average to exceptional in the case of a half dozen or so overachievers.
Aging potential:	Over 95% of every bottle of generic Côtes du Rhône, whether red, white, or rosé, should be drunk early; the whites and rosés within two years of the vintage, and the reds within two to four years of the vintage. However,

General characteristics:	some of the seriously endowed wines from the top estates can age for 20 + years.
	At the top levels, the white wines have made tremendous progress in quality as a result of modern cold fermentation and the introduction of Viognier and Roussanne in the blend. Even with these improvements, these are wines that are fresh, lively, and meant to be drunk quickly. The red wines vary enormously. A well-made Côtes du Rhône should be bursting with red and black fruits, have a peppery, Provençal herb-scented nose, a supple, velvety texture, and a heady, lusty, spicy finish.
Greatest recent vintages:	1995, 1990, 1989.
Price range:	$7–$15, except for the single-vineyard and old-vine cuvées of a handful of estates.

The Côtes du Rhône appellation's most profound wines:

Coudoulet de Beaucastel Côtes du Rhône
Domaine de Beaurenard †
Domaine de l'Espigouette Plan de Dieu
Château de Fonsalette
Château de Fonsalette Cuvée Syrah
Domaine Gramenon Cuvée des Ceps Centenaires
Domaine Gramenon Cuvée des Laurentides
Domaine du Grand Moulas Côtes du Rhône

Domaine de la Guichard Cuvée Genet
Domaine de la Janasse Les Garrigues †
Jean-Marie Lombard Cuvée Eugène de Monicault
Roger Perrin Réserve des Vieilles Vignes †
Domaine Réméjeanne Les Genevrières
Château St.-Estève d'Uchaux Grande Réserve
Château St.-Estève d'Uchaux Vieilles Vignes

RATING THE CÔTES DU RHÔNE PRODUCERS

* * * * *(OUTSTANDING)

Coudoulet de Beaucastel
Château de Fonsalette
Château de Fonsalette Cuvée Syrah

Domaine Gramenon (Ceps Centenaire)
Domaine Gramenon (Cuvée de Laurentides)

* * * *(EXCELLENT)

Domaine de la Becassonne †
Domaine A. Brunel
Domaine de la Cabasse
De la Canorgue
Domaine du Couroulu
Cros de la Mure
Domaine Gramenon (various cuvées)
Château du Grand Moulas
Château du Grand Prébois †
Domaine des Grands Devers †
Domaine de la Guichard
Guigal
Paul Jaboulet-Aîné Parallel 45 †
Domaine de la Janasse †

Jean-Marie Lombard
Plan Dei †
Rabasse-Charavin †
Domaine de la Réméjeanne
Domaine des Richards †
Domaine St.-Gayan†
Château St.-Maurice †
Domaine St.-Apollinaire †
Domaine Santa Duc †
Domaine de la Solitude †
Tardieu-Laurent
Château des Tours
Domaine des Treilles †
Vidal-Fleury †

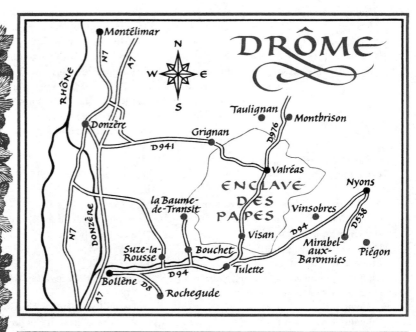

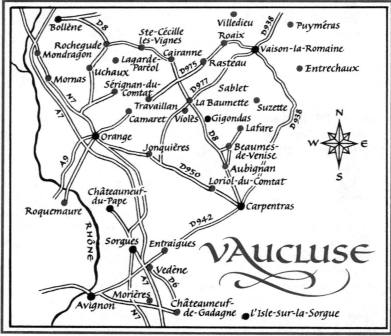

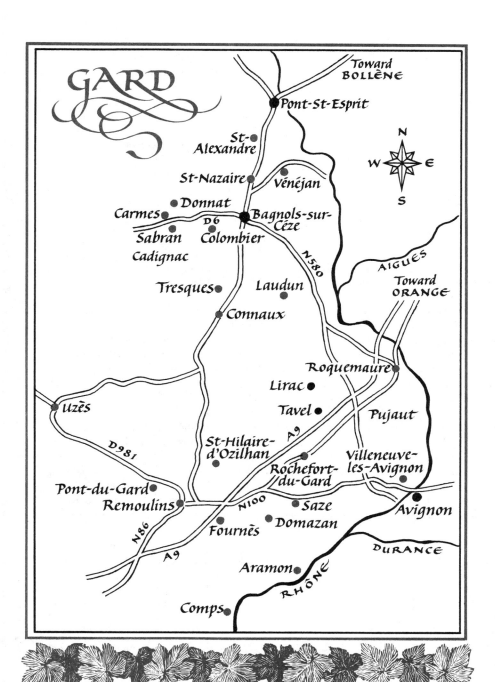

GARD

Toward BOLLÈNE

Pont-St-Esprit

St-Alexandre

St-Nazaire

Vénéjan

Donnat

Carmes

Bagnols-sur-Cèze

Sabran

D6

Colombier

Cadignac

N580

AIGUES

Tresques

Laudun

Toward ORANGE

Connaux

Roquemaure

Lirac

Tavel

Pujaut

Uzès

D981

St-Hilaire-d'Ozilhan

A9

Villeneuve-les-Avignon

Rochefort-du-Gard

Pont-du-Gard

Remoulins

N100

Saze

Avignon

N86

Fournès

Domazan

A9

DURANCE

Aramon

RHÔNE

Comps

RATING THE CÔTES DU RHÔNE PRODUCERS (cont.)

* * * *(EXCELLENT) (cont.)

La Vieille Ferme (Perrin Réserve de   Domaine du Vieux Chêne
   Vieilles Vignes) †   (various cuvées)

* * *(GOOD)

Domaine des Aires Vieilles	Domaine des Moulins***/****
Domaine Clos du Caillou †	Domaines Mousset †
Daniel Combe †	Nero-Pinchon Ste.-Agathe †
Château de Domazan	Domaine de la Présidente
Domaine de l'Espigouette***/****	Domaine de la Renjarde †
Domaine les Goubert †	Château St.-Estève d'Uchaux
Domaine de la Millière †	Domaine St.-Michel †
Domaine Mireille et Vincent †	Domaine St.-Pierré†
Domaine Mitan	Château de Trignon †
Domaine de Mont Redon †	La Vieille Ferme (other cuvées) †

† The Rhône Valley producers are most frequently associated with wines from other Rhône appellations, but also produce good to excellent wines under the Côtes du Rhône appellation.

Officially, Côtes du Rhône is at the bottom of the Rhône Valley wine hierarchy, notwithstanding the fact that these wines represent nearly 90% of the entire wine production between Ampuis, in Côte Rôtie, and Avignon, just south of Châteauneuf du Pape. It is the best-known wine of the Rhône Valley, if only because so much is produced. Côtes du Rhône can range from shabbily made, oxidized, alcoholic, out-of-balance wines, to the increasing numbers of stunningly rich, exceptional wines with a decade's worth of cellaring potential. The bulk of the wines tend to be sound, fruity, well made, and satisfying to both the palate and the purse, if somewhat one-dimensional and lacking complexity.

The Côtes du Rhône appellation, much like the Côtes du Rhône-Villages appellation, is dominated by cooperatives, which account for nearly 75% of the wine produced. Yet there are a multitude of fine estates and/or domaines run by committed individuals who turn out very serious wines. The challenge I have faced for more than 20 years is to find those unheralded estates producing vinous treasures that taste like $30 or $40 bottles of wine, but cost one-third to one-fourth that. What is so fascinating about the Côtes du Rhône appellation is that each year new stars emerge, adding to the growing numbers of fine estate bottlers.

This chapter includes a detailed profile of the three finest Côtes du Rhône producers, Château de Fonsalette, Coudoulet de Beaucastel, and Domaine Gramenon. It also provides a profile of other top estates where readers are likely to enjoy a degree of pleasure far beyond what they might expect from this deceptively humble appellation.

With the exception of Fonsalette, Coudoulet de Beaucastel, and to a certain extent Domaine Gramenon, and a handful of Syrah cuvées, these are wines to drink within 5–6 years of the vintage.

Of the recent vintages, the 1995, 1990, and 1989 are the three most impressive recent years. The finest cuvées will drink well for 10 years, and Fonsalette will last for two decades or more. Nineteen ninety-four is a good, but soft, easygoing vintage that will need to be drunk within 6–7 years.

DOMAINE DES AIRES VIEILLES (GEORGES DUBOEUF) (VAUCLUSE)* * *

Address: 75150 Romanèche Thorins
Tel: 4-85-35-34-20
Fax: 4-85-35-34-25
Wines produced: Côtes du Rhône (red)
Surface area: 62 acres
Production: 15,000 cases
Upbringing: Fermentation of 3 weeks in cement vats and bottling after 6 months. The grapes
    are destemmed, and there is a fining and filtration.
Average age of vines: 35 years
Blend: 40% Grenache, 30% Syrah, 15% Cinsault, 10% Carignan, and 5% other varietals

Known as the king of Beaujolais for his consistently excellent selections from that
appellation, Georges Duboeuf has also recognized the potential for high quality in the
southern Rhône Valley. The Domaine des Aires Vieilles is a fruity, light- to medium-bodied,
elegant Côtes du Rhône that is bottled quickly to preserve its freshness and fruit. A wine to
drink within 2–3 years of the vintage, it offers a less powerful, more finesse-styled Côtes du
Rhône when compared to Georges Duboeuf's Domaine des Moulins Côtes du Rhône.

DOMAINE A. BRUNEL (VAUCLUSE)* * * *

Address: Les Cailloux
        6, chemin du Bois de la Ville
        84230 Châteauneuf du Pape
Tel: 4-90-83-72-62
Wines produced: Côtes du Rhône Domaine Becassone (white), Côtes du Rhône Domaine A.
    Brunel (red)
Surface area (white): Domaine Becassone—6.2 acres
             (red): Domaine A. Brunel—27 acres
Production (white): Domaine Becassone—1,562 cases
           (red): Domaine A. Brunel—6,250 cases
Upbringing (white): Domaine Becassone—Fermentation of 15 days to 3 weeks at low
            temperatures in stainless steel tanks. Malolactic is stopped with sul-
            fites; bottling is done after 4 months; no filtration.
           (red): Domaine A. Brunel—Fermentation of 15 days to 3 weeks in enamel
            tanks, followed by one year in stainless steel tanks. There is no fining or
            filtration.
Average age of vines (white:) Domaine Becassone—20 years
                     (red): Domaine A. Brunel—30 years
Blend (white): Domaine Becassone—50% Roussanne, 40% Clairette, 10% Grenache Blanc
      (red): Domaine A. Brunel—85% Grenache, 12% Syrah, 3% Mourvèdre

André Brunel is more renowned as a progressive producer of high-quality Châteauneuf
du Pape, where he fashions the superb Les Cailloux. But readers looking for a value-priced
introduction to his fine winemaking should seek out his red Côtes du Rhône, bottled under
the name Domaine A. Brunel, and his white Côtes du Rhône, Domaine Becassone. These
are forward, rich, fruity wines that are meant to be drunk early. The red Côtes du Rhône is
a delicious, peppery, complex wine that will drink well for 5–6 years. Desiring to capture
the full pleasures of his vineyard, Brunel bottles this wine without fining or filtration.

The white wine from the Domaine Becassone has improved immensely over the last five
years. It is now one of the finest examples of a dry white Côtes du Rhône. It is a gutsy wine

with a robust, honeysuckle-like nose and flavors. This boldly styled, rich, flavorful wine should be drunk within 2–3 years of the vintage.

COUDOULET DE BEAUCASTEL (VAUCLUSE)* * * * *

Address: Domaine de Beaucastel
           84350 Courthézon
Tel: 4-90-70-70-60
Fax: 4-90-70-25-24
Wines produced: Coudoulet de Beaucastel Côtes du Rhône (red and white)
Surface area (white): 12.35 acres
             (red): 74 acres
Production (white): 1,875 cases
             (red): 12,500 cases
Upbringing (white): 8–10 months total, with 90% of the yield fermented and aged in enamel
             vats, and 10% in 2-year-old oak barrels; malolactic is allowed to occur
           (red): 20 months total, with 2–3 weeks' fermentation in enamel tanks, and aging
             for 8–16 months in oak casks; there is no filtration
Average age of vines (white): 12 years
                       (red): 40 years
Blend (white): 30% Viognier, 30% Bourboulenc, 30% Marsanne, 10% Clairette
       (red): 30% Mourvèdre, 30% Grenache, 20% Syrah, 20% Cinsault

The vineyard soils of Coudoulet are very similar to those of the Beaucastel estate in Châteauneuf du Pape. Only a highway separates Coudoulet's vineyard from that of Beaucastel. Formerly, Coudoulet produced only red wine, from a 30% Mourvèdre, 30% Grenache, 20% Syrah, 20% Cinsault blend, which resembled Beaucastel but without the same intensity and structure. Coudoulet is capable of lasting 10–12 years. For example, the 1978 remains a strong effort, and even the soft, forward 1985 is still an excellent wine. The wine's strong Mourvèdre character is softened by the greater percentage of Cinsault in Coudoulet than in Beaucastel.

While always one of the reference point red wines of the Côtes du Rhône (and better than many producer's Gigondas or Châteauneuf du Pape), Coudoulet has recently introduced a high-quality white wine that is proving to be one of the finest examples from Côtes du Rhône, offering up a Viognier nose of honeysuckle, peaches, and apricots. It is a rich, lush, low-acid, fleshy, dry white that is put through full malolactic fermentation.

VINTAGES

1995—Côtes du Rhône (red)   The 1995 Coudoulet Côtes du Rhône is, as they say in the
   ·   wine trade, "packed and stacked." The wine exhibits a dense ruby/purple color
   91   and a superb nose of smoky herbs, barbecue spices, and sweet, rich black-cherry
             jam. Full-bodied, dense, and thick, with outstanding concentration, low acidity,
             and fine purity, this is a gorgeously rich Coudoulet that should drink well for a
             decade. Last tasted 6/96.

1995—Côtes du Rhône (white)   Made from a vineyard situated just outside Château
   ·   Beaucastel's border, in a sector known as Coudoulet, the white wine offers convinc-
   90   ing evidence of the heights that can be achieved in the southern Rhône. Made from
             a blend of 30% Viognier, 30% Marsanne, 30% Bourboulenc, and 10% Clairette,
             the 1995 Côtes du Rhône blanc is rich and concentrated, with the apricot/peach-
             like fragrance of the Viognier dominating the wine's personality. It is low in acidity,

and thus comes across as sumptuous, rich, and chewy. Drink it over the next 2–3 years. Last tasted 6/96.

1994—Côtes du Rhône (red)   The 1994 Côtes du Rhône is also outstanding. It offers
· up a sweet, fragrant nose of new saddle leather, black cherries, smoke, olives, and
90 herbs. Lush, ripe, and full-bodied, with outstanding concentration, this velvety fruit bomb should drink well for 10–12 + years. The 1994 and 1995 are two of the finest examples of Coudoulet since the great 1989 and 1985. Last tasted 6/96.

1994—Côtes du Rhône (white)   The 1994 Côtes du Rhône blanc reveals good fat and
· ripeness, as well as an opulent, unctuous texture. The nose has begun to shut down,
89 so it is less expressive than the 1995. Nevertheless, it is a full-bodied, powerful, Viognier-dominated wine that should drink well for 3–4 years, possibly longer. Last tasted 6/96.

1993—Côtes du Rhône (red)   The terrific 1993 possesses good grip and structure (typical
· of the vintage), as well as a deep ruby/purple color and a sweet nose of black fruits,
90 tree bark, earth, pepper, and spices. Full-bodied, with outstanding concentration, this beautifully made Coudoulet could easily be mistaken for a top Beaucastel. Drink it over the next 10–12 + years. Last tasted 6/96.

1992—Côtes du Rhône (red)   The 1992 Coudoulet de Beaucastel is more austere and
· tannic than the 1993. It possesses structure, gobs of ripe, leathery black-fruit
87 aromas, and a spicy, firm finish. Drink it over the next 7–10 years. Last tasted 6/95.

1990—Côtes du Rhône (red)   The 1990 offers a big, leathery, beefy, peppery, violet- and
· cassis-scented nose, deep, supple, heady flavors, soft tannins, and low acidity. It
88 exhibits the telltale spice and fragrance of the so-called "brett" yeast so readers who do not like animal smells in their wine will no doubt find this offering objectionable. Anticipated maturity: now–2002. Last tasted 11/95.

1989—Côtes du Rhône (red)   The 1989 is softer than the 1990. The wine exhibits a
· forward, fleshy personality, with peppery and plum scents, excellent flavor concen-
88 tration, plenty of glycerin, and a smooth, spicy finish. Anticipated maturity: now– 2000. Last tasted 6/96.

1988—Côtes du Rhône (red)   The 1988 combines the richness of the 1989, but with even
· more clarity and focus, layer upon layer of rich, peppery, black-raspberry fruit,
90 plenty of body, and a remarkably long finish. Anticipated maturity: now–2000. Last tasted 6/96.

Older Vintages

The 1985 and 1983 are fully mature and should be drunk before the end of the century. The 1981 is an explosive wine (much like this vintage of Beaucastel), with smoky, earthy, animal, berry aromas intertwined with gobs of fruit and heady alcohol. This lush, large-scaled Coudoulet needs to be drunk up, but it is still intact. Among very old vintages, the 1978 is a firmly structured, fully mature, austere wine that is capable of lasting another 5–7 years.

CROS DE LA MURE (VAUCLUSE)* * * *

Address: Hameau de Derboux
          84430 Mondragon
Tel: 4-90-30-12-40
Fax: 4-90-30-46-58
Wines produced: Côtes du Rhône (red and white)
Surface area: 15 acres
Production: 2,000 cases
Upbringing: in tank and foudre

Average age of vines: 30 years
Blend (white): 36% Viognier, 34% Grenache Blanc, 30% Roussanne
  (red): 50% Grenache, 40% Syrah, 5% Mourvèdre, 5% Cinsault

Proprietor Eric Michel turns out one of the most opulently textured, gloriously fruity, seductive Côtes du Rhônes I have ever tasted. It is bursting with gorgeous levels of unadulterated, gorgeously proportioned, fleshy black fruits (due no doubt to the 40% Syrah in the blend) that reveal no evidence of oak. The wine is undeniably one of the most hedonistic and decadent of the Côtes du Rhône, and is best drunk within the first 5–7 years of the vintage.

This estate also turns out a tiny quantity of very well-made, fragrant, juicy dry white wine from a blend of Roussanne, Viognier, and Grenache Blanc.

This is an excellent, though tiny estate situated close to my favorite restaurant in the southern Rhône, La Beaugravière, in Mondragon.

CHÂTEAU DE DOMAZAN (GARD)* * *

Address: 30390 Domazan
Tel: 4-66-57-07-37
Wines produced: Côtes du Rhône (red)
Surface area: 111 acres
Production: 25,000 cases
Upbringing: Fermentation of 10 days in cement vats, followed by 9 months in stainless steel
        tanks before bottling. There is a fining and filtration.
Average age of vines: 25 years
Blend: 50% Grenache, 20% Syrah, 30% Cinsault and other varietals

Domazan, a small Côtes du Rhône village southwest of Avignon, is well known for having several high-quality domaines, the best of which is Christian Chauderac's Château de Domazan. The Chauderacs have been producing wine at this property since the fourteenth century, making it among the oldest family-run estates in France. The wine is consistently a fruity, cherry, Côtes du Rhône with flavors and scents of *garrigue* and herbes de Provence, meant to be drunk within 2–4 years of the vintage. Made in a modern style, it possesses character, spice, and plenty of fruit.

DOMAINE DE L'ESPIGOUETTE (VAUCLUSE)* * */* * * *

Address: 84150 Violès
Tel: 4-90-70-95-48
Fax: 4-90-70-96-06
Wines produced: Côtes du Rhône (red), Côtes du Rhône Plan de Dieu (red), Vin de Pays
        Vaucluse (red)
Surface area (Côtes du Rhône): 22 acres
        (Plan de Dieu): 17.3 acres
        (Vin de Pays): 12.4 acres
Production (Côtes du Rhône): 4,400 cases
(Plan de Dieu): 2,500 cases
(Vin de Pays): 3,125 cases
Upbringing (Côtes du Rhône): Traditional fermentation of 8 days; 30% of the yield then
                spends 9–12 months in old oak casks and the rest in tanks
                for 12 months prior to bottling. There is no fining and only
                a slight filtration.
        (Plan de Dieu): Fermentation of 10–12 days at 30–32° centigrade. The wines
                spend 6–9 months in oak casks and are bottled unfined, but
                with a slight filtration.

(Vin de Pays): Fermentation of 4–5 days followed by 6–9 months in vats. There is no fining, but there is a slight filtration.

Average age of vines (Côtes du Rhône): 40 years
(Plan de Dieu): 30 years
(Vin de Pays): 25 years

Blend (Côtes du Rhône): 80% Grenache, 20% Syrah, Cinsault, and Carignan
(Plan de Dieu): 85% Grenache, 15% Syrah and Mourvèdre
(Vin de Pays): 70% Grenache, 30% Syrah, Cinsault, and Carignan

This 52-acre estate is run by the warm, inviting, open Edmonde Latour. The bulk of the estate is located on the mistral-swept part of the Vaucluse known as the Plan de Dieu, which has a particularly hot climate and precocious terroir. The wines of Domaine de l'Espigouette have been estate-bottled for just over two decades, and have shown increasing quality with every good vintage. There are multiple cuvées, all of which are rustic, peppery, flavorful, robust, mouthfilling, textbook Côtes du Rhônes. I generally find the Côtes du Rhône Plan de Dieu slightly richer and more intense than the regular Côtes du Rhône. The best value is often the low-priced, chunky, fleshy Vin de Pays Vaucluse.

Domaine de l'Espigouette's recent top vintages have been 1989, 1990, 1994, and 1995. These traditional old-style Côtes du Rhône can easily age for six or more years.

CHÂTEAU DE FONSALETTE (VAUCLUSE)* * * * *

Address: Château Rayas
84230 Châteauneuf du Pape
Tel: 4-90-83-73-09
Fax: 4-90-83-51-17
Wines produced: Fonsalette Côtes du Rhône (red and white), Fonsalette Cuvée Syrah (red)
Surface area (white): 7.5 acres
(red): 19.8 acres
Production (white): 500 cases
(red): 1,666 cases
Upbringing (white): 9 months in stainless steel vats
(red): 2 years total; fermentation in cement vats followed by 12–24 months in old oak casks
Average age of vines (white): 35 years
(red): 35 years
Blend (white): 50% Grenache Blanc, 30% Marsanne, 20% Clairette
(red): 50% Grenache, 35% Cinsault, 15% Syrah

Although the Fonsalette wines are made at the cellars of Jacques Reynaud's Château Rayas, the estate is located near Lagarde-Paréol. This large 321-acre property, planted by Jacques's father, Louis, at the end of World War II, has only 27 acres under vine. The largest part of the property is a huge park that surrounds a dilapidated, unusual-looking edifice that might pass for a castle in a B horror movie.

Two extraordinary red wines emerge from this domaine. The remarkable Fonsalette, a 50% Grenache, 35% Cinsault, 15% Syrah blend, is better than the great majority of Châteauneuf du Papes. It is made in the exact same manner as Rayas, from yields that are amazingly low (about five barrels of wine per acre are produced from yields well under 2 tons of fruit per acre). There is also a legendary Cuvée Syrah that is made in microscopic quantities from what Jacques Reynaud does not blend in with Fonsalette. It is made from a Syrah vineyard planted with a northern orientation, which gives it a cooler microclimate than other vineyards in the south. The Syrah came from cuttings that Jacques's father,

Louis, obtained from Gérard Chave in Hermitage. It is a remarkably dense, concentrated, opaque-colored wine that often needs 15–20 years to begin to evolve (the 1978 is just beginning to emerge from its infancy).

The most controversial wine in Fonsalette's portfolio is the white wine, a 50% Grenache Blanc, 30% Marsanne, 20% Clairette, blend that seems to be made in whatever style Jacques Reynaud deems acceptable for a given vintage. In some years malolactic fermentation is blocked, and in others it is encouraged. The wine is thick, oily, and rich, as well as slightly oxidized at times, but it is always a distinctive, noteworthy, traditional, heavyweight, old-style dry white.

Another wine sometimes produced by Fonsalette is La Pialade, which is simply a blend of whatever remnants are left in the Rayas cellars after all the other wines are produced. It is a pleasant but undistinguished wine.

The red cuvées of Fonsalette Côtes du Rhône and Côtes du Rhône Cuvée Syrah can easily last for two decades, with the Syrah probably having 30–40 years of ageability. That this estate produces the singularly greatest, most monumental Côtes du Rhône is uncontestable. It always confounds me that this wine is largely ignored by the trophy hunters in the wine commerce—so much the better, I suppose.

VINTAGES

1995—Côtes du Rhône (red)   The 1995 Côtes du Rhône Fonsalette was made from yields of under 2 tons per acre. It exhibits a sweet, expansive personality with gobs of
· **90** fruit, surprisingly crisp acidity for such ripeness and intensity, full body, and spectacular concentration and purity. The cuvées of Grenache and Cinsault were oozing with ripeness and that seductive, exotic, decadent richness this estate achieves in great vintages. Anticipated maturity: 1998–2015. Last tasted 6/96.

1995—Côtes du Rhône Cuvée Syrah (red)   The 1995 Fonsalette Cuvée Syrah should turn out to rival other great vintages of this wine, i.e., 1978, 1979, 1983, 1985, 1988,
· **94** 1989, 1990, and 1994. This parcel of Syrah (from clones taken from Gérard Chave's parcels on the hill of Hermitage) is now 30 years old. The wine's opaque black color is accompanied by celestial aromas of cassis and smoke. Full-bodied, with magnificent purity, a layered, viscous texture, and awesome richness and length, this monster Syrah will need at least a decade to become civilized. It could last 30–40 years, which may seem outrageously long, but keep in mind that the 1978 in my cellar is still not ready for prime-time drinking. Last tasted 6/96.

1994—Côtes du Rhône (red)   The 1994 Côtes du Rhône Fonsalette is a gorgeously rich wine with a deep ruby/purple color, a peppery, spicy, herb, and jammy black-
· **90** cherry nose, moderate tannin, full body, and super intensity and length. This wine has turned out to be an outstanding example of Côtes du Rhône that should drink well for 15+ years. Last tasted 6/96.

1994—Côtes du Rhône Cuvée Syrah (red)   The 1994 Fonsalette Cuvée Syrah (only 4,000 bottles produced) achieved 14.5% alcohol naturally. This black-colored, stagger-
· **94** ingly rich wine is not far behind the otherworldly 1995. It hits the palate with a crescendo of massive portions of cassis fruit, smoke, earth, and Asian spices. Extremely thick, unctuous, and moderately tannic, this is an enormously endowed, gargantuan Syrah that will require 7–10 years of cellaring. It is another 30-year wine. Last tasted 6/96.

1993—Côtes du Rhône (red)   The solidly made 1993 Fonsalette Côtes du Rhône will offer delicious drinking over the next decade. It reveals a healthy dark ruby color,
· **87** a robust, roasted-herb, black-cherry, and peppery nose, and good ripeness and richness. Anticipated maturity: now–2004. Last tasted 6/96.

1993—Côtes du Rhône Cuvée Syrah (red)   This closed Syrah requires 5–6 more years
·   of cellaring. An opaque black/purple-colored wine with considerable tannin and
88+   intensity, it is immensely weighty and powerful on the palate. There is a degree of
        austerity in the 1993, but it is a well-endowed, rich, structured wine. Anticipated
        maturity: 2000–2015. Last tasted 6/95.

1991—Côtes du Rhône (red)   The loosely knit 1991 Fonsalette Côtes du Rhône is tasty
·   in a monolithic manner, soft, medium-bodied, and pleasant. Drink it up. Last tasted
83   6/95.

1991—Côtes du Rhône Cuvée Syrah (red)   The profound 1991 Cuvée Syrah offers an
·   amazing opaque, black/purple color, followed by a huge nose of roasted herbs and
92+   cassis that roars from the glass. With a natural alcohol of more than 14% (from
        yields of 20–25 hectoliters per hectare), this massive, phenomenally extracted,
        gigantic wine needs 8–10 years of cellaring. Anticipated maturity: 2000–2018.
        Last tasted 12/95.

1990—Côtes du Rhône (red)   This dark ruby/purple-colored wine displays the essence of
·   cherry, kirsch, and Provençal herbs in its nose. Quite full-bodied, this large, fleshy
92   wine reveals corpulent, sweet, expansive, rich flavors that linger on the palate. It is
        a lavishly rich Côtes du Rhône, with a thick texture and enough alcohol and soft
        tannin to keep it going. Anticipated maturity: 1999–2012. Last tasted 12/95.

1990—Côtes du Rhône Cuvée Syrah (red)   The opaque black-colored 1990 Cuvée Syrah
·   offers an extraordinary perfume of hickory wood, chocolate, cassis, and black fruits,
95   staggering richness, astonishing opulence, plenty of alcohol, and gobs of tannin. A
        massive wine, it will need plenty of cellaring to reach its zenith. This dazzling wine
        does require discipline, as it must be cellared. Anticipated maturity: 2002–2025.
        Last tasted 12/95.

1989—Côtes du Rhône (red)   The 1989 Fonsalette Côtes du Rhône is a beautifully made,
·   seductive mouthful of wine. It is all velvet and silk, and there is a whopping de-
92   gree of alcohol in the finish. Along with the huge 1990, it appears to be the
        finest Fonsalette since the late 1970s. The tannin is soft and the acidity is low, yet
        the wine's concentration and magical flavors (overripe, jammy cherries, truffles,
        grilled meats, and thyme) are dazzling. Anticipated maturity: now–2010. Last tasted
        9/95.

1989—Côtes du Rhône Cuvée Syrah (red)   The 1989 Cuvée Syrah is similar to the 1990,
·   exhibiting exceptional intensity, a black/ruby/purple color, a huge perfume of
93   black raspberries, and a whoppingly long, moderately tannic finish. Typically, it is
        extracted, large-scaled, and capable of lasting for another 20+ years. Anticipated
        maturity: 2002–2016. Last tasted 9/95.

1988—Côtes du Rhône (red)   The spicy 1988 Fonsalette Côtes du Rhône is a rich,
·   intense, powerful wine with plenty of alcohol in its heady finish. Full-bodied and
87   supple, it should drink well for another decade. Last tasted 9/95.

1988—Côtes du Rhône Cuvée Syrah (red)   The 1988 Cuvée Syrah is a riveting wine,
·   with a splendid dark ruby/purple color, a spicy Provençal herb and superripe
92   cassis-scented bouquet, highly extracted flavors, and a rich, full-bodied, velvety
        texture. Anticipated maturity: 1999–2018. Last tasted 9/95.

1986—Côtes du Rhône (red)—Much like the 1986 Rayas, the 1986 Fonsalette exhibited
·   far more fat, appeal, and quality when it was young than it does at present. The
78   baby fat has melted away to reveal a vegetal, hollow, austere style of wine that is
        past its peak. It is losing its fruit and should be drunk up. Last tasted 9/95.

1985—Côtes du Rhône (red)   A textbook Côtes du Rhône, the 1985 Fonsalette exhibits
·   a healthy dark ruby color with purple nuances, a peppery, licorice, earthy, black-
88   raspberry-scented nose, full body, juicy, plump flavors, and a soft, robust finish.

Although drinkable since bottling, it reveals no signs of fruit loss or color deterioration. Anticipated maturity: now–2002. Last tasted 9/95.

1985—Côtes du Rhône Cuvée Syrah (red)   A backward, soft, inky/purple-colored wine, the 1985 Cuvée Syrah remains monolithic and youthful. It is still thick and juicy, · with tremendous quantities of black fruits, particularly cassis, but there are no **92** signs of evolution. Owners are advised either to drink it (if you like grapy, exuberant, uncomplicated, mouth-filling red wines), or continue to cellar it for more complexity will emerge from this big, beefy wine. Anticipated maturity: 1998–2015. Last tasted 9/95.

1983—Côtes du Rhône (red)   This dark garnet-colored wine has been fully mature for a · number of years. It exhibits an attractive, fragrant, earthy, mushroomy nose filled **87** with scents of Provençal herbs, pepper, and red fruits. Soft, round, medium- to full-bodied, and revealing considerable rust in its color, this wine requires consumption before the end of the century. Mature now. Last tasted 9/95.

1983—Côtes du Rhône Cuvée Syrah (red)   An unqualified success, this saturated dark · ruby/purple-colored wine remains an infant in terms of its development. Still thick, **90** juicy, intense, and full-bodied, with few signs of development other than the change in color from opaque purple to opaque garnet, this structured, broad-flavored, sweet, jammy Syrah will continue to benefit from further cellaring. It is a weighty, husky wine. Anticipated maturity: 2000–2015. Last tasted 9/95.

1982—Côtes du Rhône (red)   No Rayas was produced in this vintage, and thus Fonsalette · contains all the Rayas juice. I do not have any tasting notes on a 1982 Cuvée **87** Syrah, but the Côtes du Rhône has always been a noteworthy success. The wine is more rustic than normal, with a dark, opaque garnet color, a vivid, savage nose of *garrigue* (Provençal herbs, pepper, earth, and black fruits). Full-bodied, tannic, and powerful, with considerable structure, this is a hefty, full-throttle wine that will last for another 5–7 years. Look elsewhere for finesse and elegance, as this is a mouth-filling wine of power and extract. Anticipated maturity: now–2003. Last tasted 9/95.

1978—Côtes du Rhône (red)   Delicious since the early eighties, it is still a beauty, · offering plenty of peppery, black-raspberry and cherry fruit, along with copious **89** quantities of earth, truffles, and spice, loads of glycerin, and a chewy, fleshy mouth feel. There is only slight amber at the edge. Fully mature now, it is a terrific Fonsalette. Last tasted 4/92.

1978—Côtes du Rhône Cuvée Syrah (red)   Will this wine ever reach full maturity? · Incredibly dense, the stain on the inside of the bottle reminds one of a 20-year-old **92 +** vintage port. A healthy dark ruby/purple color with no signs of amber or lightening is followed by a huge, smoky, peppery, cassis-scented nose, and equally impressive, highly concentrated flavors. It is powerful, rich, and thick, with another 15–20 years of evolution ahead. The only question is, will it develop the majestic perfume of a great Hermitage or Côte Rôtie? Anticipated maturity: 2000–2015. Last tasted 4/92.

1969—Côtes du Rhône (red)   Considerable amber and rust at the edge of this wine's · color are misleading given the sweet, berry fruit that jumps from the glass. Tinged **88** with scents of pepper, smoke, and Provençal herbs, this intact, full-bodied, supple Côtes du Rhône remains delicious after 26 years of aging. I purchased this wine for a song, along with an elder sibling, the 1966. Not one bottle has been less than delicious. I suspect this wine has been fully mature for much of its life, so there is no reason to hold on to it should readers still have a bottle or two languishing in their cellars. Drink it up. Last tasted 1/96.

1966—Côtes du Rhône (red)   Light ruby/garnet-colored with considerable amber at the
·   edge, the 1966 offers an herbal and sweet, jammy-scented nose with more definition
88   and fewer smoky notes than its younger sibling. Full-bodied, sweet, velvety, and
delicious, with an expansive mid-palate and a soft, heady, alcoholic finish, this
wine has been delicious since I first tasted it in the mid-seventies. I usually opt for
drinking Fonsalette's Côtes du Rhônes within their first 10–15 years of life, but
the 1966 and 1969 authoritatively prove that the finest vintages of Fonsalette can
age brilliantly. Mature now. Last tasted 1/96.

DOMAINE GRAMENON (DRÔME)* * * * *

Address: 26770 Montbrison-sur-Lez
Tel: 4-75-53-57-08
Fax: 4-75-53-68-92
Wines produced: Côtes du Rhône (white), Côtes du Rhône Cuvée des Ceps Centenaires
(red), Côtes du Rhône Cuvée des Laurentides (red), Côtes du Rhône Le
Gramenon (red); other red wine cuvées
Surface area (white): 5 acres
(red): Cuvée des Ceps Centenaires—5 acres
Cuvée des Laurentides—12.4 acres
Le Gramenon red—25 acres
other red wine cuvées: 15 acres
Production (white): 750 cases
(red): Cuvée des Ceps Centenaires—438 cases
Cuvée des Laurentides—2,500 cases
Le Gramenon—5,625 cases
Upbringing (white): Half of the yield is fermented and brought up in 1-year-old barrels, and
half in stainless steel vats. Malolactic is allowed to occur, and the wines
are bottled after 10 months.
(red): Cuvée des Ceps Centenaires—Fermentation of 4 weeks, followed by 12
months in 1-year-old oak casks. There is no fining or filtration.
Cuvée des Laurentides and Le Gramenon—Destemming is followed by a
traditional fermentation lasting 20 days; then 10–12 months in tanks.
There is no fining or filtration.
Average age of vines (white): 8–15 years
(red): Cuvée des Ceps Centenaires—100 + years
Cuvée des Laurentides—40–50 years
Le Gramenon—10 and 30 years
Blend (white): 100% Viognier
(red): Cuvée des Ceps Centenaires—100% Grenache
Cuvée des Laurentides and Le Gramenon—70–80% Grenache, 20–30% Syrah
Note: In some vintages a Cuvée Sagesse, from 95% Grenache and 5% Syrah, and a Cuvée
Pascal (made only in 1995 as an homage to a dear friend), and a 100% late harvested
Grenache are also made.

I have written affectionately about Domaine Gramenon in *The Wine Advocate*. It is one of
the greatest estates in the southern Rhône. In the most northern sector of the southern
Rhône, not far from the Côtes du Rhône-Village of Vinsobres, the husband-and-wife team of
Philippe and Michelle Laurent organically farm a 37-acre vineyard that may be expanded to
60 acres. Philippe Laurent, who could be the twin of the famous New York restaurateur Drew
Nierporent, makes some of the most sumptuous, honest, and compelling Côtes du Rhône wines
readers are likely to find. Virtually everything is made from extremely ripe fruit, and is bottled

by hand with no fining or filtration, in addition to extremely low sulfur levels. These are wines of a true artist. I have served them blind to guests who think they are drinking either a great grand cru Burgundy or one of the top Rhône wines selling for six times the price. Interestingly, the rusty sign hanging outside Gramenon's farmhouse simply says "Vin du Raisin," a simplistic statement that in many ways mirrors the Laurents' noninterventionist, minimalist philosophy of winemaking. A tour of the vineyards poignantly demonstrates why so much wonderful wine is produced from this northerly Côtes du Rhône location—low yields and incredibly old vines, with one large parcel of Grenache more than 100 years old.

What is so astonishing about Domaine Gramenon is that Michelle and Philippe Laurent's debut vintage was only 1990. Previously this estate sold its production to Marcel Guigal, among others, and to a lesser extent the huge négociant Paul Jaboulet-Aîné. The 1990s were superb and piqued my interest in this estate. Domaine Gramenon is in the Drôme département, not far from Valence, the city that represents the southern boundary of the northern Rhône. A visit to this fascinating property reveals not only extraordinary parcels of old vines but a family dedicated to being totally self-sufficient, raising their own produce, as well as chickens and ducks. The damp, traditional cellars contain no high-tech equipment. Everything is essentially done by gravity, with aging of all the cuvées of red wine in old casks and demi-muids. This is a totally organic approach to life as well as to winemaking. Virtually no sulfur is used, except for an extremely low touch at bottling. Everything is fermented with indigenous yeasts, and the wines are bottled without fining or filtration. All the red wines are loaded with flavor, as well as that unmistakable thick, rich, chewy texture that can come only from low yields and/or old vines.

A small quantity of white wine has begun to be produced. It is made from mostly Viognier that is blended with small quantities of Clairette. It is a typical Laurent product—rich, full-bodied, loaded with flavor, and high in alcohol. It is a lusty example of an impeccably made southern Rhône dry white.

Success has come quickly to the Laurents, but they seem totally unfazed by all the people who want to visit, taste, and buy their wines. This couple, who have three children, exhibit a remarkable joie de vivre that seems to be reflected in all their wines. Readers looking for great wines at modest prices from a humble origin need look no further than Domaine Gramenon.

VINTAGES

1995—Côtes du Rhône (red)   Gramenon's 1995s are the most successful wines produced
·   since the great 1990s. The 1995 Côtes du Rhône is a 100% Grenache wine with a
87   Burgundian, smoky, animal, Pinot Noir–scented nose, as well as gobs of black-
        cherry fruit, an expansive, soft texture, superb purity, and a refreshing, deliciously
        fruity, velvety mouth feel. It should drink well for 2–3 years. Last tasted 6/96.

1995—Côtes du Rhône Cuvée des Ceps Centenaires (red)   The 1995 Côtes du Rhône
·   Ceps Centenaire (made from a 100-year-old Grenache vineyard on an elevated
92   plateau) is an exotic, decadently rich Côtes du Rhône that resembles the great
        Jacques Reynaud's Château Rayas. The wine takes hedonism, decadence, ripeness,
        and richness to the limit. There is a kirsch liqueur intensity to its fruit, as well as
        a layered mouth feel. An extremely pure wine of astonishing ripeness and richness,
        it is an unbelievably sumptuous and thrilling wine to taste. Unfortunately, only
        about 100 cases of this cuvée make it to America. It should drink well for 5–7
        years. Last tasted 6/96.

1995—Côtes du Rhône Cuvée des Laurentides (red)   The 1995 Cuvée Laurentides is
·   made from 70% Grenache and 30% Syrah. The wine exhibits a deep ruby/purple
90   color, followed by sweet aromas of overripe black cherries, Provençal herbs, miner-
        als, and flowers. Dense, full-bodied, and chewy, with a superb midsection and a

lush texture, this sumptuous Côtes du Rhône should drink well for 5–6 years. Last tasted 6/96.

1995—Côtes du Rhône Cuvée Pascal (red)   In 1995, Philippe and Michelle Laurent
   ·   produced a special Côtes du Rhône Cuvée Pascal as an *hommage* to a close friend
   93   who passed away. Made from 100% Grenache and harvested on November 1, 1995, it contains an element of *surmaturité*. Readers unaccustomed to drinking Côtes du Rhône this rich, ripe, and concentrated might compare it to some of the block-buster, late-harvest Zinfandels being made in California. Although it reached 16.5% natural alcohol, the wine does not taste hot because of its extraordinary richness and ripeness of fruit. I was knocked over by the copious quantities of luscious black-cherry fruit. This silky wine possesses astonishing purity and a multilayered texture. Lamentably, only tiny quantities are available in the United States. Anticipated maturity: now–2007. Last tasted 6/96.

1995—Côtes du Rhône Cuvée Sagesse (red)   The 1995 Cuvée Sagesse is a blend of 95%
   ·   Grenache and 5% Syrah. The wine reveals the expansive, intensely fragrant style
   89   that is so much a part of the Domaine Gramenon winemaking philosophy. It hits the palate with a luscious display of berries. Rich, silky, and velvety, with full body, loads of fruit, great purity and expressiveness, and no hard edges, this is a delicious, round, gorgeously proportioned Côtes du Rhône to drink over the next 4–5 years. Last tasted 6/96.

1995—Côtes du Rhône Cuvée Syrah (red)   The 1995 Cuvée Syrah reveals a deep, opaque
   ·   ruby/purple color, and an attractive nose of ripe cassis fruit with a touch of prunes,
   90   and a hint of that herbes de Provence/*garrigue* smell. Sweet and expansive, with admirable lushness and opulence, this is a full-bodied, pure, multilayered Côtes du Rhône for drinking over the next 5–6 years. Last tasted 6/96.

Older Vintages

1994 was a very successful vintage at Domaine Gramenon, and 1990 was a great vintage. The last bottle from my case of 1990 Cuvée des Ceps Centenaires was drunk in September 1996, and the wine was still a young, vigorous, gloriously rich, hedonistic example of Côtes du Rhône.

CHÂTEAU DU GRAND MOULAS (VAUCLUSE)* * * *

Address: 84420 Mornas
Tel: 4-90-37-00-13
Fax: 4-90-37-05-89
Wines produced: Côtes du Rhône (red and white)
Surface area (white): 4.4 acres
      (red): 67 acres
Production (white): 875 cases
      (red): 12,500 cases
Upbringing (white): fermentation of 15 days to 3 weeks in stainless steel vats and bottling
      after 4–5 months
      (red): fermentation of 8 days in stainless steel vats followed by 6 months in tank;
      there is both fining and filtration
Average age of vines (white): 12 years
      (red): 25 years
Blend (white): 75% Marsanne and Roussanne, 25% Grenache Blanc and Clairette
      (red): 50% Grenache, 50% Syrah
Note: In top vintages—1989, 1990, and 1995—a 100% Syrah Cuvée Clos l'Ecu is produced with the same upbringing as the red Côtes du Rhône.

In 1958, Marcel Ryckwaert immigrated from Algeria and founded this estate of nearly 72 acres in the tiny village of Mornas, along Route Nationale 7, north of Orange and south of Bollène. It offers a convenient place to stop and taste wines on the way to the superb restaurant La Beaugravière in nearby Mondragon. Brothers Marc and Yves Ryckwaert have built this estate into one of the top producers of red Côtes du Rhône, and have increasingly improved the quality of the dry white, which is now an intriguing blend of Marsanne, Roussanne, Grenache Blanc, and Clairette. The red wine is a supple, deliciously fruity, pure Côtes du Rhône, with plenty of black cassis character, no doubt because of the 50% Syrah utilized in the blend, along with 50% Grenache. It is usually low in acidity, yet capable of lasting for 5–7 years. In top vintages there are also small quantities of a 100% Syrah cuvée called Clos l'Ecu, an impressive, high-class wine characterized by smoke, tar, and cassis scents and flavors.

DOMAINE DE LA GUICHARD (VAUCLUSE)* * * *

Address: 84430 Mondragon
Tel: 4-90-30-17-84
Fax: 4-90-40-05-69
Wines produced: Côtes du Rhône (white), Côtes du Rhône Cuvée Genet (red)
Surface area (white): 8.6 acres
       (red): Cuvée Genet—25 acres
Production (white): 1,375 cases
       (red): Cuvée Genet—2,500 cases
Upbringing (white): 3–6 months in cement vats, with malolactic stopped
       (red): Cuvée Genet—Fermentation of 7–9 days followed by 5–12 months in
           cement vats. The grapes are destemmed.
Average age of vines (white): 30 years
       (red): Cuvée Genet—30 years
Blend (white): 100% Grenache Blanc
       (red): Cuvée Genet—80% Grenache, 20% Syrah

Proprietor Armand Guichard has burst on the scene with deliciously fruity, ripe, round, generous red Côtes du Rhône made from 80% Grenache and 20% Syrah. Although I have never tasted Guichard's white wine, the red wine, particularly the cuvée bottled unfiltered especially for the American importer, is a generous, well-endowed Côtes du Rhône that is meant to be drunk within 4–6 years of the vintage. It is deeply colored, with a peppery, spicy, richly fruity nose, and fine body, especially in top years such as 1990 and 1995.

GUIGAL (NÉGOCIANT)* * * *

Address: 1, route de Taquières or Château d'Ampuis
       69420 Ampuis
Tel: 4-74-56-10-22
Fax: 4-74-56-18-76
Wines produced: Côtes du Rhône (red and white)
Production (white): 17,000 cases
       (red): 70,000 cases
Upbringing (white): Fermentation at low temperatures followed by 8 months in stainless
           steel vats. There is slight fining and filtration.
       (red): Fermentation of 15–21 days followed by 1 year in oak casks. All the
           Mourvèdre and some of the Syrah and Grenache are destemmed. There
           is no fining or filtration.
Blend (white): approximately 30% Bourboulenc, 25% Roussanne, 18–20% Viognier, 10%
       Grenache Blanc and 10% Clairette is the desired blend

(red): approximately 50% Grenache, 25% Mourvèdre, 25% Syrah, with small quantities of other varietals

Note: These wines are blends from purchased juice, not grapes, aged in Guigal's cellars in Ampuis.

Additional information on the Guigal firm can be found in the chapter on Côte Rôtie. Perhaps the best introduction to the marvelous winemaking and upbringing abilities of Guigal are his Côtes du Rhônes. These wines, which represent the largest production of this renowned négociant and vineyard owner, are among the best wine values in France. Guigal has increasingly improved his white Côtes du Rhône, which used to be a bland, innocuous wine. It is now fresh, lively, and perfumed, and wins high marks from both critics and consumers. The blend incorporates approximately 18–20% Viognier, 25% Roussanne, and the rest the standard old-style varietals from the southern Rhône—Bourboulenc, Grenache Blanc, and Clairette. Bottled early to preserve its freshness, it is a perfumed, dry, medium-bodied, delicious white wine to drink within 1–2 years of the vintage.

Guigal's red Côtes du Rhône has always been a deeply colored, spicy, structured, Syrah- and Mourvèdre-dominated wine. Made from a blend of 25% Syrah, 25% Mourvèdre, and 50% Grenache, it is a mouth-filling, high-quality Côtes du Rhône that in top vintages (1989, 1990, 1995) can drink well for 7–8 years. Otherwise, it should be drunk within 3–4 years of the vintage. These are reliable wines that are also reasonably priced.

JEAN-MARIE LOMBARD (DRÔME)* * * *

Address: Quartier Piquet
　　　　 26250 Livron
Tel: 4-75-61-64-90
Wines produced: Côtes du Rhône (white), Côtes du Rhône Cuvée du Grand Chêne (red),
　　　　 Côtes du Rhône Cuvée Eugène de Monicault (red)
Surface area (white): 1.5 acres
　　　　 (red): Cuvée du Grand Chêne—6.2 acres
　　　　　　 Cuvée Eugène de Monicault—3.7 acres
Production (white): 150 cases
　　　　 (red): Cuvée du Grand Chêne—1,375 cases
　　　　　　 Cuvée Eugène de Monicault—812 cases
Upbringing (white): Fermentation in 2-year-old oak barrels; the wines remain on their lees
　　　　 for 6 months before bottling; malolactic is not stopped.
　　　　 (red): Cuvée du Grand Chêne—20 months total; fermentation of 12 days in
　　　　　　 cement tanks, followed by 12–14 months in old oak casks. At times a
　　　　　　 light fining and filtration are done.
　　　　　　 Cuvée Eugène de Monicault—Fermentation of 15 days in cement vats,
　　　　　　 where malolactic also occurs, followed by 14 months in 2-year-old oak
　　　　　　 barrels.
Average age of vines (white): 5–6 years
　　　　　　 (red): Cuvée du Grand Chêne—15 years
　　　　　　　　 Cuvée Eugène de Monicault—22 years
Blend (white): 75% Marsanne, 25% Viognier
　　　 (red): Cuvée du Grand Chêne—100% Syrah
　　　　　　 Cuvée Eugène de Monicault—100% Syrah

In a game of Trivial Wine Pursuit, the estate of Jean-Marie Lombard would make one of the more interesting and challenging subjects. This tiny appellation, neither a Côtes du Rhône-Villages nor Côtes du Rhône, but simply Brézème-Côtes du Rhône, was created in

1974. The 11-acre Lombard estate produces a tiny quantity of white wine, from an intriguing blend of 75% Marsanne and 25% Viognier that is rich and full, but perhaps too heavy for most modern-day palates.

The real glories of Lombard are his two cuvées of 100% Syrah (a distinctive component of wines from this northerly region of the Côtes du Rhône only 12 miles from Valence). In truth, these wines have more in common with Cornas and Hermitage than with anything produced in the south. Lombard spares nothing when turning out these dense, dark-colored, intense wines. The Cuvée du Grand Chêne, made from a 15-year-old vineyard, is kept in old wood casks for 12–14 months, and is bottled with very little processing. The top cuvée, the Eugène de Monicault, is 100% Syrah from 22-year-old vines. My experience has shown that these wines have a tendency, especially during the decade of the eighties, to display the vegetal side of Syrah. In very ripe years, that characteristic is less apparent. Moreover, about five years ago Lombard began to destem his Syrah, aiming for wines with less herbaceousness and a more civilized tannin level.

These are serious, muscular, ambitious wines that are likely to please fans of gutsy Syrah more than those looking for the easy-to-drink, lusty Provençal style of the southern Côtes du Rhône. In top vintages, such as 1990, the red wines can keep for a decade, but in most years, in spite of the tannin level, Jean-Marie Lombard's wines should be drunk within 5–7 years of the vintage.

CHÂTEAU MALIJAY (VAUCLUSE)* */* * *

Address: 84150 Jonquières
Tel: 4-90-70-33-44
Fax: 4-90-70-36-07
Wines produced: Côtes du Rhône (red and white)
Surface area (white): 2.47 acres
　　　　　　　(red): 2,470 acres
Production (white): 400 cases
　　　　　　　(red): 45,000 cases
Upbringing (white): Fermentation of 1 month in refrigerated tanks with bottling after 6
　　　　　　　months. Malolactic is stopped, and there is a slight fining and filtration.
　　　　　　　(red): a modern vinification with early bottling, fining, and filtration
Average age of vines (white): 20 years
　　　　　　　(red): 35 years
Blend (white): 70% Grenache Blanc, 30% Viognier
　　　　　　　(red): 50% Grenache, 30% Syrah, 2–3% Mourvèdre, and the rest other varietals

This lavish château, reconstructed on the site of the original eleventh-century castle that stood on the property, produces an enormous quantity of highly commercial, soft, fruity red wine, and small quantities of a bland white. The red Côtes du Rhône is pleasant, but one-dimensional. However, the property and château, only a five-mile drive east of Orange, near the well-known Vaucluse Côtes du Rhône village of Jonquières, are noteworthy tourist attractions. Run by the Baron de Malijay, the property exports its wines to almost every civilized country in the world, reflecting the huge commercial success of this straightforward wine. Everything here is immaculately clean, state of the art, and well run under administrator Henri Chavernac. However, do not expect a great deal of complexity, as nothing is produced at Château Malijay without being intensely sterile-filtered.

DOMAINE MITAN (VAUCLUSE)* * *

Address: Rue du Felibrige
84270 Védène
Tel: 4-90-31-07-12
Wines produced: Côtes du Rhône (red)
Surface area: 15 acres
Production: 2,800 cases
Upbringing: 2 years total. Fermentation of 1 week in cement vats; storage in tanks and demi-muids for 12 months. There is no fining, but there is a light filtration.
Average age of vines: 30 years
Blend: 60% Grenache, 20% Syrah, 10% Cinsault, 10% Mourvèdre

This low-profile, underrated estate produces traditional, full-flavored, muscular Côtes du Rhône. The wines are mouth-filling, cleanly made, and meant to last for 5–8 years. Unfortunately, the estate is small, but proprietor Frédéric Mitan is a serious vigneron.

DOMAINE DES MOULINS (GEORGES DUBOEUF) (GARD)* * */* * * *

Address: 75150 Romanèche-Thorins
Tel: 4-85-35-34-20
Fax: 4-85-35-34-25
Wines produced: Côtes du Rhône (red)
Surface area: 49 acres
Production: 10,000 cases
Upbringing: 100% destemming; vinification in temperature-controlled stainless steel tanks, followed by 6 months in tanks before bottling
Average age of vines: 30 years
Blend: 40% Grenache, 20% each Cinsault, Mourvèdre, and Syrah

The Domaine des Moulins is Duboeuf's most full-bodied, rich, and deeply extracted Côtes du Rhône. It is a chewy, fleshy, supple red wine meant to be drunk within 2–4 years of the vintage.

DOMAINE DE LA PRÉSIDENTE (VAUCLUSE)* * *

Address: 84290 Ste.-Cécile-les-Vignes
Tel: 4-90-30-80-34
Fax: 4-90-30-72-77
Wines produced: Côtes du Rhône Domaine de la Présidente (red), Côtes du Rhône Cuvée 20 (red)
Surface area (Domaine de la Présidente): 62 acres
(Cuvée 20): 12.4 acres
Production (Domaine de la Présidente): 9,000 cases
(Cuvée 20): 700–800 cases
Upbringing (Domaine de la Présidente): fermentation of 12 days in stainless steel vats, followed by 12 months aging in tank; there is destemming
(Cuvée 20): The Syrah receives carbonic maceration for 16 days and the other varietals receive a traditional fermentation for 12–15 days, followed by 2 years in stainless steel tanks. This cuvée is produced only in top vintages.
Average age of vines (Domaine de la Présidente): 25 years
(Cuvée 20): 35 years

Blend (Domaine de la Présidente): 70% Grenache, 20% Syrah, 10% Carignan
(Cuvée 20): 50% Syrah, 40% Grenache, 10% Carignan

Max Aubert produces both a high-quality Châteauneuf du Pape (see that chapter), as well as a very good Cairanne, but the bulk of his production is in Côtes du Rhône. There are two cuvées, the Domaine de la Présidente, which is a solid, rustic wine, and his Cuvée 20, previously called Cuvée Goutillonné. This is an attractive, fleshy, full-flavored Côtes du Rhône that benefits from the carbonic maceration given the Syrah, which represents 50% of the blend. It is produced only in the best vintages. The most recent vintage I tasted was the excellent 1990.

DOMAINE DE LA RÉMÉJEANNE (GARD)* * * *

Address: Cadignac
      30200 Sabran
Tel: 4-66-89-44-51
Fax: 4-66-89-64-22
Wines produced: Côtes du Rhône Les Arbousiers (white), Vin de Pays du Gard Les Genevrières (white), Côtes du Rhône Les Arbousiers (red), Côtes du Rhône Les Chevrefeuilles (red), Côtes du Rhône Les Eglantiers (100% Syrah) (red)
Surface area: 67 acres
Production: 6,000 cases
Upbringing: aging takes place in tank, foudre and smaller barrels, depending on the cuve of wine
Average age of vines: 20–40 years
Blend (white): 60% Clairette, 20% Roussanne, 10% Marsanne, 10% Ugni Blanc
    (red): 40% Grenache, 20% Syrah, 15% Carignan, 14% Cinsault, 10% Counoise, 1% Mourvèdre

Rémy Klein and his wife, Ouahi, who took over the family estate in 1988, can take credit for developing it into one of the finest and most consistent Côtes du Rhône vineyards. The red wines are delicious, and in an area not known for top-flight white wines, the Domaine de la Réméjeanne's whites are increasingly well made. This highly morsellated property situated in the Gard, not far from Bagnols-sur-Cèze, has a cooler than usual terroir, and thus favors Syrah.

The white wines, which exhibit wonderful fresh fruit as well as a honeyed, buttery character (no doubt because of the Roussanne in the blend) are among the finest of the southern Rhône Valley.

As fine as they are, the white wines are surpassed by the delicious bevy of red wine cuvées, which are made partially by carbonic maceration and part by classical vinification techniques. The red wine cuvées include a Côtes du Rhône Les Chevrefeuilles, a lighter, Burgundy-styled wine with cherry fruit; the Côtes du Rhône Les Arbousiers; a textbook, Provençal herb–scented, smoky, black-cherry-flavored, fleshy Côtes du Rhône Les Genevrières; and a 100% Syrah, the Côtes du Rhône Les Eglantiers, a fleshy, thick, juicy, opaque-colored wine bursting with Syrah fruit.

The white wines need to be drunk within 1–2 years of the vintage, and the red wine cuvées, except for Les Eglantiers, within 4–5 years of the vintage. In vintages such as 1995 and 1990, Les Eglantiers can last up to a decade. This is an impeccably run estate turning out delicious, modern-style wines filled with personality and pleasure.

CHÂTEAU ST.-ESTÈVE D'UCHAUX (VAUCLUSE)* * *

Address: Route de Sérignan
        84100 Uchaux
Tel: 4-90-19-19-44
Fax: 4-90-40-63-49
Wines produced: Côtes du Rhône Château St.-Estève (white), Côtes du Rhône Viognier
        (white), Côtes du Rhône Cuvée Friande (red), Côtes du Rhône Cuvée
        Tradition (red), Côtes du Rhône-Villages Grande Réserve (red), Côtes du
        Rhône-Villages Vieilles Vignes (red)
Surface area (white): St.-Estève—14.8 acres
        Viognier—14.8 acres
    (red): Cuvée Friande—19.8 acres
        Cuvée Tradition—62 acres
        Grande Réserve—12.4 acres
        Vieilles Vignes—10 acres
Production (white): St.-Estève—3,750 cases
        Viognier—1,200 cases
    (red): Cuvée Friande—5,000 cases
        Cuvée Tradition—15,000 cases
        Grande Réserve—2,500 cases
        Vieilles Vignes—1,625 cases
Upbringing (white): St.-Estève—Fermentation of 15 days in temperature-controlled stain-
        less steel vats; malolactic is stopped by cold and the addition of sulfites.
        Fining and filtration are done. Bottling is done after 6–8 months.
        Viognier—Same as for the St.-Estève cuvée.
    (red): Cuvée Friande—Fermentation of 7 days in stainless steel and cement
        tanks, where the wines remains for 6–12 months. There is a fining and a
        filtration.
        Cuvée Tradition—Same as the Cuvée Friande except the fermentation
        lasts 8–10 days.
        Grande Réserve—Same as the Cuvée Friande except the fermentation
        lasts 10–15 days.
        Vieilles Vignes—Fermentation of 10–15 days in cement and stainless
        steel vats, then 30% of the yield is transferred to 3-year-old oak barrels
        for 1 year. There is no fining and only a slight filtration.
Average age of vines (white): St.-Estève—15 and 30 years
        Viognier—13 years
    (red): Cuvée Friande—15–20 years
        Cuvée Tradition—20–25 years
        Grande Réserve—25 years
        Vieilles Vignes—30–35 years
Blend (white): St.-Estève—60% Grenache Blanc, 30% Roussanne, 10% other varietals
        Viognier—100% Viognier
    (red): Cuvée Friande—50% Grenache, 50% Cinsault
        Cuvée Tradition—80% Grenache, 20% Syrah
        Grande Réserve—60% Grenache, 40% Syrah
        Vieilles Vignes—60% Syrah, 40% Grenache

Just north of the old Roman city of Orange is the huge estate of Château St.-Estève d'Uchaux. Owned by the Français family, this estate is run with considerable care by Marc Français. It is a textbook, modern, well-equipped, impeccably clean winemaking facility that has more in common with a new world winery than with some of the old, rustic cellars in the Rhône Valley. From machine harvesting, centrifuges, temperature-controlled stainless steel tanks, and sterile filtration, this estate turns out clean, correct, fruity whites and reds that offer ideal drinking in their first two to four years of life.

The Côtes du Rhône Viognier, which is made from relatively young vines, is a good rather than exciting Viognier.

The red wines range from the light, fruity Cuvée Tradition and Cuvée Friande to the more substantial Côtes du Rhône-Villages Grande Réserve (60% Grenache and 40% Syrah), and the Côtes du Rhône-Villages Vieilles Vignes (60% Syrah, 40% Grenache). The latter wine, which represents the estate's smallest red wine production, is head and shoulders above the other Château St.-Estève cuvées. It is a more intense wine that sees some aging in oak casks, and is bottled with less processing.

These are reliable, consistently well-made red and white Côtes du Rhônes that are not likely to disappoint, but neither are they likely to provide the "thrill a sip" joys of a Domaine Gramenon, Château de Fonsalette, or Coudoulet de Beaucastel.

TARDIEU-LAURENT (NÉGOCIANT)* * * *

Address: Chemin de la Marquette
       84360 Lauris
Tel: 4-90-08-32-07
Fax: 4-90-08-26-57

This négociant operation, run by Michel Tardieu and Dominique Laurent, is dedicated to producing concentrated wines that are bottled with minimal intervention, and extremely low levels of SO_2. The first two vintages of Côtes de Rhône-Cuvée Guy Louis certainly suggest that this is a four-star producer. These wines, aged in small oak casks, of which 50% were new in 1995, contain at least 50% Grenache, as well as copious quantities of Syrah (for example, 40% in 1995), along with some Mourvèdre. They are deep purple-colored, chewy, multilayered Côtes de Rhônes to drink in their first 5–8 years of life. This is an impressive newcomer to the Côtes de Rhône sweepstakes.

CHÂTEAU DES TOURS (VAUCLUSE)* * * *

Address: Quartier des Sablons
       84260 Sarrians
Tel: 4-90-65-41-75
Wines produced: Côtes du Rhône (white and red), Vin du Pays de Vaucluse (red)
Surface area (white): 3.7 acres
       (red): 25 acres
       Vin du Pays de Vaucluse—25 acres
Production (white): 812 cases
       (red): 6,250 cases
       Vin du Pays de Vaucluse—6,250 cases
Upbringing (white): fermentation of 8–10 days in stainless steel tanks; bottling after 2 years; malolactic is allowed to occur
       (red): fermentation of 8–10 days in stainless steel tanks followed by 18 months in cement vats, with a small percentage of the yield aged in oak casks
       Vin du Pays de Vaucluse—the same upbringing as for the red Côtes du Rhône
Average age of vines (white): 15 and 50 years
       (red): 45 years
       Vin du Pays de Vaucluse—15 and 50 years

Blend (white): 80% Grenache Blanc, 20% Clairette
(red): 40% Grenache, 40% Cinsault, 20% Syrah
Vin du Pays de Vaucluse—40% Grenache, 35% Cinsault, 25% Syrah

Château des Tours is also covered in the chapter on Vacqueyras. This estate is owned by Emmanuel Reynaud, the nephew of Châteauneuf du Pape's recently deceased Jacques Reynaud. It is a property to watch carefully as very high-quality wines are emerging under all appellations. The white wine is slightly funky and unusual, but the red wine cuvées are full-flavored, spicy, peppery wines with a lot of character and intensity. The Côtes du Rhône, a blend of 40% Grenache, 40% old-vine Cinsault, and 20% Syrah, is a scaled-down version of the great Fonsalette. Even the Vin du Pays de Vaucluse is an intriguing, surprisingly rich, intense wine that sells for a song. These Côtes du Rhônes are not made in the light, fruity, commercial style, but rather in a full-bodied, powerful, highly extracted manner that gives them the ability to age for 7–10 years. This is a very serious producer.

DOMAINE DU VIEUX CHÊNE (VAUCLUSE)* * * *
Address: Rue Buisseron
Route de Vaison-la-Romaine
84850 Camaret
Tel: 4-90-37-25-07
Fax: 4-90-37-76-84
Wines produced: Côtes du Rhône-Villages (white), Côtes du Rhône (red), Côtes du Rhône Cuvée des Capucines (red), Côtes du Rhône Aux Haie des Grives (red), Vin de Pays Vaucluse (red)
Surface area (white): Côtes du Rhône-Villages—2.47 acres
(red): Côtes du Rhône (all cuvées)—60 acres
Vin de Pays Vaucluse—37 acres
Production (white): Côtes du Rhône-Villages—375 cases
(red): Côtes du Rhône (all cuvées)—8,000 cases
Upbringing (white): Côtes du Rhône-Villages—fermentation of 3 weeks in stainless steel vats at low temperatures; malolactic is allowed to occur; bottling after 6 months
(red): Côtes du Rhône (all cuvées)—Fermentation of 20 days in cement tanks, followed by 10 months' storage in cement vats. There is no destemming, but there are both fining and filtration.
Average age of vines (white): Côtes du Rhône-Villages—50 years
(red): (all cuvées) Côtes du Rhône—40 years
Blend (white): Côtes du Rhône-Villages—40% Picpoul, 20% Viognier, 20% Roussanne, 20% Clairette
(red): Côtes du Rhône (all cuvées)—80% Grenache, 20% Syrah
Cuvée des Capucines—90% Grenache, 10% Syrah
Aux Haie des Grives—60% Grenache, 40% Syrah
Vin de Pays Vaucluse—80% Grenache, 10% Syrah, 10% Muscardin and Carignan

This has been a popular Côtes du Rhône estate that consistently turns out enjoyable, fleshy, purely made red wines and, recently, a tiny quantity of white wine. Brothers Jean-Claude and Dominique Bouché, aided by Madame Béatrice Bouché, broke away from the local coop at Sérignan and began estate-bottling in the late seventies.

Four cuvées of red wine emerge from Vieux Chêne: Côtes du Rhône, Côtes du Rhône

Cuvée des Capucines, Côtes du Rhône Aux Haie des Grives, and Vin de Pays Vaucluse. In general, the red wines are heavily Grenache-based since the total vineyard area is planted with 85% Grenache and 15% Syrah. These wines are consistently well made, with the Cuvée des Capucines the lighter cuvée, and the Haie des Grives more Syrah dominated, as well as richer, fuller, and heavier.

The white wines have improved immensely over recent years, particularly with the new plantations of Viognier and Roussanne coming into production. Traditionally the wine was made from equal parts Picpoul and Roussanne, but it is moving toward a blend of Viognier, Picpoul, Roussanne, and Clairette.

Vieux Chêne's winemaking is completely traditional, yet the wines reflect a progressive mentality, with emphasis on purity and forward, supple, rich fruit. In top vintages, such as 1989, 1990, 1994, and 1995, the red wines are best drunk within 5–6 years of the vintage. The whites require drinking within 12–18 months.

OTHER RECOMMENDED CÔTES DU RHÔNE WINES
(Listed in alphabetical order)

Note: Those marked with an asterisk are more consistently superior.

Château d'Aigueville (Uchaux)
Domaine de l'Amandier (Carmes)*
Paul Autard (Châteauneuf du Pape)
Domaine de Beaurenard (Châteauneuf du Pape)*
Domaine la Berthet (Camaret)
Château la Borie (Suze-la-Rousse)
Château de Boussargues (Colombier)
Cave Jaume (Vinsobres)
Domaine de la Chapelle (Châteauneuf-de-Gadagne)
Gérard Charvin (Châteauneuf du Pape)*
Auguste Clape (Cornas)*
Clos du Caillou (Courthézon)
Domaine de Cocol (Donnat)
Domaine de l'Enclos (Courthézon)*
Château de l'Estagnol (Suze-la-Rousse)
Château de Farel (Comps)
Domaine les Goubert (Gigondas)
Château Gourdon (Bollène)
Château du Grand Prébois (Courthézon)*
Domaine Grand Veneur (Châteauneuf du Pape)*
Paul Jaboulet-Ainé (Côtes du Rhône Parallel 45) (Tain l'Hermitage)*
Domaine de la Janasse (Côtes du Rhône) (Châteauneuf du Pape)*

Domaine de la Janasse (Côtes du Rhône Les Garrigues) (Châteauneuf du Pape)*
Domaine Martin (Travaillan)
Domaine A. Mazurd et Fils (Tulette)
Domaine de Mont Redon (Châteauneuf du Pape)
Domaine de la Mordorée (Lirac)*
Domaine de Perillière (Loumarin)*
Domaine Piredon (Loumarin)
Domaine de la Renjarde (Sérignan)*
Domaine des Richards (Violès)
Domaine St.-Gayan (Vacqueyras)
Domaine St.-Pierre (Violès)
Domaine Ste.-Apollinaire (Puyneras)
Santa Duc (Gigondas)*
Domaine la Taurelle (Mirabel-aux-Baronnies)
Domaine des Trielles (Montbris-sur-Lez)
Château du Trignon (Gigondas)
Vidal-Fleury (Ampuis)*
La Vieille Ferme (Perrin Réserve) (Orange)*
Domaine de la Vieille Julienne (Châteauneuf du Pape)
Vignobles de la Jasse (Violès)
La Vignonnerie Plan Dei (Travaillan)

ESOTERIC
RHÔNE WINES

Clairette de Die, Côtes du Vivarais,
Coteaux du Tricastin, Côtes du Ventoux,
Costières de Nîmes

CLAIRETTE DE DIE AT A GLANCE

Types of wine produced:	Dry and sweet white sparkling wine, and dry still white wine.
Grape varieties planted:	Muscat and Clairette.
Acres currently under vine:	2,950.
Quality level:	Mediocre to good.
Aging potential:	1–4 years.
General characteristics:	The best sparkling wines, because of the high quality of Muscat in the blend, can be fragrant and tasty; most, however, are bland.
Price range:	$15–$20.
Best producers:	Claude Achard, Achard-Vincent, Buffardel Frères, Henri Grangeron, Georges Poulet, Pierre Salabelle, and Jean-Claude Vincent.

Few wine enthusiasts seem to claim any experience or even knowledge of Clairette de Die, an area that has been making sparkling wine longer than Champagne. There are historical references to the wine of this region as far back as A.D. 77, but it is not an easy area with which to become familiar.

The Die vineyards, an appendage of the main Rhône viticultural district, are isolated in the mountain countryside east of Valence, over 40 miles of labyrinthine roads. It can take half a day to traverse these switchback-laden roads. As one begins to encounter more and more forbidding mountains, a patchwork carpet of vines and walnut tree orchards announces to the visitor that Clairette de Die, the least-known Rhône wine appellation, has been reached. There are three types of white wine made here. The still wine, usually a rather bland, innocuous drink, is made from 100% Clairette. The second type of wine is a sparkling wine simply called Clairette de Die Brut. It must be made from 100% Clairette also, and it, too, is a bit dull. The best wine of this appellation is the Clairette de Die Tradition, a sparkling wine made from a blend of Muscat (usually 50–75%) and Clairette. The Clairette de Die Tradition is an exuberant, delightful wine that has a particularly perfumed character to its bouquet. It comes in both the dry brut style or the sweeter demi-sec style. Given its broad commercial appeal, I am surprised that the wine has not become better known.

Among the growers, the sparkling Clairette de Die of **Claude Achard, Achard-Vincent, Buffardel Frères, Henri Grangeron, Georges Poulet, Pierre Salabelle,** and **Jean-Claude Vincent,** especially their cuvées of Tradition with their high percentage of Muscat grapes, offer surprisingly good drinking.

CÔTES DU VIVARAIS AT A GLANCE

Type of wine produced:	Red, white, and rosé.
Grape varieties planted:	Both vinifera and hybrid grapes, but largely Grenache, Syrah, Cinsault, Mourvèdre, Picpoul, Chardonnay, Cabernet Sauvignon, Merlot, and Viognier.
Acres currently under vine:	2,200 acres (of a potential vineyard area of 20,000 acres).
Quality level:	Poor to pleasant.
Aging potential:	1–3 years.
General characteristics:	Cheap, light-bodied, generally well-made, fruity white and red wines.
Price range:	$6–$10.
Best producers:	Domaine Belvezet, Hervé Boullé, Domaine Gallety, Louis Latour's Chardonnay l'Ardèche, Domaine de Vigier, Caves Coopératives Vignerons de St.-Montan.

On the right or western bank of the Rhône, between the noisy little half-horse town of Viviers in the north and Pont St.-Esprit to the south, is the emerging viticultural region of the Côtes de Vivarais.

More than two decades ago my wife and I spent a week in this area, enjoying its primitive wilderness and splendid landscape studded with gorges. Until recently, this remained a region largely known for dull, inexpensive white, red, and rosé wine. My experience with the white and rosé wines has been disappointing, although the huge Burgundian négociant Louis Latour has consistently produced a very good Chardonnay that is priced under $10 a bottle. The red wines are more interesting, as well as inexpensive. They are made in a light-bodied, fruity style that is meant to be consumed within three to four years of the vintage. To date, the best red wines have come from the **Domaine de Belvezet** and **Domaine Gallety.**

Aside from these two domaines, virtually the entire production of Côtes du Vivarais is dominated by large cooperatives that produce numerous cuvées sold under brand names by both négociants and specialty importers.

COTEAUX DU TRICASTIN AT A GLANCE

Types of wine produced:	Red wine (95%); some white and rosé are also produced.
Grape varieties planted	(Red wine): Grenache, Cinsault, Mourvèdre, Syrah, Picpoul, Carignan.
	(White wine): Grenache Blanc, Clairette, Picpoul Blanc, Bourboulenc, Ugni Blanc.
Acres currently under vine:	5,500.
Quality level:	Mediocre to very good for the red wines.
Aging potential:	1–4 years.
General characteristics:	The white wine is heavy; the rosé fruity and decent; the red wine richly scented, supple, and potentially very good, but it must be drunk young.
Price range:	$8–$12.
Best producers:	Château la Decelle, Château Guery, Château des Estubiers, Domaine de Grangeneuve, Domaine de l'Orgeat, Domaine de Rieu-Frais, Domaine St.-Luc, Domaine du Serre Rouge, Domaine de la Tour d'Elyssas.

Tricastin is the fastest-growing viticultural region of the Rhône Valley. Thirty-five years ago this area, beaten by the mistral wind more severely than the rest of the southern Rhône, was known only for its barren, moonlike landscape and late fall and early winter truffle harvest. Following the French relinquishment of autonomy over Algeria and Tunisia, and to a lesser extent, Morocco, many French natives of these countries, uncertain of their future in these newly independent former French possessions, came to the southern Rhône and began to establish vineyards. Many of them settled in Tricastin, and in the last three decades have elevated this vast area from a vin de pays to a VDQS, and finally to a full-fledged appellation contrôlée wine.

The Tricastin viticultural area is located between Bollène and Montélimar, and takes its name from a tribe of warriors called the Tricastin, who battled unsuccessfully with the Romans during their conquest of Gaul. As mentioned, the area is famous for its black truffles as well as tomato, melon, and asparagus crops.

The producers have wisely not attempted to compete with nearby Châteauneuf du Pape and Gigondas, and aim for large-scaled, full-bodied wines of power and depth. The style of red wine that has emerged from Tricastin is one in which the intense, supple aromas and flavors of strawberry and cherry fruit are emphasized. These are deliciously round, fresh wines that might well become the Rhône Valley's alternative to the hedonistic appeal offered by the wines of Beaujolais.

One of the most interesting developments in Tricastin over recent vintages is the movement by a handful of growers to break away from the appellation system and offer single-varietal wines with such internationally recognized superstar grapes as Chardonnay, Cabernet Sauvignon, Syrah, and Viognier. The reason is simple. Historically, Tricastin fetches very low prices and growers need to increase cash flow in order to maintain their vineyards. Therefore, increasing numbers of growers think that producing varietal-named wines, so much a part of wine commerce in the new world (California, Australia, South America, etc.), is the way to increase sales and profits.

In spite of what may be a new direction in how the wines of Tricastin are presented in the international marketplace, the finest Tricastin red wine continues to be made at the **Domaine de la Tour d'Elyssas**, which was run with great visionary zeal by the late Pierre LaBeye. This estate has 346 acres and produces two vineyard-designated Tricastins called

Le Devroy and Les Echirousses. There is also a 100% Syrah cuvée that is even deeper and more concentrated, but still in full possession of its wonderful fruitiness and supple, generous texture. Domaine de la Tour d'Elyssas's rosé is also the best of the appellation.

The other well-known Tricastin estate is the **Domaine de Grangeneuve.** Run by Odette and Henri Bours and her lovely daughter, this property of 247 acres produces a very fruity, soft, easy-to-drink, understated wine that offers immediate gratification. The finest two red wine cuvées are the Cuvée Speciale and the even richer Cuvée de la Truffière (a 100% Syrah aged 12 months in new oak). The latter wine may be the finest wine made in Tricastin. A decent, dry fruity rosé is also made.

Another top grower in Tricastin is **Château des Estubiers.** A 227-acre property run by Hector Roth and Léopold Morel, Estubiers applies the same winemaking philosophy as the other domaines mentioned above. It eschews wood aging and bottles its wines early to preserve all of their fruit and charm. Their vineyards are planted with 55% Grenache, 18% Syrah, 9% Mourvèdre, 9% Cinsault, and 9% Carignan.

CÔTES DU VENTOUX AT A GLANCE

Type of wine produced:	Light, fruity red, white, and rosé.
Grape varieties planted:	Primarily Grenache, Carignan, Cinsault, and Syrah for the red wine; Clairette and Bourboulenc for the white wine.
Acres currently under vine:	17,500.
Quality level:	Good.
Aging potential:	1–3 years.
General characteristics:	Soft, light, fruity wines meant for very early consumption.
Price range:	$6–$10.
Best producers:	Domaine des Anges, Domaine de Champaga, Domaine Fondrèche, Paul Jaboulet-Ainé, Château Pésquié, Domaine Ste.-Sauveur, Château de Valcombe, Domaine de la Verrière, Vidal-Fleury, La Vieille Ferme.

This giant appellation has just over 17,500 acres of vineyard spread out over an enormous area, with the majority of the vineyards situated on Mont Ventoux. This is one of the most gorgeous areas of Provence, with nearly 4,000 growers producing wine from a region extending from Vaison-la-Romaine in the north, south through Carpentras to L'Isle-sur-la-Sorgue, all in the shadow of the Ventoux mountain range that forms the scenic backdrop for these vineyards. The region's 16 cooperatives account for 90% of the production. The good news is that the reference point firm of **La Vieille Ferme**, run by Jean-Pierre Perrin, that has dominated quality wine production in the Côtes du Ventoux for over two decades, is now being joined by a handful of other estates making top-class Côtes du Ventoux that sells for a song. The best wines now being made in this region come from Englishman Malcolm Swan, whose 45-acre estate at Mormoiron is called **Domaine des Anges.** Swan's offerings include round, fruity, carbonic maceration red wines, as well as intense, concentrated cuvées that can age for 10 years. The terrific 1990s from Domaine des Anges possessed a decade's worth of aging potential.

Other estates that have produced high-quality wine include Gildas D'Ollone's **Domaine des Champaga.** This estate, run by the D'Ollone family (Gildas is the administrator at Château Pichon Longueville Comtesse de Lalande in Pauillac), is producing deliciously fruity, round, soft, velvety-textured wines of very high quality. Other promising wines have emerged from **Domaine de la Verrière, Domaine Ste.-Sauveur,** and the excellent selections made by the two northern Rhône negociants, **Paul Jaboulet-Aîné** and **Vidal-Fleury.**

There is considerable diversity in style of the Côtes du Ventoux wines, although the great majority are fruity, soft, refreshing wines to be drunk within two to three years of the vintage. However, Domaine des Anges and La Vieille Ferme produce cuvées that can handle significantly more aging. One of the interesting trends in Côtes du Ventoux has been to incorporate more Syrah in the blend, recognizing that Grenache and Cinsault grown in this area tend to oxidize very quickly.

The Côtes du Ventoux is a treasure trove for fine values, particularly from the estates mentioned above.

COSTIÈRES DE NÎMES AT A GLANCE

Type of wine produced:	Increasingly high-quality, delicious, midweight reds, crisp, fragrant whites, and a small amount of rosé.
Grape varieties planted:	Grenache, Mourvèdre, Syrah, Cinsault, Carignan for the reds, and Clairette, Grenache Blanc, Bourboulenc, Ugni Blanc, Marsanne, Roussanne, Maccabeo, and Rolle for the whites.
Acres currently under vine:	24,700.
Quality level:	Good and getting better.
Aging potential:	1–3 years for the whites; 2–6 years or more for the reds.
General characteristics:	The white wines are crisp, fragrant, vibrant, and delicious; the red wines vary from light-bodied, fruity wines to those with more substantial concentration and flavor.
Price range:	$8–$15.
Best producers:	Château Beaubois, Château de Campuget, Mas des Bressades, Château Mas Neuf, Mourgues du Grès, Château de Nages, Château de la Tuilerie.

Costières de Nîmes, situated in a sun-drenched, windswept area that was once a Roman outpost, as evidenced by the ancient Roman cities of Nîmes and Arles, the two leading tourist attractions of this region, is unquestionably an up-and-coming appellation. The wines quickly moved from vin de pays to VDQS to a full appellation contrôlée area in 1986. In 1989, it was given permission to change its name from Costières du Gard to Costières de Nîmes. It is now considered to be part of the Rhône Valley, although the producers essentially think of themselves as a totally different region, sandwiched between the Rhône Valley to the north and the Languedoc-Roussillon to the south.

This is one of the most exciting viticultural areas in France, largely because of the efforts of some young, visionary producers who are turning out excellent high-quality wines that are remarkably undervalued, something readers should put to good use as it is just a matter of time before Costières de Nîmes is held in the same regard as some of the Rhône Valley's more prestigious appellations. An old-line estate that still turns out a bevy of exceptionally good wines is **Château de la Tuilerie.** They produce two cuvées of white and two of red, all of it excellent, with the more ambitious cuvées spending some time in wood. The property is superbly run by Madame Chantal Comte. As anyone who has tasted these wines can attest, both the white and red wines are impeccably vinified, modern-style wines made without compromising the typicity of the local area, or the character and pleasure of the wine.

Two other up-and-coming stars of this appellation are Château de Campuget and Mourgues du Grès. Both are names to memorize. **Château de Campuget** has received considerable coverage in my journal, *The Wine Advocate*, for its superb red and white wine values. This large estate of 247 acres produces a red wine made from 40% Syrah, 40% Grenache, 10% Cinsault, and 10% Carignan. The white wine is made from 50% Grenache Blanc, 25% Roussanne, 15% Clairette, and 10% Marsanne. Campuget is also fashioning one of the best Merlots of the southern Rhône, as well as incorporating increasing amounts of Cabernet Sauvignon into their red wine blend, along with Grenache and Syrah. All of Château de Campuget's offerings have represented exceptional values over recent years. Château de Campuget and Château de la Tuilerie have considerable competition from **Château Mourgues du Grès.** This property is brilliantly run by François Collard. It is a 75-acre estate dedicated to producing two cuvées of red wine. The vineyard, planted with 70% Syrah and 30% Grenache, produces what are probably the most concentrated, intense, full-bodied wines of the appellation. Both wines are aged in small casks, and the normal cuvée is a concoction of delicious red and black fruits. The special cuvée, Terre d'Argence, is a candidate for the best red wine of the appellation. It can easily age for 5–10 years in top vintages. Bottled carefully, with minimal intervention, these wines are "must purchases" for readers looking for excitement, quality, and pleasure at a very reasonable price. Another excellent estate is **Mas des Bressades.** Most of this estate's production is marketed under a vin de pays designation since their white is a Roussanne/Viognier blend and their red a Cabernet Sauvignon/Syrah blend. However, they do produce a small quantity of excellent wine under the appellation of Costières de Nîmes.

Just below this bevy of producers who are committed to making the world recognize the exciting level of quality that exists in Costières de Nîmes are **Château de Nages,** run by the négociant Michel Bernard from his headquarters in Orange, the Tremblay family's **Château de Belle-Coste,** and Hubert Sendra's **Domaine des Aveylans.**

I recognize how easy it is for readers to think that this part of Provence exists primarily to showcase the exquisite old Roman cities of Nîmes and Arles, but Costières de Nîmes, the wine-producing appellation, is a name to remember.

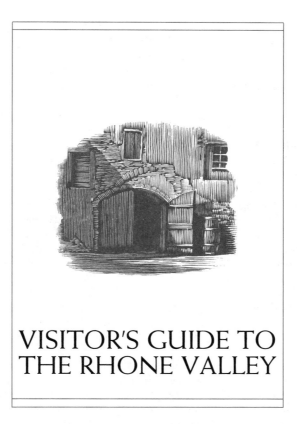

VISITOR'S GUIDE TO THE RHONE VALLEY

In addition to the obvious attraction of the wines of the Rhône, this area is loaded with wonderful restaurants, hotels, and inns that do justice to the spectacular natural scenery. Since the Rhône Valley is one of the most traveled regions of western Europe, reservations are a must during the peak travel season of May through September. My hotel and restaurant recommendations are arranged by viticultural areas, beginning in the north at Vienne and concluding in the south at Avignon. As a general guide, the price of a meal for two people with one bottle of good wine, based on a relatively weak dollar trading at five francs to a dollar, is as follows:

WHAT A MEAL FOR TWO WILL COST

Very expensive	$200–$400
Expensive	$100–$200
Moderate	$ 50–$150

Visiting Côte Rôtie and Condrieu

For visiting the most northern of the Rhône Valley's vineyards, Condrieu is the best place to use as a base since Côte Rôtie is only a five-minute drive to the north. However, Vienne, which is 15 or 20 minutes north of Condrieu and Côte Rôtie, is also a possibility. This more urban city is more congested and noisy than either Condrieu or Ampuis.

Condrieu: Restaurant and Hôtel Beau Rivage (tel. 4-74-59-52-24; fax 4-74-59-59-36) This lovely inn right on the Rhône River offers 20 very comfortable rooms, classic cuisine, a superb wine list, and a friendly reception. It is one of the most lavishly appointed and deluxe establishments in the northern Rhône Valley. The food is very good, and the wine list, filled with Condrieu, Côte Rôtie, and other northern Rhônes, is top-notch. Very expensive.

Les Roches de Condrieu: Bellevue (tel. 4-74-56-41-42; fax 4-74-56-47-56) Located across the river from Condrieu on a noisy, sharp curve, the splendidly situated Les Roches de Condrieu has adequate rooms, but the delicious, country-style cooking is excellent, especially the fish dishes. Be sure to try the pike quenelles in a nantua sauce with a bottle of Condrieu. The wine list is excellent. Expensive.

Vienne: Pyramide (tel. 4-74-53-01-96; fax 4-74-85-69-73) This hotel/restaurant is famous because the legendary chef, Fernand Point, reigned here earlier this century, influencing many of the present giants of French cuisine. After losing several stars, it has regained one and serves refined, modern French cuisine that is quite good, but very expensive. The wine list may not be what it was when I first ate here in 1975, but it is still filled with plenty of treasures. This is also a hotel, with 20 rooms and 4 apartments. Very expensive.

Chasse-sur-Rhône: Hôtel Mercure (tel. 4-72-24-29-29; fax 4-78-07-04-43) This modern hotel is about six miles south of Vienne, and 15 minutes north of Condrieu and Côte Rôtie. It has 103 sparsely decorated rooms, and makes a decent base for those requiring a modern facility. It is directly beside Autoroute A 7, so access is excellent. Moderate.

Ampuis: Restaurant Le Côte Rôtie (tel. 4-74-56-12-05; fax 4-74-56-00-20) There are two restaurants called Le Côte Rôtie in Ampuis, one terrible and one (this one) excellent and fairly priced. Be sure you go to the one located at 18 boulevard des Allées. It offers country-style cooking with four to five *dozen* Côte Rôties on the wine list—can you believe that? Prices are low, and the food substantial, flavorful, and well prepared. This is an excellent place to take in lunch or dinner in the heart of Côte Rôtie. Moderate.

Ampuis: Hôtel Alice and Gilles Barge (tel. 4-74-56-13-90; fax 4-74-56-10-98) Yes, Gilles Barge is president of the Côte Rôtie Syndicate, and one of the talented young growers in that appellation. Readers looking for a small, intimate, guest house with two rooms with a fabulous view of the Côte Rôtie terraces, should give this hotel a call. Inexpensive.

Visiting Hermitage, Cornas, Crozes-Hermitage, St.-Joseph, or St.-Péray

For visiting the southern part of the northern Rhône viticultural region, the distance from Vienne or Côte Rôtie is only 40–45 miles. However, it makes sense to make your base for this area in and around the large commercial city of Valence, which puts you within a 15-minute drive of St.-Péray and Cornas, and only 11 miles from the heart of Hermitage. This area has some excellent restaurants and plenty of hotels, so lodging is not nearly as difficult to find as it is in Côte Rôtie and Condrieu.

Valence: Pic (tel. 4-75-44-15-32; fax 4-75-40-96-03) This was once the finest restaurant in the Rhône Valley under the inspired as well as remarkably consistent cooking of Jacques Pic. However, Pic, one of the few Michelin Guide's three star chefs who preferred to stay in the kitchen rather than promote himself or become a traveling salesman for a brand of products, passed away several years ago. The kitchen was turned over to Pic's immensely talented son, Alain. Things seem to have become less consistent, and several friends I sent there complained of bad service and irregular cooking. I have eaten at this restaurant twice under Alain Pic, and though Michelin justifiably dropped the restaurant from its lofty three-star rating to two stars, the cuisine is still imaginative, excellent, occasionally superb, with very fine service. Although very expensive, the wine list remains among the finest of the Rhône Valley. It appears to me that restaurant Pic deserves its two-star Michelin rating, but it does not merit elevation to three-star status, although that could come with only a few refinements. There are also five rooms above the restaurant, which are convenient if you are going to do the famous *menu rabelais* at Pic. Very, very expensive.

Pont de l'Isère: Michel Chabran (tel. 4-75-84-60-09; fax 4-75-84-59-65) There is little reason to stop in Pont de l'Isère, a tiny, dull village six miles north of Valence, except to eat and/or stay at the restaurant and hotel Chabran. Fifteen years ago, Chabran seemed like a sure bet to win three stars from Michelin, but he began doing too many tours and not spending enough time in his kitchen. After losing a star, he rediscovered himself by the end of the eighties. Since then, Michel Chabran, an enormously talented chef, has regained the magic that makes this small, intimate restaurant the best candidate for three-star cuisine in this part of the Rhône Valley. The cooking is immensely imaginative, satisfying, and always beautifully presented and prepared. Once again, if you love Rhône wines, the wine list is remarkable. The hotel has small, modern, air-conditioned rooms—a luxury that is especially appreciated in this area during the torrid summers. Chabran may have two stars, but his cooking often approaches three stars. Moreover, he is rarely absent from the kitchen these days. This restaurant should not be missed when traveling in the Rhône Valley. Very expensive.

Valence: Novôtel (tel. 4-75-42-20-15; fax 4-75-43-56-29) This modern hotel situated next to the Autoroute A 7, at the southern exit for Valence, has 107 modernly equipped, air-conditioned rooms. I have often used it as a convenient spot for visiting northern Rhône vineyards, especially those between Tain l'Hermitage and St.-Péray. Moreover, the restaurant Pic is only a five-minute drive, and Chabran 15–20 minutes away. Expensive.

Granges-les-Beaumont: Restaurant Les Cèdres (tel. 4-75-71-50-67; fax 4-75-71-64-39) To find the restaurant Les Cèdres, follow the directions to Romans-sur-Isère from Valence and proceed about three miles in the direction of Granges-les-Beaumont. With a fabulous cellar full of not only young but old vintages of Côte Rôtie and Hermitage, this would be a worthy choice just to drink some great bottles off the wine list. However, the cuisine of Chef Bertrand is top-class, so much so that he has already earned one star in the *Guide Michelin,* although his cooking is closer to two-star quality. Reservations are essential since this is a tiny restaurant. Expensive.

Cornas: Restaurant Ollier (tel. 4-75-40-32-17) It can't get any more traditional and rustic than the Restaurant Ollier, which serves up plenty of gutsy, earthy French food that is meant to accompany the huge selection of Cornas wines available. The hangout for local winemakers, the food is substantial and flavorful, and there are at least 20 Cornas selections on the wine list. It is just south of the cellars of Auguste Clape, right on N 86. Moderate.

Tournon-sur-Rhône: Hôtel and Restaurant du Château (tel. 4-75-08-60-22; fax 4-75-07-02-95) The rooms in this small nineteenth-century house overlooking the Hermitage vineyards may be functional and sober, but they offer splendid views of Hermitage's huge dome of granite. The restaurant is a good bargain, with fine, traditional Rhône Valley and Provençal dishes. Servings are abundant and well prepared, but the wine list could be improved. Moderate.

Roche-de-Glun: Restaurant Gilbert et Charlotte (tel. 4-75-84-60-45) This inexpensive restaurant proved to be quite a find as it is located on the water and next to a flowering garden. The food is fashionable country cooking that is both abundant and moderately priced. Inexpensive.

Tournon: Restaurant le Chaudron (tel. 4-75-08-17-90) Tournon is a quaint town that sits across the Rhône River from and facing the immensely impressive terraced vineyards of Hermitage. Le Chaudron, a small restaurant in the town's old section, is attractive, with a good wine list (reasonably priced as well), and serves rustic Rhône/Lyonnais cooking. The address is 7, rue St.-Antoine. Moderate.

Tain l'Hermitage: Hôtel Mercure (tel. 4-75-08-65-00; fax 4-75-08-66-05) This newly renovated hotel has become part of the Mercure chain located throughout France. It is air-conditioned and has a swimming pool and, believe it or not, a surprisingly competent restaurant. It is the perfect place to stay when visiting Hermitage, Crozes-Hermitage, Cornas, or St.-Joseph. Moderate.

Tain l'Hermitage: Restaurant Reynaud (tel. 4-75-07-22-10; fax 4-75-08-03-53) This traditional, old-style restaurant on the outskirts of Tain l'Hermitage in the direction of Valence is known for its rich, rather heavy but excellent cooking. I enjoy eating here, but visitors should not expect nouvelle cuisine. The wine list is impressive, as well as expensive. There are also ten moderately priced rooms. Expensive.

Rive-de-Gier: Restaurant la Renaissance (tel. 4-77-75-04-31; fax 4-77-83-68-58) This country restaurant, 15 miles south of Vienne, serves excellent food that deserves far more attention than it has received. There is also a small six-room hotel, but utilize this venue for a Saturday or Sunday lunch rather than a base for touring Rhône vineyards.

Charmes-sur-Rhône: Autour d'une Fontaine (La Vieille Auberge) (tel. 4-75-60-80-10; fax 4-75-60-87-47) This popular country restaurant is six miles south of Valence. It serves excellent local cuisine at very reasonable prices. There are also seven rooms available for a modest price. Moderate.

Montmeyran: La Vieille Ferme (tel. 4-75-59-31-64) Offering a rustic country setting and excellent cuisine served without pretension at modest prices, this restaurant nine miles from Valence features the rich and bountiful cuisine of the countryside. Moderate.

St.-Hilaire-du-Rosier: Bouvarel (tel. 4-76-64-50-87; fax 4-76-64-58-47) This attractive restaurant northeast of Valence (about 32 miles) is a noteworthy destination for food enthusiasts. The *Guide Michelin* gives it one star, but the cooking is often closer to two-star quality. It remains a well-kept secret among foreigners, although European insiders are well aware of the high-class cooking that takes place in these kitchens. Prices are expensive. There are also fourteen rooms available at moderately expensive prices. It is an excellent place to spend the weekend after too many visits to the wineries. Expensive.

Granges-les-Valence: Auberge des Trois Canards (tel. 4-75-44-43-24; fax 4-75-41-64-48) Just west of Valence, but before passing into St.-Péray on the west bank of the Rhône, is the little town of Granges-les-Valence. This inexpensive, always packed, smoky bistro serves generous portions of very good food from the former chef of a famous Paris restaurant. It is an ideal spot for lunch. Moderate.

Visiting Châteauneuf du Pape and Avignon

Readers who find no value to a bright sun and/or gusty winds may well want to pass quickly through this region, which enjoys an abundance of both. Châteauneuf du Pape is, however, among the easiest places to visit as virtually all of the châteaux or domaines are accustomed to the hordes of summertime tourists who descend on this tiny village. Therefore, there are free tastings set up by many of the châteaus right in the town (look for the signs that say CAVEAU-DEGUSTATION). Châteauneuf du Pape has only three good hotels, the Hostellerie des Fines Roches, Logis d'Arnavel, and Le Sommellèrie, but the fascination of the hallowed walled city of Avignon is only 10 miles away. Avignon is an ideal base for exploring the southern Rhône provided readers can tolerate the traffic congestion.

Châteauneuf du Pape: Hostellerie des Fines Roches (tel. 4-90-83-70-23; fax 4-90-83-78-42) This quiet place in the middle of the vineyards is south of the village in the direction of Sorgues and Avignon. You can't miss the faux château, which looks like the Hotel Excalibur on Las Vegas's strip. The rooms are old-fashioned but spacious. Moreover, guests get to sleep in the middle of some of the oldest vineyards in Châteauneuf du Pape. The regional cuisine, prepared by one of Provence's most memorable personalities (and most talented chefs of the village) Monsieur Estevenin, is easily one-star quality, and sometimes two stars. The wine list consists largely of Châteauneuf du Papes with moderate prices and high quality.

Châteauneuf du Pape: La Sommellèrie (tel. 4-90-83-50-00; fax 4-90-83-51-85)
Under a new ownership, this has become the hot new spot in Châteauneuf du Pape largely because of the excellent cuisine of Pierre Paumel and the beauty of the renovated hotel. It is a modern, modestly priced, country hotel two or three minutes outside Châteauneuf du Pape in the direction of Roquemaure. There is a large swimming pool, and comfortable, beautifully appointed rooms. The excellent cooking is among the best of the area. Moderate to expensive.

Châteauneuf du Pape: La Mule des Papes (tel. 4-90-83-73-30) This second-floor restaurant does plenty of business since it is located in the middle of the village, but the wine list is inexcusably limited only to the wines produced by the négociant Père Anselme. The generous portions of food are good and cheap. Moderate.

Châteauneuf du Pape: Le Pistou (tel. 4-90-83-71-75) I adore this tiny hole-in-the-wall restaurant on the same street where the great Henri Bonneau lives. It offers many Provençal specialties at remarkably low prices. The food and service have flair and personality. Moderate.

Châteauneuf du Pape: Le Verger des Papes (tel. 4-90-83-50-40; fax 4-90-83-50-94) This small bistro has the finest ambience and setting in Châteauneuf du Pape. It is located at the top of the village just two minutes' walk down the hill from the ruined château. One of the village's great personalities, Henri Estevenin, is the chef. (His son is the chef at Hostellerier des Fines Roches.) Visitors are sure to enjoy a true Provençal meal and a great deal of fun if Henri is present. His personality is bigger than life, and he is also a fine cook, but he has a penchant for carousing with the clients rather than remaining in the kitchen. Moderate.

Châteauneuf du Pape: La Mère Germaine (tel. 4-90-83-70-72; fax 4-90-83-53-20) This is primarily a restaurant, although there are six rooms above the eating facilities. Many Châteauneuf du Pape old-timers seem to hang out at La Mère Germaine, telling stories and drinking glasses of full-bodied red Châteauneuf du Pape. The cooking is rustic Provençal, with enough lamb, garlic, tomatoes, eggplant, and olives to satiate aficionados of southern French cooking. Moderate.

Avignon: Hiely-Lucullus (tel. 4-90-86-17-07; fax 4-90-86-32-38) This famous restaurant's look and cuisine have remained unchanged since my wife and I first ate there in 1971. This second-floor restaurant inside the walls of Avignon is known for its rotund matronly waitresses who perform flawlessly. The cuisine is never adventurous, which may be why Michelin dropped one of its two stars, but it is always immensely satisfying, and the wine list is chock-full of treasures. For its pedigree, I have always found the prices reasonable. Moderate.

Pontet: Auberge de Cassagne (tel. 4-90-31-04-18; fax 4-90-32-25-09) This attractive, quiet, family-owned auberge is four miles north of Avignon in the suburb of Pontet. There are 22 attractive rooms, as well as excellent cooking at this inn known for its beautiful gardens. Moderate.

Montfavet: Hôtel les Frênes (tel. 4-90-31-17-93; fax 4-90-23-95-03) Located in a quiet park 10 minutes outside Avignon in the suburb of Montfavet, this fine hotel complex, with a superb swimming pool and nice rooms, has seen its kitchen become more irregular, as well as, inexplicably, more expensive. I used to be a regular diner, but recent meals have been disappointing. Expensive.

Avignon: Hôtel-Restaurant la Mirande (tel. 4-90-85-93-93; fax 4-90-86-26-85)
This luxury hotel is the top spot to stay in Avignon. Located adjacent to the Palais des Papes, the rooms are spectacular (and very expensive), and the cooking, which merits one star from Michelin, is often closer to two-star quality. It is Provençal cuisine at its best, innovative, not gimmicky, and rustic enough to satisfy big eaters. I have enjoyed several terrific meals at this venue. The wine list is expensive, but good buys can be found. Very expensive.

Avignon: Restaurant Christian Etienne (tel. 4-90-86-16-50; fax 4-90-86-67-09)
Recent meals have been inconsistent, but this restaurant still offers Avignon's most refined cooking. When the chef is on, he is very good, but the unevenness is inexplicable. Moderate to expensive.

Avignon: Novôtel Avignon Nord (tel. 4-90-31-16-43; fax 4-90-32-22-21) This excellent, modern hotel has 100 air-conditioned rooms (although the last time I was there it was 100° outside and the air-conditioning system behaved as if it consisted of nothing more than a chimp blowing on a fan in the basement). It is well located just north of Avignon, next to the Autoroute, making it easy to plunge into the countryside. Expensive.

Avignon: Restaurant les Domaines (tel. 4-90-82-58-86; fax 4-90-86-26-31)
This is a superb Provençal venue where a formidable wine list has been put together by Christophe Tassan. The cooking is quintessentially Provençal, and Tassan has an astonishing three to four dozen top quality Châteauneuf du Papes on the wine list that can be purchased for a song. Restaurants such as this should exist all over France, but, unfortunately, there are too few of them. This is a must for wine lovers and fanciers of good, earthy, Provençal cooking. Moderate.

Avignon: Restaurant le Caveau du Théâtre (tel. 4-90-82-60-91) Some of the finest, bargain-priced Provençal cuisine can be found at this tiny, nicely decorated, warm restaurant. There is an intelligent selection of good-value wines, and the cooking is simple but flavorful and remarkably cheap. Inexpensive.

Courthézon: Restaurant la Jardinière (tel. 4-90-70-84-49) This is another simple Provençal kitchen that offers well-prepared regional specialties at very fair prices. There is also a good selection of Châteauneuf du Pape and Côtes du Rhône wines fine enough for even the most discriminating drinking.

Villeneuve-les-Avignon: Le Prieuré (tel. 4-90-25-18-20; fax 4-90-25-45-39)
Splendidly located at the back of an alley, this gorgeously furnished hotel and restaurant offers good food and warm service in a marvelous medieval, vaulted stone priory. The setting is hard to beat. Expensive.

Visiting Tavel and Lirac

Tavel and Lirac are to the west of Avignon and one could easily remain in the city of the popes since neither Tavel nor Lirac is more than 30 minutes away by car. But if you want to bed down in the countryside, the following spots are recommended.

Tavel: Auberge de Tavel (tel. 4-66-50-03-41) The food is good, not excellent enough to merit its one star, but regional in orientation and well presented. The rooms are adequate. Moderate.

Tavel: Hostellerie du Seigneur (tel. 4-66-50-04-26) Less renowned than the Auberge de Tavel, this charming bistro has excellent cooking and very attractive prices, plus an array of Tavels on the wine list. Moderate.

Castillon-du-Gard: Le Vieux Castillon (tel. 4-66-37-00-77; fax 4-66-37-28-17)
This spare-no-expense establishment near the stunning Roman aqueduct the Pont du Gard has only one star from the *Guide Michelin*, but often deserves two. It is one of the most luxurious hotels and restaurants in this part of France. The cuisine is inspired, the wine list

outstanding, the views over the valley memorable, and the 11 rooms fit for the rich and famous. Take plenty of money to Le Vieux Castillon. Very expensive.

Visiting Gigondas, Vacqueyras, and the Côtes du Rhône-Villages

The eastern flank of the Rhône Valley is studded with medieval Provençal hill towns, tiny, charming, rustic restaurants, and red-faced vignerons offering a free taste of their wines.

Mondragon: La Beaugravière (tel. 4-90-40-82-54) I have eaten many meals at Beaugravière, the simple family restaurant in the small village of Mondragon, located just off the Bollène exit of France's A 7 (Autoroute du Soleil). This is a marvelous spot for the finest country French cooking of Provence. Chef Jullien is known as the truffle king of southern France, and in addition to offering a multitude of truffle dishes between December and May, he is a purveyor of these black nuggets to many of France's renowned chefs. The restaurant's cooking, from its spectacular omelette with truffles, to the local leg of lamb, is delicious. La Beaugravière also has the world's most prodigious Rhône wine list, with vintages of Chave's Hermitage back to 1929, Jaboulet's Hermitage La Chapelle back to the twenties, Château Rayas back to 1945, and Beaucastel back to the late forties. For an example of the breadth of this extraordinary wine cellar, consider the fact that there were 48 separate Châteauneuf du Pape estates represented, with more than 300 separate offerings on the wine list when I last ate there in summer 1996. But diners don't have to buy an expensive 30-year-old bottle of Hermitage to find a great wine. Jullien has a selection of fabulous Côtes du Rhône-Villages and Côtes du Rhônes that will boggle the mind. This is a must place to eat and drink (leisurely for sure) for any enthusiast of Provence cuisine or Rhône wines. Moderately expensive.

Gigondas: Les Florets (tel. 4-90-65-85-01; fax 4-90-65-83-80) This family-run restaurant on the lower slopes of the Dentelles de Montmirail is beautifully appointed. In the summer, it is the equivalent of dining in a heavenly garden of flowers. It serves husky proportions of skillfully prepared regional cuisine. The wine list has a selection of Gigondas staggering in its depth. The prices are unbelievably modest. Moderate.

Gigondas: L'Oustalet (tel. 4-90-65-85-30) My favorite restaurant in Gigondas is Les Florets, but I have plenty of affection for this simple, rustic, country restaurant right on the square in the old village of Gigondas. They offer numerous Provençal dishes at bargain-basement prices. Don't expect to drink anything other than a Côtes du Rhône or Gigondas from one of the local producers—which is the way it should be.

Séguret: La Table du Comtat (tel. 4-90-46-91-49; fax 4-90-46-94-27) A fabulous place to stay and dine, La Table du Comtat, which sits in the tiny hilltop village of Séguret, is a required stop, if only to have a meal while looking over the endless miles of Côtes du Rhône vineyards during a radiant Provençal sunset. The eight rooms are lovely and the pool refreshing. Moderate.

Séguret: Domaine de la Cabasse (tel. 4-90-46-91-12; fax 4-90-46-94-01) There is no menu, only Madame Nadine Latour's excellent daily fare to keep you contented. Her wines are served directly from the tanks in carafes, and her cooking is excellent, but you must take whatever she is cooking that day. It is well worth the risk. Moderate.

Rochegude: Château de Rochegude (tel. 4-75-04-81-88; fax 4-75-04-89-87) This marvelous château is enchantingly situated among an ocean of vineyards, as well as a large park. This is one of the famed Relais et Châteaux restaurants/hotels (there are 25 rooms) situated in the heart of the Côtes du Rhône appellation, about 15 minutes north of Orange on D 11. The rooms are magnificent, and the cooking of very high quality, although very refined and perhaps more internationally styled than I prefer in this part of Provence. Nevertheless, if your pockets are deep, Château de Rochegude is a marvelous venue for a special occasion. Very expensive.

Joucas: Mas des Herbes Blanches (tel. 4-90-05-79-79; fax 4-90-95-71-96) A meal here overlooking the Lubéron Mountains on the open-air deck is memorable by any standard. This luxury resort is hidden away on a hillside. The food is excellent and the view of the valley below and the mountains at sunset are unforgettable. Very expensive.

Vaison-la-Romaine: Le Bateleur (tel. 4-90-36-28-04) Looking for some of the most honest cooking in Provence? This small restaurant in one of the more fascinating Provençal hill towns, Vaison-la-Romaine, turns out regional cooking at bargain-basement prices. Moderate.

Loumarin: La Fenière (tel. 4-90-68-11-79; fax 4-90-68-18-60) In Loumarin, one of the loveliest Provençal hill towns (about one hour east of Avignon), is the restaurant La Fenière run by the immensely talented Madame Sammut. Her husband, Guy, is responsible for the excellent wine selections that offer high quality at reasonable prices. Many culinary enthusiasts consider La Fenière's cooking, only a one-star restaurant in the most recent *Guide Michelin*, to be among the very best in southern France. I enthusiastically agree, as this is a must stop in southern France. The loup (sea bass stuffed with truffles and sautéed in olive oil) and the grilled rougets (small red mullet) are remarkably fresh. This is a great restaurant, with a terrific chef at the top of her game. The *Michelin* rating is inexcusable. Not to be missed! Expensive.

Cairanne: Auberge Castel Mireio (tel. 4-90-30-82-20) This lovely restaurant has an excellent wine list and serves up generous portions of very reasonably priced Provençal cuisine. It is a satisfying restaurant for the eye, palate, and purse. Moderate.

Sorgues: Davico (tel. 4-90-39-11-02; fax 4-90-83-48-42) This hotel/restaurant in Sorgues turns out gutsy, earthy, Provençal cooking at very attractive prices. There are also 28 rooms in the comfortable hotel. Moderate.

Valréas: Le Grand Hôtel (tel. 4-90-35-00-26; fax 4-90-35-60-93) This is a classic country hotel/restaurant where the locals eat Saturday lunch. The food is very good, especially if you stick to the Provençal specialties, anything with truffles, and the wonderful eggplant and lamb dishes. Moderate.

Gordes: Restaurant les Vordenses (tel. 4-90-72-10-12; fax 4-90-72-11-63) Chef Patrick Gracia turns out classic Provençal dishes for reasonable prices at this beautifully situated restaurant in one of the most touristed Provençal hill towns. Although there are better-known restaurants in Gordes, Les Vordenses has the best cooking for the money. If you visit when the weather is fine, be sure and ask for a table on the terrace overlooking the marvelous view of the Lubéron mountains. Moderate.

FOOD SPECIALTIES
OF THE RHÔNE
VALLEY

Aïoli   This is a sauce made of egg yolks, garlic, and olive oil, often served with the region's fish dishes.

Anchoïade   A pasty anchovy and garlic vinaigrette.

Bourride   A hearty fish chowder that comes in endless variations.

Brandade de morue   It may sound terrible, but this is a delicious treat composed of salt cod reduced to a paste and blended with olive oil and garlic.

Brouillade d'oeuf aux truffles   It may be impossible to pronounce for most Americans, but this classic Provençal dish is essentially scrambled eggs with diced black truffles. If you like eggs and have an addiction for truffles (as I do), this is heavenly.

Daube de (boeuf, agneau, porc) Provençal   A substantial, long-simmered stew cooked in red wine with an assortment of vegetables. Think of it as Provence's answer to beef bourgignon, although pork and lamb are often substituted for beef.

Fougasse   This is the spicy flat bread of Provence that is studded with onions, black olives, and anchovies.

Gigot d'agneau d'Alpilles (or Sisteron)   A remarkably tasty leg of lamb from the two most desired areas for raising this animal, the Alpilles south of Avignon and the Sisteron region in the mountainous gorge-laden area east of the Côtes du Ventoux.

Picodon   Very fashionable at the moment, this soft goat cheese is made in small discs and has a pronounced fresh, nutty flavor.

Pissaladière   This is essentially Provence's answer to pizza, a light-crusted, pizza-shaped pie garnished with onions, tomatoes, olives, and anchovies. Go into any *boulangerie* in Provence and you will see it prominently displayed.

Pistou   A hearty vegetable soup loaded with aromatic herbs and garlic.

Quenelles de brochet, sauce nantua   Pikefish dumplings with a sauce made from freshwater crayfish sounds terrible in English, but just try them.

Ratatouille   This concoction/stew is a marvelous aromatic, heavy-duty soup/vegetable dish made of onions, eggplants, zucchini, tomatoes, and peppers and cooked slowly for hours in olive oil and garlic.

Rigotte de Condrieu   As the name implies, this cheese is regularly encountered in the northern Rhône. Made from cow's milk, it is a firm, creamy cheese.

St.-Marcellin   One of the region's most famous cheeses, made from cow's milk in the Isère area, with a creamy texture and mild flavor.

Soupe à l'ail   Garlic soup.

Tapenade   A paste made from black olives, garlic, herbs, and olive oil.

Tomme   A mountain cheese made from either goat's or sheep's milk, it has a distinctive flavor.

Truffles   Black truffles from Tricastin are not as famous as those from Périgord, but they taste every bit as good. They are in season during the late fall, but most restaurants preserve enough of them to last for six to eight months.

A GLOSSARY
OF WINE TERMS

acetic: Wines, no matter how well made, contain quantities of acetic acidity that have a vinegary smell. If there is an excessive amount of acetic acidity, the wine will have a vinegary smell and be a flawed, acetic wine.

acidic: Wines need natural acidity to taste fresh and lively, but an excess of acidity results in an acidic wine that is tart and sour.

acidity: The acidity level in a wine is critical to its enjoyment and livelihood. The natural acids that appear in wine are citric, tartaric, malic, and lactic. Wines from hot years tend to be lower in acidity, whereas wines from cool, rainy years tend to be high in acidity. Acidity in a wine can preserve the wine's freshness and keep the wine lively, but too much acidity, which masks the wines flavors and compresses its texture, is a flaw.

aftertaste: As the term suggests, the taste left in the mouth when one swallows is the aftertaste. This word is a synonym for length or finish. The longer the aftertaste lingers in the mouth (assuming it is a pleasant taste), the finer the quality of the wine.

aggressive: Aggressive is usually applied to wines that are either high in acidity or have harsh tannins, or both.

angular: Angular wines are wines that lack roundness, generosity, and depth. Wine from poor vintages or wines that are too acidic are often described as being angular.

aroma: Aroma is the smell of a young wine before it has had sufficient time to develop nuances of smell that are then called its bouquet. The word aroma is commonly used to mean the smell of a relatively young, unevolved wine.

astringent: Wines that are astringent are not necessarily bad or good wines. Astringent wines are harsh and coarse to taste, either because they are too young and tannic and just need time to develop, or because they are not well made. The level of tannins (if it is harsh) in a wine contributes to its degree of astringence.

austere: Wines that are austere are generally not terribly pleasant wines to drink. An austere wine is a hard, rather dry wine that lacks richness and generosity. However, young Rhônes are not as austere as young Bordeaux.

balance: One of the most desired traits in a wine is good balance, where the concentration of fruit, level of tannins, and acidity are in total harmony. Well-balanced wines are symmetrical and tend to age gracefully.

barnyard: An unclean, farmyard, fecal aroma that is imparted to a wine because of unclean barrels or unsanitary winemaking facilities.

berrylike: As this descriptive term implies, most red wines have an intense berry fruit character that can suggest blackberries, raspberries, black cherries, mulberries, or even strawberries and cranberries.

big: A big wine is a large-framed, full-bodied wine with an intense and concentrated feel on the palate. Most red Rhône wines are big wines.

blackcurrant: A pronounced smell of blackcurrant fruit is commonly associated with certain Rhône wines. It can vary in intensity from faint to very deep and rich.

body: Body is the weight and fullness of a wine that can be sensed as it crosses the palate. Full-bodied wines tend to have a lot of alcohol, concentration, and glycerin.

Botrytis cinerea: The fungus that attacks the grape skins under specific climatic conditions (usually alternating periods of moisture and sunny weather). It causes the grape to become superconcentrated because it causes a natural dehydration. Botrytis cinerea is essential for the great sweet white wines of Barsac and Sauternes. It rarely occurs in the Rhône Valley because of the dry, constant sunshine and gusty winds.

bouquet: As a wine's aroma becomes more developed from bottle aging, the aroma is transformed into a bouquet that is hopefully more than just the smell of the grape.

brawny: A hefty, muscular, full-bodied wine with plenty of weight and flavor, although not always the most elegant or refined sort of wine.

briery: I think of California Zinfandel when the term briery comes into play, denoting that the wine is aggressive and rather spicy.

brilliant: Brilliant relates to the color of the wine. A brilliant wine is one that s clear, with no haze or cloudiness to the color.

browning: As red wines age, their color changes from ruby/purple to dark ruby, to medium ruby, to ruby with an amber edge, to ruby with a brown edge. When a wine is browning it is usually fully mature and not likely to get better.

carbonic maceration: This vinification method is used to make soft, fruity, very accessible wines. Whole clusters of grapes are put into a vat that is then filled with carbonic gas. This system is used when fruit is to be emphasized in the final wine in contrast to structure and tannin.

cedar: Rhône reds can have a bouquet that suggests either faintly or overtly the smell of cedarwood. It is a complex aspect of the bouquet.

chewy: If a wine has a rather dense, viscous texture from a high glycerin content, it is often referred to as being chewy. High-extract wines from great vintages can often be chewy, largely because they have higher alcohol hence high levels of glycerin, which imparts a fleshy mouthfeel.

closed: The term closed is used to denote that the wine is not showing its potential, which remains locked in because it is too young. Young wines often close up about 12–18 months after bottling, and depending on the vintage and storage conditions, remain in such a state for several years to more than a decade.

complex: One of the most subjective descriptive terms used, a complex wine is a wine that the taster never gets bored with and finds interesting to drink. Complex wines tend to have a variety of subtle scents and flavors that hold one's interest in the wine.

concentrated: Fine wines, whether they are light-, medium-, or full-bodied, should have concentrated flavors. Concentrated denotes that the wine has a depth and richness of fruit that gives it appeal and interest. Deep is a synonym for concentrated.

corked: A corked wine is a flawed wine that has taken on the smell of cork as a result of an unclean or faulty cork. It is perceptible in a bouquet that shows no fruit, only the smell of musty cork, which reminds me of wet cardboard.

cuvée: Many producers in the Rhône Valley produce special, deluxe lots of wine or a lot of wine from a specific grape variety that they bottle separately. These lots are often referred to as cuvées.

decadent: If you are an ice cream and chocolate lover, you know the feeling of eating a huge sundae of rich vanilla ice cream lavished with hot fudge and real whipped cream. If you are a wine enthusiast, a wine loaded with opulent, even unctuous layers of fruit, with a huge bouquet, and a plump, luxurious texture can be said to be decadent.

deep: Essentially the same as concentrated, expressing the fact that the wine is rich, full of extract, and mouth filling.

delicate: As this word implies, delicate wines are light, subtle, understated wines that are prized for their shyness rather than for an extroverted, robust character. White wines are usually more delicate than red wines. Few Rhône red wines can correctly be called delicate.

diffuse: Wines that smell and taste unstructured and unfocused are said to be diffuse. When red wines are served at too warm a temperature they often become diffuse.

dumb: A dumb wine is also a closed wine, but the term dumb is used more pejoratively. Closed wines may need only time to reveal their richness and intensity. Dumb wines may never get any better.

earthy: May be used in both a negative and a positive sense; however, I prefer to use earthy to denote a positive aroma of fresh, rich, clean soil. Earthy is a more intense smell than woody or truffle scents.

elegant: Although more white wines than red are described as being elegant, lighter-styled, graceful, well-balanced red wines can be elegant.

extract: This is everything in a wine besides water, sugar, alcohol, and acidity.

exuberant: Like extroverted, somewhat hyper people, wines too can be gushing with fruit and seem nervous and intensely vigorous.

fat: When the Rhône has an exceptionally hot year for its crop and the wines attain a super sort of maturity, they are often quite rich and concentrated, with low to average acidity. Often such wines are said to be fat, which is a prized commodity. If they become too fat, that is a flaw and they are then called flabby.

flabby: A wine that is too fat or obese is a flabby wine. Flabby wines lack structure and are heavy to taste.

fleshy: Fleshy is a synonym for chewy, meaty, or beefy. It denotes that the wine has a lot of body, alcohol, and extract, and usually a high glycerin content. Châteauneuf-du-Pape and Hermitage are particularly fleshy wines.

floral: Wines made from the Muscat or Viognier grape have a flowery component, and occasionally a red wine will have a floral scent.

focused: Both a fine wine's bouquet and flavor should be focused. Focused simply means that the scents, aromas, and flavors are precise and clearly delineated. If they are not, the wine is like an out-of-focus picture—diffuse, hazy, and possibly problematic.

forward: A wine is said to be forward when its charm and character are fully revealed. While it may not be fully mature yet, a forward wine is generally quite enjoyable and drinkable. Forward is the opposite of backward. Accessible is a synonym for forward.

foudre: Large oak barrels that vary enormously in size but are significantly larger than the normal oak barrel used in Bordeaux or the *pièce* used in Burgundy. They are widely used in the Rhône Valley.

fresh: Freshness in both young and old wines is a welcome and pleasing component. A wine is said to be fresh when it is lively and cleanly made. The opposite of fresh is stale.

fruity: A very good wine should have enough concentration of fruit so that it can be said to be fruity. Fortunately, the best wines will have more than just a fruity personality.

full-bodied: Wines rich in extract, alcohol, and glycerin are full-bodied wines. Most Rhône wines are full-bodied.

garrigue: In the southern Rhône Valley and Provence, this is the landscape of small slopes and plateaus. This Provençal word applies to these windswept hilltops/slopes inhabited by scrub-brush and Provençal herb outcroppings. The smell of *garrigue* is often attributed to southern Rhône Valley wines. Suggesting more than the smell of herbes de Provence, it encompasses an earthy/herbal concoction of varying degrees of intensity.

green: Green wines are wines made from underripe grapes; they lack richness and generosity as well as having a vegetal character. Green wines are infrequently made in the Rhône, although vintages such as 1977 were characterized by a lack of ripening.

hard: Wines with abrasive, astringent tannins or high acidity are said to be hard. Young vintages of Rhône wines can be hard, but they should never be harsh.

harsh: If a wine is too hard it is said to be harsh. Harshness in a wine, young or old, is a flaw.

hedonistic: Certain styles of wine are meant to be inspected; they are introspective and intellectual wines. Others are designed to provide sheer delight, joy, and euphoria. Hedonistic wines can be criticized because in one sense they provide so much ecstasy that they can be called obvious, but in essence, they are totally gratifying wines meant to fascinate and enthrall—pleasure at its best.

herbaceous: Many wines have a distinctive herbal smell that is generally said to be herbaceous. Specific herbal smells can be of thyme, lavender, rosemary, oregano, fennel, or basil and are common in Rhône wines.

herbes de Provence: Provence is known for the wild herbs that grow prolifically throughout the region. These include lavender, thyme, sage, rosemary, and oregano. It is not just an olfactory fancy to smell many of these herbs in Rhône Valley wines, particularly those made in the south.

hollow: Also known as shallow, hollow wines are diluted and lack depth and concentration.

honeyed: A common personality trait of specific white Rhône wines, a honeyed wine is one that has the smell and taste of bee's honey.

hot: Rather than meaning that the temperature of the wine is too warm to drink, hot denotes that the wine is too high in alcohol and therefore leaves a burning sensation in the back of the throat when swallowed. Wines with alcohol levels in excess of 14.5% often taste hot if the requisite depth of fruit is not present.

inox vats: This is the French term for stainless steel vats that are used for both fermentation and storage of wine.

intensity: Intensity is one of the most desirable traits of a high-quality wine. Wines of great intensity must also have balance. They should never be heavy or cloying. Intensely concentrated great wines are alive, vibrant, aromatic, layered, and texturally compelling. Their intensity adds to their character, rather than detracting from it.

jammy: When wines have a great intensity of fruit from excellent ripeness they can be jammy, which is a very concentrated, flavorful wine with superb extract. In great vintages such as 1961, 1978, 1985, 1989, 1990, and 1995, some of the wines are so concentrated that they are said to be jammy.

Kisselguhr filtration system: This is a filtration system using diatomaceous earth as the filtering material, rather than cellulose, or in the past, before it was banned, asbestos.

leafy: A leafy character in a wine is similar to a herbaceous character only in that it refers to the smell of leaves rather than herbs. A wine that is too leafy is a vegetal or green wine.

lean: Lean wines are slim, rather streamlined wines that lack generosity and fatness but can still be enjoyable and pleasant.

lively: A synonym for fresh or exuberant, a lively wine is usually young wine with good acidity and a thirst-quenching personality.

long: A very desirable trait in any fine wine is that it be long in the mouth. Long (or length) relates to a wine's finish, meaning that after you swallow the wine, you sense its presence for a long time. (Thirty seconds to several minutes is great length.) In a young wine, the difference between something good and something great is the length of the wine.

lush: Lush wines are velvety, soft, richly fruity wines that are both concentrated and fat. A lush wine can never be an astringent or hard wine.

massive: In great vintages where there is a high degree of ripeness and superb concentration, some wines can turn out to be so big, full-bodied, and rich that they are called massive. A great wine such as the 1961 or 1990 Hermitage La Chapelle is a textbook example of a massive wine.

meaty: A chewy, fleshy wine is also said to be meaty.

monocépage: This term describes a wine made totally of one specific varietal.

monopole: Used to denote a vineyard owned exclusively by one proprietor, the word *monopole* appears on the label of a wine made from such a vineyard.

morsellated: Many vineyards are fragmented, with multiple growers owning a portion of the same vineyard. Such a vineyard is often referred to as a morsellated vineyard.

mouth-filling: Big, rich, concentrated wines that are filled with fruit extract and are high in alcohol and glycerin are wines that tend to texturally fill the mouth. A mouth-filling wine is also a chewy, fleshy, fat wine.

musty: Wines aged in dirty barrels or unkept cellars or exposed to a bad cork take on a damp, musty character that is a flaw.

nose: The general smell and aroma of a wine as sensed through one's nose and olfactory senses is often called the wine's nose.

oaky: Many red Rhône wines are aged from 6 months to 30 months in various sizes of oak barrels. At some properties, a percentage of the oak barrels may be new, and these barrels impart a toasty, vanillin flavor and smell to the wine. If the wine is not rich and concentrated, the barrels can overwhelm the wine, making it taste overly oaky. Where the wine is rich and concentrated and the winemaker has made a judicious use of barrels, however, the results are a wonderful marriage of fruit and oak.

off: If a wine is not showing its true character, or is flawed or spoiled in some way, it is said to be "off."

overripe: An undesirable characteristic; grapes left too long on the vine become too ripe, lose their acidity, and produce wines that are heavy and unbalanced. This can happen frequently in the hot viticultural areas of the Rhône Valley if the growers harvest too late.

oxidized: If a wine has been excessively exposed to air during either its making or aging, the wine loses freshness and takes on a stale, old smell and taste. Such a wine is said to be oxidized.

peppery: A peppery quality to a wine is usually noticeable in many Rhône wines that have an aroma of black or white pepper and a pungent flavor.

perfumed: This term usually is more applicable to fragrant, aromatic white wines than to red wines. However, some of the dry white wines (particularly Condrieu) and sweet white wines can have a strong perfumed smell.

pigéage: A winemaking technique of punching down the cap of grape skins that forms during the beginning of the wine's fermentation. This is done several times a day, occasionally more frequently, to extract color, flavor, and tannin from the fermenting juice.

plummy: Rich, concentrated wines can often have the smell and taste of ripe plums. When they do, the term plummy is applicable.

ponderous: Ponderous is often used as a synonym for massive, but in my usage a massive wine is simply a big, rich, very concentrated wine with balance, whereas a ponderous wine is a wine that has become heavy and tiring to drink.

precocious: Wines that mature quickly are precocious. However the term also applies to wines that may last and evolve gracefully over a long period of time, but taste as if they are aging quickly because of their tastiness and soft, early charms.

pruney: Wines produced from grapes that are overripe take on the character of prunes. Pruney wines are flawed wines.

raisiny: Late-harvest wines that are meant to be drunk at the end of a meal can often be slightly raisiny, which in some ports and sherries is desirable. However, a raisiny quality is a major flaw in a dinner wine.

rich: Wines that are high in extract, flavor, and intensity of fruit.

ripe: A wine is ripe when its grapes have reached the optimum level of maturity. Less than fully mature grapes produce wines that are underripe, and overly mature grapes produce wines that are overripe.

round: A very desirable character of wines, roundness occurs in fully mature wines that have lost their youthful, astringent tannins, and also in young wines that have soft tannins and low acidity.

savory: A general descriptive term that denotes that the wine is round, flavorful, and interesting to drink.

shallow: A weak, feeble, watery or diluted wine lacking concentration is said to be shallow.

sharp: An undesirable trait, sharp wines are bitter and unpleasant with hard, pointed edges.

silky: A synonym for velvety or lush, silky wines are soft, sometimes fat, but never hard or angular.

smoky: Some wines, either because of the soil or because of the barrels used to age the wine, have a distinctive smoky character. Côte Rôtie and Hermitage often have a roasted or smoky quality.

soft: A soft wine is one that is round and fruity, low in acidity, and has an absence of aggressive, hard tannins.

spicy: Wines often smell quite spicy with aromas of pepper, cinnamon, and other well-known spices. These pungent aromas are usually lumped together and called spicy.

stale: Dull, heavy wines that are oxidized or lack balancing acidity for freshness are called stale.

stalky: A synonym for vegetal, but used more frequently to denote that the wine has probably had too much contact with the stems, resulting in a green, vegetal, or stalky character to the wine.

supple: A supple wine is one that is soft, lush, velvety, and very attractively round and tasty. It is a highly desirable characteristic because it suggests that the wine is harmonious.

tannic: The tannins of a wine, which are extracted from the grape skins and stems, are, along with a wine's acidity and alcohol, its lifeline. Tannins give a wine firmness and some roughness when young, but gradually fall away and dissipate. A tannic wine is one that is young and unready to drink.

tart: Sharp, acidic, lean, unripe wines are called tart. In general, a wine that is tart is not pleasurable.

thick: Rich, ripe, concentrated wines that are low in acidity are often said to be thick.

thin: A synonym for shallow; it is an undesirable characteristic for a wine to be thin, meaning that it is watery, lacking in body, and just diluted.

tightly knit: Young wines that have good acidity levels, good tannin levels, and are well made are called tightly knit, meaning they have yet to open up and develop.

toasty: A smell of grilled toast can often be found in wines because the barrels the wines are aged in are charred or toasted on the inside.

tobacco: Some red wines have the scent of fresh tobacco. It is a distinctive and wonderful smell in wine.

troncais oak: This type of oak comes from the forest of Troncais in central France.

unctuous: Rich, lush, intense wines with layers of concentrated, soft, velvety fruit are said to be unctuous.

vegetal: An undesirable characteristic, wines that smell and taste vegetal are usually made from unripe grapes. In some wines, a subtle vegetable garden smell is pleasant and adds complexity, but if it is the predominant character, it is a major flaw.

velvety: A textural description and synonym for lush or silky, a velvety wine is a rich, soft, smooth wine to taste. It is a very desirable characteristic.

viscous: Viscous wines tend to be relatively concentrated, fat, almost thick wines with a great density of fruit extract, plenty of glycerin, and high alcohol content. If they have balancing acidity, they can be tremendously flavorful and exciting wines. If they lack acidity, they are often flabby and heavy.

volatile: A volatile wine is one that smells of vinegar as a result of an excessive amount of acetic bacteria present. It is a seriously flawed wine.

woody: When a wine is overly oaky it is often said to be woody. Oakiness in a wine's bouquet and taste is good up to a point. Once past that point, the wine is woody and its fruity qualities are masked by excessive oak aging.

INDEX

(Page numbers in **boldface** *refer to main entries for producers and growers. Page numbers in* italic *refer to illustrations.)*

Much of the material in this book is based upon tastings and research done in conjunction with the publishing of *The Wine Advocate*, an independent consumer's guide to fine wines, which is issued six times a year. A one-year subscription to *The Wine Advocate* costs $40.00 for delivery in the continental United States, $50.00 for Canada, and $70.00 for air-mail delivery anywhere in the world. Subscriptions or a sample copy may be obtained by writing to *The Wine Advocate*, P.O. Box 311, Monkton, MD 21111, or by sending a fax to 410-357-4504.